Brink's Modern
Internal Auditing

SUBSCRIPTION NOTICE

This Wiley product is updated on a periodic basis with supplements to reflect important changes in the subject matter. If you purchased this product directly from John Wiley & Sons, Inc., we have already recorded your subscription for this update service.

If, however, you purchased this product from a bookstore and wish to receive (1) the current update at no additional charge, and (2) future updates and revised or related volumes billed separately with a 30-day examination review, please send your name, company name (if applicable), address, and the title of the product to:

Supplement Department
John Wiley & Sons, Inc.
One Wiley Drive
Somerset, NJ 08875
1-800-225-5945

For customers outside the United States, please contact the Wiley office nearest you:

Professional & Reference Division
John Wiley & Sons Canada, Ltd.
22 Worcester Road
Rexdale, Ontario M9W 1L1
CANADA
(416) 675-3580
1-800-567-4797
FAX (416) 675-6599

John Wiley & Sons, Ltd.
Baffins Lane
Chichester
West Sussex, PO19 1UD
UNITED KINGDOM
(44) (243) 779777

Jacaranda Wiley Ltd.
PRT Division
P.O. Box 174
North Ryde, NSW 2113
AUSTRALIA
(02) 805-1100
FAX (02) 805-1597

John Wiley & Sons (SEA) Pte. Ltd.
37 Jalan Pemimpin
Block B # 05-04
Union Industrial Building
SINGAPORE 2057
(65) 258-1157

Brink's Modern Internal Auditing

Fifth Edition

ROBERT MOELLER

HERBERT WITT

JOHN WILEY & SONS, INC.
New York • Chichester • Weinheim • Brisbane • Singapore • Toronto

This book is printed on acid-free paper. ∞

Copyright © 1999 by John Wiley & Sons, Inc. All rights reserved.

Published simultaneously in Canada.

This publication is designed to provide accurate and authoritative information in regard to the subject matter covered. It is sold with the understanding that the publisher is not engaged in rendering legal, accounting, or other professional services. If legal advice or other expert assistance is required, the services of a competent professional person should be sought.

Library of Congress Cataloging-in-Publication Data:

Moeller, Robert R.
    Brink's modern internal auditing.—5th ed. / Robert R. Moeller,
Herbert Witt, Victor Z. Brink.
      p. cm.
    Rev. ed. of: Modern internal auditing / Herbert Witt. 4th ed. c1982.
    Includes bibliographical references and index.
    ISBN 0-471-52132-9 (cloth : alk. paper)
    1. Auditing, Internal. I. Brink, Victor Zinn, 1906–   .
II. Brink, Victor Zinn, 1906–   Modern internal auditing.
III. Title.
HF5668.25.B74   1998
657′.458—dc21   98-20229

Printed in the United States of America

10 9 8 7 6 5 4 3

ABOUT THE AUTHORS

Robert R. Moeller has over 25 years experience in internal auditing, ranging from launching new internal audit functions in several companies to serving as audit director for a Fortune 50 corporation.

Moeller has an MBA in finance from the University of Chicago and an undergraduate degree in engineering; he has accumulated a wide range of professional certifications including the CPA. He was appointed the National Director of Computer Auditing for the major public accounting firm of Grant Thornton. There he developed firm-wide audit procedures and directly managed information systems audits. He eventually assumed responsibility for their Chicago office information systems consulting practice, leading projects to build and install systems for a wide range of clients.

In 1989, Moeller was recruited to build and organize the first corporate information systems audit function for Sears Roebuck. He went on to become their audit director, initiating numerous new practices to their internal audit department. He has been active professionally in both the Institute of Internal Auditors and the AICPA. He was president of the IIA's Chicago chapter, served on its International Advanced Technology Committee, and was chair of the AICPA's Computer Audit Subcommittee.

In 1996, Moeller launched his own corporation, Compliance and Control Systems Associates, Inc., and presented seminars on internal controls and corporate governance throughout the United States. He has worked as a consultant and project manager, specializing in the telecommunications industry; has helped develop controls for a major cellular telephone billing system; has managed a year 2000 project for AT&T; and most recently managed a cellular telephone financial system project on a worldwide basis.

Herbert Witt was formerly with Price Waterhouse and with the Department of Health and Human Services Office of Inspector General. He received an MBA degree from the University of California, Berkeley, and is a Certified Public Accountant, a Certified Internal Auditor, and a Certified Government Financial Manager. He was co-author of the American Institute of Certified Public Accountants course in Operational Auditing. Witt is the former Regional Vice-President, Regional Director, and National Director of the Institute of Internal Auditors. He also served as Chairman of the IIA's International Research Committee and the International Education Committee.

PREFACE

In 1941, the clouds of war—initiated by such dictators as Hitler, Mussolini, and Stalin—were surrounding much of the world. At the same time, Victor Z. Brink completed his New York University Ph.D. thesis. While the "maximum leader" dictators were predicting one kind of violent revolution, Brink's Ph.D. thesis outlined a much more benign revolution, a revolution in the way that internal auditors should perform their work. Prior to the 1940s, internal auditors were essentially in-house assistants to their company's public accounting firms, performing little more than clerical financial auditing support duties for those external auditors. Brink's thesis argued that a much better role for internal auditors should be as servants to management, not as external auditor assistants.

Vic Brink then went off to service in World War II, but not before the wheels were put in place to publish his thesis as a book for business leaders. Its title was *Modern Internal Auditing*. With the United States gearing up for total war and looking to better utilize every scarce resouce, the first edition of *Modern Internal Auditing* (1942) caused many managers to consider how they might better organize their internal audit functions. Brink's book strongly proposed that internal auditors could and should be much more significant members of an organization's management team. The *modern* internal auditor that Brink envisioned served management by going beyond routine accounting verification procedures and taking a broader approach of *supplying service to management* as part of their internal audit activities. This approach came to be known as *operational auditing*.

Brink returned from the war and became director of internal audit for the Ford Motor Company. He also worked with others, such as Brad Cadmus and Larry Sawyer, to expand and better define this new professional called the modern internal auditor. A final result of the work of Brink and others was the establishment of the Institute of Internal Auditors (IIA), now a major professional accounting organization, responsible for setting standards and providing guidance to the profession of internal auditing.

Often, authors of significant and groundbreaking business books "go to sleep" after their first or second editions. However, Brink kept active in the profession, revising his original 1942 edition three times over the years, either by himself or in collaboration with Herbert Witt in the last editions. Because Herbert Witt worked on the two most recent revisions, some of his ideas and expression remain in the book and his name properly continues its association with this edition. Although Brink introduced new concepts and technologies in the subsequent editions, he never lost his basic philosophy that internal auditing should provide a basic and essential *service to management* in the modern organization. In this edition of *Modern Internal Auditing*, author Robert Moeller takes full responsibility for taking Brink's philosophy into today's world.

Until his death in 1992, Brink continued to be alert and professionally active. I met Brink at an IIA annual international conference as well as several times after this new edition was launched. He was an impressive, interesting man, with an ongoing concern for the practice of internal auditing. This fifth edition preserves Brink's important concept of internal audit's responsibility to management but also introduces many of the changes and concepts that continue to make internal auditing exciting and important.

Although changes have taken place in many areas, it's the growth of computers and information systems that perhaps best illustrates how changes have impacted internal auditors over the last 50 to 60 years. At the time of the first edition of *Modern Internal Auditing*, the digital computer did not exist and companies were just beginning to use 80- or 90-column punched-card tabulating equipment for some of their elementary statistical record-keeping applications. There was no need to mention these machines in the first edition of this book because they were just not that important to businesses.

Mainframe computers, behemoths that weighed tons and occupied major areas of floor space, were introduced in larger companies starting in the 1960s, but internal auditors were not concerned with them. This was the era in which audits were performed *around* the computer; that is, if a total had been generated by the computer and printed on some report, it was assumed to be correct because "the computer figured it out." Auditors were primarily concerned that the input controls were adequate. Internal auditors had little to do with these computer systems besides perhaps checking to see if the door to the computer room was locked or that candy and soft drinks were not being consumed in the computer room.

Business data processing systems became more pervasive with IBM's introduction of its 360 series in the mid-1960s, and internal auditors began to pay a little more attention to them. They began to pay a *lot* more attention when news broke of a computer-based fraud in the early 1970s involving a company called Equity Funding. Suddenly, the profession of computer auditing was launched, but these specialized computer auditors were viewed as out of the mainstream of normal internal audit activities. Previous editions of *Modern Internal Auditing* gave little attention to computer systems and their controls.

By the late 1970s, the classic mainframe computer was common to larger organizations and smaller "minicomputers" were beginning to be introduced to others. Internal auditors, through their use of audit retrieval languages and their greater understanding of information systems controls, began auditing and testing the adequacy of controls surrounding these new business tools. This was the era when an organization's security function was primarily involved with parking lot slots and building gates. Management began to view internal auditors as computer security experts, an example of how internal audit's service to management has yielded positive results.

Mainframes and their smaller micro- and minicomputer versions became pervasive by the end of the 1980s. The modern internal auditor had to better understand these machines and their control risks. The fourth edition of *Modern Internal Auditing* (1982) devoted a whole chapter to computer systems, although the material seems elementary today. By that time, internal auditors were concerned with computer system control issues in their accounting and general business audit areas, but were still not generally using computer systems to automate internal audit practices.

As we enter the next millennium, automation in all of its forms has become common for all areas of operations. Networks of computer systems are used throughout the organization, and today's modern internal auditor will typically go on an audit assignment armed with a laptop computer that will allow the auditor to: (1) record workpaper interviews; (2) perform various financial and statistical analyses; (3) communicate with the home office via modem; and (4) look up reference information on the Internet. As a result, this new edition has five chapters devoted to information systems and their impact on internal auditors.

This edition is divided into six major parts, organized as follows:

Part One—Foundations of Internal Auditing.   Four chapters here describe what internal auditing is really all about. The origins of the profession are discussed in Chapter 1 and the basic or fundamental concepts of internal control in Chapter 2. The broader definition of internal control, as defined in what has been called the Committee of Sponsoring Organizations (COSO) report, is discussed here. Part One in general, and Chapter 3 in particular, describes the importance of internal audit's service to management as part of its overall approach. Chapter 4 describes the operational approach of an internal auditor, as opposed to the more traditional "Do the debits equal the credits?" approaches of many traditional financial auditors. Of course, as the reader will discover throughout this edition, this more operational approach of assessing and evaluating controls is being more frequently used by all auditors, whether they be internal or external. Finally, Chapter 5 covers the Standards for the Professional Practice of Internal Auditing, issued by the Institute of Internal Auditors. These are the standards that should govern activities of *all* internal auditors. They are important for understanding the basic foundations of the profession of internal auditing. While earlier editions contained the complete text, Chapter 5 contains extracts from the actual text of the standards as well as explanatory comments; references to these standards will be found throughout the other chapters of this edition.

The chapters in Part One should give the reader a general understanding of what internal audit is and what an internal audit function can do for an organization. Taken by itself, this part can be useful reading for the nonauditor (for example, a member of senior management) who wants to have a general understanding of internal audit's purposes and objectives. Even though internal auditors have been in the modern organization since about the time of Vic Brink's first edition, there are still some managers who do not fully understand the purpose and roles of the modern internal auditor. Things have become, perhaps, even more confusing with other professions now having specialists who call themselves "auditors."

Part Two—Administering Internal Audit Activities.   The 10 chapters in this Part all discuss alternatives and recommended practices of how a modern internal audit function should be organized. The modern internal audit organization is an independent entity within the company and should be of service to all levels of the organization. Internal audit reports problems, suggests solutions, and acts as an overall evaluator. In order to maintain its independence, internal audit should report not to the CFO or some other member of management. Rather, the board of directors' audit committee is often the best independent authority to oversee a modern internal audit function, and Chapter 6 provides guidance on how to set up that reporting relationship, along with sample board-authorizing resolutions and internal audit reports.

Chapters 7, 8, and 9 discuss, respectively, organizing the internal audit activity, evaluating various risks to allow internal audit to better plan audit projects, and staffing the internal audit function. These chapters provide some basic guidance on building an effective internal audit organization, evaluating organizational and audit risks, and recruiting and training an internal audit staff. Evaluating audit risk, as covered in Chapter 8, is an important concept for all professionals involved in the audit process. Whether an audit manager looking at all entities and activities in the organization and developing an overall annual audit plan from this analysis or a staff member on a field assignment deciding on specific areas to investigate, internal auditors need a consistent approach to evaluating risks. Risk analysis allows internal audit to devote its always limited audit resources to the higher, more significant risk areas.

The effective internal audit function must spend significant amounts of its audit evaluation time in the ''field''—the various local and remote locations and organization activities. Although much can be accomplished through review of records on computerized databases and published reports, the effective internal auditor still needs to observe operations. Chapter 9 discusses ways to select people with appropriate skills to build an effective internal audit organization, approaches to provide them with ongoing training, and considerations for evaluating auditor effectiveness. Chapter 10 then provides approaches to managing that internal audit organization, particularly when auditors are working in the field. These two chapters are valuable for audit managers, from supervisor to director, as well as for staff auditors who have management aspirations.

A crucial part of the audit process is the auditor's documentation, which should include records of interviews, the results of tests performed, and other evidence supporting the audit work. This documentation is gathered together in what are called auditor ''workpapers,'' whether they be handwritten notes or computer-based files and reports. Chapter 11 discusses several approaches to prepare workpapers that effectively document all audits.

The computer is an invaluable tool for internal auditors. Chapter 12 discusses ways to develop computer-assisted audit procedures to allow the internal auditor to better analyze and evaluate computerized data. Even when using computer-assisted audit techniques, auditors are often faced with large volumes of audit evidence. Rather than examining all of this material or making arbitrary selections from it for audit tests, Chapter 13 discusses how to use audit or statistical sampling techniques to select appropriate samples of the audit data and then how to develop conclusions based upon the sample results. Finally, internal auditors historically have not taken advantage of computerized tools to better manage their own internal audit administrative work. Chapter 14 provides both suggestions and examples of reports developed to automate internal audit processes.

A formal report of an internal auditor's work—an audit report summarizing what was observed and what was found, and giving recommendations for improvement—is one of the most important functions of the internal audit process. Chapter 15 discusses different formats for audit reports and good, general techniques for communicating internal audit efforts. This chapter contains several examples of effective audit reports.

The ten chapters in this part should be useful for all members of the internal audit organization. They build on material found in the previous editions and provide guidance on building an effective internal audit department.

Part Three—Impact of Information Systems on Internal Auditing. The internal control implications of computer systems in the modern organization is an example of how this edition has changed from previous editions. The five chapters in Part Three provide background and help for internal auditors in this rapidly evolving field.

Chapter 16 covers reviews of data processing operations, reviews that were once limited to classic mainframe computer systems. This chapter discusses changes in these review techniques due to newer hardware and processing technologies, the growth of telecommunications, and the use of sophisticated systems in all areas of operations.

Computer hardware or equipment is of little value unless it uses effective computer programs, or applications. Chapter 17 discusses approaches to reviewing and evaluating controls in computer business applications while Chapter 18 discusses approaches for auditing newer systems under development. Although the concept of developing applications was once thought of as the process of writing programs from scratch—such as an organization writing its own payroll program—today we normally purchase software components. Auditors continue to have an important role in reviewing the controls that are built into these applications as well as the management controls over the projects necessary to implement them.

Chapter 19 discusses audit procedures for reviewing physical security, logical security such as the use of passwords, and contingency planning procedures. Contingency planning refers to the procedures that should be in place to get an organization's information systems back in operation after an unexpected and extended outage of some sort. This chapter discusses contingency planning both for the classic mainframe or centralized computer systems as well as for the newer networked or client-server systems.

Part Three ends with a chapter on new and evolving computer systems technologies and some of the internal audit concerns associated with these technologies. This message is always difficult in this type of book as technologies evolve and in some cases all but disappear very quickly. Chapter 20 looks at a series of issues that appear to be on the horizon and which may soon impact internal auditors in their reviews of internal controls.

Part Four—Areas for Operational Auditing. As discussed, Brink's original book introduced the concept of operational auditing to a world where people known as internal auditors did little more than test fairly basic financial controls. Prior editions—as well as this one—introduce operational concepts in various functional areas to help the internal auditor hone in on specific areas of potential control concern. Part Four contains ten chapters that provide some specific internal audit control review guidance in important areas of operations. After Chapter 21, which provides a general introduction to planning and performing an operational review, the chapters in Part Four are as follows: Chapter 22, Accounting Systems and Controls; Chapter 23, Manufacturing Production Planning; Chapter 24, Purchases, Receipts, and Electronic Data Interchange; Chapter 25, Distribution and Transportation; Chapter 26, Engineering, Research, Quality, and Quality Control; Chapter 27, Fixed Assets and Capital Projects; Chapter 28, Sales, Marketing, and Advertising; Chapter 29, Payroll and Personnel; and Chapter 30, Financial Management.

Each of these chapters provides a description of the specific operational areas and then takes on the audit issues associated with the area, dividing them between financial, operational, and information systems audit concerns. Tables of suggested audit procedures or questionnaires, as appropriate, are included in each chapter. In addition, most chapters contain suggested audit report findings and recommendations in specific operational areas. The audit report comments should help internal auditors to develop better report comments in their own operational reviews.

These materials represent a major addition to this new edition; prior editions provided more general guidance, but this new editon gives some detailed materials that the staff or senior internal auditors can use to develop specific audit programs.

Part Five—Special Audit Activities. The world of internal auditing is constantly changing and expanding. Part Five covers three of these areas. Chapter 31 discusses loss prevention and fraud investigations. Historically, internal auditors did not get much involved with fraud-related investigations. With the elimination of traditional company security functions in today's leaner, more efficient organization, internal audit is often called in to help with loss prevention and fraud-related activities. Chapter 32 then discusses coordination with external auditors. These two audit groups have always worked together, but today standards are in place on both sides to make this process more formal and expansive. Finally, Chapter 33 discusses internal audit quality assurance reviews. This chapter tries to answer the old question, "But who audits the auditor?"

Part Six—Internal Audit Future Directions.   The scope of modern internal audit activities is always changing and often expanding. This Part examines it from three directions. Chapter 34 considers the overall changing role of audit activities. Internal audit was once essentially limited to formal audit activities, resulting in traditional audit reports; this chapter looks at how the role of internal auditing is expanding. Vic Brink's *service to management* concept is readily accepted at face value today, and auditors are being asked to operate in a variety of expanded roles. In addition, the public today takes a much more critical view of business practices than in the past. Finally, Chapter 35 discusses the evolving field of business ethics and the social responsibilities of organizations as well as the potential role of internal auditors in this whole process.

There have been many changes in the profession of internal auditing in the over 50 years since Vic Brink published his first edition. Brink's emphasis on *service to management* and the efforts of others in the profession to promote this type of duty have done much to make internal auditing a vital, important part of the modern organization. An objective of this edition is to promote that concept and to provide help for internal auditors to build and develop new tools and skills to allow them to be even more effective in internal audit activities.

CONTENTS

PART ONE

FOUNDATIONS OF INTERNAL AUDITING

CHAPTER 1

Foundations of Internal Auditing

1-1 WHAT IS INTERNAL AUDITING?

There is no better way to begin this book about modern internal auditing than to refer to the Institute of Internal Auditors (IIA), the professional association of internal auditors. The IIA's Standards for the Professional Practice of Internal Auditing contain the following definition:

> *Internal auditing is an independent appraisal function established within an organization to examine and evaluate its activities as a service to the organization.*

This statement becomes more meaningful when one focuses on the key terms. *Auditing* suggests a variety of ideas. It can be viewed very narrowly, as the checking of arithmetic accuracy or physical existence of accounting records, or more broadly, as a thoughtful review and appraisal at the highest organizational level. In this book, we use the term *auditing* to include this total range of levels of service, from detailed checking to high-level appraisals.

The term *internal* defines work carried on within the organization by its own employees. Internal auditing work is distinguished from such audit-related work carried on by outside public accountants or other parties (such as government regulators) who are not directly a part of the particular organization.

The remainder of the IIA's statement covers a number of important terms that apply to internal auditing work. For example:

- *Independent* is used for auditing that is free of restrictions that could significantly limit the scope and effectiveness of the review or the later reporting of resultant findings and conclusions.

- *Appraisal* confirms the need for an evaluation that is the thrust of internal auditors as they develop their conclusions.

- *Established* confirms that internal audit is a formal, definitive function in the modern organization.

- *Examine and evaluate* describe the active roles of internal auditors, first for fact-finding inquiries and then for judgmental evaluations.

- *Its activities* confirm the broad jurisdictional scope of internal audit work that applies to all of the activities of the modern organization.

- *Service* reveals that help and assistance to management and other members of the organization are the end products of all internal auditing work.

- *To the organization* confirms that internal audit's total service scope pertains to the entire organization, including all personnel, the board of directors and their audit committee, stockholders, and other owners.

A better understanding of internal auditing can be obtained by recognizing that it is an organizational control that functions by measuring and evaluating the effectiveness of other controls. When an organization establishes its planning and then proceeds to implement its plans in terms of operations, it must do something to monitor the operations to assure the achievement of its established objectives. These further efforts can be thought of as *controls.* While the internal audit function is itself one of the types of controls used, there is a wide range of other controls. The special role of internal audit is to help measure and evaluate those other controls. Thus, internal auditors must understand both their own role as a control function and the nature and scope of other types of controls in the organization.

Internal auditors who do their job effectively become experts in what makes for the best possible design and implementation of all types of controls. This expertise includes understanding the interrelationships of various controls and their best possible integration in the total system of internal control. It is thus through the control door that internal auditors come to examine and evaluate all organizational activities and to provide maximum service to the organization. Internal auditors cannot be expected to equal—let alone exceed—the technical and operational expertise pertaining to the various activities of the organization. However, internal auditors can help the responsible individuals achieve more effective results by appraising existing controls and providing a basis for helping to improve those controls.

1-2 HISTORY

It is normal for any activity—including a control activity such as internal auditing—to come into being as a result of emerging needs. The business organization of 1942, when modern internal auditing was just getting started, had no need for computer systems specialists. Aside from some electromechanical devices and activities in research laboratories, the computer system did not exist. Organizations had no need for computer programmers until these machines started to become useful for various record-keeping and other computational functions. Similarly, organizations had very rudimentary telephone connections where switchboard operators routed all incoming calls to a limited number of desktop telephones. Today, we are all connected through a vast, automated worldwide web of telecommunications. The increasing complexity of modern business and other organizations has created the need for a similar specialist in various business controls: the internal auditor.

We can also understand better the nature of internal auditing today if we know something about the changing conditions in the past and the different needs these changes created. What is the simplest or most primitive form of internal auditing and how did it come into existence? How has internal auditing responded to changing needs?

At its most primitive level, a self-assessment or internal auditing function can exist when any single person sits back and surveys something that he or she has done. At that point, the individual asks him- or herself how well a particular task has been accomplished and, perhaps, how it might be done better if it were to be done again. If a second person is involved in this activity, the assessment function would be expanded to include an evaluation of the second person's participation in the endeavor. In a small business, the owner or manager will be doing this review to some extent for all of the employees. In all of these situations, the assessment or internal audit function is being carried out directly as a part of a basic management role. However, as the operations of an organization become more voluminous and complex, it is no longer practicable for the owner or top manager to have enough contact with all operations to satisfactorily review the effectiveness of performance. These responsibilities need to be delegated.

Although this hypothetical senior manager could build a supervisory system to try to provide a personal overview of operations, that same manager will find it increasingly difficult to know whether the interests of the organization are being properly served as the organization grows larger and more complex. Are established procedures being complied with? Are assets being properly safeguarded? Are the various employees functioning efficiently? Are the current approaches still effective in the light of changing conditions?

The ultimate response to these questions is that the manager must obtain further help by assigning one or more individuals to be directly responsible for reviewing activities and reporting on the above-mentioned types of questions. It is here that the internal auditing activity comes into being in a formal and explicit sense. The first internal auditing assignments usually originated to satisfy very basic and sharply defined operational needs. The earliest special concern of management was whether the assets of the organization were being properly protected, whether company procedures and policies were being complied with, and whether financial records were being accurately maintained. There was also considerable emphasis on maintenance of the status quo. To a great extent, this internal auditing effort was viewed as a closely related extension of the work of external auditors.

The result of all of these factors was that early internal auditors were viewed as playing a relatively narrow role in their organizations, with relatively limited responsibility in the total managerial spectrum. An early internal auditor was viewed as a financially oriented checker of records and more of a police officer than a coworker. In some organizations, internal auditors had major responsibilities for reconciling canceled payroll checks with bank statements or checking the mathematics in regular business documents. In retail organizations, internal auditors often were responsible for reconciling daily cash sales to register receipts.

Understanding the history of internal auditing is important because the old image still exists to some extent for modern internal auditors. This is so even though the character of the internal auditing function is now very different. Over a period of time, the operations of various organizations increased in volume and complexity, creating managerial problems and new pressures on senior management. In response to these pressures, management recognized the possibilities for better utilization of their internal auditors. Here were individuals already set up in an audit function, and there seemed to be every good reason for getting greater value from these individuals with relatively little increase in cost.

At the same time, internal auditors perceived these opportunities and initiated new types of services themselves. Thus, internal auditors gradually took on broader and more management-oriented responsibilities in their work efforts. Because internal auditing was initially accounting-oriented, this upward trend was felt first in the accounting and financial-control areas. Rather than just report the same accounting-related exceptions—such as some documentation lacking a supervisor's initial—internal auditors began to question the overall control process they were reviewing. Subsequently, internal audit evaluation work was extended to include many nonfinancial areas in the organization.

In 1942, IIA was launched. Its first membership chapter was started in New York City, with Chicago soon to follow. The IIA was formed by people who were given the title internal auditor by their organizations and wanted to both share experiences and gain knowledge with others in this new professional field. A profession was born that has undergone many changes over subsequent years and has resulted in the type of modern internal auditor discussed in this edition of Brink's original book.

New business initiatives, such as the COSO internal control standards discussed in Chapter 2 or the Foreign Corrupt Practices Act of the late 1970s, have caused a continuing increase in the need for the services of internal auditors. In addition, some newer environmental forces have created needs in such areas as protection from industrial hazards, support of quality-control programs, and different levels of business responsibility, including ethical standards. The need for ethical standards includes higher standards for corporate management, greater involvement of boards of directors (including their audit committees), a more active role for stockholders, and greater independence of the outside public accountant. Ethics and social responsibility issues will be discussed in Chapter 35. As a result of these new pressures, the services of internal auditors have become more important to all interested parties. There are now more and better-qualified internal auditing personnel and a higher level of organization status and importance attached to the position. The IIA has grown from its first, 25-member charter chapter in 1942, to an international association with over 60,000 members and 200 local chapters worldwide. At the same time, the importance of internal audit has been recognized by external auditors through their auditing standards, as will be discussed in Chapter 32. The internal audit profession has reached a major level of maturity and is well positioned for continuing dynamic growth.

Internal auditing today involves a broad spectrum of types of operational activity and levels of coverage. In most organizations today, internal auditing has moved beyond being a staff activity roughly tied to the controller's organization, although internal audit's role is constantly being redefined. In some other organizations, internal audit is functioning at just a routine compliance level. In other situations, internal audit still suffers from being integrated too closely with regular accounting activities and limits virtually all of its audit work to strictly financial areas. These are all exceptions that do not reflect the potential capabilities of the modern internal audit organization. They may also reflect the lack of progressive attitudes in the overall organization.

Today, internal audit has expanded its activities to all operational areas of the organization and has established itself as a valued and respected part of the top management effort. To an increasing extent, the modern internal auditor is actively serving the board of directors, usually via its audit committee. While internal audit organizations once had an almost nonexistent, dotted line reporting relationship to the audit committee—with little direct communication—the director of internal audit in many organizations today has an active level of communication with that same audit committee. This overall situation reflects major progress in the scope of internal audit's coverage and level of service to all areas of the organization. The internal auditing profession itself, through its own self-development and dedication, has contributed to this progress and has set the stage for a continuing upward trend. Internal audit's service responsibilities to the audit committee will be discussed in Chapter 6.

(a) COMPOSITE NATURE OF OPERATIONAL AND FINANCIAL AUDITING

During the 1960s, there was a strong tendency for many to adopt the label of *operational auditing* in place of the traditional *internal auditing*. The rationale was that *internal auditing* was a term tied too closely with basic financial auditing, including the review of both financial control activities and financial statements. Internal auditors called themselves operational auditors because of their desire to focus more of their efforts on the other operational activities in the organization that could potentially point to areas for increased profit and overall management service. In its most extreme form, the so-called operational auditing function would disassociate itself entirely from the so-called financial areas. They would claim, for example, to have no expertise on the financial controls surrounding an accounts receivable operation. Rather, they might look at procedural controls and ignore the issue of whether the cash received was properly recorded in correct accounts. Management often became confused and dismayed when their internal auditors all but ignored important accounting or financial-related issues.

This separation of responsibility involved matters of both substance and self-interest for the *operational audit*–oriented internal auditors. Traditionally, internal auditors had been concerned with accounting and financial matters, and some expertise in these areas had generally been considered to be essential. The coverage of these matters had also served to provide an opportunity for expanding the range of internal audit services into the broader operational areas. Since accounting or financial records directly or indirectly reflect all operational activities, financially oriented reviews performed by internal auditors open the door to the other activities. This type of extension has been most advantageous, and the combination of operational and financial as well as information systems auditing will be considered throughout this book.

In terms of strategy, an internal audit abandonment of accounting and financial areas can create a vacuum that would invite the emergence of other audit-type functions. Chapter 26, for example, will discuss how many traditional internal auditors ignored the International Standards Organization (ISO) ''quality'' movement in its early days, leading to an almost separate profession of quality standards auditors. An organization certainly needs to have someone covering the accounting and financial areas, and the responsibilities of whomever does that will inevitably spill over into an overview of broader operational areas. The failure to cover key financial areas is one of the arguments external audit firms may make to senior management when they seek to provide internal audit outsourcing services. Therefore, internal audit needs to cover accounting and financial areas for their own self-interest, if for no other reason. Internal audit outsourcing will be discussed in Chapter 34, which deals with internal audit's changing role and future prospects.

Some internal audit functions will feel that a continuing connection with financial auditing hinders their effort to adequately reach the potentials of operational auditing. They will argue that external auditors can more appropriately cover areas of financial control risk. Other internal audit functions prefer to perform work in both areas but to deal with them separately. On balance, however, there is an important linkage between the so-called financial and nonfinancial areas, and it is desirable to recognize and to take advantage of that linkage. Similarly, what were once called *EDP auditors* (or information systems auditors) should not operate separately and independently from other internal audit activities. All internal audit efforts should be shaped, with specialized types of emphasis, to serve overall organizational needs in the most effective manner possible. Therefore, operational, financial, and information systems auditing should be able to find a full expression within the framework of modern internal auditing. There should no longer be operational, financial, or computer auditors, but only good modern internal auditors.

1-3 INTERNAL AUDITING IN TODAY'S ORGANIZATION

A better understanding of the nature of internal auditing comes by examining the relationship between internal auditing and the organization's other activities. The work of internal audit needs to be detached from the regular day-to-day operations of the organization. A good practical test is that if internal auditing activity were to be temporarily inactivated, either partially or completely, regular organization operations should be able to continue in their normal manner. The reasons for detachment are very practical. To the extent that the internal auditing group is charged with day-to-day activities such as validating disbursements, reconciling bank accounts, approving movements of assets, and the like, internal audit's separate and supplementary review has ceased to exist. Instead, internal audit activities have simply taken the place of regular accounting or other operational responsibilities.

At times, management may be tempted to assign operational responsibilities to internal audit, but when this is done, the result is the loss of internal audit's independent review. The effective modern internal audit function must recognize its relation as an important *independent* entity with strong relationships to the audit committee of the board of directors, to the external auditors who are hired by the board and who have special responsibilities to the outside, and to organization management.

(a) RELATIONSHIP OF INTERNAL AUDIT WITH THE BOARD OF DIRECTORS

As a result of the previously mentioned environmental pressures, boards of directors today play a more active role and assume increased responsibilities in their relationships with organization management, the stockholders, and other stakeholders. One of the ways in which the board has coped with its increased responsibilities is through the expansion of the role of its audit committee. Although this role is continually evolving, it normally includes an overview of the completeness and integrity of the financial statements, the effectiveness of the system of internal control, and the adequacy of the total audit effort. Assessing the total audit effect requires relations with both the independent auditors and internal audit. Although the more usual arrangement is for internal audit to report administratively to either the chief executive officer or chief financial officer, the need also exists for defined reporting and assistance to the audit committee. As will be discussed in more detail in Chapter 6 and other chapters, internal audit customarily has a dual relationship with organization management and the audit committee. In both relationships, internal audit must appropriately coordinate its work with that of the independent public accountant—the external auditors.

(b) RELATIONSHIP OF INTERNAL AUDIT WITH THE EXTERNAL AUDITORS

As previously discussed, the earlier view of internal auditing was as an extension of the external audit effort. In many cases, early internal auditing programs were designed by the organization's external auditors primarily to assist the needs of that outside audit function. Internal auditing personnel were frequently recruited from the public accounting profession and their approach was often oriented to public accounting auditing standards and interests. Internal audit and their management now generally recognize that despite certain common interests, internal and external audit priorities are quite different. External auditors have a primary responsibility to parties outside the client organization, while internal auditors have a primary responsibility to the organization. An external audit is interested more specifically in the soundness of the financial statements, whereas an internal audit is concerned predominantly with the overall effectiveness of the company operations, its control procedures, and resulting profitability. The situation becomes a little more complex, however, when senior management contracts with an external auditing firm to provide them with internal audit services through an outsourcing arrangement. Internal audit outsourcing will be discussed in Chapter 34.

Although both audit groups have different primary missions, there are many common interests that provide the basis for extensive coordination efforts, which will be discussed in more detail in Chapter 32. These common interests stem from the fact that the soundness of the organization's system of internal control is an important basis for each group's achieving its primary mission. This relationship has become especially important because of such actions as the requirement in the Foreign Corrupt Practices Act of 1977 (FCPA) that corporations maintain a system of sound internal accounting control, and the U.S. Securities and Exchange Commission requirements for a report from management covering the adequacy of their system of internal control. Newer internal control requirements, often called COSO report standards, as well as the FCPA and other internal control standards, will be discussed in Chapter 2.

(c) RELATIONSHIP OF INTERNAL AUDIT WITH ORGANIZATION MANAGEMENT

Internal auditors must recognize that they occupy a staff function in the organization, and should never attempt to usurp the roles and responsibilities of other departments or individuals. Line management should have the basic responsibility for their own particular sphere of the operations and this responsibility should never be shifted to internal audit. This does not mean that internal audit should be without responsibility. Internal audit has a strong responsibility to do a job that is competent in a professional sense. If internal audit were to relieve line personnel of their responsibilities, this would weaken the motivation of the line managers and lessen the value of their roles. Thus, the findings and recommendations of internal audit should always be informative and advisory, and should in no way carry any direct authority to command specific actions. Such authority must be determined by the line personnel, based on the soundness and persuasiveness of the particular audit findings and recommendations.

There will always be an unavoidable overlap of internal audit's role with other organization activities. In principle, all personnel in an organization should be committed to doing their particular jobs effectively and helping to achieve maximum organization welfare. This commitment increases as one goes up the organizational ladder, including the various staff areas. Thus, a financial analysis group, a quality assurance group, or some other staff function might be very much concerned with operational analysis and assistance. Frequently, special task forces will be created as well to study designated organizational problems. What, then, is so unique about the role of internal audit in providing analysis and service? The answer here is that internal audit is the *one function* in the modern organization that is completely detached from both the operational components and functional staff groups (such as finance or marketing), and that can look at the various problems independently and in terms of overall control procedures.

Internal audit's competence in the analysis of internal control systems, as well as their understanding of the design and implementation of controls, gives them a needed credential to round out their overall professional capabilities. No other group in the organization so well combines the fact of detachment, the objectives of organizational service to the organization, and the major competence in the field of control.

1-4 FUTURE DIRECTIONS

The development of the profession of internal auditing has largely been centered in business organizations. Although this tie continues in the treatment of many internal control problems within the framework of business organizations, it unduly denies the universal applicability of internal auditing to all types of organizations. Moreover, this view fails to recognize that some of the most progressive internal auditing is now being done by nonbusiness types of organizations. The federal government auditors in the General Accounting Office (GAO) as well as defense contract auditors both conduct sophisticated audits. Subsequent chapters will attempt to incorporate and discuss some of these techniques, where appropriate.

A related fact here is that many organizations are a blend of business and nonbusiness activities. For example, a governmental entity such as the New York Port Authority has been created and charged with the responsibility for operating public-service facilities as a business. Other similar examples exist within the U.S. federal government. All of these developments confirm that the need for internal auditing exists in all types of organizations where the complexity of the activities, the volume of transactions, and the dependence on large numbers of people exist in some combination to create operational problems. Organizations can exist for a variety of purposes, but there are always tasks to be performed and objectives to be achieved. All organizations should have a common objective to utilize their available resources in the most productive manner possible to achieve overall organizational objectives. In that endeavor, all responsible managers require effective internal control mechanisms and can utilize the assistance of internal audit.

Thus, all types of organizations have a need for internal auditing services, and there is a common body of professional knowledge that applies to all of these varied internal audit activities. Another aspect of internal audit's universal applicability is that there is potentially a need for the services of internal audit at any organizational level in any particular organization. This means there are legitimate needs for internal auditing services by the stockholders, the board of directors, and by the responsible management. The controlling principle here is that whenever organizational responsibilities are established, there are potential needs for internal auditing services, which should be provided in some way and at some level.

All of an organization's needs might be served by a central internal audit group, provided that the central group can structure and administer the total operation in a sufficiently competent manner. In other cases, organizational components may be best served by an internal auditing group of their own that is directly responsible to the central group. What is important, however, is that internal auditing needs are directly linked to all organizational components. The organization of internal audit activities will be discussed in Chapter 7, Evaluating Organization and Audit Risk.

   This chapter has described the background and development of the profession of internal auditing, how the modern internal auditor serves management at all levels, and how this management service should apply to all organizational activities. The following chapters will discuss how an internal audit function might be organized and how modern internal auditors can perform effective reviews in a large variety of areas.

CHAPTER 2

Fundamentals of Control

2-1 IMPORTANCE OF INTERNAL CONTROL

Internal control is the most important and fundamental concept that an internal auditor must understand. An internal auditor reviews both operational and financial areas of the organization with an objective of evaluating internal controls. Virtually all internal audit procedures focus on some form of this evaluation of internal controls. Although internal control has been defined in different ways, the effective internal auditor must use a consistent definition of internal control and have a good understanding of the concepts of internal control evaluations. This chapter discusses the importance of controls in the total management process and provides a framework for such evaluations.

Lawrence (Larry) Sawyer, a contemporary of Vic Brink, has called control evaluations the auditor's "Open Sesame."[1] That is, an internal auditor's skills at evaluating internal controls in various specialized areas of an organization will open doors throughout the organization. The examination and appraisal of controls are normally components, either directly or indirectly, of every type of internal auditing assignment. An internal auditor's special competence in the control-evaluation area justifies reviews covering a wide range of operational activities, even though the auditor may not possess specialized knowledge about the operational details surrounding those activities. The chapter considers both the basic fundamentals of control and the underlying concepts and definition of internal controls. That definition is used by a wide group of interested parties, internal and external auditors, management, regulators, and others. All levels of management will accept this special role of internal audit and will look to their skills to both evaluate strengths and weaknesses of their controls and to suggest any improvements.

The Introduction described internal auditing as an organizational control itself, one that functions by measuring and evaluating the effectiveness of other controls operating elsewhere within the organization. The understanding of basic control concepts and evaluating systems of internal control should be the major concern and interest of all internal auditors.

---

[1] Lawrence B. Sawyer, *The Practice of Modern Internal Auditing* (Altamonte Springs, Fl.: The Institute of Internal Auditors, 1988).

2-2 BASIC NATURE OF CONTROL

An internal auditor is faced with two challenges in attempting to review controls in the organization. First, the internal auditor needs to have a good understanding of the nature of controls, *a definition of a control system*. Next, the internal auditor needs to understand the overall concept of the types and nature of an organization's operating internal controls. The first of these two concepts, the idea of a control system, is perhaps the easier. This concept goes back to the basic principles of mechanical and paperwork procedures that exist throughout one's everyday life. The following discussion will provide some definitions of a control system. Following this, we will provide a definition of the objectives and components of an internal control system, a key component of many audit review activities.

Control systems are needed in all areas of activity, both inside and outside the organization. In most respects, the concepts and principles used are the same no matter where the control system is encountered. The automobile can provide a good analogy of a control system. When the accelerator is pressed, the automobile goes faster. When the brake is pressed, the automobile slows or stops. When the steering wheel is turned, the vehicle turns. The driver *controls* the automobile. If the driver does not use the accelerator, brake, or steering wheel properly, the automobile will operate *out of control.*

An organization is similar to an automobile. There are a variety of systems at work, such as the manufacturing and sales process, computer information systems, and the accounting system. If management does not operate or direct these systems properly, the organization may operate out of control. The control of an organization, of course, is much more complicated. The internal auditor first develops an understanding of these control systems and then assesses them to determine if the components of the system are properly connected and if management is properly operating the controls that allow it to manage the system. This type of system or process is often referred to as the organization's *internal control* or *control* system.

(a) A SIMPLE CONTROL SYSTEM

The concept of internal control is not particularly complex, and simple control processes and procedures are often ignored. Internal audit is often called on to describe control systems to management and to convince them of the importance of controls even when management has other priorities. The internal auditor must be a spokesperson for the importance of control. To be effective, an auditor must have a good understanding of basic control system concepts as well as internal control objectives and components.

Another very simple illustration of the control system is a sailboat that sets sail for a given port with a planned arrival date. At interim points, progress is determined through the use of various navigational aids. Because of prevailing winds, or weather conditions, the boat may travel off course or schedule. As a result, changes in direction are made necessary, sail settings may have to be modified, and there will be a revision of the scheduled arrival. The captain of the boat operates the control system here by considering and evaluating the impact of the new developments in actual progress, and then providing proper adjustments in sail settings or other supplementary actions. The captain's control system contributes to the boat reaching its destination on a timely basis and in the most efficient manner practicable. However, unforeseen weather conditions can cause significant scheduling problems.

The purpose of any control system is to attain or maintain a desired state or condition. The system of internal control should be able to satisfy various objectives established by management for that control area. A basic control system has four elements.

1. *Detector or Sensor.* There must be some type of measuring device that detects what is happening in the particular element of the system being controlled—for example, a thermostat in the home that connects to the furnace. An internal auditor often is the sensor who observes some problem while working on some other issue.

2. *Selector or Standard.* The detector that reports on current conditions must have some type of a standard to compare what is actually happening to what should be happening. The thermostat is set to a desired temperature linked to a thermometer that measures the actual temperature. Fluctuation in temperature above or below the user-supplied setting causes the furnace to take action. Internal audit standards that serve that purpose are discussed in Chapter 5.

3. *Effector or Controller.* The control system element alters the behavior of the area under control based on the comparison of detector and standard results. The thermostat turns off the furnace when the heat reaches some certain predetermined level and restarts the furnace again when the level drops.

4. *Communications Network.* The control system communications network is simply a vehicle for transmitting messages between the control sensor and the entity being controlled. A home heating thermostat has a connection between the sensor on the furnace—usually away from the living area—and the measuring unit in the home living space.

These four elements can be called a control system because they are separate but interrelated components of an overall control process. Figure 2.1 illustrates such a concep-

Figure 2.1   Elements of a Control System

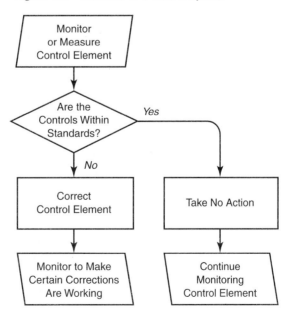

tual control system. There are many other examples of these types of control systems in everyday life. The same elements repeat themselves in more complex systems. Many processes in a business organization do not have the level of automatic control system because formal detection devices are not in place. However, even manual systems have control elements. For example, the approval system for reviewing documentation, approving, and paying employee travel expenses has the elements of a control system. Also internal auditors often serve as a type of control system detection device, as described above, by helping to make sure that the control system is working effectively. This chapter discusses the components of an internal control system as installed in the modern organization.

(b) ELEMENTS OF A CONTROL SYSTEM

All too often, people think of control systems in terms of complex mechanical devices or computer information systems. This limited perspective is not correct. Different types of control systems or processes exist at all levels in the organization and in everyday activities. Any established automated or manual process can be considered a control system. The basic nature of these systems can be understood in terms of the major elements or phases of the total management process. An internal auditor often needs to look at a process—such as the ordering of goods to be placed in stores inventory—and needs to understand how that process works. That understanding begins with planning the audit review and the related establishment of audit objectives. Planning is supported by data developed from ongoing operations as well as through overall management strategies and external information. The planning element of the control system provides input to the next element, budgeting, which in turn feeds the operating, measurement, reporting, and analysis phases of the management control system. A management control system for the approval of travel expense reports is shown in Figure 2.2. This and most complete business processes generally contain the following elements:

- *Planning*. This is the process for deciding on appropriate control programs for the organization, both for continuing and new efforts. The planning of changes to ongoing control processes should be modified through reviews of the results of past activities. The planning process is also influenced by overall management strategies as well as by information from various external sources. An internal audit report discussing a control weakness in some area might be such an external source.

- *Budgeting*. A control budget is a plan expressed in monetary or related quantitative terms. The budget provides a standard or selector for measuring ongoing performance. Due to changes in conditions over the operating period, a control budget may be subject to revisions.

- *Operating and Measurement*. This is the element in the control system that covers what the organization actually does. In a manufacturing organization, for example, resources are used to produce a product that is then sold. Records of costs and performance are maintained in order to monitor the progress of the operation. Control is influenced in this phase by internal and external sources. Internal audit is one of those sources to this phase. An internal audit report can describe control weaknesses that may require immediate corrective action.

Figure 2.2   Control System Example

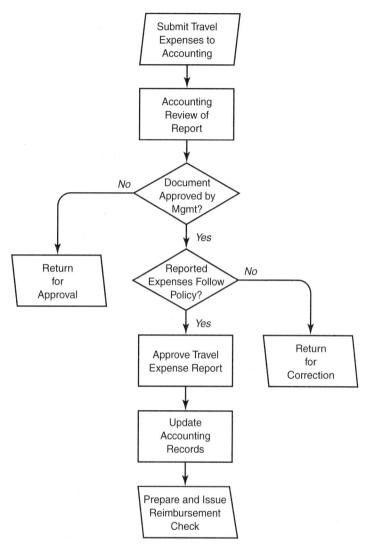

- *Reporting and Analysis.* This is the effector and controller element in the control system. Operating results are compared to budgeted standards and adjustments are made as required. This phase also provides communication links to other elements of the control system in order to allow corrective action if required.

The control system illustrated in Figure 2.2 describes a basic management process for approving employee travel expense reports. This figure describes a process that typically has many variations or exceptions, since things seldom work out exactly as planned. That is, not all documents will flow from the approver's desk to the processing station. Questions or exceptions may route the travel expense documents on different paths. The underlying details or documentation may be incomplete, and errors may be made. Supplementary measures and actions provide appropriate measures on progress and provide the basis for further corrective action to better assure the achievement of objectives. The control function supplied by internal audit is concerned with providing these supplementary measures, actions, and procedures.

(c) DETECTIVE AND PROTECTIVE CORRECTIVE CONTROL TECHNIQUES

Following the control system illustrated in Figure 2.1, control techniques can be further categorized as *preventive, detective, corrective,* or a combination of the three. The sum of these three basic control techniques should provide management with reasonable assurance that a particular process is operating properly.

- *Preventive controls* are built into a system to prevent an error or undetected event from happening. A very elementary type of preventive control is an organization structure that establishes a separation of duties over certain functions. Another preventive control is a locked door to prevent unauthorized access to critical equipment.
- *Detective controls* are designed to alert management of errors or problems as they occur, or shortly after. A cash count and reconciliation of cash register sales at the end of the day is an example of such a detective control. An alarm that sounds when the locked door is forced open is another detective control technique.
- *Corrective controls* are used in conjunction with detective controls to recover from the consequences of the undesired events. An insurance policy to pay for losses is one type of corrective control. A guard to apprehend the intruder who forced open the locked door and sounded the alarm is a corrective control technique.

Preventive, detective, and corrective control techniques are important elements in an overall system of control. While it is often more cost-effective to install preventive controls in a system, detective controls are also needed, and detective controls are of little value unless some form of corrective action or control is also in place. In many instances, internal audit acts as a type of detective control to determine, among other things, that the preventive controls are working properly. Because internal auditors are not ''police officers,'' however, management must implement the corrective actions to respond to any reported control findings. Since these controls should always be tied directly or indirectly to control objectives that may vary widely in nature and scope, the manner in which control is exercised can also vary. Preventive, detective, and corrective controls can be considered to operate on three different levels.

1. *Steering Controls.* One level of control is through the identification of events that will prompt interim action contributory to the achievement of larger objectives. These interim events can be very precise or very broad. The common characteristic of steering controls is that they are usually preventive and call attention to the need to take managerial action on a timely basis. In the case of the skipper of the sailboat previously mentioned, the drift of the boat to one side due to winds indicates the need for some steering action. Various types of gauges in a manufacturing process indicate conditions that require particular processing actions. A drop in dealer orders

may highlight the problem of declining market acceptance and the related need to adjust production schedules. In other cases, a broad index of economic trends can alert management to changing conditions that should spark protective or other opportunity-oriented actions.

2. *Yes-No Controls.* These controls are designed to function more automatically, to be protective, and to assure the accomplishment of desired results. In their simplest form, a yes-no control could be a quality-control gauge on a mechanized assembly line that checks product parts for exact specifications. Parts that are out of tolerance are routed to a rework area. This control could also be a required approval signature on a business form to help ensure that an authorized individual has reviewed the document. The common element here is a preestablished control device or arrangement that, under normal conditions, will more or less automatically assure desired protective or improved actions.

3. *Post-Action Controls.* A third control somewhat overlaps with the other two controls discussed, but is distinctive because managerial action comes later and takes the form of after-the-fact corrective action. The action may be taken to repair a product that has been damaged or to dismiss or reassign an employee. That after-the-fact action happens immediately or may require extended analysis. The analyses done by internal auditors are typically directed to recommending the most effective type of after-the-fact action, even though that action may be very much future-oriented. This recommendation can be directed to correcting established preventive, detective, or corrective types of control.

The modern internal auditor needs to understand these very basic control system concepts. This will be useful whenever the auditor is asked to document and understand a system or process. If the auditor is unfamiliar with this type of control system thinking, it is often a good idea to try documenting some very simple processes in order to understand the types of controls in place for those purposes.

2-3 INTERNAL CONTROL AND INTERNAL AUDIT

The preceding sections described control systems, a very important concept for the modern internal auditor. The discussion following defines internal control in the modern organization. This definition can be used by internal auditors asked to assess whether internal controls are adequate in an organization. In order to successfully perform an audit review and to report to management that internal controls are adequate in a given area, all parties need to use a consistent definition for internal control.

This section briefly describes some of the past definitions used for internal control and presents a definition of internal control that was introduced in the United States in 1992 and has been accepted by virtually all professional auditing and accounting organizations. This definition should provide the internal auditor with a general understanding of the objectives and components of a system of internal control. These internal control concepts are very important for the modern internal auditor and will be used in other chapters in this book.

(a) EARLY DEFINITIONS OF INTERNAL CONTROL SYSTEMS

The concept of control or internal control has been used by auditors since the very early days of auditing to define the process of how management mechanisms work. In the first edition of this book, Brink talked about the importance of understanding and evaluating internal control systems and provided the basis of a definition of internal control that was used to launch the internal audit profession. Other interested parties, such as external auditors, each developed their own definitions of internal control, which were similar but not totally consistent.

The definitions of internal control used by both the American Institute of Certified Public Accountants (AICPA) and the Canadian Institute of Chartered Accountants (CICA) are of special interest to internal auditors because of the role of certified public accountants (CPAs) or, in Canada, Chartered Accountants (CAs), who express independent opinions as to the fairness of the financial statements of their clients. For example, in the United States, these definitions have been used as a guide by the Securities and Exchange Commission (SEC) in developing regulations covering the enforcement of the Securities Exchange Act of 1934 and later, the Foreign Corrupt Practices Act of 1977. Although there have been changes over the years, the AICPA's first codified standards were called the Statement on Auditing Standards (SAS No. 1[2]). This standard covered the practice of financial statement auditing in the United States for many years and used the following definition for internal control.

> *Internal control comprises the plan of organization and all of the coordinate methods and measures adopted with a business to safeguard its assets, check the accuracy and reliabililty of its accounting data, promote operational efficiency, and encourage adherence to prescribed managerial policies.*

Other earlier clarifications and definitions in the original AICPA SAS No. 1 then further defined two elements of that internal control plan.

> Administrative control *includes, but is not limited to, the plan of organization and the procedures and records that are concerned with the decision processes leading to management's authorization of transactions. Such authorization is a management function directly associated with the responsibility for achieving the objectives of the organization and is the starting point for establishing accounting control of transactions.*

> Accounting control *comprises the plan of organization and the procedures and records that are concerned with the safeguarding of assets and the reliability of financial records and consequently are designed to provide reasonable assurance that:*

> a. *Transactions are executed in accordance with management's general or specific authorization.*
> b. *Transactions are recorded as necessary (1) to permit preparation of financial statements in conformity with generally accepted accounting principles or any other criteria applicable to such statement and (2) to maintain accountability for assets.*

---

[2] American Institute of Certified Public Accountants, "Statement on Auditing Standards No. 1" (New York: AICPA).

    c. Access to assets is permitted only in accordance with management's authorization.

    d. The recorded accountability for assets is compared with the existing assets at reasonable intervals and appropriate action is taken with respect to any differences.

The overlapping relationship of these two types of internal control was then further clarified in these pre-1988 AICPA standards:

> *The foregoing definitions are not necessarily mutually exclusive because some of the procedures and records comprehended in accounting control may also be involved in administrative control. For example, sales and cost records classified by products may be used for accounting control purposes and also in making management decisions concerning unit prices or other aspects of operations. Such multiple uses of procedures or records, however, are not critical for the purposes of this section because it is concerned primarily with clarifying the outer boundary of accounting control. Examples of records used solely for administrative control are those pertaining to customers contacted by salesmen and to defective work by production employees maintained only for evaluation personnel per performance.*

These earlier AICPA standards stress that the system of internal control extends beyond those matters that relate directly to the accounting and financial statements, but also that the CPA's primary interest for purposes of the review of financial statements is with internal accounting control. The standards specifically state that accounting control is within the scope of the study and evaluation of internal control contemplated by generally accepted auditing standards, but administrative control is not.

    The interests of internal auditors have always extended beyond internal accounting control to the effectiveness of the total system of internal control. Internal auditors have historically believed that internal accounting control is part of a larger control system, with the lines of demarcation as to where internal accounting control fits in the total system never exactly clear. As a result, interpretations by both the SEC and AICPA relate to the system of internal accounting control, as do voluminous interpretations and guidelines developed by major CPA firms.

    The definition of internal control has changed and evolved in recent years. While older interpretations are not incorrect, they have been expanded and clarified since 1992. This new definition is discussed in the section on the Committee of Sponsoring Organizations (COSO) report. An internal auditor will find it useful to understand this historical evolution of these definitions. If for no other reason, this background should be useful for the internal auditor who encounters someone in organization operations who went to school many years ago and has never opened an accounting book since.

(b) FOREIGN CORRUPT PRACTICES ACT OF 1977

The period of 1974 through 1977 was a time of extreme social and political turmoil in the United States. The 1972 presidential election was surrounded by allegations of a series of illegal and questionable acts that eventually led to the president's resignation. The events were first precipitated by a burglary of the Democratic party headquarters, then located in a building complex known as Watergate. The resulting scandal and related investigations became known as the Watergate affair. Investigators found, among other matters, that various bribes and other questionable practices had occurred that were not covered by legislation.

In 1976, the SEC submitted to the U.S. Senate Committee on Banking, Housing, and Urban Affairs a report on its Watergate-related investigations into various questionable or potentially illegal corporate payments and practices. (The phrase ''potentially illegal'' is used because many legal statutes in place at the time were somewhat vague regarding these activities.) The Senate report recommended federal legislation to prohibit these bribes and other questionable payments. In response to the recommendation, the Foreign Corrupt Practices Act (FCPA) was enacted in December 1977. The act contains provisions requiring the maintenance of accurate books and records and the implementation of systems of internal accounting control, and prohibitions against bribery. The FCPA provisions apply to virtually all U.S. companies with SEC-registered securities. Using terminology taken directly from the Act, SEC regulated organizations must:

- Make and keep books, records, and accounts, which, in reasonable detail, accurately and fairly reflect the transactions and dispositions of the assets of the issuers

- Devise and maintain a system of internal accounting controls sufficient to provide reasonable assurances that:
  - Transactions are executed in accordance with management's general or specific authorization
  - Transactions are recorded as necessary both to permit the preparation of financial statements in conformity with generally accepted accounting principles or any other criteria applicable to such statements, and also to maintain accountability for assets
  - Access to assets is permitted only in accordance with management's general or specific authorization, and
  - The recorded accountability for assets is compared with the existing assets at reasonable intervals, and appropriate action is taken with respect to any differences.

The special significance of FCPA requirements is that, for the first time, management was made responsible for an adequate system of internal accounting control. This responsibility overlapped with, but went beyond, the external auditor's reliance on just internal accounting control to support an opinion on the fairness of the financial statements of the organization. However, it was significant that the FCPA requirements used word-for-word the AICPA's internal control definition.

The act requires organizations to ''make and keep books, records, and accounts, which in reasonable detail, accurately and fairly reflect the transactions and dispositions of the assets of the issuer.'' This provision applies to organizations that have securities registered under Section 12 of the Securities Exchange Act of 1934 and does not apply to nonpublic companies. It was adopted as a result of SEC comments that illegal payments disclosed in SEC filings were often hidden by either falsification of records or maintenance of incomplete records. The FCPA requires that organizations keep records that accurately reflect their transactions. The phase ''in reasonable detail'' was added during congressional deliberations to address concerns that no accounting system could achieve complete freedom from error. While there is no exact definition of ''in reasonable detail,'' the intent of the rule appears to be that records should reflect transactions in conformity with accepted methods of recording economic events, preventing off-the-books "slush funds" and payments of bribes. The fraud provisions of the FCPA are discussed further in Chapter 31, on loss prevention and fraud investigation.

The FCPA also requires that companies with registered securities maintain a system of internal accounting controls. These controls should be sufficient to provide reasonable assurances that transactions are authorized and recorded to permit preparation of financial statements in conformity with generally accepted accounting principles. Accountability is to be maintained for assets, and access to the assets permitted only as authorized. Also, recorded assets are to be physically inventoried periodically, with any significant differences analyzed.

Because the cost for fully controlling individual organization transactions cannot be justified in the face of existing risks, the act uses the term "reasonable assurances" when mandating accounting control requirements. This same term is encountered later in this chapter. Management must estimate and evaluate these cost-versus-benefit relationships and judge the appropriate steps to be taken. Although the concept of cost-versus-benefit decisions is not mentioned in the FCPA, based on the conference committee's minutes, Congress apparently intended that management have the right to make such decisions as to controls.

The bribery provisions of the act, which are applicable to both issuers of securities and all other U.S. domestic concerns, prohibit bribes to a foreign official. The maximum penalty for violation of the bribery prohibitions by an organization is $1 million, or imprisonment for not more than five years, or both. The purpose of the bribery payment must be to influence a foreign official to assist an organization in obtaining business. The offer or gift must be intended to induce the recipient to misuse an official position, such as to direct business to the payer or a client. Excluded from the definition of foreign official are government employees whose functions are clerical or ministerial in nature. Thus, so-called grease payments to minor officials to get their help in expediting some process are permissible.

The act suggests that various groups may be involved in determining an organization's compliance with FCPA standards. The controller or vice president of finance would be responsible for the financial control system. External auditors are involved through reviewing management's representations of its control system. Legal counsel would be interested because of the need for interpretations of compliance with the act. Internal audit, of course, would be involved because of its responsibilities for the evaluation of internal control. Because of the FCPA, many companies' boards of directors and their audit committees began to take an active part in directing reviews of internal controls. Although these activities were initiated to assure compliance with the FCPA, they have continued because of a general management recognition of the importance of good internal controls.

When enacted, the FCPA resulted in a flurry of activity among major U.S. corporations. In the years immediately following its enactment, many organizations initiated major efforts to assess and document their systems of internal control. Organizations that had never formally documented procedures, despite a long chain of internal audit reports pointing out that weakness, now embarked on major documentation efforts. This responsibility for FCPA documentation was usually given to internal audit departments who used their best efforts to comply with the internal control provisions of the act. Internal auditors worked with management and their external auditors to complete the documentation requirements of the act properly. Considerable efforts were expended in these efforts, and many consultants and seminar presenters became wealthier in the process. One of the major public accounting firms at that time ran a series of advertisements in major business publications showing a small flowchart template with a message that this public accounting firm could use its template to help client organizations solve their FCPA problems. Of course, much more was needed than a flowchart template. Even though systems and procedures change over relatively short periods of time, many large organizations developed extensive sets of paper-based systems documentation with no provisions, once they had been completed, to update them. As a result of the FCPA, many organizations also strengthened their internal audit departments significantly.

Many writers anticipated a wave of additional regulations or legal initiatives following the enactment of the FCPA. However, this did not occur. Legal actions were relatively minor, no one came looking for the files of assembled documentation, and the FCPA dropped off of the list of current ''hot'' management topics. The FCPA is still in force, a U.S. law requiring corporate compliance. Internal audits should be aware of FCPA requirements and always determine that their organizations have complied with the provisions of this law. The FCPA did emphasize the importance of internal control and many initiatives then were launched to improve internal control evaluations in the modern organization.

(c) TREADWAY COMMISSION, COSO, AND OTHER INTERNAL CONTROL INITIATIVES

With all of the various published approaches for documenting internal controls, it soon became obvious to the accounting profession that the various parties involved in this FCPA documentation process, including business and financial managers, did not have a clear and consistent understanding of what was meant by the term ''internal control.'' As discussed previously, external auditors thought in terms of ''internal accounting control'' while internal auditors had their own broader definition of internal control. Internal control is defined in the IIA standards, discussed in Chapter 5.

Concurrent with these internal control definition concerns, the financial press and others in the United States began to discuss the need for external auditors to express an opinion on an organization's internal controls as part of their audits of financial statements. At that time, in the late 1970s, external auditors merely reported that an organization's financial statements were ''fairly presented.'' There was no attention given to any mention made of the internal control procedures supporting those financial statements. The FCPA put the requirement on the reporting organizations to document their internal controls but did not ask independent public accountants to attest to whether the organizations under audit were in compliance with any internal control reporting requirements. The SEC, which regulates publicly held companies in the United States, began to study whether external audit reports were adequate. As a result, a series of studies and reports were completed over about a 10-year period in the United States to define better both internal control and the external auditor's responsibility for reporting on the adequacy of those controls.

(i) AICPA and CICA Commissions on Auditor Responsibilities. The AICPA formed a high-level Commission on Auditor's Responsibilities in 1974 to study the issue of the external auditor's responsibility for reporting on internal controls. This group, better known then as the Cohen Commission, released its report in 1978, recommending that

corporate management present a statement on the condition of the company's internal controls along with the financial statements. These Cohen Commission intiatives were taking place concurrently with the development and initial publication of the FCPA. At about the same time, the CICA's Commission on Auditor Expectations released a report in 1978 with similar conclusions.

In the United States, the Cohen Commission's report initially ran into a torrent of criticism. In particular, the report's recommendations were not precise on what was meant by "reporting on internal controls," and external auditors expressed concerns about their roles in this reporting process. Many external auditors were concerned about potential liabilities if their reports on internal control gave inconsistent signals due to a lack of understanding over what were internal control standards. Although auditors were accustomed to attesting to the fairness of financial statements, the Cohen Commission report suggested that they should express an audit opinion on the fairness of the management control assertions in the proposed financial statement internal control letter. The issue was again raised that management did not have a consistent definition of internal control. Organizations might use the same terms regarding the quality of their internal controls, with each term meaning something a little different. If an organization reported that its controls were "adequate" and if the auditors "blessed" the assertions in that controls report, the external auditors could later be criticized or even suffer potential litigation if some significant control problem appeared at a later date.

The Financial Executives Institute (FEI) then got involved in this reporting proposal controversy. Just as the IIA is the professional organization for internal auditors and the AICPA or CICA represents the public accountants in the United States and Canada, respectively, the FEI represents senior financial officers in organizations. The FEI released a letter to its members in the late 1970s endorsing the Cohen Commission's recommendations on internal control reports. They suggested that publicly held organizations should report on the status of their internal accounting controls.

As a result, publicly held corporations in the United States began to discuss the adequacy of their internal controls as part of the management letters typically included as part of annual reports. These internal control letters were not required and those issued did not follow any standard format. They were an entirely voluntary initiative and often were included in annual report management letters summarizing operations. They typically included comments stating that management, through its internal auditors, periodically assessed the quality of its internal controls. The same letters sometimes included "negative assurance" comments indicating that nothing was found to indicate that there might be an internal control problem in the organization's operations.

This term *negative assurance* will return again in the discussion of internal controls. Because an external auditor cannot detect all problems and because of the risk of potential litigation, external audit reports often have been stated in terms of a negative assurance. That is, rather than saying that they "found no problems" in an area under review, they have tended to report that they did not find anything that would lead them to believe that there was a problem. This is a subtle but important difference.

(ii) SEC 1979 Internal Control Reporting Proposal. The SEC subsequently took the Cohen Commission and the FEI's recommendations and issued proposed rules calling for *mandatory* management reports on an entity's internal accounting control system. The SEC suggested that information on the effectiveness of an entity's internal control system was necessary to allow investors to evaluate better both management's performance and the integrity of published financial reports.

The SEC proposal raised a storm of controversy. First, many senior managers felt that this was an onerous requirement on top of the newly released FCPA regulations. Questions were once again raised regarding the definition of internal accounting control, and while organizations might agree to voluntary reporting, they did not want to subject themselves to the civil and legal penalties associated with a violation of SEC regulations.

The SEC soon dropped this 1979 internal control reporting proposal. They promised to rerelease the regulations at a later date. The SEC proposal was important, however, in that it emphasized the need for a separate management report on internal accounting controls as part of the annual report to shareholders and the required SEC filings. This tentative regulation caused larger public companies to issue voluntary internal control comments or letters in their annual reports.

(iii) Minahan Committee and Financial Executives Research Foundation.

In parallel with the SEC's proposed rules on internal control reporting, the AICPA formed another committee, the Special Advisory Committee on Internal Control, also called the Minahan Committee. Their 1979 report pointed out the lack of management guidance on internal control procedures and acknowledged that most of the published guidance on internal controls was found in the accounting and auditing literature. This guidance would not necessarily come to the attention of or to be completely relevant to a business manager in other areas of an organization, such as operations, who had a need to understand internal control concepts.

At about the same time, the FEI Research Foundation (FERF) commissioned two studies in this area. The first researched published literature and considered definitions used for the characteristics, conditions, practices, and procedures that define internal control systems. This report,[3] published in 1980, pointed out the vast differences in the definitions of various professional standards-setting groups in what constitutes an effective system of internal control. FERF also released a related research study in 1980[4] that attempted to define the broad, conceptual criteria for evaluating internal control.

These two efforts pointed out the need to find a better and more consistent meaning of internal controls. A regulatory group such as the SEC could not realistically draft requirements for reporting for internal control unless both the organizations developing those reports and the investors who read them all had a consistent understanding of the concept.

(iv) Earlier AICPA Standards: SAS No. 55.

The AICPA's definition of internal control is of special interest because this understanding supports the external auditor's expression of an opinion as to the fairness of the financial statements. As discussed below, these definitions have also been used as a guide in developing regulations covering the enforcement of the Securities Exchange Act of 1934 and the Foreign Corrupt Practices Act of 1977.

---

[3] Kenneth A. Merchant, *Fraudulent and Questionable Financial Reporting: A Corporate Perspective* (Morristown, N.J.: Financial Executives Research Foundation, 1980).

[4] R. K. Mautz and J. Winjum, *Criteria for Management Control Systems* (Morristown, N.J.: Financial Executives Research Foundation, 1981).

The AICPA's audit standards are defined through a series of Statements on Auditing Standards (SASs) that are released from time to time and are also codified in an overall set of professional standards.[5] As discussed previously regarding SAS No. 1, these standards were once almost engraved in stone, with little change for many years. They formed the basis of the external auditor's review and evaluation of financial statements. During this same period of the 1970s and 1980s, the public accounting profession, in general, and the AICPA were criticized that their standards did not provide adequate guidance to either external auditors or the users of these reports. This problem was called the ''expectations gap,'' in that public accounting standards did not meet the expectations of investors. To answer this need, the AICPA released a series of new SASs on internal control audit standards during the period of 1980 to 1985.

- SAS No 30, *Reporting on Internal Accounting Control,* 1980, provided guidance for terminology in internal accounting control reports. The SAS did not provide much help, however, on defining the underlying concepts of internal control.
- SAS No. 43, *Omnibus Statement on Auditing Standards,* 1982, revised some of the basic guidance for the independent auditor's study and evaluation of its internal control as defined in their first standard, SAS No. 1.
- SAS No. 48, *The Effects of Computer Processing on the Examination of Financial Statements,* 1984, provided guidance on the need to review both the computer systems applications controls and such general controls as physical security. Although there had been massive technological changes in the way computer systems were constructed, at the time SAS No. 48 was issued external auditors were still using guidance from the early 1970s.

The AICPA subsequently released a whole new series of auditing standards that better defined many problem areas facing the external auditor. One of these, SAS No. 55, defined internal control from the perspective of the external auditor.

SAS No. 55, *Consideration of the Internal Control Structure in a Financial Statement Audit,* 1988, provided the AICPA's definition of internal control in terms of an entity's overall control structure, which consists of three elements:

1. The control environment
2. The accounting system
3. The control procedures

SAS No. 55 presented a somewhat different approach to understanding internal control than had been used by the AICPA in the past, as well as by other standards setting groups, such as the IIA.

An organization generally has other internal control structure policies and procedures that are not relevant to a financial statement audit and therefore are not considered by the external auditors. Examples include policies and procedures concerning the effectiveness, economy, and efficiency of certain management decision-making processes, such as setting of an appropriate price for products or deciding whether to make expenditures for certain

---

[5] AICPA Professional Standards, Volumes 1 & 2 (New York: AICPA, updated annually).

research and development activities. Although these processes are certainly important to the organization, they do not ordinarily relate to the external auditor's financial statement audit.

SAS No. 55 defined internal control in much broader scope than had been traditionally taken by external auditors. However, this was still a narrower view than the scope traditionally taken by internal auditors. This AICPA definition, however, provided a basis for the COSO report definition of internal control and SAS No. 78, both discussed later in this chapter. The interests of internal auditors extend beyond internal accounting control to the effectiveness of the total system of internal control, and that internal accounting control is part of a larger system. SAS No. 55 became effective in 1990 and represented a major stride toward providing external auditors with an appropriate definition of internal control.

(v) Treadway Committee Report.   The later 1970s and early 1980s were a period of many major organization failures in the United States due to factors such as high inflation, the resultant high interest rates, and high energy costs due to excessive government regulation. Organizations sometimes reported adequate earnings in their financial reports, and their external auditors attested that these same financial reports were fairly stated, only to have the organization suffer a financial collapse shortly after the release of such reports. Some of these failures were caused by fraudulent financial reporting, although many others were caused by high inflation or other factors causing organization instability. Several members of Congress proposed legislation to ''correct'' these potential business and audit failures. Bills were drafted and congressional hearings held, but no legislation was passed.

In response to these concerns, the National Commission on Fraudulent Financial Reporting was formed. Five professional organizations sponsored the Commission: the IIA, the AICPA, and the FEI, all discussed previously, as well as the American Accounting Association (AAA) and the Institute of Management Accountants (IMA). The AAA is the academic professional accountants organization. The IMA is the professional organization for managerial or cost accountants. This organization, formerly called the National Association of Accountants, sponsors the Certificate in Management Accounting (CMA). The National Commission on Fraudulent Reporting, called the Treadway Commission after its chairperson, had as its major objectives the identification of the causal factors that allowed fraudulent financial reporting and the making of recommendations to reduce the incidence. The Treadway Commission's final report was issued in 1987[6] and included recommendations to management, boards of directors of public companies, the public accounting profession, and others.

The Treadway Commission report again called for management reports on the effectiveness of their internal control systems. It emphasized some key elements in what it felt should be an effective system of internal control, including a strong control environment, codes of conduct, a competent and involved audit committee, and a strong internal audit function. The Treadway Commission report again pointed out the lack of a consistent definition of internal control, suggesting further work was needed. The same organizations that managed the Treadway report, the Committee of Sponsoring Organizations (COSO), subsequently contracted with outside specialists and embarked on a new project to define

---

[6] *Report of the National Commission on Fraudulent Financial Reporting* (National Commission on Fraudulent Financial Reporting, 1987).

internal control. Although it defined no standards, the Treadway report was important as it raised the level of concern and attention regarding reporting on internal control.

Other internal control–related activities took place about the time the Treadway Commission's report was released. As discussed earlier, the AICPA initially released its SAS No. 55 auditing standard on internal control. The SEC responded to the Treadway recommendations by proposing additional management reporting on internal control. In addition, the AICPA began an effort to modify its auditing to conform with the COSO recommendations (see next section).

The internal control–reporting efforts discussed earlier are presented as if they were a series of sequential events. In reality, many of the internal control–related committees and report efforts took place in almost a parallel fashion. This massive effort over nearly a 20-year period redefined internal control, a basic concept for all auditors, and increased the responsibility of many other participants in an organization's control structure.

(d) COSO REPORT DEFINITION OF INTERNAL CONTROL

As mentioned earlier, COSO stands for the five professional auditing and accounting organizations that developed this internal control report; its official title is *Integrated Control–Integrated Framework*. Throughout this book, it is referred to as the COSO report, its commonly accepted name.

The sponsoring organizations contracted with the public accounting firm of Coopers and Lybrand to manage the development of the actual report. A large number of volunteers helped research issues and develop the final report. The COSO development group first released a draft report in 1990 for public exposure and comment. More than 40,000 copies of this draft version were sent to corporate officers, internal and external auditors, legislators, academics, and other interested parties. Formal comments regarding this draft were requested. Based on these comments, a revised draft was circulated to a more limited group for additional comment. In addition, the internal control review procedures portion of the study, discussed later, was field-tested by five public accounting firms.

The final COSO report was released in September 1992. The report proposes a common framework for the definition of internal control, as well as procedures to evaluate those controls. The document was released in four separate sections or books.

1. An *Internal Control Framework* document that provides the overall definition of internal control, as well as criteria to assess those internal controls

2. An *Evaluation Tools* document with checklists and other guidance for conducting evaluation reviews of systems of internal controls

3. A section called *Guidance on Reporting to External Parties* that provides help for developing public or outside reports on internal controls

4. An *Executive Summary* to highlight the overall COSO report

While the report does not have the authority of a standards-setting document such as an AICPA auditing standard or a government agency regulation, all significant parties involved in the process of evaluating internal control standards have endorsed the COSO report and its internal control framework definition. For example, the AICPA subsequently modified its internal control standards (such as SAS No. 55, discussed previously) to bring them in compliance with the terminology of COSO. The report has also been used to develop new laws and regulations, such as the Federal Deposit Insurance Corporation Improvement Act of 1991 (FDICIA), which contains regulations for larger banks. The 1993 regulations for FDICIA used the COSO definition of internal control with no modifications. Over time, it can be expected that the Internal Audit Standards, discussed in Chapter 5, will be modified to reflect COSO terminology and procedures.

The COSO report provides a good general definition of internal control. Internal control concepts, based on this description, are discussed throughout the other chapters of this book. The following sections describe that COSO definition in greater detail. Internal auditors should be aware of the COSO report and its overall description of the components and objectives of a system of internal control.

2-4 INTERNAL CONTROL COMPONENTS AND OBJECTIVES

With the exception of very small proprietorships, the modern organization usually has a complex control procedures structure. Following the description of a classic organization chart, there are levels of senior and middle management in its multiple operating units or within different activities. In addition, control concerns may be different at each of these levels and components. For example, one operating unit may operate in a regulated business where control concerns are very high, while another will be an entrepreneurial start-up operation with less formal procedures. Different levels of management in these organizations will have different control concern perspectives. The question ''How do you describe your system of internal controls?'' would receive different answers from persons in different levels and components in the organization.

The COSO report introduced a good description of this multidimensional concept of internal control. It defined internal control as follows.

> Internal control is a *process,* effected by an entity's board of directors, management, and other personnel, designed to provide reasonable assurance regarding the achievement of objectives in the following categories:
> * Effectiveness and efficiency of operations
> * Reliability of financial reporting
> * Compliance with applicable laws and regulations

This is the official COSO report definition of internal control and a very good definition for use by internal auditors. The definition is very similar to Brink's definition of internal auditing in his first edition of this book. While external auditors focused on financial reporting controls, Brink used the broader definition of service to management to define what was then the new profession of internal auditing. That definition is still important today.

Using the above definition for internal control, the COSO report uses diagrams to describe a three-dimensional view of the internal control system in an organization. Figure 2.3 defines the five COSO components of an internal control system. These are shown as a pyramid with the Control Environment component serving as the foundation for the entire structure. While four of these components are horizontal layers, the communication and information component of internal control acts as an interface channel for the other four layers. Each of these components is described in greater detail in the following sections.

Figure 2.3   COSO Components of Internal Control

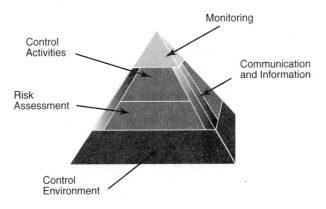

The three internal control objectives included in the definition—effectiveness of operations, reliability of financial reporting, and compliance with laws and regulations—all are related to the four internal control objectives. There are risk-assessment and monitoring components, COSO terminology, for each of these objectives.

There is a third dimension to this model. These are the units or activities of the entity to which this internal control system relates. The number or type of these activities or units may vary from one organization to another. These three dimensions of internal control are shown in Figure 2.4, which shows the COSO internal control model and the relationship between internal control objectives and components for each activity in the organization. These figures should become clearer to the auditor as they are described in greater detail in the following sections.

Figure 2.4   COSO Internal Control Model

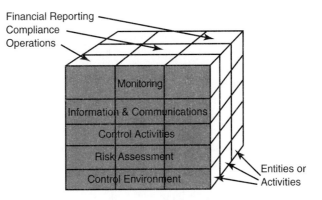

Relationship Between Control Components, Objectives, and Organization Entities

(a) CONTROL ENVIRONMENT COMPONENT OF INTERNAL CONTROL

The COSO report emphasized that the control environment in an organization has a pervasive influence on how business activities are structured and risks are assessed. It serves as a foundation for all other components of internal control and has an influence on each of the three objectives and all activities. The control environment reflects the overall attitude, awareness, and actions by the board of directors, management, and others concerning the importance of internal control in the organization.

Organization history and culture often play a major role in forming the control environment. An organization like Motorola has had a strong management emphasis on producing error-free products. Top management has emphasized the importance of producing high-quality products, and the message has been communicated to all levels of the organization. This becomes a major control environment factor for Motorola. Similar messages communicated by management will establish this control environment for an organization. If top management has had a reputation of looking the other way at violations of policy or other matters, this message will be similarly communicated to other levels in the organization. A positive tone at the top by senior management will establish the control environment for the organization.

The following sections outline some of the major elements of the control environment component of internal control. Internal auditors should always understand the overall control environment when performing reviews of various organization activities or units. In some instances, they may want to perform specific reviews of some or all of these control environment factors covering the overall organization. In smaller organizations, the control environment factors will be much more informal. However, the internal auditor should still look for the appropriate control environment factors in any entity and should consider them as essential components of internal control.

(i) Integrity and Ethical Values. The collective integrity and ethical values of an organization are essential elements of its control environment. These factors are often defined by the ''tone at the top'' message communicated by senior management. If the organization has developed a strong code of conduct emphasizing integrity and ethical values, and if all elements of management appear to follow that code, the internal auditor will have assurances that the organization has a good set of values.

The code of conduct is an important component of organizational governance. There is no one model to follow that outlines the preferred contents or length of a code for a given organization. Some organizations have very detailed, lengthy codes describing all areas of their business. Others may have very short but meaningful messages that set the moral tone for the organization. An example of the latter, Johnson & Johnson, the medical products company, has defined their values in a very short credo statement, as shown in Figure 2.5. This message has guided corporate actions when they faced some tough product integrity questions in the later 1980s. A very small organization may not even have a formal code of conduct, but its senior management should be directly communicating a message to employees on a regular basis.

Although an organization may have a strong code of conduct, its principles can often be violated through ignorance rather than by deliberate employee malfeasance. In many instances, employees may not know that they are doing something wrong or may erroneously believe that their actions are in the organization's best interests. This ignorance is often caused by poor moral guidance by senior management rather than by any employee

Figure 2.5   Johnson & Johnson Credo

We believe our first responsibility is to the doctors, nurses and patients,
to mothers and all others who use our products and services.
In meeting their needs everything we do must be of high quality.
We must constantly strive to reduce our costs
in order to maintain reasonable prices.
Cutomers' orders must be serviced promptly and accurately.
Our suppliers and distributors must have an opportunity
to make a fair profit.

We are responsible to our employees,
the men and women who work with us throughout the world.
Everyone must be considered as an individual.
We must respect their dignity and recognize their merit.
They must have a sense of security in their jobs.
Compensation must be fair and adequate,
and working conditions clean, orderly and safe.
Employees must feel free to make suggestions and complaints.
There must be equal opportunity for employment, development
and advancement for those qualified.
We must provide competent management,
and their actions must be just and ethical.

We are responsible to the communities in which we live and work
and to the world community as well.
We must be good citizens—support good works and charities
and bear our fair share of taxes.
We must encourage civic improvements and better health and education.
We must maintain in good order
the property we are privileged to use,
protecting the environment and natural resources.

Our final responsibility is to our stockholders.
Business must make a sound profit.
We must experiment with new ideas.
Research must be carried on, innovative programs developed
and mistakes paid for.
New equipment must be purchased, new facilities provided
and new products launched.
Reserves must be created to provide for adverse times.
When we operate according to these principles,
the stockholders should realize a fair return.

Johnson & Johnson

Source: Used by permission of Johnson & Johnson. Copyright Johnson & Johnson.

intent to deceive. An organization's policies and values must be communicated to all levels of the organization. While there can always be "bad apples" in any organization, a strong moral message will encourage everyone to act correctly. When performing a review in a given area, the internal auditor should always ask questions to determine if appropriate messages or signals have been transmitted throughout the organization.

The internal auditors should have a good understanding of the organization's code of conduct and how it is applied throughout the organization. The auditor would, or at least should, have been asked to sign that code as an employee of the organization. If the code is out-of-date, if it does not appear to address important ethical issues facing an overall organization, or if management does not appear to be communicating the code to all employees on a recurring basis, internal audit should remind management of the significance of this deficiency, both in the course of audits in other areas and as a special message to management. If the organization does not have a formal ethics office function, internal audit may often be asked to suggest changes and to help in the dissemination of the organization's code of conduct. Although a code of conduct can take many forms, Figure 2.6 is an example of an abbreviated code of conduct for a smaller manufacturing organization. This sample code emphasizes the important aspects of fair dealing with both customers and suppliers, as well as the responsibilities of employees to follow appropriate standards in the conduct of organization business and in their dealings with fellow employees. An organization should have procedures in place that require all employees to acknowledge their acceptance of such a code on a periodic—often annual—basis.

While the code of conduct describes the rules for ethical behavior in an organization and while senior members of management can transmit the proper ethical message throughout their organizations, other incentives and temptations can erode the overall control environment. Individuals in the organization may engage in dishonest, illegal, or unethical acts if their organization gives them strong incentives or temptations to do so. For example, an organization may establish very high, unrealistic performance targets for areas such as sales or production quotas. If there are strong rewards for the achievement of these performance goals—or worse, strong threats for missed targets—employees may be encouraged to engage in fraudulent or questionable practices to achieve those goals. As part of the studies regarding why fraudulent financial reporting occurs, the before-mentioned 1987 FERF study cited a series of "temptations" for employees to engage in improper acts:

- Nonexistent or ineffective controls, such as poor segregation of duties in sensitive areas, that offer temptations to steal or to conceal poor performance
- High decentralization that leaves top management unaware of actions taken at lower organization levels and thereby reduces the chances of getting caught
- A weak internal audit function that has neither the ability nor the authority to detect and report improper behavior
- Penalties for improper behavior that are insignificant or unpublicized and thus lose their value as deterrents

There is a strong message here both for internal auditors performing their various reviews and for the internal audit organization in total. First, the internal auditor should always consider these control environment factors when performing reviews. A good internal auditor should always be skeptical and perform appropriate levels of tests when reviewing various areas of operations. When things look "too good," the auditor might

Figure 2.6 Code of Conduct Example

ExampleCo Corporation

Our Values

ExampleCo employees must exercise a commitment to the highest ethical standards in order to safeguard the company's reputation and credibility. No one, regardless of position or title, is ever expected to commit an improper, unethical, or illegal act or to ask anyone else to do so.

Adherence to the Law: We believe in the concept of good corporate citizenship, and employees are expected to conduct business in accordance with the laws where we do business. Use of ExampleCo assets or resources for personal gain or benefit for illegal purposes is strictly prohibited.

Conflict of Interest: Employees at all levels must be free at all times of any interest, influence, or relationship that conflicts with the best interests of the company.

Insider Trading: Employees are prohibited from trading in company securities when material inside information is known to them which could influence the market price of those securities.

Confidential Information: Employees are responsible for protecting any information that is proprietary or confidential. No such information should be given to any individual or outside organization without proper authorization.

Integrity of Records and Reporting: Accurate and reliable records are critical to the business. Every company transaction must be reflected on our books and records promptly, accurately, and in accordance with legal and accepted accounting standards. No undisclosed or unrecorded funds, assets, or accounts will be established for any reason.

Gifts or Favors: Employees should neither receive nor give money, gifts, or favors that in any way could influence or appear to influence company business dealings.

Nondiscrimination: Discrimination in employment is illegal and morally wrong. Such discrimination is to be avoided in all aspects of business operations.

Harassment of Employees: ExampleCo will not condone, permit, or tolerate any harassment or intimidation based on race, color, religion, sex, age, national origin, handicap, or veteran status, or marital status.

Bribery: The payment of bribes is dishonest, unfair, and usually illegal. The company and its employees will not indulge in bribery.

Political Contributions: No illegal political contributions, either directly through donations of company funds or indirectly through rendering services or company goods, will be permitted.

---

want to look a bit harder. This is not just to find something in the course of a review but to assess whether deficiencies in the control environment may lead to possible fraudulent activities. Procedures for fraud investigations are discussed in Chapter 31.

The second message from the above FERF study is the importance of a strong internal audit function. The internal audit department that follows the guidance presented in the chapters of this book should be able to operate as a strong component of an organization's control environment. If internal audit finds that management is placing constraints on the internal audit function, the director of internal audit should remind management of the importance of internal audit as part of the organization's overall internal control structure and should go to the board of director's audit committee, if necessary, to achieve corrective action.

(ii) Commitment to Competence.   Sometimes a person has been assigned to a particular job but does not seem to have the appropriate skills, training, or intelligence to perform that job. Because all humans have different levels of skills and abilities, internal auditors will encounter this situation from time to time. If someone is new and learning the job requirements, adequate supervision should be available to help the person until proper skills are acquired. However, an organization's control environment can be seriously eroded if a significant number of positions are filled with persons who do not have the required skills.

An organization needs to specify the required competence levels for its various job tasks and to translate those requirements into necessary levels of knowledge and skill. By placing the proper people in the proper jobs or giving adequate training when required, the organization is making an overall commitment to competence. This is an important element in the organization's overall control environment. Internal auditors often find it valuable when reviewing a given area to assess whether adequate position descriptions have been created for the various functions under review, whether procedures are in operation to place appropriate people in those positions, and whether training and supervision are adequate.

While an important portion of the control environment, an assessment of staff competence can be a difficult internal audit review area. How does an auditor determine that the staff is "competent" with regards to its assigned work duties? If an internal auditor visits a remote subsidiary operation and finds that no one in the accounting department there seems to have any knowledge of how to record and report financial transactions, and also that no training program exists to help these "accountants," the auditor easily can raise control environment issues for this operating unit. However, the auditor should exercise extreme caution before attempting to check on the background and training of some individual manager at the headquarters facility. A personality conflict or difference of opinion is no reason to question someone's competence.

(iii) Board of Directors and Audit Committee.   The control environment is very much influenced by the actions of an organization's board of directors and its audit committee. In previous years, boards and their audit committees have been dominated by senior management with only limited, minority representation from outside members. This created situations where the boards were not totally independent of management. Company officers sat on the board and were, in effect, managing themselves with less concern for the outside investors. There has been increasing pressure over recent years to make boards and their audit committees more independent of management, including 1977 requirements for companies registered by the New York Stock Exchange. The Federal Deposit Insurance Corporation Improvement Act, as mentioned earlier, requires that larger regulated banks have an audit committee composed of outside directors that are independent of management. Other monitoring groups, such as outside shareholder committees, have pressured organizations to increase the number of outside members on their boards. Audit committees and their relationship with internal audit are discussed in Chapter 6.

An active and independent board is an essential component of an organization's control environment. These persons should ask appropriate questions to top management and should give all aspects of the organization a detailed scrutiny. By setting high-level policies and by reviewing overall organization conduct, the board and its audit committee have the ultimate responsibility for setting this "tone at the top." This same principle applies to the board of directors of a publicly held organization or boards of trustees for not-for-profit and other public bodies.

(iv) Management's Philosophy and Operating Style.   The philosophy and operating style of top management has a considerable influence over an organization's control environment. Some top-level managers frequently take significant organization risks in their new business or product ventures while others are very cautious or conservative. Some managers operate by the seat of the pants while others insist that everything must be properly approved and documented. Still other managers take very aggressive approaches in their interpretations of tax and financial-reporting rules while others go by the book. These comments do not necessarily mean that one approach is always good and the other bad. A small, entrepreneurial organization may be forced to take certain business risks to remain competitive while one in a highly regulated industry would be risk-averse.

These management philosophy and operational style considerations are all part of the control environment for an organization. Internal auditors and others responsible for assessing internal controls should understand these factors and take them into consideration when evaluating the effectiveness of internal controls. While no one set of styles and philosophies is always the best for all organizations, these factors are important when considering the other components of internal control in an organization.

(v) Organization Structure.   The organization structure component of the internal control environment provides a framework for planning, executing, controlling, and monitoring activities for achieving overall objectives. This is an aspect of the control environment that relates to the way various functions are managed and organized, following the classic organization chart. Some organizations are highly centralized while others are decentralized by product or geography. Still others are organized in a matrix manner with no single direct lines of reporting. Organizational structure is a very important aspect of the organization's control environment.

No one structure provides a preferred level of control. There are many ways in which the various components of an organization can be assembled. Organizational control is a part of a larger control process. The term *organization* is often used interchangeably with the term *organizing* and means about the same thing to many people. *Organization* sometimes refers to hierarchical relationships between people but is also used broadly to include all of the problems of management. This book and other sources generally use the term organization to refer to the organizational entity, such as a corporation, a not-for-profit association, or any organized group. This section considers the organization as the set of *organizational arrangements* developed as a result of the organizing process.

An organization can be described as the way individual work efforts are both assigned and subsequently integrated for the achievement of overall goals. While in a sense this concept could be applied to the manner in which a single individual organizes individual efforts, it is more applicable when a number of people are involved in a group effort. For a large modern corporation, a strong plan of organization control is an important component of the system of internal control. Individuals and subgroups must have an understanding of the total goals and objectives of the group or entity of which they are a part. Without such an understanding by members of the organization, there can be significant control weaknesses.

Every organization or entity—whether a business, government, philanthropic organization, or other type of unit—needs an effective plan of organization. The effective internal auditor needs to have a good understanding of organizational structure and reporting relationships that should be considered in a given organization under audit. Often, a weakness in organization controls can have a pervasive effect throughout the total control environment.

Although organizations come in all sizes and shapes, they generally follow three basic organizational structures.

1. Functional organization
2. Divisional or decentralized organization
3. Matrix organization

Simplified organization charts showing these three are shown in Figures 2.7, 2.8, and 2.9. Each of these structures has its own control and efficiency advantages and disadvantages. The auditor should be aware of these basic structures and should understand the basic control strengths and weaknesses associated with each. Some of the strengths and weaknesses of these different organization structures are discussed in the following sections.

Functional Organizations

In a functional organization, each manager is responsible for one specific function that collectively supports the next higher level in the organization. For example, Figure 2.7 can be considered as describing a small manufacturing organization. One manager may be responsible for designing products, another for building them, and still another for marketing. Staff directly responsible for these functions will report to each of these managers, who all report to a central authority. Each manager—as well as the central authority, typically the president—may have a limited staff function that supports the functional organizations under that chain of command. For example, the finance function may provide staff support to the office of the president. However, most specialized functions are the responsibility of a line organization for that area.

Functional organizations have the potential for major efficiencies. Each functional unit should be designed to operate in its own area of responsibility and expertise. For example, one manager in a multiproduct manufacturing operation might be responsible for all machining operations. All products manufactured by the organization would pass through control of the manager for machining operations. That manufacturing department should have established a high level of efficiency and knowledge over its area of responsibility but will not have the experience or authority over other areas. In a functional organi-

Figure 2.7 Functional Organization Chart Example

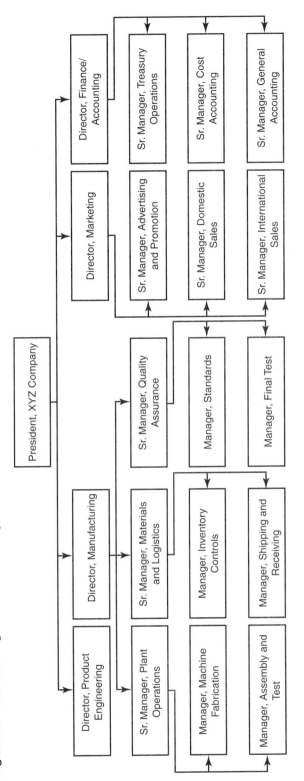

Figure 2.8   Decentralized Organization Chart Example

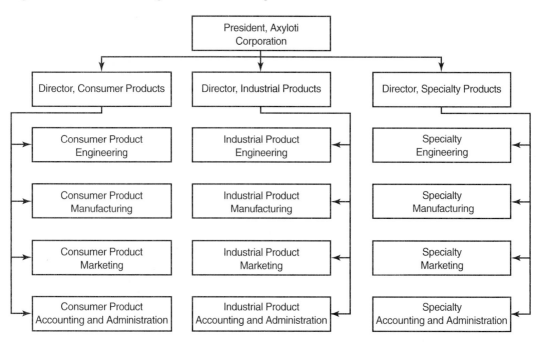

zation, policy and direction come down from higher levels and problems requiring resolution flow up to appropriate levels.

Despite their clear lines of authority, functional organizations often have some built-in inefficiencies that become greater as the size of the organization expands. These inefficiencies, summarized next, can often cause control procedures to break down, and the auditor should be aware of them when evaluating the organizational control environment in the functional organization.

- *Inconsistent Organization Goals.* The overall organization may have a goal to be profitable and to increase market share for its products. Such a goal can be directly communicated to some functional units such as marketing. However, management sometimes finds it difficult to communicate such goals to specialized functional units such as engineering. A manager of an engineering unit may be primarily interested in providing a specialized and technically ''interesting'' engineering design for the product. Because the technically interesting design may not be all that cost-effective, the effort will not be totally consistent with overall organization goals.

- *Inefficient Decision-Making Processes.* When a manager in a manufacturing function wishes to request an engineering product design change in a pure functional organization, it is sometimes necessary to route the request up through manufacturing management to upper management, where it then flows down through the ranks to the appropriate level within the engineering organization. While Figure

Figure 2.9 Matrix Organization Chart Example

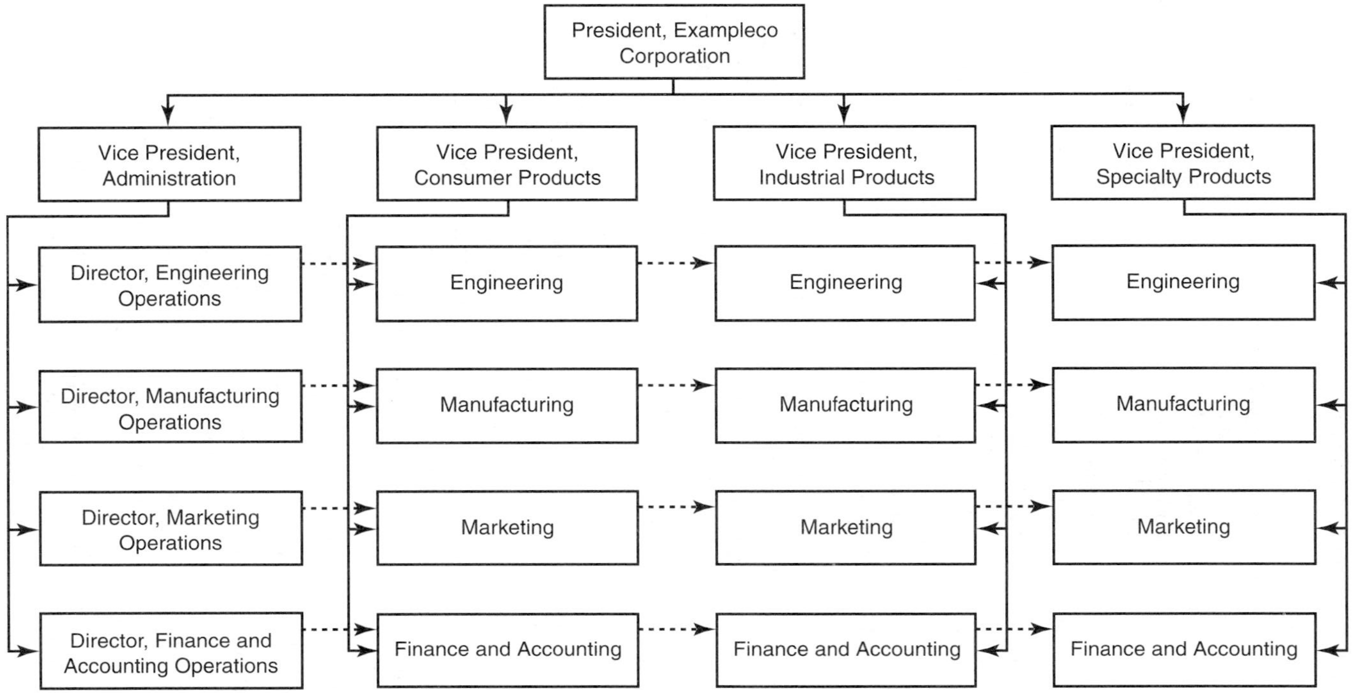

2.7 shows a relatively small organization where communication should travel fast, this type of decision-making can be both slow and inefficient in a large organization with many levels. In addition, top management in such an organization often takes the responsibility for making many decisions, and subordinates may be reluctant to make decisions until they have cleared them with high levels.

- *Excessive Bureaucracies.* Because of problems with communicating with other functional units as well as setting and interpreting upper management policies, functional organizations sometimes have a tendency to create staff level groups to perform needed specialized tasks at multiple levels. However, if a staff function such as an information systems service is formed for each functional unit, there may be duplicative efforts and overall wasted resources. If that same staff function is combined and reports at a high level, it may be too distant from actual operations and may become bureaucratic.

In many respects, the auditor may find the functional organization one of the easiest in which to plan and perform audits. In an operational review of the engineering function, as described in Chapter 26, the internal auditor need only to be concerned with one centralized area of activity. In addition, there will be clear lines of authority for setting policies, approval levels, and procedures.

Decentralized Organizations

Many larger private and government organizations, dating back to the nineteenth century, were highly centralized, functional organizations with well-defined reporting structures. However, in the early years of the twentieth century, General Motors Corporation, faced with the challenge of manufacturing and marketing multiple lines of automobiles over large geographic areas, devised the concept of decentralized management. Here, major organization responsibility was divided up among separate divisions based on product or some other activity areas. Upper management was responsible only for overall goals and strategies. The person who "invented" the decentralized organization, Alfred P. Sloan, Jr., then president of General Motors, described that philosophy in his biography, *My Years with General Motors.*[7] Although many events have changed General Motors's organization structure over time, the book is still an excellent source for understanding the basic management philosophy that was used to build the company. The key concept associated with decentralized management is that many managerial responsibilities are moved down to a more direct level. For example, a divisional general manager in a multidivision organization may have decision responsibility for all day-to-day operations within that division. There is no need to go back to upper management for many decisions. In his book, Sloan described this process at General Motors as follows:

> *The role of the division manager is an important one in our continuing efforts to maintain both efficiency and adaptability. These managers make almost all of the divisional operating decisions, subject, however, to some important qualification. Their decisions must be consistent with the corporation's general policies; the results of the division's operations must be reported to the central management; and the*

---

[7] Garden City, N.Y.: Doubleday, 1964.

division officers must "sell" central management on any substantial changes in operating policies and be open to suggestions from the general officers.

This concept of decentralization can go down multiple numbers of levels within the organization. Sometimes, individual products or locations within a division of an organization will have their own sets of responsibilities. The brand manager in a consumer products organization, for example, may have a wide range of responsibilities, including manufacturing, advertising, and finance for their products or brands. A highly decentralized organization can promote a very strong entrepreneurial spirit within its unit managers. Each is responsible for managing and making the most efficient use of resources. Higher levels of organization management are used for such matters as allocating and managing capital.

A potential disadvantage with a highly decentralized organization is that overall policies and management directives may not be followed in a consistent manner. Also, a decentralized division may be organized on functional lines itself, with all of the same problems, as discussed, of a functional organization.

Internal auditors often have an important role in performing reviews within a decentralized organization. Because of its ultimate reporting relationship to the audit committee of the board of directors, the internal audit department often reports at a senior management level rather than to divisional management. Those senior management policies may not always be appropriately communicated to functional management at lower levels or more remote locations within a decentralized organization. The auditor should be aware of those overall policies and should determine that there is compliance at lower levels within the autonomous units of the organization.

Matrix Organizations

A matrix organization is really the result of two organizations, one functional and one decentralized, superimposed on one another. A major shipyard might be a good example of such an organization. There are functional responsibilities within the yard, such as sheet metal, electrical, plumbing, and component fabrication. However, each ship is a major project that is independently managed separately from the other ships under construction. The project manager is responsible for moving the ship through each of the functional areas and resolving any problems as they pertain to that project. Any operating unit at one of the Figure 2.9 organizational intersections has responsibilities both to the project and to functional management.

Aircraft and aerospace equipment manufacturers, consulting firms, construction companies, and many other related companies often have complex matrix organization structures. The functional side of the organization is responsible for providing and managing resources. The other dimension of the matrix is responsible for products or other transactions. Management-control problems in a matrix organization are usually much more complex than those found in either a functional or decentralized organization. The requirements of the projects must be meshed with the available resources within functional units. Coordination is often difficult because of the different objectives of each side of the matrix, and also because many unit managers within a matrix are effectively serving two bosses.

Internal auditors often face a greater challenge when performing operational reviews of matrix organizations. Because of differing pressures and incentives, control procedures can tend to vary within the different elements of a matrix organization. An internal auditor must assure that a certain minimum level of control, consistent with the wishes of management, is in place throughout the matrix organization. With both vertical and horizontal lines of control to examine, an internal auditor can easily look in the wrong direction within the matrix organization structure.

(vi) Assignment of Authority and Responsibility.

This area of the control environment, as defined in the COSO report, is similar to the organization structure area previously discussed. An organization's structure defines the assignment and integration of the total work effort. Each of these aspects can be considered separately. The first, assignment of authority, is essentially the way responsibilities are initially defined in terms of job descriptions and then are structured in terms of organization charts. Although job assignments can never fully escape some overlapping or joint responsibilities, the more definitely and precisely these responsibilities can be stated, the better. The decision of how responsibilities will be assigned is often concerned with avoiding confusion and conflict between individual and group work efforts. The second aspect of the organizational process, integration, brings together the defined individual job responsibilities with the total work effort. This integration also has its own special problems, including a need for specific organizational arrangement to assure most effectively the needed job-task integration. In addition to the formal organization chart, examples are the various types of coordinating committees, requirements for review and approval, and specific assignments for the responsibility for relating and integrating the results of different types of activities.

In order to streamline operations within organizations, the 1980s and 1990s saw an increasing tendency in organizations of all types and sizes to push the decision-making authority downward and closer to the front-line personnel required to make the decisions. The idea is that these front-line employees should have the knowledge and power to make important decisions in their own area of operations rather than be required to pass the request for a decision up through organization channels.

The critical challenge that goes with this delegation or empowerment is that although it can delegate some authority in order to achieve some organizational objectives, senior management is ultimately responsible for any decisions made by those subordinates. An organization can place itself at risk if too many decisions involving higher-level objectives are assigned at inappropriately lower levels without adequate management review. In addition, each person in the organization must have a good understanding of the organization's overall objectives as well as how his/her individual actions interrelate to achieve those objectives. The framework section of the COSO report describes this very important area of the control environment as follows:

> *The control environment is greatly influenced by the extent to which individuals recognize that they will be held accountable. This holds true all the way to the chief executive, who has ultimate responsibility for all activities within an entity, including internal control system.*

(vii) Human Resources Policies and Practices.

Human resource practices cover such areas as hiring, orientation, training, evaluating, counseling, promoting, compensating, and taking appropriate remedial actions. While the human resources organization should have adequate published policies in these areas, their actual practice areas send strong messages to employees regarding their expected levels of ethical behavior and competence. The higher-level employee who openly abuses a human resources policy, such as a plant smoking ban, quickly sends a message to other levels in the organization. The message grows even louder when a lower-level employee is disciplined for the same unauthorized cigarette while everyone looks the other way at the higher-level violator.

Areas where these human resources policies and practices are particularly important include:

- *Recruitment and Hiring.* The organization should take steps to hire the best, most qualified candidates for new positions. Potential employee backgrounds should be checked to verify their education backgrounds, prior work experiences, and other references. Interviews should be well organized and in-depth. They should also transmit a message to the prospective candidate regarding the organization's values, culture, and operating style.

- *New Employee Orientation.* The organization needs to give a clear signal to new employees regarding its value system as well as the consequences of not complying with those values. This is the appropriate time to introduce new employees to the code for conduct and to obtain their formal acknowledgment of that code. Without these messages, new employees will join the organization lacking an appropriate understanding of organization values.

- *Evaluation, Promotion, and Compensation.* The organization should have a fair performance-evaluation program that is not subject to an excessive amount of managerial discretion. Because issues such as evaluation and compensation can violate employee confidentiality, the overall system should be established in a manner that appears to be fair to all members of the organization. Bonus incentive programs are often useful tools to motivate and reinforce outstanding performance by all employees.

- *Disciplinary Actions.* Consistent and well-understood policies for disciplinary actions should be in place. All employees should know that if they violate certain rules, they will be subject to a progression of disciplinary actions leading up to dismissal. The organization should take care to ensure that no double standard exists for disciplinary actions—or, if any such double standard does exist, that higher-level employees are subject to even more severe disciplinary actions.

Effective human resource policies and procedures are a critical component in the overall control environment. Messages from the top of strong organization structures will accomplish little if the organization does not have strong human resource policies and procedures in place to send appropriate messages to all members of the organization. The internal auditor should always consider this element of the control environment when performing reviews of other elements of the internal control framework.

(viii) Control Environment in Perspective.   Figure 2.3 showed the components of internal control as a pyramid, with the control environment as the lowest or foundation component. This concept of the control environment acting as the foundation is very appropriate. Just as a strong foundation is necessary for a multistory building, the control environment provides the foundation for the other components of internal control. An organization that is building a strong internal control structure should give special attention to placing solid foundation bricks in this control environment foundation.

Internal auditors should always be aware of the control environment components in place when performing reviews of their organizations. In many instances, internal audit may find internal control exceptions in other areas of their review that are attributable to the lack of a strong control environment foundation. For example, they may find that employees in a given unit are violating some travel expense rule that is defined in a company policy statement. The excuse by local management may be that the rule doesn't apply to them or that everyone is doing what the auditors found. Depending on the nature of the issue, this may be a situation where internal audit should talk with appropriate persons in senior management and point out the control environment problem here.

(b) INTERNAL CONTROL RISK-ASSESSMENT FACTORS

All organizations, regardless of their size, structure, or nature, encounter various risks at all levels of their operations. Because an organization may be impacted by both internal and external events that they cannot fully anticipate, they face risks in every element of their activities. No area of operation is 100% certain; if it were, the risk-free organization would be flooded with competition to take advantage of this risk-free opportunity for profit. That competition would add a new level of risk, and the environment would cease to be risk-free. The COSO report places risk-assessment as an important component of the internal control structure, located just above the control environment.

A first step to performing an organizational risk-assessment is to establish risk objectives. These must be linked to different activities in the organization and should be internally consistent. Risk-assessment is then the process of identifying and managing pertinent risks to allow the organization to achieve its established objectives. Because many external factors change on an ongoing basis, the organization needs to have procedures in place to assess the special risks associated with change.

This section discusses the risk-assessment process as it applies to the overall internal control structure. Internal auditors need to understand this process when evaluating the overall internal control environment as part of reviewing an activity. They also have another very important risk-assessment task: to determine which areas to select for an internal audit review. Those internal audit planning procedures—which include some specific, quantitative measurement techniques—are discussed in Chapter 7, "Evaluating Organization and Audit Risk." The internal auditor should consider that chapter and this section as complementary.

(i) Risk-Assessment Objectives.

Objective-setting is the first step to establishing an effective risk-assessment program as a component of internal control. This objective-setting process can be a highly structured, formal process (as discussed in Chapter 7) for internal audit planning purposes, or it can be a rather informal process. An organization's values treatment or the chairperson's message covering strategy can represent the organization's broad objectives. For example, the chairperson of an organization may state an objective for the organization to be "the market leader for product XYZ." All other more specific objectives and strategies would flow from this broad objective statement.

The above broad objective statement would typically result in linked but very specific objectives covering various areas of organization activities, such as engineering and marketing. These more specific objectives might be defined in terms of critical success factors at various levels. For example, in order to be a market leader for product XYZ, the manufacturing department might establish a performance goal that a minimum of 99.9% of the products will leave the production line with no inspection defects. Although objectives and goals can cover many areas of operations, this example would relate to the organization's total quality management initiative, again discussed in Chapter 33.

Internal control objectives normally fit into one of three broad categories: operations objectives, financial-reporting objectives, and compliance objectives. These are the same objective areas that were introduced in our overall definition of internal control, discussed previously. While these objectives should be considered when evaluating any internal control component or activity, they are particularly relevant here when considering internal control risks.

Operations Objectives

Operations objectives refer to an organization's basic mission, its purpose for existence. The prior example statement about being a market leader for product XYZ is such an operations objective. Similarly, the inspection rate objective mentioned in connection with XYZ is such an operations objective. A clear set of overall operational objectives coupled with appropriately linked subobjectives, is critical for success. A manufacturing subobjective to reduce costs only may be in conflict with the overall market leader objective if the result is a high rate of faulty products.

Objectives must reflect the industry and economic environment in which the organization operates. Management should change these objectives from time to time to reflect new conditions, such as changes in technology or new competitors. Operational objectives accomplish little if they do not reflect current and attainable reality. An organization can state an objective to have an annual 20% return on investment (ROI); however, if they have never been close to that goal and if there have been no other lower-level plans or objectives made to achieve that 20% ROI, it becomes an almost hollow statement that could be treated with derision by both the public and the members of the organization.

Internal auditors should always keep operations objectives in mind when performing their review. This key component of the operational approach to internal auditing is discussed in Chapter 4.

Financial-Reporting Objectives

Financial-reporting objectives cover that part of internal control that had been called internal *accounting* control by external auditors. Objectives here cover published financial statements, such as publicly reported earning statements, as well as various interim reports. Although the emphasis on financial reporting often is considered only in terms of publicly owned entities, the objectives here apply to all entities. Private organizations must have fairly presented, accurate financial statements for purposes of requesting credit from their bank or for filing accurate tax returns. Similarly, not-for-profit organizations have a need for financial-reporting objectives. All interested parties, such as investors, creditors, customers, or suppliers, depend on reliable financial statements.

The standards established by the AICPA are of help in defining financial statement objectives. A key component of any financial-reporting objective is that the financial statements must be reliable. That is, the financial statements must be fairly presented in conformity with generally accepted or other relevant accounting principles and should comply with any regulatory agency accounting statement requirements. Although the concepts apply to all types of financial reporting, the AICPA's SAS No. 69[8] defines this concept of fair presentation as follows:

- The accounting principles selected and applied have general acceptance.
- The accounting principles are appropriate in the circumstances.
- The financial statements are informative of the matters that may affect their use, understanding, and interpretation.
- The information presented is classified and summarized in a reasonable manner, such that it is neither too detailed or too condensed.
- The financial statements reflect the underlying transactions and events in a manner that presents the financial position, results of operations, and cash flows stated within a range of acceptable limits; that is, limits that are reasonable and practical to attain in financial statements.

The internal auditor with primarily an operational background and training may read the above quote from SAS No. 69 and say, "I'm an operational auditor, and this only applies to the CPA-type external auditors." That is not really true for the modern internal auditor! The concepts for fair presentation of financial-related reports should apply to all other reports used within the organization. The internal auditor who does not have a strong accounting background should look at all financial reports encountered through the course of an audit and ask similar questions of the nature of the report's presentation. For example, the auditor may find that a manufacturing division is sending a report on scrap materials costs to a central headquarters office. Due to the manner in which the use of scrap materials is reported, an internal auditor may question the fairness of these reported results. This is a valid area for internal audit to suggest the need for better financial-reporting objectives.

Compliance Objectives

The modern organization today is subjected to a large and increasing number of laws and regulations. Organizations must establish objectives and take actions to remain in compliance with these rules. This is an area where the organization should establish specific objectives to assure compliance in these special operational areas. For example, the organization may need to establish specific objectives regarding compliance with environmental laws and regulations.

In the United States, compliance with laws and regulations has become critical since the early 1990s due to an increasing tendency to criminalize violations that were once subject to fines and other civil penalties. A company that once might have been given a slap on the wrist for some violation might today find that the company officers could now be subject to criminal proceedings and the company to an onerous fine of hundreds of millions of dollars. The Organizational Sentencing Guidelines outlines these penalties, as well as potential corrective action to lower them. These matters are discussed in Chapter 31, "Loss Prevention and Fraud Security," and in Chapter 34, "Changing Role of Audit Activities."

---

[8] American Institute of Certified Public Accountants, *The Meaning of "Presented Fairly in Conformity with Generally Accepted Accounting Principles" in the Independent Auditor's Report* (New York: AICPA, 1992).

An organization's level of compliance with applicable laws and regulations can have a significant impact, both positively and negatively, on other operations. As part of its overall control objective–setting process, the organization should establish strong performance objectives in this area. Internal audit should consider periodic reviews of legal and regulatory compliance, such as those discussed in Chapter 35, on business ethics.

Overlap and Achievement of Objectives

An objective in one category may overlap or support one in another area. The COSO report gives as an example the goal ''Close quarterly within 10 workdays,'' which supports both operations and financial-reporting needs. Management and internal auditors should realize that these various objectives may very well overlap in their purposes. This should present no problem to either the organization's overall internal control structure or to the internal auditor reviewing these various internal control objectives. A more serious problem, however, occurs when objectives somewhat overlap but contain ''holes'' or inconsistencies. A financial objective may be in place covering all operating divisions while some, but not all, of these operating divisions may have a complementary operations objective. Such inconsistencies would require management attention.

The COSO report emphasizes that the establishment of objectives is ''a prerequisite for effective internal control.'' Those objectives provide targets that management can use to measure its own performance and should be expressed in consistent terms throughout the organization. Key success factors and other measures should be installed to measure whether management is achieving the goals, and a reporting system should alert appropriate levels of management when there is a risk that significant objectives will be missed. Internal audit should be part of that reporting.

(ii) Risk Identification and Assessment. An organization's ability to achieve its objectives can be at risk due to a variety of internal and external factors. As part of its overall control structure, the effective organization should have a process in place to evaluate the potential risks that may impact attainment of its various stated objectives. While this type of risk-assessment process is less formal than the quantitative risk-assessment process discussed as part of the internal audit planning process in Chapter 8, there should be some level of formality or action in the process. An organization that has an informal objective of ''no changes'' in its marketing plans may want to assess the risk of not achieving that objective due to the entry of new competitors that may place pressures on the objective of doing the same as in the prior year.

Risk assessment should be a forward-looking process. That is, many organizations have found that the best time and place to assess their various levels of risks is during annual or periodic planning process. This risk-assessment process should be performed at all levels and for virtually all activities within the organization. As described in the COSO report, this risk analysis is a three-step process:

1. Estimate the significance of the risk.
2. Assess the likelihood of frequency of the risk occurring.
3. Consider how the risk should be managed and assess what actions must be taken.

This process puts the responsibility on management to go through the steps to assess whether a risk is significant and then to take appropriate actions. This is a process that has been used frequently by internal auditors. For example, Chapter 19 discusses computer security risk assessment issues, including contingency planning. This is the process where an auditor might assess both whether a computerized application is critical to the organization and whether it has an adequate disaster-recovery backup plan. Internal audit can assist members of management who are not familiar with this type of a risk-assessment process.

The COSO report emphasizes that risk analysis is not a theoretical process, and it often can be critical to an entity's overall success. As part of its overall assessment of internal control, management should take steps to assess the risks that may impact the overall organization as well as the risks over various organization activities or entities.

Organization Levels of Risks

Certain risks may affect the overall organization and could be caused by either internal or external sources. The COSO report has a series of very appropriate examples that, by their nature, explain these types of risks.

Organization Risks Due to External Factors

- Technological developments can affect the nature and timing of research and development, or lead to changes in procurement
- Changing customer needs or expectations can affect product development, production processing, customer service, pricing, or warranties.
- Competition can alter marketing or service activities.
- New legislation or regulations can force changes in operating policies or strategies.
- Natural catastrophes can lead to changes in operations or information systems and highlight the need for contingency planning.
- Economic changes can have an impact on decisions related to financing, capital expenditures, or expansion.

Organization Risks Due to Internal Factors

- A disruption in information systems processing can adversely affect the entity's operations.
- The quality of personnel hired and methods of training and motivation can influence the level of control consciousness within the entity.
- A change in management responsibilities can affect the way certain controls are effected.
- The nature of the organization's activities, and the extent of employee accessibility to assets, can contribute to misappropriation of resources.
- An unassertive or ineffective board or audit committee can provide opportunities for indiscretions.

The above examples were taken directly from the COSO report and illustrate the wide range and variety of potential risks that might impact an organization. Some of the above examples might be identified by management teams or internal audit. Others, such as the potential problem of the inactive board audit committee, are really the responsibility of an external source to highlight these concerns to appropriate levels of senior management. However, all have a responsibility to identify appropriate levels of organization-wide risks and to take steps for corrective action where appropriate.

Activity-Level Risks

In addition to the organization-wide risks, risks should also be assessed at an individual business unity or activity level. Risks should be considered at each significant business unit as well as for key activities such as the marketing function or information systems. In many instances, these activity-level concerns contribute to the organization-wide risks. The lack of effective contingency planning for new computer applications as they are placed into production may contribute to an organization-wide risk.

While organization-wide risks are often best assessed as part of the annual planning process, activity-level risks should be identified on an ongoing basis, depending on the overall process with the risk. That is, a risk-assessment procedure should be built into various planning processes throughout the organization. Examples might include the introduction of a new product or a proposal to embark on a new computer systems development project. In all cases, the organization should attempt to have some type of risk-assessment process in place. Appropriate actions or provisions for the risk should be initiated as part of the management planning process for the activity.

Internal auditors should be aware of the risk-assessment process in place for various activities and should assess its effectiveness when performing reviews over these activities. Where no such risk-assessment process exists, internal audit should highlight this need as an audit report finding and recommendation. All too often, management may have a process in place that gives the appearance of risk-assessment but lacks any substance. For example, a new product authorization approval form will have a box for the requester to describe the risks associated with the proposed product. Local management may consistently describe them as ''low,'' with no further analysis. This assessment may not even be questioned until there is some type of massive failure. When performing reviews in these areas, internal auditors should ask to see the analysis or to discuss the reasoning behind the ''low'' assessment. If nothing exists, the auditor will have an issue to report to senior management.

(iii) Managing Change in the Organization.   The objective-setting and risk-assessment processes discussed earlier typically take place at a single point in time, normally annually but sometimes more frequently. However, the various external and internal events that can impact the organization can occur on a continuous basis, and some type of process should be in place to detect those changes and to take appropriate actions in response to them. The nature of these changes can include new legislation, a legal ruling that may require some action, new competition, or new technological developments. Rather than waiting for the annual planning cycle to recur, the organization should have a mechanism in place to respond to these changes that includes, per the COSO report, ''identifying potential causes of achieving or failing to achieve an objective, assessing the likelihood that such causes will occur, evaluating the probable effect on achievement of the objectives and considering the degree to which the risk can be controlled or the opportunity exploited.''

The COSO report also identifies a series of specific change circumstances that should

Figure 2.10   Change Circumstances Requiring Special Attention

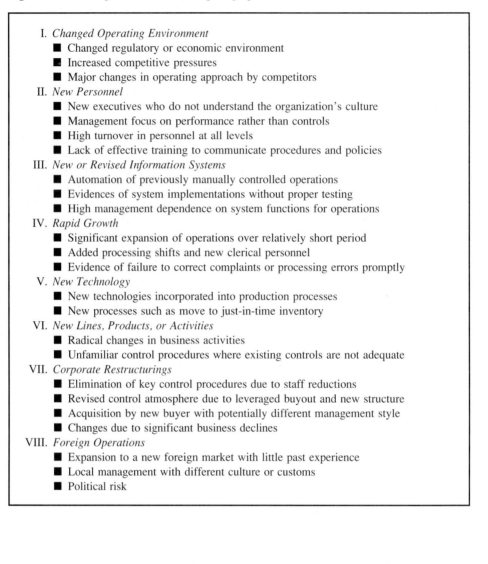

I. *Changed Operating Environment*
- Changed regulatory or economic environment
- Increased competitive pressures
- Major changes in operating approach by competitors

II. *New Personnel*
- New executives who do not understand the organization's culture
- Management focus on performance rather than controls
- High turnover in personnel at all levels
- Lack of effective training to communicate procedures and policies

III. *New or Revised Information Systems*
- Automation of previously manually controlled operations
- Evidences of system implementations without proper testing
- High management dependence on system functions for operations

IV. *Rapid Growth*
- Significant expansion of operations over relatively short period
- Added processing shifts and new clerical personnel
- Evidence of failure to correct complaints or processing errors promptly

V. *New Technology*
- New technologies incorporated into production processes
- New processes such as move to just-in-time inventory

VI. *New Lines, Products, or Activities*
- Radical changes in business activities
- Unfamiliar control procedures where existing controls are not adequate

VII. *Corporate Restructurings*
- Elimination of key control procedures due to staff reductions
- Revised control atmosphere due to leveraged buyout and new structure
- Acquisition by new buyer with potentially different management style
- Changes due to significant business declines

VIII. *Foreign Operations*
- Expansion to a new foreign market with little past experience
- Local management with different culture or customs
- Political risk

demand the special attention of management. These have been summarized in Figure 2.10. While this table should not be considered all-inclusive, it points to some of the special circumstances that can impact both internal control objective-setting and the risk-assessment process.

This type of overall risk-assessment component of internal control should be in place in all organizations, no matter what their size. This component is just as important for a small, private, not-for-profit association as for a large corporation. Also, to the extent practicable, this risk-assessment component of internal control should be forward-looking in order to anticipate changes that might occur and to plan for appropriate changes. Strong information systems can play a significant role in helping to predict these potential future risks. As highlighted in the COSO report, ''No one can foresee the future with certainty, but the better an entity can anticipate changes and their effects, the fewer the unpleasant surprises.''

(c) CONTROL ACTIVITY INTERNAL CONTROL COMPONENTS

The COSO report defines control activities as the policies and procedures that help ensure that management actions identified to address risks are carried out. While the term ''activities'' is used in the COSO definition of internal control, this component includes a wide range of activities and procedures, from establishing organization standards with appropriate segregation of duties to reviewing and approving key operations reports properly. Control activities should exist at all levels and activities within the organization. In many cases, these activities may overlap one another. A control activity, however, should exist to help the organization achieve a control objective in a given area.

The concept of control activities should be familiar to the modern internal auditor. Although the COSO report talks of objectives and control activities, internal auditors have often used the terms *control objective* and *audit procedures* when developing an audit program to perform a review in a given area. Chapter 21 through 30 contain such audit objectives and procedures for many operational areas. An internal auditor might develop a procedure to sample a set of invoice records from an accounts payable system to test whether the invoice was properly coded and the discount properly calculated. The audit objective is to determine if the invoices were correctly handled. The audit procedure is to use the sampling techniques to review a representative set of these invoice records.

Just as the internal auditor performs certain audit procedures, other levels of management should have control activities installed to ascertain that their control objectives in various areas are being achieved. Although oriented toward specific internal audit procedures, many chapters in this book discuss other control activities in the modern organization. This section discusses how COSO has defined the types of control activities. A particularly important aspect of this section of the COSO report is the emphasis given to controls over information systems. These are discussed in greater detail in Chapters 16 through 20.

(i) Types of Control Activities. Many different definitions of controls have been used, including manual, computer system, or management controls. Chapter 4 discusses controls in preventive, corrective, and detective terms. No one set of control definitions is correct for all management situations or for all organizations. While the definitions used in the subsequent chapters of this book should provide guidance to internal auditors, the important point made by COSO is that all members of management should think of the importance of various controls and control activities to achieve objectives, no matter what their business function. The COSO report suggests a series of control activities that might be installed by the organization. While the report certainly does not suggest that this is an all-inclusive list, these control activities represent the range and variety of control activities in the modern organization.

- *Top-Level Reviews.* Management at various levels should review the results of various areas of performance, contrasting those results with budgets, competitive statistics, and other benchmark measurements. Management actions to follow up on the results of these reviews and to take corrective action represent a control activity.

- *Direct Functional or Activity Management.* Managers at various levels of the organization should review the operational reports from their control systems and take corrective action as appropriate. Many management systems have been built to produce a series of exception reports covering various activities. For example, a computer security system will have a mechanism to report unauthorized access attempts. The control activity here is the management process of following up on these reported events and taking appropriate corrective action.

- *Information Processing.* Modern automated systems contain many control areas where systems check for compliance with a variety of control areas and then report any exceptions. Those reported exception items in need of follow-up should receive corrective action by systems operational personnel or by management. Other areas of information systems control activities include controls over the development of new systems or over access to data and program files.

- *Physical Controls.* An organization should have appropriate control over its physical assets, including fixtures, inventories, and negotiable securities. An active program of physical inventories represents a major control activity.

- *Performance Indicators.* Management should relate various sets of data, both operational and financial, to one another and should take appropriate analytical, investigative, and corrective action. This process represents an important control activity to the organization that can also satisfy financial- and operational-reporting requirements.

- *Segregation of Duties.* Duties should be divided or segregated among different people to reduce the risk of error or inappropriate actions. This is a basic internal control discussed throughout this book as part of specific internal control procedures.

This list, included in the COSO report, represents only a small number of the many control procedures that can be performed as part of the normal course of business in the modern organization. These activities will keep the organization on track toward achieving its many objectives.

Control activities usually involve both a policy establishing what should be done and procedures to effect those policies. The COSO report recognizes that policies sometimes may only be communicated orally by appropriate levels of management. However, COSO points out that no matter how communicated, the policy should be implemented ''thoughtfully, conscientiously, and consistently.'' This is a strong message for internal auditors reviewing control activities. Even through an organization may have a published policy covering a given area, an internal auditor should review the established control procedure that supports the policy.

Procedures are of little use unless there is a sharp focus on the condition to which the policy is directed. All too often, an organization may establish an exception report as part of an automated system that receives little more than a cursory review by the report recipients. However, depending on the types of conditions reported, those reported exceptions should receive appropriate follow-up actions, which may vary depending on the size of the organization and the activity reported in the exception report.

(ii) Integration of Control Activities with Risk Assessment. Control activities should be closely related to the identified risks discussed as part of that component of the internal control framework. Internal control is a process, and appropriate control activities should be installed to address identified risks. Control activities should not be installed just because they seem to be the "right thing to do" if management has identified no significant risks in the area where the control activity would be installed. All too often, management may still have control activities or procedures in place that perhaps once served some control-risk concern, although the concerns have largely gone away. A control activity or procedure should not be discarded because there have not been control violation incidents in recent years, but management needs periodically to reevaluate the relative risks. All control activities should contribute to the overall control structure.

The comments above refer to what might be called "dumb" control activities that once may have had a purpose but currently accomplish little. For example, business data-processing computer operations centers, up through the 1970s, had input-output clerks who manually checked file-record count reports from various programs in automated systems. Computer operating system facilities effectively automated the need for those control procedures by the early 1980s. However, some organizations continued to employ these input-output clerks long after they were needed. They logged in their record counts and never found an exception. If there had been an exception, the operating system would have flagged the problem and would have initiated corrective action long before any reports were delivered to the input-output desk. This became a "dumb" control because it now accomplishes little or nothing in the overall control environment. While some controls will cease in their relative importance, other basic controls, such as the importance of strong separation-of-duties controls over incompatible functions, should always remain in effect.

(iii) Controls over Information Systems. The COSO report emphasizes that control procedures are needed over all significant information systems—financial, operational, and compliance-related. The COSO report places a much stronger emphasis on the importance of information systems controls than had been the case for earlier internal control–related standards. The earlier AICPA standards, for example, treated data-processing controls as a separate area with special control standards. AICPA auditing standards only recognized the need to include information systems controls as part of the overall control structure when they released SAS No. 55 in 1988, as discussed earlier.

The COSO report goes even further in recognizing the importance of information systems controls as a key activity in the overall control environment. The report then breaks down information systems controls into the broad classifications of general and application controls. The first of these two apply to many, if not all, of the applications processed within the information systems function to help ensure adequate control procedures over all applications.

A physical security lock on the door to the computer center is a general control. The locked door serves as a general control for applications running at that data center. Application controls refer to the controls built into or around a specific information systems application. A program control in a weekly payroll application program that prevents any employee from being paid for over 100 hours in a given week is an example of an application reasonableness control.

Information systems controls will be discussed in Chapters 16 through 20. Although discussed in greater detail in those chapters, the COSO report highlights a series of information systems control areas for consideration by persons evaluating the overall adequacy of internal controls.

- *Data Center Operations General Controls.* Control here includes all centralized data center or computer systems controls, including job scheduling, storage management, and disaster-recovery planning. These controls typically are the responsibility of data operations specialists in centralized computer or server centers. However, with newer, more modern systems connected to one another through telecommunications links, these controls can be distributed across a network of server-based systems.

- *Systems Software General Controls.* Modern data-processing operations use complex operating systems, database management tools, computer language processors, and other specialized software products that support most if not all applications in the data centers. General controls should be in place for these types of software, including procedures to protect against improper use or alteration of the system's internal tables.

- *Access Security General Controls.* The modern data center may be accessed by many users over a network of telecommunication links. Computer systems need passwords and related controls to prevent unauthorized users. Although access controls can be built into a specific computer application, these are normally classified as general controls to monitor access for all systems users.

- *Application System Development and Maintenance Controls.* Whether an information systems organization purchases software to build its applications or designs and programs them in-house, controls over the development process are needed. These are to assure that new applications are implemented with proper controls and according to user needs. Once placed into production, controls over the application-development process are also important. These types of controls are discussed in Chapter 18, on auditing new applications under development.

- *Application Controls.* These are the controls built into specific applications to help ensure the completeness and accuracy of transaction processing. The COSO report talks about the importance of individual application controls to the overall control structure. Application controls are discussed in greater detail in Chapter 17.

The COSO report stresses that general information systems controls and application controls are interrelated, and that both must be considered. In the early days of what was then called ''computer auditing,'' reviewers sometimes focused only on one side of these controls, often the overall general controls. For example, they would review various data center operations general controls—such as physical security—and often paid little attention to the controls over the applications operating in those data centers. General controls are needed to support the functioning of specific application controls, but both are needed to ensure the completeness and accuracy of information processing. Strong data center physical security controls contribute little to the control environment if controls over specific applications are generally weak.

This section of the COSO report concludes with a discussion on the need to consider the impact of evolving technologies, such as computer-aided systems engineering (CASE) and expert systems. The impact of these newer evolving technologies always should be considered when evaluating information systems control activities. Due to the rapid introduction of new technologies, what is new today will be considered mature tomorrow, soon to be replaced by something else. New technology controls will be discussed in greater detail in Chapter 20.

(d) INFORMATION AND COMMUNICATION INTERNAL CONTROL COMPONENTS

The COSO model of internal control describes most of its components as layers, one on top of another. The control environment component was the first layer of the foundation. Monitoring, introduced later in this chapter, is the upper layer of the model. The information and communication component, however, is different. As illustrated in Figure 2.1, this component is not a horizontal layer but spans across all of the other components.

In the original draft of the COSO report, information and communication were treated as two separate components. In order to make the final report less complex, the two were combined in the final draft. Information and communications are related, but are really very distinct internal control components. Both are important portions of the internal control framework. Appropriate information must be communicated up and down through the organization in a manner and time frame that allow people to carry out their various responsibilities. These information flows are supported by automated systems. In addition to formal and informal communication systems, organizations must have effective procedures in place to communicate with internal and external parties. As part of their evaluation of internal controls, internal auditors should develop a good understanding of the information and communication flows or processes in the organization.

(i) Relationship of Information and Internal Control.
Various types of information are needed at all levels of the organization in order to achieve operational, financial-reporting, and compliance objectives. The organization, for example, needs proper information in order to prepare the financial reports that are communicated to outside investors. It also needs both internal cost information and external market preference information in order to make correct marketing decisions. This information must flow both from the top levels of the organization on down and upward from lower levels. Figure 2.11 shows the information flow for an example product marketing decision in a medium-sized organization. This diagram simplifies the process because many more parties may become involved in larger organizations. An internal auditor should always attempt to understand and to document this information flow when reviewing a process and evaluating its controls.

Although Figure 2.11 shows the information flow as essentially a manual process, these processes are typically highly automated in the modern organization. COSO takes a very broad approach to the concept of an information system. The report recognizes the importance of automated systems but makes the point that information systems can be manual, automated, or conceptual. Any of these information systems can be either formal or informal. COSO uses the example of conversations with customers or suppliers, who can be highly important sources of information. These often informal types of information systems may not be documented but should still operate as some form of process. That is, the effective organizations should have some information system in place to listen to customer requests or complaints and to forward that customer-initiated information to appropriate personnel.

COSO also emphasizes the importance of keeping its information and supporting systems consistent with overall organization needs. Information systems adapt to support changes on many levels. Internal auditors often encounter cases where an information system was implemented many years ago to support different needs. Although its application controls may be good, the information system does not support the current needs of the organization. Chapter 17 discusses how an internal auditor should evaluate the

Figure 2.11 Product Marketing Decision Information Flowchart

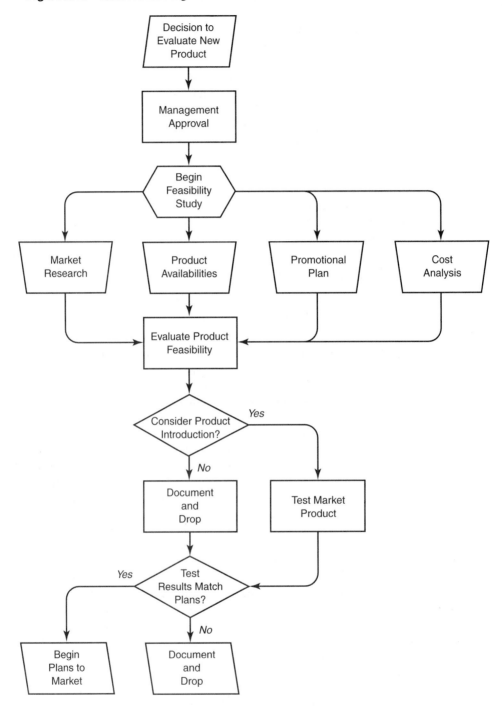

effectiveness of an automated information system. The COSO report takes a much broader view of information systems, both automated and manual, than has been discussed in previous auditing standards. This broadening viewpoint points to the need for all internal auditors to become competent in understanding both manual information systems processes and computer processing technologies.

Strategic and Integrated Systems

Accounting and financial processes were the first automated systems in organizations, starting with the unit record or ''IBM card'' accounting machines in the 1950s and then moving to the earliest computer systems. Some organizations may have upgraded their automated systems over time with the introduction of new computer technologies, but their basic mix of supporting automated applications has not changed significantly. An organization will have its general ledger, payroll, inventory, accounts receivable, accounts payable, and related financial-based processes as core information systems, without too much else. The COSO report suggests that the effective organization should go a step further and implement both strategic and integrated information systems.

By a strategic system, the report suggests that management should consider the planning, design, and implementation of its information systems as part of its overall organization strategy. These strategic systems then support the organization's overall business and help it to carry out its overall business missions. There have been many examples of companies that developed strategic information systems to support their business strategies—systems that moved them even further forward. An example might be American Airlines, which developed its SABRE automated reservation system in the 1960s, greatly enhancing its ability to sell tickets and make more effective use of its resources. Then, the same airline developed the first frequent-flyer program in the early 1980s, again giving it a business edge. Other airlines developed similar or even better information systems subsequently, but American Airlines' systems gave them an initial marketing and customer-acceptance edge for a time.

The effective organization should develop strategic information systems, whether automated or even manual. Not every organization has the resources or needs to develop systems of the nature or scale of SABRE; however, even smaller systems should be designed and developed to support the organization's strategies. These strategic systems will allow organizations to understand and to respond better to changes in their marketplaces and control environments.

The COSO report also talks about the importance of integrating automated information systems with other operations. Examples would be a full-automated manufacturing system that controls both production machines and equipment inventories or a highly automated distribution system that controls inventory and schedules shipments. The report uses electronic data interchange (EDI) systems as an example of the type of automated system that provides for operations integration. The audit implications of EDI systems are discussed in Chapter 24.

These comments about strategic information systems are a step forward or into the future when contrasted with the information systems–related comments from earlier internal control standards. COSO makes the point, however, that it is a mistake to assume that just because a system is new, it will provide better control. Older systems have presumably been tried and tested through use while the new system can have unknown or untested control weaknesses. The internal auditor can play a significant role in assessing whether controls are adequate in new automated systems by reviewing these new systems while under development. Audit procedures here will be discussed in Chapter 18.

Quality of Information

The COSO report has a brief section on the importance of the quality of information. Poor-quality information systems, filled with errors and omissions, affect management's ability to make appropriate decisions. Reports should contain enough data and information to support effective control activities. The COSO report points out that this concept of quality of information includes ascertaining whether:

- The content of reported information is appropriate
- The information is timely and available when required
- The information is current or at least the latest available
- The data and information are correct
- The information is accessible to appropriate parties

These points all mention issues that should be covered in overall systems design. If an information system does not meet these quality issues, it is possible that the system will not meet management requirements. The internal auditor should always be aware of the quality of the information produced by all systems, in particular an automated system. This concern goes beyond the traditional role of auditors, who have historically looked only at systems controls and given little attention to quality-related issues.

(ii) The Communications Aspect of Internal Control. The COSO report highlights communications as an element of internal control that is separate from information when describing this component of COSO's internal control framework. Communication channels are inherent in information systems that provide the details to individuals to carry out their financial reporting, operational, and compliance responsibilities. The report emphasizes that communication must take place in a broader sense in dealing with various individuals and groups and their expectations.

The existence of appropriate channels of communication is an important element in the overall framework of internal control. An organization needs to establish these communication channels throughout its various organization levels and activities, and between the organization and various interested outsiders. Although communication channels can have many dimensions, the COSO report highlights the separate components of internal and external communications.

Internal auditors have always looked at communication channels in their reviews. However, auditors have focused on formal channels of communication such as procedure manuals or published systems documentation. Internal audit reports frequently cite entities for a lack of documentation in their reviews. While that documentation is a very important element of communication, the COSO report takes an expanded view when considering internal control.

Communications: Internal Components

According to COSO, perhaps the most important component of communication is the need that all personnel should periodically receive a message from senior management reminding them that their internal control responsibilities must be taken seriously. The clarity of this message is important to ensure that the overall organization follows effective internal control principles. This message is part of the ''tone at the top,'' discussed earlier as part of the control environment, and should be communicated throughout the organization.

In addition to these overall messages, all members of the organization need to understand how their specific duties and actions fit into the total internal control system. If this understanding is not present, various parties in the organization will ignore errors and make decisions thinking no one cares. The COSO report gives an example of unit heads in a large organization who were asked to sign a periodic report indicating that monthly reconciliation had been performed by their units. Because the reconciliation process had not been adequately communicated to these managers, they approved the report only indicating that differences had been identified. No one was attempting to correct the errors. Management did not communicate the appropriate message to these unit managers about what was expected of them when they approved the monthly reports. Personnel need to know that certain of their activities may be unethical, illegal, or otherwise improper.

People also need to know how to respond to errors or other unexpected events in the course of performing their duties. They typically require communication in terms of messages from management, procedure documentation, and adequate training. Internal auditors often encounter these issues in the course of their review. However, while auditors may have historically presented a finding about the lack of documentation as a fairly minor point, the COSO report points out that this lack of documentation may mean a lack of appropriate internal control communication channels.

Communication must flow in two directions, and the COSO report emphasizes that personnel must have a mechanism to report matters upward throughout the organization. This upward communication has two components: communication through normal organization channels and special, confidential reporting channels. Normal reporting refers to the management process in which members of the organizations are expected to report status information, errors, or problems up through their supervisors. This communication should be freely encouraged, and the organization should avoid shooting the messenger when bad news is reported. Otherwise, it will be understood throughout the organization that employees should report only good news, and managers may not become aware of significant problems.

Because personnel may sometimes be reluctant to report matters to their immediate supervisors, COSO suggests that organizations also need to install mechanisms to report information outside of normal organization channels. This can be accomplished through a toll-free telephone line set up to receive anonymous calls, or through an evening open-office-door policy by senior managers, who allocate time to talk to personnel. The nature of this type of communication channel will depend on the size and style of the organization, but COSO considers these channels important. In addition to allowing employees to communicate their complaints or concerns, the organization should establish procedures to act on these reported matters. All must understand that there will be no reprisals for reporting such information outside of normal communication channels.

This section of the COSO report concludes with the importance of communication channels between top management and the board of directors. Management must inform the board of major developments, risks, and occurrences. The board, in turn, must independently review operations and communicate their concerns and decisions to management. Internal audit has a key roll in this communication channel, as is discussed in Chapter 6, ''Serving the Audit Committee of the Board.'' While this type of two-way communication is not very common today, more instances should occur in the future, and the modern internal auditor should be prepared to play a key role in facilitating that communication.

External Communications

An organization needs to establish appropriate communication channels with interested outside parties. Today, these parties can include customers, suppliers, shareholders, bankers, regulators, and others. This communication should go beyond the public relations–type of function that large organizations have established to talk about themselves. As with internal communication channels, external information must flow in two directions. The information provided to outside parties should be relevant to their needs so they can better understand an organization and the challenges it faces. The organization that sends out highly optimistic reports to outsiders when many inside the organization realize there are problems is also giving an inappropriate message to its own employees.

    External communications can be a very important mechanism for identifying potential control problems. Customer complaints (involving such matters as service, billings, or product quality) often can point out significant operating and control problems. The organization should establish independent mechanisms to receive these messages and to appropriately act on them. This form of communication should be investigated and corrective action taken when necessary.

    Management should establish appropriate communication channels with outside parties such as financial analysts or even regulators. Open and frank two-way communications may alert the organization to potential communication problems or allow it to discuss and solve problems in advance of adverse publicity. One of these outside parties, often considered to be almost an insider, is the independent public accountant or external auditor. He or she can provide an important channel of communication, particularly with regard to control problems. Senior management and the board should encourage open, two-way communication with the independent public accountant.

Means and Methods of Communication

There is no one correct means of communicating internal control information within the organization. The modern organization can communicate its messages through many vehicles, including bulletin board announcements, procedure manuals, videotaped presentation, or speeches by members of management. Often, however, the action taken by the communicator either before or after the message will give a stronger signal to the recipients of that communication. The COSO report summarizes this internal control element as follows:

> *An entity with a long and rich history of operating with integrity, and whose culture is well understood by people through the organization, will likely find little difficulty in communicating its message. An entity without such a tradition will likely need to put more into the way the messages are communicated.*

(e) MONITORING COMPONENT OF INTERNAL CONTROL

The capstone of the internal control framework model, as shown in Figure 2.3, is the monitoring component. While internal control systems will work effectively with proper support from management, control procedures, and both information and communication linkages, a process must be in place to monitor these activities. Monitoring activities has long been the role of internal auditors, who perform reviews to assess compliance with established procedures; however, the COSO report takes a broader view of monitoring while still reserving a significant portion of that activity to internal audit.

COSO recognizes that control procedures and other systems change over time. What appeared to be effective when it was installed may not be that effective in the future due to changing external conditions, new personnel, new systems and procedures, and a variety of other factors. A process must be in place to assess the effectiveness of established internal control components and to take corrective action when appropriate. While this certainly points to the role of internal audit, this internal control component cannot be relegated to the auditors while management remains somewhat oblivious to potential control problems. An organization needs to establish a variety of monitoring activities to measure the effectiveness of its internal controls.

Monitoring can be accomplished through a series of separate special evaluations as well as through ongoing activities. The latter—ongoing activities—refer to processes that monitor performance and make corrective action when required. The classic control system described at the beginning of this chapter and illustrated in Figure 2.1 is an example of how a system, such as a home thermostat, will monitor its activities and initiate corrective action.

(i) Ongoing Monitor Activities.   Many routine business functions can be characterized as monitoring activities. Although auditors and others do not always think of these as monitoring activities, the COSO report gives the following examples of the ongoing monitoring component of internal control.

- *Operating Management Normal Functions.* Normal management reviews over operations and financial reports constitute an important ongoing monitoring activity. However, special attention should be given to reported exceptions and potential internal control deviations. Internal control is enhanced if reports are reviewed on a regular basis and corrective action initiated for any reported exceptions.

- *Communications from External Parties.* This element of monitoring is closely related to the component of communication from external parties discussed earlier. External communication measuring monitors, such as a customer complaint telephone number, are important; however, the organization needs to monitor closely these calls and then initiate corrective action when appropriate.

- *Organization Structure and Supervisory Activities.* While more senior management should review summary reports and take corrective action, the first level of supervision and the related organization structure often plays an even more significant role in monitoring. Direct supervision of clerical activities, for example, should routinely review and correct lower-level errors and should assure clerical employee performance. This review is also an area in which the importance of an adequate separation of duties is emphasized by COSO. Dividing duties between employees allows them to serve as a monitoring check on one another.

- *Internal and External Audit Reports.* As mentioned earlier, both internal and external auditors play an important monitoring role in the organization's control structure. As will be discussed in subsequent chapters of this book, audit reports should both identify control weaknesses and suggest corrective actions.

- *Physical Inventories and Asset Reconciliations.* Periodic physical inventories, whether of store room stock or negotiable securities, are an important monitoring activity. An annual inventory in a retail store, for example, may indicate a significant merchandise loss. A possible reason for this loss could be theft, pointing to the need for better security controls.

These are examples from a longer list in the COSO report. They illustrate procedures that are often in place in organizations but are not thought of as ongoing monitoring activities. Any activity that reviews organization activities on an ongoing basis and then suggests potential corrective action can be thought of as a monitoring activity.

(ii) Separate Internal Control Evaluation.   While COSO points out the importance of ongoing monitoring activities to support the internal control framework, the report also suggests that ''it may be useful to take a fresh look from time to time'' at the effectiveness of internal controls through separate evaluations. The frequency and nature of these separate special reviews will greatly depend on the nature of the organization and the significance of the risks it must control. While management may want to initiate from time to time an evaluation of its entire internal control system, most reviews should be initiated to assess a specific area of control. These reviews may often be initiated when there has been an acquisition, a significant change in business, or some other significant activity. This is often the time that internal audit will be requested to perform a special review, as discussed in Chapter 8, on planning and organizing.

COSO also emphasizes that these evaluations can be performed by direct line management through self-assessment types of reviews. Internal audit is not required to perform the review unless requested by senior management; the scheduling of these will be dependent on audit's risk-assessment process and the resources available to schedule and perform reviews. Considerable time may pass before internal audit may have scheduled a normal review in a given area of operation. However, responsible management in that area should consider scheduling and performing its own self-assessments on a more regular basis. The internally generated review can point out potential control problems and cause operating management to implement corrective action. Because these self-assessment reviews will typically not be as comprehensive as a normal internal audit, internal audit can be requested to perform a more comprehensive review over the same general area if potentially significant problems are encountered through such a limited review.

Internal Control Evaluation Process

The COSO report talks about the evaluation process for reviewing a system of internal controls. The report advises the evaluator first to develop an understanding of the system design, to identify its controls, to test those controls, and then to develop conclusions on the basis of the test results. This is really the internal audit process that will be discussed in some detail throughout the balance of this book. Although the experienced internal auditor should have a good understanding of this process, the COSO report does a good job summarizing the internal audit process in a few paragraphs for the benefit of management.

COSO also mentions another approach for evaluation called *benchmarking,* an approach that is not yet commonly performed by internal auditors. Benchmarking is the process of comparing an organization's processes, control procedures, and other activities with those of peer organizations.

Comparisons may be made with specific similar organizations or against published statistics from similar industry groups. This approach is convenient for some types of measure but filled with dangers for others. For example, it is fairly easy to benchmark the organization size, staffing levels, and average compensations of a sales function against comparable organizations in the same general industry; however, the evaluator may encounter difficulties in trying to compare other factors due to the many small differences that make all organizations unique. Because of their contacts with many organizations, public accounting firms can often help to supply benchmarking data.

Evaluation Action Plans

The COSO report describes the importance of control documentation, particularly when statements about controls are made to outside parties. However, the report recognizes that not all control procedures lend themselves to formal documentation. Many are informal and undocumented although both are regularly performed and highly effective. COSO makes the point that these undocumented controls can be tested and evaluated in the same manner as documented ones. While an appropriate level of documentation makes any evaluation of internal control more efficient and facilitates employees' understanding of how the process works, that documentation is not always essential.

These comments about system documentation seem to run almost contrary to the provisions of the Foreign Corrupt Practices Act (FCPA), discussed earlier in this chapter. When enacted, the FCPA mandated the documentation of all systems. As discussed, for many organizations this resulted in the generation of extensive files of not particularly effective documentation. While the COSO report certainly does not override the FCPA, its description places a reality check on the earlier FCPA documentation requirements.

The COSO report then suggests an action plan for the steps necessary to perform a specific evaluation of internal control. That control-evaluation action plan is summarized in Figure 2.12. While it should not replace the internal control evaluation guidance found

Figure 2.12 Evaluation of Internal Control Action Plan

I. Decide on the evaluation's scope, in terms of the categories of objectives, internal control components, and activities to be addressed.

II. Identify ongoing monitoring activities that routinely provide assurance that internal controls are effective.

III. Analyze control evaluation work and findings by both internal and external auditors.

IV. Prioritize by operating unit, departmental component, or some other means the higher-risk areas that warrant immediate attention.

V. Based on the step IV risk prioritization, develop an evaluation program with short- and long-range segments.

VI. Bring together the parties who will carry out the evaluation. Together, consider not only the scope and time frames, but also the methodology tools to be used; input from the law department, external auditors, and others; means of reporting findings; and expected documentation.

VII. Monitor progress and review findings.

VIII. Take necessary follow-up actions and modify subsequent evaluation segments as necessary.

---

throughout the chapters of this book, the table provides internal audit with a good guide to give to management to explain the controls-review evaluation process.

(iii) Reporting Internal Control Deficiencies.

Whether internal control deficiencies are identified through processes in the internal control system itself, through monitoring activities, or through other external events, these internal control deficiencies should be reported to appropriate levels of management in the organization. The monitoring component of internal control should have identified the deficiencies. The key questions for the evaluator—such as internal audit—is to determine what should be reported given the large body of details that may be encountered, and to whom the reports should be directed.

COSO states that "all internal control deficiencies that can affect the entity's attaining its objectives should be reported to those who can take necessary action." While this statement initially makes sense, the experienced internal auditor will realize that this directive is difficult to implement. The modern organization, no matter how well organized, will be guilty of a variety of internal control errors or omissions. COSO suggests that all of these should be identified and reported, and that even the most minor of errors should be investigated to understand if they were caused by any overall control deficiencies. The report uses the example of an employee's taking a few dollars from the petty cash fund. While the amount may not be significant, COSO urges that the matter be investigated rather than ignored, since "such apparent condoning personal use of the entity's money might send an unintended message to employees." External auditors regularly apply the concept of materiality when performing their reviews. That is, they may decide that some errors are so small that they are not material to the overall conclusion that the external auditor will reach. While the operational efficiency of administrative control is of prime importance, materiality should also be considered when evaluating internal controls in general.

The COSO report then discusses to whom to report internal control deficiencies in the organization. In one paragraph, COSO provides guidance that is useful for evaluations of internal control following COSO and for all internal audit review activities, as discussed in other chapters.

Findings on internal control deficiencies usually should be reported not only to the individual responsible for the function or activity involved, who is in the position to take corrective action, but also to at least one level of management above the directly responsible person. This process enables that individual to provide needed support or oversight for taking corrective action, and to communicate with others in the organization whose activities may be affected. Where findings cut across organizational boundaries, the reporting should cross over as well and be directed to a sufficiently high level to ensure appropriate action.

This is very useful guidance that is mentioned again in Chapter 15 on internal audit reporting techniques. The organization should also develop other reporting procedures such that all control deficiencies, whether encountered through special reviews or through reviews of ongoing operations, are reported to appropriate persons in the organization. Management reporting and monitoring is a highly important aspect of internal control.

2-5 RELATIONSHIP BETWEEN CONTROL OBJECTIVES AND COMPONENTS

The discussion above summarizes the COSO description of an internal control framework. This is a much more complex module than has been described in earlier, pre-COSO internal control definitions. The internal auditor should remember that internal control can be viewed as a three-dimensional model, with separate and independent x, y, and z axes, to use common mathematical notation. The internal control components are the horizontal layers on the y-scale. The three internal control objectives—financial reporting, operations, and compliance with laws and regulations—lay on the x-axis and divide the model with vertical lines. Finally, the z-axis divides the model into the separate activities and entities in the organization. The internal control structure for any area in the organization can be separately viewed using this three-dimensional model approach first illustrated in Figure 2.4.

The model might allow the auditor to think it is possible to consider as a separate unit, for example, the internal control structure for the control procedures component in a ''Division A'' with regard to financial reporting objectives. Internal control, however, is not that simple. While the internal control evaluator can focus on one particular element in this three-dimensional model, each element must be considered with respect to all of the other components in the total framework.

This narrow view of looking at only one element caused the failure of earlier approaches for evaluating internal controls. An auditor might have looked at financial accounting controls and procedures for this same independent Division A while paying little attention to the other related components. If Division A was a separate reporting entity, the external auditor might have stated that the financial reports from Division A were fairly stated, and given little consideration to Division A operational or legal-compliance issues, to control environment or risk-assessment issues, or to other entities in the total organization. This narrow view sometimes caused internal control evaluators to miss significant, interrelated internal control issues.

The COSO report provides an excellent description of the components of an internal control framework, as well as an integrated model that ties these components together. Internal auditors should always keep this broad picture of internal controls in mind when evaluating controls in any area of operations. This does not mean that the internal auditor must test and evaluate every element on every axis of the model when performing an evaluation of internal control for a given element. Rather, the internal auditor should be knowledgeable of the framework and related components that might impact an evaluation of any given element.

Many of the following COSO report chapters discuss procedures for performing reviews and evaluating controls in some given area of the modern organization. They focus on a specific area, such as distribution and shipping controls, discussed in Chapter 25. However, the effective modern internal auditor should consider each of them, with consideration given to the overall internal control framework in the entity reviewed.

2-6 ASSESSING INTERNAL CONTROL EFFECTIVENESS

The COSO report concludes with several sections that express some words of caution about the whole process of installing effective internal controls. The report reminds us that internal control can only provide reasonable but not absolute assurance that an organization will achieve its objectives. For example, a financial institution can have a good set of controls in place to provide management with assurance that the organization is in compliance with significant laws and regulations. A determined rogue employee, however, might be able to circumvent those controls and cause the financial institution to violate some significant regulation. While procedures can be improved to prevent this from happening again, it is very difficult to make control totally fault-free.

These inherent internal control limitations make the role of internal audit even more important in the modern organization. The internal auditor often schedules control reviews in areas where management has reported no problems. Internal audit should continue with these scheduled reviews, reminding management of the limitations of internal control and internal audit's very important role in evaluating those controls.

(a) LIMITATIONS OF INTERNAL CONTROL

The COSO report devotes considerable attention to reminding management that good internal controls will only provide *reasonable assurance* that the entity will achieve its objectives. The report reminds readers that ''internal control is not a panacea.'' These are rather strong words, but the report tries to emphasize that management should not operate under the false assurance that because its internal controls are good, it will not face any significant risks or exposures. Internal control, no matter how effective, will operate somewhat differently with respect to each of the established control objectives.

Failures in human judgment can cause any system of internal controls to break down. These breakdowns can be caused by poor information available at the time, improper training, carelessness, or a wide variety of other factors. It is easy for internal audit to review an entity after such a failure and to easily identify these internal control failures. This kind of analysis is what has sometimes given internal auditors a reputation as the persons who visit the battlefield after the war is over in order to shoot the wounded. This reputation can be avoided through constructive, positive recommendations. When there has been a failure in judgment or a breakdown in internal control, the effective modern internal auditor should look for ways to improve or tighten controls to prevent a recurrence. Nevertheless, the COSO report points out several factors that could prevent internal controls from operating as intended.

(i) Management Overrides or Collusion.

Internal control can only be as effective as the people who are responsible for its operations. Even if the system of internal controls is well constructed and appears effective, a member of management with the authority to do so can override those controls. A very simple or minor example could be found in an organization where all employees are required to wear and show their identification badges when entering the facility. A very senior officer, who is well known and recognized by most employees, could override that rule by not showing her badge when entering the facility. Although probably a fairly trivial matter, the officer is overriding a control by not complying with an established rule. The guard at the door is also at fault by not asking to see the badge. The control override breakdown would be even more serious here if the officer had dressed down the guard for insisting on seeing the badge. Although probably a relatively minor manner, this is an example of management overriding an internal control.

Management has the ability to override certain controls to enhance or protect the entity or to provide the manager with an opportunity for personal gain. The COSO report provides some examples of management overrides.

- A division manager might override a control system to report increased revenue to cover an unanticipated decrease in market share.
- A senior manager might report incorrect earning projections to increase the value of the stock in an upcoming public offering.
- Management might make deliberate misrepresentations to their outside auditors regarding the estimated collectability of a sales contract.

Many more examples of these types of overrides are possible. They generally result in deliberate misrepresentation to the public or to other members of the organization. In most cases, more than one person will be involved in this override. They will be engaging in a collective activity. That is, the more senior manager might insist on making the incorrect earnings statement. A lower-level employee may be asked either to look the other way or actually to violate controls to make the false report. In both instances, controls are being violated due to collusion.

Internal auditors may often find instances where a control has been violated due to collusion. An example would be in a cash receipts operation where one employee opens the mail, removing any cash, and another employee takes the cash to make bank deposits. This is a classic separation-of-duties control. If the two collude to withhold some of the cash for their personal gain, it will be very difficult to detect this control breakdown. These types of control breakdowns are discussed in Chapter 31, "Loss Prevention and Fraud Security."

(ii) Internal Control Costs versus Benefits.   The COSO report cautions that the costs required to implement controls should not exceed the benefits to be received from those controls. Consideration should always be given to risk of a control failure, along with the related costs of installing an effective control. The report gives the example of a decision as to whether an organization should install a sophisticated raw material inventory-control system given that the inventory does not represent a high element of cost, is not perishable, and is readily available. These factors together would suggest that the cost of the control system is too high given the potential risks.

Cost-versus-benefit analyses often present difficulties to all persons evaluating controls. While it is often easier to estimate the cost to install a control than to estimate its expected benefits, both represent a very inexact science. The process is made even more difficult by the interrelationship of certain control with business operations. The types and nature of controls can also vary depending upon the very nature of the business. A manufacturer of pumps to be installed in medical equipment may have a need for much more comprehensive quality-control programs than would a similar pump manufacturer selling to an industrial market. The medical equipment supplier can and should expect to spend more on installing adequate quality controls.

The COSO report provides some good general guidance here. It emphasizes that an organization is faced with a challenge to find the right cost-versus-benefit balance. Excessive control can be too costly and counterproductive. Internal auditors, as a key component in the internal control framework, should always keep this balance of internal control costs and benefits in mind when making their recommendations.

(b) INTERNAL CONTROL ROLES AND RESPONSIBILITIES

COSO makes the point that everyone involved with an organization has *some responsibility* for internal control. The chief executive officer (CEO), in particular, is described as ultimately responsible and should assume the "ownership" of this process. This is a particularly important message for internal auditors in many organizations. All too often, some members of management assume that the auditors who review controls are in some way responsible for making sure that appropriate controls are installed. All parties involved with the organization have responsibilities to assure that effective internal controls have been implemented. Members of the organization, no matter what their level of responsibility, should not assume that internal control issues are not their job. Although appropriate management structures are needed to distribute the various internal control duties and responsibilities, all members of an organization have some level of responsibility to assure that internal controls are in place and are working. Internal auditors should always feel comfortable recommending appropriate internal control improvements in the course of their reviews.

(i) Responsible Parties inside the Organization.   The COSO report outlines the internal control responsibilities for parties both inside and outside of the organization. Within the organization, it further details internal control responsibilities for organization management, the board of directors, internal auditors, and other parties. These groups play an important part in the system of internal control in an organization. Each should contribute in differing ways to provide reasonable assurance that various specified objectives are being achieved.

This portion of COSO strongly emphasizes the importance of the modern internal audit function in the overall control structure of the modern organization. Internal audit has a more important role than just reviewing specific controls and reporting deficiencies to lower levels of management, which may not be too interested in internal audit's findings. In addition to the board of directors and other members of management, internal audit has key internal control responsibilities in the organization.

Management Roles and Responsibilities

COSO is very strong in stating that the CEO of the organization has ultimate responsibility for the effectiveness of its internal control systems. Once again, this section of the report talks about how the CEO should take a "the buck stops here" type of responsibility for that system of internal control and set the overall tone at the top for the organization. This is a message that is heard throughout the COSO report.

COSO reminds us that the CEO should have a more significant responsibility than essentially any other person in the organization. The CEO, for example, typically exercises a major influence in selecting members of the board of directors. The CEO with high ethical values can help assure that the board also shares those values. Although members of the board are elected by the shareholders and although any shareholder, theoretically, can nominate a candidate for the board, the CEO typically takes the major initiative here. Similarly, the CEO will have a major influence in selecting the public accounting firm that will audit the books and records of the organization.

The CEO has a responsibility to see that all components of the system of internal control are in place. This is usually accomplished by the CEO working with various senior managers to set overall policies and procedures, to define the overall organization structure, and to design the overall objectives for planning and reporting systems. The senior managers then should delegate appropriate responsibilities to other functions within their organizations, performing adequate reviews as necessary to determine that control procedures are effective. Rather than be the distant, high-level person who has minimal contact with others in the organization, the COSO report suggests that the CEO must play a fairly active role in the management of the organization.

In addition to the role of the CEO, the COSO reports also specifically talk about the internal control responsibilities of financial officers. Managers and their staff involved in finance and controller functions should operate at all levels of the organization to track and analyze performance and to compile and report results. These financial officers should be involved with tracking operations and compliance performance as well as with financial reporting. The finance function in the organization is typically headed by the chief financial officer (CFO), whose role is discussed in greater detail in Chapter 22, "Accounting Systems and Controls."

The CFO has an important role in preventing and detecting fraudulent financial reporting. Although the COSO report used the title *chief accounting officer* rather than CFO, this responsibility was also emphasized in the original Treadway report: "As a member of top management, the chief accounting officer helps set the tone of the organization's ethical conduct; is responsible for the financial statement; generally has primary responsibility for designing, implementing and monitoring the company's financial reporting system; and is in a unique position regarding identification of unusual situations caused by fraudulent reporting." Although the CFO sometimes plays a less important role, almost as the "bookkeeper" in some organizations, COSO emphasizes that the CFO should have an equal role with other senior managers under the CEO.

The COSO report outlines some important responsibilities for officers in the organization and for the CEO and CFO in particular. The internal audit department may find that this description is not always true in its organization. Sometimes, the CFO and perhaps a small group of senior staff officers will have isolated themselves in an ivory tower type of office somewhat remote from many other members of line management. While there is nothing wrong with senior management being in a separate facility, COSO points out that they should have ongoing responsibilities to manage the entity actively. If not properly managed, this isolation can lead internal audit to the identification of internal control concerns.

What can an internal auditor do in this situation? Suggesting that the CEO is not fulfilling his or her responsibilities will not work. However, as will be discussed in other chapters, the director of internal audit should express these concerns to the audit committee of the board. Internal audit is then fulfilling its responsibility to provide counsel to management at a very high level.

Board of Directors and Its Committees

The board of directors and its committees have a very significant, high-level responsibility in providing organization guidance and oversight. Although the board may only meet a limited number of times during the year, members should provide a very high level of oversight to management activities. Although the CEO, as has been previously discussed, plays a major role in identifying appropriate persons as candidates for board positions, the board will have ultimate management responsibility for the CEO and all other senior managers. The effective board should play a role in high-level objective-setting and management guidance.

Because boards of directors have limited time, much of their work takes place through committees. These include the compensation committee, which sets overall compensation arrangements for senior officers; the finance committee, which makes major fund investment decisions; and the audit committee. While the types and responsibilities of board committees generally vary, the responsibilities of the audit committee have been established by several regulatory groups. An audit committee consists of outside directors. It has the authority to question the actions of senior management regarding their financial-reporting responsibilities and to ensure that corrective action has been taken. In most organizations, the director of internal audit has a direct reporting responsibility to the audit committee. This relationship and the responsibilities of internal audit to serve the audit committee are discussed in Chapter 6.

COSO Definition of Internal Audit Responsibilities

The COSO report gives a very major responsibility to the internal audit function for monitoring the system of internal control. COSO recognizes that the standards for internal auditing define internal audit's responsibilities for reviews of internal controls. These standards are presented and discussed in Chapter 5. Internal audit standards call for internal auditors to go beyond reviews of financial accounting in their work. Internal audit work, per the standards, covers reviews of such areas as the economy and efficiency of operations, the safeguarding of assets, and compliance with significant laws and regulations. Other chapters will discuss these very important internal audit review areas.

The report specifically emphasizes that internal audit does *not* have the primary responsibility for establishing or maintaining the internal control system. COSO specifically gives that responsibility to the CEO and other key senior officers. Internal audit plays its own important role in establishing an effective system of internal control by independently evaluating the effectiveness of the organization's internal control systems. Many aspects of that role will be discussed in other chapters of this book.

Other Parties in the Organization

Although the CEO, financial officers, and internal auditors play a significant role in maintaining internal control, virtually all other employees of the organization also have some responsibility for internal control as well. Most employees have some responsibility for recordkeeping and for communicating that information. This might include recording stockroom inventory disbursements, ringing up retail sales, initialing the receipt of incoming goods, or even completing a weekly timecard. In addition, all personnel should be responsible for communicating to higher organization levels problems in operations, violations of the code of conduct, or other improper activities. Each of these employee activities has a small part in the overall internal control structure.

Internal control in the modern organization is everyone's responsibility, and the roles and responsibilities of all employees should be effectively communicated. Personnel at all levels should be encouraged to resist any pressure from supervisors who may ask them to participate in improper activities. All members of the organization should realize that they have a role in the overall internal control system. They should never be encouraged to look the other way when they observe improper activities. All members of the organization, starting with the CEO, have a responsibility to practice good internal control procedures.

(ii) External Parties Internal Control Responsibilities. A variety of parties outside of the organization have some responsibility for internal controls within the organization. The most obvious of these is the independent public accountant who has been hired by the board of directors to review internal accounting controls and to express an opinion on the fairness of the organization's financial statements. This is a vital component in an organization's internal control framework. Some internal auditors who have been working with the same outside public accounting firm for many years may argue that these external auditors are almost part of the internal structure of the organization. However, external auditors have an important internal control responsibility due to their ability to exercise independent opinions. Even though they may seem almost part of the organization, their professional standards require independence. Internal and external audit coordination are discussed in Chapter 32.

The COSO report highlights three other groups outside of the organization who have a responsibility for internal control within the organization: legislators and regulators, customers and vendors, and financial analysts. The first of these can directly impact the internal controls in an organization through the enactment of laws or through regulatory reviews. The Foreign Corrupt Practices Act of 1977, discussed previously, is an example of the former. Regulated industries—such as banks—will be subject to external reviews by regulatory auditors.

Customers, vendors, and other parties interacting with the organization can be an important source of information regarding internal controls. An organization should establish channels for these parties to register complaints or to inform appropriate levels of management of improper activities. The organization should develop mechanisms to receive these types of messages through the use of toll-free telephone lines, surveys, and newsletters. Mechanisms should be in place to communicate this need for outside information, to process messages received, and to take corrective action.

The third major group of outside persons are financial analysts, bond rating agencies, and the news media. Although their roles are well understood by senior management, internal auditors often overlook the very important internal control responsibility of these outside groups. Analysts and rating agencies review objectives and strategies, the financial strength of the organization compared to that of its peers, and actions taken in response to market and economic changes. The news media—and the financial press, in particular—may look at some of the same issues as rating agencies but may also report on other matters that come to the public attention. That reporting can be an embarrassment to senior management if it emphasizes problems such as faulty product or excessive behavior such as a lavish party for key contractors. These gadfly reports should enhance the organization's internal controls, however, if corrective action is taken in response to them.

2-7 CHARACTERISTICS OF EFFECTIVE INTERNAL CONTROLS

The concept of internal control is sometimes difficult for an internal auditor, particularly the beginning auditor, to understand properly. While internal control is the basis for virtually all audit work, internal auditors sometimes have difficulty identifying effective controls when evaluating a system or organization structure. A 1988 study by the President's Council on Management Improvement[9] defined the characteristics of effective controls. The report stated that such controls must be:

---

[9] President's Council on Management Improvement, *Model Framework for Management Control Over Automated Information Systems* (Washington, D.C.: U.S. Government Printing Office, January 1988).

- *Clear in Purpose.* If not understood, control procedures may not be used and if they do not have a clear purpose or address a known vulnerability, they are of little or no value.

- *Developed in Partnership.* Controls must be developed by personnel knowledgeable in the process to be controlled and should understand related control techniques. It is unlikely that effective, feasible controls can be selected and implemented unilaterally by a user, an information systems analyst, or an internal auditor.

- *Cost-Effective.* As mentioned previously, the cost of a control should not, in general, exceed the expected benefits. Stated another way, there should be reasonable assurance that the system is protected from known risks. If total assurance of control were possible, it would be prohibitively expensive. More simply, spending $100 to protect against a one time $80 loss makes little sense. While many controls might be obviously cost-effective, the consideration of other controls may require a detailed cost-versus-benefit analysis.

- *Documented.* The documentation process should be simple and understandable, clearly link risks to controls, and provide management with assurance that all reasonable controls are in place. Without some form of documentation, there is no assurance that all known vulnerabilities are addressed or that controls are in place.

- *Tested and Reviewed.* There must be assurance that the installed controls function as originally intended. This assurance is needed when the control procedure first becomes operational and also during its ongoing operation. Initial controls testing should normally be done when all aspects of the system are tested. Ongoing testing and review might be done as part of a general system review, an audit, or another management initiative.

- *Manageable.* Management must have a means to change, delete, evaluate cost, upgrade, and review the components of the internal control system under its purview.

Reviewing and understanding internal controls requires a wide variety of auditor understanding. For example, techniques to ensure data are complete are quite unlike methods to ensure that good personnel practices are employed. The approach an internal auditor takes to evaluating controls will vary greatly, just as management approaches to implementing these controls also vary.

As discussed at the beginning of this chapter, when an internal auditor has a good understanding of controls, it is an ''open sesame'' that will allow the auditor to review and access many areas within the organization. As long as management realizes that its internal audit department is composed of a group of professional control experts, management will welcome and even invite internal audit to perform reviews in a large variety of operational areas.

2-8 INTERNAL CONTROL COMPLIANCE FUTURE DIRECTIONS

The internal control framework outlined in the COSO report and discussed in this chapter defines the concept of internal controls for auditors and all other persons associated in the organization. Just as the effective internal auditor should have a good understanding of internal audit standards as defined in Chapter 5, the effective internal auditor also needs to consider internal controls in the manner that they are described in the COSO report. The AICPA has accepted COSO through its SAS No. 78 internal control auditing standard, and internal auditors will see changes in internal audit standards to reflect COSO's language and terminology.

The effective internal auditor does not need to purchase a copy of the COSO report package in order to perform effective reviews. However, an internal auditor should develop a good understanding of the COSO internal control framework and terminology as discussed in this chapter. This knowledge, coupled with the various specific audit procedures discussed in other chapters of this book, should arm internal audit with some powerful tools to be of appropriate service to management.

While the COSO report will almost certainly be reflected in future legislation and revised auditing standards, it currently provides the internal auditor with an effective framework to use to understand and evaluate internal control in the modern organization. The modern internal auditor should have a good understanding of internal control fundamentals, as outlined in COSO, in order to effectively serve management.

CHAPTER 3

Understanding Management Needs

3-1 INTERNAL AUDIT'S MANAGEMENT FOCUS

The first editions of this book, starting in 1942, emphasized that *service to management* should be the major mission of internal audit. These mission concerns were fairly narrow and emphasized the needs of middle to senior management. Over time, internal audit's mission has expanded to cover the board of directors, stockholders, all levels of employees, government, and society. The controlling mission of internal audit today is service to the overall organization, including those responsible for the governance of that organization. However, that mission still must have a strong internal management focus.

While many recipients of internal auditing services have special needs, management effectiveness is a major concern of all parties of interest. If an organization is not well managed, all members of society associated with it suffer. Management's tasks are becoming more complex at the same time because of a rapidly changing external environment with regards to technology, markets, regulatory factors, and societal values. These factors make it important that internal audit takes a broad approach to the concept of service and assists the organization at every level and in every way.

In order to properly assist management, an internal auditor must continuously strive to understand management needs, both in terms of general concepts and in the unique characteristics of a particular organization. Auditors need to understand management theory and its process, how managers set their objectives, and how they identify and solve problems to achieve those objectives. All internal auditors must learn to think like managers in order to form a partnership relationship with them. They also must establish communication links with management in order receive information on management needs and concerns.

Another important reason to understand management theory and practice is because internal auditors themselves are managers. Their roles include supervising audit projects or directing overall internal audit functions. Internal auditors must be able to develop objectives and strategies to achieve those objectives, working through people and with other resources, just as other managers. Auditors cannot be qualified counselors to managers if they cannot effectively manage their own operations. Internal auditors should provide a model that can be observed and followed by others in the organization. In this way, internal auditors will also be viewed as likely candidates for other management-level positions in their overall organizations.

This chapter considers some of the more general concepts of management. It also discusses communication techniques that may help an auditor gain a better understanding of management needs. This chapter should be read in conjunction with the other audit management chapters of this book. Chapter 2 considers the fundamentals of control necessary for all management systems, Chapter 6 examines the services rendered to the audit committee of the board of directors, and Chapter 35 discusses the larger social responsibilities of internal auditors. Effective internal auditing involves understanding management needs and working with management to serve those needs. That understanding is an essential ingredient for establishing internal audit credibility such that management will then respect and listen to internal audit's counsel. Working together, managers and internal auditors can achieve increased effectiveness in many operational areas and promote overall organizational welfare.

3-2 WHAT IS MANAGEMENT?

The words *management* or *manager* suggest a variety of different concepts to people. Most people are aware, however, that management requires abilities distinct from those needed to perform work tasks. An excellent product development engineer may be unable to successfully manage an engineering organization or even a small engineering project-development group. In its most simplistic form, management presents an image of someone getting a job done and doing it in an effective manner. Management often suggests an individual or a group of individuals who are dealing with large and complicated problems. A common thread of any management activity is a systematic approach to accomplish some defined organizational objective.

Experts in the field use a wide range of concepts, in terms of nature and scope, to develop formal definitions of management. Some view management as a science while others feel that good management is almost an art. A compact and useful definition for the internal auditor is: *Management is the process of achieving the effective utilization of resources.* This definition recognizes that management is an active process, that it deals with human and other resources, and that its end objective is the effective utilization of those resources. This process is the most basic aspect of what management is all about. Managers attempt to get the best possible results in the best possible manner. In business, this normally means maximum profitability, based on long-run standards and giving fair consideration to the rights of all parties.

(a) FUNCTIONS OF MANAGEMENT

The basic definition of management described above requires both decision-making and the ability to get things done through other people. The manager must decide on the objectives to be accomplished and select the resources needed to accomplish these objectives. This management process is broken down into detailed areas in which necessary decisions are made.

The basic functions of management have really not changed much throughout our industrial age. While technologies and business practices change, good management concepts generally have remained unchanged. As a very early definition, Gulick and Urwick described the functions of management in 1937 as planning, organizing, staffing, directing, coordinating, reporting, and budgeting.[1] With some modifications, combinations, and additions, these management functions are still valid today. The effective internal auditor should keep these concepts in mind when managing all aspects of the internal audit function or department as well as when evaluating management controls as part of internal audit projects. A detailed description of these concepts follows.

- *Planning.* A manager must decide what needs to be done and must set short- and long-term goals to achieve those objectives. In order to do this, the manager must make his or her best effort to understand the economic, social, and political environment in which the organization will be operating and the resources available to make the plans work out. As one example, plans entirely feasible in a time of prosperity may be utterly impractical in a time of recession. Planning also includes the management function of *budgeting,* since a budget is a plan to spend a certain amount of money to accomplish certain objectives. Planning is the foundation for all the other functions and is a necessary component in all levels of an organization.

- *Organizing.* This involves breaking down any work effort into distinct pieces and then bringing them back together to accomplish total work requirements. Management objectives and the work necessary to attain them dictate the skills needed. In organizing, the manager must decide on the positions to be filled and on the related duties and responsibilities. That is, what positions or functions will be responsible for performing the planned work? Because the work done by individual members of the organization will necessarily be interrelated, some means of coordinating these efforts must be provided. *Coordinating* is, in fact, an essential part or subset of organizing rather than a management function in itself.

- *Staffing.* In organizing, the manager establishes position descriptions and decides which skills are required for each. Staffing is the management function of attempting to find the right persons for required jobs. An established organization, of course, already should have both a structure and appropriate people to fill the authorized positions. Nevertheless, both organization and staffing are likely to be continuing management tasks since changes in plans and objectives often require changes in the organization and may occasionally necessitate a complete reorganization. Staffing is not a one-time effort. People are continually leaving, getting terminated, or retiring while changes or growth in the organization create new or different positions. While many of these activities are to a major extent part of the modern human resources or personnel function, all managers must be deeply involved.

- *Directing.* Since no one can predict just what problems and opportunities will arise in day-to-day work activities, position descriptions must naturally be couched in rather general terms. The manager must, therefore, provide ongoing direction for subordinates. The manager must make sure that subordinates are aware of the results expected in each situation, must help them improve skills, and in some cases tell them exactly how and when to perform certain tasks. A good manager makes subordinates feel they want to do the best possible job, not merely work well enough to just get by.

---

[1] Lester Gulick & Lyndall Urwick, "Notes on the Theory of Organization," *Papers on the Science of Administration* (New York: Institute of Public Administration, 1937).

- *Controlling.* Current work accomplishments are affected by changing conditions and varying human capabilities. Controlling is a function where the manager must determine how well jobs have been done, identify deviations from plans, and make changes if the organization is deviating from its overall goals. Although sometimes considered a separate function, *reporting* is a means of controlling. Reports are made so that the manager, as well as superiors and subordinates, may see what is happening in order to change course if necessary. Controlling is also the area in which internal audit has special expertise. This important management function was discussed in greater detail in Chapter 2.

(b) ADDITIONAL FUNCTIONS OF THE MODERN MANAGER

The functions discussed previously focus on the administrative aspects of management. Indeed, internal audit often focuses review activities in these areas. However, the modern manager must also be a leader in moving the organization in new directions. As Peter Drucker wrote many years back in his classic description of management, ''Managing a business can not be bureaucratic, an administrative, or even a policy-making job. . . . [It] must be a creative rather than adaptive task.''[2] In other words, the real manager is always an innovator.

Innovating should be considered an additional key function of the manager. A second function is representing the organization to outside groups. There are other additional functions that could be mentioned, but they are essentially subfunctions. For example, communicating is often considered a major part of a manager's job. Unless the manager can communicate with subordinates, important ideas and concepts may be missed. However, achieving good communications is really part of the *directing* function in which the manager attempts to ensure the overall success of the organization through communication with subordinates. The two additional management functions are:

1. *Innovating.* When a manager attempts to merely continue what has been done in the past, making the best possible showing in view of external or available resources, the organization will tend to be static at best. If in a competitive field, the organization is more likely to decline over time. Innovation is a key management function. The manager must innovate by combining new ideas into existing practices or by acting as a catalyst to stimulate others to innovate. The function of innovating is similar but different from the *planning* function described previously. Innovation covers all areas and functions of an organization.

2. *Representing.* The manager's job includes representing the organization in dealings with other groups within the organization as well as with outside groups, including government officials, financial institutions, unions, customers, suppliers, civic groups, and others. Sometimes this function only requires the manager to become accessible to outsiders while at other times it requires strong negotiating skills. All levels of management are typically involved with representing their organization at some level. The factory foremen must represent the organization in discussions with the union steward while the chief executive officer may represent the organization in front of a legislative committee.

---

[2] Peter Drucker, *The Practice of Management* (New York: Harper & Row, 1954), 47.

Management can also be considered in terms of its responsibility for the various functional areas of a typical organization. These areas refer to the various groups of work activity that are similar in character. Typical areas include research, engineering, production, marketing, administration, personnel, and finance. Although they will vary depending on their importance in a given organization, the management process in each area follows the same functions of management previously discussed. However, the focus in each will be on achieving performance in the designated area in the most effective manner practicable. That is, a manager in a finance or accounting area has some specific technical responsibilities for accounting-related issues as well as overall management. The functional management in these areas, combined with general management, comprise the total management of the organization. Because each of these functional areas has its own relatively unique problems, some separate management and control concerns are discussed in the separate operational audit chapters of this book.

3-3 NATURE OF THE ORGANIZATION ENVIRONMENT

The individual organization operates in a complicated environment. Many years ago, organizations were often isolated, with their markets local or restrained by limitations in communications and transportation systems. Nevertheless, communications and transportation systems had an influence even though things traveled at a much slower pace. For example, as early as the 1880s, the price of grain in Kansas was influenced by grain prices in Kiev and Argentina.

It took a few days for that price information to travel to the market in Kansas and much longer for grain to actually be transported to these other markets. Similar examples can be found going back to Roman times. However, speed of communications and other factors have increased the environmental complexity today. Modern environmental factors include economic, competitive, technological, political, and social matters.

Economic Factors

A major portion of the external environment for any organization has to do with economic factors, including dimensions of the state of world, national, and regional economies. Within this framework are more specific factors that relate to the organization's products or services. Who uses the products and why? How strong is that demand in terms of other needs? Where are the users of the product? Are there other, competitive products or services? There are also factors relating to the supply of the product or service. Where do the materials come from that are needed to produce the aforementioned products, and what is their availability? What kinds of facilities are needed and what kind of production processes are involved? What are the requirements in terms of capital, specialized knowledge, and marketing? Finally, factors relating to demand and supply must be considered in terms of whether there are acceptable profit potentials.

Economic factors impact all organizations, whether a private-sector industrial organization, a not-for-profit service organization, or a governmental unit. For example, the United Parcel Service (UPS) in the United States has largely taken over small parcel delivery from the U.S. Postal Service due to UPS's ability to provide better service at a lower cost structure. The U.S. Postal Service, once a virtual monopoly, could not effectively compete when faced with these economic factors. Similarly, International Business Machines (IBM) lost a significant share of the computer systems market starting in the mid-1980's when organizations converted from their traditional mainframe or legacy computers, where IBM held a significant share of the market, to smaller client-server computer systems. The auditor should always consider the role of economic factors when considering an organization and how it fits in its overall political economy. That understanding will be valuable for a better understanding of management needs.

Competitive Factors

The existing competitive situation is a factor closely coupled with the economic factors just described. Who are the competitors? How many are there and what are their respective shares of the overall market? What are their unique competitive strengths? How easily can competitors enter and withdraw from the market? What is the overall market? The answers to these questions determine the character of the competitive environment. Very often, the competitive relationship has a number of dimensions. A maker of metal can containers for example, is subject to the competition of other can makers as well as to makers of other types of containers—glass, plastic, paper, and the like. At a still broader level, there is competition because certain products packaged in a can or some other container may also be marketed in an entirely different manner. For example, foods may be packaged in a can or bottle, or they may be sold frozen or fresh. The effective manager understands competitive factors and their impact on organizations.

Technological Factors

All organizations are subject to technological factors in some way. Advances in microelectronics and computers, for example, have impacted virtually all organizations. Financial services, with its strong dependence on computer systems and telecommunications, is an example of an industry where there have been major technological changes. There are other organizations where the impact is relatively low, an example of which might be a not-for-profit service organization. However, technology can present both major risks and major opportunities. The auditor should always be aware of the technological factors that may impact a given industry and organization. They may cause changes in processes and in products. They may also point to areas where the auditor may want to emphasize review activities.

Political Factors

Laws, regulations, and outside political or societal pressures may have important bearings on the operation of the organization. These will vary with the industry and location. For a public utility, this regulatory aspect is often very significant. In the automobile industry, regulations covering safety and emissions are a legislative constraint. In other industries, organizations may be subject to the pressure of ''public interest'' types of political operatives who are able to manipulate the press and others to promote their causes. All organizations are subject to controls and political constraints of various types. These issues are discussed in greater detail in Chapter 35.

Social Factors

The force of the society, expressed ultimately through the political process and in the enactment of various laws, can be a significant factor. While the U.S. railroad barons in the 1880s could say, ''The public be damned,'' today the attitudes and views of society are an important factor influencing management decisions. There is a wide spectrum of developments here, including the rights of minority groups, attitudes toward pollution, and changing social expectations as to various types of business ethics. These social factors are often some of the more difficult problems an organization may face.

This discussion of environmental factors has been from the standpoint of the entire organization. However, management entities also exist at lower levels, including subsidiaries, divisions, departments, and the like. The environmental factors previously discussed also include the authority and controls of the higher organizational levels, to which lower-level management entities are accountable. Also included are the resources available from upper-level management that augment and better define the environmental factors as well as constraints of various kinds that may be imposed by the senior-level management.

3-4 ATTRIBUTES OF MANAGEMENT

In addition to environmental factors, the auditor also needs to understand other key attributes concerning the management process. These attributes help to define the overall process of management and will be of help to the auditor in developing an understanding of management's needs. Some of the more important of these include:

Dependence on People

People are perhaps the most important resources the effective manager must utilize. People are important resources to the manager in terms of their knowledge, skills, and experience; however, people have a unique importance that goes far beyond those considerations because all management action is carried out by and through people. An effective manager, therefore, is directly dependent on people to make plans and to implement them through definitive actions. Thus, an internal auditor must understand how people, or the human resources of an organization, can operate in an effective manner to provide a maximum contribution toward the achievement of managerial goals and objectives.

Understanding the human resources of an organization and how they contribute to management is not a simple accomplishment. People as individuals have feelings and emotions, and they must be properly motivated. In other words, management has a continuing challenge to find the best possible fit and integration of individuals within overall organizational goals. These human resources may range from the top management support staff to the overall labor pool in a larger manufacturing organization. Each of these groups has its own general interests, motivations, and needs. Management needs to understand these factors in order to best utilize the human resources of the organization.

Focus on Decision-Making

Managerial action is based on various types of decisions. Some are at a very high level, such as a major strategic policy decision involving the entry into a new line of business. Other decisions are at relatively lower levels. They all have common elements in their decision-making process with respect to decision principles and methodology. The problem must be identified, alternatives explored using all information available, and a decision made as to the type of action to be taken.

This decision-making process is similar for managers at all levels, but it differs in individual situations due to the magnitude of the problem, the extent to which information is available, the available decision alternatives, and the potential risks associated with the decision outcomes. The factors of time available, risk levels that are acceptable, and the costs of improving the basis for the actual final decision all affect this management process. The effective manager surveys a variety of issues and then identifies the most significant issues in order to make the best decisions. Internal auditors need to understand this management decision-making process to help assemble the correct supporting data when making a recommendation. It will also help the auditor to better understand how management reacts to audit report findings and recommendations.

Effect of Risk Level

There are risks associated with every management decision. If the manager makes the wrong decision, there is the risk that the manager will be responsible for the many potential costs associated with that wrong decision. These could include wasted resources, diminished future performance, or even legal liability for the organization or manager. To a considerable extent, risk can be reduced by better management information about operational and environmental factors. Of course, every decision could be risk-free if the manager had what is hypothetically called perfect information. There are costs associated with obtaining the various types and levels of information desired, and probability factors will affect the desired results. As a result, total certainty is impossible because of both practical and absolute limitations. This means that management decisions reflect the levels of risk deemed to be acceptable to the particular responsible manager. Managers and their overall organization have varying inclinations to take risk, and each manager must make evaluations within the parameters of decision authority and risk preferences.

The effective internal auditor should have a good understanding of this risk assessment process. Chapter 7 discusses the entire process of evaluating risk in the context of audit planning. In order to understand management needs, an internal auditor also needs to understand management's willingness to accept or avoid risks. Management may ignore certain audit recommendations if they are not presented properly and if management does not see the risks that the audit findings expose. The auditor who understands this risk-taking process will do a better job of presenting audit findings and recommendations. Of course, the auditor is sometimes in a situation where management is willing to take an unreasonably high level of risk and is willing to ignore audit findings and recommendations. This situation moves auditors from a position of attempting to understand management needs to larger ethics issue, as will be discussed in Chapter 35.

Management Is Judged by Results

Virtually everything a manager does is judged by how that manager's actions further the achievement of established organization goals and objectives. Managers should be primarily interested in results as opposed to letting an intermediate process be an end in itself. However, the significance of this management attribute goes deeper, since there are different ways to achieve managerial objectives, and different approaches in individual situations can achieve the same desired results. At the same time, similar approaches to solving management problems can end up with completely different measures of success.

This attribute of judging overall management effectiveness by results was a subject of controversy during the various hostile management takeovers of the 1980's. The controversy has continued into the present. Corporate raiders took over many otherwise successful companies with the argument that they could achieve better short-term financial results by selling off underperforming assets and undertaking other restructuring actions. Although an organization might have been considered otherwise successful, these raiders promised better results and often took over the organization and then reported improved short-term results. The costs to personnel, to the communities where the companies were located, and to society in total as a result of these restructurings have been mixed. Only time will be the best judge of some of these actions.

There are always decision variables that cannot be fully predicted or adequately evaluated. As a result, the merits of particular managerial decisions or approaches are often extremely controversial. While management competence is judged mostly by the results achieved, good results actually achieved in a particular situation might have been even better with a different management approach. On balance, managerial excellence is measured by the quality of its results. Auditors must be aware of these issues when attempting to understand management needs. If management wishes to achieve the best results for the overall organization, the auditor should attempt to support and corroborate those decisions.

Time Span for Appraising Results

This judgment of management by its results raises questions as to the time frame in which the particular results are to be evaluated. In many situations, a manager can show short-term results such as profitability, but he or she buys that profitability by undermining the longer-run profits of the organization. For example, quality can be temporarily sacrificed with resulting short-term profits, but this action can be so damaging to customer satisfaction that future products are no longer purchased.

Good managers should think in terms of longer-term factors and resist the often tempting shortcuts that may endanger longer-term potentials.

When management understands these factors, the correct judgments should be clear. Often, however, the evaluation may be complicated by such matters as how long of a time span should be allowed for decisions made today and how willing upper management or stockholders are to wait for longer-run rewards. A further complicating factor is the difficulty of measuring long-run effects. Managers often innocently make bad estimates in these areas and also are victims of wishful thinking. In other cases, lower-level managers ignore long-run consequences because they will not be directly involved when final outcomes become evident. There are many published accounts of this practice, where a manager achieves short-term results at a unit and either is promoted or leaves to join a different organization. The successors must deal with the long-term results of these short-term decisions.

Auditors can often play a very important role in this short-term versus long-term results decision process. An internal auditor frequently identifies operational issues that may have long-term negative implications for an organization even though the short-term results are not nearly as obvious. Through an audit of manufacturing job costing practices, including comparisons with past periods, an auditor may find that the substitution of a lower-cost part has increased the profit margins on a certain component. However, a subsequent audit of the marketing department, as discussed in Chapter 28, might detect a growing level of customer dissatisfaction with the new, low-cost component. The auditor should highlight these situations to management. The marketing department might not even be aware of this if they have not taken the time to analyze customer complaint letters.

(a) CHANGE AND REGULARITY

A central truth of management is that conditions are always changing. A valued employee leaves the organization, a new invention obsoletes existing practices, consumer preferences shift, or something else unforeseen develops. As a result, many dimensions of the management process must be reappraised or redirected. An organization's capacity to foresee such possibilities and to adapt to them is a measure of its ability to survive and prosper. This adaptive approach often takes a rather unstructured management style. At the same time, however, there are potential benefits to standardization and regularity, including lower costs and a more effective supervisory effort. This creates a conflict because change is needed for growth or even organizational survival, and management has a continuing challenge to find the proper balance between these two pressures.

To what extent should capital investment be made in a single-purpose machine when a change in product design may make that machine obsolete? The capital investment will allow the organization to continue to produce the same, known product. The investment in a new machine, which may have some risk, might launch the organization in a new direction but also might make the current product obsolete. This problem is never properly solved at any one point in time and the reconciliation continues to be complex as conditions continue to change. The ability to cope with this kind of challenge identifies and measures managerial competence.

(b) IS MANAGEMENT AN ART, SCIENCE, OR PROFESSION?

All the variables discussed lead to the question of whether management is an art or a science. The correct answer is "probably both." To the extent that scientific surveys, analyses, and methodologies can be developed—as, for example, with the tools of management science or sophisticated information systems—the practice of management moves in the direction of being a science. However, information can never be complete and there are always variables that are too complicated, diverse, and uncontrollable to be adequately assessed quantitatively. At some point, therefore, management must depend on judgment and personal effectiveness. To that extent, management remains an art. Obviously, there are continual attempts to expand the scientific dimensions and thereby reduce the impact of variables and their related risks. However, the world continues to become increasingly complex and management is usually hard pressed just to keep even.

A related question is whether management is a profession. The answer here is a very definite yes. Managers increasingly develop the kinds of capabilities that enable them to move relatively freely from one organization to another and from industry to industry. Managers can often move beyond their original professional or industry backgrounds. While a manager may come from a specific area such as finance, professional managers increasingly exhibit a breadth of responsibility for general management. A very good example of this is an internal auditor who has developed strong management skills in managing audit projects. That internal auditor is often a candidate for some management position elsewhere in the organization.

3-5 GENERAL CONCEPTS OF MANAGEMENT FOR THE INTERNAL AUDITOR

All of the theoretical and practical concepts of management need to be applied to individual managerial situations in a manner that recognizes the unique factors associated with a particular situation. While the basic principles and concepts of management are generally applicable to all managerial situations, it is sometimes difficult to see how they apply in certain special situations. Whether working in a large private-sector business, in government, or in any not-for-profit type of organization, the auditor should always keep general management concepts in mind. The problems in principle are the same in that all managerial concepts and practices are of use in evaluating resources and considering how to best achieve managerial objectives. This is true even though the character of the individual situation may require a different application of these concepts.

The successful auditor needs to have a general understanding of these management concepts. While some of this understanding can come from the college training the auditor receives, it should also come from exposure to experienced managers on audit assignments within the organization, or from professional contacts. Finally, it can come from an ongoing program of auditor self-education. There are numerous trendy books on management published from year to year. Many of these receive a lot of attention for a year or two and then are quickly forgotten. However, there are also some other classic books on management that will provide the auditor with a better understanding of management fundamentals. An internal auditor might want to talk with a professor of management at a local graduate school of business for some recommendations. An extended reading program will greatly enhance an internal auditor's knowledge and skills in the important practice of management.

In the typical business organization, success is measured by the ability to grow and be profitable. In our free enterprise system, a business organization that is not generally profitable over a period of time is either not providing needed products or services or is not effectively managed. Although this profit measure does not exist in government or in some not-for-profit organizations, there are comparable yardsticks available for these, including the achievements of various types of service levels rendered or the quantity or quality of services delivered.

The determination and evaluation of economic or other measurable goals can also be affected by personal goals. These are the real—though often denied—desires of managers to do something personally satisfying for themselves. Having the most impressive office facilities, being number-one in unit or dollar volume, or favoring relatives for staff appointments over better-qualified people are all common examples. Sometimes managers have the power to make such personal goals prevail, but in any event their cost should be known in terms of its effect on fully economic or other more rational goals.

The more significant conflict, however, exists in relation to socially oriented goals. Increasingly, there is the pressure from society on the business organization to act in a manner that achieves so-called social objectives. Examples are conservation of natural resources, improving the physical environment, special assistance for minority groups, and pressuring a country that violates human rights—all involving actions that may often go beyond existing legal requirements. The rationale here is that these are major responsibilities of a business organization in this modern world. As a result, the manager is subject to conflicting pressures but must somehow also assure the growth and profitability of the organization.

3-6 UNDERSTANDING OUR OWN MANAGEMENT

Thus far, this chapter has discussed principles and concepts of a very general nature that apply to every managerial situation in all kinds of business and nonbusiness activities.

These principles and concepts are basic and need to become a foundation for all managerial activities. How they are applied, however, depends on the kind of business or nonbusiness activity in the particular organization. Varying physical factors, technologies used, the nature and scope of processes to produce the product or service offered, capital investment, types of facilities, distribution, sales, maintenance, conditions of product usage, extent of risk, social visibility, and a host of other factors combine to make managing different in individual situations. As a result, the various aspects of the management process need different kinds of attention with differing priorities and considerations. Effective managers must understand these factors in order to properly manage their organizations. The modern internal auditor also needs to have a strong understanding of the same factors.

The effective auditor must understand the special factors surrounding any organization. This is often a key difference between external and internal auditors. The external auditor works with a variety of clients and should be an expert on generally accepted accounting principles and how they apply to a particular organization. However, while that external auditor should have a good general understanding of the client organization, it is internal audit that better understands management's day-to-day needs.

Granted the importance of adequately understanding these factors, how do internal auditors acquire the needed knowledge and understanding? Related questions include how much one needs to independently know and how much time should be devoted to the pursuit of such expertise. The resolution of these questions necessitates judgment in the light of changing conditions. This resolution is also different for each auditor in terms of ongoing career aspirations and utilization of auditor resources in the most effective manner over future periods.

(a) DEVELOPING COMMUNICATION LINKS WITH MANAGEMENT

The most important way an internal auditor can understand the needs of management is to develop ongoing channels of communications with organization management. This process is often both quite easy and quite difficult for the auditor. It is easy because internal audit often has communication links with the highest levels of management. Internal audit, as described in Chapter 6, typically reports to the audit committee of the board of directors. Thus, internal audit has an ability to communicate face to face with senior members of management. Because of this high level of communication, internal auditors can contact almost any level of management within the organization to establish a meeting and to discuss matters of audit interest.

This same high level of communication often makes communication with management somewhat difficult. Although internal audit generally reports at a high level, communications with the audit committee and members of very senior management can become very formal and essentially one-way channels. Internal audit may report on its plans and on significant audit findings. Senior management may ask questions but may not provide internal audit with enough additional insights to allow them to fully understand management needs. At the same time, other members of management may be wary of frank communications with internal audit because of fear that the wrong information or impressions might just end up as a critical audit report. Although internal audit standards, as will be discussed in Chapter 5, call for strict confidentiality of this type of information, some members of senior management may not be aware of internal audit's professional standards.

Internal audit must take specific steps to establish communication links with all levels of management in order to better understand their needs. Many of the operational audit projects described in other chapters of this book require this understanding of management needs. For example, internal audit cannot perform an effective audit of the capital projects function, as discussed in Chapter 27, unless the auditor is aware of management concerns and approaches in this area. Internal audit must establish communication channels through its planning process, through participation in various advisory meetings and boards, and through frank discussions with management over the results of audits.

The Audit-Planning Process

Chapter 7 covers procedures for evaluating organizational risk to allow an auditor to develop a more effective program while Chapter 8 discusses the overall audit-planning process. Both of those chapters emphasize the need to communicate plans with management. Feedback or responses as a result of this communication is important to better understand the needs of management. The effective internal auditor will present such plans to management along with a rationale of why given audit projects were scheduled or deferred. The auditor should then ask management to provide some additional insights on the scheduled projects as well as to communicate additional needs. This planning and risk-assessment process, as discussed in subsequent chapters, is an excellent means of better understanding the needs of management.

Establishing Effective Communication Channels

Although a separate and independent function, internal auditors must also continually think of themselves as members of the management team. This requires that appropriate levels of the internal audit department are sitting in various status and advisory meetings within the organization. Many larger organizations have a variety of committees, both formal and fairly informal, to discuss and resolve various problems. These range from the controller's monthly status meetings to the information systems department's user advisory board to manufacturing and engineering coordination meetings. As much as is practicable, appropriate members of the internal audit organization should secure invitations to sit in on these various committee meetings. These can be valuable sources for securing background information on various management needs and concerns. Of course, internal audit must participate in these meetings only as an observer, maintaining an attitude of independence.

Even when time resources do not allow direct participation, internal audit should ask to be placed on the distribution lists for various internal status reports or advisory committee minutes. This information will also help internal audit to better understand the needs of management. Many larger organizations have a public affairs or related function that prepares packages of news articles from outside published sources for senior managers. Internal audit should request to become a recipient of this information to gain insight into management concerns.

Audit Results Communications

Chapter 15 discusses the process of issuing effective audit reports that summarize internal audit's findings and recommendations. Since such reports usually require a formal management response, this is another means of receiving input on management needs and concerns. However, the effective auditor can also use these reports as a further vehicle of communication to better understand management needs. Often, it is effective to prepare significant findings in summary reports for review with top management. These often become a vehicle where management can respond to audit findings and point out areas where audit may be off target with regard to changing situations or where audit needs to place increased emphasis.

Communications is really the key element to understanding the needs of management. The auditor can work with management through effective audits or ongoing discussions. While it is often said that internal audit is the eyes and ears of an organization, the internal audit department will be much more valuable if it can observe and listen with an understanding of management needs in mind.

(b) ALTERNATIVE APPROACHES FOR DEVELOPING EXPERTISE

Perhaps the best of the alternative approaches for understanding the nature and scope of particular types of operations is actual experience as a worker on the job. To the extent that an individual can have direct responsibility for particular types of operational activities, the more likely that individual is to become familiar with the types of problems that arise. The drawbacks are the amount of time required and the fact that much experience can become unduly repetitive.

It is sometimes very effective to bring an individual into an internal audit organization with previous work experience in the specialized area of concern. For example, an internal audit department in a manufacturing company might find it useful to add a member to the staff with experience in a manufacturing activity such as industrial engineering. That individual should be able to provide some important insights to the organization and to audit its activities. Of course, this will only work if internal audit has a strong, ongoing program of such operational audits and if an appropriate, interested candidate can be selected. Special consideration may need to be given for the training and career planning for such an individual.

A second alternative approach is through the observation of operations. Such observations may take the form of deliberately planned tours and visits or they can be byproducts of other audit projects. One could also study production operations, the use of particular products, or other matters in a wide and varying range of focus. Some industries have their own professional organizations that offer educational programs. The insurance industry, for example, has a trade group that offers specialized related insurance training to employees of member companies. These programs are often good ways to increase internal audit understanding.

3-7 PARTNERSHIP ROLE OF INTERNAL AUDIT

The basic internal audit role of service to management starts with understanding management problems and needs. It then goes on to involve a partnership role between the manager and internal audit at all operational levels—a partnership role that extends to helping management achieve its goals and objectives to the maximum extent possible. Such an effective partnership role can be achieved in many ways. The following are essential ingredients of a sound program to achieve these desired results.

- Internal audit must provide basic audit protective services but, at the same time, help management achieve desired improvement. Moreover, protective contributions often provide an important foundation for making constructive contributions.

- Internal audit should be continuously alert to use its independence from actual operational responsibilities to identify, evaluate, and support issues of significant management interest.

- The capacity to interface in a persuasive manner with managers at all levels should be exercised whenever practicable. This requires a combination of having a strong operational understanding plus having appropriate personal contacts and conduct.

- Auditors must avoid the inherent temptation to use their potential power with management and other auditees. Such actions generate auditee resistance that later will block ongoing constructive relationships.

- Internal audit's strategic focus on internal controls should be used as the credential for the analysis and review of many operational areas. Since the technical expertise of the auditee is typically superior, the auditor's focus on control provides a more acceptable justification of the audit assistance offered.

- There must be respect given at all times for the responsibility that managers have for operational results. Audit recommendations must stand on their own merits, as judged by those who have operational responsibility.

- There must be a blending of the objectives of the audit at operational levels with the necessity for upward disclosure within the framework of total organizational welfare. This focus should help to neutralize any lower-level audit conflicts due to their more senior management exposure.

Service to the organization through assistance to management at all levels is a major goal for internal auditors. This justifies the efforts of internal audit to see its job through the eyes of management and to render all possible assistance for maximum management goal achievement. The problems of management are complex and continually changing in light of both internal and external environmental factors. This means that management increasingly needs the assistance of internal auditors and will, in many cases, welcome it when the ability and credibility of the internal audit function is established. It is a continuing challenge to internal auditors to render assistance to management through effective and significant audit recommendations.

CHAPTER 4

Operational Approach of Internal Audit

4-1 INTRODUCTION: OPERATIONAL AUDITING

The preceding chapters have considered the nature and scope of the internal auditing function. This chapter focuses on internal auditors as individuals and how they should view this profession. Despite discussions in previous chapters, some persons unfamiliar with the profession may still consider internal auditing to be a variant of financial or external auditing. This chapter emphasizes internal audit's operational approach, including its differences from traditional, financial statement–oriented external auditors. In addition, this discussion of internal audit's operational approach includes guidance on how to define the scope and nature of an operational review, its phases, and some problems common to all operational reviews.

The importance of internal audit's role in the modern organization has increased considerably since Brink's first edition, published in 1942. Then, the new profession of modern internal auditing was defining itself and, in some instances, was attempting to convince management of the importance of the services it could offer. In those days of some 60 years ago, many organizations viewed internal auditors as little more than a support function for their external auditors. When not helping the external auditors in their financial statement reviews, internal auditors spent their time on accounting-related functions such as reconciling organization bank accounts. Today, this concept has totally changed, starting with the Federal Corrupt Practices Act of 1977: requirements and standards have been established to make management responsible for the adequacy of their systems of internal controls. Internal audit has been designated as a key component in that overall system of internal control. Internal control standards were briefly discussed in Chapter 2, but this chapter will focus on the professional attitude necessary for an internal auditor to better perform internal control–oriented operational reviews.

The materials in this chapter should be particularly useful to the internal auditor who has joined this profession as a new college graduate, as a transfer from public accounting, or from some other professional position. Internal audit's interests go beyond the system of internal *accounting* control to include controls throughout the auditor's organization. An internal auditor is a key member of the modern organization, whether a major corporation, a government agency, or a not-for-profit enterprise. Although internal auditors may perform reviews in a variety of areas, their operational approach is an important distinction that sets them apart from others in the modern organization.

4-2 INTERNAL AND EXTERNAL AUDITORS: A COMPARISON

Internal auditors sometimes suffer from an identity problem because other members of their organization, often in middle management, do not realize the approach differences between internal auditors, external auditors, and other persons in the organization who may carry the title "auditor." Regarding the latter, some organizations have assigned administrative or clerical persons whose primary job has been to balance cash accounts, such as point-of-sale (POS) terminals in a retail store. These persons often were given the title of "retail auditors," and some internal auditors today still have a responsibility for those types of functions. However, modern internal auditors today have many other more important responsibilities in their overall service to management.

A more common area of confusion in the eyes of outsiders is the difference of purpose and function between internal and external auditors. One way to help explain this difference in approach is to compare the operational approach of internal auditors with the way external auditors perform their work. The two groups have very different missions even though some managers may announce to their staffs that "the auditors are coming," with little thought to whether they are their own internal or the external auditors. External auditors are associated with a public accounting firm that is separate and independent from the organization they audit. An organization's stockholders and board of directors make the decision to engage or hire the external audit firm, and the external auditors act independently of management in performing their reviews.

External auditors have only one major mission or goal when they perform an audit: to be able to express an opinion as to whether the organization's financial statements fairly present its current financial condition and the results of the operations over the preceding year. External auditors are, therefore, more concerned with the fairness of financial statement balances, and they work backward from the completed statements for the evidence to support the validity of those balances. This can be a very large role, of course, since virtually all activities in the organization have an impact on the control procedures supporting those financial statements.

An example of the type of account reviewed by external auditors is the reported accounts receivable balance or the moneys due the organization from credit sales. Both cash and credit sales are reported on the income statement as sales. The cash received is recorded as a cash asset, and the credit sales will be recorded as accounts receivable. However, not all credit customers pay their bills on time or sometimes even at all. The organization also sets up an account, often called the "allowance for doubtful accounts," which reduces the accounts receivable balance to estimate for those accounts that will not be collected. In their enthusiasm to boost profits, management sometimes sells to poor credit risks but does not make the allowance for doubtful accounts large enough to consider these potential bad credit risk customers. The external investor or banker is not able to determine the adequacy of this account through a review of published financial statements. External auditors look at such an account in detail, perform tests to determine whether it was fairly presented, and possibly insist on adjustments before the financial statements are presented. If they cannot resolve the matter, they might give an unfavorable audit opinion on the overall fairness of the financial statements. This is an extreme step that can result in the organization losing its lines of credit with banks and with other investors until the matter is corrected.

While external auditors start with this financial statement ending result, internal auditors start with the basic activities and work forward to achieve organizational service objectives. Internal audit might review the overall credit-granting policies to determine if credit is given to appropriate customers. They might also look at overdue account and write-off procedures to determine if any control problems exist. In total, they emphasize the controls that allow the allowance for doubtful accounts balance to be created.

Although statements about working backward or forward are oversimplifications of the audit process, they do have a certain amount of substance. Internal audit is more concerned with the effectiveness of basic operational activities and how those operational activities contribute to the total organization's economic welfare and profitability. All of this means that the two auditing groups approach information sources with different priorities, in somewhat different sequences, and with quite different end objectives.

The work of external auditors is often described as *financial auditing,* and this title has perhaps partially contributed to the movement of some modern internal auditors away from so-called financial auditing toward *operational* or *management auditing.* As discussed in Chapter 1, the separation of these two types of auditing is not that simple. There are some strong linkages between financial and operational auditing at several different levels and in various situations. The first is when internal audit is asked by management or by its external auditing firm to perform a financial review of a division subsidiary or some other operational entity. If internal audit is performing this work in support of the organization's external auditors, they are essentially working as external auditors, following the standards and procedures of that external auditing firm. However, internal audit cannot attest to the fairness of those financial records in the same manner as external auditors. Internal audit also can perform the same type of financial audit review at the request of management, independent of the external auditors. Here, the same financial review procedures may be used by internal audit, but they do not directly contribute to the financial statement audit.

At another level, internal auditors review operating activities that relate primarily to a financial or accounting function—for example, records retention activities, as well as security over those records. External auditors would typically only review the financial controls in this area, with minimal attention given to the operational issues. In many situations, internal audit's review focuses directly upon a regular operating activity such as materials-receiving operations or the custody and control of some portable fixed-asset equipment. While these types of reviews are primarily operational, the audit activities may extend into other matters that are financial in character, such as expense and revenue controls. Although operational auditing can deal almost entirely with nonaccounting activities, in many situations there are important linkages from operational procedures to so-called financial auditing procedures.

(a) GOING BEHIND FINANCIAL STATEMENTS

Any consideration of the requirements of financial auditing and operational auditing provides the basis for bringing these two audit functions—as well as information systems auditing—into the concept of integrated, or modern, internal auditing. Financial auditing in its most fundamental sense focuses on the fairness of presentation and the reliability of financial statement balances, including such aspects as their compliance with authoritative rules and standards.

These financial auditing objectives are only a component and starting point for other objectives of the typical organization. The modern internal auditor should have a combination of financial, operational, and information systems auditing skills, and audits should go behind financial results to examine all aspects of the manual and automated processes where those balances were created and maintained. The internal auditor can then give full recognition to the ever-present overlapping relationships between various assets and liabilities on the balance sheet and the different types of revenue and expenses that comprise the income statement. A modern internal auditor is concerned with the policies, decisions, procedures, and performance issues that affect those financial statement balances.

In this sense, financial auditing is an important but limited component of the total internal audit mission, which is expanded through operational auditing to cover an overall objective of maximizing organizational welfare. While the degree of emphasis on final statement balances and related operational issues can vary significantly in individual audit assignments, financial and operational auditing, as well as information systems auditing, should be fully integrated in well-designed internal audit procedures. Audit programs and activities must continuously focus on this broader, total internal audit mission.

(i) Organizational Service Approach. As we saw in Chapter 1, the mission of internal audit is to serve the organization from the board of directors and its audit committee through all levels of management. The practical effect of this extended range of internal audit services is that different audit service recipients may have similar needs at the same time, but with varying degrees of emphasis. All audit service recipients should have some interest in operational effectiveness or profitability, but in differing degrees of intensity and detail. Recipients also should have a need for internal audit protective services, such as the protection of physical assets, but in varying degrees and emphasis depending upon individual responsibilities. Members of the board of directors are more concerned than middle-level management with such issues as the legality of organization practices, its public relations, and their own personal professional liability. The internal audit service needs of an assistant controller responsible for manufacturing cost accounting are considerably different.

Because of these varying needs, internal audit's approach must be broad enough to properly serve all recipients. The approach throughout this book will be to first emphasize operational audit needs, then follow with information systems controls needs, and finally consider financial needs—to somewhat less a degree. This does not mean that protective needs can or will be neglected. This approach reflects a belief that the organization's highest-level need is for strong operational effectiveness, with adequate consideration given at the same time to protective internal control needs.

While internal audit should be concerned with internal control—and internal *accounting* controls in particular—modern internal auditors have other objectives in their service to management in the organization. Although certainly related to the concepts of internal control discussed in Chapter 2, internal audit should always focus on the specific needs of management and strive to contribute to the overall profitability and success of the organization. These two objectives place internal audit in a somewhat different position from the very important but more limited mission of the external auditors who serve an organization.

(ii) Internal Audit's Management Service Focus. The wide range of management service that can be provided by internal audit was outlined in the preceding chapters. The tie to this operational approach is that all aspects of internal audit's initial direction, the actual execution of review efforts, and the subsequent reporting of conclusions and recommendations are conditioned by the overall objective of helping management at all levels to do their jobs most effectively. Internal auditors who look at things as if they are the organization's owners can thus directly gather the needed facts for the solution of managerial problems. The focus here is on maximum organization welfare, and internal audit should represent the owners in situations where the limitations of time and energy preclude both owners and responsible managers from being directly exposed to some aspects of organization operations. Internal audit in this role has often properly been called the eyes and ears of management.

This service-to-management focus is one of the major areas that defines the overall operational approach of internal audit. The following also discusses the importance of a focus on profitability in the organization and on internal audit's reliance on a strong set of professional standards. All of these components combine to define the role of the modern internal auditor.

(iii) Internal Audit's Profitability Focus.

A good way to understand this operational approach is to recognize its primary focus on profitability. This has sometimes been called a business approach, to place the emphasis on doing what is good business for the organization. This does not mean that internal audit is only important in commercial, for-profit organizations as opposed to not-for-profit enterprises such as government agencies. The typical for-profit enterprise, whether publicly held or privately owned, measures a large component of its success in terms of the amount of profit generated. The not-for-profit organization measures its success in terms of other measures, such as the level of service performed to clients. Whether working within a typical organization concerned with profitability or a not-for-profit group that has other measures of success, internal audit should always understand these measures and focus its service activities along those lines.

Internal audit should attempt to find ways and sponsor the types of actions that will enhance the long-run profitability or success of a particular organization. This long-run profitability merges into a total management objective for internal audit for achieving the most productive utilization of organizational resources, thus providing a focus that is equally applicable to all types of organizations, whether commercial, public, or not-for-profit.

Profitability as a term itself is much more complicated than it first appears, and needs further clarification. First, profitability is the net result of cost and revenue factors, which are both generally independent but often closely interrelated. For example, reducing costs may increase profitability, but additional costs might also be the basis for generating revenues greater in amount than the additional cost. Illustrative of this could be increased advertising expenditures. An organization might decrease its costs by slashing expenditures for advertising; however, that advertising may have attracted significant additional revenues. With no advertising, sales and profits will probably go down as well. Reduced costs could in some cases lead to a still greater reduction in revenue. An excessive cutback in service could generate customer complaints and ultimately reduce sales. Because of these types of interrelationships, internal audit should think in terms of effective cost performance. Consideration should be given to the level of higher or lower cost which, after taking into consideration their impact on revenue, yields the greatest profit.

Profitability also has a time dimension that must be evaluated. Management actions often do not have a major impact until sometime in the future. As a result, internal audit is faced with two types of problems. First, time dimensions should be extended far enough into the future so that the cost revenue effects are properly matched in a sound evaluation.

The second problem is that the longer the period necessary for that type of evaluation, the more speculative becomes the estimate of the longer-run benefit. We often see this phenomena in U.S. federal government programs. A government official may predict that an X% tax increase to finance training programs will yield future benefits of reduced welfare costs. The expected benefits are often far into the future and assume many other variable factors that are difficult to estimate. As a result, this type of prediction is often of little value. All in all, it is difficult to properly evaluate the effectiveness of cost-revenue relationships and to determine whether present actions are really in the long-term interests of the enterprise. However, this is just what the business manager and owner must do, and in turn what internal audit must do in order to provide useful help and counsel.

Any examination of this operational approach leads directly to the problem of the various ways in which internal auditors should define the coverage of their reviews. The major issue here is whether the review should deal with a given function or with the total operational responsibilities of a given organizational entity. The function reviewed may be something like purchasing or receiving, and can involve a single operational unit or extend through all organization levels or through particular levels. In an entity approach, the review may cover all of the activities carried on by an particular entity, regardless of how many functions are involved. The entity involved can be the entire organization or a division or other operational unit. If a particular operational entity is responsible only for a single function, the two approaches, of course, become the same. Both functional and organizational-type reviews can vary greatly in complexity, depending on the volume of operations and the number of people involved.

Although most internal audit reviews have the characteristics of either a functional or organizational type, others will also have a defined scope that is determined by the specific request of management. Such requests can have to do with the verification of a particular fact or set of facts, the determination of the cause for a particular development, the correction of a specific deficiency, or gathering information about any managerial question. Thus, internal audit's operational activities can be broken down in any way desired as a basis for establishing what is wanted for the audit work. In the last analysis, the scope of particular review is determined by a combination of what management wants and what internal audit sees professionally as both significant control risks and the needs of management.

(iv) IIA Standards Approach. Chapter 5 discusses the professional standards for internal auditing. We refer to these standards here because they provide an excellent framework for the operational approach of internal audit. That standards framework includes the following broad areas of potential emphasis in designing and performing an operational review.

1. Reliability and integrity of information
2. Compliance with policies, plans, procedures, laws, and regulations
3. Safeguarding of assets
4. Economical and efficient use of resources
5. Accomplishment of established objectives and goals for operations or programs

An analysis surrounding this standards framework is discussed in more detail in Chapter 5. That analysis and the comments in this chapter point to internal audits emphasis on helping management to *better utilize* its resources in terms of profitability and related management welfare. Assistance to management in maximizing their effectiveness is indeed the central core of modern internal auditing. This is in every respect internal audit's most rewarding level of service to management.

4-3 TECHNICAL APPROACH OF THE INTERNAL AUDITOR

Up to this point, we have dealt with the various attitudes an internal auditor should possess and alternative ways to define the scope of an internal audit review. We turn now to the way in which the internal auditor proceeds to carry out these activities. The concern here is with the various technical approaches that have general application to all types of internal audit reviews. These approaches provide a framework into which an internal auditor can inject the audit programs that apply to individual review activities. A broader and more detailed discussion on administering internal audit activities in various areas of operations are discussed in Chapters 6 through 15.

We have divided this technical approach into four broad areas: internal audit familiarization, verification and analysis, the evaluation of audit results, and reporting the results of audit activities. These activities are discussed here in terms of the operational approach of the internal auditor. The same themes will return in later chapters in terms of both administering internal audit activities and performing specific internal audits in various areas.

(a) INTERNAL AUDIT FAMILIARIZATION NEEDS

An internal auditor's first and perhaps most basic activity is to become informed about the operational activity to be reviewed, an audit phase commonly referred to as *familiarization*. There are two broad levels of familiarization. The first includes defining the steps necessary, or the information needed, prior to arriving at a field or departmental audit site location. The second includes what should be done at the location of the review. Before going to a field location, audit management and the assigned internal audit team should perform the following types of familiarization activities.

- *Definition of the Overall Purpose of the Review.* This statement of audit purpose might be developed by the director of the internal audit or a member of the audit management team. Even if the review had been requested by some other level of management, the scope of the planned audit should be formally agreed upon by internal audit and organization management at an appropriate level.
- *Discussions of Audit Plans with Other Interested Personnel.* These discussions should include others at various levels of responsibility, including management at the field location to be visited. This familiarization exercise should also include other staff managers and key personnel to the extent that they are involved in the definition of the scope of the audit assignment. While familiarization discussions can serve a number of purposes, they primarily alert these individuals to the fact that a review is to be made and get from them either questions for internal audit's attention or information that may be useful in connection with the review.
- *Accumulation of All Pertinent Data.* The internal audit team should obtain and review any kind of information that could be applicable to the planned audit. They

may wish to review the working papers and reports from the last audit and obtain and inspect any other types of reports or materials from other sources that may be relevant.

- *Advance Arrangements with Field Location.* Unless there are special reasons that dictate the review should be performed on a surprise basis, internal audit should normally communicate with the field location and advise the responsible head of the function of the planned review. At the same time, necessary preparatory and administrative arrangements can be handled and internal audit can become familiar with any local conditions requiring modification of audit plans and procedures.

Once internal audit has completed its central familiarization activities, the assigned audit team should be ready to move to the field location—which, of course, can be held at either a geographically distant site or at an office where internal audit is located. The familiarization steps in this phase are similar to the types of activity done prior to arriving at the field location and includes the following:

- *Discussions with the Responsible Field Site Manager.* Internal audit should meet with the local manager responsible for the site to be reviewed, who often is the person to whom the final audit report will ultimately be directed. Internal audit should request from that manager a description of the operational activities, organizational relationships, potential problem areas, and other points of interest. The familiarization discussion here would also normally include internal audit's discussion of the overall purpose of the review, its timing plans, and other special arrangements.

- *Discussions with Other Key Personnel.* The discussions with the responsible field site managers should be supplemented by discussions with other key personnel. These discussions will normally provide additional details about the various subactivities and at the same time serve as a cross-check against the information previously obtained.

- *Reviews of Policies and Procedures.* Discussions with personnel at all levels should also be supplemented by reviews of written policies and procedures of all kinds that bear on the administration and control of the various types of operational activities carried on by the organizational group.

This familiarization phase should extend into the actual internal audit review. This is to say that a regular review program involves a further familiarization with detailed activities not completely covered by other key personnel. Included here would be further discussions with personnel, actual observations, and documentation of procedures, including the preparation of flow charts. Familiarization enables the internal auditor to know what the operational activity involves, how it is supposed to be managed, and the inherent control risks.

(b) VERIFICATION AND ANALYSIS

Starting from the base level of familiarization, an internal auditor would next move to the verification and analysis phases of a review. These two activities are interwoven as the internal auditor moves downward through the organizational levels and performs necessary review procedures. Conceptually, verification is the independent determination of the extent to which assertions made in the familiarization phase prove true. For example, the internal audit review team may be advised during its familiarization phase that all new information systems placed into production are fully documented. Internal auditors might verify through examination whether, and how fully, a sample set of these new systems actually is documented.

Verification can be achieved in a number of ways, but there must be sufficient credible evidence. This evidence can be gathered through oral inquiries, observations, written confirmations, the tracing of the processing of data, tests, and in other ways. The quality of the evidence gathered will vary, not only with the type, but also with the manner in which individual efforts are carried out. All of these aspects have a highly judgmental character, both as to the quality of the particular evidence and as to how much effort should be expended by internal audit in obtaining additional evidence. The application of the necessary judgment in turn depends on the level of professional competence possessed by the internal auditors responsible for the review.

Analysis, a related phase of internal audit's approach, is the more detailed examination of the data and information gathered during the review in terms of its component elements. It is frequently carried out as part of the verification process, such as in the detailed analysis of an account balance, which might also serve to help verify the correctness of the account. In an operational situation, the detailed breakdown of performance under different types of operating conditions can provide the basis for determining better ways to control the particular type of performance. In all types of analysis, there can be highly judgmental aspects both in terms of making a decision as to how a particular type of information or operational activity should be analyzed and, subsequently, in defining any potential benefits as the analysis is completed. The analysis phase of an internal audit review provides an especially fine opportunity to both observe the evolving elements and to perceive relationships or other matters of managerial interest. Analysis is, indeed, the major route to effective internal auditing service.

(c) EVALUATION OF AUDIT RESULTS

The familiarization, verification, and analysis phases have now set the stage for an evaluation of the results on an operational audit. This is the critical phase of operational audit work, when the auditor reviews results and seeks to draw conclusions that may provide a basis for recommendations and definitive management service. Its scope, as described in Figure 4.1, can best be understood by viewing audit results as being carried out at three levels.

1. *How good are the results of the review presently being achieved?* This may be a fairly narrow question on the level of compliance with a particular procedure, or it may be a more serious question as to how efficiently the given operational activity is carried out. This step would often include an overall assessment of the effectiveness of the performance of the operational activity under review.

2. *Why are the results of the review what they are?* Why is the performance identified in the review good or bad? If any problems were found, why were the results not better? This step involves an evaluation of the causal factors behind any reported audit findings. Internal audit should give particular attention to the extent to which those factors might have been more effectively controlled.

Figure 4.1   Evaluation of Audit Results

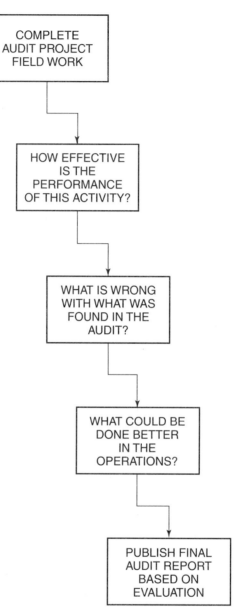

3. *What could be done better?* Internal audit should ask questions such as whether the procedures could be made more effective. Should a particular policy be changed or even abandoned? Are the proper people involved in the process and are they adequately trained and supervised? Some of these conclusions may be reasonably clear and can become the basis for specific recommendations. In other cases, more information, or, if not practicable, the recommendation may simply be that further study

is needed. These determinations as to the scope of the recommendation are, of course, highly dependent on the situation and the capabilities of the internal audit group.

During all phases of the work, internal audit should strive to achieve maximum effectiveness. This work should never be done in a routine or mechanical manner. Whether examining documents, talking with individuals, or observing various operational activities, an internal auditor should always be thinking of the underlying conditions pertaining to the situation observed during all parts of a review. What is right? How responsibly was a particularly action carried out? How valid are the audit results? What else could be done as part of the review? These are typical questions that should always be in an internal auditor's mind. While an internal auditor should never have a distorted belief that everything is wrong or that some disaster is imminent, an auditor should never be a naive optimist. Internal auditors should always take an inquiring and challenging approach to their review and interview questions and should have a relatively greater need to be convinced than other persons in the organization. While an internal auditor should always strive to be open-minded and fair, the auditor should exhibit natural skepticism and a need to understand all relevant information bearing on the objectives of a review and its related conclusions. Internal audit's alertness helps provide greater protective services to management and also aids in a continuing search for improvement.

(d) REPORTING THE RESULTS OF AUDIT ACTIVITIES

The final phase of internal audit's work results in the development of audit conclusions and recommendations. Internal audit should now consider a range of possible actions at the end of a review. At one extreme, internal audit can simply report their findings while making no recommendations or taking other steps to determine if there has been corrective actions. Internal audit would simply report its findings, allowing the audit report recipient to decide exactly what actions to take, and when. At the other extreme, internal audit can attempt to oversee the implementation of the recommended action while still at the field site. While this book generally suggests that internal audit report its findings, make recommendations for corrective action, and allow management to take appropriate action, internal auditors will sometimes become very involved in helping to implement the corrective actions. This approaches a fine line where internal audit wants to continue to be independent. If too involved in overseeing the implementation of a recommendation, internal audit risks losing objectivity. The real issue is often the extent to which it is possible to move individual matters toward completed action. In many cases, the particular matter may clearly be something that should be handled immediately. This could be the correction of an error, or perhaps a more informed interpretation of a company policy.

Other cases may be more controversial and may require decisions or a review at higher organizational levels. The important thing, however, is that all parties should be committed to the concept of taking maximum corrective action in response to internal audit's reported findings. The reasons for this approach is that earlier action accelerates the achievement of the expected benefits. Furthermore, the partnership relationship of internal audit and the responsible management can be more effectively implemented. Internal audit and management can work more closely together and can agree as to what needs to be done. This allows internal audit to demonstrate more realistically its intention to help local management, not to police them, as well as its overall interest in the organization.

The audit process normally ends with a reporting phase where internal audit summarizes what has been accomplished and makes this information available to higher-level management and other interested parties through a formal audit report. The content of the audit report will, of course, be determined directly by the extent of the completed actions and what matters still require further consideration and possible action. Chapter 15 discusses the preparation of audit reports, including alternative ways in which reports can be developed. Formal audit reports are the major means through which internal audit communicates findings, recommendations, and activities to all interested personnel, especially organization senior management.

Audit reports need to be handled with special care. However, the modern internal auditor should concentrate more on what can be accomplished at the field site and less on what goes into reports. Internal audit will serve organization interests better in most situations by helping responsible management at the field level rather than just by reporting matters to senior management. Under these circumstances, the reporting of completed actions may need not be as elaborate as when the basis for a recommended action is presented. At the same time, senior management should both understand this audit approach and support it.

4-4 QUALIFICATIONS OF AN INTERNAL AUDITOR

As mentioned, some members of an organization may not understand or even accept internal audit's important and very unique roles. This lack of understanding may range from the lowest-level employee in the operational area being reviewed to the higher-level executives. Some managers responsible for an area to be reviewed may question whether the effort required to accommodate an internal audit is justified in relation to the benefits to be received. The department or functional manager may even feel that the internal audit activity is counterproductive to the achievement of the manager's own operational objectives. While various human factors can contribute to that attitude, our interest at this point is in identifying the problem and determining the rationale for overcoming these obstacles. Managers want to maximize their own interests in terms of a greater achievement of objectives, but they often do not see internal audit as being able to contribute to those ends in a worthwhile manner.

To reconcile this dilemma, the internal audit team assigned to a review area must make it clear that they do not claim to have all the technical knowledge or experience to tell the manager what the manager's operational objectives should be or how those objectives should be achieved in an operational sense. Instead, internal audit should convey the message that all operational activities have common needs in the manner in which objectives are established and in the manner in which implementing actions are planned and controlled. Internal audit's major area of competence is in understanding how the planning and operational activities can implement the best possible and most effective operational controls. These approaches require the modern internal auditor to understand both underlying management concepts and more detailed procedures that assure desired levels of performance and final results. Once internal audit has been given the opportunity to demonstrate what it can do in providing such assistance, the credentials and related acceptability of internal audit rise steadily.

In order to demonstrate these operational auditing skills to management, the modern internal auditor must exhibit strong professional and technical skills. An internal auditor will not be viewed by management as a key member of their team just because the auditor has an MBA or is either a Certified Internal Auditor (CIA) or a Certified Public Accountant.

Management also will expect members of the audit team to have strong personal and professional qualifications.

(a) PERSONAL QUALIFICATIONS OF THE MODERN INTERNAL AUDITOR

While internal auditors must have strong technical qualifications, as will be discussed below, their personal qualifications also play a major role. Although a lengthy list of desirable personal qualifications can be developed, the problem is complicated because the identification and evaluation of these individual qualifications can be at best very subjective. The most useful approach here is to look at internal audit personal qualifications in terms of the major end objectives:

1. To achieve a good first impression when performing any audit
2. To develop a more enduring relationship with auditees over a longer period of time
3. To provide an additional basis for sound professional results

These three end objectives are, of course, closely related, but they do emphasize particular types of personal qualifications necessary in the successful modern internal auditor. Directors of internal audit responsible for recruiting new members to the audit staff should keep these objectives in mind when evaluating potential candidates. Internal auditors, themselves, should always keep these in mind when performing their various audit tasks.

(i) Achieving a Good First Impression. First impressions can be, as we know, both good and bad. When an internal auditor begins a field audit assignment, a good first impression by management of the auditor should help to get things off to a good start and to avoid future conflicts. In many situations, this first impression is gained through a very limited contact. For example, an internal auditor may initially just make some inquiries regarding a planned review. If auditee management has had no prior contact with that auditor, relationships can be very much damaged if the auditor asking the questions has a poor professional style or appearance. An internal auditor's emphasis should be on making a good impression in a short time. What can be done to contribute to a successful first impression? The answer is a combination of both personal and professional image and the ability to capitalize quickly on limited opportunities.

With respect to image or appearance, standards of dress and grooming should be consistent with the organization's dress code and in the middle range between extreme conservatism and high style. In order to capitalize more effectively on opportunities, the modern internal auditor should be able to respond quickly to questions, and be able to enter into discussions with courtesy and professional competence. The internal auditor's objective should be to engender respect and confidence.

(ii) Building Long-Term Internal Audit Relationships. While short-term impressions are important, the modern internal auditor often has a greater opportunity to develop effective personal relationships over a longer period of time. Internal auditors often have the time to develop professional relationships of mutual respect with both personnel in the operational activities reviewed and managerial personnel at all levels. In these situations,

Figure 4.2   Necessary Attributes for the Successful Internal Auditor

1.   *Basic Fairness and Integrity*

2.   *Dedication to the Organization's Interests*

3.   *Reasonable Humility*

4.   *Professional Poise*

5.   *Empathy*

6.   *Role Consistency*

7.   *Curiosity*

8.   *Critical Attitude*

9.   *Alertness*

10. *Persistence*

11. *Energy*

12. *Self-Confidence*

13. *Courage*

14. *Ability to Make Sound Judgments*

individual auditor qualifications become especially important. Figure 4.2 outlines some of these attributes which are necessary for the successful internal auditor to earn the respect and cooperation of other members of the organization.

While these concepts of basic fairness, dedication to organizational interests, and professional attitude are important in establishing an effective relationship throughout the organization, other personal qualifications also bear directly on an internal auditor's competence. These relate particularly to the way an internal auditor goes about performing actual audit and review activities. Some critical success factors for the modern internal auditor include:

- *Curiosity*. An internal auditor should have a natural curiosity to probe for the possible underlying explanations of observed conditions and should not be satisfied with generalizations or types of explanations that ignore the concerns raised.

- *Critical Attitude*. An internal auditor should be critical by making careful judgments about the areas reviewed. The auditor must have high standards for evaluating the adequacy of information reviewed or observed.

- *Alertness*. An internal auditor needs to be alert to all possible sources of information that may bear on the issues surrounding a review. An internal auditor should be alert to the significant facts, innumerable interrelationships, and the "fuzzy" information which always comes with individual audit review situations.

- *Persistence*. An internal auditor should not give up easily when blocked in the pursuit of needed information or an answer to a question, or for possible solutions to problems that have been identified.

- *Energy.* This is an important backup quality that keeps a good internal auditor going when others would give up and settle for whatever has already been found. Energy is a combination of temperament, dedication, and good health.

- *Self-Confidence.* Confidence in one's self generates confidence in others. This is the inward conviction that one knows what one is doing and that it is the right thing to do.

- *Courage.* The quality of courage, which is related to self-confidence, goes further and involves the willingness to stand one's ground in the face of pressures and risks. This personal qualification adds status to an internal auditor, especially when that courage has been demonstrated. All internal auditors may face the challenge of having their courage tested at one time or another.

- *Ability to Make Sound Judgments.* Faced with conflicting factors of all types, judgment is the ability to weigh conflicting factors calmly, including the impact of varying time dimensions. Here, the goal is not for a ''perfect record'' but rather for how many more correct judgments are made versus the ones in error.

- *Integrity.* An internal auditor's personal reputation for integrity allows others to rely on audit findings and conclusions. This reliance includes the belief in the professional competence, fairness, and honesty with which the material has been presented.

- *Independence.* Closely interrelated with all of these attributes is the need to be independent and not to compromise unduly in the face of various pressures.

(b) INTERNAL AUDIT TECHNICAL AND PROFESSIONAL QUALIFICATIONS

To be effective, an internal auditor must have a certain level of technical and professional competence. An internal auditor needs an understanding of internal control concepts, of information systems, and a good knowledge of the operational issues in the auditor's organization. A major purpose of this book is to provide the modern internal auditor with this necessary information.

Every internal auditor needs to have certain basic skills, ranging from a good general understanding of internal control principles to a basic understanding of the audit process. The latter can include such things as the process of risk assessment, the preparation of workpapers, and the performance of necessary audit tests to develop audit conclusions. Again, these topics are all covered in various chapters of this book. When assessing their technical needs and qualifications, internal audit management and individual internal auditors should ask themselves three basic questions.

1. What basic technical qualifications are needed?
2. To what extent are special types of technical qualifications needed?
3. When are these skills needed?

Individual internal auditors must be prepared to deal with a wide range of operational situations, and technical qualifications in the broadest possible sense are needed. These can be obtained through both education and experience. For education, an internal auditor might acquire a college degree in an established school of business, although many other degree programs and courses of study will still provide the necessary level of technical education to qualify as an internal auditor. While a college degree may not be necessary, it helps.

Regarding experience, an internal auditor often can operate more effectively with some previous involvement in operational activities or at least a reasonable exposure to them. The activities most useful may vary with the individual organization, but they should preferably have been in situations where a number of people were involved and where there were issues of administrative direction and control. A second useful qualification would be some experience in or understanding of the accounting and financial control processes. This type of qualification does not necessarily require direct work of an accounting nature but should at least involve the kind of exposure that provides a reasonable understanding of this area. This need for an understanding of accounting controls is consistent with the view that the financial control dimension can be an effective starting point for an examination of the broader types of internal controls.

In many operational activities, internal auditors often find it helpful if not necessary to have some special expertise with respect to those particular areas. Illustrative of this would be reviews of manufacturing process activities, various kinds of engineering activities, or organizations involved in specialized accounting control areas. Depending on the organization, the need for this special expertise can vary. Internal audit may want either to recruit or to develop, through training, staff members with those needed special skills. Internal audit, however, may be faced with some very real practical limitations. First, it is often impossible and impracticable for all personnel to have all of the types of technical skill that might be needed at one time or another. At best, internal audit should seek to have a balanced staff with some personnel having certain skills and others having different ones. At some level of excellence with regard to a particular skill, a question might be raised whether a highly skilled auditor might not be more useful to the organization if assigned directly to those operations. Issues surrounding the staffing and training of internal auditors are discussed in Chapter 9.

In addition to the problem of agreeing on what kinds of general and special technical internal audit skills are needed, management always must schedule internal audit resources when they are available. The director of internal auditing needs to have personnel available who already meet requirements. Even though they may initially lack some of the necessary standards, others can be recruited assuming they have the potential to acquire them. As Chapter 9 points out, internal audit management can start to develop a new college graduate, or perhaps another employee who has been working in some other area of organization operations. Through experience and perhaps some special training, internal audit management can expand the competence of these recruits. What is important is that the personnel capabilities in total meet the needs of actual internal audit assignments. In addition, there is always the possibility of going outside the department to obtain special expertise, either within the organization or from outside.

The desire on the part of the internal auditing profession to maximize its effectiveness in serving management leads naturally to the desire to develop standards by which there can be some better measure as to how well internal auditors are carrying out their functions. Moreover, internal auditors have a basic professional interest in achieving effective control, and the use of internal audit standards in that effort suggests that these activities can be better controlled and measured. In the early days of internal auditing and when the first editions of this book were published, the profession had no standards of its own. Internal auditors then relied on public accounting standards, even though they were not all that relevant to internal auditors.

In response to this lack of standards, The Institute of Internal Auditors authorized a major study effort and in 1978 published its "Standards for the Professional Practice of Internal Auditing." These Standards are discussed in some detail in Chapter 5. For internal auditors, they have provided an important base of reference in the practice of modern internal auditing. For all others—including management, boards of directors, public accountants, government, businessmen, and educators—the standards have provided more definitive information about what they should expect from internal auditors. While the Standards have limitations, they do provide a solid basis for the practice of modern internal auditing.

The Institute of Internal Auditors also developed a certification program with the designation of Certified Internal Auditor (CIA). The foundation for this program was a major study of what constituted a needed "common body of knowledge for the internal auditor." Subsequently, an examination program was established that has been administered by the IIA on a regular basis. The number of persons sitting for the examination has steadily increased, and a large number of internal auditors now have the CIA designation.

A continuing problem of the certification program has been the difficulty of defining and evaluating the knowledge that internal auditors should have. This is because the operational activities covered by internal auditors in actual practice are so broad. However, that problem has been dealt with in a most commendable manner and the major benefits of the CIA certification program have been amply demonstrated. Professionals who wish to establish their credentials as internal auditors should strongly consider sitting for the CIA examination.

An ongoing problem pertaining to the CIA program is that a large number of IIA members are still not certified. This mixed-membership mode is in contrast to the approach taken by the American Institute of Certified Public Accountants, where the holding of a CPA certificate is generally a requirement of AICPA membership. One contributing factor to this problem is that the movement of individuals in and out of internal auditing practice is often very great, thus reducing their incentive to make the effort needed to achieve CIA certification. All internal auditors should strongly support this increased internal audit professionalism, the related greater career commitment, and the resulting potentially longer tenure in internal auditing practice. At the same time, management's interests can often be best served by moving individuals in and out of the internal auditing department. While it is not practicable today to require new internal auditors to complete the CIA examination program before they join the profession, at the same time all internal auditors are encouraged to qualify for the CIA certificate.

4-5 OPERATIONAL REVIEWS OF INTERNAL CONTROLS

We have previously defined a major mission of internal auditors is to assist their organizations to achieve an effective use of its resources. This mission is achieved primarily through reviews of the adequacy of all types of internal controls, including the integrity of financial procedures and appropriate laws and regulations. However, an internal auditor must use this internal control–related material and at the same time carry out the previously described broader objectives of operational auditing. Put in other words, internal auditors must best utilize the results of their total operational reviews as a means of achieving a full range of service to the organization.

While it is neither feasible nor appropriate in this book to develop still another set of guidelines, it is useful to suggest an overall framework for operational reviews on the adequacy of individual internal control systems and then to supplement that framework through further brief comments. The following is an overall framework for internal audit operational reviews.

1. *Review and evaluate the background environment.* This includes an understanding of the kind of business (or businesses) carried on by the particular organization, its goals and objectives, and the current status of operations. The review step includes gaining a reasonable understanding of the major activities, policies, key computer systems, and organizational arrangements. The focus should consistently be on the extent of potential controls, as discussed in Chapter 8.

2. *Acquire an understanding of the existing system of internal control.* An internal auditor should both gain this understanding and document it through a combination of observations, inquiries, and transaction analyses. The focus should emphasize the extent of control risk.

3. *Undertake a preliminary evaluation of the adequacy of design of the existing system.* This step includes the extent to which the organization has defined its internal control objectives and the manner in which it perceives the achievement of them. A cost/benefit analysis can be performed in a preliminary manner based on professional judgment and experience.

4. *Test compliance with the aforementioned existing systems.* This is a detailed audit determination of whether the system is functioning in the manner intended. This step includes the verification of results through observations, interrogations, or audit sampling. The focus here should be on the nature and scope of any errors identified. Audit sampling is discussed in Chapter 13.

5. *Reevaluate the entire system in terms of both current design and actual implementation.* This step includes a definitive evaluation of all significant controls, both individually and in combination, based upon the results of the audit testing. The evaluation should cover both the goodness of the design and the quality of implementation singly and in all combinations. This step should extensively use cost/benefit analyses to allow internal audit to develop practicable recommendations.

6. *Summarize and report on deficiencies and present appropriate recommendations.* In this final phase, internal audit judgments should be made regarding the significance and materiality of any audit findings. These conclusions and recommendations should recognize the prerogatives of management to make final decisions depending on the extent they wish to incur costs to take corrective actions or to accept risks. However, management should have views and recommendations that are consistent with those of internal audit.

The framework outlined above represents the basic operational steps that should be followed by internal auditors in any review. The steps are generally repeated in the various operational auditing topics discussed in Chapters 21–30. Internal auditors should recognize that these steps are often subject to certain important collateral considerations regarding the internal auditor's review approach. All evaluations involve factors that range from those very direct and immediate to those that are more indirect, and hence more difficult to perceive. For example, when evaluating the environmental factors surrounding an operational system, internal auditors should evaluate what the responsible people do and how they do it, as well as what those same people assert. Management can assert their desire for strong controls but then not respond vigorously or decisively to disclosed deficiencies. A further example involves the causes of faulty compliance with a procedural control. The deficiency may be caused by such direct factors as inadequate design of the control system, unusual operating conditions, or inadequate training of personnel. However, the deficiency may be due more to basic environmental factors.

An internal auditor should always prepare adequate documentation of any audit findings. Such documentation is desirable both to assure a more systematic and thorough review and to provide backup evidence if the adequacy of the review is later challenged. However, documentation can become too elaborate and too costly to prepare. Internal audit can incur a continuing cost to maintain such documentation to reflect changing conditions accurately. An example here could be an overly elaborate transaction analysis and related flowcharts. Clearly, good judgment is very much needed as to where to strike a practical balance. Internal audit documentation and the preparation of workpapers are discussed in Chapter 11.

Internal auditors can use different approaches in sequencing and combining review steps in an operational review. There is no single one best approach. The problems here stem from the fact that an evaluation normally proceeds at various levels and is unavoidably interwoven to some extent with the checking of audit compliance. The recommendations in this book are subject to these same limitations. Design considerations often overlap with those of implementation. It is important, however, to try to draw the line between design and implementation while performing an operational review. This allows an internal auditor to focus on the sources of existing significant system strengths and weaknesses. In most situations, the remedial action is quite different for correcting a system design as compared to implementing it.

Responsibilities for the environmental conditions, the design of controls, and the implementation of those controls exist at various levels in the organization. At the same time, basic responsibilities for internal controls vary. It is important that internal audit review and evaluation procedures be compatible with the underlying responsibilities as defined for particular individuals and groups of individuals in the organization.

In all phases of an operational review and in evaluating each activity level, the central focus of the review and evaluation of internal controls should be on potential risks and the related evaluation of costs versus benefits. This is simply to say that internal audit should attempt to minimize risk, but the desired minimization must be in balance with the costs incurred. Here, internal audit should recognize that all kinds of costs must be considered to the extent that they may be significant. Auditors are always faced with the question of how accurately they can measure the current and future impact of alternative procedural approaches. There is also the question of the level of risk acceptable to management. The evaluation of organizational risk is discussed in Chapter 7.

These considerations have been outlined not to emphasize the inherent limitations of every review of internal accounting control, but rather to help internal auditors to better understand the problems and thus to induce the level of competence and care that is necessary. All participants in the total review process, including the internal audit team, can make important contributions in helping to generate the needed capabilities.

4-6 OPERATIONAL APPROACH IN PERSPECTIVE

Having the proper operational approach is a necessary basis for effective internal auditing. As we have seen, the starting point is the development of professional competence where the important ingredients are personal and technical qualifications combined with a reasonable understanding of human relations issues and problems. The major thrust of internal audit's operational approach is to see the operations of the organization through the eyes of management, and to appraise all operational situations as the responsible manager would do if actually there. In doing this, an internal auditor does not take the place of management nor relieves individual managers of their own responsibilities. Rather, the modern internal auditor should do everything possible to provide the means by which management can have both the backup it desires and the basis for ongoing management determinations. This represents the management service focus of internal audit, which properly envelops and conditions the total internal audit effort. This is the hallmark of the operational approach of internal audit.

Historically, the narrower focus of internal accounting control has also always been part of internal audit's concern but in many cases is taking an increasingly smaller proportion of the total internal auditing effort. This changing proportion has been a natural result of the expanded role of operational auditing in terms of both scope and management level. At the present time, the special concern for the more protective internal control, as reinforced by the COSO report guidelines and the Foreign Corrupt Practices Act, has supported this operational auditing trend. In light of the perceived needs of management, this operational approach is needed and is a proper concern for internal auditors. At the same time, however, these needs for reviews of internal control should not limit internal audit's broader service roles. Ideally, internal audit should take special care to consider the special needs for achieving sound internal control, so that there will be no diminution of broader management services. This approach is consistent with our own belief in the potential for a high-level contribution to the organization through modern internal auditing.

PART TWO

ADMINISTERING INTERNAL AUDIT ACTIVITIES

CHAPTER 5

Professional Standards

5-1 INTRODUCTION: UNDERSTANDING INTERNAL AUDIT STANDARDS

For a practice to qualify as a profession, certain requirements are necessary. These include a recognized and well-defined area of service to society, special knowledge and skills for providing that service, standards of performance, a code of ethics, and a procedure by which the members can be disciplined. The Institute of Internal Auditors (IIA) has developed such a set of Standards for the Professional Practice of Internal Auditing.[1]

These Standards serve both the members of The Institute of Internal Auditors and the larger society served by internal auditors, and provide a benchmark against which to measure the level and quality of individual and overall internal auditing activities. At the same time, IIA Standards provides a basis for education and training to achieve desired levels of professional excellence. For those outside the internal auditing profession—including management, boards of directors, external auditors, and regulatory bodies—the Standards serve as a useful measure of what they all should expect to receive in the way of internal auditing services.

All internal auditors should understand and subscribe to these professional standards. This chapter contains annotated extracts of the Statements on Internal Auditing Standards (SIAS) as issued by The Institute of Internal Auditors and a detailed explanation and discussion of the Standards. In addition, comments and clarifications are offered which should help the modern internal auditor to operate more effectively. Because the various internal audit procedures and techniques discussed in later chapters of this book are based on these Standards, the reader should develop a general understanding of these standards before moving on to the various other chapters in this book.

5-2 WHY INTERNAL AUDIT STANDARDS?

Internal auditors work in a large variety of organizations and are asked to perform internal audit reviews in a diverse number of operational and financial areas. Because of this diversity, internal audit is faced with a wide spectrum of professional challenges, including

---

[1] *Standards for the Professional Practice of Internal Auditing* (Altamonte Springs, Fl.: The Institute of Internal Auditors, 1995.

that management expects internal auditors to perform reviews in a competent and consistent manner. The Standards aid in this process; they provide a guideline for management to measure their internal auditors as well as for internal auditors to measure themselves. The Standards also set some constraints upon internal audit activity.

The professional auditor today may be asked to follow several sets of standards. For example, if an internal auditor originally came from a public accounting firm and is a Certified Public Accountant (CPA), that internal auditor would be required to understand and follow certain standards established by the American Institute of Certified Public Accountants (AICPA). Some of these standards apply to ethical conduct and will continue to apply to internal auditors holding a CPA. Other AICPA standards apply only to the independent audits of financial statements performed by external auditors and are not applicable to internal audit.

Internal auditors may have also come from some other professional audit area, such as banking. Many such disciplines have professional organizations with their own standards that, generally, will not be in conflict with the IIA Standards. They may use slightly different terminology but should follow audit practices that generally fit under the IIA Standards.

As a matter of practice, however, the IIA's Standards for the Practice of Internal Auditing will govern the work of internal audit. When there appears to be a conflict and when the individual questioning that conflict is working as an internal auditor, the IIA's Standards will take precedence over any conflicting professional standards. If there appears to be a question, the individual now working as an internal auditor should address the standards-setting body, which has created the conflict, for a clarification.

(a) BACKGROUND OF THE IIA STANDARDS

As stated in its own materials, the Institute of Internal Auditors issued these Standards for the Professional Practice of Internal Auditing in 1978 "to serve the entire profession in all types of business, in various levels of government, and in all other organizations where internal auditors are found . . . to represent the practice of internal auditing as it should be . . . ." Prior to the approval of these Standards, the most authoritative document was the Statement of Responsibilities of internal audit, originally issued by the IIA in 1947 and subsequently revised over the years until the current Standards. The 1978 IIA Standards are described in their published foreword as "the criteria by which the operations of an internal auditing department are evaluated and measured." The foreword goes on to state, "Compliance with the concepts enunciated by the Standards is essential before the responsibilities of the internal auditor can be met."

The Standards were developed by the IIA's Professional Standards Committee based upon their own professional expertise as well as comments received from IIA members and other interested parties. Because of the diverse group of participants who developed the Standards, the final language has some overlap, compromise, and incompleteness. As a result, individual standards and guidelines may be subject to varying interpretations. These matters will be discussed in subsequent sections of this chapter.

Although the language of the Standards is sufficiently broad to cover current and changing conditions, it has been necessary for the IIA over time to issue updates or clarifications covering specific internal audit issues. These pronouncements are called Statements on Internal Auditing Standards (SIAS) and are issued by the IIA's Professional

Standards Committee after public exposure and comments through a formal exposure draft.

SIASs are official, authoritative interpretations of the Standards. They provide internal audit with interpretations of existing Standards in areas of concern, question, or current interest. For example, in the mid-1980s there was a significant concern over management frauds and the internal auditor's responsibility for deterring, detecting, investigating, and reporting such acts. While the internal auditor's responsibility in this area was covered in a very general sense by the existing Standards, SIAS No. 3, "Deterrence, Detection, Investigation, and Reporting of Fraud," was issued in 1985 to interpret and provide guidance in this area. An SIAS covers a broad area requiring interpretation or guidance that will be eventually incorporated into the full body of Standards. The IIA does not issue SIASs simply to answer a member's question or to interpret narrow specialized areas.

While SIASs are initially issued as freestanding notification documents, they are promptly codified in the Standards. As of 1997, all of the SIASs have been incorporated into the IIA Standards and are discussed here as part of our overall discussion of the various Standards.

More specific Standards-related questions are answered through Professional Standards Bulletins (PSB) published in the IIA's journal, *"Internal Auditor."* Individuals address technical questions about the intention, implementation, or interpretation of the Standards to the Professional Standards Committee. A PSB response is then published which represents the opinions of the committee member assigned to answer the question but not the overall opinion of the IIA. A PSB is not an official amendment to the Standards, nor is it an official pronouncement. However, PSBs provide members guidance in specific areas as required.

(b) AUTHORITY OF THE IIA STANDARDS

The IIA Standards provide a guideline for internal auditors and the overall internal audit department. Other entities and internal levels of management may judge the professional adequacy of an internal audit department by its compliance with IIA Standards. For example, as discussed in Chapter 6, the audit committee of the board will often insist the internal audit department *formally* adopt the IIA Standards as part of its charter.

External auditors, when deciding to rely upon the work of internal auditors, will include the internal auditor's compliance with the Standards as a measure to help in that decision. This is documented in the AICPA's Statement on Auditing Standards (SAS) No. 65, "Internal Auditors' Relationships with Independent Outside Auditors," and discussed in Chapter 32. The IIA Standards do not apply just to members of The Institute of Internal Auditors. They provide a guideline for *all* internal auditors, although members of the IIA and Certified Internal Auditors, in particular, are expected to follow them.

5-3 STRUCTURE OF THE IIA STANDARDS

The Standards are organized with a foreword, an introduction, a summary of general and specific standards, and five chapters covering applicable general and specific standards along with supporting guidelines. The contents of the Standards are considered here. The chapter is organized by quotations from the major sections of the Standards, with explanations and discussion of how those sections apply to the practice of internal auditing.

Two points worthy of attention from the foreword section have already been quoted, the definition of internal auditing at the beginning of Chapter 1 and in the Standards background section of this chapter. A third is the indication of the intent to modify the standards from time to time in response to continuing changes in business and society. These modifications occur through the (previously discussed) SIASs which are integrated into the Standards sections to which they relate.

The Standards were developed by IIA committee members based on their individual thinking as well as comments received from many other interested parties, both inside and outside the internal auditing profession. With such a committee development approach, there has been, quite obviously, a varying range of expertise, experience, and values incorporated in the standards. As a result, individual standards and guidelines may be subject to interpretations. This chapter quotes significant portions of each Standard, and then provides an interpretation of the particular issues involved. The overall objective of this chapter is to develop the best possible conceptual foundation for modern internal auditing. These concepts are again introduced in further chapters along with specific audit procedures which follow the general standards.

(a) THE STANDARDS AS EDITED IN THE CHAPTER

The published standards are clear, precise documents designed to minimize any misinterpretations or ambiguities. In this chapter, we have directly cited many of the standards, preserving those same words as published in the official IIA Standards. However, over time, certain sections of the IIA Standards have been expanded to almost textbook-length chapters to describe internal audit practices in various areas. For example, specific Standard 520 on planning has an extensive section on internal audit risk assessment. This material was added when there was little published internal audit material on this subject. In these situations, this chapter has heavily summarized the IIA Standards material with a reference to the chapter of this book where the topic is covered in greater detail.

In the interest of space and for clarity, this chapter also has edited or condensed portions of many of the standards. Some of these changes are minor. For example, the Standards uses the term ''director of internal auditing'' throughout, which we have reduced to ''director of internal audit'' or ''audit director'' as appropriate. Similarly, the official term ''independent outside auditor'' has been changed to ''external auditor.'' We have made a series of other small changes of this nature. They are in no way intended to revise the IIA Standards but only to provide a condensed, edited version for the purposes of this book.

This chapter is designed to capture the flavor of the Standards for the Professional Practice of Internal Auditing. However, if the reader is interested in securing the exact wording of some detailed guideline or is interested in the specific bullet points following some standard guideline, the official IIA standards should be referenced.

5-4 THE INTRODUCTION TO THE STANDARDS

The published standards start out with the following introductory statement: *Internal auditing is an independent appraisal function established within an organization to examine and evaluate its activities as a service to the organization. The objective of internal auditing is to assist members of the organization in the effective discharge of their responsibilities. To this end, internal auditing furnishes them with analyses, appraisals, recommendations, counsel, and information concerning the activities reviewed. The audit objective includes promoting effective control at a reasonable cost.*

The Introduction is, of course, the definition of internal auditing. It recognizes that the way for internal audit to serve the organization is to assist others in the organization. Internal audit can render this service in many different ways including, but not limited to, the examination and evaluation of organization control procedures. Helping the organization achieve a best possible utilization of its resources is another central role of the modern internal auditor.

This first paragraph of the Standards provides a broad statement explaining what an internal auditor actually does. The remaining paragraphs here highlight issues that are discussed more thoroughly in the detailed Standards:

The members of the organization assisted by internal auditing include those in management and the board of directors. Internal auditors owe a responsibility to both, providing them with information about the adequacy and effectiveness of the organization's system of internal control and the quality of performance. The information furnished to each may differ in format and detail, depending upon the requirements and requests of management and the board.

The internal auditing department is an integral part of the organization and functions under the policies established by senior management and the board. The statement of purpose, authority, and responsibility (charter) for the internal auditing department, approved by senior management and accepted by the board, should be consistent with these Standards for the Professional Practice of Internal Auditing.

The charter should make clear the purposes of the internal auditing department, specify the unrestricted scope of its work, and declare that auditors are to have no authority or responsibility for the activities they audit.

Especially important here is the clear statement that the organization served by internal audit includes both senior management and the board of directors. It is necessary that any internal audit department charter be consistent with these Standards.

An internal audit charter is a statement of purpose or objectives that an internal audit department would develop to define its purpose based upon the approval by senior management. Internal audit charters are discussed in greater detail later in this chapter as well as in Chapter 6.

The Standards requirement that auditors should have no authority or responsibility for the activities they audit is an important concept for both internal audit and management. Internal audit will review an activity's processes and its controls, and then will make recommendations for improvement. However, internal audit should never have the responsibility for managing the implementation of those recommendations.

The introduction discusses the impact of the environment surrounding an auditor:

Throughout the world, internal auditing is performed in diverse environments and within organizations which vary in purpose, size, and structure. In addition, the laws and customs within various countries differ from one another. These differences may affect the practice of internal auditing in each environment. The implementation of these Standards, therefore, will be governed by the environment in which the internal auditing department carries out its assigned responsibilities. Compliance with the concepts enunciated by these Standards is essential before the responsibilities of internal auditors can be met. As stated in the Code of Ethics, Members of the Institute of Internal Auditors and Certified Internal Auditors shall adopt suitable means to comply with the Standards.

The above recognizes the wide range of situations and environmental influences encountered by individual internal auditors, and the detailed implementation of these Standards may vary. While the differences must not extend to the fundamental concepts of internal auditing, there can be questions as to what is a fundamental concept of internal auditing that must not be violated, and where that concept starts and stops in practice. Identifying that line often requires professional judgment. This chapter and others provide some guidance and suggestions in this area.

The sixth paragraph of the introduction emphasizes the importance of auditor independence. Auditor independence is discussed in much greater detail throughout the Standards, but this paragraph links independence to the results or product of internal audit:

"Independence," as used in these Standards, requires clarification. Internal auditors should be independent of the activities they audit. Such independence permits internal auditors to perform their work freely and objectively. Without independence, the desired results of internal auditing cannot be realized.

The two subsequent paragraphs in the introduction provide background on the external developments that encouraged these Standards as well as an outline of the purposes of the Standards. The considerations mentioned, such as the external auditor's use of the work of internal audit, are only increasing. These subsequent paragraphs provide an introduction to the development of the Standards:

In establishing the Standards, the following matters were considered:

1. *Boards of directors are being held accountable for the adequacy and effectiveness of their organizations' systems of internal control and quality of performance.*

2. *Members of management are relying upon internal auditing as a means of supplying objective analyses, appraisals, recommendations, counsel, and information on the organization's controls and performance.*

3. *External auditors are using the results of internal audits to complement their own work where the internal auditors have provided suitable evidence of independence and adequate, professional audit work.*

In the light of such matters, the purposes of these Standards are to:

1. *Impart an understanding of the role and responsibilities of internal auditing to all levels of management, boards of directors, public bodies, external auditors, and related professional organizations.*

2. *Establish the basis for the guidance and measurement of internal auditing performance.*

3. *Improve the practice of internal auditing.*

This portion of the Standards recognizes internal audit's unique impacts on all entities affected, and that the term "internal auditor" covers a wide range of practitioners whose responsibilities may vary greatly.

The Introduction concludes with a description of the format of the main body of the Standards as well as additional definitions, as follows:

The Standards encompass:

1. *The independence of the internal auditing department from the activities audited and the objectivity of internal auditors*

2. *The proficiency of internal auditors and the professional care they should exercise*

3. *The scope of internal auditing work*

4. *The performance of internal auditing assignments*

5. *The management of the internal auditing department*

The Standards and the accompanying guidelines employ seven terms that have been given specific meanings. These are as follows:

1. *The term "board" includes boards of directors, audit committees of such boards, heads of agencies or legislative bodies to whom internal auditors report, boards of governors or trustees of nonprofit organizations, and any other designated governing bodies of organizations.*

2. *The terms "director of internal auditing" and "director" identify the top position in an internal auditing department.*

3. *The term "internal auditing department" includes any unit of activity within an organization which performs internal auditing functions.*

4. *The term "auditee" includes any units or activity within an organization that is audited.*

5. *The term "management" includes anyone in an organization with responsibilities for setting and/or achieving objectives.*

6. *The term "senior management" refers to those individuals in management to whom the director of internal auditing is responsible.*

7. *The term "external auditors" refers to those audit professionals who perform independent annual audits of an organization's financial statements.*

The designation "director of internal auditing" is somewhat cumbersome in its repetitive use within this book, while the single term "director" alone is not sufficiently precise. In actual practice, the term "general auditor" is frequently used to identify the head of the internal auditing departments in many organizations and will also be used as well. This introduction to the more formal Standards also stands by itself. It provides a broad definition of internal auditing, as discussed in the opening paragraph; background regarding the purposes of the Standards; basic definitions; and other substantive statements that introduce and further extend the standards. While the Introduction does not have the same authority as the formal Standards, it provides useful information to provide management and others with a brief introduction to the definition and function of internal auditing.

5-5 THE PROFESSIONAL STANDARDS

The remainder of this chapter contains extracts from major portions of the Standards along with discussions of major sections or important paragraphs within them. As with the introduction sections, all direct excerpts from the Standards are shown here in italics. The same standards and guideline reference numbers—for example, Guideline 560.03—are also used in these references. The supporting SIASs are discussed along with appropriate sections of the Standards.

The Standards are organized into five general standards covering major areas and functions of internal auditing, as follows:

100	Independence
200	Professional Proficiency
300	Scope of Work
400	Performance of Audit Work
500	Management of the Internal Auditing Department

This discussion of the Standards is organized around the five general standards and the specific standards and guidelines under each. For example, Section 400, on Performance, includes the following specific Standards:

410	Planning the Audit
420	Examining and Evaluating Information
430	Communicating Results
440	Following Up

These steps form the basis for performing an internal audit in any of a wide variety of areas. For example, the Standards will guide internal audit in a review of payroll and personnel, as discussed in Chapter 29; distribution and shipping, as described in Chapter 25; and audits of information systems operations, as discussed in Chapter 16.

Each of the sections following will contain an outline of that section of the Standards, edited versions of portions of these Standards sections, and comments regarding the Standards when helpful to an internal auditor.

(a) INTERNAL AUDIT STANDARDS FOR INDEPENDENCE

The general Standard 100 on Independence and 110 on Organizational Status are the most basic or fundamental Standards guiding modern internal auditing.

100.   *Internal auditors should be independent of the activities they audit.*

100.01   *Internal auditors are independent when they can carry out their work freely and objectively. Independence permits internal auditors to render the impartial and unbiased judgments essential to the proper conduct of audits. It is achieved through organizational status and objectivity.*

Independence for the professional practice of internal auditing means being independent of the activities audited. While part of the overall organization, internal audit must be independent of the specific area where an audit is performed. This general standard is basic to all other specific standards and supporting guidelines. The supporting guideline (.01) more clearly links the existence of independence for internal auditors to whether they can carry out their work freely and objectively. This independence is essential to the proper conduct of audits and is achieved through organizational status and objectivity.

Internal auditors should always keep the important concept of independence in mind when performing reviews in various areas and when providing suggestions for improvement to management. Although an internal auditor may be asked to serve on a task force or some other management committee from time to time, internal audit always must consider this professional standard of independence when providing management with observations and recommendations to perform other audit procedures in this same area in an unbiased manner.

(i) Standard 110—Organizational Status

110.   *The organizational status of the internal auditing department should be sufficient to permit the accomplishment of its audit responsibilities.*

110.01   *Internal auditors should have the support of senior management and of the board to gain the cooperation of auditees and perform their work free from interference*

110.01.1   *The director of internal auditing should be responsible to an individual in the organization with sufficient authority to promote independence and to ensure broad audit coverage, adequate consideration of audit reports, and appropriate action on audit recommendations.*

110.01.2   *The director should have direct communication with the board to assure independence and provide a means for each other to keep informed on matters of mutual interest.*

110.01.3   *Independence is enhanced when the board concurs in the appointment or removal of the director of the internal auditing department.*

110.01.4   *The purpose, authority, and responsibility of the internal auditing department should be defined in a formal written document (charter). The director should seek approval of the charter by management as well as acceptance by the board. The charter should (a) establish the department's position within the organization; (b) authorize access to records, personnel, and physical properties relevant to the performance of audits; and (c) define the scope of internal auditing activities.*

110.01.5   *The director of internal auditing should submit annually to senior management for approval and to the board for its information a summary of the department's audit work schedule, staffing plan, and financial budget. The director should also submit all significant interim changes for approval and information. Audit work schedules, staffing plans, and financial budgets should inform management and the board of the scope of internal auditing work and of any limitations placed on that scope.*

110.01.6   *The director of internal auditing should submit activity reports to senior management and to the board annually or more frequently as necessary. Activity reports should highlight significant audit findings and recommendations and should inform senior management and the board of any significant deviations from approved audit work schedules, staffing plans, and financial budgets, and the reasons for them.*

This standard establishes minimum requirements for internal audit department organizational independence. The key phrase regarding organizational status is that the status of the audit function or department in the organization *should be sufficient* to allow the internal auditors to work independently. The Standards establish no firm rule requiring, for example, that internal audit must be independent of the organization's controller function. Rather, internal audit's organizational status should allow it a sufficient level of organizational independence to the internal audit to operate independently of the activities audited.

The (.01) guideline identifies the need for senior management and board of directors support as a necessary basis for gaining the cooperation of auditees to perform audits free from interference. The six supporting guidelines then interpret that more general guideline, including the criteria for evaluating the adequacy of the authority of the individual to whom the director of internal auditing reports. He/she should report to someone sufficiently powerful to assure backing for internal audit in the organization as necessary.

This reporting status guideline is often easier to establish in theory than in specific practice. An audit director may report at a sufficiently high level in the organization, but, because management either does not understand the function or is otherwise reluctant to press certain issues, the director of internal audit may have difficulty establishing the proper level of support and authority. In order to establish a level of support, the audit director needs the backing of the organization's board.

The term "board," as used in the Standards and generally in this book includes boards of directors, their audit committees, heads of agencies or legislative bodies to whom internal audit reports, boards of governors or trustees of nonprofit organizations, and any other designated governing bodies of organizations. The effective relationship of internal audit to any of these bodies is key to the internal auditor's independence.

The Standards establish the requirement of "direct" and regular communication between the director of the internal auditing and the board, helping assure independence and providing a means of keeping both parties informed as to matters of mutual interest:

a. *Direct communication occurs when the director regularly attends and participates in those meetings of the board which relate to its oversight responsibilities for auditing, financial reporting, organizational governance, and control. The director's attendance at these meetings and the presentation of written and/or oral reports provides for an exchange of information concerning the plans and activities of the internal auditing department. The director of internal auditing should meet privately with the board, at least annually.*

Communications with the board is discussed in greater detail in Chapter 6. This communications link is essential for complete internal audit department independence. The supporting guideline then strengthens this link in another manner. It recommends the board have the opportunity to review the appointment of the director of internal auditing. When the board concurs in the audit director's appointment or removal, the result enhances the independence for the director. The Standard uses the term "concurs" instead of "approves" to recognize that the director's primary reporting responsibility is more likely to be to management than to the board. This requirement of concurrence is important as it gives the board an opportunity to question any appointment or removal actions and thus to have a better basis for evaluating the judgment of management pertaining to the action. A further advantage is that the board is alerted to the need to establish a proper relationship with a new director of internal auditing.

An internal audit charter (.3) is an important document that should be approved by an appropriate level of management and accepted by the board. The term "acceptance" used to define the board's involvement follows the same logic previously discussed for "concurrence." Because the internal audit charter covers responsibilities to both management and the audit committee, approvals by both parties are equally important. Internal audit charters are discussed in Chapter 6.

An internal audit charter should be a dynamic document that keeps current with changing conditions. A clarification of the Standards states:

a. *The director of internal auditing should periodically assess whether the purpose, authority, and responsibility, as defined in the charter, continue to be adequate to enable the internal auditing department to accomplish its objectives. The result of the periodic assessment should be communicated to senior management and the board.*

The next organizational independence guideline (.5) clarifies the director of internal auditing's reporting to management and the board, areas discussed further in Chapter 6 on board reporting, and Chapter 15, on general internal audit reporting. The language in the standard about reporting ''to senior management for approval and to the board for its information'' emphasizes internal audit's primary reporting responsibility to management. There is a very great need for keeping both management and the board informed of internal audit activities. Although the information provided to the audit committee would typically be in less detail, it should be sufficient to provide a needed understanding and an opportunity to raise questions. The mention in this guideline, however, of possible ''limitations'' imposed upon internal audit is a serious matter. SIAS No. 7 provided four additional guidelines regarding communication of the plan and, more importantly, potential internal audit scope limitations:

a. *The approved audit work schedule plan, staffing plans, and financial budget, along with all significant interim changes, should contain sufficient information to enable the board to ascertain whether the internal auditing department's objectives and plans support those of the organization and the board. This information should be communicated, preferably in writing.*
b. *A scope limitation is a restriction placed upon internal audit that precludes the department from accomplishing its objectives and plans. Among other things, a scope limitation may restrict the:*
   - *Scope defined in the charter.*
   - *Department's access to records, personnel, and physical properties relevant to the performance of audits.*
   - *Approved audit work schedule.*
   - *Performance of necessary auditing procedures.*
   - *Approved staffing plan and financial budget.*
c. *A scope limitation along with its potential effect should be communicated, preferably in writing, to the board.*
d. *The director of internal auditing should consider whether it is appropriate to inform the board regarding scope limitations which were previously communicated and accepted by the board. This may be necessary particularly when there have been organization, board, senior management, or other changes.*

The above four interpretive guidelines provide additional guidance on this important area of communications with the board with an emphasis on raising a red flag on any limitations in the audit process. An internal auditor hopes that no management scope limitations over audit activities will be encountered. Although the guidelines to the Standards direct the auditor to communicate with the board, bypassing management and communicating directly with the board, this poses serious pressures upon the director of internal auditing and often leads to some form of confrontation.

The (.6) guideline also deals with reporting to management and the board regarding audit results and conformance to established plans. Although the guideline again does not say whether the volume and detail of such reports should vary as between management and the board, the effective internal audit department will report them to the board in a more summarized form. This detailed (.6) reporting guidance includes:

a.   *Activity reports should be communicated, preferably in writing.*

b.   *Significant audit findings are those conditions which, in the judgment of the director of internal auditing, could adversely affect the organization. Significant audit findings may include conditions dealing with irregularities, illegal acts, errors, inefficiency, waste, ineffectiveness, conflicts of interest, and control weaknesses. After reviewing such findings with senior management, the director of internal auditing should communicate significant audit findings to the board, whether or not they have been satisfactorily resolved.*

c.   *Management's responsibility is to make decisions on the appropriate actions to be taken regarding significant audit findings. Senior management may decide to assume the risk of not correcting the reported condition because of cost or other considerations. The board should be informed of senior management's decision on all significant audit findings.*

d.   *The director of internal auditing should consider whether it is appropriate to inform the board regarding previously reported significant audit findings in those instances when senior management and the board assumed the risk of not correcting the reported condition. This may be necessary, particularly when there have been organization, board, senior management, or other changes.*

e.   *The reasons for significant deviations from approved audit work schedules, staffing plans, and financial budgets that may require information include:*
   * *Organization and management changes.*
   * *Economic conditions.*
   * *Legal and regulatory requirements.*
   * *Internal auditing staff changes.*
   * *Expansion or reduction of audit scope as determined by the director of internal auditing.*

These guidelines show the manner in which senior management and the board of directors can provide support to internal auditors as well as how audit findings should be communicated to them. The identification of significant audit findings is one of the most important duties of internal audit, and senior management and the board have to regularly review audit reports of such findings and take appropriate actions.

Internal audit needs to recognize that support can also be provided in other ways beyond official organizational materials, such as organization charts, charters, and other formal reports. These include the extent to which senior management and the board demonstrate their interest in ongoing internal audit activities and how they interpret the formal arrangements as defined by the Standards and the organization's internal audit charter. Individuals at all levels in the organization will directly or indirectly continue to test whether formally stated arrangements have adequate higher-level support sufficient to be taken seriously. Senior management and the board should be alert to this danger and continuously reaffirm their support for the internal audit. This support is especially critical when, as often happens, a particular manager resists a planned internal audit review or tries to convince senior management that internal audit activities may have a detrimental impact on the achievement of that manager's organizational objectives. Such problems need to be promptly resolved so that obstacles to effective internal auditing are eliminated.

(ii) Standard 120—Objectivity

120. *Internal auditors should be objective in performing audits.*

129.01 *Objectivity is an independent mental attitude which internal auditors should maintain in performing audits. Internal auditors are not to subordinate their judgment on audit matters to that of others.*

129.02 *Objectivity requires internal auditors to work in a manner that they have an honest belief in their work product and that no significant quality compromises are made. Internal auditors are not to be placed in situations in which they feel unable to make objective professional judgments.*

129.02.1 *Staff assignments should be made to avoid potential and actual conflicts of interest and bias. The director should periodically obtain from the audit staff information concerning potential conflicts of interest and bias.*

129.02.2 *Internal auditors should report to the director any situations in which a conflict of interest or bias is present or may reasonably be inferred. The director should then reassign such auditors.*

129.02.3 *Staff assignments of internal auditors should be rotated periodically whenever it is practicable to do so.*

129.02.4 *Internal auditors should not assume operating responsibilities. But if on occasion management directs internal auditors to perform non audit work, it should be understood that they are not functioning as internal auditors. Moreover, objectivity is presumed to be impaired when internal auditors audit any activity for which they had authority or responsibility. This impairment should be considered when reporting audit results.*

129.02.5 *Persons transferred to or temporarily engaged by the internal auditing department should not be assigned to audit those activities they previously performed until a reasonable period of time has elapsed. Such assignments are presumed to impair objectivity and should be considered when supervising the audit work and reporting audit results.*

129.02.6 *The results of an audit should be reviewed before the related audit report is released to provide reasonable assurance that the work was performed objectively.*

129.03 *Internal audit objectivity is not adversely affected by procedure reviews or control recommendations regarding systems before they are implemented. Designing, installing, and operating systems as well as the drafting of procedures for systems are not audit functions. Performing such activities is presumed to impair audit objectivity.*

This Standard establishes the very key and broad requirement that internal auditors ''should be objective in performing audits''; it is one of the most important to the practicing internal auditor. An auditor must be objective in performing audit procedures, analyzing results, and making effective recommendations.

This quality of objectivity is important in every phase of an internal auditor's activities. The Standard's general guidelines first (.01) recognize that internal audit must have an *independent mental attitude,* something that is the responsibility of the individual internal auditor, irrespective of organizational status. The guideline then stipulates that internal audit, having reached its conclusions with independent mental attitude, must not compromise by yielding to the pressures of other affected parties. These pressures can come from people at all levels who either have strong contrary views about the judgment of an internal auditor or who see possible embarrassment from the visibility that will result from the internal auditor's findings and conclusions. While an internal auditor may consider these other views, he/she must not bend under pressure and should do what is necessary and proper.

The focus of the second guideline (.02) is on the way internal auditors carry out audit assignments. An audit should be made in a manner that makes internal audit professionally proud of the work product. That is, an internal auditor must avoid shortcuts and compromises that may block or dilute the adequate basis needed for the auditor's "honest belief" in the audit results. The guideline also makes a related point that internal auditors should avoid situations where their making objective professional judgments is not possible.

Six specific guidelines identify the 129.02 requirements bearing on objective professional judgements. The first (.1) emphasizes that staff assignments should be made to avoid conflicts of interest or bias. While an internal auditor should have enough character and objectivity to avoid a conflict of interest or bias, audit project assignments should be made to avoid any possibility of conflicts of interest or bias. The director of internal auditing should obtain information about any existing conflicts or potential bias by individual staff members. For example, if an internal auditor's relative works in a given department, there is a very strong danger of conflict. The director of internal auditing must make a subjective judgment, and this information should be given appropriate consideration when actual staff assignments are made.

In the second requirement (.2), the same problem is directed to individual auditors who are specifically charged with the responsibility to report any situation involving either actual or reasonably inferable conflict of interest or bias. Audit management should consider reassigning that internal auditor since any suggestions of a conflict of interest can damage the credibility of an individual auditor and the entire department. Audit management and staff have a joint responsibility to prevent the existence of potential conflict or bias.

In the third requirement (.3), the director is charged with the responsibility of periodically rotating audit staff assignments. While the practicability of rotation in certain specialized areas may be limited, rotation of audit assignments is beneficial solely on the grounds of providing fresh and often more effective approaches to particular audit assignments. The ongoing assignment of an individual auditor to the same audit task may result in personal relationships that may dilute the auditor's independence and related objectivity. Auditees very often prefer the relative comfort of dealing with the same internal auditor and may exert pressure for the continuation of that arrangement. However, rotation is a desirable practice for both the professional development of individual auditors and for the total interest of the organization. These staffing issues are further discussed in Chapter 9.

The fourth requirement (.4) covers a number of different and important aspects of the objectivity requirement. First, the standard recognizes that internal auditors generally should not assume operating responsibilities since an internal auditor with operating decision responsibilities can easily become an integral part of the organization and no longer function as an independent auditor. However, due to a death or some sudden departmental management change, an auditor may be asked to take over the temporary management of that department due to the auditor's knowledge of its operations. In that situation, all interested persons should understand that the assigned internal auditor *is not functioning as an internal auditor*. Under those conditions, other staff personnel should be assigned to provide regular internal auditing services in this area.

The same requirement highlights a related but different objectivity problem when an auditor goes back to audit a particular organizational component for which that person previously had some level of authority or responsibility. Even if the auditor did not have that much authority and responsibility in the prior assignment, he/she may still have various biases or grudges, causing problems for all concerned. While sometimes a prior employee may be the best person in the audit department with a proper understanding of a complex process or department, the assigned auditor must be especially careful of the possibility of loss of objectivity.

The fifth requirement (.5) builds on the threat to objectivity just discussed and emphasizes that auditor assignments in previous work activities should not be made until after a reasonable time has elapsed. Whether the auditor previously held some responsibilities or just operational participation, the key factor is the intervening elapsed time. A too strict interpretation here can unduly limit the availability of an auditor, and there can also be some real benefits in using such individuals because of their better understanding of the activity. Nevertheless, both audit management and staff should be aware of the potential danger of a loss of objectivity and guard against it.

The final requirement in this group (.6) stresses the need for a review of the results of the audit before the release of the audit report. Except in cases of special investigations performed at the request of management, internal auditors should never just do their work and publish the audit findings without appropriate auditee review. This important point is discussed in Section 200 of the Standards.

Guideline .03 under the Objectivity Standard covers the special problem when internal audit performs preimplementation reviews of major systems under development. Once a typical automated system or major manual procedure has been implemented, it usually becomes very costly—in terms of time, resource requirements, and organization impact—to correct deficiencies identified by internal audit in a later, postimplementation review. It makes far greater sense for auditors to perform preimplementation reviews of new systems under development.

While internal auditors should provide counsel on standards of control in these preimplementation situations, they should not impair their objectivity by getting directly involved in designing, installing, or operating those systems, or in drafting procedures. As a practical consideration, such involvement is time-consuming and can be a drain on overall audit resources. However, it is often difficult to draw the line when internal audit interfaces with the individuals directly charged with the development of new systems. Good sense and sound judgment are essential. Internal auditors most frequently become involved in these types of reviews when management requests a review of controls of a new information system under development. These preimplementation reviews of systems under development are discussed in Chapter 18.

(iii) Independence and Objectivity in Perspective.   Auditor independence is essential for the performance of effective internal audits. While independence is achieved both by the conditions imposed upon internal auditing by the organization and through the objectivity of the individual internal auditors, a continuing effort must be made to maintain and improve both of these basic needed independence conditions. However, because of various organizational constraints, complete independence can never be achieved. For example, a board of directors is subject to the constraints of its accountability to government and society, and a chief executive officer has the same constraints plus the constraint of the board itself. The outside public accountant can never fully forget that the client pays his fees and that these fees are necessary to maintain a viable public accounting firm. Internal audit reports to and is dependent upon someone in the organization. In addition, internal auditors also must face the problem of resisting pressures from organizational colleagues with whom they wish to maintain good working relationships. What this means is that no person is an island and that independence is always a relative term, greater or less but never absolute.

These comments about independence in no sense depreciate the value of auditor independence or detract from efforts to upgrade the extent and quality of desired internal auditor independence. There must be continuing efforts to strengthen needed independence even though there are, and always will be, substantive limitations to that independence. Internal audit does this, first, by doing effective work and having the courage to stand up for its convictions, and second, by exerting every effort practicable to induce and obtain the organizational arrangements that will best assure independence. Effective internal audit management provides support for all members of the audit organization in this goal of independence.

While there is a general agreement as to the desirability of internal auditor objectivity, the means of achieving objectivity is primarily in the hands of internal auditors themselves. Where the arrangements that assure needed objectivity are in the hands of other individuals or functions in the organization, internal auditors must utilize every possible means to inform and guide others in the organization about their impact on auditor objectivity. By so doing, internal auditors can best assure the needed setting for achieving the proper levels of objectivity. In the last analysis, of course, objectivity is a state of mind; the ability to develop that needed state of mind is one of the greatest challenges to the truly professional internal auditor.

(b) INTERNAL AUDIT STANDARDS FOR AUDIT DEPARTMENT PROFICIENCY

Professional proficiency standards cover both the audit departments and individual internal auditors. General Standard 200 covers Professional Proficiency and detailed Standards 210 through 230 cover the internal audit department. Standards 240 through 280, discussed in the next section, apply to the individual internal auditor. Standard 280, on due professional care, carries important guidance on fraud-related audit investigations. This dual assignment is important because the department and the individual each has its own roles to play and each has differing opportunities to further professional proficiency.

200.   *INTERNAL AUDITS SHOULD BE PERFORMED WITH PROFICIENCY AND
          DUE PROFESSIONAL CARE.*

200.01   *Professional proficiency is the responsibility of the internal auditing department
          and each internal auditor. The department should assign to each audit those*

persons who collectively possess the necessary knowledge, skills, and disciplines to conduct the audit properly.

210.   *The internal auditing department should provide assurance that the technical proficiency and educational background of auditors are appropriate.*

210.01 *The director of internal auditing should establish suitable criteria of education and experience for filling internal auditing positions, giving due consideration to scope of work and level of responsibility.*

210.02 *Reasonable assurance should be obtained as to each prospective auditor's qualifications and proficiency.*

220.   *The internal auditing department should possess or should obtain the knowledge, skills, and disciplines needed to carry out its audit responsibilities.*

220.01 *The internal auditing staff should collectively possess the knowledge and skills, including proficiency in applying internal auditing standards, procedures, and techniques, essential to the practice of the profession within the organization.*

220.02 *The internal audit department should have employees or use consultants who are qualified in such disciplines as accounting, economics, finance, statistics, information systems, engineering, taxation, and law as needed to meet audit responsibilities. Each auditor, however, need not be qualified in all of these disciplines.*

230.   *The internal auditing department should provide assurance that all work is properly supervised.*

230.01 *The director of internal auditing is responsible for providing appropriate audit supervision, a continuing process, beginning with planning and ending with the conclusion of the audit assignment.*

230.02 *Internal Audit supervision includes:*
   .1 Providing suitable instructions to subordinates at the outset of the audit and approving the audit program.
   .2 Seeing that the approved audit program is carried out unless deviations are both justified and authorized.
   .3 Determining that audit workpapers adequately support the audit findings, conclusions, and reports.
   .4 Making sure that audit reports are accurate, objective, clear, concise, constructive, and timely.
   .5 Determining that audit objectives are being met.

230.03 *Appropriate evidence of supervision should be documented and retained.*

230.04 *The extent of supervision required will depend on the proficiency of the internal auditors and the difficulty of the audit assignment.*

230.05 *All internal auditing assignments, whether performed by or for the internal auditing department, remain the responsibility of its director.*

These Standards sections 210 through 230 deal with internal audit department responsibilities to provide assurances that the internal auditors have the technical proficiency and educational background appropriate for audits performed. Personnel assigned should be capable of doing the required jobs.

To fulfill these standards, the director of internal auditing should consider the criteria needed for filling audit staff positions after giving consideration to the scope of work to be performed and level of responsibilities pertaining to those positions. Procedures should be in place to provide assurance that individual audit assignments are carried out by properly qualified auditors.

The nature and scope of audits are always changing and audit staff personnel previously having adequate qualifications may no longer satisfy new needs. A manual procedure may become highly automated, and auditors who previously reviewed those manual systems may no longer have the necessary skills or training to review and test the new automated system. Thus, the effort to assure the proper staff skills is ongoing. Internal audit must provide assurances to management and others that auditor staff qualifications are appropriate for the audits to be performed. In order to "provide assurance" as mentioned in the Standard, the director of internal auditing should develop adequate documentation covering the manner in which that matching is made in terms of individual capabilities and work assignments.

The internal audit department should possess or obtain personnel with those particular capabilities as necessary to carry out its audit responsibilities. The focus on these essential knowledge areas and skills uses the word "collectively," meaning that a particular needed knowledge or skill should be somewhere among the staff members. The knowledge and skills qualifications include proficiency in applying internal audit standards, procedures, and techniques.

The second interpretative guideline on the kinds of audit disciplines required cites accounting, economics, finance, statistics, information systems technologies, engineering, taxation, and law as examples. Required disciplines must be reappraised in light of the nature of the organization and its particular audit needs. For example, if an organization had agricultural operations, the director of internal auditing might want internal auditors with knowledge or skills in such areas as crop storage inventory controls. The Standards guideline allows that consultants may be used if the needed capabilities are not available from audit staff personnel. Any one auditor does not need to be qualified in all of these relevant disciplines.

The .03 detailed Standard for professional proficiency and responsibility deals with the proper supervision of internal audits. Supervision includes the total span of responsibility from the initial planning to the conclusion of the audit assignment. Audit planning, including the need for planning by the director, is discussed in Chapter 8.

The second guideline (.02) identifies five aspects of the supervisory process which is discussed further in Chapter 10. It should be noted that there is no specific identification of the personnel involved in the planning phase, even though these personnel would also need to be supervised.

The third guideline (.03) emphasizes the need for adequate documentation, and for the retention of that documentation, to provide evidence of proper supervision. In addition to just good audit documentation procedures, adequate documentation is essential for any human resources administration function.

The fourth guideline (.04) recognizes that the need for supervision is directly dependent on two key variables: the proficiency of the audit personnel involved in audit assignments and the varying difficulties of individual assignments. Relevant also is the significance of the activity reviewed in terms of its impact on overall organizational welfare.

The fifth guideline (.05) here emphasizes that persons responsible for any group can never escape ultimate responsibility, irrespective of delegations to subordinates. This joint interresponsibility also extends to the director of internal auditing. This standard has the requirement to provide assurance of such proper supervision. Procedures for documenting that assurance and other audit staff matters are discussed in Chapter 9.

(i) Individual Auditor Professional Proficiency Standards

240.   *Internal auditors should comply with professional standards of conduct.*

240.01   *The Code of Ethics of The Institute of Internal Auditors sets forth standards of honesty, objectivity, diligence, and loyalty to which internal auditors should conform and provides a basis for enforcement of the standards among its members.*

250.   *Internal auditors should possess the knowledge, skills, and disciplines essential to the performance of internal audits.*

250.01   *Each internal auditor should possess certain knowledge and skills as follows:*

    .1 *Proficiency in applying internal auditing standards, procedures, and techniques. Proficiency means the ability to apply knowledge to situations likely to be encountered and to deal with them without extensive recourse to technical research and assistance.*

    .2 *Proficiency in accounting principles and techniques for auditors who work extensively with financial records and reports.*

    .3 *An understanding of management principles in order to recognize and evaluate the materiality and significance of deviations from good business practice. An understanding means the ability to apply broad knowledge to situations likely to be encountered, to recognize significant deviations, and to be able to carry out the research necessary to arrive at reasonable solutions.*

    .4 *An appreciation of the fundamentals of such subjects as accounting, economics, commercial law, taxation, finance, quantitative methods, and computerized information systems. An appreciation means the ability to recognize the existence of problems or potential problems and to determine the further research to be undertaken or the assistance to be obtained.*

260.   *Internal auditors should be skilled in dealing with people and in communicating effectively.*

260.01   *Internal auditors should understand human relations and maintain satisfactory relationships with auditees.*

260.02   *Internal auditors should be skilled in oral and written communications in order to clearly and effectively convey audit objectives, evaluations, conclusions, and recommendations.*

270.   *Internal auditors should maintain their technical competence through continuing education.*

270.01   *Internal auditors are responsible for continuing their education in order to maintain their proficiency. They should keep informed about improvements and current developments in internal auditing standards, procedures, and techniques. Continuing education may be obtained through membership and participation in professional societies; attendance of conferences, seminars, college courses, and in-house training programs; and participation in research projects.*

280.   *Internal auditors should exercise due professional care in performing internal audits.*

280.01   *Due professional care calls for the same care and skill expected of a reasonably prudent and competent internal auditor in the same or similar circum-*

stances; it should, therefore, be appropriate to the complexities of the audit being performed. In exercising due professional care, internal auditors should be alert to the possibility of those conditions and activities where irregularities are most likely to occur and should identify inadequate controls and recommend improvements to promote compliance with acceptable procedures and practices.

280.01.1 *Fraud encompasses an array of irregularities and illegal acts characterized by intentional deception. It can be perpetuated for the benefit of or to the detriment of the organization and by persons outside as well as inside the organization.*

280.01.2 *Fraud designed to benefit the organization generally produces such benefit by exploiting an unfair or dishonest advantage that also may deceive an outside party. Perpetrators of such frauds usually benefit indirectly, since personal benefit usually accrues when the organization is aided by the act.*

280.01.3 *Fraud perpetrated to the detriment of the organization generally is for the direct or indirect benefit of an employee, outside individual, or another organization. Some examples are:*

a. *Acceptance of bribes or kickbacks.*

b. *Diversion to an employee or outsider of a potentially profitable transaction that would normally generate profits for the organization.*

c. *Embezzlement, by the misappropriation of money or property, and falsification of financial records to cover up the act.*

d. *Intentional concealment or misrepresentation of events or data.*

e. *Claims submitted for services or goods not actually provided to the organization.*

280.03.4 *Deterrence of fraud consists of actions taken to discourage its perpetration and to limit the exposure if fraud does occur. Adequate control is the principal mechanism for deterring fraud and limiting its exposure, and the primary responsibility for establishing and maintaining control rests with management.*

280.03.5 *Internal auditors are responsible for assisting in the deterrence of fraud by examining and evaluating the adequacy and effectiveness of the system of internal control, commensurate with the extent of the potential exposure/risk in the organization's operations. In carrying out this responsibility, internal auditors should determine whether:*

a. *The organizational environment fosters control consciousness.*

b. *Realistic organizational goals and objectives are set.*

c. *Written policies (e.g., code of conduct) exist that describe prohibited activities and the action required whenever violations are discovered.*

d. *Appropriate authorization policies for transactions are established and maintained.*

e. *Policies, practices, procedures, reports, and other mechanisms are developed to monitor activities and safeguard assets, particularly in high-risk areas.*

f. *Communication channels provide management with adequate and reliable information.*

g. *Recommendations are made for the establishment of cost-effective controls to help deter fraud.*

280.04   *Due care implies reasonable care and competence, not infallibility or extraordinary performance. Due care requires the auditor to conduct examinations and verifications to a reasonable extent, but does not require detailed audits of all transactions. Accordingly, internal auditors cannot achieve absolute assurance that noncompliance or irregularities do not exist. Nevertheless, the possibility of material irregularities or noncompliance should always be considered during audit assignments.*

280.04.1 *Detection of fraud consists of identifying indicators of fraud sufficient to warrant recommending an investigation. These may arise as a result of controls established by management, tests conducted by auditors, and other sources both within and outside the organization.*

280.04.2 *An internal auditor's responsibilities for detecting fraud are to:*

    a. *Have sufficient knowledge of the characteristics of fraud, the techniques used to commit fraud, and the types of frauds associated with the activities audited to be able to identify indicators that fraud may have been committed.*

    b. *Be alert to opportunities, such as control weaknesses, that could allow fraud. If significant control weaknesses are detected, additional procedures should include tests directed toward identification of other indicators of fraud, such as unauthorized transactions, overrides of controls, unexplained pricing exceptions, and unusually large product losses. Internal auditors should recognize that the presence of more than one indicator at any time increases the probability that fraud may have occurred.*

    c. *Evaluate the indicators that fraud may have been committed and decide whether any further action is necessary or whether an investigation should be recommended.*

    d. *Notify the appropriate authorities within the organization if there are sufficient indicators of the commission of a fraud to recommend an investigation.*

280.04.3 *Internal auditors are not expected to have knowledge equivalent to that of a person whose primary responsibility is detecting and investigating fraud. Also, audit procedures alone, even when carried out with due professional care, do not guarantee that fraud will be detected.*

280.05   *When an internal auditor suspects wrongdoing, the appropriate authorities within the organization should be informed. Internal audit may recommend whatever investigation is considered necessary in the circumstances. Thereafter, the auditor should follow up to see that the internal auditing department's responsibilities have been met.*

280.05.1 *Investigation of fraud consists of performing extended procedures necessary to determine whether fraud, as suggested by the indicators, has occurred. It includes gathering sufficient information about the specific details of a discovered fraud. Internal auditors, lawyers, investigators, security personnel, and other specialists from inside or outside the organization are the parties that usually conduct or participate in fraud investigations.*

280.05.2 *When conducting fraud investigations, internal auditors should:*

    a. *Assess the probable level and the extent of complicity within the organization. This can be critical to ensuring that internal audit avoids providing information to or obtaining misleading information from persons who may be involved.*

    b.   Determine the knowledge, skills, and disciplines needed to effectively carry out the investigation. An assessment of the qualifications and the skills of internal auditors and of the specialists available to participate in the investigation should be performed to ensure the investigation is conducted by individuals having the appropriate type and level of technical expertise, including their professional certifications, licenses, reputation, and whether there is any relationship to those investigated or to any other employees or management of the organization.

    c.   Design procedures to follow in attempting to identify the perpetrators, extent of the fraud, techniques used, and cause of the fraud.

    d.   Coordinate activities with management personnel, legal counsel, and other specialists as appropriate throughout the course of the investigation.

    e.   Be cognizant of the rights of alleged perpetrators and personnel within the scope of the investigation and the reputation of the organization itself.

280.05.3   *Once a fraud investigation is concluded, internal auditors should assess the facts known in order to:*

    a.   Determine if controls need to be implemented or strengthened to reduce future vulnerability.

    b.   Design audit tests to help disclose the existence of similar frauds in the future.

    c.   Help meet the internal auditor's responsibility to maintain sufficient knowledge of fraud and thereby be able to identify future indicators of fraud.

280.05.4   *Reporting of fraud consists of the various oral or written, interim or final communications to management regarding the status and results of fraud investigations.*

280.05.5   *A preliminary or final report may be desirable at the conclusion of the detection phase with the internal auditor's assessment whether sufficient information exists to conduct an investigation. It should also summarize findings that serve as the basis for such decisions.*

280.05.6   *Section 430 provides interpretations for internal audit reports issued as a result of fraud investigations. Additional interpretive guidelines on reporting of fraud are:*

    a.   When the incidence of significant fraud has been established to a reasonable certainty, senior management and the board should be notified immediately.

    b.   The results of a fraud investigation may indicate it has had a previously undiscovered significant adverse effect on the financial position and results of operations of an organization for one or more prior years. Internal auditors should inform senior management and the board of such a discovery.

    c.   A written report should be issued at the conclusion of the investigation phase, including all findings, conclusions, recommendations, and corrective action taken.

    d.   A draft of the proposed report on fraud should be submitted to legal counsel for review. In those cases in which internal audit wants to invoke client privilege, consideration should be given to addressing the report to legal counsel.

These detailed Standards 240 through 280, deal with the responsibilities for professional proficiency attributable to the individual internal auditor. The first of this group of Standards is compliance with professional standards of conduct. The supporting guideline is self-explanatory in its reference to the IIA Code of Ethics as the standards of conduct to which internal audit is required to conform. The Code of Ethics was introduced in Chapter 1, is mentioned throughout other chapters, and will be further discussed in terms of business ethics in Chapter 36. A complete text of the Code of Ethics can be found in Figure 5.1.

The specific Standard 250 reemphasizes the importance of matching professional knowledge, skills, and disciplines with audit assignment needs. However, the Standard here focuses on these responsibilities with respect to the individual internal auditor.

The first Standards specification (.1) here states there should be proficiency in applying internal auditing standards, procedures, and techniques, meaning the ability to apply internal audit knowledge to individual audit situations encountered and to deal with them without extensive technical research and assistance. Equally important is the ability to recognize when further technical research and assistance may be needed.

The second specification (.2) covers the requirement for proficiency in accounting principles and techniques when an internal auditor works extensively with financial records. Because most auditors today perform work that at some point relates to financial records, at least some understanding of accounting principles is essential. Even if a particular internal auditor does not often work in areas requiring a knowledge of accounting principles, many members of management may expect, just because the individual is "an auditor," that he/she will have some accounting skills.

The third specification (.3) recognizes that internal auditors need to understand general principles of management and how they apply to varying operational situations. That understanding is a basic foundation for carrying out internal audit assignments in a manner that best contributes to management needs. Chapter 3 deals with that type of knowledge and with understanding the needs of management.

Finally, the last guideline specification in this section (.4) outlines knowledge requirements in terms of the individual internal auditor. While an internal auditor need not have expertise in all of these technical areas, each auditor should have a general understanding of both control fundamentals and related organizational issues. This enables an internal auditor to know when actual or potential problems may exist in areas reviewed and when further information or special assistance may be required.

The specific Standard 260, on human relations, and its supporting guidelines highlight the importance of these skills. Understanding people and communicating with them is a basic requirement in all internal audit activities.

Although perhaps more of an objective than a standard to be followed, the first supporting guideline (.01) states that internal auditors should both understand human relations and maintain satisfactory relationships with auditees. Understanding human relation is something exceedingly complex and probably never fully achieved. The reference to maintaining satisfactory relations with auditees should also include all other persons with whom internal audit has contact during an audit project. While a standard of internal auditing, communication is always a two-way street. The individual internal auditor should

Figure 5.1 Code of Ethics

The Institute of Internal Auditors
Code of Ethics

PURPOSE: A distinguishing mark of a profession is acceptance by its members of responsibility to the interests of those it serves. Members of The Institute of Internal Auditors (Members) and Certified Internal Auditors (CIAs) must maintain high standards of conduct in order to effectively discharge this responsibility. The Institute of Internal Auditors (Institute) adopts this *Code of Ethics* for Members and CIAs.

APPLICABILITY: This *Code of Ethics* is applicable to all Members and CIA's. Membership in The Institute and acceptance of the ''Certified Internal Auditor'' designation are voluntary actions. By acceptance, Members and CIAs assume an obligation of self-discipline above and beyond the requirements of laws and regulations.

The standards of conduct set forth in this *Code of Ethics* provide basic principles in the practice of internal auditing. Members and CIAs should realize that their individual judgment is required in the application of these principles.

CIAs shall use the ''Certified Internal Auditor'' designation with discretion and in a dignified manner, fully aware of what the designation denotes. The designation shall also be used in a manner consistent with all statutory requirements.

Members who are judged by the Board of Directors of The Institute to be in violation of the standards of conduct of the *Code of Ethics* shall be subject to forteiture of their membership in The Institute. CIAs who are similarly judged also shall be subject to forfeiture of the ''Certified Internal Auditor'' designation.

STANDARDS OF CONDUCT

   I. Members and CIAs shall exercise honesty, objectivity, and diligence in the performance of their duties and responsibilities.

   II. Members and CIAs shall exhibit loyalty in all matters pertaining to the affairs of their organization or to whomever they may be rendering a service. However, Members and CIAs shall not knowingly be a party to any illegal or improper activity.

   III. Members and CIAs shall not knowingly engage in acts or activities which are discreditable to the profession of internal auditing or to their organization.

   IV. Members and CIAs shall refrain from entering into any activity which may be in conflict with the interest of their organization or which would prejudice their ability to carry out objectively their duties and responsibilities.

   V. Members and CIAs shall not accept anything of value from an employee, client, customer, supplier, or business associate of their organization which would impair or be presumed to impair their professional judgment.

   VI. Members and CIAs shall undertake only those services which they can reasonably expect to complete with professional competence.

   VII. Members and CIAs shall adopt suitable means to comply with the *Standards for the Professional Practice of Internal Auditing.*

   VIII. Members and CIAs shall be prudent in the use of information acquired in the course of their duties. They shall not use confidential information for any personal gain nor in any manner which would be contrary to law or detrimental to the welfare of their organization.

   IX. Members and CIAs, when reporting on the results of their work, shall reveal all material facts known to them which, if not revealed, could either distort reports of operations under review or conceal unlawful practices.

   X. Members and CIAs shall continually strive for improvement in their proficiency, and in the effectiveness and quality of their service.

   XI. Members and CIAs, in the practice of their profession, shall be ever mindful of the obligation to maintain the high standards of competence, morality, and dignity promulgated by The Institute. Members shall abide by the *Bylaws* and uphold the objectives of The Institute.

Adopted by Board of Directors July 1988.

always work to maintain this type of a satisfactory level of communication with auditees, management, and all others.

The second human relations guideline (.02) focuses on both oral and written communications skills, a need that applies to all individuals involved in internal auditing. Although Standard 250 calls for internal audit to have a good understanding of various specialized technical areas, this knowledge is of little value if the auditor lacks proper oral and written communication skills. The importance of such skills cannot be overemphasized. Chapter 15 discusses internal audit human relations and communication skills and also discusses the important element of communication through formal audit reports. There may also be situations when an internal auditor will need to seek special assistance from communications specialists.

Standard 270 emphasizes the need to maintain technical competence through continuing education. In our dynamic and changing world, this is the only way for the modern internal auditor to avoid becoming obsolete or ineffective. The supporting guideline reaffirms the need for continuing education but in terms of "proficiency," a somewhat broader term than "technical competence." The guideline mentions continuing education in terms of internal audit techniques but does not mention other important educational areas. However, continuing education should also extend to many other nontechnical but related areas that can improve the effectiveness of internal auditors. Although the guideline mentions specific means by which the continuing education can be obtained, other ways would also certainly be acceptable.

Continuing education is important to all professionals. Internal auditors who hold professional certifications such as the CIA or CISA have specific requirements for obtaining continuing professional education credit hours. Internal auditors who are also CPAs now also have very tight continuing education requirements. However, even if an internal auditor does not have such a professional certificate requirement, the auditor should still strive to build skills through an ongoing program of continuing education.

The last specific Standard under the Professional Proficiency Standard is 280, covering the important requirement that an auditor exercise what is called "due professional care" in performing audits. Due professional care is a basic component of the internal auditor's professional effectiveness. While the definition, measurement, and final evaluation of that due professional care is often subjective, it is a standard for measuring an auditor's performance and procedures.

The guidelines associated with the due professional care Standard address this issue in several different ways. Although .01 talks about the proper utilization of professional care, much of this standard provides guidance on identifying and reporting errors, omissions, or wrongdoing. This is an issue that became increasingly important starting in the 1970s, when there seemed to be an increasing amount of organizational fraud but limited standards calling for internal auditors to look for potentially fraudulent acts.

The guidelines here provide an extensive outline of the auditor's responsibility for deterring, detecting, investigating, and reporting fraud. The guidelines make an important point by containing no statement about the auditor's responsibility to *deter* fraud. Deterrence is the responsibility of management, while internal auditors are responsible for evaluating the adequacy and effectiveness of the actions taken by management in this area.

The Standards guideline includes some examples of fraud, including:

- Sale or assignment of fictitious or misrepresented assets
- Improper payments, such as illegal political contributions, bribes, kickbacks, and payoffs to government officials or their intermediaries, customers, or suppliers

- Intentional, improper representation or valuation of transactions, assets, liabilities, or income

- Intentional, improper transfer pricing (e.g., valuation of goods exchanged between related organizations) in order to improve the operating results of one organization involved to the detriment of the others

- Intentional, improper related-party transactions in which one party receives some benefit not obtainable in an arm's-length transaction

- Intentional failure to record or disclose significant information to improve the financial picture of the organization to outside parties

- Prohibited activities violating government statutes, rules, regulations, or contracts

- Tax fraud

The guidelines recognize that all internal audits have limitations and cannot provide complete assurance that all noncompliance and irregularities have been disclosed. There are numerous reasons for these limitations, including that the extent of audit work must be guided by an evaluation of costs and potential benefits, that audits of an expanded scope will still not always detect all irregularities, and that internal auditing work is subject to human limitations. However, internal audit should always keep in mind the possibilities of material irregularities or noncompliance. The internal auditor's responsibilities in the area of fraud and fraud investigations are discussed in more detail in Chapter 31.

The third due professional care guideline deals with a somewhat different matter: procedures when wrongdoing is suspected. While there is a requirement to inform the appropriate authorities when a potential wrongdoing is encountered, the auditor must make some judgments as to its significance, the extent of the belief that such a wrongdoing in fact exists, and the identification of the appropriate reporting authority. Based on professional judgment, an internal auditor may make a recommendation for an investigation where wrongdoing is suspected.

The internal auditor's responsibility to identify and detect fraud and wrongdoing has become a quite important issue in recent years. Sometimes, however, management has almost too high of an expectation of an auditor's ability to detect fraud. Chapter 31 provides guidance on detecting and reporting fraud, and Chapter 35 discusses some ethical issues facing internal auditors in this area.

(ii) Professional Proficiency in Perspective. ''Professional proficiency'' is one of those interesting terms that can be viewed at varying levels. At its highest level, the term encompasses the achievement of total internal auditing effectiveness. As used in the preceding paragraphs, however, the term relates more to how internal audit work is carried out for particular assignments. As such, professional efficiency becomes the responsibility of both the internal auditing department and of the individual auditor. Professional proficiency includes the objective of matching staff personnel with audit assignments in a manner that best assures a high level of internal auditing service to the organization. To achieve this objective, there must be both adequate audit department capabilities as well as a strong sensitivity for exercising due professional care. Of course, measurement and evaluation in these areas is very difficult, so consideration must be given to the concepts of reasonableness, the significance of activities being audited, the costs of audit work, and the expected benefits. Thus, judgment becomes the final determinant.

The Standards guidelines relating to due professional care focus on concerns in such areas as fraud, compliance, and conservation of assets. Despite this protective orientation, however, an internal auditor should not forget the relevance of due professional care in carrying out the broader management-improvement types of audits. The needs for proper due professional care are just as important for identifying and properly recommending opportunities for greater management effectiveness and profitability. These dual objectives of protection and improvement often distinguish the internal from the external auditor.

(c) GENERAL STANDARD 300: SCOPE OF WORK

300.   *THE SCOPE OF THE INTERNAL AUDIT SHOULD ENCOMPASS THE EXAM-INATION AND EVALUATION OF THE ADEQUACY AND EFFECTIVENESS OF THE ORGANIZATION'S SYSTEM OF INTERNAL CONTROL AND THE QUALITY OF PERFORMANCE IN CARRYING OUT ASSIGNED RESPONSI-BILITIES.*

300.01   *The scope of internal auditing work, as specified in this standard, encompasses what audit work should be performed; however, senior management and the board may provide a general direction as to the scope of work and the activities to be audited.*

300.02   *The purpose of the review for adequacy of the system of internal control is to ascertain whether the system established provides reasonable assurance that the organization's objectives and goals will be met efficiently and economically.*

300.02.1 *Objectives are the broadest statements of what the organization chooses to accomplish, and their establishment precedes the selection of goals and the design, implementation, and maintenance of systems whose purpose is to meet the organization's objectives and goals.*

300.02.2 *Goals are objectives of specific systems and otherwise referred to as operating or program objectives or goals, operating standards, performance levels, targets, or expected results. Goals should be clearly defined, measurable, attainable, and consistent with established broader objectives; they should explicitly recognize the risks associated with not achieving those objectives.*

300.02.3 *A system (process, operation, function, or activity) is an arrangement, a set, or a collection of concepts, parts, activities, and/or people that are connected or interrelated to achieve objectives and goals. A system may also be a collection of subsystems operating together for a common objective or goal.*

300.02.4 *Adequate control is present if planned and organized in a manner which provides reasonable assurance that the objectives and goals will be achieved efficiently and economically. The system design process begins with the establishment of objectives and goals followed by connecting or interrelating concepts, parts, activities, and/or people in a manner to operate together to achieve them. If system design is properly performed, planned activities should be executed as designed and expected results should be attained.*

300.02.5 *Reasonable assurance is provided when cost-effective actions are taken to restrict deviations to a tolerable level. This implies that material errors and improper or illegal acts will be prevented or detected and corrected within a timely period by employees in the normal course of their assigned duties. This cost-benefit relationship is considered by management during the design of systems.*

300.02.6   *Efficient performance accomplishes objectives and goals in an accurate and timely fashion with minimal use of resources.*

300.02.7   *Economical performance accomplishes objectives and goals at a cost commensurate with the risk. The term* efficient *incorporates the concept of economical performance.*

300.03   *The purpose of the review for effectiveness of the system of internal control is to ascertain whether the system is functioning as intended.*

300.03.1   *Effective control is present when management directs systems in a manner to provide reasonable assurance that objectives and goals will be achieved.*

300.03.2   *Directing involves, in addition to accomplishing objectives and planned activities, authorizing and monitoring performance, periodically comparing actual with planned performance, and documenting these activities to provide assurance that systems operate as planned.*

300.04   *The purpose of the review for quality of performance is to ascertain whether the organization's objectives and goals have been achieved.*

300.05   *The primary objectives of internal control are to ensure:*
  .1   *The reliability and integrity of information*
  .2   *Compliance with policies, plans, procedures, laws, and regulations*
  .3   *The safeguarding of assets*
  .4   *The economical and efficient use of resources*
  .5   *The accomplishment of objectives and goals for operations or programs*

300.06   *A control is any action taken by management to enhance the likelihood that established objectives and goals will be achieved. Management plans, organizes, and directs the performance of sufficient actions to provide reasonable assurance that objectives and goals will be achieved. Thus, control is the result of proper planning, organizing, and directing by management.*

300.06.1   *Controls may be preventive (to deter undesirable events from occurring), detective (to detect and correct undesirable events which have occurred), or directive (to cause or encourage a desirable event to occur).*

300.06.2   *All variants of the term* control *(administrative control, internal accounting control, operational control, output control, preventive control, etc.) can be incorporated within the generic term. These variants differ primarily in terms of the objectives to be achieved; since they are useful in describing specific control applications, auditors should be familiar with the terms as well as their applications. The methodology followed by internal auditing in evaluating controls is consistent for all of the variants.*

300.06.3   *The variant "internal control" came into use to distinguish controls from those existing externally (such as laws). Since internal auditors operate within an organization and, among other responsibilities, evaluate management's response to external stimuli (such as laws), no such distinction between internal and external controls is necessary. Internal controls are activities which attempt to ensure the accomplishment of the organization's objectives and goals and are considered synonymous with control within the organization.*

300.06.4   *The overall system of control is conceptual in nature, the integrated collection of controlled systems used by an organization to achieve its objectives and goals.*

300.07   *Management plans, organizes, and directs in such a fashion as to provide reasonable assurance that established objectives and goals will be achieved.*

300.07.1   *Planning and organizing involve the establishment of objectives and goals and the use of such tools as organization charts, flowcharts, procedures, records, and reports to establish the flow of data and the responsibilities of individuals for performing activities, establishing information trails, and setting standards of performance.*

300.07.2   *Directing involves activities to provide additional assurance that systems operate as planned, including authorizing and monitoring performance, periodically comparing actual with planned performance, and appropriately documenting activities.*

300.07.3   *Management ensures that its objectives and goals remain appropriate and that its systems remain current through periodic reviews of its objectives and goals and modification of its systems to accommodate changes in internal and external conditions.*

300.07.4   *Management establishes and maintains an environment that fosters control.*

300.08   *Internal auditors examine and evaluate the planning, organizing, and directing processes to determine whether reasonable assurance exists that objectives and goals will be achieved. Such evaluations, in the aggregate, provide information to appraise the overall system of internal control.*

300.08.1   *All systems, processes, operations, functions, and activities within the organization are subject to the internal auditor's evaluations.*

300.08.2   *Such evaluations should encompass whether reasonable assurance exists that:*
   a.   *Objectives and goals have been established.*
   b.   *Authorizing, monitoring, and periodic comparison activities have been planned, performed, and documented as necessary to attain objectives and goals.*
   c.   *Planned objectives and goals have been achieved.*

300.08.3   *Internal auditing performs evaluations at specific points in time but should be alert to actual or potential changes in conditions which affect the ability to provide assurance from a forward-looking perspective. In those cases, internal auditing should address the risk that performance may deteriorate.*

The General Standard 300 above covers the total scope of internal auditing but emphasizes two key aspects: the examination and evaluation of the organization's system of internal control and the quality of performance in carrying out assigned audit responsibilities. The first deals with the kind of work to be performed and the second with the quality of performance. The two have distinctive characteristics that are closely interrelated.

There are five specific Standards under General Standard 300 as well as eight guidelines supporting it. The first guideline (.01) ties the scope of work to the General Standard. It includes the qualification that the scope of audit work and activities to be audited are subject to the general direction of management and the board of directors. This qualification might be interpreted as endorsing a situation where the internal auditing department is restricted in exercising its own judgment as to what kind of an internal audit program is appropriate. However, the use of the word ''general direction'' provides a basis for such management direction in a manner that is not inconsistent with the Standards. Without that assumption, the guideline would point to a potential threat to the independence of internal audit.

The second guideline goes on to define the purpose of the auditor's review. They define the purposes of the auditor's reviews emphasizing the adequacy, effectiveness, and quality of performance, and the above supporting Standard outlines some of the important elements in internal audit risk analysis, used to analyze and select audit projects for review. (Chapter 7 discusses the process for evaluating and assessing audit risk.) This guideline ties the accomplishment of the organization's objectives and goals directly to the adequacy of its system of internal control, the prime means of assuring the efficient and economical accomplishment of the objectives and goals of the organization.

The third guideline (.03) defines the purpose of a review for internal control system effectiveness, to ascertain that the system is functioning as intended. This guideline is rather narrowly structured since an internal auditor is also concerned with identifying additional means by which the system can be improved. That is, internal auditors should always search for systems betterment in addition to just determining whether systems are working as originally defined.

The fourth guideline (.04) defines the purpose of reviews for quality of performance as ascertaining whether the objectives and goals of the organization have been achieved. While the quality of performance pertains to the level of contribution made for the achievement of the objectives and goals, management also utilizes many other means to achieve those objectives and goals. When following this guideline, the auditor should recognize that goals and objectives are an ongoing process and never fully achieved.

In the fifth guideline (.05), the primary objectives of internal control are defined as assuring the five different types of results. In the first three of these, desired results pertain to the more protective internal audit procedures, while the final two refer to constructive procedures.

These five important objectives provide a good basis for understanding internal control. They essentially follow the internal control model of Chapter 2 and will be referenced again in Chapter 21 on operational auditing. The internal auditor's review of internal control should always consider these five objectives. At the same time, internal audit often has a broader mission. In addition to the review of internal control, the auditor endeavors to assist management to achieve maximum effectiveness in the use of resources with proper consideration given to economy and efficiency.

This sixth Standards guideline (.06) provides a rather detailed description of internal control. The first specification establishes three types of controls: preventive, detective, and corrective. Corrective controls remedy existing problems while directive controls look to correcting future problems. The second specification combines a wide variety of controls under the generic concept of controls. This is a useful concept for the internal auditor, who should think of all controls as having some of the same general concepts.

The two remaining guidelines define, first, management responsibilities for internal controls (.07) and then internal audit's related responsibilities in this area (.08). An internal auditor should have a good understanding of the proper roles for each. Management establishes and promotes the environment that allows the overall control system to operate while internal audit reviews and evaluates those controls. Although an internal auditor can recommend improvements in controls systems, internal audit should not be responsible for establishing or implementing internal control systems.

The above Management Responsibilities guideline section of the Standards defines an overall approach or ideal that an internal auditor can use to measure management processes. However, while these Standards provide definitive guidance, management in a given organization may not follow all of the procedures outlined in this guideline. The Standards describe what management *should* do, even though senior management is not subject to nor may be aware of these Standards. For example, the first specification discusses management's responsibility to document their procedures, including the use of flowcharts. In many otherwise well-managed organizations, internal audit may not find such documented procedures. The auditor may then make appropriate recommendations for such documentation, as outlined in guideline .08. Chapter 3 discusses some of these management needs and responsibilities. These particular standards tie quite closely to the guidelines in the COSO report and the requirements of the Foreign Corrupt Practices Act (FCPA), both of which were discussed in Chapter 2.

This final guideline under the Scope of Work Standard provides an excellent statement of the responsibilities and activities of an internal auditing department. The guideline stresses that *all* operations or activities within an organization can be subject to audit and that these reviews might take place at various specific points in time.

Although basic concepts remain the same, the term ''system of internal control'' is changing. While internal auditors have used this term, external auditors who are primarily interested in attesting to the fairness of financial statements had used the related term ''system of internal accounting control.'' In 1990, the AICPA released Statement on Auditing Standards (SAS) No. 55, which redefined these terms. They were greatly broadened in 1996 through SAS No. 78, which follows the COSO model of internal control discussed in Chapter 2. Because of the strong influence of external auditors on many internal audit activities and because the COSO report also uses these concepts, the COSO and SAS No. 78 terms will replace the internal control definitions now used in the Internal Audit Standards.

(i) Standard 310—Reliability and Integrity of Information.

310.   *Internal auditors should review the reliability and integrity of financial and operating information and the means used to identify, measure, classify, and report such information.*

310.01   *Information systems provide data for decision-making, control, and compliance with external requirements. Therefore, internal auditors should examine information systems and, as appropriate, ascertain whether:*

    .1   *Financial and operating records and reports contain accurate, reliable, timely, complete, and useful information.*

    .2   *Controls over record keeping and reporting are adequate and effective.*

Standard 300 discussed the internal auditor's concern for the reliability and integrity of financial and operating information as well as the means used to identify, measure, classify, and report such information. Now, this mandate to ensure reliability and integrity is made directly to internal auditors through this specific Standard.

Although the Standard makes a distinction between ''financial'' and ''operating'' records and reports, in practice both types of records are closely interrelated and frequently either overlap or are integrated. Many operational records eventually also affect or become a part of other financial records.

This supporting guideline here describes the implementation of reliability and integrity objectives and emphasizes the importance of the data provided by information systems. Since systems can be manual or automated, two internal auditor approaches are identified. The first focuses on the records and reports produced by the system while the second considers the adequacy and effectiveness of the underlying controls. In automated system applications, as discussed in Chapter 17, these approaches are sometimes called ''auditing around the computer'' versus ''auditing through the computer.'' The modern internal auditor should endeavor to develop internal audit procedures to consider all aspects of the control process including computer systems controls, implementing procedures to assess all aspects of a process and considering computer systems controls as part of any review.

(ii) Compliance with Laws and Regulations and Safeguarding of Assets.

320. *Internal auditors should review the systems established to ensure compliance with those policies, plans, procedures, laws, and regulations which could have a significant impact on operations, and should determine whether the organization is in compliance.*

320.01 *Management is responsible for establishing the systems designed to ensure compliance with policies, plans, procedures, and applicable laws and regulations. Internal auditors are responsible for determining whether the systems are adequate and effective and whether the activities audited are complying with the appropriate requirements.*

330. *Internal auditors should review the means of safeguarding assets and, as appropriate, verify the existence of such assets.*

330.01 *Internal auditors should review the means used to safeguard assets from such potential losses as theft, fire, improper or illegal activities, and exposure to the elements.*

330.02 *Internal auditors should use appropriate procedures when verifying the existence of assets.*

Internal auditors employ a variety of measures for evaluating effectiveness, such as the use of generally accepted accounting principles to help determine whether accounting processes are functioning correctly. Laws and regulations are another type of standard covering all aspects of an organization's operations, and, increasingly, auditors must measure performance against them.

Specific Standard 320 deals with the auditor's review of the organization's compliance with existing policies, plans, procedures, laws, and regulations. Two means to accomplish this are reviews of supporting systems or a confirmation of compliance by external sources. Compliance reviews have always been a basic review approach for internal auditors.

The supporting guideline here reaffirms the basic responsibility of management for establishing the systems designed to ensure the various types of compliance. An internal auditor is responsible for determining both the adequacy and effectiveness of supporting systems and the appropriate compliance actions involving policies, plans, procedures, laws, and regulations, plus other specified actions authorized by management, formally or implicitly. Compliance actions can apply to any level of organizational activity.

While not expected to be an expert in the details of all laws or regulations, an internal auditor should have a general knowledge and know when to seek help. Compliance audits are increasingly important for internal auditors working in heavily regulated industries.

Specific Standard 330 focuses on and expands upon the third objective of 300.05, stated above. It recognizes two types of audit approaches through reviews of the means employed to safeguard assets and through the direct verification of the existence of the assets involved. Activities to support the safeguarding of assets have always been a responsibility of internal auditors. As mentioned in Chapter 1, this and the two previous objectives of reliability and compliance initially helped establish internal auditing in the early days of internal auditing.

The wide range of safeguarding activities is, of course, directly dependent on the particular type of asset involved. The importance of safeguarding assets is directly dependent on the extent and significance of the risk of loss to the organization. For example, cash is especially vulnerable and requires safeguarding actions that should generally be very detailed and intensive. Conversely, the risk may be very low for an asset that is bulky and relatively immobile. Judgment is required to determine the extent of risk and how best to deal with the related problems.

The second guideline here calls for direct verification of the existence of assets and that "appropriate procedures" should be used in carrying out that verification. The significance of the term "appropriate" is that different types of procedures can be used depending upon the type of assets and the related risks. For example, various procedures are discussed in Chapter 22 on accounting systems controls, and in Chapter 27, on fixed asset and capital project controls.

(iii) Standard 340—Economical and Efficient Use of Resources

340. *Internal auditors should appraise the economy and efficiency with which resources are employed.*

340.01 *Management is responsible for setting operating standards to measure an activity's economical and efficient use of resources. Internal auditors are responsible for determining whether:*

　.1 *Operating standards have been established for measuring economy and efficiency.*

　.2 *Established operating standards are understood and are being met.*

　.3 *Deviations from operating standards are identified, analyzed, and communicated to those responsible for corrective action.*

　.4 *Corrective action has been taken.*

340.02 *Audits related to the economical and efficient use of resources should identify such conditions as:*

　.1 *Underutilized facilities*

　.2 *Nonproductive work*

　.3 *Procedures which are not cost justified*

　.4 *Overstaffing or understaffing*

This specific Standard and its two supporting guidelines cover the responsibility of internal audit to help achieve economical and efficient uses of the organization's resources. The key word in this Standard is the internal auditor's "appraisal" to assist management in this important aspect of total organizational welfare.

The first guideline here clarifies the respective responsibilities of both management and internal audit. The overall control cycle is the responsibility of management, and the internal auditor's role is to assist by providing information on how economically and efficiently the various parts of the control cycle are actually being carried out and how the control system can be improved. This guideline should at no point give the impression that internal audit has some special responsibility that either conflicts with or dilutes basic management responsibilities.

The second guideline mentions specific conditions that should be identified and appraised by internal audit. All of the conditions mentioned are potential causes of the organization falling short in making economical and efficient use of its resources. Of course, there can also be other causes. An internal auditor must identify and establish priorities to best assist management to achieve their objectives and goals of the best utilization of resources. As was discussed in Chapter 3, the effective utilization of resources should be a basic objective of all management efforts.

(iv) Establishing Objectives and Goals for Operations and Programs

350.   *Internal auditors should review operations or programs to ascertain whether results are consistent with established objectives and goals and whether they are being carried out as planned.*

350.01   *Management is responsible for establishing program objectives and goals, developing and implementing control procedures, and accomplishing desired results. Internal auditors should ascertain whether such objectives and goals conform with those of the organization and are being met.*

350.01.1 *The term "operations" refers to recurring activities directed toward producing a product or rendering a service and may include, but are not limited to, marketing, sales, production, purchasing, human resources, finance, and accounting. An operation's results may be measured against established objectives and goals, including budgets, time or production schedules, and/or operating plans.*

350.01.2 *The term "programs" refers to special purpose activities including the raising of capital, sale of a facility, fundraising campaigns, capital expenditures, and special purpose government grants. They may be short-term or long-term, spanning several years, but when a program is completed, it generally ceases to exist. Program results may be measured against established programs, objectives, and goals.*

350.01.3 *Management is responsible for establishing criteria to determine if objectives and goals have been accomplished.*

350.01.4 *Internal auditors should ascertain whether criteria have been established, and if so, should use such criteria for an evaluation of their adequacy.*

350.01.5 *If management has not established criteria, or if the established criteria, in the internal auditor's opinion, are less than adequate, the conditions should be reported to the appropriate levels of management including recommendations for appropriate courses of action depending on the circumstances.*

350.01.6 *Internal auditors may recommend alternative sources of criteria to management including acceptable industry standards, government regulations, or standards developed by professional associations.*

350.01.7 *If adequate criteria are not established by management, internal auditors may still formulate criteria they believe to be adequate in order to perform an audit, and form an opinion on the accomplishment of objectives and goals.*

350.01.8 *An internal auditors' evaluation of the accomplishment of established objectives and goals may be carried out with respect to an entire operation or program or only a portion of it and may include determining whether:*
a.   The objectives and goals established by management for a proposed, new, or existing operation or program are adequate and have been effectively communicated.

    b. The operation or program achieves its desired level of results.

    c. The factors which inhibit satisfactory performance are identified, evaluated, and controlled appropriately.

    d. Management has considered alternatives for directing an operation or program which may yield more effective and efficient results.

    e. An operation or program complements, duplicates, overlaps, or conflicts with other operations or programs.

    f. Controls for measuring and reporting the accomplishments of objectives and goals are established and are adequate.

    g. An operation or program is in compliance with policies, plans, procedures, laws, and regulations.

350.01.09 *Internal auditors should communicate the audit results to the appropriate levels of management. Their report should state the criteria established by management and employed by internal auditors and disclose the nonexistence or inadequacy of any needed criteria. If internal auditors formulated criteria by which to measure the accomplishments of objectives and goals, the report should clearly state that internal auditors formulated the criteria, when presenting audit results.*

350.02 *Internal auditors can provide assistance to managers who are developing objectives, goals, and systems by determining whether the underlying assumptions are appropriate; whether accurate, current, and relevant information is being used; and whether suitable controls have been incorporated into the operations or programs.*

Internal auditors are often given information about future management plans or objectives designed to correct areas of auditor concern. This specific Standard covers the auditor's review of these planned objectives and goals for operations or programs. Internal audit has a specific concern that results are consistent with these objectives and goals and that operations or programs are implemented as planned. This Standard is closely related to the preceding one, covering the economical and efficient use of resources.

As in the preceding Standard, the first guideline distinguishes between the responsibilities of management and internal audit. Management is responsible for establishing operating or program objectives and goals, developing and implementing control procedures, and accomplishing desired results. Internal audit ascertains whether such objectives and goals conform with management plans and whether they are being met. Internal audit's role is to assist management in establishing better policies and procedures.

The second guideline supports internal audit's role in providing assistance to management in developing objectives, goals, and systems. The first two types of assistance must not go so far as to undermine basic management responsibilities, while the third concerning the suitability of controls, involves the questions discussed previously with guideline 120.03.

(v) Scope of Internal Audit Work Standard in Perspective. The central point regarding the Scope of Work Standard is that internal audit accomplishes objectives of assisting management through the review and evaluation of various internal controls. Although management can alter that scope, any alterations should not prevent internal audit's basic concentration on the system of internal control. The higher-level objectives achieved are the protective services of the safeguarding of assets and the contribution to the improvement of resource utilization in terms of economy, efficiency, and effectiveness. Of course, the role of internal audit is always advisory, never to relieve management of its basic responsibility for utilizing the resources for maximum organizational welfare.

The Scope of Work Standard provides a general map describing the activities of internal audit. From time to time, an internal auditor may want to review this Standard with management to emphasize the important rule of internal audit in the organization. An internal audit department should consider this Standard particularly when assessing its own activities, such as when internal audit is involved in a quality assurance review, discussed in Chapter 33.

(d) STANDARD 400: PERFORMANCE OF AUDIT WORK

400. *AUDIT WORK SHOULD INCLUDE PLANNING THE AUDIT, EXAMINING AND EVALUATING INFORMATION, COMMUNICATING RESULTS, AND FOLLOWING UP.*

400.01 *Internal audit is responsible for planning and conducting the audit assignment, subject to supervisory review and approval.*

The fourth section of the Standards deals with the actual performance of the work segment components of an individual internal audit project. The specific Standards following cover all of the individual phases of an audit project. These are discussed in greater detail in the Part III chapters covering the administration of internal auditing activities.

(i) Standard 410—Planning the Audit

410. *Internal auditors should plan each audit.*

410.01 *Planning should be documented and include:*

410.01.1 *Establishing audit objectives and scope of work.*

    a. Audit objectives are broad statements developed by internal audit to define intended audit accomplishments. Audit procedures are the means to attain audit objectives. Auditor objectives and procedures, taken together, define the scope of the internal auditor's work.

    b. Audit objectives and procedures should address the risks associated with the activity under audit. The term "risk" is the probability that an event or action may adversely affect the activity under audit. The section 520.04.1–.14 Standards guidelines discuss risk assessment for individual audits.

410.01.2. *Obtaining background information about the activities to be audited.*

    a. A review of background information, with an emphasis on audit impact, should be performed including:

       • Mission statements, goals, and plans.

       • Organization information, including the names of key employees, job descriptions, policy and procedure manuals, and details about any recent changes in the organization or major systems.

       • Budget information, operating results, and financial data of the activity to be audited.

       • Prior audit workpapers.

- *Results of other audits, including external auditors, completed or in process.*
- *Correspondence files to determine potential significant audit issues.*
- *Authoritative and technical literature appropriate to the activity.*

b.   *Other audit requirements, such as the period covered and estimated completion dates, should be considered, in order to coordinate release of the final audit report.*

410.01.3   *Determining the resources necessary to perform the audit.*

.a   *The number and experience level of the internal auditing staff required should be based on an evaluation of the nature and complexity of the audit assignment, time constraints, and available resources.*

.b   *Knowledge, skills, and disciplines of the audit staff should be considered in making audit assignments.*

.c   *Auditor training needs should be considered, since each audit assignment serves as a basis for meeting staff developmental needs.*

.d   *Consideration of using external resources in instances where additional knowledge, skills, and disciplines are needed.*

410.01.4   *Communicating with all who need to know about the audit.*

.a   *Meetings should be held with management responsible for the activity being examined; meeting topics may include:*
- *Planned audit objectives and scope of work.*
- *The timing of the audit work.*
- *Communications throughout the audit, including the methods, time frames, and individuals responsible.*
- *Business conditions and operations of the activity audited, including any recent changes.*
- *Concerns or any requests of management.*
- *Matters of particular interest or concern to internal audit.*
- *Internal audit's reporting procedures and follow-up process.*

.b   *A summary of matters discussed at meetings and conclusions reached should be prepared, distributed as appropriate, and retained in the workpapers.*

410.01.5   *Performing an on-site survey to become familiar with the activities, risks, and controls to identify areas for audit emphasis, and to invite auditee comments and suggestions.*

.a   *A survey gathers information, without detailed verification, on the activity being examined with objectives to:*
- *Understand the activity under review.*
- *Identify significant areas warranting special emphasis.*
- *Obtain information for use in performing the audit.*
- *Determine whether further auditing is necessary.*

.b   *A survey permits an informed approach to planning and carrying out audit work, and is an effective tool for deciding where audit resources can be used most effectively.*

.c   *The focus of a survey will vary depending upon the nature of the audit.*

.d   *The scope of work and the time requirements of a survey will vary based on the auditor's experience, knowledge of the activity being examined, the type of audit, and whether the survey is part of a recurring or follow-up assignment. Time requirements are also influenced by the size and complexity of the activity being examined, and by its geographical dispersion.*

.e *A survey may involve discussions with the auditee or its users, on-site observations, reviews of management reports and studies, analytical procedures, flowcharts, or functional "walk-throughs."*

.f *A summary should be prepared at the conclusion of the survey including:*

- *Significant audit issues identified.*
- *Pertinent information developed during the survey.*
- *Audit objectives and planned audit procedures such as computer assisted audit techniques.*
- *Potential critical control points, deficiencies, and/or excess controls.*
- *Preliminary estimates of audit time and resource requirements.*
- *Revised dates for reporting phases and completing the audit.*
- *When applicable, reasons for not continuing the audit.*

410.01.6 *The audit program should include a) the objectives of the audit, b) procedures for collecting, analyzing, interpreting, and documenting audit information, c) the scope and degree of testing required to achieve the audit objectives, and d) any technical aspects, risks, processes, and transactions requiring audit examination.*

410.01.7 *The director of internal auditing is responsible for determining how, when, and to whom audit results will be communicated. This determination should be documented and communicated to management, to the extent deemed practical, during the planning phase of the audit with any subsequent changes affecting the timing or reporting of results also communicated if appropriate.*

410.01.8 *Audit work plans and adjustments to plans should be approved in writing by the director of internal auditing or designee prior to the commencement of audit work. Initial approval may be obtained orally, if factors preclude obtaining written approval prior to commencing audit work.*

Planning is an essential component of any management process, and this specific Standard confirms the necessity for planning each audit. The supporting guideline provides considerable detail on the scope of that planning, including the essential first step of establishing audit objectives and scope of work, important preparatory activities, appropriate on-site reviews, and determining the audit program. While much of this can be viewed as preliminary work, it is also an integral phase of the audit itself. The final audit-planning steps include determining how, when, and to whom audit results will be communicated and obtaining appropriate approval for the work plan. Planning and organizing audit activities are discussed in Chapter 7.

(ii) Standard 420—Examining and Evaluating Information.   This Standard, perhaps in greater detail than the other Standards, describes the process of performing an internal audit. As published by the IIA, 420 is more a detailed checklist than a concise standard. At the beginning of this chapter, we mentioned that our description of the official IIA Standards have been edited for some sections. Because this is a very detailed Standard, and because many of these same issues are discussed in greater detail throughout this book, significant editing changes have been made to Standard 420. The reader is encouraged to read the official IIA standards for the actual text.

420. *Internal auditors should collect, analyze, interpret, and document information to support audit results.*

420.01.1 *Information should be collected on all matters related to the audit objectives and scope of work.*

.a *Analytical auditing procedures are used when examining and evaluating both financial and nonfinancial information and relationships.*

.b *Analytical auditing assumes that, in the absence of conditions to the contrary, relationships among information may reasonably be expected to exist and continue except in the case of contrary conditions such as: i) unusual or nonrecurring transactions or events, ii) accounting, organizational, environmental, and technological changes, iii) errors and irregularities, or iv) illegal acts.*

.c *Analytical auditing procedures provide efficient and effective means of making an assessment of information collected in an audit; analytical auditing procedures are useful in identifying i) differences that either are not expected or the absence of differences when they are expected, ii) potential errors, irregularities, or illegal acts, or iii) unusual or nonrecurring transactions.*

.d *Analytical auditing procedures may include:*
   - *Comparisons of current period information with similar information for prior periods or with budgets or forecasts.*
   - *Relationships of financial with the appropriate nonfinancial information (e.g. recorded payroll expense compared to changes in average number of employees).*
   - *Relationships among elements of information (e.g. fluctuations in interest expense compared to changes in related debt balances).*
   - *Comparisons with similar information for other organizational units or for the industry in which the organization operates.*

.e *Analytical auditing procedures may be performed using monetary amounts, physical quantities, ratios, or percentages.*

.f *Specific analytical auditing procedures include, but are not limited to, ratio, trend, and regression analysis, reasonableness tests, period-to-period comparisons, comparisons with budgets, forecasts, and external information.*

.g *Factors to consider when determining the extent to which analytical auditing procedures should be used:*
   - *The significance of the area examined and the adequacy of the system of internal control.*
   - *The availability and reliability of financial and nonfinancial information.*
   - *The precision with which the results of analytical auditing procedures can be predicted.*
   - *The availability and comparability of industry information in which the organization operates.*

.h *When analytical audit procedures identify unexpected relationships, internal auditors should examine and evaluate such results including inquiries of management and the application of other auditing procedures until the results or relationships are sufficiently explained.*

.i   *Unexplained results or relationships from analytical audit procedures may indicate a significant condition such as an error, irregularity, or illegal act.*

.j   *Results or relationships from analytical audit procedures that are not sufficiently explained should be communicated to appropriate levels of management, including recommendations for appropriate actions.*

420.01.2   *Information should be sufficient, competent, relevant, and useful to provide a sound basis for audit findings and recommendations.*

.a   *Sufficient information is factual, adequate, and convincing so that a prudent, informed person would reach the same conclusions as the auditor.*

.b   *Competent information is reliable and the best attainable through the use of appropriate audit techniques.*

.c   *Relevant information supports audit findings and recommendations and is consistent with the objectives for the audit.*

.d   *Useful information helps the organization meet its goals.*

420.01.3   *Audit procedures, including testing and sampling techniques, should be selected in advance, where practicable, and expanded or altered if circumstances warrant.*

420.01.4   *The process of collecting, analyzing, interpreting, and documenting information should be supervised to provide reasonable assurance that auditor objectivity is maintained and audit goals are met.*

420.01.5   *Workpapers that document the audit information obtained and the analyses made should be prepared by the auditor and reviewed by audit management.*

.a   *Audit workpapers: i) document whether the audit objectives were achieved, ii) provide the principal support for the internal audit report, iii) aid in the planning, performance, and review of audits, iv) facilitate third party reviews and provide a basis for evaluating the internal audit quality assurance program, v) provide support for insurance claims, fraud cases, and lawsuits, and vi) aid in the professional development of the internal audit staff.*

.b   *The organization, design, and content of audit workpapers will depend on the nature of the audit, and workpapers should document the audit process including: i) audit planning, ii) an evaluation of the adequacy and effectiveness of the system of internal control, iii) audit procedures performed, information obtained, and conclusions reached, iv) evidence of workpaper review, v) the audit report, and vi) follow-up actions.*

.c   *Audit workpapers should be complete and include support for audit conclusions reached including:*

• *Planning documents and audit programs.*
• *Control questionnaires, flowcharts, checklists, and narratives.*
• *Notes and memoranda from interviews.*
• *Organization data, such as organization charts and job descriptions.*
• *Copies of significant contracts and agreements.*
• *Information about operating and financial policies.*
• *Letters of confirmation and representation.*
• *Analysis and tests of transactions, processes, and account balances.*
• *Results of analytical auditing procedures.*
• *Correspondence documenting audit conclusions reached.*

.d *Audit workpapers may be in the form of paper, diskettes, films, or other media, but if other than paper, backup copies should be retained.*

.e *If reporting on financial information, the workpapers should document whether the accounting records agree or reconcile with such financial information.*

.f *Some workpapers, containing information of continuing importance, may be categorized as permanent audit files.*

.g *The director of internal audit should establish policies for the types of audit workpaper files maintained, standardized questionnaires and audit programs, indexing, and related matters to improve efficiency and facilitate the delegation of audit work.*

.h *Each audit workpaper sheet should contain a heading, consisting of the name of the organization being examined, a title or description of the contents or purpose of the workpaper, and the date or period covered by the audit.*

.i *Each audit workpaper should be signed (or initialed) and dated by the audit, all audit verification symbols (tick marks) should be explained, and sources of data should be clearly identified.*

.j *All audit workpapers should be reviewed, initialed, and dated to ensure they properly support the audit report and that all necessary auditing procedures have been performed. The director of internal audit has overall responsibility for review but may designate others to perform the review. However, the review should be conducted at a level of responsibility higher than that of the preparer of the audit workpapers.*

.k *Reviewers may make a written record (review notes) of questions arising from the review process. When clearing review notes, care should be taken to ensure the workpapers provide adequate evidence that questions raised have been resolved. Acceptable alternatives with respect to disposition of review notes include retaining them as a record of the questions raised and the steps taken in their resolution, or discarding the review notes after the questions have been resolved and the appropriate workpapers amended to provide the additional information requested.*

.l *Audit workpapers are the property of the organization but should be accessible only to authorized personnel. While management and other members of the organization may request access to audit workpapers to substantiate or explain audit findings or to utilize audit documentation for other business purposes, these requests for access should be subject to the approval of the director of internal audit. While it is common practice for internal and external auditors to grant access to each other's audit workpapers, access by external auditors should be subject to the approval of the director of internal auditing.*

.m *There are circumstances where requests for access to audit workpapers and reports are made by parties outside the organization other than external auditors. Prior to releasing such documentation, the director of internal auditing should obtain the approval of senior management and/or legal counsel, as appropriate.*

.n *The director of internal auditing should develop retention requirements for audit workpapers, consistent with the organization's guidelines and any pertinent legal or other requirements.*

This specific Standard covers the collection, analysis, interpretation, and documentation of information to support audit results, allowing for the development of audit conclusions as well as backup support for those conclusions. That is, data must be first analyzed and interpreted as a basis of developing audit findings and related conclusions. As these conclusions and recommendations are developed, there must be adequate backup documentation to support them. Such backup is especially important because the audit conclusions and resultant recommendations may be possibly challenged at a later time.

The first of these five components (.1) prescribes the concept of audit objectives and scope of work. The materials outline the concept of analytical auditing procedures, an important tool that internal auditors should use on a regular basis. Often, an internal auditor can identify a potential problem through such procedures as measuring changes in certain key ratios from period to period or comparing certain results in the auditor's organization with other entities in the same industry.

The second section of this Standard has an important statement (420.01.2) on the qualities of audit information. The key attributes are sufficiency, competence, relevance, and usefulness, which fall back on the previously introduced concepts of due care and reasonableness of content. The concept of *competent* evidence is particularly important for auditors. This means that the evidence gathered must be sufficient and adequate enough to properly support the audit conclusions. The quality of *useful* overlaps the other three more definitive qualities and is more of a supporting point.

The third component of this guideline (.3) recognizes the need to expand or alter audit procedures in the light of evolving circumstances. No matter how well planned, internal audit will typically encounter circumstances that require some adjustment in the preliminary audit plan. The fourth component (.4) reaffirms the importance of supervision in the audit process, to assure objectivity and the accomplishment of audit goals. These areas are discussed in Chapter 10, on directing audit field activities.

Finally, the fifth component (.5) covers the importance of properly prepared and reviewed workpapers. These interpretations are discussed in Chapter 11, on the preparation of audit workpapers. The rather extensive standards for workpapers are examples of the current direction and thrust of Internal Audit Standards. While once similar to high-level policy statements, the standards statements are evolving into a much more detailed set of procedures. (As mentioned, the materials in this chapter have been edited.)

The five components of guideline 420.01 constitute the basis for an effective examination and evaluation of audit information, the development of appropriate audit conclusions, and the supporting documentation necessary for work done and conclusions reached.

(iii) Standard 430—Communicating Results

430.   *Internal auditors should report the results of their audit work.*

430.01   *A signed, written report should be issued after the audit examination is completed. Interim reports may be written or oral and may be transmitted formally or informally.*

430.01.1   *Interim reports may be used to communicate information requiring immediate attention, changes in audit scope for the activity under review, or to keep management informed of progress when audits extend over a long period. The use of interim reports does not diminish or eliminate the need for a final report.*

430.01.2   *Summary reports highlighting audit results may be appropriate for levels of management above the head of the audited unit and may be issued separately from or in conjunction with the final report.*

430.01.3   *The term ''signed'' means that authorized internal auditor, designated by the director of internal audit, should manually sign in the audit report or, alternatively, a cover letter.*

430.01.4   *If audit reports are distributed by electronic means, a signed version of the report should be kept on file in the internal audit department.*

430.02   *Internal audit should discuss conclusions and recommendations at appropriate levels of management before issuing final written reports.*

430.02.1   *Discussion of the audit conclusions and recommendations is usually accomplished during the course of the audit, through postaudit meetings (exit interviews), or the review of draft audit reports by the head of each audited unit. These discussions and reviews help ensure that there have been no misunderstandings or misinterpretations of fact by providing the opportunity for the auditees to clarify specific items and to express views of the findings, conclusions, and recommendations.*

430.02.2   *Although the participants in an audit review meeting may vary by organizations and by the nature of the report, they should generally include individuals who are knowledgeable of the detailed operations audited and who can authorize the implementation of corrective action.*

430.03   *Audit reports should be objective, clear, concise, constructive, and timely.*

430.03.1   *Audit reports should be factual, unbiased, and free from distortion, with findings, conclusions, and recommendations included without prejudice.*

    .a   *If an issued final audit report contains an error, the director of internal auditing should consider the need to issue an amended report which identifies the information being corrected, and the amended audit report should be distributed to all individuals who received the report being corrected.*

    .b   *An ''error'' is defined as an unintentional misstatement or omission of significant information in the final audit report.*

430.03.2   *Audit reports should be easily understood and logical, with a minimum of unnecessary technical language and sufficient supportive information.*

430.03.3   *Concise reports should be to the point, avoid unnecessary detail, and express thoughts completely in the fewest possible words.*

430.03.4   *Constructive reports, as a result of their content and tone, help auditees and the organization and lead to improvements where needed.*

430.03.5   *Timely reports are those issued without undue delay, to enable prompt effective action.*

430.04   *Reports should present the purpose, scope, and results of the audit and, where appropriate, reports should contain an expression of the auditor's opinion.*

430.04.1   *Audit report format and content may vary by organization or type of audit, but should contain, at a minimum, the purpose, scope, and results of the audit.*

430.04.2   *Audit reports may include background information and summaries to organizational units and functions reviewed and provide relevant explanatory information. They may also include the status of findings, conclusions, and recommendations from prior reports and may also indicate whether the report covers a* scheduled audit or the response to a request. Summaries, if included, should be balanced representations of the audit report content.

430.04.3   Purpose statements should describe the audit objectives and may disclose why the audit was conducted and what it was expected to achieve.

430.04.4   Scope statements should identify the audited activities, the time period audited, when appropriate, and related activities not audited to delineate the boundaries of the audit. The nature and extent of auditing performed also should be described.

430.04.5   Results may include findings, conclusions (opinions), and recommendations.

430.04.6   Audit findings, included in the final audit, are pertinent statements of fact which support internal audit's conclusions and recommendations. Less significant information or findings may be communicated orally or through informal correspondence.

430.04.7   Audit findings emerge by a process of comparing "what should be" with "what is." Whether or not there is a difference, internal audit has a foundation on which to build the report, and acknowledgment in the audit report of satisfactory performance may be appropriate. Findings should be based on the attributes:

.a   Criteria: The standards, measures, or expectations used in making an evaluation and/or verification (what should exist).

.b   Condition: The factual evidence which internal audit found in the course of the examination (what does exist).

.c   Cause: The reason for the difference between the expected and actual conditions (why the difference exists).

.d   Effect: The risk the auditees' organization may encounter because the condition is not the same as the criteria (the impact of the difference). In determining the degree of risk, internal auditors should consider the effect the findings may have on the organization's financial statements.

.e   The reported finding may include recommendations, recognition of auditee accomplishments, and supportive information if not included elsewhere.

430.04.8   Conclusions (opinions) are internal audit's evaluations of the effects of the findings on activities reviewed. Audit conclusions, if included in the audit report, should be clearly identified as such, and may encompass the entire scope of an audit or specific aspects. They may cover but are not limited to whether program objectives and goals conform with those of the organization, whether those objectives and goals are being met, and whether the activity under review is functioning as intended.

430.05   Reports may include recommendations for potential improvements and acknowledge satisfactory performance and corrective action.

430.05.1   Recommendations are based on internal audit's findings and conclusions and should call for action to correct existing conditions and improve operations. Recommendations may suggest approaches to correcting or enhancing performance as a guide for management in achieving desired results and may be general or specific. It may be appropriate to recommend a general course of action and specific suggestions for implementation or only to suggest further investigation or study.

430.05.2   Auditee accomplishments, including improvements since the last audit or the establishment of well-controlled operations, may be included in the audit re-

port, particularly to fairly represent existing conditions and to provide a proper perspective and appropriate balance to the audit report.

430.06 *The auditee's responses to the audit conclusions or recommendations may be included in the audit report.*

430.06.1 *As part of the conclusion of the audit, internal audit should try to obtain agreement on its results and the plan of action to improve operations, as needed. If internal audit and auditee disagree about the audit results, the audit report may state both positions and the reasons for disagreement. The auditee's written comments may be included as an appendix to the audit report, or alternatively, may be presented in the body of the report or cover letter.*

430.07 *The director of internal auditing or designee should review and approve the final audit report before issuance and decide to whom the report will be distributed.*

430.07.1 *The director of internal audit should approve and sign all final reports, or if circumstances warrant, the auditor-in-charge, supervisor, or lead auditor may sign the report as a representative of the director.*

430.07.2 *Audit reports should be distributed to those who are in a position to take or ensure that corrective actions are taken. The final audit report should be distributed to the head of each audited unit while higher level members in the organization may receive only a summary report. Reports may also be distributed to other interested or affected parties such as external auditors or the board.*

430.07.3 *Information that may not be appropriate for disclosure to all report recipients, because it is privileged, proprietary, or related to improper or illegal acts, may be disclosed in a separate report. If the conditions reported involve senior management, report distribution should be to the audit committee of the board or a similar high level entity within the organization.*

Standard 430 summarizes internal audit's responsibility to report the results of audit fieldwork. Audit findings and conclusions are of little value unless reported to members of management who have the authority to take necessary actions. This very important supporting Standard and its seven supporting guidelines outline the form and content of audit reports as well as the manner of their preparation and distribution. Chapter 15 also discusses internal audit communications procedures, including the preparation of audit reports.

The guidelines emphasize the need for a signed written report plus possible interim reports, written or oral, formal or informal, depending on the significance of the contents and the degree of urgency. The audit report is the primary internal audit work product available to outsiders. Internal audit has a responsibility to issue a final report documenting the conclusions of any audit.

The guidelines here call for a preliminary discussion, with appropriate levels of management at the conclusion of the audit. This very key communications step assures that management has had opportunity to review audit report conclusions and to provide any additional relevant input. The expression ''appropriate levels of management'' is important here. Due to the nature of some audit projects, such as any involving potential fraud or other improper acts, internal audit should review draft report findings with appropriate higher levels of management.

The third guideline describes the four desired qualities of audit reports: to be objective, clear, concise, and timely. The quality that internal audit should incorporate into audit reports should reflect the Standards for due professional care and for the scope of internal auditing work discussed in earlier sections of the Standards.

While many think of an "audit opinion" as something found only in external audit reports, the Standards guideline here (.04) highlights the frequent need for that opinion. Even if there is no formal opinion statement, however, the report's overall conclusions are to some extent an opinion.

In the past, some outside observers have felt that internal auditors should not act as "consultants" to management and should not make recommendations for management actions. While it might be better to recognize that internal auditors should always seek to identify potential improvements, the Standards guideline here encourages appropriate audit recommendations.

The .06 guideline Standard deals with whether the auditee's views about audit conclusions or recommendations should be included in an audit report. Ideally, internal audit should reach agreement with the auditee on all matters, and any remaining areas of disagreement suggest that the auditors may not have adequately reviewed the facts. However, there may be good reasons why an auditee has different views from internal audit and why those different views should be reported. While internal audit and management "may agree to disagree," the application of this guideline needs to be handled with care and objectivity.

The importance of an appropriate supervisory review of the audit report before issuance is emphasized. While there is often a standard report distribution, the unique findings and recommendations from a particular audit may justify a special distribution of all or part of the particular report.

The supporting Standard provides excellent guidance on the development and issuance of audit reports. While we have again condensed the actual IIA standards, this section, along with the discussion in Chapter 15, should help an internal auditor to prepare effective reports at the conclusion of audit assignments.

(iv) Standard 440—Following Up

440.   *Internal auditors should follow up to ascertain that appropriate action is taken on reported audit findings.*

440.01   *Internal audit should determine that corrective action was taken and is achieving the desired results, or that management or the board has assumed the risk of not taking corrective action on reported findings.*

440.01.1   *Internal audit follow-up is a process to determine the adequacy, effectiveness, and timeliness of actions taken by management on reported audit findings, including relevant findings made by external auditors and others.*

440.01.2   *Responsibility for audit report follow-up should be defined in internal audit's written charter.*

440.01.3   *Management is responsible for deciding the appropriate actions taken in response to audit report findings. The director of internal audit is responsible for assessing such management action for the timely resolution of audit findings. In deciding the extent of follow-up, internal auditors should consider similar follow-up nature procedures performed by others in the organization.*

440.01.4   *Senior management may decide to assume the risk of not correcting the re-*

ported condition because of cost or other considerations, but the board should be informed of this action for all significant audit findings.

440.01.5 *The nature, timing, and extent of follow-up should be determined by the director of internal auditing.*

440.01.6 *Factors to be considered in determining appropriate follow-up procedures are: .a) the significance of the reported finding, .b) the degree of effort and cost needed to correct the finding, .c) risks that may occur should the corrective actions fail, .d) the complexity of the corrective action, and .e) the time period involved.*

440.01.7 *Certain reported findings may be so significant as to require immediate action by management; these conditions should be monitored by internal audit until corrected because of their effect.*

440.01.8 *In instances where the director of internal audit judges that management's oral or written response shows that action already taken is sufficient when weighed against the relative importance of the audit finding, follow-up may be performed as part of the next audit.*

440.01.9 *Internal auditors should ascertain that actions taken on audit findings remedy the underlying conditions.*

440.01.10 *The director of internal audit is responsible for scheduling follow-up activities as part of developing work schedules.*

440.01.11 *Scheduling of follow-up should be based on the risk and exposure involved, as well as the degree of difficulty and the significance of timing in implementing corrective action.*

440.01.12 *The director of internal auditing should establish procedures to include the following:*

.a *A time frame within which management's response to the audit findings is required.*

.b *An evaluation of management's response.*

.c *A verification of the audit report response and scheduling a follow-up audit, if appropriate.*

.d *A reporting procedure that escalates unsatisfactory responses/actions, including the assumption of risk, to the appropriate levels of management.*

440.01.13 *Techniques used to effectively accomplish follow-up include:*

.a *Addressing audit report findings to the appropriate levels of management responsible for taking corrective action.*

.b *Receiving and evaluating management responses to findings, with information on corrective actions planned, during the audit or within a reasonable time period after the report is issued.*

.c *Receiving periodic updates from management in order to evaluate the status of efforts to correct previously reported conditions.*

.d *Receiving and evaluating reports from other organizational units assigned responsibility for follow-up procedures.*

.e *Reporting to senior management or the board on the status of responses to audit findings.*

This last specific standard under Performance of Audit Work calls for internal audit to follow up to ascertain that appropriate actions have been taken on reported audit findings. Of course, management may decide not to take the recommended corrective action, but instead assume the related risk. This is a similar issue to that discussed under Standard 340; internal audit has an interest in the utilization of its findings and recommendations and should assist in assuring that utilization in every practicable manner. That assistance must not, however, become so structured, or administered in such a way, that it undermines the basic responsibility of management to give proper consideration to audit results and to take appropriate actions. Of course, appropriate action may, in management's judgment, be no action at all. Typically, management will use one of its regular line or staff components to administer a formal program of monitoring audit responses, actions, and the ultimate clearance of all audit recommendations, including the recommendations of both internal and external auditors. Internal audit should then periodically reappraise the effectiveness of that procedural program. As a part of the next audit, internal audit should also review corrective actions on previous audit reports and incorporate any noncompliance findings in the current audit evaluations. This procedure is consistent with the roles and responsibilities of internal audit and also avoids having internal audit taking on too much of a police image.

(v) Performance of Audit Work Standard in Perspective.   This section on performing audit work focuses on the four sequential phases of an audit: (1) planning the audit, (2) examining and evaluating information, (3) communicating results, and (4) following up. This process, of course, builds on the standards of independence, and as a result, unavoidably overlaps with the Standards on professional efficiency and the scope of work. It is not surprising, therefore, that these Standards occasionally seem to repeat on these same basic points. There are also situations where the coverage of a particular Standard could logically be in either one or another of the other sections. This is not a serious problem, but it does mean that these Standards must be viewed as an integrated whole. Together, the proper base is established for the final section of the Standards, dealing with management of the internal audit department.

(e) GENERAL STANDARD 500: THE MANAGEMENT OF INTERNAL AUDITING

500.   *THE DIRECTOR OF INTERNAL AUDITING SHOULD PROPERLY MANAGE THE INTERNAL AUDITING DEPARTMENT.*

500.01   *The director of internal auditing is responsible for properly managing the department so that: .1) Audit work fulfills the general purposes and responsibilities approved by management and the board, .2) the resources of the internal audit department are efficiently and effectively employed, and .3) all audit work conforms to the Standards for the Professional Practice of Internal Auditing as summarized in the chapter.*

The final section of the Standards concerns the management of the internal auditing department. The mandate included in this Standard is that the director of internal auditing should properly manage that function, subject to the approval of senior management and the audit committee. The director of internal audit has the same responsibilities that exist for all managers—to make effective use of assigned resources. However, in addition, the director must perform audit work that is consistent with these Standards. This ties to earlier statements that the Standards are intended to represent all aspects of the practice of internal auditing.

(i) Standards 510 and 520—Purpose, Authority, Responsibility, and Planning

510.   *The director of internal auditing should have a charter, a statement of purpose, authority, and responsibility for the internal auditing department.*

510.01 *The director is responsible for seeking the approval of management and the board for a formal charter for the internal auditing department.*

520.   *The director of internal audit should establish plans to carry out the responsibilities of the internal audit department.*

520.01 *Audit plans should be consistent with the internal audit's charter and the goals of the organization.*

520.02 *The planning process involves establishing: .1) goals, .2) audit work schedules, .3) staffing plans and financial budgets, and .4) activity reports.*

520.03 *The goals of the internal audit department should be capable of being accomplished within specified operating plans and budgets and, to the extent possible, should be measurable through established criteria and targeted dates of accomplishment.*

520.04 *Audit work plans should include the activities to be audited, audit start times, and estimated time requirements, taking into account the scope of the audit work planned. Matters to be considered in establishing audit plan priorities include: .a) the date and results of the last audit, .b) financial exposures and other risks, .c) requests by management, .d) major changes in operations, programs, systems, and controls, .e) opportunities to achieve operating benefits, and f) changes in the audit staff. The internal audit plan should be sufficiently flexible to cover unanticipated demands or events.*

520.05 *Staffing plans and financial budgets, including the number of auditors and the knowledge, skills, and disciplines required to perform their work, should be determined from audit work schedules, administrative activities, education and training requirements, and audit research and development efforts.*

520.06 *Activity reports, explaining the reasons for major variances and actions taken or needed, should be submitted periodically to management and to the board to compare .a) performance with the department's goals and work schedules and .b) expenditures with financial budgets.*

This section of the Standards establishes the responsibility of the director to have an audit charter, a statement of purpose, authority, and internal audit responsibility. The content of this charter should be consistent with the Standards in total, and should also specify the unrestricted scope of internal audit's work. The charter should state the objectives of internal audit, as stated in the Scope of Work Standard 300.05, including services in the areas of economical and efficient use of resources and the accomplishment of objectives and goals for operations or programs. The charter should be of sufficiently high level in terms of its purpose, authority, and responsibility. Internal audit charters are discussed in Chapter 6.

Planning is the basis for achieving effective results in every organization, and the specific Standard requires the director of internal audit to establish plans to carry out internal audit responsibilities. Those plans should be consistent with the internal audit department and the goals of the overall organization. The planning process includes both establishing goals and establishing a framework for the implementation, as covered in greater detail in Chapter 8 to 15, covering the administration of the internal auditing department.

Guideline .04 of this Standard provides a detailed explanation of the procedures necessary for internal audit's risk assessment process. This section is almost textbook-length and was incorporated into the Standards in 1991, when there was not a great deal of published material on the internal audit risk-assessment process. We have not even included an edited, abridged version of this section here. Rather, the reader can refer to Chapter 7, on evaluating risk, as well as to the actual IIA Standards.

(ii) Standard 530 and 540—Procedures, Human Resource Development

530. *The director of internal auditing should provide written policies and procedures to guide the audit staff.*

530.01 *The form and content of audit policies and procedures should be appropriate to the size and structure of the audit department and the complexity of its work. Formal administrative and technical audit manuals may not be needed by all, and a small internal audit department may be managed informally through daily, close supervision and written memoranda. In a large internal audit department, more formal and comprehensive policies and procedures are essential to guide the staff in the consistent compliance with its standards of performance.*

540. *The director of internal audit should establish a program for selecting and developing internal audit's human resources including: .1) developing written job descriptions for each level of the audit staff, .2) selecting qualified and competent individuals, .3) training and providing continuing educational opportunities, .4) appraising each internal auditor's performance at least annually, and .5) providing counsel to internal auditors on their performance and professional development.*

These specific Standard recognize the importance of both written policies and procedures for guidance to the audit staff, as well as strong human resource policies. The policies and procedures described here can be implemented at either a planning or an implementation level. At the former level, higher-level policies and procedures become the basis for more detailed action plans.

All too often, published standards attempt to fit everyone into the same mold. The IIA standards recognize that larger and smaller organizations have different needs and requirements. This is because in smaller organizations, administrative matters can usually be accomplished through closer supervision, without the need to refer to a detailed set of "rules." Internal audit policies and procedures, in accordance with these Standards, are discussed in Chapter 8, on planning and organizing.

Managerial results are accomplished through people. The director of internal audit, like any manager, must accomplish objectives through people. The human resources–specific Standard calls for the director to establish a program for selecting and developing internal audit human resources. This entire area is covered in Chapters 7 and 9. Several broad observations are, however, appropriate. First, the human resources management process actually begins with the determination of personnel needs for the internal audit department, based on the total needs of the organization; this extends to career planning when individuals leave the internal audit department. This implies that internal audit personnel-management activities should be related to those of the overall organization of which internal audit is a part. In some cases, personnel activities for internal audit are handled by the overall human resources function while in other instances they're handled separately by the internal audit department. In all instances, the policies of the overall organization, such as health benefits and vacations, will apply to internal audit. This means that the director of internal audit must determine what is needed to supplement the policies and procedures of the organization to achieve proper internal audit objectives. At the same time, these activities must conform to established organization policies.

(iii) Standard 550—External Auditors

550. *The director of internal auditing should coordinate internal and external audit efforts.*

550.01 *Internal and external audit work should be coordinated to ensure adequate audit coverage and to minimize duplicate efforts.*

550.01.1 *The scope of internal audit work encompasses both financial and operational objectives and activities while the outside auditors' ordinary examination is designed to obtain sufficient evidential matter to support an opinion on the fairness of the financial statements. The scope of the work of independent or external auditors is determined by their professional standards, and they are responsible for judging the adequacy of procedures performed and evidence obtained for purposes of expressing their opinion on the annual financial statements.*

550.01.2 *Oversight of the work of independent auditors, including coordination with internal audit, is generally the responsibility of the audit committee while actual coordination should be the responsibility of the director of internal auditing. The director of internal audit will require the support of the audit committee to achieve effective coordination of audit work.*

550.01.3 *In coordinating the work of internal and external auditors, the director of internal audit should ensure that work to be performed by internal audit does not duplicate the work of external auditors. To the extent that professional and organizational reporting responsibilities allow, internal auditors should conduct examinations in a manner that allows coordination and efficiency.*

550.01.4 *Internal audit may agree to perform work for external auditors in connection with their annual audit of financial statements, but this work is subject to all relevant provisions of the* Standards for the Professional Practice of Internal Auditing.

550.01.5 *The director of internal audit should make regular evaluations of the coordination between internal and external auditors, including assessments of overall efficiency of the audit work and aggregate audit costs.*

550.01.6 *In exercising its oversight role, the board may ask the director of internal auditing to assess the performance of the independent outside auditors. Any assessment provided by the director of internal audit should be based on sufficient evidence of the efficiency and effectiveness of the work of the external auditors.*

550.01.7 *The director of internal audit should communicate the results of evaluations of this audit coordination to senior management and the board along with any relevant comments about the performance of external auditors.*

550.01.8 *While external auditors may be required by their professional standards to ensure that certain matters are communicated to the board, the director of internal auditing should communicate with external auditors and have an understanding of the issues. These matters may include: a) significant control weaknesses, .b) errors, irregularities, and illegal acts, .c) management judgments and accounting estimates, .d) significant audit adjustments, .e) disagreements with management, and .f) difficulties encountered in performing the audit.*

550.02   *Coordination of audit efforts involves:*

550.02.1 *Periodic meetings to discuss matters of mutual interest and to assure audit coverage is coordinated and duplicate efforts are minimized. Sufficient meetings should be scheduled during the audit to assure coordination of work, and to determine whether findings from work performed to date require that the scope of planned work be adjusted.*

550.02.2 *Access to each other's audit programs and workpapers may be important in order for internal audit to be satisfied in the propriety of relying on the external auditor's work. Such access carries with it the responsibility for internal audit to respect the confidentiality of those programs and workpapers. Similarly, access to the internal auditors' programs and workpapers should be given to the independent outside auditors in order for external auditors to be satisfied of the internal auditors' work.*

550.02.3 *Internal audit reports including management responses and subsequent internal audit follow-up reviews should be made available to external auditors for determining and adjusting the scope of work.*

550.02.4 *The director of internal audit should understand the scope of the work planned by the external auditors and should be satisfied that the independent outside auditors' planned work, in conjunction with internal auditing's planned work, requires an understanding of (a) the best level of materiality used by the independent outside auditors for planning, and (b) the nature and extent of the independent outside auditor's planned procedures.*

    .a *The director of internal audit should ensure that the external auditors' techniques, methods, and terminology are sufficiently understood by internal audit to: i) coordinate the internal and external audit work, ii) evaluate, for purpose of reliance, the external auditors' work, and iii) ensure that internal auditors who are to perform work for external auditors can communicate effectively with them.*

    .b *The director of internal auditing should provide sufficient information to enable external auditors to understand internal auditor techniques, methods, and terminology to facilitate reliance by external auditors on work performed using such work.*

    .c *It may be more efficient for internal and external auditors to use similar techniques, methods, and terminology to effectively coordinate their work and to rely on the work of one another.*

This specific Standard outlines the responsibilities of the director of internal audit to coordinate efforts with external auditors, an area that is becoming increasingly important as external auditors place increasing reliance on the work of internal auditors. Coordination with external auditors, including both these Standards and external auditor standards, is discussed in Chapter 32, while, in addition, Chapter 34 briefly discusses a new and evolving role where an external audit firm takes over the entire internal audit process through what is called *outsourcing*. While the overall coordination of the two audit efforts is often the responsibility of the audit committee, the director of internal auditing has a day-to-day coordination responsibility to assure the best possible two-way coordination of the two audit efforts. A similar responsibility exists for external auditors, and internal auditors working under the supervision of external auditors must also follow these internal audit Standards. While external auditors have their own audit standards (the SAS series), these are not in conflict with the Standards for the Professional Practice of Internal Auditing. Internal auditors should remind their external auditors of these complementary Standards requirements if necessary.

Effective audit coordination begins with advance planning between the two audit groups, internal and external, and also requires the understanding and recognition by each audit group of the other's primary roles and responsibilities. Internal audit should understand these major common interests in understanding the effectiveness of the system of internal accounting control and accept the environment in which two mutually respected partners work together.

Over the years, the relationship between internal and external auditors has been, in some situations, an uneasy truce. This has changed with the AICPA's release of an auditing standard, SAS No. 65, on coordination with internal auditors. Chapter 32 discusses this external audit standard and these IIA Standards guidelines to provide guidance for better coordination of efforts.

(iv) Standard 560—Quality Assurance. The final specific Standard deals with an aspect that has become an important dimension of the internal auditor's Standards for Professional Practice: the establishment of a quality-assurance program to evaluate the effectiveness of the operations of the individual internal auditing department. Although quality is an objective that should always be in the mind of any manager, a formal quality-assurance program provides a definite effort to measure, protect, and generate desired high levels of audit quality. As with many of the later Standards, 560 has been amended through the SIAS process to be almost textbook in length. Here, we only summarize the set of supporting standards covering quality assurance.

560.   *The director of internal auditing should establish and maintain a quality assurance program to evaluate the operations of the internal auditing department.*

560.01   *The purpose of a quality assurance program is to provide reasonable assurance that audit work conforms with these Standards, the internal auditing department's charter, and other applicable standards. A quality assurance program should include the elements of appropriate supervision, internal and external review of internal audit work.*

560.02   *Supervision of the work of the internal auditors should be carried out continually to assure conformance with auditing standards, departmental policies, and audit programs.*

560.03   *Internal reviews should be performed periodically, and in the same manner as any other internal audit, by members of the internal auditing staff to appraise the quality of the audit work performed.*

560.04   *External reviews of the internal audit department should be performed by quali-*
fied independent persons—who do not have either a real or an apparent conflict
of interest—to appraise the quality of its operations. Such reviews should be
conducted at least once every three years, and on completion of a review, a
formal, written report should be issued. The report should express an opinion
as to the department's compliance with the Standards for the Professional Prac-
tice of Internal Auditing and, as appropriate, should include recommendations
for improvement.

The above are only the major, supporting standards covering this important internal audit process. Guidance on the implementation of a formal quality assurance program within the internal audit department, is discussed in Chapter 33.

5-6 INTERNAL AUDIT STANDARDS IN PERSPECTIVE

This chapter has endeavored to provide an understanding of internal auditing as a total professional activity. This understanding can best be achieved through a knowledge of the Standards for the Professional Practice of Internal Auditing as issued by The Institute of Internal Auditors. These Standards are the basis for many of the concepts and practices in internal auditing described in this book. Where appropriate, specific sections of these standards are referenced. However, in many cases the subsequent chapters discuss the practice of modern internal auditing in general without specific section-by-section refer-ences to the Standards.

In using these Standards, subsequent chapters may go beyond them to develop related principles, concepts, and approaches. In so doing, areas may be identified where the coverage in the Standards appears to be incomplete or where further interpretation appears to be needed. Such conditions should be expected when one considers that the Standards were a joint effort of many practitioners and necessarily involved compromise and adjust-ment. However, this in no way detracts from the monumental significance of the Standards and the level of achievement on the part of those who produced them. Further interpreta-tions will be issued over time to cover areas where guidelines may now require definition.

CHAPTER 6

Serving the Audit Committee of the Board

6-1 INTRODUCTION: ROLE OF THE AUDIT COMMITTEE

Prior chapters have discussed fundamentals of control, internal audit's operational approach, and professional standards for internal auditing. A significant first step in the process of organizing an effective internal audit function process is the authorization and approval of the function by the audit committee of the board. It provides broad authorization for internal audit through an audit charter as well as approving internal audit's overall plans for continuing activities through the current period and beyond.

The audit committee is one of several operating committees established by the board of directors and to some extent guided by the full range of board responsibilities. As discussed in Chapter 2, on fundamentals of control, the audit committee has a rather unique role compared to other board committees. It consists of only outside directors—giving it independence from management—and should be composed of a specially qualified group of outside directors who understand, monitor, coordinate, and interpret the internal control and related financial activities for the entire board. In order to fulfill its responsibilities to the overall board of directors and to the stockholders of the organization, an audit committee needs other independent ''eyes and ears'' inside of the organization to provide its board committee members with assessments of internal controls and other matters. While external auditors play this role in attesting to the accuracy and fairness of financial statements, internal audit has an even larger role in assessing controls over the reliability of financial reporting, the effectiveness and efficiency of operations, and the organization's compliance with applicable laws and regulations.

This chapter discusses the expanding role of an audit committee and how internal audit can serve that audit committee. Although the committee has most of its contacts with the director of internal audit, all internal auditors should have an understanding of this very important relationship. This understanding will help both to provide added purpose to internal audit efforts and to allow internal audit to better focus its internal control assessment efforts.

6-2 AUDIT COMMITTEE ORGANIZATION

An audit committee consists of members of the board of directors of the organization. Outside parties who are not stockholder-elected members of the board do not serve on audit committees as voting members. An audit committee is not like a professional or charitable organization where members are selected based upon their service to the organization, financial contributions, or outside reputation. This does not mean that outside persons cannot attend audit committee meetings. An audit committee may invite members of management or others to attend audit committees and even to join in on the committee's deliberations. However, invited outside guests are not voting members.

An organization's board of directors is a formal entity given the responsibility for the overall governance of that organization for its investors or lenders. Because all members of the board can be subsequently questioned and even penalized regarding their actions on any issue, a board tends to enact most of its formal business through resolutions, which become matters of organization record. The organization of the board's various committees, including the audit committee, is established through such a resolution. Figure 6.1 is a sample resolution to establish an audit committee. This type of resolution is documented in the records of the organization and not revised unless some circumstances require a change.

An internal audit director who has questions regarding the authority of an audit committee can secure a copy of the board's authorizing resolution through the corporate secretary or some such responsible officer. Beyond the board-authorizing resolution, an internal auditor should also be interested in the board's membership, the nature and frequency of its meetings, and its overall operating style. With this understanding, the internal audit function in an organization can more effectively serve its audit committee.

(a) MEMBERSHIP

Organizations have no requirements as to the size or makeup of their boards of directors. One corporation may have eight persons on its board of directors while another corporation of similar size and in a similar industry may have 25 persons on its board. Similarly, one organization's board may be composed primarily of corporation insiders, including current and retired officers or members of the original founding family. Other corporations may look to outsiders such as executives from other organizations or persons in law firms or other public organizations. No matter what the board organization structure, the audit committees of publicly traded companies in the United States and many other countries will usually consist of only outside directors.

Investors in and lenders to an organization expect that outside members of a board of directors will serve on its audit committee. This provides them with some protection from improper management actions regarding financial reporting, internal control, or other issues. Those shareholders do not want the CEO and other key officers on an audit committee that receives reports, often of a confidential nature, from internal and external auditors. While those insiders can serve on the overall board, audit- and control-related critical matters should be restricted to the outside directors. Companies listed on the New York Stock Exchange are *required* to have their audit committees be composed of just outside directors. Similarly, banks that operate within the strictures of the Federal Deposit Insurance Corporation Improvement Act (FDICIA) must have only outside directors on their audit committees.

Depending upon the size of the overall board, the audit committee may consist of four or more board members with one designated as the chair. An internal auditor or any investor can identify who serves on the audit committee of an organization by reading its annual report or proxy statement. Membership is always indicated. The chair of the audit

Figure 6.1   Audit Committee Authorization

ExampleCo Corp Board of Directors
Board Resolution No. XX, MM DD, 19YY

The Board of Directors authorizes an audit committee to consist of five directors who are not officers of ExampleCo. The Board will elect one member of the Audit Committee to serve as its chair for a term of three years. The ExampleCo Chief Executive Officer may attend all Audit Committee meetings as a non-voting member at the invitation of the Audit Committee.

The Audit Committee is responsible for:

* Determining that ExampleCo internal controls are effective and reporting on the status of those controls on an annual basis.
* Recommending an outside auditor to be selected on an annual basis through a vote by the shareholders.
* Approving an annual audit plan to be submitted by the outside auditor.
* Approving the appointment and ongoing service of the Director of Internal Auditing.
* Approving the annual internal audit plan and recommending areas for additional audit work as appropriate.
* Reviewing and distributing the audited financial statements submitted by the outside auditor.
* Initiating appropriate actions based upon any recommendations by the outside auditor or the Director of Internal Audit.

An Audit Committee meeting will be held at least concurrently with each Board meeting. The Audit Committee will meet privately with the outside auditor or the Director of Internal Auditing to assess the control environment and to evaluate the independence of the audit function.

Approved: <u>Corporate Secretary</u>

committee is responsible for conducting audit committee meetings and should typically be in close contact with the director of internal audit.

(b) MEETINGS

An audit committee normally meets at about the same time as the formal board of directors meetings. This is because outside directors, in particular, must take time off from their other activities to attend normal board meetings. It is just not efficient for them to fly in for an audit committee on one week and for the full board meeting a week later. Although it is often efficient for audit committees to meet directly before the full board so that they can report any items of interest to the board, audit committees have no requirements either to meet directly before the full board or to meet only at that time. The chair of the audit committee also might call special meetings to investigate matters of particular interest.

An audit committee does have special agenda responsibilities over the course of a financial reporting year. For example, it nominates the outside auditing firm whose selection will be voted on by the shareholders at the annual meeting; it approves the budget and annual plan of the external auditors; finally, it meets with the outside auditors at the conclusion of the fiscal year to review both the results of that audit and the financial statements in the annual report. While these responsibilities would suggest that the audit committee is primarily involved with just the external auditors, internal audit also has a close relationship with the audit committee. The director of internal audit, although not a formal member of the audit committee, typically is involved in virtually all audit committee meetings. In some organizations, the director of internal audit serves as the ex officio secretary of the audit committee, with responsibilities for keeping minutes and helping to arrange the meeting agendas. The director of internal audit can play a very strong role in helping the audit committee achieve its internal control and financial reporting responsibilities.

(c) OPERATING STYLES

As has been emphasized in other chapters, rendering effective internal auditing services always combines both responding to needs expressed by responsible members of the organization and initiating service to cover other perceived needs of those same individuals. This dual approach is especially important in the case of the audit committee. Members typically are busy with their own organizations or other professional careers and often have other company board of director responsibilities. Some members also may be new to this committee task and not certain of their roles. Although each committee will have its own operating style, internal auditors should take the initiative in understanding, expanding, and refining the nature and scope of their service roles to their audit committee.

Admittedly, there may be various types of barriers to developing effective audit committee service roles. In some cases the problem is one of the adequacy of internal audit's basic charter, whereas in others it is one of better implementation of an existing charter. In all instances, the director of internal auditing needs to make audit's service relationship effective with the audit committee, and with the board of which that committee is a part. Internal audit should be flexible and determine the best manner in which to report to the audit committee given the style of its chair and members. Some audit committee members may have served on audit committees for other organizations and become accustomed to certain internal audit reporting styles. Even if it had not been the practice for a given organization, the director of internal audit should modify procedures to meet the collective wishes of the audit committee.

The director of internal audit can often determine the style of the audit committee through a series of meetings or discussions with its chair. Some members may want formal presentations by internal audit at periodic meetings while others may only want the director of internal audit to be present and to respond to questions when asked. If the audit committee does take advantage of the services internal audit can offer, the director of internal audit should make constructive suggestions to improve the flow of important internal control–related information from internal audit to the audit committee.

6-3 AUDIT COMMITTEE RESPONSIBILITIES

The responsibilities of an audit committee can also be best understood by recognizing both the protective and constructive aspects of their roles in organization governance. An audit committee's first responsibility is to protect all board members from developments that are either illegal or otherwise so damaging that they threaten the public standing and welfare of the organization. An organization also must effectively utilize its resources to continue to remain healthy and profitable. Although those broader profitability objectives are the responsibility of the total board, the audit committee shares them. What this means is that the committee must administer its protective role in such a way that it does not unduly inhibit the capability of the organization for profitability. This requires a sensitive blending and balancing of the protective services with broader organization objectives. It is in this area where the relationships with internal audit can be especially helpful.

Through the formal review and approval of an internal audit charter, the audit committee effectively authorizes the internal audit function for the organization and its stockholders. It aids in the nomination of the director of internal audit and provides guidance on where internal audit should focus its review activities. Finally and most importantly, the audit committee acts as a "court of last resort" where internal audit can potentially communicate any concerns that go beyond the responsibilities of senior management in the organization.

(a) INTERNAL AUDIT CHARTER

As discussed in Chapter 1, an adequate internal audit charter serves as a basis or authorization for every effective internal audit program. An adequate charter is particularly important to define the roles and responsibilities of the internal audit group and its responsibility to serve the audit committee properly. It is here that the mission of internal audit must clearly provide for service to the audit committee as well as to senior management. An internal audit charter is a very broad and general document; Figure 6.2 is an example. There is no fixed content or format to an internal audit charter, but it should define the responsibilities of internal audit in very broad terms, describe the standards followed, and define the relationship between the audit committee and internal audit. The latter point is particularly important as it sends a special message to senior management that the director of internal audit can go to a higher authority—the audit committee—in the event of a significant controversy or controls issue.

Who is responsible for drafting this internal audit charter? In theory, perhaps, the audit committee might draft the document as a board committee activity. In reality, the director of internal audit will usually take the lead in drafting this charter and/or suggesting appropriate updates to an existing charter to the chair of the audit committee. While the charter authorizes the work that should be performed by internal audit, the audit committee members may not be in a position to draft detailed audit charter requirements. The director of internal audit typically works closely with the chair of the audit committee to draft this document for audit committee and overall board approval. The organization's external auditors should also have an opportunity to review this document.

In addition to the charter, the specific nature and scope of internal audit's service responsibilities to the audit committee should be formalized and outlined. These responsibilities could include periodic written audit status reports, regularly scheduled meetings with the audit committee, and both the right and obligation of internal audit's direct access

Figure 6.2   Internal Audit Department Charter

ExampleCo Corp. has established a Corporate Internal Audit Department to apprise management and the Audit Committee of the Board of Directors concerning the adequacy and effectiveness of the system of internal controls in all phases of the business. The system of internal controls encompasses the policies, systems, and procedures pertaining to accounting, administration, and operations. The Internal Audit department is charged with the responsibility of independently appraising all phases of the Company's business, and it is authorized unrestricted access to all Company records, properties, and personnel. Internal Audit shall have no direct authority or responsibility for activities they audit. The attainment of the overall Internal Audit Department objectives involves, but is not limited to, activities such as:

- Reviewing and appraising the adequacy and application of accounting, financial, information systems, administrative, and operating controls.
- Reviewing compliance with established policies, plans, procedures, and regulations.
- Ascertaining the reliability and timeliness of management information.
- Performing special analyses and projects for the Audit Committee and management.
- Coordinating the internal and external audit efforts to ensure adequate audit coverage and to minimize duplication of efforts.

The results of the reviews made by the Internal Audit Department, the opinions which they form, and the recommendations which they make will be promptly reported to appropriate management personnel. Management is responsible for resolving reported conditions.

The Corporate Internal Audit Department has sole responsibility for all Corporate internal audit activities. It may authorize separate internal audit functions at individual operating units, but the Corporate Internal Audit Department is responsible for the management, administration, and performance of any separate internal audit functions.

Approved by the Audit Committee
MM DD, YYYY

to the audit committee. While this understanding typically does not require a formal audit committee action or resolution, both parties should have a clear understanding of the responsibilities of internal audit to present reports and to attend audit committee meetings.

The acceptance of the internal audit charter and related provisions by all parties of interest means that internal audit is freed from barriers that might otherwise prevent it from making needed disclosures to the audit committee, even those of a very sensitive nature. In fact, the charter should outline a specific obligation to make such disclosures. This charter statement of internal audit's relationship to the audit committee is especially important since internal audit's day-to-day reporting responsibility is to organization management. That is, senior management typically selects and hires the director of internal audit. All members of the audit team are hired and paid by the organization, not the independent audit committee. Senior management often may forget that internal audit also

Figure 6.3   Internal Audit Reporting Policy

The ExampleCo Corp. Internal Audit Department has a special reporting relationship within the company. The department reports administratively to the Vice President of Administration and reports functionally to the Audit Committee of the Board of Directors, who will approve their annual plans and budget. From time to time, the Audit Committee of the Board may authorize the Internal Audit Department to initiate special projects. The Director of Internal Audit or a designate will present a periodic report on the progress of all internal audit projects as well as significant audit findings and recommendations. The Director of Internal Audit may also meet privately with the Audit Committee of the Board of Directors. These meetings may be initiated by the Audit Committee or by the Director of Internal Audit.

has this special reporting relationship to the audit committee. These activities might be documented in a formal policy statement, developed by internal audit and approved by senior management, which outlines internal audit services to its audit committee. Figure 6.3 provides an example of this type of policy statement, which is particularly important when there are significant changes in management, the composition of the audit committee, or even internal audit management.

The need for an adequate charter or services policy statement is sometimes discounted by organization management on the grounds that there are *no restrictions* to internal audit's independence. An audit charter provision establishing separate, periodic internal audit private meetings with the audit committee may be questioned by management on the grounds that the internal audit function can have such meetings whenever it wants. But without a charter provision mandating audit committee meetings, both sides may be reluctant to schedule formal meetings. Even when such meetings are scheduled, the director of internal audit may be reluctant to speak independently to the audit committee. The director of internal audit needs to have the propriety of this freedom of action formally confirmed. Even if this freedom of action in fact exists, it is important, in terms of long-run organization interests, to protect that freedom from successive management, who might not be similarly inclined.

(b) NOMINATION OF THE DIRECTOR OF INTERNAL AUDIT

The director of internal audit typically reports administratively to organization management. The audit committee does not directly recruit new internal audit directors, nor do they fund the salaries and other expenses of internal audit. The board may only be involved with the audit director's compensation through its compensation committee if the director of internal audit is designated as an officer of the organization. Nevertheless, the audit committee often participates in some manner in the hiring and/or dismissal of the internal audit director. The objective here is not to deny organization management the right to name the person who will administer the internal auditing department, which serves the combined needs of organization management and the audit committee. Rather, the significance of the audit committee's participation is to provide mutual assurances that there will be good internal audit services to satisfy their needs. At the same time, this participation better assures the independence of the internal audit function when there is a need to speak out regarding issues identified in the review and appraisal of internal controls and other organization activities.

The actual participation of the audit committee in the selection of the audit director can take a number of forms but typically involves a review of the proposed director's credentials followed by a formal written concurrence to organization management. At a minimum, organization management—often the CFO—advises the chair of the audit committee of any intended actions regarding the director of internal audit, allowing the audit committee time to review and comment before the personnel change is actually made. In most situations, the audit committee defers to management's decision.

In many instances, the organization will be faced with the need to name a new director of internal auditing because the existing director has resigned or has been promoted. This is a relatively easy task for all concerned. Management may elect to promote someone from within the organization or to recruit an outsider. Agreement on the adequacy of the qualifications to serve the needs of both management and the board of directors is an essential condition of an ongoing effective relationship between senior management and the audit committee. This aspect of that ongoing relationship warrants the most careful kind of joint review and discussion.

This participative role should also extend to actions involving the outgoing director of internal auditing. In many cases, the incumbent may be receiving a promotion or given a planned exposure to other organization responsibilities as a part of a management-development program. In other instances, the director may be transferred or terminated because of the unwillingness of management to accept the impact of a sound internal auditing approach. In the latter situation, the audit committee should review the particular planned personnel action. In this way, the audit committee provides an opportunity for the affected director to have a fair hearing on the issues involved, and the audit committee is thus better protected from potentially significant internal control deficiencies.

The audit committee may feel that the director of internal audit is not doing an adequate job in either complying with the audit committee's requests or in directing the internal audit function, or both. This is certainly an extreme situation that rarely occurs. In such a case, the chair of the audit committee typically expresses those concerns to organization management and suggests a change in personnel. In an extreme case where management disagrees with the audit committee regarding the director of internal audit, the audit committee can always hire an outsider to perform the audit review work desired by the committee or can direct management, through board directives, to make a change. The most common result of this type of disagreement, however, is that other parties—such as the external auditors—will see the same problem and changes will be made.

(c) APPROVAL OF INTERNAL AUDIT PLANS AND BUDGETS

As previously discussed, the audit committee should ideally have developed an overall understanding of the total audit needs of the organization. This high-level appraisal covers various special control and financial-reporting issues, allowing the audit committee to determine the portion of audit needs to be performed by either the internal or external auditors. This committee decision is consistent with its role as the ultimate coordinator of the total audit effort. At the same time, organization management may have its own ideas about the total audit effort and how it should be carried out. In addition, the director of internal auditing has views as to what needs to be done. It is therefore essential that the varying views of the key parties be jointly considered and appropriately reconciled.

Normally also, that overall reconciliation will include the decisions as to the scope of external audit's review and their related fees.

The review of all audit plans by the committee is essential if the policies and plans for the future are to be determined most effectively. Of equal importance, all interested parties should understand the nature of the total audit plan so that they have a basis for later involvement in the implementation of those plans. Organization management, internal auditors, and external audit alike then will know what to expect from the suppliers of audit services. The committee also then can assume a high-level coordination role. Although there are practical limitations as to how actively the audit committee can become involved in the detailed planning process, some involvement has a demonstrated high value. Typically, the chair of the audit committee is the most active person in this plan review, but even this person is subject to time limitations.

Internal audit should prepare a comprehensive set of annual planning documents for the committee which give detailed plans for the upcoming year as well as longer range plans for the future. Suggested formats for these documents are discussed in Chapter 7, on risk analysis, and Chapter 8, on planning audit activities. In addition, internal audit should prepare a summarized report of past audit activities and reassessments of its coverage to give the audit committee an understanding of significant areas covered in past reviews. Although internal audit should report its activities to the audit committee on a regular basis, this summary report of past activity gives an overview of past areas for audit emphasis as well as highlighting any potential gaps in audit coverage. Figure 6.4 is an example of a past audit activities report for a multi-unit organization, and Figure 6.5 is a one-year audit plan for presentation to the audit committee. The director of internal audit presents these types of reports to the committee, prepared to answer questions and to discuss their supporting details. The summary report on past activities is particularly important in that it shows the areas that had been scheduled in the prior year's plan and the accomplishments against that plan.

In many organizations, the annual audit plan is developed through both internal audit's risk analysis process and discussions with both senior management and the audit

Figure 6.4 Audit Committee Past Audit Activities

Unit	Audit	Status	Audit Rpt #
WhizBang Sales Div.	Sales Commissions Procedures	Completed 1st Qtr	A-6604
WhizBang Sales Div.	Order Entry System	Scheduled 3rd Qtr	
WhizBang Sales Div.	EDI Customer Contracts	Postponed	
Axylotl Manufacturing	Work in Process Inventory	Completed 1st Qtr	A-6703
Axylotl Manufacturing	Plant Security	In Process	
Axylotl Manufacturing	Annual Physical Inventory Observation	Scheduled 4th Qtr	
Axylotl Manufacturing	Special Audit: Components Fraud	Completed 2nd Qtr	Special
SE Asia Operations	Assembly Plant Operations Review	In Process	
SE Asia Operations	New Systems Preimplementation	Cancelled	

Figure 6.5 Internal Audit Annual Plan Example

EXAMPLECO CORPORATION 1997 SUMMARIZED AUDIT PLAN

Division	Audit	Risk Rank	Est. Start	Planned Finish	Total Hours	Total Costs	Comments
Electro	Inv. Planning Cntrls.	8.4	11/10/96	03/05/97	500	$1,200	Carry-over—'96
Electro	Phys. Inv. Observation	9.5	01/20/97	02/15/97	90	$2,600	
Electro	B-Plant Security	7.4	02/15/97	03/31/97	220	$900	Physical & Logical Security
Electro	Materials Receiving	6.2	04/22/97	05/25/97	520	$1,200	Operational Assessment
Electro	Procurement Controls	6.8	07/25/97	10/05/97	340	$200	Operational & I/S
Electro	New Marketing System	7.8	09/20/97	01/15/98	440		I/S Review Thru 1998
Electro	Q/A Lab. Controls	5.9	04/15/97	06/01/97	290	$1,200	Operational Review
Distribution	EDI Order Controls	9.1	03/25/97	05/20/97	520	$250	First Audit of Process
Distribution	Whse. Physical Security	7.9	08/10/97	09/25/97	90	$120	Operational Controls
Distribution	Factory Labor Reporting	8.2	10/20/97	11/15/97	470	$290	Financial Controls
Distribution	Product Incentive System	5.8	04/25/97	06/15/97	200		Audit Committee Request
Distribution	Prod. Warranty Returns	6.7	08/10/97	10/15/97	310		Operational Controls
Distribution	LAN Contingency Planng.	7.9	11/10/97	12/15/97	190		
Distribution	A/R Control Proced.	9.2	11/05/97	02/20/98	440	$80	1997 Hours Only
Asia Pacific	G/L System Integrity		05/20/97	06/30/97	360	$3,600	First Review of Unit
Asia Pacific	Labor Relations Stds.		06/10/97	06/30/97	180	$3,600	First Review of Unit
Asia Pacific	Mfg. Control System		05/05/97	06/30/97	300	$3,600	First Review of Unit
Corporate	Government Relations Dpt.		10/15/97	11/20/97	250		COSO Related Review
Corporate	Ext. Audit Yr. End Support		01/20/97	04/12/98	440	$400	1997 Hours Only
Corporate	Construction Contracts		05/15/97	07/25/97	580		Major Plant Review
Total Direct	Internal Audit				6730	$19,240	
Non-Audit	Holidays & Vacation				880		
Non-Audit	Company & Staff Meetings				210	$500	
Non-Audit	Training				160	$8,200	
Non-Audit	Audit Administration				440	$1,500	
Total Planned 1997 Internal Audit Hours					8420	$29,440	

committee. Management and the committee may suggest areas for potential internal audit review. Audit will then develop plans within the constraints of budget and resource limitations. If the audit committee has suggested a review of some specialized area but internal audit is unable to perform the planned audit due to some known constraints, the director of internal audit should clearly communicate that deficiency to the audit committee.

(d) PARTICIPATION IN INTERNAL AUDIT BUDGETARY AUTHORIZATION

The kind of broad planning just discussed provides the basis for the presentation and approval of the annual budget for internal audit. Normally, that budget is a part of the total organization budgetary process and is administered under the same rules as for all organization components. This budget phase is important because now the levels of spending for personnel and related auditing service activities are precisely established. The audit committee therefore needs to satisfy itself that resources actually committed by management are consistent with the previously agreed upon policies and plans. The budgetary process is also important because it provides the format within which internal audit activities during the year are to be reported and controlled. The committee can thus establish itself in a meaningful monitoring and audit-coordination role in the budgetary process. The audit committee and the director of internal auditing can now understand each other's needs and relate effectively to each other.

The director of internal audit should present this budget at about the same time as the annual plan is presented to the audit committee. If management has restricted audit activities through budget restraints, the director of internal audit should present these concerns to the audit committee in a scheduled private meeting, as discussed below. While the audit committee does approve the budget, they can communicate any of their questions or concerns to proper members of senior management.

6-4 INTERNAL AUDIT SERVICES TO THE AUDIT COMMITTEE

The preceding paragraphs discussed the responsibilities of the audit committee to authorize and govern the internal audit function. Once constituted through the internal audit charter and once staffed and fully organized, internal audit can perform important services to the audit committee to aid them in their organization governance role. Most of these cover internal audit's role as being a set of ''eyes and ears'' for the committee to monitor internal controls and to report significant concerns to them. These services are typically performed by internal audit in their meetings with the committee as well as through periodic reports. In addition, internal audit may perform special reviews or investigations under the direct supervision of the committee, participate in activities with the external auditors, and make recommendations to the committee regarding external and internal audit coordination.

(a) SCHEDULED AUDIT COMMITTEE MEETINGS

Normally, the audit committee holds a number of scheduled meetings during the year. In some organizations the director of internal auditing attends all meetings while in others the director may be asked to attend only specific meetings. The latter situation is an exception in the modern organization. As discussed previously, the director of internal auditing often acts as the secretary of those audit committee meetings, an arrangement that assures a close tie between the audit committee and internal audit. Ideally, the director of internal auditing should attend all meetings, but there will sometimes be portions of individual meetings when the committee will wish to excuse all and/or specific parties.

As discussed, a variety of parties, including members of senior management and external audit, may be invited to attend audit committee meetings. At least once a year, the director of internal audit should meet alone with the committee for an open discussion on audit issues and concerns. In this meeting, the director of internal audit can discuss any concerns or answer any committee questions in a frank and open manner without being concerned with offending management. The director can discuss any constraints that may have been placed over internal audit through budget limitations or audit scope restrictions. If an organization's audit committee does not have these regularly scheduled meetings with the director, the need for these meetings should be privately discussed with the chair of the audit committee.

Because the internal and external auditors have so many common interests and potential activity overlaps, the two audit groups will participate jointly in some of the audit committee meetings. In some cases, these joint meetings will be initiated by the audit committee as a part of its basic audit integration responsibility; at other times, the initiative may come from the CEO or CFO. In still other cases the initiative will come from the internal and external auditors themselves. Chapter 32 discusses approaches for effective coordination between the internal and external auditors, leading in many instances to joint reviews and presentations by the two audit groups.

(b) PERIODIC REPORTS TO AUDIT COMMITTEE DURING THE YEAR

The extent of the formal reporting during the year to the audit committee by internal audit can vary considerably based upon committee operating styles. In some instances, the audit committee receives a copy of all reports covering completed audits. Since copies of all completed audit reports can result in a large volume of materials, executive summaries of each report are more typically distributed to the committee. In still other instances, internal audit develops summary reports of its audits on a quarterly, semiannual, or annual basis. Such reports can cover both audit activity statistics and highlights of audit findings and recommendations. These reports should keep the committee informed of significant audit findings, the extent to which the audit plan is being achieved, and the reasons for any significant variance from that plan. Normally, these reports are for information only and the committee would expect internal audit to bring to its specific attention anything requiring special consideration or action by the committee or its chair. Figure 6.6 is an example of such a quarterly report.

Periodic summarized reports of internal audit activities enable the audit committee to ask appropriate questions regarding internal control developments. The total internal audit reporting to the audit committee should be a combination of written and oral presentations in sufficient depth to keep the committee properly informed. Such ongoing communication is particularly important in more critical situations when the support of the audit committee is specifically needed. Internal audit's relationship with the committee should be developed and consistently maintained both to satisfy current needs and to serve as a foundation for potentially serious developments. The internal audit director needs to assume this responsibility for maintaining an adequate relationship with the committee.

(c) EXTERNAL AUDITOR NOMINATIONS AND PLAN APPROVALS

The audit committee is responsible for the nomination of the organization's external auditors. The recommendation is communicated to shareholders through the annual proxy statement. The shareholders will then have the opportunity to confirm that external auditor

Figure 6.6 Audit Committee Quarterly Report Example

ExampleCo Corporation

Audit Committee of the Board of Directors

Internal Audit Quarterly Activities—March 31, 20XX

Regularly Planned Audits Completed During Period
  4 Scheduled Field Operations Reviews Completed—Reports Issued
  2 Scheduled Field Operations Reviews Completed—Responses Due
  1 Scheduled Year End Audit Completed—No Report

Audits Completed Due to Special Request
  1 Inventory Observation Completed—External Audit Request

Audits Scheduled and Not Completed
  2 Manufacturing Operations Review Still in Process
  1 Information Systems Security Review Still in Process

Planned Audits Canceled
  2 New Fixed Asset Accounting System Audits Canceled—New Automated System
    Postponed to 4th Qtr.
  1 Retirement System Audit Postponed—Personnel Shortage

Status of Audits Remaining from Prior Period
  4 Audits Still Open—Awaiting Report Responses
  2 Prior Quarter Audits in Process
  1 Audit Canceled—Operating Unit Closed

Audit Department Personnel Status
  Authorized head count—1 Jan   37
  Actual head count—1 Jan   35
  Resignations / Transfers   3
  New Hires   1
  Head count 31 March   33

---

selection. Once the external audit firm has been selected through a vote of the shareholders at the annual meeting, the audit committee approves the external audit firm's annual plans as well as its budget recommendations for the entire audit effort. That annual budget often includes an allowance for the number of hours internal audit will be expected to supply for the external auditors. Recommendations and observations regarding the nominations of external auditors and the approval of the annual external audit plan are areas where internal audit can provide significant support and service to the audit committee.

Organizations tend to keep the same auditing firm on a regular, continuing basis. They will typically only recommend changes in their external auditors if there has been some substantial disagreement regarding audit or accounting issues, annual audit fees, or general management disagreements regarding the external audit services. Although they are asked to vote on the external auditors, it is extremely unusual for the shareholders to reject the external auditor nomination. In the United States, any changes in auditors and the reasons for such changes must be reported to the SEC. As a result, organizations are reluctant to change their external auditors. Even if the published report to the SEC regarding the change in auditors states that the existing firm was dropped for totally valid reasons, investors may question whether there were other issues not disclosed.

Internal and external auditors often work closely together as partners in the audit efforts for the organization. Both have their own separate as well as mutual objectives. Because they are jointly responsible for the overall audit process, internal audit should not normally keep track of the external auditors and report problems regarding their services to the audit committee. However, the director of internal audit may be asked from time to time to comment on the performance of the external auditors. This is particularly true if the committee feels that they are not receiving adequate services from their external auditors. Internal audit may be asked to comment on the external auditor's level of service during internal audit's private audit committee meetings. Internal audit's assessments here should be done with fairness. Per auditing standards, the external auditors are required to comment on the adequacy of the internal auditors on a periodic basis. Little will be accomplished if one group just comments on perceived problems with the other.

A much more important area where internal audit can serve the audit committee is in a detailed review of the external auditor's proposed audit plan and budget. The director of internal audit can perform a significant service to the audit committee by reviewing this annual plan and suggesting areas where the external auditors have failed to recognize a similar internal audit review in a proposed area, situations where external audit has reviewed an area in the past and found no problem, or cases where external audit is not making the best use of its resources. Regarding the latter, external audit firms sometimes advertise some new labor-saving software package they have developed, but then do not use it on the particular engagement. Members of the audit committee do not necessarily review this type of material or make these connections. Internal audit can serve the audit committee by pointing out these discrepancies.

While internal audit does not have a direct responsibility for selecting the external auditors or for approving its proposed budget, internal audit is close enough to this process to advise the audit committee. While the chair of the committee—an outside director—will often defer to the counsel of the partner responsible for the external audit engagement, internal audit can potentially be an important influence.

(d) SPECIAL ASSIGNMENTS FROM THE AUDIT COMMITTEE

The regular internal program carried out for management should at the same time fully serve the interests of the audit committee. Nevertheless, situations may arise when the audit committee initiates special audit assignments. This often occurs when the committee feels that management has not appropriately managed a situation and when a special review is needed. Because the committee has no staff of its own, they often in these situations look either to the external or internal auditors for such further audit services. Although these assignments are more typically given to external auditors, the performance of such supplementary work by internal audit is in no sense inconsistent with the fact that the primary responsibility of internal audit is to internal management.

Typically, supplementary audit assignments are requested by the audit committee if there is a suspicion of management fraud or some other malfeasance. This type of fraud investigation review is discussed in Chapter 31. Other special reviews may result from other audit committee initiatives and will be known to all parties, including senior management. These special assignments are exceptions and generally not of enough frequency or magnitude to handicap internal audit in carrying out its regular program. In the event of such a request, the director of internal audit should demonstrate a willingness to satisfy such supplementary audit committee needs.

(e) OTHER COMMUNICATIONS BETWEEN THE AUDIT COMMITTEE AND THE INTERNAL AUDIT

An important aspect of the internal auditing services rendered to the audit committee is the open communication between the chair of the committee and the director of internal auditing whenever there are questions that need to be answered or significant information to be shared. This continuing availability is basic to an effective utilization of internal auditing services by the committee. What is needed is that the chair of the committee clearly declare a desire for this kind of relationship and then demonstrate support by communicating with the director of internal audit from time to time. The director then should feel an obligation to keep the audit committee chair properly informed.

At the same time, the committee must demonstrate to management that this kind of continuing contact is maintained with internal audit. However, the internal audit organization should not unduly burden the audit committee with matters that should properly be resolved with management. What is important is establishing an atmosphere where all parties of interest understand that internal audit is expected by the audit committee to keep it informed and to communicate with the chair whenever the total organizational welfare can be best served.

(f) EVALUATION OF INTERNAL AUDIT SERVICES

Scheduled year-end reports and meetings provide an appropriate time for the audit committee to look back over the year and to make summary judgments as to the overall effectiveness of the internal auditing services provided. The results of an internal audit quality assurance review, as will be discussed in Chapter 33, can be a very useful input to the audit committee. These evaluations can also become important inputs for determining optimum internal audit budget levels as well as the rank and compensation of the director of internal auditing, a matter in which the audit committee and its chair should also participate.

Internal audit should recognize the committee's need for this kind of in-depth evaluation and welcome all types of useful input generated from the committee. Indeed, when internal audit has adequate confidence in the quality of its performance, it should welcome every possible opportunity for encouraging the various types of cross-evaluation. At the same time, internal audit will better achieve all possible improvements in services.

6-5 AUDIT COMMITTEE MEETING FORMATS

The choice of format and frequency of reporting will be the decision of the audit committee. However, the director of internal audit can often play a major role in influencing the audit committee as to what they should seek for internal audit reporting. The audit committee should not be burdened with too much minutiae but should have sufficient detail to understand important control issues.

Internal audit summary level reports can cover both activity statistics and highlights from selected audits, including significant findings and recommendations. Figure 6.6 is an example of one of many alternative formats. In any case, the audit committee should be kept informed as to the extent to which the audit plan is being achieved, the reasons for any major variances from that plan, and significant audit findings. In addition to the periodic summary reports, internal audit may want to develop a summary report of significant audit findings, which describes the findings and ongoing corrective actions to remedy the audit finding. Figure 6.7 is an example of this type of significant findings report. Normally, these audit activity summary and significant findings reports are for information only and the audit committee would expect the director of internal audit to call specific attention to any matter requiring special consideration or audit committee action. These reports enable the audit committee to raise questions of any kind relative to the audit developments.

The total extent of reporting to the audit committee of course needs to be a combination of written and oral presentations and in such depth as will keep them properly informed. Such ongoing communication becomes all the more important in more critical situations when the support of the audit committee is specifically needed. All this means that a relationship with the committee needs to be developed and consistently maintained both to satisfy current needs and as a foundation for more serious developments. The director of internal audit needs to recognize this responsibility for maintaining an adequate relationship with the audit committee.

6-6 ACHIEVING EFFECTIVE AUDIT COMMITTEE RELATIONSHIPS

An understanding of the underlying needs of the audit committee and related internal auditing services, together with a review of the operational components of those services, are not in themselves enough. To make them all work in an effective manner also requires

Figure 6.7   Audit Committee Significant Audit Findings Status

ExampleCo Corporation

Audit Committee of the Board of Directors

Internal Audit Significant Audit Findings—May 31, 20XY

Status of Findings Reported in Prior Periods

- Jan XX—Disaster recovery plans have not been tested   —Open
- Jul XX—Physical security of abc plant poor   —Final rest
- Oct XX—Federal form S-1's not completed   —Corrected
- Nov XX—Poor project planning for Maxx Div   —In process
- Poor accounting controls over plant scrap   —Corrected

New Significant Audit Findings Added

- Mar XY—Poor controls over new WIP system   —Open
- Mar XY—Federal EEOC reports not filed   —Open

a combination of understanding, competence, and cooperation by all of the major parties of interest—internal audit, management, external auditors, and the audit committee itself. Senior management, from the CEO on down, needs to recognize that their own interests are best served when internal audit fully serves audit committee needs, even though the primary reporting responsibility of internal audit is to the CEO or CFO. Total organizational welfare then becomes the standard by which to judge all internal audit services, as opposed to more provincial views that the interests of management and the audit committee may be to some extent conflicting.

The same considerations apply for the organization's CFO but go beyond to include the possible direct interests of that officer. This sometimes causes difficult situations because an organization's CFO has traditionally thought of internal audit as part of the CFO's own domain. In the case of the audit committee, which may be viewed through the eyes of its chair, a similar need exists to view overall auditing activity in terms of total organization interests. This means that the audit committee must understand management's operational needs and not be unduly motivated by its own often narrower protective needs. This somewhat statesmanlike approach avoids excessive control over internal auditing services, including any belief that the primary reporting role of that group should run to the audit committee.

In the case of the independent public accountant, a somewhat different situation exists. Here too, external audit needs to see its own self-interest as best achieved through total client organization welfare. Quite clearly, independent public accountants must protect their own primary responsibilities, including the adequacy of their audit procedures and the integrity of their independent opinion. External auditors need at the same time to understand the other organizational objectives fully and to work cooperatively toward their maximum achievement. They must also at times take a statesmanlike view of their own professional interests and resist shorter-range revenue potentials that might not be properly justified over the long run.

Internal auditors, and especially the director of internal auditing, must have both the technical competence and the broader capabilities to work effectively with all parties of interest at all levels. In these relationships, internal audit needs to demonstrate its own dedication to total organization welfare as opposed to the special interests of the internal audit organization. All interested parties should be kept informed of the potential impact of activities that internal audit is pursuing. Internal audit rights, established by charters and supporting policy statements, should be used with care and made more acceptable through adequate coordination. Internal audit is certainly entitled to the kind of independence that allows for a full range of auditing services in accordance with the highest professional standards. It is important to recognize, however, that such power improperly used endangers the substance of that power and instead generates hostility and resistance. Most important, such a misuse of authority and power gets in the way of accomplishing overall needed results and thus deprives the organization of valuable benefits. The special challenge to internal audit is to focus on the right priorities and administer relationships in a manner that will continue to command respect and cooperation.

6-7   SERVING AUDIT COMMITTEES IN PERSPECTIVE

The broad acceleration of social expectations, the resulting impact on the areas of organization responsibility, and the related growth of audit committees have generated new and expanded needs for the organization. As a result, there are new and expanding needs for internal auditing services that constitute both challenges and opportunities for internal auditors. There is especially the greater emphasis on the evaluations of internal control, as was discussed in Chapter 2, as well as protective services caused by COSO and the Foreign Corrupt Practices Act. The overall challenge to internal auditors is to understand these needs and to develop the composite capabilities of dealing with them effectively. Because of these new opportunities and challenges, the modern internal auditor should understand audit committee needs and how to provide effective services to them. Internal auditors should both respond to those existing service needs and at the same time help shape the roles of audit committees as part of an overall objective to provide maximum service to the organization.

CHAPTER 7

Evaluating Organization and Audit Risk

7-1 UNDERSTANDING RISK

Earlier editions of this book did not discuss risk in depth. Internal auditors have always encountered some level of risk in their work, whether it be the risk that the auditor will review some materials and miss a significant error, that the auditor may decide not to review some entity or process even though it turns out to have significant problems, or that the auditor may fail to report some significant control weakness due to poor audit procedures or a mistake. While internal auditors always understood that they faced these issues when performing reviews, they often viewed them as singular mistakes rather than looking at the entire situation from the perspective of risk.

This chapter discusses risk and how to assess it when performing actual audit tests or when making a decision of which area to audit, given a large selection of audit candidates and limited resources. Understanding the concept of risk can help internal audit to better determine which areas to include in a review, where to concentrate audit resources when performing reviews in some areas, and how better to report to management the results of the audit work performed. Some background is given on the concept of risk along with the various types of risk an auditor will encounter when performing audits and developing conclusions, and how to consider risk when building an audit plan, deciding which areas to review, and reviewing audit evidence.

(a) CHANCE, CHOICE, AND DEFINITION OF RISK

Although the concept of risk is originally Italian in origin, it came to England from France in the seventeenth century and to the United States in the early 1800s. Originally, the French spelling *risqué* and the English word *risk* were used interchangeably. The former, of course, now refers to rather ribald language or actions that risk offending someone.

The dictionary definition of risk is "to expose to chance of injury or loss"; in other words, we face some level of risk every time we become involved in an activity where we might incur a loss. While management may not directly punish an internal auditor if there has been some mistake in an internal audit review, all audit conclusions contain some risks both for the auditor making the assessment and for the overall organization. The injury or loss may be to the auditor's professional credentials and reputation as well as to the overall organization.

In general, actions or decisions do not present risks unless there is *some loss* associated with making the wrong decision or taking the wrong action. An organization that makes an investment in a new plant or new venture faces the possibility that it may lose money, reputation, or both. Therefore, that investment is considered risky. If the company had invested cash in U.S. government bonds, for example, there would be no question as to the outcome of that decision and no risk. If we know the outcome of an action *for certain,* we are not taking a risk.

Risks in general or a loss in particular is dependent upon one's point of view. While some people may be concerned with the consequences of a risk, others may view the same situation and either see no risk or see very little to be concerned about. Posted highway automobile speed limits are an example of this difference in perception. Back when the United States had the nationwide 55 miles per hour (mph) speed limit, some risk-averse drivers consistently drove within this limit even though they were driving on highways designed for much higher speeds and even though most drivers on the same highways were operating their cars at higher speeds. Others drove in the fast lane and above 55 mph, passing legal-limit drivers and seeing no risk in driving beyond the posted limits. Because almost everyone was driving somewhat faster than 55 mph, the police usually just ignored all but the really high-speed drivers. The point here is that not everyone views risks in the same manner. While some may be worried about the consequences of their actions, others see no risk and take advantage of a situation.

Another key concept necessary to understand risk is to recognize that there will always be a chance associated with the risk. Because a citation and fine might result if one was stopped for driving beyond that 55 mph limit—although the drivers also realized that there were hardly ever any highway patrol officers in a given stretch of highway—the driver always faced an uncertainty about whether a police officer just might be parked on the road and just might stop some car for speeding traveling above 55 mph. Because the driver did not have complete information about possible outcomes from speeding, there was an element of chance in this process. Similarly, a company can place its funds in AAA-rated corporate bonds rather than U.S. Treasury securities. Although the risk is small in the short run, there is a *chance* that one of those AAA companies will go bankrupt and not redeem the investment. In the longer term, those risks are much greater. One need only look at a list of Fortune 500 companies of perhaps 50 or 75 years ago to see those risks. Many of that earlier era, such as Baldwin Locomotive, have long since dissolved.

While it is easy to say that there is uncertainty surrounding nearly all decisions and all risky decisions in particular, the auditor should have a better understanding of this uncertainty and its implications. When dealing with risky situations, the internal auditor faces different levels and types of uncertainty. There are three basic types of uncertainty surrounding risky decisions:

1. *Descriptive or Structural Uncertainty.* The auditor does not have complete information about all of the variables that should be considered when reviewing some area. Even though reviews of documentation or interviews provide considerable data or audit evidence, there is always the uncertainty that the internal auditor will miss something. This situation is true when an auditee does not want to reveal certain "bad news" to an internal auditor. Even though the auditor has asked twenty questions and received correct if vague answers for each, that twenty-first question might reveal the problem.

2. *Measurement Uncertainty.* We are often uncertain about how good or bad the audit

results are. It is sometimes easy for an internal auditor to view certain audit evidence as presenting no problem even though a different summary and analysis of that same material could point to a significant error. We sometimes lack the tools or the complete knowledge to measure the results properly.

3. *Event Outcome Uncertainty.* Even though an internal auditor may have gathered an appropriate level of audit evidence, limited the structural uncertainty, and limited the measurement uncertainty through a detailed review of the materials, the conclusions drawn from the audit work may still be uncertain. Internal auditors sometimes make recommendations without full knowledge of what will happen if they are carried out to the letter. Experienced auditors have often looked at the results of audit recommendations made in the past and found that the results were not as expected.

These three factors should be included when examining the uncertainty associated with risk. While an internal auditor will never have complete knowledge, an audit project should start with some knowledge and certainty. An internal auditor will almost always have some information about a situation and will not start an audit assignment in the dark. Audits often start somewhere in the middle of this spectrum and move toward greater certainty during the audit. Even when the audit has been completed, the internal auditor will not have complete knowledge but will have moved closer to that status than before the audit started. Figure 7.1 shows this spectrum in an audit situation. On the far left, there is complete uncertainty.

The third important concept behind risk is *choice.* While we are all exposed to certain levels of risk, such as ''act of God'' events where there really is no choice, an internal auditor normally can select from a variety of choices when making audit decisions. If an auditor chooses to review 100 percent of the evidence, any conclusion based on this evidence will entail very low risk, assuming the auditor understands the evidence gathered and the expected results from the audit recommendations. However, that 100 percent examination destroys audit efficiency. An auditor needs to accept some risk when making

Figure 7.1 Spectrum of Audit Uncertainty

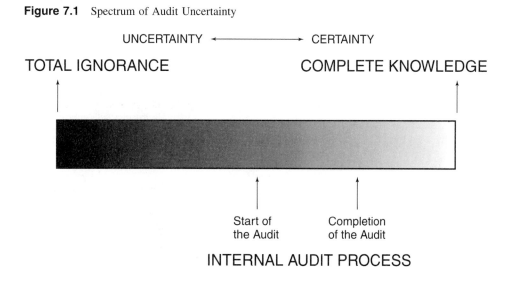

UNCERTAINTY ←——————→ CERTAINTY

TOTAL IGNORANCE   COMPLETE KNOWLEDGE

Start of   Completion
the Audit   of the Audit

INTERNAL AUDIT PROCESS

a choice of how much evidence to examine. This concept of choice extends to all risk-based decisions. If we do not have a choice to accept or reject some decision that might result in a loss, we are not facing a risk.

These three elements that define risk—the associated loss, the uncertainty element, and a choice of alternatives—always should be considered, whether in an internal audit–related situation or in a wider range of other business or personal matters.

(b) RISK ANALYSIS AND THE INTERNAL AUDITOR

Internal auditors face a level of risk in all elements of their work. The two most important areas where an internal auditor encounters risk are in deciding which areas to select for audit and, having made that decision, how to interpret appropriately the results of the audit evidence gathered. In other areas, an internal auditor needs to know the risks associated from alternative actions, the probability of losses from those actions, alternative actions to reduce or eliminate risks, and other risks associated with the alternatives. In order to understand these options better, the effective internal auditor should go through a process called risk analysis, where the auditor looks at the various alternative risks, considers the probabilities of those various risks occurring, and selects alternatives that have only the most acceptable risks.

Figure 7.2 describes this process of risk analysis. This is the same basic process used by the defense industry and in other processes requiring making decisions when faced with multiple alternatives. Often, this risk analysis flowchart approach is coupled with detailed tables of alternative probabilities on what can go wrong, the likelihood of the alternative events happening, and an evaluation of potential damage if events do go

Figure 7.2   Risk Analysis Process

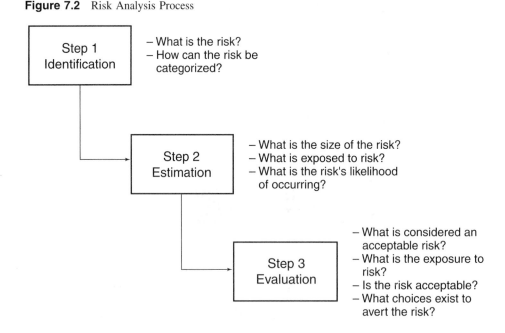

wrong. A numbers-oriented, specific probability-based approach to risk analysis will be introduced later in this chapter. While a detailed probability and mathematical approach is useful for some internal audit activities, it is normally sufficient for an internal auditor just to remember the general process of categorization, estimation, and evaluation of results.

The risk-analysis process in Figure 7.2 uses very general measures to help an auditor sort out alternatives. Step 2 in this figure asks the auditor to estimate the risk's likelihood of occurrence. While we can assign specific probability values here, those measures also can be stated in rather vague terms such as ''Probably not a problem,'' ''This may cause a problem,'' or ''This could cause trouble!'' The whole idea is not to get buried in details but to understand how to go through this type of formal risk-analysis process when making internal audit decisions.

Internal auditors sometimes become too buried in statistical values when attempting to do a formal risk analysis. Effective internal audit risk analysis should not get buried in specific probability values, nor cause worry over whether some event had a 39.7 percent or a 42.5 percent probability of occurring. Rather, the effective internal auditor should understand the basic process and estimate relative values. A specific, numerical approach, described in this chapter, can be performed later if needed. This general, nonmathematical concept of risk analysis is mentioned throughout this book.

7-2 AUDIT EVIDENCE AND RISK

The concepts of risk and risk analysis presented in the first paragraphs of this chapter are important for all internal auditors, whether the director of internal audit or an audit manager developing a plan from a large variety of audit candidates, the audit project manager understanding the risk issues associated with a specific review, or the internal auditor faced with a task to measure relative probabilities for a special project such as an information system disaster-recovery plan. The comments on evaluating risk for developing an effective audit plan also can be applied to the discussions in Chapter 8 on building an internal audit annual plan. The process of performing a risk analysis for evaluating audit evidence is useful for all internal audit field procedures, and these concepts are mentioned, implicitly or explicitly, throughout this book. Finally, specialized contingency planning risk analysis approaches are discussed in Chapter 19 with references to this chapter.

This section looks at risk assessment from two levels. First, we consider understanding and evaluating risk when assessing various alternative audit results. This discussion is based on an analysis of the results of an audit of a sales and distribution system. We next explore the use of risk analysis for selecting audits from a wide range of alternatives when building an audit plan. After our discussion of a typical audit risk-analysis process, we conclude with an introduction to a more probability oriented, mathematical approach to risk analysis. While our informal approach is useful for most internal audit situations, the more formal, mathematical approach may be necessary in some situations.

(a) AUDIT RISK WHEN RELYING ON INTERNAL CONTROLS

Internal auditors perform most reviews with an objective to detect errors that may be large enough, individually or in the aggregate, to be significant or material. This tends to be true whether an auditor is performing a financially oriented review of transactions, a review of an operational process, or an information systems review of some newly implemented application. As mentioned, there is always a risk the auditor's procedures will not detect significant errors or irregularities or that the auditor will fail to observe or understand, for better or worse, how some process or control is supposed to operate.

In many instances, due to information gathered from other audit projects, limited time to do specific audit work requiring summarization, or a basic understanding of the area reviewed, an internal auditor may develop a general understanding of the controls in place without performing any further tests. This is a common and in many instances correct procedure given limited audit resources. An example of this kind of action is a review of a business process supported by an automated accounting system. If overall control procedures appear adequate and if the auditor concludes that there are more important areas to include in the review, the internal auditor may rely upon the reported results from the automated accounting system without any further testing of that system. The auditor's conclusion may be that the automated system controls *appear* to be good and that this is a low-risk area of the total process being reviewed. As an example, auditors often rely upon numbers maintained in a general ledger system even though that system may not have been reviewed for some time.

When just relying upon the outputs from the automated application and not performing any further tests of system or application controls, an internal auditor may face a risk that errors, irregularities, or systems weaknesses in the overall process will not be detected. In the example cited, the auditor may conclude that the risk of some undetected error in the supporting general ledger automated accounting system is low, and, further, that any errors would be readily detected through other controls. However, if the risk appears to be sufficiently high, the auditor should probably expand procedures to perform detailed testing in addition to just placing reliance upon an application's internal controls. In this example, those expanded procedures might include detailed application testing or other evidence-gathering.

The American Institute of Certified Public Accountants (AICPA) has done a good job of defining risk through its auditing standards.[1] Although used by external auditors in performing their attest oriented audit work, an understanding of these risk concepts is also useful for non-CPA internal auditors as well. The AICPA, in its Generally Accepted Auditing Standards, has broken down risk into the following three elements:

Inherent Risk. Even if there were no related internal control considerations, there is a greater risk of error of audit concern in some transactions than in others. There is a greater inherent risk of errors or irregularities in an accounts-receivables system—which handles cash—than, for example, in a manufacturing scrap-materials reporting system. Similarly, an application that performs complex calculations is more likely to be misstated than a simple bookkeeping process. When deciding if an automated application should be a candidate for detailed, substantive testing, the auditor should consider its inherent risk.

Control Risk. There is always a risk that the internal controls for some process or application will not prevent or detect an error or irregularity on a timely basis. The auditor may have found that there are good controls over a given process but will nevertheless want to do some detailed evidence-gathering and testing to minimize the control risks. This is because some control risk will always exist due to the inherent limitations of any system of internal controls (see Chapter 2).

---

[1] SAS No. 47, Audit Risk and Materiality When Conducting an Audit, AICPA, New York, 1983.

Detection Risk. There will always be some detection risk even when the auditor examines 100 percent of the transactions in an application. This is because inappropriate auditing procedures may have been used or the results may have been misinterpreted. However, detailed sampling and evidence-gathering of an application's transactions and balances can help to reduce detection risk.

The internal auditor should consider all three of these risk elements when deciding whether or not to perform detailed tests of a process or area. These risk factors are not realistically quantifiable but, rather, require the auditor's judgment. The nature of the process, the quality of the controls surrounding it, and the type of evidence-gathering procedures to be used will all enter into this assessment. In addition, the concept of risk should be considered in terms of the three factors above: risk of loss, element of uncertainty, and some choice among alternatives.

While this risk-evaluation approach is normally used by external auditors when planning their procedures, it is equally appropriate for internal auditors performing operational reviews of nonfinancial applications. For example, management may ask internal audit to review controls for a new manufacturing shop floor-scheduling system. Based upon the above three types of risk, internal audit may decide that detailed testing of that application is necessary before advising management that the controls in that automated application are adequate.

Virtually no area in which an auditor works will be without some risk. To better understand this whole risk-analysis concept, we will consider risk analysis in terms of a review of a distribution and shipping process. Operational audit procedures for shipping and distribution will be discussed in greater detail in Chapter 25. This chapter takes relatively simple audit processes and discusses the related risk analysis approaches.

(i) Risk Analysis in a Distribution Audit: "Burning Stump" Example.   In this section, we consider how an auditor can use risk-analysis approaches to decide what areas to review in a hypothetical company situation and how to analyze the audit findings from this sample review, highlighting the more significant findings. The risk-analysis approaches discussed allow us to review the distribution function for a smaller, remote branch office. This same basic approach can be used for a wide variety of internal audit projects.

Assume that an internal audit team has been asked to perform an operational review of a remote warehousing and shipping unit of a company. Although most products are manufactured at headquarters, the company utilizes remote offices to handle some sales and distribution because of a need for locally added and tested components to the main products as well as a need to supply spare parts on an emergency basis. While the need to have local spare parts supply warehouses has largely disappeared due to improved shipping and communications channels, the company has elected to keep its network of branch offices. This particular facility is located in the town of Burning Stump and is a three-hour flight from headquarters. This has been the first scheduled audit of Burning Stump operations.

The internal audit team has been asked to perform a complete review of Burning Stump processes and operations, and assume you have been asked to lead the review of their local sales and distribution function. Internal audit has programs and procedures available from home office operations but has been advised that local management may do things "differently" in Burning Stump. To gain an understanding of local operations

Figure 7.3   ''Burning Stump'' Example: Sales and Distribution Risks

R_1	Orders may be shipped without proper credit authorization.
R_2	Orders may be shipped with improper discount or freight terms.
R_3	Orders may be shipped without proper salesperson credits.
R_4	Orders may be shipped lacking properly recorded sales invoices.
R_5	Incorrect goods may be shipped.
R_6	Duplicate orders will be shipped.
R_7	Shipments may not be recorded in inventory.
R_8	Damaged or soiled goods may be shipped.
R_9	Returns may be accepted without proper authorization.
R_{10}	Goods may leave without proper shipping papers.
R_{11}	Customer sales history records may not be recorded.
R_{12}	Home office accounting records may not be properly recorded.

the auditors should first meet with local management as well as persons directly responsible for the local sales and distribution system. After follow-up discussions with headquarters sales and distribution, and Burning Stump local management, a next step in this review might be to list the significant risks surrounding these sales and distribution operations. Although not all-inclusive, Figure 7.3 shows the types of risks that have been identified. They are listed in an R_i format that will be used later in this chapter. The internal auditor should take care to not make this type of a list of risks too long. It is easy to get carried away trying to identify every possible risk in the operation being reviewed, even though some of them are very remote. A meteor could fall from the sky and land on the Burning Stump facility; however, we need not worry about improbable events. Too long a list will divert the audit team from identifying significant problem areas and developing effective review approaches for those risk areas.

The fact that something has been identified as a risk does not necessarily mean that it is a significant problem in the entity reviewed. The list of risks should include common risks for the particular operational area as well as impressions gained through visits and reviews of summary reports. The R_1 through R_{12} risks in Figure 7.3 represent things that could go wrong in this distribution and shipping operation. Once a reasonable list has been built, the next step is to assign relative probability values representing an estimate of each risk. Information gathered during the review of controls at the Burning Stump facility will be of value. Even a walk-through observation, mentioned in Chapter 4 on the operational approach to auditing, and discussed further in Chapter 21, will be of help in assigning these values. For example, the auditor may take a tour of the Burning Stump distribution operations area and observe that personnel do not follow the proper customer order paperwork procedures properly. As a result, the auditor could decide there may be a risk that incorrect goods will be shipped.

A single walk through the operations area, in this example, would not necessarily give the internal auditor enough information to assign specific, numerical probabilities for expected exposures to these risks. However, other related information can help an auditor to detect a problem and assign relative probabilities such as ''high risk.'' For example, a review of customer complaint records may support the possible risk that incorrect or damaged goods are being shipped. This whole process does not call for detailed analyses. This is only preliminary information that will help an auditor to develop more detailed and comprehensive audit plans and procedures later in the audit.

As was shown in the risk-analysis process described in Figure 7.2, each of the risks identified here should be analyzed for the expected size of the risk and its likelihood of occurring. While later in this chapter we will talk about this process in terms of estimated relative probabilities, the easiest way to handle this is to classify each risk and its range of probabilities as follows:

Likelihood	Probability
I Very High	0.75 to 1.00
II High	0.50 to 0.75
III Possible	0.25 to 0.50
IV Low	0.05 to 0.25
V Very Low	0.00 to 0.05

In reality, we will almost never find risks at 0 percent or at 100 percent. In general, if the likelihood probability for some significant risk is greater than 25 percent, the organization probably has a significant internal control problem. While these preliminary estimates are often guesses at best, these relative probabilities allow an internal auditor to define possible risks. The ranges of probabilities allow the internal audit team as well as the management group being reviewed to agree on some rough probability estimates. The internal auditor who made the initial observation of poor order-shipping procedures may suggest that there is a high likelihood, possibly over a 10 percent probability, that orders will be shipped incorrectly. A local facility manager may argue that things really are ''not that bad'' and will point to a not-too-thick customer complaint file. After some discussion and further analysis of the controls in place, internal audit may decide that there is still a high likelihood of error in this area and will assign a probability value of 5 percent. These probabilities should then be assigned to each risk, as shown in Figure 7.4. In actual practice, this will be a much more extensive list of risks, and internal audit should make adjustments to the probabilities as necessary. Also in actual practice, the probabilities should all be quite low. If any significant control has an error rate of even more than perhaps 10 percent, the overall organization has a significant problem!

The next step is to analyze separately the exposures associated with each of the risks. If we have agreed that there may be a 5 percent risk that Burning Stump operations may ship incorrect goods, what is the volume of goods shipped that might be subject to this error? While this exposure could be the same if all shipments were the same, it will often vary as different classes of goods may or may not be subject to some specific risk. This estimation process is perhaps the most difficult step in the risk-analysis process. With total annual sales for the operation at $750,000, the internal auditor performing this analysis should ask questions along the lines of:

Figure 7.4   "Burning Stump Example": Sales and Distribution Risk Analysis

Risks	Relative Risk	Likelihood of Occurrence	Potential Exposure	Expected Loss	Rank
R01	Low	0.18	$150,000	$27,000	9
R02	High	0.33	$750,000	$247,500	1
R03	Low	0.08	$750,000	$60,000	5
R04	Low	0.10	$300,000	$30,000	8
R05	Low	0.08	$250,000	$20,000	10
R06	Very Low	0.05	$150,000	$7,500	11
R07	Low	0.15	$400,000	$60,000	5
R08	Low	0.15	$250,000	$37,500	7
R09	Possible	0.40	$125,000	$50,000	6
R10	High	0.70	$125,000	$87,500	3
R11	Low	0.15	$500,000	$75,000	4
R12	Low	0.22	$750,000	$165,000	2

- What are the classes of goods shipped under special credit terms that could be released without credit authorization?
- What is our annual cost of shipping duplicate orders? Are all shipments subject to this risk?
- What is our cost of not maintaining customer sales records?

These types of estimates, usually in terms of annual dollars, should be made for each of the identified risks. As much as possible, this analysis should be kept separate from the loss probabilities assigned previously to allow these estimates to be made independently. They also should be entered in the appropriate column of the risk-analysis process table, Figure 7.4.

Arbitrary values have been assigned for each of the sales and distribution risks in the figure. The final step in the risk analysis is to multiply the probabilities of occurrence with the monetary loss exposures to come up with the *expected* losses. Based on the estimated expected losses, the hypothetical numbers in Figure 7.4 would indicate that risk R_2—that orders may be shipped with improper discount and freight terms—presents the greatest potential expected loss to the Burning Stump branch office operation. Internal audit should plan expanded audit procedures in this area at least to confirm or deny the risk-analysis estimates.

This risk-analysis process can be useful in a variety of audit review situations. The process allows internal auditors to identify the whole range of risks in the area reviewed and then to concentrate audit efforts in the more significant areas. Although the process can easily generate bad information if the various probabilities or loss estimations are way off target, the process can allow auditors and management to focus on these estimates and decide whether they point to the correct audit actions to be taken. This type of risk analysis can be useful and help internal auditors to make better decisions.

(b) RISK ANALYSIS AND AUDIT PROJECT PLANNING

Many internal audit groups are faced with the process of developing an annual and perhaps a five-year plan outlining the activities and areas where internal audit will perform its reviews. The basic risk-analysis process can allow internal audit to make effective and appropriate audit plans. While the specific risk-analysis matrix outlined in Figure 7.4 is not the correct tool for developing annual project plans, this basic approach is still very useful for internal audit project planning.

Internal audit functions are typically faced with a large number of candidates or areas they could audit but they just cannot audit everything in a given year. Nevertheless, there are always high-risk areas that perhaps should be visited annually, some that should only be reviewed because of significant control problems identified through prior audits or operations, and some that should not be reviewed during a current period due to an audit that was recently completed and found no significant control problems. The basic risk-analysis process described here can help internal audit decide which areas to review.

Chapter 8 describes the process of planning audit activities through the development of annual and five-year plans. Neither of these time periods is ''magic'' since internal audit could, for example, develop short-term six-month and then ten-year plans. The one- and five-year time periods are useful, however, since most organizations budget and plan on an annual basis, making a one-year planning window very useful. The five-year period also is useful because it stretches into the future but not so far that internal audit would have no understanding of what might happen. Technology developments and economic factors always cause major future changes that we cannot easily predict.

Internal auditors should develop a risk-analysis worksheet to allow them to perform their annual plans. First, the auditor needs to identify all auditable entities within the organization. While this list will change from year to year, such a list provides internal audit with an opportunity to identify every activity within the organization that could be audited. This list should include mainstream activities that are reviewed every year or two as well as some of the more remote or obscure operations in the organization that never have and may never be subject to an internal audit.

In order to develop an audit plan of higher-risk entities, each audit population area should be evaluated and scored for exposure and risk. To accomplish this, internal audit needs to develop a risk-assessment scoring model to aid in the planning process. The idea is to rate or score each auditable entity against a series of audit-risk and planning factors. For example, if the area was audited within the last year and if control problems were moderate, the auditable entity would receive a lower score. If the area is a work-in-process manufacturing area that controls significant business assets, it would receive a higher risk score than an accounting area that is primarily responsible for only record-keeping. Figure 7.5 is an example of this type of risk-analysis scoring sheet. Only a few of the questions that might be included in this type of analysis are shown, and the questions asked and the factors assigned will vary depending upon the organization. However, the idea here is to rank what is often called the organization's audit universe—all of the potential areas subject to audit in the organization. Those areas can then be scored and ranked on a worksheet, as shown in Figure 7.6. A series of audit projects have been included on this schedule to show how the scores might be calculated and tabulated. This exercise will highlight the higher-risk areas that should be included in an annual internal audit plan.

The whole idea here is to rank all entities in the organization for their potential audit risk. The higher-risk items should be considered for the annual audit plan. Of course, this

Figure 7.5 Internal Audit Planning Risk-Analysis Sample Scoresheet

---

Every entity in the Potential Audit Universe should be subject to the following analysis. Assign scores and tabulate using a microcomputer spreadsheet.

1. When was the entity last audited?

Last year:	1 point
Last 1 to 5 years:	3 "
Over 5 years ago:	5 "
Never audited.	8 "

2. During last audit, were findings significant?

   Depending upon level of findings: 0 to 10 points

3. If there were past audit findings, is there evidence of corrective action taken?

   Depending upon information/observations of actions: 5 to 0 points

   (5 if not working, 3 if partial implementation, 0 if implemented)

4. What level of assets are controlled by entity?

   Depending upon size of entity and organization: 0 to 25 points

5. What level of sales/liabilities are controlled by entity?

   Depending upon the relative size of entity: 0 to 25 points

6. How does auditable entity relate to central management / the Board of Directors

Headquarters / core operations unit:	10 points
Plant or operation key to business operations:	20 "
Sales or supporting operations	5 "
Overseas / offshore operation	15 "
Consolidated separately owned operation	5 to 10 points
Significant investment only	5 to 20 points

7. Who requested new audit?

Senior management / board	25 points
External audit firm	20 "
Local / Operations management	10 "
Not requested	0 "

8. Is the entity information systems technology dependent?

   Based on level / type of automation: 0 to 15 points

Note. The above survey questions are only examples. Depending upon the organization and overall audit risks, this type of list will typically be much more extensive.

Figure 7.6 Audit Planning Risk-Analysis Project Scores

Auditable Unit	Last Audit	Past Findings	Assets	Sales Liabilities	Reporting Structure	Audit Request	New Technology	New FASB STDS	Legal Concerns	Complexity	Total Score	Norm	Risk Rank
Corp. Accounting	1	2	25	10	10	0	0	0	0	0	48	0.102	5
Pension/Profit Sharing	3	3	15	15	10	25	2	15	0	3	91	0.193	1
Fixed Asset Controls	3	5	15	7	10	0	0	0	0	2	42	0.089	6
New Mfg. System	8	0	5	2	20	20	15	0	0	8	78	0.166	2
Engineering Decision Supprt	8	0	5	2	20	0	12	0	3	10	60	0.127	3
Finished Goods Inventory	1	1	8	6	10	0	5	10	0	0	41	0.087	7
Branch Sales Offices	3	5	12	2	10	0	3	0	0	0	35	0.074	8
Indonesia Sales	8	0	8	5	15	0	5	0	5	3	49	0.104	4
Sales Representatives	5	5	3	1	10	0	0	0	1	2	27	0.057	9

exercise can be subject to ongoing revision and adjustment in terms of the basic risk-scoring factors and the scores assigned to various entities. All too often, the first time this type of exercise is used by an internal audit organization, some surprises appear, such as areas that have not received much audit attention in the past, or areas not appropriate for inclusion in the annual audit plan. After careful review as well as discussions with management, the audit-planning risk-scoring model should be adjusted both in terms of the risk-scoring factors assigned and the values that were assigned to various entities. While the idea is not to adjust the model to project the pre-established audit assumptions, the adjustment to scoring factors and the values assigned will help internal audit develop more effective and efficient internal audit plans.

7-3 QUANTITATIVE APPROACHES TO RISK ANALYSIS

Earlier in this chapter, we discussed how a quantitative risk-analysis approach, using detailed probability estimates and the like, is often not necessary. It simply involves too much calculation and analysis in many audit situations. Nevertheless, there may be times when an internal auditor needs to do this detailed analysis—for example, when a government regulator or legal prosecutor challenges the overall organization and the work that internal audit has done in some area. This happens when there may be questions about why internal audit did or did not perform review procedures in some area. Of course, a quantitative approach will do no good after the fact. If internal auditors are working in an area where they feel that they may be questioned, a quantitative risk analysis should be considered. Even if after the fact, the documentation covering a formal, quantitative risk analysis can serve to justify internal audit's position in those situations. This section briefly discusses formal, quantitative approaches to risk analysis.

Quantitative audit risk analysis requires internal auditors to go through a fairly formal statistical analysis that identifies all auditable entities in the organization, identifies all threats to those entities or processes, assigns the probability of occurrence for each of the identified threats to those assets, and ranks probable expected losses as a result of the threats. This is the same basic approach used earlier in this chapter; however, here we are making the process somewhat more formal. Quantitative risk analysis has its origins in product-safety analysis techniques, and there have been many published variations to this same basic quantitative risk-analysis approach.

The approach is based on calculating or estimating the risk (R) that some threat will occur. Risk is determined from the probability (P) of a security exposure occurring a given number of times per year, and the exposure (E) cost attributed to any such loss. The risk is then stated in terms of probable-loss dollars per year according to the relationship:

$$R = P \times E$$

This is essentially the same approach used previously in this chapter. However, here more attention is devoted to the mathematical calculations and the quantitative expressions of risk and expected losses.

(a) ASSIGNING RISK EXPOSURE PROBABILITIES

The first step in any risk analysis is to assign probabilities of occurrence to all of the significant exposures identified. As discussed in the earlier distribution and shipping processes audit example, these probabilities should be stated in terms of the expected annualized loss per year. That is, if an event is expected to occur once per year, the annualized probability of loss will be 1.0 or 100 percent. If a loss is expected to occur once every three years, the annualized probability of loss will be 0.333 or one third.

Developing a table of expected probability values is probably the most difficult part in the whole formal analysis. We generally do not have enough information, data, or historical records to provide any basis for probable values. As a result, auditors and all members of management tend to forget history and base probable expectations on recent events. For example, assume a building sits on what is called a ''one hundred years flood plain.'' This means that the site may be flooded within that interval. If the facility has not experienced a flood in anyone's recent memory, we tend to forget the flood plain problem and assume that such a flood will never happen. Conversely, if one of those ''every hundred years'' floods has taken place the past spring, people generally give future floods a much higher occurrence probability rate than they deserve.

Ignoring the probabilities at this time, internal audit should next try to list all of the significant risks or events. This will typically become a long list of normal as well as ''can't happen'' types of risks. The distribution systems example in Figure 7.4 showed a schedule of these types of risks. A difference with the quantitative approach is that internal audit should attempt to assign more accurate relative probabilities to each of those risks. The key element to this approach is to derive accurate values that are more than just ''blue sky.''

Often the best approach here is for internal audit not to assign the values itself but to ask the user personnel involved to guess at some probabilities. Often, of course, operations area managers will have no idea of the probability of a significant breakdown in a system or of a flood, a major defalcation, or the like. The best approach is often for internal audit to assign a set of values and to present them to various managers. Using a table of probabilities developed by internal audit, managers can be asked to agree or disagree. For example, internal audit might ask information systems personnel for their estimates of the probability of one of a computer system's disk drives crashing once per day, once every 10 days, once every 100 days, and so forth. If there are significant differences in models or types of equipment, the analysis should be performed separately for each system. In this type of area, internal audit could talk to a variety of technical personnel who might be able to give more reliable estimates. Where available, actual statistics can be used to support these probabilities. When there are differing probability estimates, internal audit should try to develop an average response to select the appropriate probability category.

The preparation of a table of this sort can be a valuable process beyond just the assignment of probabilities. To avoid needless speculation, the internal auditor compiling the probabilities should avoid asking subjective estimate questions about events such as natural disasters where personnel have no particular expert knowledge. That is, it is reasonable to ask an information-systems operations manager for an estimate of disk head crash probabilities. It accomplishes little to ask that same individual for the probability of occurrence of a major earthquake!

The assigning of an expected loss probability in this type of exercise is very subjective at best. As discussed, we tend to base our estimates of future performance on recent past history. One method that has been used for determining better expected-loss probabilities is the use of *Delphi techniques.* This method was developed by the RAND Corporation in the late 1960s and is sometimes an effective method of obtaining an independent consensus opinion from experts on future outcomes. The concept requires a panel of experts who,

Figure 7.7 Example Estimated Loss Probabilities

	Per Year Prob.	Probability Per Day
Every Week	5200%	14.2466%
Two Times Every Month	2400%	6.5753%
Once Every Month	1200%	3.2877%
Once Every Six Months	200%	0.5479%
Once Every Year	100%	0.2740%
Once Every Two Years	50%	0.1370%
Once Every Three Years	33%	0.0913%
Once Every Ten Years	10%	0.0274%
Once Every Hundred Years	1%	0.0027%

having reviewed a set of estimation-related questions, are asked individually to submit written answers to an independent analyst. Names are removed from these answers, they are tabulated and sent back to the experts who are asked to revise their original answers based on the anonymous responses of all of the others. The process is repeated until a consensus is reached.

Delphi techniques can be effective exercises to obtain consensus opinions on such unknowns as risk-analysis expected-loss probabilities. However, the exercise can be expensive in terms of the time and effort required. In addition, the technique would appear to work best for more global issues, such as questions about the state of organization automation in the year 2020 than more specialized problems, such as asking about the expected probabilities of disk failures due to human mistakes.

Regardless of the method used, this step in the risk-analysis process should result in a list of expected probabilities for each of the significant exposures that were identified. These probabilities can be annualized on a per-year or per-day basis, as illustrated in Figure 7.7. Although some of these annualized exposure probabilities may appear very small, they should not be discarded from the list at this point. If the probability issues are very high, this is really not an audit analysis issue, but a problem that needs to be fixed. Expected exposure losses should be calculated next.

(b) ESTIMATING EXPECTED EXPOSURE LOSSES

The next step in quantitative risk analysis is to calculate expected exposure costs or losses for each of the exposures identified. These estimates should include both the cost of replacing an asset and the more intangible costs of business interruption, extra personnel, and opportunity losses. They can include such things as recognizing that the original or current book value of an asset does not represent the true cost for replacing that asset. Similarly, the loss of a productive asset may reduce business in other areas. While it may be easy to carry such estimates to extremes, the total lost business costs associated with a productive asset should be considered.

Just as a fair amount of subjectivity is involved in assigning the expected loss probabilities, this cost-estimating process is equally as difficult. It is fairly easy to estimate the expected replacement cost, net of insurance proceeds, for the loss of a small client-server computer system due to a fire. However, estimating the cost of business loss due to the unavailability of the equipment is much more difficult. For example, if some computer hardware is no longer manufactured, much of the software may have to be rewritten in order to work on any more modern replacement machine.

Internal auditors compiling these exposure-cost estimates should take care to document all estimates and computations. Once the results of the risk analysis are compiled and released to management, audit's results may be challenged. This documentation will allow the estimate to be supported or be modified with additional new data.

Using the costs of expected losses calculated here and the annualized loss probabilities calculated previously, risks can be calculated for all of the expected exposures using the $R = P \times E$ relationship. The result will be a series of expected dollar losses per year for each of the exposures evaluated. When calculating these values, internal audit should keep in mind that it is only necessary to state risks in terms of rounded values. It is of little value to multiply two very subjective estimates together and then to present the expected joint probability result stated in terms of five decimal places! The calculated results can be ranked in order of descending values to highlight higher risk areas in the schedule similar to the more informal one shown previously in Figure 7.4.

(c) USING QUANTITATIVE RISK-ANALYSIS RESULTS

The purpose of the risk analysis and computation is to identify those exposures with the highest probable expected annualized losses. This can be quite a powerful method for identifying areas where corrective action should be taken to protect the organization from potential risks and losses. Quantitative risk analysis is a fairly common technique used by many agencies of the U.S. federal government and financial institutions. However, because of the computations required, the exercise can become quite time-consuming and difficult. In addition, the method described here is a rather abbreviated approach. Many of the more formal procedures used—for example, in federal government agencies—employ much more complex statistical analyses which sometimes raise more questions than they provide answers.

Quantitative risk analysis can be a useful tool for identifying and quantifying various types of audit exposures. However, it should be recognized that the calculated risks are only as good as the underlying estimates of costs and probabilities, and the rough, qualitative approach discussed earlier in this chapter is also quite useful. Many of the calculated values are difficult, if not impossible to estimate, and considerable management time can be spent in attempting to estimate the probabilities of events where there is no historical data.

7-4 RISK EVALUATION IN THE MODERN ORGANIZATION

The prior sections have discussed several approaches to risk analysis in the modern organization. Internal auditors involved in a risk analysis should select an approach that appears to be best for the organization under review. Each of these risk-analysis approaches has its own advantages and disadvantages. Generally, the quantitative approach is best suited to the larger, centralized environment, while a management-oriented, more qualitative approach works best for a smaller or more decentralized organization.

Risk analysis is a useful approach both in deciding what to audit and then in fine tuning audit testing and analysis strategies. It is also a very useful tool to help better explain to management why internal audit did or did not perform audit work in some area. However, auditors often will find it necessary to simplify their risk assumptions and calculations to an even more easily understandable manner when presenting them to management. This is not because upper management does not understand such complex computations; rather, upper levels of management in most organizations are generally both generalists and risk takers. Auditors should keep these two concepts in mind when presenting risk analysis findings to management.

The typical upper-level manager is not particularly interested in complex charts or tables of subjective probabilities when reviewing the results of an auditor's risk analysis. Rather, that typical manager will recognize that risks should be minimized when possible. Auditors should consider presenting their risk-analysis findings in the context of this question: What would be the costs to the organization if there were major process or control-system failures and what would it take to prevent them from occurring?

Auditors will generally find it effective to use risk-analysis findings with the above general questions in mind. Care should be taken to avoid ''for want of a nail'' types of arguments when using risk analysis. While it is often easy for an internal auditor to develop such scenarios regarding various risks, senior management is accustomed to accepting a level of risk in many of its decisions and will often have trouble accepting such arguments.

Properly implemented, risk analysis is an important tool that should be used by all internal auditors, whether a director developing a five-year plan or an in-charge auditor making an audit-evidence decision.

CHAPTER 8

Organizing and Planning Internal Audit Activities

8-1 INTRODUCTION: INTERNAL AUDIT ORGANIZATION AND PLANNING

Previous chapters have dealt with the foundations and standards of internal auditing, the nature of controls, and the operational approach of internal auditing. This chapter offers approaches to bring these efforts together for meaningful audit results. An effective plan of organization is a key component of a successful internal audit function. Once organized, the internal audit function needs to identify and plan its activities.

The director of internal auditing should initiate internal organization auditing and planning strategies. Internal audit management, of course, is responsible for implementing the best solutions and should always develop solutions with consideration given to the five components or framework of the management process: planning, organizing, providing resources, administering, and controlling. This framework was discussed in Chapter 3, Understanding Management Needs, and this chapter discusses the specific application of this management process.

A series of high-level internal audit management activities must take place in order to achieve the overall goals and objectives of the internal audit effort. A number of supporting policies and procedures revolve around the organization of the internal audit function. That organization impacts administrative direction, which includes assigning responsibilities and establishing accountabilities. This chapter describes alternative internal audit organization approaches.

8-2 ORGANIZING THE INTERNAL AUDIT EFFORT

There is no single or optimal way to organize an internal audit function in a modern organization. A director of internal audit who has been given the challenge to establish a new internal audit function has a variety of options, depending upon the organization's overall business, its geographic and logistical structures, the various control risks it faces, and its overall culture. This section will discuss some of the elements required to build and manage an effective internal audit organization.

A key requirement for effective organizations is a strong leader, a director of internal audit who understands the needs of the organization and its potential control risks. This audit director must have the support of both senior management and the audit committee of the board of directors. The roles and responsibilities of the director of internal audit were discussed in Chapter 1, with the important supporting role of the audit committee discussed in Chapter 6.

Most larger organizations today have multiple units or operations. They may be spread across the world or may consist of diverse operations all under one roof. Even if geographically located in one location, the larger modern organization today will almost always have multiple specialty functions with individual control risks potentially requiring separate internal audit emphasis. The effective internal audit department must be organized in a manner that serves senior management and the audit committee by providing the best, most cost-effective audit services to the entire organization. We will consider the benefits and difficulties in having either a centralized or a decentralized internal audit organization as well as some alternative internal audit organization structures.

(a) ALTERNATIVE INTERNAL AUDIT ORGANIZATION STRUCTURES

In a larger, diverse organization, a basic question facing the director of internal audit is whether to have a centralized internal audit function or to decentralize it along one of several lines to be discussed later. The alternative approaches for developing an internal audit organization will support internal audit management's philosophy for the centralization or decentralization of authority. However, this management philosophy issue is really independent, as virtually any type of internal audit organization can be administered on either a very centralized or decentralized basis. The central question is the extent to which individual decisions should be made and actions taken at lower organizational levels, as opposed to requiring clearance or approval by various levels of a centralized internal audit headquarters management.

The kinds of decisions and actions involved include the modification of required audit procedures, the need to report certain types of audit deficiencies, negotiations regarding actions to be taken on audit findings, the manner of reporting findings, the completion of reports and signing of audit reports, and the follow-up on corrective actions taken covering reported deficiencies.

(i) Centralized vs. Decentralized Internal Audit Organizations. Over one hundred years ago, many business organizations were managed and organized in a highly centralized manner. That is, major decisions were made by a central authority, and lower levels in the organization did little more than pass materials up through the ranks for central office approvals. Perhaps the best, or most absurd, example of this form of a highly centralized organization would be the government of the Soviet Union before its collapse in the late 1980s. There, all planning and economic decisions theoretically were made by a limited number of central authorities. A plant wishing to order pencils as part of its office supplies would have to put its requirements for pencils into an annual production plan. Assuming that plan was approved by the central authorities, the plant would then file supply requisitions in order to request its needs for pencils over the course of the planning cycle, often as long as five years. The central planning authority would look at all planned requests for pencils across the country and then decide both how many pencils were to be manufactured in order to supply everyone and even how many trees would be cut down to supply raw materials for those pencils.

This type of central planning may sound very efficient to the student or theorist; however, it just does not work! Large economic units find it difficult—if not impossible—to develop appropriate centralized plans that correctly define the requirements or set the rules for everyone. Too many persons spend time processing forms, and the ultimate users of the services do not see much value from the process. This centralized approach creates little more than bureaucracy! We also saw a similar example of the failure of central planning when the United States federal government tried to regulate prices and allocate the supply of gasoline in the late 1970s. The result was high prices, long lines due to local shortages, and an army of bureaucrats trying to regulate everything. Prices went down and supplies increased only after central controls were abolished in the early 1980s.

As a result of these inefficiencies, many once highly centralized organizations have pushed decision-making authority down and have decentralized their processes. Today, many larger organizations have developed this overall style or philosophy of operating in a decentralized manner. Some are extremely decentralized, with each operating unit responsible for making most of its business decisions, including securing its own financing. To increase the level of decentralization, major operating units may each have their own decentralized operations.

Whether the internal audit function or the total organization—any organizational unit can be administered on a centralized or decentralized basis—the main question is the extent to which individual decisions should be made and actions taken at lower organizational levels, as opposed to those requiring clearance or approval by the central or intermediary organizational levels. For internal audit, the kinds of decisions and actions involved will include the modification of required audit procedures, procedures necessary to report given types of deficiencies, negotiations necessary in order to take actions on audit findings, the manner of reporting audit findings, and internal audit's follow-up on the corrective action covering reported deficiencies.

The arguments or benefits that support decentralization generally include:

- Freeing up higher-level personnel from minor decisions so that they can deal with other important matters. Senior management does not always need to review or approve all levels of organizational details. It can become mired in these lower-level details and miss making important overall decisions.

- Lower-level personnel in the organization often have a better understanding of local problems. Rather than summarizing problem situations and passing them up to higher levels for the decisions, lower-level management can often act directly and in a more intelligent manner.

- Delays involved in passing decisions up for approval can be avoided. In addition, the lower-level personnel are often better motivated to solve problems at their own level of the organization and will often have the opportunity to develop more appropriate decisions.

- Lower-level personnel who are empowered, through delegations of authority, to make decisions are often viewed with more respect by persons at those levels. Unit-level managers who make their own decisions will typically receive more respect than unit managers who must pass all approval questions to headquarters to wait for decisions.

Some managers, and certainly some directors of internal audit, may feel that a decentralized organization is not always the most effective. Internal audit organizations in particular can operate efficiently as centralized or "corporate" functions where members from a single headquarters staff perform audits throughout the organization. Some of the arguments in favor of a highly centralized rather than a decentralized internal audit organization structure include the following:

- Lower-level personnel may not know the full implications of particular types of judgments and decisions. This is particularly true for decentralized-organization field auditors who may be asked to explain the rationale behind certain central policy decisions. They may have trouble adequately communicating how those decisions may impact all units in the organization.

- A highly decentralized organization will find it difficult to maintain uniform, organization-wide standards. While this may be acceptable for some functions in the organization, the internal audit effort may be improperly presented. Despite strong common policies and procedures, decentralized functions typically will almost always vary slightly in their approaches.

- Senior management responsible for coordinating the decentralized parts run the risk of being charged with abdicating responsibility for important unit-level organization activities, especially when something goes wrong. In a centralized organization, senior management, including the director of internal audit, can take a "buck stops here" responsibility for all major decisions.

- Higher-level corporate management can easily get out of touch with current developments in the decentralized components of their organization. Their only contact with the decentralized units may be through periodic budget-planning and performance meetings. With greater central control, management may not have sufficient time to spend with operating units.

- Valuable communications links can be lost for coordination and personnel-administration purposes. A centralized organization can more easily transfer personnel to appropriate assignments throughout the overall organization rather than restricting movement to individual operating units.

This discussion assumes that an organization is either highly centralized or decentralized. There are, of course, numerous in-between positions possible where some matters are delegated and others not. Some internal audit organizations will delegate authority subject to a post-review of the actions taken pursuant to the delegation and with automatic ratification after some given period of time. It is not practicable to suggest a single best solution to these alternatives, and the director of internal audit should have the final responsibility for all organization staff actions. Similarly, the persons at each organizational level should have a responsibility for the actions of their subordinates.

Granted that there must be delegations of authority, a basic necessity is that the higher-level personnel, starting with the director of internal audit, must weigh carefully the merits of each type of delegation and the effectiveness of related supplementary controls. Management must be satisfied that, on balance, the particular mode of delegation or centralization of authority is best for total organization interests. The delegator must also be prepared to amend that delegation when developments indicate that the existing organization arrangement is not working out satisfactorily.

(ii) Decentralization on a Functional Basis.   A special kind of decentralization of authority exists when separate internal audit groups exist in the overall organization that are not part of the regular or central internal audit organization. These separate internal audit functions, which may result from restructuring or acquisitions, often report directly to the management of individual subsidiaries and divisions. The responsibility of the central internal audit function here is often only to serve in an advisory capacity, and many of the administrative considerations discussed in this chapter are not directly involved. This kind of situation can occur when an organization A owns 75 percent of organization B, with the other 25 percent held by other stockholders. Organization B will probably have its own audit committee and director of internal audit. However, A's 75 percent ownership of B means that A's director of internal audit has some responsibility for the audit function at B.

   The director of internal audit for the parent organization (A in the above example) should have a special professional concern as to the effectiveness of the semiautonomous internal audit groups (B's) that goes beyond the normal interest in the effectiveness of all organization operations. The special relationship to any semiautonomous internal audit groups will normally be indicated on a complete internal audit organization chart that shows these other groups as reporting to the central director of internal audit on a dotted-line basis. In these situations, the existence of the semiautonomous internal audit group's responsibility to local management does not preclude the regular or "corporate" internal audit department from making supplementary reviews of these subsidiaries and divisions, as deemed necessary. The central internal audit organization cannot be responsible for organization-wide internal audit results unless it has both access and line control over all supplementary internal audit work. The central director of internal audit has a responsibility to make any dotted-line reporting relationships to other internal audit groups sufficiently strong or as weak as necessary given overall organization considerations.

(b) TYPES OF INTERNAL AUDIT ORGANIZATIONS

An internal audit function in a small organization presents a smaller number of organizational challenges. One person—the director—will be given responsibility for internal audit, and depending upon the size of the staff needed, a group of managers or supervisors responsible for the staff internal auditors may report to that director. In a very small organization, all of the staff may report directly to that director. While many of the internal audit planning and administration topics covered throughout this book still apply to the very small internal audit organization, the director of a very small audit organization does not need to give much consideration to internal audit organization variations. All of internal audit will be reporting to that one director with not enough staff to provide many organizational variations.

   Most organizations will have an internal audit function large enough for the director of internal audit to consider the best way to organize internal audit given a variety of factors impacting the overall organization. Although there may be many minor variations, internal audit functions are commonly organized following one of four overall approaches: the types of audits performed; internal audit conformance to the general structure of the organization; organization by geographical area; and combinations of the aforementioned approaches with a headquarters staff.

(i) Organization by Type of Audit.   Internal audit functions are frequently organized by the types of audits to be performed. An audit department might be divided into three groups of specialists: computer or information systems auditors, financial audit specialists, and purely operational auditors. This approach rests on the logic that individual internal auditors may be most effective if given responsibility for an area in which they have expertise and experience, recognizing that efficiency is often achieved through specialization. The problems and control risks pertaining to a particular audit area can often be best handled through the assignment of internal auditors who have the necessary special expertise. For example, an organization may have a great number of district and regional sales offices having the same kind of operations. That internal audit function may want to develop a special internal auditing group that does nothing but audit these sales offices. The practical benefits here can be substantial.

At the same time, internal audit management should recognize that there are disadvantages to this type-of-audit approach. Where several types of audits exist at a given field location, it may be necessary for each specialist internal auditor to travel to that location. This extra cost in time and money should be clearly offset by the added efficiency gained from the several specialist internal auditors. Figure 8.1 is an organization chart from this type of internal audit organization. It shows that specialized groups have been established for information systems, financial auditing, and several operational areas. A risk with this approach is that specialist internal auditors may spend too much time on their own specialty areas and miss the big picture in the process. This has been particularly true with technical, computer-audit areas, which may spend too much time on technical control issues and miss significant control-concern risks in the process. It is often very difficult for the director of internal audit to create a team of integrated auditors with this type of approach.

Although tight, specific definition of audit tasks can promote efficiency and allow for more effective, specialized audits, a variety of assignments keeps an internal auditor from getting in a rut and performing audit reviews in too mechanical a fashion. Here, the audit staff is alert and well motivated and can bring a fresh approach to old problems, something that frequently pays good dividends. Mixed assignments for individual internal auditors lend themselves best to growth and professional development. They help to create *the integrated auditor*. This integrated audit approach promotes adequate education and training opportunities to all members of the audit staff.

On the balance, any gains through audit specialization may be more than offset by the factors just discussed. Internal audit management faces the danger that these gains will appear to be more substantial than they actually are. The specialist approach should be used cautiously and only when the organization has strong needs for auditors with unique abilities. In many instances, the type of audit approach for an internal audit organizational structure is at odds with the objectives of achieving maximum quality of the audit effort, especially as the concern of internal audit moves further away from reviewing lower-level procedures and towards broader managerial issues.

(ii) Internal Audit Organization Parallel to Overall Organization Structure.

In a large organization, a practical alternative is to align audit responsibilities along the same lines as the organization structure. Individual internal audit groups can be assigned to specific organizational components such as operating divisions or affiliated subsidiaries. When these organization operating units are in specialized lines of business or geographical areas, internal audit may benefit from the previously discussed advantage of an understanding of audit and control issues for the particular types of operational activities and the related development of greater internal audit expertise. An example might be a large

Figure 8.1 "Type of Audit" Organization

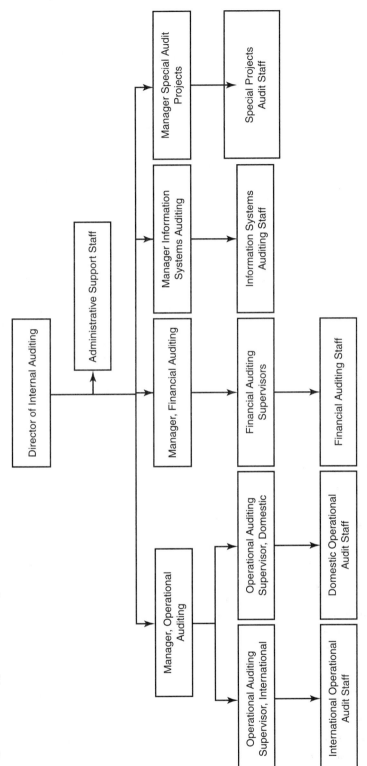

manufacturing organization that has a separate finance subsidiary responsible for financing equipment leases. Because of significant differences in control issues between manufacturing operations and those of the finance operations, internal audit management might find it effective to have two separate audit groups, one to cover manufacturing operations and the other for the financial subsidiary.

An advantage in this internal audit organizational approach is that management in charge of the various operations, and other operating personnel as well, can develop more effective working relationships with the responsible internal audit personnel. The separate internal audit groups should come to speak the language of the particular operation and can become more useful to the individual management groups. Internal audit can also develop more effective working relationships with responsible managers at all levels. Figure 8.2 shows this type of internal audit organization structure.

There are often certain disadvantages to this separate form of internal audit organization structure, similar to those of the type-of-audit approach just discussed. Just as separate information systems and manufacturing auditors might travel to and perform audits of the same general area, here a manufacturing division and a finance division auditor might each be asked to review the same general area if multiple operating divisions are located there. Although organization operating units are often separate and autonomous, this approach can result in duplication of field travel, diminished internal audit staff motivation, and reduced opportunities for management development. A given operating division can be considered to be less important to the overall organization, and members of the internal audit team assigned there may feel that their career opportunities are hampered.

Another potential danger with this approach is that the separate internal audit groups can develop too close of an alliance with the particular divisional or staff personnel they audit, which can sometimes undermine the independence and objectivity of the individual internal auditors.

This effectiveness of this organizational structure approach for internal audit is more controversial than it first appears and perhaps should be used cautiously. Even a very large organization, with many different operating units, may find it more effective to have a central group of *corporate auditors* who perform their reviews at all units, despite the line of business. The organization with multiple internal audit groups, each serving separate lines of business, may find it difficult to conduct audits throughout the organization that speak in the same voice, no matter how strong the central internal audit policies and procedures.

(iii) Geographical Approach to the Internal Audit Organization.   Under the geographical approach, all organization operations in a given geographical area are assigned to a particular auditor or group of internal auditors. In some cases this geographical approach can automatically, to some extent, become a type-of-audit or organization-structure approach when particular types of operations are concentrated in separate geographic areas, but usually there will be some diversity of audit assignments in the individual areas. Figure 8.3 shows an internal audit function organized by geographical area.

The advantages and disadvantages of an area approach to an internal audit organization are reasonably well indicated by the evaluation of the first two organization structures discussed previously. On balance, a geographic approach often seems to be best and is commonly used in practice. The number of separate audit offices to be established will depend on the scope of the organization's operations. In some organizations, there may be a number of separate audit offices within the United States, with international operations

Figure 8.2 Parallel Organization Internal Audit Function

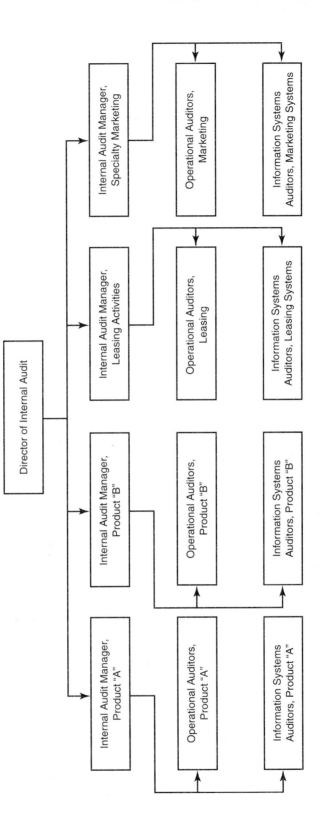

Figure 8.3 Area Approach Internal Audit Organization

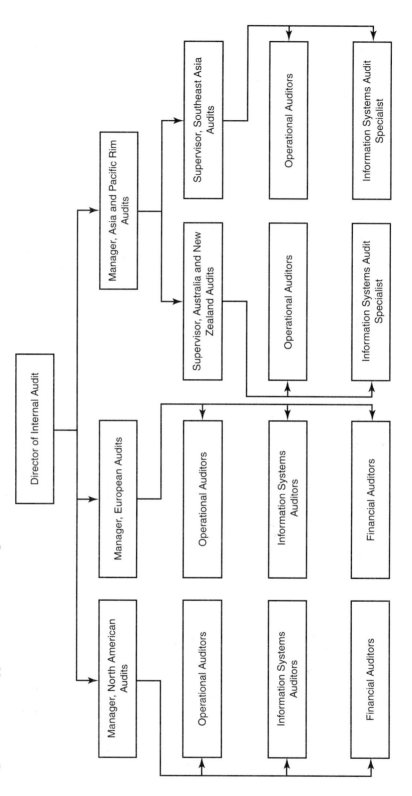

located in one separate office, often at a prominent offshore location. Organizations with a large, diverse number of international operations may have multiple international internal audit offices.

(iv) Use of a Headquarters Internal Audit Staff.   The three approaches to the organization of internal audit field activities just discussed should always be supplemented by some kind of headquarters organization. Each of the organization charts shown in Figures 8.1, 8.2, and 8.3 shows some type of central internal audit staff support function. At its minimum, this headquarters will consist of the director of internal audit and a very limited administrative support staff. Any expansion of the central internal audit organization above this minimum depends on what work is delegated to the line components and what types of internal audit services are provided by the central unit. In a typical situation, all or almost all audit reports may be reviewed and approved at the central headquarters. Other matters requiring centralized attention, such as common internal audit policies and procedures, may be developed, or at least finalized and distributed, by the headquarters internal audit function. There may also be some planning and administrative work that either must be done, or is preferably done, at the organization headquarters. Most of these activities will require some administrative support. Other activities may be performed in part by the corporate director of internal audit, but will usually require additional professional internal audit assistance, which might be provided by one or more headquarters internal audit managers or other planning and administrative personnel. Normally, the director of internal audit will want one individual to have the authority to act in the director's absence, thus ensuring a needed continuity of operations.

With a highly decentralized organization where most of the internal audit activity takes place by division, by type of audit, or by geographic area, this central internal audit function may be viewed as little more than a central ''corporate overhead'' type of function that contributes to expenses of the operating unit but provides little value. Although the director of internal audit may speak to senior management and the audit committee of the board, both may question how familiar that director is with field or operating-unit audit activities. A centralized internal audit function may not be particularly effective if the headquarters function does not add value to total internal audit efforts.

(v) Non-Audit and Informal Staff Assignments.   Internal auditors are frequently asked to carry out special financial or operational activities at the request of senior management, even though those activities are so much a part of the regular day-to-day organization activities that they do not satisfactorily meet the test of true internal auditing. These are often task force projects of limited duration, such as solving an overall inventory control problem. The internal auditors assigned may be pulled from their regular audit assignments to participate on the project and then return back to internal audit when complete.

Although such activities may delay completion of the audit plan and cause some organization control problems, these short-term special projects are generally good for internal audit as a whole and for the individual auditors assigned. Senior management's desire to have members of the internal audit staff participate on a special project represents an endorsement of the professionalism of all members of the internal audit organization. The director of internal audit should actively encourage these types of projects from time to time to give members of the staff additional experiences and potentially to groom them for other positions within the organization.

A different problem arises when management asks internal audit to assume some non-audit function on a regular basis. Illustrative would be the responsibility for reviewing and approving current cash disbursements before those disbursements are actually made. Management may assume that because internal audit has certain special control skills, it is the best suited in the organization to perform these special tasks. These types of ongoing special projects generally take resources away from regular internal audit activities and may even place internal audit in a position where its independence could be compromised. The director of internal audit should strenuously object to such ongoing assignments.

Assuming that internal audit has no alternative other than to accept such an assignment, the recommended organizational approach should be to segregate these additional activities from the normal internal audit activities, and to subject them to periodic reviews by the regular internal audit group. Wherever possible, this kind of a situation should be avoided. The dual responsibilities tend to infringe on the time for internal audit management activities. In addition, there is the very real danger that the dual responsibilities will weaken the image of the director of internal audit to others in the organization.

The discussion of organizational arrangements in this chapter has dealt chiefly with formal types of structures and the essential guidelines for efficient operations. For many organizations, there may also be various kinds of interrelationships in the internal audit department that cut across the established organizational lines. Such interrelationships are informal and take place as necessary to meet current operational needs. They will exist under all types of formal arrangements. Within reasonable limits, these informal organizational arrangements serve a useful operational purpose and often point the way to needed formal organization modifications. If carried too far, however, they can undermine the effectiveness of internal audit's basic organizational approach. The important thing, therefore, is to recognize their necessity but to keep them within sensible bounds.

(c) REVIEWS OF THE INTERNAL AUDIT ORGANIZATION

In closing this discussion of organizational arrangements, it is important to emphasize the changing nature of internal audit organizational needs. These needs should be a reflection of the changing structure of the entire organization. As organization operations change, both in terms of size and basic nature, the approach followed by internal audit also needs to be reappraised. Organizational arrangements in the last analysis are a means to an end, never an end in themselves. Although this reappraisal can and should be made on a rather continuous basis, the preparation of the annual internal audit budget provides an especially good opportunity to carry out a more complete organization reevaluation. At this same time, consideration can be given to the matters of staff administration and control and is discussed in Chapter 10.

8-3 THE INTERNAL AUDIT ORGANIZATION PLAN

Planning can be defined as the formulation of goals and objectives that provide for the matching of opportunities with available resources to achieve the most effective utilization of those resources. To an internal audit organization, these resources include the staff, budget, and the reputation the internal audit has earned among other organization personnel. Resources include both what internal audit actually has in hand and what it can reasonably expect to get as a result of additional management support.

The director of internal audit should always consider the environment of which the internal audit function is a part. This includes the overall organization and, in a broader sense, the world of which the organization is a part. Within the organization, the environment includes management and other personnel at all levels, including executives responsible for the various operational components audited, intermediate managers, and the rank and file personnel. A portion of these individuals will be supportive, some hostile, and some relatively indifferent. Some individuals will be in such a position that their attitudes are very important, while in other cases the relationship is more detached. Internal audit must attempt to appraise this environment as it currently exists and as it might change over time. Through the study and evaluation of internal audit resources and of the environment, internal audit goals and objectives can be formulated in an intelligent manner.

Internal audit planning is vitally concerned with this process of formulating objectives, but it goes still further. Planning has to do with developing the supporting strategies, policies, procedures, and programs that will best assure that actions carried out currently will move the internal audit department toward the achievement of its future objectives. Thus, to internal audit, planning means projecting where to go in the future and then devising the means that will help to best get there. Like every other manager, the director of internal audit must be concerned about the present and future role of the internal audit function.

(a) ESTABLISHING INTERNAL AUDIT PLAN GOALS AND OBJECTIVES

Internal audit's role should be a dynamic one, continually changing to meet the needs of the organization. There is often a need to change audit plans as circumstances warrant. These changes may include the coverage of new areas, assistance to management in solving problems, and the development of new internal audit techniques. Planning is especially important in the face of uncertainty. The demands of the modern organization make it important that internal audit change plans as the needs arise. When management's needs change, internal audit must analyze these trends and have the flexibility to adjust to the new conditions.

An internal audit function must have a clear understanding of its objectives when formalizing its plan. What does management expect of internal audit? What types of coverage and findings are desired? Preceding chapters of this book considered the role that internal auditors could and should play in the organizations of which they are a part. These concepts must be defined in specific terms by the individuals responsible for internal audit activities.

This high-level or conceptual planning of internal audit activities is not an easy task and hence is frequently not done adequately. However, the more carefully and sharply this planning is done, the more likely it is that the supporting activities will be carried out effectively. Additionally, the goals and objectives established through a planning process are not constant for all time. As conditions change, they should be reappraised and modified as is appropriate. The following issues should be considered.

- *Type of Managerial Assistance.* Will it be limited to ascertaining compliance, and to what extent should efforts be made to search out and report possibilities for improvement? In the latter case, does improvement mean the operational efficiency of existing policies and procedures and/or the reappraisal of these underlying policies and decisions?
- *Level of Managerial Assistance.* What is the scope or the extent to which internal

audit's reappraisal role will involve specific organizational levels? How far up in the organization should internal audit go in carrying out this review role? Internal audit may review controls at a field location level that may point to potential control problems within a more senior management group. Internal audit may have to seek support and assistance from various levels of management to follow up on this type of control problem. Access to senior officers holds the greatest promise for internal audit management service.

- *Degree of Independence.* To what extent, both in terms of access to various parts of the organization's operations and in its authority to report on all matters pertaining to the organization's welfare, should internal audit seek independence?

- *Resources to Be Provided.* Goals and objectives should also include an identification of the kind of internal audit efforts necessary, its organization structure, the size of the department, its composition in terms of people and their qualifications, and the level of budgetary support. These determinations will necessarily be linked to projections of the growth of the overall organization.

- *Quality of Service.* Internal audit should strive to improve the value of its audits in terms of such factors as the depth of coverage or quality of audit analysis. Compliance with the standards of the profession, discussed in Chapter 4, will help to achieve this coverage. In addition, internal audit should experiment with new techniques and reexamine how best to satisfy management expectations.

- *Quality of Internal Audit Staff.* The selection and training of staff are crucial for productive and high-quality audit results. Internal audit goals and objectives must properly consider an appropriate level to staff development and training. Chapter 9 discusses these issues.

Internal audit should review the above considerations before it embarks on any level of organization planning. Of course, any internal audit plan must reflect the potential risks that internal audit will face. Risk analysis, which is an essential element in the internal audit planning process, was discussed in Chapter 7.

(i) Developing a Planning Strategy.   A managerial strategy is necessary to define the major operational approaches by which an organization's goals and objectives are achieved over time. Goals and objectives describe where one wants to go and are concerned with what is to be achieved, whereas strategies outline a means of accomplishing desired results. Strategies are sometimes also called *major policies*, the term *major* distinguishing these higher-level determinations from the more routine supporting policies pertaining to the implementation actions. Internal audit groups should consider the following strategies.

- *Manner of Organizing the Internal Audit Staff.* For many organizations, this is a question of the desired level of internal audit staff centralization or decentralization and physical dispersion discussed previously.

- *Staffing Policies.* At the highest level, staffing has to do with the qualification requirements as well as the required numbers of personnel. These considerations are discussed in more detail in Chapter 9.

- *Manner of Administering the Internal Audit Function.* Administration is a combination of issuing instructions, coordinating the efforts of individual persons, and providing effective leadership. The major strategy or policy issue here is the manner in which responsibilities are delegated within the framework of the selected organizational approach. Another strategic concern is the extent to which the director will be participative. In a modern internal audit organization, the trend is toward greater delegation and a more democratic approach.

- *Extent of Formal Auditing Procedures.* Related closely to the broader issue of directing is the extent to which internal audit procedures should be formally documented and the degree of latitude allowed in their use. In this book we generally emphasize the importance of formal, documented procedures whenever possible. Nevertheless, the nature of many internal audit activities is such that internal audit management must weigh the costs of developing formal documented procedures in a new area against management pressures to complete the task using basic internal audit practices.

- *Manner of Reporting.* The manner in which findings resulting from the audit work are disseminated to the various interested parties—including the subsidiary questions of reporting format, timing, and substance—are discussed in more detail in Chapter 15.

- *Flexible Audit Project Planning and Programming.* Unforeseen audit requirements and management requests can create the need for changes in both audit programs and overall plans. Although these cannot be predicted with any accuracy, a flexible approach ensures maximum service with existing resources. Nevertheless, the director of internal audit should not develop a plan and then abandon it shortly thereafter due to ''other requests.'' The difficult decision is to decide what is necessary.

- *Level of Aggressiveness.* The flexibility to be imaginative and innovative in their reviews, and to press strongly for new and higher levels of management service, enables internal audit to maintain the highest standards. Even though certain levels of management may not request a review in a given area, internal audit may see a potential control problem and schedule a review. Such an aggressive review approach may require courage to face criticism on various levels.

- *Action on Recommendations.* Internal audit should be interested in the actions taken, based on their recommendations, beyond reporting the conditions leading to the recommendations. All too often, certain managers may thank the internal auditors for their findings and recommendations but then take no positive actions to correct the problems and implement their recommendations. A well-written audit report serves no useful purpose unless it is used as a framework for appropriate action. Internal audit needs a strategy to assure that actions are taken on reported audit findings and recommendations.

- *Identification of Time Periods.* All of the previously discussed aspects of internal audit goals and objectives need to be related to specific time periods, normally in months or years. In certain cases, the accomplishment of the individual goals and objectives should be sought after in specific phases, a portion in nine months, a second phase in two years, and the like.

Internal audit strategies must combine their own goals and objectives with those of management. Agreement between management and internal audit is more likely to be achieved if internal audit first thinks through the issues carefully, considers the risks, and develops an audit plan in a proper manner. To the extent that management will not accept internal audit's views, two sets of goals and objectives then emerge: those accepted by management—which then become part of internal audit's published plans—and those temporarily held in abeyance by internal audit. The latter serve as a useful base point for subsequent negotiation with management as conditions change.

In some instances, the director of internal audit may feel very strongly about an audit strategy that senior management rejects. For example, the director may have some information indicating that certain officers of the organization are improperly accounting for their travel expenses. The director of internal auditing may propose such an audit with senior management and be discouraged from initiating the review. Depending upon the potential seriousness of these concerns and the nature of the management rejection, the director may next want to take the matter to the chair of the audit committee of the board of directors. As discussed in Chapter 6, the director of internal audit has every right as well as an obligation to bring an issue to that level. However, both sides of the issue should be reexamined before requesting any reversal of a management decision.

Objective measurements should be developed to report the progress of internal audit goals and accomplishments in reported periods. This type of reporting will enable internal audit to measure performance and evaluate progress to date. Specific projects should be developed, where feasible, to accomplish each of the internal audit objectives. Figure 8.4 is an example of a report on the status of projects initiated under one internal audit objective.

(ii) Short- and Long-Range Internal Audit Planning. The director of internal audit today cannot develop an audit plan based solely on such factors as last year's plan and current available resources, publish the plan, and proceed with audit activities. Many factors impact the type of audit activities that should be planned, and various functions and individuals within the modern organization will have some input into that planning process. These factors are discussed in various chapters throughout this book. Some of the groups who will play an important influence on the development of the audit plan include:

- *Management Requests.* Organization management at all levels can and should request internal audit assistance in various internal control–related areas. This request process was discussed in Chapter 3, ''Understanding Management Needs.''
- *Board of Directors–Initiated Requests.* Even though internal audit functionally reports to senior management, it also reports to the audit committee of the board of directors. That group may initiate certain high-level requests for internal audit services outside of normal management request channels. This process, which can very much impact audit plans, was discussed in Chapter 6.
- *External Auditor–Initiated Requests.* Internal audit should work closely with the organization's external auditors. In order to realize economies or to take advantage of internal audit's particular skills in performing operational reviews of key controls, the external auditors may often request internal audit assistance. This relationship is discussed in Chapter 32, ''Coordination with External Auditors.''

In order to develop short- and long-range audit plans, internal audit needs to take into account these outside requests for internal audit services, along with information

Figure 8.4 Progress Against Audit Objectives Special Report

MAXXAM CORP. INTERNAL AUDIT
SPECIAL TRAVEL ACCOUNTING AUDIT STATUS REPORT
March XX, XXXX
PERFORMANCE AGAINST AUDIT BUDGET

	PLANNED	ACTUAL
Operational Audit Hours	360	432
Information Systems Audit Hours	120	146
Financial Audit Hours	4	12
Total Hours	484	590

START AND COMPLETION DATES

Planned	Oct XX, XXXX	to	Nov XX, XXXX
Actual	Nov XX, XXXX	to	Jan XX, XXXX

BUSINESS UNITS AND TRAVEL VOUCHERS REVIEWED

Planned	XXX	XXXX
Actual	XXX	XXXX

AUDIT OBJECTIVES ACHIEVED: XXXX

INTERNAL CONTROL ASSESSMENT: Adequate

COMMENTS:

regarding audit needs based upon the results of other audits, internal audit control assessments, and other inputs. A key factor in developing these plans is audit's assessments of control risk, discussed in Chapter 7. As noted, risk assessment allows internal audit to review various potential audit candidates throughout the organization and to allocate the always limited audit resources to higher-risk areas.

Long-Range Planning

It is a normal practice in any well-run internal audit organization to develop a long-range audit plan. In its final form, this long-term audit plan represents the agreement among internal audit, the audit committee of the board of directors, and senior management as to the planned activities for each component of the internal audit organization, subject to later change in accordance with specified procedures. An internal audit long-range plan is an important tool to manage the internal audit function, to communicate planned internal audit activities to other interested parties, and to measure the performance of internal audit on a periodic basis. These plans are often prepared on two levels:

- *Annual Internal Audit Plan.* A detailed plan is generally prepared on a one-year basis to outline the planned audit activities for the upcoming year. The plan is limited by the current audit department budget and planned resource levels. Figure 8.5 is an example of an annual audit plan.

- *Multi-Year Future Periods Audit Plan.* An internal audit function typically does not have the resources to complete audits for all higher-risk audits in a given year. In addition, they may perform a review in a given area and may want to revisit that area at some future period. A multi-year (usually five-year) audit plan outlines those future planned internal audit activities. Just as an annual plan is created at least once per year, the five-year plan is updated or rolled forward annually. Figure 8.6 shows a five-year plan.

There is no one correct format for an annual audit plan. However, it should be organized to show organization management the area where internal audit plans to concentrate its efforts over an upcoming period. The plan should show the area to be reviewed for each planned audit, the relative risk assessed for the audit, the type of audit, its location, the planned hours, and any other planned costs. Depending upon the size and complexity of the overall organization, the plan as shown can be summarized and broken into a variety of different sequences. This will allow various levels of management to understand the breadth and scope of audit coverage in their areas.

Prior to developing its annual plan, internal audit should request suggestions from management for areas of audit emphasis. This request should be directed to selected middle as well as senior management because of their familiarity with operations. Audit managers who have the responsibility for individual operational areas should also be requested to submit their proposals for audit coverage. In addition, other key members of the audit staff should also be contacted to obtain innovative ideas for audits. The preparation of the annual plan thus stimulates the staff to reexamine objectives and select those audits of most importance.

Benefits are also derived from coordinating with other audit groups. In addition to the public accountants, government auditors may perform reviews of certain operational and financial matters. Information should be obtained, when possible, as to their reported areas of concern and planned future audits. The annual plan should be distributed to various management and audit groups.

In selecting audits for the annual work program, the audit risk analysis should also be considered. Some criteria to be applied in reviewing potential audit areas include:

- *Prior Findings.* Deficiencies may have been reported in a prior audit, indicating the need for follow-up review. This is especially important where significant findings were reported in more than one prior audit.

- *Management Requests.* The chief executive officer or other high official may request specific audits. In addition, the audit committee of the board of directors may ask for coverage of various areas. These requests must, of course, be given priority. Also, various levels of management—such as department heads or branch managers—may ask for audits.

Figure 8.5 Internal Audit Annual Plan Example

EXAMPLECO CORPORATION 2000 INTERNAL AUDIT PLAN

Division	Audit	Risk Rank	Est. Start	Planned Finish	Est. Hours Oper.	Est. Hours I/S	Est. Hours Finan.	Total Hours	Travel Costs	Other Costs	Comments
ELECTRO	INV. PLANNING CNTRLS.	8.4	11/10/00	03/05/00	420	80		500	$1,200		CARRYOVER—'99
ELECTRO	PHYS. INV. OBSERVATION	9.5	01/20/00	02/15/00	60		30	90	$2,200	$400	
ELECTRO	B-PLANT SECURITY	7.4	02/15/00	03/31/00	170	50		220	$900		
ELECTRO	MATERIALS RECEIVING	6.2	04/22/00	05/25/00	340	80	100	520	$1,200		
ELECTRO	PROCUREMENT CONTROLS	6.8	07/25/00	10/05/00	240	100		340	$200		
ELECTRO	NEW MARKETING SYSTEM	7.8	09/20/00	01/15/01	100	340		440			1997 HOURS ONLY
ELECTRO	Q/A LAB. CONTROLS	5.9	04/15/00	06/01/00	210		80	290	$1,200		
DISTRIBUTION	EDI ORDER CONTROLS	9.1	03/25/00	05/20/00	240	180		420		$250	
DISTRIBUTION	WHSE. PHYSICAL SECURITY	7.9	08/10/00	09/25/00	90			90	$120		
DISTRIBUTION	FACTORY LABOR REPORTING	8.2	10/20/00	11/15/00	280	80	110	470	$50	$240	
DISTRIBUTION	PRODUCT INCENTIVE SYSTEM	5.8	04/25/00	06/15/00	80		120	200			
DISTRIBUTION	PROD. WARRANTY RETURNS	6.7	08/10/00	10/15/00	270		40	310			
DISTRIBUTION	LAN CONTINGENCY PLANNING	7.9	11/10/00	12/15/00	40	150		190			
DISTRIBUTION	A/R CONTROL PROCEDURE	9.2	11/05/00	02/20/00		120	320	440		$80	1997 HOURS ONLY
ASIA PACIFIC	G/L SYSTEM INTEGRITY		05/20/00	06/30/00		180	180	360	$3,600		
ASIA PACIFIC	LABOR RELATIONS STDS.		06/10/00	06/30/00	180			180	$3,600		
ASIA PACIFIC	MFG. CONTROL SYSTEM		05/05/00	06/30/00	100	100	100	300	$3,600		
CORPORATE	GOVERNMENT RELATIONS DEPT.		10/15/00	11/20/00	150		100	250			
CORPORATE	EXT. AUDIT YR.-END SUPPORT		01/20/00	04/12/01		160	280	440		$400	1997 HOURS ONLY
CORPORATE	CONSTRUCTION CONTRACTS		05/15/00	07/25/00	340	150	90	580			
TOTAL DIRECT INTERNAL AUDIT					3310	1770	1550	6630	$17,870	$1,370	
NON-AUDIT	HOLIDAYS AND VACATION							880			
	COMPANY AND STAFF MEETINGS							210		$500	
NON-AUDIT	TRAINING							160	$4,800	$3,400	
NON-AUDIT	AUDIT ADMINISTRATION							440		$1,500	
TOTAL PLANNED 1997 INTERNAL AUDIT HOURS								8320			

Figure 8.6 Internal Audit Five-Year Plan Example

MAXXAM CORP 2000 INTERNAL AUDIT FIVE YEAR PLAN

DIVISION	AUDIT	RISK RANK	2000 HOURS	2001 HOURS	2002 HOURS	2003 HOURS	2004 HOURS
ELECTRO	SYSTEM DEVELOPMENT CNTR.	9.7			250		250
ELECTRO	NEW SYSTEMS UNDER DEV.	9.5		500	500	500	500
ELECTRO	PHYS. INV. OBSERVATION	9.5	90	90	90	100	100
ELECTRO	ACCOUNTS PAYABLE SYSTEM	9.1			350		
ELECTRO	UNSCHEDULED OPERATIONAL	8.9		1200	1200	1500	1500
ELECTRO	UNSCHEDULED SYSTEM AUDIT	8.9		750	1000	1000	1000
ELECTRO	INV. PLANNING CONTROLS	8.4	500	80			200
ELECTRO	RAW MATERIALS SCHEDULING	8.3			200	80	
ELECTRO	EQUIPMENT FIXED ASSETS	8.2		250		250	
ELECTRO	NEW MARKETING SYSTEM	7.8	440				
ELECTRO	A-PLANT SECURITY	7.4		220			200
ELECTRO	B-PLANT SECURITY	7.4	220			200	
ELECTRO	PROCUREMENT CONTROLS	6.8	340				
ELECTRO	MATERIALS RECEIVING	6.2	520				500
ELECTRO	PLANT LABOR REPORTING	6.2		400	100		300
ELECTRO	R-PLANT SECURITY	6.2			150		
ELECTRO	Q/A LAB. CONTROLS	5.9	290		150		150
ELECTRO	PRODUCT SHIPPING	5.7		220			220
ELECTRO	PAYROLL AND PERSONNEL REVIEW	5.2		360			360
TOTAL ELECTRO ANNUAL AUDIT COVERAGE			2400	4070	3990	3630	5280
DISTRIBUTION INV. CONTROLS		9.3			300	100	
DISTRIBUTION A/R CONTROL PROCED.		9.2	440	40			400
DISTRIBUTION EDI ORDER CONTROLS		9.1	420		120		400
DISTRIBUTION UNSCHEDULED OPERATIONAL		8.9		1200	1200	1500	1500
DISTRIBUTION UNSCHEDULED SYSTEM AUDIT		8.9		800	800	1000	1000
DISTRIBUTION DELIVERY SCHEDULING		8.2		450	100		450
DISTRIBUTION FACTORY LABOR REPORTING		8.2	470		150		500
DISTRIBUTION PHYSICAL INVENTORY OBSER.		8.1		90		90	
DISTRIBUTION LAN CONTINGENCY PLANNING		7.9	190	40	40	40	40
DISTRIBUTION WHSE. PHYSICAL SECURITY		7.9	90			100	
DISTRIBUTION PRODUCT TESTING		7.5		240			200
DISTRIBUTION PROD. WARRANTY RETURNS		6.7	310		300		200
DISTRIBUTION PRODUCT INCENTIVE SYSTEM		5.8	200				

- *Prior Audit Coverage.* Significant delays may have occurred in auditing an area because of higher priorities. As the time between audits increases, additional weight has to be assigned in this area for audit coverage.

- *Required Internal Audits.* Compliance with certain legislative or other governmental requirements may have been assigned to the internal audit department. Also, internal audit may have a fixed role to play in providing assistance to the outside public accounting firm in its annual financial statement audit. These audit assignments represent fixed requirements that have to be budgeted.

- *Sensitive Areas.* Sensitive areas may change in view of revised conditions, or may be inherent in the nature of the organization's operation. An example might be the review of conflicts of interest in the aftermath of some unfavorable publicity.

Internal audit should prepare a formal analysis as part of its annual planning process, showing accomplishments against the past one-year and five-year plans. This document will allow internal audit to explain why a given audit project may have run over schedule due to expanded audit scope requirements and why others may have been dropped. While these matters are reported on a month-by-month basis, an annual report shows performance for the period and provides some support for the new multi-year audit plan. Figure 8.7 shows an example of an annual-plan performance report.

The audit plan examples described in Figures 8.5, 8.6, and 8.7 show audit projects along with their estimated time and expense requirements. A financial budget to support these plans may be of even greater significance. In order to support budget requirements, internal audit must estimate the costs involved with the total auditing program to be carried out over the year ahead. This will include how internal audit plans to implement its annual plan in terms of the number of personnel, travel, and supporting services required to perform the planned audits and to support other internal audit activities, such as staff training. Internal audit must justify both the overall validity of the proposed audit plan and the efficiency with which internal audit plans to carry out the program. Other questions necessary to build the budget include: What locations are to be covered? What kind of audit work is to be done? How long will it take to do the job? What staff will be required? What will be the travel costs? and, What supporting services need to be provided? The answers to these questions may require an in-depth analysis of the major factors pertaining to the operations of the internal audit department. The overall budgeting process will be discussed in Chapter 22, "Accounting Systems and Controls."

Internal audit plans, as finally approved and supported by financial budgets, provide a major basis for administering and controlling the day-to-day operations of internal audit during the budget year. How tight that control will be depends on how much flexibility has been allowed in the final budget, and on the overall policies of the organization as to budgetary compliance. Under best practices, the budget should be viewed as a major guideline but one that is subject to change when it is agreed that new developments warrant such change.

Short-Range Planning

Short-term work plans play an important role in a successful internal audit operation. Without a plan, efforts may drift and be overly subject to various pressures. Basically, these short-term planning documents show the audit projects in process as well as those selected for audit coverage for the next period, generally one month. In some instances, a longer period can be used, such as three months or a quarter. However, it is frequently difficult to plan these short-term activities more than a month or two in advance because of special requests by management, changes in business operations, losses of personnel, and delays in completing audits. Sometimes scheduled areas are preempted by special audits with higher priority. Because of changes during the year, it is often desirable to schedule monthly meetings to revise the short-term plan for the ensuing month or three-month period. Chapter 10, "Directing and Performing Internal Audits," provides more information on short-term audit planning. The chapter discusses the planning memos and

Figure 8.7 Annual Plan Performance Report

MAXXAM CORP 2000 INTERNAL AUDIT PERFORMANCE

01/16/01

DIVISION	AUDIT PROJECT	PLANNED END DATE	ACTUAL END DATE	COMMENTS	PLANNED HOURS	ACTUAL HOURS	COMMENTS	PLANNED TRAVEL/ EXP.	ACTUAL TRAVEL/ EXP.	COMMENTS	AUDIT STATUS
ELECTRO	INV. PLANNING CONTROLS	02/15/00	02/12/00		500	542		$2,585	$2,490		COMPLETE
ELECTRO	NEW MARKETING SYSTEM	03/22/00	03/28/00		440	385					COMPLETE
ELECTRO	B-PLANT SECURITY	01/15/00	01/30/00		220	245		$7,550	$6,954		COMPLETE
ELECTRO	PROCUREMENT CONTROLS	09/12/00	11/09/00	MGMT. REQ. DELAY	340		IN PROCESS	$5,370	$1,366		IN PROCESS
ELECTRO	MATERIALS RECEIVING	06/20/00		DELAYED	520			$14,323	$0		DELAYED
ELECTRO	Q/A LAB CONTROLS	05/12/00	07/30/00		290	485		$8,459	$12,856	ADDED TRAVEL	COMPLETE
DISTRIBUTION	A/R CONTROL PROCEDURES	08/10/00	08/22/00		440	531		$100	$225		COMPLETE
DISTRIBUTION	EDI ORDER CONTROLS	06/15/00	07/22/00	RESOURCE PROBS.	420	452		$0	$0		COMPLETE
DISTRIBUTION	FACTORY LABOR REPORTING	11/10/00		IN PROCESS	470			$14,865	$9,655		IN PROCESS

detailed schedules necessary to develop effective short-term audit plans. These short-term plans, however, should always be closely linked to the longer-term one- and five-year plans discussed above.

(iii) Squpporting Policies and Procedures for Internal Audit Planning.

The higher-level internal audit strategies and major policies must be backed up by a great number of supporting policies and operational procedures. Many of these will relate to the areas of organizing and planning internal audit activities. Some will relate to the current day-to-day administration of current internal audit matters to be discussed in more detail in Chapter 10. Others will have to do with audit staffing, the preparation of workpapers, and audit reports.

An important consideration is the way in which these policies and procedures come into existence. Where no formal policy or procedure exists, the basis of action may be an independent determination of what should be done each time a particular problem arises. The advantage of this approach is a fresh appraisal of the problem based on the specific situation. The disadvantages are, first, that a great deal of valuable time is consumed over and over again while wrestling with the same kind of problem; second, there is the lack of consistency that is bound to result when different people are dealing with the same type of problem, or even when the same individual is examining the problem over a period of time. The practical needs, therefore, at some point lead to the development of written internal audit policies and procedures.

Another significant aspect of all policies and procedures is the extent to which they rigidly provide for particular types of action or, on the contrary, leave some flexibility in their application. A related factor here is the extent to which the policy or the procedure is detailed. More detailed statements generally tend to be more restrictive. The determinations here, of course, need to be made with care, with appropriate consideration of the importance of exact compliance with the matter being covered, the stage of development of the particular problem, and the effect on the motivation and overall effectiveness of the users.

Internal audit–developed policies and procedures covering their own activities must be closely linked to, and not be in conflict with, existing overall organization policies and procedures. In many instances, organization policy covers certain matters for everyone—such as, for example, the employee vacation policy. In other cases, organization policy or procedure may need some supplementary materials. For example, the organization might have some general position descriptions, but internal audit might want to develop its own specific descriptions within the framework of those general job descriptions. In still other instances, the needs for policies or procedures are unique to internal audit. Illustrative would be policies and procedures covering the actual audit reviews and the reporting of results.

The basic policy statement under which internal audit functions is the charter, or formal written document for the internal audit department. The Standards issued by The Institute of Internal Auditors, discussed in Chapter 5, state: ''The director of internal audit shall have a statement of purpose, authority, and responsibility for the internal audit department.'' The director is responsible for seeking a statement that is approved by management and accepted by the board of directors. As official company policy, this statement serves not only as a guide to the internal audit function but as a clarifying document for various levels of managers as to the role of internal audit.

8-4 IMPORTANCE OF ORGANIZING AND PLANNING

An effective internal audit function must be built around an effective plan of organization that considers both the needs of management and the overall structure of the organization. Without such a plan, understood by all members of the organization, internal audit may be viewed as a weak link in the chain of internal controls supporting the organization. In addition, internal audit needs an effective set of procedures for short- and long-range planning. These plans will allow internal audit to demonstrate to others in the organization that it is proceeding with various audit projects in a planned and orderly manner.

CHAPTER 9

Internal Audit Staffing, Training, and Evaluating

9-1 INTRODUCTION: THE INTERNAL AUDIT STAFF

The strength of any internal audit function lies in its staff. Internal audit is effective only if there is a strong professional staff in place to review operational areas, to perform tests as appropriate, to develop conclusions as a result of those tests, and to describe to management both the findings of the audit efforts and recommendations for corrective action. While tools such as auditor laptop computer systems, described in Chapter 14, and strong audit sampling procedures, discussed in Chapter 13, help the process, a skilled audit staff is really the critical element for a strong internal audit function. An organization must not only attract competent and enthusiastic people but also must provide training to build necessary skills. Finally, it must coach the staff, evaluate their performances, and provide them with proper professional and career guidance.

This chapter discusses effective procedures for building and increasing the professionalism of the internal audit staff. Because the internal audit function is often unique when compared to the remainder of a given organization, special emphasis must be placed on building effective internal audit staff procedures. Although internal audit management is most involved with staff recruiting and training, all members of the internal audit staff should have an understanding of the processes necessary to build and develop an effective internal audit team.

9-2 BUILDING THE INTERNAL AUDIT STAFF

Frequently, in a new start-up organization, internal audit professionals are asked to build an entirely new internal audit staff. In other instances, management may request that a separate internal audit organization be established in an organizational unit that management wants to keep organizationally separate. The necessary requirement to build and manage such an internal audit function starts with obtaining adequate authorization so that needed resources can be recruited. In addition, there is also a need for office facilities and equipment, proper clerical and administrative support, supplies, funds for travel, and the like. The major challenge for procuring internal audit resources, however, has to do with department staffing. This section discusses options for recruiting and building this major resource into an effective internal audit department.

Staffing requirements should be based upon the overall internal audit organization plan as discussed in Chapter 8 and upon the assessment of control risk within the environment to be reviewed, as discussed in Chapter 7. The decisions made and approved by management in building that audit plan will determine internal audit's organizational responsibilities, the general level of staff qualifications needed, and the number of people required. These staffing needs must go beyond the current situation and look to the future plans of the overall organization. Future audit staffing needs must be properly projected and programs developed to provide necessary additional personnel.

Internal audit staffing activities, with a central focus on providing needed personnel, cover a spectrum that runs from the recruitment, training, and development of personnel, to policies relating to their ongoing careers within the organization, and to decisions on when internal auditors voluntarily or involuntarily leave the department. The specific internal audit–related activities carried out in these areas should supplement and are interrelated with the overall human resources department of the organization. (Personnel or human resource department procedures are discussed from an audit and control-review perspective in Chapter 29.)

(a) STAFF RECRUITMENT

The initial step to building an internal audit staff is the recruitment of properly qualified personnel. Recruitment procedures are dependent upon the status of personnel in the present audit organization, any additional technical staff or other audit needs due to planned organization changes, and the level of management-requested authorizations. Based upon the overall internal organization plan, discussed in Chapter 8, the internal audit department should have some authorized staff level. When there are shortages, the audit department will have a need to recruit additional staff to the audit function.

Internal audit management must initially make some decisions as to what levels of staff to recruit. As discussed in Chapter 8, internal audit should have developed position descriptions for all of the audit positions in the organization. Such descriptions, which can follow the same formats and use the same standards and pay levels as defined by the organization's human resources department, provide a basis for seeking candidates. The director of internal audit and other members of audit management may be able to provide some helpful guidance as to competitive pay ranges for various classes of internal auditors within the immediate geographic area and within similar industry groups. Audit management in other organizations will often informally share this information, provided there is a level of reciprocity.

Audit management can choose to find the audit staff recruits either from within the organization or outside. There are advantages and challenges to either overall recruiting approach.

(i) Staff Recruiting from Within the Organization.   Some internal audit departments prefer to fill staff vacancies from other personnel in the organization who have a level of familiarity with their in-house operations and procedures as well as with the organization's culture. Such transfers are usually structured as promotions for the individuals recruited, making them good moves for both the individuals and the overall organization. Also, if the audit position is open due to an internal promotion out of internal audit,

other organization staff members may seek internal audit positions with similar expectations of future promotion.

The sources for candidates from within the organization may include other members of the audit staff, experienced personnel from other departments, or newly hired management trainees. The internal audit organization, of course, does not need only to follow one or another of these approaches. Depending upon the particular staff need, any of these approaches can be used from time to time. Promotion from within generally improves the morale within the internal audit staff. Also, recruitment is often easy if an internal audit department has a record of progressive advancement from within.

There are other strong advantages to promoting internal auditors from within the existing staff. An emphasis on internal development and promotion will mean that most higher-level openings would be filled from the ranks. This practice allows staff members to see that there is room for growth within the audit organization.

While members of the general audit staff may not have certain specialized audit skills, such as a knowledge of computer operating system software controls, there are often persons within the audit staff who might qualify for most promotional positions. A strong training program where internal audit staff personnel are continually given more challenging assignments to prepare them for higher-level work can prepare and groom personnel. Managers have the opportunity to observe an auditor's work and know the candidate's capabilities firsthand. Performance evaluations from prior audits can form a basis for this promotional decision. Training and evaluation procedures are discussed later in this chapter.

Another widely used source of recruitment is the transfer of experienced personnel from other organization components. The candidate is known, and his/her experience and work qualifications can be more precisely evaluated. In this connection, the candidate's familiarity with a specific component of the organization's activities can be matched to the staffing need. Since that experience is in the organization, it also includes a familiarity with organization policies and practices. This approach can be especially advantageous from an overall organization point of view. The movement of organization personnel into the internal audit group can provide both special training and a broader perspective of organization operations. Of course, this should be a two-way street, with people leaving the internal audit department to go back into other various organization assignments. This outward flow can be useful in establishing a better understanding of internal audit's role with other components of the organization. It also builds good staff morale because of the greater number of career opportunities provided to internal auditors, not only within the department but in other organization management positions.

(ii) Recruiting Internal Auditors from Outside of the Organization. Many internal audit departments find it to their advantage to recruit from outside of the organization. Such decision may be due to the lack of qualified persons within the organization; often, however, the internal audit department is a good place to start persons in the organization and to introduce the new auditors to the organization. If they learn the organization and perform well, they can be promoted out of internal audit after a period of time and on to other positions in the organization. The internal audit department would then act as a feeder source for other components of the organization. Several well-respected organizations, such as General Electric, have successfully used this approach. Depending upon overall organization culture, audit management must carefully weigh the advantages and disadvantages of this type of recruitment in filling audit vacancies. This approach also requires the ongoing support of senior management.

Many sources are available for locating suitable internal audit candidates. Internal audit management must consider internal audit skill needs when deciding where to look for candidates. Some good sources for internal audit candidates are:

- *Public Accountants.* Public accounting–based candidates should probably have been awarded a CPA and have some accounting and strong financial audit–related skills. Their experience in carrying out audit procedures in accordance with professional standards is a useful asset in making the transition to internal audit. A public accounting background is often a good qualification for entry-level internal audit positions. In addition, there often is close coordination between public accountants and internal auditors, and each should be familiar with the other's work and capabilities. When vacancies occur in the internal audit department, many organizations look to public accounting firms as a source for able candidates. Public accounting firms also often identify members of their firms who, they feel, may not be suited to public accounting but would be excellent candidates for other positions. However, internal audit management should not look to public accounting firms as the only source for internal audit candidates.

- *Universities and Colleges.* The employment of new college graduates depends in part on the college's programs for training and development. Many universities emphasize a career in public accounting to their accounting students, but there is an increasing tendency for schools to emphasize internal audit as a career direction as well. The Institute of Internal Auditors has worked very closely with selected educational institutions to help them develop strong internal audit programs. Candidates can also be found from both undergraduate and graduate-level programs in business and other disciplines. This recruiting may be done as part of a larger organization program. For internal audit, college recruits have up-to-date competence in skills such as computer systems networks, are familiar with Internet use, are familiar with new research on human behavior, and the like. The new graduate hire in internal audit has the opportunity to learn about all the organization's operations, with the option at a future time of deciding what direction the new auditor's career might take, either in that organization or elsewhere.

    In order to hire outstanding candidates, it is helpful to interview students at the college, establish strong relations with faculty members, give speeches before accounting clubs and other student groups, and attend employer-student functions sponsored by some colleges. This relationship allows the faculty and students an opportunity to become familiar with the organization's internal audit function, and gives internal audit management an opportunity to know the students.

- *Experienced Internal Auditors.* Experienced candidates can bring in skills in various specialized areas that they have learned elsewhere. For example, the organization may be embarking upon a specialized new business area. Experienced internal auditors with skills in those areas, learned from another respected employer, can be very useful. However, screening and evaluating these candidates can be a daunting task. If the candidate is still employed, the current employer cannot be asked about the candidate, and the internal audit department must rely upon a substantial number of candidate representations. The candidate's credentials can be very important here. For example, the Certified Internal Auditor certificate has become the badge of the profession and is evidence that the applicant has a good understanding of internal audit concepts and procedures.

• *Outside Candidates with Other Skills.* The broad scope of the internal audit activities has increased the need for internal audit candidates who have various specialized backgrounds and qualifications in addition to traditional accounting and auditing skills. Individuals with various combinations of education and experience are often needed in specialized operational audit areas such as computer operating systems, production, construction, quality control, legal, and the like. Such audit staff additions can strengthen the capabilities of the internal audit group and enable it to expand its range of management services. These special capabilities can be especially advantageous when the candidate can combine them with financial and internal-control skills. Recruiting these auditor candidates can be a challenge. Internal audit management needs to advertise these open positions or work through outside recruiters.

A good approach for hiring new entry-level employees into the audit department is to make use of management trainees. Sometimes, assistants are hired directly from colleges and universities as management trainees. They are enrolled in a formal management-training program but may not have a formal job until their skills and potentials are evaluated. Under this type of program, the management trainees are given an opportunity to rotate through various departments of the organization before being given a permanent assignment. A tour of duty in internal audit could provide the new employees with excellent training in analyzing and evaluating controls. If the overall organization has such a training program, internal audit management should request that these trainees be rotated through assignments in internal audit similar to any other department. The program can give potential future managers who might not have a career plan to work in internal audit an introduction to internal audit and provide the internal audit department with a valuable resource.

The Institute of Internal Auditors' target-schools program, discussed above, can be an even better source for new internal audit candidates. In these programs, undergraduate students are trained to be internal audit candidates. The students coming out of these programs typically have a good understanding of the internal audit process and are very good candidates for entry-level internal audit positions. The specific designated schools may change from time to time, so the director of internal audit should make inquiries regarding the current schools and auditor candidate availability.

The important point in discussing these potential sources for internal auditors is that a wide range of skills is needed for internal audit, and the recruitment effort should focus on those needed skills wherever they can be located. While the internal audit group can never be expected to have a specialist in every type of its operational activities, a reasonable balance and coverage is needed. The risk-assessment process discussed in Chapter 7, coupled with an evaluation of the current internal audit staff, can help internal audit management to determine where audit skills are needed. Staff-development plans, criteria for promotions, and normal turnover expectations all help management to plan for future audit-staff needs.

(b) INTERNAL AUDIT ORGANIZATION STRUCTURES

Many factors impact how an internal audit department should be organized. These can include the size of the overall organization, special audit needs, and senior management preferences. Organizations operating in diverse types of businesses or in different geographic locations have different internal audit organization structure needs than ones where all operations are in a single location. A basic audit organization rule, however, is that the director of internal audit must have a management and reporting structure that allows that director to have an overall understanding of all internal control issues and audits in process at any point in time. This does not imply that the audit director must be personally involved in all audits—that is often not necessary and certainly not feasible for larger audit organizations. Rather, the director of internal audit should have a sufficient number of managers directly overseeing all audits in process, who can then report audit progress to the director.

Internal audit organizations are typically organized into either a traditional structure, where auditors are responsible for different business activities, or an ''audit specialist'' structure, where auditors have specialized skills such as finance, manufacturing, and information systems. The alternative audit organization is called an *integrated audit* structure, where audits are not devoted to technical specialty areas, such as information systems application controls, but cover all risk areas in the entity under review. Audit staff members with special skills would be drawn from a pool of available resources to serve as staff members on the various audits. Figure 8.1 from the previous chapter, describes the first of these approaches while Figure 9.1 shows the pooled approach. These different organization structures can be further divided into separate groups responsible for various divisions or geographic areas.

In an audit-specialist type of organization, auditors work on projects where they have the best skills. For example, the department may have a separate information systems audit group composed of specialists who will plan their own projects under the overall guidance of the director of internal auditing. Similarly, another section in the department may be composed of financial auditors. The advantage to this type of organization is that the audits are focused on the particular area reviewed. The disadvantage is that the separate groups are often not coordinated very well. For example, the information systems auditors can perform a purely technical review of a client-server application, ignoring important financial or operational control issues. The other audit groups may be working on different projects and never get to the area surrounding that same application.

In an integrated organization, as illustrated in the Figure 9.1 organization chart, all auditors are assigned to an administrative manager. Separate managers are responsible for overall areas of audit activity, such as manufacturing operations versus marketing operations. An audit of a manufacturing process would be performed by a team of financial, operational, and computer-audit specialists, all working together to assess risks and to develop coordinated audit findings. The individual auditors work for an assigned supervisor on one project but may be assigned to another supervisor for another type of audit project. The supervisors will evaluate auditor performance for each individual project, but the administrative manager has overall responsibility for the pool of internal auditors.

Which one of these organization structures is best for the modern internal audit department? The pooled-resource approach allows the audit department to focus on all aspects of control risks during an audit and may be better—however, this approach can be difficult to manage. For example, under the pooled approach, a computer-audit specialist may be assigned to review specialized technical controls as part of an overall audit effort. However, if the manager directly responsible for that team-audit approach does not understand the control ramifications raised by the computer-audit specialist, important audit points may be lost. Specialists can often better focus on unique control-risk areas but

Figure 9.1 Internal Audit Pooled Resources Organization Chart

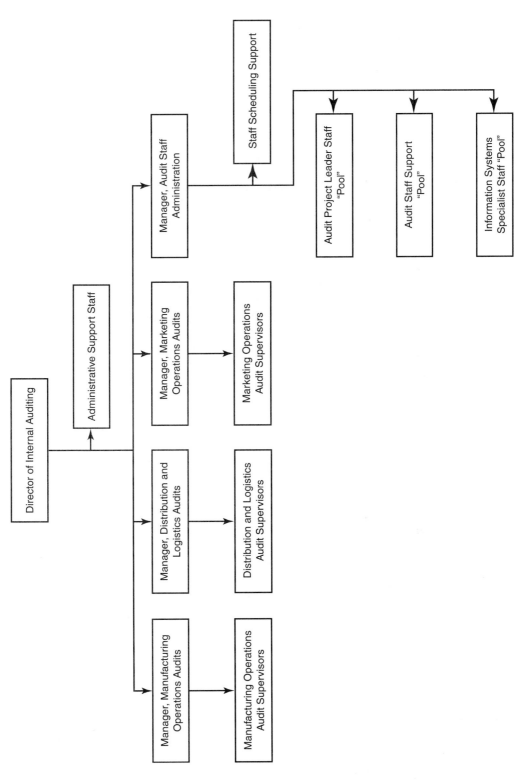

become lost in their specialty areas and ignore other areas of potential audit concern. For example, an information systems audit group may assign its technical specialists to review certain technically interesting areas while the main operational audit group performs reviews without the benefit of the information systems specialists. The pooled approach usually yields better, more comprehensive audits if closely managed.

(c) INTERNAL AUDIT TYPICAL JOB DESCRIPTIONS

To be useful, job descriptions must be specific. If stated in general terms, they serve only as a description of functions rather than as a statement of job responsibilities. Critical elements of the job should be pinpointed and performance standards separately stated so that the employee can be rated realistically. Working with the organization's human resources department, job descriptions should be prepared for all positions in the internal audit department.

The types and titles of the various audit positions depend upon the overall organization structure, described in the previous section. Examples of internal audit job titles include the Director of Internal Audit, Audit Managers, Audit Supervisors, Senior Auditors, and Systems Auditors. Examples of job descriptions for the various levels from staff auditors to audit manager as well as for a systems auditor are shown in Figures 9.2

Figure 9.2 Staff Internal Auditor Position Description

Position Title: *Internal Auditor*

Responsibilities:

1. Based upon established audit objectives and scope, perform assigned audits in accordance with IIA and department standards.

2. Obtain, evaluate, and document audit evidence to support conclusions.

3. Develop appropriate audit tests based upon audit department and other recognized audit procedures, conduct audit tests based upon those procedures, and evaluate the results of those tests.

4. Evaluate operational and financial controls for assigned audits and provide input to other members of the internal audit staff on how those controls may impact other audit procedures.

5. Develop and communicate audit findings and recommendations.

Work Experience Requirements

• One or two years of internal audit or public accounting experience.

Education and Professional Requirements

• Bachelors degree required and advanced degree preferred.

• CIA or CPA preferred.

Figure 9.3 Senior Internal Auditor Position Description

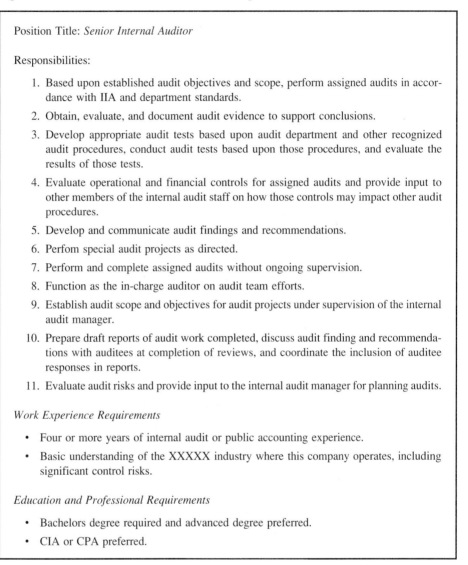

Position Title: *Senior Internal Auditor*

Responsibilities:

1. Based upon established audit objectives and scope, perform assigned audits in accordance with IIA and department standards.
2. Obtain, evaluate, and document audit evidence to support conclusions.
3. Develop appropriate audit tests based upon audit department and other recognized audit procedures, conduct audit tests based upon those procedures, and evaluate the results of those tests.
4. Evaluate operational and financial controls for assigned audits and provide input to other members of the internal audit staff on how those controls may impact other audit procedures.
5. Develop and communicate audit findings and recommendations.
6. Perfom special audit projects as directed.
7. Perform and complete assigned audits without ongoing supervision.
8. Function as the in-charge auditor on audit team efforts.
9. Establish audit scope and objectives for audit projects under supervision of the internal audit manager.
10. Prepare draft reports of audit work completed, discuss audit finding and recommendations with auditees at completion of reviews, and coordinate the inclusion of auditee responses in reports.
11. Evaluate audit risks and provide input to the internal audit manager for planning audits.

Work Experience Requirements

- Four or more years of internal audit or public accounting experience.
- Basic understanding of the XXXXX industry where this company operates, including significant control risks.

Education and Professional Requirements

- Bachelors degree required and advanced degree preferred.
- CIA or CPA preferred.

Figure 9.4   Internal Audit Manager Position Description

Position Title: *Internal Audit Manager*

Responsibilities:

1. Based upon established audit objectives and scope, perform assigned audits in accordance with IIA and department standards.
2. Obtain, evaluate, and document audit evidence to support conclusions.
3. Develop appropriate audit tests based upon audit department and other recognized audit procedures, conduct audit tests based upon those procedures, and evaluate the results of those tests.
4. Evaluate operational, financial, and information systems controls for assigned audits and provide input to other members of the internal audit staff on how those controls may impact other audit procedures.
5. Develop and communicate audit findings and recommendations.
6. Perform special audit projects as directed.
7. Perform and complete assigned audits without ongoing supervision.
8. Function as the in-charge auditor on audit team efforts.
9. Establish audit scope and objectives for audit projects.
10. Prepare draft reports of audit work completed, discuss audit finding and recommendations with auditees at completion of reviews, appraise auditee responses for reports, and issue final audit reports.
11. Evaluate audit risks and provide input to the director of internal audit for planning audits.
12. Develop annual audit plan and monitor performance against the plan.
13. Coordinate annual audit plan with external auditors.
14. Provide functional guidance and support to the director of internal audit.

Work Experience Requirements

- Six or more years of internal audit or public accounting experience.
- Senior auditor or supervisory experience required.
- Strong understanding of the XXXXX industry where this company operates, including significant control risks.

Education and Professional Requirements

- Bachelors degree and advanced degree required.
- CIA or CPA required.

Figure 9.5 Information Systems Auditor Position Description

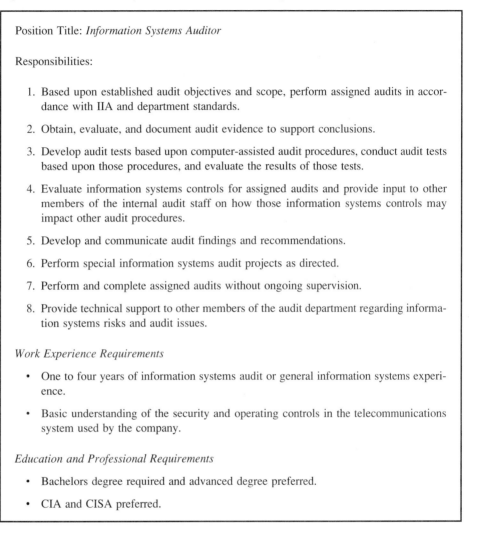

Position Title: *Information Systems Auditor*

Responsibilities:

1. Based upon established audit objectives and scope, perform assigned audits in accordance with IIA and department standards.

2. Obtain, evaluate, and document audit evidence to support conclusions.

3. Develop audit tests based upon computer-assisted audit procedures, conduct audit tests based upon those procedures, and evaluate the results of those tests.

4. Evaluate information systems controls for assigned audits and provide input to other members of the internal audit staff on how those information systems controls may impact other audit procedures.

5. Develop and communicate audit findings and recommendations.

6. Perform special information systems audit projects as directed.

7. Perform and complete assigned audits without ongoing supervision.

8. Provide technical support to other members of the audit department regarding information systems risks and audit issues.

Work Experience Requirements

• One to four years of information systems audit or general information systems experience.

• Basic understanding of the security and operating controls in the telecommunications system used by the company.

Education and Professional Requirements

• Bachelors degree required and advanced degree preferred.

• CIA and CISA preferred.

through 9.5. Each of these descriptions describes the duties, responsibilities, and reporting relationships for that job. They provide both the individual auditor and management with a clear understanding of each job position and how it relates to the others in the organization.

In order to determine that the responsibilities of various members of the audit staff are clearly differentiated—a senior auditor versus a staff auditor, for example—the organization should develop a summary matrix describing all positions in the organization and the major responsibilities and requirements of each. This will provide members of the organization with an understanding of where they fit in the overall department and what is required to move to the next level. Figure 9.6 is an example of this type of audit organization matrix.

Figure 9.6   Internal Audit Organization Matrix

RESPONSIBILITY	Audit Manager	Senior Auditor	Info Sys Auditor	Staff Auditor
Provide support for director of internal audit	X			
Coordinate audit plan with external auditors	X			
Develop annual audit plan and monitor performance	X			
Evaluate audit risks	X	X		
Issue final audit reports	X	X		
Prepare draft reports and coordinate responses	X	X		
Provide technical support to internal audit	X		X	
Perform special information systems projects	X	X	X	
Establish audit scope and objectives for audits	X	X	X	
Function as in-charge auditor	X	X	X	
Perform and complete audits without supervision	X	X	X	
Develop and communicate audit findings	X	X	X	X
Evaluate operational and financial controls	X	X	X	X
Evaluate information systems controls	X	X	X	
Develop appropriate audit tests including CAATs	X	X	X	X
Obtain, evaluate, and document audit evidence	X	X	X	X
Perform assigned audits in accordance with standards	X	X	X	X
WORK EXPERIENCE REQUIREMENTS				
Six or more years	X			
Four or more years	X	X	X	
One or two years	X	X	X	X
Relevant industry experience	X	X	X	
Relevant technical experience			X	
EDUCATION AND PROFESSIONAL REQUIREMENTS				
Bachelors degree	R	R	R	R
Advanced degree	R	D	D	D
CIA or CPA	R	D	D	D
CISA			R	

9-3 INTERNAL AUDIT STAFF TRAINING AND DEVELOPMENT

An internal audit department needs to reexamine continuously the quality of its training program. Sometimes training activities fall into a fixed pattern that is not sufficiently responsive to changing conditions. Other times, training is relegated to a minor role so as not to interfere with current demand for audit services. In times of pressures to reduce budgets, training is sometimes viewed as an employee perquisite that can be dropped or deferred. However, a meaningful program of staff training is necessary to maintain and enhance the skills of the internal audit staff. This on-the-job and off-the-job training needs to be continually updated to meet the current and expected needs of the overall audit department as well as individual members of the audit staff.

(a) INDIVIDUAL AUDITOR TRAINING OBJECTIVES

Chapter 8 discussed how planning and organizing were the first essential steps in performing both an individual audit and an overall program of internal audits. This same concept is true for developing an auditor training program. Individual and overall audit department training objectives must be established and constantly reevaluated as a first step in audit training. Audit management must establish clear training and improvement objectives for all members of the audit staff. These can often be based upon what audit management would like to have changed based upon an evaluation of each auditor's work and career-assessment discussions with members of the staff. Audit management should plan as clearly as possible the kind of individual auditor performance toward which it is aiming.

Individual differences must necessarily be recognized when setting training objectives. The audit staff has varied educational and experience backgrounds, as well as different capacities, or learning curves, in their ability to benefit from specific experiences. Training objectives should thus be set for each auditor based on individual needs as well as the needs of the organization. These objectives should not be static but should change in accordance with progress made by the auditor during the course of various assignments.

Someone, preferably a member of audit management, should act as training coordinator for the entire department. The task should not be assigned to a staff member as an ad hoc type of responsibility due to the need to evaluate individual staff weaknesses and training needs as part of establishing the overall audit training program. Charges of conflicts or favoritism could occur if a staff member were given this task.

The training coordinator should work with each member of the audit staff and attempt to develop a unique plan for each built on strengthening skills in areas where the individual auditor has a perceived weakness. These can be defined by the individual auditor, by management, or through evaluation comments developed over the course of past audit projects. The idea, however, is that the training plan should specify immediate and long-term objectives for each member of the staff. Figure 9.7 is an example of an individual training plan prepared for a staff member and based on specific developmental needs. This type of plan should be reviewed and updated at least once a year.

Individual auditor training objectives should be considered as part of overall audit objectives used in planning assignments. Sometimes, it may be necessary that time be made available for a staff member to leave a job to attend a specific training course. Also, sufficient time should be budgeted to allow for the training defined in the audit department objectives document. Short-run considerations may have to give way to long-run improvements through training in individual performance.

(b) FORMAL AUDITOR TRAINING PROGRAMS

Although the on-the-job training provided in the course of audits is ongoing and contributes the most in shaping individual progress, there is also a need for more formal, structured classroom instruction. These can be classes developed internally or presented by outside providers. Attendance at these training classes should be arranged for staff members according to the training plans and recurring auditor needs, such as strengthening report-writing. Newer technological developments, such as EDI or Internet-based security issues, and changes in professional standards can be studied for application in day-to-day assignments. Successful approaches for performing audits should be disseminated to the entire staff. Because many of these topics may be specific to the organization, outside seminar

Figure 9.7   Individual Auditor Training Plan Example

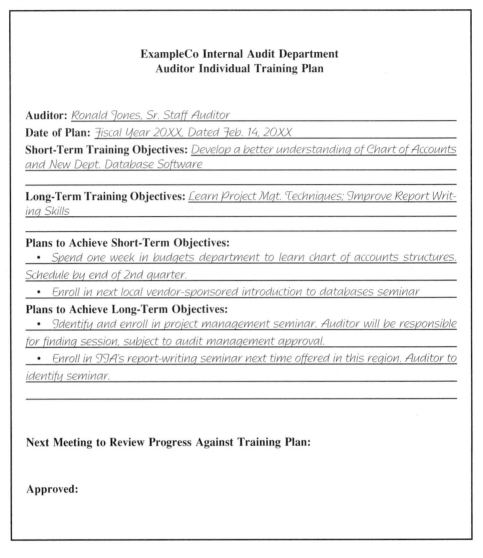

ExampleCo Internal Audit Department
Auditor Individual Training Plan

Auditor: *Ronald Jones, Sr. Staff Auditor*

Date of Plan: *Fiscal Year 20XX, Dated Feb. 14, 20XX*

Short-Term Training Objectives: *Develop a better understanding of Chart of Accounts and New Dept. Database Software*

Long-Term Training Objectives: *Learn Project Mgt. Techniques; Improve Report Writing Skills*

Plans to Achieve Short-Term Objectives:
- *Spend one week in budgets department to learn chart of accounts structures. Schedule by end of 2nd quarter.*
- *Enroll in next local vendor-sponsored introduction to databases seminar*

Plans to Achieve Long-Term Objectives:
- *Identify and enroll in project management seminar. Auditor will be responsible for finding session, subject to audit management approval.*
- *Enroll in IIA's report-writing seminar next time offered in this region. Auditor to identify seminar.*

Next Meeting to Review Progress Against Training Plan:

Approved:

providers can not always totally satisfy all audit department training needs. For these and other reasons, each internal audit department should have its own program of formal training.

Larger departments have found it desirable to sponsor some internally developed and delivered training classes. In addition to being cost effective, the training can be tailored to meet the specific needs of the overall audit department. In many cases, internal auditors in the department can be used as instructors working with standardized training material. In other instances, outside instructors can be contracted to provide training classes in selected subjects, such as statistical sampling. In-house capability can then be developed for teaching subsequent courses.

Several of the major public accounting firms as well as specialized providers have offered good internal audit–oriented seminars. Professional courses available in the community also should be periodically screened. In some instances local colleges schedule courses that are applicable to internal audit, such as business writing or communication skills. Professional organizations also offer seminars of interest to auditors. Some of the organizations sponsoring classes of internal audit interest are: The Institute of Internal Auditors, American Institute of Certified Public Accountants, Institute for Management Accounting, Information Systems Audit and Control Association, American Management Association, and Association of Government Auditors.

(i) New Auditor Orientation Programs.   Once candidates have been identified and recruited to join an internal audit department, they should be introduced to the overall organization and trained in internal audit departmental procedures through an orientation program. All too often, internal audit hires new candidates, gives them some procedural manuals and the like to read during their first days on the job, and then assigns them to an audit project even though they have little or no understanding of the overall organization or of departmental standards. This is a poor use of new auditor resources!

The scope and extent of this program will depend upon the size of the internal audit department, the frequency of new auditors joining it, and the backgrounds of those new candidates. A smaller internal audit department that adds perhaps one or two new auditors per year has a far different need for an orientation program than a large department that recruits a new class of auditors annually from the ranks of college graduates. Similarly, an audit department that generally promotes from within, bringing current employees from other departments into internal audit, has different employee-orientation needs than does an audit department that generally hires experienced internal auditors from outside of the organization.

Whether new employees joining the audit department are new college graduates, experienced internal auditors from other organizations, internal transfers from other departments in the organization, or recruits from public accounting firms, all require some form of new-auditor orientation training. Each group has a different level of experience in internal audit techniques; however, all need an introduction to the procedures unique to their new organization (for example, how to complete a travel expense report).

The audit department should develop an outline of a new-auditor orientation so that key elements are not forgotten during lapses of time when new employees are not brought into the organization. Orientation programs should take a period of perhaps two to three days. When multiple auditors are hired at the same time—such as a group of recent college graduates—the orientation can be provided to them as a group.

Topics for an auditor orientation program are listed below. Areas may not be covered comprehensively, but should sufficiently inform the new auditor employee as well as highlight audit department differences and similarities for the new employee with internal audit experience.

- *Auditing Standards.* The new employee, even if an experienced auditor, should be introduced or reminded of the key standards covering the profession discussed in Chapter 5. These standards describe the overall activities and practices of internal audit.

- *Organization Charter for Internal Audit.* A charter is the top management statement that gives the audit department its general marching orders. The new auditor should have an understanding of the importance that organization senior management gives to its internal audit function. Internal audit charters were discussed in Chapter 6.

- *Introduction to the Organization, Its Personnel, and Its Policies.* The orientation program should provide some fairly detailed materials concerning the auditor's new organization. This introduction can include facility tours and detailed discussions of operations by key members of management, as well as an introduction to key organization policies.

- *Administrative Matters.* These can range from how to complete a travel expense report to how to obtain office supplies.

- *Audit Department Approaches and Procedures.* Even though new auditors joining the organization may have gained their experience through work in other internal audit departments, the orientation program should emphasize the particular audit department standards, such as the planning and preparation of new audits, guidelines for workpaper documentation, and audit sampling. While these standards are covered in many of the chapters of this book, each director of internal audit may want to make certain minor adjustments to conform with preferences and various requests. This material would be much more extensive for new auditors.

- *Data Processing Systems and Audit Automation Tools.* Many systems may require the internal auditor to understand a specialized software package or a retrieval language to access reports and data. In addition, the audit department may have a variety of its own computer-assisted automation tools (discussed in Chapter 14). Classes with both demonstrations and hands-on exercises are valuable.

- *Planning and Performing an Audit.* The new auditor should be introduced to the entire audit process, starting with the overall audit planning steps discussed in Chapter 8 and the risk assessment process described in Chapter 7. The overview should include audit program development and workpaper documentation techniques, as discussed in Chapter 11.

- *Review of a Set of Workpapers.* A good way to help the new auditor understand how audits are performed, documented, and reported is to walk the new employees through a set of workpapers from a recently completed review.

- *Overview of Training.* This orientation will be the first audit department training session for new auditors. They should be introduced to the department auditor training program, including the use of individual training plans, as described in Figure 9.7, which will be developed for them.

- *Auditor Career Paths.* Although it is certainly premature to talk about specific career advancement opportunities with the new employee, the orientation should describe the process for evaluation and potential advancement.

A larger internal audit department with a fair degree of staff turnover should have a formal staff training program that goes through constant adjustments and improvements based on the previous orientations. A training and orientation program is also particularly important for the smaller department with little staff turnover. The department that only adds a single new candidate once every two or three years will find it difficult to maintain an effective training program. If new auditors are only added infrequently, audit management may easily forget all of the important elements needed in the orientation program unless that program is formally documented.

A member of internal audit department management should be assigned responsibility for developing the new auditor orientation program. Such responsibility may include the delivery of actual orientation sessions as described above, as well as reviews of the new auditor's progress on various tasks. The best way for a new internal auditor to understand how audits are performed in a new audit job is to participate in an actual internal audit. Depending upon experience, the new auditor can participate as just an observer, as a junior-level audit assistant performing limited tasks, or as a more active member of the audit team.

After new staff members have been with the department for about six months to a year, it is advantageous to have an off-the-job training class to synthesize their learning to date. This class can discuss such matters as how audit objectives are established, general audit procedures, methods of analyzing evidence, clearing open items in working papers, and report-writing. The new staff members would have worked as part of the team on several audits by this time. They may have questions that they no not want to cover with their in-charge auditors. The off-the-job class provides staff members the opportunity to ask questions, digest what has been learned to date, discuss mutual areas of concern, and learn how to solve problems in the field.

(ii) Other Topics for New Auditor Training.   Due to the relative complexity of the topics and the backgrounds of many newer members of the typical internal audit staff, the audit department should develop some more detailed, follow-up training sessions on specialized topics that were only introduced in the orientation sessions. This approach will allow the new auditor to understand these specialized and technical topics better. Areas for this follow-up training might include:

- *Audit Sampling.* With the widespread use of statistical and other audit sampling techniques by internal auditors, it is especially important that all staff members become familiar with these concepts at an early date. Instructions should include when to apply statistical and other audit sampling techniques, how to select the best method, and how to evaluate the results of the sample. The class should also cover the use of any audit software in use. Chapter 13 outlines the elements of such a class.

- *Information Systems Audit Tools and Techniques.* Information on the audit software packages used and the department's recommended computer audit methods should be given. If several alternative methods are used, such as a microcomputer-based file download package and relational database query tools, the auditor should be given guidance for deciding which method is most appropriate. Hands-on experience should be provided.

- *Report-Writing.* Because developing and writing effective audit reports is often a major challenge for many auditors, and because audit reports represent a final product distributed to many members of management, new auditors should be given experience in writing as soon as they develop their first audit project findings. In addition to this on-the-job experience, report-writing case studies should be developed for use in a specialized report-writing training session. These case studies will help an auditor to understand basic attributes of an audit report finding, its condition, criteria, cause, effect, and auditor recommendation. See Chapter 15 for techniques on preparing effective audit reports.

The above classes are designed to enhance and reinforce the skills of the newly hired internal auditor. They are also topics that may be worthwhile for other, more experienced members of the audit staff when needs are identified through audit performance evaluations. As an internal auditor advances in the organization, training also should be provided in audit supervision. It is often difficult to progress from the technical aspects of performing an audit to supervising a staff of subordinates. As an aid to making the transition, a course can be provided to cover such areas as ways to motivate subordinates, management styles, methods of delegating and controlling, and human-relations problems. A course developed in-house can focus on unique problems associated with supervising a particular organization's internal audit projects.

(c) AUDITOR ON-THE-JOB TRAINING

In addition to the need for extensive education and training classes in modern internal audit practice, on-the-job training is also of utmost importance. Although classrooms try to simulate reality, they cannot take the place of day-to-day experience. It is on the job that an auditor has the opportunity to solve problems under tight time pressures, analyze various data, work with management to arrive at conclusions, and gain acceptance of findings. When a new auditor is assigned to an on-the-job training project, the success of an auditor in making a qualitative appraisal comes into management focus. What are the standards for satisfactory experience for internal auditors? How well do the practices of my department meet these standards? What can internal audit management do to improve the experience and training that are given its staff members?

Whenever practicable, on-the-job training assignments should not be made on a piecemeal basis, but in accordance with a plan that results in the continuing development of the auditor as well as in timely completion of audits. Often, this cannot be done because of the exigencies of workloads, rush assignments, and the problem of obtaining personnel to perform them. However, much can be accomplished by a deliberate intent by audit management to make assignments purposeful.

The assignment of an auditor to different supervisors is recognized as a valuable learning tool. However, unless each supervisor becomes familiar with the manner in which the staff auditor has performed in the past and the areas in which improvement is needed, the benefits from these assignments may be lessened. A review of prior performance appraisals and discussion with other staff members can provide an audit supervisor with information that will assist in carrying out both the audit assignment and the desired training.

The development of a staff member into a topflight senior auditor or manager requires training in the ability to handle increasingly more complex problems. It is through a diversification of audit assignments that the staff member becomes familiar with problems in the audits of various parts of the overall organization. The auditor who has worked for a year on the audit of inventory and receiving operations, for example, is going to obtain a specialized knowledge of these areas only. On the other hand, the staff member who has been assigned to the audit of various operational areas on a planned basis over a period of time will have a better opportunity to obtain the wide experience needed to advance. Internal audit management should keep a record of types of assignments by staff as a basis for future assignments and advancement in the organization.

(d) NEW AUDITOR SUPERVISION AND COUNSELING

There are many opportunities for the in-charge auditor to aid in on-the-job training in the course of planning, organizing, and controlling the performance of audit assignments. The supervisor must always keep in mind the responsibility for the field training of staff assigned. This responsibility is easily overlooked with the pressures of the job. The supervisor should, however, realize that his or her own position is strengthened by an ability to develop subordinates. This training may take several forms, including a combination of instruction, demonstration, encouragement, criticism, and advice. The subordinates should be made to feel that criticism is given in a constructive manner, with the object of helping them improve.

In general, the method of giving instruction to subordinates plays an important part in on-the-job training. Communication of objectives down through the organization—such as explaining the meaning and purpose of the work to be undertaken—is very important. Specific assignments should be related to the overall audit program. Each subordinate should thoroughly understand instructions given. Supervised study of prior years' reports and working papers, or working papers prepared on similar audits, will assist the auditor in this development.

The importance of counseling must be emphasized as a device for augmenting and strengthening the learning process in on-the-job training. An effective counseling program helps to point out an individual's weaknesses and suggest ways to correct them. Counseling serves to obtain the staff member's viewpoint, and thus furthers participation in shaping the auditor's own training program. It may also assist in the staff member's personal adjustment to the firm's culture—its work practices and personnel matters. Through use of effective counseling techniques, the staff members can thus be motivated to accelerate their learning and ability to advance.

The personal development of an internal auditor is an important element of the on-the-job training program. The new auditor's ability to get along well with others should be emphasized, as should the ability to talk intelligently and sell ideas. The effective leadership of other staff auditors should also be an integral part of this development. There typically are many opportunities for an audit supervisor to develop these traits on the job. Audit staff members should be encouraged to express themselves in various job situations. They should be encouraged to participate in discussions with department heads and superiors. The developing auditor should be stimulated to arrive at independent decisions and gather sufficient evidence to support positions. The ability to plan, organize, and control the work of subordinates should be emphasized, including the ability to get along with all members of the audit staff.

It is primarily through the assumption of additional responsibilities and challenges that the internal auditor develops. Supervisors must be alert to the strengths and weaknesses of all members of the staff and continually try to assign them more difficult work. The final product should be that of the in-charge auditor who, in turn, should learn to delegate work to subordinates to develop their capabilities.

(e) AUDITOR SELF-IMPROVEMENT PROGRAMS

The ambitious and effective internal auditor will not develop skills by just waiting to be assigned to some training program or class. Auditor self-improvement programs are typically the most effective way for individual auditors to develop skills and special areas of technical knowledge may take one of the following forms:

- *The Certified Internal Auditor (CIA) Examination.* This examination, directed by The Institute of Internal Auditors, tests the candidate on such subjects as internal audit concepts, standards, and procedures. The certificate has become accepted in many companies as a requirement for advancement to higher levels. Review study manuals and courses are available. An understanding of many of the materials in this book should help the candidate with preparation for the examination.

- *Professional Reading.* Ongoing new developments in the accounting and auditing profession make it important that an internal auditor follow a professional reading program that includes professional journals, new books in the field, literature of public accounting firms, and tax and other government regulations.

- *Advanced Degree Programs Such As a Masters of Business Administration (MBA).* An advanced business education curriculum typically provides the auditor with a broad base of management and business theory, quantitative and computer techniques, and advanced accounting and auditing concepts.

- *The Certified Information Systems Auditor (CISA) Examination.* This examination, sponsored by the Information Systems Audit and Control Association (ISACA), tests the auditor's knowledge of information systems controls and related technical audit topics. Completion of the CISA program is particularly important for information systems auditors.

- *Certified Public Accountant (CPA) Examination.* Passing this examination has long been a goal for many auditors, both in private work and in public accounting. There are a large number of books and coaching courses available. The examination emphasizes financial accounting, financial statement audit, and tax-related issues. This CPA training should, however, be viewed as a supplement to CIA training, not as a substitute.

Internal audit management should encourage members of the staff to embark upon self-improvement programs such as those above. In particular, staff members should be encouraged to enroll in an advanced degree program or to pass an examination such as the CIA. While a program such as professional reading is also important, the effort required to pass the CIA, for example, can be more easily measured.

9-4 EVALUATING INTERNAL AUDIT STAFF PERFORMANCE

Performance appraisals serve to inform various levels of management and supervisors as to staff member abilities and accomplishments. Appraisals thus provide an important input for the consideration of auditor promotion, compensation, transfer, or employment termination. They also serve as a useful tool in staff training through:

- Establishing requirements for periodic appraisal and documentation of strengths and weaknesses
- Helping to determine basic training needs and planning methods of improving performance

- Providing a basis for assignment of staff to individual jobs
- Acting as an aid to counseling an auditor as to his or her ability to meet performance standards

Performance appraisals should usually be completed at the end of each significant job assignment. In addition, composite ratings should be prepared, usually on an annual basis, to provide an overall evaluation of work under various audit supervisors. The value of the appraisals can be significantly increased if proper instruction is given to supervisors on how to fill them out, including some guidance on how to conduct review meetings with the auditor being evaluated. This involves, on one hand, the understanding by supervisors that criticism on an appraisal is meant to help the subordinate. Conversely, there should be an understanding by the audit staff that criticisms shown in appraisals are constructive in nature and are used as a basis for helping with auditor progress and advancement. An example of an audit project performance appraisal form is given in Figure 9.8.

An essential component of an effective performance-appraisal system is the need for formal auditor-performance standards. These permit the objective, accurate evaluation of job performance. When possible, performance standards should be stated in quantifiable terms that can be easily interpreted. Members of the audit staff should be encouraged to participate in establishing these quantified standards, both to gain support for the system and to assure fair and equitable treatment.

In order to develop auditor performance standards, the various auditor job descriptions should first be reviewed and a list made of major responsibilities. One or more objectives for each responsibility can then be identified, followed by several standards of performance for each objective, either in quantitative or qualitative terms. Finally, performance points can be assigned to each objective if desired.

Because of the many responsibilities reported in audit appraisals, audit management may find that it is not practicable to develop standards for each rating element Figure 9.9 is an example of standards for planning and directing an audit, stated in qualitative terms for an audit supervisor. This same concept can be used for developing standards for other members of the audit staff.

9-5 INTERNAL AUDIT STAFF PROCEDURES

The effective internal audit organization needs to develop other important organization procedures to build an effective audit team in which members communicate well with one another and work towards common goals. Communication is the real key here. Too often, an internal audit department is composed of staff members who travel extensively. Procedures should be established to enhance the overall communication and effectiveness of the audit staff. Several examples are as follows.

- *Staff Meetings.* Periodic (monthly or at least quarterly) staff meetings are an important training device for staff members. The meetings serve as a basis for discussing overall organization news, changes in audit plans, and new audit techniques and procedures. Formal lectures may be given or intensive staff participation invited. Staff members can be selected to handle certain subjects such as actual audit field problems and their solutions. Staff meetings are especially useful in exchanging ideas and providing information on current developments.

Figure 9.8 Individual Auditor Performance Appraisal Form

Audit Staff Member Name: _____ Date: _____

Audit Assignment Rated: _____ Location: _____

	POOR	AVERAGE	GOOD	SUPERIOR
Completion of Assigned Audit Engagement				
1. Developed understanding of audit objectives?				
2. Understand key auditee processes and systems?				
3. Completion of audit program as developed?				
4. Appropriate suggestions to improve audit steps?				
5. Appropriate relations with auditees?				
Documentation of Audit Work				
1. Workpapers prepared according to department standards?				
2. Flowcharts used to describe key processes?				
3. Cross-reference between audit program and workpapers?				
4. Audit findings described?				
5. Appropriate sections of draft audit reports completed?				
Technical Competence				
1. Review completed in a competent manner?				
2. Statistical sampling procedures used if appropriate?				
3. Understanding of information systems controls?				
4. Overall technical performance of audit?				
Audit Project Management				
1. Audit segment completed within assigned hours budget?				
2. Audit segment completed within assigned time budget?				
3. Overall auditor project management skills?				

Figure 9.9 Internal Audit Performance Standards Example

STANDARDS for PLANNING and DIRECTING AUDITS

AUDIT SUPERVISOR STANDARDS

Auditor _____ Location _____ Date _____

AUDITOR PERFORMANCE STANDARD	YES	NO	N/A
1. Was plan consistent with long-range audit plans?			
2. Was an engagement memo prepared?			
3. Was the engagement memo reviewed with audit management, senior management, and auditee?			
4. Did supervisor review past audit workpapers and other materials as applicable?			
5. Was there a walk-through prior to start of audit?			
6. Was the walk-through documented?			
7. Did the actual audit time requirements planning and staff assignments reflect information gained from walk-through?			
8. If audit planning requirements were different from long-range plan, were differences discussed with audit management?			
9. If specialized auditor resources were needed, were arrangements made prior to start of audit?			
10. Was audit fieldwork adequately supervised?			
11. Were all issues resolved in a timely manner?			
12. Did supervisor review work over course of audit through use of workpaper point sheets?			
13. Were preliminary audit findings discussed with auditee?			
14. Was all audit documentation reviewed by supervisor?			

- *Audit Newsletters.* This is a good vehicle to discuss informal audit-development issues as well as staff activities such as marriages or promotions. Because many of the staff members may be on the road, the newsletter can be mailed to home addresses or written in electronic media so that all staff members can access it. Rather than making the newsletter another audit-management duty, the editorial task should be assigned to a staff member.

- *Annual Audit Conferences.* A more extended version of the staff meeting is the annual conference. When an audit departmental staff is geographically dispersed to a number of field offices, an annual audit conference is an especially important way to bring everyone together face-to-face. On the technical side, the conference provides all members of the audit staff the opportunity to achieve a broader technical understanding of existing policies, procedures, and problems. As part of the conference, internal audit management should consider the use of various qualified educators, practitioners, specialists, and other authorities. These individuals can come both from within and outside the organization. At the same time, presentations by members of senior management can provide an important opportunity to develop a better understanding of common interests and to make those organization officials more receptive to future internal audit services. All of these inputs, combined with personal contacts, can build better departmental morale throughout the entire internal audit staff.

Internal audit management should always look for ways to increase communications within the internal audit department. A strong network of people who communicate with one another is essential to the successful internal audit organization.

9-6 IMPORTANCE OF PEOPLE IN THE AUDIT ORGANIZATION

This chapter and others throughout this book have emphasized the importance of people in every kind of operational activity that directly or indirectly concerns management and in turn the internal auditor. In a true management sense, people are resources that need to be utilized properly, and all managerial activities are carried out by and through people. Whether those managerial activities involve planning, organizing, providing resources, administering, or controlling, we do things through people. It is therefore quite clear that internal auditors need to do everything practical to understand people and be better able to deal with the especially difficult problems of utilizing them. The importance of people in internal auditing can be identified in three major areas.

1. *All operational activities reviewed by internal auditors involve people.* Every major issue dealt with and every conclusion reached requires consideration of its impact on people. In most operational judgments, the way people are used and the way they perform become critical elements.

2. *Internal audit effectiveness directly depends on how successful the auditor is in influencing people and receiving information from them.* As internal auditors carry out audit work at all levels, the understanding of people enables auditors to get the necessary responses and support that helps them best achieve their professional objectives.

3. *Internal auditors must also be concerned with the management of their own internal audit department.* Like every operational manager, an internal auditor selects and supervises people. An understanding of people enables the internal auditor to work with audit teams and staff personnel effectively and to promote the professional interests of the internal auditing group.

A question might be raised as to whether the effective utilization of people involves pressures or other types of excessive influence that border on unacceptable manipulation. At some point, a focus on end results can conceivably lead to an undue justification of the means. Although there are ethical and moral standards that must be respected, the line of demarcation between acceptable and unacceptable means is often difficult to draw. However, there are legitimate areas for influencing people to serve proper organizational goals that are good for both the organization and the individual. When there is that mutual benefit, the process is especially proper and acceptable. Relations with people and efforts to achieve a better understanding of people combine to promote the best possible utilization of all personnel in a proper professional sense.

Internal audit management must recognize that there are wide variations among individuals as to their capabilities, traits, and intensity of feelings. There are, however, also certain characteristics that are common to every individual. A management review of these common characteristics can be useful, and internal audit management's recognition of their existence can often enable the kind of human relationships that are the foundation for the most effective utilization of people in the internal audit organization. The following types of common characteristics exist in a wide range of levels of intensity.

- *To Be Productive.* In strong organizations with well-qualified people, the normal individual wants to be busy rather than idle and wants to do something meaningful rather than wasteful or without purpose. This characteristic is especially true with auditors who have been exposed to the opposite experience.

- *Urge for Dedication.* The typical internal auditor tends to respond to a cause and derives real satisfaction from expending efforts in the active support of that cause. Strong leaders have utilized this human characteristic even when the cause itself was not really valid.

- *Desire to Serve.* This urge is closely allied to productive work and to the urge for dedication, but it goes beyond these to include the urge to provide genuine assistance to another individual. The source of the motivation can be the need of the other individual, a natural love of humankind, or a basic quality of kindness.

- *To Be Free to Choose.* Most people resent conditions that restrict their independence and freedom of choice. Although individuals may not later elect a particular alternative, they resist being deprived of the right to make that choice. Americans especially take pride in their relatively high freedom of choice.

- *Fairness and Honesty.* The average individual wishes everyone to be dealt with fairly, and is resentful of any action that is at odds with that fairness. Although this need applies mostly to how other people treat each other, it does carry over to concerns about actions affecting other individuals. This fairness then blends into the need for related honesty.

- *Bias Toward Self.* Some individuals are said to be their own worst critics, but others are not fully objective in evaluating their own qualifications or performance. Often, people tend to expect more in the way of praise than criticism, and are often defensive against criticism from others. Although typically we are reasonably objective regarding matters involving others, that objectivity does not extend to ourselves in the same manner. We frequently blame others for deficiencies for which we are partially or fully responsible.

- *Satisfaction of Ego.* A closely related characteristic is that all individuals typically like to be complimented and praised, especially if that praise is visible to other persons. We are hungry for legitimate self-respect, and hence seek all possible reinforcement of that self-respect through the evaluation of others. Even when we know that the praise is not fully warranted, we still respond favorably to those from whom we receive it.

- *Desire to Get Value.* Most people want very much to get their own money's worth. This judgment is of course different for different people and in each case takes into consideration the elements that are of special worth for the individual evaluator. Conversely, people resent not getting their money's worth, especially if they are somehow tricked or otherwise unduly influenced to take the action hastily.

- *Habit.* To a major extent, we are all creatures of habit. In the first place, we tend to welcome familiar situations to which we can respond in the same manner and with minimal effort. Then, having enjoyed that repetitive response, we resent all the more any developments that disturb or threaten that habit.

- *To Be Part of a Team.* This characteristic overlaps some of the previously mentioned characteristics. Team membership, however, is such a powerful motivation that it deserves special emphasis. An individual, such as an internal auditor, who is part of a team derives direct satisfaction in sharing in the team effort. The fact that this membership is in a team—especially when that team is successful—reinforces the individualism's ego image.

- *To Have Compassion.* Individuals often are compassionate and respond to the distress of others. Most people want to help those in distress once they are sufficiently conscious of that distress.

- *Self-Interest.* Although people tend to give of themselves, a basic truth is that the typical individual is guided by self-interest. It is, of course, true that many individuals are very generous, but more often that generosity is operative only after certain levels of self-interest have been achieved, or where there are other overriding needs.

- *Sensitivity.* Most individuals take pride in their ability to keep calm in the face of distress. Whether or not the responsive feelings are visible to others, most people often have feelings of dissatisfaction and resentment. These feelings may be well controlled or they may be volatile in nature. In all forms, however, they usually impede rational thought and tend to induce actions that may later be regretted. This sensitivity of feeling is perhaps the most dynamic ingredient of human behavior.

Understanding individuals and relating to them effectively constitutes a continuing challenge. As we have seen, there are major variations in basic capabilities and in the response to all types of developments. Because of the mix of reason and emotion, the understanding of every individual in the internal audit department represents a unique challenge. Knowledge, patience, care, and alertness are needed for anyone who seeks to work effectively with other individuals. At the same time, internal audit management should seek to understand and thus be a more productive recipient of and responder to the actions of others. The entire problem is complicated because as all individuals know more about all aspects of human relations, they become more sophisticated in their evaluations and responses. Thus effective relations with individuals are always changing and are consequently a never-ending challenge. What makes this all the more important for internal audit management is that all individuals have wide ranges of emotional receptivity, a range that is not necessarily diminished by either greater knowledge or higher-level organizational status. Hence, there are major opportunities for achieving more effective human relations at all organizational levels that well justify the efforts required.

CHAPTER 10

Directing and Performing Internal Audits

10-1 ORGANIZING AND PERFORMING INTERNAL AUDITS

While the effective internal auditor serves as the eyes and ears of top management, it is not sufficient just to review documentation and procedures from the auditor's office. The internal auditor must visit the department, facility, or location where the actual work is performed or where records are maintained. The auditor can then observe and develop an understanding of the procedures and practices in place and design and perform appropriate tests to evaluate controls.

Chapter 7 discussed the process of selecting areas or projects for internal audit review through a formal risk analysis. Once higher-risk audit candidates have been identified and audits planned, the next step is to organize and direct the audit staff to perform the audits. This chapter introduces procedures to direct and perform internal audits, including the field survey, documentation of systems, workpaper documentation, and administrative controls for managing the field audit. These procedures are appropriate whether the audit covers an operational area such as manufacturing resource planning or a financial area such as an accounts payable function. The same procedures are also appropriate for specialized audits, such as reviews of telecommunications or data-processing controls.

The basic steps to perform internal audits discussed in this chapter—such as the preliminary survey to evaluate audit evidence and documentation techniques, with an emphasis on flowcharting—are useful for performing most internal audits.

An internal audit department will be more effective if all members of the audit staff follow consistent, professional procedures in performing their reviews. They will also be much more effective in the eyes of general management, who will come to expect a consistent, quality approach from the audit staff in the ongoing performance of internal audits.

10-2 AUDIT PLANNING PREPARATORY ACTIVITIES

Each audit assignment should be planned carefully prior to its start. Much of this general planning work should be accomplished as part of internal audit's annual planning and risk-assessment process, as discussed in Chapters 7 and 8. Even with time factored in for unscheduled or special reviews, other requests may come from management or other situations may bring attention to a potential problem (such as the results of other audits or a report about another organization). Sometimes, there are pressures to begin special audits immediately. However, a better audit will result from a properly planned project. In addition, internal audit can obtain significant savings in time and effort with adequate advance planning and preparatory work.

Although some of the preparatory activities described in this chapter can be performed during the audit itself, many of them are normally done in advance of visiting the actual audit site. These activities define the objectives, scope, and procedures used in an audit. This is particularly important in larger organizations performing multiple, concurrent audits with different mixes of audit personnel assigned to each.

The following sections discuss the actual steps required to plan and perform a typical audit. Of course, no single audit is really typical. The planning outlined in these paragraphs normally is done well in advance. Relative risks, as discussed in Chapter 7, have been considered, and based on this risk evaluation, a long-range audit plan has been developed. The next step is to develop detailed plans, starting with the definition of specific audit objectives.

(a) DETERMINING AUDIT OBJECTIVES

The need to establish specific audit objectives is the most important aspect of audit planning. The scope of operational auditing may be as broad as the management process itself. Management's desires, the various audit approaches available, audit staff capabilities, the nature of prior audit work, available resources and time, and the specific objectives and limitations of an audit project are all considered at the beginning of each assignment.

General objectives are part of the overall audit plan discussed in Chapter 8. They define high-risk areas for internal audit consideration and, based upon this risk identification, allow broad audit objectives to be established. When the individual audits included in that long-range plan are scheduled, these stated original audit objectives should be reexamined and defined in more detail as necessary. The objectives also should be reviewed with management or others requesting the audit. For example, the original audit plan may have identified controls over an order-entry process to be a high-risk area considered for an audit. A new system with improved controls may limit the original need for the order-processing and shipping review or change the potential emphasis of that review. Once an overall audit purpose is defined, the scope of specific audits can be established.

Internal audit management sets forth this scope and these objectives and planned procedures in an engagement-planning memo. Although it may be altered later through the preliminary audit investigation process, a formal statement of scope and objectives communicates the general intentions of the planned audit to the staff members who will be assigned to the review. Figure 10.1 shows a sample audit planning memo.

(b) AUDIT SCHEDULING AND TIME ESTIMATES

The annual internal audit plan, discussed in Chapter 8, is used to decide which audits are to be performed in the next period, sometimes designating plans by specific auditors or by auditor job grade. Key staff members, generally audit managers, should have participated in this planning process and be aware of any subsequent adjustments. Preliminary time estimates are established and time frames set for performing each audit. However, changes are often made to this annual plan during the course of the year due to the increased

Figure 10.1 Sample Audit Planning Memo

Date: Mar 15, 20XXX

To: Workpaper Files

From: L. C. Tuttle, Audit Supervisor

Subj: Accounts Payables System Audit Planning Memo

The memo is to document the planned review of the accounts payables process at the ExampleCo Corp. manufacturing headquarters facility. The review is planned to begin on about April 15, 20XX and will be staffed with four members of the internal audit organization; Henry Hollerith for information systems controls, two regular or senior internal audit staff members, and L. C. Tuttle as project leader.

The review will include internal accounting controls at the headquarters accounting facility, controls over linkage with the purchasing system at multiple facilities, the management of the cash discount system, and overall controls surrounding the Electronic Data Interchange (EDI) function for receiving advices of shipments to the plants and for paying remittances due. The review will perform both manual and computer systems–based tests to assess the overall process as appropriate.

The audit is scheduled to begin on about April 22, 20XX and has been budgeted to require a total of XX hours of time from the overall audit team. A detailed audit plan, including an estimate of expected hours by auditor, will be prepared prior to the actual start of the review.

The review will emphasize controls over the EDI process at the specific request of X, Y, & Z, our external audit firm. Alex Ponzi from X, Y, & Z will supply a detailed schedule of their audit objectives prior to the start of the review. All findings surrounding this review will be communicated to X, Y, & Z and they will have no opportunity to review the workpapers per normal internal audit procedures. All audit findings and recommendations will be reported in a normal internal audit department report.

L. C. Tuttle, Audit Supervisor

S. J. Smyth, Audit Manager

resource requirements of other audits in progress, revised audit scopes due to other audit findings, personnel changes, and other management priorities.

In addition to the annual plan and any revisions, individual audit schedules, based on this plan, should be prepared. Depending upon the nature of the audits performed and audit staff size, these individual schedules may cover a month, a quarter, or even a longer period. For a larger internal audit department, detailed audit schedules should be prepared for both the entire audit department and the individual auditors and reviewed at least monthly to reflect changes or adjustments. For example, an audit specialist in a key area may be unavailable for several weeks or months. This might require an overall shift in audit department plans.

Figure 10.2 shows a sample detailed schedule of audit activity for the entire department over a three-month period. The same type of plan can be reorganized to show project assignments for each auditor over a similar multi-month period. It also can be used to show scheduled vacations, supervisory and administrative time, and formal training. As a control device, a detailed audit plan can serve as a tool for the reconciliation of available auditor days with scheduled audit requirements. Figure 10.2 is prepared using a spreadsheet package. While an internal auditor can easily develop such a plan tailored to meet individual audit department needs, commercial software packages as discussed in Chapter 14, are readily available.

The number and level of staff required for various audits depends upon an evaluation of the nature and complexity of the audit projects as well as auditor abilities and time constraints. Audit projects should be broken down into individual tasks for making these audit project hour estimates. Overall estimates are then more reliable and can serve as a benchmark for comparing actual with budgeted audit performance. Of course, the plans developed at an early stage of the audit are preliminary and must be adjusted once more information is obtained.

Auditor skills and developmental needs should be considered in selecting personnel for any audit project assignment. After deciding upon the individual audit segments, the talents needed to perform the audit tasks must be determined. For example, one segment of a planned audit may require an information systems audit specialist to evaluate certain information systems controls, as illustrated by the Test EDI Controls step shown in Figure 10.2. Another segment may require an auditor with audit-sampling skills to construct and evaluate a statistical test.

(c) PRELIMINARY SURVEY

The annual and long-range audit plans discussed in Chapter 8 should be made with some knowledge of the expected area to be audited. For example, audit management would realize that a branch office review should take *about* X hours to complete based on past experience; however, risk analysis for annual audit planning is often performed at a high or overview level. Steps beyond those risk-analysis and annual-plan-hours estimates are taken before starting the actual audit. The first step should be a preliminary survey that gathers background materials regarding the entity to be audited. This survey is often the responsibility of audit management or the designated in-charge auditor and is followed by the field survey discussed later in this chapter. Prior to starting actual fieldwork, it is essential there be some review of background and other pertinent materials covering the planned audit.

Some of this background information may be available in prior audit files or corre-

Figure 10.2 Audit Department Detailed Schedule

EXAMPLECO CORP. INTERNAL AUDIT DEPARTMENT
APRIL–JUNE AUDIT PROJECT SCHEDULE

PROJECT #	AUDIT	AUDITOR	ACTIVITY	APR	MAY	JUNE
A23-O6	AP— EDI REVIEW	H. HOLLERITH	TEST EDI CONTROLS	20	80	45
A23-O6	A/P—EDI REVIEW	J. JONES	DOCUMENT PAYMENT PROCEDURES	110	24	12
A23-O6	A/P—EDI REVIEW	T. SCHMIDT	TESTS OF TRANSACTIONS	36	80	8
A23-O6	A/P—EDI REVIEW	T. SCHMIDT	TESTS OF TRANSACTIONS	36	80	8
A23-O6	A/P—EDI REVIEW	L. TUTTLE	MANAGE AUDIT	12	18	12
A28-78	BRANCH SALES OFFICES	J. DOE	LOCATIONS G34, F21, R45	120	145	30
A28-78	BRANCH SALES OFFICES	M. LESTER	LOCATIONS E33, G34, N16	0	65	160
A31-01	JOB COSTING REVIEW	F. BUSHMAN	COMPLETE REVIEW / ISSUE REPORT	80	16	0
A31-01	JOB COSTING REVIEW	L. TUTTLE	RESOLVE ISSUES, MANAGE AUDIT	12	4	0
E04-00	FIREWALL SECURITY REV	H. HOLLERITH	TEST AND DOCUMENT CONTROLS	0	64	80
E04-00	FIREWALL SECURITY REV	J. HOOVER	REVIEW SECURITY PROCEDURES	0	40	60

spondence. The following items should, generally, be reviewed if available during an internal audit preliminary survey:

- *Review of Prior Workpapers.* The prior audit objectives and scope, audit workpapers, and programs used should be reviewed to gain familiarity with approaches used and the results of those audits. Some organizations prepare an audit critique at the conclusion of each review to better understand the approaches used and the alternatives available for future audits. Special attention should be given to any problems encountered in the prior audit and the suggested methods of solving them. The organization of workpaper permanent files, which often contains this material, is discussed in Chapter 11.

  Knowing the amount of time the prior audit took as well as any problems encountered can help determine the planned resources needed. The results of prior tests performed should be reviewed, deciding whether any should be reduced, eliminated, expanded, or performed on a rotating basis in future audits. Prior workpapers may indicate a large sample of test-count items was included as part of an inventory review, but due to generally good control procedures, few problems were encountered. Planning for the upcoming audit should focus on whether those same control procedures are still in place, potentially allowing sample sizes to be reduced.

- *Review of Prior Audit Reports.* Past audit findings and their significance should be considered, as well as the extent of management commitments to take corrective actions. To obtain leads to other sensitive areas, the auditor should also study reports on similar entities or functions in the organization. For example, if a branch-level audit is planned in a multi-branch organization, recent audit reports covering other branches may point to potential problem areas in the branch planned for review. Related findings in other areas may also be useful.

  Particular attention should be given if substantial corrective actions were required. The upcoming planned audit may want to include an examination of these areas. Attention should also be directed to any disputed items from a prior report. Although internal audit management should have an objective of clearing up all disputed items in an audit report, there may be situations where the auditor and auditee agree to disagree. These matters are discussed in Chapter 15. The auditor should note any such areas as a suggestion for a planned audit in an upcoming period.

- *Organization of Entity.* The auditor should obtain an organization chart of the entity to be audited to understand its structure and responsibilities. Particular attention should be given to areas where there may represent a potential separation of duties problem. In addition, the number of employees and the names of key employee contacts by major departments or sections should be obtained. This should include, if possible, the name of a key liaison person for contacts during the audit. The entity's mission statement or similar functional descriptions should be obtained to better understand its purpose. Budgets and financial-performance data should be reviewed as background material. The audit manager may want to gain this information through a telephone request and should advise the auditee that the requested information is to help in the planning of the potential audit.

  The areas reviewed when gaining an understanding of the organization of the entity will vary somewhat depending upon the type of audit planned. In an operational audit of a manufacturing area, as discussed in Chapter 23, the auditor might want to gain an overall understanding of the manufacturing process. Similarly, a planned data-processing legacy computer system general-controls review, as discussed in Chapter 16, would require the auditor to gain some background information about the type of computer equipment used, the telecommunications network, and the applications processed.

- *Other Related Audit Materials.* Materials from related audits completed, planned, or in process should also be studied. This may include audits by the outside public accountant, with an emphasis on its management letters, or any reviews by governmental regulatory auditors. The results of internal reviews by departmental or other organization officials, trip reports, and other related reports provide additional useful background material. Any indication of known problem areas from these reviews should be noted. In some instances, it is beneficial to review articles in the professional literature—such as the IIA's monthly publications—to discuss successful approaches used by other internal auditors.

10-3 STARTING THE AUDIT

The next step in starting most internal audits is to inform the organization to be audited—the auditee—that the review has been scheduled. This is often done through an informal telephone call or conversation followed by a formal engagement letter notifying auditee management of the planned review. This engagement letter should inform the auditee of when the audit is scheduled, who will be performing the review, and why the audit has been planned (regularly scheduled, management or external auditor request, etc.). This who, what, and why approach should be used for all engagement letters. A sample engagement letter is shown in Figure 10.3. This letter should notify auditee management of the following.

1. Addressee. The letter should be addressed to the manager directly responsible for the unit being audited.
2. Objectives and Scope of the Audit. The auditee should be clearly advised of the purpose of the review and the areas it will cover. For example, a letter might advise that internal audit plans to review internal controls over the shop floor labor collection system and that the review will only include main-plant shop floor operations.
3. Expected Start Date and Planned Duration of the Audit. As much as possible, the engagement letter should give the auditee some understanding of the timing of the audit.
4. Persons Responsible for Performing the Review. At a minimum, the in-charge auditor should be identified. This will help auditee management to identify the key person when a team of auditors arrives on site.
5. Advance Preparation Needs. Any requirements needed in advance of the field visit or at the audit site should be outlined. This might include copies of certain reports in advance of the visit. This is also an appropriate place to request field audit office space, computer systems network access, or access to office microcomputers.
6. Appropriate Engagement Letter Carbon Copies. Copies of the engagement letter should be directed to appropriate levels of management.

Figure 10.3 Audit Engagement Letter Sample

March 15, 20XX

To: Red Buttons, Dept. 7702

From: Sam Smyth, Internal Audit

Subj: Accounts Payable System Audit

The internal audit department has scheduled a review of your accounts payable processes. Our review will include your general accounting procedures, communications and interfaces with the purchasing department, and the procedures for accepting cash discounts. We also plan to perform a detailed review of your EDI procedures. This review has been scheduled through our annual internal audit planning process and has also been requested by our external auditors.

We expect to start our review during the week of April 22, 20XX, and we plan to conclude our work, including the issuance of an audit report, in June. Lester Tuttle will be directly responsible for this review; he will contact you to discuss our review plans in greater detail. Lester will be assisted by two other members of our regular audit staff as well as by Herman Hollerith, who will do some EDI system detailed testing.

We will need access to your regular accounts payable records and accounting reports. In addition, please inform your EDI value-added vendor that we plan to perform some automated testing over ExampleCo files. Please arrange for systems access in advance of our visit. We will also require some working space in your office area.

Please contract me at ext. 9999 if you have any questions.

CC: G. Busch
        A. Ponzi, X, Y, & Z Co.
        L. Tuttle

Financial, statistical, and other reports relating to the entity being audited should also be requested in advance. Reports of this nature can help identify trends or patterns. Also, comparisons can readily be performed between entities to determine any significant variances. Appropriate levels of management should also be copied on this engagement memo.

Although it is usually appropriate to inform auditee management that an internal audit has been scheduled, there may be circumstances where no formal engagement letter is released. For example, if the audit is fraud-related, the review might be performed on a surprise basis and only scheduled through appropriate levels of senior management. Small retail locations are also good candidates for surprise audits. In most instances, however, auditee management should be informed of the planned audit visit and made aware of its planned objectives.

Some internal audit professionals have taken different stands on whether or not audits should be announced in advance. Some argue that a surprise audit allows the auditor to review actual conditions without giving the auditee the benefit of cleaning up records, documentation, and other matters. However, the arrival of an audit team for an unannounced audit can cause some serious disruptions to the auditee organization, with the possibility that the prime auditee may be on vacation or away at a seminar. Unless there is a suspected fraud or a need for a surprise cash count, unannounced audits should generally be avoided.

There may be reasons to postpone or reschedule the review as announced in the engagement letter. For example, a key manager or technical support person may have a pre-scheduled vacation during the period of the planned audit. If that person is a key source of information for the review and if there are no special reasons for the audit's planned time schedule, audit management should reschedule it to accommodate local management. In many situations, however, the unit management may inform internal audit that "this is a bad time," with no strong reasons for postponing the audit. Because internal audit has a comprehensive schedule of planned audits and its own scheduling problems, it may sometimes be necessary to refuse such requests for postponement and insist on initiating the audit as planned.

Once the audit has been scheduled and auditee management informed, the assigned audit team should be ready to begin work at the auditee site. This is called *fieldwork* even though the audit may not take place at a remote site and possibly will just start down the hall from internal audit. At this point, the internal audit team has gathered such background information as relevant policies and procedures. Internal audit would next perform a field survey to improve the assigned audit team's understanding of the areas to be reviewed as well as to establish preliminary audit documentation of those procedures.

(a) FIELD SURVEY

This survey, like the preparatory planning survey discussed above, is critically important in determining the direction, detailed scope, and extent of the audit effort; it is the first step taken at the site. The auditor cannot just rush in with no clear purpose or objectives and begin examining documents and observing operations. The field survey allows auditors to: (1) familiarize themselves with systems and (2) evaluate the control structure and level of control risk (see Chapter 2) in the various systems to be included within the audit. If members of the audit team are unfamiliar with the audit location and its management, this is the point to make introductions and to clarify any questions that may have been raised through the engagement letter. It is also the appropriate time for the in-charge auditor to outline planned interview requirements and to establish a preliminary schedule.

The following elements should be considered by the in-charge auditor and other members of the team during a typical field survey.

- *Organization.* During the field survey, the auditors should confirm that organization charts, including the names of key personnel, are correct. The auditor should become familiar with functional responsibilities and key people involved in the operations. Often, a title on an organization chart does not reflect the true responsibilities of that position. Formal position descriptions should be requested whenever the auditor feels they may be appropriate. If the function does not have prepared charts available at the time of the preliminary survey, the auditor should draft a rough organization chart and review its assumptions with auditee management.

- *Manuals and Directives.* Copies of applicable policy and procedure manuals, extracting data of interest for the audit workpapers, may be available through an on-line system, and appropriate access should be obtained. Applicable federal and state laws and regulations should be studied, as well as management directives to comply with them. Depending upon the overall objectives of the audit, departmental correspondence files should also be screened for applicable materials.

- *Reports.* Relevant management reports and minutes of meetings covering areas appropriate to the audit—such as budgeting, operations, cost studies, and personnel matters, and the results of any external inspections or management reviews as well as actions taken—should be analyzed. Examples might include manufacturing cost performance reports or a fire inspector's review of computer room physical security. Such reports may provide leads for the audit, as well as a summary of problems faced, recommendations made, and progress made in their implementation.

- *Personal Observation.* A tour or walk-through of the activity familiarizes internal auditors with the entity audited, its basic operations, personnel, and space utilization. It also provides the audit team with an opportunity to ask questions and to observe operations. Auditors are sometimes guilty of visiting an operation, spending all of their time in an accounting or administrative office, and completing the audit without a clear understanding of the actual activity performed. This can result in serious omissions in the final audit work. The impressions gained from this tour should be documented in the audit workpapers as a narrative. Compliance with company procedures can also be sometimes observed.

- *Discussions with Key Personnel.* Discussions with key personnel help to determine any known problem areas, the current results of the unit's operations, and any planned changes or reorganizations. Questions should be raised based on preliminary data reviewed or tour observations.

The field survey is the initial direct auditee contact phase of any review, where management meets the audit team and where the assigned auditors may have their first exposure to the entity to be reviewed. Problems or misunderstandings may arise at this point. Although these matters should have been resolved at the time of the engagement letter release, unit management may not always understand what the internal auditors want, or internal audit may not have developed a correct understanding of the entity through the preliminary planning. The result may point to a need to adjust the scope of the planned review, the planned audit procedures, or even the overall audit. If so, the assigned in-charge auditor should contact internal audit management for guidance.

This section has referred to both ''the internal auditor'' and ''the in-charge auditor.'' Depending upon the size of the overall internal audit staff and the audit engagement, the review may be performed by one or several internal auditors. One of these auditors should be designated as the ''in-charge'' auditor, with responsibility for making most on-site audit decisions. In-charge responsibilities are usually assigned to the more senior members of the audit staff, but the responsibility should be rotated throughout the staff to give less experienced auditors some management experience.

(b) DOCUMENTING THE AUDIT FIELD SURVEY

Normally, this survey will occupy the first day or two at the audit site. For large reviews, the survey can be performed during a separate visit in advance of the auditor's detailed testing and analysis work. In either case, the work performed and summaries of data gathered through the field survey should be documented in audit workpapers. Copies of key reports and published procedures should be obtained, summary notes and observations recorded from all interviews and tours, and flowcharts prepared for all systems or processes. This section discusses procedures for documenting the understanding gained during the auditor field survey. These will be part of the auditor's workpapers as discussed in Chapter 11.

The auditor's field survey also serves as a means for identifying new and innovative approaches to performing the audit. New techniques should be considered in the light of changed procedures or operating conditions. For example, a function that was once processed manually may now be automated.

Flowcharts should be prepared describing major processes, control risks, and internal control points. Through their graphic summary of the flow of operations and data, flowcharts illustrate the complexities and control points in a system or process. The old adage that ''a picture is worth a thousand years'' very much applies here!

The concept of developing flowcharts for all major transaction processes will become clearer to the reader in later chapters, where major organization functions or processes are described. For example, Chapter 28 discusses sales, marketing, and advertising processes. (Figure 28.9 from that chapter provides an example of the order-entry, shipping, and billing functions in an example organization. An internal auditor assigned to review a shipping and billing function at a unit of the organization might prepare this type of document.) The flowchart shows the relationships between different operational elements and where the control points exist in the process. Once completed, flowcharts become part of the auditor's permanent workpaper file for that entity. They also support the requirement in the United States under the Foreign Corrupt Practices Act (FCPA), as discussed in Chapter 2, that organizations maintain documentation covering their internal controls.

In many instances, internal audit may have prepared flowcharts as part of an earlier review, and these may need only to be updated. Similarly, flowcharts may have been prepared by the organization's external auditors and should be available for use in the audit. Sometimes, an organization will have prepared its own internal flowcharts to document procedures. These should certainly be used, although the auditor will want to determine that they are correct and current. No matter what the source, process flowcharts should be assembled for all major processes in the area to be reviewed.

Despite the need to have flowcharts for major processes, they may not be needed for small or relatively simple operations. In some cases, the internal auditor can describe a process through abbreviated workpaper notes. In most internal audit projects, however, the implementation of flowcharts should be a standard method for audit documentation and should utilize any automated tools available. Usage should also be coordinated with external auditors to prevent duplication and to standardize the flowcharting approach.

Although the approaches to developing internal audit flowcharts are described here as part of the auditor's field survey procedures, flowcharting techniques are useful for supporting many other internal audit procedures. The successful internal auditor should develop strong flowcharting skills, which can be used throughout the internal auditor's career.

(i) Flowcharting Approaches.   Flowcharts are a pictorial or symbolic representation of a process. They have been used for years by procedures analysts and computer programmers to describe how a given process will function or how the various programs in an information system will function together. They are also very useful in describing general business procedures. Non–data processing flowcharts generally follow one of three formats: process, paperwork, or functional. The internal auditor should develop a general understanding of all three and use the one that best describes the area reviewed.

A process flowchart describes the flow of information or the significant steps in various organization operations. For example, Figure 10.4 describes the various steps necessary to process incoming mail. These process steps have been discussed in this and previous chapters. A similar process flowchart could be developed for manufacturing operations to show how materials move through various machines and combine with other assemblies to make the completed component. Process flowcharts are often used for describing automated systems.

Paperwork or procedural flowcharts track the manual flow of paperwork, including where copies are filed or who approves or amends a given copy. This type of flowchart was very common prior to the now almost universal use of automated systems with limited paper trails. Through the 1960s, larger organizations even employed what were called *systems and procedures specialists* to document these paperwork processes. Although not common today, this type of flowchart is still useful for documenting the flow of manual paper documents through a process. Figure 10.5 is an example of a paperwork flowchart showing the approval of employee travel expense forms.

A functional flowchart documents the progress of a document through various departmental entities in an organization. It is really a special version of either of the above two flowchart types and places its emphasis on organizational boundaries. Figure 10.6 is an example of a functional flowchart showing the steps necessary for management to process an employee pay increase in an organization.

These three similar but somewhat different flowchart approaches raise the question of which style is best for internal auditors. Each has its uses, but an internal auditor may find the process flowchart style to be most useful for audit documentation. The paperwork flowchart is most useful when the auditor has the challenge of describing a complex paperwork process with numerous document approval steps and filing requirements. The functional flowchart is useful when the auditor wants to describe procedures or operations across various organizational or department boundaries. Paperwork may flow across various departments in the organization or data from a distributed system may actually leave the organization and return for subsequent processing. The functional flowchart also can be used to describe these paperwork steps and organization boundary issues, but the other two types are more effective when these issues are important.

Two general approaches are commonly used for developing process-oriented flowcharts: the *method approach* and the *end-result approach*. The method approach places emphasis on the system, including an analysis of controls to prevent errors, rather than describe system outputs. Under this approach, the auditor describes and documents system processes; if there are acceptable controls, the assumption is that the end results are acceptable. The end-result approach, on the other hand, starts with documenting from the final information product, such as an accounting month-end budget performance report. The data elements that feed into this report are traced back to their sources, and only data that affect the final product need to be identified. In a typical set of financial systems, it is not necessary to describe all information flows; the final product budget performance report is an example. In contrast, under the method approach, the flowchart describes all procedural steps, including some programs, decision branches, or reports that are irrelevant to the auditor's concerns over final budget performance. The end-result approach may

Figure 10.4   Auditor Process Flowchart Example: Incoming Mail

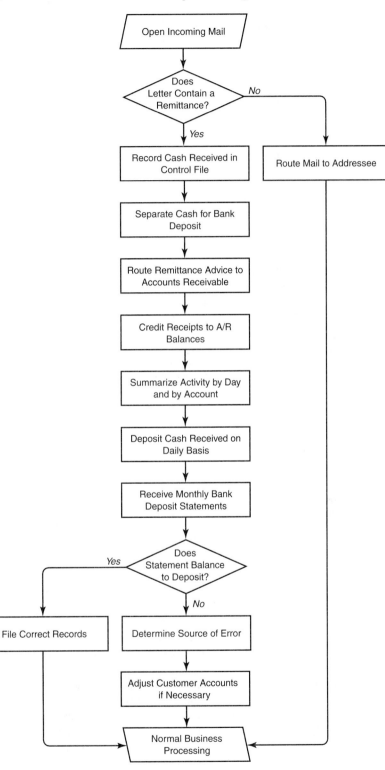

Figure 10.5   Travel Expenses Procedural Flowchart

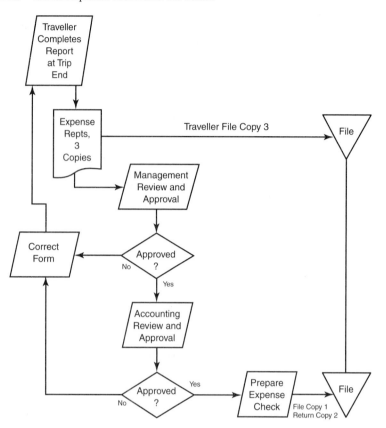

save some time and money in researching and preparing the flowchart; however, an internal auditor faces a risk that other control issues may be missed.

An example might better explain these two approaches. A factory labor payroll system might collect time card data from the factory floor with inputs going to payroll, personnel, external tax reporting, factory labor efficiency, and cost-accounting systems. A flowchart of this system following the method approach would document information flows to all of the subsystems along with the relevant controls for those supporting systems. The internal auditor might find it necessary to look at past audit history, for example, for a job order costing system, consider any past audit findings, and divert efforts in considerations of that related system.

In an end result–oriented flowchart, where the auditor was only interested in the factory payroll system, the review might start with pay registers and just trace them back to their time card sources. Figures 10.7 and 10.8 are examples of each of these flowchart approaches. In an actual audit, each of these flowcharts could be much more extensive, but the method approach will almost always require more steps and areas for consideration than will an end-results style flowchart.

Although an internal auditor should be aware of each of these flowcharting approaches, many internal audit departments will find the method approach the most useful for documenting operational procedures. They may be modified, if required by circumstances, to eliminate the details of extraneous processes. This flowchart approach will generally be used in the Part IV operational auditing chapters of this book.

Figure 10.4 is a process flowchart prepared for describing the controls over incoming mail receipts from customers. Major control points illustrated in the flowchart are:

- The mail clerk lists cash received as a control for cash accountability.
- Remittance advices are used for recording receipts in a receipts cash book as well as inputs to the microcomputer-based accounts receivable system, thus providing a control for entries made.
- Deposits are made on a daily basis.
- The automated system generates reports weekly on aging and extent of accounts receivable balances to provide a control over collection activities.
- Receipted deposit slips and later bank statements provide control over final disposition of money received.

The internal auditor who lacks experience in developing flowcharts should build these skills by developing similar flowcharts of simple processes. An auditor can then test these by reviewing them with other, more experienced members of the internal audit department, who should be able to offer helpful suggestions. Over time, an internal auditor will be able to flowchart more complex processes to support audits in various areas.

Figure 10.6   Functional Flowchart Example: Pay Increases

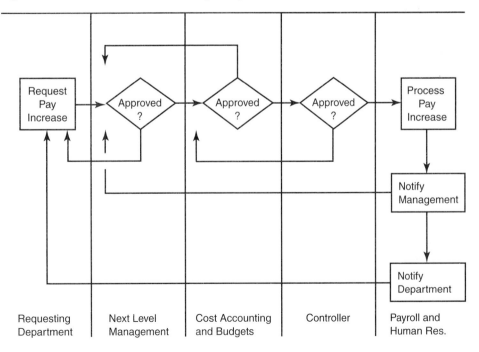

Figure 10.7 Method Approach Flowchart: Payroll

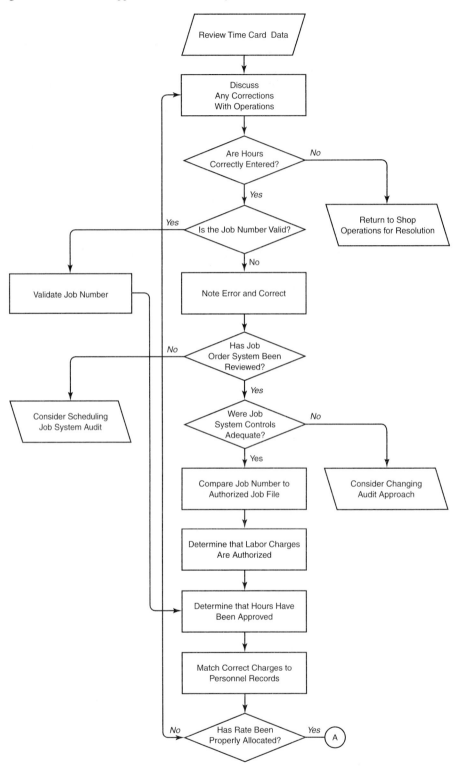

(ii) Flowcharting Symbols and Tools. The flowcharts in the preceding figures use fairly standard symbols as well as commentary to describe the various steps being documented. These symbols are recognized by many professionals. Figure 10.9 shows some typical symbols used in preparing flowcharts for manual or automated processes. Templates for pencil-draft flowcharts are available in office-supply shops or from external audit firms.

At one time, most internal auditors developed their flowcharts with pencil and paper using these plastic symbol templates. While this was a convenient way initially to draw the flowcharts, it was difficult to make changes or modifications to manually prepared documents. As a result, auditors sometimes avoided preparing and then updating detailed flowcharts. Automation changed this. Just as most auditors now use automated spreadsheet software rather than pencils and fourteen-column paper forms, various automated tools

Figure 10.7 (*Continued*)

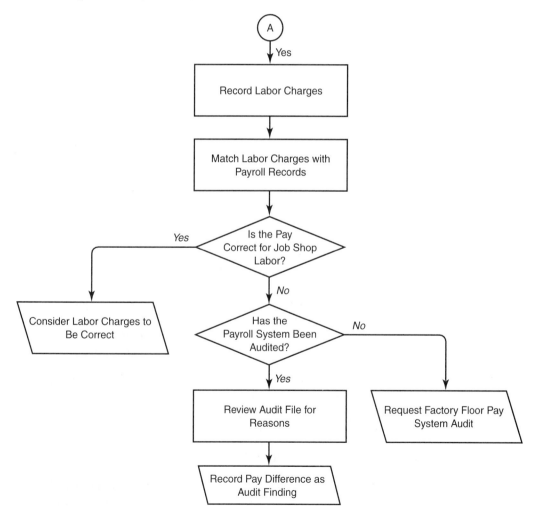

Figure 10.8 End Result Approach Flowchart

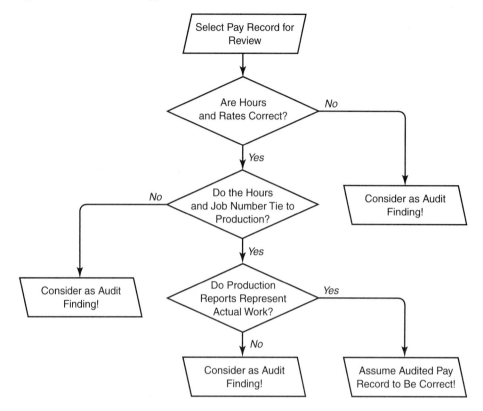

are available to help develop auditor flowcharts. This software can be installed on a microcomputer located in the internal audit department or on laptop computers assigned to auditors in the field. Earlier versions of these flowcharts can be stored and later retrieved for easy modification. Software is discussed in Chapter 14, on the automation of internal audit processes.

There is also a variety of other computer system–based flowcharting tools that may be available to internal auditors. Most of these are used primarily by information systems departments for their own systems projects. These software tools are subsets of the Computer Assisted Systems Engineering (CASE) tools used by many information systems organizations. CASE tools are described in more detail in Chapter 18. Internal audit should discuss its flowcharting needs with information systems management and then evaluate the applicability of any possible information systems department flowcharting tools for its potential use.

(c) FIELD SURVEY AUDITOR CONCLUSIONS

The purpose of the field survey is to confirm the assumptions gained from the preliminary audit planning and to develop an understanding of key systems and processes. Because the information that supports the preliminary audit planning is often imperfect, this is an important point where the assigned audit team can make adjustments to their planned audit scope and objectives. For larger audits, it is often a good idea for a member of audit management to visit the team performing the field survey and review its results. This way, any necessary management-approved scope changes can be made. This on-site presence can clear up any potential questions that could be raised later.

An internal auditor may encounter instances where the information gathered from a field survey may cause the audit team either to adjust the planned audit scope substantially or even to cancel the detailed audit work. Sometimes, the audit team involved in the

Figure 10.9 Typical Flowcharting Symbols

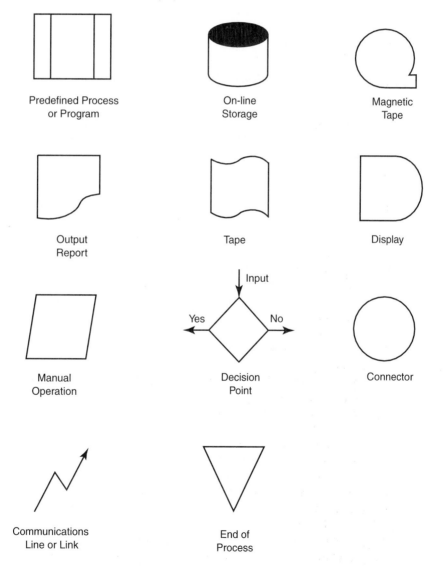

Predefined Process
or Program

On-line
Storage

Magnetic
Tape

Output
Report

Tape

Display

Manual
Operation

Decision
Point

Connector

Communications
Line or Link

End of
Process

preliminary planning may call the auditee at a remote location and be advised that there are "no changes" in the area of the auditor's interest. When the audit team arrives, the field survey could point out significant changes, such as the introduction of a new information system, which changes the overall control environment and may require the internal audit team to add another specialist to the project, causing both staffing and audit test strategy adjustments. In other cases, the audit team may find that changes are so substantial that the planned audit should be canceled or postponed. In most instances, however, the field survey provides the audit team with additional data to help them adjust their planned procedures.

The materials gathered in the field survey should be used either to document or to update a workpaper permanent file. If a member of audit management is not on site, the results of the survey should be summarized in written form, communicated through fax or e-mail, and reviewed with internal audit management before proceeding with the audit. Figure 10.10 is an example of a report on field survey conclusions. This document is particularly important if the in-charge auditor feels there is a need to change audit scope or planned procedures.

10-4 AUDIT PROGRAMS TO AID IN PLANNING THE AUDIT

Auditors should perform their test and evaluation procedures in a consistent manner with an objective of minimizing arbitrary or unnecessary procedures. Of course, an internal auditor will not necessarily know what those arbitrary or unnecessary procedures are until some experience has been gained in performing reviews. To provide some help, internal auditors should use what is called an *audit program* to perform what has proven to be their more effective audit procedures consistently. The term *program* makes the auditor's procedures seem similar to the steps in a computer program, which goes through the same instructions or steps every time the process is run. For example, a computer program to calculate pay will read the time card file of hours worked, look up the employee's rate stored in another file, and then calculate the gross pay. The same steps apply for every employee unless there are exceptions such as overtime rates coded into the payroll program. Similarly, an audit program is a set of preestablished steps the internal auditor performs.

An audit program is a tool for planning, directing, and controlling audit work and a blueprint for action, specifying the procedures to be followed and delineating steps to be performed to meet audit objectives. It represents the auditor's selection of the best methods of getting the job done. It also serves as a basis for recording the work steps performed.

As was discussed in Chapter 7, the internal audit department may have a series of generalized audit programs prepared for recurring audit activities. Many of these programs, such as one covering an observation of the taking of physical inventories, can often be used from year to year and entity to entity with little change. In other situations, the auditor may only have to modify a standard program to the unique aspects of a particular audit.

In many other situations, a standard audit program will not be applicable. For example, the internal auditor may want to review controls in a new business entity with some unique control characteristics, or audit management may want to take a different approach because of problems encountered with similar reviews. Based on planned audit objectives and data gathered in the preliminary and field surveys, the in-charge auditor will want to prepare a customized audit program for guiding the review. This may be little more than a standardized program with minimal local changes, or it may be a unique set of audit

Figure 10.10   Audit Field Survey Conclusions Report

April 5, 20XX

To: Sandra Smyth, Audit Manager

From: Lester Tuttle

Subject: Accounts Payable Field Survey Conclusions

We have just concluded our preliminary meetings with local management as well as a review of documentation and an observation of operations over the ExampleCo accounts payable operations. While most of our preliminary audit plans to review accounts payable controls were correct, we identified two areas where our audit scope and planned audit procedures should be modified:

1. *Cash Discount System* We were advised that, with the low interest rates we have been experiencing in recent years, the company has found little advantage to taking cash discounts for prompt payment. As a result, we were advised this system is not normally used today.

   I suggest we reduce Jane Jones's planned 40 hours in this area to 20 hours and either utilize her for other matters or end her role early.

2. *EDI Controls* The use of EDI is much more extensive than anticipated, and A/P does not appear to be doing a very good job in handling this growth. A much more extensive effort at controls documentation and transaction testing is needed.

   I suggest we ask Hollerith to return for an extra week during the month of May. That would increase his hours for that month to 120. We discussed this, and he is open to changing his schedule.

Please advise if these proposed changes are acceptable.

Lester C. Tuttle

---

procedures based upon the preliminary planning and the results from the field survey. In order to prepare this program, the internal auditor first should have an understanding of the characteristics of what constitutes an adequate audit program.

(a) AUDIT PROGRAM FORMAT AND PREPARATION

An audit program is a procedure, usually published internally by internal audit, describing the audit steps and tests to be performed by the auditor when actually doing the fieldwork. The program should be finalized after the completion of the preliminary and field surveys and before starting the actual audit fieldwork. It should be constructed with several criteria in mind, the most important of which is that the program should identify the aspects of the area to be further examined and the sensitive areas that require audit emphasis.

A second important purpose of an audit program is that it guides both less experienced and more experienced auditors. For example, management may request that an internal audit department observe the taking of the annual physical inventory. This type of review consists of fairly standard procedures, such as those outlined in Chapter 24, to assure, among other matters, that shipping and receiving cutoff procedures are proper. A less experienced internal auditor may not be aware of these procedure steps, and even the most experienced of internal auditors may forget one or another. An audit program outlines the required audit steps.

An established internal audit department will probably have built a library of programs, established over time, for tasks such as a physical inventory observation or a review of fixed assets. When planning a review where such established programs exist, audit management needs only to review this established program in light of any changed conditions that have been discovered through the preliminary or field surveys. The audit program is revised as necessary, with the changes approved by audit management prior to the start of the review.

For many internal audit departments, appropriate established audit programs may not be available for many potentially auditable areas. This is because internal auditors are typically faced with a wide and diverse set of areas for review. They will not have the time or resources to review every area on a frequent basis, such as every year. Established programs prepared for prior audits often become out of date due to new systems or changed processes. The auditor responsible for the field survey or another member of audit management should update any existing audit program or prepare a set of procedures for the planned review. Depending upon the type of planned audit, programs usually follow one of three general formats: a set of general audit procedures, audit procedures with detailed instructions for the auditor, and a checklist for compliance reviews.

Some examples may better illustrate these audit program types. Figure 10.11 is an audit program for a review of petty cash controls at a branch unit. It consists of general procedures to review cash at any unit of a larger, multi-facility organization. The specific area covered by this Figure 10.11 audit program highlights a key difference between the old, traditional auditor and the modern internal auditor. In the past, internal auditors spent far too much time reviewing such areas as petty cash, with little attention given to the more significant operational areas. While we hopefully have moved beyond this, there still is a need to review these types of areas as part of overall operational audits.

Typically, internal audit would have developed these general audit programs for many of its related units. The audit team visiting a unit could then use standard programs to review cash controls in a consistent manner from one unit to the next. This is particularly important in a multi-unit organization where audit management wants to have assurance that controls over the area were reviewed and evaluated in a consistent manner, no matter who was the assigned auditor or at which location.

The Figure 10.11 type of audit program form would normally have space on the document for the initials of the auditor who performs the step, as well as a cross-reference to the workpaper page. This cross-referencing process is discussed in more detail in Chapter 11, on auditor workpapers. This sample audit program is shown as a printed document that might be developed and controlled in the internal audit department. In other instances, the in-charge auditor might prepare a custom program to evaluate certain special procedures encountered during the field survey. This handwritten program document might be

Figure 10.11   General Audit Program Example: Petty Cash

1. Prior to review, determine who is the cashier responsible for the petty cash fund, the authorized fund balances, receipt requirements, replenishment procedures, and guidelines for authorized disbursements.

2. Perform the petty cash review on a "surprise" basis. Identify yourself to the cashier, ask that the cashier function be closed during your initial review, and make a detailed count of the cash in the account as well as any personal checks included. Perform this count in the presence of the cashier and ask the cashier to acknowledge your results.

3. If personal checks were included, inquire why they were not deposited on a prompt basis. If the fund is being used as an employee short-term loan fund, with checks held as collateral, assess the propriety of this practice.

4. Reconcile the cash count with the fund's disbursement register, noting any differences.

5. Determine that all disbursements recorded have been made to valid employees for authorized purposes.

6. Observe office security procedures covering the fund. Determine that the funds are locked or otherwise secured.

7. Review procedures for fund replenishments. Select a prior period, review supporting documentation, and reconcile to purchases journal.

8. Assess the overall control procedures, propriety, and efficiency of the petty cash process. Determine that the function is used only for authorized small cash disbursements rather than as a change or short-term loan fund.

given to a member of the audit staff or used by the supervising auditor who prepared the program.

An audit program with detailed instructions or procedures assumes that the auditor using it lacks some of the technical knowledge necessary to perform the review. It is usually developed for a one-time review of some fairly specialized area and prepared by audit management or a knowledgeable audit specialist Figure 10.12 is an example page from an audit program containing more detailed instructions for a review of cartridge and tape management procedures in a legacy or mainframe computer data center. The staff auditor with inadequate knowledge to plan all of the procedures outlined can perform them given some guidance. This is a useful audit program format when a centralized audit management group with remote auditors in the field wishes to have all of those field auditors perform the same general procedures.

The checklist audit program was once the most common of formats. The auditor would be given an audit program composed of a long list of questions requiring "yes," "no," or "not applicable" responses. The auditor would complete these program steps either through examinations of documents or through interviews. Figure 10.13 is an example of a checklist audit program for reviewing ethics and business compliance policy. Yes and no responses, when asked in an information-gathering context, are often appropriate. A checklist-format audit program has two weaknesses, however. First, while a series of auditee yes-or-no type interview responses can lead an experienced auditor to look at

Figure 10.12 Detailed Audit Program Example: Tape Management

Audit_____ Location_____ Date_____		
AUDIT STEP	**INITIAL**	**W/P**
1. Develop a general understanding of tape/cartridge management operations including inventory system, records, and procedures for assigning media to library.		
2. Tour storage facilities, observing media assignment and retrieval processes.		
3. Observe library security facilities, including procedures to restrict access into the facility by non–library personnel.		
4. Select two production applications and note the current and most recent backup tape reel numbers from job control records. Trace these tape reels to physical library locations to verify their existence.		
5. From the step 4 reels found in the library, use production utility programs to verify that the contents of the tapes are consistent with production process.		
6. Select a sample of reel numbers from the library and trace them to production records. Note any potential questions or problems.		
7. Review procedures for releasing tapes to any outside requesters. Review records for selected distributions to determine that procedures were followed.		
8. Review procedures for transferring media to off-site locations. Determine procedures are consistent with disaster-recovery plan procedures.		
9. Review procedures to protect media from malicious or accidental destruction.		
a. Verify storage area is equipped with fire detection and protection devices.		
b. Assure the area is environmentally controlled consistent with other data-processing operations areas.		
c. Assure that the library area is protected against water damage.		
SAMPLE PROGRAM PAGE ONLY—SEE CHAPTER 16		

problem areas or to ask other questions, these same points may be missed when a less experienced auditor is just completing the questionnaire and not going beyond the yes's and no's and where they might lead. A procedures-oriented audit program better encourages follow-up inquiries in other areas where information gathered may raise questions. Second, the questionnaire audit program tends to cause the auditor to miss examining necessary evidential matter when just asking only the questions. The more inexperienced auditor can too easily check "yes" on the questionnaire without determining, for example, whether that yes response is properly supported by audit evidence. An example would be a question regarding whether some critical document is regularly approved. It is easy to ask the question, receive an answer of "yes," and never follow up to see if those documents were actually approved.

    Each of these audit program formats will work for different types of reviews provided

Figure 10.13   Internal Audit Questionnaire: Business Ethics & Conduct

Audit _____ Location _____ Auditor _____ Date _____			
INTERNAL CONTROL CONCERN	**YES**	**NO**	**N/A**
1. Does the company have a written code of business ethics and business conduct?			
2. Is the code distributed to all employees?			
3. Are new employees provided orientation to the code?			
4. Does the code assign responsibility to operating personnel and others for compliance with the code?			
5. Are all employees required to acknowledge that they have read, understood, and agree to abide by the code?			
6. Are training programs delivered to all employees regarding compliance with the code?			
7. Does the code address standards that govern employee conduct in their dealings with suppliers and customers?			
8. Is there an effective mechanism in place to allow employees to confidentially report suspected violations of the code?			
9. Is there an appropriate mechanism in place to follow-up on reports of suspected violations of the code?			
10. Is there an appropriate mechanism to allow employees to find out the results of their reported concerns?			
11. Is compliance with the code's provisions a standard used for measuring employee performance at all levels?			
12. Is there a procedure in place to update the code on a periodic basis?			

the internal auditor gives some thought to the program questions. The key concern is that all audits should be supported by some type of audit program that documents the review steps performed. This approach allows audit management to recognize what procedures the auditors did or did not perform in a given review. Strong and consistent audit programs are an important step to improving the overall quality of the internal audits performed.

The reliability of the evidence to be reviewed and various types of other information available should also be considered when developing the final audit program. There is little value in keeping steps in an established audit program that call for reviews of systems and procedures no longer in use. An internal auditor, in developing an audit program, should try to select audit steps that are meaningful and that will produce reliable forms of audit evidence. For example, the audit program often needs to call for detailed tests in a given critical, high-risk area rather than suggesting that the information can be gathered through interviews.

Advanced audit techniques also should be incorporated into audit programs wherever practicable. For example, computer-assisted audit techniques (CAATs), discussed in Chapter 12, can perform selected audit steps—similarly, the use of more advanced audit procedures such as statistical sampling procedures to allow the auditor to extract data easily from larger populations. Members of the audit staff who have information systems audit or other technical skills should be consulted when preparing these audit program steps.

There is no best or set format for an audit program; however, the program should be a document that auditors can use to guide their efforts as well as to record activities. This audit program will then be included in the workpapers to serve as almost a table of contents of the audit activities described in those workpapers. Word-processing packages and other related software, discussed in Chapter 14, can be used to prepare audit programs.

(b) TYPES OF AUDIT EVIDENCE WHEN EXAMINING INFORMATION

As discussed in Chapter 5, IIA Standards state that an internal auditor should examine and evaluate information on all matters related to the planned audit objective. The auditor should gather information or audit evidence in support of the evaluation. This audit evidence should be what the internal audit Standards call *sufficient, competent, relevant*, and *useful*. An audit program, properly constructed, should guide the auditor in this evidence-gathering process.

An internal auditor will encounter a variety of different types of evidence that can be useful in developing audit conclusions. If an auditor actually observes an action or obtains an independent confirmation, this is one of the strongest forms of evidence. On the other hand, an auditee response to an auditor's question covering the same area will be the weakest. It is not that an auditor thinks the auditee is not telling the truth, but actually observing some event is far superior to just hearing about it. Internal auditors will encounter different levels of audit evidence and should attempt to design their audit procedures to look for and rely upon the best available audit evidence. Figure 10.14 provides some ranges of best evidence for different classifications of materials.

The field survey and the subsequent development of an audit program are preliminary activities to performing the actual audit. It is often more efficient to have supervisory personnel complete these preliminary steps before assigning staff auditors for the actual review. These supervisory auditors, either audit management or experienced in-charge auditors, usually have the experience to make quick assessments of field situations and to fine-tune the overall audit approach. However, once the survey and final audit program

Figure 10.14 Audit "Best Evidence" Classifications

Evidence Classification	Strongest	Weakest
Audit Technique	Observation/Confirmation	Inquiry
Origin of Evidence	Corroborative	Underlying Statistics
Relationship to Auditee	External Department	Internal
Form of Evidence	Written	Oral
Sophistication of Evidence	Formal/Documented	Informal
Location of Evidence	Actual System	Derived/Supporting System
Source of Audit Evidence	Personal Audit Work	Others

are complete and have been reviewed and approved by internal audit management, internal audit is faced with the challenge of performing the actual audit, which attempts to meet the desired audit objectives. The preparatory work from the survey will play an important role in assuring the audit's success; however, the internal auditor will now be faced with the day-to-day problems of performing the actual audit.

The actual audit steps performed will depend upon the characteristics of the entity audited. A financially oriented audit of a credit and collection function will be quite different from an operational review of a design engineering function. The financial audit might include independent confirmations of account balances while the operational audit might include extensive interviews with management and supporting documentation to assess key controls. Despite these differences, all internal audits should be performed and supervised following a general set of principles or standards. This will assure that internal audits are properly directed and controlled.

10-5 PERFORMING THE AUDIT

This section will discuss the general steps necessary to perform any internal audit, and should be used in conjunction with the specific audit procedures discussed in later chapters. While Chapters 21 through 30 discuss audit procedures for various types of operational audits, the general audit steps described here can be used to perform most audits following the specific audit considerations discussed in those operational audit chapters. Other chapters cover computer systems controls audits or special audits, but these same preliminary steps also are applicable.

(a) PRELIMINARY PROCEDURES: STARTING THE ACTUAL AUDIT

The preliminary survey has been discussed as the first step in an actual audit, and Figure 10.3 showed an engagement letter, the important first step in announcing the audit. That letter announced the planned audit, its objectives, the assigned audit team, and the approximate time periods. A single engagement letter is usually sufficient; however, in some audit situations there may be a considerable time interval between an initial field survey and the actual audit. A second engagement letter would then be useful.

Even though a separate letter may have been released for the earlier field survey, the engagement letter outlines the arrangements for the formal audit. As discussed previously, unannounced audits may be justified in cases where there is a suspicion of fraud or when a unit is very small, with records that can be easily altered. In most instances, however, audit management should start the review with this formal engagement letter to alert local and line management of the planned review, allowing them to adjust their schedules as appropriate. In some instances, auditee management may request a postponement due to any number of reasons. Internal audit management should always try to be flexible here.

The auditors assigned also have some advance work prior to actual fieldwork. If there was a separate field survey, those results should be reviewed, as should any audit permanent file workpapers. (The latter are discussed in Chapter 11.) For larger audits with multiple auditors, audit program assignments should be made in advance. Travel and lodging arrangements should be made in accordance with organization policies.

Travel costs can be a major expense for an internal audit department, particularly if it has numerous, scattered audit locations, either domestic or worldwide. Significant travel savings can often be realized by taking advantage of discount airfares and making other cost-effective travel arrangements. Internal audit management must recognize, however, that travel always will be a major budget expense and should not eliminate trips to higher audit-risk locations just because of the cost of travel. Internal audit has a responsibility to its senior management to report on the status of the organization's internal control structure. Field visits should not be postponed or eliminated because of the cost of travel to remote locations.

(b) AUDIT FIELDWORK PROCEDURES

An audit can cause interruptions and problems in the day-to-day operations of the auditee organization. The in-charge auditor and members of the audit team should begin by meeting with appropriate members of auditee management to outline preliminary plans for the audit, including areas to be tested and personnel to be interviewed. This also is an appropriate time for the internal audit team to tour the unit and to meet other personnel in the unit to be reviewed. The auditors should request that management contact all affected members of the auditee organization to provide them with an auditor-prepared tentative schedule of the planned audit work. This will eliminate potential problems in securing the cooperation of auditee personnel.

Problems can still occur while conducting the audit. For example, a key section supervisor may claim to be too busy to talk to internal audit and will not supply necessary information. Similarly, a key computer system file that was to have been saved for audit tests may have been deleted. These types of problems can either slow progress or require a revised testing and analysis strategy. Any problems should be detected early in the assignment and solved as soon as possible. Difficulties in obtaining cooperation of one department's personnel, for example, may slow work in that area and delay the completion of the entire audit.

The in-charge auditor should meet with management to discuss any problems and to find solutions. If local management appears to be uncooperative, the in-charge auditor may have to contact internal audit management to resolve the problem at a different level. If a key component of the audit is missing, such as a missing data file, audit management should develop a revised strategy to get around the problem. This might include:

- Revising audit procedures to perform additional tests in other areas. This type of change, however, should only be performed with care. If there was a strong reason for selecting the now missing file—such as the need to tie it to some other data—it may be necessary to reconstruct the missing balances.

- Completing the audit without the missing data file. The workpapers and the final report would indicate internal audit's inability to perform the planned tests. The in-charge auditor should always gain approval from internal audit management for this approach.

- Complete other portions of the audit and reschedule a later visit to perform tests. (This is only an option if the missing data file can be reconstructed or if a different cycle of data would be sufficient.) Management should be informed, of course, of audit budget overruns because of this problem.

These or similar types of problems will be encountered in many field audits. It is important that the problems be detected and resolved as early in the audit as possible. If the internal audit team faces a total lack of cooperation, management should be informed at appropriate levels to resolve the matter. Both the internal auditors and auditees should always remember that both parties are members of the same overall organization with, hopefully, common general interests and goals.

The actual audit fieldwork should follow the established audit program. As each step is completed, the responsible auditor should initial and date the audit program. Documentation gathered from each audit step, as well as any audit analyses, should be organized and forwarded to the in-charge auditor, who performs a preliminary review of the audit work. The in-charge auditor monitors the performance of the audit work in progress and reviews workpapers as they are completed for each step. Figure 10.15 shows a field audit point sheet where the in-charge auditor has signed off on key audit program steps and suggested areas for additional work.

The results of many audit steps will not yield specific audit findings but may raise questions for further investigation. The conditions in many areas reviewed can be subject to explanations or interpretations by local management. Rather than just writing them up, the field audit team should generally discuss preliminary audit observations with the persons responsible for the area. The auditor can sometimes misinterpret something that is easily resolved. If questions still remain, the matter may become a preliminary audit finding, as discussed in the paragraphs following.

(c) AUDIT FIELDWORK TECHNICAL ASSISTANCE

The field survey or the audit program development process should have identified any need for specialized technical help to perform the audit; however, other complex problems requiring technical support may arise in the course of the audit fieldwork. For example, the assigned auditor may question the accounting treatment of a certain set of transactions and want to get better information about normal practices for them. Similarly, the auditors may encounter a specialized computer application, with unique control considerations, that was not sufficiently identified or described in the survey.

If a technical issue is not familiar to the auditor in the field, the in-charge auditor should seek technical assistance as soon as possible. An internal audit supervisor or specialist may have to research the audit or technical issue in order to provide the answer. In

Figure 10.15   Preliminary Audit Findings ''Point Sheet''

Name of Audit: **Physical Inventory Reconciliation**   Date: _____

Potential Finding #: **3**   Title: **Excess Inventory Write-Offs**   W/P Ref: _____

   Source of Audit Concern—Where Were Conditions Found:

      Audit adjustments at end of year

   Statement of Audit Condition Observed:

      Inventory write-offs during current year increased by XX% of previous year

   Potential Cause of Error:

      Computer system errors, poor physical security, and inventory location errors

   Effect of Audit Errors:

      Production shortages, excessive insurance claims, erroneous interim reports

   Preliminary Audit Recommendation:

      Set W/P _____

   Results of Discussion with Management:

      See W/P _____, which discusses acceptance of preliminary findings

   Comments and Recommended Final Disposition:

other instances, it may be necessary to bring an internal audit expert in the area in question to the field site to resolve the concern or problem. However, a typical internal audit department does not have resident experts in the audit department, ready to travel out to the field site to resolve a problem. If the matter cannot be resolved through telephone calls, emails, or exchanges of documentation, the in-charge auditor may need to develop an alternative strategy.

The important message that audit management should communicate to staff is that all technical audit problems should be brought to the attention of the in-charge auditor for resolution as soon as possible during the fieldwork. Any cost and extra time requirements caused by these technical problems should be documented. If the technical problem cannot be promptly resolved, it may be necessary to reschedule the audit or to revise the strategy, as described above.

(d) AUDIT MANAGEMENT FIELDWORK MONITORING

Supervisory visits by internal audit management should be made frequently to review progress and provide technical direction. These reviews supplement the ongoing reviews made by the in-charge auditor, who is part of the field staff. The frequency and extent of these visits will depend upon the criticality of the review, the experience of the assigned staff, and the size of the review. A medium-sized review headed by an experienced in-charge auditor and covering familiar areas may not require a management review if communication lines are good. However, if the audit covers a critical area, if a new program or new techniques are used, or if the assigned in-charge auditor lacks appropriate experience in the area reviewed, an experienced member of audit management should visit the fieldwork project periodically.

The purpose of these visits should be to review the work in progress and to help resolve problems encountered. While audit management may feel that this is also an appropriate time to take the assigned field staff out to lunch or dinner to thank them for their efforts, all should realize this is not the purpose of audit field visits. Audit management should take this opportunity to understand any evolving issues in the audit and to suggest changes as appropriate. This is also a good time for management to start the review of completed audit workpapers, as discussed in Chapter 11.

Audit workpapers document the work performed and provide a link between the procedures documented in the audit program and the results of audit tests. Because they will become the basis for findings and recommendations in final audit reports, the workpapers should appropriately document all audit work. While the in-charge auditor should have been reviewing and commenting on workpapers for larger audits and audit point sheets (as illustrated in Figure 10.15), smaller reviews without a separate auditor will not have this type of feedback. The member of audit management visiting the field site should spend some time reviewing and approving the workpapers and preliminary finding sheets then prepared.

These workpaper-review comments should be in writing, cover such areas as additional work or explanations required, and suggest adjustments to the audit program if appropriate. The management review should typically not result in major changes to the audit approach. However, internal audit management can often bring some additional guidance or understanding to the audit in process.

The review comments should be documented in a review comment sheet that references pages or items in the workpapers where the management reviewer has questions or identifies missing items of audit documentation. This review process is discussed more fully in Chapter 11, with an example shown in Figure 11.13. Based upon these review comments, the staff auditors should then perform the additional audit work required and make necessary changes to the workpapers, indicating the action taken on the review sheet. After completion of internal audit's comments, the additional work done, or corrections, the supervisor indicates on the review comment sheet his or her clearance of all items as well as any further actions to be taken.

(e) POTENTIAL AUDIT POINT-SHEET FINDINGS

Whenever the internal auditor discovers a potential audit deficiency, a brief summary of the conditions and possible findings should be prepared. This summary is sometimes called an *audit point sheet* (see Figure 10.15). Whether or not the conditions described in such a document result in a final audit report finding depends on the results of additional review and analysis. A point-sheet deficiency would not necessarily become an audit finding in the final report, but the sheet can be used to document potential audit report findings.

A point sheet describes any deficiency or an opportunity for improvement identified during the audit fieldwork. These matters must be documented by the auditors in the field as soon as there is an indication that a potentially substantive audit issue exists. This facilitates bringing these issues to the attention of all levels of internal audit and auditee management at an early point in the review. It also serves as a control to assure that all leads are followed up. In addition, the various auditor point sheets, developed by individual staff members, may bring out a number of minor issues that fall into a pattern, indicating a more serious overall condition. The use of point sheets also starts the preliminary report-writing process early in the audit, and helps to assure that the essential facts for developing an audit report finding have been obtained.

Although the contents of a specific point sheet can vary depending upon the needs of the individual internal audit department, a point sheet typically has the following elements.

- *Identification of the Finding.* This is just an identification number and description of the potential finding as well as the name of the audit.

- *The Conditions.* The description is generally brief but sufficient to give local management an understanding of the conditions found.

- *References to the Documented Audit Work.* The audit point sheet should contain cross-references to the step in the audit program that initiated the comment, as well as where it is documented in the audit workpapers.

- *Auditor's Preliminary Recommendations.* Audit report space should be used to document the nature of the potential audit finding, and what was wrong. This might become the basis for a potential future audit report finding. Some notes on potential auditor-recommended corrective actions might be included here.

- *Results of Discussing the Finding with Management.* The in-charge auditor should discuss all potential findings on an informal basis with the manager directly responsible for the matter. The results of this conversation should be documented here.

- *Recommended Disposition of the Matter.* On the basis of the conversation with management, the in-charge auditor should include comments on the recommended disposition of the finding. It might be recommended for inclusion in the audit report, dropped for a variety of reasons, or deferred until more information can be gathered.

Audit point sheets are a good method of documenting potential audit findings. Some audit organizations may even have a space on this document for the auditee to respond to the auditor's suggested finding and recommendation. Both can be published in the final audit report. The advantages and disadvantages of this approach are discussed as part of the overall discussion on audit reports in Chapter 15. Point sheets should always be supported by and cross-referenced to the specific audit workpapers, and the status of the points raised should be documented to show their eventual disposition. If developed into a finding, the point sheet can also be cross-referenced to that audit report finding. If the point-sheet potential finding is dropped during the fieldwork or later, the reasons should be documented.

(f) AUDIT PROGRAM AND SCHEDULE MODIFICATIONS

The audit program is the overall guide for conducting the audit. Developed from preliminary survey data and from past programs on file in the audit department, they may be subject to adjustment during the course of the review. Auditors must be responsive to new evidence, changes in supporting systems, and other changes in conditions. In the early stages of an audit, it may be necessary to redirect some of the planned audit staff assignments as well as to modify some audit program steps. The in-charge auditor should always obtain approval from audit management before making any such changes.

   The need for audit program modifications is most common when internal audit has developed a common audit program for use in reviews of similar but not identical units. For example, an audit program may have been developed to cover controls over the purchasing function for an organization with multiple independent manufacturing units, each with separate purchasing functions. Those purchasing functions should all adhere to some general controls, as discussed in Chapter 24, and the audit programs used should reflect both organization policy and those general control principles. Due to local differences, however, this audit program may contain steps that are not applicable to one or another specific purchasing area under audit. Any such steps that are bypassed on the individual audit program should be approved and documented as to the reasons.

   Changes are often required in the audit schedule and plan as work progresses. Some flexibility should be factored into plans to meet unforeseen requirements. During the field audit assignment, situations may be encountered that affect the progress of its audit, such as an unexpected problem or event, the need to modify or drop an audit program segment, the discovery of a new area for review, or changes in audit personnel. In other instances, there may be slippage in the plan due to additional time requirements to finish an audit program step. In these circumstances, revised budgets are needed. Proper approvals for these changes should always be obtained from internal audit management.

(g) REPORTING PRELIMINARY FINDINGS TO MANAGEMENT

A major area of emphasis in any audit is the identification of areas where the unit reviewed is not in compliance with policies and procedures, or where improvement is needed. These areas would have been documented during the course of the audit through the use of a point or findings sheet type of document, as was illustrated in Figure 10.15. Although these potential audit items should have been discussed with the supervisors directly responsible, the audit team should also review them with unit management before leaving the field audit assignment.

   Potential audit findings should be reviewed with unit management during the audit to determine if they are factual. Depending upon the scope and size of the audit, these potential findings should be reviewed at several points during the course of the review. If an audit is scheduled over multiple weeks, the in-charge auditor might schedule a meeting with unit management at the end of each week to discuss all findings that developed over the course of that week. If the findings are of a minor, procedural nature, management can take necessary corrective actions at once. They can then be deemphasized or deleted in any final audit report. For other findings, the in-charge auditor should review proposed findings to ascertain that cost savings are indicated and properly reported and that findings are related to operational effectiveness.

   Even though the audit's duration may be too short to have weekly status meetings, the field audit team should almost always review all potential findings with management before leaving the location. This will allow internal audit to present its preliminary findings and recommendations to local management to obtain their reactions and comments. It also gives both parties an opportunity to correct any errors in the preliminary audit report findings before internal audit leaves the location. This type of audit review communication and the preparation of the final audit report are discussed in Chapter 15.

10-6 PLANNING AND CONTROLLING THE AUDIT FIELDWORK ASSIGNMENT

An internal audit project should be managed in the same manner as any large project that requires personnel time and other resources and that results in a defined deliverable. That is, both personnel resources and other costs should be planned and budgeted on a detailed level. The actual performance should be recorded and measured against established time- and cost-based budgets in order to analyze and correct for any significant variances. Significant project milestones, such as the completion of fieldwork or of the draft audit report, should also be tracked against plans. In many respects, this is similar to the process used for an engineering development project or a related research effort, as will be discussed in Chapter 26 and illustrated in Figure 26.1.

Chapter 8 discussed the development of the annual audit plan and this chapter considers the need for detailed plans for individual audit projects. All aspects of audit projects should be budgeted with time and other costs measured against those plans. No matter how large or small the internal audit function, an audit project performance-reporting system should be established.

For audits greater than about two weeks duration, or those performed in multiple locations at the same time, progress reports should be required on a weekly or biweekly basis. These reports should be based upon the time summaries from the assigned audit staff as well as commentaries from the in-charge auditor at the location. They can include such information as budgeted and actual time to date, estimated time to complete, and a summarized description of progress against the audit program. Figure 10.16 illustrates such a status report. This data should be gathered by the supervising auditor at the field site and transmitted or faxed to the central internal audit department. The in-charge auditor should take responsibility for explaining any significant variances in audit actual versus budget performance. In addition to reporting on a single field audit project, this report also provides input to the audit department's project status system, as was discussed in Chapter 8.

The time expended on individual audit projects should be further summarized by internal audit management to provide the director with an overview of all audits in process or scheduled. A three-month period is often a good time period for planned future activities, given the various senior management requests and other factors that can impact an internal audit plan. While summarized in a three-month manner, this report should follow the general format of Figure 10.16. This type of report is used to provide control over audits scheduled or in process while a separate, more detailed report can be completed for each individual audit to assure that they are started and completed on a timely basis.

Any increases in audit time requirements should be carefully monitored, identifying changes necessary due to changed circumstances. Audit project monitoring indicates any not started on time or which are outside of budget parameters. In some cases, the problem may be inaccurate budgets; in others, the problem may lie in auditor performance. Close

Figure 10.16 Audit Project Weekly Status Report

Audit Project	Audit Description	Actual Budgeted Hours	Actual Hours To Date	Est. Hours To Complete	Total Budgeted Cost	Actual Cost To Date	Current Audit Status	In-Charge Auditor

control of the audit will prevent slippage caused by inadequacies in staff, delays in solving problems, insufficient supervision, and excessive attention to detail.

As discussed in Chapter 14, an internal audit department should make use of automated techniques to develop and maintain this reporting and control system. Spreadsheet or database packages can provide a powerful structure for building such systems. Many paper-based reports can be eliminated, and the field auditors can transmit their time summaries and status report information to a central internal audit project-reporting system.

10-7 DIRECTING AND PERFORMING FIELD AUDITS

As discussed throughout this book, internal auditing is a large and complex process with many activities. The most important values the internal audit process provides to management are the detailed audits performed in the field or as part of overall operations. Gathering initial evidence, performing the audit, and reporting initial findings to management are all part off the process. Figure 10.17 summarizes these steps for performing internal audits up through the completion of the fieldwork. Other chapters will describe this audit process for specific operational and financial areas of the organization. Once the fieldwork has been completed, the next step will be the preparation of the actual audit report, as discussed in Chapter 17.

Figure 10.17   The Internal Audit Process—Through Field Work

    I. Perform risk analysis to identify potential control risks.

   II. Based on results of risk analysis and audit resource constraints, develop overall annual and long-range plans to perform audits.

  III. Schedule audit and allocate resources.

  IV. Prepare engagement letter for auditee.

   V. Perform field survey covering area of audit.

  VI. Prepare or refine workpapers based on department standards and field survey.

 VII. Begin field work and perform audit procedures.

VIII. Document procedures and perform audit tests of key controls.

  IX. Develop point sheets covering potential audit findings.

   X. Complete field work and review proposed findings with auditee.

CHAPTER 11

Preparing Workpapers to Document Audit Activity

11-1 THE IMPORTANCE OF WORKPAPERS

Workpapers are the *written records kept by the auditor* to document the evidential matter accumulated during the audit. The term *workpaper* includes the various schedules, analyses, and memoranda prepared and, in many cases, copies of documents secured from the auditee organization or outside sources. The common characteristic of all workpapers, however, is that they describe the results of the audit work performed and are formally retained for subsequent reference and substantiation of reported audit conclusions and recommendations.

Workpapers are the bridge between the actual audit procedures and the reports issued. Not an end in themselves but a means to an end, workpapers are created to fit particular audit tasks and are subject to a great deal of flexibility. They must support and document the purposes and activities of the internal auditor, regardless of their specific form. Thus, workpaper principles and concepts are more important than specific formats.

In recent years, internal audit workpapers have also taken on a legal significance. In certain investigations, they have been handed over, through court orders, to government, legal, or regulatory authorities. When scrutinized by outsiders in this context, inappropriate workpaper notes or schedules can easily be taken in the wrong context. They form the documented record of both those who performed the audit and those who reviewed the auditor's work. As time passes, members of the audit department go on to other activities or organizations. Even those still on the audit staff may forget details of the work performed. The workpapers are the only record of that audit work performed, and they may provide future testimony about what did or did not happen in an organization.

This chapter provides some general guidance for preparing, organizing, reviewing, and retaining workpapers. These workpapers are prepared by internal auditors to support all of the audit activities described in subsequent chapters. As a side note, this chapter and the remainder of the book uses the term *workpaper*. Others have used *working paper* or *work paper*. All mean the same thing.

11-2 FUNCTIONS OF WORKPAPERS

Auditing is a process of reviewing reports, forms, and other forms of business documentation as well as interviewing various members of the organization to gather information about an activity or transaction. The auditor then considers the status of the material examined or information from interviews to determine if various standards and procedures are being properly followed. Based upon this examination, the auditor forms an opinion that is reported to management, usually in the form of findings and recommendations published in an internal audit report. The internal auditor, however, cannot just give management informal impressions of what was found. The evidence, documented in the auditor's workpapers, must be sufficient to support the auditor's assertions.

The overall objective of workpapers is to document that an adequate audit was conducted following professional standards. The auditor can perhaps better understand the overall role of workpapers in the audit process by considering the major functions these papers serve:

- *Basis for Planning an Audit.* Workpapers from a prior audit provide the auditor with background information for conducting a current review in the same overall area. They may contain descriptions of the entity, evaluations of internal control, time budgets, audit programs used, and other results of past audit work.

- *Record of Audit Work Performed.* Workpapers describe the current audit work performed and reference it to an established audit program. Even if the audit is of a special nature, such as a fraud investigation where there may not be a formal audit program, a record should be established of the auditing work actually carried out. This workpaper record should include a description of activities reviewed, copies of representative documents, the extent of the audit coverage, and the results obtained.

- *Use During the Audit.* In many instances, the workpapers prepared play a direct role in carrying out the specific audit effort. For example, the workpapers can contain various control logs used by members of the audit team for such areas as the controls over responses received as part of an accounts receivable customer balance independent confirmation audit. Similarly, a flowchart might be prepared and then used to provide guidance for a further review of the actual activities in some process. Each of these would have been included in the workpapers in a previous audit step.

- *Description of Situations of Special Interest.* As the audit work is carried out, situations may occur that have special significance in such areas as compliance with established policies and procedures, accuracy, efficiency, personnel performance, or potential cost savings.

- *Support for Specific Audit Conclusions.* The final product of most internal audits is a formal audit report containing findings and recommendations. The findings may be actual evidence, such as a copy of a purchase order lacking a required signature, or derived evidence, such as the output report from a computer-assisted procedure against a data file or notes from an interview. The workpapers should provide sufficient evidential matter to support the specific audit findings that would be included in an audit report.

- *Reference Source.* Workpapers can answer additional questions raised by management or by external auditors. Such questions may be in connection with a particular audit report finding or recommendation, or they may relate to other inquiries. For example, management may ask internal audit if a reported problem also exists at another location that is not part of the current audit. The workpapers from that review may provide the answer. Workpapers also provide basic background materials that may be applicable to future audits of the particular entity or activity.

- *Staff Appraisal.* The performance of a staff member during an audit—including the auditor's ability to gather and organize data, evaluate it, and arrive at conclusions—is reflected in the workpapers.

- *Audit Coordination.* The internal auditor frequently exchanges workpapers with external auditors, each relying on the other's work. In addition, government auditors, in their regulatory reviews of internal controls, may demand to examine the internal auditor's workpapers.

In some respects, audit workpapers are no different from the formal files of correspondence and notes that are part of any well-managed organization. A manager would keep files of incoming and outgoing correspondence, notes based on telephone conversations, and the like. However, these files are based on just good practices and may vary from one manager to another in an organization. The manager may never be called upon to retrieve these personal files to support some organization decision or other action.

Internal audit workpapers are different in that they may also be used to support or defend the conclusions reached from the audit. They may be reviewed by others for various reasons. Members of an internal audit organization may work on common projects and need to share workpapers to support their individual components of a larger audit project or to take over an audit performed previously by another member of the audit staff. It is essential that an internal audit department have a set of standards to assure consistent workpaper preparation.

(a) WORKPAPER STANDARDS

The institute of Internal Auditors (IIA) provides guidance in the preparation and use of audit workpapers through its Statement on Internal Auditing Standards (SIAS) No. 6, "Audit Working Papers.[1]" (See Chapter 5 for an in-depth discussion of these Standards.) This standard provides overall guidance on the functions, contents, preparation, and ownership of internal audit workpapers. The actual style and format of the workpapers can vary from one internal audit department to another and, to a lesser extent, from one audit to another.

An internal audit department should develop its own workpaper standards that are consistent with the IIA standards. This chapter provides guidance to help conform to those standards. The organization's external auditors can suggest standard workpaper formats that are consistent with theirs; however, internal audit should always recognize the differences between the financial statement attestation work of external auditors and the operational aspects of internal auditing. There may often be no compelling reason to adopt external audit workpaper standards to meet the operational needs of internal audit.

Workpaper standards fall generally into two broad groups: those pertaining to workpaper substance and those pertaining to form.

---

[1] The Institute of Internal Auditors, SIAS No. 6—Audit Working Papers (Altamonte Springs, Fl.: IIA, 1995).

- *Standards of Substance*. The workpapers should be able to stand alone so that an outside party such as an external auditor can read through them and understand the objectives of the audit, the work performed, and any outstanding issues or findings. From this substance standpoint, internal audit workpapers should be concerned with the following areas:
  - *Relevance to Audit Objectives*. The content of workpapers must be relevant to both the total audit assignment and the specific objectives of the particular portion of the review. There is no need for materials that do not contribute to the objectives of the specific audit performed.
  - *Condensation of Detail*. Condensation and careful summarization of detail reduces the bulk of workpapers and makes their later use more efficient. An audit may make use of computer-assisted audit techniques (CAATs) to confirm balances on a data file, but it is often not necessary to include the entire CAAT-produced output in the workpapers. The total page with the test results, some sample detail pages, and a copy of the computer program used may be sufficient.
  - *Clarity of Presentation*. To present clear and understandable material, audit supervisors should review workpaper presentations on an ongoing basis and make recommendations for improvements.
  - *Accuracy*. Accuracy is an essential standard of all audit schedules and other quantitative workpaper data. Workpapers may be used at any time in the future to answer questions and to substantiate later internal audit representations.
  - *Action on Open Items*. Questions are frequently raised in an audit or information is disclosed that require follow-up. There should be no open items in workpapers upon completion of the audit. All items should either be cleared or formally documented for future audit actions.
- *Standards of Form*. For workpapers to accurately describe the audit work performed, they must be prepared in a consistent format within any audit workpaper or from one to another within the internal audit department. An internal audit manager would, for example, know where to find the hours schedule covering the audit in any workpaper binder reviewed. The standards of form should include the following:
  - *Preparation of Headings*. The individual page heading typically includes the title of the total audit, the particular aspect of that total assignment contained in a given workpaper sheet, and the date. A smaller heading on one side should indicate the name or initials of the person who prepared the workpaper and the date of preparation.
  - *Organization*. The use of appropriate headings, spacing, and adequacy of margins will facilitate reading and understanding. The auditor might think of this organization along the lines of the manner in which a textbook is organized.
  - *Neatness and Legibility*. These qualities not only make the workpapers more useful to all readers, they also confirm the care that went into their preparation.
  - *Cross-Indexing*. All workpapers should be indexed and cross-indexed. Cross-indexing provides a trail for the auditor and assures the accuracy of information in the workpapers, as well as in the subsequent audit report.

    Figure 11.1 shows a manually prepared workpaper from an operational audit of a physical inventory observation. This form can stand on its own. The

Figure 11.1   Manually Prepared Workpaper Example

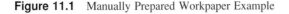

> *ExampleCo Internal Audit*   *RRM*
>
> AR-2-5.1   *Audit: MAXXAM Plant Inventory Observation*
>   *Location: South Bluff Date: March 4, 1999*   *3/4/99*
>
> *Internal audit observed the taking of finished goods physical
> inventory at the MAXXAM division plant in South Bluff, OH. We reviewed
> the physical inventory instructions issued by the plant controller's office (See
> X-Ref 01) and found them to be complete and satisfactory. Plant personnel
> started the inventory at 8:00 A.M. on March 3. Internal audit observed that
> all other activities were shut down during the inventory taking, and that
> the counting proceeded in an orderly manner.*
>
> *Worksheets for recording the counts were prepared by ExampleCo's
> inventory system—they listed the parts assigned to designated store
> locations but with no actual quantities (See X-Ref 02). A representative
> from the plant controller's office headed the control desk, issued the count
> sheets, and logged them in upon receipt.*
>
> *As part of this inventory observation, internal audit selected a series
> of random stock keeping numbers and independently took test counts. We
> compared these counts to the counts recorded by the inventory team. Test
> counts and results were summarized on X-Ref 02. We generally found . . .*

reader can determine the entity it covers, who did the work and when, and how this workpaper sheet relates to others in the audit. This basic format will be used in other figures in this chapter and in examples throughout the book.

The auditor must be particularly careful to document all work steps and all audit decisions. For example, if an audit program had a work step which the in-charge auditor determined was not appropriate for a given review, the auditor should explain why that step was deleted rather than just marking it ''N/A.'' In some situations, the initial of the audit supervisor who approved the change should also be included. Similarly, if the auditor was following up on a matter from a prior audit, the workpapers should document the manner in which the problem was corrected or else who advised the auditor that it had been fixed. It is not sufficient just to mark it ''corrected'' with no further references.

The auditor should always remember that situations may change and the auditor's workpapers may be called into question many years after they have been prepared. It is not unusual for a regulatory agency, such as the Federal Securities and Exchange Commission, to demand to see a set of workpapers prepared years ago as part of an investigation. They might ask further questions or take other steps based on the audit work and observations recorded in those quite old workpapers. Memories often fade, and in this type of situation the audit workpapers may be the only credible record.

11-3 WORKPAPER CONTENT AND ORGANIZATION

Internal auditors often follow the general workpaper format established by their own. For many, this has meant that workpapers are prepared on legal-sized sheets bound at the top. There is no particular advantage in using this format, and in the future many auditors will probably move to more conventional $8\frac{1}{2} \times 11$–inch sheets secured in three-ring binders. As discussed later in this chapter and in Chapter 14, auditors are increasingly moving toward paperless workpaper formats where many of their commentaries and schedules are maintained on microcomputer diskettes.

Regardless of page size or media, the purpose of a workpaper sheet is to provide a standard framework for documenting audit activities. As discussed above, pages should be titled, dated, initialed by the preparer, and prepared in a neat and orderly manner. While Figure 11.1 is a typical workpaper sheet illustrating substance and format standards, an audit has many requirements where that example workpaper format will not work. The paragraphs following expand upon that basic workpaper format.

(a) WORKPAPER DOCUMENT ORGANIZATION

A typical audit will involve gathering a large amount of material to document that audit process. With the wide range of operational activities reviewed and the equally wide range of audit procedures carried out, the form and content of those individual workpapers may vary greatly.

The major categories depend upon the nature of the audit materials and the work performed. For most internal audits, the workpapers can be separated into the following broad audit areas:

- Permanent Files
- Administrative Files
- Audit Procedures Files
- Specialized Computer-Assisted Audit Procedures Files
- Bulk Files of Voluminous Materials
- Audit Reports and Follow-Up Matters

An internal audit department's workpaper standards should be built around these types of files. This chapter refers to these as *files* while some internal audit departments use the term *binders* to refer to these different workpaper groupings. Just as in any manual filing system, workpaper materials are classified by their basic type and grouped together in a file or bound together in a binder in a manner that aids their retrieval.

Permanent Files

Many audits are performed on a periodic basis and follow repetitive procedures. Rather than capture all of the data necessary every time each audit is performed, certain data can be gathered from what is called a permanent workpaper file, which contains data of a *historical or continuing nature* pertinent to current audits. Some of this data include:

- Overall organization charts of the audit unit
- Charts of accounts (if a financial audit) and copies of major policies and procedures

- Copies of the last audit report, the audit program used, and any follow-up comments
- Financial statements about the entity as well as other potentially useful analytical data
- Information about the audit unit (descriptions of major products, production processes, and other newsworthy matters)
- Logistical information to help the next auditors, including notes regarding travel arrangements

A permanent file is not meant to be *permanent* in that it will never change; rather, it provides the auditor starting a new assignment a source of background material to help plan the new audit. Chapter 10 discussed the need to review the permanent file when planning a new audit. Over the course of a new audit, the supervising auditor may come across other materials to update or include in the permanent file. The permanent file is a source of continuity to tie audits together over time. Figure 11.2 shows an index or table of contents from an audit permanent file binder.

Auditors are sometimes guilty of loading up their audit permanent files with materials that do not deserve permanent file status—for example, copies of various procedures that will have changed by the time of the next audit. Materials readily available at the time of the next audit need not be retained in permanent files unless certain ongoing procedures were based upon those earlier materials. Similarly, auditors sometimes fill up permanent files for out-of-town locations with maps and menus of local restaurants. These units will change as will both individual auditor preferences and department policies. This administrative planning material should be kept to a minimum.

Figure 11.2   Workpaper Permanent File Index

ExampleCo Internal Audit MAXXAM Plant Division Permanent File Index		RRM 04/01/01
INDEX	PERMANENT FILE	DATE
A-13	MAXXAM Div. Audit Reports & Responses—1998	02/11/99
A-14	MAXXAM Div. Audit Reports & Responses—1999	02/02/00
B-02	MAXXAM Accounting Policy	09/06/98
B-17	MAXXAM Chart of Accounts	11/06/99
C-01	Product Descriptions—MAXXAM Div.	05/02/00
E-12	Press Releases—MAXXAM Div.	11/13/00
G-02	Internal Audit Plant Visit Background Notes	09/12/00

Administrative Files

This is a special type of administrative workpaper used by the supervising auditor in the field to control the audit work performed. It might include:

- The complete audit program for the review
- Checklists describing work that must be accomplished in advance of the actual fieldwork
- Detailed budgets by audit program section and assigned auditors
- Daily manpower analyses of audit actual time for each audit step, with completions noted
- Findings sheets turned in by assigned auditors on their audit work
- Budget records of any costs incurred during the course of the fieldwork
- Inventory records of items such as manuals assigned to auditors, as well as items such as tape files turned in to the supervising auditor for retention purposes

Although a separate workpaper administrative file may not be necessary for a smaller audit, the same general administrative workpaper materials should be incorporated somewhere in all audit workpaper sets. If only a single auditor or limited review, this material may be incorporated into the single workpaper.

Audit Procedures Files

These files record the actual audit work performed. They may vary with the type and nature of the audit assignment. For example, a financial audit may contain detailed spreadsheet schedules with auditor commentary on tests performed. An operational audit may contain interview notes and commentary on auditor observations. This file is generally the largest for any audit. Most internal audit procedure files contain the following elements:

1. *Listings of Completed Audit Procedures.* Workpapers are a central repository documenting the audit procedures, and include copies of the audit programs along with the initials of the auditors and the dates of the audit steps. Commentary notes may be on the programs or attached as cross-referenced supplementary notes. (Figure 11.3 shows a completed audit program filed in the workpapers.)

2. *Completed Questionnaires.* Some internal audit functions use standard questionnaires covering particular types of internal control procedures. These questionnaires normally provide for *yes* and *no* answers and appropriate supplementary comments.

3. *Descriptions of Operational Procedures.* Workpapers frequently describe briefly the nature and scope of a specific type of operational activity. This description can provide a basis for later audit management probing and evaluation. It can be in flowchart or narrative form. The auditor should always note on the workpaper the source of information to develop this description. A member of auditee management may have described the process or the auditor may have gathered this information through observation.

4. *Review Activities.* Many operational audit workpapers cover specific investigations that appraise selected activities. These can include testing of data, observation of

Figure 11.3 Workpaper Audit Program Example

B25	ExampleCo Internal Audit Audit: Headquarters Direct Sales AUDIT PROGRAM—CASH	*JAS* *10/31/01*
Ref.	Audit Procedure	Disposition
1.a	Review sources of cash and appraise the possibilities of reducing difficult-to-control cash conditions.	*WIP B32—JAS* *10/30/01*
1.b	Determine physical safeguards for providing adequate cash at all stages.	
1.c	Review procedures to keep cash on hand—in all forms and levels.	
2.a	Determine that petty cash and branch funds are utilized and operated on an imprest basis.	*WIP B27—JAS* *10/30/01*
2.b	Assess adequacy of documentary support for petty or miscellaneous cash disbursements.	
2.c	Review controls surrounding issuance and use of company credit cards.	
3.a	Determine that all employees who handle or have direct or indirect access to cash are adequately bonded.	

performance, inquiries to designated individuals, and the like. This is perhaps the most common type of workpaper prepared by the internal auditor. It follows no one form but only serves to describe the audit activities performed and the results. Figure 11.4 shows a workpaper covering tests of an audit of travel and entertainment expenses.

5. *Analyses and Schedules Pertaining to Financial Statements.* In a financially oriented audit, a special variety of workpapers relates to attesting to the accuracy of financial statement or account balances. This type is more typical for external auditors who attest to the fairness of the financial statements. Figure 11.5 is such a workpaper schedule. Fairness and accuracy statements may also include:

- Schedules relating to particular general ledger accounts
- Analyses of individual accounts, such as accruals
- Details of backup data and supporting physical counts
- Results of specific kinds of verification
- Explanations of adjustments to accounts
- Notes as to pertinent supplementary information
- Summaries of statement balances and adjustments

6. *Organization Documents.* There are often basic organization documents such as

Figure 11.4   Travel Audit Workpaper Example

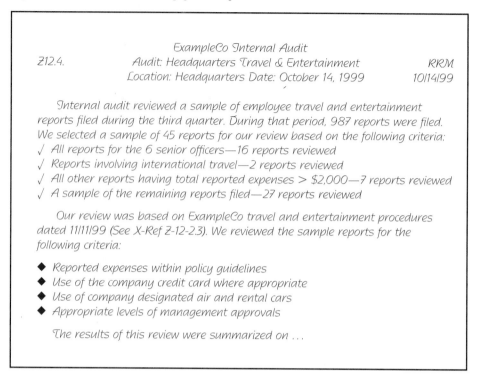

ExampleCo Internal Audit
Z12.4.   *Audit: Headquarters Travel & Entertainment*   *RRM*
Location: Headquarters Date: October 14, 1999   *10/14/99*

Internal audit reviewed a sample of employee travel and entertainment reports filed during the third quarter. During that period, 987 reports were filed. We selected a sample of 45 reports for our review based on the following criteria:
√ All reports for the 6 senior officers—16 reports reviewed
√ Reports involving international travel—2 reports reviewed
√ All other reports having total reported expenses > $2,000—7 reports reviewed
√ A sample of the remaining reports filed—27 reports reviewed

Our review was based on ExampleCo travel and entertainment procedures dated 11/11/99 (See X-Ref Z-12-2.3). We reviewed the sample reports for the following criteria:

♦ Reported expenses within policy guidelines
♦ Use of the company credit card where appropriate
♦ Use of company designated air and rental cars
♦ Appropriate levels of management approvals

The results of this review were summarized on ...

organization charts, minutes of meetings, particular policy statements or procedures, contracts, and the like. While some of these might be more appropriate for the permanent file, others are unique to a particular audit. However, the auditor should not include all material in the workpapers. For example, it may be sufficient to include a table of contents and have relevant extracts rather than incorporating an entire procedures manual in the workpapers. The purpose of these documents is to help future auditors in their decisions or processes.

7. *Findings Point Sheets or Drafts of Reports.* Point sheets describing the nature of the audit finding as well as reference to the detailed audit work should be included in audit procedures files even though a copy has been forwarded to the administrative file. A workpaper point sheet is shown in Figure 11.6. For smaller audits that do not have an administrative file, several draft versions of the written report should be included. These drafts can be annotated to show major changes, the persons responsible for authorizing those changes, and in some cases the reasons for the changes.

8. *Supervisor's Notes.* During an audit, the in-charge auditor or audit supervisor prepares review comments that may require explanation by the auditor. In some cases, further audit work is needed. Figure 11.7 is an example of such a review sheet.

9. *Audit Bulk Files.* Internal audits often produce large amounts of evidential materials, which should be retained but not included in the primary workpapers. For example,

Figure 11.5 Financial Workpaper Example

MAXXAM, Inc.
Working Trial Balance—Balance Sheet
December 31, 19X1

Prepared by: _RRM_ Date: 2/10/X1
Reviewed by: _LCT_ Date: 2/18/X1

WIP Ref.	Acct. No.	Description	Ledger Bal. 12/31/X0	Ledger Bal. 12/31/X1	Adjustments Adj. Ref.	Adjustments Debit (Credit)	Final Balance 12/31/X1
A–23	153	Cash	392,000	427,000	Z22	50,000	477,000
B–12	170	Marketable Securities	52,200	62,200			62,200
B–14	181	Receivables (net)	1,601,400	1,715,000	Z23.1	(50,000)	1,665,000
C–02	240	Inventories	2,542,500	2,810,200	Z32	133,000	2,943,200
D–12	275	Prepaid Expenses	27,900	19,500			19,500

Figure 11.6 Workpaper Point Sheet Example

B25	ExampleCo Internal Audit Audit: Headquarters Travel & Entertainment SUMMARY POINT SHEET	*LCL* *10/14/02*
W/P Ref.	**Finding Description**	**Disposition**
A422	Twelve managers consistently exceeded expense limits for daily meals, often over $50/day. All reports were approved by managers.	Audit Report–RJK
A512	Many reports were not filed within three days per policy. Fifteen percent of reports reviewed were filed more than seven days after business trip.	Pass–Check reasonableness of 3 day rule–RJK
A517	Two managers in purchasing consistently did not use the company designated travel agent and frequently purchased first class tickets.	Audit Report–RJK
A585	Meals on travel expense reports were not classified per U.S. income tax rules.	Audit Report–RJK
A633	Three employees in engineering did not properly document local seminars attended.	Pass–RJK

internal audit may perform a survey that results in a large number of returned questionnaires. These materials are classified as workpapers and can be retrieved from the bulk file as necessary.

Workpapers are the method of documentation for communication within the audit department from one audit or auditor to the next. They are also a means of communication with the organization's external auditors. An internal audit department should establish some overall standards covering the style, format, and content of the workpapers used in various audits. Some specific details do not need to be ''frozen'' given the various types of audits performed and evolving audit automation procedures, as discussed later. However, workpaper contents should be prepared consistently for all audits. The audit procedures workpaper file, for example, should contain materials covering each of the above areas.

(i) Specialized Computer-Assisted Audit Workpapers. In most respects, workpapers prepared by computer audit specialists should be no different than workpapers for any other review. There are still the same requirements to document all work performed. However, workpapers covering the development and use of computer-assisted audit techniques (CAATs) may be somewhat different in format. The major problem here is that CAAT procedures may generate fairly voluminous output reports. While some example

Figure 11.7 Workpaper Supervisor Review Example

A.4.2	*ExampleCo Internal Audit* *Audit: Axylotl Plant Production Control* *Workpaper Review Notes*	*RRM* *11108101*
WIP Ref.	**Supervisor Review Notes**	**Auditor Action**
B-12, C-21	Missing WIP X-references.	Corrected
B-16	Schedule does not crossfoot to D-02 Summary. Please revise or correct.	OK—See D-02.1
D-20	Does the ref. point to a larger control problem?	
D-21	WIP sheet was not signed or dated.	Corrected
D-36	Evidence does not support your recommendation—clarify!	See D36.3
D-41 to 5	Missing WIP X-references.	Corrected
—	Where is the X-Cat software located?	See XCM binder

pages and summary sheets should be included with the regular audit procedures workpaper files, the auditor should also capture complete versions of the output reports, the audit-retrieval programs used, and sometimes copies of source data files.

If an internal audit department is tied into using the older manual format, $8\frac{1}{2} \times 14$ binders for workpapers historically preferred by external auditors, the format often will not work very well for computer outputs since some CAAT outputs may be on diskettes or even computer tape cartridges. The internal auditor needs to develop a slightly different standard for documenting the results of CAAT work. These workpaper procedures are discussed in more detail in Chapter 12, but they generally should have the following elements:

- Program documentation describing procedures to develop and test the CAAT
- A copy of the actual programs used for the CAATs in both a paper listing and as machine-readable format (the latter should be available on tape or diskette and stored in a secure area)
- Outputs from the CAAT processing (this can be retained as a paper file using a computer forms binder or on machine-readable media)
- A reconciliation of the outputs from CAAT processing to the results reported by the system being audited (such a schedule can follow the same format as other audit procedures workpapers)

Just like regular audit workpapers, CAAT workpapers should be able to stand on their own. This is often a more difficult task for the specialist preparing them, as they may contain technical matters not readily understood by outsiders. The internal auditor must exercise care to describe and document all CAAT procedures properly.

(ii) Audit Reports and Follow-Up Matters.   Often, audit reports and related follow-up notes are included initially in the administrative file for later inclusion in the permanent file at the completion of a given audit. For larger, more complex audits with many findings, however, it is sometimes beneficial to include audit reports, management responses, point sheets used to develop the report, and follow-up matters in a separate workpaper binder. This is particularly convenient if the auditor has an ongoing series of meetings with various levels of management to discuss various aspects of the audit. While the auditor may be asked to provide details regarding the nature of one or another controversial audit finding, it may not be convenient to bring the entire set of workpaper files to each of these meetings to verify a given finding; summary data is usually sufficient.

Audit management should also maintain files of summarized audit findings, recommendations, and management responses in order to monitor the ongoing quality of the entities audited and their responsiveness to audit recommendations. They should also maintain separate files of audit reports completed within various units or organization components. Audit recommendation follow-up procedures as well as audit reports are discussed in Chapter 15.

11-4 WORKPAPER PREPARATION TECHNIQUES

Much of the process of preparing workpapers involves drafting audit comments and developing schedules to describe audit work and support audit conclusions. This is a detailed process which requires that the internal auditor follow standards both of form and of substance, as described above. In addition to overall audit department standards for the preparation of workpapers, auditors also need techniques to make workpapers easy to follow and understand.

The most important aspect is to ensure that all members of the internal audit staff have an understanding of the purposes and the criticality of their audit workpapers. They will be reviewed by internal audit management and others, who may question the type and extent of the work performed based on whatever is documented in the workpapers.

This section discusses some of the basic techniques needed for preparing adequate workpapers. These comments are largely based upon the more traditional, manually prepared workpapers used by auditors for many years. However, laptop computers and powerful software are rapidly changing these approaches. The section following discusses some of these changes. However, whether prepared manually or using microcomputer software, audit workpapers should be prepared with certain indexing and notation standards that will allow for their easy review by other interested audit professionals.

(a) INDEXING AND CROSS-REFERENCING

Similar to those in reference textbooks, sufficient cross-references and notations allow the reader to take a significant reference and trace it back to its original citation or source. For example, a workpaper document describing a financial review of fixed assets might mention that the automated system that calculates depreciation has adequate controls. It is sufficient to provide a cross-reference so that the interested reader could easily find those depreciation computation controls review workpapers.

Index numbers on workpapers are the same as volume and page numbers in a published book. Figure 11.1 showed a workpaper page with an index number in the upper left corner. That number should also tie into a table of contents, which usually appears on the first page of the workpaper binder. The number identifies the specific page in the specific workpaper binder. A reference to this number elsewhere in the audit allow the auditor to select immediately the correct workpaper binder and page.

The system used for index numbers in a set of workpapers can be as simple or complex as desired. Many internal audit departments adopt the same indexing system used by their external auditors so that all members of the audit staff can understand the correct reference to a volume in a given workpaper set. A method for indexing internal audit workpapers might follow a set of three digits so that ''AP-5-26'' would mean the 26th page section of the 5th step in a given set of audit procedures. If multiple pages were required for page 26, they would be expressed as AP-5-26.01, -26.02, and so forth. Any numbering system should be easy to use and adaptable to change.

Cross-referencing refers to placing other reference workpaper index numbers within a given workpaper schedule. For example, a workpaper schedule may discuss controls over fixed-asset additions and state that all additions above some specified limit receive proper approval by management. That workpaper statement would parenthetically reference another workpaper index number denoting fixed-asset tests and indicating evidence of management approvals. Cross-reference numbers are particularly important in financial audits where all numbers on various schedules should be tied together to assure consistency.

(b) TICK MARKS

Auditors often prepare a financial or statistical schedule and then select various numbers from that schedule to perform one or more additional tests. For example, an auditor may review a sample of purchase orders to determine if they (1) represent vendors on the approved list, (2) are subject to competitive bids, (3) are computed correctly, and so forth. Rather than list this sample of purchase orders on multiple workpaper sheets for each of the tests, auditors normally use one schedule and employ *tick marks* to footnote various tests performed.

Tick marks are a form of auditor shorthand notation that have evolved over the years, particularly for financial audits. An auditor can develop a particular check mark to indicate that a given value on the financial schedule cross-foots to other related values and another tick mark to indicate that it ties to the trial balance. The auditor need only note somewhere in the workpapers the tick mark used for each. Rather than asking the auditor to develop a legend, many internal audit departments use a standard set of tick mark symbols in all workpapers. For example, a check mark with a line through it may mean that the workpaper item was traced to a supporting schedule and the numbers tied. These standard tick marks should be used by all members of the audit staff for all audits. Standard tick marks improve communication as audit management can easily review and understand workpapers. Figure 11.8 illustrates a set of typical tick marks. In developing these tick marks, the internal audit department might want to adopt the notation used by its external auditors. Of course, the auditor might develop another mark to indicate some other type of cross-check performed in the course of an individual audit, which would then be clearly explained.

Figure 11.8   Workpaper Tick Mark Examples

⟋	Agreed to mm/dd/yy workpapers
〰	Confirmed with maker of transaction—no exceptions
✓	Examined during audit procedures
Ŧ	Footed
ŦŦ	Footed and cross-footed
^	Traced to ledger balance
CR	Traced to cash receipts deposit slips
Ω	Verified computation

(c) REFERENCES TO EXTERNAL SOURCES

Auditors often record information taken from outside sources. For example, an auditor may gather an understanding of an operational area through an interview with a member of management. The auditor would record that interview through workpaper notes and rely on what was told to the auditor as the basis of further audit tests or conclusions. It is important to always record the source of such commentary directly on the workpaper. For example, a workpaper exhibit could show how the auditor gained an understanding of a sample system. The source who provided that information to the auditor should be documented.

Auditors may need to reference an external law or regulation to support their audit work. Similarly, they may perform a vendor-related review and access a telephone book to verify vendor existence. It is usually not necessary to include in the workpapers a copy of what may be a voluminous regulation, nor a copy of a page from the telephone book. However, workpapers should clearly indicate the title and source of all external references. Extract page copies can be included to make a specific point when necessary, but a reference notation is normally sufficient.

(d) WORKPAPER ROUGH NOTES

When conducting interviews, internal auditors often make very rough notes, often written in a personal form of shorthand easily readable only by the author. Auditors subsequently should rewrite these rough notes into workpaper commentary. Because there may be a reason to rereview them, these original note sheets should also be included in the workpapers, placed in the back of the workpaper binder or even in a separate bulk file.

11-5 CHANGING NATURE OF WORKPAPERS

Historically, most workpapers were prepared in pencil. Schedules were recorded on accounting spreadsheet forms, commentaries were written in longhand, and any exhibits were attached. Many internal audit departments now automate their workpapers through the use of spreadsheet and word-processing software. This automation does not change the standards of form or substance; it usually makes the workpapers easier to read and to access. Workpaper automation is discussed in Chapter 14.

The typical workpaper today may use a mix of manual and automated schedules and audit commentaries. However, the essential workpaper binder at this stage is usually still a paper document with computer-generated materials included within it. In the future, a greater amount of this audit material will be in machine-readable format and workpaper binders prepared on diskettes.

Technology is rapidly changing, and we may be seeing quite different formats of audit evidence supporting audit workpapers in future years. Digital image scanners are quickly becoming quite inexpensive. They can be passed over a paper document, creating a digital image of that document for later retrieval. Similarly, some computers are now equipped with a pen stylus for the user to ''write'' directly on the computer screen. The data is captured on computer files. While these and other evolving technologies offer potential future opportunities for audit automation, it is perhaps too early to discuss building workpapers using these technologies at the present time. Evolving technologies are discussed in Chapter 34, on changes in audit evidence.

11-6 WORKPAPER REVIEW PROCESS

All workpapers should go through an independent review process to assure that all necessary audit work has been performed, that it is properly described, and that audit report findings are adequately supported. The director of the internal audit function has the overall responsibility for this review but may delegate that responsibility to supervisory members of the internal audit department. Depending upon the size of the audit staff and the relative importance of a given audit, there may be multiple reviews of a set of workpapers, one by the in-charge auditor and another by a more senior member of internal audit management.

Evidence of this supervisory review should consist of the reviewer's initials and dates on each sheet. Some internal audit organizations prepare a memorandum or workpaper review checklist to document the nature and extent of the reviews. In any case, there should be documented evidence that all workpapers have received a proper level of supervisory review.

In addition to initialing completed workpapers, the supervisory reviewer should prepare a set of review notes with questions raised during the review process. Any questions or problems should be given to the auditor for resolution. Some of these review points or questions may simply highlight clerical errors such as missing cross-references. Others may be of a more significant nature and may require the auditor to do some additional follow-up work. Review questions should be cleared promptly, and the reviewer should take the responsibility to assure that all open questions are resolved. This workpaper review process should always take place prior to the issuance of the audit report. This will assure that all report findings have been properly supported by audit evidence as documented in the workpapers.

11-7 WORKPAPER OWNERSHIP, CUSTODY, AND RETENTION

Audit workpapers are the property of the overall organization, but they should generally remain under the custody of the internal audit department. Access to these workpapers should be controlled by the internal audit department and be limited to only authorized individuals. Management and other members of the organization may request access to workpapers to substantiate or explain an audit finding, but that workpaper should be reviewed in a supervised manner. Internal audit can share copies of certain documentation with others but never give them the complete workpaper binder to copy or modify. In other instances, non–internal auditors may wish to utilize documentation prepared in the workpapers for other business purposes. In all events, however, the internal audit department should approve these requests and maintain control over the process.

Internal and external auditors will typically grant access to each other's audit workpapers. While this access should always be approved by both sets of audit management, it is often a useful way to increase overall audit efficiency. There is often no reason, for example, for the external auditor to review a given area if such a review has been adequately performed by internal auditors and if the external auditors can rely on that work through a workpaper review. These matters are discussed in Chapter 32, on coordination with external auditors.

As discussed previously, there may be circumstances when legal or regulatory authorities request access to audit workpapers or reports. Prior to any release, internal audit should obtain formal approval from senior management and/or legal counsel as appropriate. This type of potential exposure illustrates the importance of internal audit workpapers to the organization and why they should be prepared with due care.

Internal audit will most frequently encounter this legal requirement when there is some type of lawsuit against the auditor's organization and the other side obtains the right to perform a discovery review of various items of documentation. The organization may be faced with a court order to hand over the original copies of all workpapers, correspondence, and other documentation covering a certain matter. While this process is more common with external auditors, internal audit also must comply with the court order. It can make copies but must otherwise turn over files for legal review. When internal audit is forced into this situation, the importance of workpaper quality and appropriate reviews becomes evident. Internal auditors may be asked to testify, under oath, why they made a statement or ignored an obvious error documented in their workpapers. Audit managers may be asked to explain why they initialed workpapers containing obvious errors.

Formal internal audit retention policies for all audit workpapers should be consistent with the organization's guidelines and any legal or other requirements that affect the organization. Care should be taken that older workpapers can be fairly easily retrieved and are given adequate protection from fire or other hazards.

11-8 CONCLUSION

Audit workpapers, along with the resultant audit reports, are the key tangible output products of internal auditors. Because the workpapers support the final audit reports, adequate audit reports are not possible without adequate supporting workpapers.

Internal auditors often encounter auditees who have failed to document some system or process. This often results in an audit report finding. The same internal auditor, however, may be guilty of the same type of control weakness by failing to prepare adequate audit workpapers. This will be revealed if the internal audit department goes through a quality-assurance review, as discussed in Chapter 33. However, the best way to assure that workpapers are prepared adequately and in accordance with department standards is to assure that internal audit management performs adequate levels of reviews of all internal audit workpapers.

CHAPTER 12

Using Computer-Assisted Audit Techniques

12-1 INTRODUCTION: AUTOMATED AUDIT TESTING

Auditors have historically gathered evidence from the organization's books and records to support their conclusions. This evidence might be in the form of manufacturing change notice documents with proper approval signatures (see Chapter 23 for other examples of manufacturing operational audits). With automation replacing many of those documents and procedures, auditors have a challenge: The systems used today can create or change that change notice file, eliminating the manual signatures. Internal audit must develop different procedures to determine that these manufacturing changes are properly approved.

At present, a large volume of data is primarily retained on computer files and listed on computer output reports. While internal audit can gather data by selecting and reviewing items from these reports, it is often more efficient to use automated techniques to examine all recorded items on the supporting computer files. An internal auditor can request that the information systems function produce a report to satisfy the auditor's requirements. However, internal auditors can act with greater independence by developing their own specialized file retrievals. This audit analysis of data is accomplished through the use of computer-assisted audit techniques (CAATs).

An internal auditor has a fundamental requirement to obtain evidence as to the validity of accounting and operational data. However, large volumes of data or the lack of paper documents often makes this review of evidence difficult or impossible in many cases. This chapter describes audit approaches to testing, analyzing, and gathering detailed evidence from data contained on automated applications through the use of CAATs. These techniques can be used with most computerized applications, ranging from accounting systems on large mainframe computers to smaller systems residing on departmental microcomputers. Although some CAATs require specialized data-processing skills, many can be designed and performed by the typical internal auditor, with no particular programming skills, through the use of powerful audit software tools.

12-2 DEFINITION OF A CAAT

A computer-assisted audit technique (CAAT) is a specialized computer program, controlled by internal audit, which is used to test or otherwise analyze data on computer files.

In the early days of data-processing systems, auditors ignored the power of these systems. They perhaps relied on the printed outputs from automated systems and used conventional audit procedures to test and analyze this computer-generated data. As computer systems became more pervasive, with large data files, auditors needed an approach to adequately evaluate controls in these large information systems. CAATs were developed by some auditors to read and analyze financial data on large computer files. Many auditors, however, continued to use conventional manual techniques. The necessity for CAAT procedures first became evident with the Equity Funding fraud in the early 1970s.

Equity Funding Corporation, an insurance company, reported very significant growth from the late 1960s up through the early 1970s. It was later determined, however, that Equity Funding's growth was based on a massive management fraud in which fictitious insurance policies were entered on Equity Funding's computerized records. The external auditors at that time relied on the printed report outputs generated by the Equity Funding computer systems rather than on the data recorded on computer files. Had the external auditors looked at the contents of those computer files, they might have detected the fraud. Equity Funding did not have a significant internal audit function; an Equity Funding employee eventually revealed the fraud.

After the fraud was discovered, many professionals pointed out that it could have been detected earlier had the computer files been analyzed by the auditors. A review of computer output reports only was not sufficient. Internal audit needed independently both to review computer procedures and to analyze the contents of computerized records. The Equity Funding fraud launched computer auditing and the use of CAATs.

A CAAT is an auditor-controlled computer program that can be run against a production data file to analyze and summarize the data and perform other audit tests. Before the days of end-user computing and microcomputers, this program was a quite advanced technique. End users typically relied upon their data-processing departments to write special retrieval programs to give them the various output reports requested. Both internal and external auditors later began to use what was called generalized audit software to develop their own programs independently for testing and analyzing data. This generalized software will be discussed later in this chapter.

We use the term "CAAT" to define specialized computer systems and procedures to assist internal audit. Others, such as some external audit firms, may use the term *computer-assisted audit procedures* (CAAP). The two expressions mean the same thing and can be used interchangeably.

An example might better clarify the concept of a typical CAAT. Assume that internal audit is interested in testing the accuracy of the aging from an automated accounts receivable computer system; however, most calculated data for that system is only stored on computer files, and the system has no significant paper reports describing the calculations. Internal audit is concerned that receivables, as reported on the aged trial balance report, may not be properly aged as to the number of days due. Thus, the receivables account may be over- or understated. Internal audit can test these agings using any of three approaches. First, internal audit could use the traditional, manual approach where items are selected from a computer output report and then are traced back to any original source documents that may exist. Internal audit can then determine if the items selected are properly entered on computer system records and if the aging calculations are correct. This will work if paper records are available. However, because of the volume of receivable records in a typical automated systems file, internal audit can only selectively trace and test these items. Some exception conditions may be missed with such a manual test. In addition, internal audit might not be able to easily determine if the dates of transaction-based agings are functioning correctly.

A second approach is to perform a controls review over the automated accounts receivable system. The idea is that if controls over the application are found to be good, internal audit can rely on system output reports. This approach is discussed in Chapter 17. A review of systems documentation and perhaps of a selected program source code determines whether the system is properly aging receivables. Internal audit would then test those controls by, for example, running some test transaction into the system, either through manual transactions or another CAAT. This is the general audit approach discussed in Chapter 4. Properly performed, this review can detect significant internal control problems as well as determine whether the system is generally working in a correct, well-controlled manner. However, internal audit would only be able to estimate the total extent of the financial statement adjustments necessary due to any account aging errors, and so, in conjunction with this test, internal audit must determine that controls over data entry and error correction are adequate.

The third approach is to use a CAAT to recalculate independently all of the agings in the accounts receivable system, develop totals for the accounts receivable balance, and produce a listing of any unusual exception items. Internal audit might perform this third, CAAT-oriented approach through the following steps:

1. *Determine CAAT objectives.* Internal audit should not just "use the computer" to test a system without a clear set of starting audit objectives for any CAAT. In the above examples, internal audit would have an objective of determining if accounts receivable agings are correctly stated.

2. *Understand the computer systems.* Internal audit should review data-processing systems documentation to determine how accounts receivable agings are calculated, where this data is stored in the system, and how items are described in system files.

3. *Develop CAAT programs.* Using generalized audit software, other retrieval packages, or a computer language processor, internal audit would write programs to recalculate accounts receivable agings and to generate totals from accounts receivable files.

4. *Test and process the CAAT.* After testing the programs, the internal auditor would arrange to have the CAATs processed against the production accounts receivable files.

5. *Develop audit conclusions from CAAT results.* Similar to any audit test, audit conclusions would be drawn from the results of the CAAT processing, documented in the workpapers and discussed in the audit report, as appropriate.

This general approach to developing and processing CAATs is discussed in more detail throughout this chapter. The basic approach follows the same steps internal audit would use for establishing audit objectives and performing appropriate tests on any system or process.

As previously discussed, a CAAT is a specialized set of computer programs or procedures that are under the control of internal audit. The CAAT can be developed through generalized audit software programs run on the production computer system, specialized software run on the auditor's own microcomputer, or specialized audit-use-only program code embedded in an otherwise normal production application. These various CAAT approaches are discussed later in this chapter.

The modern internal auditor should have a good understanding of when CAATs should be used to enhance the audit process, the types of CAATs available to an internal auditor, and how to use a CAAT in an audit. Although some CAATs require an internal auditor to have specialized programming knowledge, most can be implemented by an auditor with only a general understanding of data processing. This chapter should give internal audit an introduction to defining, developing, and using CAATs.

12-3 DETERMINING NEEDS FOR COMPUTER-ASSISTED AUDIT TECHNIQUES

CAATs are powerful tools that can enhance the audit process, and, in turn, internal auditor independence. However, these procedures can sometimes be time-consuming to develop and will not always be cost-effective. Internal audit needs to understand when a CAAT might increase overall audit efficiencies or independence and when it will not. This section discusses areas where CAATs will enhance an audit and areas to consider when developing and implementing a CAAT. Other sections will discuss alternative CAAT approaches and procedures for implementing them.

Before selecting a specific CAAT, however, an internal auditor must first determine if a CAAT approach is appropriate. All too often, a member of management may have attended a seminar about the use of CAATs and then will direct an assigned audit team to ''do something'' using the computer in an audit. This type of decision will often result in disappointments for all parties. Similarly, a highly technical auditor may sometimes develop a CAAT as part of an audit even though the CAAT really does not support the objectives of that review. The result may be interesting but will not contribute to the overall effectiveness of the internal audit's objectives.

The decision to develop and implement a CAAT in support of an internal audit will depend upon the nature of the data and production programs being reviewed in the audit, the CAAT tools available to internal audit, and the objectives of the audit. Internal audit needs an overall understanding of CAAT procedures in order to make this decision, and should consider the following.

- *The Nature or Objectives of the Audit.* Internal audit should initially evaluate the data to be reviewed in the audit and how it is maintained. Audits based upon values or attributes of computerized data are typically good candidates for CAATs. For example, the above-mentioned accounts receivable audit is a good CAAT candidate because there is generally a large volume of transactions but minimal paper records. Many of the operational and financial audit areas discussed in Chapters 22 to 30 are good candidates for CAATs, and those chapters contain numerous examples. However, a business ethics policy audit, as discussed in Chapter 35, requires an examination of records usually only maintained in manual files and published procedures, may not be a good candidate for a CAAT. While a computerized database can summarize the ethics policy data, as discussed in Chapter 35, it provides only indirect support for the prime audit procedures.

- *The Nature of the Data to Be Reviewed.* CAATs are most effective when data is stored on computer files and when most decision-dependent information about that data is based on the computer system. For example, a manufacturing inventory system might have most of the descriptive information about its inventory on computer system files. Inventory-related data is input directly, and inventory status information is based on computer reports or output screens. There are only limited paper-based original records. Typical audit procedures for inventory might include an analysis of manufacturing costs (see Chapter 23). Inventory system attributes can be summarized and analyzed through a CAAT. In addition, because they are maintained on a centralized system at the main data center, the inventory data might be a good candidate for CAAT procedures. Conversely, the inventory might be located on branch office microcomputers that cannot be easily accessed through CAATs. Other computer systems are comprised of little more than log files which organize otherwise manual records. An engineering project authorization system might have summary data stored on a computer file but most of the information about the projects in manual, paper-based files. CAATs might not be all that effective in these latter areas because internal audit would also need to review the manual data. Any audit over areas where there is heavy dependence upon computerized data might be a good potential candidate for a CAAT.

- *The Available CAAT Tools and Audit Skills.* Internal audit must develop its CAAT systems using the automation tools available within the audit department or information systems function. If the internal audit department does not have or has not budgeted for specialized CAAT software, an internal auditor cannot develop a CAAT that requires such software. Some audit software products are written for IBM classic mainframe hardware and software. If the organization uses another type of equipment where such CAAT software is not available, it might be quite difficult to develop a specialized CAAT. Internal audit needs to consider the types of audit software available before embarking on any CAAT projects. That availability may be based on both audit budget constraints and product limitations. Auditor skills must also be considered. Although training materials are available, the in-charge auditor must assess whether technical audit specialists are needed and are available for the CAAT-development project.

The above three points are stated in very general terms, but they are areas to be considered when planning the overall strategy for making the decision to use CAATs. These comments point to many areas where a CAAT will be difficult or not particularly cost-effective. However, internal audit should keep an open mind and always consider using CAATs to enhance the effectiveness of an audit. Given the lack of paper-based audit trails in many automated systems today, the internal auditor has little choice but to use computer-assisted audit procedures. The challenge to an internal auditor is to identify appropriate areas for CAATs.

Computer systems technology has changed extensively over recent years. The batch-oriented systems of not that many years ago, based upon punched card inputs and magnetic tape files, have been replaced by on-line, database-oriented systems. Large centralized computer hardware has been replaced, in many respects, by networked client-server workstations. Despite these changes, however, the auditor's basic approach for defining CAATs has not really changed. For example, in 1979 the American Institute of Certified Public Accountants (AICPA) published an Audit Guide, *Computer-Assisted Audit Techniques,* which provided some basic direction to auditors on the use of CAATs.[1] Although

---

[1] American Institute of Certified Public Accountants, *Computer-Assisted Audit Techniques* (New York: AICPA, 1979).

now out of date, it contains a good list of the types of audit procedures that can be performed through the use of CAATs.

- *Examining Records Based on Criteria Specified by Internal Audit.* Because the records in a manual system are visible, internal audit can scan for inconsistencies or inaccuracies without difficulty. For records on computer data files, internal audit can specify audit software instructions to scan and print these records that are exceptions to the criteria, so that follow-up actions can be taken. Examples of specified areas are:
  - Accounts receivable balances for amounts over the credit limit
  - Inventory quantities for negative and unreasonably large balances
  - Payroll files for terminated employees
  - Bank demand deposit files for unusually large deposits or withdrawals
- *Testing Calculations and Making Computations.* Internal audit can use software to perform quantitative analyses to evaluate the reasonableness of auditee representations. Such analyses might be for:
  - The extensions of inventory items
  - Depreciation amounts
  - The accuracy of sales discounts
  - Interest calculations
  - Employees' net pay computations
- *Comparing Data on Separate Files.* When records on separate files should contain compatible information, software can determine if the information agrees. Comparisons could be:
  - Changes in accounts receivable balances between two dates, comparing the details of sales and cash receipts on transaction files
  - Payroll details with personnel files
  - Current and prior period inventory files to assist in reviewing for obsolete or slow-moving items
- *Selecting and Printing Audit Samples.* Multiple criteria may be used for selection, such as a judgmental sample of high-dollar and old items and a random sample of all other items, which can be printed in the auditor's workpaper format or on special confirmation forms. Examples are:
  - Accounts receivables balances for confirmations
  - Inventory items for observations
  - Fixed-asset additions for vouching
  - Paid voucher records for review of expenses
  - Vendor records for accounts payable recircularizations
- *Summarizing and Resequencing Data and Performing Analyses.* Audit software can reformat and aggregate data in a variety of ways to simulate processing or to determine the reasonableness of output results. Examples are:
  - Totaling transactions on an account file
  - Testing accounts receivables aging
  - Preparing general ledger trial balances
  - Summarizing inventory turnover statistics for obsolescence analysis

- Resequencing inventory items by location to facilitate physical observations
- *Comparing Data Obtained through Other Audit Procedures with Computer System Data Files.* Audit evidence gathered manually can be converted to a machine-readable form and compared to other data files. Examples are:
  - Inventory test counts with perpetual records
  - Creditor statements with accounts payable files

Although the above were originally developed for external auditors and date before the days of integrated database files, these techniques are generally still applicable for internal auditors. The number and sophistication of these CAATs increases as the individual auditor becomes more experienced in their use.

12-4 TYPES OF COMPUTER AUDIT SOFTWARE

In the early days of computer systems, most systems users had to submit a request to the programming department for a special report or analysis program. Programming was considered difficult and was controlled by specialists in the information systems department. Auditors, however, were suspicious of that approach. An auditor interested in some manual account balance would not ask the auditee for the balance but would examine the records to calculate the total. Similarly, an auditor would want to use programs controlled by internal audit to analyze computer-based data. This led to the development of what has been called generalized audit software.

There are several common standard categories or types of computer audit software.

- Generalized Audit Software Products
- Report Generators and Fourth-Generation Languages
- Microcomputer Audit Software Tools
- Test Data Techniques
- Specialized Audit Test and Analysis Software
- Expert Systems and Inference-Based Software
- Embedded Audit Procedures

Depending upon the overall data-processing environment and the objectives of internal audit, one or more of these tools may be used in a given audit situation. Some require specialized technical skills, but most can be implemented by the generalist internal auditor. Some type of audit software should be used by an effective internal audit department operating in today's highly computerized environments.

(a) GENERALIZED AUDIT SOFTWARE

In the early days of computer auditing, most applications were written in languages such as COBOL or assembler languages. Auditors usually had neither the technical skills nor the time required to write their own retrieval programs to independently access data. The increasingly large computer applications—and organization dependence upon them—

required auditors to total sample or extract data from these files through the data-processing department—the auditees in many instances—limiting the auditor's independence.

This lack of auditor independence problem was solved in the early 1970s by the major public accounting firms, who developed simple audit retrieval programs. In addition to convenient retrieval capabilities, this software often contained other common audit functions such as sequence number gap detection or audit sampling procedures.

Many internal audit departments today use the newer microcomputer audit software packages or fourth-generation languages (4GLs), discussed below, for audit retrieval tasks. However, the older generalized audit software can be used for many systems and offer internal auditors some of the following advantages:

- *Reliance on Data Processing.* Generalized audit software allows internal audit to perform tests of an application without asking the information systems function to write the necessary retrieval software, giving auditors the independence they need.

- *Increased Audit Efficiencies.* Computer audit software can more efficiently confirm accounts receivable records and produce confirmation letters. In addition, such a CAAT will almost certainly be used over multiple years, so its development costs can be spread over time.

- *Opportunity to Observe Other Controls.* By using an independent set of programs on the auditee's systems operations, internal audit can observe and develop a better understanding of other information systems controls. For example, internal audit may observe procedural weaknesses in work schedules or tape cartridge retrievals from the data center library. While not related to the planned tests of given data files, these observations can often point to areas for subsequent audit work.

Figure 12.1 shows the necessary programming steps to develop a CAAT to test balances and interest rates for a financial institution loan file. It shows this generalized software program code as batch transactions much more easily constructed than a conventional program written in a language such as COBOL or C++.

Generalized audit software was originally introduced in the mainframe computer era where there were few other easy-to-use retrieval packages available. Today, auditors can also use other software retrieval tools or 4GLs, which are available on many computer systems.

(b) REPORT GENERATORS AND FOURTH-GENERATION LANGUAGES

When information systems departments used compiler-based languages such as COBOL, end users did no hands-on applications development and relied upon the information systems department for all reports. This former dependency on COBOL-type languages has very much changed in today's modern information systems department. Today, end users with minimal training regularly produce special reports or perform complex file manipulations in addition to conventionally programmed applications with report-generator languages.

Internal audit needs an understanding of the types of generalized retrieval languages available at the auditee location. They are generally available for most types and sizes of vendors' hardware, from larger mainframes to microcomputers. Some of these software

Figure 12.1 Programming Steps to Developing a CAAT

1. Define overall audit objectives—What do we want to test and why?

2. Identify files and cycle dates that will test the audit objective.

3. Identify an audit software tool for performing the test.

4. Identify specific files and their format data contents that will be tested.

5. Code audit retrieval software to perform the desired audit test.

6. Test audit software against sample set of production files. Modify audit software until the audit test appears to be working correctly. If problems exist, correct audit program coding.

7. Determine availability and perform actual audit test.

8. Follow up on any unusual or unexpected results. Make further corrections as necessary.

9. Report audit results.

10. Document results of audit test.

products are designed to operate only as a query language for a given database or vendor's application software package. These are called *report-generators* or *query languages.* Others are quite general and can be used with many applications. The most general and flexible of these fall under the general title of *fourth-generation languages* (4GLs).

The term "fourth-generation languages," or 4GL, refers to a computer language where only very general instructions are necessary to produce a desired report rather than the detailed steps in a complete computer program. For example, the program author needs only to specify a list of items to be selected to produce a fairly professional looking output report. The 4GL takes care of most other report editing and formatting functions.

Software that comes with some form of a query or report-generator language can satisfy the many reporting needs of typical end users. For example, a fixed-assets control application may have a report-generator subsystem to allow customized fixed assets reports. Auditors should consider the use of these same report generators for audit retrieval purposes. Many are quite easy to use. Otherwise, vendors will provide training in the use of the software at the time it is installed. Even if internal audit plans to use generalized audit software or other retrieval tools, these report-generator products can be very helpful for special analysis projects.

Since the early 1980s, there have been numerous 4GL-type products, some for end-user report-retrieval purposes and others primarily for use by the information systems function such as overall applications generators. Any can be a powerful tool for auditor-developed CAATs. While it is difficult to give a single definition of a 4GL, most exhibit one or more of the following characteristics:

- *Non-Procedural Language.* Earlier programming languages required the programmer to follow a fixed sequence of instructions to accomplish a given task. For example, a COBOL program producing an output report must first open and read the input file, then select and sort items of interest to finally produce the report. This same sequence of steps is not required with a 4GL. The same example report could be produced with the single instruction, "List data sorted by. . . ." This facility makes the software easy to learn.

- *Environmental Independence.* Many 4GLs can be used on a variety of different computer systems. They are portable, from microcomputers to mainframes, operating under different types of computer hardware, operating systems, and telecommunications monitors.

- *Powerful Application-Development Facilities.* Although not necessary for auditors, most 4GLs have powerful facilities to help application developers to design entire systems, including database accesses, "paint" procedures to program retrieval screens, and graphical output reports.

A 4GL offers greater flexibility and ease of use. However, such software products may be expensive and difficult to justify for internal audit department use only. Internal audit should investigate and consider using 4GLs installed elsewhere within the organization. This software is typically licensed to the overall organization and internal audit would be one additional user.

If such tools are not in use, internal audit may recommend their consideration and use in conjunction with a review of information systems applications (see Chapter 17).

Generalized retrieval software can almost always be used for audit retrieval purposes. It has the disadvantage that it does not have such built-in audit software functions as statistical sample selections or serial number gap detection. However, it will work quite well for item selections, recalculations, file matching, or data-reporting purposes. Many specialized audit functions can generally be coded into the retrieval language with little difficulty.

Many software products come delivered with some type of vendor-supplied retrieval package. For example, accounting software packages for general ledger accounting often come with their own report-retrieval packages. Even specialized commercial software today, such as a system to control inventory in a computer center media library, comes with its own specialized retrieval software. These are often useful to an internal auditor for accessing and analyzing the particular data records.

A major disadvantage with the various retrieval products included in other commercial software is that an internal auditor, in a larger organization, may be required to learn the report-generation language from multiple software products, none of which may follow a consistent syntax. There may be one or several installed on the main computers, with additional ones on divisional or local workstations. Even though the learning curve for writing audit retrievals with these products is typically short, internal audit may encounter both training and logistical difficulties. Mainframe-based generalized audit software, discussed previously, or microcomputer audit packages, discussed below, can provide internal audit with a single software retrieval product for use throughout the organization. However, audit objectives will determine what type of audit software is best used.

(c) MICROCOMPUTER AUDIT SOFTWARE TOOLS

The microcomputer has had a very significant impact on information systems since its introduction in the early 1980s. These computer systems are found in most organizations either as freestanding devices or, more typically, networked together and to central mainframe computers. Chapter 14, for example, discusses approaches to automating the internal audit function primarily through the use of microcomputers connected through a local area network (LAN).

The microcomputer can also be a useful tool for developing CAATs. Several very excellent microcomputer-based audit-retrieval products are available to aid internal auditors. While perhaps designed more with the external auditor in mind, these microcomputer audit-retrieval packages are also very useful to the typical internal auditor. In addition, other certain standard microcomputer software products can also be used for audit retrieval purposes. All of these microcomputer audit tools are designed to access or download data from larger computer systems to bring them to internal audit's microcomputer.

(i) Specialized Microcomputer-Based Audit Software.   Internal audit often may wish to examine and analyze the contents of data files located on various remote computer systems within the organization where generalized audit software or other retrieval tools are not available for processing at each of these remote locations. For example, due to software license restrictions or computer systems incompatibilities, internal audit's generalized audit software may only be able to be used on the central computer system. Data files from other locations would have to be transported to that central site using the organization's communications network. Even if retrieval languages were available at all locations, it might be necessary for internal audit to spend increased travel time and additional resources processing CAATs at these remote locations. Microcomputer-based audit software tools can solve many of these problems.

Microcomputer audit software is a type of generalized audit software with many of the functions and features typically found on mainframe systems but implemented on a business microcomputer. It is not designed to perform audit retrievals against other microcomputer systems but against original or extract files from larger computer system applications. This software was originally developed for external auditors who are faced with the need to access files from many different clients and computer systems, and therefore, many products currently on the market have an external auditor emphasis. Public accounting firms have developed software which they sometimes make available to their clients; the AICPA has marketed its own version of microcomputer audit software; and commercial vendors market others. One software product that this author has found to be quite useful in an internal audit department is called Audit Command Language (ACL).[2]

Internal audit often must extract and analyze data from very large files on mainframe systems with thousands or millions of records. Although an internal auditor needs to access these larger files, sometimes it is more convenient for internal audit to process this data on an audit department microcomputer rather than directly on mainframe systems. This larger volume of data can be processed on a typically much smaller audit microcomputer equipped with a very high-capacity hard disc of 5.0 gigabytes or more.

The audit microcomputer also needs a mechanism to read files from mainframe

---

[2] ACL Services Ltd., Vancouver, B.C., Canada.

systems, such as a modern or other communications port to access the mainframe processors. This will be effective provided the mainframe files are not too large or the microcomputer has a sufficient hard disc capacity. An alternative and often better approach is to equip the audit microcomputer with a standard "9 track" tape or cartridge drive. These drives are not extremely expensive and can be a good addition to a centralized internal audit department machine. The microcomputer can then read from mainframe tapes to process data for the computer audit test. Although many larger data centers are now converting to cartridge formats, the 9-track reel tape should continue to be used for some time.

Figure 12.2 illustrates an audit microcomputer configuration used for computer-assisted auditing. The actual audit software programs used for the computer-assisted audit procedures have similar functions and capabilities as the mainframe-based generalized audit software discussed previously. Most of the types of CAAT procedures discussed previously, such as testing agings or recalculating balances, can be used with audit microcomputers. The only limitation is the memory and storage capacity of the microcomputer. Thus, if a large number of data files are to be compared as part of the CAAT, the microcomputer will not be that efficient because only one tape drive would typically be available.

Figure 12.3 illustrates the programming steps necessary to recalculate the agings of invoice records on an accounts receivable file using the ACL product. In this example, an internal auditor would have secured a copy or extract of the organization's accounts receivable master. Using the audit command language, internal audit can quite easily perform this common financial audit task.

(ii) Microcomputer Audit Retrievals.   Just as 4GLs and report generators can take the place of generalized audit software, standard audit software tools can, for some audit projects, substitute for microcomputer audit software. This standard software includes spreadsheet and database packages, as described in Chapter 14. Using a communications line connected to a mainframe or a modern to a remote system, internal audit can download data to an audit microcomputer. The difference with standard audit software is that this data would be downloaded into a spreadsheet or database program format. Internal audit can then analyze the data and perform CAATs using the functions of that standard software.

Figure 12.2   Audit Microcomputer Configuration

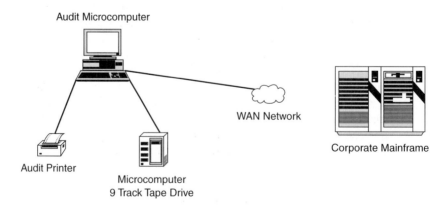

Figure 12.3   ACL Programming Example

ACL is a conversational easy-to-use interactive command audit language that the auditor can load onto the microcomputer to access a fairly universal set of computer file structures. Files can be accessed either through an on-line connection or from a tape file, extracted from the data center that the auditor would access through a special, 9-track tape drive.

As an example of using ACL, assume an internal auditor wanted to recalculate taxes payable account for a situation where the tax rates would be 20, 30, or 50 percent depending upon the income level. Income less than $5,000 would result in no taxes, and the other income breaks are $10,000, $30,000, and above. An audit analysis program to recalculate those taxes would first require codes to indicate where annual income was located on the tax file. The taxes payable could then be calculated with the following ACL command statements:

TAXES_PAYABLE_COMPUTED

0				IF INCOME < 5000
	.2	*	(INCOME − 5000)	IF INCOME < 10000
1000	+ .3	*	(INCOME − 10000)	IF INCOME < 30000
7000	+ .5	*	(INCOME − 30000)	

These four commands would read through the file and produce an audit total.

The most common software used for these CAATs is the microcomputer spreadsheet, no matter what brand. An internal auditor can use a spreadsheet to, for example, capture portions of a downloaded file for summation or analysis. Internal audit would define which portions of a larger data file to extract and submit a request through a mainframe program for that data. Mainframe-to-microcomputer file extraction routines are often available as utility programs within the information systems department. The requested data is downloaded to a microcomputer hard disc file in what is called an ASCII or standard data file format. The data fields are defined, incorporated into the spreadsheet program, and then analyzed by an internal auditor using many of the functions available with the spreadsheet or database software.

(d) TEST DATA OR "TEST DECK" APPROACHES

The term "test deck" is an old computer audit–related term that dates back to the earliest days of information systems, when applications operated in a batch mode and used punched cards as input media. In order to test a computer application, internal auditors developed a series of test transactions that achieved known results. These transactions were prepared on a set of input punched cards or a "test deck." The term *test deck* is dated given technology today but it describes a very useful CAAT approach where an internal auditor submits a series of test transactions against a live production system to determine if controls are adequate. (A better expression for this approach is *test data*, although we will continue to use the traditional name of test deck.)

For example, internal audit might use a test deck CAAT approach to test controls in a batch payroll system. Internal audit would submit transactions for known employees showing standard hours of work, for others showing some overtime hours, and for a third group showing an excessive number of hours that should trigger an error report. A special, controlled run of the payroll system would then be arranged using these test transactions. Internal audit would subsequently verify that the pay was correctly computed, the files were correctly updated, and that all expected error and transaction reports were correct. The audit test transactions would then be purged from the updated files. Through this test deck, internal audit could gain a level of assurance that the payroll system, in this example, was working correctly.

Test deck approaches fell into disuse by auditors as systems ceased to be batch-oriented and became more complex. However, this approach—which calls for the submission of audit test transactions to a copy of a live application—is still a viable CAAT tool for testing modern information systems applications. An actual deck of test transaction cards is not necessary. Test decks—or, more properly, test data approaches—can be very useful for gathering audit evidence. Even though an internal auditor will almost certainly not prepare a deck of test cards for the modern computer application, the approach uses a predetermined set of on-line transactions as the test deck. The CAAT approach allows internal audit to input a series of test transactions through an application input screen to achieve the following objectives:

- A general understanding of the program logic associated with a complex system
- A determination that valid transactions are being correctly processed by the application
- A determination that invalid or incorrect transactions are being correctly identified and flagged by the application's program controls.

There are limitations in this testing approach. If a given transaction type has not been prepared for the test, internal audit cannot affirm that the application works correctly in respect to that transaction. If the documentation is incomplete or incorrect, internal audit may miss a key transaction test.

Test data CAATs can also be developed by tracing user-initiated transactions through a normal production cycle or by inputting a series of audit test transactions through a special test run of the application. There are advantages and disadvantages to each of these approaches.

(i) Tracing User-Initiated Transactions.   An internal auditor sometimes must review and gather evidence of transaction controls for complex, on-line information systems applications. For example, internal audit may want to verify that an on-line manufacturing resource planning system, as described in Chapter 23, is operating with proper controls. Such a system generally has numerous programs to:

1. Control the receipt of materials into the plant
2. Place them in inventory
3. Later retrieve them from stores and assign them to manufacturing work orders
4. Add labor and other parts to complete the manufacturing process

These numerous and various transaction types, which update or impact multiple programs, are difficult to assess through sample processing. When faced with a complex application, an internal auditor will often be unable to identify single points in the application process to develop comprehensive CAATs. A formal test data approach, where internal audit sets up a separate system process, is also difficult due to the overall complexity of the system.

The most reasonable approach to testing may be to trace a representative sample of normal transactions initiated through the production application. Following the example of a manufacturing materials control system, an internal auditor should first identify key control points in the overall system. The next step is to observe and record transactions being entered at each of these points such that they can be subsequently traced to the appropriate on-line screens or reports. As part of this observation, internal audit may also want to ask users to input certain invalid transactions to ascertain that they have been correctly rejected. Figure 12.4 shows this user test data CAAT approach.

The tracing of user-initiated transactions is quite similar to the transaction walk-through approach for computer applications described in Chapter 17. The difference here, however, is that an internal auditor captures a more substantial number of normal transactions for tracing and verification. This approach is not a true CAAT. However, it can often be combined with the use of other CAATs at key points in the application to gain a better understanding of the application's processing procedures and of its controls. For example, internal audit can trace inventory transactions input through the on-line screens of a manufacturing system. Combined with a CAAT, these could then be used to compare beginning and ending period inventory status files to highlight the differences caused by the production on-line transactions.

This procedure is more of a manual testing technique than a true CAAT. It also places emphasis on transaction input processing and the resultant outputs around the computer system rather than the actual operations of the component programs. It is often not the best way to gain positive assurance that an application is working with all of the proper controls. However, it can be an effective approach to gaining a level of assurance that the application appears to be working with no obvious errors. While individual programs can be tested in some detail, this may be the only way to test an entire operational application.

(ii) Application Tests Using Test Data. This CAAT approach uses auditor-prepared test data transaction or test files. If an application has only one key input point, auditor-initiated test data entered through that point for processing in a special run can often be an effective CAAT. For example, an organization may have an on-line labor-hours collection system where employees input hours on a single-screen format for recording time and allocating the hours to various projects. Internal audit may be interested in verifying the integrity and correctness of the output data from such a system.

An approach to testing this type of system is to build an audit file of representative test transactions for input to a special test run. These transactions represent differing valid and error conditions to allow internal audit to test as many conditions as possible through a special run of the application under review. Live files or copies of live files can be used for all processing. The auditor's file of test transactions is input to this test run, and internal audit subsequently verifies the results of the systems processing. This type of test data CAAT approach for application testing is illustrated in Figure 12.5.

The test data approach can be an effective type of CAAT to gather evidence about smaller, self-contained information systems applications. Rather than using audit software

Figure 12.4   Test Data Computer-Assisted Audit Approach—User-Initiated Transactions

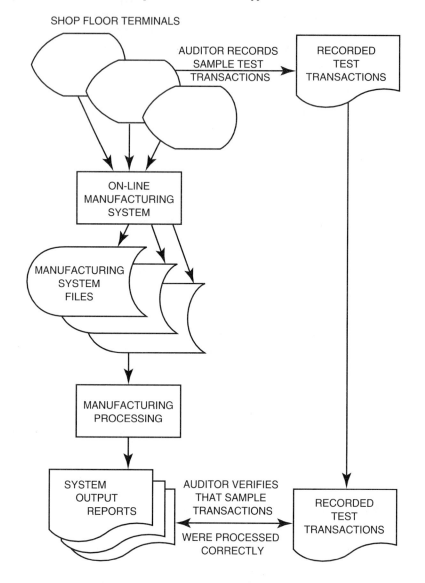

to develop retrieval reports showing file contents, this technique allows internal audit to test program logic by passing test transactions against a set of live data files and production programs to verify the correctness of application processing. While the user-initiated transaction approach discussed previously has an internal auditor reviewing the results of an actual production transaction, this approach allows the auditor to develop a series of ''can't happen'' transactions to determine how systems controls are working in these extraordinary situations. The approach has some limitations:

- Data-processing operations will sometimes object to internal audit's request to process a special run of one of their production applications for fear that the audit test data will somehow become intermingled with and corrupt the normal production data.

- Test data can only effectively test one cycle of an application. Due to the information systems operations disruptions this CAAT generally causes, it is usually difficult to schedule multiple test cycles.

- The approach is really only cost-effective for more self-contained applications since it is difficult to design test data covering multiple input points.

- The preparation of a comprehensive set of test data can be more time-consuming than the preparation of a conventional CAAT retrieval program.

Despite the above limitations, a test data approach is often useful when internal audit reviews an application that has been implemented at multiple locations within the organization. By developing a standard set of test data and using it at each of the locations, internal audit can verify, among other things, that there have been no unauthorized changes to the application programs at the various remote locations.

Figure 12.5   Test Data Computer-Assisted Audit Approach—Auditor-Initiated Transactions

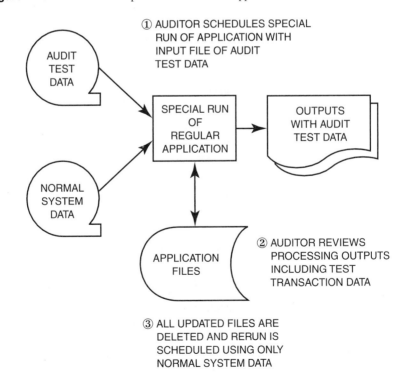

(e) SPECIALIZED AUDIT TEST AND ANALYSIS SOFTWARE

Internal audit often has a need to review specialized computer files, such as those associated with the computer operating system or on-line transaction log files. This requires a very different type of CAAT than internal audit would develop for financial and operational application audit tests. Because computer operating systems and related files generally are of a very complex nature, generalized audit software or 4GLs will often not work. Generalized audit software works best with conventional files defined in fixed record and field lengths; this is often not true for systems software files which use very specialized file format structures.

An internal auditor is sometimes interested in monitoring the integrity of the mainframe computer's operating system or related parameter files. For example, IBM's MVS operating system, used on their system 390 architecture mainframe computers, contains numerous library files and parameter tables, which could be improperly manipulated to allow security and integrity violations. Specialized audit-analysis software, discussed in Chapter 19, can be used both to access these files and to identify potential operating system integrity exposures.

There are other specialized software tools which a creative and technically skilled auditor can use to develop unique CAATs. Many are not specifically designed for auditors but for normal computer systems developers or end-users. However, internal audit can often make very effective use of them; examples include the following:

- Manufacturing production and materials scheduling software packages often contain ad hoc reporting subsystems to analyze these manufacturing files. Internal audit can use them to extract a sample of production part numbers for further testing.
- Software to control the movement of computer tapes and cartridges in and out of the library also often has an ad hoc reporting capability. With minimal training, an internal auditor can use these report-generator packages to test library operational and media-management controls.
- Applications programmers frequently use computer-aided systems engineering (CASE) software to help them build more effective new applications. CASE software, discussed in Chapter 19, can also be a very effective audit tool for developing process flowcharts and documenting applications.

Although typically not considered as CAAT software, there are numerous ad hoc retrieval or analysis software packages that can aid internal audit. Because such software is often quite easy to learn and use, internal audit need only to ask if such software is available when reviewing a specialized area or application. In other instances, internal audit may need to acquire certain specialized software tools to support audit efforts.

(f) EXPERT SYSTEMS AND INFERENCE-BASED SOFTWARE

Expert systems are a new direction for information systems applications and for CAAT software tools. Many manual processes are not only based on just the fixed rules found in a computer program but on fuzzy "best guess" judgments that are best performed by human experts in a given field. Conventional computer programs have been based on fixed rules with no allowance for "fuzzy" issues that an expert can properly analyze. Although internal auditors have not done very much in this area at present, expert systems represent a discipline where there will be considerable opportunities for CAAT development in the future. Expert systems represent a type of application often called an artificial intelligence system.

The concept of ''fuzzy'' issues relates to the knowledge that any expert, including an ''expert'' internal auditor, can add some insight to a decision process. An inexperienced auditor might review an operational area, such as manufacturing shop floor operations, and see no internal control problems based on the internal auditor's textbook knowledge. The experienced auditor might look at the same area and see a variety of potential problems based on that internal auditor's overall experience. This type of knowledge, based upon what are called ''fuzzy'' rules and inferences, cannot be directly gleaned from a textbook. However, these same rules and inference decision processes can be built into what is called an expert system.

An internal auditor should consider the many areas where there are no clear yes or no answers. For example, internal audit is often faced with a decision as to whether or not to include an item in a published audit report. Some factors will push an auditor towards a yes decision while others point to a no. There are often no clear-cut rules that point to one correct decision. An internal auditor will use what is called a ''fuzzy logic'' reasoning process to determine whether to publish the audit report item. An expert system will help to make these ''fuzzy'' logic decisions.

The Institute of Internal Auditors (IIA) has published a brief introduction to artificial intelligence and expert systems; it explains why they differ from conventionally programmed computer systems.[3] To better explain an expert system, the IIA publication provides an example of a conventionally programmed accounting system that might contain these rules:

>   *SALES REVENUE*
>   *LESS COST OF GOODS SOLD*
>   *LESS GENERAL AND ADMINISTRATIVE EXPENSES*
>   *EQUALS NET PROFIT BEFORE TAXES*

This is the conventional type of programming logic that can be written in a language such as COBOL. Net profit will always be calculated in the same manner. These programmed rules, however, will not predict profits in a future period. A set of expert systems rules can be formulated to predict potential future profitability. An analyst might program these future potential outcomes as follows:

>   *IF THE ORGANIZATION IS PROFITABLE, AND*
>   *IF THE BOARD HAS DECLARED A DIVIDEND INCREASE, AND*
>   *IF OFFICERS ARE EXERCISING OPTIONS TO BUY SHARES,*
>   *THEN, THE NET PROFIT WILL PROBABLY INCREASE IN THE NEXT PERIOD*

The above example is based on a series of ''if-then'' rules relating to a variety of factors, which often are predictive measures of future profitability. These rules provide a best guess or probable result. Chapter 8 also briefly discussed the use of expert systems for

---

[3] Robert R. Moeller, *Artificial Intelligence: A Primer* (Altamonte Springs, Fl., The Institute of Internal Auditors, 1987).

internal audit risk analysis. Expert systems have been developed for all sizes of computers, ranging from microcomputers to mainframes. While initially developed as special, free-standing applications, they are now often built into conventional computer systems applications.

Expert systems software can be a useful tool for various types of CAATs. Internal audit can use this software to develop inference-based inquiries rather than the conventional programming logic rules used with a 4GL or generalized audit software. This can be a very powerful tool for an internal auditor who often knows in general what to request but does not understand a specific data file's content. An example of an expert system CAAT is one with logic rules for an account reconciliation. Based on generalized expert systems logic rather than on a specific program product, this type of system would allow an internal auditor to survey a large population of accounts from a general ledger file and to identify those where there may have been questionable transactions.

Expert systems also have the capability to guide auditors through complex audit decision procedures. For example, expert systems have been implemented to help an auditor draw a conclusion based upon the auditee responses and other materials gathered, as outlined in an audit's questionnaire. This use of an expert system to automate the audit decision process is discussed in Chapter 14.

CAAT-based expert systems are a newer technology for many internal auditors. As these expert systems and inference-based software tools become more readily available, they can allow an internal auditor the flexibility to develop a set of rules to identify conditions that cause internal control concerns. The expert systems software can then be used to apply its if-then rules to a file to determine if the conditions exist and the extent that there may be an audit concern.

(g) EMBEDDED AUDIT PROCEDURES

Most conventional CAATs require an internal auditor to initiate some action to start the testing process. The CAAT will identify the condition only when it is processed as part of a scheduled, periodic audit. However, auditors often are interested in monitoring exception transactions within an application on an ongoing basis. Embedding audit software into a production application can provide continual monitoring for activities of interest and to report them for immediate or subsequent audit analysis. Earlier audit literature has referred to one of these approaches as the System Control Audit Review File (SCARF) method. A second, related approach is called an Integrated Test Facility (ITF), an internal audit–established, built-in test data facility. Both are embedded audit procedures.

In many respects, a continuous, embedded audit monitor is similar to the error- or exception-reporting mechanisms built into many conventional applications. It is also quite similar to the log file approach used for monitoring activities through a computer operating system. The major difference is that conventional application exception reports usually log all such problems and system log files record all activities. A continuous audit monitor only logs and reports items of predetermined audit interest. Also, application exception reports and system logs typically have a wide distribution while the audit monitors are reports for the exclusive use of internal audit.

Both continuous audit monitors and ITFs allow internals auditors to have access to certain automated system conditions on an ongoing, continuous basis. The internal audit department needs management support and commitment to devote audit resources to this type of effort. If audit management decides to implement these types of embedded audit procedures, they will have an expanded role in the organization's overall system of internal accounting controls.

(i) Continuous Audit Monitor Design and Implementation.

As an example of a continuous audit monitor, assume that an auditor is working in a multi-branch financial organization with numerous transactions between the branches. Internal audit has reviewed the significant financial applications to test internal controls and has used generalized audit software to test key elements of the financial applications. However, the internal auditor is interested in monitoring and following up on certain exception transactions that may be initiated by various branch users from time to time.

The example application has a large number of exception reports for user follow-up; internal audit is only interested in reviewing certain interbranch transactions above a specified dollar limit. While normal operational personnel also follow up on such transactions, an internal auditor is interested in the nature of such transactions and the level of follow-up activity. A continuous audit monitor CAAT can allow internal audit to review these ongoing exception transactions.

A continuous audit monitor CAAT is special, auditor-defined program code or software that gathers continuous evidence about transaction exceptions or potentially unauthorized items that may require auditor follow-up. This type of a monitor will not allow internal audit to perform detailed tests of an application but will collect the transaction data for subsequent testing and analysis. Because it must be built into a production set of programs, a continuous audit monitor CAAT should be installed only where internal audit has a strong, ongoing review interest.

Continuing with the above example, an internal auditor gains a detailed understanding of the application and identifies where the interbranch transactions of interest can be captured in the application. The information systems function then inserts program code into the application to monitor and capture all such transactions of interest. These are normally written onto a protected log file for later audit review and analysis. Figure 12.6 illustrates how such a continuous audit monitor might be constructed.

Because a continuous audit monitor is an embedded set of program code, it cannot be easily changed. Internal audit should carefully design the objectives and selection criteria associated with any such monitor. Properly constructed, however, it can be an effective tool to independently monitor applications where internal audit has an ongoing interest.

There are some potential problems with this approach. First, internal audit is generally not able to implement such a procedure independently, and needs the assistance of the information systems department to build the monitor into a production application. The other CAATs discussed previously in this chapter can often be established fairly independently by internal audit. Given an understanding of file structures, internal audit can use generalized audit software or a 4GL to perform various tests. Similarly, many test data procedures can be established independently. This is not true for the continuous audit monitor, which must be embedded into a normal production application.

It is usually necessary for internal audit to work with the information systems application development and programming function to define the requirements of a monitor that can then be incorporated into the production application design. The most efficient time to suggest the implementation of such a monitor is when an application is being developed. If appropriate, an internal auditor can request a continuous audit monitor to be installed as part of the auditor's review of the system under development (as discussed in Chapter

Figure 12.6 Continuous Audit Monitor Computer-Assisted Audit Approach

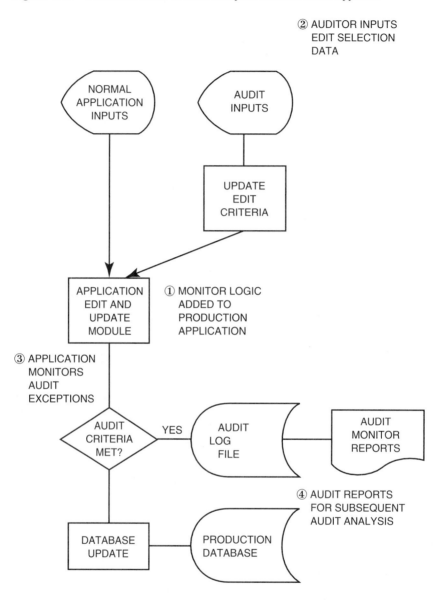

18). Installing a continuous audit monitor in an application already operational is more difficult because it will require an application modification often requiring changes to all associated procedures.

Internal audit should also recognize that because the information systems function installs such a monitor, they will be aware of it and potentially have the ability to bypass its monitoring functions. Nevertheless, a continuous audit monitor can be a powerful tool to review certain exception items associated with critical transactions. Although the example cited was for a financial application, the procedure is also applicable to many other types of nonfinancial applications. In a manufacturing organization, internal audit could install such a monitor to log and report, for example, all scrap disposals above a specified limit.

(ii) Integrated Test Facilities.   An integrated test facility (ITF) is an embedded audit module that allows an auditor to test an application on an ongoing or random basis. It differs from the continuous audit monitor which records all production transactions of a certain activity or type. An ITF records only special test transactions that internal audit has independently input to the application.

An example might better explain how an ITF is constructed and used. Similar to the continuous audit monitor example, assume that internal audit is interested in reviewing controls over a central financial system covering a large, multi-division organization. That central financial system receives transactions from its operating entities for both internal and interdivision financial entries. Each division included in the financial application is identified by a unique division code. In addition, the central organizational accounting function initiates transactions that affect all operating entities. An internal auditor is interested in the controls over these various transactions as well as in any potentially improper accounting items.

An ITF allows internal audit to review this application on an ongoing basis. Internal audit might set up a dummy division number—such as ''Division Code 99''—in the application's authorization files. All system reports for this Division Code 99 are then routed to the audit department. Internal audit inputs test transactions against this Division Code 99 to test the accuracy of the system and to verify program integrity. In addition, if other normal transactions impact all divisions, internal audit would be able to review them on their Division Code 99 reports. Figure 12.7 illustrates how such an ITF might be constructed.

An ITF can be an effective test data type of CAAT for many forms of applications. A special test run is not normally required as auditor transactions are entered with other normal transactions. Just as with other audit test CAATs, however, ITF transactions can then be compared to predetermined processing results in order to gather evidence about the application being tested.

Internal audit can construct an ITF using two alternative approaches. First, the basic information systems application can remain unchanged, with auditors only inputting transactions against the designated auditor code—such as the Division Code 99 mentioned above. It is then necessary to purge these transactions from the system only after the testing has been completed. For an accounting application, this can sometimes be as simple as entering reversal transactions to the system. However, this reversal process is often much more complex. For example, many accounting systems have allocation processes that may affect all balances in the system; it is important that internal audit's ITF test data does not cause other account balances to be altered.

A second approach to building the ITF is to add a program or modify existing programs to filter out any audit transactions. This way, internal audit's test transactions can be transparent to other users of the system. The problem with this method is the special programming required to build the filter. If the information systems department is one of the functions being examined, the integrity of the tests could be compromised.

In either event, an ITF is an advanced approach to testing and gathering evidence about an automated application. Because of the program coding and logistics required to

Figure 12.7   Integrated Test Facility (ITF) Computer-Assisted Audit Approach

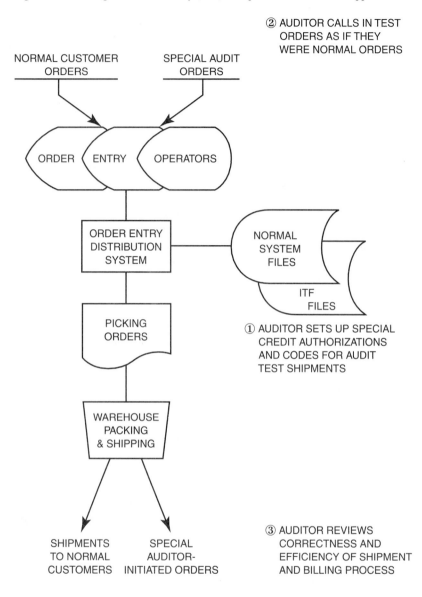

establish an ITF, the technique is difficult to establish and should be used only when internal audit has a strong, ongoing interest in reviewing an application. In addition, an internal auditor responsible for implementing the procedure should have a thorough understanding of all aspects of the target application before starting the ITF. Otherwise, internal audit's ITF transaction activities may have unintended effects.

Several other areas of caution should be considered before constructing an ITF. In some regulated industries—such as financial institutions—auditors may be in violation of state or federal statutes by establishing fictitious accounts in financial applications. Internal audit should discuss any ITF plans with the organization's consul, if appropriate. Internal audit should also take care to make certain that only a limited number of personnel are aware of the ITF. If it is generally known, for example, that Division Code 99 is internal audit's number, anyone making improper transactions will see that the code is bypassed.

12-5 SELECTING THE APPROPRIATE CAAT SOFTWARE PACKAGE

In a very general sense, any program developed or controlled by internal audit is a type of audit software. However, internal audit generally does not want to develop programs in a compiler language such as COBOL or C + + because of the development time requirements. Because of concerns with efficiency, internal audit should use generalized audit software or similar 4GL retrieval software for many of its CAATs. Which approach to use depends very much upon the computer hardware and software environment, the current availability of software tools, auditor technical knowledge, and, most importantly, internal audit's CAAT objectives.

In a larger information systems environment with centralized computer systems, generalized audit software is often the preferred alternative. It offers some of the following advantages:

- *Fast Learning Curves.* Auditors with even limited data-processing knowledge can easily build audit test and retrieval applications.
- *Preprogrammed Audit Functions.* The software generally has functions of audit interest—such as gap sequence number checking—built into the software.
- *Limited Coding Requirements.* Although the software is primarily designed for simple, ''quick and dirty'' retrieval reports, these can be produced with very few coding steps.
- *Specialized File-Processing Capabilities.* Many generalized audit software packages have the ability to read specialized system's files, such as the SMF log files found on large-scale IBM systems.

As can be expected, there are also some severe disadvantages in the use of generalized audit software, mostly because it was originally developed for larger, mainframe types of computer systems using batch-oriented simple file structures. The software often cannot easily read more complex files structures. Other disadvantages include:

- *Limited Equipment and Software Availability.* In addition to the unavailability for non-IBM larger computers, the software often cannot directly access many types of database systems.
- *Relatively High Cost.* A generalized audit software package may cost an audit department from $15,000 to 20,000, or more, with an annual maintenance fee from $5,000 to 8,000 per year. If only limited usage is planned, this may seem too expensive.
- *Limited Transportability.* Auditors in many larger organizations are faced with multiple computer sites having differing operating environments. Equipment dif-

ferences or software license restrictions may prevent transporting the audit software package to multiple sites.

A report generator or 4GL is often the most cost-effective mainframe-oriented audit software tool for many audit organizations today. Internal audit can use and share the costs of a software package used in various other parts of the organization. Often, the 4GL can accomplish most of internal audit's CAAT objectives despite its lack of specialized audit functions.

Microcomputer audit software provides some unique advantages in many situations. Files can be downloaded to a microcomputer within the audit department rather than having an internal auditor work directly in information systems operations. Although this tool was developed for external auditors, new microcomputer hardware and audit products are making it increasingly attractive for internal auditors.

The decision of which CAAT software to use depends very much upon overall audit objectives. Internal audit should consider the appropriate type of audit software, depending upon overall audit objectives, the equipment environment, auditor information systems skill levels, and budget constraints.

12-6 STEPS TO BUILDING EFFECTIVE CAATS

Internal audit should follow the same approach for developing CAATs whether using generalized audit software, a 4GL retrieval language, or downloaded data on a microcomputer. This approach is similar to the systems development methodology (SDM) approach discussed in Chapter 17. The difference here is that an internal auditor may develop a CAAT for a one-time or limited-use effort rather than for an ongoing production application.

Because internal audit often draws conclusions and makes rather significant recommendations based upon the results of a CAAT, it is important to use good systems techniques to design and test CAATs. Following is a four-step approach to develop a CAAT.

1. *Determine Audit Objectives of the Application.* It is not sufficient for internal audit just to audit the automated accounting system. The desired audit objectives should be clearly defined; this will make the subsequent identification of testing procedures a much easier task.

   Once internal audit has defined CAAT objectives, file layouts and systems flowcharts should be obtained to select the appropriate data sources for testing. Sometimes, an internal auditor at this point encounters technical problems that might impede further progress. An application documentation file or workpaper should also be started along with this step.

2. *Design the Computer-Assisted Application.* The CAAT software tool used must be well documented, including the overall program logic and any report formats. Any special codes or other data characteristics must be discussed with persons responsible for the computer application. Consideration should also be given to how internal audit will prove the results of audit tests by, for example, balancing to production application control totals. These matters should be outlined in the documentation workpapers.

3. *Program and Test the Application.* This step usually follows step 2 very closely.

Programming is performed using the generalized audit software, the 4GL, the microcomputer software, or some other selected software tool. Once the CAAT has been programmed, internal audit should arrange to test it on a limited population of data. The results must be verified for both correctness of program logic and the achievement of desired audit objectives. This activity should also be documented in the workpapers.

4. *Process and Complete the CAAT.* Making arrangements for processing the CAAT often requires schedule coordination between internal audit and information systems operations. Internal audit is often interested in a specific generation of a data file, and it is necessary to arrange access to it. During the actual processing, internal audit must take steps to assure that the files tested are the correct versions.

Depending upon the nature of the CAAT, an internal auditor should prove the results and follow up on any exceptions as required. If there are problems with the CAAT logic, internal audit should make corrections as required and repeat the steps. The CAAT application workpapers should be completed at this point, including follow-up points for improving the CAAT for future periods.

Computer-assisted audit techniques are powerful tools that can be used by any auditor, and should not be solely the responsibility of the computer audit specialist in the audit department. Just as end-users make increasing use of retrieval tools for their own information systems needs, all members of an audit department should gain an understanding of available audit tools to allow them to develop their own CAATs.

12-7 EVIDENCE-GATHERING IN A PAPERLESS ENVIRONMENT

As more and more automated processes become paperless, the auditor's need to build and use CAATs will increase. That is, the traditional paper trails, as discussed in Chapter 4, that auditors use to trace and validate transactions are reduced or even eliminated in the modern automated system. Audit tools ranging from generalized audit software to continuous audit monitors will increasingly become the only options available to test and gather evidence about these paperless systems.

Many modern operational systems, such as those discussed in Chapters 22 to 30, have some very strong paperless elements. For example, the electronic data interchange (EDI) systems discussed in Chapter 24 have very limited paper trails, as do the automatic teller machines (ATMs) used by financial institutions.

Internal audit frequently encounters paperless or limited-paper-trail accounting systems in a microcomputer environment. For example, an organization with a network of external sales representative may have their field representatives input sales activity to portable laptop computers for subsequent transmission of their orders to a central system for actual order processing. In other implementations, field personnel may not even input part numbers of the items to be ordered but will use bar code scanners to read stock labels to set up the order.

Although an internal auditor must be creative when designing a CAAT to gather evidence regarding these newer, paperless applications, many of the techniques described in this chapter can still apply. For example, the microcomputer field order system could be tested through an ITF on the central computer system. A continuous audit monitor can also be installed to record and report to internal audit all unusual order activity outside of some predefined audit parameters. (See also Chapter 20 for a discussion on new technologies.)

12-8 THE IMPORTANCE OF CAATS FOR AUDIT EVIDENCE-GATHERING

Many auditors do not give proper attention to the need to gather evidence when reviewing computer applications. It is often an interesting and challenging audit task to gain an understanding of an automated application and to evaluate its internal controls. However, detailed confirmations of account balances or other types of evidence-gathering tests are sometimes viewed as not as interesting and just as time-consuming. However, these evidence-gathering procedures often provide internal audit with opportunities to implement the most creative portion of the audit project.

Assume, for example, that internal audit has performed a detailed internal controls–oriented review of a large fixed-asset capital budgeting application where transactions are initiated from a variety of subsidiary systems and where the application eventually provides general ledger financial statement balances. Internal audit has tested system-to-system controls and concludes that they are adequate and has also manually recalculated the depreciation expenses for several selected transactions and found them to be correct. Can an internal auditor conclude that the fixed assets and accumulated depreciation numbers produced by this sample system are accurate?

In a large organization, where fixed assets may represent a substantial portion of the balance sheet, an internal auditor may decide that there is far too great of a risk in relying solely on just this internal controls review. The several transactions selected for a recalculation compliance test may not be representative of the entire population, and there may be an error in certain classes of these transactions. Although application-to-application controls may have appeared proper, some types of transactions may be assigned to incorrect account groups. Without detailed testing of this example fixed-assets system, it is quite possible that these errors could go undetected.

Auditors should have an understanding of when it is cost-effective and appropriate to perform detailed tests of information systems applications in order to verify the correctness of transactions or account balances. Some of the circumstances when internal audit will want to do this more detailed applications evidence-gathering and testing include the following:

- There is a perception that the risk of relying just on internal controls is too high.
- Although internal audit may have performed limited walk-through or compliance types of tests, the results of these tests may be somewhat inconclusive and will suggest a need for more detailed tests.
- In some instances, certain internal controls may be weak or difficult to identify; internal audit may want to perform detailed tests of the automated applications.
- Some complex or large automated applications are involved. (The continuous audit monitoring techniques described earlier in this chapter would be useful here.)

In many instances, the decision whether to rely just on internal accounting controls and limited compliance testing or to perform detailed tests of transactions will be a decision of audit management. The nature of the audit tests to be performed, the extent of data, the complexity of the application, and the tools and skills available to internal audit should all be factors in this decision.

Internal audit should become familiar with the various software products and techniques available for analyzing and testing computer system files. The implementation and processing of CAATs should not just be delegated to the computer audit specialist in the audit department but should be part of the skill set requirement for all auditors.

CHAPTER 13

Gathering Evidence Through Audit Sampling

13-1 INTRODUCTION: ROLE OF SAMPLING IN AUDITING

The extensive responsibilities of the modern internal auditor require the use of many different audit approaches. In a particular assignment, an internal auditor may review the policies and procedures of the organization to assess their adequacy or may perform surveys of data to identify unusual trends. This work supports the internal auditor's study and evaluation of the systems of internal control. When an internal control system appears to be satisfactory in principle, a next step is to examine transactions or other records to determine the effectiveness of the internal control system in practice. An initial review of a purchasing system, for example, may indicate that effective controls appear to exist and that the organization's interests are protected. It is only by testing actual purchase documents, however, that an internal auditor has assurances that the system is working and employees are not bypassing the controls built into the system.

In the early days of internal auditing, 100% examinations of transactions or documents were commonly performed to test compliance with control procedures. As organizations grew larger and more complex, this 100% examination approach was often not feasible, so auditors examined a portion of the transactions. Because of the large number of invoices, reports, inventory items, and other documents to be reviewed, internal auditors would typically select a sample to develop an audit conclusion. The challenge is to find a sample representative of the entire population. If there are 100,000 transactions and an internal auditor looks at 50 of them, finding 10 exceptions (20%), can the auditor conclude that 20% of the total transactions, or 20,000, are exceptions? This assumption is true only if the sample drawn is representative of the entire population. Audit sampling techniques can help an auditor determine an appropriate sample size and develop an opinion for this type of audit task.

Audit sampling has two major branches: statistical and nonstatistical. Statistical sampling is a mathematics-based method of selecting representative items that reflect the characteristics of the entire population. Using the results of audit tests on the statistically sampled items, an auditor can express an opinion on the entire group. For example, an auditor could develop a statistical sample of items in an inventory, test those items in that sample for their physical quantity or value, and then express an opinion on the value or accuracy of status quantity for the entire inventory.

Non-statistical sampling, also called judgmental sampling, is not supported by mathematical theory and does not allow an auditor to express *precise* opinions on the entire population. Nevertheless, non-statistical or judgmental sampling is a useful audit tool.

This chapter introduces the concepts of both types of sampling. It includes procedures for determining appropriate sample sizes based upon the size and characteristics of the overall population, performing sampling tests, and evaluating the results. Several different methods for sampling will be introduced along with suggestions for the best methods to use in performing various sample tests. Although statistical sampling once required strong mathematical skills, newer procedures using improved manual and automated tools make audit sampling powerful and easy to use. All internal auditors should have an understanding of sampling procedures and should use them when appropriate.

13-2 AUDIT SAMPLING DECISION

When planning an audit that includes the examination of a large number of transactions or other evidence, the modern internal auditor should always ask the question, "Should I use audit sampling?" The correct answer here is often not just a simple Yes or No but may be complicated due to such factors as the number or location of items to be sampled, a lack of technical expertise or computer software availability at a field location, the potential nonacceptance of the results from sampling by auditee management, or a shortage of appropriate audit resources. Because the selection of audit procedures is a matter of judgment, the auditor must carefully weigh the advantages of the various alternative audit procedures in a particular situation, with audit sampling as one of the options.

Why use sampling? We are all familiar with the use of statistical sampling, whether in consumer opinion polls or in the quality-control testing on a production assembly line. If an internal audit department has often relied on 100% examinations or has never used formal sampling techniques, the transition to considering audit sampling for each significant test may initially appear difficult. However, with education and some practice, internal auditors can easily and effectively use sampling procedures. The result should be better and more efficient audits. The following are reasons that encourage the use of audit sampling and statistical sampling in particular.

- *Conclusions may be needed regarding an entire population of data.* If a statistical sampling method is used, information can be accurately projected over the entire population without performing a 100% check on the population, no matter how large. For example, an internal auditor may be interested in the occurrence of some error condition in a large volume of incoming product freight bills. The auditor could select a statistical sample of these freight bill documents, test the sample for the error condition, and then be able to make a 98% certain estimate about the occurrence of that error condition in the entire population of freight bills. This technique typically will result in a strong audit position and significant audit savings.

- *Sample Results are Objective and Defensible.* Internal control errors often occur on a random basis over the total items subject to error, and each error condition should have an equal opportunity of selection in a random sample. An audit test based upon random selection is thus objective and even defensible in a court of law. Conversely, a sample based upon auditor judgment could be distorted due to intentional or unintentional bias in the selection process. An auditor looking for potential problems might examine only the larger or sensitive items, ignoring others.

- *Less Sampling May Be Required through the Use of Audit Sampling.* Using mathematics-based statistics, auditors need not increase the size of a sample directly in proportion to increases in the size of the population to be sampled. Even though a sample of 60 items may be needed to express an audit opinion over a population of 500 items, that same sample of 60 may still be sufficient for a population of 5,000. An internal auditor who does not use statistical approaches often will oversample large populations because of the incorrect belief that larger populations require proportionately larger samples. By using statistics-based sampling procedures, less testing may be required.

- *Statistical Sampling May Provide for Greater Accuracy than a 100% Test.* When voluminous amounts of data items are counted in their entirety, the risk of significant clerical or audit errors increases. However, a small sample will typically receive very close scrutiny and analysis. The more limited sample would be primarily subject only to sampling errors resulting from the statistical projection.

- *Audit Coverage of Multiple Locations Is Often More Convenient.* Audits can be performed at multiple locations with small samples taken at individual sites to complete an overall sampling plan. In addition, an audit using comprehensive statistical sampling may be started by one auditor and subsequently continued by another. Each of their sample results can be combined to yield one set of audit results.

- *Sampling Procedures Are Simple to Apply.* In the past, an internal auditor often was required to use tables published in sampling manuals or to use complex mainframe computer systems in order to develop a sampling plan and sample selection. With the availability of easier-to-use client-server-based software packages, the application of audit sampling has been simplified. The sampling tools and techniques discussed in this chapter should help to explain the process for internal auditors.

Despite the advantages of audit sampling, an internal auditor must keep in mind that *exact information* cannot be obtained about a population of items based on just a sample, whether it be judgmental or statistical. It is only through making a 100% test and following good audit procedures that an internal auditor can obtain exact information. With non-statistical, judgmental sampling, information is only obtained about those items examined. With statistical sampling, regardless of the number of items examined, positive information can be obtained about all of the items in the population within a level of statistical confidence.

13-3 JUDGMENTAL SAMPLING

Although the merits of audit sampling are generally accepted, the auditing standards of the American Institute of Certified Public Accountants (AICPA) state only that statistical sampling is *permitted* rather than mandatory. In judgmental sampling, an auditor uses his or her good judgment to pull a sample. No statistical decision rules are used and the auditor only selects a large enough sample to provide an impression as to whether the internal controls reviewed are in place or procedures examined are being followed.

Judgmental sampling requires an internal auditor to select representative samples of items in a population of data or transactions for audit review. The sample is something less than 100% of the entire group of items included in the review. For internal auditors, the method of the audit selection may take many forms, including:

- An examination of a fixed percentage—such as 10%—of the items or dollars in an audit population. These sample items are often selected haphazardly, with the auditor opening a file drawer, for example, and selecting one or two account files as audit sample items, often because they looked ''interesting.''
- A selection of all or part of the items active during a time period, such as one month in an audit covering a year's transactions. Alternatively, an auditor could select all items having a common characteristic, such as all accounts ending in a particular letter of the alphabet, as part of a review of vendor invoices.
- A selection for audit review of just those items with a large monetary or other significant balances.
- An examination of only items readily available, such as those stored in a particular file drawer.
- A review of only sensitive items or items with some other attribute of audit concern. In a review for inactive or obsolete inventory items, an auditor might select for review only those items that appear to be dusty or located in out-of-way locations in the inventory stores area.

Although useful data may be obtained from judgmental samples, the results can be misleading or inaccurate regarding overall conclusions about the whole population or account. An internal auditor may look at the accuracy of finance charges for the largest 10% of some account under the assumption that these are the most significant. Even though no significant problems were found for the 10% sampled, the auditor will not know of any significant control problems over the remaining accounts representing the other 90%.

An internal auditor must make three audit judgment decisions. First, the internal auditor must develop a method of selection, and decide what types of items to examine. Internal auditors can be subject to criticism if problems are encountered later that were not included in the sample selection. An examination of all account names starting with the arbitrary first letters *A* and *M* will not reveal a problem with an account name starting with *S*.

The size of the sample is the second audit judgment decision. Auditors can incorrectly select only two or three items located off the top of the deck, review them, and state that the results are based upon an audit sample. This can be misleading, as audit report readers may assume a far larger sample was reviewed. The sample size should be reasonable compared to the entire population. Too small of a sample will often not represent the overall population, while too large of a sample may be too time-consuming or otherwise expensive to evaluate.

The third decision is how to interpret and report the audit results from the limited judgmental sample. An internal audit review of excess and obsolete inventory that selects 20 dusty and dirty items from the stores area, finding that 10 are obsolete, cannot conclude that 50% of the entire inventory is obsolete. The bulk of the stores inventory may be active and appear to be clean. If those active items were not considered in the selection, conclusions from the judgmental sample may be inaccurate. Even though 50% of the dusty and dirty items examined may be obsolete, this does not mean that *all* of the inventory is obsolete. The results from a judgmental sample must be stated very carefully. Figure 13.1 lists some ambiguous audit report conclusions based upon incomplete judgmental

Figure 13.1   Judgmental Sampling Problem Audit Findings

Finding 1: Based on our sample of inventory items, we found three items that were incorrectly labeled. Controls need to be improved to …

What's Wrong Here: No reference to the number of items in the inventory, the size of the sample, or the implications of the sample results.

Finding 2: Based on our statistical sample of accounts receivable accounts, we found …

What's Wrong Here: No reference to what is meant by a "statistical sample" and how the conclusion was developed.

Finding 3: We found seven incorrectly valued items in our sample of fixed asset items; based on the results of our sample, we recommend …

What's Wrong Here: Again, no clarification on what is meant by "items in our sample."

samples. All of these examples point out that the findings were based upon some level of judgmental sample. The problem here is that auditors frequently refer to their audit sample and draw conclusions from the results even though there has been little statistical foundation in the sample process.

(a) JUDGMENTAL SAMPLING EXAMPLE

Judgmental sampling is often effective because in many instances internal auditors will find it impractical to take statistically correct samples. Time and other logistical constraints may prevent a true random sample where every item in the population class should have an equal chance of selection. A well-thought-out judgmental sample allows an internal auditor to draw meaningful conclusions based on a limited sample. Below is an example where a judgmental sample is often appropriate.

Consider an internal auditor working for a large convenience store chain called Quick Bite Stores, with 1,400 units located throughout the United States and Canada. About 15% of the units have relatively large sales volumes. All units, both large and small, are widely scattered, with some in such places as Hawaii, Alaska, Puerto Rico, and Nova Scotia. The demographics of these units are described in Figure 13.2. Although the stores are organizationally divided into nine separate regions, many controls and procedures are administered centrally from the Phoenix, Arizona, corporate headquarters. Corporate-developed control procedures are the same, whether for a large or small unit. Due to some reported problems, management has requested that internal audit test compliance with certain procedures at various remote locations and provide the results of its audit at an upcoming board meeting.

Figure 13.2 Quick Bite Store Demographics

Region	Total Units	Large Units
NW U.S. & Alaska	131	12
SW U.S. & Hawaii	239	122
Mountain States	194	6
SE U.S. & Puerto Rico	86	36
Midwest U.S.	162	0
New England	249	23
Western Canada	168	9
Central Canada	103	0
Eastern Canada	68	2
	1400	210

From past audits, internal audit knows that individual store compliance with various centrally directed procedures will vary. Those units close to headquarters receive more frequent visitors, and store compliance is often well implemented. Those in remote locations may not always follow the rules as closely. To comply with management's request, internal audit would want to review a representative sample of all units throughout the United States and Canada. One approach would be to take a statistical sample from a population of all of the units. First, internal audit could decide on a sample size and then randomly select the units to be visited. This approach has several potential problems if internal audit wants to present some meaningful conclusions to Quick Bite management:

- Although management has requested that all units be reviewed, internal audit knows that more attention should be given to the 210 larger units. If a true random sample selection approach is used, the sample selection might not include enough of the larger units to satisfy management. While there are formal statistical methods to solve this, internal audit should design a sample that emphasizes the larger units.

- Audit travel and time logistics must be considered when selecting the units to review, and a random draw might include some of the more difficult-to-reach locations (such as both Alaska and Puerto Rico in the same draw). Although geographically distant locations might be eliminated, internal audit still might want to review a representative sample across all of Quick Bite's territories. While there are statistical approaches to stratify the population across locations as well as by size, the statistical selection mathematics becomes complex.

Given the above situation, an internal auditor might develop a judgmental sampling plan that would examine an arbitrarily selected sample. The auditor might arbitrarily decide to visit 4% (or 56) of the total Quick Bite units, with six or seven units reviewed in each of the nine regional areas in the United States and Canada. Geographically distant locations, such as Hawaii and Alaska, would be eliminated from potential selection for logistical reasons. Internal audit might then decide to visit two larger units in each of the regions where there are larger units. Having developed this sampling plan, internal audit should first discuss it with management to make certain they understand and accept the sampling approach. There is no statistical precision behind this selection approach, just good auditor judgment.

There could be true random draw in the selection of larger units from each of the regions with larger units by placing names of each larger unit within a region in a box and drawing two. Some judgmental bias could technically be introduced into this process. Assume there are three larger units in the Seattle area with another nine scattered throughout the northwest United States and Alaska. If the random draw by region happened to select two of the larger Seattle units (possible with a true random draw), internal audit might reject one of the Seattle units and select another to give a more representative selection from this region. The point to remember is that this is a *judgmental sample.* If the internal auditor assigned to the midwest region has relatives in the Minneapolis area, there would be no harm in selecting Minneapolis as one of the sites to visit, allowing the assigned auditor to spend an evening with relatives, provided there is no other reason not to select Minneapolis.

Next, internal audit may select four smaller units from each of the regions where the larger units were selected, as well as six from the two regions with no larger units. Here, auditor travel logistics should be considered. If one larger unit was selected in Seattle and one in the Portland area for the northwestern draw, it might be best to select smaller units that are easily visited as part of a visit to the selected larger units. Random selection techniques might choose a small Quick Bite northwestern-region location (such as western Montana or Sitka, Alaska), but it would not be cost- and time-efficient to visit either of these smaller units while also visiting the larger ones in Seattle and Portland; instead, internal audit could take a judgmental sample of two smaller units in each region that are nearby the larger unit selected. Figure 13.3 shows this judgmental sampling plan for the northwest and Alaska region.

Internal audit then uses the judgmental sample to perform the planned audit procedures. Although the results will not be based upon a truly random sample that can be projected across all of the stores with statistical accuracy, management will generally understand when internal audit makes some arbitrary decisions when developing its sample, such as rejecting certain geographically remote units from the population to be selected, as long as the sample appears to represent the population. Figure 13.4 shows some sample

Figure 13.3 Quick Bite Northwest Region Judgmental Sample Plan

Location	Large	Small	Judgemental sample selection
Seattle area	4	29	1 Large + 2 Small
Spokane area	1	13	
Other WA	0	9	
Portland area	4	21	1 Large
Other OR	0	12	
Boise area	1	8	
Other ID	0	6	
Anchorage	2	9	2 Small
Other AK	0	12	
	12	119	2 Large + 4 Small

Figure 13.4 Quick Bite Stores Audit Findings (Based on a Judgmental Sample Selection)

---

1. **Store Inventory Controls Need Improvement.** Quick Bite procedures require that each store should take a detailed count of perishable inventory items on a daily basis and should use the summarized results for monthly reporting. We reviewed these procedures at 56 different units throughout the U.S. and Canadian regions. Our sample was judgmentally selected to represent both large and small Quick Bite units. Based on the units visited, we found that perishable inventory procedures are generally not being followed.

2. **Federal Labor Notices Are Not Posted.** The U.S. government requires that certain notices about overtime rules and minimum wages must be posted in all workplaces. We visited two of the 122 large units and four of the 239 small units in the Southeast and Puerto Rico region and found that these signs were generally not posted. While other units in that region may be in compliance with the law, our limited sample indicated that these requirements are not being followed for the region. We did not encounter this problem in the other regions visited.

3. **Cash Count Procedures Are Weak.** Quick Bite procedures call for a formal cash count, including a reconciliation of any differences, for all units. We visited 56 units throughout the organization, including a total of 14 larger units. Based on the units selected, we found that cash count controls are generally good for the larger units but are weak for the others.

---

findings from the Quick Bite audit report based upon these judgmental sampling results. Internal audit has been careful in this example report to qualify the results of the findings and to not suggest they can be easily projected across the remainder of the population. Management often is not interested in the statistical integrity of the sample as long as the results appear to represent the entire population. Non-statistical sampling is useful for many audit situations. However, internal audit should take care to not claim that their audit results are based upon a ''statistical sample,'' a term that implies much more precision.

13-4 STATISTICAL SAMPLING

Despite the ease of use of nonstatistical sampling, internal audit often will want to project the results of an audit sample over the entire population with a strong degree of accuracy. This is where statistical sampling becomes a powerful internal audit tool. Based upon the rules of probability, which in turn allow internal auditors to develop stronger conclusions, statistical sampling is more than simply taking a sample on a random basis. Rather, it requires a precise, controlled sample based upon established mathematical selection relationships. The results of statistical sampling can be then projected over the entire population in a manner that will be accepted by the courts, government regulators, and others.

Statistical sampling was once a fairly complex process for most internal auditors, requiring a high degree of mathematical and computational skills. Sampling results were subject to computational errors and could be easily challenged. Today, the process is quite different. Microcomputer software tools are available to eliminate much of the computational difficulty once encountered with statistical sampling. In addition, mathematical concepts have advanced to make the process easier. The following sections discuss some of the statistical concepts supporting statistical sampling as well as more common approaches to internal audit statistical sampling. Examples are presented to help an internal auditor more effectively use statistical sampling.

(a) ELEMENTARY STATISTICAL SAMPLING CONCEPTS

An important first step in the use of statistical sampling is to gain a general understanding of probability and statistical concepts. While this chapter does not attempt to be a textbook on the subject, the paragraphs following introduce some of these basic statistical concepts and terminology. Although an internal auditor can draw a statistical sample just by following the rules and not having any understanding of statistical concepts, there is always a risk of error. An interested internal auditor should consult a more detailed book on statistical auditing.[1] Some concepts are fairly easy and are used in examples discussed in this chapter. This very general understanding is important!

We start by defining some of the important statistical sampling terms. A *random sample* gives each unit in a population an equal probability of selection. When a sample is selected on a random basis from a group or population of transactions, it represents one of many groups of samples that could be selected from the same population. The item characteristics of a random sample drawn by one auditor may be different from the characteristics of the sample item drawn by another, and both may be different from the results of an examination of all the transactions. To determine how far a sample result differs from that of a 100% test, an internal auditor should have an understanding of the behavior of all possible samples that might be drawn from the population.

It is also important to understand the measures of central tendency over the data. In audit sampling or statistics, specialized terms such as *average value* are used to describe or measure data. We will look at these data measurements in terms of both an example and the mathematical descriptions. Consider the population of 25 accounts receivable balances with a total value of $86,345.24 shown in Table 13.1. Auditors typically encounter much larger populations of data. Six different measures are commonly used by statisticians to look at the central tendencies of this data or the degree that the various values are dispersed around a central average. The most common measure for looking at how data is organized is to consider the statistical measures called the *mean,* the *mode,* the *range of data values,* the *variance,* the *standard deviation,* and the *skewness of the data.* Although the calculation of these central-tendency measures can now be performed today by pressing a function key on the auditor's business calculator, the effective modern internal auditor should understand their meaning, use, and how they are calculated.

The Mean.   The mean is the simple average of the values of items in a population. It is calculated by adding up the total amount in the population of interest—in this example,

---

[1] Two very good but older audit-oriented statistical sampling reference books are: A. A. Arens and J. K. Loebbecke, *Applications of Statistical Sampling to Auditing* (Englewood Cliffs, N.J.: Prentice-Hall, 1981), and A. D. Bailey, Jr., *Statistical Auditing: Review Concepts and Problems* (New York: Harcourt Brace, 1981).

Table 13.1 Sample Population of A/R Balances

Item#	A/R Balance	Rank
1	$275.00	3
2	$1,059.25	8
3	$2,564.78	15
4	$9,032.00	22
5	$1,750.00	12
6	$17,110.40	25
7	$1,713.99	11
8	$6,245.32	20
9	$534.89	5
10	$534.89	6
11	$2,564.78	16
12	$1,122.05	9
13	$3,025.88	17
14	$514.99	4
15	$10,554.58	24
16	$1,988.63	13
17	$7,026.50	23
18	$978.00	7
19	$1,654.54	10
20	$3,066.00	18
21	$35.87	1
22	$78.99	2
23	$2,003.00	14
24	$6,995.41	21
25	$3,915.50	19
	$86,345.24	

25 individual balances for $86,345.24—and then dividing this total by the total number of observed items in the population. The Greek μ symbol is often used to report the mean. In this example, the mean is:

$$\mu = 86,345.24/25 = \$3,453.81$$

The Median.   The median is the middle amount value when all of the items in the population are ranked by size. Table 13.1 contains a column on the right side, rank, which shows the ranking of each item by its value or size. Item #21 has been ranked as #1 because it is the smallest value in the population at $35.87. Item #22 is ranked as #2 because it is the next smallest. The median is calculated by counting the number of individual items in the population and selecting the one where 50% are larger and the other 50% are smaller. In this example, item #16 has been ranked as #13 and $1,988.63 is the median for this population. Twelve items are smaller and twelve larger. The median is rarely the same value as the mean. Here, the median value is smaller than the mean because there are more items of smaller value in the population.

Figure 13.5 Accounts Receivables Balances Histogram

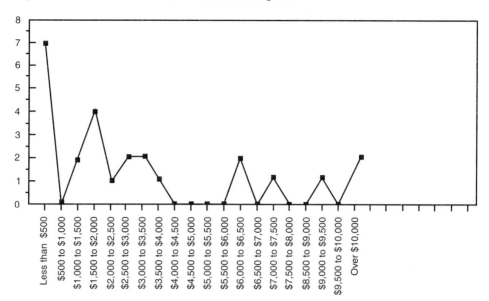

The Mode. The mode is the amount or value that occurs most frequently in a population. In this example, two items—numbers 9 and 10—each have a value of $534.89. The mode is generally not a very meaningful measure of statistics. While sometimes useful when there is a larger population with many items bunched around the same general values, a mode is more useful when the data is summarized into a histogram. The Figure 13.5 histogram for this sample shows that the most common value for the sample data is less than $500.

The Range. The range is the difference between the largest and the smallest values in the population. In this example, the range is the difference between item #6 ($17,110.40) and item #21 ($35.87 or $17,074.53). This measure is primarily useful as an indicator of the breadth of the population data. The range will also be discussed as part of measuring dispersion through what is called the standard deviation.

Standard Deviation. Each of the measures discussed until now—such as mean and median—should be fairly easy to understand for most professionals, even those who may not have not had much background in statistics. In contrast, many find the concept of standard deviation more difficult even though it is an important measure of the dispersion or distribution of data around a central mean.

The standard deviation is a statistical measure of the *variability* of values of the individual items in a population. The symbol σ, or sigma, is often used for the standard deviation where:

$$\sigma = \sqrt{\frac{\Sigma(X - \bar{X})^2}{n - 1}}$$

Table 13.2   Standard Deviation Example Calculations

n	x_i	$x_i - \bar{X}$	$(x_i - \bar{X})^2$
1	275.00	(3,178.81)	10,104,833.02
2	1,059.25	(2,394.56)	5,733,917.59
3	2,564.78	(889.03)	790,374.34
4	9,032.00	5,578.19	31,116,203.68
5	1,750.00	(1,703.81)	2,902,968.52
6	17,110.40	13,656.59	186,502,450.43
7	1,713.99	(1,739.82)	3,026,973.63
8	6,245.32	2,791.51	7,792,528.08
9	534.89	(2,918.92)	8,520,093.97
10	534.89	(2,918.92)	8,520,093.97
11	2,564.78	(889.03)	790,374.34
12	1,122.05	(2,331.76)	5,437,104.70
13	3,025.88	(427.93)	183,124.08
14	514.99	(2,938.82)	8,636,662.99
15	10,554.58	7,100.77	50,420,934.59
16	1,988.63	(1,465.18)	2,146,752.43
17	7,026.50	3,572.69	12,764,113.84
18	978.00	(2,475.81)	6,129,635.16
19	1,654.54	(1,799.27)	3,237,372.53
20	3,066.00	(387.81)	150,396.60
21	35.87	(3,417.94)	11,682,313.84
22	78.99	(3,374.82)	11,389,410.03
23	2,003.00	(1,450.81)	2,104,849.66
24	6,995.41	3,541.60	12,542,930.56
25	3,915.50	461.69	213,157.66
Sum	86,345.24		392,839,570.23
Average, $\bar{X}$	3,453.81		16,368,315.43
		Std. Dev.	4045.78

Standard deviation tells the auditor how much variation of values exists around the mean or central point. (See Table 13.2.) One column in Table 13.2 shows the $X_i - X$ differences, and the next shows differences as squared values of those differences. Following the above formula, we divide the sum of these squared differences by the population size minus one (a correction because this is a sample) to compute the standard deviation of $4,045.78

The properly skeptical internal auditor may ask ''What is all of this good for?'' Standard deviation, which will be used later in this chapter, is a measure of the central tendency of a normally distributed population of data. All this means is that the standard deviation tells us how far the items in the population are from the mean or central point. A population of 50 items all with values of about $1,000 each as well as a population of another 50 with average values of less than $1 would have about the same mean value as a different population of 100, with 50 around $450 and the other 50 of around $550. Although the mean for each would be around $500, they would be very different populations of data, and the standard deviation would help to explain those differences.

Normal Distributions.   A normal distribution is the bell-shaped diagram used to show data; it is often organized with a few values very high, a few very low, and most in the middle. If a large supply of small pebbles were to be dropped, one by one, onto a flat surface, the pebbles would form in a mound the shape of a bell curve. Much of the data an internal auditor will deal with also follows this bell-curve shape. If we look at the population of an average large city and plot the number of people by age, a few will be either very old or newborn at any point in time—with perhaps an equal number less than five years and greater than 90 years—but the average or mean age will be 45. These ages will be distributed into a bell-curve shape or what is called a normal distribution.

The assumption that most populations follow a normal distribution is important for internal auditors involved in sampling. Populations of data may take other shapes. In Figure 13.6 the distribution shown as A follows this normal distribution where the mean,

Figure 13.6   Normal and Other Distribution Examples

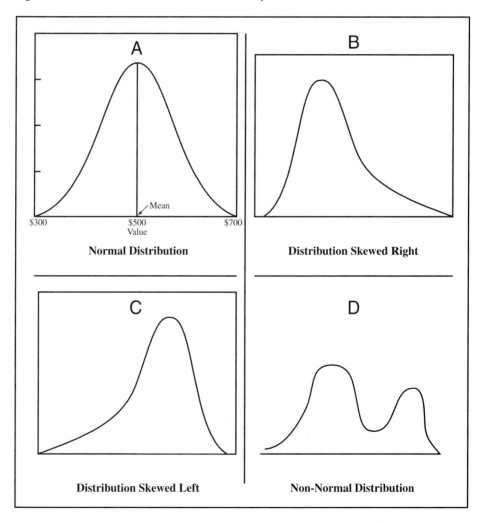

median, and mode are all the same. Distribution D does not follow that normal curve in shape.

The standard deviation is a measure of how many items in a population will be disbursed around the central or mean point in a standard distribution. Statistical theory says that 68.2% of a normally distributed population will reside plus or minus one standard deviation around the mean; 95.4% will be within two standard deviations.

How the items in the population are distributed around those central measures of mean and standard deviation is also of interest to the internal auditor. Is there an equal distribution of large and small values around the central measures? At times, a population will *not* follow this normal or symmetrical shape. If plotted by age, the population of a retirement community would be heavily weighted to older persons. We would say that this distribution by age is *skewed*. Curves B and C in Figure 13.6 are examples of skewed populations—skewed to either the right or left. Many accounting populations follow the C type of distribution, with a few items with very large values. It is important for an internal auditor to understand when a population of data is skewed to either the right or left. Audit testing and evaluation procedures are often modified by how the auditor reviews this distribution of skewed data.

(i) Standard Deviations.   Because of its rather complex-looking formula, the importance of standard deviations does not seem that apparent, and the calculation of standard deviation may seem rather difficult or at least tedious to many internal auditors—however, paper-and-pencil spreadsheets are generally not needed. Various tools are available to perform these calculations, ranging from the audit software discussed in Chapter 12 to spreadsheet software to handheld calculators. An internal auditor who needs a better understanding of these concepts should reference one of the statistical textbooks mentioned earlier.

Consider a very small population of five audit items with values that have been found to be either correct or incorrect. We can think of these five items as expense vouchers, and in this example, the term *correct* is as an indication of some audit test, such as whether the document was properly calculated, coded, or approved. Assume an internal auditor has reviewed these five vouchers and has found them to be either correct or incorrect as follows: (1) Voucher A—Amount Correct; (2) Voucher B—Amount Correct; (3) Voucher C—Amount Incorrect; (4) Voucher D—Amount Correct; and (5) Voucher E—Amount Incorrect. Two of the five items (40% of the vouchers audited) were found to be incorrect. While an internal auditor would certainly not want to draw a sample from such a very small population of five items, a random sample of two items *could* be selected from this population. As a way to make this random selection, five balls marked A through E could be placed in a box, with a series of samples of two items drawn from this population. A total of 10 combinations of samples would be possible: A and B, A and C, A and D, A and E, B and C, etc. The first of these possible sample draws—A and B—might result in two correct vouchers, a second potential sample of A and C could show one item correct. Three sample combinations—A and B, A and D, and B and D—would yield samples of only correct vouchers. Just one sample would result in all incorrect items with the remaining six (or 60%) of the combinations with mixed results. Thus, 60% of the time when an auditor pulled a sample from this population, the auditor could conclude that 50% of the population was incorrect. This statement is not totally accurate, but this sampling procedures gives some indication about the rate of incorrect vouchers in the population.

A total population of five items is quite unrealistic for most audit projects. An internal auditor will more often encounter populations of 5,000 or more. However, even though a two-out-of-five (or 40%) ratio was used as the sample size in the above example, internal auditors generally would not want to pull a sample of 2,000 but a much smaller amount—perhaps as few as 30 items. If the sample error rate from all possible samples from this 5,000-item population were determined and plotted, the distribution should approximate the bell curve (or, a normal distribution) discussed previously. The properties of a normal distribution can be mathematically determined and both statistical experimentation and theory will prove that 68% of the individual members of the larger distribution lie within plus or minus one standard deviation of the arithmetic mean of the total distribution, and 95.5% lie within plus or minus two standard deviations. Expressed another way, 90% of the members will lie within plus or minus 1.65 standard deviations and 95% within plus or minus 1.96 standard deviations. Based on this, if one sample were drawn at random from a fairly large population with a known or calculated standard distribution, an internal auditor could calculate the probability that the sample mean would fall within a certain range. For example, with a mean of $100 and a standard deviation of $10, 95% of the observations would fall within plus or minus 1.96 standard deviations, or plus or minus $19.60. Thus, there is a 95% probability that the sample mean (different from the mean of the full or actual population) drawn at random would be within the range $80.40 to $119.60. If there are 1,000 items in the population, the point estimate (or estimated parameter of the population) would be $100,000, and the range at the 95% probability would be between $80,400 and $119,600. Figure 13.7 is an example of how to look at the distribution of the differences around a standard deviation.

(b) STATISTICAL SAMPLING: DEVELOPING THE SAMPLING PLAN

To obtain the advantages of audit sampling, an internal auditor must first develop a sampling plan to make the selection, developing a sample selection approach where each item in the population will have an equal probability of selection. This involves a much more precise approach than that used in the judgmental sampling discussed previously. In order to evaluate the results of any statistical sample with some confidence, internal audit must remove any bias in the selection of items to assure that the items selected are representative of the total population.

An internal auditor is often faced with the challenge of attempting to understand a large amount of data, whether inventory records, accounts receivable payment histories, actual physical locations of assets, or other types of audit evidence. Statistical sampling allows an internal auditor to pull a representative sample of this data and to develop an audit conclusion over the entire population of data based on the audited results of the sample. However, before attempting to pull any sample of audit data, the internal auditor must understand the nature of the data to be reviewed. Following are some of the key points necessary to consider when developing this sample selection strategy or audit plan.

- *The population (or universe or field) to be sampled must be clearly defined.* The *population* is the total number of units from which a sample can be drawn, including the scope or nature of items to be reviewed, such as *all accounts payable vouchers for a year* and the specific characteristics of audit interest. An example would be a large number of accounts payables vouchers where internal audit is only interested in materials purchases. Payables for other things—such as travel reimbursements or telecommunications charges—would not be included in this example audit population.
- *The population should be divided or stratified into groups if major variations exist*

Figure 13.7 Percentage of Observations Around a Standard Deviation

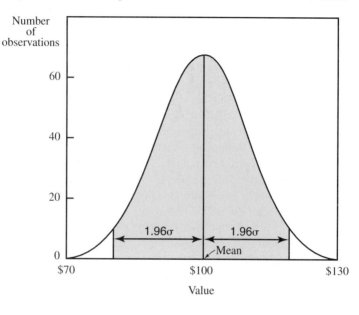

Distance from mean in terms of ± standard deviations on both sides of mean.	Percentage of observations included.
± 1.00 std. deviations	68.26%
± 1.65 std. deviations	90.00%
± 1.96 std. deviations	95.00%
± 2.33 std. deviations	98.00%
± 2.58 std. deviations	99.00%
± 3.00 std. deviations	99.73%
± 3.30 std. deviations	99.90%

between population items. A population of items such as an inventory often includes a few items of very high value and many others of smaller values. This population might not follow a normal distribution. When the population covers such a wide range with a few very large but significant items and many other very small amounts, statistical conclusions based upon the entire population often will not be sufficiently precise. In addition, internal audit may be more interested in whether the large items are fairly valued but may only have a general interest in the other, smaller items. When there is a wide diversity in the population, internal audit should consider stratifying the sample into separate sample groups such as by placing the smaller set of high-value items in one population and the balance of the lower-valued items in a separate population. Separate samples could be drawn from each.

- *Every item in a particular population must have an equal chance of being selected in the sample.* Every attempt must be made to eliminate bias in a sample selection when there is limited availability or even lack of availability of particular items of interest. Auditors are sometimes guilty of bias when deciding to restrict some items from the sample selection even though the audit conclusions are expressed in terms of the total population. They may decide arbitrarily to ignore certain items in a population because of lack of easy access. They will pull the sample from readily available items and then state their audit conclusions as if they had looked at the entire population. If certain items must be ignored for logistical or other valid reasons, internal audit should always reveal that fact when reporting results.

- *There should be no bias in making the sample selection from the population.* Similar to the above situation, an auditor may be faced with a population of items stored at both local and remote storage facilities and only look at the items in the local facility. The auditor can then draw an audit conclusion based only on the items stored locally. Those items stored in remote warehouses that have been ignored may have different attributes than the central warehouse items. Sample result conclusions from the local items reviewed may not represent the remote warehouses.

The sampling plan to be used should be clearly documented and discussed with management as part of the audit planning process. Often, members of management who understand the items to be reviewed suggest adjustments to the sampling plan that internal audit should consider.

(c) SELECTING THE SAMPLE

There are four common methods for selecting an audit sample: *random number, interval, stratified,* and *cluster selection.* The latter two are also often referred to as types of sampling, but they are more properly identified as optional selection techniques. The paragraphs following discuss very briefly each of these techniques. The modern internal auditor should have a general understanding of the most appropriate technique for a given audit situation. In many instances, the larger internal audit department may have one or several specialists who can provide strong technical guidance regarding these various sample selection methods.

(i) Random Number Selection.   As its name implies, random number selection's basic requirement is that the sample should be selected *at random,* with each item in the population having an equal chance to be selected as a part of the sample. If practicable, an internal auditor theoretically could place all the items, or numbers that would identify particular items, in a container, mix them thoroughly, and independently draw the individual items for the sample from the container. Since this is generally not feasible, an internal auditor must find other means to draw the random sample. One way is to use the random number tables. These types of tables are published in statistical sampling books or can be generated through microcomputer spreadsheets or even on handheld calculators.

Figure 13.8   Random Number Table Extract

	1	2	3	4	5	6	7	8	9
56	97998	85049	43598	52551	25225	79671	57697	87618	79050
57	31323	47498	54059	17902	58705	84566	07427	51966	76188
58	10433	34130	42521	22762	98955	94218	14975	06177	29190
59	26208	04624	91057	33665	89863	24706	90978	79731	28042
60	85953	02926	42521	22762	98955	94218	46797	16177	10916
61	19925	78883	90273	03382	54341	39612	76233	27066	88678
62	16640	07711	65004	99634	20737	61695	16210	66773	017784
63	80884	82213	20738	94462	22377	46238	46550	80601	35683
64	07358	11255	71734	10254	33066	85111	29493	84039	54722
65	71557	45733	46900	87393	03096	81015	96802	02713	95120
66	13921	44221	56051	49705	99863	59562	61894	90026	35573
67	20480	46038	61258	04600	68623	82369	80279	57265	80906
68	80320	05600	80568	65007	08970	34019	81518	13627	55902
69	60767	75141	39591	13032	73032	78418	82492	94034	02160
70	87541	84023	44412	69067	06707	20018	92351	35811	97574

Figure 13.8 is a sample of a page from a random number table, consisting of a column of item numbers followed by seven columns of five-digit random numbers. To select even larger samples, these tables often cover many pages. To use a random number table an internal auditor must relate the table to the items in the population. For example, if an auditor had a population of 5,000 items starting at number 1 and a need to select 25 items from this population, Figure 13.8 could allow the auditor to pull these 25 items at random. The auditor should arbitrarily select a starting point from this table, perhaps line 61 of column 4, or number 03382. The lower four digits of this number would indicate that item 3382 should be selected from the population. The auditor should then move down the selected column, identifying all items in the range. The next item in the column is 99634 and should be bypassed since it is larger than 5,000. Bypassing that item, the next entry in the table is 94462 defining item 4462 as the next to be selected. The auditor would then go through the table selecting items until the total of 25 items has been selected.

Prior to our use of computers, random numbers were the only practicable way to select a random sample. The random-number table is still a useful audit sampling technique; however, internal auditors sometimes encounter three problems with its use: (1) relating items in the population to numbers in the tables, (2) determining a starting point in using the tables, and then (3) selecting the route to take after the determination of this table starting point. An internal auditor should take the following steps to use a random number table:

1. *Establish numbering system for population to be sampled.* Each item in the population to be sampled must be identified with a unique identifying number. This can

be the voucher number on a paper document, the part numbers for an inventory, or just some sequential number. For example, if the population is described on a multiple page computer-generated report, items can be identified on the basis of page number and line number per page. An inventory of 1,625 items could be printed on a 30-page report since about 55 lines are printed on a standard 11″ × 14″ page. Since the individual inventory items in a such a computer-generated report generally will not be numbered, they can be identified by their placement on this report. The items on page one would range from page 1, line 1 (or 0101 to 0155), followed by 0201 to 0255 for the entries on page two. This scheme will define the items in the population subject to selection. That is, if the first random number selected was 0199, the number should be rejected because the highest number in this series would be 0155.

2. *Relate individual audit items to the random number tables.* When the audit items in the population to be evaluated are already numbered, their numbers provide a ready basis for use of the random-number table. It is only necessary to work with the table in a way that will provide random numbers with the same number of digits. The columnar data can be used in any manner desired, provided that the particular selection approach is used consistently. Numbers encountered that are outside the limits of the audit sequence should be ignored. For example, in the preceding paragraphs, 91245 was used but 58492 was ignored. Similarly, if the audit items are in a broken series, the auditor should ignore the random numbers encountered that do not apply to the actual audit sequences. Where the audit items are controlled by a letter sequence, the letters can be converted to a numerical equivalent. Similarly, audit items lacking any formal sequencing designation must be provided with some kind of a numerical equivalent. If by chance the same random number comes up again, repeating the identification of the same audit item, the duplicate number should be ignored, and the next applicable number used. There is clearly no point in auditing the same item twice.

3. *Establish random number table starting point and route.* A starting point should be established in the table on a random basis. Although people tend to start this exercise at the top left position, this could introduce bias in the results. A practical method is not to look at the table and simply let one's finger find a starting point on a blind-thrust basis. Once the starting point has been established and the number of digits related to the table in some way, the identification of the random numbers to be used can proceed in any direction. In the prior example, the auditor started with 91245, moved down that column selecting items, and could then have moved to the first item of the next column to select additional items. The only condition is that the use of the columns and the selected direction be maintained on a consistent basis.

A random number or a computer system that generates lists of random numbers provides an auditor with a powerful tool to draw a random sample. Frequently, the size of the sample may have to be increased or decreased. In the case of an increase, the internal auditor should go back to the previous stopping point in the random number selection and then continue. If the sample needs to be reduced, the random numbers last selected should be eliminated in reverse sequence. Normally, it is more convenient to err on the overselection side. A second problem with selection from a table of random numbers has to do with putting the random numbers selected in a sequence to make it convenient to proceed sequentially to locate the actual audit items. The simplest solution is to rearrange the random numbers sequentially after they have been selected or to line up the selected numbers on a sequential basis during the actual process of selection. A very easy way to accomplish this is to enter the numbers selected in a microcomputer spreadsheet and then simply sort the numbers once the sample is complete. This spreadsheet can later serve as a control document for the actual sample audit.

The final step in any random number selection is to document the manner in which the random selection process was actually carried out. If a table of random numbers was used, the workpapers should document the source of the tables and the starting random number "seed." One humorous approach by auditors was to develop the starting random number seed based upon the serial number of a $1 bill with that bill included in the workpaper documentation. The documentation, whether the $1 bill or normal audit work-paper descriptions, then serves to confirm the basis for the sample selection, and can in fact be auditable, if such proof is ever necessary.

This same basic procedure can be performed through the use of a handheld financial calculator. The more powerful of these have a key marked RAN, RND, or the like, which generates a random number of perhaps three or four digits whenever depressed. These digits follow the same concept as a table of random numbers in a printed table. The auditor just needs to press this key and record the random numbers generated for the sequence. A problem with the individual use of a calculator key function, however, is that an auditor may arbitrarily bypass items, claiming they were never selected. To minimize that type of bias, an independent member of the audit staff might pull the random numbers and give them to the auditor actually pulling the sample.

Determining the Correct Sample Size

Although many public accounting firms have developed a theoretical minimum sample size for their tests (often 60 or even 30), for internal auditors there should be *no minimum sample size* for use in an audit. On the one hand, an internal auditor may conservatively select a very large sample—say 1,000—on the basis that this will provide better results and management will be more apt to accept the results if a large sample is selected. Alternatively, the internal auditor may choose a sample size of 25 on the theory that the auditor should be able to arrive at adequate conclusions based on a limited amount of work. These sample-size decisions are sometimes made strictly on the basis of audit judgment without regard to formal statistical sampling rules. The objectives of the audit, of course, determine the extent of sampling. If the audit calls for survey work, tests to determine acceptability of the system may be minimal. If significant weaknesses are expected to be found, however, and the test is to determine the extent and magnitude of the deficiency, then the auditor should perform appropriate statistical analysis to determine the number to be tested. This provides auditors and management with an assurance that conclusions reached are valid.

The formal approach for determining an optimal sample size requires a fairly precise computational exercise. For a variables sample, an internal auditor must consider four factors:

1. An estimate of the upper and lower error bounds. This is an estimate of how large or small an error will be tolerated, based on an established precision limit.

2. The estimated average percent of errors for population items containing errors. For example, the auditor may estimate that 3% of the items in the population may contain some error.

3. Percentage of confidence level. This is an estimate of how certain the auditor wants to be that the statistical estimates are correct. Often numbers such as 98% sure or 95% sure are used here.

4. Determination of the recorded value of the population evaluated.

The idea is to use these four values to calculate an optimal sample size. The approach will be presented in the detailed explanation of different sampling techniques in the paragraphs following; however, the internal auditor should refer to a detailed statistical sampling text for more information.

Non-Normal Distributions

We have assumed that most populations of data follow normal or bell-curve distribution. Many actual populations do not follow such a normal distribution, raising a question on the feasibility of using audit sampling. Often, a population may contain a small but significant group of very large items with the remainder having small balances distributed over a wide range. In other cases, most items, whether as errors or not, may be all nearly equal with respect to the audit attribute to be examined. They do not follow a standard distribution even though the basis of many of the statistical sampling methods discussed assumes that the distribution is in the form of a normal distribution. If the population is positively skewed to the right, certain statistical estimates will be understated if a normal distribution is assumed. Similarly, if the population is negatively skewed to the left, other estimates might be overstated. Populations of accounting data are almost always skewed to the right.

The procedures discussed through this chapter assume normal distributions. While there are mathematical techniques to get around non-normal distribution and to still take a valid sample, they are mathematically complex and not necessary for the typical internal auditor. However, one method of assuring more accurate results when a sample is drawn from a badly skewed population is to increase the sample size. Mathematical theory says that as the sample size gets larger, the shape of the sampling distribution becomes closer to a normal distribution. If the skewness is not known and large sample sizes are impracticable, other approaches may be needed.

(ii) Interval Selection. Another technique for selecting sample items in a statistically sound manner is through what is called *interval selection* or *systematic sampling*. This approach requires the selection of individual items based on uniform intervals from the series of items in the total population. This technique is especially useful for monetary unit sampling, as discussed below, or when the particular population does not have an assigned value that makes it practicable to work from the items selected on the basis of random table numbers. In an interval sample, an internal auditor would develop a sample by selecting every n^{th} item in the population, such as an inventory listing. It is necessary that there be a reasonably homogeneous population, in terms of type of item, and no bias in the arrangement of the population, which would result in the interval approach coming up with a sample that is not statistically representative.

It is also crucial that interval selection is properly related to the size of the sample and the size of the total population. Where necessary, the population can be estimated. The planned sample size divided into the population size then establishes the interval. Thus, a population of 5,000 and a needed sample of 200 would yield an interval requirement of 5000/200 or 25. An internal auditor would then examine every twenty-fifth item in the population series with the starting point in the first interval group established on a random basis, preferably from a random-numbers table. In the event the actual population turns out to be larger than was estimated, a practical solution is to increase the sample by extending the interval selection on the same basis. If the actual population is less than estimated, it will be necessary to complete the sample through a new interval selection based on the number of items short in relation to the total population size. This problem can be avoided by always having a safety margin through a larger than needed sample estimate.

An interval selection where every nth item is selected is perhaps the easiest way to draw a sample from a population; however, the very nature of the method introduces the possibility of bias in the sample selection. For example, in a sample of daily transactions with an interval selection of every thirty days, if the starting random number pointed to the beginning of the month, a compliance error that normally took place later in the month might not be detected. The internal auditor could select day five of month one, then move forward on the interval of 30 to perhaps day six of month two and so on. Based upon this start, items from day 15 to about 30 will never be selected. Because of this bias, some public accounting firms have discouraged the use of interval selection techniques in their work.

(iii) Stratified Selection.   Stratified selection allows an internal auditor to divide a particular population into two or more subgroups or strata with each subgroup handled independently. Stratified selection can be considered an extension of random- or interval-selection techniques because either can be applied to the smaller strata of the population. In some cases, one of the strata may be examined 100% while the balance would be subject to random selection. The basic justification for stratification is that one strata of items has significantly different characteristics, and internal audit wishes to evaluate that subgroup on a more individual and precise basis. Through reducing variability, stratification can decrease the standard deviation, and help to reduce sample sizes.

The data presented in the Table 13.1 example show where stratification might be useful. Internal audit might decide that all items in the population with balances greater than $10,000 should be examined 100%. In a purely random selection, using a random number table and a sample size of five, none of the three large items might be selected. Using stratification, internal audit could divide this population into two strata: items over $10,000 and items under. The strata less than $10,000 would be subject to random selection, as discussed previously. The strata greater than $10,000 would receive 100% selection.

The most common populations requiring stratification are those that have a few items of very high value, such as inventories, accounts receivable, or invoices. Since these high-value items have much greater significance, internal audit may wish to subject them to higher standards of scrutiny. In other cases, the need for stratification may arise from the fact that individual subgroups are processed in different ways, or by different groups, and the nature of the items may call for different standards of audit scrutiny, such as certain inventory subject to theft. Under these conditions the larger variability in the total population makes a single type of testing and evaluation inapplicable.

These stratified sampling principles have long been recognized. The special importance in audit sampling is that stratification provides more meaningful statistical measures together with the possibility of smaller sample sizes. Once the stratification selection technique has been adopted and the subgroups subjected to different standards of audit scrutiny, the results of each evaluation can be used independently, based on the sampling of the separate populations, or can be brought together to support a consolidated conclusion relative to the total population.

(iv) Cluster Selection.   Another sampling approach is called *cluster selection;* here, the sample is made by systematically selecting subgroups or clusters from the total population. Cluster selection is useful when items are filed in shelves or in drawers, and it is physically more convenient to select subgroups based on the physical shelf area or individual file drawers. The rationale is that the items on particular portions of the shelf areas or in designated drawers are substantially similar in their nature and that a sample thus selected will be representative of the total population. However, the variability *within* the individual samples is frequently less than the variability *among* the samples. Hence, it is customary to use a larger sample when using the cluster selection approach to offset this lesser variability. A variation of the cluster selection approach, called *multistage sampling,* involves sampling the individual clusters instead of examining the sample as a whole.

Assume a population of 60,000 warehouse items located on 2,000 feet of shelves. If internal audit decides to review a sample of 600, the plan might be to divide the population into 20 clusters where each cluster would have 30 items. Since the average number of items on the shelves is 30 per linear foot (60,000/2,000), each cluster would cover an area of one foot (30/30). These individual clusters would then be selected at intervals of 100 feet (2,000/20) and with a random start. It should be recognized that the validity for this type of sample selection is dependent on the consistency of the population. That is, random number selection or regular interval selection would presumably assure a better representative sample. While sometimes useful, cluster sampling generally must be used with special care.

13-5 AUDIT SAMPLING APPROACHES

Several approaches can be used by an internal auditor to complete the sampling, depending upon the audit objectives, upon whether internal audit wants to performs tests of compliance or wants to verify balances such as in a financial statement, and upon any special conditions. Three common approaches are: *attribute sampling, variables sampling* (including monetary unit sampling), and *discovery sampling.*

Attributes sampling is a common approach used to measure the extent or level of occurrence of various conditions or attributes. For example, an internal auditor might want to test for the attribute of whether invoice documents have received proper approval signatures. An invoice will either be correctly approved or not—a ''yes'' or ''no'' qualitative condition. Normally, the attribute measured is the frequency of an error or other type of deficiency. The extent of the existence of the particular deficiency, such as improperly approved documents, determines the seriousness of the situation and how internal audit will report its findings and recommendations. Attributes or characteristics can be applied to any physical item, financial record, internal procedure, or operational activity. Attributes sampling often deals with compliance with a designated policy, procedure, or established standard.

The key point is that attributes sampling is a test for internal controls. A control is either determined to be working or not working. "Sort of working" is not an appropriate determination! The auditor tests conditions in the selected items and then assesses whether the overall population is in compliance with the control attribute.

Variables sampling deals with the size of a specified population, such as an account balance, and tests of balances in individual sample items. Here the auditor's focus is on "how much" as opposed to the "yes or no" focus of attributes sampling. The objective of variables sampling is to project total estimated quantities for some account or adjustments to the account on the basis of the auditor's statistical sample. Illustrative would be a sample that allows an internal auditor to estimate the total value of an inventory based upon sample results. Variables sampling is concerned with absolute amounts as opposed to the number or extent of a particular type of error.

Two important variations to variables sampling are *stratified sampling* and the now very common *monetary unit sampling*. Variables sampling procedures are closely related to attributes sampling, but include additional concepts and calculations. Because of the more complicated nature of the variables sampling approach, a step-by-step analysis is given below for single-stage variables sampling. The example is based on a simplified manual estimate of the standard deviation when computer support tools or other information on the standard deviation are not available.

The third type of statistical sampling, *discovery sampling,* in many respects is similar to the non-statistical judgmental sampling discussed earlier. Discovery sampling is used when an internal auditor wants to pull a sample from a large volume of data without the statistical and mathematical controls associated with variables and attribute sampling methods.

The paragraphs following discuss all of these various sampling methods in some detail; however, the information contained in this chapter may be just enough to make an internal auditor "dangerous." That is, this chapter provides a discussion of these sampling methods but does not equip an internal auditor with enough information to master statistical sampling concepts. Appropriate training, experience, and specialized books and computer software tools are necessary.

13-6 ATTRIBUTES SAMPLING PROCEDURES

The purpose of attributes sampling is to estimate the *proportions* of items in a population containing some characteristic or attribute of interest. For example, an internal auditor may be interested in the rate of occurrence of some monetary error or compliance exception that might exist in a population of accounts payable disbursement vouchers. The auditor here would be interested in the number of items that have some type of significant error, not the total monetary value of all of the errors. This type of test is very appropriate for assessing the level of internal control in a population such as an account.

The starting point in attributes sampling is to estimate an expected rate of errors—that is, how many errors will internal audit and management tolerate? Depending upon the items sampled and the culture of the organization, this expected error rate may be as little as 0.01% or as large as 5% or even more. Even if senior management states that no errors will be allowed in some highly critical operation, all parties often recognize that there may be a small or very small possibility of an error, and depending upon the criticality of the operation, a very small error rate will be accepted. An expected error rate is the recognition that certain types of operations contain errors no matter how good are the other controls and procedures. If internal audit were to perform a 100% examination of an account but only find a small number of errors—say, 0.5%—it might be difficult to convince management that its controls are weak. Management, however, might expect and tolerate a 1% error rate and not express much concern at internal audit's findings. In an attribute-sampling test, internal audit must estimate the expected rate of errors in the population sampled. This can be based upon management's stated expectations, other audit tests, or just internal audit assumptions.

Along with estimating the expected error rate, internal audit must decide upon the acceptable precision limits and the degree of wanted confidence for the sample. In other words, an internal auditor would like to be able to say, "I am 99% confident that the error rate of this account is less than 1%." These estimates will allow an internal auditor to determine the size of a sample that will provide a reliable conclusion regarding the condition tested. This determination is made through statistical methods and can be obtained from various microcomputer statistical software packages or even from manual tables found in statistical sampling books. These factors provide an initial basis for the size of the sample to be reviewed. The internal auditor now selects this sample and examines the items sampled to determine the number of errors that exist in the sample.

As can be expected, the error rate in a sample is normally higher or lower than the previously estimated acceptable error rate. If lower, the internal auditor has established that the condition tested is safely within the limits selected. If the sample shows a higher error rate, the auditor must determine whether the results are satisfactory and what further action, if any, is needed. Conceivably, the sample can be expanded, but internal audit will often feel there is an adequate basis for arriving at a conclusion. The key to meaningful attribute sampling is to take an appropriate sample and properly develop an audit conclusion based upon the sample results.

Attributes sampling, once commonly used by both internal and external auditors, is now used less frequently because of the computational requirements and statistical knowledge required. However, it remains an effective tool to report to management on the status of some control procedure. This section will describe attribute procedures in some detail. However, the internal auditor who wishes to obtain a greater understanding is encouraged to seek out a detailed book on the subject. Unfortunately, there have not been many recent books. The two books that contain good backgrounds are Arens and Loebbecke's *Applications of Statistical Sampling to Auditing* and Andrew Bailey's *Statistical Auditing*, previously referenced.

(a) PERFORMING THE ATTRIBUTE SAMPLING TEST

An attribute sampling test is perhaps the best tool available to an internal auditor who is faced with a rather large number of items to be examined and wants to test whether certain controls are working or not working. An attribute sample can be performed following four basic steps.

1. Understand the nature of the items to be sampled.
2. Establish statistical parameters for the attribute-sampling test
3. Select the sample and perform audit procedures.
4. Evaluate the results of the attribute sampling test.

Figure 13.9   Attribute Sampling Test Examples

---

1. In a test of expense account documents, the auditor may want to test whether all reports have been approved by a person at least one level above the person submitting the report. In this audit, anything that has not been so approved would be classified as an error.

2. If computer security rules require that all passwords must be changed every 30 days or sooner, any password that had not been changed within the 30-day limit would be treated as an error in an attributes test. Even if a password had been changed after 31 or 32 days, it would still be considered an error for attributes test purposes.

3. Internal auditors reviewing control procedures in manufacturing production environment may be asked whether controls over that area are adequate or are not adequate. Although there may be many shades of gray in such a real-life situation, an internal auditor would be required to make a yes/no decision for an attributes test of these controls.

Each of these steps, of course, have many additional substeps. This type of sampling, for example, is used by governmental regulatory agencies, and its results are acceptable in a court of law. Although it may seem that the process takes more work than nonstatistical procedures, when properly performed, this relatively easy-to-use technique will allow the auditor to express an opinion over the presence of some condition with a high degree of statistical authority.

(i) Understanding the Nature of the Items to be Sampled.   As with an operational audit, an internal auditor must first define what is to be evaluated or tested before embarking upon any audit involving audit sampling. As discussed in previous chapters, an internal auditor should carefully define the objectives of the audit. In the case of attributes sampling, an internal auditor needs to understand the specific nature of the compliance tests to be performed, the nature of the sampling units, and the population. Each of these is critical for performing an attributes sampling test and will be discussed in the sections following.

> • *Defining the Nature of the Compliance Tests to be Performed.* As discussed previously, a compliance test is a yes-no type of audit test. That is, the attribute sampled must either be correct or incorrect. There can be no measures of "almost correct" or "close enough." For example, an internal auditor may be testing travel report approvals. If organization procedures state that the manager responsible for a department must approve all travel reports greater than $100, any voucher not approved by the responsible department manager would be considered a compliance or control error. Internal audit should carefully define the types of tests to be performed as well as the acceptance and rejection rules. Figure 13.9 contains some examples of typical attribute sampling tests. As demonstrated in this figure, all tests should be carefully defined. While it is possible to separately sample for two or more different attributes, each statistical test will concentrate on compliance

with one such test criteria. If multiple ones are used in a single test, the failure of any one would mean that the entire item sampled is out of compliance.

• *Understanding the Population to Be Sampled.* The population is the body of data or items from which an internal auditor will draw a sample. Internal audit should have a clear understanding of the number and location of the items to be sampled. If internal audit initially plans to sample *all* travel accounting reports, those reports must be available in one central source or must be readily accessible if located elsewhere. If certain of those reports are filed at a remote, international location, internal audit may not be able to sample all such reports unless it gains access to the remote, international reports as well as the national items filed centrally. Otherwise, internal audit should reduce the scope of the population sampled and look at only domestic travel accounting reports. The size of this population will impact the number of items to be sampled. In addition, any audit results should clearly disclose that international travel reports were not sampled.

• *Defining the Sampling Unit.* If the population of interest is travel expense reports and the audit test performed is whether these expense reports have or have not been approved, the sampling unit is the individual travel expense report. In some instances, this can be a more complex measure. For example, if an auditor is testing to see whether certain codes have been correctly entered on a purchase order, the audit test may be to check on two different purchase order codes. An internal auditor can define each purchase order to be an individual unit with the test whether both codes are correct. However, internal audit could define the two codes tested on a purchase order separately, making each purchase order two units. A single purchase order could have one, two, or no errors. This latter approach of performing separate attribute tests against the same overall population is usually not very practical or effective.

(ii) Establishing Statistical Parameters for the Attribute Sampling Test. The auditor first makes some preliminary estimates, based on observations and other audits, of what is expected from the sample results and, second, evaluates the results of an actual audit sample based upon those expectations. If a fairly high level of errors in the population is expected, the auditor should select a sample that is sufficient to confirm or refute those initial expectations. Internal auditors need to estimate the maximum tolerable error rate, the desired *confidence level* of the sample, the estimated population error rate, and then the initial sample size.

• *Maximum Tolerable Error Rate.* Statisticians also call this estimate the *desired upper precision limit.* This is the error rate an internal auditor will allow while still accepting the overall controls in the system. Most likely, a typical population of items may have some errors. In the previously discussed travel expense reports, which were reviewed for departmental management approvals, a realistic internal auditor recognizes that there may be *some* errors, such as vouchers that have not been properly approved or correctly coded. An employee may have had another manager or a peer employee sign for approval. These are errors, but an internal auditor should recognize that this situation might happen from time to time and that there may be logistical reasons why some other person had approved an expense report. Although these are internal control error exceptions, an internal auditor might accept a certain number of such errors and still feel that internal controls are generally adequate.

The maximum tolerable error rate is normally expressed as a percentage that can vary based upon the nature of the items reviewed. In the above example, an auditor might accept a 5% tolerable error rate or upper precision limit. In other instances, a smaller or larger estimate can be used. However, this estimate should never be more than 10%. Such an estimate indicates major internal control problems, and the resultant attribute sample may provide little further information. If an internal auditor knows that internal controls are very bad, it is of little value to take an attribute sample to verify what the internal auditor has already determined through other audit procedures. Similarly, an internal auditor should normally expect some errors and should establish some reasonable value for this rate, perhaps 1% or 2%.

• *Desired Confidence Level.* This is a measure of the auditor's confidence on the results of a sample. That is, internal auditors would like 95 or 98% certainty that the results of the sample are representative of the actual population. An internal auditor will never be 100% certain that a condition exists unless the auditor reviews essentially 100% of the items in the population. If a population of 100 items contains one error, an auditor might look at a sample of 10 items and find no errors. He or she may look at 20, 30, 50, or even 90 items and still not find that one error. The only way an internal auditor can be 100% certain that the population contains a 1% error rate is to look at 100% of the items. However, based upon the laws of probability, an internal auditor can look at a much smaller sample and still state that he or she is 95 or 98% certain that the error rate is no more than 1%.

The assumed confidence level value, usually 95 or 98%, along with the estimated population size discussed previously, will determine the size of the sample needed to test the estimated population. Too large of a confidence level may require too large of a sample. Too low of a confidence level may reduce the size of the sample, but the results may be questionable. Management typically would not accept an internal audit finding that states they are "75% confident" that some condition is true.

• *Estimated Population Error Rate.* In attributes sampling, an internal auditor estimates the level of errors in population and then takes a statistical sample to confirm or refute those assumptions. In order to calculate the sample size, the internal auditor also needs to estimate the expected rate of occurrence of errors in the population. This estimate, together with the confidence level and the maximum tolerable error rate, determines the size of the sample. For example, if the confidence level is 95% and the maximum tolerable error rate is 5%, the auditor should look at a sample of 1,000 items in a very large population if the estimated population error rate is 4%. A smaller estimated population error rate will reduce the sample size. Given the same parameters, an estimated population error rate of 1% will drive the sample size down from 1,000 to 100 items. If the expected population error rate is very large—greater than 50%—the required sample size will become very large. Generally, the larger the difference between the maximum tolerable error rate and the estimated population error rate, the smaller the necessary sample size.

• *Initial Sample Size.* The above three factors, along with some other correction factors, combine to determine the necessary sample size. Although a statistical textbook will provide the formulas, internal auditors have historically used published tables to determine sample sizes. Today, even these table are not necessary as an internal auditor can access a statistical sample software package and only provide the maximum tolerable error rate, the confidence level, the estimated population error rate, and the approximate sample size. The software will then provide the required sample size for the attributes test. Table 13.2 contains some attributes sample sizes estimated using values for all three factors discussed here. The table illustrates that if the confidence level is 99%, the maximum tolerable error rate is not over 5%, and the estimated error rate is 4%, an internal auditor should examine 142 items for an attributes test over a population of about 500 items. The size of the sample here can be adjusted by modifying the auditor's various parameter estimates.

The above is only a brief introduction to the process of selecting a sample size when performing an attributes test. The real difficulty in performing an attributes test is that sample sizes tend to be quite large. Because judgmental tests often sample perhaps only 50 items, it may be difficult to initially justify the larger sample sizes needed to perform a statistically correct attributes test. While in many instances an internal auditor can modify the sample size by modifying sampling assumptions, this becomes part of the overall audit conclusions. In the Table 13.3 illustration, the 142-item sample for a 500-item population based upon 99% confidence, 5% tolerable error rate, and 4% estimated error rate using a different table goes down to a sample size of 102 or 30% if the confidence level is lowered from 99% to 95%. In such cases, there is the possibility that management may question audit findings with a 95% certainty, particularly when the auditee disagrees with the findings and is looking for a way to refute the sampling results.

(iii) Selecting the Sample to Perform Audit Procedures. Having made some audit sample assumptions and determined the sample size, the next step is to pull the actual items for review. The random number tables described previously or some similar means can pull the number of items called for through the sample calculations. Reserving extra audit items through the random number selection can avoid the possibility of drawing duplicate random numbers or finding that an actual item does not legitimately exist within an otherwise valid range of items. Multiple attributes can be tested using the same set of sample items. The concept to remember is that the internal auditor will be performing a separate yes/no type test for each of the individual attributes on each of the items in the sample.

The internal auditor should document all items selected to be part of the attribute test. Again, spreadsheet software, as shown in the example following, is useful here. The auditor should list all items and then use that same spreadsheet to record the results of the audit tests. The actual audit tests must be performed with great care. If an audit fails to recognize an error condition in the selected sample items, that fact will throw off the conclusions reached as part of the overall sample. With a large population, each sample item may speak for hundreds or even thousands of actual items.

The auditor should evaluate each item carefully and consistently against the established attributes. They should never be "close enough." If it appears that some attribute measurement is too stringent for certain items, internal audit should consider reevaluating

Table 13.3   Sample Sizes for Sampling Random Sample Attributes

Confidence Level 99%
Expected Error Rate Not Over 5%

Population Size	Sample Size for Reliability of:					
	± 1%	± 1.5%	± 2%	± 2.5%	± 3%	± 4%
200						99
250						110
300						119
350					175	126
400					187	132
450					197	137
500					206	142
550				263	214	145
600				274	221	148
650				284	228	151
700				293	234	154
750				302	239	156
800			397	310	244	158
850			409	318	248	160
900			420	324	252	162
950			431	330	256	163
1000			441	336	260	165
1050			450	341	263	166
1100			459	346	266	167

the entire sample set. An internal auditor may be looking for several error conditions but then find another error not included in the original test design. If significant, internal audit may want to redefine the overall attribute test. Other problems with a sample can be corrected and adjusted as follows:

- *Voided or Unused Sample Items.* Sometimes the random number sample selection may point to an item, such as a document, that has either been properly voided or is otherwise unused. Such an item should not be counted as an error and should be replaced with another random number sample item. Neither of these should be counted as errors or included in the total count of the population.

- *Definition Problems in Counting Errors.* A clear definition can eliminate or lessen the chances of an error being considered significant if it occurs only rarely. The internal auditor must be very careful in attempting to define these types of error conditions in advance of the statistical test.

- *Nonapplicable Sample Items.* Sometimes, in a review of selected items through perhaps a manual filing system, the auditor may find some items that are misfiled and not even applicable to the audit test performed. For example, internal audit may be reviewing certain conditions in a series of capital expenditures during a fixed assets review. The sample may call for the selection of a specific file folder that turns out to be a misfiled architect's worksheet file. Should this be considered an error? In this type of condition, internal audit would probably reject the incorrect file from the sample and select another. The misfiled materials might only be noted as an internal control problem.

After the completion of the attribute sampling test procedures, internal audit next must evaluate the results of the sample to determine if the auditor's test assumptions are correct.

(iv) Evaluating the Results of the Attribute Sampling Test. As discussed, prior to actually selecting and evaluating the sample items, the internal auditor has made some initial assumptions regarding the maximum tolerable error rate, the reliability, and the level of confidence, as well as about how many compliance errors would be tolerated while still maintaining that controls are adequate. The next key step is to evaluate the sample results against those assumptions to determine if a control problem exists.

Recall that an upper precision limit or maximum tolerable error rate and a confidence level formed the standards used to determine the sample size and perform the sampling test. The auditor should now determine the error rate of the sampled items and calculate an upper precision limit based upon those sample errors. That precision limit, computed on the basis of the actual sample, must be less than or equal to the desired precision limits established at the beginning of the sample exercise in order for the auditor to report favorable results from the sample.

Normally, if the results of the sample do not meet the preliminary criteria, the internal auditor has a major audit finding. These audit criteria should have been well thought out and approved by auditee management before beginning the test. However, sometimes internal audit or management may decide that the original assumptions were too conservative. A new upper precision limit or confidence level could be used and the sample results measured against it. This approach should only be used with the greatest caution. In effect, the auditor here is attempting to justify some bad results. Were the matter ever to reach a court of law, internal audit would have a tough time justifying why it had altered its assumptions to make the sample results look good.

A better approach when the results are unfavorable is to expand the sample size. Frequently, when attribute sampling results turn out unfavorably, auditee management will claim that internal audit only looked at some *very unusual* items and that the remainder of the population is not that bad. An increase in the sample size will have the effect of decreasing the computed upper precision limit, assuming that the auditor does not find a substantial number of additional errors. Both internal audit and management should weigh the relative costs and benefits of this approach. A better approach is to report the internal control problem based upon the current results and to expand the sample size in a subsequent audit review. Management should, hopefully, take steps during the interim to improve internal controls in the area of interest.

Attribute sampling is a very useful technique for assessing one or several internal controls in an area of audit interest. Because estimates of such things as the maximum tolerable error rate are made in advance, it is difficult to dispute the audit test assumptions when compared to sample results. Similarly, because random number or similar techniques are typically used to select the sample items, it would be difficult to claim auditor bias in the selections. To better explain the attribute sampling process, an example follows.

(b) ATTRIBUTE SAMPLING AUDIT EXAMPLE

Internal audit at Gnossis, Inc., a large research and development organization, is interested in whether controls over organization of its human resource records are correct. Certain employees have complained that they did not receive their scheduled increases on a timely basis, and Gnossis was recently fined in a court action when human resources records deficiencies were found during a legal discovery action. Senior management has asked internal audit to review payroll department internal controls. Gnossis has about 4,000 employees, and internal audit has decided to perform an attributes test to assess internal controls covering human resource records.

The Gnossis human resources function uses two computer systems for employee records—one for pay calculations and one for benefits—and maintains a centralized manual system for all employees where such matters as health insurance declarations are filed. Through a review of the human resources record-keeping process, internal audit found some 30 different record-keeping control issues, ranging from such major matters as whether pay is properly withheld for tax purposes to more minor items such as whether monthly deductions to pay for an employee credit union loan are correct. Internal audit could combine all of these 30 record-keeping issues as a single attribute. Then, the attribute sample would check for all of these as a single yes/no test. The problem here is that a few minor problems would force internal audit to conclude that internal controls are not working even though no problems were found over the major issues. This will often be difficult to communicate to management.

A strategy is to test Gnossis human resource records for separate attributes. Although internal audit could have tested separately for all 30 attributes, a better approach is to decide which are the most significant and to only test for those separate attributes. Assume that internal audit has decided to test human resource records for the following five attributes.

1. Pay grade and status on the automated system is same as in manual files.
2. Authorizations for withholdings are signed and dated by employees.
3. Preemployment background checks were completed.
4. If no life insurance deductions, employee-signed waivers are recorded.
5. Pay increases are according to guidelines and are properly authorized.

The above are certainly not all of the areas where audit can test to determine if controls are adequate; however, in this example, internal audit has determined that it will statistically test employee records internal controls based upon these five attributes. Internal audit can then discuss this approach with Gnossis management to obtain their consent.

The next step is to establish sampling parameters and develop a sample plan. Based on the prior year's experience and staff projections for the coming year, it was estimated that there would be approximately 4,000 employees in Gnossis payroll records. Using statistical sampling software, internal audit assumed an expected error rate of 2%, a desired precision of 1.25%, and a 90% confidence level to select a sample size of 339 items. The item of interest here would be an employee payroll file, and internal audit would separately review employee files for each of these five attributes.

Internal audit's next challenge is to select the 339 plus perhaps 40 extra payroll files for audit inspection. The actual records are stored alphabetically in human resource department files and the eight-character employee numbers are not sequential but assigned when an employee joins the organization. Because of turnover over the years, internal audit was not able to directly select the sample by matching selections from a random number table to a list of employees in sequence by their employee number. Rather, the sample employees were selected from a printed list of employees, a report 75 pages long and with about 55 items per page, using four-character random numbers 0101 through 0155 by page to 7555.

The sample items selected were listed on spreadsheets, as shown in the Figure 13.10 example, with space to list the results of each attribute test. Although largely manual procedures were used here to select the sample, internal audit could have made this selection using automated procedures. The automated procedures would be as follows.

1. Use a random number program to generate 379 numbers for the 339-count desired sample size, along with 40 extras. The range of these random number should be between 1 and 4,000.

2. Output the selected random numbers to a file and sort them in ascending order.

3. Using a utility program, match the sequential random numbers with the record counts on the employee master file. Thus, if the first random number is 0137, the program would select the 137th record on the employee master file.

4. Output the selected record data to a spreadsheet file similar to the data shown in Figure 13.11.

This automated approach to attributes sample selection will take more initial effort but will reduce auditor clerical time. This type of approach is best if internal audit also contemplates additional audit sampling procedures against the employee records files.

Once the statistical sample is selected, these attributes are tested by pulling the designated employee personnel file. The procedures here are essentially the same as for any audit. The internal auditor checks each employee record selected against each attribute and then indicates on the worksheet whether the attribute is in compliance. After reviewing these attributes for the 339 sample items, the final step is just to tabulate the exceptions or error rates. For Attribute #1 as described previously, internal audit finds that 10% of the employees in the sample had data errors between their manual payroll files and automated payroll records. At the 90% confidence level, this represents 7.3 to 13.3% of the total number of employees at Gnossis. Because sample results show an extensive error rate for this one important attribute, the results are immediately disclosed to management without the need for further sampling.

Summary information on the results of these five attributes tests is provided to management in a formal audit report. A sample finding is shown in Figure 13.12. Only minor or insignificant problems appear for three of the five attributes tested, while for the other two, Attributes #1 and #3, significant internal control problems are found. In internal audit's opinion, the internal control breakdown over these two attributes is sufficient to suggest major problems within the human resources record-keeping process. Based on these internal audit recommendations, management has the responsibility to analyze the entire file to determine the extent and frequency of these and other attribute errors throughout the system.

Figure 13.10 Attribute Test Worksheet for Human Resource Test of Records

Random Number Selected	Matching Employee #	Employee Name	Audit Attribute Test Result					Auditor Initials	Date Reviewed
			# 1	# 2	# 3	# 4	# 5		
0137	0266812	Archer, James Q.							
0402	0342201	Aston, Robert							
0988	0466587	Djuruick, Mary Jo							
1003	0502298	Eggbert, Katheran P.							
1256	0629870	Fitzgerald, Edward K.							
1298	030029	Gaddi, Emron							
1489	0687702	Horen, Rupert D.							
1788	1038321	Issac, Stanley L.							
1902	1189654	Jackson-Smith, Susan							
2263	1250982	Jerico, John							

Figure 13.11 Attribute Test for Human Resource Internal Controls

Random Number Selected	Matching Employee #	Employee Name	Audit Attribute Test Results					Auditor Initials	Date Reviewed
			#1	#2	#3	#4	#5		
0137	0266812	Archer, James Q.	OK	OK	OK	OK	OK	RJK	11/16
0402	0342201	Aston, Robert	NO-12.3	OK	NO-14.02	OK	OK	RJK	11/17
0988	0466587	Djuruick, Mary Jo	OK	OK	NO-14.12	OK	OK	RJK	11/16
1003	0502298	Eggbert, Katheran P.	OK	OK	OK	OK	OK	RJK	11/16
1256	0629870	Fitzgerald, Edward K.	OK	OK	OK	OK	OK	RJK	11/16
1298	030029	Gaddi, Emron	OK	NO-13.2	NO-14.32	OK	OK	RJK	11/16
1489	0687702	Horen, Rupert D.	OK	OK	OK	OK	OK	RJK	11/16
1788	1038321	Issac, Stanley L.	OK	OK	OK	OK	OK	RJK	11/16
1902	1189654	Jackson-Smith, Susan	OK	OK	OK	OK	OK	RJK	11/16
2263	1250982	Jerico, John	NO-12.5	OK	OK	NO-25.23	OK	RJK	11/16

Figure 13.12 Attribute Test Audit Findings

> **Finding # 1–Pay Grade Status Differences.** We used attribute sampling procedures to assess whether employee pay grade and job grade status data included in the automated system was the same as recorded in departmental manual files. Approximately 10% of the items included in our attribute sample had differences between these two files, indicating errors. Based on the results of our attribute statistical sample, we are 90% confident that a significant internal control problem exists over the pay and job grade data recorded on manual records and maintained on the automated payroll file. This attribute sampling finding indicates there *is a significant internal control problem* over this area of employee records.

(c) ATTRIBUTES SAMPLING ADVANTAGES AND LIMITATIONS

When there is a need to review a large number of items, attributes sampling procedures best provide a statistically accurate assessment of a control feature or attribute. Although statistical theory requires a relatively large sample size, internal audit can review some control or condition within a sample of that data and then can state that it is confident, within a preestablished confidence value or percentage, that the number of errors in a total population will not exceed a designated value or that the control is working adequately.

Attributes sampling is not useful for determining the estimated correct value on an account such as an inventory book value but is an extremely useful tool for reviewing control procedures in a variety of operational areas. Some auditors feel the technique has some negatives or impediments to its use, including the following:

- *Attributes sampling computations are complex.* This chapter has only introduced some very basic attributes sampling concepts. The actual review and analysis of sample results can be very complex and require the use of sampling software or complex statistical tables. An internal auditor needs to have a good understanding of the process or could be in danger of interpreting results incorrectly.

- *Appropriate definitions of attributes may be difficult.* In the previous human resources records example, the internal auditors sampled and evaluated controls on five attributes selected from a set of 30 actual attributes. The selection of attributes to be tested was based upon either auditor judgment or management requests. However, an auditor may have missed one or another important attribute when analyzing the data.

- *Attributes sample results may be subject to misinterpretation.* Properly presented, the results of an attributes sample are stated very precisely, such as, ''We are 95% confident that the percentage of error items in the account is between 2% and 7.3%.'' Despite this precision, people may hear these results and interpret them incorrectly, such as ''There is over a 7% error rate in the account.'' That is not what was communicated, but many listeners prefer easier answers.

- *Imperfect data requires corrections.* The basic theory surrounding an attributes sample assumes the population of data follows a bell-curve type of normal distribution, with no other unusual complications. While nonstandard data distributions can be corrected through adjustments in the sample size selection and evaluations, non-normal distributions complicate the process.

Despite these problems, attributes sampling equips internal audit with a very powerful tool to evaluate internal controls in a large population of data through the evaluation of a limited sample. While the technique is too time-consuming or complex for many audit problems, the modern internal auditor should develop a basic understanding of attributes sampling and make use of it when appropriate. The technique is particularly appropriate when the initial, judgmental results of an internal controls review indicate problems in an area and when management disputes the preliminary results from audit's limited, judgmental sample as being ''unrepresentative.'' A follow-up attributes sample will allow internal audit to take another look at the data and come back making a stronger statement about the status of internal controls surrounding the area in dispute.

13-7 MONETARY UNIT SAMPLING

The initial discussion on statistical sample divided the approach between the previously discussed attributes sampling, which measures the extent of some condition, and variables sampling, which estimates the value of an account. Variables sampling is further divided between the more traditional stratified sampling methods, discussed later in this chapter, and what is called *monetary unit sampling*. Although these sampling procedures can also be used for attributes sampling, monetary unit sampling is more commonly used to review an account described in monetary values to determine if the account is fairly stated. It is a particularly good method for estimating the amount of any overstatement of accounts.

This variables sampling technique is alternatively called monetary unit sampling, dollar unit sampling, or probabilities proportional to size (PPS) sampling. Here, every dollar or other unit of currency in an account is a member of the population and each has an equal chance of selection. A $1,000 voucher for an account will have 1,000 units of population while a $100 voucher for the same account will have 100. Thus, a $1,000 item in a population has a thousand times greater chance of selection than a $1 item has. This is a very popular form of sampling, particularly for public accounting firms, and although various texts and sources use different names, we will here call this approach monetary unit sampling.

As stated, the sampling unit is *each dollar* rather than a physical unit such as an invoice or payroll check. For example, if purchases are being tested for a year, the monetary unit sampling population will consist of the total dollar value of purchases made, and the sampling unit will be each dollar of purchases. If errors are found in the invoices, they are related to individual dollars in these invoices using various evaluation methods. One method, called *tainting*, determines the ratio of dollar errors to the amount of the invoice. This ratio is then applied to the dollar sampling unit. Another approach uses what is called a fixed decision rule, where if there is an error, the last dollar unit within the physical unit or account sampled, to the extent of the errors, may be considered wrong.

This section will give an overview of monetary unit sampling. Although monetary unit sampling is discussed in many of the sampling books previously referenced, an older book by Leslie, Teitlebaum, and Anderson[2] provides one of the more detailed descriptions

---

[2] D. A. Leslie, A. D. Teitelbaum, and R. J. Anderson, *Dollar-unit Sampling* (Toronto: Copp Clark Pitmen, 1979).

of the process for auditors. The authors are the fathers of monetary unit sampling for auditors.

(a) SELECTING THE MONETARY UNIT SAMPLE: AN EXAMPLE

Assume that internal audit wants to review a series of accounts receivable balances to determine if they are fairly stated or recorded. There are 1,364 items or customer balances in this account, with a total recorded balance of $54,902.25. The balances are both large and very small, with the first 30 of them listed in Table 13.4. Although the determination of sample sizes will be discussed later, assume that internal audit has decided on a sample size of 60, or to look at only 60 individual dollars and the items these dollars represent. With a sample size of 60, the auditor can look at $54.902.25/60 = 915.034 or every 915th dollar in the account balance. Each time the items included in one of those dollars are selected, the auditor will examine that entire item.

Table 13.4 has columns for the account numbers (here numbered from 1 to 30), the balance for each of these accounts, and the cumulative total. The additional columns in this table show the process of making a monetary unit selection, as follows:

1. Although the auditor will select every 915th dollar, a starting point is needed somewhere between $1 and $915. To select the starting point, a starting random number between 1 and 915 was selected; in this case, the number was 37.

2. The starting random number, 37, is then added to the first invoice at 124 to yield 161. All values have been rounded to avoid pennies. Since 161 is less than 915, the next item, 754, is added to the accumulated value to yield 1039. Here, the auditor will encounter the 915th dollar, and this item will be selected for review.

3. A new starting number is now needed, and 915 is subtracted from the 1039 to compute a starting number for the next item of 124. This is added to the third item of 589 to yield 713, not enough for selection.

4. The fourth item in this sample is large, 2056. The interval of 915 appears twice in this stream of dollars (915 × 2 = 1830) and the item is selection for two of the sample items.

5. The sample selection procedures are shown in Table 13.4. The auditor can walk through these calculations using a pocket calculator.

The selection of items for a monetary unit sample is generally just as easy as that shown in Table 13.4. An auditor can select a sample using a spreadsheet software package or even through a manual calculation using a desk calculator. The purpose is simply to determine the monetary interval based upon the calculated sample size.

Two key points and limitations of monetary unit sampling should be mentioned here. First, monetary unit sampling is only useful for testing for the presence of *overstatement*. In the extreme, monetary unit sampling will never select an account that has been incorrectly recorded at a zero value. If the auditor has selected dollars in a population that is understated, the selection method may never find those dollars.

Second, the selection method described does not handle credit amounts correctly. The sample selection procedure would not work correctly if the account included a large number of credit items. The best solution here is to pull out all recorded credit balances and treat them as a separate population to be evaluated. If there are only a small number,

Table 13.4   Monetary Unit Sampling Selection Example

Acct. No.	Balance	Cum. Total	Start	Int. Tot.	-I-Mus Selects			-II-
1	$123.58	$123.58	37 +	124 =	161			
2	$754.22	$877.80	161 +	878 =	1039 SELECT	1039 −	915 =	124
3	$588.85	$1,466.65	124 +	589 =	713			
4	$2,055.95	$3,522.60	713 +	2056 =	2769 SELECT (2)	2769 −	1830 =	939
5	$341.00	$3,863.60	939 +	341 =	1280 SELECT	1280 −	915 =	365
6	$855.20	$4,718.80	360 +	855 =	1215 SELECT	1215 −	915 =	300
7	$12.55	$4,731.35	300 +	13 =	313			
8	$89.00	$4,820.35	313 +	89 =	402			
9	$250.00	$5,070.35	402 +	250 =	652			
10	$1,099.30	$6,169.65	652 +	1099 =	1751 SELECT	1751 −	915 =	836
11	$87.33	$6,256.98	836 +	87 =	923 SELECT	923 −	915 =	8
12	$788.99	$7,045.97	8 +	789 =	797			
13	$5,892.10	$12,938.07	797 +	5892 =	6689 SELECT (7)	6689 −	6405 =	284
14	$669.90	$13,607.97	284 +	670 =	954 SELECT	954 −	915 =	39
15	$24.89	$13,632.86	39 +	25 =	64			
16	$123.00	$13,755.86	64 +	123 =	187			
17	$123.00	$13,878.86	187 +	123 =	310			
18	$6.00	$13,884.86	310 +	6 =	316			
19	$540.90	$14,425.76	316 +	541 =	857			
20	$100.50	$14,526.26	857 +	101 =	958 SELECT	958 −	915 =	43
21	$66.89	$14,593.15	43 +	67 =	110			
22	$39.00	$14,632.15	110 +	39 =	149			
23	$35.00	$14,667.15	149 +	35 =	184			
24	$89.00	$14,756.15	184 +	89 =	273			
25	$100.00	$14,856.15	273 +	100 =	373			
26	$53.90	$14,910.05	373 +	54 =	427			
27	$436.09	$15,346.14	427 +	436 =	863			
28	$237.76	$15,583.90	863 +	238 =	1101 SELECT	1101 −	915 =	186
29	$209.91	$15,793.81	186 +	210 =	396			
30	$28.89	$15,822.70	396 +	29 =	425			

Starting Random Seed = 37
Interval Selection = 915
Total Sample Items Selected = 10

they might be ignored. Despite these limitations, monetary unit sampling is an effective way to evaluate the recorded balance in a large monetary account.

(b) PERFORMING THE MONETARY UNIT SAMPLING TEST

The first step here is to determine the sample size, the number of dollars to be examined in the population. Similar to attributes sampling, the monetary test requires that four things be known regarding the account to be sampled.

1. Maximum percentage of the recorded population value that the auditor will tolerate for errors. This is the same upper precision limit discussed previously for attributes sampling.

2. The expected confidence level.

3. An expected error rate for sampling errors.

4. Recorded value of the account to be evaluated.

The first of these calculations is the dollar value of the populations that may contain allowable errors divided by the recorded book value of the population. This is the same estimate discussed previously for attributes sampling, an error rate that an internal auditor could tolerate and still accept the overall controls in the system. Using public accounting terminology, an internal auditor should first think of the total amount of *material errors* that would be accepted. Although this can be calculated, generally a small percentage rate of perhaps 2% is used.

The estimated confidence level follows the same general rule for attributes. An internal auditor does not want to say that he or she is 100% confident unless the sample size is 100%. Anything too small, such as 80%, will cause management concern. Often 98% or 95% are good assumptions.

These three factors provide data to determine the recommended sample size, which again, can be obtained from a table or from statistical sampling software. The values in Figure 13.11, based on a 95% confidence level, can be used here. As discussed previously, this is also an area where some public accounting firms use a fixed sample size of 60, arguing that the mathematics do not require larger sample sizes.

The monetary unit sample size is then used to calculate the monetary interval. The recorded book value of the account is divided by the sample size to determine every n^{th} dollar interval. This interval sets a selection limit for larger items and all items greater than or equal to this interval will be selected. Table 13.3 shows the process for selecting items through monetary unit sampling.

Each item represented by a selected dollar is then evaluated by the auditor to determine if it is correctly stated. The auditor calculates the correct amount for each selected account and records both that amount and the correct audited amount. This will point out how much each account is overstated.

(c) EVALUATING MONETARY UNIT SAMPLE RESULTS

Monetary unit sampling is a popular approach for evaluating account balances to determine if they have been overstated. Since every dollar in every item in an account will be subject to sample selection, if an item is overstated, it may be discovered during the sampling process. The evaluation of the monetary unit sampling results to estimate the total error in the account is a more complex process. The basic idea is to document the recorded amounts and the audited amounts for each item selected and then to calculate the error percentage for each. Upper precision limits are calculated for each error item to determine the suggested amount of any audit adjustment.

The computations for a formal monetary unit sample evaluation have a series of statistical or theoretical options that go beyond the scope of this chapter. The process is often of more interest to external auditors, who can use this to propose a formal adjustment to a client's audited financial statements. For internal auditors, it is often sufficient to use the results of items selected through monetary unit sampling to gain an overall assessment as to whether an account is correctly stated. Books such as Leslie and Teitelbaum, referenced previously, can walk the interested internal auditor through the formal sample evaluation process.

(d) MONETARY UNIT SAMPLING ADVANTAGES AND LIMITATIONS

The most important advantage of monetary unit sampling is that it focuses on the larger value unit items in a population. A purely random sample could bypass large dollar value items in a population based on the random nature of the selection. Because monetary unit sampling selects units in a sample proportional to their dollar values, there is less risk of failing to detect a material error since all the large dollar units are subject to selection based on the size of each. Any item in a population that is larger than the monetary interval will *always be selected.* Even though management will, on one hand, expect internal audit to take an unbiased, random sample, it might express concern if an audit bypassed certain large-value items using other sample selection techniques. Monetary unit sampling assures there will be a greater coverage of the larger value items in a population.

Another advantage of monetary unit sampling is that if no errors are found in an initial sample and a very low expected error rate is established, relatively small sample sizes may be used. An internal auditor can readily determine the maximum possible overstatements and restrict the sample sizes in these circumstances. As discussed, many of the public accounting firms limit their monetary unit sample sizes to either 60 or 30 items. In addition, an internal auditor obtains the benefits of unlimited stratification by use of a monetary sampling unit.

Monetary unit sampling is also attractive because the item selection is computationally easy. As has been illustrated in the previous example, an internal auditor can effectively select a sample from a relatively large population using a spreadsheet program or even a pocket calculator, making it a good choice when an internal auditor is at a field location and decides to pull a representative sample but lacks computer-assisted audit tools.

The main disadvantage of monetary unit sampling is that the procedure does not adequately test for financial statement understatements. Missing documents or transactions are a common controls problem in many poorly controlled systems, and if items are missing from a population, dollar unit sampling procedures do not detect the missing items. They cannot be sampled. Accordingly, an internal auditor cannot project a value of the population using monetary unit sampling.

Another drawback to this method is that zero or negative values would have to be sampled using a physical unit approach. Since there are no dollar values included in these, there is no chance that zero or negative values would be sampled. Further, since the projection is made to a universe of dollars, a total book value must be known. The method cannot provide estimates of unknown population values. Also, under monetary unit sampling it is necessary to accumulate the dollars progressively in drawing the sample.

Finally, because monetary unit sampling is a relatively new concept for use by internal auditors, there is currently less training available than for traditional methods such as attributes sampling.

Despite these concerns and limitations, monetary unit sampling is often the best method for internal auditors auditing errors in some recorded book value. It can also be useful as a selection method for an internal control attributes test when all items in the population have some recorded monetary value. The approach replaces the random number selection previously discussed and will result in a very appropriate selection.

13-8 VARIABLES AND STRATIFIED VARIABLES SAMPLING

Variables sampling is one of the basic types of audit sampling where the auditor's objective is to test the detailed items that support some account total in order to assess whether that total is fairly stated. Monetary unit sampling is a type of variables sampling. In a variables sample, an auditor selects individual *items* in a population and estimates the total population based on whether the items selected were fairly valued. A variation of pure variables sampling is called *stratified sampling*. In this method, the population is divided into various levels by their values or extended values. Items within each strata are selected, often with differing sampling plans for various strata. The highest value strata may have 100% inspection while the selection for lower value strata will be based upon random selections.

Judgmental sampling was once the method primarily used in testing, and an internal auditor often performed a preliminary analysis before deciding which items to select. This analysis was based on review of correspondence in the files, discussions with auditee's staff to obtain explanations and leads, review of prior audit findings, comparison of operations and data, and an analysis to determine the larger or sensitive items for test. When sampling was first introduced into auditing, simple random sampling was generally used. This method was relatively easy to learn and apply, especially under manual methods. When there was an area to test, an internal auditor often took a random or *probe* sample of the population to find out more about the items before developing a sampling plan. The results of the probe sample were then used to arrive at final conclusions as to the acceptability of the area tested.

(a) STRATIFIED SAMPLING

When computer systems and software first became available to simplify sample selection and the projection of results, stratified variables sampling became more feasible and useful. Often, the only practical method for selecting a stratified sample was by use of a computer. Also, as auditors gained in sophistication in applying audit sampling, they experimented with more advanced techniques to get better precision. Prior to the widespread adoption of monetary unit sampling in the 1980s, external and internal auditors used stratified variables sampling for many auditing applications. Although in some cases it may not be practicable to stratify a population, or to identify the items for which differences will occur, these situations are rare.

Stratified sampling allows internal auditors to place a greater concentration on larger items in a population when they are included as separate strata. However, by placing them in a separate population subject to random selection, the auditor is not forced to examine all of these items. A major advantage of stratification is that it improves the efficiency of the testing. When the population variability or standard deviation is high, sample sizes may be reduced for the desired levels of precision and reliability by using stratified random sampling. If a sufficient number of strata are selected, the sampling error can often be reduced substantially. With the use of modern statistical sampling software, this becomes a very feasible internal audit approach. Another advantage is that emphasis can be given to sensitive areas that require audit. Often, an internal auditor's preliminary analysis will disclose areas with potential errors or problems. These can be classified in separate strata and audited 100% or on a sampling basis, as warranted.

Stratification provides an internal auditor with a tool for reviewing sensitive areas in a very systematic manner. The computation to perform stratified variables sampling properly is complex and usually supported through computer software. Due to space limitations and other reasons, this chapter will not attempt to present all aspects of stratified sampling, only to introduce the concepts and general approach.

(b) PERFORMING THE VARIABLES SAMPLING TEST

The total application of variables sampling can best be understood by listing and discussing the sequential steps that must be carried out. The following are some factors to consider when developing a stratified sampling test and, in some instances, any statistical sampling test:

1. *Determination of Audit Objective.* A first audit step is to decide the desired level of confidence and the desired degree of precision. As discussed with attributes sampling, the latter is normally first expressed as a percentage, but is then converted into a dollar amount. This dollar amount can then be translated into the average amount per inventory item. The precision can be called the sampling error.

2. *Selection of Preliminary Sample.* Through a proper selection process, discussed later in the chapter, a preliminary sample of perhaps 50 items should be selected.

3. *Arrangement of Preliminary Sample.* The preliminary sample should be arranged in groups of six, seven, or eight items, but subject to the requirement that the total of the items is a multiple of both the number of groups and the number in each group in the preliminary sample. For example, a preliminary sample of 48 items would be composed of eight groups of six each.

4. *Determination of the Average Range.* In each of the above-mentioned groups, the difference between the highest and lowest item constitutes the range. The ranges of all groups are then added and an average computed.

5. *Calculation of the Estimated Standard Deviation of Population.* The estimated standard deviation of the total population can now be calculated through a simplified method by dividing the average range, just computed, by an amount that is known in statistics as the d_2 factor.[3] For a group content of 6, 7, and 8 items, the d_2 factor is, respectively, 2.534, 2.704, and 2.847. The estimated standard deviation is the average range divided by the d_2 factor.

6. *Computation of the Stipulated Sampling Error.* The sampling error per average inventory item, as expressed in dollars, is now divided by the previously calculated estimated standard deviation. This will yield a new ratio called the *stipulated sampling error.*

7. *Determination of the Complete Sample Size.* Using the previously established level of confidence and the just computed ratio of sampling error, statistical sampling tables are available to show the size of the complete sample to be used. This type can be found in a statistical sampling handbook.

---

[3] The d_2 for estimating standard deviations is widely used in statistical quality-control work. An internal audit need only reference the above factors for groups of 6, 7, and 8.

8. *Reevaluation of the Calculated Sample Size.* At this point, internal audit should take an opportunity to reevaluate the suggested sample size in light of established audit objectives. It may be that the sample indicated is so large that the auditor may wish to reevaluate the confidence level and level of precision (the amount of the sampling error). It is possible by decreasing the former and/or increasing the latter to decrease the size of the needed sample.

9. *Examination of Sample.* The indicated sample, based on the above criteria, should now be examined in complete detail and the sampling error determined for this now more-complete sample.

10. *Reevaluation of Sampling Error.* The reliability of the complete sample can be further established by recomputing the stipulated sampling error for the complete sample in the same manner as was done for the preliminary sample. Again, tables are available to measure the significance of the variance from the error shown by the preliminary sample, and a reevaluation of the audit objectives may be necessary.

11. *Projection to Total Population.* The results obtained from the complete sample are finally projected to the total population. In some cases the conclusion or recommendation developed may be of a general nature such as a control weakness. In others, the final action may be a definitive adjustment of the account sampled, such as an inventory recorded balance.

In a stratified sample, the above procedures would be used for each strata selected. The internal auditor with a limited hours-and-cost budget or a management desire for fast results generally finds this type of manual procedure too labor-intensive. However, with computer software the auditor can more easily perform these tasks by answering the defining questions for the selection. Available software tools should always be considered.

We have talked about computer statistical sampling software in a general manner here, not recommending any package over another because software and related technology change so fast that any package recommended could soon be obsolete. For suggestions on appropriate software to use, the internal auditor might contact The Institute of Internal Auditors or an external audit firm.

(c) EVALUATING SAMPLE RESULTS

The real strength of variables sampling come from the auditor's ability to suggest a projected book value for the account sampled. For example, internal audit can perform a stratified variables sample of an inventory and then report the results to management, stating, ''We are 95% confident that the correct book value of the inventory should be between X_{LOW} and Y_{HIGH}. Since the recorded book value of the inventory at the time of our sample was Z, we recommended an adjustment of + or − W dollars.'' This is a very powerful internal audit decision tool.

Using variables sampling, an internal auditor can decide how to report the projection of dollar amounts, whether for adjustments or for estimates of the effect of a particular deficiency. The projection is normally stated as a range of values for a given confidence level. Management, however, often prefers a specific dollar amount or point estimate.

The point estimate is calculated by multiplying the sample mean times the number of items in the universe. This estimate is generally used when the range of values, or confidence interval, around the point estimate is small. For example, the point estimate based on a statistical projection of the results of audit is $100,000. The precision at a 95% confidence level could be stated as plus or minus $4,000, giving a range of final audit results between $96,000 and $104,000. Under these circumstances, management will accept such a range, and the use of the point estimate would generally be warranted.

If the calculated range were between $60,000 and $140,000, management would probably never accept these results and an internal auditor would have to either increase the sample size or use a different method of reporting. One method of reporting here would be to state: "We estimate with a probability of 95% that the recorded inventory value of $2.5 million is overstated between $60,000 and $140,000, and is most likely overstated by $100,000."

The projected results can be presented in terms of the upper limit, where the internal auditor reports the assurance that the amount of error or deficiency is *not greater than* this amount. For example, in a statistical review of equipment on hand, an internal auditor projects at the 95% confidence level that the maximum overstatement of the equipment is $30,000. Since this amount is not material in relation to the $5 million of equipment owned by the organization, the auditor can conclude that the amount of error is not significant. However, the auditor could also analyze the causes of errors found in the sample to determine procedural weaknesses that required correction. The upper limit is frequently used by internal audit to determine the validity of account balances for financial statement purposes. A tolerable error rate is first determined for the population. If the projected error rate using the upper limit does not exceed the tolerable error rate, the account is considered reasonably stated for financial statement purposes.

A one-sided confidence limit can be used to demonstrate that the total universe value *is not less than* some amount at a given confidence level. For example, in a statistical sample of fixed asset acquisitions, it is found that equipment costing over $1,000 was being expensed rather than capitalized. The projection shows a 95% confidence that the amount expensed in error is at least $150,000.

Audit samples are typically based upon the amounts of individual inventory items. Frequently, it is practicable instead to deal with the differences between the book and actual (as determined by an internal auditor). Under this approach, a similar procedure is followed but all of the samples and computations pertain to the differences data. The advantage is that smaller amounts (and thus smaller standard deviations)—and, therefore, smaller samples—will be required to achieve the same levels of confidence and precision. It is, of course, possible that the differences will be as great or almost as great as the absolute values and, therefore, the advantages may disappear. However, the use of differences is a good technique and can often be used as a first approach. A second type of evaluation is the ratio estimate. Here, the auditor works with ratios instead of absolute values. Computations of the standard deviations under this method are more complicated, but computers can effect significant time savings. The ratio estimates method is preferable to the use of the difference estimates method when the errors found are related in size to the value of individual items being tested.

The above discussion of variables sampling is very brief and does not describe many of the mathematics typically required in such an exercise and also typically embedded into statistical sampling programs. For more information, the auditor should consult some of the previously referenced statistical sampling books. See Table 13.2 for examples of standard deviation calculations.

13-9 OTHER AUDIT SAMPLING TECHNIQUES

A fair amount of study, training, or experience is necessary to gain more than a minimum level of proficiency in any or all of the methods discussed above. Although an internal auditor who plans on using audit sampling will almost always use these techniques, a variety of other methods can be used under certain circumstances. The following sections briefly describe some of these other sampling methods.

These additional sampling techniques are not that common, and the sampling books referenced in this chapter generally make little mention of them. Where does an auditor get more information if one or another of these techniques seems to fit an audit problem or is otherwise intriguing? The auditor might consult a good library for a reference. A better approach might be to contact the statistics department of a local university. Since alternative methods of statistical sampling are not topics of high general interest, the internal auditor may very well find some professor who would love to talk about some alternative sampling technique and discuss its good and bad points.

(a) MULTISTAGE SAMPLING

Multistage sampling involves sampling at several levels. A random sample is first selected for some group of units and then another random sample is pulled from the population in each unit sampled. For example, each of 200 retail stores maintains its own inventory records, sending only summarized results to a headquarters office. Internal audit, interested in the age or condition of the inventory, might first select a sample of the stores and then at each store select a random sample of their inventory items. When all of the sampling units at a given location are examined, the result is a cluster sample. When all locations are examined with a sample selected at each location, the result can be treated as a variables or attributes sample.

Multistage sampling assumes that each primary sampling unit is homogeneous. This assumption can cause problems. If the auditor assumes that all Quick Bite stores are essentially the same, and the audit subsequently finds that one or two of the units is very different from the others, such failure to consider those unusual stores in the overall audit test can bias any overall sample projection.

The technique can be useful for a retail chain store environment. However, the formal mathematics for calculating sample sizes and reliability, and in particular for estimating the sampling error, are quite complex. While practical for the chain store situation, the method can break down if the internal auditor wants to project the results of the sample test statistically. The previously referenced book by Arkin contains a detailed discussion of this process.

(b) REPLICATED SAMPLING

Replicated sampling is a variation to cluster and multistage sampling in that it requires the drawing of one overall random sample of size X. Y random subsamples of size X/Y then should be obtained. If a sample of 150 items is to be taken from a very large population, rather than drawing a single sample, the auditor would select 15 samples of 10 items each. These primary samples from the overall population would be pulled from a series of random numbers. Then, the same random numbers used to select each of the primary items would be used to select subsamples or items within those groups. The first random number would be assigned to subsample #1, the second to subsample #2, and so forth until a sufficient number have been apportioned.

Why would an internal auditor want to use replicated sampling rather than the cluster or multistage sampling previously described? The main reason is that the mathematics are easier.

Again, this chapter will not devote space to a detailed discussion of this sampling procedure.

(c) BAYESIAN SAMPLING

A technique rarely used or even mentioned in the audit sampling literature but which appears to have great potential promise is *Bayesian sampling*. The procedure is named after the mathematician Bayes, and is based on revised probabilities of sample sizes and the like, based on what are called *subjective probabilities* acquired from the results of prior tests.

Very simply put, Bayesian sampling allows an auditor to adjust sample assumptions and probability factors based upon the results of a prior audit. In other words, even though the size of the population is the same and the auditor's risks are unchanged, the sample can be modified based upon the results of past audit work. While auditors tend to do this as a matter of course, Bayesian sampling allows an auditor to *formally* modify the sampling plan based upon the results gathered in past audit tests.

The purpose of this section is only to mention the concept. The modern internal auditor will probably not encounter Bayesian sampling either in internal audit publications or by contact with external auditors. However, the evolving internal control model, defined in the COSO report and as described in Chapter 2, makes a Bayesian sampling approach potentially attractive. Internal auditors will probably encounter Bayesian sampling in the future!

13-10 INTEGRATING SAMPLING INTO INTERNAL AUDIT PROCEDURES

Audit sampling should be considered a key, important part of the internal auditor's "tool-kit," but should not be viewed as an essential requirement to be included in all audits. An internal auditor may or may not decide to test transactions in performing an audit. The auditor may, for example, either decide on the basis of overall comparisons and other auditing procedures that a test of transactions is unnecessary, or that the amounts involved are not sufficiently material to warrant testing. However, an internal auditor is often faced with situations that require sampling of transactions. The best of control systems cannot eliminate errors resulting from system breakdowns, and overall reviews or tests of a few transactions may not be sufficient to disclose whether internal controls are operating effectively. The organization's procedures may appear to be adequate, but an internal auditor generally must test actual transactions to determine whether the procedures have been followed in practice. If tests are made, audit sampling should be considered as a basis for arriving at more valid conclusions. If the test of transactions generated through the audit sample indicates that operations are acceptable, no further work may be required. Where errors are found, an internal auditor is generally faced with the decisions described below in order to arrive at an audit conclusion.

- *Isolating Errors.* Through a review of the types of errors and their causes, an internal auditor may be able to isolate the total amount of errors. For example, one vendor may be submitting erroneous invoices, and a review of all of the vendor's invoices may pinpoint all the errors. As another example, a particular automated system may appear to be causing the errors, and a special review of that system may be required. Either type of analysis can determine the amount of deficiency as well as the basic cause.

- *Reporting Only on Items Examined.* When an internal auditor encounters significant errors, it may only be necessary to report the results of the tests to operating personnel. The nature of the errors may be such that it is the responsibility of operational managers to strengthen procedures and determine the magnitude of errors. As part of this review, an internal auditor should attempt to determine the causes for the condition and make specific recommendations for corrective action. Unless an internal auditor projects the results of a statistical sample, management is provided only with errors or amounts pertaining to the items examined.

- *Performing 100% Audits.* Although an internal auditor is not expected to perform a detailed examination of all transactions, in some instances there may be a need for an extended examination when significant errors are found. An example is where certain recoveries are due from vendors but where specific vendors and amounts have to be identified in order to file the claims. If not 100% examinations, the auditor's sampling plan must be based on a very high confidence level, perhaps greater than 99%, and a low risk of perhaps 1%. The result will be a very large sample but with a very high acceptability of sample results. This large sample size or 100% examination may not be justified in terms of the costs involved, and a more conventional statistical sampling plan may suffice.

- *Projecting Results of Sample.* If the selection of items for the test is made on a random basis, the results can be evaluated using statistical tables. The number and dollar amount of errors can be projected to determine the range of errors in the entire field at a given confidence level. The projection can be used to make an adjustment, or as a basis for decisions of the kind described in the preceding paragraphs.

Internal auditors often experiment with audit sampling, such as in the review of equipment operating records to assure effective utilization, or tests of purchase requisitions to determine the timeliness of filling requests. An internal auditor often uses such procedures as inquiry, observation, vouching, confirmation, computation, and analysis. As a basis for extending the use of audit sampling, internal audit can review areas in which testing was performed in prior reviews along with an analysis of the objective of each test, the period covered, the effective use of judgmental or audit sampling, the number of items in both the field and the sample, results of these tests, and the feasibility of using these audit sampling procedures in subsequent audits. A review of this nature can have the following benefits:

- The analysis may pinpoint areas where auditors have been overauditing on the basis of their larger-than-necessary judgmental sample sizes.

- Discover common weaknesses where testing has been performed for short periods such as one month even though the audit report issued implied a period of the entire year.

- Examine areas where auditors have not been testing the entire population and only concentrating on sensitive or high-dollar items; this is only a problem when the audit report implies that the entire population had been reviewed.
- Identify areas where audit sampling is practicable in light of the objectives of the test, number of items in the population, and the results of the prior testing performed.

This type of detailed analysis makes more efficient and effective use of audit sampling techniques. A strong internal audit quality assurance process, as discussed in Chapter 33, is often the best time to identify opportunities for the extended use of audit sampling procedures. Of course, internal auditors should become familiar with these procedures and incorporate them as part of the planning process rather than waiting for a quality assurance function to catch them for any failure after the audit work has been planned and completed.

13-11 MAKING EFFICIENT AND EFFECTIVE USE OF AUDIT SAMPLING

For many years, audit sampling was a difficult process both to understand and to use. Auditors needed to reference published handbooks filled with extensive tables and then to use this tabled data to perform fairly detailed sample selection and test results calculations. The process was comparatively difficult and certainly was not understood by many auditors. Computerized sampling software has changed all of that. The computer has proved to be an invaluable tool to auditors in applying audit sampling. It simplifies the necessary calculations, eliminating the need for reference to formulas or tables. In addition, it facilitates the use of sophisticated techniques, thus enabling an internal auditor to obtain more precise and unbiased results. An internal auditor can, of course, use the time-consuming manual calculation procedures to determine the sample size and to evaluate results in the rare situation when a computer is not available. Today, an auditor can usually take a laptop computer to the site, or the auditee may have a computer available for auditor use. In other cases the data may be transmitted or mailed to a central location.

When the modern internal audit embeds audit sampling procedures into other general audit procedures, a better, more effective audit review results. The following techniques will facilitate the use of audit sampling for many audit procedures:

- *Combine audit steps.* Savings in audit time can be achieved if various audit steps are performed as part of the same statistical sample. This can be done by testing for as many attributes or characteristics as possible in the sample. For instance, in a review of purchases, the primary audit objective may be to determine whether there is adequate documentary support. In addition, an internal auditor may decide to include tests as part of the statistical sample, to determine whether excess materials are being acquired.
- *Use a preliminary sample.* Auditors can devote considerable effort to developing a sampling plan based on an estimated confidence level, precision, and expected error rate or standard deviation; however, in many cases there is insufficient information on which to develop the sampling plan—as, for example, in a first audit. By taking a preliminary sample of from 50 to 100 items, an internal auditor is in a better position to make decisions on the extent of sampling required. The prelimi-

nary sample can then be included as part of the final sample. Also, the results of the preliminary sample may lead an internal auditor to conclude that no further testing is required.

- *Perform interim audits.* When a sampling plan is prepared in advance—such as for a year—the items to be tested can be examined on a monthly or other interim basis without waiting until the end of the year. Thus staff auditors can be utilized when available to perform the audit sampling on an interim basis. For example, if the sample plan calls for examination of every hundredth voucher, these can be selected for examination as the transaction is processed.

- *Enlarge the field size.* A basic consideration in audit sampling is that the sample size should not vary to a great extent with an increase in field size. Thus, savings can be obtained by sampling for longer periods of time, or from a field composed of more than one department or division. In some cases an internal auditor may decide to test a particular account for a two-year period, with selection of items during the first year on an interim basis as part of that two-year test.

- *Use a mix of attributes and variables sampling.* In some cases, an internal auditor does not know in advance whether variables sampling is required. Since variables sampling is often more complex to apply, the auditor may pick a random sample for attributes, evaluate the results, and decide at that point, on the basis of dollar errors, whether variables sampling is required. If it is, the sample can then be projected or incorporated in an extended sample selected for variables. The important point is that once a sample is taken on a random basis, it can be evaluated using different sampling methods.

- *Apply simple audit sampling methods.* Some auditors believe that they must use complex methods of sampling and spend considerable effort and study in arriving at the method to use. In most instances, a simple estimation sample will provide adequate results, without the need for techniques that are difficult to understand, apply, and explain. This does not mean that an internal auditor can overlook judgment in the audit tests. Sensitive items should be examined in addition to a random selection of items, if required. These can be examined on a 100% basis or sampled as part of a separate stratum.

- *Achieve an effective balance of audit costs and benefits.* An internal auditor should consider the costs of examining each sampling unit when considering extending a sample. The costs of additional work should be compared with benefits from obtaining increased confidence or precision in the final results.

As the modern internal auditor first tries and then effectively uses some of the audit sampling techniques discussed in this chapter, the auditor will subsequently find other useful areas to use sampling in the course of operational audit, including:

- *Production Activities.* The production function in the modern organization has always been one of the major areas for statistical applications. One of the most common of these is the use of statistical tests by quality control groups that show which individual manufacturing units are completing particular parts or processing operations in accordance with desired specifications. The same problem exists in connection with purchased parts, materials, and partial assemblies. Other applica-

tions include the forecasting of machine capacity needs and continuing maintenance needs. The same procedures can be applied as either a review of production
functions or as an independent test.

- *Inventory Management.* While variables sampling can be used for such things as
  the valuation of an inventory, attributes sampling is useful for testing inventory-
  related internal controls, such as whether estimates for inventory obsolescence are
  correct, or testing to determine if needed inventory levels by individual items are
  correct.

- *Marketing.* Combined with various types of statistical analysis, marketing functions sometimes use attributes sampling procedures to measure and evaluate consumer preferences. Major applications include the evaluation of advertising approaches, promotional activities, sales techniques, and the like.

- *Personnel or Human Resources.* Common attributes sampling in this area include
  the analysis and evaluation of record-keeping requirements, recruitment policies,
  training methods, employee turnover, compensation policies, and other compliance
  tests. As illustrated by the example earlier in this chapter, attributes sampling can
  be useful for testing compliance with various procedural requirements.

- *Finance-Related Attributes Tests.* Variables sampling is much more common in
  the financial area as it is normally used to test the value of an account or the like.
  However, there is also a strong need for attributes sampling as part of the auditor's
  assessments of internal control procedures. Attributes sampling can include reviews of pricing policy, capital project evaluations, and all types of cost and
  revenue projections.

Many organizational activities besides internal audit make use of statistical methods
and concepts to some extent. The key questions are, first, whether they are being as fully
utilized as they can be, and second, whether those uses are carried out in an effective
fashion. Internal auditors should be interested in both of these questions. While the answers
may require counsel from persons with specialized expertise, much can be done by internal
audit in evaluating how operations managers are developing orderly procedures and good
administration over these activities.

13-12 AUDIT SAMPLING FOR THE MODERN INTERNAL AUDITOR

Audit sampling is a powerful tool that is all too often ignored by some internal auditors.
At one time auditors did not use it because it was viewed by many as being too difficult
and too theoretical. Auditors found it easier to say, ''You have a problem here'' rather
than say ''Based on our audit sample, we are 95% certain that we have identified a control
problem. Findings based on appropriate audit samples allow internal auditors to express
concerns or opinions on a more solid basis.

Computer tools now make statistical sampling a simpler task. In older days, auditors
relied on extensive tables of values and difficult formulae. Today, the effective modern
internal auditor must learn the basics of audit sampling and use it when appropriate.

CHAPTER 14

Automating Internal Audit Processes

14-1 INTRODUCTION: NEW TOOLS AND TECHNOLOGIES

Today, the documents that the auditor might wish to examine will often be available only on computer files. Computerized systems are so common that manual, paper-intensive applications tend to be the exceptions. Chapter 12 discussed the use of computer-assisted audit techniques (CAATs) to review various automated systems and to extract data of audit interest from them. An internal auditor can no longer rely on just paper-based reports but often must use computerized tools and procedures to help analyze the data on automated files and the controls within information systems. This chapter suggests ways to automate these internal audit procedures to gain better efficiencies in the entire audit process.

There are many easy-to-implement automation tools available to internal auditors involving the use of portable or office microcomputers and powerful software. This chapter provides an overview of hardware and software tools for internal audit automation. Examples of typical internal audit automated systems are presented, as are potential steps for implementing a program of internal audit automation. Internal auditors must always recognize that technologies change very fast and concepts discussed in this chapter may soon change due to technology or new product introductions.

14-2 OPPORTUNITIES FOR INTERNAL AUDIT AUTOMATION

The various chapters of this book provide an overview of all internal audit activities. These include planning the audit, gathering evidence through fieldwork, documenting and reporting on that audit work, and administering the overall audit activity. Each of these is a candidate for some form of internal audit automation. The microcomputer, client-server computing, and the supporting software available are the components of most internal audit automation projects.

Most organizations have separate information systems or data-processing functions to design and develop automated applications for their various organization departments or functions. Because an internal audit function is small in comparison to other organization functions, it is difficult to justify centrally developed information systems for audit purposes only, and audit often must share in such centralized accounting information systems as the organization's budgeting system. However, internal audit will probably have its own microcomputer-based systems for such areas as audit decision support or workpaper documentation. Because of the reduced costs and efficiencies associated with microcomputer-based systems, internal audit can usually justify specialized information systems. However, manual systems and procedures often continue to be used in many internal audit departments.

Internal audit management and administrative processes can often be automated through microcomputer- or local area network (LAN)–based systems within the internal audit. These automation projects usually do not require major investments in time or capital due to the many off-the-shelf software tools available. They do require a few creative internal auditors who are willing to spend some time to develop and implement automation tools to improve their overall audit function efficiency.

Because the needs of any internal audit department may vary, the first step for automating internal audit processes is to evaluate the potential areas within an audit function that may be automation candidates. The following sections discuss some of these potential automation opportunities.

(a) AUDIT PLANNING AND ADMINISTRATIVE SYSTEMS

Internal audit is faced with some unique planning and administrative requirements often not found in other business areas. First, internal audit needs to understand the potential universe of audit candidates and then to evaluate the relative risks associated with each. For higher-risk candidates, audits must be planned and reviews scheduled. Low-risk areas can be deferred. Chapter 7 covered the evaluation of audit risk, and Chapter 8 discussed this internal audit planning process. Besides identifying the task requirements for preliminary surveys, auditor fieldwork visits, and other analysis work, internal audit management must also take into account the mix of other audit projects, the availability of audit staff, and individual auditor skills required. In addition to these developed schedules, management will often request special reviews, or a fraud-related action will require immediate audit attention. Finally, the auditor must capture actual times and costs associated with each of these projects in order to compare actual results with budgeted plans. This entire process can be difficult and time-consuming using manual techniques.

Microcomputer software tools can provide significant help in automating these planning and administrative audit functions. Spreadsheet software, such as Lotus 1-2-3 or Microsoft Excel, organizes data in rows and columns similar to the multiple-column paper worksheets once used by accountants and auditors. Those older paper-based worksheets typically had 14 columns and about 30 lines or rows down the page. An electronic spreadsheet can have an almost unlimited number of rows and columns, which the user can access and change electronically. On paper spreadsheets, a change required erasures and a recalculation of footing and crossfooting totals, both of which happen automatically with an electronic spreadsheet.

Figure 14.1 shows how an automated spreadsheet works for a simple financial budgeting application. However, this example does not illustrate the power of these automation software products. Electronic spreadsheets are discussed again later in this chapter. They have been common since the early 1980s, and many auditors have learned to use them even when they had no other experience with internal audit automation tools. It is fairly easy to build internal audit planning and administration tools through the use of spreadsheets. Examples of these types of audit automation tools follow.

(i) Spreadsheet-Based Risk-Analysis Models.   Chapter 7 discusses the audit risk-analysis process in detail and several approaches to building risk-evaluation models. One

Figure 14.1 ExampleCo Internal Audit Department FY 20XX Annual Budget

	JAN	FEB	MAR	APR	MAY	JUNE	JULY	AUG	SEP	OCT	NOV	DEC	TOTAL
Salaries & Overhead	$93,750	$93,750	$94,580	$95,664	$95,664	$96,525	$96,525	$97,035	$97,035	$97,588	$97,588	$98,320	$1,154,024
Travel: Tickets & Lodging	$3,255	$3,600	$4,500	$1,250	$6,525	$7,285	$1,875	$4,500	$5,250	$3,900	$4,500	$1,200	$47,640
Travel: Meals	$391	$432	$540	$150	$783	$874	$225	$540	$630	$468	$540	$144	$5,717
Computer Equipment	$0	$6,500	$0	$0	$7,500	$0	$0	$14,500	$0	$0	$0	$0	$28,500
Office Supplies	$609	$609	$615	$622	$622	$627	$627	$631	$631	$634	$634	$639	$7,501
Subscriptions & Reference	$600	$300	$300	$750	$300	$600	$750	$300	$300	$600	$600	$300	$5,700
Professional & Tuition	$0	$2,675	$2,675	$250	$250	$1,050	$1,755	$4,250	$250	$250	$2,660	$250	$16,315
General Office Expenses	$12,500	$12,500	$12,500	$12,500	$12,500	$12,500	$12,500	$12,500	$12,500	$12,500	$12,500	$12,500	$150,000
Internal Audit Expenses	$111,105	$120,366	$115,710	$111,186	$124,144	$119,462	$114,257	$134,256	$116,596	$115,940	$119,022	$113,353	$1,415,397

example of such risk-related questions and the assigned factor values model used to select candidates for future audits might be:

Factor 1: How many years since the last audit?

Less than 2 years   Assign 0.2

2 to 5 years   Assign 0.5

Over 5 years   Assign 0.8

Never   Assign 1.0

Factor 2: Significance of prior audit findings?

Never audited   Assign 0.0

Minor procedural concerns   Assign 0.1 to 0.3

Internal control problems   Assign 0.3 to 0.7

Significant problems   Assign 0.7 to 1.0

An audit risk-analysis model typically requires a large number of such questions and assigned risk factors. Each potential audit candidate is evaluated with relative risk values assigned per responses to the risk-evaluation questions. Risk scores are then calculated for all candidates to identify those for the potential scheduling of audits.

Audit risk models are excellent candidates for spreadsheet applications. Columns can be established for each risk factor with potential audit candidates evaluated row by row across these columns for relative risk. Figure 7.6 is an example of such an audit risk matrix.

Spreadsheet-based risk models can be easily adjusted to reflect corrections or additional analysis as well as to produce audit management reports in a variety of formats and sequences. Although commercial software products are available to help the internal auditor perform such a risk analysis, simpler models can easily be built through spreadsheet software. The commercial products are sometimes best in a larger audit organization with many complex projects.

(ii) Audit Planning Tools.   Once an area has been identified as a potential audit candidate through the risk-analysis process, the logical next step is to plan that audit, as discussed in Chapter 8. Audit management needs to develop three levels of those plans as follows:

- A total audit department plan that shows all planned activities, including both audits and activities such as training for a given period
- Individual detailed plans for each audit showing estimated personnel staff and time requirements
- Period-by-period individual plans for the audit staff

These three plan levels, also discussed in Chapter 8, need to be tied together. It is of little value to plan an aggressive schedule of audits for the department if there are not enough personnel or time resources available. Internal audit management must balance the time requirements of individual audits and available audit resources with other limitations, such as scheduled auditor educational offerings or vacations. A change to any one of these plans will cause changes to all of the others. An audit staff resignation or a management request for a special review may require all of the plans to be adjusted. An automated planning system will allow internal audit management to easily make adjustments to existing plans. The following are four approaches to automating the internal audit planning process:

- *Spreadsheet-Based Planning Models.* The same spreadsheets used for risk analysis can develop audit plans. Separate schedules can be built for each of the basic plans discussed above. The spreadsheet software will take care of adding columns containing the hours requirements for any period, adding the rows to total resources over a project plan, and performing other necessary computations. Spreadsheet software packages allow individual project plans to be linked together.

  Figure 14.2 is an example of an audit plan developed through spreadsheet software. Although fairly easy to learn, the software may lack sufficient flexibility for making substantial changes, depending upon the overall design of the plans.

- *Microcomputer Database Software.* A variety of microcomputer software products fall under the general category of database software. A database has the ability to store and manipulate larger volumes of data. An integrated planning database can be built to incorporate all three of the above-mentioned levels of audit plans. A change made to one element in the plan, such as an auditor reassignment to a special project, will be reflected in each of the other plan schedules.

  While database software offers more flexibility, it typically requires practice and training to build the database, to maintain it, and to develop appropriate planning status reports. Internal audit management might want to designate a member of the audit staff for a special project to build such an audit-planning database. In some organizations, there may be resources within the information systems or end-user computing groups to help with such a database project. Database planning models are particularly useful for larger audit organizations with many staff members or planned audit projects. The overall audit plan can be divided up among the various audit managers and then consolidated for overall audit department reporting purposes.

- *Specialized Planning Software.* There are a limited number of specialized planning software products available designed specifically for internal audit departments. The Institute of Internal Auditors has marketed a product called AuditMasterplan for multiple levels of internal audit planning and risk analysis. The input requirements are fairly extensive and may be best suited for only a large internal audit organization.

  Many generalized planning software packages are not that useful for an internal audit-planning process. They are typically designed more for major projects with many interrelated tasks rather than for typical internal audit projects. That is, they are designed to plan projects such as the construction of a large building and can produce detailed, critical, plan-type charts as well as other resource-utilization outputs. However, input setup steps with this software may be onerous and its output not useful for typical smaller audit projects involving only four or fewer auditors over shorter periods such as several weeks or months.

- *Other Planning Automation Tools.* Internal audit should inquire about other soft-

Figure 14.2 ExampleCo Internal Audit Department FY 20XX Annual Budget

	JAN	FEB	MAR	APR	MAY	JUNE	JULY	AUG	SEP	OCT	NOV	DEC	TOTAL HRS
XYZ Plant Distribution Controls													
Audit Planning	30												30
Initial Field Survey Visits			60										60
Develop and Test CAATs				30									30
Distribution Audit Procedures				60	440	240							740
Complete Fieldwork & Report						160	20						180
Exit Meetings & Report Prep.							20	20					40
Follow-Up											16		16
Total Audit Project Hours	30		1620	2430	11880	10800	1080	540	0	0	432	0	28812
													0
Info. Systems Logical Security													
Audit Planning					24								24
Initial Field Survey Visits					36								36
Develop and Test CAATs						40							40
Logical Security Audit Procedures						40	160	60					260
Complete Fieldwork & Report								20					20
Exit Meetings & Report Prep.								36					36
Follow-Up										36			36
Total Audit Project Hours					60	80	160	116	0	36	0	0	452

ware planning products in use by other departments within the organization. Depending upon the overall business functions of the organization, there may be a planning software package installed in engineering, real estate, or other departments. Internal audit management should survey other organization functions, investigate any potential candidates to determine if they are appropriate, and arrange to install any candidates for detailed evaluation. In some instances, this software may be implemented on a mainframe or on other computer systems; it would also be necessary to arrange for access to the relevant computer.

(iii) Internal Audit Accounting and Reporting Systems. Internal audit departments have cost-accounting requirements similar to all other units in the organization. These systems provide inputs to the centralized general ledger system and receive output reports from it. In addition, an internal audit department typically has its own internal accounting requirements. It is often necessary to gather costs for individual audit projects, to measure actual costs against budgeted plans, to allocate those costs back to benefiting auditees, and to assemble data for input to centralized accounting systems.

This is an area closely related to the above-mentioned planning systems. Any of the planning system approaches, spreadsheets, databases, or specialized software may have the capability to capture actual costs. Figure 14.3 shows a sample individual auditor time sheet for reporting hours spent on direct and indirect projects. Data to develop such a report can be captured from auditor time and expense reports. While the figure shows a template from a spreadsheet-based file, a database system might be more useful because

Figure 14.3 Auditor Project Timesheet: ExampleCo Internal Audit Weekly Project Time-Sheet

Name: Sarah Tweedie Department: Internal Audit					Starting Date: 03/18/02 Ending Date: 03/24/02			
Billable Time	03/18 Mon	03/19 Tue	03/20 Wed	03/21 Thu	03/22 Fri	03/23 Sat	03/24 Sun	Weekly Totals
SlickStuff Div. Inventory	8.00	6.00	2.00					16.00
Corp. Ethics Dept.				6.00	8.00			14.00
Daily Totals (hrs)	8.00	6.00	2.00	6.00	8.00	0.00	0.00	30.00
Nonbillable Time	03/18 Mon	03/19 Tue	03/20 Wed	03/21 Thu	03/22 Fri	03/23 Sat	03/24 Sun	Weekly Totals
IIA Seminar			8.00					8.00
Internal Audit Admin		2.00		2.00				4.00
Daily Total (hrs)	0.00	2.00	8.00	2.00	0.00	0.00	0.00	12.00
TOTAL HOURS	8.00	8.00	10.00	8.00	8.00	0.00	0.00	42.00
Misc. Expenses								Amount
Total								$36.25

historical cost and performance data can easily be separately retained. Spreadsheet software is usually sufficient for all but very large internal audit organizations.

Although this chapter discusses mostly microcomputer tools such as spreadsheets, other organizations may find that they have similar software available on their mainframe legacy computer systems. Internal audit management should contact their information systems resource to determine what types of software tools are available and whether they are appropriate for internal audit administration purposes.

Even though end-user oriented tools may not be available on central mainframe systems, internal audit management should consider implementing appropriate planning and administrative tools on their own departmental microcomputers. A good way to start this process is to investigate a specialized internal audit planning package or to begin to use a spreadsheet package.

(b) AUTOMATED WORKPAPER APPLICATIONS

Workpapers are the documented records of auditor activities. Chapter 11 discussed the process of preparing and assembling auditor workpapers. Some in that chapter were prepared in the traditional manner, manually. However, workpaper automation can help the auditor achieve improvements in both productivity and efficiency.

Automated workpapers typically require the use of several types of software as well as portable computers issued to auditors. The numerous types of portable microcomputers discussed later in this chapter range in size from small, notebook-sized devices to machines about the size of a large briefcase. It is almost *essential* that portable computers be issued to auditors on remote, field audit assignments. The auditor can enter workpaper data and commentaries directly into the computer while performing the fieldwork. It is inefficient to record such audit data manually for subsequent entry into an automated system back in the internal audit home office.

Nearly every organization today has a telecommunications network where an internal auditor can gain access to a centralized system as part of any field audit through the use of portable audit computers equipped with modems using normal telephone lines. However, there must be adequate security controls over centralized systems and the network (as discussed in Chapter 18) to preserve the confidentiality and integrity of the auditor's fieldwork. If the organization has a network of LAN microcomputers installed at each operating unit, with connections to central locations, the auditor can use or borrow such departmental machines while performing the field audits. However, it will be necessary to load the auditor's workpaper software onto the field machine and to record all workpaper data on removable diskettes. Full-time terminal or machine availability during the period of the audit may also be a problem. It is generally best to equip internal auditors with their own portable microcomputers.

There are four basic types of software that can be used for automating workpapers: spreadsheet-analysis software, wordprocessing software for commentaries, financial statement software, and flowcharting or diagramming software.

(i) Spreadsheet-Analysis Software for Workpapers.   Automated spreadsheets are another ideal application for workpaper automation. Often, the auditor is required to test a selected sample against a series of audit attributes. For example, the auditor might select a sample of purchase orders and test them for attributes such as whether they have been properly approved, whether an approved vendor was used, whether terms are

Figure 14.4 Travel Expense Audit Spreadsheet

AUDIT TEST	MATERIALS REVIEWED	ITEMS REVIEWED	EXCEPTIONS	ERROR RATE
A. Expense report mathematical accuracy	Filed Reports AP Division, May and June 20XX	149	3	2.01%
B. Proper expense report approvals	Filed Reports AP Division, May and June, 20XX	149	1	0.67%
C. Expense report completed in a timely manner	Filed Reports—AP & BZ Divs, April 20XX	223	15	6.73%
D. Approved air and hotel vendors used	Three months study—Corp, AP & BZ Divs, Apr–June	415	37	8.92%
E. Evidence of "luxury" travel—i.e., first-class air or hotels	Three month study—Corp, AP & BZ Divs, Apr–June	415	12	2.89%

consistent with organization policy, and the like. This is the type of audit analysis traditionally recorded on manual spreadsheets. An electronic spreadsheet can automate this type of process. Once the auditor is trained in the use of the software, a simple spreadsheet format can be set up on a microcomputer in about the same time as it takes to lay out a manual form. However, the automated spreadsheet has the ability to better tabulate and summarize auditor data.

Figure 14.4 shows a computer spreadsheet for a series of personnel travel expense audit tests. Such a spreadsheet format could be set up in the audit department prior to starting fieldwork. If the audit sample is selected in advance, that data could also be entered prior to the start of fieldwork. The cross-references on this example sheet would refer to separate file names containing audit commentary. The audit supervisor reviewing the automated workpapers need only reference the file names to call up commentary descriptions. Many spreadsheet software packages today have built-in documentation tools that integrate the data gathered with internal auditor comments.

(ii) Workpaper Commentary Software. A considerable amount of fieldwork involves internal audit interviews with other parties, observations of operations, and documented observations and meeting notes. This recording process can be accomplished more easily through the use of word-processing software rather than through the traditionally manual preparation.

Word-processing software allows the auditor to type commentaries directly into a computer file and then print those results for a paper record, if desired. Because of its electronic medium, words can be easily changed or entire paragraphs shifted with only a few keystrokes. Many packages have spell checking for misspelled or mistyped words. Audit management generally finds it much easier to review such commentaries since the problems of different handwriting and sloppy page format composition styles are eliminated. Commentaries can also easily be exported directly to audit report files. Figure 14.5 is an example of audit workpaper commentary made using word-processing software. A standard header block has been established for workpaper identification. The other information would have been typed in by the field auditor. These workpapers would have been based on auditor interviews or observations. The auditor should retain the rough notes taken during the audit as well.

(iii) Financial Statement Software.   Several products are available to prepare financial statement audit workpapers. This type of software is often used by external auditors for their financial statement attest work. The external auditor initially loads a client's trial balance into this ''lead schedule'' software and reviews each of the financial statement lines, calling up appropriate files in the software to enter any financial statement adjustments. For example, an external auditor reviewing recorded inventory balances may determine that certain items were not shipped as of the day of the physical inventory and cannot be recorded as sales. An adjustment would be necessary. When the auditor has completed entering these adjustments, the financial statement software would produce a revised set of financial statements.

Financial statement software products are available commercially or through public

Figure 14.5   Audit Workpaper Commentary Sheet

ExampleCo Internal Audit
Audit: Manufacturing Quality   Location: Burning Stump   Date: 04/12/03

W/P Reference	Exception	Disposition
	Cross-Reference Missing	Corrected
04-10/11	Exception item schedule appears to be an exception, but is not mentioned as an audit finding.	Open
04-13	No attachments or x-ref to support items described.	Open
05-03	Analysis does not adequately support Finding #3 - Need names, times of meetings, etc.	Open
06-03 to 07	03-16	Corrected

Figure 14.6 Lead Schedule Examples

			ExampleCo Cash Lead Schedule			
W/P REF	Acct. No.	Account	Final 12/31/99	Ledger 12/31/00	Adjusted Entry	Final 12/31/00
A-12	1230	Petty Cash	1,000	1,000		1,000
A-13	1231	Cash in Bank	391,000	426,000 (2.3)	50,000	476,000
		Total	392,000	427,000	50,000	477,000

accounting firms. They often contain features that are not applicable to most internal auditors, such as corporate income tax computations. However, they can also be very powerful automated workpaper tools for internal audit performing financially oriented audits. Figure 14.6 shows an example of this type of financial statement ''lead schedule'' audit software.

Internal audit should discuss any such financial statement software needs with the organization's external auditors. They may supply a copy of their software to internal audit. Internal audit may have used that same software in the past when performing external audit support projects.

(iv) Flowcharting and Diagramming Software. Auditors frequently have a need to describe a process or system through a flowchart—often the best way to document a given process. The traditional manual method for preparing these flowcharts was to use a plastic template with various flowchart symbols and to draw a diagram (see Chapter 10). However, if there were any changes, the document had to be erased where necessary or totally redrawn.

The flowcharting software products available for auditor documentation are generally easy to use, and flowcharts can easily be modified when there are changes. Completed flowcharts can be displayed on microcomputer monitors or printed. Many of the figures in this book were created using this type of software.

In addition to flowcharting software, some organizations have installed systems-development software for their information systems organizations. These products are often called Computer Aided Systems Engineering (CASE) software. Although designed for systems developers, CASE software can also be used for audit documentation. The main disadvantages to the auditor is that CASE software often has too many features, is more difficult to learn, and the auditor may require special rights to gain access to this software. CASE tools are discussed in Chapter 18 as part of the section on auditing new computer applications under development.

Although flowcharting software may not be used in manual workpaper documentation procedures, it can be a powerful tool for automated workpapers. Flowcharting allows an auditor to understand processes and to identify controls better. Massive files of workpapers can be replaced with files on diskettes, which can then easily be updated from year to year. However, the internal audit function may need to invest in portable microcomputers, will need to select a set of software tools to accomplish required audit objectives, and will need to train auditors in the use of these tools.

(c) DECISION-SUPPORT AUTOMATED AUDIT TOOLS

Internal auditors are often required to perform numerous detailed analyses or computations. In the example described in Chapter 13, internal auditors may wish to develop an audit sampling plan based on risk parameters and the expected attributes of the population to be sampled. They will later need to analyze the audit results of that sample. Although these computations can be performed manually using published tables and formulae, this task is very much simplified through the use of statistical sampling software.

Most of the other automated audit tools for simplifying audit procedures while also improving auditor effectiveness are available as easily installed microcomputer software. Although the types of software to be used will depend upon the needs of both the internal audit department and the overall organization, these software tools can generally be broken down into the following broad categories: audit program generators, statistical sampling tools, analytical review and analysis tools, decision-support expert systems, and specialized information databases.

(i) Audit Program Generators.   Chapter 10 discussed the preparation of audit programs, the sets of procedures or steps an internal auditor will follow in performing a review. For some repetitive audits, the internal audit department can rely upon programs prepared from a previous audit with only minor modifications. For others, as was discussed in Chapter 10, a specialized, tailored program should be prepared from audit's preliminary survey. In either case, the process of audit program preparation and maintenance is a good candidate for automation.

As noted, word-processing software is an effective tool for developing and maintaining internal audit programs. Spreadsheets are also useful for building audit program skeletons. In either case, the auditor can draft the audit program directly using a microcomputer system. Once the program has been approved, a permanent copy can be saved on an archival file and another copy used for the actual audit. Program step completion information and workpaper cross-references can then be entered directly onto the microcomputer-based programs.

Sometimes, machine-readable audit programs are available along with published reference books. *Computer Audit, Control, and Security*[1] comes with an ASCII file diskette that contains a copy of all of the audit programs in the book. The reader can load them into a word-processing package to make any necessary local modifications. There are currently other examples of these machine-readable audit programs from various published sources.

(ii) Statistical Sampling Tools.   Chapter 13 discussed the process of gathering audit evidence through audit or statistical sampling. When designing a sampling plan, the auditor needs to establish sampling parameters, such as the expected error rate, and then must calculate the sample size. This sample size calculation can be a fairly laborious task using tables and a desk calculator. However, there are numerous statistical software tools available to help an internal auditor select the proper sample size. Similar software tools are available to assist the auditor in evaluating the results of such a sample. This software has essentially replaced the manual tables in the same manner that electronic calculators have replaced manual computation procedures.

---

[1] Robert R. Moeller, *Computer Audit, Control, and Security* (New York: John Wiley, 1989).

Many organizations have statistical software on their primary computer systems. Internal auditors should inquire about the availability of such software tools. There are also numerous statistical sampling software tools available for microcomputers. Some of this software is available commercially while other programs can be located through public domain sources, as discussed briefly later in this chapter.

(iii) Analytical Review and Analysis Tools.   Auditors frequently perform specialized mathematical computations in the course of their efforts. While these computations can be performed manually, microcomputer software tools increase audit efficiency. The tools to be used depend upon the nature of the audits that are performed. The following are some examples of these automated tools.

- *Special Computation Programs.* Some audits require specialized financial computations such as recomputations of interest accruals or of present values. These are most often used for financial instrument or fixed asset–related audits. These auditor computations can be complex but can be simplified through the use of microcomputer software. Depending upon computational needs, commercial and public-domain software packages are available. In some instances, the computation can be developed through a spreadsheet program that can be tested and then distributed to field auditors.
- *Analytical Review Computations.* Auditors frequently have a need to perform ratio computations to assess overall operations at a location. For example, they might perform a series of ratio measures at one branch location in order to assess the performance of that branch in comparison to others. Spreadsheet software is a useful tool for this work. Computations can be prepared as part of preaudit work or can be performed by the field auditor at the branch location. Figure 14.7 is an example of an analytical review computation performed by an auditor at a branch retail location using a spreadsheet.

(iv) Decision Support Expert Systems Audit Tools.   Expert systems are a relatively new application that can make some human-like decisions based upon a set of rules

Figure 14.7 Analytical Review

Analytical Measure	Average All Branches	Branch #34 Audit DT: 08/15	Branch #34 Performance
ExampleCo Branch Performance Audit			
Total 2001 Sales	$9,123,525	$8,795,466	96.40%
2001 Gross Margin	$1,033,254	$888,332	85.68%
Total Inventory Items Yr Ending 12/31/00	3,754	4,622	123.12%
Inventory Turnover	3.45	1.22	35.36%
Employees/Branch	9.25	11	118.92%

that a human expert would follow. Chapter 35 discusses this technology and potential audit applications in greater detail. In the future, auditors may increasingly use expert systems applications to improve the audit decision process.

As an example, expert systems have been developed to assess control risk in a classic mainframe data center. This type of system is constructed like an audit checklist, with an opportunity for "Yes" or "No" responses. When an experienced auditor uses such a checklist, the auditor may receive a "No" to a given auditee question and will then go on to ask a series of clarifying questions. An inexperienced auditor may just record the response and go on to the next question. An expert system can prompt the inexperienced auditor to ask the additional clarifying questions that the expert might ask.

(v) Specialized Information Databases.   Auditors frequently look up various reference materials to aid in the audit. This may include a stock quote for a securities valuation, a bibliographic reference, or even the airline schedule in order to book a return flight. Some are free and available through the Internet, using Internet browser software, while others require a subscription fee. There are a variety of databases available with these types of information, all easily accessed through a microcomputer equipped with a modem.

Internal audit management should consider the various types of specialized information databases available for internal audit functions. Some Internet databases are more research-oriented and contain detailed bibliographic references. Others are financially oriented and contain stock quotes, company financial reports, and investor-related information. Still others are much more consumer-oriented, including airline schedules, consumer product offerings, and special interest group conversational sessions. Users can typically access these databases through a local telephone call to a value-added carrier often known as an ISP (Internet Service Provider).

(d) AUDIT REPORTING SOFTWARE

Most audit departments have long since automated the process of producing their audit reports through the use of word-processing software. In many organizations, however, there are still numerous manual steps associated with this audit report production process. Some audit managers still write their report drafts in longhand, submit them to a clerical support person for entry, and then correct or proofread the drafts using pencil for subsequent word-processing reentry.

The audit report production process is simplified and made more efficient when those word-processing tasks are shifted to the internal auditors responsible for drafting the report. Initial reports should be produced by the responsible auditor using the same word-processing software used for report production. They can perform spelling and grammar checks against the rough drafts using software functions and then place them into the correct format. Supervisors would then review the report draft texts via a computer screen and make any suggested changes directly to the draft files. The automation idea here is to *totally automate* the report production process and to make it almost paperless until the final report versions.

An internal audit department will produce better, more effective audit reports if it goes beyond text-based reports and uses some of the readily available graphics software. Audit findings often gather much more management attention when presented in a format that combines text with appropriate graphs. That same software can also be used to prepare

Figure 14.8   Audit Report with Graphics

As part of our annual safety compliance review at all 81 ExampleCo branches, internal audit again reviewed branch compliance with various government procedures. We assessed the current status on five levels:

   A: Branches where required safety warning signs were not properly posted.

   B: Branches lacking required hazardous material procedures.

   C: Branches lacking safety training programs.

   D: Branches with required safety equipment installed.

   E: Number of reported significant safety accidents.

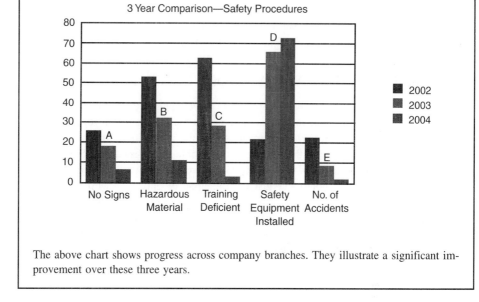

The above chart shows progress across company branches. They illustrate a significant improvement over these three years.

slides for audit-related presentations to management. There are many easy-to-learn micro-computer software tools available for graphics. These graphics can also be incorporated directly into the audit report's word-processing text. Figure 14.8 shows a chart of audit findings, developed from spreadsheet software, incorporated into the text of a sample audit report.

(e) INTERNAL AUDIT COMMUNICATIONS TOOLS

An internal audit organization has a variety of communication requirements. Auditors in the field may need to communicate preliminary reports back to audit management to obtain approval before auditee review meetings. Once they are back in the home office audit department, the in-charge auditors need to communicate their draft audit reports back to auditees for review. Finally, auditees need to communicate preliminary responses back to the in-charge auditor.

There are a variety of electronic tools available to assist in internal audit communications. Many organizations today have electronic e-mail systems used throughout their organization. Such systems typically have password controls to protect the integrity of messages. If such a system has been installed, the internal audit organization should consider using it for communication between the field and the audit department and for communications with auditees. It is only important that the auditor remember to archive or take copies of all e-mail messages for workpaper documentation purposes.

If the organization does not have a formal e-mail system, auditor microcomputers equipped with modems can often accomplish the same function. With one microcomputer in the audit department acting as a central node, field auditors can dial into that machine to send and receive messages. Workpaper findings can be communicated along with other audit communications. This approach will not work, of course, for communicating with auditees who do not have access to the same private system. Otherwise, an audit department e-mail system will increase communications with the field until such time that the internal audit department can become part of the overall organization e-mail system.

14-3 COMPUTER HARDWARE TOOLS FOR INTERNAL AUDIT

Although there have been references in this chapter to the use of the organization's central mainframe computer resources to automate the internal audit function, the most frequent reference has been to the auditor's use of microcomputers. Microcomputers and powerful software to operate on them have been available since the early 1980s. Machine capabilities as well as the features of available software are constantly changing. The internal audit manager should not select just one machine or approach with expectations that it will serve internal audit purposes for many years into the future. Rather, internal audit should develop an overall hardware strategy that will allow it to grow in the future.

This section gives some very limited guidance on the selection of microcomputer hardware for an internal audit department. There are numerous books and magazines that will provide much more detail on the capabilities of current microcomputer hardware. A local dealer or the end-user computing function in the auditor's organization is also a good source. The purpose of this section is to give the neophyte internal audit manager some guidance to ask the right questions when taking steps to acquire microcomputer hardware.

(a) INTERNAL AUDIT CENTRAL OFFICE MICROCOMPUTERS

Many of the opportunities for audit department automation discussed previously, such as planning and audit administration functions, require the availability of microcomputers in the audit department at all levels. There are a large number of brands of such machines available and virtually all use one of two operating systems. Many of the applications discussed above can be implemented on any such system.

The characteristic that distinguishes one type of microcomputer hardware from another is its operating system master program. The most common today are Microsoft's Windows operating systems, with Apple's Macintosh a distant second in popularity. Virtually all microcomputers today are designed to operate primarily on one or the other, although some have the capability to operate both. Windows and the Mac each have their own advantages, and it is not the purpose of this book to recommend one over the other for internal audit use. When making any initial decision, internal audit should research its needs and discuss this decision with members of the information systems organization to obtain guidance.

When selecting the type of equipment to install, the best choice for the internal audit department is to select a machine that follows any overall standard within the organization. This way, internal audit will be assured of better prices and improved support if there are problems. If there is no one system standard, internal audit should select equipment that is compatible with the departments where internal audit most frequently operates. In many organizations, this means using the same equipment as that in the controller's department. While systems are becoming increasingly generic, the use of the same style of equipment as is used in the majority of the organization will help internal audit with small problem-solving situations. If most other departments in the organization use the XYZ operating system and internal audit uses a fully compatible ZYX operating system, internal audit may receive responses along the lines of "it's a ZYX problem, not a XYZ problem."

While not all office microcomputers need to have the same configuration, some of the features that should be incorporated into one or more of the internal audit department's microcomputers include:

- *Expanded Memory.* Many of the first microcomputers were equipped with 640k (640,000) bytes or less of random access memory. Most new software today requires much more memory, and new machines should be configured with at least 16MB (16,000,000) of memory or more. Additional memory can be added through the introduction of memory chips.

- *Increased Hard Disk Capacity.* Hard disks are used to store both program and data files. An internal audit department planning to use one of the microcomputer-based, computer-assisted audit tools, as discussed in Chapter 12, should have hard disk of at least 200MB (200,000,000). Today, 2.0 gigabytes (2,000,000,000) or larger is common.

- *Better Graphics Capabilities.* Graphics capabilities refers to the resolution or number of dots per square inch used to display outputs on a computer monitor screen. Because the audit department will use its computers for flowcharting and other graphics presentation work requiring high-resolution screens, departmental machines should have strong graphics capabilities.

There are, of course, many other hardware features available. Internal audit management should discuss options with members of the information systems organization familiar with microcomputers, with internal audit professionals from other organizations, or with knowledgeable dealers. Internal audit management must realize, however, that the best and most current technology can become obsolete in only a few years. However, it is never a good idea to wait for something better because with each new introduction there still will be something better to come in the future.

(b) NOTEBOOK MICROCOMPUTERS FOR AUDIT FIELDWORK

Notebook-size portable computers have been subject to major technological improvements in recent years. Machines are now available that weigh five pounds or less; have full functions including hard disks, CD ROM drives, and modems; and are small enough to fit into a briefcase. An internal audit function with multiple remote locations within its audit universe should consider equipping field auditors with notebook computers. While it may not be necessary to assign a machine to each auditor, there should be at least one for each team. The features available with these machines are constantly increasing. The machine should be small enough to be easily carried to remote sites, have sufficient hard disk capacity and have an easy-to-read screen and easy-to-use keyboard. Some features, such as extended battery power, may not be needed if most internal audit fieldwork is taking place where regular power is available and where there are not many long air trips where auditors could work on board. Many of the newer portable machines are notebook-sized or even fit in the palm of the hand. However, these often have very small keyboards and may not be appropriate for efficient internal audit fieldwork.

The portable computer is a key component necessary to fully automate internal audit activities. Just as public accounting firms have achieved some major efficiencies with their portable computer financial or audit software, internal auditors should be able to achieve significant automation efficiencies through the use of portable machines equipped with productivity-improvement software.

(c) TELECOMMUNICATIONS AND LOCAL AREA NETWORKS

Freestanding microcomputers in the internal audit department and portable computers in the field should be linked together such that information can be shared. Office microcomputers can be linked together through a local area network (LAN), which will allow all machines to share some resources, such as large capacity storage server and laser printers, and to communicate with one another. One individual in the internal audit department should be designated LAN administrator, along with another as the backup, and one larger machine should be given overall control responsibility as the LAN server machine. Some of the operational logistics considerations for building an internal audit department LAN are the same as the control considerations for auditing a LAN. These are discussed in Chapter 16.

A computer equipped with a modem that can dial into another machine through a normal telephone line to transmit or extract data can be a powerful tool for sending report drafts from the field to headquarters or for downloading data from central databases. There are also some risks involved. Without proper security software installed on a microcomputer, files can be subject to improper access attempts. Chapter 19 discusses some of these controls.

14-4 AUDIT AUTOMATION SOFTWARE TOOLS

In addition to the variety of approaches and techniques discussed, there are many software products available today, with new ones constantly being introduced. Information about these software products is available through published reviews, discussions with other internal audit professionals, and discussions with information systems professionals within the organization. The internal audit department should consider its needs, experiment with several software products if appropriate, and select a set of software tools to automate the internal audit function. Although some internal auditors tried to write their own software in the early days of microcomputers, almost all have found that it is more efficient to use commercial package software.

It is beyond the scope of this book to suggest specific software products for internal audit automation. In addition, anything suggested may become quickly dated with ongoing new product introductions or improvements. However, the internal audit department that is beginning to automate its functions should select software products from a group of general categories.

- *Spreadsheet Software.* The electronic spreadsheet is perhaps the most powerful software tool available for internal audit automation. There are a variety of excellent competing products on the market. Internal audit should select a package that is compatible with others in the organization and that can easily be loaded into portable field machines.

- *Word-processing Software.* Word-processing software can be easily learned and used by auditors as well as by administrative personnel. The software should be able to import data from spreadsheet packages as well as graphics, and should have a good grammar, spelling, and style checker to allow internal audit to create better, more consistent audit reports.

- *Graphics Software.* Many spreadsheet and word-processing software packages have the ability to make simple line and bar charts. However, internal audit often has a need to produce more formal graphics for presentations to management or for inclusion in audit reports. Specialized software packages provide this capability.

- *Database Software.* Database packages can often perform many of the same functions that spreadsheets can accomplish. In addition, they are useful for tasks such as maintaining repositories of data (such as files of auditee responses to audit findings) for subsequent follow-up. These database capabilities go beyond those found in spreadsheet software.

The above four categories of software will initially fulfill the needs of an internal audit department starting automation. These, as well as some other productivity tools, are often sold as an integrated software "suite." Various specialized software packages, such as tools to transport data from other applications to spreadsheets and statistical-analysis software, can be added later. Many of the above types of software also have additional features that will satisfy other needs. For example, some word-processing packages have built-in telecommunications functions, while many spreadsheet packages have fairly good graphics capabilities.

Provided the auditor has selected appropriate brands of software, many packages have the ability to "talk" to each other. For example, spreadsheet data can be downloaded to a word-processing package in order to incorporate tabular data in a formal report. Database data can be communicated to a spreadsheet package as well as spreadsheet data to the database software. To obtain help in selecting software with the appropriate features, the auditor should consult the end-user or any information center support function in the organization, if such a function exists. The auditor will want to research other users or dealers to determine that the software selected has the appropriate compatibility features.

14-5 IMPLEMENTING INTERNAL AUDIT AUTOMATION TOOLS

In order to realize the efficiencies that can result from automation, the internal audit department needs to take some properly planned steps, including an audit automation implementation plan. Without proper planning, staff training, and quality assurance, automation efforts may end in failure. When developing an automation implementation plan, internal audit should consider some of the planning controls that they look for when performing operational reviews of software implementation projects in other areas of the organization. For example, Chapter 18 discusses audits of new computer applications under development. The auditor, in that situation, looks for certain plans and other documentation. Internal audit should follow these same or similar steps when implementing automated procedures within the audit department.

(a) AUDIT AUTOMATION PLANNING AND BUDGETING

Internal audit management needs to prepare an overall audit automation plan and a budget for all expected costs, including hardware, software, training, supplies, and other costs. The first step to building such a plan, however, is to decide on an automation strategy. This will typically require some reading, attendance at professional conferences, discussions with peers in other internal audit departments, and discussions with others within the organization. An analysis of the types of audits typically performed as well as the time spent on various aspects of those audits will also be of help. Based on these discussions, internal audit management can identify opportunities for potential audit automation.

The internal audit automation strategic plan is a document that the director of internal auditing can present to management for preliminary approval and a funding request if appropriate. Of course, the plan should also be reviewed with key members of the internal audit staff as well as with other members of the organization, such as the information systems group. This plan may be modified with experience or new product introductions over time. However, it should provide internal audit with a map to automate the function.

Once the plan has been developed, a next step is to review various hardware and software products to determine which can potentially satisfy requirements. Sometimes, information gathered during this step may cause some overall strategy changes. For example, internal audit management may find that the organization is primarily tied to a mainframe computing strategy built around one vendor and that required software tools are not available. This may require internal audit to modify its strategy or to seek upper management permission to use different computing tools. In most instances, however, the automation strategy will be consistent with other automation requirements within the organization.

Internal audit may want to experiment with various hardware and software tools before making final decisions. Given the prospect of a large computer-related purchase, some dealers or vendors will lend hardware and provide demonstration copies of hardware or software tools. Internal audit management should assign one or more members of the internal audit staff to help in this research project. This will involve evaluating automation products to determine whether they appear to meet requirements. The main consideration should be compatibility with other hardware and software in the organization, functionality to achieve automation goals, and efficiency to allow them to be easily used by staff auditors.

Based on these experiments, internal audit management should prepare an implementation plan for its internal audit automation project. This plan should take into account the time required to install equipment, including any network cable requirements. It should also consider time required for staff training in the use of the equipment and software.

The plan should then be presented to management for their final approval. It is often helpful if the information systems department as well as the organization's external auditors are fully aware of the plan and are in agreement with its assumptions.

(b) AUDIT AUTOMATION IMPLEMENTATION AND STAFF TRAINING

Any aspect of the audit automation plan, such as workpaper automation or the use of portable computers, may represent a very major change for the internal audit department in the manner in which it performs its audits. In order to be successful, internal audit needs to establish new procedures and to train auditors in the use of the new tools. The new internal audit procedures, in particular, may represent major changes to the organization. For example, auditors who have been accustomed to paper-based records may now have to rely on machine-readable documents with less reliance on printed documents.

An internal auditor at a supervisor level or above should be given the responsibility for implementing the automation project. This usually involves several key elements, as follows.

- *Software Customization.* The new software will often work much better if there has been some streamlining of its functions for the audit staff. For example, a menu screen can be created to help guide auditors to the correct program selections.

- *Hardware and Software Training.* While tutorial programs are available for many software packages, hands-on, instructor-led classes are usually best for first-time introductions. Some of these training considerations were discussed in Chapter 9.

- *Internal Audit Procedure Revisions.* In order to take advantage of the automation tools, procedures need to be revised in many areas. These may range from transmitting project hours through the new automated timekeeping system to correctly use the new statistical software.

- *Solving Field Automation Problems.* No matter how good the training or comprehensive the procedures, auditors in the field will undoubtedly encounter many areas where they have problems or questions regarding the new software. An audit automation coordinator should be assigned to take the role of a help desk. This role may involve using the coordinator's own knowledge or acting as a central source to call vendors with any questions.

- *Software Revision Control.* The coordinator should be responsible for maintaining revision control over the software loaded onto portable field computers and on office machines. When vendors supply updates, the coordinator should ascertain that they are installed in a timely manner. This type of revision control is similar to the types of revision controls that internal audit would expect to find when reviewing purchased computer application packages, as discussed in Chapter 17.

- *Backup and Retention Procedures.* Perhaps the most important role of the coordinator is making sure that auditors are properly backing up files and programs. Procedures should be established for all users of the systems to back up their files on a regular basis. The coordinator should take the responsibility for determining that these backups are taking place. Arrangements should be made to store certain copies of audit documentation in a secure off-site location as well.

The objective of internal audit automation is to introduce efficiencies to the internal audit organization and to improve the overall quality of audit procedures. Internal audit management should closely monitor audit automation efforts to determine areas where procedures can be improved or where different software tools may be required. This is an ongoing effort where all staff members should have an opportunity to provide their input to this process. As discussed in Chapter 33, a review of audit automation efforts should be included in the periodic internal audit quality assurance review.

14-6 FUTURE DIRECTIONS FOR INTERNAL AUDIT AUTOMATION

With increasingly powerful and easy-to-use software tools, areas for potential internal audit automation are constantly increasing. For example, we are beginning to see effective expert systems applications to aid in internal audit decision support. There will almost certainly be many more software products available in the future. Internal audit automation will also be aided by staff members with increasing computer literacy skills. The typical college graduate today has a general familiarity with tools such as microcomputer spreadsheets.

This chapter has discussed approaches to automating internal audit functions. While there are many ways to implement such a program, internal audit management needs to begin an ongoing program of identifying opportunities for automation, keeping informed of the tools available and what others are doing, and implementing audit automation tools where these appear to improve audit quality and efficiency.

CHAPTER 15

Audit Reports and Internal Audit Communication Techniques

15-1 INTRODUCTION: REPORTS AND COMMUNICATIONS

The development and issuance of reports are perhaps the most important phase of the total internal auditing process and the major means by which persons both inside and outside the organization are apprised of internal audit's work. Audit reports constitute the most enduring type of evidence about the professional character of internal audit activities and allow others to evaluate this contribution. Effective audit reports, of course, must be supported by high-quality audit fieldwork, but that same audit fieldwork can be nullified by poorly written or prepared reports. Preparation of clear and effective reports are a major concern for internal auditors at all levels, from the director of internal audit—who is ultimately responsible for the total internal auditing program—to staff members of the auditing team who did the detailed work and wish to report their audit results.

Good reporting is more than just report preparation and appearance. Audit reports should reflect the basic philosophy and related concepts of the organization's total audit approach, including its underlying review objectives, supporting strategies and major policies, procedures covering the audit work, and the professional performance of the audit staff. Internal audit reporting provides a good opportunity to integrate total internal auditing efforts and to provide a basis for overall appraisal.

While the audit report is a major means of communication, the modern internal auditor will not be effective if communications with the rest of the organization are limited to published reports. Communication with other members of the organization must be effected daily through interviews during the course of fieldwork, closing meetings when audit findings are first presented, meetings with senior management to apprise them of the results of audits, and through many other contacts throughout the organization. All members of the internal audit organization must be effective communicators in both their written and spoken words.

This chapter will discuss the purpose and presentation styles of audit reports, including various formats and methods of presenting the results of audit work to management and other members of the organization. We'll discuss relations with people and basic communication techniques.

15-2 PURPOSE AND TYPES OF AUDIT REPORTS

Internal audit reports have several important functions, both for the auditor and management, which should always be considered when completing audit work and communicating the results. Whether it is a formal written document circulated to many organizational levels or an informal or verbal presentation at the end of the audit fieldwork, internal audit reports should always have four basic objectives:

1. *Disclosure of Findings.* The audit report should summarize and outline the conditions observed or found, both good and bad, and can thus be viewed as an information device for management concerning the operations of the organization.

2. *Description of Findings.* Based upon the conditions mentioned above, the report should describe what, if anything, is wrong with the conditions found, as well as why it is wrong.

3. *Suggestions for Corrections.* Audit recommendations serve as a framework for action for correcting the conditions and their causes, with an objective to improve operations.

4. *Documentation of Plans and Clarification of Views of Auditee.* The auditee may wish to state mitigating circumstances or provide a clarification of issues for any reported matters in disagreement. Depending upon the report format, this is also a place where the auditee can formally state plans for corrective actions in response to the audit findings and recommendations.

This four-step process—(1) what is wrong, (2) why is it wrong, (3) what should be done to correct the matter, and (4) what will be done—forms the basis of virtually all audit reports. Internal auditors should always keep these four steps in mind when drafting complete audit reports and the separate audit findings that provide the basis of audit reports.

(a) FOR WHOM IS THE REPORT PREPARED?

An internal audit organization can spend considerable time in preparing its audit reports. Nevertheless, internal audit can often lose sight of who is the report reader. At first glance, the answer seems very simple: It is being prepared for management. But management exists at all levels, including the management of the organizational component reviewed and management at the higher levels to which the component is responsible. Each management group has special needs and interests, and the question becomes one of which needs best serve overall organization interests. In more specific terms, the question comes down to what internal audit's respective responsibilities are to the auditee versus to the auditee's bosses.

The auditee—that is, the organizational staff and its responsible management group who was audited—will be motivated by a combination of organization and local entity interests. Direct auditee management knows that its ultimate welfare is closely related to the total organization welfare but knows also that these rewards are largely determined by its own performance. This perception of performance is a combination of the operational results achieved and how upper-level management thinks the directly responsible managers actually contributed. In everyday parlance, local management strives to look good to upper-level management. What this all means in terms of internal audit is that the local managers want help, but want it on a basis that does not discredit them with more senior level management. Ideally, they might like to have internal audit work with them on a private consultant basis but not report finding any ''dirty linen'' to headquarters senior management.

Internal audit tries to help local management do a more effective job and knows that in order to identify control problems and recommend potential solutions, internal audit must have the full cooperation and a near-partnership relationship with local management. However, this cooperative attitude can place pressure on internal audit if it is asked to pull its punches in audit reports with copies that go to senior management. Internal audit may feel that its reported concerns will be implemented sooner if it does not criticize local management too harshly in its published audit reports. While providing service to local management, internal audit's obligations reach all the way up to the audit committee of the board of directors.

As a starting point for resolving these potentially conflicting demands, both management groups must be provided with a comprehensive understanding of each other's needs and also of the desire of internal audit to serve both. There is a need to increase the level of tolerance and flexibility for each. A second way to minimize the problem is through raising the level of findings and issues considered sufficiently significant to warrant inclusion in an audit report. This way, internal audit can eliminate many of the more minor matters that should be, and can be, finalized at the local level without involving higher-level managers. Third, a more determined joint effort is needed between the local managers and internal audit to work out needed follow-up actions during the course of the audit. The general effect of all these actions is to push internal audit more toward the ''service to local management'' concept and away from being viewed as a headquarters spy. This approach must continue to recognize that internal audit still has an important final reporting responsibility to senior management and the audit committee.

15-3 FORMAL WRITTEN AUDIT REPORTS

Although we have discussed audit reports as almost a single concept, internal audit reports can take a variety of different formats and styles. Some of these are formal printed reports of internal audit's concerns and recommendations following the four objectives discussed previously. In some instances, management may place restrictions or constraints on internal audit that may limit it from preparing effective audit reports. For example, a senior member of management may declare that all audit reports must be one page or less in size. This may be a difficult but not insurmountable challenge, and internal audit should attempt to meet that requirement. If it proves too great of a problem given certain internal-control situations that need to be explained, the director of internal audit should meet with senior management to discuss the problem or, if necessary, should bring the matter to the attention of the audit committee of the board.

Audit results can be reported in a wide spectrum of formats. Later, this chapter will describe a standard written audit report format in some detail. This is a multipage document that describes the audit work performed, the situations found, internal audit's recommendations, and published management responses to those findings. Some of the less formal and more abbreviated alternative means by which internal audit can report the results of its work include:

- *Oral Reports.* In some situations, internal audit may want to report the results of its work and any recommendations on an oral basis. To some extent this will always occur when the audit team assigned reports the results of their work as part of a closing conference at the end of audit fieldwork. In other cases, an oral report may be the result of emergency action needs. An oral presentation may also be a prelude to a more formal written report. To some extent there may always be oral reporting as a means of supplementing or explaining written reports, especially when individuals being served have special needs. Oral reporting, therefore, often serves as a useful and legitimate form of audit reporting.

An oral report has a major limitation as there generally is no permanent record. The auditor may think that local management agrees to correct some problem, but management may not really say that. As a result there are more likely to be later misunderstandings unless detailed, contemporaneous notes are taken for workpaper documentation or the meeting is taped. However, the appearance of a tape recorder usually causes distrust. Oral audit reports should be used carefully and not in lieu of later written reports.

- *Interim or Informal Memo Reports.* In situations where it is deemed advisable to inform management of significant developments during the course of the audit, or at least preceding the release of the regular report, internal audit may want to prepare some kind of interim written report. These reports may only pertain to especially significant problems where there is a need for prompt corrective action, or the reports may be a type of progress report. A memo report should be used, at a minimum to describe the results of an oral presentation, as discussed previously. Figure 15.1 is an example of an interim memo which was released to record the results of an oral presentation and to call local management's attention to a potential audit finding. The material discussed in this example report will eventually be included in a more formal audit report discussing the total results of an internal audit.

- *Questionnaire-Type Audit Reports.* The usual procedure is that some kind of a written report is prepared at the completion of an individual audit assignment. One alternative type of final report is built around the format of a completed questionnaire. This format works best where the scope of the audit review deals with fairly specific procedural matters, and usually at a fairly low operational level. This type of report usually has a fairly limited range of overall usefulness. Figure 15.2 is an example of a questionnaire audit report. It is perhaps best used as an educational tool to inform management of internal audit's concerns.

- *Regular Descriptive Audit Reports.* In most audit assignments, the work should be concluded with the preparation of a formal descriptive audit report. The exact form and certainly the content of such written reports will vary widely, both as between individual audit assignments and individual internal audit departments. They may be short or long. They may be presented in many different ways, including the extent to which quantitative or financial data are included. Problems and alternatives associated with this regular written type of audit report are discussed in more detail later in the chapter.

- *Summary Audit Reports.* Some organizations issue an annual or more frequent report summarizing the various individual reports issued, and describing the range of their content. These summary reports are often primarily prepared for the audit committees or other members of senior management. Figure 6.4 shows an example of this type of summary report as part of the Chapter 6 discussion on serving the

Figure 15.1 Informal Memo Format Audit Report Example

MEMO

To: Sam Sneed, Purchasing Dept.

From: Samantha Smith, Internal Audit

Date: Thursday, October 10, 20XX

Subject: Audit of Purchasing, Interim Report

ExampleCo Internal Audit has completed its review of the Heavy Iron Division purchasing function. Our fieldwork was started on September 5 and included visits to the Heavy Iron offices and additional testing as we found necessary. We have concluded our fieldwork for this review as of October 5, and this memo represents an interim audit report covering said fieldwork. A formal audit report, requiring your plans for corrective actions, will be released after we complete certain additional audit work, including purchase order confirmations.

We generally found internal controls over Heavy Iron purchasing function operations to be adequate. However, we also found certain internal control weaknesses requiring additional Heavy Iron Division investigation and correction actions. Although these comments may be subject to revision when we complete all of our audit work in this area, we have initially identified the following control weaknesses.

- Despite frequent, multiple use of certain parts, blanket purchase orders allowing for price/volume discounts are not used.
- There appears to be little effort to seek bids from multiple vendors for some common commodities. Multiple vendors might yield lower prices.
- Security over purchasing files is weak. Although the function is largely automated, many product lines still use substantial paper records. There is no effort to protect those records during nonbusiness hours.
- The automated purchasing system needs an upgrade or overhaul. The system now in use is over 15 years old, has poor documentation, and cannot interface with several other key systems.

These comments are very preliminary and will be discussed in greater detail, along with our recommendations for corrective action, in our draft audit report to be issued after the completion of our final audit work. If there are any questions during the interim, please contact me.

Figure 15.2   Questionnaire-type Audit Report Example

ExampleCo Heavy Iron Division
Audit of Purchasing, October 29, 20XX
Summary of Internal Control Strengths and Weaknesses

1. Are departmental operating procedures current and adequate?	**YES**
2. Are purchasing requirements properly specified by requesting departments?	**YES**
3. Are multiple bids sought for all regular, non-custom purchases? *Multiple bid procedures are regularly ignored.*	**NO**
4. Do requesting groups regularly send specifications with purchase requests?	**YES**
5. Are blanket purchase orders used for volume use parts? *Although procedures exist, blanket purchase order procedures are often ignored.*	**NO**
6. Have dollar-based authorization limits been set for all P/Os and are they followed?	**YES**

Note: The above is only a sample of what would be a much larger ''Yes'' and ''No'' type of audit questionnaire report. Additional sheets could be attached to better explain ''No'' control weakness responses.

audit committee of the board. Summary reports are especially useful to top-level managers who do not actively review the individual reports. In a larger internal audit organization, summary reports also allow the director of internal auditing to see the total reporting effort with more perspective, and on an integrated basis.

(a) APPROACHES TO PUBLISHED AUDIT REPORTS

As discussed previously, the form and content of regular written audit reports will vary widely. The operational auditing chapters in this book (starting with Chapter 22 on accounting systems and controls through Chapter 30 on financial management) all cover topics that might be the subjects of formal internal audit reports. For example, Chapter 24 on purchases, receipts, and electronic data interchange describes operational controls in these areas.

Figures 15.3 and 15.4 are examples of introductory pages of a formal audit report covering a review of the purchasing function in a manufacturing organization. This report's introductory page or pages should have the following elements:

- *Report Addressees and Carbonees.* An audit report should always be addressed to one person, usually at least one organizational level above the auditee, as well as to a selected list of carbonees, as determined by internal audit. The latter will include the auditee manager who was responsible for the audit responses included in the report, members of senior management, and other interested persons such as the partner in charge of the external audit team.

- *Title of Report and Objectives of Review.* A brief, definitive title tells the reader what is contained in the audit report and also will be useful for various summary reports. Similarly, an audit report should have a brief but clear statement of the objectives of the review.
- *Audit Scope and Date of Fieldwork.* Usually included with the statement of audit objectives is some abbreviated information on the general scope of the audit and the approximate date of the audit fieldwork. A statement that a given report covers a review of the ''purchasing function for electronic components at the XYZ division'' will lead the report reader to expect a different report than a statement that the audit covered the overall purchasing function.

Figure 15.3   Formal Audit Report Introductory Page

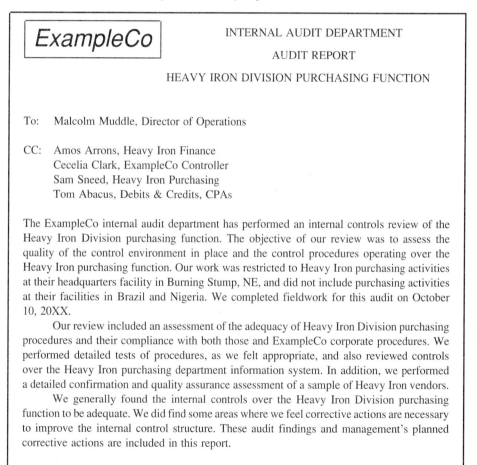

ExampleCo   INTERNAL AUDIT DEPARTMENT

                                          AUDIT REPORT

                    HEAVY IRON DIVISION PURCHASING FUNCTION

To: Malcolm Muddle, Director of Operations

CC: Amos Arrons, Heavy Iron Finance
          Cecelia Clark, ExampleCo Controller
          Sam Sneed, Heavy Iron Purchasing
          Tom Abacus, Debits & Credits, CPAs

The ExampleCo internal audit department has performed an internal controls review of the Heavy Iron Division purchasing function. The objective of our review was to assess the quality of the control environment in place and the control procedures operating over the Heavy Iron purchasing function. Our work was restricted to Heavy Iron purchasing activities at their headquarters facility in Burning Stump, NE, and did not include purchasing activities at their facilities in Brazil and Nigeria. We completed fieldwork for this audit on October 10, 20XX.

Our review included an assessment of the adequacy of Heavy Iron Division purchasing procedures and their compliance with both those and ExampleCo corporate procedures. We performed detailed tests of procedures, as we felt appropriate, and also reviewed controls over the Heavy Iron purchasing department information system. In addition, we performed a detailed confirmation and quality assurance assessment of a sample of Heavy Iron vendors.

We generally found the internal controls over the Heavy Iron Division purchasing function to be adequate. We did find some areas where we feel corrective actions are necessary to improve the internal control structure. These audit findings and management's planned corrective actions are included in this report.

Samantha Smith
Internal Audit, Nov. 7, 20XX

Figure 15.4   Summary Format Report Introductory Page

ExampleCo	INTERNAL AUDIT DEPARTMENT

AUDIT REPORT

HEAVY IRON DIVISION PURCHASING FUNCTION

To: Malcolm Muddle, Director of Operations

CC: Amos Arrons, Heavy Iron Finance
        Cecelia Clark, ExampleCo Controller
        Sam Sneed, Heavy Iron Purchasing
        Tom Abacus, Debits & Credits, CPAs

The ExampleCo internal audit department has performed an internal controls review of the Heavy Iron Division purchasing function. Our review was completed on October 10, 20XX. We generally found the internal controls over the Heavy Iron Division purchasing function to be adequate. We found certain areas where controls could be improved. The Heavy Iron purchasing function has agreed to initiate corrective actions to improve those controls.

Samantha Smith
Internal Audit, Nov. 7, 20XX

- *Locations Visited and Timing of Audit.* Because of potential timing delays in wrapping up audit reports due to a whole range of reasons, time may pass between the time of the fieldwork and the final published audit report. The cover page of a report should clearly state when the audit fieldwork was performed and also should mention the locations visited.
- *Audit Procedures Performed.* A brief paragraph describing the audit procedures performed is often very helpful to the report reader. This information is particularly useful if internal audit has performed some special testing procedures in order to arrive at its opinion.
- *Auditor's Opinion Based upon the Results of the Review.* An internal audit report should *always* have some fairly general assessment of the overall adequacy of the controls in the area reviewed. For example, the opinion statement might be worded as follows.
  - "We found the controls in the area reviewed to be adequate except for . . ."
  - "We found that most controls were good and were operating as installed . . ."
  - "We identified significant control problems in the areas reviewed. Our findings . . ."

    The statement of the auditor's opinion can take many forms. However, it generally points to the detailed audit findings and recommendations, which follow these first pages of the full audit report. Figure 15.5 contains some examples of

Figure 15.5 Audit Report Findings and Recommendations Examples

I. *Blank Purchase Orders*

Blanket purchase orders would allow the organization to receive supplies of frequently used common parts without the need to issue a separate purchase order for each commodity replenishment. Company purchase department policies allow and even encourage the use of these blanket orders, at buyer discretion. We found that several buyers of small commodity parts have never used the blanket purchase order concept. They generally advised us they thought they could get better prices by negotiating each purchase separately.

We reviewed the pattern of purchase orders for several frequently purchased commodities and found opportunities for potential savings. For example, separate purchase order arrangements with different vendors were made for certain electronic switch units. Vendor prices varied up or down by about 5% over the nine months reviewed. A blanket purchase order might have provided a guaranteed price, based on total aggregate quantities purchased.

Recommendation. A program of blanket purchase orders should be initiated for frequently used commodity type parts. Price versus total quantity agreements should be negotiated with key supplying vendors. The purchasing department should monitor the cost savings and other benefits from the program.

II. *Professional Travel Expenses*

The company travel policy specifies that all employees should work with the company travel agent to find the lowest airfares for business travel. In addition, policy specifies that travelling employees should always attempt to be at their business destinations by 12:00 noon on the first business day of their trips. We found that this travel policy is largely ignored by employees in certain company departments. For example, almost all air travel arrangements for employees of department 22-88 were made individually by employees, ignoring the travel agent. Expenses were charged to corporate charge cards with no evidence of efforts to seek minimal air travel cost. Similarly, in our review of travel records over the past six months, we found over 5% of employees ignored the lowest-cost recommendation of the agent and selected higher-cost air tickets. Frequently, these same employees made air travel arrangements that brought them to their destination late on the first day of the trip.

Recommendation. Policies should be strengthened to encourage least-cost air travel. A revised policy statement should be developed and issued to all travel-mode employees, emphasizing the need for lowest-cost travel. When employees do not accept the travel agent's least-cost recommendation, the fact should be printed on the air ticket travel itinerary included with the employee's expense report. Departmental managers should be assigned first-tier responsibility to reduce their employee's air ticket travel expenses.

III. *After-Hours Office Security*

Company policy specifies that all office employees should clear their desks of all reports, memos, and other business papers at the end of the business day and also should sign-off from their desktop computers. In a review of office areas on three successive evenings during the period of our fieldwork, we found numerous desks covered with work materials and numerous computer systems still left running. These practices compromise company security due to the possibility of unauthorized persons viewing materials left in desk areas.

Recommendation. All employees should be reminded of after-hours desktop policies. The security department should visit office areas from time to time in the evening. Persons not in compliance with after-hours policy should be reminded with a desktop security department note.

other auditor findings, including an opinion statement. No one form is "right" and the audit department's style should be consistent with management's wishes.

Internal audit reports often follow one of several different common approaches. Given the type of organization, its overall management style, the skills of the internal audit staff, and many other factors, each has certain merits as well as disadvantages. Internal audit wants to communicate what it did, what it found, and what needs to be corrected. All professionals are faced with a barrage of paper documents as well as electronic communications, which they are asked to read, understand, and act on. Internal audit wants to provide the readers of its reports with enough information to explain the issues but not so much that members of management will place the report on an office credenza with little more than good intentions of reading it later. Without enough information, the reader may not know if a serious problem or other issues requiring action exist given the summarized report format. In an overly detailed report, the reader may miss significant points given the large volume of the materials presented. Some approaches might include:

- *Audit Reports with "Encyclopedic" Coverage.* Some internal audit reports strive to present a great deal of information about the activity that has been reviewed. Their objective is to provide an in-depth reference source to the report user. The information can be of a historical nature or pertain to the current situation. It may cover operational practices and results or may deal with financial information. An example here might be a review of a complex finance-oriented automated system.

- *Description of the Audit Procedures Performed.* Audit reports sometimes provide a great deal of information about the audit procedures actually performed. Audit steps may be described in some detail, as might the scope of actual verification and testing. To some extent, this audit report coverage overlaps with statements of procedures contained in audit procedural manuals, as discussed in Chapter 10. In this case, the question may be how interested the reader of the report is in these procedural details and what purpose it really serves. Most users of audit reports are willing to rely on the competence of internal audit for those technical dimensions. These detailed descriptions are only of value when internal audit needs to describe a complex procedure such as the decision logic forming an opinion based upon audit sampling. On balance, such detailed accounts of technical auditing procedures should be excluded, or at least minimized.

- *Detailed Explanations of Audit Findings.* Some internal audit reports go into fairly voluminous detail about the results of the various audit efforts. Although the coverage here may look impressive, it is doubtful whether a large number of audit findings or an extensive amount of detail describing the findings serve a sufficiently useful purpose. With a very large audit report "book," the reader may be turned off and thus miss important materials. Audit reports should give a sufficient amount of information about audit findings and allow the reader to understand the issues involved.

- A *Highly Summarized Report.* In the other extreme, some internal audit departments release very summarized reports that only provide information that internal audit has reviewed the topic area of a report and found no control exceptions of significance. These reports often do little more than state that internal audit has reviewed an area and found some minor items, which were not included in the report even though they might be interesting to a reader. Unless these summarized reports support a longer, more detailed report (as discussed later in this chapter), they are not effective for most internal audit reporting needs.

- *Focus on Significant Issues.* The more common format—often the best—is one that focuses only on significant issues. "Significant issues," as used here, are those that have potentially important bearings on policies, operational approaches, the utilization of resources, employee performance, and the results achieved or achievable. More senior organization managers are interested primarily in problems that are of such a nature and scope and they typically wish to be informed and given the opportunity to contribute to solutions. If these significant issues relate to completed actions, the issues would have to be still more significant to merit the reporting. The advantage of this focus on significant issues is that senior managers can get the information they need without wading through excessive detail. This is the type of audit report approach that the modern internal auditor should try to follow, and is discussed later in this chapter, with an example shown in Figure 15.8.

The actual audit report format and method of presentation will vary from one organization to another. Once, audit reports were formally typed documents. Word-processing software on microcomputers has changed the style and format of many reports today. Audit reports can now be issued with interesting typeface fonts, with supporting graphics, or even in a totally electronic format over a proprietary intranet. The use of graphs and charts will be discussed in the following paragraphs on audit report findings. However, no matter what the basic format, an audit report should always contain the elements of what internal audit did, when they did the work, and what they found. A very key portion of the internal audit report should be the auditor's findings and recommendations.

(b) ELEMENTS OF AN AUDIT REPORT FINDING

In the course of a review, the auditors assigned to the project may encounter exceptions to many of the areas to review as outlined in the established audit program. (See Chapter 10 on how to prepare an audit program.) Those audit program exceptions are the subject of the audit findings. For example, the audit program may direct the auditor to review a sample of travel expense vouchers to check that they are properly approved and to verify that the reported expenses are consistent with published travel policies. If internal audit finds that some of the sample selected are not properly approved or are not in compliance with travel policy, internal audit will have one or more potential audit findings to report.

Auditors will encounter a large number and variety of these exceptions in the course of almost any review. Some may be important—such as the discovery of significant numbers of vouchers submitted for payment lacking proper approval signatures. Others may be relatively minor—such as the discovery of an employee who reported $25.50 for meal expenses when policy requires that expenses must be less than $25.00. While the latter is a violation of policy, senior management may not be too interested in an audit report that is filled with these relatively minor infractions. This is not to say that an internal auditor should look the other way at such "minor" internal control infractions. Such smaller internal control exceptions should be discussed with management at the conclusion of fieldwork (discussed in Chapter 10) but they may not necessarily be the type of issues to report to senior management through a formal audit report. Only if there were a large number might internal audit consider reporting them in a summarized finding.

An internal auditor must analyze the bits and pieces of information gathered during a review to select those for inclusion in the final report. At the conclusion of the audit fieldwork, internal audit should always ask itself whether there was sufficient information to develop an audit finding, and, if so, how these matters of audit concern should be presented. Options for the latter range from informal discussions with local management to a formal presentation in the audit report.

Audit report findings presented in a common format allow the reader to understand the audit issues easily. No matter what the nature of the audit work or the finding, readers should be able to scan an audit finding and quickly decide what is wrong and what needs to be corrected. While important to both the internal auditors who drafted a finding and to report readers, audit report findings are sometimes not that well constructed. In our years of experience in reviewing draft internal audit reports, we have seen some very poor examples of audit findings. They often make the report reader question what the problem is, and make he or she wonder why they should be concerned. Good audit report findings should contain the following:

- *Statement of Condition.* The first sentence should usually summarize the results of internal audit's review of the area of concern. It can give a comparison of ''what is'' with ''what should be.'' The ''what is'' summarizes the condition or appraisal made by internal audit based on the facts disclosed in the review. The purpose is to capture the report reader's attention. Examples of audit report finding statements of condition include:
    - ''Obsolete production equipment is being sold at bargain rates and in a manner that does not follow fixed asset disposition policies.''
    - ''The backup and contingency plan for the new customer billing system has not been tested and does not follow organization security standards.''
    - ''The ABC division work-in-process inventory is not correctly valued according to generally accepted accounting principles.''
- *What Was Found.* The finding should discuss both the procedures and the results of those procedures. Depending upon its complexity, the finding can be summarized in little more than one sentence or may require an extensive discussion describing the audit procedures. This ''what was found'' statement can be as simple as, ''Based upon a sample of employee expense reports filed for fourth quarter 200X, the preferred organization rental car agency was not used for over 65% of the expense reports reviewed.'' Often, this portion of the finding will be much more extensive, as internal audit describes the procedures performed and what was found. Examples can be found in the Figure 15.6 sample audit report findings.
- *Internal Audit's Criteria for Presenting the Finding.* The finding should always have a criteria, or a statement of ''what should be'' to be used in judging the statement of condition. Without strong criteria there cannot be an audit finding. Criteria vary according to the area audited and the audit objectives. The criteria may be the policies, procedures, and standards of an organization.

    In some instances, internal audit must develop the criteria. In an audit of

Figure 15.6 Audit Report Preparation Steps

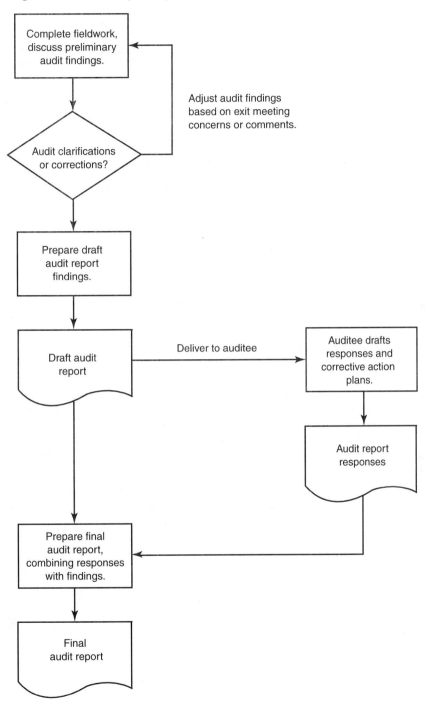

the effectiveness of some procedure, there may not be preestablished targets or measurements which can be used as indicators, and standards may be couched in general or vague terms. Internal audit should consider the following:

- *Criteria of Extremes.* Clearly inadequate or outstanding performance is relatively easy to appraise. However, when performance moves closer to the average, it becomes more difficult to judge. Internal audit can sometimes use extreme cases of inadequate performance as a criteria for the report finding. This might cause internal audit to state that some observed condition was ''almost as bad as . . .''

- *Criteria of Comparables.* Comparisons can be made between similar operations or activities, determining their success or lack of success and causes for the differences. While it is never good to state specifically that Department A is X% worse than Department B, the report might compare the conditions found to average or typical conditions throughout the organization.

- *Criteria of the Elements.* In some cases, internal auditors incorrectly state their performance criteria in such broad terms that it is impossible to evaluate the reported condition. This is the type of criteria that states ''all managers should make good decisions.'' While ideal, we all know exceptions exist regularly. The reported measure should be broken down on a functional, organizational basis, or by elements of cost related to specific activities.

- *Criteria of Expertise.* In some cases, internal audit may find it useful to rely on other experts to evaluate an activity. These experts may be outside the organization or may be part of the audited organization's staff. This type of supporting reference often strengthens the overall audit finding.

- *The Effect of the Reported Finding.* Internal audit should always consider the question of ''How important?'' when deciding whether to include an item in the audit report. Internal audit must weigh materiality—if the finding is of no significance, it may not be a finding at all. Once the decision has been made to include it as a finding in the audit report, the effect of the reported condition should be communicated. Findings that will result in monetary savings or that affect organization operations and achievement of goals are always of special interest to management.

- *The Cause or Reason for the Audit Deviation.* The answer to the question ''Why?'' is especially important to management when reading an audit report. The reasons for a deviation from requirements or standards or policy should be explained as well as possible. Identifying a cause for the condition gives a basis for taking needed management action.

- *Internal Audit's Recommendation.* Audit report findings should conclude by recommending appropriate corrective actions. This is the audit finding conclusion ''What should be done?''

Although internal audit's description of objectives, audit procedures performed, and the opinion of the controls as a result of the review are all important elements in an internal audit report, members of management will evaluate the quality of the report on the basis of the reported findings and recommendations. If any facts reported in an audit finding are incorrect, no matter how close to the real truth, the auditee will typically challenge the credibility of the overall audit report. Any misstatement can place the entire audit report into question. Internal audit should *take extreme care* to report its audit findings factually and accurately. Otherwise, a significant amount of good internal audit work can be ignored.

Care should also be taken in developing strong, meaningful, and realistic recommendations. The recommendations should generally give some consideration to the costs and benefits of various alternative recommended action. Of course, if the audit finding is highlighting a potential violation of the law, the recommendation should always be to take prompt and complete corrective action.

Figure 15-6 contains examples of audit report findings and recommendations in an audit report format. In addition, Chapters 21 through 30 (on operational auditing topics) contain other examples of audit findings and recommendations. An internal auditor should consider these examples when developing a report.

(c) BALANCED AUDIT REPORT PRESENTATION GUIDELINES

An important part of internal audit's efforts is to evaluate the efficiency, economy, and effectiveness by which management has accomplished its objectives. This involves the disclosure of both satisfactory and unsatisfactory conditions disclosed during an audit. While conditions needing improvement should always be described, communications here should minimize the description of audit findings in totally negative terms. Internal audit should strive to encourage management to take needed corrective action and to produce results. An internal audit report cannot be fully successful if the auditee is not receptive to the results of the audit. Also a report with findings that just talk about what was right provide little help to management. Consequently, internal audit should adopt a positive reporting style that is balanced with a mixture of favorable as well as appropriate unfavorable comments, always presents matters in perspective, and emphasizes constructive rather than just negative comments.

To provide a level of balance, internal audit must sort through the various positive and negative data gathered during the course of a review and ask itself the question, "What should be the type and extent of favorable comments to be reported as a result of this audit?" The answer cannot be laid down in precise terms. The same criteria used in identifying significant findings can be used to report items considered significant based on standards of performance. For example, assume that an audit objective was to evaluate the timeliness of filling purchase requisitions. Comments in a report finding should relate to the organization's ability or inability to fill purchase requisitions in a timely manner and ignore other unrelated issues. Some techniques to provide balance are:

- *Provide Audit Reports with Perspective.* Internal audit should avoid the temptation to cite only those factors that support internal audit's conclusions and to ignore those that distract from it. Perspective is always added when listing the monetary effect of a finding as well as the value of the entire account under review. A $1,000 error sounds much more severe when it is part of a $100,000 account than it does for a $10,000,000 account.

  The report finding should disclose, as appropriate, the total monetary amount audited or recorded in relationship to the total value of errors encountered. The significance of the finding is made evident by this procedure. Also, when deficiencies are disclosed in only part of the area examined, balance will be added to the report by identifying those areas examined that did not contain deficiencies. This practice should be in accordance with an internal audit policy of disclosing accomplishments as well as deficiencies.

- *Report Auditee Accomplishments.* Since the evaluation process involves weighing both satisfactory and unsatisfactory aspects of the auditee's operations in light of the audit objectives, mentioning the auditee's accomplishments in improving controls or correcting errors together with the noted deficiencies or aspects in need of improvement can add much to the usefulness of the audit report as a management tool. The auditee's accomplishments should be disclosed in the summary of the report when the conclusions of the audit may be affected by the significance of the accomplishments, and in the findings when a detailed disclosure of the accomplishments is desired or necessary.

- *Show Planned Actions.* In situations where the auditee has taken, or has made plans to take, corrective action prior to the completion of the audit, the audit report should disclose this fact. In addition, other steps taken by the auditee in an attempt to correct a reported deficiency may not be so obvious but nevertheless should be considered as a positive reportable action. For example, the auditee may have contracted with an outside consultant to help implement the internal controls needed in a computer system covered in an audit report. Such arrangements should be included in the report along with those control weaknesses.

- *Report Mitigating Circumstances.* Mitigating circumstances generally consist of factors relating to the problems or conditions discussed in the audit report over which management has little or no control. Since these factors lessen management responsibility for the condition, they should be reported as part of cause. Mitigating circumstances, for example, may include the very short time frame in which a program was required to be implemented, business conditions requiring immediate changes, or a lack of adequate funds for adding personnel or other resources to accomplish objectives.

- *Include the Audit Responses as Part of the Audit Report.* The auditee's response to a finding may contain information that provides additional balance to an audit report. In addition to planned corrective action, the auditee may indicate other related accomplishments or cite additional facts and other circumstances. In instances where agreement has not been reached on the finding or recommendation, the auditee should be given the opportunity to explain the basis for nonoccurrence.

- *Improving Audit Report Tonal Quality.* The use of positive and constructive words and ideas rather than negative and condemning language will give a positive tone to the report. Audit reports should avoid phrases indicating that the auditee ''failed to accomplish,'' ''did not perform,'' or ''was not adequate,'' and should state audit report ideas in a positive and constructive manner. Table 15.1 contains a few examples of how negative opening statements in an audit report can be rephrased to a more positive and constructive tone. Similarly, negative titles and captions should be avoided since they do not add to the finding and may even misrepresent the actual situation. Thus, a negative-sounding title for a finding such as ''Inadequate Controls over Company Cash Controls'' might be replaced by ''Cash Controls Improvement'' or ''Cash Collection Procedures.''

Table 15.1   Audit Report Negative and Positive Statement Examples

Negative Audit Findings	Positive Audit Findings
1a. We found that controls in the area were generally poor.	1b. We identified areas where controls need improvements.
2a. Little management attention has been given to keeping documentation current.	2b. The documentation was not current and other priorities have prevented it from being updated.
3a. The failure to reconcile these accounts was caused by a lack of management attention.	3b. We observed that these accounts had not been reconciled for several past periods.
4a. Documentation was either out of date or nonexistent.	4b. We found only minimal current documentation in this area.
5a. The new inventory system is poorly designed.	5b. The inventory system has some major control weaknesses. More attention should have been given to its design.
6a. This failure to protect passwords could result in a management fraud.	6b. Poor password controls are a weak internal control.
7a. No attention has been given to protecting stockroom inventories.	7b. Better controls should be established over stockroom inventories.
8a. The responsible manager did not seem to understand company procedures in this area.	8b. Training in the use of these procedures needs to be strengthened.
9a. The department failed in several of its training program operations.	9b. Several opportunities exist for strengthening controls in training program operations.
10a. The budgetary system was not adequate to assist management in the control of project funds.	10b. The establishment of a proper budgetary system would assist management in the control of project funds.

These comments are not meant to suggest that all audit reports should be sugar-coated and that internal audit should never make strong critical statements about auditees. An audit and the subsequent audit report can often be a very critical process where internal audit investigates an area that perhaps has not received much management attention. If internal audit finds serious problems in the area reviewed, it should clearly identify problems that might be significant unless prompt corrective actions are taken. When possible, however, internal audit should give credit where due and discuss either positive or mitigating circumstances as would be appropriate.

15-4 AUDIT REPORTING CYCLE

During the early stages of an audit, it is often desirable to develop a framework for the final report, filling in as much of it as possible. Information and statistics on the area to be audited can be gathered during the survey stage and included in the audit workpapers, discussed in Chapter 11. This process will assure that needed information is obtained early in the audit, and will prevent delays in the final report-writing process. In addition, the objectives and scope of the review should be defined clearly at the start of the audit. These serve as useful guides for the audit staff in planning and carrying out the audit assignment. As findings are developed and completed, they can be inserted in the proper sections of the report, together with any comments by the auditee.

The completed audit report is just one step—though a very important one—in internal audit's overall process of evaluating and commenting on the adequacy of internal controls in order to serve management needs. The audit report process starts with the identification of findings, the preparation of a draft report to discuss those findings and their related recommendations, the discussion of the audit issues identified with management along with the presentation of the draft report, the completion of management responses to audit report findings, and the publication of the formal audit report covering the area under review. Figure 15.7 outlines these critical phases for the preparation of an audit report. Although a given internal audit department may alter some of these steps slightly to modify its own needs, this generally should be the process necessary to issue an appropriate internal audit report.

As findings are developed, the internal audit team in the field should review them with members of auditee management, soliciting ideas as to their validity. Possible causes for the audit finding should also be discussed and additional information gathered to prove or disprove the potential audit condition. In some instances, organization personnel will assist in obtaining information to develop the findings. They will often provide useful feedback as to whether internal audit's facts are correct or whether they are on the right track. Areas of disagreement can be pinpointed and resolved. Discussing findings with organization personnel at a staff level has another benefit: It helps to get agreement and encourages implementing actions. When agreement is reached, internal audit may be able to limit the amount of detail included in the audit report finding, thus shortening the writing process and the audit report.

(a) DRAFT AUDIT REPORTS

Once the audit fieldwork has been completed and internal audit has discussed its proposed audit findings with the auditee, a draft audit report should generally be prepared. We have used the term ''generally'' since sometimes a draft report will not be necessary if a special report is to be made to management. In other cases, internal audit should prepare a report draft with their proposed findings and recommendations along with a space for management responses. The draft is then sent to the manager directly responsible for the area audited, who responds and outlines the corrective actions to be taken. Internal audit will then combine these auditee responses with the original report header pages and the draft findings and recommendations to produce the final audit report, as is shown in Figure 15.8.

The closing meetings and the draft report are important steps intended to validate the adequacy and accuracy of the reported findings and the soundness of the related recommendations prior to the release of the final audit report. While the major foundation for this validation is the audit work performed by the internal audit staff, work needs to

Figure 15.7 Audit Report Critical Phases

A.   Development of Finding Outline

A.1   Determine if there is sufficient support to warrant the findings.
A.2   Review to determine where additional evidence may be needed.
A.3   Ascertain that the causes and effects of findings are considered.
A.4   Determine whether there is a pattern of deficiencies requiring procedural changes or whether the findings are an isolated case.
A.5   Review plans to assure that audit budgets are revised as necessary to assure the adequate development of findings.

B.   Preparation of First Draft

B.1   Review findings for adequate development.
B.2   Ascertain whether the findings are stated in specific rather than in general terms.
B.3   Assure that figures and other facts have been checked to the working papers.
B.4   Review working papers supporting all findings for adequacy of support and disclosure of items of significance.
B.5   Check for adequacy of tone, punctuation, and spelling.
B.6   Ascertain whether there is sufficient support for the expression of opinion or whether a qualification or disclaimer is needed.
B.7   Determine whether the cause, effect, and recommendations are adequately developed.
B.8   Discuss methods of improving content and writing style with subordinates.

C.   Discussion with Management

C.1   Determine whether management was aware of the problem and was taking corrective action.
C.2   Find out management's reasons for the conditions.
C.3   Ascertain whether there are facts or mitigating circumstances of which the auditor was unaware.
C.4   Determine management's ideas on how to correct the conditions.
C.5   Assure that management is aware of all significant items that will be present in the report.
C.6   Assure that efforts are made to obtain agreement on the facts and conditions.

D.   Preparation of Final Draft

D.1   Ascertain that all prior recommendations for changes in report have been made.
D.2   Assure that management's viewpoints have been adequately considered.
D.3   Determine that the report is well written and easily understood.
D.4   Ascertain that summaries are consistent with the body of the report.
D.5   Assure that recommendations are based on conditions and causes stated in the findings.
D.6   See that management's viewpoints are fairly stated and adequately rebutted, if necessary.
D.7   Review report for use of graphics, tables, and schedules to clarify conditions presented.
D.8   Assure that auditors who wrote the findings agree with any changes made.

E.   Closing Conference

E.1   Assure that management has had an opportunity to study the final report.
E.2   Attempt to obtain agreement on any points of difference.
E.3   Consider any suggestions for changing content of report, including specific wording.
E.4   Obtain current plans for follow-up action from management.

Figure 15.7   *(Continued)*

F.   Issuance of Final Report

F.1   Assure that final changes are made in accordance with the closing conference.
F.2   Check report for typographical errors.
F.3   Review report for a balanced presentation, with positive comments included on results of audit when applicable.
F.4   Make final reading of report for content, clarity, consistency, and compliance with professional standards.

Figure 15.8   Complete Audit Report Example

April 20, 20X2   Report No. X2-36

Mr. Bruce R. Weston, General Manager
Bright Products Division
The Wonder Corporation

Dear Mr. Weston:

The corporate audit department has completed an operational review of the internal control structure for the Bright Products Division engineering organization. Bright Products engineering has a FY 20X2 budget of $13,000,000 and is responsible for technical research, product design, and development of the Whatzit product line. As of March 30, 20X2, engineering had 1,018 employees, of which 916 were direct.

The objective of our review was to evaluate the controls over equipment resource planning and utilization, compliance with policy, and the effectiveness and efficiency of the current plan of organization. Our audit included, but was not limited to, reviews of the following.

• General organization controls over engineering projects
• Controls over company utilization of capital equipment
• Controls over the accuracy of the reporting of indirect labor charges
• Departmental expenses, including a review of travel expense reports

This review covered operations during the period January 1 to December 31, 20X1. The review was made by Roger G. Wilson and his assistant, Connie Rodriguez, during the period February 13 to March 31, 20X2.

Our review found that the Bright Products engineering department is well managed, with generally good controls over its resources. However, we found that controls over capital equipment inventory should be strengthened. Our audit findings and Bright Products Division's plans for corrective actions are summarized below.

The internal auditing department wishes to express its appreciation for the very fine cooperation received during the review by the divisional management and personnel.

Respectfully submitted,
Charles W. Reiber, general auditor

Figure 15.8   *(Continued)*

Findings and Recommendations

Capital Equipment Inventory

Capital equipment is not under proper administrative control within the Bright Products engineering organization. The Equipment Capitalization Report, maintained by property accounting, is not used by the engineering organization on a regular basis. Although engineering has responsibility for the assets assigned to them, they have not taken a capital equipment inventory of that equipment for over one year.

We selected 50 units from the most current Equipment Capitalization Report and found the following:

- Three units with an original capitalized value of $119,402 could not be located during our fieldwork. One of these was found after the release of our draft report.
- Nine units were found to have no capital equipment serial number identification tags.

The cause for these expectations is the lack of sufficient capital equipment inventory verification procedures and the failure to consistently use serial number identification tag procedures.

Recommendations

Engineering should utilize the existing property accounting reports to better control its capital equipment. All section managers installing engineering capital equipment should be reminded of the need to properly install identification tags on all newly installed equipment. In addition, engineering should take a full wall-to-wall inventory of its capital equipment and schedule period limited inventory reviews on an ongoing basis.

Management Responses

Copies of the Equipment Capitalization Report will be circulated to responsible managers on a regular basis. Procedures have been issued to remind engineering managers of the need to review that report and to assure that identification tags are properly installed.

A full inventory of installed capital equipment will be taken in June 20X2. Procedures will be developed to regularly cycle-count installed capital equipment.

be supplemented by certain types of review and confirmation involving auditee personnel—including, ultimately, auditee senior management. The benefits of this supplementary validation are twofold. First, this provides a cross-check on the accuracy, completeness, and quality of the audit work. Important facts may have been overlooked or erroneously interpreted. There may also be other factors affecting the particular matter that are known only to certain people. The exposure to the auditee thus provides an important check on whether the findings and recommendation will stand up under later scrutiny. The second benefit is to help promote a partnership relationship with local management. The opportunity for this kind of participation creates both a cooperative spirit and a commitment to working out adequate solutions.

While the above-mentioned type of validation should go on during all stages of a review, one of the most important ways this is effected is through the presentation of the draft report to auditee management. Depending upon the nature of the audit objectives and the complexity of the audit findings, the draft report can be presented at either the closing conference at the end of the fieldwork, just preceding the departure of the field audit personnel, or delivered to the auditee after the completion of the fieldwork. Strategies for the timing of the draft report delivery include:

- *At the Exit Conference.* Most audits are too complex or there may be too many final questions or clarifications to allow draft audit reports to be delivered at the time of the exit conference. This strategy typically only works for compliance-type audits of smaller field or branch locations where the recommendations are to correct a less significant local compliance problem, such as mispriced goods at a retail branch.
- *Before Departure of the Field Audit Team.* Here, the audit team has discussed its concerns with local management in a formal exit conference and then prepares the draft report, including any additional comments or clarifications that may result from that conference. In most situations, this approach is more realistic than a strategy of presenting the draft report at the time of the exit conference. However, the pressure to wrap up the audit work and ''get home'' may cause the audit team to take shortcuts in their desire to complete the field engagement. This strategy again works best with relatively simple audit assignments.
- *After the Completion of Fieldwork.* With this strategy, the audit team has its exit conference but returns to the office to draft the audit report over the next few days or even weeks. Many internal audit organizations find this approach works best. Audit management has an opportunity to review the field team's work and to make adjustments, as appropriate, to the draft audit report. The risk here is that the internal audit team responsible for the review will be pulled in other directions and will not complete the draft audit report in a timely fashion.

Audit exit or closing conferences include members of the audit group and the local management responsible for the area reviewed. At the conference, major findings and proposed recommendations are reviewed and, to the extent that an agreement has already been reached between audit and local organization personnel on particular matters, an opportunity is provided to inform responsible management in the area reviewed and to secure further agreement on audit findings and recommendations.

The closing conference provides internal audit with a major opportunity to confirm the soundness of the audit results and to make any necessary modifications to the audit report draft as justified. This is also a major opportunity to demonstrate the constructive and professional type of service internal audit can provide. These meetings, although sometimes contentious, can be a major means for building sound partnership relations with the auditee. The objective should be to get as much agreement as possible so that the audit report can indicate the completed actions.

In many situations, the draft report is forwarded to the local management for their review and comment prior to the finalization of the report. Local management and the actual auditees will typically be given a limited amount of time to review this draft report, to suggest changes to its overall tone or to specific findings, and to prepare their audit responses. While internal audit should encourage auditee management to request changes to the draft report, the emphasis should be on the substantive issues in the draft report rather than on its wording.

Internal audit should request formal responses within perhaps 14 days after the receipt of the draft report. Although this is a relatively short time period given the time that the audit team spent on its fieldwork and draft report preparation, auditee management should be in a position to develop a rather rapid response since they are aware of the findings and suggested recommendations from the exit conference. However, both internal audit and auditee management should try to operate in the same general time frame. That is, if internal audit spends an inordinate amount of time preparing their draft report, they should give auditee management a greater amount of time to prepare their audit report responses.

The submission of draft reports to auditee management at a later stage has merit through the demonstration of genuine consideration for the auditee. However, internal audit should work with auditee management to avoid excessive delay in finalizing the report. A major part of the effectiveness of the report is the extent to which it is issued promptly.

(b) AUDIT REPORTS: FOLLOW-UP AND SUMMARIZATION

Once management has submitted its audit report responses, internal audit should combine these responses with its draft findings and recommendations to release the final audit report. This report will be addressed to management at least one level above auditee management, with copies to other appropriate officers of the organization. An example of such a brief but complete audit report is shown in Figure 15.8. While many other potential areas for operational audits are discussed in later chapters, this shows a representative audit report.

Once the final audit report has been issued, internal audit should subsequently schedule a follow-up review to ensure that needed actions based on the audit were actually taken. In some cases, management may request this procedure. While the desirability of follow-up action in itself is very clear, questions can be raised whether this is the proper responsibility of internal audit, and whether such action by internal audit will undermine the basic responsibilities of the managers in charge of the particular activities. Although standards call for follow-up reviews, they can put internal audit more in the role of a policeman, which could conflict with its ongoing partnership relationship with the auditee. In many organizations, therefore, internal audit plays a limited specific role after the audit report has been released, such as making itself available to respond to questions, and to review again the situation at the time of the next scheduled audit in the area.

Many organizations have adopted an intermediate type of approach where the coordination for audit report recommendation follow-up is placed in the hands of another office—usually within the controller's organization or some more neutral administrative services group. The corrective actions are then initiated by the responsible line or staff manager, but responses are made to the coordinating group. If there are undue delays in dealing with the recommendation, the coordinating office can issue a follow-up status report. Under this approach, copies of these responses can also be supplied to internal audit for information, or internal audit can maintain a liaison with the coordinating group. There is no single best answer as to how this follow-up effort should be handled, but on balance it seems best to subordinate internal audit's formal role in it. Internal audit's help can always be requested on a special basis, either by the coordinating office or by individual managers. In addition, any lack of action can be highlighted at the time of the next scheduled internal audit review.

Internal audit has a responsibility to produce audit reports that are readable, understandable, and persuasive. The objective is to issue reports that will command the attention of the managers who have the responsibilities for the various operational activities, and to induce them to take appropriate corrective action. A secondary objective is for reports that will build respect for the internal auditing effort. Internal audit reports should be released with attention given to the following 10 criteria:

1. Professional tone
2. Accuracy
3. Courtesy and tact
4. Consideration to auditees
5. Persuasiveness
6. Clear sentence structures
7. Logical paragraphing
8. An appropriate choice of words
9. Good grammar and spelling
10. Physical processing and binding

Internal audit receives a final payoff in its knowledge of the actions taken by auditees based upon the internal audit report recommendations. A combination of internal audit technical skills and the ability to communicate results to people in a way that will best assure their acceptance and active support are elements of good audit reporting. The importance of this part of internal audit's work underlines the need for the internal audit director to give audit reports careful attention. It means especially that the director should be actively involved in the report process, and all levels of the internal audit staff should think in terms of ultimate report needs. In this connection, the problems of report development should also be given proper attention in internal audit training programs. The reports become a statement of internal audit's credentials when reports are subsequently circulated, referred to, and implemented. Audit reports are usually the major factor by which the reputation of an internal audit department is established.

15-5 EFFECTIVE AUDIT COMMUNICATION OPPORTUNITIES

Communications are an important element of every phase of internal audit activities. Internal auditors communicate with others through formal audit reports, through face to face encounters such as in audit fieldwork or meetings, and through a wide range of other formal and informal communications. When there is a misunderstanding or conflict on an audit assignment or when the auditor's recommendations are not correctly understood, a subsequent analysis of the difficulty usually points to some type of communication problem. Internal auditors should always keep in mind that communications with people are a basic ingredient of almost every type of audit activity. All auditors, and internal audit managers in particular, should understand how to maximize job satisfaction, improve communications, and handle organizational conflicts.

(a) MAXIMIZING JOB SATISFACTION

Job satisfaction comes first from expected things such as reasonably pleasant working conditions, fair compensation (including reasonable benefits), and qualified supervision.

Because these satisfactions are *expected,* they are not major motivating factors to employees. If they are *not* provided, however, they can be a major source of irritation and dissatisfaction. The second kind of job satisfaction comes from higher levels of self-expression and self-fulfillment. Included here would be the assignment of greater job responsibilities, more authority, the opportunity to learn and develop, the opening of broader career opportunities, and being given greater freedom to achieve results without burdensome restrictions. This second kind of job satisfaction is achieved through strong managerial competence in its planning, organizing, administering, and controlling activities, and in the way it provides resources. Employees typically take pleasure in being part of an organization that is well managed, as evidenced by its above-average reputation, profitability, and growth. They also associate such organizations with offering expanded opportunities for qualified people.

At lower organization levels, efforts to provide maximum job satisfaction are often called ''job enrichment.'' The worker in an automotive assembly line who attaches a small part as the partially assembled car moves down the line provides a classic example of a job that can be boring and potentially disturbing. Job enrichment comes when a worker is given other duties that provide some variety and that expand the nature and scope of responsibilities. Unfortunately, there are limitations to that job enrichment because some cost savings are more often directly dependent on automated production processes.

When a worker joins to some extent in the planning of the work and in the development of policies and procedures by which that work is actually accomplished and administered, the potential benefits can affect both employer and employee. All levels of the organization can benefit through the input that comes from experience and firsthand exposure to actual operations. Management benefits from the greater commitment of employees, and the employee benefits because of greater job satisfaction and a basis for claiming the rewards of any resulting greater productivity.

Participative management can be practiced successfully in connection with all phases of the management process—planning, organizing, providing resources, administering, and controlling—especially in connection with making key decisions about goals, policies, and procedures. At the same time, there must be a continuing awareness of the problems. If a participative management effort is perceived by the lower-level subordinates as being superficial—for example, when views submitted are not fairly or adequately considered—then the entire managerial approach can do more harm than if never attempted. Other limitations include the lack of available managerial time and the need to withhold certain vital information. Internal auditors should keep participative management concepts in mind when making audit recommendations and when organizing their own internal audit organization efforts.

The establishment of proper standards for the rewards and related penalties is an essential part of the management of people. The rules governing those rewards and penalties must be defined, properly interpreted, and administered throughout the organization. Internal auditors need to recognize the importance of these standards in human relations and the need that they be administered in a manner that demonstrates genuine concern and fairness to all participants. Because of the sensitive nature of any human relations system of rewards and penalties and the varying objectivity of individuals in evaluating fairness, there are bound to be differences of opinion and some resulting dissatisfaction surrounding any system. Individuals will tend to judge the system in terms of the impact on themselves, and their criteria will be the fairness of the system as designed and as administered.

(b) EFFECTIVE COMMUNICATIONS

Effective communication both on a person-to-person basis and with larger groups in the organization is a key component to internal audit success. The modern internal auditor should have a good understanding of some of the problems associated with effective communications and an understanding of how to cope with those problems. Situations continuously arise in the operations of an organization when two individuals need to communicate with each other. These include giving an oral instruction to a staff auditor, discussing an operational problem during an audit exit meeting, counseling a subordinate, interviewing a prospective employee, or conducting a staff performance review. All of these situations involve differing personal relationships, but consist of a continuing two-way flow of messages that follows a definable technical model, as outlined in Figure 15.9.

That model can be portrayed as follows: The sender is the first speaker who has a message, which must put it into some kind of a code, symbols, or words that can then be transmitted by voice or via some other channel. The symbols are then decoded by the receiver. When the receiver replies, a similar process takes place as the message flows back to the first speaker. An internal auditor should understand this process in order to identify the kinds of problems that can distort or actually prevent effective communications. These problems affect all steps in the Figure 15.9 model and include:

- Not giving proper consideration to the power relationship of sender and receiver. Communication with a line supervisor will be different than with a senior officer.

- Ignoring temporary emotional stress by either the sender or receiver. An audit exit meeting can often turn into an emotional situation unless the internal audit communicator takes care to consider potential emotional stress.

- Not properly evaluating the capacity of the recipient to receive and understand the message. If internal audit encounters a severe control problem in a technical area in the course of its work, it must be communicated properly.

- Use of words that can have multiple meanings and which therefore can convey unintended meanings. We have discussed this problem previously in our discussion on preparing audit reports. This is all the more critical in verbal communications.

Figure 15.9   Sender and Receiver Communication Model

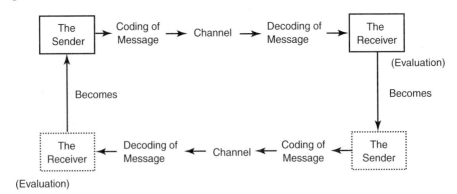

- Undue haste in the transmission of messages that undermine clarity and/or credibility.

- Temptations of the sender to satisfy personal needs, thus inducing emotional resistance and blocks. Often an internal auditor will be viewed by others as having a personal agenda. Others quickly recognize this and communication may become blocked.

- Failure to build needed foundations for the core message and related bad timing. Internal audit concerns are not effectively communicated when they are just thrown in the lap of the auditee.

- Lack of clarity or conviction because of a reluctance to cause the receiver dissatisfaction. While an internal auditor must build a case to describe a concern convincingly, the auditor should never mince words to avoid describing a problem situation. The internal auditor should always understand and clearly communicate a control concern.

- Impact of nonverbal actions such as tone of voice, facial expressions, and manner of communication. In some parts of the world, a crossed leg with the sole of the foot pointing to the listener can be viewed as an extreme insult.

- Not giving consideration to the perceptions and related feelings of the recipient. Auditors should try to understand how messages will be received and decoded by their receivers.

All of these problems are part of the larger need for an internal auditor to put him- or herself in the receiver's perspective and to consider how a message will be received. (This is sometimes referred to as "empathy.") When done with sensitivity and judgment, the result is a foundation for effective two-way conversation. The communicator must do everything practicable to understand how the receiver thinks and feels and then to communicate in a manner that gives all possible consideration to that knowledge. While the communicator often has conflicting higher-priority needs that prevent fully satisfying the receiver, it is still important to have a good understanding of the total communication process in order to make choices that are most consistent with overall organizational welfare.

Both parties—especially the main activator—learn from the questions and comments made by the receiver in response to a series of messages. This is called "feedback." Part of effectively continuing two-way communication is the capacity to induce that feedback to the maximum extent so that the main activator has the best possible basis for determining whether managerial objectives are achieved. Different approaches may be necessary to induce and utilize good feedback.

A related component—listening—is important in order to utilize any feedback better and to demonstrate interest in the other person's views. Otherwise, the result can be to create an emotional response that significantly blocks the receiver's acceptance and understanding of the sender's intended message.

(c) CONFLICT AND ORGANIZATION CHANGE

People have varying needs that relate alternatively to competition, conflict, and cooperation. Traditionally, conflict has been viewed as destructive and hence undesirable. However, when properly administered, conflict can be useful in achieving organizational welfare. This does not mean that conflict cannot get out of control. Internal auditors need to learn to utilize conflict to the point where it is constructive and to control it when it threatens to get out of hand. To do this effectively depends upon a good understanding of people and a great deal of practical judgment.

Internal audit task and group responsibilities unavoidably generate situations that set the stage for competition and potential conflict. Individuals continuously compete in terms of job performance for the rewards of personal recognition, better jobs, and higher compensation. Organizational units similarly compete for recognition and resources, common services, and other management support. To a major extent, that competition should induce imaginative and sound thinking and high-level work performance. At the same time, the forces generated can be so intensive that the competitors seek any means to win, irrespective of the questionable propriety and legitimacy of those means. At that point, competition ceases to benefit the organization and appropriate corrective actions are needed. Management then has a challenge to exploit the benefits of competition and healthy conflict in a legitimate professional sense but to control the process to avoid excesses. (See Chapter 2 on ''Fundamentals of Control,'' which discusses management pressures that can cause members of the staff to take inappropriate actions.)

Internal audit becomes very much part of this set of competition and conflict concerns. In the course of their review, auditors often find themselves in conflict with various elements of an organization. This can cause auditees to lose a level of competitive standing within their organizations. Auditees may disagree with the audit team on just that basis. In the course of a review, conflict will occur. The effective auditor should use this conflict to communicate with management and convince it to take appropriate actions. However, the effective auditor needs to understand how to control that conflict.

Although the achievement of the immediate goal—that is, to win—is an important and desirable motivation, it is the responsibility of every manager to make subordinates understand that there are other things more important to the larger organizational welfare than that particular victory. Put in other terms, people need to understand that how one wins is more important than the fact of winning. These principles also need to be reinforced continuously by the rejection of approaches that are not in the common interest. This means that management and internal audit must both be continuously involved and alert. Internal audit should always watch for red flags that indicate potential problems.

When problem situations are observed, decisive actions may be necessary. Rules may be amended, particular individuals disciplined, personnel assignments readjusted, and the like. Ideally, conflict should not be allowed to develop to the point where these more dramatic direct actions are necessary. There is the managerial challenge to utilize this conflict but not to let it get out of control to such an extent that it is counterproductive. This requires good leadership qualities coupled with good judgment based on a proper understanding of people.

In the typical organization, there is a continuing need for properly balancing stabilization and change. On the one hand, management seeks stabilization through developing policies and procedures whereby operations are standardized to improve internal controls and to assure the best handling of recurring similar types of events. On the other hand, changing conditions call for amended policies and procedures. The problem is to find a proper balance between stabilization and needed change. This is complicated because the perception and resolution of needed changes are often very difficult and controversial—that is, the factors involved are usually hard to analyze and measure. Change must be effected by people with the required expertise, adequate funds, and strong managerial direction. One obstacle is that organizations often become used to the existing policies and procedures and tend to become biased in their favor, thus making them unaware of and unresponsive to need for change. Internal audit often encounters this when it recommends extensive policy or procedural changes. Additionally, people typically do not like to accept change even when the need for it is reasonably clear. Somehow, convenience tends to triumph over objectivity. This means that internal auditors often face a great deal of resistance when suggesting changes, irrespective of the real merits.

At the highest level, the need for change may involve new strategies, new business ventures, changes in products, or new supporting policies. Related changes may involve new organizational structure, relocation of plants, new production processes, or changes in people. Internal auditors often do not make recommendations for change at that level. While they certainly can recommend that an overall management strategy should be changed, more typically internal audit recommendations might cover the need for a new information system that involves drastic changes in the way operations are controlled, or, at a lower level, minor modifications in work assignments. In some cases, these changes involve only established habits or convenience, while others require more substantial adjustments. From our understanding of people, it naturally follows that there would be some built-in resistance to change ranging from minor attitudes to deliberate defensive action—including, in its most extreme form, sabotage. The managerial challenge is that when a decision involving change has been properly made, any resistance, whatever it may be, should be minimized, eliminated, or at least reasonably controlled.

When making their recommendations, internal auditors should understand how the organization will deal with the change. How can internal audit achieve needed change in a manner that will best serve higher-level organizational welfare? In all cases, the nature and scope of the different types of actions depend on the significance of the particular recommended change.

Chapter 2 discussed the problems of developing effective systems of internal control. Because individuals place such a high priority on their freedom of action, the design and implementation of controls is an area where human considerations are especially important. Since all managers to some extent are responsible for internal controls and at the same time are subject to them, the impact of recommended control improvements on people should be carefully considered. Perhaps in no phase of the management process is an understanding and consideration of people so critical.

15-6 UNDERSTANDING PEOPLE IN INTERNAL AUDITING

This discussion on human relations has focused on the interests of all managers in connection with their relations to each other, including both at a higher level and with subordinates. While all of this is of interest to internal auditors as a part of their review and analysis of internal controls, it should also be of interest as internal auditors manage their own subordinates. In addition, some unique and specific problems confront internal auditors in their activities. The overall burden all internal auditors carry is that they often have an image problem. To some extent, this image problem may be due to the term ''auditor'' as part of our professional title. That term is often thought of as focusing excessively on detail and compliance or control issues and is viewed as threatening. As has been discussed in earlier chapters, this image may have been earned in the past because of the manner in which internal auditors were once used in organizations. To some extent, the image has also resulted because some internal auditors today do not do enough through their audit work and mode of personal relations to build a better image.

The modern internal auditor faces some serious problems in changing this image. Internal audit is charged with certain protective-type responsibilities that tend to make other members of the organization see them in the role of an antagonist. Internal audit's total role goes far beyond the narrow role of providing protective service. The modern internal auditor is no longer the ''policeman'' as such or the person with the green eyeshade who buries himself in detail. Instead, the modern internal auditor is concerned with total organizational welfare at all levels and in relation to all organizational activities.

Internal auditors are specialists in analyzing and promoting the effectiveness of internal controls. The challenge is to broaden the image of internal audit as a profession serving total organizational welfare. In the course of its review activities, internal audit must demonstrate that it is part of an overall program mandated by senior management to meet organizational needs for both protection and maximum organizational benefits. Internal audit should focus on these objectives to emphasize its importance in terms of people relationships. At this point, major benefits can be achieved or hostile relationships established.

The benefits to the organization will include a better understanding of internal audit's role and the personal understanding by members of the organization that internal audit is concerned about their feelings. What is basic is that people have apprehensions about the impact of an audit and need, as far as is possible, to be put at ease. Internal audit often needs to go out of its way to establish good person-to-person relationships.

The overall importance of developing effective internal audit communication techniques and good human relations procedures cannot be overemphasized. When communicating through formal audit reports or face-to-face meetings, there must first be a recognition that people as individuals are important and continuously need to be considered as key factors in all organizational activities. Internal auditors need to strive to find the best possible balance between broader organizational welfare and accommodating to human needs.

In all aspects, communications and relations with people are continuing challenges that involve a kind of a target that is always moving forward. At the same time, internal audit's success in meeting that challenge provides one of the greatest available opportunities to serve the organization and to achieve its maximum welfare.

PART THREE

IMPACT OF INFORMATION SYSTEMS ON INTERNAL AUDITING

CHAPTER 16

Information Systems Operations Controls

16-1 INTRODUCTION

Auditors became involved with computers and data-processing controls as manual and punched card accounting applications were first installed on early computer systems. These early systems were often impressively installed in glass-walled rooms within corporate lobbies. Those early applications were not particularly sophisticated, and internal auditors unfamiliar with data-processing technology would ''audit around the computer.'' That is, the auditor might look at input controls procedures, applications outputs, and whether the inputs balanced to the output reports. The auditor would just go around the actual computer program processing procedures. In the early 1970s, a company called Equity Funding changed all of this. Equity Funding Corporation was a California-based insurance company that initiated a rather massive management fraud. Its computer systems were used for a portion of that fraud. Under management direction, fictitious insurance policy data was entered on computer files. Equity Funding's public accountants audited around the computer system, relying upon printed and output reports from those computer systems, and did not use procedures to verify the correctness of supporting computer programs and files. A massive fraud was eventually discovered. In the aftermath of the Equity Funding affair, organizations such as the American Institute of Certified Public Accountants (AICPA) and The Institute of Internal Auditors (IIA) began to emphasize the importance of reviewing data-processing operations and application controls. A new professional specialty, called *computer auditing,* was launched!

In those early days of business data-processing, most computer systems were expensive and considered to be ''large.'' Fairly standard sets of auditor control objectives and procedures were developed for reviewing controls. While many are still applicable for computer systems today, internal auditors must look at these information systems control objectives from a somewhat different perspective when reviewing controls in the modern computer environment. This chapter emphasizes controls over data-processing operations. The four chapters following cover other important areas of information systems controls. Chapter 17 discusses reviews of applications for both larger computer systems and for smaller, networked systems, often called client-server systems. Chapter 18 focuses on reviews of new applications under development and Chapter 19 covers systems security and systems contingency planning. Finally, Chapter 20 discusses new or evolving computer systems technologies and their impact on audit professionals.

In this chapter, we discuss three important areas of data-processing operations: Classic "mainframe" or "legacy" systems operations controls; a discussion of networked systems (ranging from personal microcomputers to the larger client-server systems) will follow; and will conclude by discussing controls over other areas of computer systems operations, such as systems programming and database administration.

Because information systems are such an important element of the control structure in the modern organization, all internal auditors should be familiar with information systems controls and not defer these controls issues to a computer audit specialist on the audit staff. While these specialists can provide significant contributions to the internal audit organization, all internal auditors today should have a good general understanding of information systems controls and their audit control procedures.

This chapter and the four that follow are adapted from the author's *Computer Audit, Control, and Security*.[1] These five chapters provide an introduction to information systems controls, a topic not included in earlier editions of this book. Readers seeking more information on control objectives and procedures over information systems are advised to consult the most current edition of *Computer Audit, Control, and Security* for more information.

16-2 MODERN, LARGER INFORMATION SYSTEMS ORGANIZATION

The UNIVAC I, the first successful business information systems computer, was introduced in 1951 and helped predict the results of the 1952 U.S. presidential election. It required a huge amount of physical space, weighed 15 tons, and cost $1.3 million (in 1950 dollars). Its central processing unit (CPU) had doors on both ends so a technician could walk through it to make any required repairs. A "bug" in those days referred to an insect that got into the CPU cabinet and perhaps blocked a relay tab. In contrast, a $1,000 personal computer system today has perhaps 50,000 times the memory and speed of the UNIVAC I—or more. Was the UNIVAC I a "large" computer system? In today's terms, although it was large, based on its cost or the floor space it occupied, with respect to its memory, speed, and functional capabilities, the answer is no.

The term *large* as it applies to computer systems becomes even more difficult today. Once described by their manufacturers as "minicomputers," some systems may appear to be "large computers" to an auditor as they will support a large variety of peripheral equipment such as multiple terminal processors, printers, and disk drives. The computer hardware may also be supported by a fairly large operations staff and will handle many varied processing tasks.

Different professionals each have their own definitions for a larger computer system. The technical programmer may define a larger computer system in terms of the central processor's internal design or architecture. Management may define the same computer system's relative size in terms of what the equipment cost and the size of the information systems staff necessary to support the system. Some auditors not familiar with computer systems may observe an older, or what is now called a legacy, computer system located inside a secure facility with a raised floor and, on that basis, will conclude that it must be large. This is particularly true if the auditor's experience is limited to small laptop or desktop machines.

---

[1] Robert R. Moeller, *Computer Audit, Control, and Security* New York: Wiley, 1989.

Auditors have typically been interested in the size of the computer system to be reviewed because it will impact internal audit's approach and the audit control procedures. This has changed with the rush forward of technology developments, and there is not always a direct relationship between machine size and audit complexity. Nevertheless, some of the controls that internal audit would expect to find in a very large computer center operation would not necessarily apply to a small business computer system. For example, a technical or systems programming staff, responsible for monitoring performance and maintaining a larger computer's operating systems, is often not necessary for a smaller and more modern computer system.

(a) EQUIPMENT CHARACTERISTICS OF LARGER INFORMATION SYSTEMS

The larger systems usually have some common characteristics, whether a classic IBM mainframe requiring a chilled-water cooling system or several interconnected UNIX file server processors. While all information systems internal control characteristics may not apply to every larger computer system, the following should help an internal auditor understand the characteristics of the larger business information systems.

- *Physical Security Controls.* A larger computer center with significant data files is usually located in a room with locked access controls and no windows to the outside. This security helps to protect the equipment as well as programs and data. Locked doors to the computer room prevent unauthorized persons, both employees and outsiders, from entering the area to pick up reports, to ask distracting questions of the operators, or to cause malicious damage.

  While all business operations are subject to fires, floods, or vandalism, a computer center has a particular vulnerability because the equipment can not easily handle these stresses. Because of the type and extent of data processed in the modern larger-scale computer system, systems operations should be located in unobtrusive locations and built to minimize exposure to fires, floods, or other acts of God. These controls are discussed further in Chapter 19, ''Physical, Logical Security and Contingency Planning.''

- *Environmental Control Requirements.* Specialized electrical power systems as well as dedicated air conditioning or water-cooling chiller systems are often necessary because miniature electrical components operating at full power generate a considerable amount of heat. Because of these special needs and because computer systems consist of multiple pieces of equipment connected by communications cables, larger systems are located in specialized rooms with dedicated environment monitoring controls and false floors that provide space for power cables and ventilation. Larger systems, vulnerable to electrical power outages or fluctuations are equipped with emergency power supplies that can smooth out power fluctuations or provide a source of emergency power to allow the computer system an orderly shutdown. Some systems may even be supported by independent generators to provide power over an extended period in the event of an outage.

  Weaknesses in environmental controls can potentially result in failures in the operation of key information systems applications. Internal audit should always be aware of control procedures in the area and make recommendations where appropriate.

• *Separate storage media libraries.* The storage or library areas for magnetic cartridges and tapes are typically adjacent to the computer equipment rather than on racks in the machine area. This separation provides extra protection for the magnetic media and for more efficient mounting and backup of tape cartridges. Automated tools are often used to schedule and call up cartridges for mounting as well as to write internal labels onto tape files and to schedule them for backup rotation. Earlier generations of magnetic media files are often rotated to another library storage facility so that, in the event of a fire or other disaster within the computer room facility, these key backup files can then be recovered for transfer to an emergency backup processing site.

• *Multi-Task Operating Systems.* Virtually all computers use some type of a master program or operating system to control the various programs run by the computer and other tasks such as reading disk files or supplying report data to a printer. Typically, these operating systems can run many programs during the same time intervals and can handle many other tasks. A multi-task operating system on a larger computer must be managed and usually requires specialized personnel, called systems programmers, to maintain the operating system.

• *In-House Programming Capabilities.* The smaller staff organizations may purchase the majority of their applications as packages from software vendors or have all of their systems supplied by an organization headquarters staff. Organizations with larger computer systems are supported by an in-house systems and programming department ranging in size from a group of perhaps several hundred employees or more to others with limited in-house programming capabilities. Programmers are different as well. Until the early 1990s, many used the COBOL language, but programmers today may only develop parameters for specialized purchased software packages or may do some custom work in languages such as C + + or JAVA. In-house programmers almost never write custom inventory control or payroll applications. A larger organization with its own programming and systems analysis staff should have a fairly formal systems-development methodology, or SDM, to develop and implement new applications. SDMs are discussed in Chapter 17. There should be specialized library files to control computer programs as well as technical documentation covering the programmers' work.

• *On-Line Telecommunications Network.* Virtually all modern systems have an extensive telecommunications network to support multiple on-line terminals, located throughout the organization, and connected either directly to the central computer system or to external networks. Telecommunications networks will be discussed later in this chapter. Chapter 19 discusses the need for specialized information security controls to prevent improper access attempts. The network may also require specialized technical personnel within the information systems organization to manage telecommunications.

• *Very Large or Critical Files.* Although a computer system may be rather small in many respects, it may have one or more applications that maintain critical data on very large databases or files. In older computer systems, these critical files often consisted of many reels of magnetic tape. Today, disk-oriented database management systems are used. Because of the criticality of such large databases or files, the computer system—whatever its actual hardware size—takes on characteristics of a larger system. The need for backup copies and the integrity of critical files is crucial to the information systems function. The organization should require strong file backup procedures and database administrators to help ensure the accuracy, integrity, and completeness of the database.

- *Input-Output Control Sections.* Some systems have an input-output control section to receive any batch input data (such as tapes mailed from remote sources), to distribute any outputs, and to schedule and set up production jobs. In the earlier days of information systems, when most production jobs were run in a batch mode, such control functions often balanced input batches to system outputs and resolved many problems. Today, users generally take responsibility for their own data, submitted through terminals in user areas with outputs transmitted back to them. Input-output sections may exist to receive any manually submitted transactions that are still processed in batch mode and to take responsibility for distributing key reports produced on data center high-quality laser printers, staging work and scheduling production jobs in the computer room. Specialized software is used to support this equipment scheduling.

- *Specialized Staff Positions.* The size of a computer system may be defined by all of the above measures. However, management may have staffed the information systems organization with other specialized personnel such as data security officers, telecommunications analysts, or quality-assurance specialists. When organized in such a manner, internal audit may want to structure their review procedures similar to those they'd use for a larger computer system.

The above characteristics, although not that specific or precise for the larger legacy system, should provide some guidance for internal auditors in determining the review procedures to be followed. There are many variations in what can be defined as a larger or smaller computer system. While internal audit's control objectives will remain essentially the same for both, control procedures will differ. Techniques for auditing smaller systems are discussed later in this chapter. If an internal auditor has doubts whether an information systems review should be tailored to a large or small system, the safest approach is to consider the system to be reviewed as a larger, more complex one.

(i) Classic "Mainframe" or "Legacy" Computer Systems. Larger information systems organizations typically have their own unique control characteristics. Although much as been published about the ''microcomputer revolution'' and the growth of small, networked systems, significant changes have also taken place over the years for larger, mainframe computer operations. For internal auditors, internal controls issues that were once frequent audit concerns are now an almost accepted part of large computer systems operating procedures. Other, newer control issues have now become part of the internal audit's review process.

In the early days of mainframe computer systems, an internal audit concern was that computer operators should neither have access to computer programs nor the knowledge to change them if they somehow gained access. Similarly, the reasoning was that if programmers could operate the equipment, they could improperly modify or run unauthorized programs. Checklists and audit programs were published that directed auditors to attest that, among other matters, computer operators did not program and programmers did not operate the equipment. Because of the complexities of modern, large information systems operating systems and the high production demands within the machine room today, this separation of duties generally exists in the larger organization, but it still can be a concern in the smaller organization or computer systems environment, as will be discussed later in this chapter. Of course, internal audit should always confirm there is an adequate separation of responsibilities within any information systems function.

There is no typical hardware configuration for the modern larger information systems organization. Often, the inexperienced auditor will be given a tour through a room filled with central processors, disk drives, printers, and other equipment and will complete the tour with little understanding of what was seen. Because IBM equipment is found in the preponderance of larger business information systems computer organizations today, an internal auditor will find most of the equipment to be colored blue because IBM has painted its equipment blue. However, a larger systems operations room can be configured similarly with Amdahl, Hitachi, or some other vendor's equipment. To the internal auditor unfamiliar with computer hardware, such an operations center will look about the same except that the equipment may be of a different color.

Because of the miniaturization of electronic components, the modern computer center increasingly takes less space than was previously required. The IBM larger legacy mainframe system is an example. Up until recently, these larger machines required water-cooling systems with a requirement for extensive plumbing. Advances in technology have all but eliminated the need for these elaborate, large, and expensive systems. In addition, there have been significant changes in the design of some computer peripheral components. Magnetic tape drives are now all but replaced, for example, by cartridges that are much smaller and have a much higher capacity. Disk drives are physically smaller but have considerably greater data storage capacity. Output printing is done on remote printers, although large, high-speed laser printers, which can replicate traditional paper forms and which operate at a very high speed, are now found in many computer operations.

An internal auditor should gain an understanding of the types of equipment in a computer center scheduled for a general controls review by requesting a hardware configuration chart from data center operations management. While internal audit will probably not be in a position to determine if the computer center has, for example, the correct models of disk drives, such a chart will indicate that management has done some planning in their computer hardware configuration. These charts are often filled with model numbers rather than explanations of the equipment. The internal auditor should always ask questions about the nature of this equipment.

While the number and type of tape drives, printers, and other equipment will vary, an internal auditor can expect to find similar characteristics in all operating facilities. The previously mentioned characteristics for a mainframe operation suggest what an internal auditor can expect to find in such a larger computer system, no matter what model of computer is actually being used. These characteristics should help internal audit to develop procedures to test the appropriate controls.

When auditors first started to review information systems general controls, they often looked for such things as locked computer room doors, fire extinguishers, and proper batch controls. These controls are now often, as a matter of course, in place in most larger computer centers. While internal audit should always keep them in mind, other general control objectives and procedures must also be considered.

(ii) Operating Systems and Software.   Early business computer systems had little more than a basic master program—what came to be called an operating system—to load the application programs into the hardware circuitry, with the application programs taking care of their own utility functions, such as tape file label checking or sorting data. The IBM 1401 computer of the mid-1960s had only 8K (eight thousand bytes) of memory to contain its operating system. The basic 1401 operating system did little more than load programs and communicate with input and output devices. The modern operating system and its associated systems software are much more complex and capable of handling many users and systems functions.

This section discusses types of systems software the auditor might expect to find on a larger or legacy computer system. Although there are multiple computer systems vendors, much of this section refers to IBM products because they represent such a large percentage of the worldwide mainframe computer market today. When planning audits of operating systems software controls for another computer vendor, the auditor should look for similarities between that equipment and IBM larger computer systems. There are many.

Operating Systems Software

Computer operating systems are the basic software tools that provide an interface among computer systems users, the application programs, and the actual computer hardware. Figure 16.1 provides a conceptual look at an operating system as installed on a larger but older IBM 3084 computer system. Smaller computer systems have many of the same functions but may not have as large a network of devices attached to them. In addition to the basic operating system, the auditor will encounter various software monitors and controllers in this class of software, including specialized software to schedule jobs or to handle logical security.

Operating systems software can be classified in four broad categories: the central

Figure 16.1   Operating System Conceptual Overview (IBM 3084 Multiprocessor System)

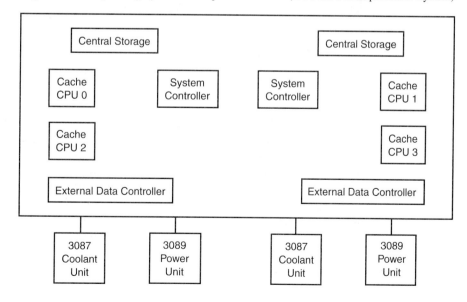

operating system, operations control programs, systems programming aids, and application-related support software. The auditor should have a general understanding of the various types of operating systems software that may be installed on a given system. While not all of these will be candidates for internal audit procedures, the auditor should be aware of the control risks associated with each.

- *Central Operating Systems.* The operating system (O/S) supervises the processing of all systems resources and programs. IBM's larger computer MVS operating system, as mentioned previously, is an example. Because they are often so closely tied to the hardware they control, operating systems traditionally have been unique by computer vendor and sometimes even by model. Digital Equipment Corporation's VAX family of computers, for example, uses the VMS operating system. VMS cannot operate on IBM equipment, and IBM's MVS will not work on DEC equipment. Although IBM is moving toward common operating systems, its large-scale ES9000 processors use a totally different operating system than its mid-sized AS/400 products.

  Today, there is a trend toward common operating systems. The AT & T-developed UNIX operating system, for example, has been implemented on virtually all sizes and models of computer systems. Although less common on larger mainframes, UNIX is found on many small to midsize computers and is a major controller for Internet systems. UNIX provides common user interface functions with the hardware where it is installed. IBM also has a variation of UNIX called AIX. There are other versions of UNIX which differ slightly.

- *System Monitors.* There are a variety of basic operating system support software products that help schedule jobs into the machine, monitor systems activities, and help solve operator problems or system errors. These products are very closely tied to the basic operating system but are usually sold and installed separately. Monitors provide internal signals to other operating system functions—that is, they are similar to a semaphore signal once found on a railroad track. Once a train enters a stretch of track, the signal detects the train and raises various semaphores to signal other trains that one is already on the track.

  Some monitors just log operating system activity for historical purposes. An example is IBM's SMF (System Maintenance Facility) utility, which monitors virtually all systems activities, including which programs are processed and the various disk file and other resources used. Operating systems memory dumps are another example of a monitor. Here, the contents of the affected system memory are reported when a program goes into an error status.

- *Network Controllers and Teleprocessing Monitors.* These are specialized operating system programs that supervise and control transmissions between the host computer system and peripheral devices. The MVS operating system sometimes uses a network controller called VTAM (Virtual Telecommunications Access Method) controller. That allows the multiple applications processing on a host computer system to communicate with multiple and differing sets of terminals.

  Software programs that support the interaction between on-line terminals and the host computer also fall into this class of operating software. IBM's on-line monitor called CICS (Customer Information Control System) allows user terminals to access and process on-line programs. An internal auditor may find the name CICS somewhat curious as it is generally used for much more than customer information applications. CICS was originally developed by IBM in the early days of its 360 series computers for a specific customer who needed a method for customers to access a central system in an on-line manner. IBM did not have such an on-line software product at the time, although its mainframe computer system competition did. So, it created CICS as a special product. It has since become IBM's basic on-line processing control product, and many have forgotten what the acronym CICS really means. Acronyms becoming names or words themselves is common in the computer industry. Over time, information systems professionals forget what the acronym once signified.

All of these special names or acronyms can cause an auditor some communications problems. Computer systems users may know what the product does but may forget what the acronym really represents. As long as the systems specialist and the auditor understand the functions of a software product, there is little need to worry about the specific meaning of the acronym. The modern internal auditor should not become discouraged by this "foreign language" of specialized computer software terms and names. When information systems technical personnel speak in their own techno-jargon, the internal auditor should always ask for clarifications when not certain of a meaning. Separate systems software products such as CICS are unique to IBM machines. Other vendors, such as DEC and Unisys, built these monitors and controllers directly into their operating systems, eliminating the need for separate software.

Application Software Administration and Control

A large class of systems software products is responsible for controlling access to system resources, monitoring application program computer resource usage, and supervising other resources such as tape files. On-line documentation tools to provide program reference listings as well as to document machine problems can be also classed in this category of application control software.

- *Access Control Programs.* These are the password-based logical security software that protects system resources. For a larger IBM machine, product names include Computer Associate's ACF-2 and Top Secret as well as IBM's RACF logical security software. The use of these products as well as audit procedures for reviewing them are discussed in Chapter 19. Access control software, which is typically centrally administered and controls the access to all applications, should be an important risk concern area for internal auditors. An internal auditor should understand how this software is administered for the entire organization as well as its use on individual applications.

- *Job Accounting Software.* Information systems operations should have a means to measure the level of computer resources used by each job processed. Specialized job accounting software provides this facility by linking back into the operating system and tracking the amount of resources each application program uses. If an organization measures computer resource usage and allocates these charges to its users, an error in the job accounting software can cause users to make improper decisions regarding the cost of their applications. Many organizations use their job accounting software to charge benefiting users for their proportionate use of computer systems resources. Although not discussed in this chapter, audits of computer billing and pricing systems are an important area where internal auditors can combine their knowledge of internal accounting controls with the technical considerations of a computer resource pricing system.

- *Library Control Software.* Media library control software logs and tracks tape or cartridge files to verify they have proper logical identification labels. This software typically defines parameters to prohibit an application from processing if the logical tape file label is incorrect. However, the same control software can also be set to bypass this control or can allow individual user groups to establish their own label rules.

    A tape or removable cartridge library control system is an example of operating software that lies between the applications program and the operating system. If not controlled properly, this type of software can present significant security and control risks. Internal audit reviews of either specific applications or operating system integrity often ignore these software products, assuming that they have adequate controls.

- *On-Line Documentation Tools.* Two types of software are usually included here. First are systems software utility products that create and maintain listings of data names, cross-reference files, and computer operator support information. The second are information logging facilities that allow operators to record machine problems for later follow-up and resolution. These utilities are several levels removed from the operating system but have the ability to access otherwise protected files in order to develop the required reference listings and, thus, are useful for audit review purposes. However, because this software is so common and used by many users, auditors typically do not review controls over this type of software.

Information-logging facilities have replaced the manually prepared shift reports and problem reports that once existed in many data centers. An example is the on-line facilities used to log console operator problems. While auditors once looked for extensive handwritten notebooks, operators can now enter their activities through an on-line screen. This has a distinct advantage over older, paper-based versions in that various historical trends and statistics can be summarized and reviewed by information system management. Auditors who have asked to review paper-based logs in the past should at least become familiar with these various new documentation tools.

This very brief list of application support software tools illustrates the massive need for internal auditors to understand the functions and controls risks surrounding this specialized and essential large systems software. Because limited time and resources create difficulties for scheduling separate reviews of these various software elements, internal auditors should be aware of the control risks associated with these products and periodically perform specialized, controls-oriented reviews.

Systems Programmer Support Tools

Software is available to help systems programmers to monitor operating systems problems and to make any necessary changes. Because this software allows highly technical systems programmers to take certain shortcuts, and because they may not formally document their work on the same level of detail often found for application programs, this software presents special audit risks. This class of systems software can be further classified into operating systems utilities, performance-management software, and capacity-planning software.

- *Operating Systems Utilities.* Utility programs allow systems programmers to make operating systems program adjustments easily. IBM's SMP/E (System Modification Program Extended), for example, is used to apply corrections to the MVS operating system. IBM may notify its customers of a small, noncritical fix and ask them to add the corrections with SMP/E. Internal audit should find out which utilities have been installed. While many are designed to perform useful functions not included in the main operating system, some may present security, integrity, or control risks. Although these products were designed to solve problems, they can be used by computer operations to get around one or another system control.

- *Performance-Management Software.* Specialized software monitors the performance of the operating system in such areas as response times, error rates, and application job load requirements. For example, Candle Computer Corp's Omegamon product is used primarily on MVS-type systems to monitor and correct operations problems. Performance-management products sometimes have powerful attributes that can modify operating system functions as well.

- *Capacity-Planning Software.* Separate software products can also monitor performance CPU (central processing unit) utilization, DASD (direct access storage device) response times, and I/O (input/output) performance. The systems programmer uses these to adjust file buffer sizes, mixes of jobs, and other variables with an objective to improve overall system performance. Many capacity-planning packages produce extensive graphical reports showing various measures of systems performance. Internal auditors can find these reports useful in reviewing the overall operations-management procedures used to monitor computer systems capacity.

The modern larger computer center will also have a variety of language processors, such as C++ or COBOL, and other specialized control programs to access files and the database-management system. These will be mentioned again in Chapter 17, on applications controls. In addition, a computer system uses numerous special programs called *utilities* to sort data, copy files, and correct file problems. Some utilities are quite powerful. For example, ZAP or Super-ZAP, found on many larger IBM systems, can modify data without leaving any sort of audit trail. Internal audit should be aware of these programs and the controls over their usage.

(b) INFORMATION SYSTEMS OPERATIONS INTERNAL AUDIT ACTIVITIES

In the older, traditional information systems organization, the computer operations area was often internal audit's prime area of control concern. The computer operator had considerable power to make changes or to bypass systems controls such as overriding tape label controls or change-program processing sequences, or inserting unauthorized program instructions into production applications. While this is still possible today, the complexity of large computer operating systems as well as the sheer volume of work passing through the modern computer operations center make this difficult. Internal audit has greater risks to consider.

Many earlier audit recommendations regarding information systems operations controls are no longer feasible. For example, auditors traditionally recommended that someone review computer console logs on a regular basis. Older business data center computers had a console printer attached to record operator commands. These logs were useful for tracing problems and also recorded any inappropriate operator activities. Today, console activity is recorded onto log files, and its data extracted only for special purposes. The sheer volume of that data would make a periodic human review of console log reports all but totally unrealistic; other tools and controls are available to help internal auditors understand operations controls.

Internal audit should initially gain an understanding of the information system organization, its established control procedures, and specialized duties and responsibilities. The distribution of control procedures in the modern information systems organization will impact how internal audit develops its procedures and the areas internal audit may want to emphasize during a particular review. Many larger organizations with specialized mainframe-type computer systems have developed information systems groups with some persons responsible for applications development, others for computer operations, and still others for such technical areas as telecommunications management, database administration, and computer systems logical security. Just as in the financial controls area, internal audit should always look for a separation of duties over such key functions. However, internal audit must first understand the information systems organization.

Formerly called the data-processing department, this function has come to be called *information systems,* as computer-based systems have become much more critical to the modern organization. Figure 16.2 shows a typical organization structure of an information systems department in a larger organization. While there can be many variations in an information systems organization structure, internal audit should look for a separation of functions between systems and programming, computer operations, and technical support functions. The technical support function will often include database administration and telecommunications control along with systems programming. However, these groups are sometimes set up as separate organizations reporting directly to the information systems director. The chart in Figure 16.2 shows a quality-assurance function with responsibilities for security, contingency planning, and overall standards. As will be discussed in Chapter 19, security and contingency planning are often separate functions.

End-user or client-server systems is another function that did not appear on earlier organization charts. This function helps users to develop their own applications on the personal microcomputers configured in local area networks (LANs) and located throughout the organization. End-user, client-server computing is sometimes attached to the applications-development function or may be separate as shown in the figure. Internal audit should be aware of how end-user computing is managed and controlled, even if it happens to be outside of the classic information systems organization. End-user information systems controls are discussed as part of the applications-development process in Chapter 17.

The person responsible for information systems, often called the chief information officer (CIO), should report to an appropriate senior management level. Before its rise in importance, information systems historically reported to financial controllers, since most computer applications then were accounting-oriented. Because it now typically supports manufacturing, purchasing, marketing, and many other types of applications, the modern information systems function now typically reports at a higher level in the organization and the CIO is part of the senior management team.

A variety of other functions may be attached to the modern information systems

Figure 16.2 Larger Information Systems Organization Chart

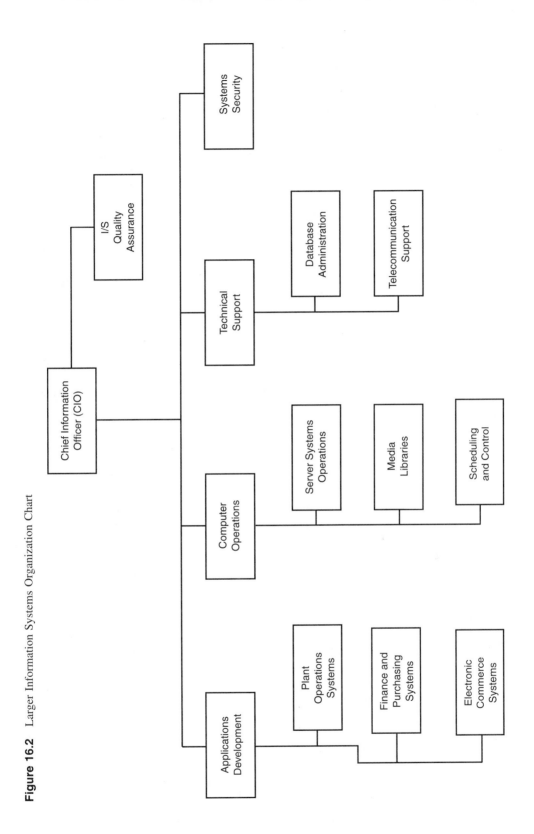

department. Some support office automation equipment and related functions while others are responsible for both voice and data telecommunications. These activities will typically be part of the technical support or the systems programming functions. Modern information systems departments are taking on these additional responsibilities because of their overall responsibilities for organizational information. Information systems management, data security, and integrity controls and procedures need to be established whether a critical document is on the mainframe computer or is transmitted through a departmental FAX machine. Quality assurance (QA) often acts as an internal computer audit function within information systems; it may be a staff function attached to the director or attached to systems and programming.

Management controls—including published policies and procedures, documented position descriptions, and programs for staff training and career development—should be as least as good as those found in the rest of the organization. That is, if the organization has overall policies and procedures, internal audit should determine that they are also followed within information systems, or should point out the deficiencies.

An important step in the review of information systems operations is to clearly define the review's objectives. All too often, a member of management or the external audit firm may ask internal audit to ''review the computer systems controls'' in the data center. Memories do not fade very fast and that request may be based upon data-processing controls as they once existed in older systems. The modern internal auditor should consider the following questions when planning the review:

- What is the purpose of the information system operations review?
- Which specific controls and procedures are expected to be in place?
- How can evidence be gathered to determine if controls work?

Based upon the results of this exercise, internal audit should develop a set of control objectives specifically tailored for the planned review rather than just use a standard set of internal control questions. This should be a standard approach, even though internal auditors use standard lists of objectives for information systems reviews more frequently than for other operational and financial types of reviews. Whether information systems or any other review, the audit objectives identified depend upon the purpose of the review. If management has requested a review of the costs and efficiency of data center operations, the audit procedures might include such areas as the chargeback and the job-scheduling systems. An outside auditor–requested review of the same data center might pay little attention to the chargeback system but would emphasize change-control procedures over program libraries.

General controls reviews of computer center operations can take several forms, but are typically organized as:

1. Preliminary reviews of information systems controls
2. Detailed general controls reviews
3. Reviews of specialized controls area
4. Reviews of compliance with laws or regulations

Although a general controls review can have a variety of purposes, it will often fit into one of these four following review types.

(i) Preliminary Reviews of Information Systems Controls. This is the type of review that outside auditors sometimes call a *preliminary survey* or an *assessment of control risk*. Its purpose is to gain a general understanding or overview of the information systems controls environment. Internal audit asks questions, observes operations, and reviews documentation, but there is typically only very limited testing, if any. For example, internal audit might inquire about the procedures for updating production program libraries and might review the forms used for the approval process. However, the auditor would probably not select a sample of the programs in the production library to determine if they had followed proper library update procedures.

A preliminary review can help determine the need for a more detailed general controls review or extended control risk assessment at a later date, or can gather preliminary controls information for a specific applications review. This type of review is limited in scope and may not cover all aspects of the information systems organization. Some areas where a preliminary review would be appropriate might include the following:

- A preliminary controls review of information systems operations at a new acquisition
- A follow-up review after a very detailed controls review from an earlier period; the review here would emphasize changes in control procedures as well as actions taken on prior audit recommendations
- An outside auditor's request for internal audit to review and document a general understanding of information systems controls

Although they can change with the specific purpose of the preliminary review, audit procedures in Figure 16.3 can be used for a preliminary review of information systems general controls. The auditor is gaining information here about the general structure of the information systems organization, how it plans and organizes resources, its management reporting tools, and procedures for security and contingency planning. These audit steps might be used when the organization is considering the acquisition of another company and management has asked internal audit to assess its information systems control environment. These audit steps will not help in assessing the types of systems in place, but will assess how that information systems function is organized and managed. Instead of presenting a formal report with its findings and recommendations, internal audit would simply give management an assessment of information systems general controls.

(ii) Detailed General Controls Reviews of Operations. A comprehensive, detailed review of information systems general or interdependent controls will typically cover all aspects of operations, including systems programming, telecommunications controls, and database administration. A detailed general controls review should also include tests of controls over program libraries, made by running specialized programs to compare source versions with production program versions.

A detailed general controls review requires good planning in order to make it effective and also requires internal audit to spend considerable fieldwork time in both the information systems operations and development functions. While the preliminary review can sometimes be performed by a less experienced auditor who is developing information systems audit skills, a detailed general controls review is best performed by a more senior audit staff member with a good understanding of information systems controls and procedures.

Figure 16.3   Information Systems (IS) Controls Preliminary Survey

Obj. 16.03.01   Obtain basic information about the environment through initial exploratory discussions with IS management.

Obj. 16.03.02   Review the organizational chart to determine that appropriate separation of functions exists.

Obj. 16.03.03   Obtain job descriptions of key IS personnel and review them for adequate and appropriate qualifications, task definitions, and responsibilities. Ensure that security and control accountability are appropriately assigned to key personnel.

Obj. 16.03.04   Based on discussion within management both inside and outside the IS organization, assess whether the organizational structure is aligned with business strategies to ensure expected IS service delivery.

Obj. 16.03.05   Review IS policies and selected procedures for completeness and relevance with specific emphasis on security, business continuity planning, operations, and new systems development.

Obj. 16.03.06   Inquire whether responsibilities have been assigned to keep the policies and procedures current, to educate/communicate them to staff members, and to monitor compliance with them.

Obj. 16.03.07   Based on discussions with senior IS management, assess whether strategic, operational, and tactical IS plans are in place to ensure alignment with the organization's overall business plans.

Obj. 16.03.08   Determine the existence of an IS steering committee and review this committee's functions through a limited review of steering committee meeting minutes.

Obj. 16.03.09   Ensure that a formal methodology is used in the development of new systems or major enhancements to systems in production. The methodology should include formal steps for definition, feasibility assessment, design, construction, testing, and implementation as well as formal approvals at every stage.

Obj. 16.03.10   Assess the uses of systems development efficiency and effectiveness tools, including joint application design (JAD), rapid application design (RAD), code generators, CASE tools, and documentation generators.

Obj. 16.03.11   Determine that a process is in place for making changes to application programs in production, including testing and documentation sign-off, and formal approvals to implement the change into production.

Obj. 16.03.12   Ensure that responsibility for physical and logical security has been appropriately apportioned and that appropriate documented procedures exist.

Obj. 16.03.13   Review procedures in place for operating and maintaining the network, in terms of device configuration and software parameter changes, and ensure that procedures for allocating and maintaining the network configuration are performed on a scheduled basis and under proper change management.

Obj. 16.03.14   Review the disaster-recovery plan to ensure that detailed plans for recovery of operations have been prepared, that the plans are documented, communicated to the appropriate personnel, and are properly tested on a periodic basis.

Based upon a preliminary review or walk-through of information systems operations, internal audit should develop an understanding of the control procedures over computer operations. The detailed audit procedures performed can be modified based upon this preliminary information. Questions internal audit might pose could include:

- *How is work scheduled?* Some computer operators do little more than initiate jobs from a production job queue file, while others have considerable authority in deciding which jobs to run. In the latter situation, internal audit might want to spend time reviewing control log reports and operator instructions. If these procedures have been automated, internal audit may want to consider a specialized review of the production control software area.

- *How are tapes, cartridges, and DASD files managed?* Automated tools are often used here. In addition, some operations have a separate library facility where production cartridges or tapes are mounted. When automated tools are not used for controlling tape libraries, there is a greater chance for mount errors. Even when software has been installed, computer operators often can bypass label controls and introduce incorrect files into a production environment.

- *What types of operator procedures or instructions are used?* Larger systems operations documentation can take a variety of formats; internal audit should have a general understanding of this documentation format and content. This will help in the design of specific audit tests.

- *How is work initiated and how does it flow through operations?* In many larger computer systems operations, production is initiated through remote job entry user terminals. In others, the production-control function funnels all necessary input data to machine operations. Some functions rely on users to initiate most inputs through their on-line terminals. The type and nature of internal audit's tests will depend upon the customary procedures.

The basic idea is for internal audit to understand how information systems operations function. The effective internal auditor should go through a set of these types of questions prior to each review. A larger systems operations function may install new procedures from time to time, changing or adding complexities to the control structure.

The audit procedures to be performed in a detailed review of general controls for a legacy computer system can be quite extensive, depending upon the size and scope of the audit. Figure 16.4 contains a limited set of control procedure areas for this type of review. Refer to the current edition of *Computer Audit, Control, and Security,* mentioned previously, which is a good source for fairly detailed sets of audit objectives and procedures.

(iii) Specialized or Limited-Scope-Oriented Reviews.   Because of management requests and perceived risks, auditors often perform limited reviews over specialized areas within an overall information systems function. These specialized reviews can be limited to one function, such as database administration, or even to one specialty area, such as output report distribution. Often, management will request that internal audit perform this type of a review due to some identified problem, such as a well-publicized security violation.

An audit of a highly specialized or technical area of information systems operations

Figure 16.4   Larger Computer System General Controls Review Procedures

Note: These audit procedures are for a general controls review of a legacy mainframe system. Figure 16.6 contains review procedures for client-server systems.

Obj. 16.4.1 Computer equipment should be located in a secure, environmentally controlled facility.

Proc. 16.4.1.1. Discuss physical and environmental control procedures with information systems management to determine current policies and future plans.

Proc. 16.4.1.2. Tour computer room facilities and observe physical security strengths and weaknesses, including:

- The existence of locking mechanisms to limit computer room access only to authorized individuals
- The placement of computer room perimeter walls and windows to limit access
- The location of power transformers, water chiller units if appropriate, and air conditioning units to provide proper protection
- The general location of the computer room facilities within the overall building to minimize traffic
- The existence of fire detection equipment, including zone-controlled heat and smoke detectors
- The existence of a zone-controlled, overall fire protection system, including local extinguishers

Proc. 16.4.1.3. Review computer room temperature, humidity, and other environmental controls and assess their adequacy.

Proc. 16.4.1.4. Briefly review maintenance records to ascertain that physical and environmental controls are regularly inspected and maintained.

Obj. 16.4.2. Production processing should be scheduled to promote efficient use of computer equipment consistent with the requirements of systems users.

Proc. 16.4.2.1. Through interviews with operations management, develop an overall understanding of computer processing demands, including on-line and batch production work as well as any end-user computing.

Proc. 16.4.2.2. Also through interviews, describe the telecommunications network surrounding the computer system, including connections to workstations, computer centers, and the outside.

Proc. 16.4.2.3. Review procedures for scheduling regular production jobs including the use of automated job scheduling tools.

Proc. 16.4.2.4. Match a limited number of scheduled production jobs against actual completion times to determine whether actual schedules are followed.

Proc. 16.4.2.5. Determine that operating system job classes or priority codes are used to give proper priority to critical production jobs, and evaluate procedures for rush or rerun jobs.

Obj. 16.4.3. Operations instructions should exist to allow operators to correctly process normal production as well as to respond to errors.

Proc. 16.4.3.1. Review documentation standards for production applications to determine that they provide operators with information regarding:

- Normal operations, including instructions for special forms, tape files, and report disposition
- Application restart and recovery procedures.

Proc. 16.4.3.2. Review procedures, automated or manual, for turning new applications or revisions over to production to determine there is a review by operations following standards.

(continued)

Figure 16.4   *(Continued)*

Obj. 16.4.4. Computer operators should not be allowed to change programs independently or initiate production jobs without authorization.

  Proc. 16.4.4.1. Determine that policies prohibit computer operations personnel from performing programming tasks or running unauthorized jobs.

  Proc. 16.4.4.2. Determine that production source libraries cannot be accessed by operations personnel.

  Proc. 16.4.4.3. Assess information systems procedures for periodically reviewing the contents of log files or otherwise monitoring improper operator use of computer equipment.

Obj. 16.4.5. Procedures should exist to allow for emergency modifications when error conditions prevent the processing of critical production work.

  Proc. 16.4.5.1. Review and document procedures for changing production programs or procedure libraries when emergency situations require special handling.

  Proc. 16.4.5.2. Determine that all emergency processing activities are properly documented and are subject to subsequent management review.

  Proc. 16.4.5.3. Select several documented emergency program fixes and determine that the necessary changes were added to production processing libraries and were documented.

Obj. 16.4.6. Logs or records of computer systems activity should exist to monitor both regular and abnormal computer operations.

  Proc. 16.4.6.1. Determine that an automated system is in place to log all computer systems activity, including all jobs and programs run, any reruns, abnormal terminations, or operator commands and data entered through system consoles.

  Proc. 16.4.6.2. Determine that computer activity logs are reviewed periodically, that exception situations are investigated, and that the results of investigations are documented.

  Proc. 16.4.6.3. Determine that files produced from the computer operating system's log monitor are retained long enough to allow investigation of unusual activities.

  Proc. 16.4.6.4. Review procedures for logging problems to determine that all abnormal software and hardware operating conditons are documented.

Obj. 16.4.7 When batch jobs are run, procedures should exist to determine that only authorized input data is transmitted or submitted at scheduled times.

  Proc. 16.4.7.1. Determine that schedules exist for the submission of critical input batch files and that procedures exist to follow up on missing data.

  Proc. 16.4.7.2. Review procedures to prohibit unauthorized input or access to production files and programs.

  Proc. 16.4.7.3. Review a limited sample of production batch applications to determine that appropriate systems control techniques are used.

Obj. 16.4.8. Controls should exist to determine that computer system outputs are correctly distributed only to authorized users.

  Proc. 16.4.8.1. Determine whether users or information systems personnel are responsible for reviewing output controls and assess whether those control reviews are being performed.

  Proc. 16.4.8.2. Assess procedures for reviewing distributed output reports to determine whether they are complete.

often takes considerable auditor creativity in planning the work. Management may be concerned about the equity of the computer chargeback system and may ask the audit department to look at it. Internal audit will need to gain a general understanding of the system used, spend time planning the additional procedures and tests to be performed, and then return to the actual testing.

As information systems departments grow in complexity and importance to the organization, auditors can expect to perform more of these specialized, limited reviews. With the information systems function a major resource in many organizations, it may be inappropriate to attempt to review *all* information systems general controls in *all* operational areas as one single detailed review. This would be the same as if internal audit attempted to perform a review of "manufacturing" in a major plant environment. Rather than cover all manufacturing functions, internal audit might review production control one year and receiving and inspection the next, and eventually cover most significant functions.

Reviews of specialized information systems technical areas will be discussed later in this chapter, and should help internal audit gain a more general understanding of potential technical information systems control areas. However, a more specialized text such as the Moeller book should be consulted. For a specialized review of a specific information systems control area, such as cartridge or DASD library management, internal audit should expand upon the procedures developed for a general controls review in that area and add additional audit tests as necessary.

(iv) Reviews to Assess Compliance with Laws or Regulations.

One of the major objectives of internal control as outlined in Chapter 2 is compliance with laws and regulations. Internal auditors should always be aware of objectives in this area and include appropriate tests in their reviews. Auditors working with governmental agencies or in organizations that do extensive governmental contracting often may be required to perform information systems–related compliance audits to determine if appropriate laws and regulations are being followed. These will differ very much from agency to agency and from one political division to another.

A compliance-related information systems review can often be combined with a preliminary or detailed general controls review, but auditors must be aware of the relevant procedures and regulations, such as those published by the governmental agency requiring the audit. Most bank-examination agencies, for example, have published information systems controls guidelines. When operating in this type of environment, internal auditors must become aware of the regulatory environment as well as any published procedures.

(c) ESTABLISHING THE REVIEW PURPOSE

Internal audit should educate their management on the various types and scopes of general controls reviews they can perform for direction as to the scope desired. All too often, management will ask for "an audit of that computer center"!

If management expects a brief, preliminary survey of the information systems function and internal audit performs a very detailed review, no one will be satisfied. Internal audit will not be able to understand why management is exerting so much pressure to complete the work in a short amount of time and, conversely, management may not be able to understand the relevance of internal audit's comments in specialized areas such as the lack of systems programming documentation.

A more common problem occurs when management requests a detailed review of the information systems function to assess perceived control or performance problems. If not properly planned and scheduled, internal audit may not be able to perform the requested extensive review. As a result, internal audit's report and findings may be quite general rather than the detailed and comprehensive review requested.

16-3 SMALLER, INFORMAL INFORMATION SYSTEMS ORGANIZATIONS

Auditors traditionally have had problems evaluating controls in smaller information systems organizations, ranging from the client-server systems of today to older mini- and microcomputer business data-processing environments. These problems arise because smaller systems are often installed with limited staffs in a more user-friendly type of environment. Internal auditors, however, typically look for controls in terms of the more traditional, larger mainframe information systems environment—that is, strong physical security controls and proper separation of duties among members of the information systems organization often just do not exist or are only partially implemented in the typical smaller systems environment. This approach was perhaps adequate when what were called minicomputers were limited to smaller operations and the microcomputer was used primarily for single office spreadsheet or similar low-audit-risk applications. The large capacity and capability of microcomputers today, the growth of telecommunications networks including the Internet and intranets, and the transition to client-server computing has made these smaller systems important parts of the information systems control framework.

When faced with evaluating controls in these smaller computer systems settings, internal auditors have sometimes reverted to the traditional, almost ''cookbook'' types of controls recommendations. That is, they have recommended that microcomputers be placed in locked rooms or that a small, two-person information systems development staff be expanded to four in order to ensure proper separation of duties. While there may be situations where such controls are appropriate, they often are not applicable in a smaller business setting. Internal audit can easily lose credibility if their control recommendations are not appropriate to the risks found in the smaller computer systems setting.

Organizations are implementing increasing numbers and networks of microcomputer systems to support smaller business units, support specific departmental computing, or provide information systems for the entire organization. Despite their smaller size, these systems often can represent significant control concerns. The paragraphs following discuss information systems controls in the small-system business information systems environment, including control procedures for local area networks (LANs) and client-server computing systems.

This chapter has discussed differences between general, interdependent controls and application controls in larger systems. These differences are equally applicable for microcomputer-based systems including LANs and client-server configurations. Internal audit should understand the general controls surrounding a smaller computer system. If no significant weaknesses are identified, the auditor can then review specific applications as discussed in Chapter 17, ''Computer Systems Applications Controls.''

(a) SMALLER COMPUTER SYSTEMS CONTROLS IN THE MODERN ORGANIZATION

Although some auditors once thought of mini- or microcomputer, and client-server systems as one generic computer system class (as opposed to larger, mainframe computers), techno-

logical and organizational changes have caused significant differences in control procedures and internal audit concerns among them. Smaller systems can be implemented in a
variety of ways, depending upon the type of system and the size of the organization. The
modern internal auditor should be able to recognize these differences and develop control
procedures to review them. Subsequent sections of this chapter will discuss controls in
terms of:

- Small business computer systems controls
- Microcomputer-based systems controls using LANs
- Client-server systems controls
- Mini- and micro-processor or nonbusiness systems controls

Internal audit may encounter all of the above types of smaller computer systems in
a single modern organization. Small business computer systems provide total information
systems support for a smaller business function or unit while microcomputers or personal
computers, often connected through LANs, will support limited, departmental computing
functions. Client-server systems, defined in greater detail later in this chapter, are often
a combination of various types and sizes of interconnected computer systems and may be
found in all types and sizes of organizations. Process or nonbusiness computers include
the numerous types of small computers used increasingly for manufacturing, distribution,
and other various operational control applications. Internal audit will frequently find these
specialized control machines in many areas of an organization's operations.

(i) Small Business Computer System Controls. This chapter previously defined
the larger computer system in terms of its computer equipment and information systems
organizational attributes. We have suggested that if a computer system is located in a
secure facility, has a multi-task operating system, or has a large programming staff, internal
audit should probably consider it to be a ''larger'' computer system for purposes of audit
planning and should review for appropriate control procedures. While not particularly
precise, this definition would have covered the typical major computer system.

The same type of attribute-based description can be more difficult in the smaller
system environment. A strict computer hardware architecture definition often does not
help internal audit to decide when to apply smaller system control procedures. For example,
Digital Equipment Corporation (DEC) was a major manufacturer of what were once called
minicomputers in the United States. DEC's larger VAX ''super-minicomputers'' are quite
powerful, with virtually all of the capabilities of a traditional mainframe computer. In
addition, a series of these VAX machines, connected together, provide more computer
power than some traditional mainframe machines. When reviewing controls in such an
environment, internal audit should consider these linked computers to be the same as the
larger, legacy mainframe systems discussed previously.

Another problem in identifying a smaller computer is that they often look like a
larger processor. For example, the older IBM 43xx series of computer systems were
generally described as on the lower end of IBM's mainframe computers, but their 4361
machine was very much a minicomputer in terms of its capacity and the way IBM literature
described them. Nevertheless, many information systems organizations implemented them
as if they were more of a mainframe processor. Similarly, IBM's AS/400 system was first
implemented in the 1980s as a small business minicomputer. The AS/400 product line

and their individual machine capacities have been expanded to make many of these systems effectively operate as classic mainframe systems.

Smaller systems, which once were known as minicomputers, have been used for business applications since about the late 1960s. They are a product of the increased miniaturization of electronic components as well as of different approaches used by computer engineers. Because they were relatively inexpensive, easy to use, and did not require elaborate power or air conditioning support, minicomputers were used for many smaller business organizations as well as for specialized information systems applications. Long before the introduction of today's microcomputers, they brought information systems capabilities to organizations that could not afford the large investments required by classic mainframe systems.

Microcomputers (also known as personal computers, or PCs) have had a much more rapid growth curve. During the mid-1970s, hobbyists began to build their own microcomputers using newly available integrated circuit chips. In the late 1970s, Apple Computer Corporation was formed and produced the Apple II microcomputer. Although the machine was initially viewed as a curious toy by many, a spreadsheet software package, VISICALC, introduced about a year later, made the Apple II a serious tool for business decision-making. Several years later, in the early 1980s, IBM introduced its personal computer and legitimized the microcomputer as a serious business-processing tool. Today, many of the machines are said to be "IBM compatible" even though IBM is a relatively minor player.

Today, microcomputers, often connected into LANs, are used for many business information systems applications. They are often the only computer system resource for a smaller company or a division of a larger organization, and often have replaced minicomputer or mainframe systems. They may also be used for specialized departmental computing even though there may also be a larger, mainframe computer capability within the organization. In particular, these specialized computers are used for such applications as research laboratory or manufacturing process control rather than for pure business information systems. These same machines may also be used for some business-processing applications in addition to their intended specialized purposes.

Ever-increasing speed and capacity has done much to promote the use of microcomputers. When the first Apple II was released, it had an internal memory of 42k, or 42,000 memory locations. By the mid-1990s, by contrast, off-the-shelf machines typically come with 32,000,000 memory locations, or 32 meg. Virtually every other measure, whether it be processing speed, capability of running multiple tasks, or disk file memory capacity, has changed dramatically. Even the term "microcomputer," which is used throughout this book, is becoming obsolete. The former "microcomputer" is now known as a desktop computer, with legacy devices having their own special names. Nevertheless, we will continue to use the term "microcomputer" in this chapter and throughout this book.

These machine-size-based definitions of computer systems often cause difficulties for internal auditors because computer systems are used for so many types of business-related applications. Internal audit may be directed by management to review the general controls surrounding "all" computer systems in the organization. Clearly, this type of directive covers the mainframe computers and freestanding divisional minicomputer systems. The directive may also cover the organization's departmental LANs or personal computers. However, internal audit may wonder if it really covers the specialized workstation computer in the engineering laboratory used for recording test results or the microcomputer at the end of the distribution line that weighs the package and routes it to the correct shipping dock. These definition problems will only get worse as such things as embedded systems take a greater role in controlling business processes. Embedded systems are the computers that reside behind such things as the dashboard of a car or on the control panel of a video recorder or even in the kitchen microwave. As consumers, we press these flat panel screens and generally do not think we are submitting computer system commands. However, embedded systems will take greater roles in business processes as their capacities and applications increase. Embedded processors will be discussed briefly in Chapter 20 on new and evolving technologies.

While all of the above are computer systems in accordance with a request to review all systems, internal audit's reviews should emphasize the computer systems used for *business information systems* purposes. To follow the above example, the processor at the end of the distribution line probably uses a standard set of embedded software that cannot be modified by the local staff. It was very possibly purchased from an outside systems vendor and, after initial installation and testing, it simply works, with no programmer interaction. Such a machine generally has limited business or control risk implications.

Internal audit will often work in an environment where only smaller business system computers are used, particularly when the auditor's organization is relatively small or does not require extensive computer systems power. An example would be a not-for-profit organization whose only systems needs are to support direct mailing and limited accounting-related applications. While these can be handled today by a network of individual microcomputers, the organization may have purchased a classic minicomputer some years ago, when that represented the best technical solution. Although it is not the most current or modern, internal audit still has an obligation to review the internal controls surrounding that older system provided it falls within internal audit's risk parameters. Internal audit should review the controls over minicomputer operation as if it were either a smaller business system or a classic, larger organization mainframe system. While the underlying concepts and objectives of internal control will not vary, the scope and nature of the internal audit review will. When internal audit has doubts, the controls review should be conducted as if it were a larger system. The following should help internal audit to understand the characteristics of the typical smaller business information system:

- *Limited Information Systems Staff.* The small business computer system, whether microcomputers on a LAN or an older minicomputer, will have a very limited dedicated information systems staff, if any. A microcomputer used to provide accounting reports for a smaller company may be maintained by a single person. A small business or LAN system may have a manager / LAN administrator, a programmer, and perhaps one or two operators as its total information systems department. The nature of the equipment, the applications processed, and the size of the total organization tends to limit information systems staff size. This small operation creates a control risk because no one person may be required to perform such functions as backing up critical files. However, a small staff size will not in itself always cause an organizational controls concern. Internal audit should be able to look for compensating controls just as it does when reviewing a smaller accounting department where a classic separation of duties is lacking.

- *Limited Programming Capability.* The typical small business computer system makes extensive use of purchased software packages. The few programmers in the department, if any, are responsible for updating the purchased packages, maintaining operating system tables or parameters, and writing simple retrieval programs. If internal audit finds a larger programming staff or extensive in-house development activity, some of the control procedures discussed previously for larger systems-development functions should be considered.

- *Limited Environmental Controls.* Larger mainframe computer systems require specialized power, temperature, and other environmental controls such as water-cooled chillers for the central processors. Small business computer systems tend to be just the opposite. They can generally be plugged into normal power systems and operate within a fairly wide range of temperatures. Because of these limited requirements, smaller systems are often installed without important, easy-to-install environmental controls such as backup drives or electrical power surge protectors. While some small business computer installations or LAN file servers may be housed in formal, environmentally controlled computer rooms, this is not a necessary attribute of a minicomputer system.

- *Limited Physical Security Controls.* Because of less need for environmental controls, mini- and microcomputer business information systems are often installed directly in office areas. The level of auditor concern regarding physical security controls depends upon the type of computer equipment and the type of applications being processed. As will be discussed later in this chapter, internal audit may sometimes recommend that physical security be improved, particularly if a LAN file server is involved or if critical applications are being processed. In many other instances, this lack of physical security controls should not present a significant control problem.

- *Extensive Telecommunications Network.* Only a limited number of business microcomputers today are freestanding devices. Most are tied together in a LAN or a much broader wide area network (WAN), or to the Internet. The typical individual network supports anywhere from a few to hundreds or more devices with most residing locally in the same general building or facility. These systems also may be linked to a mainframe as part of a distributed processing network where files are both uploaded and downloaded. All of these issues add different levels of control considerations to the system under review.

The previous characteristics certainly do not define a mini- or microcomputer system. They only explain common system attributes. However, they should help internal audit to better decide upon the control procedures to be used. As noted, when in doubt, internal audit should consider the system to be a larger, more complex one.

(ii) Smaller LAN Systems in Larger, Traditional Organizations. LANs have been discussed as a type of computer system often found in smaller size businesses as opposed to the large organization classic mainframe system with its centralized processor and the network of terminals connected to it. In our rapidly changing information systems environment today, this configuration is no longer always true. Separate LANs are often found at a departmental or separate operating division level in the larger organization. These may operate as dual systems, separate from the mainframe central system, used for a specialized departmental database or information system necessary for that unit's operations. Often, this dedicated LAN may have evolved through one or several groups placing their unique applications on an office microcomputer when they were unable to get priorities for a mainframe system development. As other departmental users saw the value in this local application or desired similar microcomputer-based power, the organizational unit may have established its own departmental LAN, separate from the traditional mainframe system. Today, that same LAN architecture will be used as almost a first choice to avoid the time and expense of placing a new application on the info-systems department-administered classic mainframe.

Because the departmental LAN is separate from traditional mainframe-based systems and often does not follow the standards established by the central information systems organization, internal audit should treat the LAN operation review similar to that in a separate, small business type of system. Control procedures here are discussed in Figure 16.7.

LANs were initially implemented as part of traditional large organization, mainframe computer system networks. The centralized computer system would have its network of attached terminals as well as multiple attached LANs. Today's workstations on LANs may be used for local, microcomputer-based data processing as well as for communication with the centralized computer system. Each of the LAN workstations sends and receives its mainframe-based transactions through the LAN server and then to the mainframe system. Although this computer system has some of the characteristics of the small business systems described previously, it is very much a component of a larger computer system, and internal audit should consider the general controls over a LAN connected to a large system mainframe essentially the same as the controls in any larger computer system.

(iii) Client-Server Computer Systems.   The term *client-server* first appeared in information systems business literature in the late 1980s. To many non–information systems specialists, including many auditors, it is one of those specialized information systems terms that is often difficult for the nonspecialist to understand, let alone describe. However, client-server architecture has become a very popular information systems configuration in all sizes of organizations and all types of modern computer systems. In a LAN environment, for example, each of the workstations on the LAN is a *client*. The centralized LAN processor, which contains common shared files and other resources, is called the *server*. The workstation user submits a request from the user's client machine to a server, which then serves that client by doing the necessary processing and then fulfilling the request.

This client-server architecture, however, goes beyond just a workstation and a LAN server. An application that queries a centralized database can be considered the client while the database that develops the view of the database is the server to all workstations requesting database service. Similarly, an application program can request services from an operating system communications server. Figure 16.5 shows a client-server system sample configuration where a single server handles requests from multiple clients across a network.

Our discussion of client-server architecture, though very general, represents the typical computer systems configuration of the future. Internal auditors should consider control objectives here similar to those found in larger computer systems along with a strong telecommunications network, as discussed in Figure 16.4.

(iv) Nonbusiness Specialized Processor Computer Systems.   In many organizations today, other systems can be found in areas beyond information systems operations. Special-purpose machines may be located in engineering laboratories, manufacturing control operation, marketing departments, and many other areas. The computer systems may be used for process control, automated design work, statistical analysis processing, or for many other applications. Some are totally dedicated to specific applications while others

Figure 16.5   Client-Server Simplified Architecture

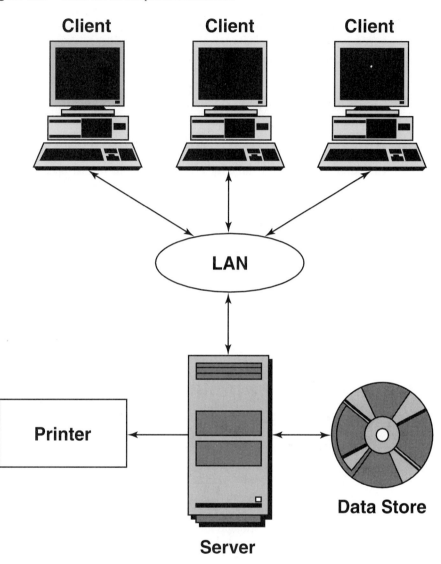

may be used for a variety of tasks within their assigned functions. This multitude of information systems machines has come about in many organizations because of the relatively low cost of such machines, the familiarity of many professionals with information systems techniques today, and because of the inability of traditional information systems departments to support specialized information systems needs.

Although these systems are not used for traditional business information needs, such as maintaining accounts receivable records, they often support critical applications for the organization. For example, an engineering computer may support new product computer-aided design (CAD) work. Systems backup and integrity concerns in this environment may be equally as great as in the typical business information systems center.

Internal audit's role in regard to specialized information systems operations will vary with both management's direction and internal audit's review objectives. While some audit organizations will have little involvement with reviews over specialized computer systems, information systems controls reviewed here can often play an important role in support of internal audit's understanding of control procedures and in other operational audit activities. Several of the operational audit chapters in Part Five of this book discuss areas where specialized computer systems may be used. For example, Chapter 26 briefly discusses computer systems used to support engineering and research activities.

Before attempting any review of such a specialized computer system, internal audit should obtain a rough familiarity with the functions of that operation. For example, an internal auditor who plans to review a dedicated computer-aided design and manufacturing (CAD/CAM) computer operation needs a general understanding of the terminology, general workings, and objectives of CAD/CAM.

Reviews of specialized computer systems are not recommended for the less experienced internal auditor. In order to find control analogies from normal business information systems situations and translate them to specialized controls environments, an auditor must be fairly experienced in reviewing business information systems computer centers, whether larger or smaller operations. Over time, internal audit will encounter more of these specialized computer operations. Most will use micro- or super-microcomputers. The creative auditor can make increasing contributions to management by performing operational reviews over these computer centers on a periodic basis.

(b) SMALLER SYSTEM OPERATIONS INTERNAL CONTROLS

As discussed, internal auditors have traditionally looked for a proper separation of duties as a first procedure for evaluating information systems general controls. This organizational control is also often lacking in a smaller business information systems department. While good information systems control objectives call for a proper separation of responsibilities between users, programmers, and operators, such strict organization controls are often difficult to establish in a small department.

When auditors first began to review general organizational controls in these smaller information systems departments and tried to apply large mainframe system control remedies, those earlier recommendations were hard to sell to a cost-conscious management; they would be treated with derision today.

The responsible manager of the smaller client-server or LAN-based information systems department today may also be the principal programmer and operate the equipment when the need arises. Because much of the programming involves manipulating simple retrieval languages, many users have some programming knowledge. The separation-of-duties control found in a larger shop just does not exist in this smaller environment, but there should be compensating controls, including:

- *Purchased Software.* Nearly all smaller computer systems today operate with purchased software packages where ''programmers'' do not have access or have very limited access to source code.
- *Increased Management Attention.* Although the management in an organization

supported by a small business computer system may have very little knowledge of information systems techniques, they often give considerable attention to the key computer-generated reports. In a small company, it is not unusual for top management to review, for example, an accounts receivable aged trial balance in detail and on a regular basis.

- *Separation of Input and Processing Duties.* In virtually all modern small business computer systems today, users submit data inputs through their individual workstations and receive outputs on their terminals or remote printers.

Even with these compensating organizational controls in the modern, small business computer system, internal audit should also be aware of potential control risks and weaknesses. Information systems departments continue to exist in which the responsible manager implements many of the applications, has reponsibility for the network management, controls all passwords, and appears to be the only person in the organization that understands the information systems applications. While a limited staff may be quite acceptable in some circumstances, the organization faces a risk if all information systems knowledge is vested in only one person.

Other control weakness symptoms in the smaller information systems organization that do not typically exist in the larger department include:

- "Loyal" employees who do not take their vacations or time off
- The use of special, undocumented programs known only to the information systems manager
- Direct information systems department participation in system input transactions, such as adjustments to the inventory system

Control risk may be a major consideration when audit procedures have identified significant control weaknesses in these smaller business systems. In larger organizations, auditors often look for documented position descriptions as evidence of good management controls over the information systems function. Many smaller organizations do not have such descriptions for *any employee*. An internal auditor will not be effective in suggesting that such position descriptions be drafted just for the information systems function while ignoring the rest of the organization when overall control risk is minimal because of the smaller size of the organization.

We have discussed how the plan of organization and related management practices are often among the strongest control procedures in a larger information systems organization. In the smaller organization, the size and informality typically associated with such a small group will tend to weaken controls. Senior management should have a good understanding of the information systems function, its plans, and its objectives.

A very important general control for the smaller information systems organization is adequate documentation over its systems and procedures. Management can be very vulnerable if systems, programs, and operating procedures are not properly documented. There have been instances where both members of a two-person information systems organization suddenly resigned due to a disagreement or better employment offer. Without adequate documentation, it is very difficult for someone else suddenly to take over. This is even true if the organization primarily runs packaged software, since there may be many special procedures associated with those packages. The risk is equally high if the organization uses microcomputers on a LAN where all users do much of their own work. The LAN administrator who configures the system and backs up files has a key control responsibility.

Sometimes, the smaller information systems organization is located at an operating unit of a larger organization with other centralized information systems facilities. Even though the smaller information systems organization is entirely freestanding, it may receive central direction as to appropriate standards and procedures. In order to ensure compliance with these standards, internal audit should have a general understanding of them and the level at which these corporate standards are expected to be followed. Sometimes, a large organization will issue mandatory standards to all of its operating units, no matter what their size, even though the standards may not be practicable for smaller units. While central management may look the other way regarding local compliance with these standards, internal audit often feels compelled to bring up violations found at a smaller unit. If such problems exist, internal audit should discuss these concerns with the central information systems management group responsible for the standards. Very little is accomplished if a field internal auditor brings up a violation of a corporate standard found at a remote unit when that central management really does not expect full compliance. This may be a topic more for a centralized review of standards!

(c) SMALLER SYSTEM OPERATIONS INTERNAL AUDIT ACTIVITIES

A smaller computer system may provide information systems support for the total organization or for a separate operating unit of a larger organization. Such systems may have many of the attributes of a larger, mainframe computer system, including a limited but formal information systems organization, production schedules, and a responsibility for implementing new applications. However, the smaller computer system organization often has no other specialized functions.

Internal audit will encounter a variety of computer hardware "brands" or product names in a smaller systems environment, but most will be "open systems" in that a common operating system generally can operate no matter what brand of hardware is used. This is quite different from classic mainframe computers, where the manufacturer generally builds the computer hardware as well as an operating system. Numerous vendors supply such small business computer systems with both improved functionality and price performance, and internal auditors will be more effective in reviewing small business computer system controls if they have an overall knowledge of some of their capabilities.

Despite the smaller and more informal nature of a typical small business computer system, internal audit should still expect to have some of the same general organizational control objectives discussed for larger systems, although some procedures may be modified due to the more informal nature of these smaller systems. Figure 16.6 provides a set of audit procedures for evaluating general organizational controls in the more modern, LAN-based small business computer system. The paragraphs following discuss some of these control concerns in greater detail.

(i) Smaller System Controls over Access to Data and Programs.   When unauthorized persons are allowed to access and modify computer files and programs, general controls are very much weakened. In the smaller information systems organization, it is much more difficult to satisfy control objectives in this area. However, internal audit should consider access to data and programs to be *the major general controls objective*

Figure 16.6   Audit Procedures for a LAN, Client-Server Environment

16.06.1. Determine there is a complete inventory of all LAN hardware, including the servers, printer(s), and modem(s), as well as a complete inventory of all LAN software, including application and systems software.

16.06.2 The LAN hardware inventory report contains unique identification numbers or model numbers for the various hardware devices.

16.06.3. Through review of a limited sample, determine items on the LAN inventory report correspond to the physical equipment and that LAN hardware components contain an asset number or other ownership identification mark that cannot be removed or altered.

16.06.4. Review policies for storing unused equipment and disposing of obsolete or badly damaged LAN equipment. Does the policy require management approval of disposal of equipment?

16.06.5. Determine that LAN hardware devices and documentation are located in a secure facility and that the LAN file-server components (keyboard lock and power on password) are restricted to the LAN administrator.

16.06.6. Observe the LAN file-server facility and verify that it is physically secured and observe the LAN file-server computer and verify that it is secured in a manner to reduce the risk of removal of computer components or the computer itself.

16.06.7. Visit the LAN file-server facility and verify that temperature and humidity are adequate, static and electric surge protectors are in place, and fire extinguishers are nearby.

16.06.8. Observe the storage methods and media for backup diskettes and tapes, verifying that they are protected from environmental damage.

16.06.9. Review the procedures in place for restricting, identifying, and reporting authorized and unauthorized users of the network. Determine that users are required to use passwords and that passwords are changed periodically. Are passwords internally encrypted and not displayed on the computer screen when entered?

16.06.10. Review procedures for monitoring access and use of the LAN. Evaluate a sample of LAN user's access/security profiles to ensure access is appropriate and authorized based on the individual's responsibilities.

16.06.11 Where the LAN is connected to an outside source through a modem or dial-up network, determine what controls are in place to secure these outgoing connections. In particular, does the security firewall function for these connections?

16.06.12. Determine that back-up copies of all LAN files created at intervals are adequate, current, and for disaster-recovery purposes. Ensure that LAN applications have been prioritized and scheduled according to their sensitivity and importance.

16.06.13. Select another sample of LAN application software and verify that they are supported by a written contingency recovery plan and are prioritized by their level of sensitivity and importance. In addition, verify that all the sensitive applications sampled have been subject to a test of the back-up files.

16.06.14. Review the log of LAN downtime for the last six months. If frequent downtime has been recorded, determine if adequate short-term and long-term measures have been implemented to resolve the problem.

16.06.15. Interview the LAN administrator to determine if this person is knowledgeable and properly trained.

16.06.16. If available, obtain the LAN application operating schedule and assess whether key LAN-based financial and operational applications, such as payroll and accounts payable, have adequate processing coverage.

16.06.17. Interview a sample of LAN users and determine if they are satisfied with response time and LAN availability.

when reviewing the smaller information systems organization. This is true whether the information systems department uses packaged software products or software developed in-house.

Controls over access to data can be considered in terms of both specific applications and general controls (see Chapter 17). However, in smaller computer systems, general controls often have a greater importance than specific application data access controls because applications operating on the same LAN or small business computer system will typically all operate under the same set of data-access controls.

In a small system or LAN, data can be improperly accessed and modified in one of three ways:

1. Improper data access attempts through user terminals

2. Unauthorized use of specialized utility programs

3. Invalid information systems requests

Of course, there may also be other ways to access data. In older small business computer systems, there may have been decks of data cards that could be manually accessed and altered. In some newer systems with telecommunications capabilities, it may be possible for outsiders to access files through uncontrolled dial-up telephone lines.

(ii) Improper Data Access through User Workstations.   Small systems, whether LAN-based microcomputer systems or a powerful server-type system, often do not have the sophisticated security found on many larger mainframe systems. Rather, these smaller systems have a user log-on/password identification coupled with menu-based information security. A systems user typically enters the assigned log-on or userid identification code onto the terminal and receives a display of a menu screen with the applications available to that code. The user can only then access the applications assigned to that menu.

For example, a small business computer system may have a series of accounting applications that some users can update and others can only access. Two series of log-on ID codes would be assigned: The first would display a menu of programs to update these various accounting applications and the second would display only the files.

This type of menu-based security, historically found in systems such as an IBM AS/ 400, can provide a fairly effective control against improper access attempts. However, these controls often tend to break down due to the informality of many smaller organizations. Log-on codes are often not changed on a regular basis, one general menu is given to virtually all employees, or terminals with more privileged IDs are left on for virtually all to use. Because users are generally not aware of potential data sensitivities and vulnerabilities, management may give only minimal attention to such security issues.

In order to review controls in this area, internal audit should first gain a general understanding of the data security system installed. Such security ranges from good password-based systems and highly structured menu systems to quite rudimentary sets of procedures. The next step is to understand how that security system has been implemented in the system under audit. Finally, internal audit should determine how that system is being used. The latter step implies that the auditor should spend some time reviewing the use of the application and its controls in user areas.

A small business computer system may not have the logging mechanisms to monitor invalid access attempts. Instead, internal audit should review the overall administration procedures covering the security system. These can include reviewing how often log-ons are changed, who has access to the system administrator's menu, and what local management's general appreciation is of information systems access controls. Computer systems logical security controls are discussed in Chapter 19.

(iii) Unauthorized Use of Utility Programs. Modern small systems often are equipped with powerful utility programs that can easily change any application data file. These programs are designed to be used for special problem-solving situations, and they often produce no audit trail report. All too often, these utilities serve as substitutes for normal production update programs or are used by an information systems manager for these special updates, and sometimes are even given to users.

For example, an organization may have installed an inventory status system. While the system normally provides proper stockkeeping records, the inventory status may become misstated from time to time due to a variety of reasons. In order to help users correct these inventory status record-keeping problems, the information systems manager or LAN administrator may have developed the practice of correcting inventory balances through the use of a utility program. While the information systems manager may be following proper management direction in the normal use of such a program, there may be no audit trails over its use.

These utility programs go by a variety of names depending upon the type of computer operating system used. For example, in a UNIX operating system environment, the *su* or super-user command has some powerful attributes that should be protected. Internal audit should understand the types of standard utility programs available for the system under review. The usage of the particular program can best be determined through inquiry and observation.

(iv) Improper Information Systems Data and Program Access Requests. The informality of smaller organizations often allows data to be accessed improperly through normal information systems operations procedures. For example, someone known to the information systems function may initiate a special computer run, which results in an improper access to confidential data. In larger, more formal organizations, such a request would often require some type of special management permission, but smaller, more informal organizations often waive such requirements. This type of access may be a greater control risk than access through use of improper programs.

Internal audit should look for controls to prevent such casual information systems requests. The best control could be a formal "request for data services" type of form, approved by management. In addition, logs should be maintained listing all production information systems activities as well as the name of the requester and the report recipient.

Many of the control concerns over improper access to data also apply to small system program libraries. Small business system mini- or microcomputers typically do not have the sophisticated software control tools over program libraries found in larger, mainframe systems. However, many do have menu-based systems that offer some security types of controls. Without such a proper menu type of security system to limit improper access, it can often be relatively easy for someone with a little knowledge to locate and potentially modify program library files. The strongest compensating control, perhaps, is that micro-computer programs, in particular, are written in languages such as C++ or JAVA, which may not be familiar to many potential perpetrators.

Internal audit may also find weak controls over program library updates. The one or two information systems personnel in a smaller information systems department who act as the LAN administrators typically can update program libraries with little concern for documenting those changes or for obtaining any type of upper management authorization. While some of these changes may be justified in order to respond to user emergency requests, others may not be properly authorized.

It is difficult, if not impossible, to install separation-of-duties organization controls over small business system program libraries. In addition, it probably will not work for internal audit to suggest that management formally review and approve all program library updates—they will neither be interested in nor have the technical skills to perform such reviews. The best control method here might be to install procedures that require the logging of all changes or software package updates to the production program library, with such logs subject to periodic internal auditor reviews.

This type of control takes advantage of the fact that many small business computer system program compilers maintain a hash[2] total count of the program size in bytes and also have the ability to retain some form of date or version number within the program name. Internal audit might then suggest a small business computer system program library control as follows:

1. Establish program naming conventions that include the date or version number included with the program name. When not available in commercially purchased software, a separate control file with this data can be established. This feature is becoming increasingly common; for example, it can be implemented within the Windows 95 or Windows NT operating systems.

2. Have the persons authorized to make program changes log in the version number, date, program size, and reason for the change in a manual listing subject to periodic management. If the application was developed in-house, the source code should contain comments explaining the change.

3. Maintain at least one backup copy of the program library and rotate a copy of the program library file to an off-site location at least once per week.

4. Strengthen access controls such that nonauthorized personnel cannot easily access program library files.

5. Perform an internal audit review of the library change log on a periodic basis. That review should match logged program versions, dates, and sizes with data reported on the program library file.

The above steps will not provide internal audit with complete assurance that all program changes have been authorized; however, if internal audit periodically reviews logged changes and questions any discrepancies, programmers will probably take care to document and log any production program changes.

(d) SMALLER SYSTEMS AND LAN OPERATIONS CONTROLS

As previously discussed, traditional information systems operations control concerns, such as a review of console log files, are not practical in the modern larger data center. Internal

---

[2] A hash total is a summation of the numeric and alphabetic values for some computer value. It is used as a control total.

audit questions about console log reviews are typically not appropriate because of the complexity of larger systems. Such control concerns may still be applicable in the smaller computer system.

Computer operators or LAN administrators can represent a significant control risk in the smaller information systems operation. Operators can often bypass system controls or can insert incorrect run parameters through console log entries. Smaller computer systems often do not have the software and hardware tools to monitor such operator activities. Internal audit, nevertheless, should have similar control objectives for smaller business systems or LAN operations as for those discussed previously as operational controls in larger systems. Because of the lack of hardware and software control tools, internal audit should spend much more time reviewing and understanding individual computer or network operations procedural controls.

Many smaller computer hardware and operating systems software packages are designed such that a traditional systems programmer function is not necessary. For example, the IBM AS/400's operating system is designed effectively to "tune" the system better than could be accomplished by most system programmers. Smaller computer systems do, however, require some type of technical person to back up files, to reset passwords, and to install program library upgrades. In a microcomputer environment, this person is often called the LAN administrator, a very key person in a LAN environment. This is a critical control area for many microcomputer systems and should be a key component of internal audit's review activities.

A prime control concern in the smaller computer center is often just whether the information systems organization is keeping the operating system and related software products properly updated. Both computer and software vendors will regularly supply upgrades for their products. If such upgrades are not installed on a fairly regular basis, the system can quickly become out-of-date and unreliable.

(e) SMALL BUSINESS COMPUTER SYSTEM CONTROLS

The informality found in many small business computer systems and discussed above often makes internal audit's task even more difficult because management often does not understand the need for controls in the smaller, user-friendly type of computer environment. Internal auditors should attempt to exercise a bit of creativity when making controls improvement recommendations for the smaller data center. That is, internal audit should consider analogies to manual control concepts and determine if those are in place. In addition, compensating control procedures should be suggested when they will tend to be more cost effective than more traditional control procedures.

16-4 SPECIALIZED INFORMATION SYSTEMS CONTROL AREAS

The larger, modern information systems operation typically has a variety of technical support functions to manage its specialized software tools. These might include a systems programming function or network specialist to maintain the operating system and related communications processors; database administration to maintain the database software, including the data dictionary; and telecommunications support to manage the various necessary hardware and software telecommunications products.

While these information systems operations functions are essential to the overall control environment of the information systems organization, they are often ignored by auditors. This is perhaps because internal auditors find it difficult to think of these functions in the same context as, for example, the controls issues surrounding an accounts receivable application that uses some newer technology. Nevertheless, there are some strong analogies between applications controls and the control procedures that should be in place in these technical support areas.

Internal audit is most effective in reviewing technical areas if not put off by the technical jargon and mystique associated with the particular function. Internal auditors do not need to know the technical issues associated with installing IBM's MVS/XA operating system to ask questions about how the project is being managed, what the procedures are for testing, and how results and progress are reported to information systems management.

(a) SYSTEMS PROGRAMMING CONTROLS

As noted, a larger information systems function will typically have a separate systems programming group or function. If information systems management has elected to place that function as part of the applications programming group, internal audit should raise separation-of-duties concerns.

A systems programming function generally has the responsibility for the following general areas:

- Installing new systems software products, operating system components, and installing the upgrades to them
- Adjusting systems parameters or "tuning" hardware and software components to improve overall performance
- Establishing and testing backup and recovery procedures
- Resolving system-level hardware and software problems
- Consulting with applications programmers with job control language (JCL) problems

The nature of many systems programming projects requires emergency procedures to fix a system problem or bug. If a major business application fails due to an operating system or related failure, systems programmers will be under severe pressure to bring the system back up with little consideration given to following documented procedures. The well-managed organization, however, should have some formalized procedures in place to correct these types of problems. In addition, systems programmers often find it necessary to interact more closely with computer operations than would be normal for applications programmers. In many respects, the larger computer systems programming function operates more like an engineering or scientific support function than one of functional information systems support. It should probably be managed as such, and internal audit should look for procedural controls to properly manage such a creative, technical support function.

Figure 16.7 contains suggested procedures for reviewing the systems programming function. Many of these are management controls, such as reviewing project planning or documentation. Since internal auditors typically do not come from systems programming or technical backgrounds, they will probably not have the necessary skills to evaluate technical materials. The audit procedures outlined in Figure 16.6 can probably be performed by inquiry and do not require specialized operating system knowledge.

Systems programming is an important element in the overall controls environment

Figure 16.7 Systems Programming Function Control Procedures

Obj. 16.7.1. The duties of the systems-programming function should be organizationally separate from the systems-development function and computer operations.

Proc. 16.7.1.1. Review the organization of the systems-programming function, including its reporting relationships, and assess the level of separation of duties.

Proc. 16.7.1.2. Determine that systems programmers are prohibited from changing production files and programs.

Proc. 16.7.1.3. Determine that systems programmers are prohibited from operating computer systems when production files or application programs are resident.

Proc. 16.7.1.4. Determine that responsibilities for various processors or software products are rotated periodically among members of the systems-programming staff.

Obj. 16.7.2. Systems-programming activities should be documented and approved by information systems management.

Proc. 16.7.2.1. Determine that all systems-programming activities are approved by proper levels of management and, when appropriate, that project budgets are established.

Proc. 16.7.2.2. Determine that documentation standards exist for all systems-programming activities including descriptions of software options selected; vendor-supplied changes, fixes, or version enhancements; special user exit routines.

Proc. 16.7.2.3. Determine that systems programmers record time against authorized projects or other activities as specified by management.

Proc. 16.7.2.4. Trace the activities logged on selected programmer timesheets to documentation records to determine that the activities were approved and documented.

Proc. 16.7.2.5. Determine that all systems software documentation, including documentation supplied by vendors, is restricted to persons with a need to know.

Proc. 16.7.2.6. Review the level of system utilities in use and assess whether such usage is appropriate.

Obj. 16.7.3. The selection and acquisition of new operating systems software and utilities should follow the same purchase justification and approval standards as used for application software.

Proc. 16.7.3.1. Describe procedures for selecting new systems software products and determine if the same standards are used as for application software.

Proc. 16.7.3.2. Review procedures used to catalog systems software products and to control their versions or release levels.

Proc. 16.7.3.3. When a systems software product is used by applications programmers, assess the adequacy of procedures to communicate the use of this product and to help with any programmer questions.

Proc. 16.7.3.4. Select several systems software products and both review documentation and discuss product usage to ensure that:
- The software product is still being used
- Vendor licenses for the product are current
- Documentation for the product is current

of a larger information systems organization. If the total information systems organization is sufficiently large, internal audit management might consider training selected members of its staff with systems programming specialized controls review skills.

(b) TELECOMMUNICATIONS SUPPORT CONTROLS

The typical larger computer center has a telecommunications network of many terminals, LANs, WANs, distributed processors, and other devices attached to central computer intranets or to the Internet. These telecommunications networks may stretch to remote facilities in other cities or even other countries. Because of the many telecommunications technologies in use, information systems organizations often have a telecommunications support facility within their information systems department.

Depending upon the organization's needs, telecommunications may be part of systems programming or may be a separate department. However, it will usually perform some of the following functions:

- Helping applications developers and users to plan the most efficient data communications networks
- Working with hardware and telecommunications vendors to promote efficiency and resolve problems
- Establishing standards and certification procedures for new devices on the network
- Helping to develop related communications networks such as LANs or even wireless links

In some organizations, the information systems telecommunications function has responsibility for voice or regular telephone communications as well as for data. In others, this function is also responsible for security over the telecommunications lines. As a first step to reviewing telecommunications operations, internal audit should understand the scope and extent of the telecommunications network.

Some very preliminary control procedures for a review of an information systems telecommunications support function are outlined in Figure 16.8. These audit procedures have been limited to inquiry and observation types of steps, and a detailed review, beyond asking general management controls–oriented questions, must be performed by someone with specialized telecommunications skills. (*Computer Audit, Control, and Security,* referenced earlier, provides more information on auditing telecommunications controls and an approach to performing audits in this area.)

(c) DATABASE ADMINISTRATION

Modern information systems, whether mainframe client-server or desktop systems, use database technologies to manage information better and to share data rather than retain it in redundant storage locations. Because database software is a specialized product that supports many users and applications, database administration is often a separate function in the larger information systems organization and may be located with the other technical support departments or may be part of applications development.

Before reviewing the database administration function, internal audit should have a general knowledge of the database product being used in the organization. This is often

Figure 16.8 Telecommunications Administration Control Procedures

Obj. 16.8.1. The information systems telecommunications network should be controlled through a central administrative function.

Proc. 16.8.1.1. Interview personnel responsible for the data-processing telecommunications network and assess their authority and responsibility for management of the function.

Proc. 16.8.1.2. Determine whether the telecommunications network management function has developed appropriate records documenting the existing network.

Proc. 16.8.1.3. Review procedures for making changes to the telecommunications network and determine if there is an appropriate level of management approval.

Proc. 16.8.1.4. Review telecommunications network management policies and procedures and assess the extent to which these are communicated to users of the network.

Proc. 16.8.1.5. Review procedures for allowing outside, Internet-type access to the network and assess whether this appears justified given business demands and security risks.

Obj. 16.8.2. Inventory and "device ID" identification controls should be maintained for all terminals on the telecommunications network.

Proc. 16.8.2.1. Obtain an inventory listing of all terminals or other devices attached to the in-house communications network.

Proc. 16.8.2.2. Determine that standards exist to assure that only authorized terminals or devices are connected to the network.

Proc. 16.8.2.3. Select several terminals from inventory listings and verify inventory information by checking the actual terminal installations.

Proc. 16.8.2.4. Select a sample of workstations or terminals in user areas and trace their attributes back to telecommunications records to determine whether records are correct.

Obj. 16.8.3. If employees or others are allowed to access the network through home computer systems or laptop devices, access should be limited to only those with a business need to use the system.

Proc. 16.8.3.1. Obtain a list of all employees and others authorized to access the system through remote devices and assess if procedures appear to be well controlled.

Proc. 16.8.3.2. Review the adequacy of software security and other authentication procedures to discourage unauthorized access from remote computer systems.

Proc. 16.8.3.3. Determine that procedures are in place to terminate access rights when employees leave the organization or accept different positions no longer requiring system access.

Obj. 16.8.4. All system access should be controlled through passwords and authorizations codes that are validated by security software.

Proc. 16.8.4.1. Review procedures for granting authorization codes to terminals and determine that access authorizations are canceled when a terminal has been inactive for a specified length of time.

Proc. 16.8.4.2. Review procedures for granting access passwords and determine that passwords are assigned to specific individuals rather than functions.

(continued)

Figure 16.8 *(Continued)*

Proc. 16.8.4.3. Review procedures for canceling passwords when an individual leaves the organization or has a change in responsibilities and assess whether these procedures are adequate.

Proc. 16.8.4.4. Select several former employees from personnel records and determine that their terminal access rights have been deleted.

Obj. 16.8.5. Appropriate levels of "fire walls" should be in place to prevent any incoming transmissions of data or programs from accessing other production files or data.

Proc. 16.8.5.1. If outside service providers are used, determine through inquiry the types of fire wall protections in place, whether a special system or used monitor, and assess adequacy.

Proc. 16.8.5.2. Determine through inquiry whether arrangements have been made with outside service providers to provide indemnification against the harmful effects of hacking.

Proc. 16.8.5.3. Select a sample of access calls to outside providers to determine if this activity is for legitimate business purposes. Access these lines to determine they are not "joke" boards or worse.

Obj. 16.8.6. All telecommunications accesses to the computer system should be logged, and logs should be reviewed periodically by data-processing or telecommunications management.

Proc. 16.8.6.1. Develop an understanding of the software tools in place to monitor telecommunications activity.

Proc. 16.8.6.2. Review telecommunications administration procedures for reviewing control logs and following up on exceptional situations.

Proc. 16.8.6.3. Review telecommunications logs for several periods and determine that any exceptions have been reviewed and resolved by appropriate levels of management.

Obj. 16.8.7. The use of dial-up lines to the computer systems should be controlled to prevent unauthorized access attempts.

Proc. 16.8.7.1. Survey the number of dial-up lines that are available within the telecommunications network and assess their relative need.

Proc. 16.8.7.2. Determine whether existing dial-up lines are necessary and have been approved by management.

Proc. 16.8.7.3. Determine if callback devices, see-through security units, and other controls have been installed on dial-up lines to prevent improper access attempts.

Proc. 16.8.7.4. Determine that the security system logs a potential user off the system after a very limited number of unsuccessful password or authorization code access attempts.

Obj. 16.8.8. Master terminals, which can change the access rights of other terminals or users, should only be located in secure locations.

Proc. 16.8.8.1. Identify the number of terminals designated as master terminals for various applications and assess whether that number appears reasonable or seems to be excessive.

Proc. 16.8.8.2. Verify that all authorized master terminals are located in secure or highly visible locations so that unauthorized individuals are blocked from easy access.

(continued)

Figure 16.8 (*Continued*)

Obj. 16.8.9. Sensitive data should be encrypted or otherwise protected when transmitted, to prevent message interception.

  Proc. 16.8.9.1. Determine whether the information systems handle any sensitive data that should be encrypted to prevent detection. If so, develop an understanding of the techniques used.

  Proc. 16.8.9.2. Determine whether procedures exist to identify risks where data should be encrypted and review encryption procedures, as discussed in Chapter 19.

Obj. 16.8.10. Manufacturer, software vendor, and third-party access lines to the computer system should be monitored, with frequent changes made to lines and their access codes.

  Proc. 16.8.10.1. When outside service providers or others have access to the computer system, determine whether those requirements appear to be justified.

  Proc. 16.8.10.2. Determine that outside user authorization codes are changed periodically.

Obj. 16.8.11. All requests for uploads or downloads of data or programs from distributed processors (such as microcomputers) should be subject to management review and approval.

  Proc. 16.8.11.1. Determine who is responsible for approving requests for uploads or downloads of data.

  Proc. 16.8.11.2. Review a list of users receiving or transmitting data to the central systems, and determine whether requests have been properly approved and appear to be justified on a need-to-know basis.

  Proc. 16.8.11.3. Determine that remote user access to program libraries is limited strictly to approved users and to read-only capabilities.

Obj. 16.8.12. Telecommunications billings should be monitored to identify potential efficiencies and to detect unauthorized users.

  Proc. 16.8.12.1. Determine that telecommunications billings are compared against authorized users to detect unauthorized usage.

---

called the database management system (DBMS). Database software is offered by many of the hardware vendors as well as by independent suppliers. All such products, however, store data in an independent, logical manner, which can be viewed in multiple perspectives and used by multiple applications. For larger systems, software that creates what is called a relational database is perhaps the most common. Figure 16.9 illustrates the structure of a typical relational database. The stored data is independent of specific applications and may be used by differing applications for differing needs.

The database administration function or department typically interacts with the programming group for new applications and also works with systems programming on database system technical problems. The functions of this department often include:

• Design of logical and physical database structures

• Operation and maintenance of the database software

• Monitoring and tuning the software to improve performance

Figure 16.9   Relational Database Conceptual View

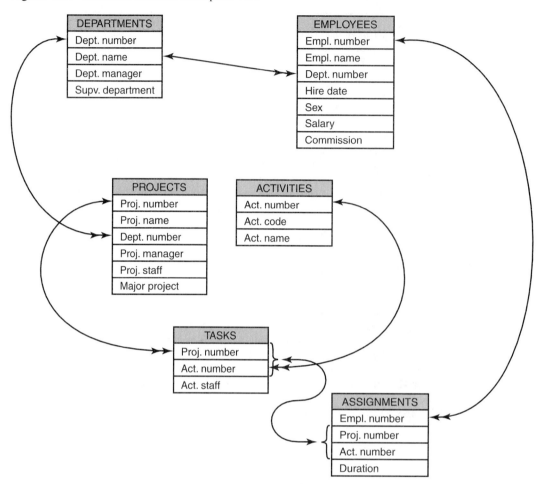

- Maintenance of a data dictionary to define data elements for applications developers
- Maintenance of procedures for the security and the recovery of the database

Database administration should be included in any overall general controls review of a larger information systems operation. An important element is the control over access to specific data elements or units of data that are shared by various users of a database. It is particularly important that there are controls over who can update or access each individual database element.

Database file structures are used by most information systems departments. An understanding of the data-administration function will help internal audit in reviewing application controls and end-user computing controls as well as general controls. Internal audit should also develop an understanding of the retrieval languages associated with individual database packages so that auditors can generate reports in support of their reviews when required.

16-5 FUTURE DIRECTIONS

The use of computer systems in virtually all aspects of the organization makes it crucial for the modern internal auditor to understand some of the control risks and audit procedures associated with computer systems operations. This understanding will allow for more effective operational audits in many areas.

This chapter offered basic information on the control procedures and risks associated with modern computer systems operations, whether classic mainframes, LAN-based client-server applications, or the Internet-connected network computer of today. The procedures described in this chapter generally do not require the knowledge of a computer audit specialist but should be within the capabilities of most if not all members of the internal audit organization. The same will be true for the materials covered in the next chapters, on other areas of information systems controls.

A portion of this chapter was devoted to the classic, large system information systems type of organization. While still very applicable, particularly for large organizations, this classic mainframe type of computer system and organization is rapidly going away. The microcomputer coupled with client-server computing, also discussed in this chapter, is the evolving trend. While the classic mainframe computer system continues to exist for larger organizations, it is rapidly being replaced by LANs, client-server systems, and Internet-based network computers. The communications networks of wire- and satellite-based networks may also be replaced in the future with wireless networks where users can access systems from handheld, personal terminals. Computer systems and computer operations controls will change with these introductions. The modern internal auditor should always survey these trends and adapt existing control procedures to assess these new risks.

CHAPTER 17

Information Systems Application Controls

17-1 INTRODUCTION: THE IMPORTANCE OF APPLICATION CONTROLS

A typical business information systems organization will process a large number of specific applications ranging from the relatively simple, such as an hourly payroll, to the highly complex, such as a manufacturing resource control system. While the general control procedures discussed in Chapter 16 apply to the entire information systems function, specific controls are also associated with each of these applications. In order to perform operational reviews in specific areas such as distribution or engineering, internal auditors must have the skills to understand, evaluate, and test the controls over their supporting information systems applications. Reviews of specific application controls can often be more critical to achieving overall audit objectives than reviews of general information systems controls.

Application controls, however, are very dependent upon the overall information systems general controls, discussed in Chapter 16. For example, if there are inadequate controls over the program library update process, it will be very difficult for an internal auditor to rely on the controls built into a specific application. Even though internal audit may find that an order-entry system, as will be discussed in Chapter 28, is properly screening sales orders for valid credit approvals, the surrounding general controls must also be considered. Without program library update controls, for example, the order-entry system's programs could be changed, without management's authorization, perhaps to accept orders without proper credit approvals.

A typical information systems organization may have a large and diverse number of production applications. They will support a wide variety of functions within the organization, starting with accounting but including such areas as manufacturing, marketing, engineering, and others. Chapters 22 through 30 cover operational audit procedures for many such areas. These chapters provide descriptions of supporting key application systems, implemented using a variety of information systems technologies, such as centralized systems with telecommunication networks, Internet-based network computer systems, client-server applications, and even older batch-processing systems. Some of these applications may have been developed in-house, but increasingly large numbers of them are based on purchased software packages. In-house-developed applications may be written in a language such as C + + or COBOL, a database report-generator language such as SQL, or the object-oriented language JAVA. Applications documentation may range from very complete to almost nonexistent. Despite the best efforts of internal audit to suggest improvements, the same can often be said about application controls.

Management is typically interested in audit findings covering specific application controls reviews. For example, while an audit finding on general controls over computer operating systems program libraries may not generate management interest, a finding of an incorrect discount calculation based on a Euro-currency conversion problem in an accounts payable application is sure to draw attention. However, because of the relative complexity of many information systems applications and because their controls often reside both within the application and in user areas, an audit of information systems applications can often be a challenge to the modern internal auditor.

This chapter discusses how internal auditors can effectively review internal accounting controls in information systems applications, including how to select applications for review, how to develop an understanding of application controls, and how to evaluate and test those controls. These application-review activities can then be used to support an overall review of selected operational areas. (The materials in this chapter are adapted from *Computer Audit, Control, and Security.*[1] Detailed references to that book were included in Chapter 16.)

17-2 INFORMATION SYSTEMS APPLICATION COMPONENTS

An internal auditor should understand the components or elements of a typical computer system application. People not familiar with information systems sometimes think of a computer application just in terms of the system output reports or the data displayed on terminal screens. However, every application, whether an older mainframe business system, a client-server application, or an office productivity package installed on a local microcomputer, has three basic components: the system inputs, the programs used for processing, and the system outputs. Each of these has an important role in the application's control structure.

Early computer systems applications could easily be separated into these three components. The traditional computerized payroll system used time cards and a personnel paymaster file as its inputs to the calculation and updating programs. The outputs from the payroll system were the printed checks, payroll register reports, and updated paymaster files. Today, that same payroll system might accept inputs from an automated plant badge reader that controls accesses and tracks attendance, a shop floor production system that performs incentive pay calculations, various other on-line inputs, and a human resources database. A series of computer programs, some located on a mainframe computer system and others distributed to remote workstations, would do the processing. The modern payroll system's outputs might include credit transactions to transmit to employee bank accounts, pay vouchers mailed to employees, input files to various tax and benefit sources, various display screens, and an updated human resources database. While the input, output, and computer processing system components may not be clear to an auditor performing an initial review, the same three elements exist; however complex the system may be, the

---

[1] Robert Moeller, *Computer Audit, Control, and Security* (New York: John Wiley, 1989).

auditor should always develop an understanding of the application by breaking down its input, output, and processing components. The following paragraphs briefly discuss some of the control aspects of these application components to give an overview on modern information systems applications. The internal auditor unfamiliar with data-processing concepts should consult a textbook or consider taking an introductory computer systems course at a local college.

(a) APPLICATION INPUT COMPONENTS

Every computerized application needs some form of input, whether it be separate transaction vouchers or data supplied from some other automated system. Think of a common hand-held calculator: the device will generate no results unless data of some sort is input through the keyboard.

Although the computer programs in an application determine the outputs and have a major impact on controls, an internal auditor should always understand the nature and sources of them. In traditional, batch-oriented systems, this was a fairly easy process as inputs were sequential records on a tape file or even punched cards. Today, inputs are often generated from various automated sources, including factory data collection devices and specialized bar code readers.

(i) Data Collection and Other Input Devices.

As mentioned, earlier computer systems used punched cards as their input source. A single card carried 80 or 90 columns of alphanumeric encoded data. Users entered their transactions on data collection sheets for keypunching onto one of these card formats. The original data collection sheet was the first step in the input chain. Auditors were concerned that all transactions were keypunched correctly. These cards were then machine-sorted or otherwise manipulated prior to entry into a computer system, being either read directly into a computer program or copied to magnetic tape for subsequent processing on a batch basis. That is, 500 lines of transactions may have been prepared on data collection sheets and processed as a batch. Because up to 500 cards were keypunched with 500 subsequently read into the computer program, concern over these input transactions was a key component of an application's controls.

Technological improvements have essentially eliminated the punched cards and separately keypunched input records. Batch-type transactions that must be entered into a computer application are typically not entered by a specialized "keypunch" or data-entry department. Rather, operational departments use on-line terminals to enter their transactions for collection and subsequent processing. Following a processing schedule, these transactions are all collected and updated in a batch mode. The data-entry programs used to capture them often have some transaction-screening capabilities to eliminate many low-level errors common to earlier batch input systems.

Transaction input data now comes from many other sources. A retail store captures sales inputs through a combination of sales entries entered on the cash register [now called a point of sale (POS) terminal] and product sales entered through bar code readers. Similarly, data is captured on a manufacturing shop floor through various tickets and badges that are entered in readers by workers directly on the shop floor. These are all input devices generating transactions for updating to some type of processing application.

Input transactions are increasingly generated not from within the organization but from applications located in other physical locations and controlled by others. Organizations today receive a wide variety of data transactions through the Internet or electronic data interchange (EDI) systems, discussed in Chapter 24. Here, another organization may submit purchase order transactions, accounts payable remittances, or other significant business transactions. Individuals may even initiate sales transactions, trade securities, and perform other business through their home microcomputers via the Internet. All of these represent input transactions to various computer systems applications. Each has its own unique control considerations.

An internal auditor reviewing input controls over these types of applications should always look for the same basic control elements found in all computer systems. There should be some means of checking that only correct input is entered. A computer program that, through its supporting validation tables, can verify that a part or employee number is or is not valid, cannot easily verify that the current quantity should have been entered as 100 as opposed to 10. The older batch systems had hash total checks to help check for these possible errors. Hash totals are given often as a nonmonetary value such as the ''sum'' of all account numbers. Modern systems need reasonableness checks built into their data-collection procedures, and the programs processing the transactions need controls to prevent errors or to provide warning signals.

(ii) Inputs from Other Automated Systems.   Computer applications are often highly integrated, with one application generating an output file of data or transactions for processing by other applications. The transaction entered into one system may impact a variety of other interrelated applications. Thus, an error or omission of an input at one point in a chain of applications may impact the processing of another connected application.

In addition to understanding the sources of the batch transactions to an application, an internal auditor should understand the nature of all other automated inputs to that same application. For example, a modern payroll system may receive inputs from a sales performance system to calculate sales commissions. The sales performance file that feeds the payroll system is another input. The input controls there are based on the input, processing, and output controls of the sales performance system. If sales performance data represent a significant input to the payroll system, the internal auditor needs to be concerned about the controls over it, as well as over any other supporting applications.

A large network of interconnected applications can present a challenge to the auditor attempting to review the input controls for just one of these. An internal auditor may be interested in understanding application input controls for application X. However, files from applications A, B, and C provide inputs to X while D and E provide inputs to A and C, respectively. In order to review input controls, an internal auditor typically does not have the time or resources to review all of these processes. The auditor must decide on the most critical of them and assume the other less critical supporting applications are generating appropriate transactions.

(iii) Files and Databases.   Although usually generated by some other supporting application or updated by the application under review itself, various files and databases represent important inputs. In some instances, these files represent tables of data used for the validation of program data. As part of gaining an understanding of an application, the internal auditor should understand the nature and content of all supporting application files. The software that controls these files generally has various record-counting and other logical controls to determine that all transactions are correctly written onto and can be retrieved from the magnetic media. Files also have their own dating and label-checking controls to prevent them from being improperly input, such as in the wrong processing cycle or to an incorrect application.

Once written as streams of sequential records on magnetic tape, today's files are input onto higher-density tape cartridges, microcomputer diskettes, or magnetic disc memory. Some of the controls surrounding those devices are covered by the general controls discussed in Chapter 16. However, the internal auditor needs a general understanding not only of the type and nature of inputs to a computer application but also of the source of the file data and any controls over it. This will be discussed in greater detail later in this chapter.

Database files can represent a particular challenge to the auditor. Although the term *database* is often misused to refer to almost every type of computer file, a database is in fact a method of organizing data in a computerized format such that all important data elements point or relate to each other. In past years, many mainframe computer systems used what were called *hierarchical databases,* where data was organized in a "family tree" type of structure. IBM's mainframe product called IMS (Integrated Management System) was the most popular type of this software. In a manufacturing organization, each product might be organized as a header record that would point to each of its parts. Those components in turn would each have a hierarchy of records comprising its individual parts. Figure 17.1 shows how a hierarchical database is organized. File integrity is very important here because a program error that breaks one of the connecting chains would make it difficult to retrieve the lost data.

The relational database is a much more common file structure found on all types and sizes of computers. A relational database is like a multi-dimensional microcomputer spreadsheet. That is, the user can retrieve data across various database rows and columns rather than having to go to the head of each tree and then search down through that tree to retrieve the desired data. Figure 16.9 in Chapter 16 illustrates a relational database structure. In addition to being a very effective way to organize input data to application systems, these databases allow for easy retrieval of end user–oriented reports.

(b) APPLICATION PROGRAMS

Applications are processed through a series of computer programs or sets of machine instructions. The payroll system example in this chapter consists of a series of computer programs. One of the programs perhaps reads the employee's time card data, stores the number of hours worked, and then uses the employee number on the input time card to look up the employee's rate and scheduled deductions. Based upon this match, the program looks up the employee's rate of pay and multiplies this by the number of hours worked to calculate the gross pay.

A computer program is a set of instructions covering every detail of a process. The process of writing a program is simply a process of writing detailed instructions and then following them to the letter. As an experiment, to comprehend the details required to write a larger program, write down each step to follow in the morning from the time the alarm goes off until arrival at the office. Do this one day, documenting all normal actions as well as alternate decision paths, such as whether to have fruit or cereal. The following morning, use these same instructions *exactly* as they are written to get up, wash and dress, and then go off to work. Most will arrive at work missing an item of clothes or worse. This is the difficulty of writing detailed computer programs! It is often not necessary for internal auditors to know how to write formal computer programs today beyond the simple audit-retrieval applications discussed in Chapter 12, but the effective internal auditor should understand how computer application programs are built and what their capabilities are, to define appropriate control procedures.

Figure 17.1 Hierarchical Database Example

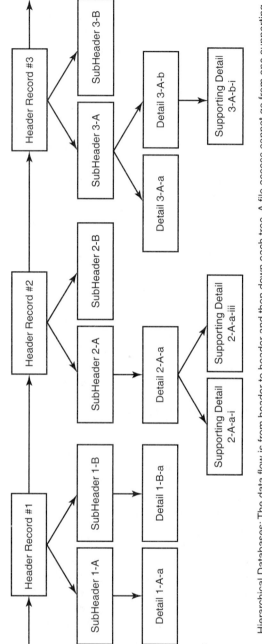

Hierarchical Databases: The data flow is from header to header and then down each tree. A file access cannot go from one supporting detail to another unless it goes up the tree structure first and then back down.

(i) Traditional Mainframe Programs.   Mainframe computers have been used extensively for business applications since the early 1960s, using a variety of programming languages. Computer systems were first programmed with the actual binary computer machine language of 1s and 0s, before computers were generally used for business applications. Machine language is called the first-generation language, while assembly language—a symbolic language with codes to represent instructions (such as to add or to store a value)—is called the second generation.

Third-generation languages soon followed. They used actual English-like instruction statements such as ''ADD A TO B'' to describe the actions to be taken. Programs called *compilers* translated these instructions into machine language. Although a large variety of these third-generation or compiler languages were introduced in the 1960s, COBOL became the almost standard language for business data processing. Illustrating its English-like character, Figure 17.2 shows examples of COBOL, which was the predominant lan-

Figure 17.2   COBOL Programming Language Styles

I. COBOL is an English-like language using verbs to describe actions to be performed and alphanumeric symbols to describe data fields. For example, employee hours worked might be carried in a data item called HOURS-WORKED and pay rates might be called just that, PAY-RATES. While pay rates would be carried in a table for all employees, the pay calculation here would be:

MULTIPLY HOURS-WORKED BY PAY-RATE GIVING GROSS-PAY ROUNDED

The above statement calculates a rounded value for GROSS-PAY which is then used for further pay processing.

II. COBOL program statements are organized almost as text where sets of instructions are grouped by paragraphs. The set of instructions to the pay calculation might be called PAY-CALC. A program can get back to these paragraph names by what is called a GO TO instruction. The very last two lines of the above pay calculation might be:

PRINT FINAL-PAY.
GO TO PAY-CALC.

These final two instructions would complete the pay calculation of pay for one employee and go back to the beginning of the paragraph for the next. However, GO TO statements can cause a problem for complex COBOL programs, with program code instructions pointing a variety of different ways.

III. A better way to organize COBOL is through what is called *structural programming*. Here, sets of instructions are organized as subroutines. The example program would call up the pay calculation subroutine by stating PERFORM PAY-CALC. Then, all of the calculations for pay would be grouped together, and rather than ending with a GO TO, the subroutine would simply terminate with an END. This would return the program control back to the statement following PERFORM PAY-CALC, perhaps PERFORM PRINT-CHECKS.

While they can be very simple, COBOL programs can also be very complex and difficult to read and understand. A strong set of programming standards should help make this process more manageable.

guage for business applications well into the 1980s. It is still quite common today for classic mainframe systems; however, specialized database and report-generator languages as well as object-oriented languages are making increasing inroads.

The manner in which COBOL business programs are written has changed over the years as well. Earlier programs followed almost no standards. A programmer might insert a variable value such as an overhead rate into the COBOL code. When that rate changed at a later date, a programmer had to search through the program listing because the language often provided insufficient index cross-references. Early programs were sometimes written with program logic that was difficult to follow and where control errors were quite possible. These practices were a major reason for the year 2000 problems starting in the mid-1990s.

As organizations realized that their programming practices needed improvement, they implemented and enforced programming standards. They also introduced a concept called *structured programming,* where program code was written in a manner to make it easier to maintain and less prone to program logic errors. Figure 17.2 shows different COBOL programming techniques up through structured programming and indicates strengths and weaknesses of each. An auditor should understand the basic differences between these programming styles and the control strengths of using structured programming techniques.

(ii) Modern Computer Program Architectures. Where in past years a business application under review would almost always be written in COBOL, today most micro-computer-based programs are associated with either object-oriented or fourth-generation programs, where reports and database manipulations take place using almost English-like instructions. Although both techniques have been used by information systems organizations for some years, they are still considered new and evolving. (See Chapter 20.)

An internal auditor with only a fundamental knowledge of a language such as BASIC or COBOL or C++ may have some initial difficulties understanding how client-server-based applications are programmed and constructed. Often, they consist of many very small program code modules that pass data to one another, sometimes over remote telecommunication lines. The internal auditor should rely on the overall application program standards in place as well as on other programming development and maintenance controls, and rather than looking for these in each given application reviewed, should review the general systems development controls in the information systems organization. These might be included in a general review of information systems operations, as was discussed in Chapter 16. Figure 17.3 contains audit procedures for a review of an applications development or programming organization.

(iii) Purchased Software. Most computer applications today are based upon purchased software. An outside vendor will supply the basic programs, and the information systems development organization only has the responsibility of building custom tables, file interfaces, and output report formats around the purchased application. The actual program source code for the purchased software is often protected by the vendor to prevent improper access and changes. Both the internal auditor and information systems should be concerned that the software vendor is reputable and has a reputation for quality, error-free software. If there is any doubt that the software vendor lacks stability, arrangements should be made at the time of the software purchase contract to place a version of the vendor's source code ''in escrow'' in the event of a vendor business failure. A bank or some

Figure 17.3   Audit Program for a Review of Applications Development Process

Audit _____   Location _____   Date _____

AUDIT STEP	INITIAL	W/P
1. Are formal requests for new or revised applications submitted with proper authorizations?		
2. Has a to-be-completed projects list been prepared and a schedule implemented for accomplishing such tasks?		
3. Do the application development objectives fit within the long-range scheduled plans of the organization?		
4. Have responsibilities for systems development been assigned and sufficient time allotted to complete the assignments?		
5. Is there a sufficient division of responsibilities within the application development function?		
6. Does the application development process contain enough user interviews to obtain an understanding of needs?		
7. Does the applications implementation process give sufficient attention to controls, such as audit trails and security?		
8. Are cost/benefit analyses regularly prepared as part of application designs?		
9. Is the overall application development project management process adequate and are all interested parties represented in key decisions?		
10. Are there adequate controls to ensure that all application data originates from approved sources?		
11. Is there adequate planning to determine that hardware and software will be sufficient when placed into production?		
12. Has sufficient attention been given to the backup and storage of the media used by the application?		
13. Are there adequate controls to provide assurances regarding the integrity of the data processed and the outputs from those applications?		
14. Does the application provide adequate tools for the identification and correction of processing errors?		
15. Does the application have an audit trail to indicate that all transactions got to their present state?		
16. Has adequate documentation been prepared for all applications systems and programming activities?		
17. Has test data been prepared according to a predefined test plan, outlining expected results, and have user groups participated in the test transaction?		

Figure 17.3   (*Continued*)

Audit _____ Location _____ Date _____		
AUDIT STEP	**INITIAL**	**W/P**
18. For a conversion from an existing application, have good control procedures been established over this conversion process?		
19. Has internal audit been invited to participate in a pre-implementation review of all critical systems?		
20. Is there a formal signoff or approval process as part of systems implementation?		

other agency would hold a version of the protected source code for release to customers if the software vendor were to fail.

Audit procedures for reviews of newly purchased software applications are discussed in Chapter 18. The internal auditor should have as good an understanding of these purchased software applications as of any other in-house-developed application.

(c) COMPUTER SYSTEMS OUTPUT DEVICES

We have briefly talked about computer application inputs and the programs to process that input data. No discussion of a system would be complete without a description of computer application outputs, which usually consist of printed reports, output screens, or updated files. This is an important area to survey in an application review, as, in many instances, the controls of internal audit concern in an application are contained on the output reports or control files.

Older applications produced large volumes of output reports indicating the results of the processing and any control or error problems. The sheer volume and frequency of these output reports prevented users giving adequate attention to any reported control problems, unless some other type of problem was discovered. Internal auditors frequently have been able to identify control concerns that users could have identified by just reviewing their output reports.

Today's application produces far fewer paper-based output reports—instead, the results of processing are often reported on on-line data-retrieval screens. In some cases, special on-line reports signal control problems and data errors; in others, the user is responsible for calling up the appropriate screen to review any problems. All too often, this step may be ignored and processing errors can go undetected. Internal auditors should always review the scope of application output reports and their user dispositions.

Reports or screens are not the only output. Often, an application produces few if any output reports but passes transactions or updated files to a variety of other integrated applications. This is essentially the same situation as was discussed previously regarding integrated application inputs. Just as a modern application system may receive its inputs from a highly integrated set of feeding application systems, it may be one more link in a chain to still others. Again and always, the internal auditor should develop a good understanding of the application reviewed as well as all of its inputs and outputs.

17-3 SELECTING APPLICATIONS FOR REVIEW

While all major computer operations centers should be subject to regular reviews, the typical internal audit organization does not have the resources or the time to review the controls for all of its information systems applications. There will be just too many given the limited time, the relative risks, and audit resources available. In addition, many of these applications will have minimal audit risk. As part of a specific operational review or as part of a general information systems controls review, internal audit should select only the more critical applications for review.

The audit process for selecting these applications should be again based on relative risk following the selection procedures outlined in Chapter 7. Because computer systems applications are so critical to the other operations of an organization, internal auditors often receive specific requests to review application controls. Some of the factors which may impact internal audit's decision to select one specific application over another may include:

- *Management Requests.* Internal audit is often asked by management to review the controls in newly installed or other significant information systems applications due to reported problems or their strategic importance to the organization. These management requests are not always made for the correct reasons, however. For example, sales analysis reports may appear to be incorrect due to bad data submitted from a reporting division, but management may consider the incorrect reports to be a "computer problem" and request an internal audit applications review. Internal audit may not initially be aware of such user input problems and would perform normal review procedures. When internal audit is aware of such mitigating circumstances, audit test strategies should be modified prior to starting the review.

- *Post-Implementation Applications Reviews.* Chapter 18, Auditing Systems Under Development, will discuss the process for selecting and reviewing applications controls prior to implementation as well as for performing a prompt post-implementation review. For some critical applications, subject to a risk analysis, auditors may also want to perform a detailed applications review some time after the actual system implementation. If an application has sufficient financial and operational controls significance, internal audit may want to schedule at least limited controls reviews on an ongoing basis.

- *Internal Control Assessment Considerations.* Chapter 2 discussed the objectives and components of the internal control framework in an organization. A computer application controls assessment is an important part of that overall controls evaluation. Internal auditors working on other projects—and external auditors—often are interested in specific information systems applications controls. In their attestation function, external auditors must assess control risk and understand these critical applications, but without the necessary skills to evaluate these controls, they will ask for help from their client internal audit departments to perform the application reviews. While senior management may have only some very general concerns over a given application, the two groups of auditors may have much more specific concerns and internal control objectives.

- *Other Audit Application Selection Criteria.* There are many other reasons why internal audit may select one application over another for a detailed, internal controls–oriented review. These are in addition to those discussed here and in Chapter 7, on audit risk, and may include some of the following considerations:

  - Does the application control significant assets?
  - Does the application represent a significant risk exposure to the organization?
  - Is the application a strategic system for organizational decision-making?
  - Does the application support a function that will be reviewed later as a scheduled internal audit operational review?
  - Have significant changes been made to the application system which were not part of any preimplementation audits?
  - Have there been significant personnel changes in the departments or functions using the application?

Internal audit is typically faced with requests for reviews of a large number of application candidates at any time, and care should be taken in documenting the reasons for selecting one application over another. This will help if internal audit is questioned subsequent to completing a series of reviews.

Audits of the controls over representative information systems applications are sometimes included as part of a general controls review of information systems function. Internal audit should develop a detailed understanding of the general controls surrounding information systems operations (see Chapter 16), and then review the controls surrounding one or more selected applications.

Internal auditors often perform reviews of the specific applications that support an overall functional area. For example, internal audit may schedule a combined operational and financial review of the purchasing department (see Chapter 24). This also may be the appropriate time to review the application controls for the major automated purchasing systems supporting that department. In this integrated audit approach, internal auditors can concentrate on both the more technical issues surrounding the applications and on other supporting operational controls.

17-4 PRELIMINARY STEPS TO PERFORMING THE APPLICATIONS REVIEW

Once an application has been selected for review, an internal auditor should gain an understanding of the purpose or objectives of that application, the computer systems technology approaches or methods used, and the relationship of that application to other automated or significant processes. It may be necessary for the assigned internal auditor to do some background reading and study special technical aspects of that application.

This auditor understanding can often be accomplished through reviews of past audit workpapers (if available), interviews with information systems and user personnel, and reviews of applications documentation. While prior audit workpapers can be very helpful and the interview process will allow an auditor to ask relevant controls-related questions, a review of applications documentation is often a quite useful first step in reviewing and evaluating the controls over an information systems application. As the second step, an internal auditor should perform a ''walk-through'' of the application to better understand how it works and how its controls function. These preliminary steps will allow an internal auditor to develop specific audit tests of the application's more significant controls.

(a) DOCUMENTATION REVIEWS TO UNDERSTAND APPLICATIONS COMPONENTS

In the early days of computerized applications, documentation often consisted of detailed program and system flowcharts and record layouts, and little else. This helped the programmer but was of little use to application users and provided only minimal help to internal auditors attempting to understand the application. In addition, these early flowcharts were often hand-prepared and became quickly out of date. When one relatively small change was subsequently added to a complex system flowchart, designers were often reluctant to erase or to redraw their charts. They remembered the change but other interested persons reviewing this documentation, such as internal auditors, would not be aware of them.

Over time, applications documentation evolved into a more text- and functional chart–oriented format. Decision tables and logic charts described the functions of individual programs while extensive amounts of text described the overall system. Although this type of documentation was more functional and less technical, it also had a tendency to become quickly out of date. Programmers and system designers often would not take the time to incorporate later changes into this systems documentation.

Powerful microcomputer- or computer-aided systems engineering (CASE)–based documentation tools are now available. Flowcharts today are usually produced on a microcomputer using a simple flowchart-generator package. Many easily maintained automation tools are available to provide this type of technical documentation. A real strength of these automated documentation tools is that detailed flowcharts can be combined into summarized versions with changes introduced on one chart updating all others.

Internal audit can expect to find various types and quantities of applications documentation depending upon the relative age of the application to be reviewed. Due to poor information systems management procedures, complex in-house-developed applications may have very limited documentation. The published documentation covering some of the popular outside vendor–supplied insurance or banking application systems, on the other hand, will sometimes cover many dozens of volumes of descriptive text. Users will treat such documentation as almost encyclopeadiatic reference materials.

A review of the published documentation should be a first step to gaining an audit understanding of an application. If aspects of the documentation are missing or out of date, the internal auditor will probably have a finding at the conclusion of the review. However, this lack of documentation should not necessarily prevent an internal auditor from performing an application review. When performing the review, internal audit should normally look for the following documentation elements:

- *Systems Development Methodology (SDM) Initiating Documents.* These refer to the initial project requests, any cost/benefit justifications, and the general systems design requirements. Although many initial assumptions may have changed during the systems design and implementation process, these documents will help internal audit understand why the application was designed and controlled in the manner it is. These documents should follow the organization's SDM procedures, described in Chapter 18.

- *Functional Design Specifications.* This documentation should describe the application in some detail. Each of the program elements, database specifications, and systems controls should be described. If major changes have been made to the application since its original implementation, these changes should also be reflected in the design documentation. Their purpose is to allow the information systems department analyst to be able to make changes or to respond to user questions regarding the application.

- *Program Change Histories.* There should be some type of log or documented record listing all program changes within an application. Some information systems departments keep this with the applications documentation while others maintain it in a central file cross-referenced to the program source code. While this type of documentation is an essential element to control program changes, it will also provide internal audit with some feeling for the application's relative stability. A large number of ongoing change requests for a given application may mean that the application system is not achieving user objectives.

- *User Documentation Manuals.* Along with the technical documentation, some form of user documentation should be prepared for the application. With a modern, on-line system, much of this user documentation may be in the form of ''HELP'' or ''READ ME'' types of on-line screens. However, this documentation should be sufficiently comprehensive to answer user questions.

Internal audit should review this documentation to gain an understanding for the application controls review to be performed and may want to use these materials to develop questions for later interviews. Copies of key or representative sections should also be taken for workpaper documentation. However, internal audit should normally not attempt to copy the entire documentation file for workpaper purposes. This is all too often done by auditors. While adding considerable bulk to workpaper files, the practice does little to accomplish audit objectives!

(b) CONDUCTING THE APPLICATION WALK-THROUGH

Once internal audit has reviewed prior workpapers and the applications documentation, and interviewed users and information systems personnel to clarify any questions raised through the applications documentation's review, a next step is to verify internal audit's understanding of the application by a *walk-through*. This term refers to the same process an internal auditor frequently will do prior to the initial review of an operational facility; the auditor would request a tour of the facility, such as a production floor. The purpose of this walk-through is to confirm internal audit's initial or general understanding about how the operational facility or computer systems application operates. Its purpose is not to test application controls; this will be covered in a subsequent audit step.

An example of a system to be reviewed might better help to explain the application walk-through process. Assume that internal audit has been asked to review the controls over an older in-house-developed on-line accounts payable application written in COBOL on the corporate mainframe computer. The organization, however, is a manufacturing firm with fairly sophisticated information systems applications. This accounts payable application was installed several years before but had never been reviewed when it was under development. Now, management has asked internal audit to review the application's internal controls.

Based upon the review of application documentation, the auditor has determined that the application receives inputs from the following sources:

- Purchase order commitments from a microcomputer-based purchasing system
- Notifications of goods received from the materials-receiving system
- Various on-line terminal payment transactions for goods and services that are not recorded through the materials-receiving system
- Payment approval transactions entered through an input screen
- Miscellaneous payables journal transactions entered as batch data

Application data is recorded on a relational database along with tables of values for validating purchase terms, including the calculation of cash discounts. Based upon the review of documentation, application outputs include the following:

- Accounts payable electronic fund transfer transactions as well as paper checks
- Transactions to the general ledger application
- Transactions to cost accounting applications
- Various control and accounting summary screens and reports

The prime users responsible for the system are general accounting department personnel as well as members of the purchasing department who set up automatic vendor payments under preagreed terms.

The example application flowchart in Figure 17.4 will be used to describe an applications walk-through and will also be referenced in other examples in this chapter. The steps to performing an application walk-through for the example on-line accounts payable application are as follows:

1. *Briefly describe the application for the audit workpapers.* Based on internal audit's review of the applications documentation, a brief description of the application should be prepared for later inclusion in the audit workpapers. This workpaper documentation follows the general format of the walk-through description except there should be greater detail and it should identify key subsystems, input screen formats, key data file names, and output report formats. (For a discussion of audit workpapers, see Chapter 11.)

2. *Develop a block diagram description of the application.* This diagram represents an abbreviated auditor-level systems or functional level flowchart for the application. It should reflect the above-written description and also illustrate some application flow concepts. This hand-drawn document will help increase auditor understanding of the application reviewed. Figure 17.4 is an example of such a system block diagram. Internal audit can use this diagram to confirm internal audit's understanding of the system with key information systems and user personnel.

3. *Select key transactions from the system.* Based on the above, one or several input transactions should be selected to walk or to trace through the application. This selection would be based on discussions with users and fellow members of the audit team. In our example accounts payable system, the auditor may select the automated transactions that the receiving system should match against the payables purchase order records to initiate payment.

4. *Walk a selected transaction through the system.* In the days of manual or simpler

Figure 17.4   Application Block Diagram Example

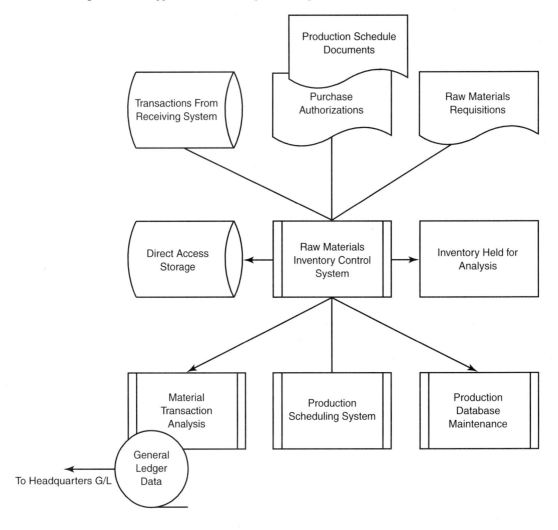

information systems application, a walk-through amounted to just what the words say. That is, an auditor would take an input transaction form and would walk it through each of the clerical desks or steps normally used to process the transaction to verify the processing procedures.

In a modern application, this walk process typically requires recording a transaction as it is entered into a terminal and then following that particular transaction through subsequent system steps. In this accounts payable example, the walk-through transaction is a receiving report entry indicating that a valid open purchase commitment had been received. Internal audit would then review the open commitments module of the system to determine whether the transaction was recorded on a transaction report or screen. It should then be traced to a properly computed accounts payable check or to a funds-transfer transaction and then to transactions given to the general ledger system for the net amount as well as for any cash discount taken.

This type of applications testing is often called *compliance testing.* That is, internal audit is verifying that the application is operating in compliance with preestablished control procedures. If internal audit wished to verify that all accounts payable checks had been input to the general ledger through a comparison of account balances or other methods, this would be called *substantive testing,* or tests of financial statement balances.

5. *Modify the system understanding as required.* Since the purpose of an application walk-through is to develop a basic understanding of its functions and controls, this preliminary review does not allow internal audit to test whether *all* transactions are working as described. However, if internal audit discovers that the walk-through transactions are not working as assumed, the preliminary auditor-prepared application documentation may need to be revised. Once revised, internal audit may want to repeat the above steps to determine that internal audit has a proper understanding of system transaction flows.

These application walk-through steps are summarized in Figure 17.5. The walk-through allows internal audit to gain a preliminary understanding of not only the application and its controls, but also its relationship with other automated systems or processes. Limited

Figure 17.5   Application Walk-Through Auditor Steps

1. Develop a general understanding of the application, its inputs and outputs, and steps requiring manual intervention.

2. For an application with a large number of steps requiring manual processing, select a sample of transactions to be processed from a normal production cycle. For workpaper documentation purposes, document identifying numbers for the transactions and work with the initial persons in the group who will be handing these transactions off to another workstation.

3. Observe the processing of each selected transaction at each workstation step, noting situations where a transaction is:

   • Input to another system or passed on to another workstation.
   • Held for further analysis or rejected for errors or other reasons.

4. Follow the selected transaction through each step in its processing, noting instances where the documented control procedures are not being followed or where the transaction causes unusual difficulties.

5. At the end of the walk-through, discuss with the administrators any unusual or unexpected problems and document internal control status.

6. For a fully automated application with no paper trail, follow essentially the same procedure. However, make appropriate inquiries on-line to determine if the application is processing as expected. Resolve any differences or questions and document the results of the walk-through test.

compliance testing allows the internal auditor to confirm that the application is operating as described. While not a substitute for detailed or substantive application testing, the walk-through allows an internal auditor to identify major control weaknesses as well as to gain a sufficient understanding of the application to define control objectives for subsequent, detailed audit testing and evaluation procedures.

(c) DEVELOPING CONTROL OBJECTIVES AND AUDIT PROCEDURES

After the review of documentation and walk-through compliance testing, the internal auditor should next develop detailed audit objectives and procedures for completing the application review. This depends upon the type of review planned, the characteristics of the application, and the results of the preliminary review steps. A given review might be concerned with the level of control risk and the ability of the application to support financial statements correctly. The procedures associated with these audit objectives would be tests of the financial statement balances built up from detailed application transactions.

An internal auditor could have other objectives in reviewing an information systems application. Management may have asked internal audit to review an application to determine if it is making efficient use of database file resources or to review another application to determine if related discount and interest calculations associated with accounts payable are correctly performed. The walk-through compliance testing may have identified significant problems, and the auditor may want to do little more than to confirm those preliminary but troubling observations. Before proceeding any further with the review, the internal auditor should now confirm or revise the specific review objectives.

Specific applications review audit objectives should be clearly defined. The auditor responsible for the detailed review might wish to summarize these objectives for the review and approval by appropriate members of management. This may help prevent an internal auditor from devoting resources to testing an area not considered significant. In the above-mentioned accounts payable system, the internal auditor may have established several specific objectives for this review:

- The accounts payable system should have adequate internal controls, such that all receipts recorded from the receiving system are correctly matched to vendor files before the preparation of disbursements.

- Vendor terms should be correctly computed with controls to eliminate potential duplicate payments.

- Controls should be in place to prevent or at least flag improper or unusual disbursements.

- All systems-generated disbursements should be recorded on general ledger files using correct account numbers and other descriptive codes.

Depending upon management's direction, internal audit might develop other objectives for performing such a review. For example, the review could focus on database integrity or on control procedures over miscellaneous disbursements. Any review may have multiple objectives. For example, if management had asked internal audit to review the accounts payable system to assure that no illegal or improper payments have been made, internal audit would probably also want to add a general objective to assess control risk and to determine that the system of internal controls is adequate.

Before actually starting any detailed applications review, internal audit should docu-

Figure 17.6 Application Review Objectives Example

> Note for the internal auditor: The following are generic test objectives that an auditor might establish when launching an application review. An understanding of the application to be reviewed is essential.

√ Determine that all transactions are accounted for in the applications—the number of transactions input in any cycle must be traceable to output files or reports.

√ Good procedures should be in place to screen for processing errors, to hold errors for correction or disposition, and to reprocess as appropriate.

√ If the application receives input or provides output to other applications, transaction and record count controls should exist between these interfaces.

√ Monetary or other mathematical calculations in the applications should work properly, with good controls for such things as rounding.

√ If the nature of the information processed has legal or accounting standards implications, the application should operate in a compliant manner.

√ If the application uses tabled data for its processing, table files must be current, secure, and regularly updated.

√ The application should be protected with appropriate physical and logical security controls.

√ Adequate application documentation at a developer or user level should be provided to describe key processes and to aid in the answering of questions.

√ Processes should be in place to revise the application or install upgraded vendor software per user requests, as appropriate.

√ Appropriate procedures should be in place to back-up key files for restoration in the event of an unexpected contingency; contingency planning processes should be regularly tested.

√ The processing performance of the application should be consistent with the other information systems standards and any problems should be monitored regularly.

---

ment the specific objectives of the review and discuss them with the management requesting the application review to determine if the planned review approach is on target and will satisfy the audit request. This same procedure should also take place even if the applications review has been initiated by the audit department as part of a total review of an information systems function. Figure 17.6 lists potential objectives for application reviews.

17-5 PROCEDURES FOR AUDITING APPLICATION CONTROLS

Usually more difficult to define than the audit's objectives, detailed audit procedures vary and depend on (1) whether the application uses purchased or in-house-developed software; (2) whether the application is integrated with others or a separate process; (3) whether it uses client-server and other more modern technologies or older, legacy computer system methods; and (4) whether it is a significant accounting application.

The exact nature of the application can also vary considerably. Although internal auditors once reviewed controls over primarily accounting-related applications such as accounts receivable, accounts payable, or fixed-asset systems, today's internal auditor may review manufacturing resource planning, marketing analysis, or other nonfinancial applications such as loan portfolio analysis. Any of these requires a knowledge of its specific attributes as well as the supporting technologies. That is, an internal auditor should understand how the application works by first documenting the computer systems applications, then defining specific audit test objectives, and finally performing a series of audit tests to verify that the application controls are in place and working as expected.

(a) UNDERSTANDING AND DOCUMENTING COMPUTER SYSTEM APPLICATIONS

Besides the review of documentation and the walk-through, discussions with key user personnel and responsible systems personnel can aid the auditor's understanding. The amount of effort spent here depends both upon the type of application reviewed and the number of users who can be of help. For example, a capital budgeting decision support application will probably have a small group of key users who have a thorough understanding of its procedures. A logistical support system, such as factory floor data collection, may be used by a large group, but it may be difficult to identify the key system users.

The next step is to complete the documentation of the application for audit purposes. Internal audit should have been making workpaper notes throughout. The documentation procedure here is largely one of summarization where workpapers describe the understanding gained and include notes for potential follow-up review work. This documentation can be examined by the key users and systems personnel for input. Examples of such application documentation should follow the workpaper procedures described in Chapter 11. (Further examples are shown in the application-review case following.)

(b) DEFINING AUDIT TEST OBJECTIVES

Clarifying the objectives of the review is often a major area where internal audit has been known to fail. Management may expect internal audit to review accounting controls but the internal audit review may have concentrated on logical security controls.

This misunderstanding of audit objectives becomes especially critical when the review is not typically in the auditor's more common realm of accounting applications. For example, if management has asked internal audit to review a new manufacturing resource planning system, its objectives could include validating internal accounting controls, or reviewing for materials parts flow efficiencies, or checking for system compliance with applicable regulations, or a combination of these. These should be summarized into a brief statement and discussed with both audit management and applications-user management.

Although the need for a clear statement of review objectives may appear an obvious early step, auditors often omit it. Of course, the objectives of an applications review may change if internal audit encounters evidence of other control problems during the course of a review that would suggest audit scope or procedure changes. In the manufacturing resource review above, the initial objective of affirming the adequacy of the system's internal controls might change to one of fraud detection if potentially invalid transactions were encountered.

(c) APPLICATION TEST PROCEDURES

Internal audit should next test the key control points within the application. Having already done limited compliance testing as part of gaining an understanding, these test procedures can now be expanded to make a more definitive assessment of the application's controls. In older and simpler batch-oriented systems, this task was fairly easy. Internal audit looked for input data acceptance controls, for any computer-processing decision points, and for output data verification controls. Since there may have been only a few programs associated with such an older batch application system, this identification of test procedures could often be accomplished with minimal analysis.

For modern applications, on-line updating, close integration with other applications, and sophisticated programming techniques all combine to make identifying test procedures difficult. Other factors include the following:

- Inputs to the application may have been generated by external sources, such as EDI transmissions, or from other computerized applications at partner organizations.
- Controls once performed by data input personnel are now built into programs.
- Modern optical scanning input devices and output documents with multi-dimensional bar codes make visual inspection difficult.
- Database files may be shared with other applications, making it difficult to determine where a change or transaction originated.
- The application may make extensive use of telecommunications and will appear to be paperless to internal audit.

There are numerous other reasons why an internal auditor may have difficulty initially identifying audit test procedures in a modern data-processing application. However, the application description, along with key user discussions, should help to identify some of these controls. As a rule of thumb, an internal auditor should look for points where system logic or control decisions are made within an application and then develop test procedures to verify that those decision points are correct. These points include such areas as checks on the completeness of transactions or on the accuracy of calculations. They often represent the key controls within an application.

Figure 17.7 lists some typical test procedures oriented both to more classic batch applications and to modern, integrated, on-line ones. The application description and the interviews can help determine which of these test procedures may be applicable.

(i) Tests of Application Inputs and Outputs.
In the very early days of computer systems and computer auditing, many audit-related tests were little more than checks to verify that all inputs to a program were correctly accounted for and that the correct number of output transactions was produced based upon these inputs. An auditor's review of an automated payroll system would be an example here. The auditor would test to determine that all time cards input were either accepted or rejected and that the number of output checks produced could be reconciled to those system input time cards. This is a test of system inputs and outputs.

Figure 17.7 Application Test Procedures Sample

Note for the internal auditor: The following are test procedures that an auditor might use when assessing application controls. These may not apply to all applications; an understanding of the application is essential.

√ Foot key files. Using computer-assisted audit techniques (CAATs), test that the data files are the same as the printed reports by using CAAT software to recalculate key file values and fields.

√ Test key application calculations. Using a sample transaction, determine that the results and totals are the same as predicted.

√ Run a special audit-only update. Prepare a set of test transactions covering all aspects of the application and arrange to run a special audit-only update. Review the results of the update for controls and processing correctness. Remove the audit-updated application from the production cycle.

√ Transaction balancing. Using the transaction totals production process, independently calculate and reconcile the control totals to the reported application totals.

√ Application logical security. Review the application's embedded security levels to determine if employees are allowed the proper levels of read and write access.

√ Document controls. Test for controls in key documents (ID #s, etc.) for determining that updates can be traced back to the point of origination.

√ Unauthorized changes. By counting the total number of characters or through other controls, determine if the application program versions on production libraries are the same as those retained in documentation files.

√ Contingency planning provisions. Depending on audit risk, review the contingency planning setup; give special attention to the last contingency test results.

Although our automated applications have become much more complex, many audit test procedures today are little more than those same tests of inputs and outputs. An internal auditor will examine the outputs generated from an application, such as invoices produced by a billing system, to determine that the input data and automated computations are correct. This type of audit test is limited in nature and will not cover all transactions or functions within an application.

The purpose of a control risk assessment or compliance test is to determine if application controls appear to be working. If all transactions or all data are to be reviewed, substantive testing procedures or tests of financial statement balances should be used. (See Chapter 13, on evidence-gathering through the use of audit sampling.) The extent of this testing depends upon the audit objectives. For example, an external auditor will tend to perform compliance tests over those aspects of an application which cover financial statement–related internal accounting controls. An internal auditor also may want to perform compliance tests over other areas of an application, such as data-processing efficiency or administrative controls.

For older applications, tests of inputs and outputs are often quite easy to perform. The auditor would select a sample of input transactions and then determine that the number of inputs was equal to the count of processed items plus any rejected or error items. This type of audit test is not nearly as easy for today's more modern applications, where the auditor will not normally encounter a one-to-one relationship between inputs and outputs. Test transaction approaches, discussed below, are often much easier to perform and even more meaningful. Nevertheless, tests of inputs and outputs are sometimes useful for reviews of applications. Audit procedures for this type of more traditional test are outlined in Figure 17.8.

(ii) Test Transaction Evaluation Approaches.   An internal auditor may want to ascertain that transactions entered into a system are correctly processed. For example, when reviewing an on-line manufacturing application, an internal auditor might record several shop materials transactions as they are entered on manufacturing floor terminals. After a typical overnight processing cycle, the auditor can verify that those transactions have correctly made adjustments to inventory records and that work-in-process cost reports have also been properly updated. This verification can take place by reviewing the output reports generated by the system or by running special retrieval reports against data files.

As part of the test transaction process, an auditor can also test whether error screening controls are operating as described. The emphasis here should be on the testing of the error-verification routines within the application. Internal audit can select transactions

Figure 17.8   Automated Purchasing System Compliance Tests Example

1. Select a series of purchase orders generated by the system and trace them back to either requirements generated by the manufacturing system or by authorized, manual purchase inputs. All new purchase order transactions should be properly authorized.

2. From the same sample above, trace the purchase orders back to established records for vendor terms and prices. Resolve any differences.

3. Trace a cycle of automated purchase orders to EDI control log records to determine if all documents were transmitted on a timely basis.

4. Using sample purchase orders that are transmitted via EDI, determine if vendors are covered by signed, current agreements.

5. Select a sample or receiving report and determine if the system is working properly by matching receipts to open purchase orders and accounts payables.

6. Select a sample of recent accounts payables checks generated for parts and materials. Trace transactions back to valid receiving reports and purchase orders.

7. Using sample transactions that were either held upon receipt for noncompliance with terms or for improper timing, verify that transactions are handled correctly, per established procedures.

8. Balance a full cycle of purchase transactions—from the manufacturing system providing inputs to control logs over both EDI transactions and printed purchase order documents.

input to an application that appear to be invalid and then trace them through the application to determine that they have been properly reported on exception reports. Internal audit can also consider submitting test error transactions to a system to verify that they are being properly rejected by the application.

(iii) Other Application-Review Techniques. The computer-assisted audit software discussed in Chapter 12 can be useful in reviewing application system controls. All too often, internal auditors use computer-assisted software to test some accounting control such as an accounts receivable billing calculation but not to evaluate other application controls. Audit software can match files from different periods, identify unusual data items, perform footings and recalculations, or simulate selected functions of an application. Other useful techniques are:

- *Reperformance of Application Functions or Calculations.* This type of test is applicable for both the automated and the manual aspects of application systems. For example, if a fixed-assets application performs automatic depreciation calculations, internal audit can use a CAAT to recalculate depreciation values for selected transactions as a compliance test.

- *Reviews of Program Source Code.* Internal audit can verify that a certain logic check is performed within a program by verifying the source code. However, this type of compliance test should be used with only the greatest amount of caution. Because of the potential complexity of trying to read and understand program source code, it is very easy to miss a program branch around the area being tested. There are specialized programs available to compare program source code with the compiled versions in production libraries.

- *Continuous Audit Monitoring Approaches.* Internal audit can sometimes arrange to build embedded audit procedures into production applications to allow those applications to flag control or other application exception problems. These techniques were discussed in Chapter 12, on computer-assisted audit techniques. This approach goes beyond just auditing an application and adding procedures to make it self-auditable on an ongoing basis.

- *Observation of Procedures.* This type of observation may be of use when reviewing an automated application as well as a manual process. For example, a remote work station receiving downloaded data from a central computer system may require extensive manual procedures in order to make the proper download connection. Internal audit can observe this on a test basis to determine if these manual procedures are being correctly performed.

(d) COMPLETING THE APPLICATION CONTROL REVIEW

Although compliance tests are powerful methods to test application controls, internal audit should be aware that their level of assurance is not absolute. There is a risk that an internal auditor may test an application control and find it to be working when, in fact, it does not normally work as tested or vice versa. Because of the risks associated with such compliance tests, therefore, internal audit should always be careful to condition its audit report to management with a comment about the risks of incorrect results due to limited audit tests. Sometimes, the controls tested do not appear to be working correctly because internal audit does not understand some aspects of the application system. Internal audit may want to review the application description and identification of controls to verify that they are correct. It may be necessary to revise internal audit's understanding of application controls and then to reperform the audit risk assessment procedures.

If internal audit finds that, through compliance testing, the application controls are not working, it will be necessary to report these findings. The nature of this report very much depends upon the severity of the control weaknesses and the nature of the review. For example, if the application is being reviewed at the request of the external auditors, the identified control weaknesses may prevent them from placing any level of reliance on the financial results produced by the application. If the control weaknesses are primarily efficiency-related or operational, internal audit may want to just report them to information systems management for future corrective action.

Applications can be primarily financial or operational. They can be implemented on minicomputers using purchased software, can be custom-developed applications located on mainframe systems using extensive database and telecommunications facilities, or can operate in a client-server environment or exist in numerous other variations. As we have noted, this diversity makes it difficult to provide just one set of audit procedures for all applications.

While internal audit can develop a general approach to reviewing most data-processing applications, it is usually necessary to tailor that approach to the specific features of a given application. The following paragraphs describe how an internal auditor might perform a review of two different data-processing applications. The first is a mainframe database application with interfaces to several other mainframe applications. The second is a client-server system using purchased software with telecommunication links through a network connection to a larger server machine.

17-6   REVIEW EXAMPLE: MAINFRAME ACCOUNTING APPLICATION

Our first example—a database on-line purchasing system with interfaces to manufacturing resource planning, receiving, and accounts payables systems—uses electronic data interchange (EDI) techniques (discussed in Chapter 24). This system is implemented on a larger mainframe computer at a highly automated manufacturing organization. The auditors have reviewed general controls within the data-processing organization and have found them to be generally good. Now, internal audit plans to perform an applications review of the automated purchasing system as well as of its interfaces with other systems.

Although implemented several years ago, the system was not reviewed while it was under development. The system is of major accounting significance, but internal audit department scheduling problems prevented a pre-implementation review (see Chapter 18). In addition, the application's title of ''New Purchasing System'' on data-processing development schedules did not attract audit attention. The external auditors who initially encountered it attempted to audit around the application in its first year of operation and have now asked internal audit to review the application's controls. The system has several paperless features that attracted their attention.

This example electronics assembly company purchases fairly high volumes of many small parts and components. Its purchasing department issues blanket purchase orders with many vendors to supply periodic shipments of parts with quantities specified by a just-in-time scheduling system. The purchasing department makes price and terms agreements with vendors in advance such that unit prices will drop as the total quantities purchased increases. To promote operational efficiency, this example system was implemented to minimize paperwork. The system operates as follows:

1. Vendor purchase order price and terms agreements are input to a purchasing database. The blanket purchase orders are entered annually and others are input as required.

2. The automated manufacturing resource planning system determines parts requirements. These are automated inputs to the purchasing database along with any other manual data inputs.

3. The system generates purchase orders on a daily basis, which, after review, are simultaneously transmitted to vendors using EDI communications and input to the automated receiving system.

4. When goods are received, the open purchase-order data is called up from the receiving database. The quantities received are entered, and the data received is automatically entered by the system.

5. The material receipts data is automatically input to the inventory system and back to the purchasing database. If the receipt is in compliance with purchase order terms, the receipt is set up for payment.

6. Parts vendors are encouraged not to send invoices. For parts receipts in compliance with purchase order terms, the purchasing system will send records to the accounts payable system authorizing an electronic funds transaction or check to be issued. If the shipment arrives early or incomplete, the payment amount or timing will reflect this. If the vendor sends an invoice, it will be essentially ignored.

The automated purchasing system described in this example is a fairly complex, paperless type of application system using EDI—a type that might be found in many larger organizations. Because this application has some fairly tight ties to other applications (including manufacturing resource planning, receiving, and accounts payable), an applications review presents internal audit with the dilemma of where to draw the review boundaries. For example, should the receiving or the accounts payable system be included in any automated purchasing applications review because they are so closely tied to that system?

Internal audit will do best to limit the scope of such an applications review. In this case, internal audit might only review the automated purchasing system and its interfaces with other applications. Internal audit can verify that the issuance of a purchase order correctly initiates a transaction to the purchasing system and that, when the receiving system indicates a receipt, a transaction is received by the automated purchasing application. However, it is not necessary to review controls within the purchasing system here—that can be the subject of another applications review.

Internal audit's objectives in a review of this sort can be many and varied. The external auditors may primarily want assurance that a receipt of goods is properly recorded as an accounts payable item. A more technically oriented internal auditor may want assurance that the purchasing system database properly maintains vendor terms and conditions.

As always, objectives should be carefully defined and discussed with all parties interested in internal audit's review. Below is a possible abbreviated set of controls objectives for a review of this purchasing system:

- Purchasing should have good controls over both inputs of purchase order and vendor terms data.

- The database should maintain purchasing data in an accurate and complete manner.
- There should be controls to prevent an improper purchase order from being created and transmitted.
- There should be adequate audit trails over transactions to or from such interface systems as manufacturing resource planning, receiving, and accounts payable.
- Only transactions for authorized and correct vendor payments should be sent to the accounts payable system.

(a) REVIEWING AUTOMATED PURCHASING SYSTEM DOCUMENTATION

The first review step—that of obtaining a good understanding of the overall application through the discussions and review of documentation, discussed above—can be fairly extensive in a system as comprehensive and integrated as this example. Internal audit may want to review purchasing department procedures, special control procedures over the use of the purchasing database system, and the application's systems and other user documentation.

In performing this documentation review, internal audit may want to also review workpapers from any past audits of related applications and recent reviews of general controls in such areas as database administration. If this is internal audit's first review of an EDI-based application, the assigned audit team should become familiar with EDI controls (which will be discussed in Chapter 24). Although interface applications may not have been reviewed previously, internal audit still may want to postpone any detailed reviews of them at this time. Any potential control questions regarding these interface systems can be documented on a "to do" list prepared in conjunction with this purchasing system review. Internal audit would expand the review to these others only if there appear to be potentially significant control problems.

(b) IDENTIFYING AUTOMATED PURCHASING SYSTEM INTERNAL CONTROLS

Internal audit's next step is to describe the automated purchasing system using verbal and pictorial flowcharts, as described previously. In this case, the flowchart should be broken down into smaller subprocesses, such as one for setting up new vendor price and terms agreements. There are many potential internal controls issues associated with such a large database application as this purchasing system. In keeping with internal audit's review objectives, many of the control concerns here deal with the interaction of this application and interrelated ones such as receiving and accounts payable. Others deal with newer technologies such as the application's use of telecommunications for the EDI transmission of purchase orders.

Audit procedures based on the preliminary set of objectives as well as the understanding gained from the documentation review phase should be in the same general format as the audit procedures shown in Figure 17.7. Because this is a larger application, more controls points should be identified here.

Internal audit next would develop a tailored set of audit procedures for each portion of the example automated purchasing system. When building these specific sets of audit procedures, internal audit may want to consult with information systems or other specialists if appropriate. For example, this application receives inputs from a manufacturing resource planning system. If an internal auditor is unfamiliar with such applications, their unique characteristics should be discussed with other members of the audit team or user personnel to gain a general understanding.

Once controls have been identified in the example application, internal audit should discuss these with management and others, such as external auditors, who may have an interest in the audit. This review of planned objectives with outside parties may help prevent internal audit from attempting to perform controls tests that would be extremely difficult or that might only yield inconclusive results.

(c) TESTING AND EVALUATING AUTOMATED PURCHASING SYSTEM CONTROLS

The final audit steps—the tests of controls—follow the procedures identified in Figure 17.7. Compliance or walk-through testing will not give internal audit an absolute assurance that the application controls are working as tested. Depending upon the overall scope of the planned review, internal audit may or may not want to test all of the controls identified in its applications overview. This decision may depend upon the audit budget and the overall criticality of the application. In any event, internal audit should attempt to perform a walk-through type of compliance test on what appears to be the application's more significant controls. When deciding which controls to test initially, it is perfectly proper to base the testing strategy on comments received from users or information systems personnel on potential control problems. These individuals will frequently make comments during an auditor interview along the lines of, ''The system would work fine except for . . . .'' Such comments will often point internal audit to potential control weaknesses.

Audit compliance tests involve such things as reverification of computations, comparisons of transactions, and the like. Figure 17.8 contains some potential compliance tests for the example application. Detailed compliance testing can be a fairly time-consuming process if a large number of application controls are to be evaluated. The experienced auditor may want to have an audit department assistant help perform these detailed testing procedures.

17-7 REVIEW EXAMPLE: CLIENT-SERVER BUDGETING APPLICATION

In our second example, internal audit has been asked to review the controls over a capital budgeting system based upon client-server architecture. The financial-planning department has developed the capital budgeting analysis portion of the application using a popular microcomputer spreadsheet software package. Although built around a purchased software spreadsheet package, the users have coded a series of macro instructions for running the programs. The workstation portion of the system communicates with a server file containing mainframe budgeting system data. Client-server systems were discussed in Chapter 16.

Internal audit has been asked by management to review general controls over their client-server computer operations and LANs. Following audit procedures in Chapter 16, internal audit found that general controls in these areas were adequate. That is, users documented their microcomputer applications; adequate backups of files and programs were performed on server files; password procedures limited access to only authorized personnel; and other good control procedures were followed. Among internal audit's recommendations was to place stronger controls over telecommunications access to the LAN and to install virus-scanning procedures. (Virus programs are discussed in Chapter 19.)

Some time after that general controls review, this capital budgeting system was implemented on the administrative office LAN. Because this system provides direct input to the corporate budgeting system, management has asked internal audit to review its application controls. After discussing this review request with senior and information systems management, internal audit developed the following review objectives:

- The microcomputer capital budgeting system should have good internal accounting controls.
- The system should properly make capital budgeting decisions based upon both the parameters input to the system and programmed macro formulas.
- The system should provide accurate inputs to the mainframe budgeting system through the LAN file server.
- The capital budgeting system should promote efficiency within the financial-planning department.

The above objectives represent the general format for objectives for this type of application. Management will typically not state their objectives in these words. It is the responsibility of internal audit to listen to management's requests and to translate them to review objectives, as in the above example.

(a) REVIEW THE CAPITAL BUDGETING SYSTEM DOCUMENTATION

Internal audit first reviews the documentation available for this example capital budgeting system. Since the application is built around a commercial spreadsheet software product, internal audit might expect to find or should ask for some of the following:

- Documentation manuals or on-line files for the spreadsheet software package
- Documentation for the programmed spreadsheet macro procedures, using, perhaps, a spreadsheet auditor type of software which documents spreadsheet formulas
- Procedures for uploading capital budget data to the mainframe budgeting application through LAN server files
- Operations procedures for accepting the microcomputer input data to the mainframe information systems function
- Procedures to ensure the integrity of the data resident on LAN server files

Internal audit will probably not find documented procedures covering exactly all of the above five elements. However, there should be documentation covering the software product used, the interfaces with other applications, and the necessary manual procedures. These materials can be reviewed by internal audit to determine that they are complete and that internal audit has gained a general understanding of the overall application.

(b) DESCRIBING THE MICROCOMPUTER CLIENT SYSTEM

After reviewing the capital budgeting system documentation and discussing the application with its financial planning users, internal audit describes the system for audit workpaper purposes. Since the application is built around a microcomputer spreadsheet product, this description primarily covers its manual interfaces. Control descriptions over file server applications and their network connections to client systems have been covered as part of the previously mentioned general controls review.

Auditors often find it convenient to describe such an application in the form of a flowchart, although a written description may be just as adequate. The purpose of this type of description is to provide internal audit with workpaper documentation of the application and to provide a basis for the identification of significant control points.

(c) IDENTIFY CAPITAL BUDGETING APPLICATION KEY CONTROLS

Although a rather simple and compact application, this example capital budgeting system has some critical control points. For example, if the spreadsheet macro procedures are incorrectly calculating capital costs, present values, and such related factors, management may very well take incorrect actions regarding their investment decisions. These types of control concerns are discussed in Chapter 27, on fixed assets and capital projects. If data is incorrectly transmitted to the mainframe budgeting system, financial statement records may be incorrect. If the microcomputer application is not properly documented, a change of key users in the financial-planning department may make the system nearly inoperable.

Based on internal audit's understanding of this example system, key system controls are now defined and documented. Here, because internal audit has recently performed a general controls review, it is not necessary to reconsider those general controls during the applications review. The audit review procedures can now be developed similar to those shown in Figure 17.9.

(d) PERFORM TESTS OF COMPLIANCE FOR THE APPLICATION

For the final step in the application review, internal audit performs tests based on the audit procedures established. Depending upon management's and internal audit's relative interest in the application, it may not be necessary to test all of the controls as listed. Many are related to one another. If no problems or weaknesses are identified in one control area, internal audit may decide to pass on the related control areas. Some of the tests of application controls might include:

- *Reperformance of Computations.* Capital budgeting is based on some very specific computations, such as the estimation of the present value of future cash flows based on discount factors. Using another spreadsheet tool or even a desk calculator, internal audit could select one or several present value computations generated by the system and recalculate them to determine the reasonableness of system processes. Any major differences should be resolved.

- *Comparison of Transactions.* Internal audit can select several sets of microcomputer budget schedules and trace them through LAN file servers to the mainframe budget system to determine that they have been correctly transmitted.

- *Proper Approval of Transactions.* Before any microcomputer-generated budget schedule is transmitted to the official mainframe budget system, it should have had proper management approvals. Internal audit can select several that were

Figure 17.9   Audit Procedures Capital Budgeting: Application Input and Output Tests

1. Develop a detailed understanding of all significant input transactions to the application—their nature, timing, and source.

2. Develop a strong understanding of transaction error correction procedures, both the nature of the tables used for verification as well as any built-in program logic. Determine that some formal turnaround procedure exists to hold error items.

3. Using documentation or database descriptions, trace all input to output data flows within the application showing how many input elements (e.g., an order from inventory) will change or modify other system elements (the order may cause inventory to be reduced, sales and accounts receivable to increase, etc.). Document this understanding through audit data flow diagrams.

4. Determine that controls exist for comparing the number of items input to those that have either been accepted or rejected. Review error identification procedures to determine if users can easily understand the nature of these errors.

5. Review procedures for the correction and resubmission of rejected items. Determine if errors are held in a suspense file allowing analysis and correction.

6. Develop a detailed understanding of all significant system output control totals, consider nature of controls for any single update cycle and for cycle to cycle.

7. Select an input update cycle for review. Determine if the number of items input, less any rejected errors, ties into system output control totals.

8. For reviewing the test cycle, determine if all error items from this cycle have been corrected and resubmitted or else properly disposed.

9. Review control totals in the subsequent processing cycle to determine if file totals have remained consistent from one cycle to the next. Investigate any discrepancies.

10. Review existing error suspense files to determine if all error items are investigated and corrected in a timely manner. Investigate any items remaining in the error recycle for more than a selected number of processing cycles. Determine reasons for delay.

transmitted to the mainframe system to verify that they were properly approved and the approvals were documented.

There are numerous other similar compliance tests that can be performed for such a microcomputer system. The imaginative auditor will be able to perform these depending upon the nature of the audit and the objectives of management. Control weaknesses should be reported to management for corrective action.

17-8 SUMMARIZING AND EVALUATING APPLICATION CONTROLS

The final steps in an applications review are to summarize audit findings, to report them to management, and to plan for any further detailed applications testing. Findings and recommendations in workpapers—and, if appropriate, in a formal audit report—provide both information systems and operations management guidance for taking corrective action to improve application controls. Workpaper documentation techniques were discussed in Chapter 11 and audit reports in Chapter 15.

When summarizing and evaluating the results of an applications review, internal audit should always be aware of the risks of concluding that a control is working when it is ineffective, as well as of the risks of coming to the opposite conclusion. If internal audit or management has any doubts that the results of a compliance test are not representative, it is always a good idea to retest the particular controls procedure or to expand the scope of the test. Statistical sampling procedures, discussed in Chapter 13, can project a rate of error in order to emphasize any control strength or weakness.

An application controls review and its related compliance tests provide internal audit with a basis of placing reliance on the results of that application. That is, internal audit may be able to conclude that the application reviewed appears to be operating as intended, with generally good controls and procedures. Internal audit may be able to stop the review at this point and go on to other information systems application review areas. In some instances, however, internal audit may want to perform more detailed or substantive tests.

17-9 REVIEWS IN SUBSEQUENT YEARS: A SYSTEMS TEST APPROACH

After performing a detailed applications review, auditors are often asked to review that same application again after a period of perhaps one or two years. The reason for this subsequent review is usually to verify that the controls improvements previously recommended have been implemented or that subsequent systems changes have not altered the overall controls environment. Internal audit need not rereview the entire application, as has been discussed in this chapter, when performing such a follow-up audit.

The idea of an applications systems test is that it is not necessary to retest all applications controls if some of the control procedures tested in a prior review were working properly at that time. Internal audit may need only to review and test those aspects of the system that have been changed. Such a review can be performed following a four-step approach:

1. *Review the application to determine which control procedures have remained unchanged and which have been modified.* This can often be accomplished by discussion with key information systems and user personnel, using internal audit's application description from the prior workpapers as a guide.

2. *Develop an understanding of any application changes.* This can often be accomplished through a review of systems development documentation materials.

3. *Update audit workpaper documentation to reflect any applications changes and identify any new controls as might be appropriate.*

4. *Perform compliance tests of key controls that may have changed due to the modifications.* Depending upon the nature of these changes, it may be necessary to also retest other existing applications controls.

The point here is that it may not be necessary to totally reevaluate an entire application every time it is subsequently reviewed. By developing an understanding of any changes that occurred after the last audit and by primarily reviewing and testing the controls associated with those changes, internal audit can continue to feel relatively confident that the application is continuing to operate as understood. This approach can help internal audit to do a more efficient job in performing repetitive applications reviews.

17-10 ROLE OF INTEGRATED AUDITS

Throughout the 1970s and into the 1980s, many audit professionals looked upon computer systems audit specialists as a separate branch of the audit profession. Audit departments established separate groups of computer audit specialists to review controls over their computer systems and automated applications. This arrangement made sense when computer knowledge and skills were not that common and when most information systems activities took place behind the essentially closed doors of the computer operations room and the information systems department. This has all changed over the years.

Much of the responsibility for information systems applications in the modern organization has been distributed to the ultimate systems user rather than keeping it with the information systems professional. This is evidenced by the client-server computing techniques and the powerful retrieval languages discussed in these chapters. These changes have arguably resulted in better applications to meet user requirements. The internal auditor's approach to reviewing these applications must also change. While many internal audit organizations may need to have specialist auditors in their organizations with knowledge of computer systems technical control issues, all internal auditors today should have sufficient knowledge and skills to review most automated application systems areas. The computer systems specialist should work with the other members of the internal audit team to perform these reviews. This approach is often called an *integrated audit*.

This integrated audit approach should work quite well for the two example application reviews discussed in this chapter. The majority of the review procedures for the client-server capital budgeting application can be performed by the generalist internal auditor who can verify such things as the correctness of the capital budget calculations. The example system was based on spreadsheet software and many, if not most, internal auditors should be familiar with microcomputer spreadsheets. A specialist information systems auditor may be needed to help with such areas as LAN controls, including logical security, and communications between the server system and the mainframe application.

Internal audit departments should attempt to schedule their applications reviews as integrated audits using both general and computer systems specialist auditors as part of the review team. They both can learn from each other and should perform more effective audits. Information systems audit specialists, however, are still needed for controls reviews in many technical areas. The pros and cons of an integrated audit approach are discussed in Chapter 21.

17-11 IMPORTANCE OF REVIEWING AUTOMATED APPLICATIONS

The effective internal auditor should place a major emphasis on reviewing the supporting information systems applications when performing operational audits in other areas of the organization. Even though good general or interdependent information systems control procedures are often in place in the modern information systems organizations, individual applications controls may not all be that strong. An organization's applications may have been developed through a series of compromises among users or without any level of proper quality assurance. To evaluate information systems applications controls properly, internal audit needs a good understanding of both information systems procedures and the specific control and procedural characteristics of each application area.

The effective internal auditor should spend a substantial amount of audit effort reviewing and testing controls over specific information systems applications. Such reviews will provide assurance to general management that applications are operating properly, and to information systems management that their design and controls standards are being followed, allowing them to place greater reliance on the output results of such applications. An understanding of application control reviews is a key component in the modern internal auditor's tool kit.

CHAPTER 18

Auditing Systems Under Development

18-1 INTRODUCTION

Both general management and many data-processing departments now recognize that it is much more efficient to ask internal audit to review an information systems application for its internal controls while it is being developed rather than after it has been implemented and placed into production. This can be somewhat of a different role for internal audit, which normally reviews processes that already have been placed in operation. The role of the internal auditor here is similar to that of a building inspector reviewing a new construction project: It would be difficult to make constructive recommendations regarding the completed building. Even if some problems were found, the inspector would be under considerable pressure not to identify problems that would require significant portions of the building to be torn down and rebuilt. Rather, the building inspector identifies problems during construction and suggests how they can be corrected before completion.

Similar to that building inspector, the effective internal auditor should also suggest corrective actions to improve system controls along the way. It is easier for the information systems function to implement changes during a systems development process than after the application has been completed and the system placed into production.

To continue with the analogy, an internal auditor must be careful not to take responsibility for *designing* the new application's controls. The building inspector points out problems but certainly does not take responsibility for their construction. The internal audit standards outlined in Chapter 5 remind internal auditors that it is their task to review and recommend but not to design or build the controls. When reviewing new applications under development, an internal auditor should simply point out control weaknesses to the application developers.

Application development groups, user management, and auditors all tend to agree that, in reviewing new information systems applications under development, internal audit provides "another set of eyes" to look at the new and soon-to-be-implemented application.

Despite the advantages, internal auditors often find it difficult to implement and execute an effective preimplementation audit program due to the dramatic, ongoing changes in techniques and approaches used to build new information systems applications. As late as the mid-1980s, many new computer applications were custom programmed to operate on central mainframe computers. As we discussed in Chapter 17, organizations today often purchase software packages or assemble modules which create today's computer systems applications. The traditional mainframe application is also almost an exception today, as systems are built on microcomputer workstations or client-server networks. This chapter offers approaches to reviewing new applications under development as well as a discussion of some of the pitfalls internal audit may encounter when attempting to audit them. For further details on information systems auditing approaches offered in this and other chapters, see Robert Moeller's book *Computer Audit, Control and Security.* Chapter 16 contains detailed references to that book. Although the title of this chapter refers to auditing new applications under development, another common term for these reviews is preimplementation auditing. Both terms will be used throughout this chapter.

18-2 SYSTEMS UNDER DEVELOPMENT: CHANGES AND AUDITOR CHALLENGES

Reviews of applications under development can often present challenges, no matter how strong the internal auditor's knowledge and technical skills, because such applications may change significantly after the preimplementation review and the system's implementation. Today, both information systems professionals and management often expect and request internal audit to review their new systems under development. All parties should have a strong interest in internal audit's preimplementation reviews and any resultant recommendations. Comprehensive reviews that cover all significant application controls are important. Even though an internal auditor may have looked at an application project in only a very limited manner, management may be aware of that review and expect that internal audit has identified all significant control problems. While well recognized and accepted, effective preimplementation reviews require both internal auditor time and special skills.

The basic idea of this type of review is that if internal audit can review an application when it is under development and can identify areas for controls improvement during these early development stages, management can implement better, more well-controlled information systems. Internal audit, however, is often faced with significant technical and systems development knowledge obstacles and must take care to carefully define the nature and objectives of any planned preimplementation review.

(a) OBSTACLES TO PREIMPLEMENTATION AUDITS

When the concept of preimplementation reviews was first proposed by the new profession of "EDP auditors" in the early 1970s, traditional internal auditors often were opposed. They argued that if an auditor reviewed an application in advance of its implementation, they would find it very difficult to come back later and review it after implementation. The argument was that if an internal auditor had "blessed" the controls of a system under development, how could that same auditor come back later and perform a critical review? Over the years, however, internal audit management and systems developers have grown to accept preimplementation reviews. There are four major obstacles when reviewing new applications under development:

1. *"Them vs. Us" Attitudes.* Although internal audit and general management may both accept the concept, information systems professionals have historically been wary of the internal auditor who asks systems analysts and project managers specific control and design-related questions. Information systems management may often

express a wariness or even resentment when internal audit announces its plan to review an application that is under development and still has many details yet to be worked out. The announcement, "Hello, I'm from internal audit, and I am here to help you" may not be received all that favorably.

Good preimplementation review procedures can establish respect for internal audit's role and add value in the development process. An internal auditor who spends many hours reviewing a complex new application with some potential control-related issues and who concludes only that "documentation needs to be improved" will not be viewed as having added much value to the process.

2. *Internal Auditor Role Problems.* The auditor's role must be clearly understood by all parties and might be defined as one of the following:

- *An Extra Member of the Design Team.* The systems design team invites the auditor to various design review meetings. However, that internal auditor will have a special interest in the projects and would not be a normal member of that design team. The auditor's objective is to gather data for the review. The auditor may use the correspondence and other materials gathered from the correspondence to identify key controls and processing procedures.

- *A Specialized Consultant.* Sometimes, an internal auditor can become so involved in the systems design and development process that the auditor is viewed as just another design team consultant making recommendations during the course of the design process. Internal audit should take care to not be viewed in that light. An internal auditor should act primarily as an independent reviewer providing help to the team, not as a specialized consultant who is part of the design process.

- *A Controls Expert.* In any review, internal audit should always make certain that a review of controls is included in the new project. However, the auditor should not be the primary designer of those controls. Otherwise, an auditor may have problems reviewing the completed application and its controls at some later date.

- *An Occupant of the "Extra Chair."* Sometimes, an internal auditor does not do a proper level of preparatory work as part of a preimplementation review. Systems management may assign the auditor to review various design materials and attend design review meetings. An internal auditor who does not prepare but simply attends these meetings provides no real contributions. Nevertheless, if problems occur in the future, management may say "But internal audit was there!"

3. *State-of-the-Art Awareness Needs.* New systems applications often involve new technologies or business processes. A general understanding of new technologies may require additional auditor homework, to read vendor manuals and other documentation.

4. *Many and Varied Preimplementation Candidates.* The typical larger organization may have a significant number of new application projects that are potential candidates for preimplementation reviews. These projects will all have different start times, durations, and completion dates. An internal auditor needs to perform an ongoing risk assessment to select the most appropriate new review candidates.

(b) OBJECTIVES OF PREIMPLEMENTATION AUDITS

Objectives for reviewing new applications under development should include:

- *An Evaluation of Controls Prior to Implementation.* The most important objective of preimplementation auditing is to identify recommended controls improvements such that they can be potentially installed during the applications-development process.
- *An Evaluation of Project Definition and Justification.* Rather than just assuming that a new information systems project is a given and then reviewing its controls, internal audit should also have an objective of reviewing the justification and definition of the new development project.
- *An Evaluation of Project-Development Controls.* Major efforts requiring considerable programmer and analyst professional time and resources should have in place a good project-management system that properly plans development steps and measures actual progress against those planned steps. For more major projects, internal audit can evaluate the adequacy of project-development controls used for the particular application.
- *An Understanding of the New System for Subsequent Audit Tests.* The preimplementation phase is an excellent time for an internal auditor to gain an understanding of the new application sufficient to design automated audit tests at some future time. In addition, this is the best time to define and suggest embedded audit modules such as integrated test facilities. (For a detailed discussion on computer-assisted audit test approaches, see Chapter 12, ''Using Computer-Assisted Audit Techniques.'')

The above four objectives emphasize that the internal auditor reviewing new applications under development should gain an overall understanding of all aspects of that application project, not just review basic application controls.

In addition to the above, some internal auditors are faced with a statutory requirement for reviewing new applications under development. Several U.S. states and other countries have legislation requiring that all new significant state agency applications be reviewed by their internal audit departments for controls prior to implementation. Auditors in state governments can expect such legislation to appear in their own states in the future.

(c) PREIMPLEMENTATION REVIEW PROBLEMS

Preimplementation reviews often present an internal auditor with some very serious implementation problems, including the following:

- *Too Many Review Candidates.* Internal auditors sometimes make the mistake of announcing their intention of reviewing all new applications and all major modifications prior to their implementation. Auditors who arrange to sign off on all new projects will often be faced with too many requests to review and approve. In a larger organization, there may be dozens or even hundreds of user requests for new or major revision applications projects initiated every week. Internal audit will find no time for comprehensive preimplementation reviews and only time for little more than nominal ''rubber stamp'' approval signatures.

- *Problems in Selecting the Right Application to Review.* Auditors are faced with the problem of selecting only those applications of audit significance. Rather than rely on a simple value judgment or an arbitrary process, the auditor should follow a risk-based, structured selection method for identifying those applications to review, similar to what was discussed in Chapter 7 and later in this chapter.

  A systems-development department, for example, may be working on applications A, B, and C. Given the relative application risks as well as limited audit time and resources, internal audit may decide to perform preimplementation reviews only for application B. However, if significant post-implementation problems appear in C, management might later second-guess internal audit and ask why system C had not been selected for review. An internal auditor with a consistent selection approach will be able to justify the decision to review B rather than C.

- *Problems in Determining the Proper Auditor's Role.* As discussed, when an application has been selected for preimplementation review, internal audit can all too often become overly involved in its systems-development and implementation processes. Particularly for applications developed with rapid application-development methods, new information systems projects require extensive user and systems-development team efforts, with numerous design review meetings. While internal audit will often be asked to participate in these design-review meetings, they may cause an auditor role problem. Actively involved in the typical design-review meetings where design compromises may be negotiated, internal audit may find it difficult to comment on these same decisions later as audit points. However, if internal and it is excluded from design meetings, it may have a hard time performing the review. To be effective in reviewing new applications under development, the internal auditor's role needs to be carefully defined.

- *Review Objectives Can Be Difficult to Define.* When an auditor informs the information systems department that a given application has been selected for preimplementation review, the department may supply hundreds of pages of requirements studies, general design review documentation, meeting minutes, and other materials. Internal audit may then be asked to review and comment on this mass of materials. An audit objectives and control procedures approach can help an auditor choose the relevant materials to review.

- *New Development Methodologies Require Greater Attention.* Object-oriented programming or computer-aided systems engineering (CASE) are among the automated, structured design tools used to build applications and their program elements. These tools allow an applications analyst to define a system and all of its data file elements through a series of automated process flow charts. When some element or relationship changes in the design, it is only necessary to make small alterations to the automated design on the workstation screen, and other related relationships will also change. Although not always quite as simple as this, structured design approaches will be discussed in Chapter 20.

  Because these tools and approaches make it easier to build and modify complex applications, they can cause problems for internal auditors performing a preimplementation review. Internal audit may be faced with a "now you see it, now you don't" situation. The auditor needs an understanding of these new structured tools and approaches and may have to operate in a constant reeducation mode.

Auditors who have been accused in an old joke as being the ones who "join the battlefield after the action is over to shoot the wounded," can now play a proactive role in the applications-development process through preimplementation reviews.

18-3 APPLICATIONS-DEVELOPMENT PROCESS

Most information systems organizations usually have a formal set of procedures for initiating and developing new information systems called the systems development life cycle process (SDLC) or the systems development methodology (SDM), and the internal auditor should understand the SDM process used.

The trend to use purchased software rather than to program new applications from scratch, as well as the use of new microcomputer-based software tools, has greatly changed the manner in which new computer systems applications are developed. Developers once designed the program modules in an application and then programmed each using a language such as COBOL. Most organizations today use more powerful development tools such as a database-development language, such as SQL, CASE design procedures, or the object-oriented languages C++ and JAVA. No matter what the system, an organization must follow certain basic steps to define its requirements, explore alternative approaches to building the new system, install and test the application, and implement with good control procedures. This section describes some of the various SDM approaches used today.

(a) TRADITIONAL SDM PROCEDURES

Formal SDM procedures evolved in response to the informal manner in which information systems were originally developed. In the early days of information systems, new applications projects were casually requested by computer systems users. An accounting manager might give the systems applications manager a brief note, for example, to redesign the accounts receivable system. The two might further discuss this request for a redesigned system over a cup of coffee. Information systems would then typically go to work on the request with little subsequent discussion, and perhaps some months or even years later, a new, redesigned system, which might or might not meet that accounting manager's needs, would be presented.

In some cases the information systems department might initiate a project without any significant user input. Because the systems analysts and programmers understood how to build computer systems, and no one else in the organization did, information systems held a strong power over these systems users. With microcomputers and end-user computing, these relationships have changed.

The lack of a long-range planning or priority-setting process often caused other problems for applications-development functions. The information systems or data-processing department frequently reported to the controller or another financial officer, who often rather arbitrarily set the priorities for new development projects. For example, an organization might very much need a new sales order-entry system to replace cumbersome manual processes; however, if the controller, who was also often in charge of the information systems department, wanted a new fixed-asset system, the sales order-entry project would probably have been placed in a hold status or moved down the priority list.

Situations like the one above often created chaos both among users and within the applications-development department, until organizations eventually developed formalized SDMs to attempt to solve some of these difficulties.

An SDM is a formalized process to define, develop, and document new information systems applications as well as major modifications. The modern organization generally uses some type of SDM for developing applications. Although there are often numerous minor variations on the procedural steps or the terminology used, a typical SDM consists of the following phases:

1. *Project Initiation and Feasibility Determination.* A formal set of procedures should be followed to allow users to request new applications or major modifications from the information systems organization, whether the system is programmed in-house or uses purchased software. Users must formally document their needs, sometimes estimate potential expected cost savings, and receive formal approval from management before any further work is initiated.

   The next step is to determine the requested project's ''feasibility'' (placed in quotes here as virtually all such projects are technically feasible). The term dates back to the early days of computer systems, when some applications were not all that feasible. The requested project is evaluated for its practicality as well as for how it would fit into the overall applications environment. This feasibility study or evaluation is documented by the development team for subsequent management review.

   The request is then either approved or rejected, with documented reasons. If accepted and if a major project, the request may go to a management steering committee for some overall priority-setting. Such a steering committee is composed of management-level users from major functional areas in the organization. They may consider the request in light of an overall information systems long-range plan. If the request was consistent with that long-range plan, the steering committee would compare its estimated costs and benefits to other applications requests and give it a relative priority for information systems action.

2. *The Requirements Definition.* This definition study requires information systems and user personnel to work together to define the project's specific objectives, prioritized for importance and cost-effectiveness.

   The requirements definition phase will usually result in a fairly detailed general design study for subsequent management review. The study defines prioritized user needs and gives a general description of the technical approach to be taken on the project. Any new or specialized systems tools, such as a database package or other software product, should be identified. Figure 18.1 is an example table of contents from an information systems requirements study.

   Application control concepts should be considered during this requirements definition phase in which the auditor can express any preliminary control-related concerns before the application is released for detailed design.

3. *Detailed Design and Program Development.* Using the above study, the new application is detailed step by step. New programs to be developed follow the department's program-documentation standards. For some organizations, automated design tools may be used in this phase to define the entity relationships, input/output logic, and data requirements of each program element. These procedures can often be defined through computer-aided systems engineering or CASE procedures, discussed in greater detail later in this chapter and in Chapter 20. Figure 18.2 is an example of

Figure 18.1   Requirements Study Table of Contents Example

Contents
New Financial Reporting System Requirements Study
Department 863-01 ExampleCo Information Systems

1.0 Introduction and Management Authorization

2.0 New Financial Systems Objectives
2.1 Controller Function Improved Report Consolidation Needs
2.2 Anticipated Financial Reporting Changes
2.3 Information Systems Network Strategies Needs

3.0 Current Systems Architecture and Transaction Volumes

4.0 Current Systems Interface Needs
4.1 Current Production and Marketing Systems
4.2 Planned Production and Marketing Systems
4.3 E-Commerce Growth Plan

5.0 ExampleCo Systems versus Competition: A Benchmarking Analysis

6.0 Software and Database Vendors Survey

7.0 Proposed New System Solution

8.0 Preliminary Time and Cost Estimates

a page from a detailed design specification that an internal auditor might expect to find when reviewing program-development documentation.

4. *Application Testing and Implementation.* This phase will consist of both program-level unit testing and overall application testing. Formalized test plans are prepared, and users typically review test results. If problems are encountered in this phase, the project may be turned back for additional programming work. This is typically what happens with applications developed under the joint application development or prototyping methods discussed later in this chapter.

     Following comprehensive testing, the users who originally requested the application are asked to approve it for implementation. A detailed, documented test and conversion plan outlines requirements such as the need for new forms, user training, or conversion steps from existing applications.

     A larger information systems organization's quality assurance (QA) function often participates in a final review at this point. Information systems QA functions were discussed in Chapter 17. Internal audit may want to rely upon the QA function to perform detailed reviews in such areas as compliance with departmental programming standards. However, internal audit should periodically review controls and procedures within its QA function (as discussed in Chapter 33).

5. *Post-Implementation Review.* The last step is a post-implementation review to determine if the new application has achieved it original objectives. If additional changes or improvements are still required, they would be documented in order to initiate a

Figure 18.2 Detailed Design Specification Example: Catalog Update Process

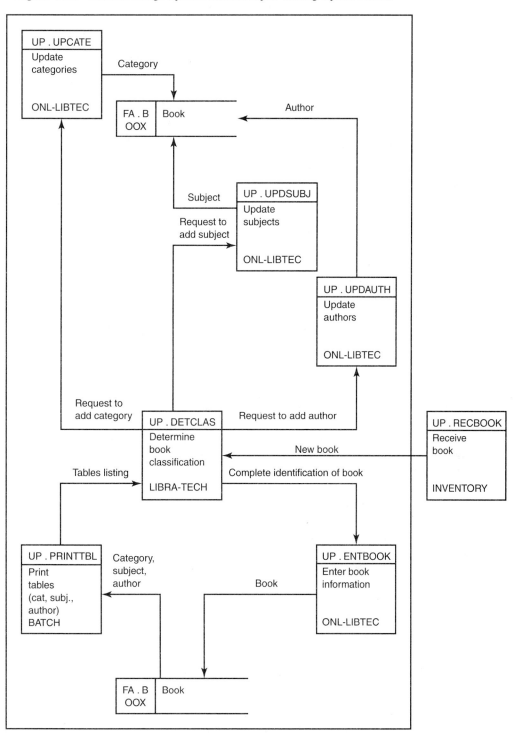

new project and SDM cycle. The post-implementation review, often ignored by development organizations, is an important part of any SDM and should be completed.

Documentation is the key to such an approach. Users document their requirements and developers document their design processes. Such documentation minimizes user and developer misunderstandings and produces better information systems. As information systems are increasingly developed through the use of purchased software elements or automated design tools, the auditor today will find less frequent use of traditional SDM approaches. If they are used, significant portions of the process may be bypassed. However, a traditional SDM approach represents a good project-management control technique.

Developed by IBM in the 1960s, the original SDM approach has been published in many variations since. Some departments implemented their SDM procedures using those original published documents and modified them over time, while others purchased packages from outside vendors, including some developed by the major public accounting firms. These packages offered standards manuals, forms, and training materials.

Today, purchased SDM packages are generally automated and follow the rapid application design or CASE approaches described in this chapter. They allow system developers and programmers to define program logic and data element requirements easily. However, some information systems developers who use primarily purchased software components will sometimes argue that the SDM is no longer appropriate. That assertion is really not true! Auditors should always look for some form of SDM methodology when reviewing in-house systems-development projects.

(b) PURCHASED SOFTWARE DEVELOPMENT PROJECTS

Today, organizations frequently purchase software packages for standard applications in order to save both time and costs. For many routine applications, it generally is not cost-effective to develop an application in-house when purchased programs packages achieve most of the desired system objectives. Many business processes, whether they are for accounts payable, general ledger accounting, or inventory management, do not differ from one organization to another or even across industries, and the software often requires only minor modifications to tailor it to the particular organization.

Similarly, some applications are just too difficult to develop and can be purchased quite inexpensively. A microcomputer spreadsheet application, with all of its extensive features, can be purchased for less than $500!

Even though a software application has been purchased, its implementation often requires strong project-management controls, programmers to make necessary changes to the software and to interface programs, and user participation to test the system. Many of the systems SDM steps for a purchased software implementation are the same as for a custom-built application.

Auditors should not ignore these purchased software system implementations when considering candidates for preimplementation review. In many instances, risks and exposures with such implementations are similar to those with in-house-developed applications. The requirements for the application may be poorly defined, the developers may add changes that do not follow good control procedures, or the conversion and testing procedures may be inadequate. There may not have been an appropriate level of review and analysis before the selection and software purchase, and the package may have some limitations that were not recognized. In addition, just because an outside vendor offers a software package for sale, one cannot assume that the application's control procedures are necessarily good!

These types of application projects generally require much more work than just loading in the new application from the vendor package and starting to work. The information systems organization must build interfaces between existing systems, convert files to adapt to the new system, build table files and parameters, and perform other in-house procedures. The systems-development organization needs to prepare detailed plans for the applications conversion and interfaces with other existing applications. However, this conversion should be documented such that it can be reviewed and approved by the requesting users. As purchased software packages play an increasingly important role, the effective auditor should participate in preimplementation reviews of these products.

(c) NEWER TOOLS AND TECHNOLOGIES

Many newer applications are developed through what are called prototyping or rapid-application-development methods. Software-development tools are available today where the applications-development specialist can point to a screen image of a system component such as file transaction update and graphically build a program or a complete system. This approach is often called object-oriented programming. Many software products are available to build these types of applications. A programmer would select those images and tie them together to build a program. Figure 18.3 is an example of this object-oriented programming approach.

These newer software tools and technologies allow information systems to develop a preliminary version using a high-level graphic language or other rapid-development software tool, review that preliminary version with the requesting user, and then make further modifications on an iterative basis until the application meets user requirements. However, if a production system, the application developed under these new software tools should still follow the information systems department's design documentation standards once the application details are formalized. In many systems-development organizations today, these rapid-application-development tools have all but eliminated the use of old classic business programming languages such as COBOL. Rather, newer programming languages such as C + + have become much more common.

Figure 18.3 Object-Oriented Programming Example

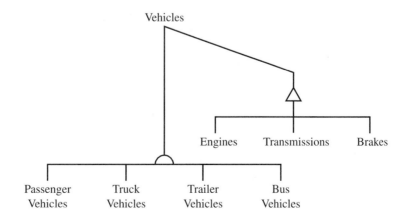

(d) USER-DEVELOPED APPLICATION PROJECTS

Many applications today are developed totally outside of the classic information systems organization. The powerful and easy-to-use microcomputer tools available make that process quite easy. As an example of this type of application development, Chapter 14, ''Automating Internal Audit Processes'' discussed a variety of reports and database files that internal audit could construct for its own use. The chapter assumed that rather than have the information systems department develop these projects, internal audit would construct them in-house.

Many user-developed applications projects today are similar to those in Chapter 14. That is, they serve the needs of a single department and have minimal interfaces or connections with other systems. Control risks are generally slight as the systems are used for departmental record-keeping or similar activities. If user-developed applications try to cross departmental boundaries or to control significant organizational assets, organization management or information systems should raise concerns or even prohibit such in-house-developed efforts, for two basic reasons. First, departmental users often do not appreciate the types of transactions and controls that may need to be built across system boundaries or interfaces. The specialized information systems function better understands these control techniques. The second reason is that a significant in-house-developed system requires considerable time and other resources to construct. Unless the overall organization does not have an information systems function, these projects would be best assigned to the applications-development specialists.

Preimplementation reviews of smaller, ad hoc systems developed within a user department are generally unnecessary, as the risk is just not that great to allocate valuable internal audit time for the review. However, if an internal auditor encounters a major user-controlled application-development effort in the course of other audit work, the auditor may want to ask questions about the appropriateness of the development effort. If it appears to be a bootleg type of application that might cause some potential control concerns, internal audit should call this development effort to the attention of appropriate members of management.

18-4 AUDITOR ROLES IN THE SYSTEMS-DEVELOPMENT PROCESS

The beginning of this chapter discussed how internal audit must be careful not to take responsibility for implementing the controls in new applications. Internal audit should be the reviewer of the controls being designed while application developers should act upon internal audit's recommendations and hopefully implement any control or project-management-oriented recommendations. Because of the varying nature of the typical systems project, internal audit can take several different approaches to reviewing new applications under development. These generally follow one of three strategies:

- Internal audit can be an active participant in the design team.
- The ongoing applications design and development effort can be externally monitored by internal audit on a constant basis.
- The application can be externally reviewed at selected intervals.

Each of the above approaches has both advantages and potential pitfalls for internal audit. As a member of the design team involved in all of the decisions and compromises that usually go into a comprehensive new applications design, the internal auditor has the best understanding of the application. However, not only can the assigned internal auditor easily lapse into becoming an integral member of the design team—thus losing independence—but this mode can sometimes turn itself into an almost full-time task for an auditor.

The design team role works best when an application is developed through a rapid-application-development approach. A version of the application may be produced, then evaluated, and subsequently modified with little lead time to produce the next version. To be effective in recommending controls improvements under this type of development approach, internal audit often needs to play an active role in the design team. Internal audit can review a preliminary design for, for instance, balancing controls while the regular design team is looking at screen formats. While they are incorporating their screen format revisions into the next version, internal audit can also suggest that improved balancing controls should also be built into the application.

In the second of the above roles, internal audit often also attends many of the same design meetings on a regular basis. However, internal audit should act only as an external, independent reviewer. This role can sometimes be quite difficult as the auditor will observe events in progress that may later lead to audit report comments and recommendations. Internal audit can easily lapse into becoming a non-independent member of the design team—or, if a less effective internal auditor, can become simply the ''occupant of the empty chair'' at design meetings.

The third approach, outlined above, is to review the application only at selected intervals during the development process. For example, the first review might occur at the conclusion of the requirements-definition phase. The next might take place early in the design phase, and that review would ascertain that internal audit's significant requirements definition control concerns have been appropriately considered as well as that good controls are being incorporated into the preliminary design.

Generally, the main problem with this third approach is in the scheduling of the audit reviews. An applications-design process is generally dynamic, with fairly constant schedule adjustments. Internal audit cannot just look at the initial project plan and then schedule subsequent reviews at future points in time. When the auditor returns from out-of-town work to review a planned requirements-definition study, for example, it may not be ready. When the study finally is ready for the preimplementation review, the auditor may be off and busy on another project.

An internal auditor must exercise scheduling flexibility when reviewing such applications under development. If an application has been rated as a relatively high risk, it may be necessary to adjust schedules for other audit projects.

18-5 PREIMPLEMENTATION RISK-ASSESSMENT PROCESSES

A typical applications-development department may be working simultaneously on a variety of large and small projects. Some may be major new applications while others will be fairly minor modifications to existing applications. Reviews of all projects in their preimplementation phases would require too many audit resources and would probably not be the best use of the internal audit's limited resources. A risk-assessment procedure for selecting which applications under development to review is somewhat different from the risk-assessment approaches discussed in Chapter 7, due to the varied and specialized nature of preimplementation projects.

Some audit departments only review all major new applications and ignore all other potential preimplementation candidates. This can be a convenient approach since a typical information systems department may be working on only one or two major new applications at a given time. The problem here is that some more minor system projects or modifications (in terms of a measure such as planned development hours) may also be of high audit significance.

Another approach is to review all new applications requests as defined through SDM procedures. However, because of the usual mass of systems-development candidates, as discussed previously, internal audit's review becomes little more than a superficial rubber stamp. It is nearly impossible to do a comprehensive review of *everything* without holding up system-development efforts. Time pressures will require internal audit to essentially just initial their approval on most of the new applications request documents and then pass them on. In addition, sometimes major purchased software projects will not use the standard SDM request forms and may go unnoticed.

A third approach is to review new applications only based on information systems management or senior management requests. Because management may not consider the application's audit risk or controls significance, and instead base its request on the application's expense, as an example, internal audit will sometimes miss reviewing new applications they should have and may also be asked to participate in other reviews that are unnecessary.

A better approach is for internal audit to develop a formal screening and evaluation approach for deciding which new applications to review. This is often called a *risk-evaluation or criticality-assessment approach,* where internal audit measures the attributes of each potential preimplementation candidate against a series of weighting factors in order to select higher scoring projects for review. Using the same basic approaches that were discussed in Chapter 7, a modified method works well for selecting preimplementation candidates for review.

(a) NEW APPLICATIONS PREIMPLEMENTATION RISK ASSESSMENT

Internal audit first needs to construct a table of measurement factors, essentially a point-scoring procedure where projects are evaluated on their technical characteristics, with those receiving high scores selected for potential preimplementation review. Criticality scoring approaches or models can be easily tailored to any risks unique or special to the organization and information systems function. The example risk-assessment process for a new application, below, is based on five broad assessment factors for evaluating the preimplementation audit candidates:

1. *Systems project status* refers to whether the applications project is a major new effort, a more minor new project, or a modification to an existing system. Perhaps the best way to determine if a project is ''major'' or ''minor'' is by using the total estimated applications and programming hours. Figure 18.4 is an example of this scoring.

2. *Audit and control significance* depends on the extent to which the project effects audit concerns. A sales order-entry system, for example, will probably have a higher level of significance than a marketing research information system because its outputs flow directly to the organization's financial statements, while the marketing system may be used for statistical purposes only.

Figure 18.4 Criticality Project Status Scoring Chart

An internal auditor should evaluate each application development project according to the following criticality scoring factors. Points should be assigned and then adjusted according to the weighting factors at the end of this chart. Each major criticality factor may receive a total score of up to 50 points. The sum of all the scores for all the factors for each application should not exceed 100 points. The highest scoring applications should be given priority as candidates for preimplementation review.

		Criticality Scores	
Criticality Factors		**Normal Range**	**Assigned Score**
I. Project Status			
A.	*Nature of the application project:*		
	New application developed in-house	8–10	_____
	Purchased application package	5–8	_____
	Major change affecting functionality	6–9	_____
	Minor change	0–5	_____
B.	*Past history of application change:*		
	Significant changes over past two years	6–10	_____
	Few changes in past two years	4–6	_____
	Two years or more since last change	2–5	_____
	New application (no changes)	0	_____
C.	*Project development team:*		
	Systems contractor, competitive bid	8–10	_____
	Systems contractor, sole source	6–8	_____
	In-house, remote location development	4–8	_____
	In-house development group	2–4	_____
	Packaged software with minor vendor changes	1–3	_____
D.	*Project management team:*		
	User group	8–10	_____
	Information systems group	4–7	_____
	Joint user and I/S management	1–4	_____
E.	*Top management interest in project:*		
	Project mandated by senior management	8–10	_____
	Division or operating unit request	6–9	_____
	Project initiated by middle management	5–7	_____
	Individual user or department request	2–5	_____
	"When time is available" request	0–3	_____
	Project Status Score		═══════

Figure 18.4   (*Continued*)

Criticality Factors	Criticality Scores Normal Range	Assigned Score
II. Audit and Control Significance		
A. *Type of application:*		
Affects financial statement balances	10	_____
Supports financial statement balances	5–9	_____
Supports major organizational operations	8–10	_____
Logistical or administrative support	2–5	_____
Statistical or research application	1–5	_____
B. *Past audit involvement with applications:*		
Prior audits including recommendations	7–10	_____
Prior audits, limited recommendations	4–8	_____
Audit reviews of related, manual areas	2–6	_____
No audit experience	0	_____
C. *Application control procedures:*		
Application-generated internal controls	8–10	_____
Run-to-run controls with other systems	6–8	_____
User-maintained on-line controls	2–6	_____
Batch controls	1–4	_____
D. *Application control responsibilities:*		
Controls handled within application	6–10	_____
Remote user control responsibility	5–8	_____
Local user control responsibility	3–7	_____
Parallel, manual control systems	0–4	_____
E. *Computer-assisted audit tools capability:*		
Candidate for embedded audit facility	8–10	_____
Standard audit software	5–8	_____
Potential use of 4GL tools	2–6	_____
No computer-assisted audit plans	0	_____
Audit and Control Significance Score		════════
III. Technical Complexity		
A. *Programming languages used:*		
Specialized Language such as Perl	8–10	_____
Mixed JAVA and other language system	6–8	_____
In-house-developed Visual Basic or C^{++} programs	5–7	_____
Programs produced by application generator	3–6	_____
Purchased software—extensive table builds	2–5	_____
Purchased software—minimal customization	0–2	_____
B. *Database procedures used:*		
Distributed client-server databases	8–10	_____
Single database, older technologies	7–9	_____
Multiple, linked relational databases	4–8	_____
Single relational database, complex tables	2–5	_____
Spreadsheet-type database	1–3	_____

Figure 18.4 *(Continued)*

		Criticality Scores	
	Criticality Factors	**Normal Range**	**Assigned Score**
C.	*Systems development methodology approach:*		
	New SDM procedures being introduced	8–10	_____
	Existing SDM procedures used	5–8	_____
	Prototyping development	3–7	_____
	Purchased software (limited SDM needs)	1–5	_____
D.	*Hardware requirements for application:*		
	New computer system	9–10	_____
	New peripheral devices	6–10	_____
	New or revised equipment configuration	3–5	_____
	Current or existing equipment	1–3	_____
E.	*Project team familiarity with technical environment:*		
	Team new to hardware or software used	7–10	_____
	Limited familiarity with environment	4–6	_____
	Strong team technical familiarity	0–4	_____
	Technical Complexity Score		═══════

IV. Interrelationship with Other Applications

A.	*Dependency on other applications:*		
	Inputs from network of polled stations	8–10	_____
	Inputs from distributed systems network	6–10	_____
	Inputs from local integrated systems	6–8	_____
	Inputs through tape or other transfer	2–5	_____
	Stand-alone application	0	_____
B.	*Requirements to supply other applications:*		
	Outputs transmitted directly to network	8–10	_____
	Direct outputs through shared databases	6–8	_____
	Outputs through file transfers	2–6	_____
	Outputs through review and reentry	1–4	_____
	Stand-alone application	0	_____
C.	*Communication relationships of application:*		
	Telecommunications through specialized network	10	_____
	Communication through dial-up lines	8–10	_____
	Use of standard remote links	5–7	_____
	Use of local links only	1–4	_____
	Stand-alone application	0	_____
D.	*Interrelationship with end-user facilities:*		
	Uploads and downloads from application files	10	_____
	Uploads and downloads from extract files	6–9	_____
	End-user downloads only	2–5	_____
	Stand-alone application	0	_____
E.	*Technical interrelationship considerations:*		
	Unique hardware and software protocols	7–10	_____
	Common hardware—unique software concerns	6–9	_____
	Common hardware and software linkages	2–5	_____
	Stand-alone applications:	0	_____
	Interrelationship Score		═══════

Figure 18.4   (*Continued*)

Criticality Factors	Normal Range	Assigned Score
V. Impact of Application Failure		
A. *Impact of incorrect outputs:*		
Potential legal liability	10	_____
Financial statement impact	9–10	_____
Potential for incorrect decisions	4–8	_____
Limited application decision support	1–4	_____
B. *Impact of incorrect files or data:*		
Incorrect results passed to other systems	8–10	_____
Corrupted data requiring reconstruction	6–9	_____
Corrupted data requiring reprocessing	1–5	_____
C. *Impact of failure on computer operations:*		
Scheduling problems with related systems	7–10	_____
Schedule adjustment for reprocessing	4–6	_____
End-user application (minimal impact)	1–5	_____
D. *Impact of failure on project management systems:*		
Requirement to reschedule planned systems	7–10	_____
Requirement to plan revised application	4–6	_____
Requirement to plan application fixes	1–5	_____
E. *Impact of application failure on personnel:*		
Need for extra management analysis time	8–10	_____
Need for extra user clerical time	6–9	_____
Need for systems or programmer efforts	2–6	_____
Purchased software vendor support	1–4	_____
Failure Impact Score		========

Summary and Weighting

Factor	Score		Weighting Factor		Weighted Score
Project Status	_____	×	0.15	=	_____
Audit and Control Significance	_____	×	0.40	=	_____
Technical Complexity	_____	×	0.05	=	_____
Interrelationship with Other Applications	_____	×	0.10	=	_____
Impact of Application Failure	_____	×	0.30	=	_____
Total Weighted Score			1.00		========

3. *Technical complexity* is based on the relative technical complexity of the application. For example, an object-oriented, graphical-interface language-based retrieval system would probably receive a lower score than an older COBOL or database on-line update system because the COBOL-based system may have a greater chance of programming errors. Similarly, a purchased software package would normally receive a lower score than an in-house-developed one.

4. *Interrelationship with other applications* directly and proportionately affects the risk factor. A stand-alone application that receives no automated inputs from other applications and supplies none would receive a relatively low risk-assessment factor score compared to a purchasing system that is part of an overall automated manufacturing system.

5. *Potential applications failure impact* should be assessed in terms of its relative impact on the organization. If an applications failure would cause the organization to cease operations in a given significant area, a much higher factor would be assigned. A system failure that merely causes some departmental inconvenience would receive a lower criticality rating.

Figure 18.5 is an example of this type of criticality scoring model. The overall approach is similar to the approaches discussed in Chapter 7. However, this model takes the unique nature of preimplementation reviews into account. Based upon the above five factors, a candidate could have a score ranging from one to fifty. The internal audit department may wish to modify some of these factors based on the overall applications environment or on the unique characteristics of internal audit's organization.

Before scoring preimplementation candidates, however, internal audit should discuss with management the approach as well as any assumptions built into the model. In addition, internal audit should evaluate it by calculating the scores for some past applications to determine if the scoring appears to be selecting the appropriate higher risk applications. Management should understand and approve of internal audit's approach to reviewing or not reviewing these new efforts.

(b) USING PREIMPLEMENTATION RISK-ASSESSMENT FACTOR SCORES

The risk-assessment scoring model is particularly useful for deciding whether new applications should be reviewed on an ongoing basis or as part of an annual audit-planning process. Although this comprehensive approach does not work as well for the smaller information systems organization that does not tie all of its development projects into an annual plan, it is still useful for internal audit. Each new systems project scheduled can be evaluated using the risk-assessment model.

Preimplementation risk-assessment should be developed using a five-step process, as follows:

1. *Assign a risk-assessment score to all review candidates.* As part of the annual audit-planning process, internal audit should assign relative risk-assessment scores to all planned new applications and modification projects. The review can be done as part of the annual audit-planning process or as individual applications are authorized. This will require discussing the proposed applications with information systems management and the requesting users.

Figure 18.5   Criticality Evaluation Scoring Chart

Using Figure 18.4, the following standard form has been filled in with scores that might be assigned by an auditor considering the criticality of a new sales and distribution system mandated by the management of a centralized consumer products company with remote locations. The relevant factors are as follows. The application is a major one for the company and will be developed in-house with user participation. The results will feed into financial statement applications, and controls with other systems will be utilized. CASE systems will be used. Programming will be in Visual BASIC. A standard database will be used, and data will be transmitted from remote locations. The existing SDM approach, which was reviewed previously by Internal Audit, will be used to develop the application. New work stations will be installed at remote locations for the first time, with dial-up lines to the central location.

Criticality Factors	Assigned Score
I. Project Status	
A. *Nature of the application project:*	
* This is a major in-house-developed application	10
B. *Past history of application change:*	
* This is a new system	0
C. *Project development team:*	
* An in-house development group will be used	3
D. *Project management team:*	
* Users and members of Information Systems will participate	2
E. *Top management interest in project:*	
* Senior management considers the application a "must" system	10
Project Status Score	25

2. *Estimate the monthly review time requirements.* Internal audit should prepare a month-by-month estimate of the audit time requirements for each of the potential review candidates. These estimates would be based upon the time expected both for application development and auditor review. The latter will be based on the preimplementation audit procedures discussed later in this chapter.

3. *Merge new candidates with current preimplementation projects.* Current plans should be merged with the plans for potential candidates.

4. *Determine hours available for review and make selections.* Internal audit should assess the hours that are available for preimplementation reviews.

5. *Review plans with management.* This will allow internal audit to explain why a given system was selected or not selected and to demonstrate why audit resource limitations may still prevent a review of some candidates.

(c) PROBLEMS WITH RISK-ASSESSMENT MEASUREMENT

In the real world, an internal auditor may encounter implementation problems with this risk-based selection process. First, the above approach is very dependent upon an annual information systems plan. If new project proposals or requests appear randomly over the course of the year, it will be necessary to continually adjust the relative risk-assessment scorings. Delays or schedule adjustments can cause internal audit to pass up reviewing other suitable candidates in process while other critical ones are delayed.

The newer structured design or prototyping approaches to applications design and development may also cause internal audit problems in applying risk-assessment measurements. Design definitions may be somewhat fluid with control concerns not all that well defined at the beginning of the project. Or, the design may happen sufficiently fast so that internal audit will not be able to evaluate it. In addition, management may decide that internal audit should review a given system even if it does not meet audit risk-assessment standards. Rather than arguing the point, the astute auditor will schedule the requested review. Some approaches to these problems are discussed in later sections of this chapter.

In order to make selection work, internal audit needs to review all selection assumptions with management on an ongoing basis. If internal audit is performing a fairly comprehensive controls review of the candidates selected, there will be fewer questions about why other applications were not reviewed.

18-6 PREIMPLEMENTATION REVIEW PROCEDURES

Audit procedures used in other reviews should be followed for new applications under development. All too often, internal auditors argue that applications under development are somehow ''different.'' However, as fluid and subject to ongoing developmental change as applications under development are, sets of control objectives and procedures are still quite appropriate for these reviews.

Preimplementation control objectives and procedures have been organized around the same SDM steps discussed earlier. The names of various phases and/or the SDM methodology may be different from one systems department to another; however, these steps can be easily tailored to fit the circumstances as required. This section initially discusses preimplementation reviews for major, in-house-developed systems. Separate sections cover preimplementation reviews of applications using newer development procedures or for purchased packages.

When the auditor has selected a given application, an important first step is to review the overall planned audit program with information systems management so that there is an understanding of what the internal auditor expects to find, as well as the review approach. Some procedures may be tailored to fit a given application, but the following objectives should apply for most preimplementation reviews.

(a) IN-HOUSE SYSTEMS-DEVELOPMENT PROJECTS

Fewer new systems are built in-house today, but even with purchased software, the typical larger information systems organization occasionally becomes involved in the design and implementation of larger systems projects. These projects most likely will be preimplementation review candidates.

The procedures discussed in this section follow the typical SDM review steps discussed previously and can be applied to other new projects such as applications with purchased software.

(i) Project Initiation and Feasibility Determination Objectives.

Usually a given applications project has been initiated and some feasibility determination has been made before it has been scheduled for development and for a potential audit preimplementation review, so the auditor will typically only have determined its criticality and selected it for review after this initiation step in the SDM.

Nevertheless, for those projects selected, consideration of feasibility is an important preimplementation review step. When a project has been selected, the auditor should determine that the project initiation request and the feasibility study have been properly prepared. Figure 18.6 provides internal audit procedures guidance for this portion of the preimplementation review. Even though the auditor may have started the review after this SDM phase has been completed, these procedures should be followed.

If internal audit determines that the initiation or feasibility determination process is flawed, suggesting to management that the given system may have been a poor choice for development can be difficult. When an application has been initiated without an adequate feasibility determination, it is often because it has a powerful sponsor. Internal audit should stress the need for a proper study and evaluation and warn management to follow its own standards.

(ii) Application Requirements Definition Objectives.

In this phase, internal audit should review the detailed requirements study to determine the overall control status of the new application. Figure 18.1 showed a table of contents from a requirements study, which provides both a general and specific controls-oriented description of the new application. If the auditor can identify control concerns during this phase of the applications development, it will be relatively easy for system designers to address and correct them.

Figure 18.7 is a set of audit procedures for the requirements definition phase of any project. Internal audit should look for similar requirements no matter how the new application is developed. Some of these procedures, of course, may require modification if the application under review is composed of specialized technologies or it will be a major modification to an existing system. However, the auditor should perform control procedures necessary to satisfy all of the control objectives listed here.

The auditor may need to decide if any special skills are required to complete the review. If the application involves the use of new or unique systems technologies and specialized supporting software, the auditor may want training on the software product to be used—such as through classes offered by the vendor to the development staff—or the auditor may bring in someone with specialized skills or training. For example, with some large projects that take years to develop and implement, it can be effective to add a specialist to the staff to cover just the review of such a large project.

Also during this requirements phase, the auditor can determine if the application will be of such audit significance that an embedded audit module should be included in the design. These techniques were discussed in Chapter 12, ''Using Computer-Assisted Audit Techniques.'' If they appear appropriate for the application under review, the auditor

Figure 18.6   Project Initiation and Feasibility Review Procedures

18.06.01	Develop a general understanding of the organization's information systems project initiation procedures including planning, budgeting, and approval procedures.
18.06.02	For the application selected for preimplementation review, initiate a review work-paper file and collect copies of all relevant project initiation documentation.
18.06.03	If the application project was initiated by the information systems function, review the analysis leading up to that new systems initiation. If the needs requirements do not appear to be particularly strong, discuss concerns with appropriate members of management.
18.06.04	If the application project was initiated by an end-user function, determine there was an appropriate level of preliminary analysis by both users and information systems. Determine that current conditions were analyzed appropriately prior to initiating the actual new systems project.
18.06.05	If the system request came from a senior management "I want . . ." type of request, ascertain whether the project appears to represent a good use of systems development resources. If there appears to be a potential problem, discuss concerns with the requesting manager as appropriate.
18.06.06	Review the analysis or preliminary feasibility work for the new project. Determine that alternatives, such as buy versus build analysis or an evaluation of alternative development approaches, were explored as part of the initiation process.
18.06.07	Review any estimated cost savings projections as well as preliminary budget estimates for the development project. Ascertain that the estimates seem to be "realistic," with attention given to all projected costs.
18.06.08	Determine that a realistic set of developed and completed application objectives, formally approved by both requesting users and information systems management, has been established for the new systems development project.
18.06.09	Review the proposed new application project in light of other organization and information systems plans. Assess whether the proposed new systems project will fit in with other existing plans.
18.06.10	Determine that the proposed project has been formally approved. Through interviews, assess whether all parties understand the nature, objectives, expected benefits, and costs of the proposed new application.

should develop requirements specifications for the module and make arrangements for development and installation.

At the completion of this phase, internal audit might write an informal audit report (discussed later). In addition, workpapers should be started to document the new application control's procedures.

(iii) Detailed Design and Program-Development Objectives.   This is typically the longest phase of a new applications project, and the auditor may want to schedule

Figure 18.7 Preimplementation Review Requirements Definition Checklist

Audit _____ Location _____ Date _____		
AUDIT STEP	**INITIAL**	**W/P**
1. Obtain a general understanding of the I/S department's SDM standards for developing a requirements definition study.		
2. Obtain feasibility study and other documentation authorizing the detailed system design.		
3. Review the system's documentation to determine that it is generally consistent with SDM standards and the nature of the feasibility study; look for specific documentation rather than vague narratives.		
4. Determine if any special skills are needed to review application controls, such as a new database platform or development approach. If appropriate, arrange for members of the audit staff to learn the new area through seminars or documentation.		
5. Identify and review significant controls surrounding new application. Discuss these controls with both the requesting users and I/S management and develop audit testing procedures.		
6. If significant portions of the application involve in-house-developed modules, assess whether appropriate consideration was given to commercial package alternatives.		
7. Assess whether the impact of non-system manual aspects of the application have been considered as part of the requirements definition.		
8. Review the preliminary project plan estimate surrounding the study. Determine if estimate appears complete and realistic.		
9. If the application appears to be a candidate for computer-assisted audit procedures, begin preliminary audit planning.		
10. Review the extent of user sign-ups on the requirements study documents. Based on selected interviews, assess whether users understand the new application and its ramifications.		

several reviews during this phase. While each of the periodic reviews should probably focus on a specific area of the new application–development project, the overall purpose should be to satisfy some of the following questions:

- Does the detailed design comply with the objectives of the general requirements definition?
- Do users understand the controls and objectives of the new application under development?
- Has proper consideration been given to application controls and security?

- Is the application being developed according to the information systems department's own SDM standards?

- Have any earlier audit recommendations been incorporated into the detailed design?

During this phase, care should be taken not to become too buried in detail. Some information systems organizations may attempt to use internal audit as a quality-assurance function for the project. However, overall audit effectiveness will be diminished if the auditor's time is spent reviewing such things as compliance with detailed programming standards. Reviews of this nature should be limited to periodic testing. Any control-related concerns encountered should be brought to the attention of management so that corrective action can be taken in a timely manner.

If the new application is purchased software, there will typically be limited in-house design and programming requirements. However, the information systems organization may have to build file-conversion programs or interfaces with existing systems or table files or report generator definitions. These can represent major efforts, and internal audit still should review controls over the purchased software before it is installed and implemented. Some of the unique auditor concerns with purchased software will be discussed later.

If the new application is being developed with prototyping or rapid-application-development methods, the auditor should review controls in the correct prototype version. Sometimes, an applications developer may decide that a control introduced in an earlier prototype version is too cumbersome and may be dropped later.

(iv) Applications Testing and Implementation Objectives. This phase includes testing of the new application, completion of documentation, user training, and conversion of data files. Internal audit often will be able to see if system controls appear to be working as expected and will want to test any embedded audit modules incorporated into the application.

Figure 18.8 contains procedures for this phase to help the auditor recommend whether the new application is ready for final implementation. Significant system control problems, coupled with management pressures to implement the application as soon as possible, can make this phase difficult. Information systems often promises to correct control problems in the new application during a ''phase two.'' Auditors often find that because of other priorities, phase two never seems to occur. The auditor should consider the severity of such control problems and either document them for follow-up review or inform management of the need for corrective action during the current implementation.

At the conclusion of the applications testing and implementation phase, the responsible auditor should prepare a final report that documents significant control issues identified by internal audit and subsequently corrected by the information systems development function. The report should also outline any outstanding control recommendations that have not been implemented. While reports up to this point have been informal, this final report should follow normal audit department reporting standards.

(v) Postimplementation Review Objectives. Although the new application is no longer in development, this phase of a preimplementation audit is still important. The postimplementation review should take place shortly after a new application has been

Figure 18.8   Preimplementation Review Application Testing Checklist

AUDIT STEP	INITIAL	W/P
Audit _____ Location _____ Date _____		
1. Determine if a formal test plan exists, including an outline by application modules detailing the data condition, the business rule tested, the type of test, and the results for each element tested.		
2. Review the results of several recent unit tests to determine if results have been mapped to the test plan, exceptions researched, and errors corrected as appropriate.		
3. Determine if the application being tested satisfies original system design requirements. If exceptions exist, determine if they were properly documented and reviewed by key users.		
4. Interview several key users to understand their participation in the testing process. Where participation is lacking, discuss the need for user participation to assure a successful application.		
5. Review the extent of overall system testing including key interfaces with other applications and outside service providers.		
6. If any original requirements have not been achieved by the completed application, assess procedures in place to determine whether to add procedures later or to otherwise allow for discrepancies.		
7. If appropriate, initiate a series of internal audit-developed test transactions that emphasize key controls defined in earlier review steps; review the test results and assess performance.		
8. Summarize the results of the testing activity and make an internal audit recommendation for the appropriateness of the application implementation.		

implemented and has time to settle down. In other words, the auditor should perform the review after the users have had an opportunity to understand the application and information systems has had time to resolve any final implementation difficulties.

A postimplementation review is different from the normal applications review discussed in Chapter 17, "Information Systems Application Controls." The postimplementation review determines if application design objectives have been met and if established applications controls are working. It also looks at project controls to determine if the application was completed within budget. Figure 18.9 contains audit procedures for such a postimplementation review. Ideally, this review should be performed by another member of the audit staff to provide an independent assessment of the new application.

(b) MAJOR SYSTEMS MODIFICATIONS

In many instances, modification projects are just as major as new systems development projects. Major modifications occur more commonly than new systems projects in order to avoid the total costs required to build or purchase a new application yet still reflect

Figure 18.9 Application Postimplementation Audit Program Steps

AUDIT STEP	INITIAL	W/P
Audit _____ Location _____ Date _____		
1. Review the current status of the new application. Does it meet requirements as originally defined?		
2. Meet with I/S and key users to assess whether new application meets their expectation. Assess procedures in place to correct any problems.		
3. Review the current status of internal audit's preimplementation review recommendations. Comment on any not implemented.		
4. Review a production cycle to assess application controls. Determine if controls appear to be operating adequately and per testing results.		
5. Review application's performance statistics to assess whether expectations have been achieved.		
6. Assess the performance of any embedded audit procedures installed during the implementation phase. Determine if procedures are working and that plans are in place to utilize them.		
7. If preimplementation review was performed by another member of the internal audit staff, assess from a quality standpoint the appropriateness of the preimplementation review.		
8. Determine that information systems has closed out of the application, documenting it per department procedures.		

changing business requirements or other needs. Because of familiarity with the current system due to past audit work, preimplementation reviews of major modifications may be easier for internal audit to perform.

Essentially the same procedures described in Figures 18.6 through 18.9 for new application preimplementation projects should be followed, with the following adjustments:

- *Project Initiation Review Procedures.* The study should not focus on why a system is needed but on why it needs to be modified, and it should also detail the justifications for modifying the existing system rather than exploring other alternatives. Sometimes internal audit has become aware of significant current control problems encountered in other audits, which may have initiated the current modification project. Both here and in the requirements portion of the review, internal audit should focus on whether these concerns have been addressed in the proposed new modification.

- *Requirements Definition Procedures.* As discussed above, internal audit should focus on whether previously identified problems with an existing system are proposed to be corrected through the modification. While not all prior recommendations can be incorporated into the modification, internal audit should assess the reasons for not including them and should note any future plans to build them into the modified application. Internal audit should carefully review the planned modifications to determine that they are not just ''window dressing'' types of changes, made to quiet various critics. If embedded audit procedures had been constructed for the existing application, this is the appropriate place to determine whether these audit procedures will work in the modified application, or if appropriate adjustments are necessary.

• *Application Detail Design Procedures.* Internal audit will typically not see the same detailed program specifications here as for a new systems design. While this phase often takes a significant portion of internal audit's budgeted time for new application reviews, the extent of work can sometimes be reduced if internal audit has a sufficient understanding of the existing application through prior audit work.

• *Testing and Implementation Procedures.* Internal audit may find this perhaps the easiest phase to cover. Often, internal audit will have the existing application to use as a benchmark to assess that the modified application continues to operate with the same general controls. The auditor performing the preimplementation review here should take particular care to determine that the controls in the modified application are at least as adequate as were those in the existing version.

• *Postimplementation Audit Procedures.* These procedures are essentially the same as for new projects. Again, internal audit should assess whether the modification project has met its stated objectives and that its controls are still functioning as intended.

Major systems modifications can cause significant changes to the control structure of established applications. All too often, information systems may describe requested modifications as ''cosmetic,'' but these small changes can modify significant systems controls. When determining candidates for preimplementation review, the auditor should ask detailed questions about the nature of the modification to determine if the change impacts control procedures. If so, those changes should be the focus of preimplementation review.

(c) REVIEWS OF PURCHASED SOFTWARE IMPLEMENTATIONS

New applications based on purchased software packages should also be considered as preimplementation review candidates. The author's review process is again essentially the same as described previously. The organization still needs to determine its needs, define requirements, install the package application, and perform appropriate tests prior to implementation. Internal audit should give particular attention to the feasibility and requirements-definition portion of this type of review. Information systems should have made some type of make-versus-buy decision before deciding to purchase the software, and they should consider pros and cons for both constructing and purchasing the software, and then review alternative packages to find the most appropriate.

We have used the term ''most appropriate'' because purchased software does not always meet the initial system requirements. Users may have some special requirements that the application may not provide. Or, the one that meets most of the requirements may be the most expensive. Users need to evaluate the cost-versus-benefit alternatives when selecting the new application package. Preimplementation reviews should determine if appropriate consideration has been given to these alternative options.

Figure 18.10 Software Contract Controls Checklist

1. Does the software appear to meet requirements definition needs?

2. Has the contract been reviewed by appropriate legal counsel?

3. Has the vendor's documentation been attached to the contract, by reference, to provide assurance that the software contract is fully described?

4. Has internal audit reviewed this documentation and does its descriptions of control procedures appear adequate?

5. Have adequate levels of vendor support been defined in the agreement?

6. Do the terms of the contract include all costs for application installation as well as some indications of upgrades and ongoing maintenance costs?

7. Has the vendor provided assurances that no organization materials will be copied or otherwise taken as part of the installation process?

8. Does the contract cover all organization units where the software will be installed and is this coverage sufficient?

9. Has the vendor offered user and information systems training on the use and operation of the software, and does this appear to be adequate?

10. Does the vendor offer some form of ''help desk'' facility for solving problems once implemented and are these defined in the contract?

11. Has the vendor made appropriate provisions to place copies of the source code in an escrow account in the event of a vendor default, and does this appear adequate?

12. Does the contract have any procedures in place for resolving disputes as well as definitions of appropriate laws?

Particular consideration should be paid to the terms of the contract negotiated to purchase or lease the software. This contract, which outlines the software vendor's responsibilities and rights, provides basic protection to the organization, including such matters as the vendor's responsibility to update the software, the organization's rights to demand the correction of software problems, and the rights and obligations of both for changes to the software source code. In addition to obtaining a review by legal counsel, internal audit should review all major new software contracts prior to final approval. Internal audit can often raise control- and security-related issues that were not considered by the information systems organization. Figure 18.10 is a checklist of key control concerns for any major software contract. Internal audit can use this list to advise both users and information systems management negotiating the contract. Major software vendors have a standard contract, but internal audit–initiated or other management-suggested changes or amendments to this standard contract are generally possible.

(d) SYSTEMS DEVELOPED USING NEWER TECHNOLOGIES

The prior sections have discussed approaches to reviewing new applications under development following the information systems department's established SDM and following a "classic" applications-development life cycle approach. However, there are increasing new methodologies and technologies whose aims are to speed up design and development, and which are tailored more to user needs.

Two such development methodologies are prototyping and the use of structured development tools, sometimes called *joint application development* (JAD). Another—fourth-generation languages—is also used for end-user computing applications and often is applicable for audit retrieval work. New methodologies may allow developers to design an application faster but may result in different documentation from that in a traditional system; however, these differences should not change the auditor's basic objectives for reviewing new applications under development. No matter what methodology is used, internal audit should still be concerned that the application is being designed with adequate controls, that it has been properly defined and justified, and that the project-development process is being properly managed.

(i) Developing New Applications Using Prototyping. The traditional SDM process works best when users know what they want in a new application and when those requirements can be easily interpreted into a new information system by the development staff. All too often, however, users have not defined their requirements all that well. They may decide that they need additional changes to their applications definition during the course of the design. In some instances, these changes also may have been caused by internal audit's preimplementation recommendations.

Systems development functions, using traditional tools such as COBOL, often have trouble reacting to a request for changes due to the inflexibilities of the development tools. Thus, design definitions are often frozen at some point during the development process. Then, when the application is finally completed, it may not meet the user's needs.

Systems developers can use the technique of prototyping, in which they give the user a test or tentative version of the new application for review shortly after the initial request is made. The user then reviews that test version, suggests changes, and the developer makes further modifications. This may result in another prototype, more changes, and still other prototypes until the final application is finally developed.

Many development groups have found prototyping an effective tool for developing new applications that better meet user requirements. Rather than going through a long development cycle, users can see a tentative version of the requested application, can suggest any additional changes which were missed in the requirements definition, and have a result much sooner that better meets their needs.

Changes in design and applications-control procedures can happen very rapidly, so internal audit usually needs to be much closer to the prototyping development process. It does not work, for example, for the auditor to review the detailed specifications and then return some time thereafter to review the results of applications testing. Prototyping could have changed many application functions and controls.

In addition, internal audit will also face other audit and control prototype implications, including:

- *Temporary versus Final Solutions.* Users will often accept one or another interim version of an application as their final system solution. Auditors should verify that the prototyping temporary solution contains all of the controls that would be expected in a final version.
- *Limited Problem Scopes.* It is very easy for applications developed under prototyp-

ing to solve limited, departmental needs but to miss major business problems. For example, a given function may request a certain type of information system that internal audit knows is also needed in other organizational units. In the rush to deliver a prototype to the requesting department, systems developers may miss the larger business problem.

- *Controls May Be Lacking.* Prototype developers and users might not give adequate consideration to access controls when working with various versions of a proposed retrieval screen, so auditors must give particular attention to these control concerns.

- *Moves to Full Production Are Sometimes Difficult.* Systems-development and operations groups often have a difficult time in bringing a prototype application into a full production status following normal operations procedures. For the application to be properly documented before being placed into a production status, the user who worked with and helped to define the prototype may end up running it in a production status as an end user.

Internal audit needs to treat preimplementation reviews of applications developed through prototyping with the above implications in mind. Figure 18.11 contains some of the unique

Figure 18.11   Preimplementation Review of Prototyping, RAD Applications

Audit _____ Location _____ Date _____		
AUDIT STEP	**INITIAL**	**W/P**
1. Develop an understanding of the rapid application development (RAD) procedures used through a review of vendor documentation or published procedures. Through interviews, determine if procedures are used as documented.		
2. For the application to be developed using RAD, assess the level of consideration given to the adequacy of controls in the design process.		
3. Determine if a level of requirements objectives has been established for the application being developed.		
4. Observe several cycles of a RAD process and determine if appropriate consideration was given to assessing controls and application performance throughout each RAD cycle.		
5. Assess whether an appropriate level of requesting users are participating in the RAD process and reviewing test results and controls.		
6. Determine if an appropriate level of documentation has been prepared for all interim RAD steps.		
7. Review user- and systems-level testing procedures in place throughout the RAD implementation steps.		
8. Determine if adequate procedures are in place to put the RAD application into a full-production status.		

procedures for auditing new applications under development when prototyping or rapid-application-development techniques are used. While much of internal audit's requirements definition and postimplementation concerns will remain essentially unchanged, prototyping will change internal audit's approach to reviewing the detailed design and program testing portion of the review.

(ii) Automated Development Tools.   A large number of automated development tools now help the information systems programmer or analyst to develop better applications faster. These tools allow applications to be developed with what is often called computer-aided systems engineering (CASE) techniques, which have some or all of the following attributes:

- *Workstation-Based.* The designer no longer needs paper and pencil to perform system design tasks. While programming code has been created through on-line terminals for some time, the applications-design process has not been that automated. Designers who formerly used flowchart templates and descriptive documentation to define their designs now have CASE and graphic user interface (GUI) tools on a workstation.

- *Structured or Object-Oriented Design Techniques.* Structured design is a procedure for defining applications through a series of data flow diagrams, showing various relationships from a very top level down. GUI design tools allow the developer to select images for various processing functions and then connect them to complete the process. CASE tools contain the graphics to produce such charts and to easily make changes to them.

- *Data-Entity Capabilities.* In addition to their GUI capabilities, CASE allows the developer to define the data entity relationships that will eventually be used in the application's data dictionary. Changes here will translate into changes in the automated structure diagrams.

- *Automatic Code Generators.* Many CASE tools can generate program code from the automated, structured design. While this facility will probably not eliminate all traditional programmers in the short run, it will greatly relieve them from such repetitive tasks as writing simple data-retrieval programs.

Such tools give the application developer much more flexibility to rapidly alter applications structures during the design phase. Control techniques have not yet become well established due to the variety of CASE approaches. Procedures that internal audit should consider when reviewing a new application under development using CASE or other GUI techniques will be described in a future edition.

(e) END-USER-DEVELOPED APPLICATION PROJECTS

In many respects, there should be no change in application controls whether they're developed through conventional techniques or through end users using modern application-generator software. However, many of the controls that may be built into end-user applications depend both upon what is available within the software products used and upon the controls knowledge and skills of the responsible end users.

There are many GUI application-development products on the market today, with a preponderance of them implemented for microcomputer workstations. The internal auditor should understand the control characteristics of the organization's end-user application-development languages used by reading documentation, using it on a test-case basis, and discussing the package with informations systems personnel.

Because of their use and ability to create ad hoc reports quickly, the auditor will often find GUI application development software in use by end users. Many are powerful tools useful for that purpose. Others, because they are mainframe-oriented and closely linked to the organization's DBMS, may be almost too powerful to give to the end user. However, these applications may sometimes be constructed by end users who lack the formal development and application controls skills found in the traditional information systems applications-development function.

(i) Understanding the GUI End-User Application.   We have previously discussed approaches for selecting traditional information systems applications for preimplementation review and suggested the types of documentation that the auditor should seek for review in order to develop an understanding of the application audit candidate. Auditors will often have a more difficult task in developing this understanding for end-user-developed applications because they often have been developed on an ad hoc basis without much documentation. However, such applications are generally not as complex as information systems department production applications.

Many end-user-developed applications, of course, are of little concern to the auditor or to management. Some may be of a personal nature, such as personal status reports or scheduling calendars. Others may be simple retrieval applications used to improve decision-making within one department or function. For example, a cost accounting department might use an end-user-developed system for special analysis reports of certain product costs. Such reports will have essentially no impact on the organization's financial statements and will present minimal risk. Others may be used for rather important strategic business decision-making and create significant control or business risks. However, unless such applications are processed with some form of information systems department involvement, it is often difficult for internal audit to even identify these critical applications.

In order to identify potential review candidates from the various end-user-developed applications, internal audit may want to consider surveying them to develop an inventory. That is, internal audit should develop an information survey form that asks users to list the types of applications that are used, the databases or files being accessed, the frequency of use, and the controls responsibility for them. A database of the completed survey would provide useful information to both internal audit and those responsible for managing the organization's information systems resources. This completed survey should help internal audit to develop demographics on the following three groupings of end-user-developed applications:

1. Applications that perform critical functions in their own areas and may be candidates for audit review

2. Applications that appear to perform significant internal control functions and should be possibly recommended for conversion to information systems–controlled production systems

3. End-user applications of little internal control risk

The first of the above are potential candidates for application reviews. Group-two candidates may also require an applications review in order to gain sufficient evidence to make a strong recommendation for conversion to a production system. The third group includes the various retrieval reports and other personal productivity applications found in many organizations. There may be little need to go beyond identifying these for statistical purposes.

(ii) Auditing End-User-Developed Applications.

Once internal audit has developed background data on the end-user-developed applications and chosen candidates for a more detailed audit review, the actual approach is similar to that for normal production applications, and includes the following steps:

1. Clearly define the objectives of the applications review.
2. Review the application with responsible key users.
3. Describe the system for audit workpaper purposes.
4. Identify system control points.
5. Test system key controls.

When working with an end-user-developed application, however, internal audit will want to emphasize areas where there may be a greater control risk. These include:

- *Poor Change Controls.* Because of the ease that users find in developing and subsequently modifying end-user-developed applications, good techniques for documenting changes to the system are often ignored. There is often little distinction between "test" and "production" versions of such an application.

- *Poor Error Controls.* End users are often not familiar with information systems procedures for error screening and detection. Novice applications developers tend to assume that there will be no data errors.

- *Application Logic Errors.* Because of the quick and dirty approach that is often taken to develop end-user applications, developers may initially process just a handful of test transactions, find that they appear to have no problems, and then assume the application will have no application logic errors. They sometimes do contain significant program logic errors!

- *Limited Documentation.* End-user applications are often developed and maintained by only a very limited number of key persons. If a certain minimum level of documentation has not been prepared, it is quite possible that the application could become difficult to maintain if those key persons are not available.

Figure 18.12 contains selected procedures for preimplementation reviews of end-user-developed applications. These procedures assume that the organization has selected GUI information system software tools, which have good controls. In addition, there should be good LAN file server controls in place to cover such matters as overall file backups. These issues were discussed in Chapter 16.

Auditors should become aware of the extent of end-user-developed applications in their organizations. While the earlier end-user retrieval languages provided little more than facilities to develop ad hoc retrieval reports, modern GUI software can allow end-

Figure 18.12   End-User-Developed Application Preimplementation Review Steps

Audit _____ Location _____ Date _____		
AUDIT STEP	**INITIAL**	**W/P**
1. Review the tools available for end-user-developed applications. Assess the user's understanding of those tools for the application to be reviewed.		
2. Determine that a level of documentation, such as management statements of objectives, exists for the application to be reviewed.		
3. Review the overall design process including the persons responsible for developing procedures, developing tests, reviewing and approving results, and turning the application over to production.		
4. Participate in several of the development cycle steps and assess whether adequate consideration was given to reviewing controls and test results.		
5. Review the application testing process and consider whether some form of test plan has been prepared to describe objectives and expected results.		
6. Review the level of documentation prepared for the application—both hard and soft copy format—and assess whether documentation is adequate to allow operation after key developers are no longer working there.		
7. Review control procedures surrounding interfaces with end-user-developed application and any other production application.		
8. Assess the data and the adequacy of security surrounding the end-user-developed application.		

user groups to implement substantial applications outside of the formal information systems function. While there can be a place for this type of development work, auditors should be aware of and include these activities with their review.

18-7 PREIMPLEMENTATION AUDITOR SKILL NEEDS

It is important that internal auditors understand computer audit, control, and security concepts, but they do not need to be highly skilled applications specialists. When reviewing new applications under development, however, internal auditors do need a somewhat higher technical skill level, as well as a general understanding of the control implications of various new technologies such as prototyping or CASE, electronic data interchange (EDI), or expert systems procedures.

Technical skill can be attained by attending some of the same vendor-offered training classes given to information systems personnel, by attending other technical seminars, and through outside technical reading. The greater an internal audit's knowledge of information systems technical areas, the greater internal audit's technical credibility when dealing with information systems specialists.

18-8 PREIMPLEMENTATION AUDIT REPORTS

Many internal audit departments have a fairly formal procedure for issuing audit reports. Draft reports are prepared, auditees prepare their responses after some discussion and negotiation on the draft, and a final audit report is issued, with copies distributed to various levels of management. (See Chapter 15.) This audit report format is often inappropriate for reviews of new applications under development.

An individual internal controls problem with a particular program or output report, which may be identified by an auditor when performing a preimplementation review, can be corrected by the applications developer almost at once. There is little need to discuss such a finding in the format of a formal audit report draft. The control concern should have been corrected long before the audit report was issued. Audit and general management, who might expect the more formal audit report with its findings and recommendations, should both understand the special report format used for preimplementation reviews.

Informal, memo-type reports should be issued after each phase of the preimplementation reviews. These memo reports should discuss the scope of review activities and document any audit concerns. If some of the prior concerns have been corrected, the actions taken and current status of the controls issue should be discussed. Figure 18.13 is an example of a memo-format preimplementation audit report. Of course, internal audit should also develop workpaper documentation covering these review activities, which will serve both to document preimplementation activities and to provide a basis for later applications reviews.

At the conclusion of the preimplementation review, internal audit should issue a formal audit report following audit department standards and the report formats discussed in Chapter 15. Where appropriate, this report can discuss preimplementation audit findings and corrective actions taken. However, the main function of this final report is to highlight outstanding control issues that still need to be corrected within the new applications system.

18-9 AUDITOR PREIMPLEMENTATION PROJECT INVOLVEMENT

Auditors have been performing preimplementation reviews of information systems applications almost since the very beginnings of computer auditing. While the concepts supporting these preimplementation reviews are attractive to both auditors and applications-development management, implementation is often difficult. For these reviews to be effective, internal audit must orient them to the organization's SDM procedures and take the role of an independent observer of controls.

The need for preimplementation reviews increases with some of the current trends in the modern information systems organization. For example, organizations typically purchase their software as a first choice for new applications. All too often, there is a tendency to blame the software vendor for control weaknesses and to take minimal further action. Internal audit can play an effective role in highlighting such deficiencies and influencing corrective actions. This need for preimplementation reviews is also of particu-

Figure 18.13   Preimplementation Review Memo Request

MEMO

July 15, 1998

To: Bob Cratchit, Excess Division Controller
             Tom Watson, Information Systems Director

From: ExampleCo Internal Audit

Re: Reporting 2001 Financial Consolidation System

Internal audit has completed a preimplementation review of the Reporting 2001 Financial Consolidation System being developed by the Excess Division. The purpose of our review was to assess the adequacy of both the system and project development controls surrounding this new application.

As part of our review, we assessed the controls built into the new application as well as the project development controls in place. We measured these project development controls against ExampleCo systems development procedures. Our review was completed in June 1998, at a time when the application was still in its final phases of testing and development.

We found that the Reporting 2001 Financial Consolidation System is generally being built with good application controls and following good project management methods. However, we found two areas that we feel need to be addressed prior to the system's implementation:

- Inadequate firewall protection. The application is linked to both plant facilities and ExampleCo headquarters through the ExampleCo intranet. We found that the firewall protection over this application was generally inadequate, leading to the risk of unauthorized data access and manipulation. Prior to implementation, procedures here need to be improved.

- Weak project management cost controls. We observed that minimal attention was given to recording the time spent on various project tasks. As a result, the costs of the completed application will be inconclusive. As much as practicable, attention should be given to reconstruction of records to assess the development costs of this project.

After attention has been given to rectifying the above two issues, internal audit sees no reason why the new application cannot be implemented as scheduled.

lar importance when new applications are being developed through prototyping methods or with portions developed by end users.

The effective auditor should devote a significant portion of review activity time to new applications under development. This will result in a more effective internal audit function as well as better-controlled information systems applications. Preimplementation reviews should be considered part of the control structure, discussed in Chapter 2.

CHAPTER 19

Physical, Logical Security, and Contingency Planning

19-1 IMPORTANCE OF INFORMATION SYSTEMS SECURITY

Information systems in the modern organization have many data and program resources that can be accessed through the telecommunication network, physical computer equipment, external files, and the attached, on-line terminals. Information systems management has come a long way from the days when computer systems were all but located in the lobbies of headquarter buildings, open to frequent visitors. Management has generally recognized today that this equipment, whether a classic mainframe, file server, or office microcomputers, should have a level of physical protection. Over time, internal audit has had a role in assessing these physical security controls and making appropriate recommendations when needed.

Logical security controls pose a greater problem to the modern organization. Large amounts of data and even programs, available through on-line terminals or networked workstations, are often either private or confidential and are usually protected through some type of logical security password-based system. If not installed with adequate controls and procedures, it will not effectively protect against improper access attempts nor monitor normal access procedures and can, therefore, represent a significant risk to an organization. Virtually every organization has some sensitive data on its computer files, including personnel records, customer lists, or proprietary engineering designs. If password controls are weak, an unauthorized person can access critical system resources and view or improperly manipulate them.

While good physical controls can prevent improper access to the equipment and logical security controls can prevent improper access to data and programs, if the information systems are subjected to some physical disaster such as a fire or flood, the organization also needs a contingency plan to allow it to return to normal operation as soon as possible.

Internal auditors should assume a major role in assessing the physical, logical security, and contingency-planning controls and procedures in the modern organization. This chapter discusses some of the risks in all three of these areas and provides procedures to allow internal audit to properly review those controls and make appropriate recommendations to management.

19-2 INFORMATION SYSTEMS PHYSICAL SECURITY

Auditors were among the first professional groups to recognize the importance of computer security controls and procedures. Today, even though formal computer security administration functions have been established in many organizations and a computer security profession is emerging, auditors are still viewed as the computer security experts in many organizations.

Computer security concerns have changed from the early days of the glass-enclosed computer rooms with batch-oriented systems. Then, internal audit was primarily interested in controls to protect expensive computer hardware from damage as well as to protect the integrity of the tapes and cards used to store data and programs. Today, an extensive network of workstations and other processors may be included with a ''classic'' mainframe processor.

Although aware of the vulnerabilities of their data-processing systems and of the need to install security controls, management often does not recognize similar vulnerabilities that may exist within such areas as telecommunications and LAN networks. Auditors can identify and evaluate computer physical security risks in all areas of data processing activity, and recommend the installation of effective controls.

The sections following discuss strategies for installing physical security controls over modern data-processing equipment. However, before recommending potentially complex and expensive physical security controls, internal audit should also understand the risks associated with *not* installing such controls. We will also discuss several approaches to computer security risk assessment and approaches for evaluating these risks.

(a) ASSESSING COMPUTER SYSTEM PHYSICAL SECURITY EXPOSURES

Physical security risks and control procedures should be included in internal audit's review of general data-processing controls, discussed in Chapter 16, and should cover the entire scope of data-processing operations—e.g., surrounding remote computing devices, telecommunications equipment, and client-server networks. These computer security exposures should be considered as well in context with similar exposures within the entire organization. An auditor's concerns about the lack of fire detection and prevention devices in a mainframe facility will accomplish little if similar controls do not exist within the rest of the organization.

Information systems physical security risks can be divided into several categories, as follows.

- Natural or catastrophic disasters
- Power and environmental failures
- Communications systems failures
- Sabotage, riots, and malicious damage
- Unintentional damage to computer systems

Some of these exposures involve low-probability, high-risk, ''can't happen'' types of situations, and some exposures that may pose significant risks to a larger organization will be of less concern to the smaller function. Understanding the range of exposures can help internal audit evaluate these risks and suggest appropriate safeguards. After reviewing the various exposures, internal audit should develop a detailed list of potential physical security exposures for evaluation, using the risk-assessment approaches discussed in Chapter 8.

(i) Natural or Catastrophic Disasters. Natural disasters include floods, earthquakes, or other "acts of God." They are probably the least common type of disaster which an information systems organization may face, but are also the most difficult to predict and generally the most devastating when they occur. For example, an organization and its data-processing operations may be located on what insurance companies call an "every hundred years" flood plain. Unpredictable weather patterns and other factors, however, can create two major floods within a three-year period, followed by none for hundreds of successive years.

Internal audit should consider remote probabilities of natural disasters that may affect the information systems facility. Data can be obtained from recent experiences with similar natural disasters, from the local weather bureau, and from historical records. The latter are important because some historical events are bound to repeat themselves. For example, recent minor seismic disturbances predict there will be a significant earthquake in the San Francisco area at some future time. However, one would have to consult history records to find that there was also a very significant earthquake in the St. Louis, Missouri, area in the early 1800s. There is certainly an exposure in both areas that such an event may be repeated.

Should internal audit or management be concerned about such natural disaster exposures? In most instances, little can be done to predict or prevent them aside from establishing some basic controls, such as a strong contingency plan, which can reduce exposures to such events. Internal audit might point out that the planned site for a new facility is in a historical flood plain, and if the decision remains to build at that location, make recommendations to construct the facility in a way that minimizes potential damage. For example, the computer center could be constructed in a place other than the ground floor or basement, such as in an "every hundred years" flood plain location. In addition, internal audit should recommend a strong disaster-recovery plan with a back-up processing site located at a remote and secure location. Disaster-recovery or contingency-planning procedures will be discussed later in this chapter.

Catastrophic disasters refer to fires, environmental failures such as a gas leak, or other disasters where man may play a role. Some controls might include housing the computer systems in a building constructed with fire-retardant materials and equipped with fire-detection and -prevention devices.

There are other types of disasters, however, where the information systems organization has little or no control. A nearby chemical or nuclear power plant or an accident with a passing train carrying chemicals could have a catastrophic accident that would render the entire nearby geographic area uninhabitable for an extended period. The probability of occurrence is probably higher than the "every hundred years" types of floods. It is quite easy to prevent and detect fires within the facility but much more difficult to prevent a major fire that starts in the building next door. It is equally difficult to prevent a chemical disaster caused by a passing train car. In the absence of a good disaster-recovery plan, few controls can be installed to limit the exposures.

(ii) Power and Environmental Failures. Because some larger and older mainframe computer systems require water-chiller systems to cool the equipment, and most larger computer systems require conditioned electrical power and strict air conditioning requirements, the risk of damage or destruction to electrical power systems or to air conditioning systems can be a major exposure to the larger, but older information systems function. Power and environmental failures represent a smaller exposure to the organization with microcomputer LAN-based systems, which often do not require specialized air conditioning or electrical power sources. However, there is an obvious need for normal power for the information systems equipment as well as for the entire facility.

A survey of the power and environmental exposures within the information systems organization requires an understanding of both the environmental requirements of the computer hardware as well as the current status of back-up sources of supply. Figure 19.1 is a checklist to help identify vulnerabilities, after which internal audit should prepare a detailed risk analysis list of probable physical security exposures for the function, as discussed in Chapter 8. This information will also help identify areas where physical security can be improved.

(iii) Communications Systems Failures.   The typical organization is highly dependent upon its communications system, whether a telecommunications network with lines connecting various remote facilities throughout the organization's operations or a local network connecting to file servers or a central computer center. The external telecommunications network is generally provided by a common carrier, leased or accessed through specialized communications lines. While the failure of such a telecommunications carrier to provide service certainly represents a physical data security exposure, the risks are typically fairly low. If an outside telecommunications organization providing lines and switching gear has an economic failure, some other organization will typically take over. Most of the communications exposures facing an organization exist within that organization and include the vulnerability of the networks and switching equipment both to failure and to malicious damage.

The most basic security exposure for communications networks is the organization's potential inability to quickly reconstruct those networks given some type of disaster. Many organizations have built their internal and even external networks on an almost ad hoc basis, with little documentation. It is necessary to have a good understanding of the existing network in order to reconstruct all or a portion of it on a short-term notice.

As part of a review of communications systems vulnerabilities, internal audit should prepare a list of potential exposures. This list should be classified by the various components of the telecommunications network that could be subject to failure. These exposures should include just those that are unique to telecommunications and should not be a duplication of other information systems exposures, such as overall natural disasters, which have been considered separately.

(iv) Riots, Sabotage, and Malicious Damage.   Once auditors expressed concerns and management realized that its older computer systems were vulnerable to a malicious intruder who could pull wires from an older mainframe's back panel to render the machine useless, a locked, limited-access computer room become necessary.

During the 1970s, many computer centers in the United States and Western Europe became targets of political insurrection, vandalism, and riots. Terrorists decided that these computer systems were symbolic of whatever it was they opposed and made them targets for destruction. Although this type of activity has very much subsided in recent years and

Figure 19.1   Physical Security Exposure Checklist: Power and Environmental Failure Risks

This checklist is designed to help identify potential electrical power, air conditioning, or related environmental risks within larger scale computer operations. Questions are designed so that a ''NO'' answer represents a potential environmental security exposure.

POTENTIAL SECURITY EXPOSURE	YES	NO	N/A
1. Are computer operations facility power sources and air conditioning facilities independent of other facilities in the building?			
2. Are exterior power transformers and air conditioning units shielded from direct exposure to outsiders?			
3. Are all power lines protected by adequate circuit breakers?			
4. Are master power switches clearly marked and located near each computer operations facility door?			
5. Is there a power conditioner installed to shield against electrical spikes?			
6. Is there an uninterruptible power supply or an emergency power system?			
7. Is the uninterruptible power supply system tested on a regular basis?			
8. Is the computer operations facility equipped with emergency, battery operated lights for use during power failures?			
9. Are any electric door locking devices also tied to the emergency power system?			
10. Are there emergency light and power systems, as required, in any nearby tape vaults or forms storage rooms?			
11. Is the computer operations facility equipped with thermostats and monitors to regulate temperature and humidity?			
12. Are there audible alarms which sound when temperature and humidity exceed defined limits?			
13. Are water cooling chiller units located to minimize damage if there is a plumbing failure?			
14. Is the computer operations facility located to minimize the danger of overhead leaks from pipes on the roof?			
15. Is the floor equipped with drains to avoid water accumulation in the event of a flood or fire?			
16. Are water level detectors installed beneath the raised floor?			
17. Is smoke and fire detection equipment approved by a recognized authority?			
18. Are supplemental heat detectors located under the false floor?			
19. Is the facility equipped with a zone fire control system?			
20. Does the fire control system both activate local audible alarms and automatically notify a nearby fire department?			
21. Is the duct system designed to exhaust smoke and combustion products to the outside?			

Figure 19.1   *(Continued)*

POTENTIAL SECURITY EXPOSURE	YES	NO	N/A
22. Are portable fire extinguishers located at every door and at other key points in the computer operations facility?			
23. Are ceiling tiles and wall surfaces constructed with a flame resistant material?			
24. Are fluorescent light fixtures designed to minimize the danger of melting or dipping?			
25. Is the computer operations facility inspected on a periodic basis by competent fire inspection authorities or insurance specialists?			
26. Are the connections to the telecommunications control facility secure and is there a backup connection in the event of a failure?			
27. If the overall facility is located in a geographic area subject to frequent weather extremes (hurricanes, floods, etc), and are there contingency plans in place in the event of such occurrences?			
28. Are there any nearby known environmental potential hazards that could cause a disruption to information systems operations?			
29. Do the providers of public utilities such as electricity and telephones represent a hazard and have backup provisions been developed?			
30. Is the information systems facility regularly inspected by governmental authorities for legal compliance and are any known issues outstanding?			

the classic mainframe computer systems are not as common, circumstances can always cause this political terrorism to erupt once again somewhere in the world.

Information systems management reacted to these threats of malicious damage or sabotage by establishing physical controls, ranging from tight access restrictions over entry to the computer operations center to placing that computer center in a separate, remote, "blockhouse" facility. While fairly good access controls have eliminated or reduced security exposures in many larger computer centers, little has often been done to reduce the physical security exposures surrounding LAN-connected microcomputers and client-server workstations. The concern surrounding these devices is often less one of malicious damage than of the potential theft of equipment such as boards and other components.

Many factors can go into the assessment of physical security exposures. As was discussed previously, these potential exposures do not necessarily mean that a control should be installed. Rather, a risk evaluation should be performed and, if management wishes, controls for the risk should then be installed.

(v) Unintentional Damage.   A significant physical security exposure in the modern information systems organization may be due to unintentional damage caused by well-meaning personnel. An employee can spill a cup of coffee over a file-server processor or can allow an unauthorized person to enter a mainframe operation room without checking for identification.

Internal auditors should consider exposures caused by human error or unintentional damage. While difficult to identify directly, day-to-day control and operational practices often indicate potential unintentional damage exposures. For example, unless there are rules prohibiting smoking, eating, and beverage-drinking around information systems equipment, there will be an exposure that the equipment may be damaged due to smoke or spilled food.

Figure 19.2 is a checklist covering unintentional damage exposures, which should be treated somewhat differently from those identified in Figures 19.1, where management may decide that the costs of installing appropriate control procedures may be sufficiently large that they will accept the risks. Controls to correct Figure 19.2 exposures can often be installed with relatively little effort. For example, a small organization may have a procedure where personnel store back-up tape cassettes in their homes for contingency-planning purposes. Since this media can be unintentionally but easily damaged, internal audit may recommend without further risk assessment that a safe deposit box be rented to store those backup files.

(b) IMPLEMENTING PHYSICAL SECURITY CONTROLS

Auditors are often in a unique position to recommend physical security improvements. Because auditors were often the first to suggest physical security improvements, management historically looked upon them as the information systems security experts. Today, information systems management often has a good understanding of physical security procedures and often employs data security professionals; however, these persons are often more involved with logical security, such as the access control software, rather than with physical security. In addition, their involvement sometimes does not extend beyond the formal business information systems function, even though there should be similar concerns with office microcomputers or network physical security.

The internal auditor, therefore, must have a good understanding of both relative security risks and effective control techniques. In addition, internal audit should keep in mind that physical security may extend beyond the formal information systems operations center to such other areas as departmental computers or office LANs.

(i) Improving Security in the Computer Room Facility.

The central information systems operations facility in the larger organization is often vital to overall operations. Whether a classic mainframe or client-server setup, the equipment is both relatively fragile and quite complex and can easily be damaged through either unintentional or malicious acts. Depending upon the relative risks and exposures, it is important to have strong computer room physical security controls covering the following broad areas.

- *Computer Room Access.* Access to computer operations should be limited to only authorized persons such as operators and management. In a smaller organization, this can often be accomplished through fairly informal procedures, such as placing the equipment in a lockable room and restricting access to only known persons who have a right to enter the facility. Controls must be much stricter in a larger organization and a larger computer facility.

Figure 19.2   Unintentional Damage Risk Security Exposures Checklist

POTENTIAL SECURITY EXPOSURE	YES	NO	N/A
1. Does the information systems operations organization have an adequate segregation of duties?			
2. Are there job descriptions for all employees and are there procedures to ensure that employees meet the requirements of those descriptions?			
3. Are background checks, within legal limits, performed for all new employees?			

4. Are new employees required to sign agreements covering:
    Nondisclosure of any organization information?
    Bonding?
    Conflicts of interest?
    Security clearances (if applicable)?			

5. Are new employees adequately trained before starting new job assignments?			
6. Is there an ongoing program of continuing education for all information systems employees within their areas of technical expertise?			
7. Are operations employees required to complete ''Problem Report'' logs in the event of any operations failure or problem?			
8. Do operations shift supervisors complete a report at the end of each shift detailing activities and problems?			
9. Are operations shift and problem reports reviewed by information systems management on a regular basis?			
10. Is there a documented procedure, known to employees, covering employee counseling or disciplining in the event of an improper employee action?			

11. Do employee resignation and dismissal procedures provide for appropriate:
    Return of access keys and badges and revocation of passwords?
    Return of confidential materials and other documentation?
    Changes to locks and combinations?			

12. Are there adequate procedures covering the access limitations and supervision of any temporary personnel working within the facility?			
13. Are fire evacuation drills conducted on a regular basis?			
14. Are key employees aware of their roles, as documented in the published disaster recovery plan?			

Figure 19.2   *(Continued)*

**Security Exposures Checklist for Evaluating
Unintentional Damage Risks**

POTENTIAL SECURITY EXPOSURE	YES	NO	N/A

15. Is there adequate off-site storage for critical applications and system media including:
   Copies of the operating system and related software?
   Source and object code versions of all programs?
   Proper versions of backup tapes to allow reconstruction of key applications?
   Database backup files and related operating software?
   Operations documentation and job control language procedures?
   Key forms and other supporting supplies?
   Copies of disaster recovery procedures?
16. Is the off-site storage area in a secure location convenient to the backup processing site?
17. Have alternative transport services to the off-site location been identified in the event of a strike, bad weather, or other problems?
18. Can the information systems center remain operational using supervisory personnel during a strike?
19. Are locked cabinets, movement logs, and related controls used to control sensitive materials within the information systems operations area?
20. Are any checkwriting signature plates and related materials stored separately from the associated documents?
21. Are logs, identification badges, and other controls used to monitor the distribution of sensitive output reports or documents?
22. Are there restrictions against food, drink, and smoking within the computer room facilities?
23. Is there a lounge or break area near the information systems facility for employee use?
24. Are there adequate policies covering personal use of information systems facilities by employees, such as for education?
25. Does the information systems organization perform periodic self-assessment reviews to evaluate the risk of unintentional damage?

Some rather sophisticated access-control devices available are:
- Cipher locks requiring a combination or code to gain entry
- Key cards, which can be matched against computer records
- Biometric devices, which match voice patterns, fingerprints, signatures, etc.

The above devices must be monitored and updated when there are personnel changes. All too often, an organization will install a sophisticated access-control device but will not update it to reflect employee terminations and the like.

- *Computer Room Location.* Location should be in a separate, blockhouse-like facility or in an unobtrusive area within the building, without windows and with secure walls. Organizations should always assess the relative vulnerabilities of their computer centers, whether classic mainframe or client-server, to terrorism, riots, or other malicious acts. If there is any potential concern about such actions, steps should be taken to limit exposures.

- *Computer Room Environment.* Larger mainframe computer systems in particular require precise environmental controls over air conditioning and electrical power, as well as a system of detection devices for fires or failures of the environmental system and preventive devices such as fire control systems. Large transformers must be mounted outside of the computer facility to supply proper power, while special compressors are required for cooling. These devices are vulnerable to both failure and malicious damage.

  These same environmental control vulnerabilities should also be assessed at smaller-system computer operations. While it may not be necessary to have a full fire-control system protecting a mid-range or LAN system, the risk of a loss of data or processing capability may still be significant. Because the cost of the fire-control equipment may be quite high relative to the cost of the computer equipment, internal audit should always consider relative risks and costs when making such evaluations.

- *Physical Security over Computer Media.* There should be proper physical security controls over computer media such as tape cartridges, files, or special forms. Some of these matters will be addressed in the data center's disaster-recovery plan, discussed later in this chapter, where arrangements can be made to store key files and other media in an off-site location. In a larger data center, some physical security over computer media may also be covered through access controls to prevent cartridges and tapes from being freely transported in and out of the computer room.

  Media backup procedures are very important in the smaller system environment. Formal, limited-access mainframe computer rooms often have controls to make it difficult to access key tapes and disk files. This is not true for many diskette-oriented LAN or microcomputer systems.

Figure 19.3 contains audit procedures for reviewing information systems' physical security controls and recommending improvements. This audit program is particularly valuable for larger system computer operations that are often used for such things as engineering automated design-processing. Although management often recognizes the importance of physical security controls for business information systems, it often ignores controls for these smaller departmental or specialized computer centers.

The effective auditor will always keep relative risks in mind when reviewing such controls and suggesting improvements. A computer center used for engineering product

Figure 19.3 Control Objectives and Procedures for Information Systems Physical Security Reviews

> **Obj. 8.7.1.** Computer equipment should be kept in a secure, environmentally controlled facility.
>
> **Proc. 8.7.1.1.** Tour computer and telecommunications physical facilities to ascertain security strengths and weaknesses including:
>
> General location within the overall facility such that it is outside heavy traffic patterns.
>
> > The placement of computer room outside walls and any windows to limit access to unauthorized individuals.
> >
> > The general structure of interior walls to determine that they are secure and are constructed from the floor to the true, not false, ceiling.
> >
> > The location of air conditioning units and power transformers to determine that they are properly protected.
>
> **Proc. 8.7.1.2.** Observe the temperature and humidity controls in place and assess the adequacy of procedures for monitoring those controls.
>
> **Proc. 8.7.1.3.** If the computer facility is located on a multi-floor facility, assess the risk of damage from plumbing failures, equipment, or occupants of upper floors.
>
> **Proc. 8.7.1.4.** Review the overall area surrounding the computer room and assess the risks of such potential nearby hazards as:
>
> Airports or airplane landing patterns
>
> Chemical plants or other hazardous facilities
>
> Warehouse buildings or other nearby structures susceptible to fire
>
> Rivers, historical flood plains, or other possible causes of flooding
>
> **Proc. 8.7.1.5.** Determine that the facility is located inconspicuously with no references or direction signs.
>
> **Obj. 8.7.2.** Access to the computer operations facility should be limited to authorized persons and that access should be controlled.
>
> **Proc. 8.7.2.1.** Observe the type of cypher lock, key lock, or badge system used to control access to the computer room and assess its adequacy.
>
> **Proc. 8.7.2.2.** Determine that locks or lock combinations to the equipment rooms are changed on a periodic basis.
>
> **Proc. 8.7.2.3.** Review the list of assigned key cards or access rights and determine that all persons on the list are still authorized employees.
>
> **Proc. 8.7.2.4.** Determine that logs or special badges are used for visitors and assess their adequacy and use.
>
> **Proc. 8.7.2.5.** Review procedures for allowing maintenance and other facilities personnel access and assess the adequacy of these procedures.
>
> **Proc. 8.7.2.6.** Visit the computer room facility on an unannounced basis during a non-prime shift and determine that access control procedures are being followed.
>
> **Proc. 8.7.2.7.** Determine that terminated employees are immediately escorted from the computer room and that their access rights are canceled.
>
> **Proc. 8.7.2.8.** Observe any supplementary doors within the computer room facility and determine that they are equipped with exit-only locks and audible alarms.

Figure 19.3   *(Continued)*

Obj. 8.7.3.   Appropriate controls should be in place in the computer operations facility to protect equipment, materials, and employees against fire or water hazards.

Proc. 8.7.3.1.   Determine that the total facility is protected by zone-controlled smoke and fire detection equipment, both above and below any raised floor, and that activation of these devices will result in an audible alarm in the computer room as well as automatic notification at the nearest fire department.

Proc. 8.7.3.2.   Determine that the computer room is equipped with an overall zone-controlled fire control system using appropriate fire suppressants as well as appropriate portable extinguishers.

Proc. 8.7.3.3.   Determine that master power switches are located at each major door to the facility.

Proc. 8.7.3.4.   Observe that fire evacuation charts are posted prominently and determine that evacuation drills take place on a periodic basis.

Proc. 8.7.3.5   Determine that the computer room facility is equipped with flame retardant, waterproof plastic covers for placement over major data processing equipment items.

Proc. 8.7.3.6.   Determine that the computer facility is inspected periodically by local fire inspectors, and review their last report to identify any open items for corrective action.

Proc. 8.7.3.7.   Discuss the computer room design with the organization's facilities manager to determine that flame resistant materials have been used for floor and ceiling tiles and that the ductwork has been constructed to minimize the risk of fire.

Proc. 8.7.3.8.   Determine that there are drainages under the raised floor to help avoid water accumulation in the event of flooding.

Proc. 8.7.3.9.   In addition to fire evacuation drills, determine that there are published procedures for an orderly shutdown of computer facilities in the event of flooding or a major weather disturbance.

Obj. 8.7.4.   Physical security controls should be in place over media storage and telecommunications controls areas.

Proc. 8.7.4.1.   Visit the prime media storage facility and determine that access, fire, and other controls are appropriate and consistent with procedures used in the main facility.

Proc. 8.7.4.2.   Review procedures for logging cartridges and tapes in and out of the library and assess the appropriateness of the controls.

Proc. 8.7.4.3.   Visit the telecommunications control area, if outside of the main computer room, and determine that access, fire, and other controls are appropriate and consistent with other computer room procedures.

Proc. 8.7.4.4.   Review cabling of telephone or local network lines from remote devices to the telecommunications facility and determine that these lines are shielded or obscured from view.

Obj. 8.7.5.   Computer operations should have adequate insurance coverage consistent with the potential risks and the desires of management.

Proc. 8.7.5.1.   Review related insurance coverage with appropriate individuals in the organization and determine whether there appears to be adequate coverage for data processing equipment and media including:

Losses from fire or flood damage
Losses from equipment breakdowns such as sprinkler system leakage
Losses from theft or vandalism
Civil commotion or riot losses.

Figure 19.3 *(Continued)*

Proc. 8.7.5.2. Review insurance coverage for business interruptions and assess adequacy given the organization's dependence upon key computer applications.

Proc. 8.7.5.3. Where there appears to be insurance-related vulnerabilities, discuss these concerns with appropriate levels of management.

Obj. 8.7.6. An effective and tested disaster recovery plan should be in place for computer operations.

Proc. 8.7.6.1. Determine that the organization has a disaster recovery plan.

Proc. 8.7.6.2. Interview several members of the disaster recovery team, as designated in the plan, and assess whether they understand their roles as outlined in the plan.

Proc. 8.7.6.3. Determine that key aspects of the plan, such as arrangements for the alternate processing site, are still current and operable.

Proc. 8.7.6.4. Determine that the disaster recovery plan is being tested periodically, and review the results of the last several tests including any documented recommendations for improvement.

Obj. 8.7.7. Backup copies of files, documentation, and critical forms should be stored in a secure, off-site location.

Proc. 8.7.7.1. Visit the off-site storage location and assess whether security and environmental controls appear to be adequate.

Proc. 8.7.7.2. Review procedures for designating files as candidates for off-site storage and assess whether proper consideration appears to be given to application criticality.

Proc. 8.7.7.3. Select several key applications and determine that key versions of files as well as documentation and special forms are stored in the off-site location.

Proc. 8.7.7.4. Secure an inventory listing of all items in the off-site location and determine whether it appears to be complete and current.

Obj. 8.7.8. Adequate procedures should be in place to record equipment failures and to maintain the equipment on a regular and emergency basis.

Proc. 8.7.8.1. Review manual and automated logging procedures for recording equipment failures and assess whether they appear to be followed.

Proc. 8.7.8.2. Determine that procedures are in place to obtain appropriate levels of approvals for calling in maintenance personnel during all operating shifts.

Proc. 8.7.8.3. If on-line remote maintenance techniques are used for hardware or software problems, determine that those activities are logged and reported to management.

Proc. 8.7.8.4 Review operations schedules to determine that equipment maintenance is performed on a regular basis consistent with equipment requirements.

Obj. 8.7.9. Controls should be in place to monitor the distribution of output reports as well as the introduction or release of tape files.

Proc. 8.7.9.1. If users pick up output reports from the operations facility, determine that a lock box or supervised, badge identification system is used such that only authorized persons may pick up their reports.

Proc. 8.7.9.2. If an office courier or mail distribution system is used for output report distribution, determine that procedures are adequate to ensure that reports go only to appropriate recipients and that confidential reports are sealed.

Proc. 8.7.9.3. Review procedures for the production and distribution of key documents, such as courier-delivered payroll transfers or printed payroll checks, and assess whether security procedures appear adequate.

Figure 19.3   (*Continued*)

> **Proc. 8.7.9.4.**   Review controls over releasing tape files to outside users and determine that adequate levels of approval are required.
>
> **Proc. 8.7.9.5.**   Review procedures for bringing data and program files into the computer system and assess management's understanding of the vulnerability to computer viruses with the introduction of such files.
>
> **Obj. 8.7.10.**   There should be adequate physical asset controls over all computer hardware and related equipment.
>
> **Proc. 8.7.10.1.**   Trace selected fixed-asset records from accounting records back to actual computer room equipment.
>
> **Proc. 8.7.10.2.**   Determine that all major items of computer equipment, if owned, are labeled with fixed-asset tags and that they appear on fixed-asset records.
>
> **Proc. 8.7.10.3.**   Using the equipment vendors' monthly lease or maintenance billings, trace a sample of selected items from the bills to actual equipment in the computer room operations area.
>
> **Proc. 8.7.10.4.**   Determine that control procedures are adequate.

design may be as critical to the organization as a small divisional business-processing system. Although a computer center may be outside of the traditional area of accounting and business information systems, it still may require strong physical security controls.

(ii) Improving Overall Information Systems Physical Security.   All too often, both internal auditors and management tend to view information systems physical security as an issue that belongs only within the computer center. Information systems extend into the office, and internal auditors should be aware of physical security concerns in such areas as the office LAN and its servers. There may be physical security exposures, risks, and areas for improved controls associated within each. While this is not to suggest that all office microcomputers should be kept in locked, limited-access facilities, they should be protected from off-hours tampering, snooping, and potential theft. It is particularly important that media and key output reports also be secured.

The same steps should be taken to keep office microcomputers secure. While mainframe machines can be subject to malicious damage, microcomputers are vulnerable to employees or others who can potentially steal component boards, microprocessor chips, or even entire units. Some fairly simple controls can be installed to enhance security, including locks that prevent the equipment from being moved or opened as well as asset identification tags consistent with tags used throughout the rest of the organization.

Internal audit should be aware of security vulnerabilities for office equipment during other operational or financial reviews. While the typical office machine does not require the formal physical security controls found in a larger mainframe environment, an important role for internal audit is that of educating office personnel in the importance of security controls. Microcomputer and client-server logical security, discussed later in this chapter, is often a much greater area of risk.

(iii) Implementing a Physical Security Policy.   As part of internal audit's findings and recommendations regarding information systems physical security vulnerabilities, it may be appropriate to suggest that the organization's security department become more involved in these issues. For example, security officers could report violations such as unlocked computers found during their evening rounds or challenge unfamiliar employees working in remote office areas during weekend hours. In other words, they could become an effective force to monitor physical security within the organization.

Internal audit should consider how security practices fit with overall organizational security policies. The latter have often not been updated to reflect the modern era of office automation and departmental LANs. In that case, internal audit should recommend that overall security policies be established to reflect both information systems physical security risks and exposures as well as good overall security practices.

19-3 INFORMATION SYSTEMS LOGICAL SECURITY

This section considers the overall administration of logical security controls in a data center and presents approaches for auditing their internal control procedures. While the emphasis will be on the logical security software tools installed on larger computer systems, many of the same concepts apply to similar logical security software installed on smaller systems, including individual microcomputers.

(a) LOGICAL SECURITY ACCESS CONTROL CONCEPTS

Logical security control systems are designed to protect data and programs from improper access. Although neither data nor programs can be completely secured as long as they are used by individuals or by other programs, a password-based logical security system usually will provide adequate levels of protection from unauthorized modification or disclosure of data and programs. Other classes of systems, such as those used on military applications, require much stronger security arrangements. Any logical security system must also be responsive to the needs of management, systems users, and others.

The logical security environment includes the relationship of the installed logical security system with other controls, password and user identification, and security adminis-trative controls. Rather than thinking about logical security as just the password system installed in a computer, internal audit must consider controls over the telecommunications network where messages are routed to the main computer; access to the computer system resources, including data and programs; firewalls to limit request transactions passing from networks; and controls over specific computer resources such as databases. Taken together, these elements represent an overall security architecture. Internal audit must always think of this overall security control environment, which includes logical security, physical security, management policies, and other elements.

(i) Understanding Logical Security Controls.   As a first step to reviewing logical security controls, an internal auditor should develop an understanding of the control envi-ronment, including the technical structure of information systems, the business or organiza-tional environment, and the status of installed security controls. While internal audit may have gathered some of this information through the materials discussed in Chapter 16, on information systems operations, and in Chapter 17, on applications controls, the auditor needs to understand the role of logical access security controls in light of other control procedures. This is similar to the process for overall risk analysis outlined in Chapter 8.

Business or organizational environment elements and external factors may impact an organization as well as the overall attitudes of all levels of management. This includes the industry in which the organization operates and the extent of interaction with other external organizations. The regulated financial institution, which could be faced with legal liabilities if it were the victim of a significant security breach, would have a much greater concern over the adequacy of its various security controls than a domestic consumer-products company.

Organizational factors include the attitudes of upper and information systems management towards security. These attitudes are demonstrated through strong policies and procedures, support for the internal audit department, and good personnel policies. Management policies and procedures over security are a particularly important control. If lacking, internal audit will have a very difficult task in getting management to recognize any logical access security exposures and to take appropriate corrective actions.

The information systems technical environment in larger organizations typically presents a rather complex picture to internal audit. In addition to a central computer system with connected remote terminals, there may be multiple interconnected computer systems platforms ranging from centralized mainframe computer centers to distributed workstations connected on local and wide area networks. Traffic over the telecommunications network may be internal or originated by outside parties. Systems software as well as major applications can have an impact on this environment.

A simple diagram, illustrated in Figure 19.4, can highlight logical security vulnerabilities that could otherwise be missed. For example, the diagram shows that electronic data interchange (EDI) activity, resulting in communications with outside sources and presenting a potential security vulnerability, is controlled through a separate, smaller computer system. Strong logical security controls over the centralized mainframe here may not include controls for these EDI-related activities.

When assessing current procedures, including physical security, logical security software, and the administration of logical security, internal audit will often find a mixed set of control strengths and weaknesses. The organization may have installed a good logical security software package on its centralized computer systems, along with good administrative controls, but there may be very limited controls on the remote, distributed machines and open access through Internet connections.

These environment assessments will help internal audit to better understand the relationship of logical security controls with other security controls in the organization. In the extreme, this assessment may point out control weaknesses in other areas that are so critical that internal audit may want to defer the logical security review until other improvements are made.

The attitude of management towards information security is crucial. Internal audit can often assess this attitude through general comments by top managers, the quality of responses to past audit report security-related findings, and the presence or lack of any employee policies in this area. Internal audit should look for some overall policy statement that reminds employees that ''information is a company asset'' and that they must actively protect all paper and computer-based files from improper access. A formal policy statement, such as in Figure 19.5, is sometimes presented to employees as part of their annual review. In this example, the employee acknowledges an understanding of the policy by

Figure 19.4 Computer Systems Security Vulnerabilities

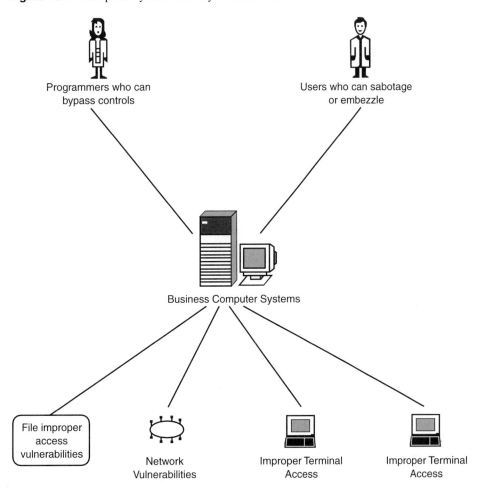

signing the document. The policy can also be covered in the code of business conduct, discussed in Chapter 33.

If the initial assessment shows that management is not particularly concerned about computer security issues, internal audit might consider a broader security review first.

(ii) Passwords and Userids. Effective password-access procedures are a major component of any system of information systems logical security controls. There are really two components to logical security passwords. First, every authorized user on a system should be assigned an identification code, often called a *userid* or log-on identification, which allows access to the various files and systems resources. The various systems resources an individual is allowed to access are tied to the userid through software in the computer system.

Userids are normally assigned on a hierarchical basis. In an accounting department,

Figure 19.5.   Automated Information Example Company Policy Statement

> The following is the type of statement that might be found in an organization's Code of Conduct or other statement of policy. All employees would be expected to sign and date it to acknowledge their compliance.

ExampleCo Company Assets and Records Policy

All employees will deal with a large and varied number of files and reports in both paper and computerized formats. Employees may be asked to prepare information reports that will be maintained on company files or to use or extract data and information from those files and records. This data and its information repositories are an ExampleCo asset to be used by employees in the performance of their work tasks. It is ExampleCo policy that:

- No employee shall use company equipment, funds, supplies, facilities, reports, or the services or labor of other employees for personal benefit.
- Employees must prepare and keep complete and accurate books and records as required for the activity involved. No employee shall knowingly make or cause any false or misleading entries in any company books or records, including computerized systems, for the purpose of misrepresenting financial reports, inventory data, travel expenses, or for any other purpose.

---

one userid might give the controller the right to view and update *all* accounting files. One level down, separate userids for managers responsible for accounts payable and accounts receivable would allow them only to view and update their respective accounts payable and receivable files. These rights would proceed down through the organization, with each level able to view only certain levels or groups of files.

User *passwords,* private codes known only to individual users, protect the various levels of data that a given userid is allowed to access. Because userids are public knowledge or may be easily determined, when used with an associated password, they allow a user to access only the systems resources assigned to that userid. While a userid will often not change over extended periods of time, passwords should be changed frequently to avoid unauthorized persons from discovering them. Many logical security control software systems automatically force users to change their passwords from time to time, often every 30 days.

The concepts of a hierarchy of userids and the associated passwords are critical to effective logical access security systems. Figure 19.6 shows userids assigned to various levels of systems resources, along with their associated passwords. Adequate control over these userids is a key component of a computer systems logical security mechanism. If a userid is allowed too much authority or if its use is not monitored, information systems logical security abuses are possible.

(b) LOGICAL SECURITY ACCESS CONTROL ADMINISTRATION

An information systems organization cannot just install a logical security software package and expect it to run by itself. There must be some type of administration function to play the role of "super user" over all userids to design an overall structure for assigning various levels of access rights, and to monitor improper access attempts. Depending upon the size of the organization and the nature of its information systems, this function can be an independent department or part of another, such as the systems programming function.

Logical security administration is the function that maintains the logical security software, assigns userids to new users, monitors improper access attempts, "resets" valid users who have been rejected from the system because they forgot their passwords, and performs similar functions. Internal audit should understand how this security administration function operates, as well as its reporting relationships and its attention to controls (such things as the procedures followed when users call in claiming they have forgotten their passwords and requesting the information or a reset). Since it can not identify that person over the telephone, a well-controlled organization may request that some known person independent of the person calling makes the reset request.

Based upon this understanding, internal audit should plan a formal review of the

Figure 19.6   Userids and Passwords

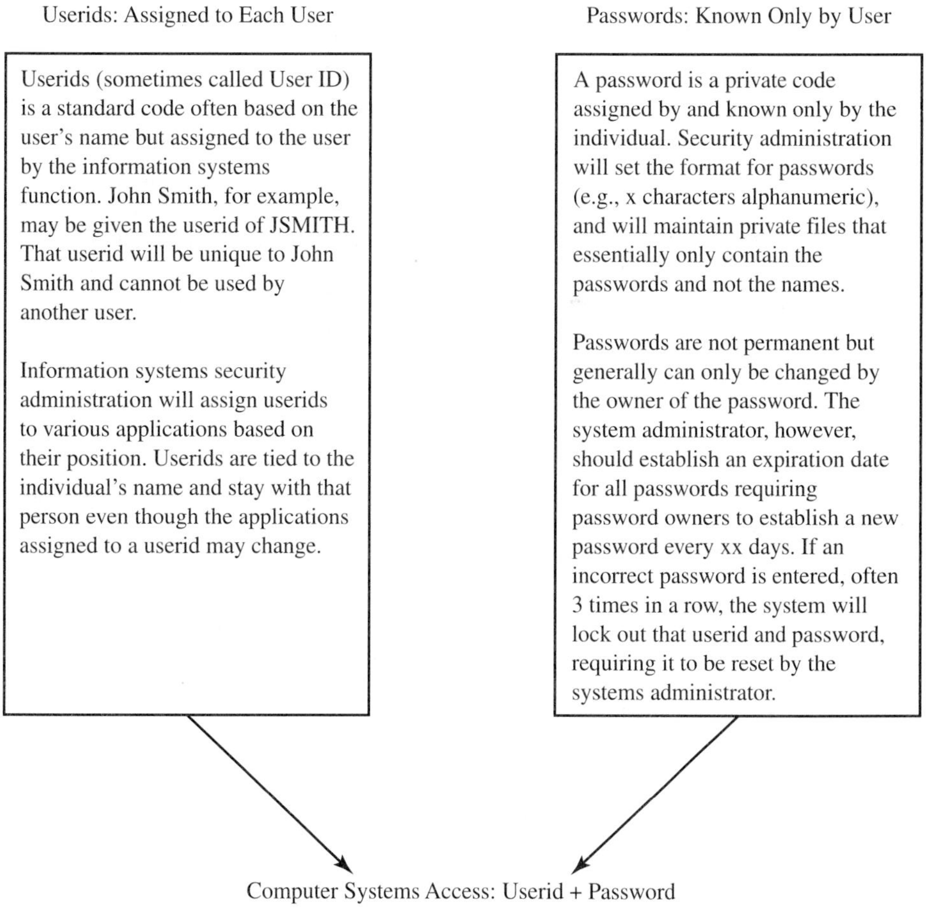

Userids: Assigned to Each User

Passwords: Known Only by User

Userids (sometimes called User ID) is a standard code often based on the user's name but assigned to the user by the information systems function. John Smith, for example, may be given the userid of JSMITH. That userid will be unique to John Smith and cannot be used by another user.

Information systems security administration will assign userids to various applications based on their position. Userids are tied to the individual's name and stay with that person even though the applications assigned to a userid may change.

A password is a private code assigned by and known only by the individual. Security administration will set the format for passwords (e.g., x characters alphanumeric), and will maintain private files that essentially only contain the passwords and not the names.

Passwords are not permanent but generally can only be changed by the owner of the password. The system administrator, however, should establish an expiration date for all passwords requiring password owners to establish a new password every xx days. If an incorrect password is entered, often 3 times in a row, the system will lock out that userid and password, requiring it to be reset by the systems administrator.

Computer Systems Access: Userid + Password

organization's logical security access control function. The audit procedures in this review depend upon the computing environment as well as the software and hardware used. The paragraphs following describe a logical security access control audit for a larger, mainframe-oriented computer environment.

19-4 LOGICAL SECURITY ACCESS CONTROL AUDIT

In addition to a specific review of the logical security administration function, internal audit can review key logical security control procedures as part of a specific application review or as a component of a general review of data center controls. However, it is often a good strategy to periodically perform separate, comprehensive reviews of overall logical security controls and related administration functions. This logical security review will allow internal audit to focus on the more detailed control issues.

Once internal audit has completed its comprehensive review of logical security access controls, the results can be used to develop audit procedures for future application reviews and overall computer center general controls reviews. As with any audit, the first steps are to determine overall audit objectives, to assess risks, and to define the detailed audit steps.

(a) ESTABLISHING LOGICAL SECURITY AUDIT OBJECTIVES

Internal auditors should carefully plan the detailed objectives of any logical security audit given the degree of attention often given to computer security issues by many members of management. A senior manager may read a news account about a network access incident at another organization and question whether the same exposure exists in his or her organization. Although the reported incident may involve hackers getting into some unsecured local area network through a dial-up connection, the audit department may be asked ''to review computer security.'' Internal audit might then use that senior management request to perform a comprehensive review of overall logical security controls, even though the organization may have little exposure to dial-up penetration. Once the review is completed, internal audit may feel that objectives have been accomplished and the requirements satisfied. Management may wonder why the audit took so long and what all of the logical security administrative control–related audit findings really mean. Because the audit may have emphasized central computer logical security, the audit still may provide no assurances that the controls to prevent outside hackers using dial-up lines are adequate or even if the organization, due to its telecommunications network structure, faces this sort of risk.

An audit of logical controls can be planned to cover a variety of differing audit scopes and objectives. These will depend upon the perceived audit risks in this area, the overall information security structure within the organization, and the relative technical skills of the audit staff. While there are numerous ways to design a logical security audit, typical review objectives might be as follows:

1. *The Adequacy of the Logical Security Software.* This type of review should focus on the integrity and use of the software. The very adequate logical security software packages available do not necessarily provide for adequate protection over computer resources. An organization may acquire a logical security software package but may implement it with weak administrative controls. Conversely, strong administrative

controls will be of little value if the logical security software has only limited or inadequate controls. For example, earlier versions of the DEC VAX/VMS security system had some well-recognized weaknesses. The review might highlight this problem and/or point out that the installed package may not be able to protect certain applications due to historical design factors or logical security software limitations. Because the adequacy of the logical security package also depends very much upon its administrative procedures, this type of review is typically combined with a review of the security administrative function.

2. *The Computer Security Administration Function.* Software with strong internal technical features and controls may have weak administrative controls installed to monitor the system. A logical security package may report improper access attempts but the security administrative function may just ignore the reported violations. This review should examine procedures for the maintenance of the installed logical security software, procedures for identifying authorized system users, and the adequacy of steps to monitor improper access attempts.

   Logical security packages generally contain user-defined options that may not be used correctly, such as parameters to specify how long a password can stay in use before the user is required to change it. Some packages are initially shipped with a default value of up to 999 days. Security administrators often do not change these defaults although the vendor documentation may recommend setting the default to perhaps 30 or 45 days. Another parameter might control the number of improper password attempts allowed. This type of review focuses on the security administration function, including the use of parameters and controls in the installed security software, and requires knowledge of the software.

3. *Security over a Specific Application.* If management has specific security concerns such as funds transfers across several outside financial institutions or to international subsidiaries, this review would focus just on the logical security controls for the application such as an electronic data interchange (EDI) including related network security controls and user controls. This type of review will rely upon a knowledge of the software and security administrative controls.

4. *Some Component of Logical Security.* This is a very focused review with specific objectives and is sometimes performed as a component of a comprehensive review of an area such as operating system integrity. It might cover logical security components such as network security, dial-up access controls, or logical security controls over some component of the operating software. In some instances, a specialized logical security review may be planned due to a security infraction or a general management concern about some component of the security environment.

The logical security audit may have been specifically requested by management or scheduled as part of the audit department's risk assessment and annual plan. In any case, the specific objectives must be clearly defined. The overall security vulnerabilities illustrated in Figure 19.4 can be quite broad, ranging from the central computer system to the data network and to various local workstations. There may be multiple, autonomous business units, each with similar architectures but also loosely connected together. Unless internal audit has extensive time and resources, the scope of any given review often should be limited to a segment of only one of these two parallel architectures.

(b) ASSESSING LOGICAL SECURITY AUDIT RISK

Assessing the level of audit risk associated with the logical security environment will require an understanding of the applications, the computer environment, the types of logical security controls in use, and overall management awareness and concerns. While audit risk is a key concern when planning any audit, it is of particular concern when planning a computer security–related review. It is very difficult to make a computer installation totally secure. Based upon the types of applications run, the organization of the information systems function, and the nature of the data files, management should assess the relative risks of security and install security procedures to provide adequate controls. With the risk-assessment tools and procedures discussed in Chapter 8, internal audit should determine if management has properly assessed risks when designing logical security controls.

(i) Understanding an Applications-Processed Risk Survey.   A financial institution will have a far higher level of both legal and management concerns about potential logical security violations than would a retail organization. Internal audit, however, must base its risk assessment not only on the type of industry but also on the types of individual applications, the potential exposures associated with the data, and any overall industry concerns, using understanding gained through previous reviews of information systems applications. The Figure 19.7 questionnaire can help internal audit understand the relative logical security risks associated with the organization's applications.

Figure 19.7   Logical Security Risk Assessment Questionnaire

1. Is there a formal security administration function or is logical security just a responsibility of network administrators?
2. Is there a userid and password-based security system with standards covering:

   • Automatic password expiration requiring new passwords on a frequent basis?
   • Lockouts after three or less improper access attempts?
   • A formal procedure for restoring only valid users due to improper passwords?
   • Size and alphanumeric requirements for passwords?

3. Are policies in effect prohibiting the sharing of passwords and have the policies been formally implemented?
4. Does the security administration function monitor on-line activity and are unusual situations investigated further?
5. What is the nature of data available through on-line sources? Beyond accounting-related statistical record-keeping files, are there files of higher sensitivity such as new product design, strategy plans, or marketing analyses?
6. Given any sensitive records as described above, are special procedures in place to prove adequate logical security over those resources?
7. Is the local network open to access through the Internet, intranets, outside sources? If so, is the logical security adequate?
8. Have software firewalls been constructed to prevent/limit unauthorized traffic?
9. Does the organization use encryption techniques to protect the integrity of transmitted data?
10. Are critical/vulnerable applications and files considered when developing strategies for contingency planning?

This risk survey does not consider the type and extent of installed logical security controls. Rather, the emphasis here is on the vulnerability of the application data. In this type of risk analysis, internal audit's concern should be to identify higher-risk applications. Although an organization may have a large variety of statistical or bookkeeping types of applications with little exposure to security violations, a single significant financial application may prove a high logical security audit risk.

(ii) Understanding Hardware and Logical Security Software. A general understanding of the hardware and the logical security software installed can be gained through interviews with the information systems department through reviews of software documentation, and by reference to other published materials. If the computer is an older, large IBM mainframe using an MVS-type operating system, this may be a fairly easy task. Several well-recognized and documented software products are available for this class of computers, such as Computer Associates' Top Secret and ACF-2 or the IBM RACF (Remote Access Control Facility) product. Internal auditors can find various specialized technical reference materials describing this software in the systems programming department or from other sources. For example, the public accounting firm Ernst & Young has published guides covering software for IBM computers, such as *Audit and Control of CICS Environments* and *Audit, Control, and Security Issues in CA TOP SECRET.*[1]

Internal auditors should review documentation describing the logical security package, available no matter what type or size of computer system. If the documentation does not appear to be adequate or if the persons responsible for logical security cannot help internal audit, it may be necessary to contact vendors who can explain the product's features and capabilities.

Figure 19.8 contains some general questions internal audit can ask. It does little good to plan an audit that looks for certain logical security software features if the installed software lacks these capabilities. If significant features are lacking, an internal auditor should focus the review on exposing risks and might suggest installing a more effective product.

(iii) Assessing Management Awareness and Concerns. In some cases, interviews with information systems and general management may yield some surprising responses. While information systems management may recognize the need for logical security, operations or senior management may not. An automatic password-expiration control, for example, may seem an annoyance. This attitude should raise audit risk levels, and management may attempt to bypass logical security controls to make their job more ''trouble free.''

Internal audit, of course, should also identify other members of management who are aware of logical security risks and of the value of the data and programs within the computer systems. These types of concerned users are often an important information source and can point to potential problem areas where internal audit may want to place increased review emphasis.

Although they often have a different perspective than users, the information systems

---

[1] Internal auditors should contact their external audit firm for these types of documents. Titles may change and different accounting firms may have different publications. Any major firm may offer help in this area.

Figure 19.8 Checklist for a Review of Access Control Software

ACCESS CONTROL SOFTWARE FEATURE	YES	NO	N/A
1. Is the information security access control software supported by an established vendor for the hardware and operating system?			
2. Is there a software vendor user group which meets periodically and requests enhancements to the security software package?			
3. Does the software vendor provide training on the use of the software package and on general information security concepts to the security administrators who will use the package?			
4. Can the security software be used to control all types of file structures and programs operating on information systems processors?			
5. Does the software provide a default level of control so that access is denied if a rule has not been established for allowing such access?			
6. Does the software provide flexibility in constructing access rules so that they will be consistent with the overall requirements of the organization?			
7. Does the software allow the security administrator the option to establish passwords of at least eight characters to allow more secure codes?			
8. Are passwords and other key elements of the security software encrypted so that they cannot be retrieved by a systems programmer or other knowledgeable persons?			
9. Does the software provide log-on protection by withholding any information until a password has been accepted?			
10. Does the software provide automatic lockout facilities so that a given number of improper password attempts will lock a perpetrator from a terminal device?			
11. Does the software have a protected logging facility such that all security-related transactions are recorded on a protected log file?			
12. Does the software provide automatic reports of actual and potential security violation attempts?			
13. Does the software have the flexibility to generate a variety of information security reports as required by the security administration function?			
14. Can status and violation reports generated by the security software be restricted such that they will be accessible only at a terminal or printer in the security administration area?			
15. Does the security software vendor provide telephone or on-line help to administrators with sufficient controls to provide such information to authorized persons only?			

department can provide some valuable insights to help in audit planning. They are responsible for maintaining the installed logical security software packages and should understand how they are being used. Due to the level of publicity on computer crime issues, internal audit can probably expect a high level of awareness.

(c) STEPS FOR REVIEWING LOGICAL SECURITY CONTROLS

The next step is to develop detailed audit procedures. An audit of logical security can often be effectively built around six general review areas:

1. Logical security administration
2. Standards for user identification codes
3. Profiles and rules for controlling systems resources
4. Reset and emergency authorization procedures
5. Security procedures for privileged users
6. Violation-reporting and follow-up procedures

While all of the above are applicable for larger mainframe systems, internal audit may limit activities based upon the size of the system and perceived audit risks. A smaller organization with a limited network may not warrant formal reset and emergency authorization procedures. If there is a separate logical security administrative function in a smaller computer system installation, internal audit can either eliminate this step or suggest this type of control.

19-5 AUDITING THE SECURITY ADMINISTRATION FUNCTION

Depending upon management, this function may range from a designated individual—who, in a smaller organization, also has other responsibilities—to a formal information systems security department, and internal audit should understand these administrative arrangements, controls, and procedures.

The size of the security administration function will depend upon the size and structure of the organization and its computer systems resources. Often assigned in a smaller organization as a part-time task to a systems programmer with the responsibility only for installing the logical security software and establishing its general rules, this function provides little more than ''window dressing'' for the computer system resources even in larger organizations. There may be no security policies, little user training, and minimal follow-up and monitoring of improper system access attempts. The result is a very weak set of administrative controls over the logical security function.

In a larger organization, there should exist a manager responsible just for information systems security or at least a formal function with defined responsibilities for information systems security, while smaller organizations typically will administer their logical security with less formality. The first step is to gain a detailed understanding of the structure, responsibilities, and activities of the computer security administrative function.

(a) SECURITY ADMINISTRATION ORGANIZATION

Logical security administration is usually independent from physical security and physical access control administration, which refers to the locking and other mechanisms to restrict access. In a smaller facility, physical security may be the responsibility of computer operations, while in a very large organization, the overall building or plant security function may handle this function. Sometimes, a building security function may also be responsible for logical security, and if this is the case, internal audit should treat them the same as a large computer operations security administration function.

The structure of security administration also depends upon the size of the organization and its industry. The larger the installed computer systems and its applications, the more extensive the network should be; the larger the organization, the more formal the computer security administration functions should be. The following describe how the logical security administration function might be organized in several example organizations.

- *Large Organization with Centralized Computer Systems.* Although there may be multiple systems-development organizations, the organization will often have a single information systems operation. A security officer reporting to the chief information officer or another member of senior management, and independent of information systems operations, would develop and administer logical security standards for all users of the centralized data center.

  This function usually involves more than a one-person responsibility with various staff members in charge of logical security software management, the monitoring of violation reporting, and other duties as discussed throughout this chapter. Internal audit should look for a strong, independent security organization, just as the internal audit function is independent.

- *Larger Organizations with Decentralized Computer Resources.* Rather than a single or small number of centralized data centers, there may be client-server interconnected systems with larger centralized systems used for major databases. The diversified nature makes it difficult to organize logical security administration around just one central function, so persons throughout the organization are given responsibility for controls and procedures on their own local systems. These distributed security functions, however, require central support and direction, including appropriate policies and procedures.

  A central security officer in a decentralized organization would be responsible for setting overall logical security standards and procedures, but individuals at each of the decentralized units would be responsible for monitoring their own sites. There should be procedures in place to assure that the decentralized security functions comply with established procedures.

- *Smaller, Midrange Computer System Organizations.* One person should have clearly designated responsibilities for logical-access control security administration. This could be the LAN administrator or even the head of information systems. Management should understand how logical security controls are structured and who has responsibility for their administration.

  A major danger with the smaller organization is the lack of effective logical security software or software installed without changing user default values or setting those values to discourage security violations.

Internal audit should use this preliminary understanding of the logical security administration function to plan other activities. At the extreme, no one will be responsible for this key area and there may be no administrative procedures in place. Given such a situation, internal audit may just bring this lack of security administration controls to the attention of management and describe the security weaknesses. Many of the steps outlined in the remaining sections of this chapter assume at least some type of administrative function over logical security.

The review of the security administration function is a more detailed information-gathering step than a normal procedure where internal audit would follow up interviews with detailed testing. Internal audit will be better able to review controls over other areas in the logical security structure.

(b) LOGICAL-ACCESS CONTROL POLICIES AND PROCEDURES

A review of logical-access control policies and procedures would be normally tied to an audit of the logical security administration function. Internal audit should look for a formal policy statement, approved by appropriate levels of management, outlining the organization's logical-access control standards. This type of document, along with the individual employee acknowledgments described in Figure 19.5, puts all users on notice that the information stored on computer files is an organization asset, and it is their responsibility to protect that asset through the use of the logical security software.

Although a policy statement outlines general management intentions, specific procedures are necessary to implement that policy. Procedures, however, can easily become out-of-date unless they are updated to reflect changes in the organization and in technology. Security administration should periodically review and update existing procedures and release final versions for management approval.

Examples of specific procedures to look for include:

- Standards for password format and expiration periods
- Standards requiring that each user on the system have a unique userid that should never be shared
- Procedures for removing an employee from the system upon termination or transfer to another function
- Procedures for restoring a user who has incorrectly input a password and has been rejected by the system
- Procedures for monitoring and reporting improper access violations

Procedures should support the logical-access control policy, provide direction to users of information systems, and keep the standards current. Figure 19.9 outlines example procedures to review logical security and monitor controls.

(c) SECURITY SOFTWARE AND IMPLEMENTATION RESTRAINTS

The type of installed logical security software as well as the way it has been implemented may cause restraints on the manner in which logical security can be controlled. For example, major logical security software packages for IBM mainframe computers such as ACF-2, Top Secret, or RACF have a full set of features that provide strong logical security controls, which other packages and types of computer hardware may not have.

The logical security software should have the ability to define files and other resources in a manner that users, after submitting their passwords, can gain access to these resources, as well as to monitor and block improper access attempts.

Figure 19.9 Logical Access Controls Audit Program Example

AUDIT STEP	INITIAL	W/P
1. Is there a formal policy statement approved by proper levels of management and communicated to all employees on logical access controls?		
2. Evaluate the security policy statement to assess whether it effectively communicates the need for strong logical security controls throughout the organization.		
3. Determine that using the installed logical security software, each user is uniquely identified to establish accountability and that the user identification (userid) remains constant once established.		
4. Determine whether policy formally prohibits any sharing of userids or passwords.		
5. Evaluate the methods in place whereby users are required to prove that they are whom they purport to be (i.e., passwords, keycards, signatures, etc.).		
6. Determine that passwords are changed periodically based on the relative criticality of the files accessed.		
7. User access to any resource should be based on documented management job-related needs and a proper segregation of duties. Use a sample of systems users to test access procedures.		
8. Assess the adequacy of the audit trail and subsequent review activities monitoring unauthorized access attempts.		
9. Based on any recent access attempts, determine that management's review of these incidents is performed on a thorough basis.		
10. Determine that the security administration function is positioned within the organization to provide appropriate segregation of duties and independence.		
11. Assess whether security facilities (i.e., databases, software, etc.) are adequately protected.		
12. Review any established information systems security classification program to identify higher risk resources. For those resources, assess whether protection measures appear adequate.		
13. Assess the adequacy of telecommunications controls, including the installation of firewalls to restrict various levels of traffic.		
14. Assess the emergency authorization procedures in place to reestablish a valid user who is locked out but with adequate ongoing security controls.		
15. Obtain a list of any users with ''privileged'' higher access rights and assess the adequacy; assess whether the assignments are appropriate.		

19-6 CONTINGENCY PLANNING

The modern organization is extremely dependent upon its information systems operations. If the order-entry terminal network goes down for just a few minutes in a sales organization, there will typically be massive chaos. Order-entry clerks can neither take orders called in nor verify the status of customer orders or check for credit approvals. When such a system is brought back on-line in a short time, there is a feeling of massive relief. The problem is much greater if the computer is down for an extended period of a day or more. While informal procedures often exist for operating during shorter-term periods of system down-time, many organizations have no plan for restoring their information systems operations in the event of an extended emergency interruption in information systems services.

An information systems disaster-recovery or contingency plan is a formal set of procedures designed to allow information systems to continue to operate at some reduced level in the event of an emergency, when normal information systems facilities are not available. A fire, flood, or some other act of God could all but wipe out an organization's central information systems facility. Without an effective plan to restore information systems operations, automated systems and the business units they support could be inoperable for an extended period of time.

Auditors can and will often be asked to help develop or review an information systems contingency plan. They have a good knowledge of the requirements and vulnerabilities for various information systems applications and also understand the need for backing up key programs and data.

This section discusses how auditors can help to build effective information systems contingency plans, including how to assemble a disaster-recovery planning team, how to evaluate information systems vulnerabilities, and how to build and test the plan. However, an effective information systems disaster-recovery plan is the responsibility of senior management, and internal audit should only act as a catalyst to see that it is developed and to evaluate the completed plan.

(a) NEED FOR AN INFORMATION SYSTEMS CONTINGENCY PLAN

In a typical larger organization, most systems are highly automated, including such areas as payroll, accounts payable, manufacturing control, and production process control. Some organizations, of course, are more heavily dependent than others. As an example, a hotel chain or airline with an on-line reservation system or a bank or other financial institution with an on-line financial accounting system could hardly operate without its computer systems.

Even though the organization depends so heavily on its information system for ongoing operations, management often fails to understand the need for effective contingency planning. Information systems are often viewed almost as a utility, along with power, telephones, and water. The difference, though, is that true outside utilities develop extensive backup facilities to allow them to continue service, and if information systems are to be viewed as a utility, they should be considered as an in-house utility that requires its own backup arrangements.

Internal auditors can play an important role in calling management's attention to the need for an effective contingency plan by emphasizing the need in their general controls review audit reports. They must educate management on the importance of such planning.

It must be emphasized that information systems contingency planning is the responsibility of management. Internal auditors can help to develop the plan and can test its effectiveness, but without an effective recovery plan, management must accept the consequences of such a loss. Some of the areas where management faces a potentially significant exposure due to the lack of an effective plan include:

- *Cash Flow Loss Potential.* The loss of information systems capabilities to record new orders, bill for order shipments, and collect open accounts will severely limit an organization's cash flow.

- *Legal Responsibilities.* A common interpretation of the Foreign Corrupt Practices Act, discussed in Chapters 2 and 31, is that the officers of an organization are personally responsible if they have not made adequate preparations to safeguard an organization's vital documents and other resources, thereby exposing themselves to litigation. Regulated industries often have a legal obligation to have proper disaster plans in place. A financial institution insured by the Federal Deposit Insurance Corporation must have a contingency plan for its information systems operations.

- *Logistics and Business-Interruption Potential Losses.* A household moving company may use an on-line system to schedule its trucks and drivers. Without such a system in place, the company could not operate competitively, if at all.

- *Public Relations Losses.* An extended interruption of information systems services could result in a major public relations and shareholder relations loss if vital functions are not restored promptly and in an orderly manner subsequent to a catastrophe or disaster.

Even if the organization has only a smaller computer system, there will almost certainly be a need for some form of contingency plan. While information systems personnel, internal auditors, and others can help to develop the plan, it must have the support of management in order to be effective.

(b) EVALUATING EXISTING CONTINGENCY PLANS

Many contingency plans, often developed as a result of earlier audit report recommendations, end up as thick books that are never again referenced, never updated, and certainly never tested. Other contingency plans are often limited to very informal, reciprocal arrangements with a nearby computer site for the right to process there if the other's computer became unavailable. Again, these plans are quite informal and generally are never tested. They usually are both ineffective and inoperable.

Internal audit should evaluate existing contingency plans and learn to recognize the types of existing plans in order to make recommendations to improve them where necessary.

(i) Evaluating Reciprocal Agreement Contingency Plans.

In the earlier days of computer systems, backup and recovery plans were relatively simple. Automated applications were often just conversions of existing paper-oriented systems and it was only necessary to use the old forms in order for the organization to return to manual operations. In addition, it was often not too difficult to informally arrange a backup processing site, because nearby organizations had computer systems that were not always that busy. Today such plans are not practical for some of the following reasons:

- *Modern applications no longer have manual backups.* Automated applications that were merely conversions of older paper-oriented systems have long since passed. Most newer applications, moreover, have no direct manual counterparts. For example, it would be almost impossible to replicate a modern materials requirements planning system using manual procedures.

- *Computer systems are usually too busy to allow backup use.* Most organizations use their computer systems on a 24-hours, six- or seven-days-a-week basis and would not be able to allow an outsider to take over a shift.

- *Telecommunications and on-line applications limit transport.* It is no longer possible to shift a given computer operation easily to another site without extensive planning. Extensive networks of terminals and telecommunication links to other sites cannot be easily moved elsewhere in a disaster situation without detailed planning.

- *Litigation concerns discourage informal arrangements.* Informal contingency-processing arrangements made in the past with a nearby organization today would have to be cleared through the legal department. Virtually no organization will formally promise to provide backup services because it may be held legally liable if it cannot provide them for some reason.

Despite these shortcomings, reciprocal agreements still exist, particularly in small remote areas. Internal audit should evaluate whether the agreement appears to be workable and whether there has been any level of testing. If neither, the contingency plan should be revised and redrafted as discussed in the paragraphs following.

There may, of course, be some instances where a contingency plan based on reciprocal agreements may be the only available alternative, such as for an organization with specialized equipment or located in a smaller city in a relatively remote area. If that is the case, internal audit should look for some evidence of disaster plan testing at the reciprocal site.

(ii) Untested or Out-of-Date Contingency Plans.

Out-of-date plans are, perhaps, more dangerous to an organization than no plans at all. The problem with an untested or out-of-date plan is that management may place a false level of assurance in the plan. Such a plan may prove inoperable because:

- *Key data sets have not been saved.* A contingency plan should identify all of the necessary data sets or files to recover key systems. If backup records have not been kept up-to-date, the published plan may not provide the proper guidance to restore key applications.

- *Recovery site configurations may have changed.* There may have been subtle changes in the hardware or operating system at the contingency planning backup site, which will not be known in out-of-date or untested plans.

- *Key personnel designated in the plan may not be available.* A properly constructed contingency plan designates various staff members to handle recovery activities. Because staff responsibilities may change or persons may leave the organization, an out-of-date plan may not properly identify recovery responsibilities.

Internal audit should review any existing contingency plan to assess whether it is current and if it has been tested recently. Sometimes, internal audit can determine that a plan is out-of-date just through simple inquiry and discussion with information systems management. In many instances, it may be necessary to perform tests in order to determine the currency of the published plan. Internal audit may find the plan to be adequate with some minor revisions or may find it to be in need of a major revision or rewrite. An adequate plan will contain many of the elements discussed later in this chapter. Internal audit should identify those elements in need of revision and suggest an update.

In many instances, the existing contingency plan will not be effective, for any of the above reasons, and internal audit should recommend the building of an updated, more effective one. This new contingency plan recommendation may require internal audit to do some "selling" to management. Any audit report including this recommendation should outline the shortcomings and deficiencies in the current plan and should discuss the potential risks of not having an effective plan. This selling is often necessary because management will look at the expense incurred to develop a revised plan, will realize that they have never had to use it, and will wonder why it is necessary to go through this effort once again.

(iii) Developing a Contingency-Planning Strategy.   If there is no contingency plan or if the existing plan is out of date or otherwise ineffective, efforts should be initiated to develop a plan following an overall strategy, with the participation of both information systems and senior management. This section discusses some of the management considerations necessary for effective contingency planning and outlines some strategies.

Figure 19.10 is an information systems vulnerabilities questionnaire to help develop management awareness. It is quite possible that the managers completing such a document will be unable to answer some of the questions. That is fully acceptable, but it does point to the need for more data-gathering and analysis. Internal audit might ask several members of senior management to complete this questionnaire. The results can be compiled and informally distributed to management, without the names of the respondees, as a stimulus for further action.

Although an organization's business information systems can be very critical, there are often other equally critical areas such as the key engineering computer-aided design files kept in a design department. In the longer run, an information systems contingency plan should be tied into a vital records program for all automated and nonautomated records. If such a vital records program does not exist, the information systems contingency plan can serve as a catalyst for developing one.

Management also needs to be aware of the roles of other supporting organizations in contingency planning, such as the in-house security function. While such a department often has limited its responsibilities to just normal guarding and fire-detection duties, it can often be of help in building an effective contingency plan for both information systems and the overall organization. For a smaller organization or one located in a more remote community, and without such a security department, other resources—such as the local fire marshal or fire department—can often provide advice on building codes and security-related issues.

Contingency Planning Strategy Alternatives.   Once management needs have been identified, the organization should consider available strategy alternatives for systems recovery.

- *Replacement with Manual Processing Procedures.* Consideration should be given to any applications that can essentially be processed without the computer and

Figure 19.10 Information Systems Vulnerabilities Checklist

This checklist is designed to assist the auditor in reviewing management's awareness of vulnerabilities and in helping management decide that there is a need for an information systems disaster recovery plan when an effective one does not exist.

INFORMATION SYSTEMS VULNERABILITIES	YES	NO	N/A

1. Does the organization have critical or strategic applications which are necessary for ongoing operations?
2. Is the organization dependent upon centralized or departmental computer systems for financial and government reporting?
3. Has there ever been a risk analysis performed covering the potential losses associated with key information systems applications?
4. Do applications, whether purchased software or developed in-house, represent a major investment to the organization?
5. Even if there are no critical applications, has there ever been an analysis performed estimating the total cost to the organization if the computer systems were not available?
6. Are all computer systems users aware of the need to back up critical files, and are they performing those backups on a regular basis?
7. Has consideration been given to the vulnerabilities of the voice or data telecommunications network?
8. Does the information systems function have a data processing disaster recovery plan?
9. Has management reviewed and critiqued that disaster recovery plan?
10. Does the disaster recovery plan include the identification of an alternate processing facility?
11. Does management understand the costs and capabilities of the alternate site processing procedures outlined in the disaster recovery plan?
12. Is there a formal program for testing the disaster recovery plan using the designated alternative facility?
13. Does information systems regularly report to management on the results of any disaster recovery plan testing?
14. Does the organization have overall security procedures regarding perimeter control and fire alarms?
15. Has the organization's security function given adequate consideration to information systems operations?
16. Has information systems security planning included both departmental computers, local client-server systems, and any other specialized computer systems?

Figure 19.10   (*Continued*)

	YES	NO	N/A
17. Has either the security function or an outside group, such as the local fire inspector, reviewed fire prevention procedures within data processing operations?			
18. Has management considered the adequacy of business interruption and loss of records insurance as part of the disaster recovery planning?			
19. Has management determined that any disaster recovery plan includes adequate backup procedures for other areas such as telecommunications?			
20. Has management reviewed disaster recovery planning for other non-data processing areas in the organization's operations?			

with manual procedures. In a larger computer environment, with database-oriented files, this is generally not a viable alternative, but it may be one in a low-transaction-volume or more recently automated mini- or microcomputer setting.

- *Identification of Alternate Processing Sites.* Such an alternate computer system may be located at another plant or division. In some very unique instances, reciprocal arrangements can be made with another organization. Outside vendors are increasingly providing computer centers for backup processing. If the computer system is older or an unusual model, alternate processing sites may be difficult to identify.

- *Identification of Critical Information Systems Functions.* Even before the identification of specific applications, general functional areas or activities should be identified for criticality. The control systems supplying goods to the manufacturing floor in a plant may be one of the more critical information systems functions. Other functions, such as sales and billings, could be handled on a more manual basis than could manufacturing operations.

- *Identification of Disaster-Planning Resources.* Key users and information systems personnel, as well as potential vendors, should be considered possible members of any contingency-planning restoration team.

This identification-of-resources step in the disaster plan development will help illustrate the magnitude of the problem as well as potential resources to solve it. At this point, it is perfectly proper not to have answers for all of these alternatives. For example, if the organization uses a less common type of mid-range computer with no readily available alternative processing site, this initial lack provides a major objective to be solved.

This identification of contingency-planning alternatives can be developed by a very limited group of personnel prior to the formal plan construction. Once completed, these alternatives should provide a basis for acquiring approval for a formal contingency plan.

(iv) Building the Contingency-Planning Team.   A first step to building such a team is to appoint a contingency plan chairperson, who should have managerial responsibilities as well as a strong knowledge of the technical issues associated with such a plan.

In a larger information systems organization, the chairperson is often the information systems department's head of data security. In other situations it may be more appropriate for a member of user management to head up the planning team, with the head of data security as a close technical advisor. Internal audit should be a member of or an advisor to this planning team. However, it is not appropriate to have the audit function head up the effort as this violates internal audit standards and internal audit may be called upon independently to evaluate the contingency plan at a later date.

In a smaller information systems organization, a key member of user management should probably head up the contingency-planning team with the head of information systems as vice chairperson.

In addition to the chairperson, a committee should be assembled to evaluate and build the contingency plan. For a larger organization, the contingency-planning committee might consist of individuals responsible for the following functions:

- Computer Operations
- Data Security Administration
- Telecommunications and Local Networks
- Systems Programming
- Database Administration
- Systems and Programming Applications Development
- Administrative Services (including risk management)
- Purchasing
- Internal Audit
- Key User Application Areas

In smaller organizations, individuals often wear multiple hats. One technical support person might be responsible for data security, telecommunications, database administration, and systems programming. That key individual should certainly be included on the contingency-planning team.

Rather than assembling an in-house team, some organizations have elected to hire outside consultants. There are consulting firms that specialize in developing contingency plans. In addition, many major public accounting firms have the necessary skills to build such a plan. The advantage of outside resources is that they have experience in building these plans for a variety of organizations and are aware of the necessary details and considerations. In addition, they will construct the plan on a priority basis, whereas insiders may require a considerable period of time to complete the plan. The disadvantage is that outside consultants do not readily know many of the organization's unique characteristics and systems-related details. As a result, their plans will often tend to be somewhat generic.

If an organization has a need to develop a contingency plan in a short time, an outside consultant is often a very cost-effective resource. However, members of the organization should participate in this effort and work to refine the document. Otherwise, these outside consultant plans can become ineffective documents that do little more than sit on the shelf.

The contingency-planning team evaluates information systems risks and then builds the actual plan. The team must determine both the applications required for disaster recovery and effective strategies to make that recovery possible. Internal audit can play a very important role in this process by performing some of the survey and analysis work.

Much of the team's work consists of information gathering. For example, while information systems management and others are aware of the organization's complex telecommunications network, the recovery team's telecommunications specialist may have to define those requirements for the network to be documented and reconstructed. Similarly, a complex application will require numerous files from feeder applications. While some system documentation may exist, a member of the planning team should review all requirements for the application to determine that they are properly documented.

(c) EVALUATING INFORMATION SYSTEMS CONTINGENCY RISKS

Evaluating potential risks due to a disaster or contingency event is the process of identifying and estimating the expected losses arising from any undesired event. The costs of installing safeguards to minimize these risks can then be considered. Although the cost of installing the safeguard should be strongly considered, some safeguards should be installed regardless of the cost to prevent loss of life or to meet legal requirements.

Some contingency-planning teams have attempted to evaluate the subjective probabilities of any one of a variety of risks potentially occurring. That is, they will attempt to evaluate the probability of a flood, a fire, a hurricane, or any one of a number of disasters occurring and causing an information systems interruption. Often, considerable but not very productive effort is put into this type of an evaluation process.

Subjective probabilities to determine, for example, that there will be a one in 10,000 chance of a flood but a one in 1,000 chance of a fire are numerical guesses at best. Whether a fire, flood, or any other type of disaster, the real concern is that information systems may be out for some extended period. In addition, the probability of variable events occurring really does not matter if any one of them can bring down the computer system.

An effective contingency-planning risk analysis should consist of the following steps:

1. Understand the potential information systems risks.
2. Evaluate the safeguards currently in place.
3. Consider the potential losses due to an interruption in services or loss of resources.
4. Evaluate the costs to continue processing in the event of various possible risks occurring.
5. Evaluate the costs to reconstruct information systems.

The sixth and final step in the above process is to develop the actual contingency plan. This final step will be discussed later in this chapter.

(i) Understanding Potential Information Systems Risks. An information systems operation faces a variety of risks, any of which could put it out of operation for an extended period. In a single mid-range computer operation, such a risk could be a hard disk crash and inadequate backup data. On a much more major scale, an earthquake could destroy the entire physical facility as well as severely limiting community support services.

The contingency-planning team should understand what types of risks are possible, including natural disasters that may affect the entire community; natural or manmade disasters that may impact the facility where information systems are located; and manmade or equipment failures local to information systems.

Although natural disasters such as earthquakes, hurricanes, or floods occur infrequently, many emergency services for the area will become unavailable when they do. Some of these natural disasters reappear with some regularity. For example, some coastal areas can expect a major hurricane or tropical storm every five or ten years. Other major disasters seldom if ever happen. Certain areas lie on geological faults where the last major earthquake occurred 100 or more years ago. The next such earthquake may not come within the lifetimes of the planning team members.

If the contingency-planning team feels there is a reasonable chance of such an area-wide disaster, recovery plans should consider facilities outside of the geographic area. It accomplishes little to have a contingency-planning computer system located in the same community if all community facilities become unavailable. However a pragmatic approach should be taken in assessing these major disaster potentialities.

Localized disasters, including fires, floods, or civil disturbances, will just impact the facility where information systems operations are located. Community-wide support services such as the fire department will remain available as the disaster would tend to be located in a single plant or organization building complex. The types of disasters that might occur depend upon the organization evaluated, such as a chemical plant.

The disaster-evaluation team should approach localized disaster risks by asking themselves a series of "what if" questions. That is, what would happen if there were a fire in the building? Are there adequate fire-protection facilities? What would happen if a water pipe were to burst and flood the basement? Would the flood impact information systems?

The localized risks that just impact the information systems department might include the failure of a power transformer, a localized fire in the telecommunications switching room, or the destruction of key data files through employee sabotage. These risks would not disable the rest of the facility, but they can cause considerable problems for the information systems function.

The contingency-planning team should rank each of the identified risks on their relative probability of occurrence—for example, whether the risk may occur within the next five years, if it may occur beyond five years, or if it probably never will happen. Figure 19.11 is an example of such a risk-ranking schedule. The 1-to-10 type of rating here is meant to only show a relative probability. There is no need to try to determine if the probability of a major flood within five years, for example, is one in 200 or one in 300. In either event, it is rather low.

As a last step, the contingency-planning team should review the risk-ranking schedule with senior management, discussing its rationale for assigning relative risks and making adjustments based on management considerations. In addition, the team may want to share its assessment rankings with community public safety personnel. Fire department, civil defense, or public safety personnel are often willing to provide some input.

(ii) Evaluating Safeguards Currently in Place. The safeguards or precautionary measures the typical organization installs may be a building fire alarm system, guards and gates to restrict access to the facility, or an emergency electrical power supply. In some instances, these safeguards may have already been factored into the risk-assessment relative

Figure 19.11   Contingency Planning Risk Ranking Schedule

This schedule allows the auditor to rank risks to information systems operations on the basis of relative probabilities. The auditor should evaluate each risk in terms of the probability of occurrence within the next five years or in the future following that five year period. For example, the probability of a flood impacting the computer center within five years may receive a rating of 2, or very low, and a rating of 7 for over five years, indicating a strong probability of a flood within that longer period.

	RELATIVE PROBABILITY (0–10)	
POTENTIAL DISASTER EVENT	**UNDER 5 YEARS**	**OVER 5 YEARS**

Area-Wide Disasters
1. Is the area subject to a major earthquake?
2. Is the area subject to hurricanes or tornadoes?
3. Is the area subject to major flooding?
4. Is the area subject to major winter storms?
5. Is the area subject to other natural disasters, such as forest fires or volcanoes?

Localized or Man-Made Disasters
1. Are nearby plants and other facilities subject to fire, explosion, or chemical contamination?
2. Are there risks of major fires in the building?
3. Are there risks of major, long term electrical power failures?
4. Are there risks of major, long term telecommunications failures?
5. Are there risks of riots or sabotage due to the type of business or of nearby businesses?

Information Systems Function Disasters
1. Are there risks of a major equipment failure due to a power or environmental system failure?
2. Are there risks of an extended equipment outage due to age or obsolescence?
3. Are there risks of intentional destruction of equipment or data through sabotage, computer viruses, or the use of destructive devices?
4. Are there risks of intentional modification of key data or programs through deleting data, improper program accesses, and the like?
5. Are there risks of accidental modification or destruction of data or programs through human or equipment errors?

probabilities, as discussed previously. In other instances, it may be necessary to reconsider the risk-assessment relative probabilities based on a safeguard evaluation.

While risks were discussed on an area-wide, organization-wide, and information-systems-function-only basis, safeguards can only realistically be considered for the organization and for the information systems function. Area-wide safeguards are the responsibility of community, state, and federal agencies, and are assumed to be in operation.

An evaluation of safeguards can best be accomplished by a series of interviews and examinations of available resources, and, here again, internal audit can play a significant role. Figure 19.12 is a questionnaire for evaluating total organizational safeguards and those specifically for the information systems function. In many instances, the audit department may already have gathered the answers to some of these questions through earlier operational audits. However, if those audits took place more than a year or two earlier, they should be updated or reconfirmed.

With this questionnaire, the contingency planning team can understand the protection measures in place and make immediate recommendations for improvement. For example, the questionnaire may find that fire alarms have not been tested in over one year. In other areas, this safeguard-evaluation process may point to areas for further audit work. The evaluators may find that certain documentation designated to be stored in a backup site does not exist. Internal audit may want to review documentation practices for the area that should have created it.

(iii) Potential Losses Due to Information Systems Failure. The third major step in the overall risk-evaluation process is to assess the potential losses that would occur, application by application, if information systems were not available for an extended period. This process again requires that a detailed survey be performed, covering all financial and operational applications. In many instances, the audit department may already have some of this information from prior application reviews.

The contingency-planning team ranks and prioritizes critical applications. Applications that are critical to an organization depend upon its size and industry. User areas should be evaluated as to whether they could function without the information systems application for limited periods of time, as well as whether such unavailability would cause a financial, operational, or legal impact.

The contingency-planning team should discuss the questionnaire responses of the principal users and modify them as appropriate. For example, the subsidiary personnel manager responsible for a 50-person payroll and operating on a mid-range computer system might state that information systems services are ''essential.'' The personnel manager responsible for a 5,000-person mainframe computer payroll system would give the same response. The former could operate for at least a limited time using manual methods, while the latter could not.

This applications-loss evaluation will help the contingency-planning team in two ways: to identify the most critical applications, which can then be prioritized, and to convince management of the importance of effective contingency planning.

(iv) Backup Processing Alternatives. The next step is to consider some of the alternatives for resuming information systems operations. This is an extremely important step for building an effective recovery plan. All too often, organizations spend considerable resources in constructing a contingency plan with no arrangements for a backup processing

Figure 19.12 Information Systems Disaster Recovery Safeguards Questionnaire

---

This questionnaire is designed to help evaluate existing safeguards within the information systems organization in order to design an effective disaster recovery plan.

POTENTIAL DATA PROCESSING SAFEGUARDS	YES	NO	N/A

1. Are data processing applications backed up as part of normal operations procedures?
2. Are backup files rotated to a secure, off-site location?
3. Are copies of operating software also rotated to the off-site location?
4. Are copies of application system and other technical documentation also rotated to the off-site location?
5. Have guidelines or standards been developed governing file backups for departmental computer systems?
6. Do computer sites have adequate environmental control facilities?
7. Is there an emergency or standby power supply system for the computer facilities?
8. Is there a zone-controlled fire and smoke detection system and a fire control system installed within the computer room?
9. Is the information systems fire control system linked to alarms at a local fire department?
10. Has adequate consideration been given to fire controls throughout any computer room raised floor system, including floor to ceiling walls and appropriate hand-held fire extinguishers?
11. Are any forms handled in a manner which minimizes the risk of fire?
12. Is the main computer facility located in a secure location with such features as:
    Limited outside windows constructed with breakage resistant materials?
    A single controlled entrance with all other doors equipped for emergency exit only?
    Limited visibility, including no signs or other unnecessary indicators?
13. Is there a separate, fire-controlled facility for the storage of cassettes and tapes?
14. Are telecommunications controls located in a secure location?
15. Is the ceiling to the computer room free of plumbing and other water sources?
16. Have sprinkler systems over sensitive resources been engineered to minimize the risk of water damage, and are plastic sheets available to protect from falling water?

Figure 19.12 *(Continued)*

	YES	NO	N/A
17. Is access to the computer room restricted to authorized individuals through the use of cipher locks, badges, or other controls?			
18. Are hiring controls in place within the information systems function to ensure that all employees have the education or experience required for their jobs?			
19. Are there procedures to control media or related materials which are taken from the computer room?			
20. Has information security software been installed to restrict access to programs and data?			
21. Are there procedures to control the distribution of output file transmissions or reports to authorized individuals?			
22. Is there a formal computer security function to monitor both physical and information security procedures?			
23. Are information systems employees trained in recovery and backup procedures and techniques?			
24. Are there provisions to monitor all alarm sources including fire, weather, and emergency radio?			
25. Are data processing safeguards consistent with those installed throughout the remainder of the organization?			

site—and with neither a computer resource nor a backup, it will be difficult to develop any reasonable strategy to resume processing.

There are numerous strategies for emergency backup processing, each with its own benefits, risks, and costs. The contingency-planning team should evaluate these alternatives, including the relative costs of each option as well as the resources required to make them effective. Based on data on the benefits, costs, and risks associated with each type of alternative evaluated (and a recommendation of the contingency planning team), management should make the decision on the preferred alternative.

Commercial Recovery Strategies.   Outside vendors offer some of the best alternatives for information systems recovery. These are organizations that have available computer systems dedicated to their client's disaster-recovery processing needs. Although such services were once available only for large-scale IBM systems, services are now offered for other vendors and equipment types. Perhaps the most expensive alternative for many organizations, a commercial recovery strategy is also often the most effective one.

The contingency-planning team should evaluate the existing vendors both in their area and, if the risk of an area-wide disaster is relatively high, outside of the geographical area. There are perhaps four different types of commercial recovery strategies:

- *"Hot Site" Recovery Centers.* In many larger metropolitan areas, vendors specializing in contingency-planning services have established "hot site" recovery rooms, equipped computer facilities ready for operations in the event of a disaster at a subscriber's site. Such recovery centers accept a limited number of subscribers, who can periodically test their applications and operating software on the contingency-planning machine. These centers also provide some technical support and telecommunications facilities.

The "hot site" contingency-planning approach is perhaps the best short-term solution for an organization with a larger mainframe computer system. It can also be the most expensive. The recovery centers typically charge a monthly standby fee plus extra fees when used for actual contingency testing and processing. If the site is located in another geographic area, there may also be costs in moving personnel to the site. Hot sites are usually only available to support the most common vendors of computer hardware, such as IBM large-scale or IBM-compatible equipment. There are also hot sites available for systems, such as HP, DEC or Unisys, but these may be located only at a few major urban areas.

• *"Empty Shell" Recovery Facilities.* Some larger mainframe computers require water-cooled chiller devices as well as special electrical power supplies. While it may not be too difficult to secure a computer from the vendor, a proper facility to house it may be difficult to locate. To answer this problem, some contingency-planning vendors offer a "shell site," an empty computer room equipped with the necessary power and environmental controls. In the event of a disaster, the vendor need only to move computer hardware and telecommunications gear into this facility.

Empty shell facilities also accept only a limited number of subscribers. They are much less expensive than a hot site. However, it will take time to have the necessary equipment installed, and a shell may not be too valuable for a shorter-term outage. In the best case, several days may be needed to restore information systems services.

• *Commercial Service Bureaus.* Although most of them are not directly in the contingency-services business, an outside commercial service bureau often offers a possible alternative site recovery strategy. They will have operational computers, telecommunications capabilities, and a ready support staff. They may also have facilities to store tapes as well as a service to courier personnel and reports. The ongoing cost of an arrangement with a service bureau will often be quite low. However, in the event of a disaster, it will be necessary to pay usage rates, which can be quite expensive. In addition, the service bureau will service its regular customers first.

• *Hardware Vendors.* Vendors of smaller, mid-range computer hardware often have marketing demonstration sites available in the event of a disaster at one of their customer sites. They typically provide information systems resources to a customer while a replacement system is being installed. There will often be little or no charge for this type of service. This capability is typically available for only smaller computer types and for limited periods of time. Vendors will usually not agree to a contract to provide this type of service and, at best, will provide their customers with a "best efforts" memo of understanding.

Cooperative Contingency-Planning Strategies.   Cooperative contingency-planning strategies require two or more organizations to work together to develop a mutual contingency-planning approach. These strategies usually work best when the organizations that enter into them are all in a geographically remote area or have some special equipment requirements, such as a unique hardware model or a specialized input/output device. These cooperative strategies generally will take one of two forms:

- *Reciprocal Processing Agreements.* Some information systems organizations have made arrangements with a similarly configured site at another organization to be each other's backup site. This can theoretically be a very mutually beneficial type of arrangement since there will be a strong equipment compatibility with few costs involved in maintaining the arrangement. Reciprocal agreements work best when they cover a specialized item of equipment—such as a unique document processor—but not when one of the parties has a long-term interruption and needs the reciprocal site over an extended period of time.

- *Cooperative Recovery Centers.* In some geographical areas or industries, data centers with common equipment have joined together to form cooperative hot site or shell site recovery centers, which work in a manner similar to that of the outside vendor hot or shell recovery centers. The advantage is that all users of the site may have some common interests or requirements. The disadvantage is that the various data operations are all partial ''owners'' of the recovery site and may become involved in their own management or priority-setting disputes within the cooperative group.

Internal Systems Recovery Strategies.   Many larger organizations decide it is most cost-effective to develop an internal strategy for recovery processing using multiple computer centers within their organization. Others may decide that the cost of having a backup facility outweighs the relative risks of not having an ongoing information systems capability. If the latter strategy is used, the contingency-planning team should give extra care to documenting the reasons for this decision. Some internal information systems recovery strategies are as follows:

- *Multiple Internal Processing Sites.* Multiple-unit organizations with a common information systems strategy can often use the computer facilities at other operating divisions or units as backup processing sites. This is true whether the organization has multiple mainframe machines in separate information systems facilities or multiple client-server networks scattered throughout the organization. Provided there is some similarity in equipment and in operating software, this can often be a fairly easy strategy to implement.

  Depending upon the culture of the organization, however, the contingency-planning team should take care when attempting to implement such an internal reciprocal agreement. Some organizations have operating units that are so autonomous that it may be easier to go to an outside recovery-services provider!

- *Shell or Computer Room Space.* The empty shell spaces available from outside providers—discussed above—can also be provided internally. A full computer room site with proper environmental controls can be constructed in a separate, remote building or in a bare room space, such as in a warehouse, where a computer could be located in an emergency. Both sites could be used for other things, such as records storage, on an interim basis. This strategy works well if the shell facility is physically remote and not exposed to the same hazards; it also works if there are some long-term plans to shift operations to that new facility in the future.

- *Service Degradation Strategies.* Sometimes, an organization will make a formal strategy decision to allow for a service degradation in the event of a disaster. If a smaller site using a micro- or mid-range computer, it may decide to revert to manual processing or to cease certain functions in the event of an extended interruption. If a larger site, it may decide to use the limited capabilities of a smaller branch machine.

  A service-degradation strategy brings with it the risk of financial loss, customer dissatisfaction, and operational inefficiencies. However, an organization may feel that the cost for recovery is too great given the perceived risks. If the contingency-planning team or senior management feels that this is the best strategy given the alternatives, it should be carefully documented.

(v) Estimating the Costs to Resume Operations.   A final step for risk evaluation is to consider the costs and requirements for resuming normal activities as well as any potential insurance recoveries. This is an information-gathering activity where the contingency-planning team starts by assembling data on the existing operating environment and the costs and logistics required to replicate it. In some instances, it may find that certain equipment is no longer available. Tentative strategies must be developed to handle this contingency.

When evaluating the costs to recover information systems operations, consideration should be given to the organization's insurance coverage. Organizations should have fire and general liability coverage as well as some form of vital records and business-interruption coverage. The contingency-planning team should make a careful evaluation of the types of coverage in place and the extent to which that coverage provides protection and helps the organization to resume its information systems capabilities.

(vi) Summarizing Risk and Recovery Strategies.   The contingency-planning team now should summarize its findings for a report to senior management. This chapter previously discussed how to summarize potential risks in order to report them to management. While those risks were presented in terms of subjective probabilities, a meaningful approach here is to discuss these risks in terms of their potentials for economic loss.

Figure 19.13 is a worksheet for calculating probable economic losses in the event of a computer disaster and if any of the several contingency-planning methods discussed were to have been used. With this worksheet, the contingency-planning team can summarize its findings and make its recommendations.

(d) BUILDING THE CONTINGENCY PLAN

Efforts at performing a contingency-planning risk assessment should provide the recovery team with sufficient data to construct an effective contingency plan, and efforts can now be directed to developing and drafting the actual plan.

The purpose of an effective information systems plan is to provide guidance for recovering information systems operations. When completed, the final document should not be a thick book to put on the shelf but a working document that is constantly revised and updated.

Figure 19.13   Probable Economic Loss Calculation Worksheet

This worksheet is designed to estimate probable economic losses if a data processing facility were unavailable for an extended period of time, as well as the most cost-effective recovery strategy. This is a three part worksheet. Part I is used to estimate recovery costs for various alternative strategies; Part II is used to estimate business losses per day when key applications are unavailable; and Part III is used to estimate the most cost-effective recovery strategy.

PART I. RECOVERY COSTS

List the various alternative recovery strategies across the columns on top. These may range from a ''hot site'' facility to taking no action. List the costs associated with each strategy. The cost categories here are only examples. Estimate the number of days to recovery for each strategy.

	RECOVERY STRATEGY #1	RECOVERY STRATEGY #2	RECOVERY STRATEGY #3
Annual facility maintenance costs	_____	_____	_____
Emergency processing costs	_____	_____	_____
Extra personnel expenses	_____	_____	_____
Telecommunications costs	_____	_____	_____
Backup storage costs	_____	_____	_____
Other out-of-pocket costs	_____	_____	_____
Total Costs:	_____	_____	_____
Days to Recover:	_____	_____	_____

PART II. APPLICATION BUSINESS LOSSES

List the organization's key data processing applications and the estimated losses, or costs to the organization, if each application were unavailable.

KEY DATA PROCESSING APPLICATIONS	ESTIMATED BUSINESS LOSS/DAY
Application #1 _____	_____
Application #2 _____	_____
Application #3 _____	_____
Total Loss per Day:	_____

PART III. RECOVERY STRATEGY ALTERNATIVES

Calculate the total losses, based on days to recover, for each strategy, to select the most cost-effective recovery method.

	DAYS TO RECOVER	ESTIMATED BUSINESS LOSS/DAY	TOTAL BUSINESS LOSS	RECOVERY COSTS	TOTAL COSTS
Recovery Strategy #1	_____	_____	_____	_____	____
Recovery Strategy #2	_____	_____	_____	_____	____
Recovery Strategy #3	_____	_____	_____	_____	____

Although it is fairly easy to recognize the vulnerability of information systems, other vulnerabilities in other areas of the organization are often ignored. Based upon the experiences gained in developing this plan, internal auditors can become aware of other areas in the organization that might benefit from such contingency planning.

While developing this plan for situations that should "never happen," the team will often gain considerable knowledge about information systems operations. As a result, other recommendations for improving procedures or saving costs may come out of the process. For example, when identifying the necessary data sets for key application backups, the team may identify data redundancies that could be corrected through minor systems enhancements. Similarly, when looking for compatible equipment for backup processing purposes, the team may find that a given item of equipment is obsolete and efficiencies would result by replacing it with a newer unit.

(i) Required Contingency-Planning Preparations. An effective contingency plan requires a considerable amount of advance data-gathering, documentation, and decision-making. Much of this is a one-time effort, and only needs to be updated on an ongoing basis. The contingency-planning team can gather much of this data and information and, when necessary, can call upon other members of the organization to assist. Some of the preparation steps for the contingency plan follow:

- *Select backup site.* Before too much other work can proceed on the plan, a decision must be made on a backup processing site. Alternative strategies were discussed previously. The use of contingency site vendors is quite expensive and requires a management commitment. Empty shell facilities will require planning for equipment to be identified and ordered for the site as soon after the emergency as possible.

- *Make contingency-planning personnel assignments.* The contingency-planning team mentioned throughout this chapter functions as something of a project-management group. Others, including computer operations supervisors, librarians, and systems programmers, will be required to actually invoke or put the plan into operation. Steps should be taken to identify these personnel, assign them responsibilities within the plan framework, and train them when necessary.

- *Identify critical applications.* While performing its risk evaluations, the planning team should have identified a series of applications that appeared critical, as well as some that might be considered as such. There now should be an effort to develop a priority list of the most critical applications. In a disaster situation with limited resources, some applications may not be able to be processed. The difficulty here is that managers responsible for each application will tend to claim that theirs is very critical. The contingency-planning team can sometimes get around this problem by allocating the costs of the contingency-planning effort to application users.

- *Inventory application data file and program requirements.* Based on the above identification, necessary data sets, programs, and database files should be identified. Steps should be taken to assure that all of these are included in the procedures for off-site backup storage.

- *Identify systems software requirements.* The operating software necessary for key applications should be identified and included in off-site backup procedures. If there are any potential differences between this software and that which is normally used at the backup computer site selected, steps should be taken to resolve potential compatibility problems.

- *Assess telecommunications needs and requirements.* Backup processing sites often may have the necessary computer power but not the required communications network. Any special equipment needs in the current network should be identified and documented. Based upon the backup processing strategy used, preliminary plans should be made for restoration of required telecommunication lines from the backup site.

- *Identify necessary documentation and supplies.* Copies of documentation covering key applications and operating software should be stored at the backup site. If any of this documentation is missing or out-of-date, steps should be initiated to bring it to a current status. Any necessary supplies—such as printed forms supporting applications—should also be identified. A sufficient stock should be retained at the backup site, and vendors should be identified such that items can be reordered with minimal difficulty.

The final item to consider is an estimation of the costs of the plan. Because not all costs will be incurred at once, these estimates should be developed on a time-based budget for management review. The contingency-planning team should propose alternatives along with associated costs. An alternative may be to construct a shell site in another facility within the organization or to subscribe to a commercial shell site facility. The costs for each should be outlined in a management proposal, along with a recommendation for the team's preferred alternative.

(ii) Completing the Actual Contingency Plan. Much of the time and effort required to develop an effective contingency plan is spent on the preliminary steps, such as risk evaluation and the gathering of data and information. Documenting all of this in an action-oriented manner will create the contingency plan. An effective contingency plan should cover the two phases of any disaster situation: the initial response to the event, and the restoration of processing at a backup facility. The first phase requires management decisions as to whether to invoke the remainder of the plan into action or to attempt to make necessary corrections and continue processing at the existing site. The second involves the necessary processing steps at the designated backup sites.

The completed plan should define the responsibilities and actions to be taken and serve as a training document for all personnel involved in contingency procedures. The size and content of the plan depends upon the information systems equipment used and the backup strategy, but many of the items listed below should be included in any such plan.

Section 1: Initial Contingency Plan Responses. This section should define the conditions that would constitute an information systems contingency event as well as the individuals responsible for initiating the plan procedures. The section should also list the home and work telephone numbers of all key response team personnel and designate a calling sequence. An initial disaster-response meeting place, such as a nearby hotel facility, should be identified for use as a potential headquarters. Figure 19.14 is an outline of this section.

Figure 19.14   Disaster Recovery Site Action Steps

Activities Within 6 Hours of Disaster Event
1. Have all members of the recovery team as well as appropriate members of management been notified?
2. Has the alternate processing site been notified that a disaster situation has occurred and that the backup site will be used?
3. Has the Control Center location been notified that the team will be occupying it on an extended basis?
4. Has the existing data processing site been secured with appropriate guards?
5. If key members of the recovery team are unreachable, have arrangements been made to assign alternate personnel to the team?
6. Do all members of the recovery team have a copy of the recovery plan and do they understand their roles?
7. Have procedures been initiated to transport all required backup files and documentation to the alternate site?
8. Have hardware and software vendors been contacted regarding the preliminary disaster assessment?
9. Have telecommunications vendors been contacted to supply voice support for the Control Center as well as data support for the backup site?
10. Have arrangements been made for administrative support such as secretaries and copy machines?

Activities Within 12 Hours of Disaster Event
1. Have key personnel arrived at the backup processing site?
2. Have backup cartridges, tapes, and documentation arrived at the backup processing site?
3. Do there appear to be any problems with system or application backups which would cause a change in backup processing strategy?
4. Have firm contacts been made with hardware vendors to initiate the ordering of any replacement hardware?
5. Have users of key applications been informed of the disaster situation and of arrangements for continued processing?

Activities Within 24 Hours of Disaster Event
1. Has the operating system been loaded on the backup equipment?
2. Have key databases been loaded on the backup equipment?
3. Has a strategy and processing schedule been established to restore applications from the backed up versions to their most current status?
4. Are all critical applications operational?
5. Are user personnel on site to verify controls in key applications?
6. Has a processing schedule been established?
7. Have any necessary job control language changes been made?
8. Are arrangements in place for installing necessary telecommunications linkages?
9. Has a more detailed damage assessment and salvage effort been performed at the original data processing site?
10. Have all key equipment, software, and supplies vendors been contacted and have orders been placed as required?
11. Has a detailed report been prepared for management as well as a briefing report for public relations?
12. Can a preliminary plan be established to move back to the organization's own facilities?

Section 2: Key Application Files and Programs. This section of a contingency plan should formally document the applications designated for emergency processing as well as the data, program, and other requirements for processing those applications. The locations of any forms or other supplies should be listed, as should the location of all backup files and program documentation.

Care should be taken that this section of the plan is prepared in a format that can easily be updated. As procedures for key systems are changed, those changes should be reflected in the contingency-plan document. A system of revision numbers or effectivity dates should be used to assure that the applications documentation is current.

Section 3: Backup Recovery Site Procedures.   This section covers the procedures to notify the designated backup site and the personnel necessary to begin operations at the site, and to begin emergency processing at that site. A major purpose of this section is to document the many steps necessary for resuming operations at the backup site, whether a vendor demonstration facility, a reciprocal arrangement site, or a hot site recovery vendor. If the contingency plan designates a shell site where new equipment must be installed, considerably more documentation is necessary for ordering and installing the necessary equipment configuration. Although team members may perform these operations almost without thinking during normal operations, the trauma caused by a disaster situation often causes otherwise responsible personnel to forget.

Section 4: Key Vendor Contacts.   This section, similar to an appendix, lists necessary vendor contacts for computer equipment, software, supplies, and all the necessary items needed to restore and continue processing. Although only one site will be designated in the plan, this section should list alternatives—the sites that were also considered—in the event that the designated backup site cannot provide the agreed level of backup processing services during the emergency period.

(e) MAINTAINING AND TESTING THE CONTINGENCY PLAN

Procedures to update the contingency plan on an ongoing basis should be established within the systems-development and the operations functions. Although the contingency-planning team will probably cease to operate once the plan is completed, a designee from that group should be assigned the ongoing task of publishing updates to the plan documents and assuring that they have actually been filed in the plan books. Internal audit should monitor this process to assure that it is taking place.

The contingency-planning team should also meet at least annually to review initial assumptions and to suggest other changes to the plan in light of other changing factors. For example, a plan may have originally been based on a reciprocal agreement with a nearby firm. However, a subsequent acquisition of a new division may provide another computer center within the organization that might be available for backup processing.

Not only will a contingency plan be of no use if out-of-date, it will also be useless if never tested. Just as an organization should periodically test its fire alarm system, it should also test its information systems contingency plan. Internal audit can play an ongoing role in reviewing the plan to assure that tests are done, as well as reviewing the results of such tests.

Contingency plan testing can take two general forms: controlled tests of selected portions of the plan, and surprise, "simulated disaster" types of tests. A controlled test simply attempts to run one or several applications at the backup recovery site. With a simulated-disaster type of test, these applications are run on somewhat of a surprise basis.

If the organization has made arrangements with a backup-recovery vendor, the contract will generally allow several tests per year as part of the subscription fee. If there is a reciprocal arrangement with another organization, some provision for reciprocal testing should be included in the agreement. The team should designate one or two applications per year to be tested at the backup site, and, together with internal audit, closely monitor the results to assure correct restoration of that application. If problems are encountered, the published plan should be corrected as necessary.

A simulated-disaster type of test does not mean that the head of information systems should rush into the computer room at month end and call out "Fire! Fire!" in order to invoke the plan. Rather, a select group of individuals should structure a test of one or several key applications covered by the plan. Confidential arrangements should be made with the backup facility and information systems should be informed on a surprise basis that the given application will be run at the backup site that day.

As much as possible, this type of test should be done on a simulated emergency basis. That is, information systems personnel would be required to use only media stored at the backup data file storage location to process the designated backup. The results of that test should be closely monitored by the contingency-planning team and by internal audit. Such a test will identify areas where files have not been properly backed up or where personnel lack proper training. Corrective action should be taken where appropriate.

Contingency-plan testing is an important component of any plan implementation. Although it takes an ongoing resource commitment to ascertain that the plan is working effectively, this is usually a small price to pay for having an effective plan.

19-7 EFFECTIVE SECURITY, CONTINGENCY PLANNING, AND INTERNAL AUDIT

The implementation of effective information systems security procedures, including a contingency plan, is not just the responsibility of internal audit, but of general management and of information systems management. However, internal audit plays an important role in helping to develop and implement those procedures and in reviewing their ongoing maintenance.

The modern internal auditor should understand information systems control and security concepts as well as the strengths and weaknesses of existing security and recovery procedures through both the applications and the general controls reviews. Internal auditors should examine existing physical and logical security procedures and contingency plans as part of ongoing review procedures. Weaknesses and vulnerabilities should be identified and reported to management when identified.

Internal auditors should also work as catalysts to improving information systems security and contingency planning. Just as they will be involved in reviewing new systems under development, they should also be involved in the development planning for information systems security and contingency issues. In this way, internal audit can have a strong level of assurance that an important set of information systems controls—physical, logical security, and contingency planning—is working effectively.

CHAPTER 20

New and Evolving Information Systems Technologies

20-1 A CONSTANTLY CHANGING WORLD

Ever since the inception of computer information systems, technology developments have been vastly expanding their functions, massively improving processing speeds, reducing costs, and expanding overall capabilities. At any point during the history of computer systems, an observer would be truly amazed with the improvements. Over the years, computer systems hardware has moved from vacuum tubes to transistors to today's highly integrated circuits. In addition, the pace of these changes is accelerating. A new generation of computer systems once had a product life of perhaps five to eight years before new developments made that product technologically obsolete; now the product life may be perhaps one year or less. These trends continue to be true for virtually all aspects of information systems technology: hardware, software, and communications.

While information systems technology is moving very fast, predicting the direction or dimension of future technology developments requires an educated guess based on a wide range of considerations. Pure technology factors are not the only determinants; economics and marketing also are very important. Even if a new computer hardware system is technically superior, the aggressive marketing of less capable competing devices may prevail. The two versions of home entertainment videotapes introduced in the 1970s, Betamax and VHS, are good examples. Both versions (or formats) were introduced at about the same time. While many considered Betamax to be technically superior, aggressive marketing and a wide mixture of economic factors caused VHS to gain a much greater market share and to soon become the de facto standard. The same can be said about mainframe computer systems. Although some of its 1960s competitors had technologically superior products, aggressive marketing caused IBM to prevail at that time with its 360 series.

Information systems technology is constantly changing, but organizations often do not adopt new technologies quickly. Even though many technology seers were predicting in the late 1980s that the mainframe computer would soon be dead, organizations continued to buy this equipment. An internal auditor will often encounter this older equipment and should continue to use the classic audit and control techniques described in previous chapters. However, the effective professional should be aware of technological trends and how they might impact other business processes and controls. This chapter discusses some of these information systems future trends, highlighting areas that may impact business processes and related controls.

20-2 IMPORTANCE OF BANDWIDTH: COMPUTER NETWORKS

Information systems and their supporting computer equipment technologies have gone through major transitions over the years. Since the 1960s, we moved first from complex, nonintegrated systems based on punched cards and magnetic tape to integrated, database-oriented systems operating on large mainframe systems, and then on to the closely connected client-server microcomputer-based systems of today. As we move into the twenty-first century, technology is on the verge of changing once again, with a greater emphasis on computer networks. Figure 20.1 shows these phases in technology development and how they overlap. While the years surrounding each could be subject to debate, the chart suggests two major future trends.

First, the classic mainframe computer, with its extensive banks of tape and cartridge drives and supporting water cooling systems, may soon become a thing of the past. They still remain important resources for large businesses and governmental units who are reticent about discarding their investments in the computer hardware and the often complex systems operating on them. However, approaches used for information systems and technology are changing. While mainframe systems will continue to be the solution of choice for large transaction-processing systems (such as for processing insurance claims), different designs will mean that these large machines will no longer need the same types of supporting water cooling systems and thus will operate more effectively. These systems will cease to be the center point for all information systems processing. Rather, they will

Figure 20.1   Technology Development Phases

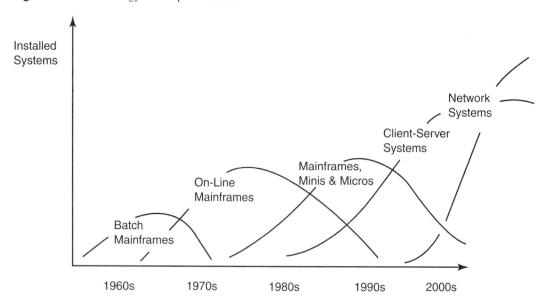

operate as large file server machines supporting extensive networks of client processors or will support data mining database operations.

The classic mainframe computer will be part of the business environment for some years, but a trend that started in the mid 1980s will only increase as the mainframe becomes less and less common and we move to the next phase of client-server systems. The era of the microcomputer was effectively launched in 1982 when IBM announced what they called a Personal Computer or PC. That machine, with 56k of RAM memory, a single floppy disk, no hard disk capability, and a very slow processing speed by today's standards, legitimatized the microcomputer as a potentially serious information systems tool. The capabilities of microcomputers or personal computers have been growing in terms of RAM (random access memory) and processing speeds ever since. By the mid 1990s, a typical microcomputer system had 130 Mb of RAM (that's millions of bytes, not thousands!), a processor speed of 200 MHz (that's microhertz or thousandths of a second in processor speed), and a hard disk of perhaps 200 gb (that's 2.0 gigabytes or 2,000,000,000 bytes or characters of memory storage capacity).

This capability has kept growing. Ever since the introduction of the first IBM personal computer, the integrated circuit chips, manufactured by Intel Corporation as well as others, that are the heart of these computers, have been subject to something called ''Moore's Law.'' As an original designer of microcomputer chips for Intel Corporation, Gordon Moore predicted that the current life of each generation of microcomputer processors will last about 18 months before their capacity and speed is approximately doubled. Once speeds moved, for example, from 64 MHz to 120 MHz with no real change in costs (a development in the middle 1990s), most users dropped their old machines and replaced them with new. Moore's prediction has proved very true over the years and it has come to be known as a law in the computer systems / technical news. As we move into the twenty-first century, a combinations of physics and manufacturing constraints may slow down this trend, and other changes may cause users to begin to drop their microprocessors and to move toward purely networked systems.

The concept, in the opinion of this author and many others, that will replace classic microcomputer systems and their connected client-server systems is the open network of Internet-based systems. The computer network known as the Internet was developed by the U.S. Department of Defense in the 1970s as a system to connect various researchers with each other, allowing them to store and share documents. Starting in the early 1990s, the Internet began to grow almost exponentially and has added capabilities to transmit pictures and sound beyond just pure document text. Through a complex highway of networks, connected together through telephone lines and ''traffic cops'' called *routers* positioned at the intersections, the Internet connects systems together worldwide. Within a given file or data screen, information can be accessed by just pointing the computer's mouse at a word, reference, or picture displayed on the screen. A double click on the mouse will connect to the source of that reference, even if the application is an international operations report of a U.S. company with international units. Using the Internet, a user can easily retrieve information, for example, about sales at their office in Milan, Italy. A double click can call up the company's local computer system in Milan. If the U.S. user reads this report and, for example, wants information on an item purchased by Milan operations from Germany, another click may retrieve the data, including, possibly, a picture or the specifications of that equipment from the German company's system.

With its extensive network, the Internet represents a very complex model for information systems. Individual systems will no longer require that much capacity on any individual machine. Rather, each machine is connected to this larger network. While any individual machine may not have that much capacity, their collective strength represents a significant capability.

The Internet, in the opinion of many industry experts, will become the dominant model for new computer systems. While there are still a wide variety of Internet problems to be solved, such as improving line and site security, the major constraint limiting the Internet's growth is something called *bandwidth,* the speed of the communications lines available to transmit data. A message composed of just words, and connected to a fairly high-speed modem, can flow across a normal voice telephone line at speeds that are acceptable to the typical computer user. However, when transmitting picture images, sound, or even multimedia presentations of motion pictures with color and full sound, the transmission can be slow. The problem is that the size of the ''pipe'' used to carry all of this information is just not big enough. This is particularly true when the needs of one user are coupled with thousand of others wishing to retrieve similar types of information at the same time. A single garden hose would be sufficient to water the front lawn, but a larger diameter pipe would be needed to supply a full block of houses simultaneously.

The solution to speeding up Internet transmission is to increase the size of the pipe that carries the computer images. The larger the diameter of a water pipe, the faster water will flow through it. Similarly, the larger the transmission path, the more information that can be transmitted at any one time. Systems users who want access to this worldwide information and who want it fast will demand higher transmission speeds.

Figure 20.2 outlines some of the considerations that may face an internal auditor as we move to this new generation or paradigm of computer systems. While many details

Figure 20.2   Internet-Related Internal Audit Issues

- Extensive Client-Server Networks Make Responsibility Difficult to Identify. With a large network of connected computer systems, some designated clients, and other various levels of central computing resource servers, responsibility for the system and individual control system processing is becoming increasingly difficult to identify. Classic auditor review approaches will not be the same.

- System Security Grows in Importance. Extensive computer networks mean that considerable amounts of key data are flowing from one destination to another. Even a Technically sophisticated individual may improperly capture this data. System security is an increasingly important factor in internal review of system integrity.

- Changing Workplaces Add New Dimensions to Controls. Auditors once did their reviews at central or branch offices, the locations of most employees and the repository of most records.With powerful laptop computers, remote or home office-based employees, and highly mobile employees, it is often necessary to look differently at control responsibilities.

- The Impact of Multimedia. Computer systems no longer are based on just tabular reports. The model today is increasingly supported by graphics, sound, and even digital video. While the classic accounting rule that the debits must equal the credits will still apply, information systems control models are changing.

could change before we get there, internal auditors will find it necessary to think about issues such as systems access and applications-development controls from a different perspective. Many computer systems based on classic mainframes will become less common, as will systems based on microcomputers in a client-server configuration. The new model will be based on individual, limited-capability machines tied via a network connection to the Internet. Some Internet problems still need to be solved, but internal auditors will almost certainly be reviewing Internet-related control procedures in the future.

20-3 LIGHTS, SOUND, MULTIMEDIA!

Microcomputer operating systems, starting with work by researchers at Xerox in the late 1970s and followed by Apple's Lisa computer system in the early 1980s, began to change the way we looked at computer operating systems. These new systems began to use graphic symbols or icons to represent computer functions. While an interesting concept, the use of graphics really was not popularized until the Apple Macintosh® (the Mac) system was introduced in the mid 1980s. The Mac changed the way many looked at and expected to use computer systems. For example, rather than forcing a user to enter a rather complex command statement to delete a file, Mac users only had to use their keyboard mouse to click on the title of a file to be deleted and then use that mouse to drag that title block to an image or icon of a garbage can. Once the file was moved to the garbage can icon, the Mac's operating system made a beeping sound, and the file was deleted. This was a very primitive first step in what is known as the systems *graphical user interface* (GUI—often called ''gooey'').

By the mid 1990s, the GUI concept had been accepted as almost a requirement for system design. After several attempts, Microsoft released its Windows 95® operating system, adopting many of the Mac concepts for the PC format. Computer systems began to be shipped with color monitors, higher-speed modems for communication with the Internet, speaker systems for both sound and discussion type information, and microphones for voice input. The network computer user in the late 1990s, using the Internet, sees input screens with color pictures and can often click on a portion of one of those pictures to bring in even greater details or information. The information may be delivered through another graphic, text, or a recorded voice message. This combination of graphics, video, and sound is called *multimedia* and will become increasingly more common in the future. By the late 1990s, even classic mainframe systems began to be modified to provide more graphical tools on user output screens.

Many are familiar with the concept of multimedia through observing or using the video games that have become very sophisticated over time. The computer video game player today may steer, using a computer joystick, an image of a high-speed automobile traveling through crowded streets. Bump a lamp post while rounding a corner, and the computer game user will hear a loud crashing sound, see images of the results of the crash, and may see a small graph to show the player's score or to assess the extent of damage. With our growing familiarity with these types of applications, we soon may see more and more business-related computer applications that use similar multimedia techniques.

Multimedia-based computer systems for business information and decision-making will change many information systems control concepts. Using the examples in Figure 30.5, Chapter 30 discusses how financial reporting information can be distorted through poorly designed graphs and charts. The same will become even more true when system designers use multimedia techniques. Some but certainly not all of the problems may include the following.

- Systems will be increasingly designed to accept voice responses. With our many variations in dialects and speech patterns, how will systems be able to maintain audit trails that trace an end user's verbal, "uh-huh" to a system "yes" or "code = 1" type of command?

- In a multimedia system, a user would be able to place an order by clicking on a series of options including the item's style, price, and color. What will be the audit trail to trace these selections to the item shipped by the system?

- Standard GUI techniques can be used to move or stretch a line from a chart as shown on a computer screen. Are there adequate security controls to prevent the manipulation of a graphic image that might cause others to make incorrect assumptions?

The previous are just a few of the types of control concerns that might result from the use of multimedia-based business systems. As creative developers make use of software tools, we can expect to see new business system paradigms in the future. Although powerful tools are being developed to help in the creation of these multimedia systems, this continues to be an uncharted territory. Information conveyed through sound and video images potentially also will require a rethinking of some basic internal control techniques.

20-4 NEW LANGUAGES AND NEW APPLICATION DEVELOPMENT TRENDS

Computer systems with high capabilities and processing speeds are of little value unless we have the tools to easily program or develop effective applications to operate on those machines. This is an area where there have been many changes over the years. Although business computer systems, for many years, were written in programming languages such as COBOL, other newer object-oriented languages such as C++ (discussed in Chapter 18) took on a much greater prominence as we moved through the 1990s. The major change or trend with these newer computer languages or processing tools is the movement to *object-oriented programming languages.* That is, the programmer is faced with a series of images or icons describing various programming processes. Rather than writing detailed program code instructions, programmers just point and click together a series of program functions to write a specialized computer application. The multimedia approach described previously follows this model.

An object-oriented approach offers some potentially dramatic savings, including:

- *Increased Productivity.* Some have estimated that development time can be reduced by one third and cost cut in half.

- *Modular Architecture with a Facility for Reuse.* A program is broken down into what are called *object modules,* whose features can be used for other applications.

- *Improved Management of Complexity.* Complex processes can be more easily defined, described, and managed.

This book is not designed to introduce object-oriented programming and systems development to internal auditors. Both will become much more common in future years, and a future edition of this book will certainly discuss object-oriented control considerations. However, object-oriented design introduces an entire new set of concepts and terminologies. Figure 20-3 summarizes these object-oriented features and terms.

Other new application-development approaches, which appeared to be evolving trends some years ago, have never really been accepted. An example would be artificial intelligence or what are called *expert systems.* Many predicted these rule-based systems would be very common by the early 1990s. Because of development complexities and output results, expert systems have never became that common. Expert systems concepts have been embedded in other systems, but they have not had a major impact in organization business information systems. They may go the way of other interesting but complex information systems development approaches of the past that have never had much acceptance. Examples are the elegant but complex CODASYL database system developed in the 1970s or some of the Computer-Aided Systems Engineering or CASE concepts of systems development. Although the CODASYL model database had a great deal of functionality and was implemented by several vendors years ago, it was never accepted in the marketplace. CASE approaches are still with us, but their real value was in the development of complex mainframe systems that used COBOL or other older development technologies.

This section briefly considers several information systems trends that may be significant in the future. While formal or specialized audit procedures have not been developed for these trends, the modern internal auditor should be aware of them.

Figure 20.3   Object Programming Concepts: Objects and Classes

A car insurance policy object

An insurance policy class

Mary's car insurance

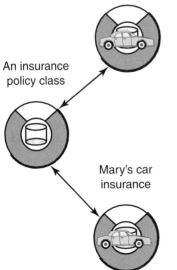

Object programming: Breaks a problem down to separate concepts of objects, classes, and entities. The programmer uses point and click procedures to tie these together.

Object: An entity that responds to a set of messages; and instance of a type or class; has state, behavior, and identity.

Class: A set of objects that share a common structure and a common behavior; inheritance.

Instantiation of an object: A specific class that is related to a specific entity.

(a) JAVA LANGUAGE

Although this chapter is devoted to future prospects, a computer language called JAVA was developed in 1996 and has quickly become the key language of the Internet. There have been numerous ''new'' computer languages over the years. Some were only described in an academic journal but never really implemented; others were implemented, often by a major vendor, and received much attention for a while. The IBM mainframe development language PL/1 is a good example here. Many large organizations made commitments to it, and it supported a large group of authors and consultants. However, while there may be some pockets where it still is used, it has all but disappeared. A long list of other casualties exists.

The JAVA language, developed by Sun Microsystems in the mid 1990s, has quickly become *the* language of the Internet. With its easy ability to combine text with graphics and its easy adaptability to multiple computer platforms, JAVA has every reason to remain as a strong component of the modern, networked computer system. The modern internal auditor should attempt, at least, to understand the JAVA language and why it may be important in the future.

Traditional object-oriented languages were essentially tied to one computer operating system, whether Windows 95, UNIX, or even mainframe MVS. A language developed for one machine could not be easily implemented on another. The JAVA language changed this. JAVA is an object-oriented language that promotes software code reuse and an easy translation of real-world processes into software modules. While other object-oriented languages are in use—notably C++—JAVA added the feature of machine independence.

While they probably will not become JAVA programmers, internal auditors should develop a general understanding of this language, some of its major concepts, and how it will be used in future applications. Unless something much better comes along in the near future, JAVA is rapidly becoming the de facto development language for Internet applications, and IBM made a major commitment to JAVA in 1997. Figure 20.4 provides a very high-level summary of the JAVA language and its major features.

Figure 20.4 JAVA Language Characteristics

- Programs are independent of the machine platform.
  - A program developed on one machine, such as a UNIX machine, can be run on another.
- Full-fledged object-oriented language.
  - Shorter learning curve.
  - Fast-growing industry acceptance.
- Addresses major O/O programming issues.
  - Portability.
  - Distributed objects
  - Integration with databases.
- The entire IT industry is investing in JAVA.
- Uses reusable software components called "JAVA Beans" that may be either GUI or "no-visual" components.

(b) GENETIC ALGORITHMS

In ancient history, when mathematicians tried to calculate some relationship such as the area of a circle, they started with some very rough estimates. Perhaps they first found the circle's area was roughly a little more than three times the length of its diameter. Over time, that factor of 3 was refined to a value of 3.142 to achieve more accurate value for the area. Finally, they discovered the mathematical relationship of what is called π or *pi*. In moving from the concept of *a little more than* to π, we have gone through a genetic process with the stronger estimations and approximations replacing the weaker.

An *algorithm* is a term once common to programmers and today much more common to mathematicians. It is just a mathematical relationship such as $A = \pi d$ for that area of a circle. Every time you define d, the algorithm will provide A, the area. Genetic algorithms are computer program routines that gradually get better over time, with the better formulas replacing the earlier, weaker formulas and approaches. A key difference here is that the programs do not get better by having some ever brighter programmer look at the code and add efficiencies. Rather, genetic algorithms modify themselves, constantly trying to operate more efficiently. Following the concepts of evolution that were originated by Charles Darwin many years ago, the stronger routines replace the weaker as computer programs go through a series of self-modifications.

At the present time, genetic algorithms are very much on the fringes of information systems. The topic currently is only found in obscure and specialized academic conferences, with no applications in the real world. However, this is a concept which, when teamed with a "pick and choose" object-based language such as JAVA, may soon regain prominence in information systems development. The implications for auditors here would be significant. Programs would attempt to modify themselves to become more efficient and, possibly, to operate with better controls.

If carried out to its fullest implications, this concept could cause both comfort and concern for the auditor. Exactly which version of the program was used? How can we be certain that the current version has the best controls? What would happen if, through the classic genetic process, some version ended up as a freak? There are no answers here, but genetic algorithms are something that internal auditors may face in the future. While they will be limited to projects by mathematicians and other researchers for the next few years, the concept may find use in business systems applications. For example, if a credit-screening system based on neural networks, as described previously, also was based on genetic algorithms, the result might be a constantly revised and improved credit screening system. However, the auditor might have no assurance of *which* version of the program ran during any processing sequence.

There are no specific audit standards today for programs' genetic algorithms, but no business applications have been developed to date using this technology. This discussion points to a possible future direction of technology and illustrates the way computer systems are changing, and their overall control implications. Software and hardware technology move in different and unexpected ways, and internal auditors should try to keep aware of these developments and their overall control implications.

20-5 WE WILL ALWAYS HAVE LEGACY SYSTEMS

The term *legacy systems* began to be used in the late 1980s. At that time, organizations were under pressure from many directions to move to the newer, microcomputer-based client-server systems. Information systems professionals and others looked at their older mainframe systems and decided, in many cases, that they were not ready to abandon them, despite their uncomfortable user interfaces and rather unappealing screen layouts and paper-based reports. Older applications, such as general ledger or inventory control systems, are often used for many years—too many employees had learned to accept their clumsiness, making any major changes too difficult and complex. These older but still operational mainframe-oriented systems came to be known as legacy systems.

Information systems represent a major investment to an organization, and a major business or government organization will not or cannot afford to discard its older systems without a strong cost or service-level justification. Because of these significant past investments, organizations will continue to patch, repair, or marginally enhance their older systems until the time when they just break under their own weight of ongoing fixes and changes. A major financial institution or a manufacturer typically may have a suite of applications developed and tailored over many years. The organization will not discard its older systems unless they have a very good reason to change. It is just too expensive to start from scratch once again and to rebuild or reengineer these systems.

The efforts and expenditures made on legacy information systems by many large organizations as they moved to get ready for the year 2000 is an example of this. Many older computer systems that used a calendar date field for various purposes originally carried those dates in a 6 numeric character, YYMMDD format. To calculate an aging or an interest-bearing amount, computer programs simply added or subtracted from this date field value. That year value was carried as YY rather than YYYY. Moving to the year 2000, that same date field moves from 99 to 00, causing many problems in the program's calculations.

These YY, two-character date fields are a result of older legacy systems and attempts to save characters of what was then comparatively expensive memory space. In many instances, the routines covering these calculations were buried in the COBOL code of older programs and were difficult to identify. However, rather than attempting to discard their older legacy systems, organizations started assembling teams in the mid 1990s to go through their libraries of programs, sometimes almost line by line, to find any YY calculations. As this edition is being initially published, just prior to the millennium, the final success of many organizations in cleaning up their year-2000 problems has not been settled. However, organizations generally did not discard their older legacy, mainframe systems and in many cases made additional Band-Aid types of changes to fix older systems because of the year-2000 problem. The result is not new or improved systems but legacy applications that will continue to operate for some years into the future.

The point here is that internal auditors will need to understand the controls and procedures surrounding these legacy systems for some years into the future. The older systems represent major investments and are very good at handling large, transaction-intense applications. Unless there is some new technical development in the upcoming years that we cannot anticipate, organizations will continue to use their legacy systems for some time. Software products, such as IBM's RACF logical security product, as discussed in Chapter 19, may go away and be replaced by new products. Similarly, requirements for classic mainframe environmental controls may change with new processors not requiring the same level of water cooling. The mainframe or larger system controls discussed in Chapters 16 and 17 will continue to be important for the modern internal auditor.

Newer and evolving tools will help to extend the life and better justify the use of older legacy systems. Two important tools or techniques are data warehousing and linkages to more modern networks. Although they will never look quite the same because of computer systems architectural constraints, there will be ongoing efforts to enhance legacy systems to make them look more like modern client-server systems.

20-6 FUTURE PROSPECTS

Information systems will continue to grow and evolve in future years. In some cases, we may face physical limits to existing technologies, limiting that particular strain or direction. As we are writing this chapter in the late 1990s, there are indications that Moore's law, predicting an 18-month product life cycle for integrated computer circuits, might change. A combination of manufacturing constraints and just plain physics may limit the growth here in the future. The integrated circuits that are the heart of a chip are produced by essentially using an etching process. Technology is approaching some limits in continually trying to reduce sizes. Today, a highly integrated circuit looks something like a very detailed street map of the city of Tokyo drawn on a surface area smaller than a postage stamp. By the next one or two generations, it will be necessary to draw that same street map on essentially the head of a pin. This presents a problem in terms of both manufacturing technology and physical principles. Does this mean that information systems technology will begin to stagnate by perhaps the year 2010? Barring some cataclysmic event, such as an earthquake pushing California into the ocean, the progress of technology will continue. However, it will take advantage of newer technologies moving in different directions.

When facing new technology developments, it is far too easy to look at a short-term new trend and use it to confidently predict the future. This often does not work! Two examples may explain. In the late 1950s, the United States military was beginning to use helicopters extensively. Several aircraft companies developed, at least up to an experimental state, small or personal helicopters. Excited by this trend, many journalists began to predict that many people would begin to use helicopters for personal purposes, such as individually commuting to work. Because of costs, the skills necessary to pilot a helicopter, and a wide range of technological factors, this prediction never occurred. Today, we do not have personal helicopters in our backyards, nor are there any prospects for this to happen.

Atomic energy is another example of what was once thought to be a promising technology that was essentially derailed and all but killed. The early 1960s saw the construction of electrical power plants worldwide based on atomic energy. They were a relatively cheap source of power with prospects as even more efficient power sources in the future. Physicists were aware of something called a ''breeder reactor'' that, once perfected, would effectively generate more fuel than it consumed. Over time, however, many realized that atomic energy posed some high potential risks. In addition, Luddite-type[1] political activists demonstrated against the use of atomic energy in all forms. The research activity stopped, the power plants largely were shut down, and these early 1960s predictions never occurred.

Many factors can change the shape and direction of technology developments. While atomic energy and helicopters are rather far removed from information systems auditing, they represent trends that everyone once thought would gain wider acceptance. They did not. Information systems technology can be caught in the same trap. New technology developments that appear to have bright futures disappear for no good reason. Others suddenly become prominent with essentially no warning. Internal auditors should keep aware of technology developments, their expected growth path, and audit implications. With this understanding, the modern internal auditor should be able to develop or adopt new audit and control techniques as required.

---

[1] The term comes from textile machine operator rioters in Yorkshire, England, in the early 1800s, who tried to fight the industrial revolution by breaking their machines. They were called Luddites after their leader, Ned Ludd.

PART FOUR

AREAS FOR OPERATIONAL AUDITING

CHAPTER 21

Introduction to Operational Auditing

Part four discusses a variety of specific audit approaches covering various operational areas in the organization, such as accounting systems controls. Others, such as engineering and research, are often ignored because auditors feel they do not understand the topic. An objective of these operational auditing chapters is to give general descriptions of these business areas to suggest some internal audit approaches for each.

These chapters do not cover *every* area that an internal auditor will encounter, but they include the key areas often found in a manufacturing company. While this guidance should be useful for many modern organizations, an internal auditor may want to consult a reference for specific information about aspects of operations of other businesses, such as banks, retailers, or other institutions. While we cover topics such as payroll or financial management, which apply to others beyond manufacturing organizations, there may be some specific control issues within a particular industry that are beyond the scope of this book.

21-1 NATURE OF OPERATIONAL AUDITING

A series of steps are necessary for an individual to become an effective internal auditor. The first building block steps include understanding the internal auditing process, the concept of internal controls and management needs, and performing basic internal audit procedures. These steps were all discussed in previous chapters. This chapter will discuss how to perform an operational audit, including its financial, information systems, and operational components. This operational audit approach can be used for the specific areas discussed in the next nine chapters as well as in many other areas of business organizations.

(a) DEFINITION

Chapter 4, "The Operational Approach of Internal Audit," discussed the differences between an internal and external auditor, with emphasis on the internal auditor's service approach, which goes beyond an attest audit of the financial statements. That chapter described how financial auditing is just one component of the overall organizational service approach.

Although other sources have defined operational reviews as "a non-financial audit whose purpose is to appraise the managerial organization and efficiency of a company," this book takes a broader approach, defining it at follows:

> *Operational auditing is an independent review including all aspects of an organization; its business functions, financial controls, and the supporting systems. It involves a systematic review of an organization's activities, or a stipulated segment of them, in relation to specified objectives. The operational auditor has an overall objective to assess the quality of internal controls for an area, including its effectiveness and efficiency of operations, reliability of the financial reporting, and compliance with applicable laws and regulations.*

With this approach, an internal auditor goes beyond a narrow range of activities and includes virtually *all* aspects of the organization in the scope of internal audit reviews. A better name for the operational audit approach might be *managerial auditing,* but we keep the term originally established by Victor Brink in the first edition of this book, as his and our current definitions are quite similar.

Although we take this broad approach to operational auditing, we will define the activity and then describe internal audit activities in terms of financial, operational, and computer systems audit objectives. These financial audit activities do not include the normal assessments of the fairness of financial statements performed by external auditors, but rather internal controls of a financial nature that do not necessarily impact the organization's overall financial statements. The sections on operational controls include physical controls over assets, the level of direct management over the activity, and the type of performance indicators in place to measure the activity. Information systems controls could quite correctly be considered a form of operational controls, but because of their technical nature and the importance and pervasive nature of information systems in the modern organization, we have treated them separately.

(b) OPERATIONAL VERSUS "INTEGRATED" AUDITING

Although the term was unknown when Victor Brink published the first edition of *Modern Internal Auditing,* "integrated auditing" has recently been used by internal audit departments to describe an audit approach where there are no financial, operational, or information systems audit specialists. The idea is that every member of the internal audit team should be able to perform reviews covering all or any areas of management interest. Under integrated auditing, an internal audit department would neither hire nor train internal auditors in a specialty area such as information systems auditing nor establish a special section within the audit department to review these areas. While the proponents of integrated auditing often claim it is a better system than operational auditing, this is not true. In fact, some integrated audit functions today may provide a lower standard of service than provided by the specialty-based, operational, internal audit organization as described throughout this book.

A major factor driving the integrated auditing movement has been the management frustrations and problems sometimes encountered in larger internal audit departments with separate audit specialties. For example, information systems auditors may have reviewed specialized, highly technical areas that were interesting but of limited audit risk, or operational auditors refused to be concerned with accounting's debits and credits because they were "operational," or financial auditors scheduled reviews with no attention given to other scheduled operational or information systems controls. One result can sometimes be a series of audit reports, all from the same audit department, that are duplicates—or, even worse—that contradict one another.

To compound the problem, internal audit departments sometimes experience troubles keeping their specialty areas fully staffed. Senior management, which sometimes still thinks that "an auditor is an auditor is an auditor," has trouble recognizing that a specialty auditor cannot easily translate those highly specialized skills to another audit task.

The response by some internal audit managers to this problem was to all but abolish audit specialties, such as information systems, and train all members of the audit staff to perform reviews that cover all areas. Specialized-topic audits were similarly eliminated. Internal audit reviewed an overall process or area, covering all aspects of the operation, including information systems and specialized operational controls, and produced a single report. Existing internal auditors were trained to understand all audit issues, and new staff members were hired as generalists, emphasizing overall rather than specific audit areas.

Concurrent with this movement to integrated auditors, others have recognized that certain areas are just so unique that specially trained auditors are needed. Perhaps the best example here is for quality management where auditors are needed for ISO 9000 and ISO 140000 quality and environmental management system standards. While these audits are often performed by outside contractors and not internal employees, a whole separate audit specialty has developed for these quality standards–certified quality auditors. While these audit specialty areas are somewhat beyond the realms of this book, Chapter 33 will introduce and briefly discuss them.

In many respects, integrated auditing is not that different from the broad "service to management" concept of internal auditing that has been promoted throughout this book. The main difference is that this book recognizes the need to provide proper attention to specific audit risks. As a result, we feel there is and will continue to be a need for specialization. The advocates of integrated auditing feel that with proper training, a single internal auditor can appropriately cover all risks, since all fit within the general model of internal control introduced in Chapter 2. While this ideal is attractive, many professionals find difficulty in achieving all of these objectives.

(i) True Integrated Auditing Weaknesses. The main difference between integrated auditing, as described by some of its proponents today, and modern operational auditing is similar to the difference between dining at either a highly efficient, limited-menu restaurant or at a full-service restaurant with an extensive menu. The limited-menu restaurant will do an adequate job on their limited menu items; however, if the diner has a special need, such as wanting no tomato sauce on some standard menu item, the limited-menu restaurant will have trouble complying.

At a full-service restaurant, the food may take longer and be more expensive. It will have a chef in the kitchen rather than someone who essentially puts preprepared dishes in the microwave or who follows strict menu instructions. If a customer has a special need, the restaurant can often more easily accommodate the request. At the limited-menu establishment, the customer knows what is offered, with no change from one visit to the next.

In the integrated audit function, auditors are trained to provide a general review covering a limited set of audit objectives. As long as members of the staff understand all aspects of that specialized audit program, they can generally do a very good job. This approach works well for an organization with a large number of essentially identical branch locations, such as a chain of retail stores or fast food restaurants. The audit team can visit any and perform a standard review covering many aspects of operations, such as a location's stock-keeping controls, the local computer system, or various financial control issues. This works well as long as senior management wants its internal auditors simply to visit those branch units to perform consistent reviews following the same audit program.

The approach may break down if any member of the integrated audit team gets into a specialty area above his or her head. An internal auditor trained in financial auditing but with minimal information systems audit training may miss key control issues surrounding the implementation of a newer technology (such as a wireless telecommunications network for local systems accounting, as discussed in Chapter 18) or may miss significant internal control issues. All too often, the integrated auditor approach can lead to lowest common denominator levels of audit quality.

(c) NATURE OF INTERNAL AUDIT REVIEWS

The modern internal auditor is primarily an operational auditor with a wide range of analysis skills. As discussed in Chapters 1 through 3, the role of the operational auditor is to provide total service to management through independent, objective assessments of operations. As noted previously, those reviews should cover effectiveness and efficiency of operations, reliability of the financial reporting, and compliance with applicable laws and regulations. This is a broad charge, which could be performed by one group of auditors having a knowledge of all aspects of operations or by a series of internal audit specialists.

A good way to think about operational auditing is to recognize that, despite technological advances and improved processes, organizations are still made up of people who do not always perform according to plans and expectations. Thus, no matter how comprehensive and complete an organization's systems and procedures, there will always be failures and breakdowns. The nature of the breakdowns may be minor, or sufficiently major to hamper organization operations. The people who design and implement these controls and procedures often fail to execute them correctly. The operational internal auditor, following an established approach and plan, independently reviews these systems and procedures, identifies areas where the controls and procedures could be improved, and reports his or her recommendations to appropriate levels of management.

21-2 PERFORMING THE OPERATIONAL AUDIT

The less-experienced internal auditor, when faced with the challenge of developing a detailed audit program, must first have a good understanding of the operation, usually accomplished through a field survey, as discussed in Chapter 10. Based upon the results from the survey and any other information gathered, the internal audit team develops a detailed review plan, including areas to be evaluated and audit tests to be performed. The audit procedures or checklists from the operational auditing chapters can be used to develop more comprehensive audit programs based on the characteristics of the area to be reviewed.

Operational audits should cover a wide area of organizational operations. A good way to look at the breadth of operational auditing is through the *Statement of Responsibilities of Internal Auditors* published by the IIA. It outlines the following objectives:

1. Reviewing and appraising the soundness, adequacy, and application of operating controls

2. Ascertaining the extent of compliance with established policies, plans, and procedures

3. Ascertaining the reliability of management data developed within the organization

4. Appraising the quality of performance in carrying out assigned responsibilities

5. Recommending operating improvements

6. Accounting for and safeguarding assets

These objectives emphasize the need to review every aspect regarding the effectiveness and efficiency of operations. However, these audits should be performed according to preestablished audit objectives, following an effective audit program. This is the operational audit process following the Standards for the Professional Practice of Internal Auditing, described in Chapter 5.

Internal auditors sometimes consider operational auditing to include all audit activities except financial and information systems. This is perhaps because external auditors and some internal auditors who support them primarily perform only financial procedures. Although external audit standards call for reviews of all activities supporting financial statement balances, their focus is primarily financial. Similarly, information systems auditors are viewed as specialists. Thus, each of the nine operational auditing chapters to follow have separate sections for financial, operational, and information systems audit procedures. The sections following describe the contents of these overall operational auditing activities.

(a) FINANCIAL AUDIT PROCEDURES FOR THE OPERATIONAL AUDITOR

Today, internal auditors involved in financial audit procedures go beyond the examination of financial statements for accuracy and fairness and assess such areas as:

- The soundness of the financial policies and procedures, and the organization's compliance with them

- The effectiveness of management over all financial assets, including cash and short- and long-term investments

- Tax management and administration, including procedures to determine that tax returns are filed in a timely manner

- Accounting controls over operations such as activity-based costing procedures or accounting systems to support major projects

- Financial analysis and statistical reporting procedures

Many of these are extensions of the basic financial audit procedures typically performed by external auditors. Chapter 24 will talk about auditing the purchasing function and Chapter 28 will discuss financial controls procedures for the management of marketing department operations.

Through these financial audit procedures, an internal auditor should understand the financial implications of the various organizational activities that have financial controls implications. Internal auditors always consider the economic and financial control implications of the areas they are reviewing. While it is one thing to identify a control problem in an automated system, identifying the overall costs due to a data-processing control problem may have a greater impact. Such costs may range from a loss of sales and the resultant loss of profits to the costs associated with the additional resources expended through unnecessary computer-processing time.

(b) IMPORTANCE OF INFORMATION SYSTEMS CONTROLS

Fifty years ago, computer systems revolutionized the manner in which business processes were organized. This automation changed and continues to change the manner in which control procedures are structured. Today, most internal auditors understand basic information systems internal control procedures. Other areas, such as appropriate information security procedures or client-server operating controls, still require a level of specialized knowledge. Because of this specialized knowledge requirement, as well as the ongoing force of technology-driven changes to business procedures, the Part Four operational auditing chapters generally have a section on information systems auditing procedures. The contents of each vary depending upon the complexity and the control risks associated with supporting information systems in each area.

Internal auditors should consider the implications of information systems controls whenever performing an operational or management audit. Years ago, auditors in general and external auditors in particular reviewed input and output controls but devoted little if any attention to the processing controls within the automated systems. Information systems audit specialists, originally called electronic data processing (EDP) auditors, filled this gap by developing specialized information systems review methods and procedures (see Chapters 16 through 20). Each of the operational chapters following has a section on information audit procedures that are more specific to that area of interest, such as the information systems controls on sales, marketing, and advertising discussed in Chapter 28.

Another area that should not be restricted to information systems auditing is the use of computer-assisted audit procedures (CAATs). (See Chapter 12 for different types of CAATs as well as steps to develop them.) Where appropriate, the forthcoming chapters discuss CAATs to support a specific internal audit area.

(c) TYPES OF OPERATIONAL AUDIT PROCEDURES

Operational audit procedures, as described in these chapters, cover perhaps everything not included with financial and information systems audit procedures. The tables of audit procedures and checklists in the following chapters should provide guidance for reviews of these areas. The real key to remember is that the auditor is always evaluating the efficiency and effectiveness of the internal controls in operation, using the following steps:

1. Understand control risks or management concerns in the area to be reviewed.
2. Perform a preliminary survey or otherwise develop an understanding of the area to be reviewed.
3. Develop an audit plan, objectives, and potential areas for test and evaluation; identify any areas where specialized help may be needed.
4. Begin the review by interviewing responsible personnel or examining appropriate audit evidence.
5. Evaluate the results of audit tests and other work and make adjustments for further tests if necessary.

6. Develop findings, conclusions, and recommendations for corrective action. Report these to appropriate levels of internal audit and general management.

We can put all of the above in focus by considering an operational audit example. This example refers to materials discussed in both prior and upcoming chapters, and presents a general idea of the operational approach an internal auditor might use in reviewing this example entity.

21-3 PERFORMING THE OPERATIONAL AUDIT: AN EXAMPLE

Assume that internal audit's organization has acquired a small company and incorporated it as a separate operating division called ExampleCo. This new unit assembles and markets a product direct to consumers through the Internet. This method of on-line computerized marketing and sales is quite different from the traditional company procedures and has raised control questions and concerns from senior financial management. Internal audit's preliminary risk analysis had called for a review of ExampleCo Division of internal controls later this year, but the CFO had requested that internal audit schedule an operational review of the ExampleCo sales and marketing processes with an emphasis on the new division.

Internal audit would first schedule the audit project following the six steps for operational auditing described above. We will not describe how to perform an operational audit of an on-line sales and marketing process but, rather, discuss how an operational audit approach is developed for any new area where internal audit does not have established audit programs or a good understanding of the area to be reviewed.

(a) STEP 1: UNDERSTANDING EXAMPLECO CONTROL RISKS

Internal audit should first reevaluate the control risks associated with ExampleCo's sales and marketing process. Following the procedures discussed in Chapter 7 on evaluating organizational risk, internal audit should reevaluate the audit risk associated with the new Internet-based ExampleCo processes of concern. There should be some general discussions with both the senior ExampleCo management who requested the review and division management. Relative risks should be evaluated and compared with other risks derived for currently scheduled audits.

If the need for a review is indicated, unless there are some extenuating circumstances, internal audit should schedule the audit depending on other audit risks and priorities. Senior management may see a new process, such as ExampleCo's selling directly to consumers through the Internet, when the organization has always sold through distributors, as a significant business or control risk. If there were nothing unusual, the director of internal audit should counsel management about the relative risks and perform or not perform the audit based upon the overall risk analysis and the annual planning procedures (see Chapter 8).

The ExampleCo on-line sales and marketing process is new, using relatively newer technology and appears to have significant control risks. Internal audit should consider these controls risks when planning the ExampleCo audit. As a courtesy, the requesting senior managers should be informed of audit plans. Figure 21.1 outlines preliminary steps for performing an operational audit, such as with ExampleCo.

Figure 21.1 Preliminary Steps for Performing an Operational Review

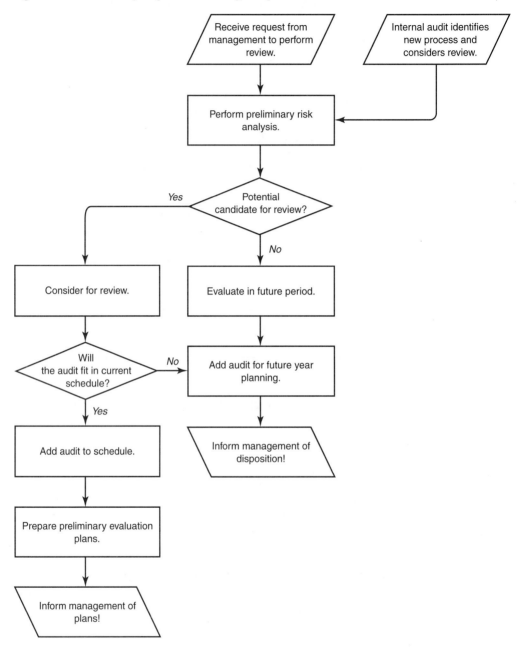

(b) STEP 2: PERFORMING THE EXAMPLECO PRELIMINARY SURVEY

Familiarization is the first and perhaps the most basic activity necessary to allow the audit team to understand the operational activity to be reviewed. There are two broad levels of this familiarization, often called the *preliminary survey*. One includes steps performed prior to arriving at the field location, ExampleCo, and the other includes activities performed at the field location. Before going to the field location, the following steps would typically be taken:

- *Definition of the Overall Purpose of the Review*. This definition might come from the director of internal audit or from one of the senior auditors. In this example, the review has been defined through a risk analysis and a request from management. The purpose might be to review the controls covering the ExampleCo sales and marketing process, not simply to ''audit ExampleCo.'' Figure 21.2 is an example of this memo.
- *Discussion with Other Interested Personnel*. Discussions with other company personnel should include staff managers and key personnel to the extent that they

Figure 21.2   ExampleCo Audit Planning Memo Example

MEMO

To: Tom Axylotl, ExampleCo Corporate Controller

From: Tom Truelove, Audit Director

Date: Thursday, August 29, 19XX

Subject: Sales and Marketing Process Planned Audit

At the request of department management, internal audit has made a preliminary analysis of the risks associated with the new sales and marketing system, PRICEWHIZ, that is scheduled for implementation at the end of the next quarter. We have determined that the new processes and procedures introduced to ExampleCo could present significant control risks if the new system were to be implemented without proper controls and user training.

We have scheduled a detailed preimplementation review of this new system starting in October of this year. Our review will be the responsibility of Herm Hollerith, our senior information systems audit specialist, along with several other members of the internal audit organization, to be determined. Our review will include detailed testing of new systems procedures as well as enrollment in one of the PRICEWHIZ training classes. Assuming that the system implementation moves ahead as planned, with full implementation scheduled for next February, we expect to complete our review and issue our audit report by January.

Please contact me if you have any questions about this planned review.

are involved with the audit assignment. These discussions serve a number of purposes, but are primarily to alert appropriate persons that an operational review is to be performed and to get from them either questions for audit attention or information that may be useful in connection with the review. For example, internal audit might determine through discussions with central information systems management if they had any particular concerns regarding ExampleCo's new Internet-based process.

- *Accumulation of All Pertinent Data.* Internal audit should examine all information which could be applicable to the planned field review. Since this is the first audit here, the assigned internal auditors should review any available working papers and reports from any related review, as well as any other types of reports or materials from other sources that may be relevant. This is a new application area, and the assigned responsible internal auditors may want to develop a better understanding of overall Internet processing procedures.

- *Advance Arrangements with Field Location.* Unless the review is to be conducted on a surprise basis, internal audit will normally communicate with the field location—the company, in this example—and would advise the responsible unit head of the planned review. At the same time, necessary preparatory and administrative arrangements can be handled.

Internal audit now visits the ExampleCo location. (See Chapter 10, ''Directing and Performing Internal Audits.'') The field location, of course, can be at a distant location or at the same home office location where internal audit is located. The familiarization phase at ExampleCo might include the following activities.

- *Discussions with the Responsible Manager.* The internal audit team should meet with the senior manager to whom the final report would normally be addressed. Because ExampleCo is a new organizational entity, care should be given to explaining procedures, the overall purpose of the review, timing plans, and other special arrangements. Internal audit will then gain a greater understanding of ExampleCo from that manager's description of operational activities, organizational relationships, problem areas, and other points of potential interest.

- *Discussions with Other Key Personnel.* Along with discussions with the responsible managers should be discussions with other key personnel—for example, the responsible supervisors for ExampleCo's sales and marketing functions. They will normally provide additional details about the various subactivities and at the same time serve as a cross-check against the information previously obtained. This is particularly important when internal audit may not have much experience regarding ExampleCo's sales and marketing activities.

- *Walk-Through of Operational Areas.* Internal audit should request a tour of all operational activities to be reviewed to observe the various procedures performed, the general work flow, and overall operations. When the entity reviewed is performing a new process (as in this case), the internal audit team might ask for a detailed demonstration of how a customer would place an on-line order and how ExampleCo would download the sales and credit card data from its Internet pro-

Figure 21.3 ExampleCo Walk-Through Flowchart Example

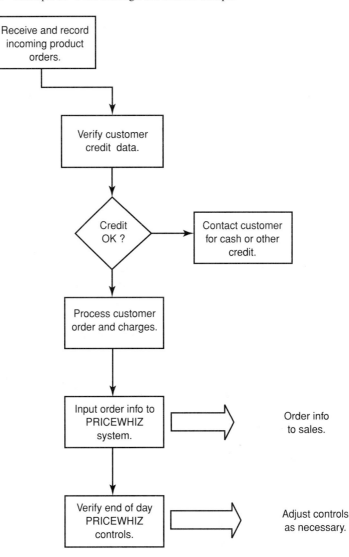

vider, process the order, and ship the merchandise. Figure 21.3 is a simplified flowchart describing the auditor's initial walk through of the area to be reviewed.

- *Review of Policies and Procedures.* The team should briefly review written policies and procedures affecting administration and control activities carried on by the total organization and for ExampleCo Division. Although this material will be covered in the formal operational audit, this information will help to complete the preliminary survey.

This familiarization phase sometimes extends into the actual review. The auditors are gathering information to help build an audit plan but also information that may provide the basis for further investigation or an actual audit finding. That is, the carrying out of the regular review involves a further familiarization with detailed activities not completely covered by other key personnel in the earlier phase. Included here would be further discussions, observations, and preparations of flow charts. The familiarization activity provides a basis for building a detailed audit plan.

(c) STEP 3: DEVELOPING THE DETAILED AUDIT PLAN

Based on the preliminary risk analysis and the preliminary survey, the in-charge auditor develops a detailed audit plan (see Chapter 10). Internal audit might initially take an existing audit program, used for a similar past review, and modify it for ExampleCo. Here, internal audit may have reviewed other standard sales and marketing systems in the past, and those audit programs can be used as starting points for the ExampleCo review.

The audit plan should give particular attention to the audit objectives and potential areas for detailed testing during the review. Those objectives may result from the request of senior management, reinforced from the information gathered during the preliminary survey.

Internal audit identifies risks and develops specific audit procedures given ExampleCo's unique sales and marketing activities. Using the general audit programs described in Chapter 10, internal audit can develop a specific program for the areas of the ExampleCo operations to be reviewed. A starting point might be the audit procedures, which will be described in Figure 28.10 (Sales Function Operational Audit Procedures), coupled with those of Figure 17.11 (Potential Application Review Objectives). The point is to develop procedures that are relevant to the operational activity reviewed. An internal auditor needs to be somewhat creative here, recognizing controls risks and overall concerns regarding the operation. If the auditor has questions regarding the appropriateness of a planned test, it might be a good idea to discuss it with local ExampleCo management.

An audit report that just talks about ''the lack of documentation'' will accomplish little if other appropriate tests have not been performed. In the case of the ExampleCo on-line sales and marketing system, some of the things that internal audit might consider could include:

- What procedures are in place to maintain the on-line system, to provide backups of orders entered, and to record those sales properly?
- Are there adequate security procedures to prevent another Internet user from intercepting sales transactions or from initiating unauthorized shipments?
- Is the marketing material contained on the on-line screens consistent with overall company policy on describing and pricing products?
- Are all sales completed through credit card transactions in a secure manner and verified and transmitted to the credit card bank promptly?

Our purpose here is not to provide a complete audit program for the ExampleCo sales and marketing function but to illustrate the types of tests that internal audit should consider. Internal audit should develop a specific audit program for the operational audit and perform tests based on that program. This is the basic audit process described in Chapter 10.

This phase is also the time to plan additional resources if needed. In this case,

Figure 21.4 ExampleCo Sample Audit Program

Audit <u>PRICEWHIZ Sales and Mktg. Sys.</u> Location _____ Date _____		
AUDIT STEP	**INITIAL**	**W/P**
1. Meet with sales and marketing personnel to develop general understanding of system and its function.		
2. Observe system operations for two one-hour periods, one during the day and one on the evening shift.		
3. Select two representative days to perform detailed tests of transactions. One should be a normal Friday high-volume day and other at end of accounting month.		
4. Arrange for I/S to save all significant files from those days selected, including telephone log files.		
5. Review sales credit card verification procedures, including controls over bank passwords and authorizations for adjustments.		
6. For two selected days, reconcile credit card receipts with recorded product sales and bank deposits. Investigate differences and document any unresolved differences.		
7.		
8. **PARTIAL SAMPLE AUDIT PROGRAM**		
9.		
10.		

ExampleCo uses the Internet, the large and widely used data network where there have been some questions about security and integrity. If internal audit has had no experience regarding Internet control procedures, arrangements should be made for specialized help. The plan should be submitted to the director of internal audit or an appropriate designee for approval. An extract of the audit program procedures is outlined in Figure 21.4.

(d) STEP 4: PERFORMING THE ACTUAL OPERATIONAL REVIEW

We need always to recognize that the two types of activity, familiarization steps and the actual audit, are interwoven as one moves through the organizational levels. Conceptually, the audit verification determines the extent to which actuality conforms to what was asserted in the familiarization phase. This verification is achieved in a number of ways, but the essence is that there is sufficiently credible evidence, acquired through oral inquiries, observations, written confirmations, computer-assisted audit procedures, the tracing of the processing of data, tests, and through other means. The quality of the evidence varies with the type and manner in which it is gathered. All of these aspects have a highly judgmental character, both as to particular evidence and how much effort should be expended in obtaining additional evidence. All judgmental decisions depend upon Internal Audit's professional competence.

It is important that the auditor be flexible and creative. In the case of ExampleCo, internal audit is turning new turf, so to speak, in an area where this audit group has little experience. The audit program should be adjusted and tests modified, as necessary.

(e) STEP 5: EVALUATION OF AUDIT RESULTS

Next, internal audit performs a detailed analysis of the information gathered in terms of the component elements. This analysis is frequently part of the audit verification process, where the detailed analysis of an ExampleCo account balance might verify its correctness. On the other hand, the detailed breakdown of performance under different types of operating conditions can determine better ways to control the particular type of performance. Both the decision of *how* to analyze a type of information or operational activity and, subsequently, the potential benefits obtained as the analysis is carried out are based on judgment. This often is a good opportunity to observe potential concerns from the preliminary review and to develop potential audit concerns and other matters of managerial interest. This type of preliminary findings summary and analysis is shown in Figure 21.5; it would be prepared at the completion of the review and prior to the preparation of the actual report. This analysis can aid in the preparation of the final audit report and can be a major tool for effective internal auditing service.

(f) STEP 6: AUDIT FINDINGS, CONCLUSIONS, AND RECOMMENDATIONS

Familiarization, verification, and analysis have now set the stage for an evaluation of the audit results to allow the audit team to draw conclusions to provide a basis for its recommendations. The scope of this process can be understood through its three levels.

1. *How good are the results presently being achieved?* This question can range from a fairly narrow one, such as how well the compliance is over a particular procedure, to how efficiently a given operational activity is being carried out. This is the place to make a preliminary judgment on the overall performance of the operational activity under review.

2. *Why is the result what it is?* At the next higher level, and interwoven with the first evaluation, is the evaluation of why the results are as they are. Why is the performance as good or bad as it is? Why is it not better? This level involves causal factors and the extent to which those causal factors might have been more effectively controlled.

3. *What could be done better?* At the highest level, and again unavoidably interwoven with other levels of the evaluation, are the auditor judgments as to what could be done to achieve better results in the future. Can processes or procedures be made more effective? Should a particular policy be changed in some respect, or even abandoned? Are the correct people in place in the area reviewed and are they properly trained and administered?

Some of these conclusions may be reasonably clear and can become the basis for specific audit recommendations. In other cases, more information may be needed, or the

Figure 21.5 ExampleCo Analysis of Audit Results Workpaper Memo

Example Internal Audit

Audit: PRICEWHIZ Sales and Mktg. Sys. Location: _____ Central Date: XX/XX/20XX

PRICEWHIZ System Preliminary Findings Analysis

I. *End-of-Day Controls Out of Balance.* We found that end-of-day activity was not reconciled between the system log file and controls sent to the sales department for 3 out of 14 days of activity tested.

II. *Rejected Customer Credit Applications.* Orders that are rejected by the credit card verification service do not always receive a proper follow-up to check errors in the account number of the like. They are just filed with no follow-up.

III. *Account Balance.* Sales were regularly reconciled to the principal general ledger accounts.

IV. *System Backups.* The PRICEWHIZ system was not included in overall contingency planning procedures. In the event of a significant contingency event, the information systems department may not be able to recover key system files.

V. *Lack of System Utilization.* Although the system has been operational for several months, its advantages and features have not been promoted to the customer base. As a result, many customers continue to use older manual procedures.

VI. *Customer Credit Card Information Security.* Input reports listing all customer credit card information are regularly left, unsecured, on staff desks during nonbusiness hours. This could compromise customer credit and cause embarrassment to ExampleCo in the event of such a compromise.

recommendation may simply be that further study is needed. These determinations are, of course, highly dependent on the situation and the capability and credibility of internal audit.

The example described covers a new technology and a new process unfamiliar to the parent organization, and the above questions should be seriously considered. The challenge for internal audit is to understand the ExampleCo control environment and to develop appropriate tests to evaluate those controls. The overall description of controls described in Chapter 2 should help the internal auditor to develop appropriate control tests and come to the appropriate audit conclusions.

The reporting phase is the final step in an internal audit where what has been accomplished is summarized and made available to higher-level management and other interested parties. The content of audit reports will, of course, be determined directly by the extent of the completed action and whatever matters still require further consideration and possible action. (See Chapter 15 on the various ways in which reports can be developed.) This point is the major means by which internal audit relates to all interested organization personnel, especially to senior management.

(g) CONCLUDING THE OPERATIONAL AUDIT

There is now a range of possibilities as to what might be done in the way of completed action. At the one extreme, there may be no action and internal audit should proceed directly to the reporting phase. At the other extreme is the completion of the recommended action in the field while internal audit is still there. The real issue is the extent to which it is possible to move matters of audit concern to completion. In many cases the particular matter will clearly be something that should be handled immediately. This could be the correction of an error, or perhaps a more informed interpretation of a company policy. Other cases may be more controversial and require decision review at higher organizational levels. The important thing, however, is that all parties should be committed to the concept of maximum compliance with the mutually agreed audit findings and recommendations. The reasons for this approach reflect the truth that earlier response to audit recommendations accelerates the timing of the achievement of the expected benefits. A further important reason is that the partnership relationship of internal audit and responsible management is more effectively implemented. Internal audit and management should work more closely and agree together on what needs to be done. It can also be more realistically demonstrated that internal audit is there to *help* local management and not to police them.

During all phases of internal audit's work, there is always the continuing need for maximum effectiveness. Nothing internal audit does can ever be done in a routine or mechanical manner. Whether internal audit is examining documents, testing computerized records, talking with individuals, or observing various operational activities, the internal audit team should always be thinking of the underlying conditions pertaining to that part of the review. What is right? How responsible was the particular action carried out? How valid are the results? What else could be done? Internal audit should neither have a distorted belief that everything is wrong and that a major disaster is imminent, nor be naive optimists. In short, internal auditors should have an inquiring and challenging approach and a relatively greater need than an ordinary person to be convinced.

21-4 FUTURE DIRECTIONS FOR OPERATIONAL AUDITING

The major mission of internal audit is to assist the organization in achieving the most effective use of its resources. This mission is achieved primarily through the review of all types of internal control, and this internal control includes the narrower internal accounting controls that focus more directly on the effectiveness and efficiency of operations, reliable financial statements, and compliance with laws and regulation. Internal auditors must utilize their operational reviews as a means of achieving the full range of service to the organization.

Having the proper operational approach is a necessary basis for effective internal auditing. The major thrust of the operational approach of internal audit is to see the operations of the organization through the eyes of management, and to seek to appraise all operational situations as the responsible manager there would. In doing this, internal audit does not take the place of management or relieve individual managers of their own responsibilities; instead, internal audit provides the means by which management can have both the backup it desires and the basis for ongoing management determinations. This focus properly envelops and conditions the total internal auditing efforts. It is the hallmark of the operational approach of internal audit.

Historically, the narrower concept of internal accounting control has also always been part of internal audit's concern; increasingly, however, it plays a smaller part in the total internal auditing effort. This changing proportion was a natural result of the expanded operational auditing role in terms of both scope and management level. At the present time, the special concern for a more protective concept of internal control, as reinforced by the Committee of Sponsoring Organizations (COSO) internal control model and the Foreign Corrupt Practices Act, has reversed the aforementioned trend. In the light of the perceived needs of management, this is a needed and proper special concern by internal auditors for a better internal control environment. At the same time, it is important that special concerns do not limit internal audit's broader service role. Ideally, internal auditing responsibilities should be increased to take care of the needs for achieving sound internal controls with no diminution of broader management services. This is consistent with our own belief that the greater service potential of the higher-level contribution is achieved through modern operational auditing. Our continuing structure of the areas of operational auditing is also consistent with that view.

CHAPTER 22

Accounting Systems and Controls

22-1 INTRODUCTION: BASIC FINANCIAL CONTROLS

This chapter deals with the accounting systems and operations that normally are the responsibility of the controllers and accounting departments in a typical organization, and considers accounting systems in terms of the overall process or flow of accounting information. These include the processes for receiving funds through an accounts receivable system, paying obligations due through accounts payable, and recording the accounting results through general ledger systems.

An understanding of basic accounting systems controls is important for all internal auditors, whether financial, operational, or even information systems oriented. The operations of accounting systems controls are important to the overall organization, and senior management usually thinks in terms of their financial impact when a control weakness is identified by auditors. Internal audit always should present audit findings with at least a partial emphasis on their financial implications.

Some operational auditors tend to look upon financial control issues as only the responsibility of their external auditors. Internal auditors often see this as a key difference between themselves, who understand operational issues, and external auditors, who primarily involve themselves with financial statement attest issues. However, the separation of interests and responsibilities is not always that clear. Internal auditors should also understand the accounting process and basic accounting controls; similarly, the effective financial statement external auditor needs to have an understanding of the related operational issues.

Internal audit needs to understand the kinds of accounting controls that should ideally be in place in individual situations. Recognizing whether those controls are actually practicable, in terms of their costs and benefits, is then a question for auditors and management. The size of the organization or of an individual account may have a major impact upon the review and subsequent recommendations. For example, in a smaller organization, a single individual might carry out activities that would be performed normally by multiple persons to achieve proper separation-of-duties in a larger organization, or the volume of a particular activity may be so small that it is simply not practical to install additional controls to achieve an ideal set of control procedures. Management may accept the risk of having only just-adequate controls in an area due to its limited materiality. Understanding these compromises should help internal audit understand the proper application of control principles in individual situations. This philosophy will be considered in this and the following operational auditing chapters.

(a) ACCOUNTING SYSTEMS TRANSACTION CYCLES

The modern organization is typically involved with different systems and transactions for its various operations. While some of these have unique features, most can be tied to basic accounting cycles involved with investing in equipment, purchasing goods or services, selling those goods, collecting and managing cash from the sales, and making payments for the goods and services, including payroll. Auditors often call these processes *transaction cycles.*

A transaction cycle approach has been used for some time by external auditors and financially oriented internal auditors to allow them to better understand the accounting processes. The same concept is also useful for the operationally oriented internal auditor. Internal auditors can identify the internal control issues surrounding each transaction cycle and then design appropriate audit procedures. The major accounting management cycles covered in this chapter as well as the operational auditing chapters following, are defined as:

- Cash Collection and Disbursement Cycles. This process covers the collection of cash, maintaining it in bank accounts, and making disbursements from those cash accounts.
- Sales and Accounts Receivable Cycles. An organization typically sells its goods or services and then sets up an accounts receivables account for future collection.
- Purchasing and Accounts Payable Cycles. Before an organization can sell its goods or services, it must first purchase the necessary items and subsequently pay for them. These actions form another overall transaction cycle.
- Payroll and Personnel Cycles. Although a variation of the accounts payable process, most organizations treat payroll as a separate transaction cycle because of its size and its unique and important aspects.
- Manufacturing and Inventory Cycles. An organization must typically go through a series of intermediate steps to add value to a product and then to prepare it prior to its final sale or disposition. Although this cycle can go by different names depending upon the nature of the business, the transactions here allocate various costs to the completed products.

An internal auditor will find it useful to think of the various accounting and business transactions encountered in the course of an audit in terms of the cycle in which they fit. This will help internal audit to better understand the process and to design appropriate tests for evaluating the internal controls surrounding those transactions.

22-2 GENERAL LEDGERS

An organization must have a place to record its various accounting transactions to allow it to summarize them and to determine if there was a profit or a loss. Using terms dating back to the very early days of business, these transactions were recorded in various special-

Figure 22.1   Double-Entry Bookkeeping Example

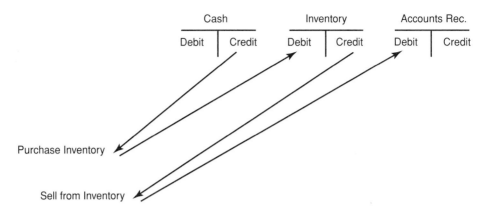

ized *journals* covering detailed purchases, receipts, and other business transactions. At the end of an accounting period, these journals were summarized and then transcribed to a *general ledger* that contained all transactions, summarized and classified to provide an overall view of results. Although the huge paper books and the quill pens once used to create these journals are long gone, business still uses these same terms. The general ledger is the basic accounting record of an organization. Transactions, either detailed or summarized, from all other accounting systems, will typically flow into the general ledger to report accounting results.

General ledgers are built around the basic double-entry accounting principles of self-balancing debits and credits. Every entry must be offset by one or more others. For example, the sale of a good requires the organization to credit the sales account and to debit the cash account for the amount of the sale. Figure 22.1 shows a simple example of double-entry bookkeeping. The general ledger is used to summarize all significant accounting transactions that should be properly authorized, accurately recorded, accumulated, and summarized.

(a) DESCRIPTION OF A GENERAL LEDGER

Although usually automated, general ledger systems typically require numerous account adjustments to allow for the many small differences and corrections necessary in any accounting system. In a larger organization, the general ledger is often the responsibility of what is called a general accounting department.

In order to understand a general ledger system and its account classifications, an internal auditor needs to understand the overall business where the general ledger is used, the accounting systems supporting that business, the controls in place to ensure the proper classification of accounting transactions, and the various administrative controls that support general ledger operations.

The following sections discuss the various accounting systems that often support a general ledger, the concepts of a chart of accounts, and the administrative operation of a general accounting function. Although the discussion is limited to general ledgers, these concepts are applicable to the subsidiary ledgers that support other accounting functions in the organization and the general ledger.

(i) Understanding the Accounting Systems.   As mentioned previously, older accounting systems used numerous sets of manually prepared subsidiary journals to record transactions for various specialized areas. Over the years, these subsidiary ledgers have been automated, starting with punched-card systems where accounting transactions were keypunched into either 80-column IBM cards or 90-column Hollerith cards. These cards could then be sorted, merged, and listed. In the early 1960s, punched-card, unit record systems represented automation for many organizations. Today, punched-card systems have disappeared and computerized accounting systems are common whether an organization is very large or small.

Whether automated or manual, the concept of subsidiary journals or ledgers feeding the general ledger remains unchanged. The major difference is the degree of automation. Early systems were primarily manual. Systems today are often highly automated, with little manual intervention required. However, often there are still some accounting processes that have not been automated due to low volumes of transactions or just a lack of management attention.

Internal audit should develop a general understanding of the various accounting systems used by the auditor's organization. This can often be accomplished by interviewing members of the accounting department and asking general questions about the types of accounting systems installed and how they relate to one another. In a manufacturing organization, for example, internal audit might ask questions such as:

- What type of system is used to record the costs of materials used in production?
- What accounting systems are used to record raw materials, semifinished goods, and completed products?
- How are the labor hours spent on this production work captured and recorded?
- What accounting systems are used to capture total production costs?
- How does the production accounting system interface with the general ledger?

The above questions cover only a limited portion of a typical production cycle. The idea, however, is to ask a series of questions that will give internal audit an understanding of significant automated and manual systems used for major organization accounting processes. These should then be documented in the form of a very general, top-level flowchart that shows the various transaction flows and system interrelationships. This type of chart will help internal audit to understand the major accounting systems used by the organization and also help to plan other audit tests and procedures.

Figure 22.2 shows a high-level accounting transaction flowchart for a manufacturing organization. The chart does not have much detail and illustrates accounting transaction flows and the information systems interrelationships. The flowchart should be prepared following the same general guidelines discussed in Chapter 11. Once these flowcharts have been completed, internal audit should discuss them with knowledgeable persons in the organization to solicit any corrections.

(ii) Chart of Accounts.   In support of its general ledger and subsidiary accounting systems, an organization needs a means of recording its transactions following a consistent

Figure 22.2 Accounting Transactions Flowchart

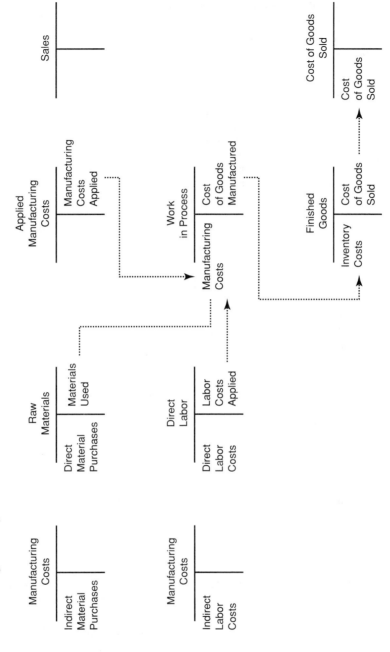

Figure 22.3 Simplified Chart of Accounts Example

Account No.	Account Description	Subsidiary Ledger
101-000	Cash	—
111-000	Notes and Interest Receivable	Notes Receivable File
112-000	Accounts Receivable	Customer Ledger
121-000	Merchandise Inventories	Stock Records
151-000	Prepaid Insurance	Insurance Policy File
152-000	Prepaid Property Taxes	—
161-000	Buildings and Equipment	Plant Records
161-500	Depreciation to Date	"
171-000	Land	—
201-000	Accounts Payable	Purchase Voucher File
211-000	Accrued Payroll	Employee Pay Records
212-000	Income Tax Withholdings	"
213-000	FICA Tax Payable	"
214-000	Unemployment Tax Payable	"
221-000	Other Taxes Payable	"
231-000	Notes and Interest Payable	Notes Payable File
231-000	Dividends Payable	Stockholder Records
235-000	Mortgages	Real Estate Files
301-000	Capital Stock	Stockholder Records
340-000	Retained Earnings	—

classification or numbering system. It would be very ineffective to use just verbal descriptions for all accounting transactions, recording them under titles such as "Purchased Goods from Supplier A" or "Labor Costs for Product B." However, account activity cannot be easily summarized or classified using such verbal descriptions. Similarly, any account numbering or coding system must have some rules. Arbitrary or just sequential account numbers would be of little value.

Organizations normally classify all of their accounting transactions into some type of consistent numbering scheme that is called a *chart of accounts*. Under a chart of accounts scheme, all fixed-asset transactions might have one identifying number, all revenue-related transactions another, and so on. Organizations typically have a published set of procedures listing their chart of accounts. An auditor should obtain this list and reaffirm an understanding of it through discussions with accounting personnel. Figure 22.3 is an example of a simplified chart of accounts scheme.

Accounting charts of accounts can be complex documents with many different accounts and subaccounts. They may form the basis of a language that some accounting personnel may use in their course of business. An organization's accounting staff, for example, may refer to a "152 transaction" as if everyone understands what they are talking about. An internal auditor generally does not need to develop that detailed an understanding of the chart of accounts, but it is useful to have a general understanding of how the various accounts are numbered and classified. This will aid in the auditor's overall understanding of accounting systems and controls.

(iii) General Ledger Accounting Department Operations. An organization's general ledger provides the basis for the monthly, upper management level financial statements as well as the overall financial records of the organization. The reports derived from the general ledger form determine if the organization was profitable during a period and provides data for the financial statements, including the balance sheet, the income statement, and summary of cash flows. Maintenance of the general ledger, often the responsibility of what is called the general accounting department or just the accounting department, normally reports to an organization controller.

Depending upon the organization's size and business functions, the accounting department may be divided into several sections, with responsibilities for such areas as general accounting, cost accounting, and fixed-asset or property accounting. Figure 22.4 shows a typical accounting department in a larger organization. In addition to general accounting (with responsibility for the general ledger) and cost accounting (with responsibility to allocate costs to various entities), the example chart has a consolidations group responsible for gathering information from various subsidiaries, a property accounting group, and a budgeting group.

General accounting normally has four broad responsibilities.

1. *Accumulating Accounting Transactions.* All accounting transactions that flow into and support the general ledger must be properly accumulated, classified, and summarized into their proper accounts. In a highly integrated automated environment, accounting personnel will place reliance on supporting systems to supply this information and should understand the controls over the systems that supply this data. When accounting procedures are not as automated, the general accounting function is responsible for reviewing these transactions for their appropriateness.

2. *Properly Consolidating Accounting Transactions.* The modern organization today typically has a large number of separate units with various accounting-related interrelationships. For example, Division A of an organization may manufacture some part that it sells to Division B. At the time it makes the shipment, it sets up an accounts receivable account for the monies due from Division B, which may have received the goods but not issued a check. Division B has an accounts payables account on its books for the same amount. Even though these transactions are proper for each of the divisions, they cancel each other out or can be eliminated when viewing the organization as a whole. Since it has an organization-wide overview, the general accounting function has the responsibility of consolidating these transactions to create a consistent set of accounts.

3. *Placing Appropriate Controls Over Closings.* An organization usually operates on an accounting calendar of monthly or scheduled periodic closings, where all transactions for that period must be properly recorded. This is also a time period when various members of the organization could improperly defer or adjust an accounting transaction to improve period ending results. For example, the paperwork for an incoming shipment of goods could be held for just a day or two at month end. This way, it would not be added as inventory or recorded as an account payable. The general accounting function has the responsibility to determine that all closing entries are recorded in proper time periods, are initiated only by responsible personnel, and are reviewed and approved by authorized personnel.

4. *Properly Preparing Accounting Reports.* The general accounting function has the

Figure 22.4 Typical Accounting Department Organization

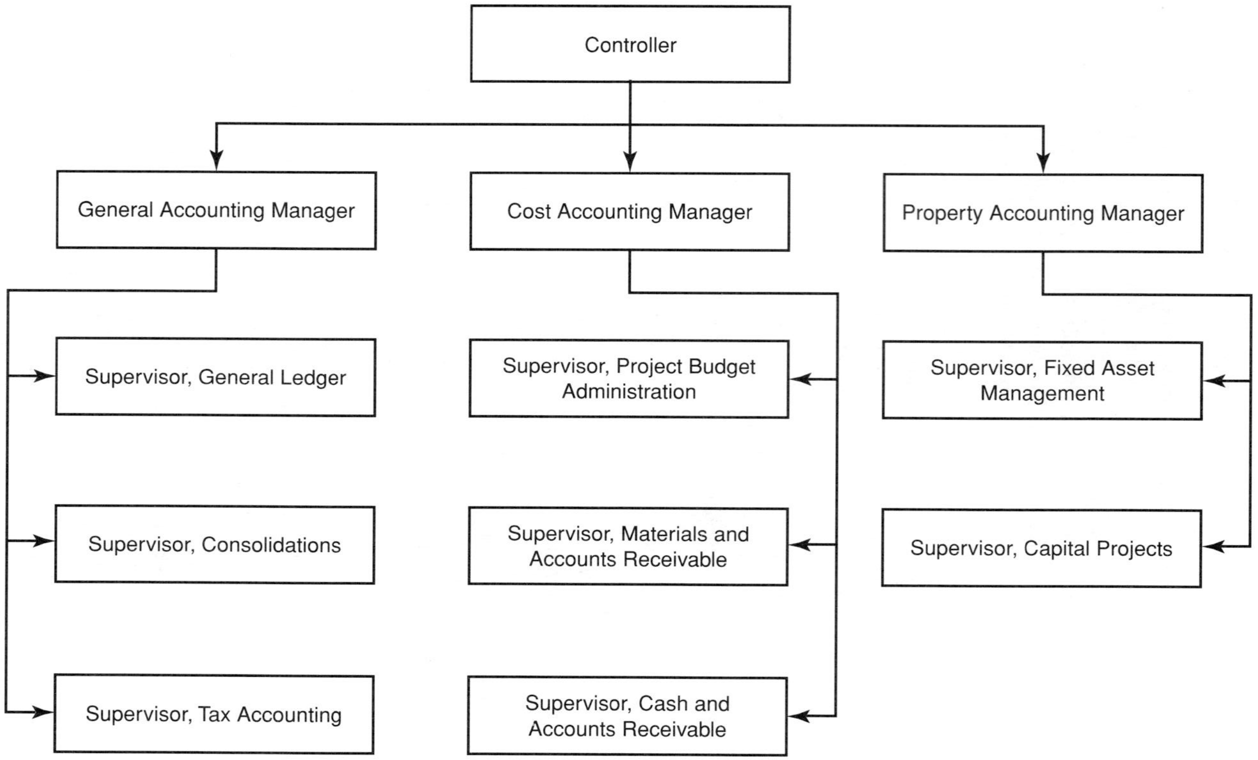

responsibility for preparing periodic financial reports based upon general ledger accounting data. They should review and approve these preliminary reports with an emphasis on determining that there is appropriate supporting documentation and approvals before report issuance.

Depending upon the nature of the organization, general accounting may be subject to various other regulations and restrictions. For example, a publicly traded organization will be subject to financial reporting requirements, a multinational organization to several different international accounting standards, and a financial institution to various regulatory requirements. The accounting transactions processed through the general ledger as well as the various financial reports produced by the department will vary depending upon these constraints. Although some of these requirements may be very specialized, an internal auditor should be aware of any such unique conditions.

The general accounting department is purely an accounting function, and some operational auditors may not bring that high of a level of accounting expertise to their jobs. Even if they are primarily operational auditors with skills in areas such as manufacturing procedures or information systems controls, they can make a strong contribution by reviewing general accounting function internal controls (as described here) or accounts payable or receivable controls (as discussed later in this chapter).

(b) GENERAL ACCOUNTING INTERNAL CONTROLS

Clearly presented and accurate financial statements are important for all types of organizations, whether publicly held businesses, private entities, or not-for-profit entities. When an organization has issued stock or other securities, stockholders as well as other investors use these financial statements to help make their investment decisions. A private organization must release financial statements to a lending institution to obtain financing. The not-for-profit entity is often required to submit financial statements to various regulatory or oversight groups. For all types of organizations, management has a need for accurate and representative financial statements to assess operations. Finally, these financial statements are used to prepare necessary tax returns.

Independent outside auditors are typically the only persons who review these financial statements to attest that they are fairly stated and represent the organization's financial condition at the time they were prepared. Although reviews of financial statements are the responsibility of external auditors, internal auditors also should have an understanding of the components of the organization's financial statements, the general ledger that supports it, and the general accounting organization's internal controls as well. There are two reasons for this internal audit involvement. First, the internal controls here are a key part of the organization's overall system of internal controls, and internal audit has a responsibility to assess them and report any control weaknesses to management. Second, internal auditors are often asked to assist external financial auditors in their preparation of financial statements, as will be discussed in Chapter 32. The internal auditor's understanding of general accounting internal controls can very much assist this process.

A general accounting function is typically a group responsible for assembling financial transactions from other sources, classifying them into proper accounts, making adjustments as considered necessary, and then publishing the completed financial statements. Chapter 2 discussed internal control fundamentals, referencing both standards of The Institute of Internal Auditors and relevant AICPA Statements on Auditing Standards

(SASs). These concepts should help any internal auditor who is attempting to gain an understanding of the internal controls over a general accounting function. In particular, an internal auditor should gain an understanding of the significant transaction types and the controls in place to insure that they are properly recorded.

Although it has been significantly amended by SAS No. 78 and others, the AICPA's original SAS No. 1[1] provides a good set of control objectives for an internal auditor reviewing internal accounting controls in a general accounting department. The SAS sets control objectives in terms of authorization for executing transactions, recording of transactions, access to assets, and asset accountability. Each will be discussed in the paragraphs following. These internal control objectives are generally applicable for other accounting areas, such as cash or accounts receivable, as will be discussed in sections following.

- *Authorization.* Transactions should be executed in accordance with management's general or specific authorization. The organization should have clearly stated procedures or organization structures that define who can or cannot execute various classes of transactions. At each higher level in the organization, employees should be granted a greater level of transaction authority along with responsibility for approving the transactions executed by their subordinates.

- *Recording of Transactions.* Transactions should be recorded as necessary to permit the proper preparation of financial statements and to maintain an accountability for assets. The key control element here is that the transactions should be recorded in accordance with what are called generally accepted accounting principles (GAAPs), as discussed below.

- *Access to Assets.* Access to assets should be permitted only in accordance with management's authorization. In an accounting organization, these assets may be negotiable instruments such as stock certificates or accounting transactions that can alter file balances or the like.

- *Asset Accountability.* Financial records should be compared with existing assets and liabilities at reasonable intervals, with appropriate action taken to resolve any differences. The taking of physical inventories is a good example of this type of comparison.

The above internal accounting control objectives reference GAAPs. There is no single published definition of all GAAP accounting treatments. Rather, GAAP refers to the "standard" accounting treatment for a given set of debit and credit transactions. For example, a manufacturing organization would enter the following transaction to transfer the cost of inventories used to product expense.

Cost of Goods Sold	$xxx,xxx.xx
Merchandise Inventory	$xxx,xxx.xx

This is GAAP treatment for this transaction. Moving the cost of merchandise inventory to the cost of goods sold account allows these costs to properly reduce income from sales and correctly state profit. Taking the costs out of inventory and moving them to

---

[1] American Institute of Certified Public Accountants, Statement on Auditing Standards No. 1.

some other account would not be consistent with GAAP unless there is some normally accepted special treatment due to some unique industry requirement. Many of these exceptions to GAAP are defined in special industry audit guides published by the AICPA.

(i) Segregation-of-Duties Internal Accounting Controls. One of the most important principles of internal accounting control is that duties should be assigned to individuals in such a way that no one individual can control all phases of the processing of a transaction. This means that, ideally, the flow of activities should be designed so that the work of one individual is either independent of or serves as a check on the work of another. Otherwise, errors of omission or commission may go undetected. For example, shipping and billing functions should be performed by separate individuals. If one individual controls both functions, an unauthorized shipment of goods could be concealed by circumventing the usual billing procedures.

It would not normally be desirable for a senior member of marketing management to be responsible for credit authorizations. In smaller organizations, however, it is often not practical to segregate all duties due to limited staff resources. In these situations, the involvement of senior management in monitoring these transactions is essential.

Internal audit should always recognize that the implementation of segregation-of-duties controls needs to be tempered by considering such characteristics as the volume, the complexity, and the significance of the different types of transactions processed, as well as the steps required to process them. These characteristics will vary from one organization to another. Because of the cost of implementing appropriate segregation-of-duties controls, an organization may accept the risks of combining various responsibilities and functions. Internal audit should always consider these costs and management concerns when making segregation-of-duties recommendations.

(ii) Transaction-Based Procedural Controls. Procedural controls include management-approved documentation explaining various systems and processes, printed forms and other documents, and supporting information systems. They are a key element in an organization's internal control structure. However, the significant variations in the physical form, design, information content, automated system complexity, and flow of documents complicates the auditor's evaluation of the adequacy of these procedural controls. No one procedure is necessarily more appropriate than another in all given situations.

An organization should have established procedural control techniques that give assurance over matters such as that all customers have been correctly billed for the quantities shipped. This type of control will vary with the organization's size and processing systems. In some organizations, for example, all incoming sales orders are still transcribed onto prenumbered, multicopy forms that are used to authorize shipping, inventory, and billing activities. Other organizations will have automated this process, eliminating the paper documents. These paper or automated documents would be assembled later to represent a complete cycle of this shipping and billing activity. General accounting should understand the control processes that feed data to them and also have their own control procedures processes in place to review and assemble this data to form the organization's financial statements. The role of the general accounting department will be essentially the same no matter whether automated or manual procedures are used.

(c) GENERAL LEDGER INTERNAL AUDIT ACTIVITIES

Whether performing financial, operational, or information systems audit procedures, or a combination thereof, the organization responsible for the general ledger is typically a critical unit that should be included in internal audit's plans, subject to audit risk assessments. All too often, the general accounting area is ignored by internal auditors because they do not view it as a direct element of operations. However, the general accounting group is important as an element in the system of internal controls. In many organizations, general accounting is responsible for reviewing and assembling the final, periodic financial statements. Internal audit should not just defer the audit responsibility here to their external auditors but should consider taking an active role in reviewing and testing appropriate controls.

(i) General Ledger–Related Financial Audit Concerns. One of the broad objectives of internal accounting control in this area is to insure that transactions are recorded in conformity with generally accepted accounting principles. This objective goes beyond just the physical recording of accounting systems in manual or automated formats and includes the management process for making estimates and other decisions related to the final preparation of financial statements. This is the broad area where external auditors often have a primary role supported by internal audit. However, internal audit needs to consider reviews of general ledger–related financial controls as well.

When internal audit provides support to external auditors in reviewing general ledger–related controls, the external auditors should provide them with some guidance in terms of what types of accounts to analyze, what types of tests to perform, and the like. This same guidance may be useful to internal audit even when it is not working in support of external auditors. Internal audit also may be asked by management to perform financial audit procedures independent of the period-end financial audit or to review financial controls in some smaller unit either acquired recently or not included in the external auditor's plan.

A financially oriented audit of a general ledger function requires some basic steps that will be repeated for other financial audit procedures discussed later in this chapter and in the others following. This is a six-step process, outlined in Figure 22.5, that starts with internal audit gaining an understanding of the accounts and systems, follows with an understanding of where financial statement errors might occur, and continues through the performance of appropriate tests to evaluate controls. The concept here is that internal audit should develop a good understanding of the organization's chart of accounts, its accounting processes, and how financial statements are derived through those accounts.

Many general accounting adjustments are necessary to fairly present the financial statements. One unit of an organization might end the accounting period with an accounts receivable on its books that is equal to an accounts payable on another unit's records. A general accounting department would make what are called "eliminating entries" to cancel out the two accounts. Another example here is what are called "reserve accounts." Management often anticipates certain contingencies, such as the obsolescence of certain inventories or the failure to collect on some accounts receivable, and to shield against these contingencies, monies are allocated to a reserve account that can be adjusted as conditions warrant. These types of accounts often can be subject to improper manipulation, and funds used for unauthorized or incorrect purposes.

Each organization, depending upon its business and industry, will have a different chart of accounts and a different set of accounting transactions. Internal audit should gain a basic understanding of these various accounts and transactions. Figure 22.6 lists some potentially significant general ledger accounts and their related audit concerns that might be found in a typical manufacturing organization. Internal audit should compile a similar

Figure 22.5 Financial Audit Procedures

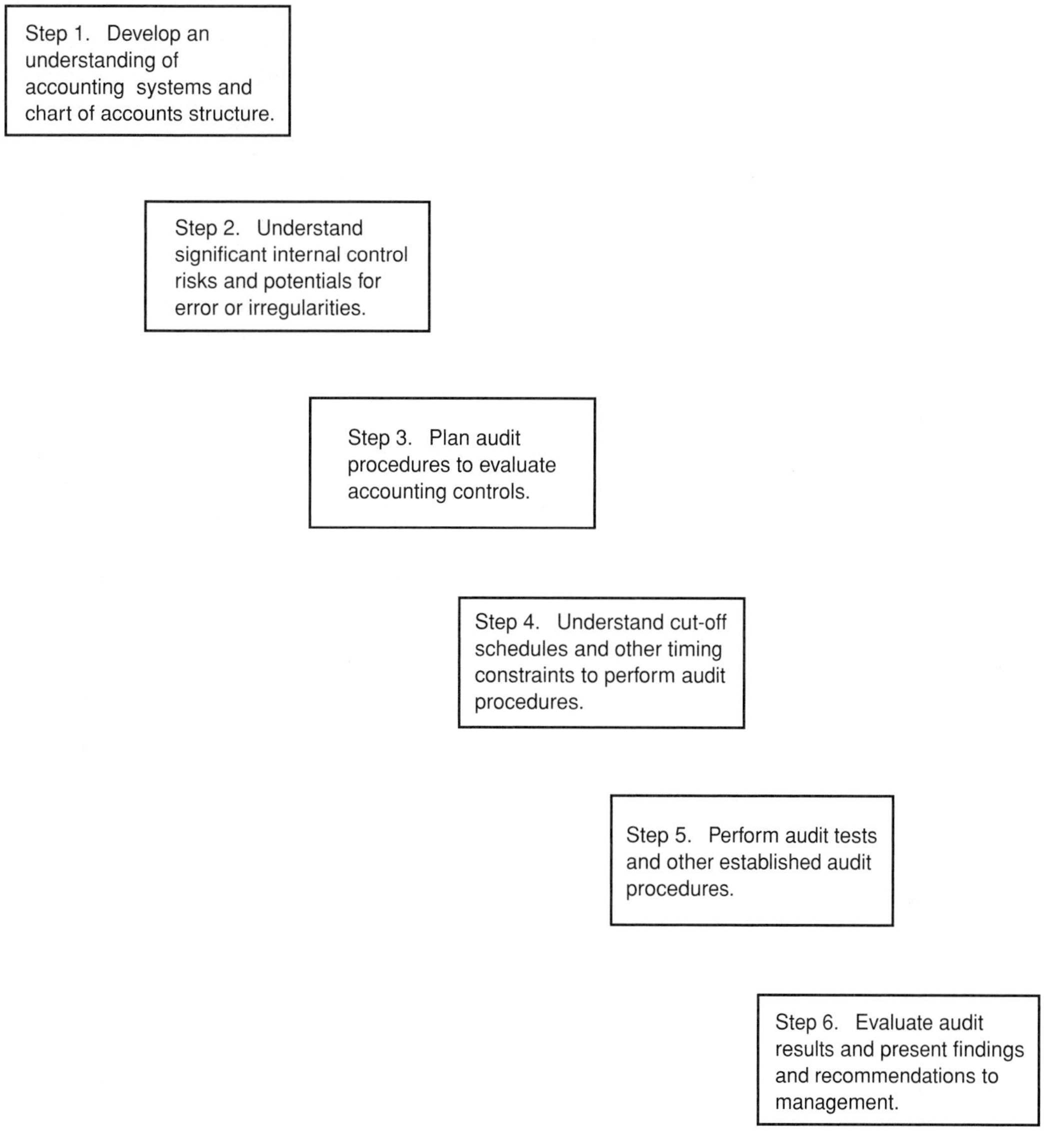

Step 1. Develop an
understanding of
accounting systems and
chart of accounts structure.

Step 2. Understand
significant internal control
risks and potentials for
error or irregularities.

Step 3. Plan audit
procedures to evaluate
accounting controls.

Step 4. Understand cut-off
schedules and other timing
constraints to perform audit
procedures.

Step 5. Perform audit tests
and other established audit
procedures.

Step 6. Evaluate audit
results and present findings
and recommendations to
management.

list for the auditor's organization and consider the risks and controls surrounding these accounts.

The next step, performing appropriate tests to evaluate whether the various accounts in the general ledger are fairly stated and are in accordance with generally accepted accounting principles, is the key procedure performed by external auditors. Internal auditors should understand this process either to support their external auditors or to perform similar reviews of other units. Figure 22.7 describes some example audit procedures for a financial audit of an organization's general ledger asset accounts. For more information on the

Figure 22.6 Significant General Ledger Accounting Concerns

Accruals—These accounts are used to recognize revenue before the related cash receipt or to recognize expenses before the actual cash payments. This requires a series of general ledger closing entries to close the books prior to the completion of these transactions.

Prior period adjustments—The correction of an error in the financial statements of a prior period or adjustments acquisition related realization of income could result in a prior period adjustment.

Foreign currency transactions—Accounting standards require adjustments to the U.S. values of various foreign currency based transactions. General ledger accounts should be in place to adjust for these mandated adjustments.

Capital accounts—These stock or ownership related accounts should be adjusted to reflect such transactions as the issuance of options or securities buy-back or other securities transactions.

Cutoff controls—Transactions that were properly dated several days before or after the cutoff dates of the general ledger should be recorded in the correct month.

Reconciliation procedure—A general ledger is derived from and relates to a series of subsidiary ledgers, such as those for production costs and for sales. Procedures should be in place to periodically reconcile these ledgers and to identify and correct any potential timing problems.

Figure 22.7 General Ledger Accounts Receivable Audit Procedures

General Objectives for Asset Accounts	Accts. Receivable Audit Objectives	Example Audit Procedures
1. Existence of assets	Determine that recorded receivables exist.	Confirm a sample of receivables by direct communication with debtors.
2. Rights to assets	Determine that the organization has the rights to these receivables.	Vouch a sample of recorded receivables to supporting sales agreements.
3. Completeness of assets	All receivables should be recorded.	Compare a sample of shipping documents with related sales agreements.
4. Clerical accuracy of asset records	General ledger records should agree with receivable records.	Reconcile ledger to aged trial balance from receivables accounts, testing clerical accuracy.
5. Valuation of assets.	Receivables should be presented at their net realizable value.	Investigate credit rating for delinquent and large balance-due accounts.
6. Financial statement presentation of assets	Receivables should be presented with proper disclosures.	Perform procedures to identify any receivables from related parties.

different types of audit procedures, internal audit should consult the type of financial auditing textbooks used for preparation for the CPA examination.

(ii) General Accounting Function Operational Audits. Although the general accounting function generally receives considerable attention from external auditors, there are many operational audit aspects surrounding this type of accounting organization. In particular, unless there are strong operational controls in place over the authorization and recording of financial transactions to the general ledger, the integrity of those financial statements may be at risk. Although external auditors often have strong skills in analyzing the various accounts in the general ledger, the operationally oriented internal auditor can provide significant support to both management and the external auditors by reviewing operational controls in the general ledger area.

As a guide to appropriate types of operational audit steps, the AICPA published an audit guide for their SAS No. 55 auditing standard[2], which defined the control procedures internal audit should consider when reviewing the controls over the preparations of financial statements. Although SAS No. 55 has been superseded by SAS No. 78, the control procedures outlined in this guide cover important areas pertaining to:

- The proper authorization of transactions and activities.
- Segregation of duties to reduce opportunities for any person to perpetrate or conceal errors or irregularities in the normal course of his or her duties. This involves assigning different people the responsibilities of authorizing transactions, recording transactions, and maintaining custody of assets.
- The design and use of adequate documents and records to help ensure proper recording of transactions and events, such as monitoring the use of prenumbered shipping documents.
- Adequate safeguards over access to and use of assets and records, such as secured facilities and computer programs and data files.
- Independent checks on performance and the proper valuation of recorded amounts, such as clerical checks, reconciliations, comparisons of assets with recorded accountability, computer-programmed controls, management review of reports that summarize account balance details, and the user review of computer-generated reports.

Although not part of current auditing standards, the above control procedures were defined by the AICPA to provide guidance for a wide range of financial accounting areas, and they will be used here and in other chapters of this book. They provide particularly useful guidance for operational reviews of a general accounting function by internal audit. More specific audit steps for operational reviews in this area are summarized in Figure 22.8. These operational audit steps are tailored for a review of a general accounting function, but can be adapted by internal audit for reviews of many other accounting areas.

(iii) General Accounting Computer Audit Procedures. There was once a time when an organization's general ledger was maintained on manual accounting books. Today

---

[2] *American Institute of Certified Public Accountants, Consideration of the Internal Control Structure in a Financial Statement* (New York: American Institute of Certified Public Accountants, 1990).

Figure 22.8 General Ledger Operational Audit Procedures

Audit _____ Location _____ Date _____

Audit Step	Initial	W/P
1. Review of nature and sources of transactions to the G/L system. If automated systems, determine if controls have been reviewed.		
2. Review procedures in place for manual transactions to the G/L system, including levels of authority to make significant financial transactions.		
3. Determine that there are appropriate segregations of responsibility between those authorized to adjust G/L accounts and those reconciling account balances.		
4. Review procedures for establishing new accounts or deleting accounts from the G/L system and determine that there is a proper level of supervision.		
5. Assess the adequacy of G/L systems processing control and balancing procedures. Select one cycle and determine that all errors have been cleared.		
6. Select several G/L system error reports from prior periods and determine that all errors have been corrected.		
7. Select a sample of G/L accounts that have been adjusted and reconciled prior to an accounting period-end. Evaluate reconciliation procedures, including the level of justification and documentation for adjustments.		
8. Review information systems password and security procedures for the G/L system. Determine whether the system has been given proper levels of protection.		

these manual systems have all but vanished, replaced by automated general ledger systems ranging from local microcomputers to large, mainframe-based applications. In order to perform either financial or operational audit procedures in this general ledger systems area, internal audit must have an understanding of the computer systems controls surrounding that general ledger application. A review of the general ledger system controls should be scheduled by internal audit.

An automated general ledger system is often not a complex, highly sophisticated data-processing application. Rather, it is only a repository of summarized accounting data from other systems, such as the payroll or accounts receivable systems. The internal auditor's emphasis in this type of automated review should be on input controls over transactions from other systems and logical security controls to detect and prevent unauthorized data manipulation. Because general ledger files are the repositories of many accounting transactions, internal audit may want to consider implementing computer-assisted audit techniques (CAATs) to better analyze file data and to support the organization's financial statements.

Account analysis retrieval software analyzing the general ledger system data are usually available from the general ledger software vendor, if a purchased package. If not, the information systems organization will often have some other type of a "report generator" package. An internal auditor should become familiar with the retrieval routine in order to support various financial-related audits that use general ledger file data.

(iv) Sample General Ledger Audit Report Findings

A: Improper Access to Critical General Ledger Accounts. We reviewed the input access rules covering the entry of transactions to general ledger files and found that a wide range of users, including members of the branch sales organization, have the ability to enter all types of transactions. That is, in addition to entering transactions that are the responsibility of their own organization, such as sales or related expense, these users can enter transactions that impact other balance sheet or income statement accounts. Although it is the responsibility of personnel in the general ledger organization to review these transactions, key transactions could be missed due to the large volume of general ledger transactions. Improper accounting transactions could distort financial statement results.

Recommendation. Controls should be established to limit general ledger access to only those persons authorized to enter transactions to specified accounts. Consideration should be given to improving logical security controls to associate each authorized user with only the accounts they are responsible for.

B: General Ledger File Retentions Need Improvement. We reviewed procedures for backing up and retaining previous versions of general ledger files. We found that general ledger files are maintained in three generations of backup files with the oldest version located in an off-site location. This procedure is appropriate for many automated systems, but we feel that better file retention procedures are needed given the historical nature of general ledger system files. Lacking a proper set of supporting backup files, the general ledger accounting organization may be unable to reconstruct transactions initiated months ago.

Recommendation. An extended backup file retention program should be established for critical general ledger system files. The three-generation procedure currently used is appropriate for the current three months, but consideration should be given to retaining key files quarterly for a period of one year with year-ending files retained for seven years. These files should be retained in the organization's off-site storage location. Procedures should also be implemented to insure that these older files remain readable given any potential future technology changes.

22-3 CASH PROCESSES

From an accounting control standpoint, cash is of special interest and concern because, in its most basic form, it is the most transferable and vulnerable of assets. Because of the risks involved here, there is always a strong need for the protection and control of cash-based assets. As technology and other processes eliminate the need to carry actual currency, there should be a continuing objective to minimize control exposures by eliminating the use of actual cash to the extent practicable.

Cash means different things to different organizations. A small retail store, for example, often sells most of its goods to outside customers for actual cash. It maintains a balance of cash to provide change for customers but otherwise deposits its cash sales in a bank account to pay for merchandise and other expenses. With the exception of bills due that are paid later, such as for rent or utilities, this type of business is operating almost entirely on a cash basis.

As organizations grow larger, their direct use of cash usually decreases. The larger version of the above-mentioned retail store may make many of its sales through the use of store-issued and bank credit cards. Although otherwise treated as cash sales, these charges are receivables due per the larger store's accounting records.

In larger organizations, virtually all business transactions are based on recorded receivables and payables, rather than through the actual handling of cash. What the larger organization considers to be cash is represented by transaction balances in their various financial accounts. Only very special legitimate business—such as a bank accepting retail customer cash deposits, or a state government lottery authority—deals in substantial amounts of cash. However, most businesses have only limited cash processes to handle the relatively small amounts of cash needed for normal business purposes, such as petty cash funds where small amounts of cash are maintained at various locations to cover various small cash payments.

Cash, of course, is essential to pay for expenses such as the payroll and other business costs (such as taxes). A publicly held corporation needs cash to pay for dividends on its stock, and banks and lending agencies will require certain levels of cash balances. Because cash in the bank has such a strong relationship with other transaction cycles such as receivables or payables, an internal auditor should have a good understanding of cash-related internal controls and processes.

(a) ACCOUNTING CONTROLS

A discussion of cash processes starts most logically with an identification of where and why cash is handled in particular organization situations. Often, this identification may lead to questions of whether a cash process is necessary or if it might be handled differently. For example, is it really necessary that a salesperson accept cash from customers or that some account collections are in cash? While cash might be best in terms of accelerating and maximizing collections, different procedures can often eliminate the handling of cash and the risk of its improper diversion. Any activities involving cash should be critically appraised to determine if control compromises are justified because of other operational considerations.

Internal audit should develop an understanding of the type and nature of the organization's cash accounts that often require special control considerations. As a matter of clarification, this cash is usually not maintained in the form of currency but as an account recording cash transactions. For many organizations, cash is maintained in five basic account types, as follows.

1. *General Cash Account.* This is the central bank account through which most receipts from sales and collections pass, as well as disbursements for purchases and expenses. Even though an organization may have a variety of specialized cash accounts, all deposits and disbursements would normally be made through this central, general account, with cash notification transactions directed to other systems.

2. *Branch Cash Accounts.* Organizations with multiple locations will typically have separate accounts at each of their outside locations. These accounts will have the same attributes as the general account but will serve local or branch operations.

3. *Imprest Payroll Accounts.* Payroll represents the major cash expense for many organizations. Aside from a minimal balance maintained in this account, at the start of each payroll period the organization would prepare a check from its general account to transfer the total amount of the payroll to the imprest payroll account. This improves controls and reduces the time necessary to reconcile payroll account balances.

4. *Imprest Petty Cash Funds.* These are normally not bank accounts but fixed amounts of cash placed under the control of various persons in the organization for special cash transactions. For example, an administrative assistant may retain a small amount of cash to dispense for such things as rolls and coffee for meetings. Petty cash funds are often relatively small, and the person in charge replenishes them by submitting receipts to cover the cash amounts disbursed.

5. *Savings Accounts.* Organizations typically place certain funds not needed for day-to-day operations in longer-term cash or cash equivalent accounts. These accounts earn interest but tie up the deposited money for limited amounts of time. For example, an organization can place monies in United States Treasury Bills that have a 90-day maturity and earn interest over that period, or they can buy what is called commercial paper, which pays interest based upon periods as short as overnight. These deposits are considered to be the same as cash because they can be easily sold with no market risk.

Cash for various purposes is usually maintained in accounts under one of the above five general categories. Cash passes through these accounts through the process of cash receipts, intermediary cash handling, and custody activities, and leaves through the process of cash disbursements. Internal audit should have a good understanding of the controls associated with each of these general cash-handling areas.

(i) Receiving of Cash. Cash receipts may be in the form of checks mailed as payments from billings, receipts from cash sales, or various types of bank transfers. This cash is captured and deposited early in the cash receipts processing cycle, and thereafter moves internally toward centralized cash controls normally exercised by the organization. A key point to consider here is that cash always has a time value. Customer checks as payments of bills should always be deposited as soon as possible. Even if they are not deposited in interest-bearing accounts, organizations may have agreed to maintain certain average daily levels of balances and should deposit cash in those accounts as soon as practicable.

Cash represents a major control risk to an organization. It can be improperly diverted, and once diverted it is often difficult to trace because the cash itself is not separately identifiable. Thus, an organization must establish strong controls over its overall cash processes, focusing both on organization outsiders, to be sure that the cash received is what should be received, and on insiders, to be sure that cash received is not improperly diverted. The sooner controls can be established over cash received, the better. Some form of receipt, such as a serially numbered document with one copy to the outside party or the entry of the transaction on a cash register with a serially numbered ticket of some kind, should be issued for the cash received.

Ideally, any receipt of the cash should be linked to the relief of a previously existing account, such as the collection of an accounts receivable with a debit to cash and a credit to the requisite receivables account. Another illustration would be the sale of merchandise controlled on an item-by-item inventory basis, where the organization must account for its inventory or cash.

Controls should be instituted to insure collection for any services provided. This might mean giving the customer a cash sales slip, without which the customer could not receive a service. It might mean physical protection over merchandise or restricted entry to areas where these services are rendered, as in the case of a theater. Appropriate internal controls over cash require a segregation of duties, and this segregation-of-duties control applies to all types of cash receipt controls.

Outside parties may be utilized as a further cash receipts control. A customer can serve as a check on the action of the employee in a retail environment, providing assurance that the employee rings up a cash receipt on a point-of-sale register.

Cash receipts must always be separated from cash disbursements. In smaller organizations, there is frequently pressure to use portions of the cash received to cover current expenditures of one kind or another. This practice should always be resisted. More effective controls and cleaner accountabilities will result when cash receipts and disbursements processes are completely separated.

Cash receipts should always be channeled intact and promptly to established central cash depositories. A day's receipts should be deposited intact as soon as possible after the cutoff for the day. If high volumes of cash are received, consideration might be given to depositing the cash at several times during the day. This is important for several reasons. First, any delay results in a greater risk of theft or improper diversion. Second, checks might be good upon receipt but not later. Third, it is important to be able to identify a particular deposit with a given period of time. Finally, and most important, undeposited cash is idle cash and is not contributing to the best use of organization resources.

When the cash received is transferred to another organization unit, the accountability of the transferor should be properly relieved and a new accountability for the transferee clearly established. This is normally accomplished by some type of a cash receipt or transfer record. Records by which the accountabilities for cash are established and controlled should be maintained by persons independent of the persons charged with the direct accountability. Checks should be made periodically by an independent person to verify that cash has been properly handled and accounted.

(ii) Cash Handling and Custody.   Cash handling is interwoven to some extent with both cash receiving and disbursements. Many of the handling and custody issues here deal with cash as it resides in the five account types described previously. When an organization has actual cash in its possession at some point during its operations, there may be other control aspects that can best be considered under the category of cash handling and custody.

Large amounts of cash retained by the organization create a risk of theft by outsiders or even by employees, and physical safeguards over the cash held within the organization should always be strong. In certain cases locked cabinets may be adequate; in others, small safes are needed; in still others, elaborate vaults may be needed. These facilities, of course, must actually be used. A safe is of little value if cash is often kept in an unlocked file and the safe is used only on an exception basis.

Access to cash-storage facilities must be controlled through keys, combination locks, and other physical protection mechanisms. If an organization has a need to disburse a fairly large volume of cash or other negotiable instruments during normal operations, a separate cashier function should be established. During operational periods, the area used by such a cashier needs to be adequately sealed off by cages or separately partitioned portions of office quarters. Finally, when cash is transferred to or from a banking facility, there must be suitable protection.

In past years, some organizations maintained large cashier facilities to cash employee payroll or personal checks or even to pay employees in cash. With the convenience of checking accounts and the ease with which pay can be transferred to checking accounts and cash withdrawn through automatic teller machines (ATMs), organizations today do not need to provide this level of a cashier facility. A larger organization can arrange to directly deposit employees' pay in their checking accounts and might even add an ATM, supplied by a local bank, to allow employees to make cash withdrawals on site. Travel advances can be handled in a similar manner. Employees can be issued company credit cards and can use these cards both for charging their expenses and for making cash withdrawals through an ATM. When these types of procedures are established, the organization needs only to provide very limited cashier facilities.

Since "cash" is a broad term that goes beyond physical cash on hand to include all types of bank accounts and negotiable instruments, the earning potential of that cash needs to be recognized, where practicable, through the placement of funds in interest-bearing accounts or under other arrangements where the time value of money will be realized. In some cases, the maintenance of given bank balances may be the basis for credit lines or other services rendered by the banks involved, even though the given account earns no interest. In other instances, funds can be placed in short-term, interest-bearing commercial paper. The objective is to exploit these potentials to the maximum extent possible.

(iii) Cash Disbursements.   Once cash is received and available in its various forms, it is ready for use for organization purposes such as the purchase of operating facilities, the payment of expenses, and for other disbursements such as paying dividends to investors. The general audit objective is that cash disbursements should be for valid and proper purposes, that fair value has been received, and that they are in the correct amounts.

Perhaps the most general control to always be considered here is that the cash receipts and cash disbursement phases of the total cash process need to be as separate as possible. Although the procedures to enforce this control may vary, internal audit should always look for an appropriate separation of responsibilities between cash receipts and disbursements.

In normal accounting operations, major expenditures are processed through the creation of a payable that is then subsequently offset by the cash disbursement. At the same time, the disbursement is normally reviewed in terms of the validity of the underlying payable plus the propriety of the timing of the liquidation of that payable. However, a number of situations will arise when small cash expenditures must be made without delay and when the amounts may be too small to justify the application of the formal disbursement procedures. In these circumstances, cash may be advanced using what is called a *petty cash fund.*

Normally, petty cash disbursements are best handled on an "imprest" basis, as discussed earlier. Under this procedure, a designated fund amount is established, cash payments are made from the fund as required, and then reimbursements are made to the fund covering exactly the total amount of expenditures, thus bringing the fund back to its original level. The size of the fund should be large enough to sustain expenditures, with allowance for the time required to process the previously described reimbursements, but no larger than necessary since the level of the fund can be changed from time to time in light of experience and new conditions.

Satisfactory evidence should always be obtained to support expenditures. If such evidence is not directly available in the form of an invoice, cash register receipt, or other documentation, a special receipt should be prepared and signed, preferably by the recipient of the cash, but at least by the person making the expenditure. These supporting documents should be canceled at the time of reimbursement to prevent their reuse. Because petty cash expenditure amounts are usually relatively small, there may be a temptation to relax controls requiring adequate documentation. Documentation should be reviewed at the time of reimbursement. Improper use, however, cannot be detected except by an actual examination and count of the fund. Both of these protective efforts need to be carried out by responsible management on a continuing basis.

The cash-disbursement process highlights the desirability of breaking down the various aspects of control activities and assigning them to different individuals. Thus, one person might review the documentation for the request, another prepare the check-processing voucher, and a third review the propriety of the combined set of documents as well as review the output from the automated accounts payable system. For larger disbursements or those not covered by an automated accounts payable system, a fourth person might provide the primary signature and another for secondary signatures for larger checks. Each of these activities serves as a cross-check on another. The organization should not overcontrol this process, however. Although multiple persons may be involved for large disbursement requests, the process should be reduced to a more cost-effective level for smaller disbursements.

All checks issued should be made payable to the specific individual or firm from which the products or services are obtained. The writing of checks to "cash" or to "bearer" should be strictly prohibited, since cash can then more easily be used for unauthorized purposes.

(iv) Other Aspects of Cash Process. A number of other matters pertaining to effective control over cash cut across the receiving, handling, and disbursement aspects of this process. These include the need to bond employees handling the organization's cash, to protect critical documents such as checks, and to independently reconcile all checking and other cash accounts.

Normal business prudence requires that all employees participating in any part of the cash processes be bonded—a company-paid insurance policy against employee malfeasance. The benefits derived are twofold. First, there is the actual protection to the organization in the case of any defalcation or other improper diversion of organization funds. Second, the knowledge of the bonding may motivate the individual employee to exercise a higher standard of care and integrity. To accomplish the latter, the bonding action should be properly publicized. The organization should also have strong, well-publicized procedures in place to obtain restitution or to force prosecution of any employee involved with any improper diversion of cash.

For all cash processes, records should be kept up-to-date as a basis for both efficient current reference and prompt periodic reporting. Delays in carrying out various parts of the cash processes can generate greater physical risk and at the same time restrict the efficient utilization of cash resources.

Although the use of paper check forms is declining due to electronic transfers and other automated payment processes, the proper control of any checks or other special forms is always important in terms of physical protection and efficient usage. The problem is complicated because modern computer printers generate the entire check document, using laser printers, from blank paper form. Control of these computer programs is also very important.

An important part of the overall cash-management process is the independent reconciliation of all bank accounts. Reconciliations should be made by persons or computer systems who are independent of the regular cash-receiving and -disbursing operations. Bank statements and canceled checks should be obtained or received directly from the depositories to insure that they have not been tampered with in any manner by any intermediary. A bank will often provide reports that help complete this process. For accounts with a smaller number of transactions, bank reconciliations also provide the opportunity to review how receipts and disbursements are handled and to identify unusual actions.

In earlier days of internal auditing, the independent reconciliation of checking accounts was once a regular internal audit task. While both internal or external auditors may want to perform this exercise as part of their annual financial audit, internal audit functions today have generally moved away from this as a regular process. Internal audit resources are too valuable, and other persons in the accounting organization can usually perform this function subject to periodic internal audit review.

(b) CASH PROCESS INTERNAL CONTROLS

Many of the cash-related internal controls discussed in this book are covered in subsequent chapters involving the receipt and disbursement of cash. This section considers cash as it applies to overall accounting operations.

Cash presents a far greater internal control risk to an organization than nearly any other operation. An organization may manufacture, for example, a product called a "widget" that has wide consumer appeal. It might be possible for dishonest employees to steal these widgets and use them or sell them for their own personal gain. However, the dishonest employee can only steal so many widgets before an astute management can see that widgets are missing from the warehouse. Without proper reconciliation procedures in place, it can be much harder to detect if cash from those widget sales is missing. This is because of the numerous transactions associated with this cash, including customer credits for returned goods, outstanding receivable balances, and payments in transit.

Cash is a dynamic commodity with its transaction balances in flux at any moment. For this reason, external auditors take strong steps at year-end to determine that the cash balances stated in financial statement balance sheets represent cash on hand, cash in transit, and cash in various general accounts. The external auditor should also be concerned that this cash has been properly classified and that any committed funds have been identified.

Management has, or should have, a strong interest in establishing adequate internal controls over its cash processes, including the following:

- Periodic reconciliation of checking accounts to recorded cash balances. This includes a review of cash deposits and checks issued, with an accounting for checks in transit.
- Examination of canceled checks on a test basis for appropriate signatures, endorsements, dates, and amounts.
- Controls over the handling of cash at all levels to ensure that controls include a proper segregation of duties.
- Physical controls over significant documents such as checks.
- Periodic follow-ups on special cash items such as checks outstanding and stop-payment notices.

Cash is such an important element in organization operations that strong internal controls are essential. These controls should be in place for all cash accounts and at all levels.

(c) CASH-RELATED INTERNAL AUDIT CONSIDERATIONS

In the early years of auditing, a major emphasis of many reviews was on the controls over cash. As the years went by, the sources of actual cash in the modern organization were limited to petty cash funds used for very small, miscellaneous purchases. With an overall objective to review controls over cash, internal auditors all too often made the reconciliation of a relatively minor petty cash fund a major component of their reviews. Even worse, they often reported a small difference in the petty cash fund as if it were a major control issue. At the same time, they may have ignored more significant control issues.

The modern internal auditor should have moved away from this overemphasis on the controls over a relatively minor petty cash account while ignoring more significant control issues. Internal audit should not ignore such areas as petty cash funds because they are viewed as too minor, but should understand where cash plays a significant role in organization operations and should review for appropriate controls.

(i) Financial Audit Considerations.   Most cash-related financial audit procedures are performed by external auditors as part of their year-end procedures. Internal auditors often become involved with these external audit procedures in their support of external auditors. They also may have a need to reconcile account balances as part of reviews of smaller units or other special audits.

Internal audit should understand how to perform a bank reconciliation. In many respects, this is similar to the process an auditor would use to reconcile a personal checking account. Internal audit starts with a statement from the bank for each account as well as internal records indicating receipts and deposits. In addition to the bank's account statement, external auditors at year-end request an independent confirmation of an organization's accounts at a given bank, revealing such matters as restrictions on withdrawals due to compensating balance requirements, liabilities to the bank related to the account, and other matters. An internal auditor might also request such a confirmation when performing a financial audit of cash at a smaller, remote unit not part of the external auditor's scope.

Figure 22.9 is an example of a bank reconciliation worksheet to test a bank account balance. This reconciliation process was once a very labor-intensive task requiring the physical handling and summation of checks. Computer systems both at the bank and within the auditor's organization have made this much easier; however, internal audit should not rely just on the printed summary reports when making the reconciliation but should also look for unusual items on a test basis. Some of these items should be physically examined in detail.

Reconciliations of petty cash funds are very similar to the process for checking accounts. However, internal audit should look for an internally prepared record of cash disbursements, including appropriate documentation, as well as a record of all deposits into the fund.

(ii) Cash-Related Operational Audit Procedures.   In any operation involving the handling of cash, internal audit should concentrate on whether cash is properly protected from theft, that it is promptly moved to appropriate accounts, and that it is managed to

Figure 22.9 Bank Account Reconciliation Worksheet

Balance per Bank		
1. Obtain balance per bank statement.		$5,236,000
2. Add deposits in transit and bank errors that understate the balance.	$ 42,126	
—Subtotal		$5,278,126
3. Deduct outstanding checks and bank errors that overstate the balance.	$136,016	
4. Calculate corrected cash balance.		$5,142,110
Balance per Books		
5. Obtain balance per books and financial records.		$5,309,461
6. Add deposits credited by the bank but not yet recorded.	$137,140	
7. Deduct book errors that understate the balance per books (e.g. a check for $10 that was recorded as $100 on the books).	$261,630	
—Subtotal		$5,184,971
8. Deduct bank charges not yet recorded by depositor (e.g. bank service charges and NSF checks).	$ 27,361	
9. Deduct book errors that overstate the balance per books (e.g. the depositor writes a check for $100 but records it as $10).	$ 15,500	
10. Correct cash balance.		$5,142,110

best serve the organization. Controls for proper protection over cash include such simple matters as keeping petty cash funds in locked, secure facilities, transporting all cash deposits in armored carriers, and discouraging any temptation through strong separation-of-duties controls. For the operational auditor, cash may include check forms, credit vouchers, negotiable securities, retail gift certificates, or any documents that could be easily converted to cash through improper procedures. Internal audit should look for appropriate controls to prevent misappropriation in any cash-related documents.

Cash always has a time value, and idle cash does not draw bank account interest or satisfy bank minimum-balance requirements. Internal audit should always look for situations where improved controls and procedures could move cash faster to appropriate banking accounts.

Figure 22.10 contains selected audit procedures for operational reviews for controls over the protection and movement of cash. These procedures cover cash or cash-equivalent functions used for operations but not cash investments, as discussed in Chapter 30 on financial management. Because actual cash processes may vary to a great extent due to the nature of the organization, these operational audit steps are very general. Internal audit should always develop an understanding of the various sources where the organization receives its cash and then concentrates on the controls over the more significant. That is, there is often little need to do a formal cash count of a petty cash fund unless that fund experiences a high volume of transactions or there is some other perceived concern.

Figure 22.10 Cash-Related Audit Procedures

22.10.01   Identify all repositories of cash or cash equivalents located throughout the organization. The surveys should include cashier functions, cash value documents such as
cash redeemable documents, and securities.

22.10.02   On a surprise basis and accompanied by a member of management, to act as a
witness, visit one or more repositories of cash and perform a formal cash count;
reconcile that count to formal accounting records, investigating any differences.

22.10.03   Review all procedures regarding cash and comment on the adequacy and attention
to controls, including separations of responsibility throughout.

22.10.04   Perform a walk-through inspection of all cash-handling areas, with an emphasis
given to security over the cash or cash equivalents.

22.10.05   Determine that procedures are in place to record the receiving, depositing, or
disbursement of all cash transactions.

22.10.06   If terminals are used for cash, determine that controls exist over the sign in / sign
out for those terminals and that procedures require a periodic review of terminal
logs.

22.10.07   Determine whether procedures require supervisory or management personnel to
review and approval all journal entries, recording cash transactions and balancing
cash routines.

22.10.08   Determine that persons involved with depositing and recording cash receipts are
covered by insurance and fidelity bonds in appropriate amounts.

22.10.09   Review the adequacy of security controls over cash functions, both monetary and
cash equivalents. On a selected basis, review security procedures in detail, noting
any potential vulnerabilities.

22.10.10   Assess overall procedures in place for the conservation of cash throughout the
organization, including:
• Use of cash discounts for early payments
• Cash concentration accounts
• Effective use of EDI and electronic fund transfers
• The use of zero-balance accounts for such matters as payroll
• The issuance of employee credit cards for travel rather than cash advances

(iii) Cash-Related Computer Audit Procedures.   The typical organization does
not have many strictly cash-oriented control systems. Cash-related transactions flow
through many processes, but internal audit is typically interested in the other transactions
related to that cash. That is, an internal auditor might review controls over a sales system
and would develop computer-assisted audit techniques (CAATs) to measure various sales-
related parameters. Internal audit would have less occasion to develop CAATs just for
the cash side of that process.

Banking or financial institutions deal with cash as their primary product and have
a large number of cash-related processes such as checking accounts, home mortgages, and
other loans outstanding. These are supported by extensive computer systems that internal
audit should consider for potential controls reviews and that lend themselves to numerous
types of CAATs. Specialized financial professional organizations such as the Bank Admin-

istration Institute[3] publish audit guides and other materials for the computer audit–related reviews of financial institution–related systems.

In a nonfinancial institution, internal audit can sometimes develop very effective CAATs covering the organization's cash-management procedures. For example, a sales organization with remote branch offices may have instructed those locations to remit all cash collected to a sweep type of account for processing in a central location. Those same branch organizations may not have appropriate control disciplines to process these remittances on a timely basis. Internal audit could possibly develop a CAAT to review reported daily sales figures and match them with reported deposits to determine if cash deposit rules are being followed. As another test, internal audit could develop a CAAT to calculate the average cash balances at these branch units. The results might reveal that management was not taking proper stewardship control over their cash management.

(iv) Cash Process Sample Audit Report Findings

A: Excessive Cash Balances in Cashier Accounts. We did a count of cash under the responsibility of the home office cashier that is used for employee travel advances, expense reimbursements, and miscellaneous expenses. We also reviewed average daily disbursements from this account over a period of six months. With the exception of two instances where there was significant employee international travel, we found that the cashier total cash balance was always greater than daily disbursements by a factor of about ten. This large cashier cash balance ties up resources that might be deposited in organization accounts.

Recommendation. The average daily balance of cash under the control of the home office cashier should be reduced by about 80%. This amount should be reevaluated periodically based on organization activities and other needs. To allow for the occasional circumstances when a large travel advance is needed, arrangements should be made with the local bank to secure travelers checks on a one-day notice.

B: Inactive Checking Accounts. The ABC and XYZ facilities were both closed about one year ago. However, the local bank accounts for each of these facilities remain open. Management advised us that the accounts are open because certain refund checks issued before closure have never cleared. Although the balances in each of these accounts is at a minimum level, the open accounts expose the organization to potential fraudulent transactions.

Recommendation. A detailed reconciliation should be performed to identify the number and nature of the outstanding checks issued from each of these accounts. Remaining balances should be reduced to the level of these outstanding checks. Consideration should be given to contacting some of these check payee parties, informing them that the accounts will be closed. In any event, the checking accounts should be closed within six months.

22-4 RECEIVABLES PROCESSES

Receivables processes cover any action that generates claims of amounts due against individuals or other organizations. These claims are usually against parties outside the

---

[3] Bank Administration Institute, 1 North Franklin Street, Chicago, IL 60606.

organization but at times can also involve employees and officers. The claims are brought into existence to allow the organization to recognize them as a future liability to be resolved later. They can be considered an intermediary phase pending their ultimate collection in the form of cash or other types of consideration. Although these claims can originate in a variety of ways, the major category has to do with the sale of products or services rendered by the organization. This section first deals with this sales-related category and then later touches on other receivable types.

The receivable processes that relate primarily to sales have a number of important relationships. There is a need for policies covering the extent to which credit is first granted and then subsequently administered. Who should be extended credit? In what amounts? How aggressive should the organization be in pressing for subsequent collection? A second type of consideration concerns customer satisfaction and continuing customer goodwill. The organization should be interested in how customers react to the modes of credit authorization, billing, and collection. The organization is also interested in learning about how the customers are reacting to organization products and policies in a broader sense. Finally, there is the specific interest of the organization in the efficiency of its various receivable activities and the effectiveness of its controls.

The modern organization faces many potential risks related to its receivables processes. If credit is granted without proper policies or customer screening, the organization may be either limiting its sales through too tight credit practices or booking sales that may be eventually uncollectible. Once a receivable is booked, the organization should handle billings in a prompt and accurate manner. Cash payments against receivables need to be properly recorded and deposited. Finally, the organization needs to establish policies to collect on late or overdue receivable accounts.

Accounts receivable are often covered by external auditors who send out independent confirmation letters asking customers with receivable balances to acknowledge the existence of those recorded receivables. This is an important step in a financial statement audit. However, there are a large number of additional and related receivables-related operational and accounting review areas that should be a key part of the internal auditor's activities.

(a) TRANSACTION CYCLE

The processes or transactions relating to accounts receivables can be grouped into three phases. The first phase has to do with the conditions under which the receivable comes into existence, including both recording the sale and determining that the customer has a proper credit history. The second covers the administration of the receivables thus created, including the processing of bills and statements as well as monitoring the overall status of all receivable accounts. The third phase consists of the means by which the receivable is finally liquidated. This includes the collection of cash to satisfy billings or the use of credit collection procedures for any overdue billings. The objective for each is to understand the general range of matters involved and to identify major control problems.

Automation and competitive business practices have changed the manner in which receivables are created and processed for many organizations. Electronic data interchange (EDI) procedures, discussed from a purchasing perspective in Chapter 24, are an example. A customer may make a purchase through an electronic transmission to the organization's order-entry system. The order is electronically acknowledged, shipped, and electronically billed. The customer may then pay through an automated electronic funds transfer (EFT) process. Using EDI, much of the traditional paper trail frequently used by auditors and others disappears. The accounts receivables process and its related controls change extensively using these newer technologies.

(i) Recording Sales and Generating Receivables. Since an account receivable normally arises out of the sale of the organization's products or services, internal audit is concerned with establishing a direct link between the actual sale and the recording of the receivable. The recorded receivable must be backed up by the shipment of the product or the performance of the service according to preestablished sales terms. These objectives are likely to be satisfied when the creation of the receivable can be directly linked with the recording of the sale and the relief of an inventory account or with a record of the performance of the service. This process usually involves three basic automated systems in the organization: sales order entry, inventory or shipping systems, and accounts receivable. The latter also links to key accounting systems including the general ledger.

Generating an account receivable creates the need for the organization to extend the required credit to the customer to cover the sale. This credit decision depends upon the general credit policy of the organization and how it is applied to a particular customer in the light of his or her credit standing and past payment experience. When credit acceptability has been determined, regular sales and billing procedures are initiated. As a part of those procedures, an invoice is prepared and the account of the customer charged.

A major control consideration applying to the generating of receivables is an independent review and approval of the customer's credit. This approval should be provided by an independent department or person within the framework of established organization policy and should consider appropriate credit-related information about the particular customer's current credit balances, payment history, and the general credit and financial standing. A credit approval by parties independent from the sales department is important since that sales function is often more interested in completing the sale rather than collecting on it in the future.

Prices and terms for the sale must be properly authorized. For billing purposes, the applicable prices, discounts, and other terms must be based on established organization policy. Any special interpretations or deviations must be approved by properly authorized individuals.

Cash discounts are usually part of standard billing terms, typically a 2% discount if the invoice is paid within 10 days with the net amount due if paid in 30 days. A penalty will usually be assessed after 30 days. These terms should be clearly stated on the invoice document using such terms as "2%-Net."

For goods shipped, invoices need to be prepared for use in several operational areas. One copy, generally with prices omitted, goes with the shipment as a packing list. Another, properly priced, goes to the customer as the official invoice. Others are used for the compilation of sales data and for accounts receivable posting. Invoice shipment data will also impact inventory and production records and may also form a basis for calculating sales commissions.

Invoices were once mostly multicopy paper documents, and proper serial number control and correct postings were critical controls. Where paper-based systems are still in place, these controls continue to be important.

(ii) Administration of Accounts Receivables. The administration phase of the receivables process starts when the receivable is recorded and continues until the receivable

Figure 22.11 Accounts Receivable Process

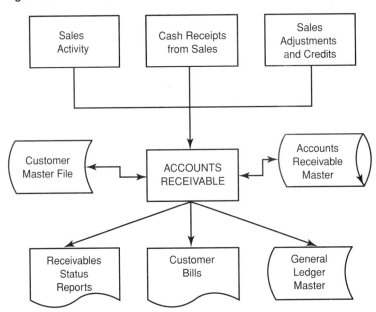

is paid or otherwise liquidated. This accounts receivable record must be tied to control accounts that support individual customer and other categories of billings.

Newly generated charges, credits from cash collections, and all other miscellaneous charges and credits should be posted on a daily basis so that up-to-date information is always available to serve the various operational needs of the organization. At the same time, accuracy must be maintained through checks on the agreement of detailed accounts with the established control. This check is normally handled by the typical automated accounts receivable system. Figure 22.11 is a flow chart showing the components of an automated accounts receivable system. Such a system could be implemented as part of a larger computer system or could be resident on a desktop microcomputer. The controls necessary for such an application were discussed in Chapter 17.

In addition to the accounts receivable information furnished regularly through on-line retrieval screens or the like, there should be periodic reports of current balances and an aging analysis. The aging analysis shows the portions of the account balances that have been unpaid for different time periods, including current, one month overdue, two months overdue, three months overdue, and so on. Figure 22.12 is an example of this type of aged receivables balance report. An analysis of this aging data is important for the administration of the ongoing credit and collection efforts. It will also allow the organization to adjust its estimates of reserves for bad debts, as discussed below.

At the end of a month or accounting period, organizations generally send statements summarizing all invoices issued during that period. Even though payment terms require that individual invoices be paid in advance of the period-end statement date, the statement provides an account summary.

A basic control here is mailing statements directly to individual customers with no opportunity for diversion or modification by others. This makes it possible for the statements to serve as a reliable cross-check on the accuracy of the individual accounts. It is also an important means of disclosing any delayed reporting of collections.

Although regular organization sales activities provide the major source of the accounts receivable, other organization activities and developments may lead to some special types of receivables, including:

- *Advances to Employees.* Sales of organization products or services are normally included in the regular accounts receivable. However, there may be advances of one kind or another for travel, special business purposes, or possibly for personal reasons. Advances for travel would normally be booked in a travel accounting system. Many other special employee advances are controlled through the payroll system and are settled over future pay periods. Advances for personal purposes would require the approval of properly authorized managers.

- *Deposits with Outsiders.* In many situations, deposits are required in connection with the establishment of utility services or for other reasons. These deposits may be of a temporary nature or may be permanent as long as the service is being utilized. The receivable record here is important so that the deposit can be recovered when the original need no longer exists. While these deposits would not be part of an accounts receivable system, other records should be established to record them.

- *Claims.* Relations with vendors, carriers, or outside service groups can lead to claims for a variety of reasons. These become a special type of receivable. Insurance claims are still another source of special receivables. Effective control is

Figure 22.12 Accounts Receivable Aging Schedule

Account	Customer Name	Current	30 to 60	60 to 90	Over 90	Total Balance Due
10046	Aacme Advertising	6,035.00	5,329.67	1,091.08	0.00	$12,455.75
10288	Arrdvark Industrial Belts	0.00	0.00	5,876.90	20,013.98	$25,890.88
10387	Axyloti Manufacturing	3,540,128.25	8,860.30	16.95	0.00	$3,549,005.50
18977	Bliely Tool Company	(1,458.56)	1,291.66	0.00	(0.00)	($166.90)
20467	Cratchit Accounting Service	6,875.00	0.00	0.00	0.00	$6,875.00
32287	Dreadlock Wig Co.	305,580.60	238,752.90	(78,082.95)	0.00	$466,250.55
33187	Enron Parts Supply	58,652.50	22,982.00	21,595.75	(185.13)	$103,045.12
40022	Faust Standards Supply	(88,089.55)	27,963.65	0.00	0.00	($60,125.90)
40573	GM Supply, Inc.	2,055.65	1,088.87	0.00	311.08	$3,455.60
53498	Hjruska Blower Corp.	12,894.00	0.00	0.00	0.00	$12,894.00
58765	Juran Scaffold Work	2,254.98	2,166.52	225.00	140.75	$4,787.25
60004	Lloyd Plumbing	20,545.00	20,854.55	20,221.78	38,878.67	$100,500.00
69813	Muffler Office Supply	0.00	0.00	0.00	678.90	$678.90
72354	Probst Computer Supply	2,689.33	0.00	0.00	0.00	$2,689.33
88904	Stearns Manufacturing	0.00	(123.45)	0.00	246.90	$123.45
95432	Ziebarth Mechanical	9,557.65	(9,557.65)	0.00	(100.00)	($100.00)
	Totals	$3,877,719.85	$319,609.02	($29,055.49)	$59,985.15	$4,228,258.53

provided by recording of the claim as a receivable, rather than recording the proceeds when received.

- *Accruals of Income.* A special type of receivable, in a very loose sense, exists when earned income is accrued prior to being due and collectible. The objective here is to recognize income in the periods it is actually earned and thus provide a better evaluation of current operational performance.

While the nature and scope of the transactions and activities that generate these miscellaneous types of receivables can vary greatly, certain minimal controls are necessary for all of them. First, policy and procedure conditions under which the particular type of receivable is created should be clearly defined. Safeguards should exist to make sure that the receivable is recorded at the earliest possible time and in the proper amount. Second, procedures must be established for the periodic review of all miscellaneous receivables, which are frequently overlooked or not given adequate attention in a regular operational review. Specific precautions must be taken to combat such tendencies.

(iii) Dispositions of Receivables and Credit Collections. Accounts receivables represent an asset claim against the particular parties involved, and these claims should be relieved only in a properly authorized manner. The four normal modes of accounts receivable account relief are cash collections, return allowances, account adjustments, or bad debt write-offs.

The most usual settlement mode is cash collections from customers to liquidate the previously generated receivables. At the time of recording the cash collections, the organization must verify that any cash or other discounts deducted are properly earned and recorded. The customer account should be properly credited and adjusted if the discount was improper.

When products sold are returned for one reason or another, the result is the reverse process of the original sale. While retailers often allow returns if a customer indicates dissatisfaction, most manufacturers, industrial distributors, and other organizations will have a requirement to determine that the shipment was somehow not in compliance with terms or was in error before returns are allowed. There should be a requirement that the actual return is authorized. A second return-related requirement is that the products returned are actually received in proper condition. Finally, the credit for the return must be in the proper amount. These three control points—proper authorization, receipt of goods, and proper amounts—provide the basis for establishing a sales return credit.

Adjustments and allowances are harder to control when a customer is granted a special credit for volume purchases, for the promotional sale of particular types of products, or to adjust for product deficiencies. Where an allowance is pursuant to a specific arrangement, controls should be in place to confirm compliance with the arrangement. In many cases, however, the authenticity of the credit may be based on judgmental factors evaluated by an executive who then approves the credit within the authorized limits.

There will always be customers who simply fail to pay. There may be bankruptcy situations, disappearance of the debtor, or other causes that leave no alternative but a write-off of the account as a bad debt. Provisions should be made for such losses through the creation of reserves for doubtful accounts. The actual bad debt write-off, properly authorized by a sufficiently high-level organization manager, is then charged to that reserve account. However, even after they are written off, these accounts written-off should be given such further collection efforts as are practicable and reasonable.

(iv) Policy Aspects of Accounts Receivable. In addition to the operational framework of the receivable process, several key policy areas relating to the handling of receivables require consideration. First, the economics of credit levels is a continuing policy question for many organizations. Management must decide how liberal an organization should be in extending credit. While it is clear that the tighter the credit granting, the lower will be the ultimate bad debt losses, sales made pursuant to a more liberal credit policy may be additional sales that otherwise would not have been made. Since these sales should yield extra profits, it may be in the organization's interests to generate higher sales with less stringent credit policies. It may be difficult to measure the incremental benefits accurately, but it is important that the auditor recognize the several dimensions of the problem when performing operational reviews in the accounts receivable area.

A second related aspect of both the operation of the credit department and the total receivable process is the impact that these activities have on good customer relations. It is usually desirable to streamline procedures and reduce the degree of personal contacts, but credit and receivable processes unavoidably involve customer contacts. These contacts must be handled in a way that minimizes customer irritation and builds positive goodwill. Real effectiveness here is to combine internal efficiency with courteous and reasonably cooperative customer relationships. Very often customer dissatisfaction, due to a cause quite independent of the receivable process, may surface through account receivable contacts. The problem can become magnified if both parties are dealing with automated billing systems that appear recalcitrant or difficult to understand. The receivable personnel must channel problems to organization personnel who will solve them and work to build greater customer goodwill.

Through a formal contract or a deferred payment, it may be the practice of an organization to make sales for its products and services on a deferred payment basis. In such cases, contracts are usually executed that specify the timing of the payments. In some cases, notes receivable may be obtained. These notes receivable are often an outgrowth of collection problems with regular accounts receivable, such as circumstances where a regular account cannot be liquidated in accordance with its payment terms. In such a situation, the organization may wish to obtain what it regards as a more precise recognition of the receivable through the use of notes receivable. This also allows an organization to define the interest that can now be charged. In all these situations, circumstances under which any notes receivable come into existence need to be defined and properly authorized. Subsequently, there is the need for a regular monitoring of the collection of the notes on the dates specified, including the collection of such interest as has been agreed upon. Notes receivable also pose a problem of custody, since the notes exist as separate documents, and there is the possibility that since the use of notes receivable is an unusual type of transaction, regular and systematic attention will not be given to them. Specific notes receivable procedures are needed for periodic review and possible action.

(b) INTERNAL CONTROLS

The monies due an organization through its accounts receivable often represent a major asset to that organization. Accounts receivable must be turned into cash collections, and because much of this process is dependent upon the actions of outside parties, internal accounting controls are critical.

A major internal control issue here is that the receivables recorded as due must be correct and collectible according to the terms of that receivable. The receivables must meet several general internal control objectives.

- *Overall Reasonableness.* The recorded value of both the receivables and any reserves must be consistent with actual collection experiences. Trade discounts and allowances should also be consistent across all recorded receivables.
- *Accounts Receivable Evidence.* The receivables must represent amounts actually due to the organization. This can be verified by the auditor's direct confirmations or through the timely receipt of cash to pay off the receivables.
- *Valuation and Classification.* The receivables must be recorded as values that are collectible. Receivables should also be properly classified as to whether they are expected to be collected in a normal span of time or are a potential bad debt. Appropriate reserves should be established for amounts estimated as uncollectible.
- *Proper Receivables Cutoffs.* Schedules need to be established to properly record sales, sales returns, and allowances. This is tied to strong controls over the proper shipping and billing of goods. Of course, there should be a segregation of duties between the shipping and billing functions in an organization.

Accounts receivable represent a major internal control issue in an organization. They must be recorded in a prudent manner that reflects their potential collectability. When the conditions surrounding those receivable accounts change, the receivable value must be adjusted through the establishment of a reserve account or through an actual write-off to reflect the anticipated collectability of that receivable.

(c) INTERNAL AUDIT PROCEDURES

Internal auditors sometimes all but ignore their organization's accounts receivable processes, often because this is one area that almost always receives extensive attention from external auditors. The generally accepted auditing standards (GAAS) developed by the AICPA contain very general directions at most, suggesting areas that auditors *should* or *may consider.* Specific procedures are usually not mentioned. However, GAAS *requires* that independent auditors *must* externally confirm their client's accounts receivable. This requirement dates back to a massive fraud of many years ago when a then-prominent organization claimed that a large number of fictitious accounts were valid and due to them. Had the auditors independently confirmed these accounts with the claimed customers, they would have found them to be invalid and would have encountered a massive fraud. Since then, independent public accountants have been required to confirm accounts receivable rather than rely upon the word of management. In addition to their confirmations activities, external auditors review the internal controls and other aspects of the organization's accounts receivable process.

Internal auditors also should have an interest in their organization's accounts receivable systems and procedures, and consider this a major risk area in their audit planning. This is an area where internal audit cannot easily separate financial, operational, and computer audit activities. Any review here may involve audit procedures in all three areas, and the following sections consider some of the separate internal audit activities in each area.

(i) Accounts Receivable Financial Audit Procedures. An internal auditor should start any review of an accounts receivable process by developing an understanding of the organization's credit policies, its methods of billing customers, the types of customers that are part of the accounts receivable, the types of transactions that would be recorded, and the procedures used for collections. Each of these factors can have a major impact on how the accounts receivable process operates and on the expected level of controls.

A good first step in developing an understanding of the accounts receivable process might be to gather some statistics about the average size of billing transactions, the frequency of adjustments, and other indicators. Figure 22.13 is a questionnaire to help internal auditors gain this understanding. There are no right or wrong answers here. Rather, an internal auditor can use this information to identify potential problems with the accounts receivable process. For example, a relatively high percentage of overdue accounts may point to collection problems. A high number of adjustment transactions during any billing period may suggest incorrect billings. Internal audit may be able to gather this data through a discussion with accounts receivable management or reviews of key reports, or it might be possible to develop a computer-assisted procedure to survey the accounts receivable file to gather performance statistics.

The major objective of any review of an accounts receivable process should be to determine that all sales are billed promptly and correctly. In addition, adequate controls should be in place to determine that any adjustments to accounts are made only with

Figure 22.13 Accounts Receivable Statistics Questionnaire

1. What is the average days outstanding for your overall accounts receivable?
2. How many accounts receivable open transactions are recorded in an average month and how many are written off or otherwise adjusted?
3. How many customer accounts have been set up on billing records and how often is the overall file reviewed or purged for inactive customers?
4. How long do accounts remain open before they are written off and are legal or other procedures used to encourage collection before write-off?
5. What is the average size of the account written-off?
6. How often are accounts adjusted, how long do they remain open prior to any adjustment, and are statistics available to describe the reasons for adjustments?
7. When credit policies suggest that credit should not be granted, how often do other levels of management override the decision and grant credit? What is the credit history of these doubtful credit accounts?
8. Are cash discounts offered and what percentage of payments take advantage of the cash discount offered?
9. Are all recorded accounts receivable subject to normal billing terms or are special, exception terms offered?
10. Are any accounts receivable goods considered to be "on loan," on consignment, or under other special billing terms?
11. Does the organization keep detailed records of all accounts receivable adjustments, write-offs, and other transactions?
12. Are accounts receivable records reconciled to the general ledger on a regular, periodic basis?

appropriate management authorization. Strong controls must also be in place to insure that remittances are controlled and applied to the correct accounts. An internal auditor can gain an understanding here through reviews of accounting records and various transaction tests.

Accounts receivable is an area closely tied to other key financial systems in the organization. Internal audit should perform various tests to determine that accounts receivable records tie to the recorded balances in other systems, and that individual receivable accounts are reconciled and balanced on a regular basis. This is an area with a high potential for fraud or error. While internal audit cannot find all types of incorrect or unapproved adjustments, audit procedures should consider controls over the overall process.

Figure 22.14 lists some financial audit procedures for a review of the accounts receivable process. These procedures can be adapted as appropriate to any special accounts receivable practices that internal audit may have discovered through a preliminary review based on the Figure 22.13 questionnaire. Before embarking upon a financial review of accounts receivable, internal audit should also consider coordinating their plans with the external auditors. While the two review objectives may not always be the same, there are benefits to this coordination.

(ii) Accounts Receivable Operational Audit Procedures.   An auditor will often find it difficult to separate financial from operational from computer audit procedures in this area. One accounts receivable audit area that has primarily operational characteristics is the collection of receivables. An organization can face significant risks if it does not properly and promptly record cash receipts and if it does not pursue good procedures for the collection of overdue accounts.

The amount of internal activity needed here depends very much upon the nature of the organization and the status of its typical accounts. If most customers remit their payments to a central bank "lock box" type of account with an immediate deposit into checking accounts and if most customers pay promptly due to good credit-granting policies, internal audit can plan minimal activities in this area. However, trends and practices should be reexamined over time to detect any changes. Internal audit should focus on three general collection areas here:

- Controls over the receipt of cash remittances, their application to customer accounts, and deposits in financial institutions
- Procedures for the ongoing review of credit policies to ascertain that customer credit limits are adjusted according to performance and other conditions
- Controls and procedures for the collection of overdue accounts, including procedures to collect on overdue problem accounts

Many of the cash receipts controls that an auditor would expect to find were discussed in the previous sections on the handling of cash and accounts receivable financial audit procedures. However, internal audit should look for any cash handling controls that are unique to organization operations.

The collection of overdue accounts is a control challenge to many organizations. It may be tempting to give established customers the benefit of doubt and not be too aggressive in pursuing overdue account collections. Nevertheless, an organization should follow

Figure 22.14 Accounts Receivable Financial Audit Procedures

Audit _____ Location _____ Date _____

Audit Step	Initial	W/P
1. Obtain a copy of the organization chart and determine that a proper separation of duties exists throughout the A/R process.		
2. Review published procedures covering the A/R function and, through discussions with management, determine that these policies are current.		
3. Select a sample of customer A/R balances and review to determine whether: • Account balances are supported by sales invoices. • Prices, extensions, footings, and contract terms are correct. • Sales invoices agree to shipping department records. • Credit has been properly reviewed and approved. • Invoices have been properly recorded in detail and control accounts.		
4. Select a sample of shipping department records and trace to A/R records to determine the accuracy and timeliness of billing.		
5. Select a sample of sales credits issued to determine that all entries were consistent with the original billing, properly recorded and with appropriate levels of approval.		
6. Select a sample of old A/R balances to determine the level of collection activities as well as management's assessment of the account's status. Review any correspondence or other data concerning selected accounts, as appropriate.		
7. Select a sample of error and control reports from the automated A/R system and assess procedures for balancing and correcting errors.		
8. Inspect facilities and procedures for the safeguarding of A/R records, critical documents, and key systems.		
9. Determine that procedures exist to issue month-end statements. Review a sample of any disputes or corrections surrounding those statements.		
10. If the status of certain A/R accounts appears to raise internal audit questions, consider issuing special positive confirmation letters for those accounts. Review the timing of any procedures with external audit to assure that the approach is consistent.		

good collection practices. When an account is disputed or becomes otherwise uncollectible, the organization should pass the matter on to the legal staff or to an outside collection agency. Internal audit should consider a review of these practices.

(iii) Accounts Receivable Computer Audit Procedures. An in-house-developed or manual accounts receivable system would be quite rare today. Accounts receivable processes are the types of procedures that lend themselves to the use of standard packaged software and are virtually always automated today.

Accounts receivable is also an area that provides opportunities for computer assisted audit techniques (CAATs). Almost as a matter of course, an auditor should consider developing two CAATs as part of any accounts receivable review. The first is to develop and produce confirmation letters to be sent to credit customers, allowing them to independently agree or disagree with recorded balances due in any account. The second accounts receivable CAAT is an aging of these accounts as a test of whether reserves for uncollectible accounts are appropriate.

An accounts receivable confirmation is an auditor-generated letter that selects customer account data from the accounts receivable file. Two basic types of confirmations are used: positive and negative confirmations. In a positive confirmation, the letter outlines the status of the customer's account and asks the recipient to acknowledge, via a signed receipt addressed to an outside location, that the amount due is correct as recorded. A negative confirmation works essentially the same way, except the recipient is asked to respond only if there is a disagreement with the amount stated in the letter. Internal audit would assume that the account is correct as recorded unless a disputed confirmation response is received. Examples of both confirmation letter formats are shown in Figure 22.15.

Typically, internal audit would not confirm all recorded accounts. Rather, statistical

Figure 22.15   Accounts Receivable Positive and Negative Confirmation Letters

Introductory Paragraph
Dear customer, ExampleCo's internal auditors are reviewing the status of our open customer accounts in support of our external auditors, Debit, Credit and Cancel, LLC. As part of our review, we request that you independently and carefully review the enclosed April 1, 2002 statement for your account.

Positive Confirmation Paragraphs
If this statement is correct, please sign and date the form included with this enclosed statement. Send this form directly to our internal auditors in the stamped, self-addressed envelope provided. If you have any disagreements with this statement, please note them directly on the statement and include this in the envelope provided.

This is not a collection letter. Its only purpose is to assess the correctness of ExampleCo's billings. Thank you for your help!

OR

Negative Confirmation Paragraphs
If this statement is correct, please follow normal procedures when paying your account. However, if you have any disagreements with this statement, please note them directly on the statement and mail it directly to our internal auditors in the stamped, self-addressed envelope provided.

Signed, ExampleCo Internal Audit

Figure 22.16 Confirmation Control Log

Acct No.	Customer	Inv. Date	Inv. Bal.	Conf. Recvd.	Exceptions	Notes	Subsequent Payment
10046	Aacme Advertising	04/01/02	$12,455.75	04/23/02	No		
10387	Axylotl Manufacturing	04/01/02	$3,549,005.50	05/09/02	Yes-3	See W/P 34.2	
18977	Bilely Tool Company	04/01/02	($166.90)	04/16/02	No		
20467	Cratchit Accounting Service	04/01/02	$6,875.00	04/10/02	No		
32287	Dreadlock Wig Co.	04/01/02	$466,250.55				05/10/02
33187	Enron Parts Supply	04/01/02	$103,045.12	04/22/02			
40022	Faust Standards Supply	04/01/02	($60,125.90)				Need Follow-up
40573	GM Supply, Inc.	04/01/02	$3,455.60	04/18/02	No		
53498	Hjruska Blower Corp.	04/01/02	$12,894.00	04/19/02	No		
58765	Juran Scaffold Workd	04/01/02	$4,787.25				04/12/02
60004	Lloyd Plumbing	04/01/02	$100,500.00	04/10/02	Yes-1	See W/P 34.3	
69813	Muffler Office Supply	04/01/02	$678.90				05/09/02
72354	Probst Computer Supply	04/01/02	$2,689.33	05/12/02			
88904	Stearns Manufacturing	04/01/02	$123.45	04/28/02	No		
95432	Ziebarth Mechanical	04/01/02	($100.00)				Need Follow-up

sampling routines would be used to allow internal audit to take a random sample of the open accounts recorded on accounts receivable files. When sending a sample of positive confirmations, internal audit needs to keep track of who did or did not respond to the letters. An accounts receivable confirmation control log is a useful tool to keep track of confirmations sent and responses. Figure 22.16 is an example of this type of log. When internal audit does not receive responses to positive confirmations, other techniques must be employed. One is to use the same CAAT software and the same input files to send a second request for a confirmation. Some customers, however, just will not respond to these types of letters. External auditors often satisfy themselves, at that time, by reviewing subsequent cash payments. That is, if a customer does not send back a response to a confirmation letter request, auditors would review the following month's receipts. If the customer paid on the account requested for confirmation, internal audit would assume that it was valid.

(iv) Accounts Receivable Sample Audit Report Findings

A: Account Adjustment Procedures Require Better Controls. The customer service department is responsible for issuing credit memos and adjusting accounts based upon customer complaints. We observed that the customer service representative made many of these credit memo adjustments by calling up the customer account from the accounts receivable system and then making the adjustment. This is simply a sales and accounts receivable adjustment with no further documentation. The customer service representative then makes a manual entry describing this adjustment. There is a risk that a customer service representative could make an inappropriate but undetected adjustment to a customer account and fail to manually record it.

Recommendation. Controls should be established so that all adjustments over a specified amount require a supervisor's approval through a systems acknowledgment before they will be processed. In addition, the accounts receivable system should be modified so that adjustments are recorded on a separate transaction log before their application to accounts receivable files. Appropriate management reports should be developed from this file.

B: Collection Agency Controls Are Lacking.   All open accounts over 120 days old are written off as uncollectible, but the accounts are given to an agency for collection or settlement. The collection agency then remits any monies collected less its commission. We observed that the accounts receivable department performs no follow-up on these referrals to the outside collection agency. They have no means of determining if the commissions paid to outside collection agencies are correct or even if collection agencies are using their best efforts to collect on overdue accounts.

Recommendation. The activities of outside collection agencies should be more closely monitored. Agencies should be required to provide detailed, account-by-account status reports on the accounts they are attempting to collect. Future contracts with outside collection agencies should grant the right to audit them.

22-5 PAYABLES PROCESSES

The operation of any organization necessarily requires that there be expenditures for necessary materials, products, equipment, salaries, and services of various kinds. All these expenditures involve the creation of organization obligations that are then either immediately liquidated—as in the case of a cash expenditure—or are liquidated at some future time through a note or financial obligation. The payables processes have to do with the recognition of all of these obligations and their subsequent control and handling. When these obligations are liquidated, control procedures over payable processes merge with the cash-disbursement procedures discussed earlier in this chapter. Payable processes are generated by the underlying operating or financial activities of the organization. They are an element of overall accounting control that is concerned with the promptness and accuracy with which obligations are formally recognized, the legitimacy and propriety of those obligations, and the procedures by which the stage is set for the final liquidation.

Payables often receive far less auditor attention than do accounts receivables because payables represent cash out. However, controls over disbursements and the accounts payables process can be a significant area of internal control concern for many organizations. Payables are the process whereby checks or other transactions are prepared to route cash out of the organization. Improperly controlled, the payables process can represent a significant control risk to the organization.

(a) TRANSACTION CYCLE

The payable processes involve activities that fit into fairly well-defined groups. In the first group are activities that cover the creation of the payables. This area raises questions about how the organization controls the amount of the payable and determines the payable's validity. In a second group are the various activities involved in administering existing payables. Various special problems are encountered here in terms of current recording and control. Finally, there are the procedures for the actual payment of individual payables, leading to the issuance of checks.

The accounts payable transaction process is a major segment of the purchasing cycle for the typical modern organization. This is a cycle wherein the organization purchases goods, receives them, and then initiates payment. Purchasing and receiving procedures and controls are discussed in Chapter 24. This section discusses the accounting or accounts payable portion of this purchasing cycle.

(i) Generating Payables. Payables can originate from a variety of sources. For many organizations, most will be a result of the purchase of products and services by an established purchasing department. These products and services relate largely to goods purchased for resale or for use in the production of products and services to be sold by the organization. The payables requirements can also be for other organizational operational needs.

In addition to payables requirements generated through the purchasing department, many products and services are, for various reasons, procured directly by other organizational line and staff activities. In terms of their importance, these can range from minor office supplies to major capital items. In all cases, a basic control is that obligations should be incurred only within authorized limits, covering the nature of the expenditure, its monetary amount, and the individual or position level incurring the particular obligation. The authorization to make these purchases and to approve payment requires the delegation of management authority. Although emergencies may develop when these authorized limits are violated, such emergencies should be carefully evaluated to ensure they are real emergencies and not just a device to get around established limits of authority.

When reviewing an accounts payable function, an internal auditor needs to understand what constitutes a valid payable. Regardless of the source of the payable, certain common accounting control criteria exist for all types of payables:

- *Is the type of expenditure reasonable?* The objective here is to ensure that any expenditure should bear a reasonable relationship to the operations of the business. Normally, this relationship is self-evident, but in other cases it may be partially or completely obscure. In the latter case, questions should be raised, and to the extent that a reasonable explanation is not available, it may be necessary to depend on the supporting documentation or the approvals recorded by responsible organization managers.

- *Are payables quantities excessive?* A related question may be whether the expenditure is of a reasonable magnitude in terms of the quantities purchased. Larger quantities may be purchased to obtain lower prices or to provide higher reserves for operational needs. In either case there is a level of judgment involved, supported by a reasonable management evaluation. The more excessive the deviation from normal levels, the greater the dependence on the judgment and approvals of responsible managers.

- *Are prices and terms correct?* There are two concerns with prices and terms. One has to do with the correctness of any previous agreements covering expenditures, including the present payable. The second is that prices and terms should be the best obtainable. In the latter case, it may be that nothing can be done about the particular payable, but there may be a possibility of affecting future expenditures. Prices and terms include list prices, trade and cash discounts, the time of payment, freight basis, warranties, guarantees, and the like.

- *Was proper value received?* One aspect of this proper value concern is whether the products or services invoiced have actually been received or rendered. A second is whether the goods or services were of the proper specifications, condition, and quality and were delivered according to agreed terms. Proper evidence is needed to cover both of these aspects. Controls must be in place to determine if the proper value was received prior to payment.

- *Are approvals and supporting evidence adequate?* The validation of payables requires that there be proper documentary evidence to back up the concerns as previously described. This evidence should consist of such documentation as purchase orders and receiving reports. If the check amount is above a specific limit, the documentation should also include the approvals by authorized managers or, if large enough, even organization officers. Payables checks produced through an automated accounts payable system should have controls to limit the generation of checks above specified monetary limits.

These basic control questions should be considered whether an accounts payable is generated manually or through an automated system. In addition, controls should be established to limit the introduction of payable transactions that are not authorized and that do not meet standards.

(ii) Administration of Accounts Payables.   The validation of a payable leads either to an immediate cash disbursement or to holding the item for later liquidation. From a control standpoint, it is desirable to recognize the payable formally at the earliest possible time. However, it may be more efficient to defer the formal accounting recognition until either the time of payment or the end of an accounting period, whichever comes first.

A key control over these disbursements is the matching of incoming records to the individual payables. These documents, whether in the form of computer records or paper, should flow directly to the accounts payable department. They include a copy of the purchase order from the purchasing department, the receiving report from the receiving department, claim forms for shortages or quality deficiencies, charges for transportation paid, and original copies or records of invoices received from vendors. All of these papers must be filed in a manner that will facilitate later assembly to support final payments.

All expenditures must ultimately be charged to their proper expense or asset accounts, as determined by existing accounting policies and procedures. The analysis of correct distributions requires an adequate knowledge of the total account structure. Automated systems often cannot provide this information, and accounts payable analysts are then charged with handling the allocation decision. This actual distribution may also require special supplementary worksheets to document any special payment cost distribution.

Once the payables are formally recognized, the overall control of payables is achieved through one or more control accounts backed up by subsidiary ledgers. The latter must be periodically checked to verify that they are in agreement with controls, and offsetting errors in individual accounts should be checked and reconciled when vendor statements are received. These detailed ledgers are commonly maintained on automated systems.

As mentioned previously, many vendors offer discount terms if bills are paid promptly. For example, an invoice might be noted "2%-10, Net-30." This means the vendor is offering a 2% discount if the invoice is paid in cash within 10 days, with the net amount due in 30 days. Where opportunities exist for taking advantage of cash discounts through timely payments, controls must be provided to exploit these benefits. Depending upon the overall "cost of money" interest rate, the failure to use cash discounts can represent a severe financial penalty in terms of current interest costs. Internal audit should always verify that management has a program or system in place to make optimal cash discount payment decisions.

In some cases, the terms of the transaction may require payment by specific dates. Good relations with vendors depend in part on making payments at the proper times. Late payments and the deduction of unearned discounts are especially irritating. All of this means that controls must be set up to insure completion of the final processing and payment in the manner and at the time intended.

(iii) Final Review and Payment.   The final phase of the payable process is to prepare the obligation for payment. The key controls at this stage are the final matching of supporting documentation, the deduction of any other claims, the preparation of the check or payment, and the final review and release of the payment.

The pertinent supporting papers—the purchase order, receiving report, and the invoice—must be brought together and checked for clerical accuracy and agreement. This set of documentation is usually physically assembled, and filed, and a request for a check is then prepared. If automated systems are highly integrated, the computer can perform much of this matching process, but some amount of manual matching and assembly is often required. There may be a risk of incorrect approvals and payments if personnel rely too much on automated controls and do not look for obvious problems.

Control procedures should be in place to identify any outstanding claims against the particular creditor that should be deducted from the payment. In some cases, amounts are to be withheld pending final inspection or usage. The payment amount approval should be appropriately modified to reflect these deductions.

A request for a check, supported by the previously described set of documents, is now subjected to review and approval by a properly authorized individual, and is routed to individuals or the automated system to prepare the actual disbursement check. This check and the supporting payable package is then ready for inspection by independent reviewers who will either provide one of the check signatures or will initial the authorization for an officer to sign. If a check has been mechanically signed, controls should be in place to insure that all remittances above a specified amount require additional approval. At this stage, the reviewers and signers should be concerned both with the completeness of the supporting papers and with the kinds of questions covered earlier as part of general payables validation. When this phase has been completed, the check number is referenced on the documents, supporting papers are marked canceled to prevent duplicate payment or reuse, and the check is mailed or transmitted directly to the vendors or bank.

The payable process as just described can vary in many individual situations, with automated systems and electronic funds transfers creating different variations. In any arrangement, the most critical accounting control is that the various processing activities are separately assigned to different individuals. With such a separation of responsibilities, the accountabilities of the individuals can be more precisely fixed.

(iv) Other Payable Processes.   While the greater part of the payable process will normally be concerned with the types of accounts payable just described, a number of operating activities generate other types of payables. Some of these are remittances between operating units and focus more directly on the correctness of the periodic financial statements. Others may have significant operational aspects. Several of the more common supplementary payable processes are notes payable and travel expenses. Others are expenses that occur regularly, such as taxes or insurance.

All of these payment cycle transactions represent an outlay of cash from the organization. From an operational and financial accounting standpoint, these expenses should be recognized as expenses applicable to the current period, even though they may not have yet been processed as regular payables. This is the process of accruing for known expenses as discussed previously. Accruals are in effect a preliminary recognition of obligations that will later be fully recognized and then liquidated. An example would be interest on notes and bonds payable, taxes, or even salaries. The control objective is to recognize all pertinent accruals and to measure them as accurately as possible.

Notes Payable

A normal payable is the last step in a good faith agreement where the organization orders the goods or services, the vendor delivers them along with an invoice, and the organization pays that invoice through its accounts payables process. Notes are a contractual obligation to pay a specified amount rather than just a bill backed by a vendor invoice. A note occurs when the organization signs a legally enforceable contract, often with interest penalties, agreeing to pay specified amounts.

In many situations, the general payable process may result directly in the creation of notes payable. This treatment is adopted usually when longer payment periods are envisioned, when the purchase represents something more valuable than normal trade goods, or when the organization does not have good credit. A note affords a vendor security over the debt. The vendor may also wish to be able to sell or discount the notes with financial institutions or to use them as collateral for loans. The notes payable may also come as a later development when accounts payable cannot be liquidated on a timely basis.

The unique control in a notes payable would be in the conditions for its creation and in the procedures that will adequately insure the meeting of future payment dates for both interest and principal. Most organizations do not incur notes payables in the normal course of their business, and a note must be handled differently from the normal document-matching process used for accounts payables. Adequate detailed supporting records are also necessary for reference and control.

Travel Expenses

Obligations incurred for travel expenses are a type of payable with special characteristics. The usual sequence is to advance funds to the individual travelers and to then credit those advances at the time properly approved expense reports are submitted. However, the personal nature of travel expenses, coupled with a distribution of cash advances, often creates operating problems. Advances may be used by the recipient for personal purposes or commingling with personal funds. In other cases, the money is used legitimately but there may be procrastination in preparing employee travel expense reports. Systematic follow-up is required to keep the submission of expense reports up to date.

Employees should report their travel expenses on a form completed immediately after the trip, or on a periodic basis for more frequent travelers. A travel expense form can be structured many different ways, but it usually allows the employee to break down expenses by category (such as transportation, lodging, meals, and others) as well as by day over the period reported. Figure 22.17 is an example of a travel expense form with some key information fields noted. Tax policies covering the deductibility of employee expenses will influence the format of a travel expense report. For example, in the late 1980s the United States began to allow only partial tax deductibility for meals. Although some organizations once required expense reporting only on a per diem basis, it became necessary for all to report separate categories for meals and lodging.

When the expense accounts are actually submitted, there is a need to validate the propriety of the expenditures claimed. Travel expense reports normally should go through multiple levels of approval with the first being the supervisor who approved the travel

Figure 22.17 Travel Expense Report Example

Name Herm Hollerith							Period Ending 10/15/05	
	10/09/2005	10/10/2005	10/11/2005	10/12/2005	10/13/2005	10/14/2005	10/15/2005	
	Sun	Mon	Tue	Wed	Thu	Fri	Sat	Totals
Miles Driven		36						36
Mileage Expense		10.44						10.44
Parking and Tolls		4.75						4.75
Auto Rental				26.85	26.85			53.70
Taxi/Limo				18.50		18.75		37.25
Other (Rail or Bus)								
Airfare			238.55		238.55			477.10
Transportation Total		15.19	257.05	26.85	284.15			583.24
Lodging				105.77	105.77			211.54
Other								
Breakfast				9.50	7.56			17.06
Lunch					9.22			9.22
Dinner			24.75	23.88				48.63
Subtotal Meals			24.75	33.38	16.78			74.91
Lodging and Meals Total			24.75	139.15	122.55			286.45
Supplies/Equipment								
Phone and Fax				1.20	3.40			4.60
Other								
Other								
Other								
Entertainment								
Total per day		15.19	281.80	167.20	410.10			874.29

(Continued)

Figure 22.17   (*Continued*)

DETAILED ENTERTAINMENT RECORD					
Date	Item	Persons Entertained/Business Relationship	Place Name and Location	Business Purpose	Amount
PURPOSE OF TRIP				SUMMARY	
Maximum Division Operational Audit				TOTAL EXPENSES	874.29
				LESS CASH ADVANCE	
				LESS COMPANY CHARGES	
				AMOUNT DUE EMPLOYEE	874.29
				AMOUNT DUE COMPANY	0.00

Herm Hollerith	10/29/2005		
PREPARED BY	DATE	APPROVED BY	DATE

and understands the nature of the travel. The travel expense form then moves to the accounts payables unit or a travel accounting group in a larger organization. They would review it for compliance with procedures, approve it, and prepare a check or cash transfer.

Most problems involved with employee travel deal with the propriety of the claimed expense. The traveler may have incurred expenses beyond established levels, or, in the absence of such established levels, in excess of prudent expenditures. Items not allowable may be claimed as expenses, or the amounts claimed may not be properly documented. Entertainment expenditures can be another problem area.

The organization must have established travel policies covering various types of allowed and disallowed expenses, expense limit amounts, as well as receipt requirements. This entire procedure should be continuously monitored and questions must be raised when established policies are unduly violated or where evidence is not sufficiently clear. These controls are necessary to provide needed support for organization expenditures and to minimize the always existing temptation for a traveler to use expense accounts for personal advantage.

The types of controls and procedures over travel accounting will depend upon the organization's overall employee travel requirements. The disbursement of cash advances followed by travel expense reports is adequate for low levels of travel, but higher levels may require better controls over the process. For example, the organization may obtain company credit cards for its frequent travelers. This eliminates much of the requirement for cash advances and provides a ready set of receipt copies. However, an organization can lose some control over the travel process if corporate travel charges are not reviewed with the same attention to detail that manually prepared travel expenses receive.

Other Accounts Payables

Any instance where the organization is issuing checks to outsiders can be viewed by internal audit as an "accounts payable" activity in their risk-based planning. Many of these activities are specialized and should have their own unique controls.

When reviewing organization activities, internal audit should understand all areas where payments are made to outsiders. Beyond such special functions as payroll or travel accounting, control is often enhanced when as much of this activity as possible is routed through a centralized accounts payable function, as has been discussed in this section.

(b) ACCOUNTS PAYABLES INTERNAL CONTROLS

Accounts payables is an area where monies are flowing out of the organization, and controls here are very important. Most payables controls fall into three very broad categories. First, all funds disbursed from an accounts payable function should only be for authorized purchases or activities in the correct amounts. As a second general control, the payables should be made only to approved entities. Finally, controls should also be in place to prevent duplicate or otherwise improper payments. Weak controls over an accounts payable operation can result in fraud and abuse.

In order to insure that the funds disbursed from an accounts payable function are for the correct amounts, there should be some type of process matching to the supporting documentation before any check is issued. For inventory and other supplies, any request for a check should be supported by an approved purchase order and an acknowledgment that the goods purchased were received in good order. Purchase orders define the agreed upon price for the goods and the receiving report provides an assurance that the goods were received in good condition in the quantities ordered.

This authorization and acknowledgment of receipt control should apply to all purchases. This means there should be a designated set of individuals who can authorize the purchase only of certain classes of goods and up to certain authorized monetary limits. An independent person should acknowledge delivery. This separation control should apply to all authorizations for payables, including such areas as heat and power for facilities. While a purchase order would not be issued for the monthly electrical bill, the amounts billed should be reviewed from time to time to insure that services have been delivered in the amounts reported on the billings.

Authorization and acknowledgment controls both become more difficult for services where the final product cannot easily be measured. For example, a consulting firm may submit a bill for services authorized by some senior manager. Controls should be in place to determine that the consulting engagement was correctly authorized and that the services were actually delivered. The accounts payable function should not necessarily question the appropriateness of these types of transactions, but they should determine that the transactions were authorized by individuals having the authority for those types of transactions.

The second general accounts payable internal control is that payments should be made only to approved entities. If a supplier has been authorized, the name and address of that supplier should have been established on a central accounts payable vendor file.

Vendors are normally established on an automated system file, and strong controls need to be established over who is authorized to add new vendors or update this file. These controls should be designed to prevent an unauthorized person from adding a fictitious vendor or making a mailing address change to a vendor's records. The risk here is that checks could be diverted to someone's personal address.

The third general area of accounts payable internal controls involves systems and accounting controls to detect and prevent duplicate payments. Due to delays in processing checks or other operational errors, more than one request for payment may go to accounts payable for the same disbursement item. The risk of duplicate payments can be minimized if all payables checks issued are tied to a purchase order or similar authorizing number. The system would then raise warning flags on requests for potential duplicate payments.

(c) PAYABLES INTERNAL AUDIT PROCEDURES

The accounts payable area is a key risk area that should be given a high level of review attention by internal audit. This review can be part of an examination of general accounting systems and controls (as discussed in this chapter) or as a review of another related function that relies upon disbursements from accounts payable. For example, a review of the purchasing and receiving process (as described in Chapter 24) might also consider a review of related accounts payable controls.

As with other internal audit review activities, any review of the accounts payable function will have elements of financial, operational, and computer audit procedures. This is another good area for the use of CAATs to analyze payments and to search for potentially improper payments. For example, if an auditor sees a risk that employees may be setting up fictitious vendors and diverting funds to them, a CAAT could be developed to match vendor disbursements by payee address to employee addresses. This type of CAAT and others will be discussed later in this section.

The earlier discussion on audits of the accounts receivable function emphasized how that function normally receives extensive attention from external auditors. This is not nearly as true for the accounts payables function. However, it is an important accounting systems and control function in the modern organization, which should be given proper attention by internal audit.

(i) Financial Audit Procedures.   An internal auditor might initiate any financial-related review of the accounts payable function by considering controls surrounding the three very general internal controls discussed in the preceding paragraphs. As with any review of this type, internal audit should first develop an understanding of the process for authorizing the issuance of accounts payables checks. One approach for obtaining this understanding, as used elsewhere in this book, is to develop a very simple flow chart that describes the accounts payable process. Figure 22.18 is an example of this type of flow chart.

The accounts payable flowchart shows significant steps in this accounting process, starting with the logging of invoices to be set up for payment and ending with the issuance of checks to vendors. Once internal audit has developed and verified the accuracy of this type of flow chart, it can be used as a basis for a series of audit tests. For example, internal audit might select a sample of invoices that have been received within the accounts payable function and then could use this sample to trace them through all of the procedures leading up to the production of checks. This type of sample, if it followed the statistical attribute sampling rules discussed in Chapter 13, would allow internal audit to make an overall

Figure 22.18 Accounts Payable Process

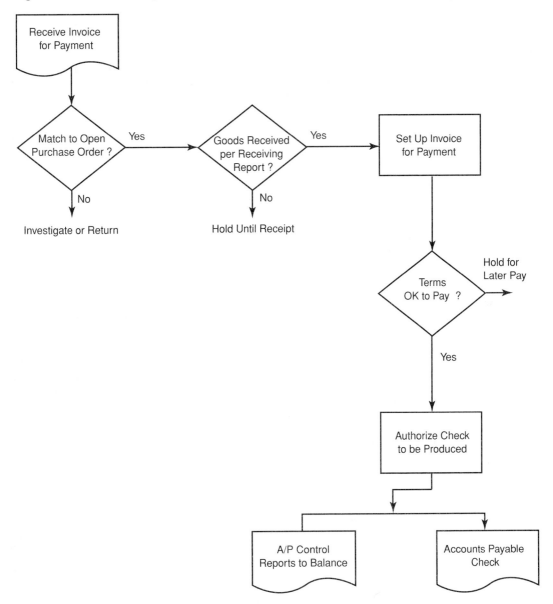

assessment of accounts payable controls. Following this flow chart, internal audit could perform financial audit procedures as are outlined in Figure 22.19.

Controls over the bank accounts used to issue payments are essentially the same as those for general checking accounts discussed earlier in this chapter. Organizations are also increasingly making payments through electronic fund transfers using electronic data interchange (EDI) systems. Although the discussion is oriented towards the purchasing function, EDI controls are discussed in Chapter 24.

Figure 22.19   Accounts Payable Audit Procedures

Audit _____   Location _____   Date _____

Audit Step	Initial	W/P
1. Obtain a listing of accounts payable as of the audit date and determine if it accurately represents account by matching records to unpaid voucher file or other general ledger account balances.		
2. Review procedures for matching invoices with approved purchase orders and receiving reports. Report any exceptions.		
3. Calculate significant activity ratios including turnover (purchase/payables) and payables/total liabilities. Investigate ratio exceptions as compared to prior year activity or published industry data.		
4. Compare expense balances to prior year or budgeted amounts for indications of possible understatement or unrecorded liabilities.		
5. Compare a sample of accounts payable transactions to supporting invoices, purchase orders, and other documents supporting the payment.		
6. Observe the number of the last check issued and mailed on the last day of a period end during the audit period and trace to accounting records.		
7. Review procedures for taking advantage of cash discounts. From a sample determine that discounts are taken when appropriate.		
8. Review procedures for approving and issuing checks to determine that controls are in place to prevent and detect unauthorized disbursements.		
9. Consider confirming accounts receivable if questions exist regarding the authenticity of the recorded payables balances.		
10. If payables not independently confirmed, reconcile a sample of recently payable checks issued to vendor statements. Investigate any differences.		
11. Review procedures to the production of A/P checks. Determine that check stocks/signature plates are properly controlled.		
12. Review procedures in place for the periodic reconciliation of check issued records with statements from banks.		

(ii) Operational Audit Procedures. Operational audit procedures for the accounts payables function should focus on an assessment of controls to safeguard assets and efficiencies in payables processing. Safeguard controls are especially important here as disputes over the timing or basis for payments typically do not take place until considerable time has passed. There is a need for strong documentation and documentation retrieval procedures to support any problem issues. Internal audit can provide a service to management by reviewing procedures and performing appropriate audit tests.

Other operational audit procedures in this area include reviews of physical procedures to safeguard the printing of checks and procedures to limit access to account entries and the processing of transactions. When an automated system is used for accounts payables, logical security controls should be in place (as were discussed in Chapter 19). Although an internal auditor may encounter situations where security controls require improvements, these controls are particularly important for an accounts payables system. Otherwise, it might be possible for a person to divert accounts payable checks to a home address or to make some other improper changes. This diversion of funds might not be detected until well after the funds are gone.

Physical controls over the printing of checks are also needed. If this printing process takes place in a central facility, internal audit's review of those controls (as discussed in Chapters 16 and 19) should provide an adequate understanding of those control procedures. However, for reasons of safeguarding check stocks or signature plates or for payables programs, accounts payable check printing has sometimes moved to the accounting office, with the check production taking place on a local printer. While this eliminates exposures over this process in a larger data-processing organization, there may be a greater risk with this operation in an unsecured office area.

(iii) Computer Audit Procedures. Most high-volume accounts payable functions use automated systems to control and generate their payments. These accounts payable systems may be freestanding applications that use an authorized vendor and other files to produce the checks, but are more commonly integrated with other control systems, including purchasing, receiving, and the general ledger. As discussed for all major systems areas, internal audit must develop an understanding of the automated systems controls over accounts payable and how they relate to other related controls. The discussions on reviews of applications controls in Chapter 17 should provide additional guidance.

As mentioned several times in this section, an accounts payable system is a particularly good candidate for CAATs. Internal audit–developed retrievals can identify areas of improper activity, duplicate payments, or just operational inefficiencies. Figures 22.20 and 22.21 illustrate two examples of internal auditor–developed accounts payable CAAT reports. Figure 22.20 was developed to highlight potential duplicate payments. Disbursements were sorted by vendor and the amount paid within a limited amount of time to highlight items for further investigation.

Figure 22.21 is a CAAT designed to detect employees who might also be on the accounts payable vendor file. Vendor and employee names were matched on address. This is a very imprecise test at best. Numerous small variations in an address can make entries look different on a computer match but will not cause a problem for postal delivery authorities.

(iv) Sample Audit Report Findings

A: Vendor Invoices Paid Outside of Accounts Payable System. We reconciled the ac-

Figure 22.20   Duplicate Payment Test CAAT

Vendor No.	Vendor Name	Invoice Ref.	Date Paid	Check No.	A/P Amt. Paid	Audit Ref.
3872254	Cratchitt & Scrooge, Inc.	XMA5922	12/05/99	985331	$12,692.27	
3872254	Cratchitt & Scrooge, Inc.	XMA5922	01/05/00	986021	$12,692.27	DUPLICATE?
6589455	Whiz Bang Corp.	5687-25	11/12/99	976621	$537.10	
6589455	Whiz Bang Corp.	5687-25	01/10/00	987234	$537.10	DUPLICATE?
6629587	Buzzey Supplies	123788	01/12/00	987388	$1,289.15	
6629587	Buzzey Supplies	123897	01/15/00	987499	$1,289.15	DUPLICATE BILLING?
6711987	XYZ Computers	88-321	12/22/99	985502	$55,382.89	
6711987	XYZ Computers	88-321	01/05/00	986211	$55,382.89	DUPLICATE?

counts payable ledger to the disbursements checking account. We found that manually prepared check forms, developed for emergency disbursement requirements, are used almost totally for vendor and supply purchases by the advertising department. This is in violation of company procedures. We also found that many of the payees on these advertising department checks were to vendors not carried in regular accounts payable vendor records. The advertising department advised that they bypassed procedures for automated accounts payable checks due to the "special" requirements of advertising. This procedure violates established accounting systems controls.

Recommendation. All advertising department normal disbursements should be processed through the automated accounts payables system. The accounts payables department should regularly review the manually prepared checking account for further occurrences of uses of manual checks for normal disbursements.

B: Duplicate Vendors on the Vendor Master File. We developed a CAAT to look for potential duplicate entries on the vendor master file. We found numerous instances where the engineering and manufacturing production control departments use identical vendors or different units of the same vendor. Since each department is responsible for submitting

Figure 22.21   Employee Improper Account CAAT

						A/P—EMPLOYEE MASTER MATCH—MARCH 1			
		QUESTIONABLE PAYMENTS					MATCHING ADDRESSES		
Date	Amount	Payee	Check #	Address	Zip	Employee	Address	Zip
03/01/01	$12,325.00	RBJ Consultants	137882	Suite 101 425 Oak Talleytown, IL	60298	Johnson, Ralph B.	425 Oak Street Talleytown, IL	60298-1269
03/15/01	$636.00	Technical Publishers	204115	823 Crawford Suite 10A Murtle, TN	35889	Ryan, Estelle A.	823 Crawford-Apt. 10A Murtle, TN	35889

requests for new vendors to accounts payable, minor changes in name or address might be accepted on the vendor master file. Multiple entries may lead to erroneous duplicate payments.

Recommendation. The accounts payable department should establish procedures to prevent duplicate entries on the accounts payable vendor file. Alphabetic lists of vendors should be consulted before entering new vendors, and suspected similarities investigated. A program should be initiated to eliminate possible duplicate entries from the current vendor file.

C: Accounts Payable System Contingency Planning.   We reviewed the accounts payable system application contingency plan for processing at an off-site location in the event of a major disruption in data-processing services. We found that the plan has not been tested, in violation of policy, and that several of the file names listed in the plan did not correspond to the current operating accounts payable system. In the event of a failure in data-processing services, there could be a severe disruption in meeting the organization's disbursement obligations.

Recommendation. The accounts payable application contingency plan should be updated to reflect the current production system. Procedures should be established to review the plan for currency on a regular basis. Tests of the accounts payable system should be scheduled at the off-site location at least once per year.

22-6 ACCOUNTING SYSTEMS AND INTERNAL AUDIT

Accounting systems and accounting transactions are a major area of concern for internal auditors in most organizations. This chapter has introduced cash and the general ledger, as well as the payables and receipts cycles. Other accounting systems, although not significant enough to represent an entire business systems cycle, will be discussed in other chapters.

Even if an internal audit describes itself as only operational, these accounting systems and their controls are significant areas for auditor review. Internal audit needs to understand major controls in an organization's accounting systems in order to perform other important operational tests, the results of which should be meaningful to organizational management. Many of the control procedures discussed in this chapter should be useful to internal auditors in their reviews of other audit areas.

CHAPTER 23

Manufacturing Production Planning

23-1 NATURE OF THE PRODUCTION PROCESS

Production, as a term, applies to all situations where materials are combined or modified in some significant manner through the use of appropriate facilities and equipment. This production process is also often referred to as the manufacturing process, covering a wide range of situations. A reflection on the various kinds of manufacturing organizations and the great number of different kinds of products and services produced makes one realize the magnitude of the range and the difficulty of generalizing the manufacturing process. However, all have common characteristics of taking inputs of material and labor and, with the use of facilities and equipment, combining these elements in such a fashion that the resulting products are ready for internal use or for sale to the outside world.

The production process will vary by the individual organization. In some cases, such as a chain of retail stores, this production process may appear to be quite insignificant. In the case of an automobile manufacturer or a refiner of metals, it is the major segment of the operations in terms of costs incurred and number of people involved. The production process is often a very complicated area because of the range of types of activities. There are, for example, various developmental activities that pertain to the way materials are obtained and processed, the facilities and equipment used, and required personnel training. On the operational side, there are the necessary movements of materials, the use of machines, supervision of people, the coordination of various subactivities, needed inspections, and the final packaging and transfer of completed units. Related are the problems of coordination with other important activities such as purchasing, finance, human resources, and marketing, as total organization operations are integrated to achieve maximum profitability. The production process normally is of vital concern to management and all other significant organization components. The challenge to internal audit is particularly interesting because of the great need for effective control over the production operations.

23-2 PRODUCTION PROCESS CYCLE

Despite the wide range of different types of production situations, which exist not only between but also within an individual organization, there is a cyclical pattern with definite stages in the production process cycle, including:

1. Estimates of the demand for needed products from the production process. That is, what is to be produced, and when?

2. The planning necessary to produce the products so specified.

3. The procurement of the needed inputs to carry out the planned production activities.

4. Receipt, installation, and testing of equipment and production processes.

5. The actual processing of the planned products.

6. The final transfer of the completed products for other organization use or for sale to customers. Included here also is the control of scrap and excess materials.

The following sections will discuss these individual stages in more detail with particular emphasis on the problems of control. The discussion includes additional aspects of the production process that cut across the entire cycle, and require more extended consideration. In order to perform any type of review over production operations, whether an operational, financial, or information systems–related review, the internal auditor needs to gain a general understanding of the process. This can often be gained through discussions with production management, walk-through tours, and asking many control and process-related questions.

(a) DETERMINATION OF NEEDS FOR PRODUCTS

The starting point for the production activity is the determination of the items that need to be produced and when they are needed. This determination includes the specifications of products, quantities, and desired delivery times, and is the responsibility of management, often in direct consultation with key customers. Production planning involves the simultaneous evaluation of many factors, including pertinent cost and revenue estimates as determined by the staff and operational groups. Other questions may include the following:

- How will the product be sold?
- What prices can be charged?
- What will be the cost of producing the product?
- What are the related procurement problems?
- What other supporting activities will be required?

Viewed narrowly and perhaps traditionally, the production activity begins only after this determination of needs has been completed. This is essentially a responding type of role for production management that is not always the approach followed today by modern manufacturing management. Rather, the modern production function is a partner in the determination of these production needs, with a role that would include at least: (1) Counseling with the management decision group as to the ability to produce desired products in terms of timing and costs, and the evaluation of possible alternatives; (2) initiating information as to new technical developments that might increase capacity and/or reduce costs, thus providing new options to the organization; and (3) conducting research and engineering studies in the area of facilities, processing, and product design which may increase production capabilities or reduce costs.

The substance of this partnership relationship is that the production function is itself an influence in the determination of the products produced. The first important control aspect is, therefore, that the production function should make its best possible contribution to the determination of production needs in the organization's best overall interests.

(b) PLANNING FOR ACTUAL PRODUCTION

Although production's participation in the determination of needs may have initiated the planning process, the detailed planning of those needs is often the basis for a more definitive planning effort. Typical considerations in this detailed planning process include:

- Evaluating existing capacity to produce the products wanted in the necessary volume within specified time periods.
- Determining how existing capacity might be expanded through more intensive use of existing equipment, additional equipment, and extra resources, with appropriate consideration of costs, timing, and quality of product.
- Potentially constructing or purchasing new production facilities, with the related factors of timing and costs of bringing the new capacity on stream.
- Determining particular types of manufacturing processes to be used, including the investigation of new methods, in relation to product specification alternatives.
- Determining needs for machine tools, specialized automated equipment, and other equipment, and scheduling programs to supply those needs.
- Planning for appropriate placement of equipment and supporting services to assure the efficient flow of production with the planned processes, facilities, and equipment.
- Determining personnel needs and planning for any necessary hiring and training.
- Determining material needs based on bills of material and coordination with the purchasing department as to procurement availability and timing.
- Arranging necessary supporting services, such as computer systems support, specialized equipment to be leased, and other special requirements.

The essential control considerations at this stage are that plans should be adequate to cover the pertinent aspects for the products needed, that supporting actions are initiated, and that procedures are established whereby the progress of those plans can be satisfactorily monitored. The latter action is especially important when there are engineering, development, or procurement requirements for individual parts or phases that are prerequisites for other parts and phases, and that must, therefore, be completed on a timely basis.

(c) PROCUREMENT OF NEEDED INPUTS

With the production input needs adequately identified, the next stage is the procurement action itself. Although the production function is normally not charged with direct responsibility for procurement, what is important is that other groups actually responsible for procurement are adequately coordinated, including the purchasing function for materials and equipment; construction for new facilities, if required; engineering for necessary technical services; and human resources for the recruitment and training or transfer of needed personnel. This coordination includes preliminary contacts during the planning stage, the transmittal of definitive requirements, and continuing liaison to deal with possible problems that might arise during the actual procurement. An internal auditor reviewing these areas should be interested that these activities are carried on in an orderly and efficient manner.

With the advent of ''just-in-time'' manufacturing techniques, planning has changed dramatically in recent years. Previously, production procurement often involved long lead times to order and build products. Materials would arrive in advance, be placed in store-rooms, and subsequently pulled when needed for actual production. Beginning in the 1980s, this changed for many manufacturing organizations. The idea today is to deliver goods, if possible, directly to the production floor just when they are needed in the production process. Manufacturers do not want to keep excess inventory in stores but to introduce it into their production cycle as quickly and efficiently as possible.

The U.S. automotive industry provides a good example of just-in-time manufacturing planning and operations. Today, many automobile components arrive at the production plant and production line only when needed. Automobile seats, for example, are built by an outside vendor and are scheduled to arrive at the plant very close to the production line process when they are needed for placement on the new automobile. The supplier manufactures them to order only as needed; there is essentially no need to keep these goods in stores inventories.

Just-in-time manufacturing and potential audit techniques to review this process require more detail than space allows in this chapter. However, other related audit procedures are discussed in Chapter 24, ''Purchases, Receipts, and Electronic Data Interchange.''

(d) RECEIVING, INSTALLATION, AND TESTING

The inputs as procured now flow to the production function. The receiving of these items may be direct from vendors, from stores, or from other internal sources. Then they must be adequately inspected to determine their conformance to previously designated quantities and specifications. Receiving will be discussed in Chapter 24. Where an installation of some type is required—as in the case of tooling and equipment—this is now carried out. Also, such equipment must be tested to determine whether its performance meets designated specifications and standards. The problems here will vary greatly depending on the complexity of the particular production process. Very often, this is the important, critical phase when errors are detected or unexpected operational problems are identified and resolved. The control focus at this stage is to carry out these important preparatory activities in a thorough and efficient manner, with strong attention given to controls and details. Failure to do so can result in excessive costs or serious delays.

(e) ACTUAL PRODUCTION

Assuming that all needed inputs, facilities, equipment, materials, people, and supporting services have been procured, made available, installed, and adequately tested, the stage is set for the actual production activities. These activities are the ultimate realization of the earlier planning activities, and in many cases are interwoven through the production process. Production activities involve many specialized subactivities and functions, including:

- Handling and effective utilization of materials
- Administration and effective utilization of labor

- Utilization and control of supporting services
- Scheduling and control of the individual production activities
- Appropriate inspection and quality-control activities at the various stages
- Maintenance of plant and equipment
- Control of the production activities in terms of levels of their physical performance
- Achieving adequate cost control
- Continuing liaison with organization activities that supply these inputs
- Coordination with ultimate users of the product to report progress and assess the need for special developments

These various production-related activities are overlapping and interrelated in many respects. Together, they combine in the processing of applicable inputs for the ultimate completion of the particular products in the form and at the times desired. These steps are fairly common, no matter what the product manufactured, whether it be building integrated circuit chips that require the etching of lines 0.000001 of an inch in width or less, or building a wide-body passenger aircraft. Basic concepts do not change all that much. Whenever embarking on any review of manufacturing activities, an internal auditor should attempt to gain a basic understanding of this process. As mentioned previously, this involves observation and many questions.

Internal auditors should always think of these common traits or characteristics when visiting a production facility and being asked to understand the process. The good internal auditor should always think of analogies when reviewing various and different types of processes. For example, the planning and placement of that 0.000001 circuit board line is, conceptually, really not all that different from the planning and building of a highway. Questions regarding planning the paths, types of equipment necessary, and control of labor and equipment costs are valid in either case.

(f) FINAL PRODUCTION OUTPUT

With the actual processing complete, the product is now ready for transfer directly to vendors, to a staging area for inclusion in other processes, or to an operational area outside of the regular production function. This completed product may now be ready for sale to the final consumer, as a component to be used in the completion of a larger product or some type of material to be used in the subsequent processing operation outside the organization. The product may also be one that is used by the organization itself—for example, in the use of electric power by an electrical utility for its own production plant purposes. The technical dividing line of where the production process actually stops is not always clear, but is generally at what has been organizationally designated as the production department.

The completed production goods would now be ready for final inspection and transfer to the parties who take custody. Control procedures here include provisions for adequate physical care and handling; the need for physical movements with reasonable promptness; accuracy of the physical counts, weights, and other pertinent measures; and the completion of documentation confirming changed accountabilities. These activities should be carried out in a controlled manner in accordance with standards appropriate to the individual situation.

23-3 MAJOR PRODUCTION PROBLEM AREAS

In developing an understanding of a production process, an internal auditor should consider production in terms of the overall operational cycle. It is useful to understand the flow of the production factors in a sequential sense, and, within the production process, the individual operations that go back and forth within the overall cycle. There are many problem areas that cut across all stages of the operational cycle and need to be examined and understood in greater depth. These problem areas in turn overlap, are interrelated, and often involve significant technical issues. This section discusses some of these problem areas to provide internal auditors with a basis for better understanding the production process and related control problems. In this connection, it is important to understand the relationships of the various production activities to other organization activities outside the production operations.

(a) PRODUCT DEVELOPMENT AND DESIGN

The production cycle begins with the determination of demand requirements for the products and services to be produced. The role of the production function is both to respond cooperatively as other organization personnel need information or assistance and to do a number of things on its own initiative. Here, the production function endeavors to employ its technical expertise in product development and design in ways that enhance organization interests. This includes the study of the properties of various types of materials—both old and new—and how they might be utilized more effectively, as well as possibilities of new approaches to the processing of these materials and new types of fabrication. All of this may apply to final end products, to components of products, or to some aspect of how components are combined or assembled. The benefits achieved may be to serve new uses or existing ones in a less costly or more efficient manner. A portion of this work includes special engineering activities, extensive testing of alternatives, and the development of prototypes. The production function should be continuously seeking new ways to improve its processes and to get more value for costs expended. The challenge here is to induce a creative and aggressive approach at all levels of production operations. What is needed is both the proper motivation of individuals and the intercommunication that makes possible the larger efforts of the total group.

While efforts should continue to search for new production approaches, management must choose between available alternatives. This decision may be based on the materials to be used, any specific production equipment, and any specialized facilities requirements. These decisions will very much depend on the nature of the production process. In a metal products fabrication industry, a decision may be based on whether the product may be made from forging or casting—these are certainly not concerns for electronic assembly! Involved here are such factors as the volume of product to be processed, the time available, and the related costs. This planning often involves a great deal of technical expertise, derived from previous production experience, as well as a good understanding of the material and labor cost alternatives.

The production planner must develop these production analyses in a comprehensive and accurate manner, with maximum objectivity. All of this must be in accordance with time schedules that will support the time requirements of the other parts of the larger production schedule.

(b) FACILITIES, EQUIPMENT, AND TOOLING

Facilities planning is a part of the decision process supporting the product design and the subsequent processing. A number of more specific problems, however, arise in connection with the actual implementation of production facilities, including the following.

- How much space is required, and of what type? What will be the penalties of compromises in these preferences?

- If there is existing production space, what is the priority of other alternative uses? What will it cost to adapt this space to the given production need?

- If space is to be acquired, what is available and what will be the costs of adapting it to the production needs?

- How important is the geographical location of the facilities in terms of such factors as labor supply, community living conditions, distance from suppliers, closeness to point of delivery for later use of the product, related availability of transportation services, cost of land, and taxes?

- If new facilities are to be constructed, what is the timing and cost? Is the organization able to provide the necessary capital? Should it, given other competing capital needs?

- To what extent should newly constructed facilities be for the current special production purpose versus being adaptable for more general usage?

- What power, telecommunications, water, and sewage-disposal type services will be required for the facilities, and to what extent will they be available?

- What provision needs to be made for special environmental controls such as lighting, humidity control, heating, and ventilation?

- What social, environmental, or community issues need to be considered?

Many of these issues will be of such significance that they must be resolved as a part of the total product and process decisions. In other cases they can be determined more independently, based on careful analysis of the pertinent factors. Always, however, will be the interrelationship with the activities and needs of other organization activities. While these are management decisions, an internal auditor should attempt to recognize these facilities-related factors and evaluate them accurately and objectively in terms of the best long-term interests of the organization. Again, there is also the necessity of following good control procedures in accordance with acceptable time schedules.

As in the case of facilities, the need for production equipment and tooling has been a part of the earlier planning of the product design and the related processing. Detailed decisions have to be made as to the types of equipment utilized, including specific operational characteristics and features. In many situations this will in effect become the determination of the vendor source, since certain features may be unique to equipment produced by particular makers. Special problems that require consideration and analysis here include the following:

- What is the economic payoff of alternative types of equipment and tooling in terms of speed of processing and reduction of labor and overhead costs?

- For the same type of machines and tooling, what is the economic payoff for different size machines and individual optional features?
- What is the right balance between special-purpose and general-purpose equipment and tooling? What factors affect this determination?
- To what extent should equipment and tooling be purchased, leased, or even made by the organization itself?
- To what extent should existing equipment and tooling be reworked?

Auditors should recognize that there is a wide range of factors to be considered which go beyond production expertise and involve marketing, personnel, and financial issues. In any event, these determinations must be made on the basis of as complete and accurate data as are available, and on a timely basis. When reviewing production operations, an internal auditor should always recognize that there is not just one right answer. While not an expert on specialized production activities, the internal auditor can serve management in these areas by asking basic questions about whether the area in question is supported by adequate control procedures.

(c) PRODUCTION LOGISTICS

In addition to planning for equipment and tooling, production management must consider the utilization of the plant layout, including the location placement of tools, storage areas, tool cribs, aisles, conveyors, and other supporting services. In addition, it should attempt to develop smooth supply chain processes such that parts and raw materials flow smoothly from suppliers to production facilities with speed and a minimum of paperwork requirements. The central objective is to facilitate the overall inflow of materials, the accomplishment of the various processing operations, the transfer of partially processed products between processing centers, necessary inspections, and the release of completed items. Achievement here is measured by the total efficiency and cost of the production process. It involves some very important decisions because once the plant layout is conceived and implemented, it is costly and time-consuming to make changes.

Plant layouts tend to be either of two types. They may follow an integrated sequential processing approach, with the placement of equipment and services supporting that approach. The automobile assembly line is a good example of this. As an alternative, the equipment may be grouped around particular types of processing—as, for example, in a departmental grouping of grinding machines.

There are numerous variations to these two approaches, which may differ at various stages of the production process. The design of the plant layout should be comprehensive, taking into consideration the various dimensions of the actual production process, with the capacity to function efficiently on a day-to-day basis. The second concern is that every reasonable effort should be made to allow the plant layout to work efficiently. A good test of this first requirement is how well the proposed plant layout has been documented to cover the various production efficiency factors. A good test of the latter is how much delay or confusion seems to exist in the actual operation. A further clue to the efficiency of the production facility is how often the plant layout has to be changed, and whether the causes for the new change could have been reasonably foreseen.

Needs for materials handling are linked to the earlier decisions involving facilities, processing, equipment, and plant layout, but with additional specific problems. The central objective here is to minimize the cost of handling materials while efficiently supporting the particular sequence of production processing.

Materials handling problems can first be viewed in terms of the different kinds of material that are normally handled, whether bulk commodities requiring physical movement or data files in need of transmission. Materials must be moved from a stores or receiving area to production. Material handling can be viewed in terms of the efficiency of the total production operations and the related scheduling activity. The latter efficiency in turn depends on the type of materials handling equipment as well as partnership agreements with key suppliers. While the materials handling function involves a substantial degree of special expertise, it offers opportunities for operational audit reviews and constructive service.

(d) PRODUCTION PLANNING AND CONTROL

Production planning and control picks up from the basic planning previously discussed and goes on to planning of the actual production, as is necessary; the transmittal of appropriate instructions to the production personnel; and the monitoring of ongoing production activities. This is a facilitating activity that has as its objectives an efficient and timely flow of the work through the production operations to make possible the scheduled delivery of completed products. The manner in which this function is carried out depends directly on the kinds of products produced and the way production activities are organized. These may vary from a job-lot production, with all operations geared to the individual production order, to continuous processing or assembly, where raw materials enter in one end of operations and finished products exit out the other. In either case, the cycle of the operations may range from very short to very long.

In any event, production planning begins with the determination of forward schedules for the day, week, month, or quarter, depending again on the type of product and the production process. While these schedules normally involve the participation of many organization activities, production personnel will be heavily involved, and in many cases top management will participate, especially to resolve the cross-pressures of the various interested groups. Based on this production planning, the quantities and timing of the various needed inputs are estimated, with consideration given to the materials on hand, items to be procured, and needed production and supporting services requirements. In some cases, plans must be made for particular machines and other needed equipment. Consideration should be given to the economies of larger runs to minimize setup costs, balanced against the cost of carrying any additional stock. Production planning is the identification of the needed inputs, dealing with them in the production process in whatever way results in the greatest efficiency in terms of costs and timing.

Once the production plan, often called a master production schedule (MPS), has been developed, specific instructions can be issued to all affected parties. This will be accomplished by various types of transmittal papers and communication devices, but in many cases this is accomplished through an automated material requirements planning (MRP) system. MRP systems are almost always automated, with the degree of system complexity and detail depending on the nature of the production process. How well an MRP system will control the production process will vary widely, but their general objective is to provide needed information as to the progress and current status of all MRP production activities. The overall results achieved reflect the adequacy of the basic implementation of the system and the promptness and accuracy with which it is maintained. The results achieved now also blend with the broader aspects of the general operational control maintained over the production activities. The design of any MRP production control system should be reasonably suited to the existing production situation, and efficiently operated. There is often a tendency to make MRP-type manufacturing-planning systems too elaborate, thus resulting in an excessive operational effort. The problems of maintaining the existing system and the extent of errors made are usually good clues to systems deficiencies.

(i) MRP Systems Introduction and Overview.   Internal auditors frequently encounter MRP systems when they review manufacturing operations. MRP systems were first developed in the mid 1960s and have proven to be key tools to help manufacturing operations to have the right parts available in the right place and time for a complex manufacturing operation. Unfortunately, MRP systems tend to take on almost mystical qualities in many organizations, with the staff referring to the behavior of their system in almost human ''he'' or ''she'' terms. That, coupled with some of the unfamiliar language of an MRP environment, may cause an internal auditor to return to something ''less complex,'' such as the information systems operations controls discussed in Chapter 16. This section provides a brief overview of MRP concepts. There have been variations and enhancements to MRP over the years, using names such as computer integrated manufacturing (CIM) techniques or MRP II, but basic concepts have not changed all that much.

To start, under MRP every item manufactured in an organization can be considered in terms of its *bill of material,* the subassemblies or parts necessary to build the final product. A bill of material for part A, along with the number of parts necessary to build part A, might look like this:

A
... B (1)
... C (3)
    ... D (2)
    ... E (2)

In this example, each part A requires one part B and three part Cs. Further, that component part C requires two part Ds as well as two part Es. Assume that the organization buys parts D and E from outside suppliers, with each requiring different supplier completion times, and that they must be assembled into C, also requiring some assembly time. In addition, this example part B is manufactured in another operation, also taking some time, with the final assembly into A requiring further manufacturing time. If an organization needs a certain number of part As at various times, it must know how long it will take to get all of the components—E, D, C, and B—ready for final assembly into part A.

Every organization manufacturing or assembling some product can define their end products through this type of bill of material. A complex, many-step, manufactured item such as an automobile will have a bill of material just as will a simple process that buys a product, affixes a label on it, and places it in a special shipping package.

Through its production schedule, an organization can forecast demand for its various products and then must be able to determine which component parts it needs, and when. Per the previous example, if it has demand for 50 completed part As every week, it must schedule its manufacturing and procurement operations to allow it to deliver those part

As, completed and tested per the production schedule. This introduces another complexity to the process. Assume that it takes two days to assemble C and B into A, but that it takes three days to build C from D and E and, further, that the supplier for part D requires 30 days from receipt of order to deliver its part Ds. The vendor that supplies part E does not require that much advance notice, but it is only economical to buy part E in larger quantities, say in lots of 1,000.

This very brief description may give an auditor some understanding of the complexity associated with a MRP system. Given that manufacturing knows its production schedules for final products, an MRP system will calculate when to build each of the components and when to place orders for the component parts or materials. On top of that, the organization would want to minimize the cost of carrying excess inventory and would prefer to maintain production operations at maximum efficiency. That is, it might not want to build subassembly C on a one-by-one basis as orders come in for A but rather to maximize the efficiency of part C production operations.

An auditor can see the complexity of this situation if an organization were building not just single part As with a two-level bill of material, but a series of products, each having multiple-level bills of materials and many subassemblies, both purchased and manufactured. The idea behind an MRP system in this type of complex environment is to allow an organization to plan backwards to determine start times. This is the same concept an auditor will use to decide when to get up in the morning. If an auditor is to be at a 9:00 A.M. meeting, and it takes x minutes to commute to work, y minutes to eat breakfast, z minutes to get dressed, and so forth, the auditor can compute the latest time to set the alarm and still make that 9:00 A.M. meeting.

When organizations first began to recognize the benefits of MRP systems and their requirements for supporting software, some larger organizations designed and programmed their own systems. This is similar to the many organizations that once programmed their own payroll systems, as was discussed in Chapter 17. Today, an organization will purchase a commercial software package to support its MRP needs. Many of these products are very complex, and production personnel will need to attend software vendor classes to even learn to build the program tables necessary to implement the system. In order to understand the MRP system in use and to effectively audit the controls surrounding that MRP system, an internal auditor should make arrangements to attend some of the various vendor-sponsored training classes for the MRP system in use.

These comments only provide a very brief introduction to MRP systems. They are used in many manufacturing organizations, particularly those requiring multistep manufacturing operations. An internal auditor seeking more information on MRP and other production-planning systems should contact an organization such as APICS,[1] which has local chapters with meetings and educational programs in most larger U.S. cities. In many respects, APICS represents production specialists similar to the role of the IIA for internal auditors.

(e) PRODUCTION OPERATIONAL CONTROLS

In addition to the underlying planning and control functions, a next step in understanding the production process is to consider the broader problems of the production operations.

---

[1] American Production and Inventory Control Society (APICS). This professional organization of about 70,000 members in the United States provides education and certification programs on production issues. Local chapters exist throughout the United States.

Our interest here is to examine the major aspects of actual operations, and to understand how they can best be controlled to achieve the most effective production results. These individual operational aspects are:

1. The utilization of material
2. The utilization of labor
3. The effective use of supporting services
4. Adequate production cost controls

These elements are brought together through good administrative management of the production function.

(i) Material Utilization Production Controls.   The effective utilization of materials is an important control concern in most production situations, although this will obviously vary greatly depending upon the nature of the particular production output. To the extent, however, that materials—raw, processed materials, or components of any type—play an important role, a key objective is to maximize the utilization at the lowest possible cost, coupled with maximum quality. Typical ways in which this can be achieved include the following:

- Insistence on receiving materials which are of the right specifications and quality, subject only to deviations that are approved at higher management levels in consideration of other organization needs and benefits.

- Requisitioning of materials in the proper quantities to permit the most efficient utilization. This requires placing orders according to MRP specifications but following economic order-quantity rules.

- Taking adequate care of materials after delivery to production areas, whether in original form or during various stages of processing, to minimize waste and spoilage.

- Where the mix of material ingredients is flexible, varying that mix to exploit current market prices for the individual ingredients while giving adequate attention to quality.

- Adequate reporting of material utilization—including scrap and spoilage—based, where possible, on established standards.

The focus from a control standpoint should be on how material needs are determined, how it is cared for after receipt, and on the prevention of losses from deterioration, spoilage, or other operational factors. Because production techniques and methods vary greatly, depending upon the type of product and its manufacturing steps, it is difficult to establish one set of audit procedures that will apply to all situations. However, Figure 23.1 contains some audit objectives for developing an understanding of materials production controls. As has been discussed, there are wide variations in manufacturing production processes as well as in the nature of the materials used. These objectives should help an auditor to gain a better understanding of this process and to develop appropriate and more detailed audit procedures.

Figure 23.1 Material Production Control Representative Audit Objectives

√ *Nature of the Production Process.* Internal audit's first object should be to understand the general nature of the production process, including such areas as the amount and type of parts and raw materials used in this process.

√ *Industry and Competitive Environment.* In a global economy, many factors can impact the production process. Internal auditors should develop a general understanding of this process and how it may impact an organization's production control process and decisions.

√ *Understanding Product Demand.* A production process is always dependent on the demands for its products, whether as sales of an end product to the ultimate users or as components to fit another manufacturing process. Internal auditors should try to obtain a general understanding of this demand and, more importantly, how the organization forecasts its demand.

√ *Understanding Component Inventory Requirements.* The production process needs additional parts and materials to continue its operations. However, that process can be very complex, with the need for one item to be dependent on the demand for another. Similarly, the production process may result in certain wasted or defective material, again impacting initial requirements. Internal auditors should understand this requirements process and how it relates to the production process.

√ *Bills of Materials.* The production process should be organized in some form or hierarchical bill of material process, showing parent-child relationships for all parts. Procedures should be in place to monitor the integrity of this process, to implement revisions when changes to the production process are necessary, and to maintain the integrity of the bill of materials records. Internal audit should understand the process used and the controls in place for maintaining bill of material integrity.

√ *Inventory Classifications.* The organization should have some type of A-B-C inventory control system where approximately 20 percent of the inventory, the A items, represent 80 percent of the total material cost (unit cost times usage quantity) with the remaining B and C items representing the middle 30 percent and the bottom 50 percent. Internal audit can perform numerous cost-related tests to determine if the procedure is operable.

√ *Enterprise Resource Planning (ERP) Processes.* While organizations once used separate systems, with interfaces between each of them, covering each of their production processes, today many organizations are installing tightly integrated ERP systems where a change to inventory, for example, may directly impact both production scheduling and procurement. Internal auditors need to understand the system in place, its linkages and interfaces, and overall controls.

√ *File Data Integrity.* A material requirements planning system will not be effective unless there is a high level of data integrity over the inventory status and bill of material data in particular. Internal audits should concentrate on this area.

(ii) Labor- and Service-Utilization Production Controls. Although the labor-related proportion of production costs will vary greatly, the cost of labor is normally a factor of great importance. Because of automation as well as technological developments, the major industrial countries no longer have many production processes requiring large pools of labor performing operations essentially by hand. Things are just not built using those older, ''hammer-to-metal'' type methods, and the cost of the production component of labor has decreased significantly. However, labor is always a significant factor in many, if not most, production operations. Even if a very highly automated operation with not that many workers involved in the production process, the small number assigned to the process will often be highly compensated technicians or engineers rather than hourly wage factory labor.

The objective of production controls here is again to achieve maximum value at the lowest possible cost, in a legitimate and long-term sense. The effective utilization of labor is particularly complex because we are dealing with human factors. Further complexities exist because all actions relating to labor have important long-term dimensions, and it is frequently hard to accurately estimate their impact. Effective utilization of labor would typically include:

- The care with which labor needs are planned to support agreed-upon schedules. This can become critical when the organization needs certain specialists, who must rotate from one task to another, or when bargaining unit contracts restrict flexibility.

- Timely recruitment and adequacy of training for the requirements of specific assignments. This can become a very critical factor when the organization has specialized needs and where the pool of available skilled labor is limited.

- Adequacy of working conditions and employee facilities.

- Assignments to meaningful work and the utilization of group efforts to the maximum extent practicable.

- Fairness of compensation, and the linkage of performance to results in every way possible. Again, bargaining unit contracts may limit an organization here, but performance-based incentive compensation is almost always desirable.

- Supervision that combines competence with effective personal relations.

- Fairly determined standards of performance, and prompt reporting against those standards.

- Transfers between production jobs in an orderly and controlled manner. The effective production operation may be involved in a variety of different production tasks; if at all possible, the labor force involved should be trained and scheduled to allow an easy transition from one job type to another.

The control aspects of labor utilization center around the way labor requirements are defined and how the application of the labor effort is administered. In many cases, the technical aspect has been determined previously through appropriate engineering analysis, and that utilization can be evaluated by someone like internal audit in a thorough manner.

Although there are many differences in the way labor is scheduled and utilized in a production environment, internal auditors can develop an understanding of those labor procedures and then make recommendations regarding the effectiveness of this resource utilization. The audit procedures described in Chapter 29, on payroll and personnel, will provide some guidance here.

In most production environments, supporting services are important both in terms of their cost and their contribution to the final production results. These supporting services should be tailored to help achieve the needed production results in the most effective manner and at the lowest cost.

Typical support services areas of interest include:

- Production support supplies and services. Just as an office environment needs such supplies as paper clips, a production environment has similar needs. With effective cost controls and prudent placement and purchasing, these supplies can be important to promoting efficient production. Without adequate controls, they can represent another excess production overhead cost.

- Prudent use of power, with provisions for adequate light for the proper execution of individual production operations. The 1970s and early 1980s were periods in the United States when energy costs became very expensive due, largely, to global economic factors and excessive governmental controls. Organizations that did not control these resources saw their costs of production increase. Today, with the increasing privatization of such resources, costs are going down or at least are in proportion to the general economic factors. However, the effective organization still needs to manage costs in this area.

- Quality of support by material-handling personnel. In many manufacturing environments, work-in-process goods move from one production workstation to another and supplies move up to production areas. Using a combination of equipment and personnel, procedures must be in place to move these goods seamlessly.

- Quality of food facilities and the adequacy of employee rest facilities. While a production facility should never be a country club, care should be exercised to building facilities to promote happy, motivated production workers.

- Overall quality of plant maintenance. A nonfunctioning air conditioner or a leaking valve can reduce the efficiency of overall plant operations. Proper attention to these details can reduce costs and raise overall production productivity.

Internal auditors can very much act as the eyes and ears of senior management when visiting a plant facility and observing production operations. Reviews of expenditure records and just observation can point to situations where costs get out of hand and where production efficiency is diminished. Manufacturing or production environments are so varied that it is difficult to suggest one or even several specific areas here for detailed review. However, Figure 23.2 describes some special instances where an internal auditor may make an observation while reviewing production operations and then can make effective recommendations to reduce cost or to improve production operations.

There is no one set of areas for auditors to review here given the wide variations in production operations. However, the effective internal auditor should observe production operations, ask questions when things do not appear to make sense, investigate the situation, and then make recommendations as appropriate. These general observation types of internal audit comments emphasize the importance of internal auditors as the ''eyes and ears'' of management in these types of situations.

23-4 PRODUCTION COSTS AND COST CONTROL

While production activities should be controlled, to the extent practicable, on a quantitative or physical basis, the basis of many of those controls is with regard to their costs. Ulti-

Figure 23.2   Representative Production Control Internal Audit Recommendations

1. *Need for Upgraded Systems.* The organization installed a "classic" MRP system some years ago but has not upgraded this system for some time; the software vendor failed to recognize that the current system was not good enough. The current system depends on planners executing or ignoring recommendations. New systems, whether MRP II or ERP, should improve production scheduling and financial controls. A detailed study of the current system should be initiated with an objective of potentially selecting an upgraded manufacturing production control system.

2. *Needs to Focus on Larger Customers.* Production control places an extensive amount of effort on forecasting demand-based patterns of orders. However, some 75 percent of the overall business is with about 10 percent of the customer base with four large customers having a major impact. Nevertheless, internal audit observed that production control made no special arrangements with these larger customers. Consideration should be given to building partnership relationships with larger customers so that the production process will better understand and anticipate customer demands.

3. *Production Control System Validity Checks.* As part of internal audit's review of the production control system, situations were observed where production planners initiated job orders for a large number of component parts. When asked about the need for such a large order, internal audit effectively was told "that's what the system says!" A more detailed analysis found that this large requirement was due to a bill of material error. The production persons receiving the system reports could have avoided this type of error by using more validity checks.

4. *Excessive Error Bias.* The detailed production forecasts in any automated production control system will never be 100 percent accurate because actual usage can be greater or lesser than systems forecasts. However, we reviewed the number of forecasting errors over the past four quarters and found a bias of forecast to actual usage by a ratio of 1.45. That is, production control forecasts have traditionally been too low.

5. *Planning Meetings.* We observed that production planning has had few, if any, cross-functional meetings with marketing or with manufacturing personnel. Production plans are developed by the system and are frequently just distributed to personnel. Overall operations would be improved if there were frequent cross-functional meetings to better coordinate the materials planning process.

mately, production activity is evaluated on the basis of what it has cost to produce products at the wanted specifications and quality. Production costs serve a number of different purposes and are developed accordingly for those varying purposes. This section discusses costs as a basis of operational control. Even more than in other areas of an organization, manufacturing cost accounting can be an important area for overall evaluations of efficiency and production effectiveness. Allocating many production expenses to some overhead account can bury true product costs and give manufacturing management wrong impressions.

This section is not at all intended to be a primer on cost accounting, but to help an internal auditor to understand why controls are important in this vital area. The idea of cost accounting is to allocate all significant costs back to areas where they can be accumulated and recognized. For example, the previous discussion of bills of materials and materials requirements planning talked about an example part A that consisted of one part B and three part Cs, and the part C that consisted of two each of parts D and E. If D and E, purchased parts, cost $1.25 and 0.50, respectively, one might assume that the cost of C = 2 × (1.25) + 2 × (0.50) = $3.50.

However, cost accounting points out that costs are not that simple. In order to build B, some production assembly time may be required, as well as some inspection time. The costs of that labor must be allocated to part C. In addition, it was mentioned that part E must be purchased in large, economical quantities. The cost of that storage either may be added to the purchase price of E or may be allocated to all production activities. Similarly, many other production costs may be allocated to this part A assembly operation.

There are no strict rules for cost accounting and these allocations. The only major exception in the U.S. is for military contracts, where a set of guideline rules called Cost Accounting Standards apply for these contracts. Normally, an internal auditor should develop an understanding of the cost accounting rules in place, assess whether they appear to consider all relevant costs, and determine whether they are applied consistently.

Even though all costs should be considered in a manufacturing operation, cost accounting is relatively simple when the production assembly consists of purchased or manufactured parts, and when each component can be traced back to either its purchase price or to the cost of raw materials plus any hours of labor added to build the item. Cost accounting remains relatively simple when the costs for such things as production scrap or inspection labor are allocated back to the completed parts. Cost accounting becomes much more complex in a process-oriented operation where, for example, a barrel of crude oil begins by entering in one end of a refinery. Through a complex refining process, various additives may be added to the oil at various stages of its production and other products, such as motor oil, extracted along the way. With various costs introduced throughout this process, the challenge is to properly assign these costs of production to the completed gasoline output from the refinery as well as the output of various auxiliary products, such as the motor oil.

As mentioned, the purpose of this chapter is not to fully educate internal auditors on the fine points of cost accounting. Because cost accounting rules will differ depending upon the internal auditor's organization—whether an oil refinery, a sawmill, an electronic assembly plant, or any number of other variations—internal auditors should first meet with their manufacturing or cost-accounting managers and acquire an understanding of how costs are applied and allocated. Figure 23.3 contains some general questions that might be useful to gain an understanding of the cost-accounting system in place. There are no right or wrong answers here, but the responses may suggest that internal audit look further in one area or another.

Two detailed areas of cost accounting are important for the internal auditor attempting to understand manufacturing operations: standard costing and activity-based costing. Each will be briefly discussed in the sections following. Standard costing is, in its simplest form, the process of taking all costs and developing a standard, average rate for purposes of developing average product costs. As a successor to standard costing, activity-based cost accounting (ABC) is the system used in many manufacturing operations today. The ABC approach places less emphasis on direct labor as a major cost component and more on other, indirect cost elements.

(a) STANDARD COSTING: AN INTRODUCTION

A manufacturing operation is faced with a variety of costs necessary to complete its product or processes. Some of these costs are tied directly to the product produced while others

Figure 23.3   General Questions to Understand Management Accounting Systems

The names and procedures for some cost accounting systems are changing. For example, the very popular activity-based costing (ABC) approach did not even exist beyond academic journals until the early 1990s. An internal auditor needs to ask some basic questions to better understand management's accounting processes and auditing procedures.

1. Does the organization have a good understanding of which costs are fixed (e.g., monthly lease payments) and which are variable? For variable costs, have costs been separated between variable costs of production and period costs, such as selling expenses?

2. If standard costs are used, what is the basis for establishing those standards and how frequently are cost volumes monitored?

3. Are manufacturing accounting systems based on traditional cost accounting measures, such as labor hours, or ABC measures, such as the number of purchase orders issued for a purchasing function? Are these measures appropriate?

4. What procedures are in place to report production cost variances? In the event of unfavorable variances, what corrective steps are taken?

5. What procedures are in place to collect and monitor plant overhead and how are these costs tolled back to the production process?

6. Does the production process have a good understanding of cost-volume relationships and are they monitored for the short- and long-term?

7. Are formal break-even budgets prepared for the manufacturing process and are adjustments made to the manufacturing process to correct a loss situation?

8. Is some type of economic order quantity (EOQ) process used for ordering new materials? Are orders monitored to determine if they are generally complete?

9. If any of the production is more process-flow oriented, what accounting systems are in place to measure and adjust costs?

10. Are appropriate procedures in place for more complex pricing issues such as joint-product costs or byproduct costs?

are fixed over extended periods. Those tied directly to the product produced are known as *variable costs*. An example there may be a part Z that costs $1 per unit added to the final product. For every unit manufactured, this part Z will add $1 to its manufactured cost. This range will only change if the quantity manufactured goes down to a very low number, where unit costs might increase, or becomes very large, where discounts may come into effect. Otherwise, the $1 charge for part Z will apply.

Fixed costs apply to the production operation no matter how many products are constructed. Even if production goes down by 10% during a given month, the organization's costs, such as rent, will remain unchanged. Except in the extreme case of closing the plant or building a new one, these costs will remain fixed.

The cost of labor may fit in either category. On one hand, the organization can look at its labor force as one that will vary with production demand; new workers can be added or others let go. However, a production facility cannot change the labor force mix on an entirely short-notice basis, and labor costs are not totally variable. What is variable is the cost of the labor that is added to the product. If a worker is paid $20 per hour and if that worker puts two hours of work into the product, this will be a variable product cost of

$40. However, if that same worker only builds one product during an eight-hour shift with nothing else to do for the production operation, the worker's remaining six hours at $20 per hour must be absorbed elsewhere. Normally, the worker will not be sent home after completing this product over two hours.

With fixed and variable elements, and the costs of labor, manufacturing costs are often classified in three major elements:

1. *Direct Materials.* These are commodities that are integral parts of the finished product. For example, the single variable cost part Z, mentioned above, will be part of direct materials costs for the final product. Other materials, such as glue, may be assigned directly to each product produced or classified as supplies and allocated across all production.

2. *Direct Labor.* When a given expenditure of labor can be traced to each product produced, this is called *direct labor.* The two hours mentioned previously is a direct labor cost for that product. Other labor cost not directly attributable to the units of product produced are called *indirect labor.* Examples of the latter include a messenger on the plant floor, bringing materials from one construction station to another, or the guard at the plant gate. It is generally impractical to track this indirect labor to each product produced, and it is allocated over all production costs.

3. *Factory Overhead.* All production costs that are not product-related direct materials or direct labor are classified as *factory overhead.* This includes the supplies mentioned with direct materials and the indirect labor mentioned above. Other overhead costs include rent, insurance, and management salaries.

A production organization should attempt to look at all of its costs and then to classify them as above. Then, the organization should attempt to decide how many units go into the production operations, and at what variable cost. That is, the previously referenced part Z may still cost $1. These costs can be accumulated and used for both budgeting and profit planning for the organization.

However, over time, the part Z vendor may raise the price of that component to $1.05, thus increasing production material costs. Even if the price stays at $1, sloppy manufacturing techniques may result in a 10% spoilage rate. It will be necessary to purchase 10 part Zs to build nine final products. The cost of the part Z component is really $(10 \times \$1)/9$ or $1.11. In either case, this differences will create production cost variances.

The idea of standard costs is that a manufacturing organization will look at its actual costs over time and establish what are called *standard costs.* If they have no reason to believe that part Z will actually change to $1.02 over the course of the year because of inflation, or other factors, the organization may assign part Z a standard cost of $(1.00 + 1.02)/2 = \$1.01$ for all production estimates over the forthcoming year. They can then track cost and usage throughout the production period by analyzing these variances.

A standard pricing or costing system allows a production analyst to first compare its budgeted inputs at standard prices with those same inputs at actual prices, providing price or rate variances. Then, the same actual inputs and standard prices can be compared to the good outputs at standard prices, giving usage or efficiency variances. Figure 23.4 is an example of this type of material rate variance calculation. The same basic principle is applied to all other manufacturing cost elements, with manufacturing operations evaluating its efficiency through a measurement of these variances. A similar type of standard cost variance analysis is used for direct labor costs as well as all indirect costs.

Figure 23.4   Material Price Variance Calculation

Assume that ExampleCo purchased 100,000 units of material XX at $306,000 ($3.06 each) and 85,000 were used in production. The standard cost for XX is $3.00. Assume further that the standard quantity of material XX is 70,000 units although 68,000 were used in this production run:

Raw Material Price Variance = (Actual Price − Standard Price) × Actual Quantity Used

Raw Material Quantity Variance = (Actual Quantity − Standard Quantity)
× Standard Cost

Price Variance = ($3.06 − $3.00) × 100,000 = $6,000 U

Raw Material Variance = (70,000 − 68,000) × $3.00 = $6,000 F

The purpose of this chapter is not to give a comprehensive explanation of cost accounting, but to explain some of these basic terms to the internal auditor. When an organization uses standard costing, the effective internal auditor should understand how this process works and what is meant by favorable or unfavorable variances. At a minimum, when an auditor sees the variance reports associated with a manufacturing operation, it is a good idea to be able to ask some question about the variances, why they have been incurred, and what management is doing in terms of corrective actions.

(b) ABC: ACTIVITY-BASED COST ACCOUNTING

Cost-accounting systems date back to the days of major production operations, where factories consisted of thousands of workers performing a wide variety of tasks. During World War II in the United States, for example, there were tens if not hundreds of thousands of workers employed in war-effort production facilities that launched an average of one major ship a day and about one aircraft every hour. Direct labor costs were a major management concern then, and a major emphasis was placed on increasing efficiency and reducing direct labor requirements. This was the era when managers placed a major emphasis on controlling and measuring costs. Labor burden or overhead, as discussed in the previous section on cost accounting, was a major measure of production efficiency.

Cost-accounting systems continued to be used by many organizations, and an understanding of cost accounting is an important internal auditor skill. However, starting in the 1950s, many academics began to question standard cost-accounting systems. There were two problems. First, manufacturing processes had changed dramatically with new types of products; significant levels of manufacturing automation, including robotics and the massive computer systems to support all types of manufacturing activities. Second, there was a recognition that traditional cost systems ignored product-specific "below-the-line" expenses such as sales, distribution, R&D, and administrative costs. In a traditional cost-accounting system, the costs associated with these elements were treated as below-the-line or fixed even though such costs often can be directly attributed to specific products. Criticisms of traditional cost-accounting systems and analyses of modern manufacturing and distribution trends evolved into what is today called activity-based costing (ABC).

ABC is based on the premise that the costs of serving various products and distribution channels varies, and accounting systems should be established to better measure and recognize those costs. Consider a manufacturer making two very similar lines of product, with one line geared for the mass market of large distributors and the second line designed for specialty, limited-distribution types of stores. As often happens in this case, the basic products are very similar, with the custom versions having only small product enhancements to add value. The overall costs for these two lines, however, can vary considerably. The manufacturing process costs for the custom line add little additional cost; however, the limited market products require a different level of direct selling, many individual customer orders with significant order-entry costs, and specialized advertising. The large distributor line requires fewer sales calls and limited order-entry activity (since many orders are placed through EDI) but demands that the larger distributors be given significant discounts.

A traditional cost-accounting system would give the wrong information here. The costs of order entry and order processing, for example, would typically all be combined into a general administrative overhead cost, applied to each product manufactured based on a common overhead or burden rate. Because these administrative costs consist of the more costly order-entry activities for the custom goods as well as the minimum EDI-based costs for the mass market, each product would have to absorb an equal proportion of cost.

The whole concept of ABC is to track costs to individual product activities such as scheduling, setups, inspection, and order entry. Whenever a product needs one of these activities, ABC says that those activity-based costs should be assigned to the product. In our mass-distribution and custom product example, an organization might find that it costs $0.85 to produce each custom invoice, but an EDI-type invoice will cost $0.26. Each type of order, specialty or mass market, will absorb either $0.85 or $0.26 based on the type of customer. The whole idea is that individual costs are applied to the products as required.

The idea is that the actual costs for each resource should be applied to the individual product or even to the individual customer. The latter comes into play when a large-volume or special customer has unique needs. In a simple example, a customer may demand that all orders be shipped by overnight mail while all others go out by two-day UPS. ABC will attempt to identify these extra costs and assign them to the special customer whenever an order is placed.

ABC seems so rational that an internal auditor might ask why everyone does not use such an approach. The reason is that ABC can require a very high level of analysis and cost-measurement complexity. More importantly, it requires quite sophisticated computer systems. ABC systems are being introduced through some of the newer enterprise resource planning (ERP) systems now being implemented in organizations; however, many have not yet shook off their older traditional cost-accounting systems.

This description is very brief, and a detailed description of auditing through an ABC system will probably be a topic in a future edition of this book. However, when an internal auditor encounters an organization with an ABC system, the auditor should realize that this is a complex type of system requiring many detailed measurements at many levels. The auditor should ask some basic but detailed questions about the assumptions surrounding the ABC approach and review cost systems to determine how costs were applied.

23-5 AUDITING PRODUCTION ACTIVITIES

Effective reviews of production facilities present internal auditors challenges because of the diverse types of production operations from one industry to another, and often within the auditor's organization, from one plant to another. An internal auditor will often have to have spent considerable time observing a manufacturing organization before it becomes possible to make effective manufacturing-related operational audit recommendations. Every industry has its own special tools, procedures, and terminologies. An internal auditor who has learned electronic assembly manufacturing procedures cannot directly bring that knowledge to a metals forging operation or to a chemical products manufacturing operation and expect to perform the same types of tests and to make the same levels of recommendations. While there are many process analogies between different production processes, a good first audit step is to really learn the operation that is to be reviewed.

Learning a production operation means that an operational auditor should spend some time on the manufacturing floor to understand operations. While a guided walk-through of the facility will help, an auditor might consider doing a little more to better understand manufacturing operations in a facility where the auditor will be performing ongoing reviews. By spending time in the production facility and observing how data is collected and processed, an internal auditor will better understand what is really going on in that facility and how the process works.

The director of internal audit can often initiate this type of learning program. If an organization has an important manufacturing operation where significant audit reviews are planned, arrangements can often be made to get all internal auditors involved in production operations. In addition to just the tour, they could be assigned to a portion of production operations to actually help for perhaps a one-week period. While they certainly would not be expected to operate heavy or specialized equipment, an auditor could be assigned to work for perhaps a week in an inventory crib area or to assist in moving materials from one workstation to another. The idea is to allow an internal auditor to get the *feel* of production operations by working with selected personnel side by side and observing their daily activities and, sometimes, frustrations. While there may be bargaining unit or other problems, this brief intern assignment should result in better, more knowledgeable auditors. The idea is to help internal auditors to become more knowledgeable about operations.

Once procedures for production operations are better understood, internal audit can perform more effective audits in this area. Many will involve assessing the effectiveness of the cost controls by the review and testing of cost performance activities. As discussed in other chapters, these audits can involve financial-, operational-, and information systems–focused reviews. The following sections discuss specific audit procedures for each.

(a) PRODUCTION PLANNING OPERATIONAL AUDIT PROCEDURES

Production operations can be one of the most important areas of potential internal audit service in a typical manufacturing-oriented organization. The scope of opportunities can be best described by identifying key levels of managerial activity in the production-oriented organization. To accomplish this, internal audit should identify the highest level of managerial planning where the production role is determined in relation to the needs and activities of other management functions, especially with respect to purchasing, marketing, and finance. This will allow internal audit to understand the role of production as a driver or follower of other organization activities. If the former, good internal control procedures become even more important.

Operational reviews here should be concerned with the managerial problems of production performance as they involve day-to-day coordination with other operational activities, and of the various components of the production function itself. In addition, audit work should consider the operational problems of the individual production units in terms of effective utilization of materials, labor, and supporting services.

The role of internal audit here is, first, to appraise the efficiency with which existing policies, procedures, and established plans are being carried out. Second, internal audit should look for new approaches that hold varying degrees of promise for ensuring more efficient and profitable production operations. The wide range of activities involved and their often large necessary expenditures make this an attractive area of management service. Although there is a major technical dimension to most of these production activities, there are still excellent opportunities for constructive audit service in supplemental ways. By working in cooperation with those who have technical expertise, a further contribution of improved controls recommendations can be made. Many areas of production operational auditing have or will be covered in other chapters on specific components of the manufacturing process. For example, Chapter 24 will discuss the receiving function, which is a very important portion of any manufacturing operation.

Internal auditors should understand product and production cost controls, as will be discussed in the section on financial-related audits for production activities. Other reviews will focus on the material requirements planning system, covered as part of our discussion on information systems auditing. However, numerous areas exist within a manufacturing or production function where an internal auditor can act as the eyes and ears for senior management, pointing out potential problem areas and making effective controls improvement recommendations.

Because of the magnitude of the production activities in most organizations, a review will often deal only with a particular type of production activity, or with the total production activities at a single field location. Figure 23.5 lists some matters of potential special audit

Figure 23.5   Areas for an Operational Review of Manufacturing

A. Manufacturing Planning and Requirements Estimation
  1. Understand the manner of receiving production requirements and how needs are transmitted to other groups who will procure such inputs.
  2. Review how production-planning criteria is established.
  3. Review controls over planning processing operations, including relations with support activities and quality control.
  4. Understand the process for maintaining and reviewing internal production records.
  5. Review the inventory-taking requirements for all production operations, including cyclical counts of stores, work-in-process, and periodic physical inventories.
  6. Understand the types and nature of reports that are produced by production and distributed to other members of the organization, either for review or action.
B. Production Planning Operations
  1. Does the production function carry out its own activities to study new manufacturing approaches for current products?
  2. Does the production function counsel with other management components as to new equipment or procedures?
  3. Does production participate in the long-term planning effort, and are they adequately provided with opportunities to make contributions in such areas as needs for facilities, equipment, personnel, and costs?
  4. Is production adequately consulted as to the feasibility and cost of newly proposed or modified products?
  5. Determine that production plan development includes active participation from all interested parties.
  6. Assess whether production has some final authority as to the feasibility of production plans. If not, are their limitations given adequate visibility?

Figure 23.5 (*Continued*)

C. Planning for Approved Production Requirements
1. Appraise the organizational status of the planning group, including its internal organizational arrangements. Assess whether they are provided with adequate opportunities to evaluate alternative approaches before facilities and equipment are committed.
2. Evaluate documentation for its adequacy in supporting processing decisions.
3. To what extent are alternative ways of satisfying facility needs adequately explored, and how adequate is the coverage of all pertinent factors in documenting a particular selection?
4. Is collaboration with other organization activities adequate?
5. Is the scheduling and subsequent control of the facilities project adequate?
6. How adequate is the evaluation of alternative types of equipment in terms of capacity, maintenance, and operations performed?
7. Are levels of authority for acquisition of equipment and tooling reasonable? Are the scheduling and subsequent control of the acquisition projects adequate?
8. Are the planning and control of the actual work adequate?
9. Appraise the adequacy of the analysis and documentation for major decisions as to how material handling needs will be satisfied, including the choice of equipment.
10. Appraise the policies and procedures by which work assignments are determined and then actually transmitted within the production department.
11. Appraise the adequacy of the system by which the production control group will maintain control of the status of production activities.
D. Current Production Operations
1. Are materials properly received and cared for pending actual processing, and is the reporting of material utilization adequate?
2. Is there excessive waste or spoilage in the processing of materials? If so, why?
3. Are spoiled materials used or salvaged in the most effective manner possible?
4. Review material usage variances to assess whether material usage is in accordance with approved bills of material.
5. How adequate is the selection and training of personnel for the particular kinds of jobs?
6. If there is excessive idle time, evaluate the causes.
7. Similarly, if there is excessive overtime, evaluate the causes.
8. Are labor standards established wherever possible? Are they fair?
9. Does morale appear to be good? If not, why not?
10. Are relations with the union satisfactory? If not, what are the problems, and how should they be dealt with?
11. Do supporting services—such as materials handling, light, temperature, work area facilities, food facilities, and rest facilities, appear adequate?
12. Is the established production-control system working effectively? If not, why not?
13. Do the various production and support groups appear to be working with each other in a cooperative fashion?
14. Are schedules being met? If not, why not?
15. Are inspection procedures adequate and carried out in a careful manner?
16. Is spoiled or defective material adequately tagged and segregated?
E. Reporting and Cost Control
1. Appraise the reporting system as it applies to the various parts of the production operations at the various levels of supervision, with particular reference to: (a) its scope; (b) adequacy of variance analysis; (c) its focus on controllable costs; and (d) the degree of summarization.
2. How effectively are the reports being used as a basis for needed managerial action—with particular reference to the promptness of reviews, probing of causes for deviation, and corrective action?

interest. However, an internal auditor should tour production facilities, review production performance reports, meet with members of production management to discuss their concerns, and then develop a detailed audit program.

(b) PRODUCTION PLANNING FINANCIAL AUDIT PROCEDURES

The major focus of many if not all financially oriented reviews of a production operation should center on the cost-accumulation and cost-accounting system in place, whether it's the previously discussed classic cost-accounting system, activity-based costing, or some other system. An initial step for internal audit is to determine that there is a *process* in place for prompt and accurate preparation of manufacturing cost-accounting reports. The frequency of these reports and their detailed coverage are related to the level of management that has direct control and responsibility. There should be evidence of prompt reviews of significant deviations and investigations of causes for deviations.

A primary interest of internal audit should be to determine whether an adequate basis for cost control exists, and whether that basis is being administered effectively. This is an area where the competence of internal audit can be especially well established. Auditors should look for evidence of vigorous management appraisals of causes for poor cost performance and the development of effective action programs to deal with those causes. All too often, an auditor will review a recent budget-variance report, see some significant unfavorable or even favorable variance, and ask for explanations only to be given far less than satisfactory answers along the lines of, "Our standard costs are bad!" These types of responses should prompt an auditor to dig deeper. Questions in response to such comments could include, "Why are the standard costs bad?" "What are we doing to correct the problem?" or "How will these bad costs affect other areas, such as profitability analysis?"

While there is no one single answer to bad standard costs as an excuse or any single audit approach given the wide range of manufacturing accounting systems and processes in place, Figure 23.6 outlines some potential areas. The key for an internal auditor is to first understand the accounting system in place for the production operation—as well as its controls—and then to evaluate and test those controls. This is really no different than the approaches discussed throughout this book.

(c) PRODUCTION PLANNING INFORMATION SYSTEMS AUDIT PROCEDURES

The key information system in any production environment is the organization's MRP: material requirements planning system. As we have discussed previously, MRP systems are regarded as having almost human qualities by staff members in some production organizations, who often refer to their system with comments about what "she" or "he" (the MRP system) decided. Today, the installed system will almost always be a purchased software package because of the complexity of these systems and the need for component integration. The system will almost certainly follow either of the MRP, MRP II, or just-in-time models. If an in-house-developed system, an auditor should question why such an in-house-developed system is needed, what its effectiveness is, and what plans are in place to keep it current.

Because of typical MRP system complexity, internal auditors will generally not have time to perform a detailed review of the controls surrounding the total MRP system—just

Figure 23.6   Audit Procedures for Selected Production Scheduling Processes

Audit_____ Location_____ Date_____		
AUDIT STEP	**INITIAL**	**W/P**
1. Develop a flowchart to describe the manufacturing production process from the initiation of sales orders/requirement to the preparation of schedules. Identify any potential control weaknesses.		
2. Are production schedules prepared to the degree of detail necessary for manufacturing operations?		
3. Review the master production schedule for operations scheduling and determine if the plan operation schedule is compatible with the master schedule.		
4. Retrace a sample of revisions from sales forecast to manufacturing production schedules. Determine if the process operates to promote efficiency and minimize disruption to manufacturing.		
5. Test a sample of production job releases and determine if they are released on a timely basis and with sufficient information to aid the production process.		
6. Review the production scheduling process to understand the process of how lead times are established. Determine if this process appears to be well controlled.		
7. Review a full cycle of reports or screens produced from a recent production process. Assess whether manufacturing operations followed up on any reported problems and assess if corrective actions were taken.		
8. Determine that safeguards exist so that workloads and requirements are scheduled in advance so that efficient planning and resource balancing can take place.		
9. Determine if problems exist with schedules exceeding production capacity; determine corrective actions taken to smooth production operations.		
10. Review the reporting process allowing the progress of manufacturing operations through the shop floor.		
11. Review the status of open production orders by a review of status reports, observations, and discussions with production personnel. Review and follow-up on any potential problems.		
12. Determine whether setup time or other regular production downtime causes significant problems to the overall manufacturing process. Suggest areas where improved scheduling might improve manufacturing efficiency.		

a review of MRP documentation will often consume considerable time. Rather, internal audit should ask some general questions about the system in place, its major components that have been implemented, and procedures in place to monitor MRP processing controls.

Today, internal auditors will often encounter a manufacturing system much more comprehensive than just the MRP types of systems. Enterprises today are attempting to tie all operations into a single comprehensive system that includes production, accounting, and other logistics operations. These new generation systems are called enterprise resource planning (ERP) systems. They are very comprehensive and often difficult to initially implement. When an organization embarks on an effort to implement this type of a comprehensive system, internal audit should get very involved in a preimplementation review to understand the controls over the new ERP system.

23-6 PRODUCTION SCRAP AND WASTE CONTROL

Waste control is a term that can be used in a very broad or in a more restricted sense. We use it here to refer to smoke or residual waste created as a result of the regular production operations. It is a problem that has always been of some significance, and in the case of certain kinds of organizations is of very serious dimensions. Waste-control costs have always had a direct relationship to total production operations and always present problems of how the disposition of waste can be achieved at minimum cost. Over time, these previously existing problems have been expanded to include the impact on the overall environment. Society has now become acutely aware of the problem of pollution of air and waterways, and is exerting major pressures on industry to find ways to reduce that pollution. To what extent these pressures may seem unreasonable is not the question for auditors to decide. The pressure is there, and the ways available to industry to deal with the problems involve major operational changes and substantial costs. How best to deal with this problem is now a major challenge to many organizations.

To a major extent, the problem of dealing with production waste is a technical problem requiring changes in the production processes. It is a problem of feasibility combined with the necessary costs to implement procedures. An attack on the problem may usually be along the following lines:

1. Changing the material content of products, processing materials, or the manner of processing to reduce the amount of waste, or to reduce its objectionable features. Using oil instead of soft coal in the production of electricity is an example.

2. Developing new ways to reuse the offending materials, such as recycling paper products.

3. Developing better ways to dispose of the waste materials or to reduce their objectionable features. Examples might include special processes for the treatment of waste or the building of special underground receptacles.

The operational concern here is to make certain that adequate steps are taken to deal with the problem. This includes finding better ways to make use of the waste and taking steps to avoid punitive governmental measures or public ill will, which can be even more costly than some kind of current action.

Production maintenance is another related but important activity. Maintenance consists of activities relating to the inspection, servicing, and repair of facilities in the organization, including buildings, equipment, and tooling used for processing, and service equipment. It may be a repetitive-type operation, or a highly sophisticated system used by management in coordination with production and facilities activities. It also includes the responsibility for making the necessary supporting arrangements with equipment suppliers and subcontractors.

Maintenance activities can be divided into four types: emergency repairs, preventive maintenance, corrective maintenance, and maintenance elimination. Emergency repairs are usually required when there is a breakdown of equipment needed currently in operations. A system of preventive maintenance or scheduled repairs serves to keep equipment in good running order and to reduce the idle time resulting from breakdowns and the time required for emergency repairs. Some organizations go beyond preventive maintenance and employ corrective maintenance. This involves the analysis of maintenance activities and costs to identify unfavorable aspects in the use of some assets. Based on this analysis, recommendations can be made for changes in use of content and design to improve productivity and decrease maintenance. The last type of maintenance is often called maintainability or maintenance elimination. It involves monitoring maintainability needs during design, production of the asset, installation, and final use. Through this approach, the nature and extent of upkeep and repair are determined in the planning phase, with specifications incorporated in the design to conform with maintenance objectives.

Managers are increasingly recognizing the need for developing plans and programs for attaining maintenance effectiveness. Maintenance costs may sometimes exceed the initial acquisition costs of assets. It is thus important that these assets be used as long as possible through added attention to maintenance. Together with this, there have been increases in the costs of maintenance labor and parts. These changes have made it increasingly necessary to plan and control maintenance expenditures to maximize benefits.

The maintenance function can also be viewed in terms of the individual stages in its total cycle. This framework is useful in evaluating the processes by which maintenance is carried out. The individual stages are:

1. Planning maintenance strategy
2. Determining needs and scheduling
3. Providing personnel and materials
4. Budgeting and controlling performance

Many organizations have broad policies and strategies for maintenance, rather than treating it as an ad hoc operation. This involves an appraisal of current maintenance practices, the need for changes in light of organization objectives, and development of a maintenance strategy based on production and other operating needs. The level of maintenance required is important in planning. The level should be selected to obtain longer equipment life without spending excessive amounts. In addition, an organization's policies should be flexible to allow for periods when maintenance may have to be deferred because of shortages of funds or other conditions. In addition to overall considerations, the organization needs to consider the operational requirements of specific assets prior to deciding on maintenance. This includes determining basic performance parameters, operating cycles, and needs as to availability. Maintenance requirements should consider personnel resource needs, the allocation of spare parts, and frequency of work. In some situations, the best policy for a unit may be to use the throwaway approach when there is a breakdown rather than using preventive maintenance. In planning for maintenance of specific assets, it is also desirable to be involved in the design stage. This enables the user to specify criteria for design in accordance with maintenance objectives.

It is important that management have procedures for determining needs for maintenance and setting priorities. Often, there are limited resources available and conflicting requests for service. Under these circumstances it is important to keep all items of equipment maintained at the optimum level. On the one hand, management wishes to maximize the useful life of an asset by an effective maintenance program. It recognizes that to optimize return on investment, excessive maintenance has to be avoided, as does insufficient maintenance. It also wishes to avoid downtime, which can be costly to the organization in terms of delays in production or lost sales. It is also faced with the necessity of making unexpected emergency repairs, which can disrupt the planned maintenance schedule. Because of these considerations, it is necessary to determine the right time to schedule maintenance work.

By considering factors of safety and economics, some unnecessary tasks can be eliminated. The organization may well determine the feasibility of deferred maintenance. However, the savings on maintenance charges may not offset the costs of lost production, spoilage, idle time of production workers, excessive wear, and overtime.

Management must, of course, have valid records and reports of maintenance needs in order to have an effective system. A significant number of items of equipment may be nonoperational although not so classified. Under these circumstances, tests may be required of equipment to determine operability. In some cases, equipment will be in running order but will have defects that could cause deterioration and breakdowns at a later time. If the defects are not reported, they represent a hidden, or unnoticed, backlog of maintenance needs that are not being given attention.

The maintenance department is a service activity that benefits other departments of the organization. As such, the department should be independent, and adequate personnel and materials should be provided to perform the function effectively. In some cases, it may be more economical to contract outside the organization to get the work done, especially if the service is needed for limited periods only. In other cases, the equipment may be highly specialized, requiring qualified technicians. It may be preferable in these circumstances to use the vendor's service personnel, even after the initial warranty period, to obtain their expertise. When contracts are entered into, the work should be adequately controlled and service charges verified. For work performed in-house, the primary element of an effective maintenance program is a well-organized and trained workforce. This should include an adequate number of craftsmen with the required skills to carry on the technical work. It should also include adequate salaries and incentive plans to retain and motivate the maintenance workers needed. The incentive plans should take into consideration the measurement of the results of the maintenance activities. As a basis for achieving effective results, management must also see that spare parts and materials are available when needed. In planning and controlling maintenance inventories, the same principles are involved as in other types of inventories. There is a need to assure that sufficient materials are available to prevent unnecessary costs and losses due to interruptions of activity. Inventory levels, however, should not be excessive because of the risk of obsolescence and unnecessary carrying costs. There are certain unique problems in maintenance inventories because the demand for some items is not repetitive. However, for preventive maintenance, the use of standard items is predictable. The use of automated systems in materials planning and control is especially beneficial in achieving effective management of maintenance materials.

There should be adequate physical inventories and storage of maintenance items. Materials and spare parts should be kept whenever possible in storerooms, readily accessible to maintenance workers. The usage experience of the items should be continually monitored to assist in determining stock levels. In addition, when there are changes in equipment, the related spare parts and materials should be disposed of if no longer needed. At the same time, there should be a coordinated approach to acquiring needed maintenance materials if a different type of equipment is acquired. For newly acquired equipment, the organization should have a system for correction of defects in parts when covered by warranties.

The many changes in fixed assets and the unknowns in technical requirements make it difficult to budget realistically for maintenance. Changes in production methods or misuse may shorten an asset's useful life. The sheer number of different types of equipment and changes in plans to replace them present problems in preparing meaningful budgets. It is important that accountability be set for preparing the budget and performing within prescribed limits. This is especially desirable in controlling the number and extent of overruns. Because of the nature of the maintenance function, overruns can frequently occur, and managers must be responsible for obtaining analyses of their causes. These analyses serve to identify areas needing additional monitoring in the maintenance process, as well as improvements needed in budgeting. They also serve to justify the costs incurred, such as when extensive overtime is used to meet production deadlines. In some instances, savings can be achieved by contracting out instead of performing the work in-house, or vice versa. For example, with a large fleet of vehicles it may be more economical to hire full-time mechanics than to have the vehicles serviced by outsiders. It is important that an organization have an accurate costing system to assure that materials and labor are charged to the right work order. Controls over transfers of costs between work orders should be instituted to prevent concealment of overruns. Also, there should be adequate control over unused materials to discourage stockpiles of material and charges to the wrong jobs. It should be recognized that costs are only a factor in evaluating performance. Management is interested in keeping equipment running, in having an effective maintenance force to handle problems, and in preventing unnecessary repairs. The operating efficiency of the maintenance department, however, is of paramount importance because of the unique nature of the maintenance role and the problems in utilizing available funds to obtain the best results.

(a) ROLE OF INTERNAL AUDIT IN MAINTENANCE

Internal audit can make a significant contribution to management through reviews of maintenance activities and the operational approaches used in reviewing production, inventories, and personnel. Also, internal audit can review the overall effectiveness and efficiency of maintenance efforts. Since maintenance is basically a service function, its contribution to facilities management and production can be reviewed and evaluated. In addition, internal audit can determine the operability of equipment through study of reports and tests made. By looking at accounting information, the auditor can analyze personnel and material costs as a basis for obtaining savings, and can review preventive maintenance schedules and determine adherence to maintenance policies in effect for various types of equipment. In total, internal audit should seek to determine how well existing maintenance-related policies, procedures, and operational activities serve the various interests of the organization. This includes, as far as practicable, an evaluation of available alternatives that might provide still greater benefits.

23-7 PRODUCTION AND MAINTENANCE ILLUSTRATIVE AUDIT FINDINGS

A: Concealment of Overruns.   We reviewed a sample of production control labor transactions for the Acme plant to determine that all transactions were appropriate. We found a significant number of transactions that indicated unsupported production labor transfers were being made between jobs to avoid overruns. These Transfers Out transactions were made after the completion of the job and often had the transaction explanation, ''to correct prior errors.'' However, we found that 17 transactions in a sample of 20 from March 20XX with this designation contained no evidence of prior errors in record-keeping. Rather, all 17 of them were initiated by two production supervisors, apparently to conceal the ineffective use of personnel on some jobs.

We have reported this matter directly to senior production management and assume that appropriate actions will be taken regarding the two supervisors. However, we also found that neither production management nor the cost-accounting department regularly reviews the reasons behind the Transfer Out transactions. In addition, the need for correct labor ticket reporting is not emphasized in supervisor training programs.

Recommendation.   Training for both production supervisors and regular production personnel should be enhanced to emphasize the importance of correctly reporting the reasons for labor adjustments. In addition, procedures should be established to require a second level of approval for all adjustments over 20 hours. Since our sample only covered the month of March, a comprehensive examination should be initiated to review all transactions over the past year and to make adjustments to accounting records where appropriate.

B: Faulty Standards for Maintaining Production Equipment.   Internal audit found that additional coordination among the sales department, the production department, and the maintenance department might potentially help to increase sales. Some cancellations in customer orders during the year were caused by delays in deliveries of essential parts. Delivery dates promised by salespeople were not being met because of lack of communication of priority needs, unrealistic production expectations, and maintenance delays. Production maintenance has been scheduled based on hours of usage for the equipment, and all production equipment parts are replaced on a time basis regardless of condition in order to assure that there would be no breakdowns. This replacement schedule applies to all parts, whether low-cost, high-usage production bushings or highly reliable electronic components. While certain component parts will regularly fail and it is better to regularly replace them, others have a much longer life. The total cost for all replacement parts at the Scimitar plant for second quarter of 20XX was $13.6 million. Significant savings might be achieved by replacing parts in a more structured manner.

Recommendation.   Production operations should develop statistics to better track equipment stoppages due to parts failures. Based on these failure statistics and their replacement cost, a specialized maintenance schedule should be developed that installs high-failure or lower-cost parts on a regular basis while scheduling others as needed.

C: Inappropriate Reviews of Material Variances.   We reviewed material cost variances for the Gee Whiz product line and found a significant number of parts had high unfavorable material cost variances. After some discussion with the accounting department, we found that there did not appear to be a systematic approach to assigning standard costs for these product line parts at the beginning of this past fiscal year. More significantly, we found that little attention appears to have been given to reviewing the cost variance report, which is produced on a monthly basis.

We interviewed members of the production cost department to determine why these large unfavorable variances had not been investigated. The answers we received ranged from ''I do not understand this report; I have not been trained in it'' to ''It doesn't matter; the standard costs are all wrong.''

Recommendation.   Since there are still two quarters remaining in the fiscal year, efforts should be made to establish correct material standard costs for the Gee Whiz product line. Once complete, appropriate members of the cost-accounting department should be trained in the analysis of cost variances as well as in actions to be taken in the event of unfavorable reported variances. Internal audit will review this area again during the third quarter to determine if the material variances are properly reported and monitored.

CHAPTER 24

Purchases, Receipts and Electronic Data Interchange

24-1 INTRODUCTION: PURCHASING CYCLE

Whether a company is a manufacturer, a distributor, or a professional services organization, goods must be purchased and received, and the suppliers paid. The purchasing cycle—which involves the purchase of goods, their receipt, and subsequent payment—is a key operational and financial control cycle for most organizations. It is also a cycle that is rapidly changing due to automation. While organizations once prepared purchase order documents and mailed them to suppliers to place orders, electronic data interchange (EDI) techniques or the Internet are now used increasingly. EDI refers to the computer-to-computer exchange of data from one organization to another to place orders and to authorize payment for them.

This chapter covers purchasing activities that are found in any organization, receiving activities with an emphasis more on a manufacturing organization, and EDI. While EDI is part of the purchasing or shipping functions of many organizations, it is still sufficiently new to many auditors and organizations to warrant a separate treatment. Over time, EDI will certainly become just another basic means of doing business. Accounts payable activities and controls, although part of the purchasing cycle, were discussed in Chapter 22, on accounting systems. They also have an electronic component, electronic funds transfer (EFT), that has some strong similarities to EDI.

Cash typically goes out of the organization to buy goods and services. Improper controls here can result in a variety of operational and financial problems. The effective internal auditor needs to develop an understanding of purchasing cycle control procedures and related audit techniques.

24-2 PURCHASING ACTIVITIES IN THE ORGANIZATION

As the starting point in this major organization operational cycle, purchasing involves the acquisition of materials and services that are to be marketed either in their existing form, or used, processed, or combined in some fashion to provide the products and services actually offered for sale. Procurement can involve raw or processed materials, parts, subassemblies, services, supplies, facilities, and money itself. Many of these procurement areas are specialized, with their own unique problems and needs for special knowledge. A large portion of purchasing activities, however, is handled by functions specifically established for this purpose. Although the scope of an organization's procurement activities will vary, the items handled by a purchasing function usually include most of the materials, parts, services, and supplies used by the organization. The purchasing activity for a manufacturing or distribution organization is very important, with purchased goods typically representing a significant part of the costs incurred for the products and services marketed. Purchasing deserves management attention because it interrelates in a significant manner with other organizational activities and often contributes to overall production efficiency. The volume of the purchases is also a determinant of inventory levels, and the investment in inventories is a major factor in the achievement of a favorable return on the capital employed. In addition, the purchasing function has direct operational relationships with such activities as receiving, warehouse operations, scrap sales, and accounts payable. For all of these reasons, purchasing is an important area for reviews by internal audit.

A basic role of the purchasing department is to provide the right products or services at the right price, at the right time, and in the right place. "Right" is used here to mean the "best possible," as judged by the long-term interests of the organization. This determination often cannot be precisely evaluated and involves a great deal of judgment because of the interrelationship of purchasing with other operational activities and the long time often required to appraise various benefits or penalties. Internal audit needs to consider these key dimensions of "right" decisions when evaluating controls and procedures in the purchasing activity.

Purchasing activities have benefited from automation over the years. Manufacturing organizations that use some form of manufacturing resource planning (MRP) system often have automated a significant portion of their purchasing requirements. The MRP system will generate purchase requirements, based on manufacturing schedules and other parameters, that are then communicated to an automated purchasing system. Here, the procurement department needs to be concerned primarily with various automated systems' parameter settings, the correct processing of the purchasing system, and situations where manual procedures are required. These linkages between the MRP system and purchasing increasingly include electronic linkages to vendors and allow suppliers to satisfy the requirements of "just in time" shipments, as was also discussed in Chapter 23 and is mentioned below.

Linkages between the purchasing organization and the seller, often called the trading partners, are increasingly using EDI or the Internet. Purchasing transmits purchase order requirements to the seller's computer system, where a subsequent return transmission acknowledges the purchase order and later transmits notice of the shipment. The purchase payable may also be handled electronically. Electronic data interchange is discussed in greater detail later in this chapter.

The internal auditor's interest in the purchasing function should exist at several levels. First, automated system controls should be in place and operations should be otherwise performed with correct controls and procedures. At another level, internal audit will be interested in the control procedures for the selection of vendors and the negotiation of prices. At another level, a concern might include the procedures and controls that allow purchasing to properly support other major management functions.

(a) NORMAL CYCLE OF THE PURCHASING FUNCTION

The purchasing function in an organization can be viewed as a cycle of activities that follow a number of fairly well-defined steps.

- *Determination of Needs.* The first step is to determine the specific need that must be satisfied through a planned purchasing action. This includes the identification of the product and its specifications, quantities, delivery requirements, and any other pertinent information. These requirements may come from a manufacturing resource planning system, as discussed in Chapter 23, or an "open to buy" authorization in a distribution environment, as will be discussed in Chapter 25.

- *Authorization of the Purchase.* Some form of authorization is needed to proceed with the purchase. Often, the level of authorization depends on the monetary size of the purchase and how it relates to normal operations. In many automated inventory-management systems, this authorization is established through systems parameters.

- *Issuance of the Purchase Order.* The purchasing function selects a vendor that appears to meet its requirements, negotiates terms, and then enters into a definitive purchase agreement called a purchase order or P/O.

- *Follow-Up Procedures.* To the extent necessary, purchasing or the ultimate users should perform follow-up actions to be sure the needed goods are delivered in the manner that will satisfy its requirements.

- *Completion of Delivery.* When the actual deliveries are made, the receiving function communicates that information to purchasing and other functions (such as accounts payables). Purchasing must determine whether there has been proper compliance with the purchase agreement, or if not, if offsetting claims exist.

- *Financial Settlement.* The settlement is made with the vendor according to the terms of the purchase agreement. The purchase transaction is now complete subject only to any continuing warranties by the vendor as part of the basic agreement.

These steps are called the purchasing cycle, an important control cycle in the operations of many organizations. Auditors should understand these basic steps and look for them when analyzing organization operations. Purchasing cycle steps are illustrated in Figure 24.1.

Each of the purchasing cycle steps has its own potential control problems. In addition, both automation and various competitive pressures are continually changing the manner in which the purchasing function is performed. The sections following discuss the control issues surrounding key operational steps in the normal purchasing cycle of a typical organization.

(i) Determination of Purchasing Needs. A basic control issue is the extent to which a determination of purchase needs is made on a sound basis and accurately communicated to the purchasing group. Functions within an organization, such as manufacturing or engineering, should have procedures in place to determine purchasing needs and communicate them to the purchasing function. Typical sources of these determinations include:

- *Manufacturing Production Schedules.* Schedules prepared by production personnel or MRP systems will identify purchasing requirements including their pertinent specifications and time requirements for delivery.

- *Inventory Stock Replenishment Requirements.* Automated inventory systems often

Figure 24.1   Purchasing Cycle Steps

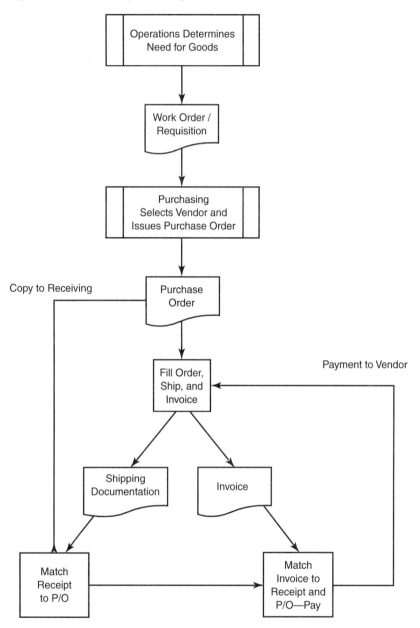

have predetermined stocking levels for individual items that then generate purchase order requirements as the stock level reaches the given minimal point.

- *Specialized Purchase Requirements.* Special projects of either a capital or operational nature may carry with them unique requirements for goods and services. The engineers and others involved with these projects determine needs and communicate them to purchasing.

- *Ongoing Operational Needs.* The modern organization has a wide variety of other operational needs, ranging from contracted services to cleaning supplies. These needs are evaluated by responsible individuals and translated into purchase requirements.

In any of these situations, questions may arise that have to be considered in a manner dependent on the significance of the particular purchased item. A first question may be the general validity of the underlying need, including both the purpose for which the items are to be used and the soundness of how basic needs are translated into definite requirements. The purchasing department should be sensitive to any unusual items reported through the supporting automated systems. In concurrence with senior management, purchasing should also establish policies, guidelines, and authorized purchase levels for various members of the organization. Unusual requests or purchase requests that exceed individual buying responsibilities should be rejected or communicated to appropriate levels of management for approval.

For many types of purchases, the determined need should be transmitted to purchasing in the form of an approved requisition or other proper documentation. How these needs are determined is usually the responsibility of other organization personnel. While these determinations initiate the purchasing process, the purchasing function often does more than just process them and is typically in a position to know what is sound in the way of an underlying method or policy for determining needs. Purchasing is also well qualified to serve as a kind of a check on unusual and abnormally high service or supply requirements.

The role of the purchasing group also extends to the determination of needs in a different way. Purchasing, through its normal activities, should be in touch with market conditions and able to appraise new developments and trends in the way of shortages or oversupply. Individual buyers also often know the situations of various vendors, especially their more important ones. Thus, purchasing personnel should be able to make an important contribution in advising other functions of changing developments and what bearing these developments might have on current ordering actions. The purchasing group thus shares in the responsibility for the proper determination of needs and often can be quite helpful.

Although the effectiveness of purchasing representatives is determined to some extent by their so-called trader skills, it also depends on basic analytical abilities. This ability is a combination of a vigorous and imaginative search for facts and the capacity to relate those facts to specific procurement situations. In a specialized product area, a buyer must know what goes into the making of the product, the nature of the manufacturing processes, and the major operational problems that affect the completion and delivery of the product.

The buyer needs to know how much things should cost and recognize what constitutes good levels of cost performance. Related also is a knowledge of how the product will be used and what types of problems can arise in that utilization. The buyer's job is to put all of this knowledge together in the most advantageous manner possible in terms of ultimate organizational interest. An illustration here is the participation by purchasing in a value analysis of finished products, where consideration is given to how alternative materials or processes might be used to take cost out of a product without impairing its quality. The buyer will often gain the cooperation of vendors, who might work with the buyer and other organization technical personnel. This capability tends to increase over time as the buyer's knowledge is augmented by further experience and breadth of contacts.

Purchase needs, once determined, must then be put into proper documentary form. In a manual environment, there will be requisition forms or other documentation that list specific needs with pertinent specifications, required approvals, and information needed for other organizational purposes. Specifications would be used for standardized components when practicable. Although today a substantial part of this procedure will be automated today, the basic input to these automated processes should have the proper information elements. In some cases, standard requisitions can be used in repetitive situations to minimize excessive clerical effort and possible human error. Important control aspects in all purchase requisitions are:

- Propriety of approvals
- Completeness of the required information
- Accuracy of the clerical and processing effort

Manually prepared requisitions will typically require detailed reviews by the purchasing department to determine if information needs are met. For automated systems, there may not be a formal requisition document because the authority to generate purchase orders would have been established at the time the automated system was reviewed and accepted. The purchase orders then produced by the automated system would be considered valid without a separate purchase requisition document.

(ii) Authorization Procedures for Purchases.   In many cases, the determination of purchasing needs will occur at the same time as the authorization to purchase. However, this is not always true because the authorization to purchase may involve further questions that are not usually the responsibility of the individuals who determine the need. Typical of these questions might be:

- *Is the item available within the organization?* The purchasing group may have knowledge of the availability of an item elsewhere in the organization. In other cases, there may be questions to justify making a specific search as to that possibility.
- *Should the item be made rather than purchased?* This is a question often under continuing scrutiny by manufacturing organizations. Changing conditions—such as increasing difficulties of procurement, increased volume, or increased cost—will sharpen interest in the "make-or-buy" decision and can be the basis of initiating more studies. The impetus for the make-or-buy investigation can come from a number of sources, and possibilities here are part of the overall concern of an effective purchasing group.
- *Can the outside purchase be made?* Conditions may have arisen where the items specified cannot be purchased or can be purchased only in a modified form. In such a situation, there must be further discussions with the requisitioning organization.

- *Are budgetary requirements complied with?* If not previously covered at the requisition stage, there will usually be a requirement for budgetary approval by appropriate levels of management. This would be particularly true if the purchase would result in an over-budget condition.

- *Are there financing problems?* Since the purchase will establish some financial obligation, the question may be whether the purchase at this time is within the organization's financial capabilities. In some cases it might be necessary to either defer the purchase, reduce the quantities, or negotiate different payment terms.

The actual authorization of the purchase can be handled either as part of the requisition or as a supplemental step. The important point is that the designated approvals have been secured and that the purchasing group has raised any questions that would be in the organization's interest before proceeding with the actual purchase. This requisition process would usually take place for larger or unusual purchases, and the approval would be handled as a supplement to the basic requisition.

(iii) Issuance of the Purchase Order. The release of purchase orders, whether in paper format or an EDI document, is the heart of overall purchasing activities. A purchase order is a contractual obligation of the organization to buy some goods according to established terms. The purchasing function or an assigned buyer is usually responsible for matching purchase requirements to appropriate vendors. This may be a decision where the purchase function coordinates requirements with others, such as manufacturing engineers or marketing personnel depending upon the nature of the business, but the purchasing function is usually responsible for the actual issuance of purchase orders.

There will often be a large number of suppliers who can satisfy the organization's needs. There is often no need to select a new vendor with every subsequent purchase of a given item, but the first such purchase requires a survey of available resources and the selection of a vendor. While there may be only a limited number of vendors available to supply certain specialized goods, the purchasing function must usually search for all vendors who would seem to be possible qualified sources. This will include both new vendors and vendors who have supplied other items.

The individual vendor's reliability in terms of past procurements, general reputation, and financial standing must be considered. In addition, purchasing should weigh such factors as price, terms, absorption of delivery costs, treatment of tooling charges, maintenance of reserve inventories, capacity to satisfy delivery requirements, quality standards, service backup, product development activities, and the like. Purchasing should also consider the extent to which the organization desires protection for supply through dual or multiple sourcing.

For some commodities or larger purchasing agreements, the purchasing function may make field contacts with potential vendors to look over facilities, to discuss operational capabilities, and to assess the vendor's ability to supply needed product. This can be a worthwhile exercise with both existing and potential vendors.

In some purchase situations, there may be supplementary considerations, such as community relations, minority contract compliance objectives, disclosure risks when working with a major supplier of a competitor, sales reciprocity arrangements, or government regulations. Foreign suppliers cause other special considerations, including currency translation risks, tariffs, customs requirements, and government trade policies. A major purchase decision with a new vendor is a complex process requiring both analysis and negotiation, and must always be handled with extreme care. An attempt to make a special allowance for one group may result in charges of discrimination by another.

The establishment of any special vendor terms in a purchase arrangement usually takes place when the price and terms are established. A basic control concern regarding the price and other purchase terms is the extent that the purchasing function has exploited market opportunities through competitive bidding. Every legitimate competitive pressure should be used to get maximum value for the organization. Of course, this usually desirable objective could conceivably be carried too far. There could be situations where a vendor needs the business so badly that the purchaser is in a position to force the price down to an unfair level. An enlightened organization recognizes that it is in their long-run interest to have solvent and reasonably prosperous key vendors, supplying quality products delivered according to schedule. The organization must consider its own problems of competitive survival and find a proper balance of toughness and fairness. To achieve these ends, it must continuously seek to have a strong and healthy competition among its vendors.

Based upon this objective of vendor competition, the solicitation of competitive bids from qualified vendors should be a standard procedure whenever practicable. The only exception may be for the special situation where there is no satisfactory second source, or where emergency pressures do not allow adequate time to get the competitive bids. These situations can be minimized by better planning and by efforts to develop alternative sources. This solicitation of competitive bids should also be done to take advantage of any new product developments, but bid solicitations should be in good faith and the basis for an actual award as opposed to a situation when they are used as a cover-up to support an already determined selection. A good purchasing group should continually strive to make effective efforts to seek competitive bids, and should be prepared to justify situations when that approach is not followed.

Despite the objective to seek competitive bidding to the maximum extent possible, in some situations vendor choice will be dictated by other factors. For example, a particular vendor alone may have the necessary know-how, experience, or patent-protected position. The choice may be dictated by a customer, as is sometimes true for government work. Under such circumstances, the vendor may have an established price, and that will be the price unless quantity discounts or other allowances can be negotiated. One approach here is to ask that the vendor provide a detailed schedule of estimated costs, plus a factor for profit. In some cases these cost estimates are subject to review, especially if there is to be any later incentive price revisions based upon actual cost experience. Cost estimates prepared by the organization's accounting function should be used to the extent possible.

In some situations, experience with a specialized product may be so limited that it is impossible to negotiate intelligently any kind of fixed-price type of contract. In that case, arrangements can be made where the payment is determined by actual costs plus an agreed-upon profit factor. Several important cost-control problems exist with this type of procurement. First is the difficulty of defining the types of costs to be reimbursed, including which costs are to be considered as direct charges and which overhead items will be proper. There may also be a further problem of how overhead costs will be allocated to particular products. Second, a vendor may lack motivation to reduce costs as compared to the fixed-price type of contract. A third difficulty is determining the profit factor. Especially to be avoided are percentage approaches that result in higher profit when costs increase, again providing the wrong kind of motivation. All this means is cost-type contracts should usually be avoided to the maximum extent possible, and if there are no other alternatives, they must be handled with extreme care. Accounting personnel should be brought in to help define the cost relationships and to review the propriety of claimed costs. Monitoring work and costs in progress is especially important in cost-type contracts.

While the procedure for handling this phase of the purchase transaction can vary, in a typical situation the purchase order process includes:

- *Recording the Purchase Request.* The requirement or authorization to purchase is initially logged in and assigned to a member of the purchasing group—usually called the buyer—depending on the size and type of the proposed transaction. This requirement may come from an authorized member of operations or be a requirement generated through an automated inventory replenishment or MRP system.

- *Determining Appropriate Vendors.* Vendor records are usually cross-referenced for the various types of items and should be consulted for possible sources. If the purchase is a regular but relatively minor repeat purchase, the buyer may reference vendor records from the last purchase and initiate another order. However, if a new item or a particularly large order, the buyer may want to review possible alternate sources.

- *Obtaining Appropriate Management Approvals.* Based on the size and nature of the purchasing request and any authority limits on purchases, the responsible buyer may need to consult with purchasing management and the requester to clarify any questions or authorization clearances for the procurement. Organizations typically have purchase authorization limits for various persons, and the buyer should check this.

- *Sending Bid Requests.* Bid requests to potential suppliers are then solicited by means of standard forms supplemented by telephone and other contacts. Many organizations today use EDI techniques here.

- *Reviewing Vendor Bid Proposals.* Bids are received and summarized so that the lowest bid, all things considered, can be determined. Factors used in the selection of the bid should be documented.

- *Making the Preliminary Vendor Selection.* The recommendation of the buyer is reviewed by a purchasing department supervisor or by the requester to the extent required. This decision will depend on the size and nature of the purchase. If the recommendation to purchase is made without competitive bidding, supporting reasons should be attached.

- *Selecting the Approved Vendor.* An authorization-to-purchase record should be completed and cross-referenced to the purchase order as listed in a register of purchase orders issued. In most instances today, this process is handled by an automated system that logs the purchase authorization data and generates the purchase order.

- *Issuing the Purchase Order.* The approved purchase order is then prepared and mailed or transmitted to the vendor. Either a paper or electronic purchase order contains an acknowledgment of the terms outlined in the vendor's winning bid, along with the quantities and delivery schedules of the purchase. The purchase order often includes a request for the vendor to acknowledge acceptance and agreement with the terms of the purchasing document.

Figure 24.2   Purchase Order Example Form

ExampleCo Corp.			PURCHASE ORDER		

3333 Corporate Square
Burning Stump, ND   800-784-8129

The following number must appear on all invoices, bills
of lading, and acknowledgments relating to this P/O:
Purchase Order: **9-7654**

TO:
John H. Doe
Maxxam Industrial Supply Co.   P/O DATE | April 15, 2000
9876 Acme Street   TERMS | 2% Ten, Net 30
Anytown, IA   F.O.B. | Anytown
                                              SHIP VIA | BigWheel VanLine

QTY	UNIT	DESCRIPTION	UNIT PRICE	AMOUNT
2	EA	Special Facilitating Product	1,322.50	$2,645.00
12	EA	Spare Parts Kit	78.50	$942.00
400	FT	Binding Cable	0.02	$8.00

A purchase order is a contractual document that allows a buyer to commit the organization to purchase goods per the specified terms and conditions. There is no one standard form for this document and practices often vary by specific industry. Figure 24.2 illustrates a typical purchase order form with various information elements such as terms and conditions noted. The purchase order is usually a numerically controlled document. In a totally manual system, it is prepared in a multicopy form so that information copies can be forwarded to other interested organization entities including the requesting user, the receiving department, and accounts payable. It contains the organization's standard contractual purchasing terms plus any approved modifications. The purchase order usually states all warranties and may provide alternative purchaser rights of rejection or repair in case the goods do not meet specifications. It may also provide a provision for damage remedies in the event the goods are defective.

Internal audit should not expect to find this detailed a set of procedures for all purchases within the organization. In many instances today, organizations make "blanket" purchase order arrangements, rather than issuing individual P/Os for each individual purchase. These blanket documents can take one of two basic forms. First, for such commodities as office services or janitorial supplies, the purchasing department, after appropriate negotiations, may issue an overall P/O to a supplier along with a list of persons authorized to place orders within the terms of that P/O. There will also be various monetary and goods restrictions.

The second form of blanket purchase order occurs when an organization has a need to purchase a given component on a continuing basis over an extended period of time. An initial order would be issued, containing some form of negotiated price based upon planned future volumes. Although automated systems usually take care of this type of purchasing arrangement, it is important that the ongoing progress of the purchase contract be closely monitored by the purchasing department.

(iv) Purchasing Follow-Up Procedures.   A continuing purchasing function concern is that the goods are actually delivered in accordance with purchase order agreements. In many situations, the dependence of other organization activities on these deliveries is so great that all possible steps must be taken to guarantee the wanted deliveries. For larger or otherwise unusual orders, it may even be desirable for a knowledgeable buyer representative to visit the vendor facilities to check on progress. Other organization personnel may also be brought into the picture to act in an advisory capacity or to verify quality performance. The emphasis here is on taking all necessary steps to insure the wanted results. In other cases, the buyer should be in touch to review any interim progress with respect to deliveries. If and when problems develop due to delays or below-standard products, the buyer can act as a liaison with the vendor to obtain corrective action.

In a larger manufacturing organization, this follow-up activity is often called ''expediting'' and may be performed by specialized individuals who are often part of manufacturing rather than purchasing. Expeditors may also travel to selected vendors to monitor critical orders, to oversee rework projects, or to deal directly with vendor technical personnel.

The extent of follow-up procedures will vary with the complexity of the goods, the delivery schedules, and the length of the delivery period. Some type of follow-up records, either in automated or manual form, should be utilized to keep the purchasing group apprised of key performance dates. Each buyer is normally responsible for monitoring the progress of his/her purchase orders, using P/O system reports as appropriate.

There normally will be a separate receiving activity to establish what has been received and in what condition. This may include inspections for conformance to agreed-upon specifications or levels of quality. As a key procedural control, the receiving and inspection activities should be organizationally independent of the purchasing group, and the records of these activities should be separately transmitted to the accounts payable activity. At that time, any records of claims of any kind should be clearly stated and communicated to accounts payable.

The financial settlement for the purchased goods is performed by the separate accounts payable group. Here, the original purchase order is matched with both the supplier's invoice and the receiving data, and, subject to any deductions or adjustments, the final approval for payment and subsequent disbursement is made. The negotiation of adjustments is usually made by the affected buyer, but in certain cases it may also be desirable to receive some guidance from accounting as part of the negotiations. At this point, the financial settlement takes place as the final step in the purchase transaction. Although the purchasing group is kept informed, this important aspect of the purchase cycle moves outside of purchasing's control.

(v) Other Purchasing-Related Matters.   The review of major control points also include a consideration of some related matters that bear importantly on effective control of the purchasing activity. These include the organizational status of the purchasing function, its purchasing jurisdiction, and various ethical issues.

Although the volume and importance of the items purchased determine, in many respects, the importance and status of the purchasing function, there could still be a question of whether the purchasing group has been accorded the level of status it really deserves. The position and organizational status of the purchasing function in the organization should be such that its management has sufficient stature and a proper degree of independence to effectively relate to others, from staff members to senior management. In addition, for separation-of-duties internal controls reasons, the responsibilities should not include collateral activities such as receiving, warehousing, and accounts payables.

A related organizational issue is the extent to which the purchasing function should be centralized at the headquarters rather than at lower-level operating units or other profit centers with a need for their own purchasing activities. The answer here depends on the overall degree of organizational decentralization. If a centralized organization, it will be logical that purchasing should also be centralized. If the organization is strongly profit-center oriented, there often will be separate purchasing groups in the individual units. Even in the latter case, there is often a need for a limited central purchasing group to develop and administer organization-wide purchasing policy and to achieve economies of scale in volume purchasing. Also, such a central group can often provide any needed central research and expertise.

In many situations, there is a need for central control of certain procurement activities on an organization-wide basis. Local purchasing groups would then report to the local management group and to the central purchasing group on a dotted line basis. It is important here that the respective jurisdictions and related responsibilities of the central purchasing group versus field purchasing be clearly stated. If done properly, it is usually possible for central purchasing operations to adequately serve the needs of both the operational components and central headquarters. This assumes the central purchasing group will exercise adequate control over the branch units through common standards and procedures as well as common information systems. Part of this control can also be built in through day-to-day operational relationships, supplemented by reviews of reports and periodic field visits.

Another organizational issue concerns defining and administering the jurisdiction of the purchasing group. This problem appears in a variety of forms, but perhaps most common is determining what types of purchases will go through the purchasing department. In some cases, an operational group may argue that it is more efficient for them to satisfy their ''special'' procurement needs through their own direct efforts. An example is an advertising department that obtains media space directly or through an outside advertising agency. In making this purchasing jurisdiction decision, the basic issue is whether the purchasing group can make a contribution, either as a result of its actual experience in a given area of procurement or because a professional purchasing approach can be expected to yield better controls.

Problems may exist when the official role of purchasing is clear enough but where there are deviations. A frequent example is when an operating department ''jumps the gun,'' so to speak and in effect carries out its own investigation of product availabilities and prices and then comes to the purchasing department only to legitimatize the effort through a perfunctory handling of the actual purchase. Here, any possibility of contribution by the regular purchasing group is precluded. While operating units may have knowledge in some fields that allow them to better understand those specialized products and their vendors, they may sometimes also make recommendations for purchase of normal types of commodities. The best remedy in this latter situation is perhaps for the purchasing department to turn back the request. The need to get the expenditure authorized properly to fit into regular accounts payable routines will then serve as a discipline to let purchasing do its proper job in the future.

Another common problem is the avoidance of regular purchasing controls by effecting the procurement through special promotional, travel expense accounts, or other types of operating funds. Such funds have presumably been set up for relatively limited purposes, usually for expenditures of a special nature. The problem arises when those funds are improperly used for the procurement of items that should go through regular purchasing channels. A result may be a loss of control for these procurements and a potential loss of the advantage that could come through consolidated purchases. Ground rules prohibiting this type of purchasing should be clearly stated and enforced through procedures under which only normal operating funds are reimbursed.

A variation of this evasion problem is through "emergency" purchases. While emergency needs are to some extent unavoidable, and there may be no choice but to complete the purchase on the best possible basis within the time constraints, emergency changes should be the exception and not the rule. In an emergency situation, prices may have to be accepted that might have been reduced through competitive bidding. This can lead also to purchase commitments being made without a price agreement; that is, the vendor is asked to proceed with the production or shipment of the item and then to advise the organization what the price will be. While emergency procurements are sometimes unavoidable due to a breakdown of equipment or an unexpected rush order, steps should be taken to eliminate the portion that is due to inefficiencies.

Others in the organization will sometimes seek help from purchasing in making their own personal purchases. This is especially likely if the items involved are the same as are purchased for organization use. This practice may be common among organization officers. Although usually not too serious a problem, it can get out of hand. Such services, if allowed, should be extended on an equitable basis to all employees at specified organizational levels, and this service should not be permitted to affect the purchasing group in discharging its regular responsibilities in an effective manner. Consideration must be given not only to the dilution of buyer's efforts, but also to the nuisance to vendors and the administrative difficulties of effecting delivery and payment. Usually, the less this practice is tolerated, the better.

A particularly troublesome operational problem in the purchasing area is the temptation for buyers to favor some vendors. Since the purchasing department's decision as to which vendor shall receive orders is one that could have an impact on the financial interest of that vendor, they will often exert a great deal of pressure on persons who can control those decisions to any significant extent. The types of pressure run from legitimate sales presentations and persistent references to friendship factors, entertainment, gifts, and even actual bribery. The line between the proper and improper is sometimes hard to draw, and the standards of what is right and wrong can easily deteriorate over time. The organization should recognize this danger and endeavor to control it through strong policies prohibiting the acceptance of all gifts or favors. These policies should be communicated to both purchasing personnel and vendors.

Purchasing is an important function in most modern organizations. Even if there is not a formal purchasing department, the organization should have some type of process within its other departmental units to purchase needed goods and services. Internal audit needs to gain an understanding of the basic controls and procedures used in order to assess purchasing function internal controls.

(b) PURCHASING FUNCTION INTERNAL CONTROL CONSIDERATIONS

As has been mentioned throughout this book, auditors often find a high degree of control risk in any function where money is leaving the organization as a result of a transaction cycle. The overall purchasing cycle very much presents this type of potential control risk environment. It also should present the same if not a greater level of concern to senior management, who are responsible for managing the cycle and installing appropriate controls. Internal audit is part of this overall control process, with a responsibility for evaluating the purchasing cycle.

Purchasing has a major responsibility in establishing controls throughout this cycle. Purchasing does not establish the purchase requirements but is responsible for establishing a consistent set of formats and procedures for submitting those requirements. Similarly, the purchasing function does not approve the purchases, but they should work with senior management to set up the rules for approval authorization. Purchasing then must have installed controls to determine that all purchases follow these established authorization rules or guidelines.

The internal controls surrounding the making of the actual purchase are a key responsibility of the purchasing function. These are controls to determine that an adequate search is made to find an appropriate vendor and that the purchase is made under the best terms and conditions. Many of the earlier paragraphs in this chapter described these control concerns. Those same sections described the role of the purchasing function in a purchase follow-up process. Purchasing has a secondary responsibility in ensuring that the vendors selected deliver the goods specified in accordance with the terms and conditions of the purchases.

The purchasing function has no direct responsibility for the receiving and payment steps in the purchasing cycle. Independent parties should take receipt of the goods after a proper inspection and initiate payment for them. The purchasing group has some control responsibilities in each of these last two steps, however. They must transmit their purchase order data to both receiving and accounts payable to complete the purchasing cycle. In addition, purchasing should monitor and control back-order situations and returns of goods. Accounts payable relies on this monitoring to control invoice settlement.

While an internal auditor sometimes has difficulty identifying specific internal controls in some specialized organization activities, this is not the case for a purchasing function. The process generally follows the control cycle steps described previously. By asking appropriate questions and reviewing the process, internal audit should be able to identify, in virtually any organization, who is responsible for these internal controls and the actual procedures used.

Although basic purchasing function internal controls should be fairly easy to identify, this is also an area with a wide variety of control risks. Members of the purchasing function are initiating transactions with outside parties that commit the organization's funds. Although the organization itself may have strong personnel and ethical standards, the best of vendor selection procedures will not ensure that those outside parties follow the same good standards. Internal auditors will often find purchasing to be an interesting and worthwhile area for review.

(c) PURCHASING FUNCTION INTERNAL AUDIT ACTIVITIES

Auditors often review accounting procedures for what they term the ''purchasing cycle'' but do not review the actual purchasing function as part of those reviews. They will review accounts payable as part of their financial reviews. They may also review the purchase requirements definition process and the receiving function in conjunction with their reviews of production operations. However, these audits frequently bypass the actual purchasing department or function. This may be because many purchasing activities involve the negotiation between buyers and their sources. Some of this negotiation may take place outside of the normal workplace, and buyer decisions may be partially based on buyer-vendor relationships.

Despite these concerns, a purchasing function should have in place a strong set of operating controls and procedures, and internal audit should design and perform reviews that evaluate the efficiency and effectiveness of the function. It may be well controlled but a poor performer. The reviews should attempt to highlight these types of issues.

As with other chapters in this book, the following paragraphs outline financial, operational, and computer systems control procedures within a typical purchasing function. However, the nature of purchasing activity often suggests that a single review should be performed covering all three of these elements.

(i) Purchasing Function Financial Control Audit Procedures.   An internal auditor should consider the two basic types of financial controls in the purchasing function. First, there should be controls to monitor the funds expended on goods and services through an authorization by the purchasing function. These expenditures can be substantial and often represent a significant portion of the organization's revenues. Purchasing will usually ensure that requisitioning areas have the budgetary funds to cover these purchase requests. The second area of financial controls covers those internal to the purchasing department itself. This really translates to controls over the buyers and others involved in the purchasing decision. While this section considers both, the emphasis here will be on controls over the purchase prices of goods or services as authorized by purchase orders.

As with other areas discussed, internal audit should initially become familiar with the characteristics of the types of sources and the stability of prices for the organization's supplies. There are many possible variations here. However, some of the basic vendor market conditions might be described as follows.

- *Large Number of Vendors and Stable Prices.* This is a type of market where many vendors supply the products but where no purchaser can dominate or manipulate the market because demand is stable over time. An example might be office supplies.

- *Large Number of Vendors but Commodity Prices.* Here, the product may be common but prices are governed by various market forces. Speculation and other forces can cause dramatic price changes. These are the types of products where demand is cyclical, such as the manufacture of cement.

- *Limited Number of Vendors.* This is perhaps the most common scenario encountered in business. A limited number of often highly competitive vendors will supply some given product. They each may be willing to offer special terms to customers to increase their own market share.

- *Near-Monopoly Vendors.* In some markets, there may be only one or a very small group of suppliers having near-monopoly control over prices. Although monopolies always collapse over time, in this situation the purchasing function does not have much flexibility to negotiate better prices in the short run.

The above are certainly not all-inclusive. There can be other market variations. For example, the type and nature of foreign market suppliers can add other variations to this mix. However, in designing audit procedures for a review of the purchasing department, an internal auditor should understand the nature of the major suppliers. Not all will fit in the same mold, but internal audit should attempt to understand the characteristics of the major suppliers.

Other major factors can influence purchasing decisions. For example, the freight costs of purchased goods can be significant in some situations. An organization purchasing structural steel for its products must consider the major cost of shipping. As a different example, a foreign supplier introduces the risk of currency fluctuations into the decision process.

Once internal audit has acquired a basic understanding of the nature of major vendor relationships, the next step is to understand the financial controls governing the negotiation of vendor prices and terms. There should be a set of purchasing department policies governing the conduct of buyers and their relationships with vendors. These relate to the overall operational controls in the purchasing department.

(ii) Purchasing Function Operational Audit Procedures.   Most purchasing function audit procedures are of an operational nature, and a purchasing function audit creates some special challenges to internal audit. Major issues revolve around potential ''less than arms length'' arrangements with vendors, authorizations for vendor terms and conditions, procedures for vendor selection, and controls over purchase order documents. In addition to concerns that the best possible prices and terms are negotiated with vendors, internal audit should try to determine that no potential conflicts of interest exist between members of the purchasing department and vendors. While internal audit can determine that the organization has established some type of conflict-of-interest policy and that all members of the purchasing department submit signed statements indicating their compliance, it is difficult to identify violations of this type of policy. Unless a buyer engages in openly questionable activities, internal auditors find it difficult to question these transactions.

The problem is even more complex in smaller, more closely held organizations when a member of top management may request that the purchasing department favor one vendor over another. Provided that this is not a significant transaction impacting outside shareholders or a transaction in violation of some contract terms, internal audit perhaps should best report these concerns as a violation of policy but recognize that management has a right to make such decisions. If internal audit encounters potential purchasing conflicts, authorized by management, that may significantly impact shareholder values, the director of internal audit should bring the matter to the attention of the audit committee of the board or to legal counsel.

The best protection against improper buyer activities is a strong conflict-of-interest policy, enforced by purchasing management through formal, signed conflict-of-interest statements, coupled with strong monitoring of buyer purchasing activity. Figure 24.3 shows an example conflict-of-interest policy. Organizations can also protect against conflict-of-interest violations through a procedure whereby vendors are encouraged to submit protests when they feel they have been wronged in a purchasing transaction. Internal audit can

Figure 24.3 Sample Conflict-of-Interest Statement

ExampleCo Corp. Conflict-Of-Interest Policy

We should never receive any improper benefit, monetary or otherwise, from an organization that is a supplier of goods or services, that seeks to do business with ExampleCo, or that is an ExampleCo competitor. We may not influence or participate in the management of any such business, except when directly authorized by ExampleCo. We may not influence any business improperly by offering them gifts or benefits.

An improper benefit may include anything of value offered to us to attempt to influence our business judgment inappropriately. We should always act in ExampleCo's best interests. Gifts exchanged or offered on a personal basis will be considered improper if the retail value exceeds $25.00 in value. All such gifts should be reported to your manager.

We are also expected to make our personal investments in a way that avoids the use, for personal gain, of any nonpublic material information obtained in the course of our work. Although we may invest in companies that do business with us, we may not do so if we are personally involved in decisions relating to those companies. We should never make a personal investment in a company when we have the ability to influence its relationship with ExampleCo.

also test for any suspicious, even potentially fraudulent buyer purchasing activities, through the computer-assisted audit techniques that are discussed in the following section.

In addition to controls to keep purchasing transactions at an arms length, internal audit reviewing purchasing department activities should look for strong procedures for establishing vendor terms and conditions. Although there can be considerable variability here depending upon the nature and quantities of the goods purchased and the nature of the market, the purchasing department should require that vendors agree to certain terms as a condition of the purchase. Although these may be separately negotiated for larger purchase contracts, these terms are often specified on the standard purchase order document or through a vendor trading partner agreement. They are often outlined in fine print on the back of the purchase order document and might include but not be limited to:

- Requirements that vendors ship according to the terms of the purchase order, with the purchaser retaining the right to reject the transaction in the event of vendor changes. Examples of these changes might be late shipments or price changes.

- Definition of the applicable laws governing the transaction. This would be true for both interstate and international transactions. If a dispute, this states that the transaction will be governed by the "Law of the State of _____," usually the purchaser's home state.

- Confidentiality requirements where the vendor must agree to not reveal any significant organization data. This is particularly important when a vendor will have access to confidential information through on-site observations or access to key records.

- Procedures for resolving disputes when goods do not appear to meet specifications.
- Assignment of responsibility in the event of damages or wartime events.

Internal audit should look for a standard set of vendor terms and conditions that are part of all purchasing function transactions. This standard should apply to common classes of goods.

The purchasing department should have standard systems in place for approving and classifying vendors. This often can be organized through a database listing authorized vendors and data on their purchase and performance histories. In times past, the buyer kept this information in his or her memory or on informal notes. However, with modern information systems, there is little reason for this informal approach. A documented file of authorized vendors will aid the purchasing department and help prevent potential questionable purchases.

In addition to approved vendor files and standardized vendor terms and conditions, internal audit should look for a consistent set of policies covering vendor selection. As discussed previously, this often means a policy requiring a minimum number of competitive bids for certain classes and sizes of purchases. Internal audit should review these matters for reasonableness, and then determine whether the policies and procedures are being followed in actual practice.

This type of audit can be a challenge. The auditor must initially advise management that, unless there is some other special request, they are not reviewing purchasing department procedures to question buyer honesty and integrity. Rather, internal audit is reviewing the controls and procedures of what is a very important function in the organization. Figure 24.4 outlines selected procedures for a review of the purchasing function, including a consideration of its efficiency and effectiveness as well as its financial and operational controls.

(iii) Purchasing Function Computer Audit Procedures.

Smaller organizations or those with minimal outside purchasing needs may have limited automated systems supporting their purchasing activities, but larger organizations and those involved in manufacturing or distribution will have extensive systems. These latter systems will typically be integrated with manufacturing scheduling or other forecasting systems to generate at least some of their purchase requirements. The automated purchasing system outputs will also support systems such as receiving and accounts payable. In addition to just generating purchase orders, the typical automated purchasing system is the source of key files containing names, addresses, and agreed-upon terms for authorized vendors.

The first automated purchasing system review task for internal audit is to gain an overall understanding of the system used, its interfaces with other systems, and the overall controls. Figure 24.5 illustrates how an automated purchasing system might be integrated with other systems in a manufacturing type of organization.

The purchasing system at the center of this purchase cycle stream of applications may be a candidate for an application controls review, as was discussed in general in Chapter 17. This review should focus on the interface controls with other systems, logical security access controls to prevent improper manipulation of system data, and contingency planning procedures to ensure that all purchasing documentation has been properly backed up.

Purchase order, vendor history, and other files from the purchasing system and elsewhere are often good areas for computer-assisted audit techniques (CAATs). For exam-

Figure 24.4 Purchasing Function Audit Procedures

24.04.01 Obtain an understanding of the purchasing function, including all persons authorized to make purchases for the organization. Document purchasing organization structure and reporting relationships.

24.04.02 Document the process for initiating a purchase. Determine that a standard purchase order form is used for all paper-based transactions.

24.04.03 Document automated purchasing systems in place as well as interfaces with other supporting systems. Assess the extent that the purchasing function is supported by electronic data interchange (EDI) and other automated techniques.

24.04.04 Determine that standard purchase orders contain appropriate terms and conditions consistent with good control procedures and organization policy.

24.04.05 Understand the vendor selection process for new and current vendors. Are new vendors reviewed for such matters as their financial strength, reputation for quality, and industry reputation? Assess the procedures in place to monitor the performance of existing vendors.

24.04.06 Determine whether procedures are in place requiring competitive bidding for selected procurements. Select a sample of recent procurements to determine that competitive bidding practices are operating.

24.04.07 Review procedures in place governing purchase limit authorizations. Based upon current purchasing organization, determine that limits are appropriate.

24.04.08 Understand the filing system in place to document purchase activities. Select several recently completed purchases and assess whether these records are complete.

24.04.09 Determine that the purchasing function uses either its own or the overall organization's conflict-of-interest procedure. Determine that all current purchasing department employees have formally acknowledged that policy.

24.04.10 Understand and evaluate procedures covering employee purchases.

24.04.11 Review procedures in place for monitoring purchasing problems such as late shipments, damaged merchandise, and the like. Assess adequacy of these procedures.

24.04.12 Review contracts in place covering blanket purchases, pricing agreements, and the like. Determine if any appear to exhibit potential control risks.

ple, internal audit can develop a CAAT to match purchase order prices with accounts payable data, recording amounts actually remitted to vendors. This type of test will reveal situations where vendors may underbid on price and then increase their revenues through contract changes, overshipments or early shipments, or other actions. While this type of CAAT measures the quality of vendors serving the organization, it is also a measure of how well the purchasing department monitors its vendor activities. Another important type of CAAT is a three-way test matching purchase orders, receiving reports, and invoiced amounts. Figure 24.6 describes this type of a three-way CAAT for operational reviews of the purchasing function.

(iv) Sample Audit Report Findings and Recommendations

A: Vendors Are Not Properly Monitored for Performance.   In our discussions with purchasing department management we were told that no formal program was in place to monitor vendor performance and that purchasing management relies upon the knowledge

Figure 24.5   Automated Purchasing System Example

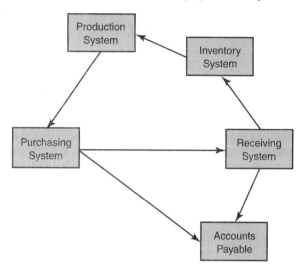

of its buyers to maintain vendor quality. We subsequently designed a CAAT to survey purchase order quantities requested as well as expected due dates for vendors in several major product classes. We found that several long-term vendors of electronic components have consistently shipped their goods from 30 to 90 days late. While their components are in short supply, these same vendors appear to be supplying the same goods to competitors. Based upon statements made by several competitors in a recent trade publication, it would appear that these vendors are not providing the same level of quality service to our organization as they do for others.

Recommendation.   The purchasing department should develop a formal program to monitor vendor quality, including their shipping performance. Vendors that exhibit below average performance should be warned that they may be dropped as approved vendors. Where there has been no improvement, the alternative sources of supply should be identified and the vendor dropped from the approved vendor list.

B: Vendor Purchases Are Bypassing the Purchasing Department.   During our review of purchasing department activities, we observed that the design engineering group had no purchase activity in the last quarter. We inquired as to the reasons and found that design engineering has established its own informal purchasing function outside of the normal purchasing department. Members of design engineering management advised us that their purchasing needs are "too specialized" for normal purchasing department procedures. We then briefly reviewed purchasing records within the design engineering group and found that their procedures were generally informal. Many if not most of the items purchased were the same as used for normal production, but only in smaller quantities.

Recommendation.   Management should require the design engineering group to use the purchasing department for all purchase activities. Purchasing should work with

Figure 24.6 Three-Way Purchasing System CAAT

ExampleCo Internal Audit Purchasing Test

Vendor #	Name	P/O #	P/O Date	P/O Amount	Received	Invoice #	Inventory Amount	Audit Check
3288	Axylotl Corp	467355	05/02/02	$3,556.35	06/25/02	A357880	$3,556.35	OK
7743	XYZ Co.	467356	05/12/02	$15,258.55	06/30/02	GB8899	$15,387.00	INV AMT DIFF
1285	Sterling Prod.	467299	05/12/02	$655.00		889911	$655.00	NO RECEIVING
5200	Modern Supply	467466	05/15/02	$12.13	06/29/02	X892188	$112.13	INV AMT DIFF
4799	Good Guys Co.	467467	05/15/02	$5,648.88	07/10/02	W213-88	$5,648.88	OK
2332	Computer Suppl	467470	05/20/02	$8,564.50	07/15/02	546XZ-12	$8,564.50	OK
9966	Smith Software	467488	05/20/02	$1,728.00	07/01/02	215	$1,728.00	OK
3288	Axylotl Corp.	467469	05/22/02	$89,251.90		3311	$89,251.90	NO RECEIVING
7743	XYZ Co.	467471	05/25/02	$15,387.00	07/21/02	13233	$5,668.00	INV AMT DIFF
6855	L. C. Tuttle Co.	467499	05/29/02	$1,555.52	07/14/02	A9988	$1,555.52	OK

engineering management to correct any problems that may have forced design engineering to do its own purchasing in the past.

24-3 RECEIVING ACTIVITIES

Receiving is a continuation of the operational cycle that began with the procurement of materials and services. Receiving starts when a supplier makes delivery to the purchaser's premises or some other designated point. The group receiving them then determines the goods are received in the quantities, specifications, and conditions covered by the underlying purchase order agreement. In addition, the receiving process includes the physical care of the goods received and their forwarding to appropriate inventory or production locations. This function provides an essential link between procurement of the goods or services and their ultimate placement where they will be available to satisfy operational needs. Delays or errors in providing this link can result in serious operational problems in the other affected activities. Proper receiving is also a basic prerequisite in establishing the validity for payments to vendors as a part of the accounts payable process. From an operational standpoint, receiving activities should be carried out with maximum efficiency.

Depending upon the nature of the business, incoming materials may be liquid or solid, packaged or in bulk, small or bulky, of low or very high value, and may have special protection or inspection requirements. The materials may arrive by rail, air, truck, or package express, emphasizing the broad range of operational problems facing a receiving department.

A key receiving function, then, is the recording of this activity, usually through automated systems, to transmit the receipts to purchasing and accounts payable. These groups will use this information to update purchase records and to initiate the payment process.

Organizational separateness from the purchasing function is particularly desirable here to minimize the risk of someone in purchasing controlling both the order and the evidence of the receipt of that order. This organizational independence is also an important check on vendor performance and should be a basis for payment by the accounts payable department. However, organizational independence should in no way lessen a cooperative relationship with other interested groups, purchasing, transportation, stores, accounts payable, and ultimate users.

Automation has caused major changes in many receiving functions. Historically, receiving was little more than a warehousing function responsible for unpacking goods and matching their contents to both the vendor-supplied packing lists and the purchase orders. This was a manual paperwork type of process, and many organizations have now adopted on-line receiving systems where incoming goods are matched against purchase order requirements, and receipts recorded for inventory status update records. Today, manual receiving procedures have been reduced even further. Suppliers are instructed to send goods with special bar-coded labels following established coding standards. The receiving department may not even open the received packages, but only record the receipts by reading the bar-coded labels with optical scanners. The packages are not opened until delivery to the designated location, and if the contents are improperly packed or counted, the differences are settled with vendors at a later time.

In some organizations today, the traditional receiving department has an even more reduced role. Goods are ordered on a continual basis using ''just-in-time'' techniques where orders are generated on a continual basis due to production requirements and shipped from suppliers to the organization's production line just as needed. The automotive industry provides a good example here. In some instances, outside vendor–supplied assemblies such as automobile seats are delivered on an almost continual flow to assembly lines, as required.

Although these newer logistical procedures have changed the receiving process, the receiving of goods is still an important part of an organization's purchasing cycle. Ordered goods must somehow be received and put into production, and vendors paid. Improved information systems, vendor agreements, and other procedures may eliminate some traditional steps here. However, the organization must still have some means to acknowledge that it received what it ordered. Internal audit should have a good understanding of the materials flow and the control aspects of this receiving process.

(a) RECEIVING DEPARTMENT CONTROL CYCLE

A receiving function usually follows a series of fairly consistent operational steps. While automation can alter the nature of some of these, a receiving function is usually responsible for the following operational steps.

- Maintaining records of open order and shipment data from purchasing
- Accepting delivery of the goods from the supplier
- A verification that the goods and quantities received are consistent with the purchase agreement
- Inspection of materials to the extent required
- Delivery of the received good to the user or to the stores department
- Reporting of receipt results to accounts payable, purchasing, and other interested groups

The above are the traditional steps that a receiving function usually follows. These steps will be performed somewhat differently depending upon the industry and the extent of automation. The following sections discuss each of these steps in the context of a smaller manufacturing organization with limited automation support. Automated receiving systems will be discussed later in the chapter. The control procedures here are applicable for most receiving functions.

(i) Receiving Department Notification.   A receiving department plays an important role in either accepting or rejecting incoming goods. If accepted, the receiving function generally is obligating the organization to pay for those goods. Therefore, the receiving function must know what orders and what quantities have been authorized, and according to what terms.

Notification is often best accomplished by the transmittal to the receiving department of a designated copy of the approved purchase order issued by the purchasing department. This document contains the vendor name, quantities ordered, and the method of shipping. The anticipated receipt date may be shown, but the receiving department copy of the purchase order would usually not show prices. The receiving function typically does not need to be concerned whether prices are correct at the time the goods are received.

Paper-based purchase order copies are filed in some kind of an open order file pending receipt of the materials. These documents can be filed by a serial number or by the vendor name, but they should be maintained in an orderly manner so that the copy can be easily retrieved upon the receipt of goods. It is essential that receiving department copies of purchase orders be forwarded promptly so they can be utilized as a continuing alert for expected goods.

Many organizations have automated this purchase order notification process where purchasing systems create a file of open purchase orders that the receiving department can access. This ensures that receiving has immediate access to all open purchase orders and eliminates the danger of paper documents becoming lost or misfiled.

(ii) Receipt of Deliveries.   While sometimes goods may arrive at a local transportation terminal and be picked up by the organization or a trucker intermediary, usually the delivery will be to the organization premises. A common control here is how the carrier obtains access to the organization's premises. A receiving area should be a fairly secured facility where deliveries must clear through a central control point before goods can be left on a dock. The receiving facility can be a wide open area with numerous shipments of goods ready for placement or inspection. Outsiders should not be allowed to enter this area unsupervised.

Plant security, which typically controls the movement of materials in and out of the organization's property, also has an important role in the receipt of deliveries. They may help to determine that trucks are directed to the correct receiving docks, or, for a much larger facility, that railroad cars are switched onto the proper sidings. The truck or railroad car should be promptly unloaded, with the materials transferred to the custody and responsibility of the organization. At this point, the receiving department would make an appropriate check of what is being delivered in terms of weight, number of packages, and the like. Empty trucks and cars, except as they may contain material for other parties, once cleared, should then leave the organization premises. Plant security is an important control here, especially for large or bulk deliveries. Receiving also has an important role in supervising the unloading in a manner that will best facilitate any subsequent verification and inspection.

(iii) Verification of Received Goods.   The receiving department would make further detailed counts of the material received as appear to be appropriate. Influencing factors here include the degree of confidence in the particular vendor, the extent to which there are sealed containers with stated quantities, the practicability of counts, and the value of goods involved. For some receiving departments, a considerable degree of judgment is required to determine the necessary level of verification. There may also be secondary checks on the quantities and conditions of materials as they are put into stores or directly into production. For bulk materials, where reliance is on weights or volumes, the role of receiving becomes one of the independent confirmation of the weights or volumes asserted by the shipper or carrier. There should be a reasonable standard of verification applied, with that verification carried out with reasonable promptness.

A question often exists as to whether the purchase order copy sent to the receiving department should show the quantities ordered. The rationale that supports omission of quantities is that the receiving personnel will then be forced to make a more independent and more accurate count of quantities received. However, this approach sometimes causes delay or confusion, especially to the accounts payable department. It also makes it impossible to identify supplier overshipment that should be returned without receiving.

Automation, coupled with the costs of opening packages and counting goods, is changing the functions of receiving departments for many organizations. Vendor quality programs can provide assurance that goods are shipped in the quantities marked or coded on package shipping labels. As previously mentioned, vendors increasingly ship goods in packages marked with bar codes to indicate purchase order number, item types, and quantities. The receiving department would then use scanning devices to read those labels for input directly into automated receiving systems. These bar code scanners are small, hand-held devices similar to the scanners found in many grocery store checkout lines. They read the bar code label and provide the inspector with a light or sound signal to indicate that label data was read. Some of these devices are plugged into receivers at the end of a shift for input to a centralized computer system. Other devices may transmit directly to a computer system through a radio frequency–based local area network (LAN) system. An increasing number of organizations—from manufacturing to distribution—are taking this type of approach for their receiving functions.

Many larger organizations have instituted penalty agreements as part of their standard purchase orders. With this type of agreement, vendors receive payment of less than the agreed-upon purchase price if the goods are shipped late, are improperly marked, or otherwise violate some significant purchase order term. These agreements are designed to improve vendor performance. Both sides must agree to the conditions, which can vary depending upon the nature of the purchasing organization. Both sides of the agreement typically prefer that a penalty deduction be charged rather than that the goods be shipped back. The receiving function must understand the nature of any penalty terms, have measures in place to check for compliance, and have systems to inform the accounts payable function of any penalty deductions.

Just-in-time manufacturing approaches or direct shipments to individual locations are also eliminating the central receiving function for some industries. Rather than receiving goods, placing them in inventory, and drawing from them later for production, organizations are demanding that only those quantities of goods needed go directly to the production line. Similarly, some retail organizations with multiple locations now ask that vendors ship goods directly to branch stores only in the quantities needed. In both instances, the receiving function has been distributed to the unit actually needing the goods at a particular point in time. Responsible persons at those units must play a receiving function role, scanning labels or otherwise providing input indicating that goods were received.

(iv) Receiving Inspection and Routing Activities.   For many materials, an inspection will be performed as a part of the counts and other verification of the goods received. In some cases, the receiver visually inspects goods to determine that there is no evident damage. In other cases, however, more elaborate and substantive types of inspection are required. Here, the inspection action is carried out by a separate inspection or quality control department that is often responsible for inspection activities at all stages of the production process in a manufacturing organization. This type of inspection is necessary when the goods must meet precise specifications or when visual inspections will not reveal potential problems. When this further inspection is necessary, the goods received are usually moved from the initial receiving area to a different area under the jurisdiction of an inspection or quality-control department. These materials should be moved with reasonable promptness and then inspected with reasonable dispatch. Because of the extra movement, organizations sometimes have control problems in keeping the individual vendor shipments separate and intact, although it is necessary that this be done. Quality-control functions and controls are discussed as part of Chapter 26.

The materials as received, or as subsequently inspected, are next ready for transfer either to stores or directly to the using department, subject to identification of any deficiencies in the way of purchase order terms, quantities, specifications, or damage. At this point, the basis for vendor payment and for all claims thus identified is established and recorded. If certain agreed standards are not in compliance and more detailed negotiations with the vendor are necessary, the items in question are typically segregated and held for later release. There may also be a need to return portions of the materials to the vendor for rework to bring them up to required standards. Important receiving and inspection internal control considerations here are as follows:

- All incoming receipts should be matched to the documentary evidence of an approved purchase order.

- Standards should be established for all major types of goods received, defining any count and inspection procedures.

- Claims against vendors for count or damage problems should be generated by a competent authority.

- Appropriate record controls should be established for all receiving activities.

- Any additional receiving-related costs that may be incurred should be properly recorded for later recovery.

- Any defective materials should be adequately tagged and segregated.

- Good items should then move promptly to their proper destinations.

With respect to the last control, there may also be a need for acceptance of the goods into the appropriate operations function for continuing accountability. However, internal audit would typically not see a formal receiving function at the loading dock followed by a duplicate function where goods are again recounted when delivered to the production line or the inventory stores area. There should be only one type of documented acknowledgment that the goods were correctly delivered to their intended destination.

The operational cycle of the receiving department is now complete except for the reporting to all interested parties of the results accomplished. For a smaller organization with manual procedures, this reporting is often accomplished through the use of multicopy receiving reports covering each incoming shipment and referencing the applicable purchase order. Copies are routed to the accounts payable department, where they are used as a basis of determining proper payments to vendors, with the purchasing department to set the stage for any negotiation of claims against vendors, and the traffic department responsible for reviewing the billings from carriers and for processing related claims. From a control standpoint, it is critical that all of these records are accurate and are promptly transmitted to the parties who will make use of them.

Many organizations today have automated receiving systems where open purchase order data is available to the receiving department on an on-line basis. Receiving calls up this data on the system and inputs or matches incoming data to that recorded on the purchase order. They may input other data—such as quantities or the date and time of receipt—if different from the computer system clock time. Organizations sometimes penalize vendors for late receipts or pay only on the basis of the agreed receipt date for any early deliveries. In any event, data from the receiving system provides input to other automated systems, such as accounts payable or inventory.

Figure 24.7 is a flowchart describing the receiving process in a typical organization. In order to develop this understanding in the organization being audited, internal audit should prepare a similar flowchart describing receiving department processes and the disposition of goods after receipt.

(v) Administrative Aspects of Receiving. The receiving department has two important but somewhat different missions. One is the prompt and accurate preparation and transmittal of information to interested parties to establish accountabilities and support financial actions. The other is the orderly handling and control of the actual materials received. The latter is especially difficult because it involves both a wide range of physical characteristics of individual items received and the pressures of fluctuating volumes, which are sometimes beyond day-to-day capacities. The two dimensions are closely interrelated in that problems that develop in the case of the second dimension can undermine the capabilities to care efficiently for the first requirement. The necessity of proper standards of orderliness and control in a physical sense in turn introduces an interest and concern in two underlying causal factors. One is the adequacy of the facilities provided for the receiving activity, including the amount of space provided, the extent to which unauthorized access to it can be prevented, and the adequacy of unloading docks and the various types of auxiliary equipment. The second factor is that of people. There should be a sufficient number of adequately trained receiving personnel, proper supervision, and a high standard of overall management direction.

The causal factors and their administrative dimensions are especially important because of their relationship to the minimization of fraud and dishonesty. In the event of collusion with purchasing or other parties, defects in receiving procedures can open up the possibilities for fraudulent payments to vendors and carriers. These defects can be in the basic design of procedures or in the laxity with which otherwise properly designed procedures are applied. Similarly, a breakdown in the orderly physical handling and control of materials can result in the fraudulent diversion of various types of materials. In the latter case, while there may be security controls to prevent materials from getting out of the facility, employees may still divert goods to improper production facilities. For example, an employee who has damaged goods in the course of the production process may seek to divert additional undamaged items to the production facility to reduce scrap counts and improve performance. This is another reason for effective receiving operations controls.

Purchasing personnel may not feel as if they are playing that important a role in total organization activities. Management needs to emphasize to them their important link in the chain of overall production processes.

Proper administrative controls over receiving present a particular dilemma for smaller organizations. While a larger manufacturing or distribution organization with ongoing receiving activity can justify a formal receiving function, some smaller organizations just do not have the volume of receipts to justify a separate function with one or more dedicated personnel. However, there should be some formal mechanism to properly acknowledge the receipt of goods, to match them to purchase orders, to verify condition and counts, and to secure them until moved to their final destination. The smaller organization should take care to designate some person or function, even on a part-time basis, to

Figure 24.7 Receiving Process Example Flowchart

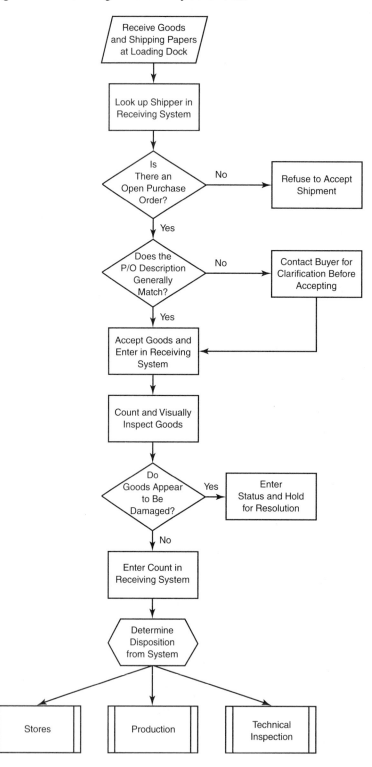

handle this receiving process. Otherwise, goods may be lost or otherwise improperly received.

Internal auditors sometimes have difficulty in making appropriate recommendations to improve the effectiveness of the receiving activity. Internal audit may want to concentrate on objectives that are the most meaningful, such as improving the level of operational efficiency, often expressed in terms of potential savings in expense and budgeted manpower costs. This approach may lead to the need for vendor agreements to properly inspect, ship, and label goods to minimize detailed package counts and inspections. Goods received would then be moved to their intended production destinations as promptly as possible to minimize costs. Because of the fairly routine nature of receiving operations, there are fewer opportunities for more innovative operational variations than is the case with other organization activities.

(b) RECEIVING FUNCTION INTERNAL CONTROL CONSIDERATIONS

The major internal control objective over the receiving function is that goods or services received should agree with the terms of the original purchase order and should be inspected, correctly counted, and properly recorded. Files or systems should be in place so that the receiving function can easily match receipts to purchase order records. As part of that match to the original purchase orders, the receiving function should compare the description of the goods on the purchase order with the goods actually received. This comparison may be relatively easy to perform for large, one-of-a-kind goods. More complex goods may require a review by a separate quality-inspection function.

Receipts should be acknowledged on some form of receiving report, copies of which go with the goods, to purchasing for control, and to accounting for payment. In addition, the receiving function also needs to prepare reports indicating the condition in which the goods were received with an emphasis on any shortages or damages. This will allow claims to be filed against the shipper or vendor.

A basis of a receiving function is that the group should perform independent counts of the goods received to ensure the accuracy of these counts. For high-value, low-volume goods, an organization may even want to assign the counting responsibility to someone in the receiving department with no advance knowledge of the expected counts. However, this type of control is difficult to impose since many vendors ship their goods with a packing slip indicating the quantities.

The classic "open the box and count the items shipped" receiving department approach is changing. Vendors may agree to ship the items and quantities ordered in boxes labeled with bar codes. The receiving department may have little more to do than look for obvious package damage, match the incoming order to the purchase order, use an optical scanner to read the labels that indicate the contents of the various packages, and then move the goods to their destination. However, some provision should be in place to open these boxes and count them on a periodic test basis.

The inspection function, which may be part of receiving or of quality control, is the final area of receiving department internal control concerns. Inspection should be an independent function that tests critical incoming goods for compliance with established component standards. The inspection function should operate independently of regular production operations. They should have appropriate standards upon which to base their tests and should keep accurate records documenting the testing activities.

(c) RECEIVING FUNCTION INTERNAL AUDIT ACTIVITIES

For many organizations, receiving is not a large enough area to justify a separate operational or financial audit of just that function. Rather, internal audit will often encounter receiving activities when reviewing the overall purchasing cycle. This section, however, focuses on potential audit activities solely over the receiving function. These can become an element of an overall purchasing cycle audit.

In some instances, the auditor's risk analysis may justify a separate review of the receiving function. More likely, management may request that internal audit review receiving as a special audit. This may be because the production function is complaining that incoming goods are improperly inspected or not arriving according to purchase order quantities, that security controls in the receiving area appear to be lax, or because of other reasons. The following sections discuss potential activities for reviews of receiving department financial controls, operational audit considerations, and related computer audit activities.

(i) Receiving Function Financial Audit Considerations. The typical receiving function exercises little direct financial control over overall organization activities. The function completes some type of receiving report that becomes the basis for payment, as well as for any claims against vendors or shippers. However, the typical receiving function does not have financial responsibility for the payment of those vendor shipments or for the resolution of any claims. If they did, internal audit might raise questions about the possibility of a separation-of-duties control weakness.

The receiving department has financial responsibilities for its own operations, including salaries and other expenses. However, these are fairly minor in terms of the overall organization and typically present only a low audit risk. One area where receiving does exercise important financial controls, however, is in the proper recording of received goods within their time periods. This is very important at both the accounting period month-end as well as at year-end. In order to improve operating results, management may request that goods received near the accounting period–end not be recorded as received until the beginning of the next period. This way, it is not necessary to add those goods to inventory balances and to increase accounts payable balances. External auditors are particularly concerned about this timing problem, but it should also be considered by internal audit when reviewing receiving function activities.

Internal audit will also encounter these same problems in the shipping department at accounting period cutoff time. Just as some members of management want to keep inventories down by not recording the receipts at period-end, goods not quite ready for shipment can be improperly recorded as sales. This will reduce inventories, increase sales, and increase accounts receivable at period-end. Internal audit should be aware of these cutoff concerns, which are particularly important when taking inventories. Figure 24.8 outlines both receiving and shipping audit cutoff procedures. Although this chapter includes only the receiving function, shipping will be discussed in Chapter 25.

(ii) Receiving Function Operational Audit Procedures. The previous paragraphs discussing receiving department functions point to many areas internal audit should consider when performing an operational review of the receiving function, whether as part of an overall review of the purchasing cycle or as a separate review, often at management's request. Figure 24.9 outlines the specific audit procedures for a review of the

Figure 24.8 Receiving and Shipping Audit Cutoff Procedures

Obj. 24.08.01   The cutoff date for the accounting and inventory close should be well publicized in operations areas, with special procedures published to document
cutoff rules.

  Proc. 24.08.01.01   Obtain a complete set of inventory instructions, noting established
date for the inventory and employee instructions for segregation of
paperwork. Comment on any problems.

  Proc. 24.08.01.02   Determine that appropriate arrangements have been made for goods
received or shipped on consignment or to other remote facilities.

Obj. 24.08.02   All ''before'' and ''after'' inventory shipping and receiving documents should
be labeled or otherwise identified to aid in establishing clean cutoffs.

  Proc. 24.08.02.01   Review procedures in place to label documents ''Before'' and ''After''
inventory to establish cutoff.

  Proc. 24.08.02.02   Physically review receiving and shipping areas to determine that areas
are clearly marked to promote a proper segregation for inventory.

  Proc. 24.08.02.03   Observe security arrangements surrounding segregated areas to ensure
that goods are not transferred from one area to another.

Obj. 24.08.03   All goods received on or before the inventory day should be recorded in
inventory.

  Proc. 24.08.03.01   Determine that all goods received prior to the cutoff date are processed
through receiving and otherwise included in inventory.

  Proc. 24.08.03.02   Observe the loading dock area and other spaces to determine that
goods are not received prior to inventory but held back from inventory
recording.

  Proc. 24.08.03.03   Review a sample of purchasing department records to determine
whether a significant amount of owned goods have been shipped FOB
but have not been received at the facility.

Obj. 24.08.04   Any goods awaiting inspection or returns to vendors should be included in
inventory unless other arrangements have been made.

  Proc. 24.08.04.01   Determine that all goods held in inspection or other similar areas have
been included with inventory.

  Proc. 24.08.04.02   Review items scheduled for return or otherwise disputed and assess
whether they should be included in inventory. For example, items
rejected during inspection but that have not received shipper credit
notices should be included, if material.

Obj. 24.08.05   Shipments must be valid sales and must take place on or before the inventory
date.

  Proc. 24.08.05.01   Determine that all goods shipped on or after the inventory cutoff are
included in inventory and not recorded as sales.

  Proc. 24.08.05.02   Observe shipping docks and other facility areas to determine that goods
are not improperly moved to warehouses or other areas but are recorded
as sales.

  Proc. 24.08.05.03   Review a sample of transactions subsequent to the inventory date to
determine that goods shipped as sales are not returned for credit or
some special arrangement.

Figure 24.9   Receiving Function Audit Procedures

24.9.01	Understand and document structure of the receiving organization, including its relationship with purchasing, inventory control, and factory scheduling.
24.9.02	Document automated receiving system, including significant controls and interfaces with other supporting systems.
24.9.03	Determine that all received goods must be supported by an authorized purchase order. Observe procedures for matching shipping documents with purchase order records and note any exceptions.
24.9.04	Observe normal receiving function operations, including the flow of goods into the receiving area and to their destinations. Assess safeguarding procedures over goods in this area.
24.9.05	Observe receiving function procedures for counting incoming goods and assess the adequacy of controls.
24.9.06	Understand organization policy for partial shipments, overshipments, and undershipments as well as for early shipments. If incorrect quantities are accepted, survey recent shipment exception history and assess financial implications.
24.9.07	Determine that the receiving function exercises an appropriate degree of inspection over received goods before acceptance.
24.9.08	Understand procedures for routing received goods to stores, production, or other areas as appropriate. Select a sample of one day's receipts and assess timeliness and controls over their movement to proper locations.
24.9.09	If there is a separate inspection department, review controls between these two functions for the prompt transfer and safeguarding of merchandise.
24.9.10	If the receiving department is responsible for third-party or consignment goods that may be returned, assess the adequacy of controls.

receiving function. These procedures are based on a receiving function with limited automation, and internal audit may have to modify them somewhat when reviewing a larger or highly automated function.

Any review of a receiving function requires that internal audit spend time within the operations area, testing and observing transactions. Any appraisal of receiving services should include an evaluation of the timeliness of processing goods and the reliability of quality and quantity checks. If audit sampling is used in these checks, internal audit should review the appropriateness of the sampling plan.

(iii) Receiving Function Computer Audit Procedures.   Organizations usually do not have freestanding "receiving systems" that internal audit would select for review. Typically, receiving department automation is part of the overall purchasing system, as described in Figure 24.5. Internal audit would usually not plan a separate review of the receiving subsystem but would evaluate receiving controls as part of the purchasing system controls.

The receiving subsystem is an area where computer-assisted audit procedures can be used to test system interfaces between receiving records and connecting systems such as accounts payable or inventory. Figure 24.10 illustrates the type of computer-assisted procedure to match receiving records to purchase order history and inventory data. If this

Figure 24.10 Receiving Function CAAT Example

ExampleCo Internal Audit
Receiving/Purchase Order/Inventory Exceptions

Month of
03/01

Date	Part #	Receiving #	P/O #	Inventory Quantity	Audit Possible Exception
03/02/01	2354-12	R2450		12	Received—No P/O on file.
03/02/01	5687-02	R2455	TY9923	5621	On-hand inventory sufficient?
03/05/01	2351-02	R2312	JJ5219	12	Receiving—P/O differences.
03/05/01	8752-00	R2319	HK8901	2	Receiving—P/O differences.
03/08/01	9682-21	R2462	JJ6923	19	Part marked obsolete.
03/09/01	4569-30	R2468	DR2354	65	Receiving—P/O differences.
03/09/01	8832-00	R2474	HK5621	1621	On-hand inventory sufficient?
03/10/01	5617-03	R2481	JJ7201	23	Receiving—P/O differences.
03/12/01	2354-03	R2492	AN0321	0	Receiving—P/O differences.

balancing was not taking place as a systems function, the purpose of this report would be to check if the receiving function is potentially recording counts to reflect purchase order quantities rather than the actual quantities as recorded in inventory. Numerous other computer-assisted procedures could be developed to test receiving department functions and activities.

(iv) Sample Receiving Audit Report Findings and Recommendations

A: Receiving department security procedures are weak.   After goods are unloaded at receiving docks, they are stored in a holding area for inspections, counts, and comparisons with open purchase orders. We found that most goods remain in this holding area for about 24 hours prior to routing to work-in-process or stores areas. However, items with count or purchase order identification problems may remain in this holding area for an extended time period. We observed that the receiving holding area does not have locked doors and that other employees frequently use this area as a short-cut to the rear employee entrance. There is a risk that goods in this holding area can be stolen or otherwise damaged.

Recommendation.   The receiving area should be physically secured through locked doors during off hours. Only authorized persons should be allowed in the receiving holding area during normal operating hours.

B: Test count deficiencies for scanned goods.   The organization has agreements with key vendors who agree to ship packages with bar-coded labels identifying their contents and quantities. These same vendors have agreed to a penalty assessment if they ship incorrectly labeled items or quantities. The receiving department usually just electronically scans these labels before forwarding them to branch distribution warehouses. However, per established procedures, they are supposed to selectively test-count these incoming packages. During our visits to the receiving area we did not observe any test-counting activities. We could also find no records of past test-counts nor of vendor-specific count plans.

Recommendation.   The receiving department should institute a program of test-counting a select group of scan-labeled packages. Systems should be installed to record these test counts and to record any penalty data to the accounts payable department.

24-4 ELECTRONIC DATA INTERCHANGE (EDI)

Electronic data interchange is the computer-to-computer electronic exchange of business or technical documents between independent organizations based on agreed-upon standards. These electronic documents are similar to such traditional documents as purchase orders, invoices, and shipping advices, once sent in a paper format. In order to use EDI, an organization must connect its computer system to the system of another, usually called a trading partner. This trading partner connection often takes place through an electronic communications network called a value-added network (VAN) or through the Internet.

Many organizations today use EDI to improve their operating efficiencies and their competitive posture, and to reduce clerical costs. The declining costs of computing and telecommunications as well as improved hardware and software capabilities have made EDI an attractive option for many organizations, both large and small. However, EDI is not that new a concept. Some larger organizations have been using EDI types of systems for years for communicating data on high-cost or short-shelf-life products. Examples would be airlines and hospital supply companies. Those pioneers each developed their own standards, while today's organizations can more easily communicate through a common set of standards governing the exchange of data.

Electronic data interchange has become a new tool for an increasingly large number of organizations today, beyond the banks or larger companies that had previously used it. Declining costs of enabling technology have allowed many additional organizations to join EDI networks in recent years. At a minimum, a personal computer equipped with a modem, along with common software for both sides of the transaction, may be all that is essentially needed. In addition, established standards and the growth of EDI VANs has made this technology easy to use and convenient. Perhaps the most important reason for this movement to EDI is the increasing need for organizations to be competitive. When a company's largest customer informs it that, in the future, all business must be transacted through EDI, the company will convert to EDI.

This section discusses EDI, including some of its potential legal, audit, and control issues. The modern internal auditor needs to have an understanding of this new and rapidly growing technology.

(a) EDI ACTIVITIES CYCLE

As a starting point to understanding how EDI works, internal audit should consider the transactions necessary between a buyer and seller—called *trading partners*—in order to complete a typical sales transaction. Figure 24.11 shows these transaction steps. After preliminary sales decisions through discussions with salespersons or advertising literature, the purchasing department of the buyer sends a formal purchase order to the order-processing department of the seller. Depending upon the nature of the product and business, the seller may acknowledge this order by sending a copy of the purchase order back to the buyer. The order is then booked for fulfillment.

Figure 24.11   EDI Activities Cycle Transaction Steps

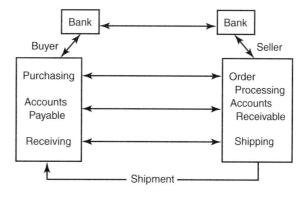

Once the order is ready, the seller's shipping department will notify the buyer that the order is ready to be shipped. Once the goods have been received per the terms of the order, the buyer's receiving department acknowledges receipt of the order. Again, this was discussed earlier in this chapter. Depending on the terms of the sale, the seller will send an invoice to the buyer, whose accounts payable department gets ready to mail a check. In addition, the check covering payment draws funds from the buyer's bank account and adds them to the seller's account. This can be a fairly complex, paper-intensive and time-consuming process.

Electronic data interchange simplifies this sales transaction process. Transactions are exchanged electronically between the buyer's and seller's systems to eliminate the amount of paper-processing required. Ideally, rather than mailing a purchase order, under EDI a transaction is extracted from the buyer's purchasing system for transmission to the seller's order-entry system. However, this process is not quite that easy. In the case of many existing systems, neither automated purchasing systems nor automated order-entry systems have been typically built to send and receive automated transactions. In addition, each may use different file format standards and representations for various data elements. For example, one may use units of measure of ``EA'' to designate the units of the commodity it is shipping while the other side may think of that same commodity in terms of its weight, ``LBS.'' The two parties, or trading partners, will follow a common set of EDI standards that contain a common language and format for automated communication, usually accomplished through the use of translator software installed at both trading partners to bring the transactions into the common format.

The remaining component necessary for this type of automated transaction is for both parties to use common-format communications software to send and receive these order transactions. This arrangement is described in Figure 24.12. Early EDI-based systems were based on specific arrangements between individual trading partners. Two closely allied organizations might decide to communicate through EDI and would agree on transaction formats and data standards. Similarly, a larger organization might inform all of its

Figure 24.12   Trading Partner EDI Transaction Arrangements

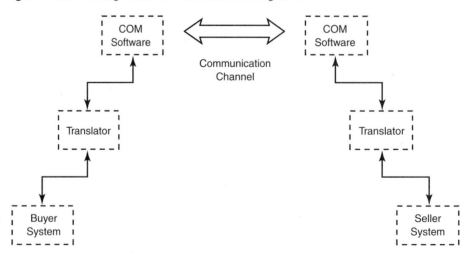

customers of the format to use for EDI communications. This was sometimes a rather coercive, "if you want to do business with us" type of standard.

Standards for EDI transactions and communications were initially established by individual industry groups. For example, the retail food industry in the United States had strong needs to communicate through EDI, and food industry standards were established. However, these common standards still did not eliminate data-communications problems. While larger organizations often run 24-hour-a-day computer and communication systems, many smaller organizations do not. Because the volume of transactions between many customers is neither constant nor large, there is little need for trading partners to stay connected over extended periods of time. To attempt such, costs would be prohibitive. The value-added network (VAN), mentioned earlier, solved this.

An EDI VAN is an electronic version of the old-fashioned small town post office system. Every resident in this small town would have his or her own post box. Incoming mail from outside sources or town residents would be placed in the recipient's mailbox; the recipient would then come to the post office to retrieve his or her mail and deliver other messages to be mailed. When someone new moved into town, a post office box would be established for them.

EDI trading partners today typically use a VAN for their communications. One side of the transaction is needed only to send transactions to the EDI mailboxes of the various trading partners. The latter can access their mailboxes from time to time to receive their messages. This expanded EDI trading arrangement using a VAN is illustrated in Figure 24.13.

As mentioned, EDI transaction standards were initially established by separate industry groups. An example is the automotive industry in the United States, which established the Automotive Industry Automation Group (AIAG), an industry-funded committee that developed a wide range of automation and information exchange standards covering such

Figure 24.13 EDI Trading Partners Using a VAN

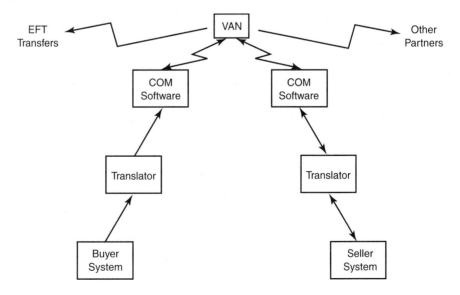

matters as the format of EDI transactions, standards codes, and the format of shipping labels. The use of these standards was mandatory for industry members and others involved in the automotive industry business. Similar standards were established by other industry groups with common needs, enabling them to communicate with one another. However, these standards still were within individual industry bounds. For example, an automobile manufacturer might not be able to communicate through EDI with a supplier primarily in the aerospace industry.

Industry groups have subsequently worked together and established common, cross-industry standards. In the United States, standards have been established by the Accredited Standards Committee (ASC) under the auspices of the American National Standards Institute (ANSI). Through negotiation with industry groups and committee efforts, ASC has established a set of standard formats for EDI transactions. These go under the name ANSI X.12 (called "X dot twelve") and define the standard transaction format for many business activities where EDI can be used. The transactions follow standard formats identified by three-digit item codes. Examples of these transaction types used for the purchase cycle described above are:

840   Request for Quotation (RFQ)
843   Response to RFQ
850   Purchase Order
855   Purchase Order Acknowledgment
856   Shipping Notice / Manifest
861   Receiving Advice
810   Invoice
820   Payment/Remittance Advice

The above is only a limited sample of what has become a large number of specialized transactions covering such matters as financial information reporting, material product safety data, and freight invoices. Any organization following these many ANSI X.12 standard transactions would use them. The standard dates back to 1986, but some organizations have taken a long time to convert their systems to the standard EDI format. And some may still use their own format. The idea of the X.12 standards is that when a seller received an 850 transaction in its EDI VAN mailbox, it would know that this represented a purchase order and would further know how to extract information from that record. The interested reader can find more information about these EDI standard transaction formats from the person responsible for EDI coordination in the auditor's organization and from national standard-setting bodies. As the use of EDI increases, the number of these X.12 transaction sets is increasing. Specialized industries have defined unique information requirements for their own special systems.

In addition to standardized formats, EDI transactions also have other identifying records. Just as letters are sent through the mail enclosed in addressed envelopes, EDI transactions are surrounded by several levels of standard format header and trailer transactions to identify the sender and the addressee. These again follow the standard format and consist of header and trailer records for each transaction type, for each functional group, and to govern the communications interchange and to transport the communication. Figure 24.14 shows these transaction communication layers of headers and trailers. Using the post office analogy, one can think of these as envelopes that are placed in larger mailbags

Figure 24.14   EDI Transaction Communication Layers

Transmitting Multiple Electronic Transaction Sets

In practice, several electronic transaction sets (e.g., invoices) may be sent together. In order to separate these documents, each is preceded by a transaction set header (code ST*) and followed by a transaction set trailer (code SE*).

Two invoices would appear as:

ST* (Header)

—Segments of Invoice—

SE* (Trailer)

ST* (Header)

—Segments of Invoice—

SE* (Trailer)

Combining different types of documents also provides for sending more than one type of transaction in the same package. In this instance, each group of the same type is placed between separators (Functional Group Header and Trailer) to differentiate the type (e.g., invoices from purchase orders).

Several groups to a single recipient may be enclosed between an Interchange Control Header and Trailer.

A complete package then would be represented by:

ICS* Interchange Header

GS* Functional Group Header

ST* Transaction Set Header

—Segments As Required—

SE* Transaction Set Trailer

—Other Transaction Sets—

GE* Functional Group Trailer

—Other Functional Groups—

ICE* Interchange Trailer

The following schematic illustrates a typical format for electronically transmitting a series of diverse business documents.

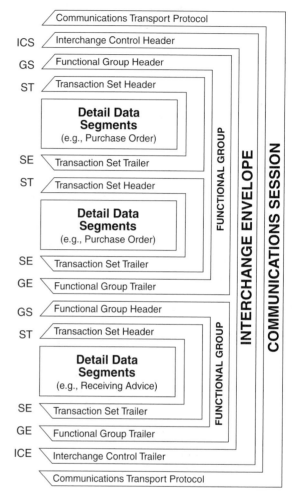

SOURCE: American National Standards Institute, ANSI No. X.12.
Used with permission.

full of letters of one purpose. These bags may be placed in separate trucks depending upon their final destination.

   When an organization moves to EDI, appropriate contractual agreements must be executed between the organization and its various EDI trading partners. The problem here is that business transactions have historically been based on paper documents with authorizing signatures. For example, a correctly signed purchase order, as discussed previously, causes the initiating organization to enter into a contractual relationship with the receiving group. If the organization issuing the purchase order later repudiated its terms and refused to pay, the holder of that signed purchase order could bring suit to recover damages. The signed purchase order would be a principle support to that suit.

With EDI, organizations exchange their transactions electronically with no paper trail and no formal authorizing signatures. This works fine as long as all parties agree to operate under these new rules of business. To avoid any future misunderstandings, organizations doing business through EDI should have all of their trading partners sign agreements to abide by the somewhat new and different rules of EDI. Trading partner agreements are essential elements of EDI control procedures and are discussed in more detail later in this chapter.

EDI is changing the manner in which many organizations are building their information systems and organizing their businesses. Although originally used primarily as a means to more rapidly send orders and to pay bills, creative organizations are using EDI for other applications where rapid responses are essential. For example, some organizations are using EDI techniques to solicit competitive bids from vendors. A request for quotation along with detailed specifications may be transmitted to a series of potential vendors through EDI distribution lists. Bids are similarly submitted through the medium of EDI, and after some negotiation, the final EDI purchase order is released.

The U.S. retailer, Wal Mart, is an example of how EDI can change the manner in which an organization handles its overall business processes and systems. Traditionally, Wal Mart's remote retail stores would contact their central office with sales data and inventory levels. Personnel in that central office would then place orders with vendors, accept shipments from those vendors, distribute the goods to stores, and make settlements with the vendors. Using EDI, the local retail unit transmits sales data back to the central office but communicates inventory levels and needs directly to vendors. The vendor ships the goods and sends EDI transactions to the central office advising them of their activities. In effect, the vendor is updating central unit files through EDI transactions. The central unit initiates EDI/EFT transactions to pay the bills. This is a very simplified description of what can be a complex set of transactions. However, it illustrates the new complexities that auditors will frequently encounter through the use of EDI.

(b) EDI INTERNAL CONTROL CONSIDERATIONS

The use of EDI introduces a whole series of new control issues to the organization. Much less reliance is placed on paper documents and much more on computer systems and electronic communications. Even though processes will still work in the same general manner, both management and auditors must rethink their control procedures when EDI is used for these processes.

The use of EDI techniques in various systems may allow an organization to gain a competitive advantage over similar organizations through improved information systems and reduced costs. However, these EDI-based systems must be built with adequate controls. An analogy can be made to the early days of computer systems. Some organizations resisted automating key processes in the 1960s and 1970s while others moved aggressively into automation. Some of those who had established significant automated systems also suffered massive internal control failures. This was not because the then ''new technology'' information systems were at fault but because these systems were built with inadequate controls. The same may be true for EDI-based systems and procedures.

Although EDI may cause some changes in many types of controls procedures and other areas, the most significant deal with the impact of the new forms of evidential matter due to paperless EDI transactions, the impact of EDI on computer systems application controls, and the impact on computer and communication systems general controls. These are discussed in the sections following.

(i) New Forms of EDI-Based Evidential Matter. The most important control aspect of an EDI-based communications message is its function as a legally binding contract. Under common law, a contract must be ''signed, sealed, and delivered'' in order to meet the requirements of a contract between parties, an agreement consisting of an offer and an acceptance. That agreement has traditionally been evidenced by a signature on a document although other forms such as Telex or FAX messages are accepted in many areas. The EDI message now becomes that contractual document. Organizations face no problems here unless there are disputes over these normal business transactions. However, because some level of disputes will be inevitable, care must be taken to make the sequence of EDI transactions serve as a legally binding contract.

A key control to building valid electronic contracts is to make sure that transactions are in proper sequence, creating a contract offer and acceptance. For example, an organization may receive a purchase order EDI transaction. Before shipping the goods ordered, it is a good idea to respond with a purchase order acknowledgment EDI transaction. This says that the organization has accepted the offer and entered into a contract to ship the goods at the proposed terms. While an organization might feel that the acknowledgment transaction is redundant, it is important as it establishes the formal contract. Both parties involved in an EDI transaction should give careful consideration to the contractual concepts of offer and acceptance when constructing their EDI processing procedures.

The previous section discussed the importance of EDI trading partner agreements. This may be an agreement between two trading partners, and to a lesser extent, between the EDI user and the VAN. The contract covers such matters as the communications protocols and standards to be used as well as the responsibility for errors. Two important elements that should also be included in every EDI trading partner agreement are:

- *Definition of ''Signed'' Documents.* The Uniform Commercial Code (UCC) in the United States requires that contracts over $500 must be executed in writing. The trading partner agreement should specify that both parties agree that certain EDI transactions constitute a signed agreement.

- *Trade Terms and Conditions.* Paper-based forms such as purchase orders usually have detailed terms and conditions outlined in fine print on the back of the documents. Since these cannot be included as part of EDI transactions, they should be defined in the trading partner agreement.

Partners trading together through EDI often rely on interchange agreements that apply to all; what are known as ''club rules.'' These binding agreements cover such matters as interchange standards, message acknowledgments, storage-of-data agreements, and prohibitions against revealing trade secrets. In a complex EDI environment, there may be a need for multiple levels of these agreements.

Procedures must also be in place to maintain records of EDI transactions. Just as organizations give proper attention to retaining copies of their paper-based documents such as purchase orders and backups of computerized records, an appropriate level of detail must be maintained for the transactions transmitted or received through EDI.

(ii) EDI Impact on Computer Application Controls.
In many respects, application controls that should be in place for an EDI application are no different from the application controls discussed in Chapter 17. However, an application used for EDI must properly translate data from established databases into standard EDI formats. This involves both what is called the mapping of data and the translation into a proper EDI format. Because these transactions are going directly to outside sources and because both parties have relied on them through their trading partner agreements, controls over these transactions are critical.

Few older applications today are designed to directly produce EDI transactions. Rather, they were developed to produce paper-based outputs, with EDI a more recent addition. Applications require what is called a mapping program, which converts internal organization data representations into standard EDI formats. This mapping process goes beyond just reformatting and involves interpreting internal data into a language that is compatible with X.12 transaction format. Gradually, as organizations move to a more total EDI environment, this mapping may not be necessary because the application will operate directly using EDI formats. However, translation software will probably still be required for the limited amount of exception-level paper-based reporting and for the different international standards that will continue to exist.

More attention should be devoted to EDI application input and output controls than is usually found in conventional applications today. Controls should be in place to ensure that all transactions are recorded in a timely manner, properly valued, correctly classified, and authorized. Internal audit can assist in evaluating these controls.

(iii) EDI Impact on Computer System General Controls.
Chapter 16 discussed computer systems controls, including such areas as backup procedures and physical access to the data center. These same control concerns do not really change once an organization begins to implement substantial EDI-based systems. Network transmission error detection controls are particularly important and should be in place over the general communications software to prevent or detect unauthorized modifications, incorrect transmissions, and unauthorized disclosures of data. These things are usually built into the VAN's systems and covered by the trading partner agreements as part of the added value gained from the use of an EDI VAN. Network control objectives and procedures that internal audit can evaluate are discussed below.

Because of the large amount of outgoing and incoming telecommunications traffic, the computer system with heavy EDI activity will need strong logical security controls over its files and programs to minimize the risk that an outside perpetrator could access computer files through an incoming line otherwise devoted to EDI traffic.

Backup and recovery procedures are particularly important in a data-processing environment with extensive EDI operations. Various EDI system files may be the only source of documentary evidence in the event of disputes with an outside organization that has received EDI transmissions. Those EDI system files should be properly backed up, with copies stored in off-site locations.

All of these EDI-related internal control comments point to one key change as a result of EDI systems: The traditional paper trail usually supporting many transactions is greatly reduced or eliminated. Organizations must build control procedures around the automated systems used for EDI rather than around traditional paper-based forms that were the basis of older automated systems. Internal auditors can assist management in evaluating these controls, but they also must have a good understanding of these EDI differences.

(c) EDI INTERNAL AUDIT ACTIVITIES

Internal audit most frequently will encounter EDI-based applications in the general area of purchasing or distribution systems. A discussion of EDI control and audit considerations has been included in this chapter for that reason. However, the same EDI control considerations apply whether EDI is used for purchasing, for soliciting competitive procurement bids, for exchanging engineering specifications, or for any other reason. Whenever significant systems using EDI technologies are included in the scope of an internal auditor's review, the control procedures discussed in the following paragraphs will generally apply.

A key concern for internal audit is to decide when the EDI-related systems included in the scope of the review are significant. Even if an organization uses more traditional systems and procedures in many areas, it still may make some use of EDI. For example, an organization using traditional automated and paper-based systems for many functions may order its office supplies through an EDI system using a local microcomputer. It uses EDI here because the office supply vendor offered favorable terms for ordering through EDI and also gave them the software. Should internal audit be concerned about the control risks associated with this use of EDI technology? Probably not, unless office supplies represents a significant portion of the organization's business.

Internal audit should always be aware of the control implications of areas where EDI is used for significant systems. The following sections outline some audit procedures for reviews of EDI applications, for reviews of the overall management of the EDI process, and for developing EDI-based, computer-assisted procedures. These can be incorporated into a purchasing-related review or any other where the use of EDI changes significant control procedures.

(i) EDI Financial Application Audit Procedures.
Audit steps for an EDI application are discussed in the following sections on EDI systems operational and computer audit procedures. However, the use of EDI applications in purchasing and other areas raises some basic control issues that, in many instances, should have been in place with conventional systems. A review of EDI controls may present a good opportunity to review overall procedural and accountability controls.

Organizations with paper-based systems should have in place controls defining who has the responsibility to request and approve purchase orders, to authorize any changes to purchase orders, and to authorize payment based upon proper receipt. Traditionally, auditors have selected a sample of purchase order copies, for example, and tested whether the signatures on those documents are on the buyer authorization lists. With EDI, internal audit will no longer find these signatures on paper documents but must determine that proper controls have been established over the ''electronic signatures'' used to initiate EDI transactions. That is, only authorized persons should have access to various EDI-related systems to authorize transactions. In addition, systems should be built with adequate transaction logs so that audit trails exist for all EDI-initiated transactions. These audit trails should be reviewed.

Chapter 19 discussed computer systems logical security controls. These types of controls are particularly significant for EDI systems and should be in place to prevent or detect unauthorized changes to programs and data because:

- An unauthorized person could improperly access an EDI system and modify records to have a shipment or payment sent to a personal address.
- Unless passwords are structured by ranges of monetary approval limits or commodity types, unauthorized persons could use the system to initiate transactions outside of their approval limits.
- A disgruntled employee could sign onto the system impersonating another for unauthorized activities.

The above risks focus on outgoing EDI transactions, but may also represent concerns over incoming transactions controls. Controls should be in place to ensure that all incoming transactions are from authorized trading partners and within established limits. All transactions should be logged with controls to ensure that these transaction sets appear to be both complete and reasonable. If trading partners are accessing other files, such as product specification file, for the purpose of completing their EDI transaction cycles, this activity should be logged. Appropriate controls should be in place to draw attention to any potentially improper activity.

Internal audit should gain an understanding of the overall flow of transactions through the system using EDI. Attention should be given to where transactions are logged and these areas screened for proper controls. The internal auditor should understand transactions between conventional production system databases and EDI communications software. With that process in mind, internal audit can develop an understanding of the significant control points in an application where EDI is used. A workpaper-type flowchart is an effective tool to describe the control points in a purchasing system that uses a combination of EDI and paper-based outputs.

Once internal audit has developed an understanding of the EDI-related application controls, the next step is to perform appropriate tests to evaluate these controls. Some of these may be computer-assisted procedures, as discussed in the sections following. Others, however, are general application review controls, as were discussed in Chapter 17. Figure 24.15 lists control review procedures of an application with significant EDI components. This should be used with appropriate application-review procedures (discussed previously in this chapter for purchasing applications and in other chapters for other EDI application types).

(ii) EDI Systems Operational Audit Procedures.   An organization will realize few benefits from the technology if it treats EDI only as some sort of exception situation, with ''business as usual'' for all other transactions. In order to successfully implement EDI, the organization must establish various operational procedures to promote and control the use of the technology. For example, internal audit should ascertain that trading partner agreements exist for all parties and that these contracts ensure that the organization's interests are protected. This can be part of an overall review of EDI operations or a part of a specific review of an EDI application.

An organization can be involved with EDI on two levels. It can respond to EDI trading partner requests from major customers or suppliers or it can develop its own EDI programs and systems. The former represents a reactive response to a limited number of

Figure 24.15 Audit Procedures for EDI Applications (Partial or Limited List)

Obj. 24.15.01 The EDI-related application should have the same general control procedures in place as should be found for any business application.

Proc. 24.15.01.01 Review for application controls, including such areas as internal balancing mechanisms, error-reporting mechanisms, and clear audit trails.

Proc. 24.15.01.02 Consider the impact of the EDI-related functions on other application controls.

Obj. 24.15.02 All EDI transactions should be properly recorded and valued by the application.

Proc. 24.15.02.01 Determine that the application uses appropriate transaction controls to only allow authorized transactions.

Proc. 24.15.02.02 Review application and VAN procedures to provide acknowledgment transactions. Develop test transactions to survey process.

Proc. 24.15.02.03 Review the adequacy of audit trail procedures, including VAN audit trail files.

Proc. 24.15.02.04 Assess adequacy of procedures in place to match transactions before transmitting; for example, P/O terms should be matched to invoice terms.

Obj. 24.15.03 All EDI transactions should be properly authorized.

Proc. 24.15.03.01 Determine there are properly controlled passwords for EDI transactions and that the passwords are stored in an encrypted manner.

Proc. 24.15.03.02 For inbound EDI, determine that appropriate screening controls exist over customer transactions, including the checking of customer-defined passwords.

Proc. 24.15.03.03 Determine that access and authority levels for all transactions are correctly defined and that all EDI system activity is logged.

Proc. 24.15.03.04 Determine that reports are delivered to appropriate persons for error-correction and -reconciliation purposes.

Proc. 24.15.03.05 Assess procedures to determine that all inbound and outbound transactions are verified against trading partner records and that errors are rejected.

Obj. 24.15.04 The application should correctly post EDI transactions in a timely manner.

Proc. 24.15.04.01 Determine there is an automated check of control totals generated by EDI function to final file output.

Proc. 24.15.04.02 Assess procedures for logging and time-stamping all inbound transactions; review a sample to test currency.

Proc. 24.15.04.03 Review the contingency plan in place for EDI application and determine whether it has been tested and provides adequate facilities for recovery.

Obj. 24.15.05. All EDI transactions should be properly supported by trading partner agreements.

Proc. 24.15.05.01 Review procedures for setting up EDI customers, including requirements for trading partner agreements.

Proc. 24.15.05.02 Select a test group of EDI customers to determine that trading partner agreements are current and complete.

Obj. 24.15.06 Application security for an EDI application should be at least as good if not better than normal application security procedures.

trading partners where many controls will be dictated by those major partners. Even data communication controls in this setting will be simplified if the organization may be directly connected rather than operating through a VAN.

An organization usually develops its own EDI program for communication with vendors or suppliers. Even if reluctant, suppliers can be forced to do business via EDI if they want to continue the business relationship. This is not the case with customers, however, who usually have other sources of supply. An organization can, nevertheless, convince both suppliers and customers to use EDI techniques if doing so results in better service and cost savings. The EDI trading arrangement described in Figure 24.13 could have been initiated by either the central organization or the supplier.

Internal audit should look for some form of central council or authority that is responsible for establishing EDI ground rules, for communicating with trading partners, for working with legal counsel to develop trading partner agreements, and for negotiating the signing of these agreements among all trading partners. This group would also be responsible for establishing technical EDI-related communication links with trading partners.

(iii) EDI Systems Computer Audit Procedures.   Before reviewing EDI application controls, internal audit should determine that general overall controls are adequate in the computer center or client-server environment where the EDI applications will be processed. Internal audit should determine that this review gave adequate attention to controls over logical security and telecommunications network security. Chapters 16 and 19 should provide some general audit guidance here.

The typical organization runs its EDI transactions through a VAN or the Internet. Either acts as a common clearing house for the EDI transactions from various trading partners. Internal audit can think of a VAN as a data-processing service bureau that provides services to multiple outside customers. Internal audit typically would not be able to visit that VAN to review its computer systems and network controls because the VAN would have just too many outside customers and could not tolerate teams of internal auditors from various customers visiting the VAN to review data-processing general controls. However, that VAN organization has an obligation to provide its customers with some assurance that its controls are adequate. This is particularly important for an EDI VAN where an organization may have significant transactions covering pricing or other matters in storage in an electronic mailbox.

In the United States, a VAN may use a service auditors report, prepared by an independent outside auditor, to provide assurance that its data-processing controls are adequate. The standards covering these reports are outlined in the AICPA's Statement on Auditing Standards No. 70.[1] Internal audit should request such a SAS No. 70 report and carefully review its contents. It may reveal control vulnerabilities at the VAN that internal audit should pass on to local management. For example, the report might reveal that the VAN does not have an adequate disaster-recovery plan, and that the organization's EDI transactions processing through that VAN might be lost in the event of an unexpected contingency situation. These concerns should be passed on to management. Either organization management or internal audit should closely question VAN management about the steps they plan to take in correcting any such weaknesses.

---

[1] SAS No. 70, Reports on the Processing of Transactions by Service Organizations, AICPA, April 1992.

There are two types of SAS No. 70 reports. What is called a *type-two report* discusses specific test procedures performed while the other, a *type-one report,* only provides general descriptions of control procedures. If the organization has a major customer relationship with the VAN, a type-two report outlining specific control tests of transactions should be requested if available. Type-one reports are often thick documents that provide only very general descriptions of VAN control procedures.

Service auditor reports covering VAN operations in the United States are not that common and not all VANs may have contracted with an outside auditor to prepare one. When the VAN has not arranged for an independent auditor's SAS No. 70 report covering VAN controls, internal audit should make contact with the VAN's internal auditors to determine their level of review activities and to request any available assurances regarding VAN controls. Figure 24.16 contains EDI VAN control objectives that should guide internal audit in either reviewing the SAS No. 70 report covering that VAN or in discussing controls with the VAN internal auditors.

Internal audit may want to test the correctness and completeness of EDI transactions sent to or received from trading partners on a periodic basis. This is particularly true if

Figure 24.16   EDI VAN Control Objectives

24.16.01	A third-party, service auditor review should have been performed to review VAN controls. Inquire as to the nature of the review, whether it was a SAS No. 70 type-one or type-two review, and the date of that review. Request a copy of the review.
24.16.02	Based on the independent auditor's report covering VAN operations, discuss any concerns raised with management. If there was no service auditor report prepared, or if the report was only a very general type-one report, consider the following control objectives starting with 16.03.
24.16.03	The VAN should maintain adequate backup for all customer EDI files.
24.16.04	A contingency plan should be in place to recover programs, data libraries, and key files in the event of an unexpected interruption in data-processing services.
24.16.05	VAN users should be aware of the contingency plan procedures and the steps necessary to maintain processing procedures.
24.16.06	VAN mailbox procedures should screen electronic mailboxes on a periodic basis to identify potential problems and to resolve them with VAN subscribers.
24.16.07	Errors and rejected items should be logged in a queue file with appropriate advice returned to senders.
24.16.08	VAN processing should have an error-recovery mechanism that includes formal identification and correction procedures.
24.16.09	Customer-defined passwords should be checked on all inbound transactions and should be encrypted if requested by the VAN customer.
24.16.10	The VAN should have appropriate controls to protect password files, including the use of encryption procedures on password validation files.
24.16.11	There should be an approrpiate segregation of duties defined through the VAN application user profiles.
24.16.12	All EDI systems activity should be logged, with log files retained for appropriate lengths of time to help resolve any problems.
24.16.13	There should be an appropriate level of segregation of duties between the VAN information security function and other VAN operations.

financial statement balances are impacted by these transactions at some point in time. Although various advanced techniques—such as the use of electronic signatures—can be used, the most effective audit procedure is the electronic confirmation of balances with trading partners through the sharing of data files.

Internal audit would contact Company X and request an extract of its EDI transactions to the organization for a test period of time. These transaction extracts should be requested from their EDI translator system files to keep them in a common EDI transaction format. Internal audit could then develop a CAAT to match these two files and to identify any differences.

An internal auditor may initially encounter some resistance in requesting a confirmation test of EDI transactions, since it is currently not a common procedure. Over time, of course, this may become as common as the independent confirmation letters now used by external auditors.

Internal audit may also encounter obstacles such as that the trading partner does not keep backup copies of translator extract files. This will change over time as EDI technology matures. Similarly, internal audit will be developing even more sophisticated EDI CAAT procedures in the future.

(iv) Sample EDI Audit Report Findings and Recommendations

A: EDI Trading Partner Agreements Not on File.   We reviewed the status of signed trading partner agreements with a sample of vendor trading partners using EDI. We found that trading partner agreements have not been executed with a significant number of these trading partners. Although requests to complete these agreements had been circulated, we also found no dedicated effort to follow up with the vendors and complete the agreements. The lack of executed trading partner agreements may expose the organization to disputes if there are ever questions about document ''signature'' or responsibility for network transaction errors.

Recommendation.   Efforts should be made to complete all EDI trading partner agreements. The EDI coordinator and a representative of the legal department should work with trading partners to resolve any questions. A deadline should be established for the completion of these agreements. Trading arrangements should be discontinued where appropriate.

B: EDI System Logical Security Controls Inadequate.   We reviewed the data-processing logical security controls over access to the purchasing system. We found that all buyers, although given individual passwords, had been placed in one logical security group and that they all had access to the same purchase order preparation standards. Although the purchasing department rules prohibit it, the system's logical security controls would not prevent a buyer from initiating a very large purchase order that is usually the responsibility of department management. Because these purchase orders would be produced as EDI transactions without the customary paper trail, they might not be detected on a timely basis.

Recommendation.   The EDI Council should work with both application management and information systems to review the logical security group's organization structures and to establish a better set of controls to divide users into access groups according to their job authorities and responsibilities.

24-5 FUTURE DIRECTIONS FOR THE PURCHASING CYCLE

The purchasing cycle is a major internal control cycle for most organizations and should receive significant internal auditor attention. With an increased use of EDI, internal audit can expect significant changes in this control cycle over time. The effective internal auditor should monitor these changes in both the auditor's organization and throughout the industry, and make certain that appropriate controls are always in place.

CHAPTER 25

Distribution and Transportation

25-1 INTRODUCTION: LOGISTICS PROCESSES

Distribution and transportation, sometimes called logistics, are often viewed as out of the "mainstream" of organization operations and not included in internal audit programs. This is in part because while distribution and transportation may represent a major cost to the organization, the individual costs are often relatively small and buried in other costs, such as production. In addition, transportation has historically been highly regulated, with the government setting rates and other rules. As a result, even when distribution and transportation costs are very large—such as for a bulk shipper of an agricultural commodity—internal auditors have performed only minimal internal audit procedures.

Distribution and transportation are areas that are often good candidates for operational reviews. However, since they are often embedded with other functions, they can be ignored in an internal auditor's risk analysis and planning process. All too often these processes are thought of only in terms of the many small transactions required to make individual shipments, and the total aggregate costs, controls, and potential efficiencies are ignored. Distribution and transportation are areas where minor process improvements can result in major cost savings. Once a heavily regulated field where organizations were subject to the whims of regulatory agencies or the then postal service monopoly, technology is rapidly changing this whole area, and the internal audit's service to management mission can be of strong value here.

This chapter considers operational, information systems, and financial audit procedures for distribution and shipping, which often involve separate processes and management procedures. Quite simply, distribution is the process of selecting the best route, the *distribution channel,* to deliver an organization's product or service to the ultimate customer. Transportation involves the way that a product moves along its selected route. Selecting optimal methods for distribution and transportation often involves different persons, who are concerned with strategy and logistics.

Because a formal shipping or transportation organizational unit is often not required for the movement of products within the organization, this transportation is often a more production-related operation. Since many strategic alternatives are available, such as the use of bar code labeling to track the goods, this function is also classified as distribution. Internal audit should understand the controls surrounding both alternative distribution and shipping methods as well as the overall transportation process. This chapter will provide an introduction to this specialized and not very often audited field.

25-2 DISTRIBUTION PROCESS

Goods or products often move through a traditional pattern, such as from the manufacturer to a distributor and then to a retailer or the ultimate customer. This distribution process is continually changing, however, with new techniques and shipping vehicles. An example here is the way microcomputer software is distributed. Software manufacturers first sold their products directly to consumers, through specialized computer software stores, and then, as computers became more popular, they began selling through general merchandising stores or mail order catalogs. Distribution requirements changed for these selling modes. When it sold through the mail to individual customers, the software developer incurred shipping charges for numerous small packages. When it began selling to more major merchandisers, distribution involved fewer shipments, though they were larger and sent to a limited number of customers.

Today, distribution channels continue to change for that same software manufacturer. The products now are often downloaded directly from the Internet to the customer's computer over public telephone lines and a modem. Documentation and everything else is provided on-line through a totally different distribution channel for the same type of product.

Distribution is primarily concerned with the alternative strategies for moving these goods, whether it be within the plant facility or to customers. This may involve such options as whether to use dealers or company-owned distributors, or to drop ship directly to customers. As with any strategic process, internal control reviews of the distribution function present a challenge. Rather than just looking for compliance with established procedures, internal audit should look for a measure of overall strategic vision. Although subjective in nature, this is an area where an internal auditor can provide thoughtful observations and recommendations.

(a) PROCEDURES

Distribution was once a fairly simple process in which an organization would promote its goods and services through a catalog or network of sales personnel and then ship them to customers. Each shipment was an individual sale initiated by the customer, based on need. With ever-increasing automation and close producer and customer partnerships, this whole concept of distribution is changing in many different dimensions. There is no longer one "best" way to distribute a product or service, and the auditor should understand the particular procedures used to distribute them for the unit being audited.

In our discussion, we first introduce some different types of distribution channels, then follow up with a discussion of what is frequently called distribution *logistics:* the process of distributing the product to the customer as efficiently as possible. A section follows on international trade and distribution. Although our world is growing ever smaller due to technology and good transportation links, the variety of currencies, national laws, and cultural differences make international trade a greater challenge.

This discussion on distribution procedures is closely tied to Chapter 23, on manufacturing production planning, and Chapter 24, on purchases, receipts, and electronic data interchange (EDI). While EDI is important for purchasing and paying for goods, it is equally important for shipping. Internal audit should reference the discussion on EDI concepts and control procedures in Chapter 24. Similarly, that same chapter briefly discusses warehousing concepts for the receipt for goods and supplies. Many of these same principles apply to the warehouses necessary for shipping finished goods.

(i) Finding the Appropriate Distribution Channels.   While the concept of transportation (discussed later in this chapter) often involves moving goods at the lowest rates in the most efficient manner, distribution is more of an overall business strategy than just a cost-minimization process. Sometimes, customers will be willing to pay more for goods or absorb greater transportation costs if they can perceive a greater value in the process. The growth of letter air freight is a good example here. Postal service mail was known to be slow or unreliable. Special courier services were an alternative but were very expensive. The air parcel services changed all of this. They offered guaranteed overnight delivery at a rate that was higher than regular postage but far less than special private couriers. Although it is not the lowest-cost distribution alternative, many found this channel to be more attractive than slower postal alternatives. This new method became almost dominant until the fax became more common. A company distributing small consumer goods from a mail-order catalog may come to the same conclusion today and ship goods via overnight air freight to boost its competitive advantage.

Selecting the best distribution channel requires a combination of understanding consumer's needs, the alternatives available, and the competitive advantages that might result from the selection of one method over another. The organization personnel who will make the selection decisions may be a combination of transportation specialists, marketing personnel, and senior management looking to gain an extra advantage in a competitive atmosphere. They are often called logistics specialists. In understanding this process, the effective internal auditor should realize that there is no one ''best'' distribution channel for any product or service. While there can be many variations in the overall distribution process, some of the more common types include:

- *Direct Sales to End Users.* The organization sells directly to the ultimate customer, either using a sales and marketing organization of in-house employees or through advertising the product and then accepting orders.

- *Direct Sales to Distributors or Dealers.* The distributor or dealer purchases the goods at an often substantial discount and provides support for the goods or service. Selling arrangements are established through contracts between the distributors and the producing organization. However, distributors are largely responsible for the terms with their dealers.

- *Indirect Sales through Agents or Brokers.* An agent is largely independent, with a contractual arrangement to represent the product or service but with little central authority or guidance. This arrangement is common for foreign sales when a company is not large enough to have its own sales network.

- *Sales through Remarketers.* The organization sells its products to an agent or merchant who will pack or mark the product according to its own specifications. While the remarketer assumes all risks, the prime supplier may be at risk if the remarketer incorrectly markets or does not support the product.

- *Piggyback Marketing.* Here, the manufacturer or service firm contracts with another company to market a product in conjunction with that company's other products. Selling and promotional expenses to the contracting organization will be minimal. This arrangement will work if the products are complementary and appeal to the same customers.

- *Pyramid Marketing.* Rather than just selling to one distributor who may sell to a limited number of dealers, any customer can become a dealer by also selling to

Figure 25.1 Pyramid Marketing

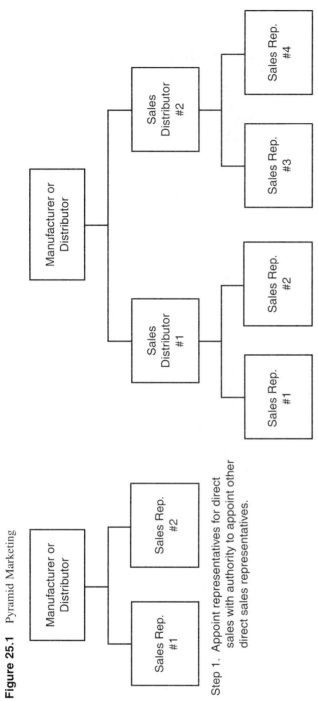

Step 1. Appoint representatives for direct sales with authority to appoint other direct sales representatives.

Step 2. Representatives appoint additional sales reps.

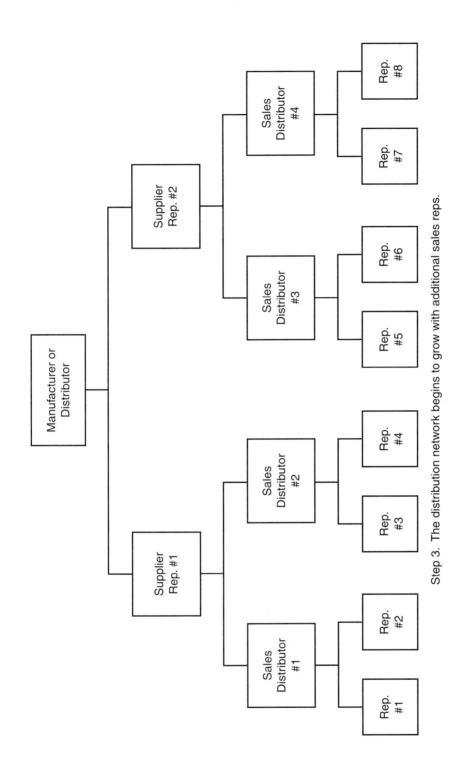

Step 3. The distribution network begins to grow with additional sales reps.

others, or can become a distributor if those customers choose to become dealers themselves. Figure 25.1 is an illustration of a pyramid marketing arrangement. This can be quite successful for consumer household products such as soaps or cosmetics. However, when abused it can become a "chain letter" type of approach where hundreds could be involved as distributors, sub-distributors, and sub-sub-distributors.

While there can be many variations, distribution patterns break down to either direct or indirect selling arrangements. While each has its unique advantages, an organization will almost always have more control over a direct selling arrangement. Direct arrangements often cost more because employees are needed to handle the sales process.

Whatever the approach used, it will become the organization's distribution channel, the road map that takes the product or service from its producer to the final or end customer. However, an organization is not restricted to one distribution channel but may use alternate methods depending upon customer desires or market factors.

Understanding those channels will help the auditor define some of the potential control strengths and weaknesses that may be found in the distribution process. The actual selection of the distribution channel will often depend on decisions by sales and marketing (as will be discussed in Chapter 28), senior management decisions, and the whole issue of how to distribute the product logistically and effectively from its source to the customer.

(ii) Distribution Logistics. Logistics refers here to the process of moving the product through the production facility, warehousing it if necessary, and then delivering to the end customer. The term or concept of logistics originated with the military, who are often faced with the logistical challenge of delivering manpower and material to various battle or defensive sites within critical time limits to meet enemy thrusts. While the process of shipping goods to a customer is not nearly so complex as a military battle plan, the effective implementation of warehousing and distribution procedures can be critical.

While sometimes the selection of the most appropriate logistical arrangements requires the use of complex mathematical modeling, many instances require just good common sense, along with an understanding of the demands of customers and suppliers. Figure 25.2 includes some of the questions that an internal auditor might ask to better understand this process. This questioning can be quite simple when an organization produces its product at one plant, then ships the product from a plant-based warehouse to a limited set of customers. Logistics can become quite complex, however, if the organization buys its goods from a worldwide network of suppliers, adds some additional value to the products, and then ships them to a large network of company-owned outlets.

After considering the responses to the questions in Figure 25.2, an internal auditor should next describe the logistical arrangements used through the workpaper documentation. The flowchart example in Figure 25.3 may point to control weaknesses or areas in which internal audit may want to emphasize audit testing. In a different example, a review may identify the fact that goods are moving to one warehouse for almost immediate "cross dock" shipments to the company's distribution stores. While there may be some good reasons for this arrangement, it might be more efficient to ship goods directly to the organization's store outlets. While this information can only be determined through detailed audit testing, in this stage internal auditors can use this type of analysis to better focus their test objectives.

Figure 25.2 Logistical Arrangements Auditor Interview Questions

1. Whom does the organization view as its customer—the end consumer, distributors, or other agents?
2. How many shipping points are needed to get the product to the customer—a network of retail stores, one central distribution point, or some other arrangements?
3. Are multiple distribution channels used? If so, what are the most significant?
4. Are there any unusual factors—such as hazardous materials, danger of spoilage, or difficulty in shipping—that would place constraints on the logistical arrangements?
5. Is the cost of insurance a factor in sorting or shipping the products?
6. Do shipping and transportation represent a significant portion of the total product or service cost?
7. Do customers pay for shipping as part of their product cost?
8. How many versions or variations of the product(s) are stocked?
9. How many warehouses or shipping points are currently in use?
10. How many stockkeeping units (SKUs) are maintained at these warehouses?
11. Do the warehouses all contain the same distribution of SKUs or are they different?
12. How many employees are involved in the distribution/logistics process?
13. Can the organization purchase the product from its suppliers and then ship it directly to customers, or is some value added? What is the nature of that added value?
14. If goods just go to a distribution center, such as a retail organization with a chain of stores, can the products be shipped directly from suppliers to stores?
15. How great has been the theft of goods from warehouses while shipping to the warehouses or distribution points?
16. Is there any risk of "piracy" or diversion of the product during shipping?
17. Are automated techniques such as EDI used in the distribution process?
18. Are bar-coded labeling techniques used?
19. Are organization-owned carriers (such as private trucks) used for distribution, or are common carriers used?
20. Is the distribution network only within national boundaries, or is it international in its scope?

(iii) International Trade Distribution Concepts.   Despite all the talk that we live in a small world and despite a growing number of free trade arrangements between countries, trade across international borders creates distribution complexities, most of which fall into one of the following areas:

- *Different Laws and Customs.* Customs and business practices are based on culture, religion, local laws, and conditions. Although the exporting country will anticipate major economic differences, management and auditors often miss minor but subtle differences in countries that otherwise seem very similar. The U.S. company exporting to Australia, for example, might encounter only some small cultural differences.

  While the western democracies practice under fairly well understood "rules of law," the rules governing dictatorships or less free governments are subject to rapid change and may appear arbitrary. In addition, laws at home can cause problems. In the United States, the Foreign Corrupt Practices Act prohibits the paying of bribes to foreign officials. In other countries, those same bribes are very much accepted and sometimes almost required as part of the cost of doing business.

Figure 25.3 Logistical Configuration Workpaper Description

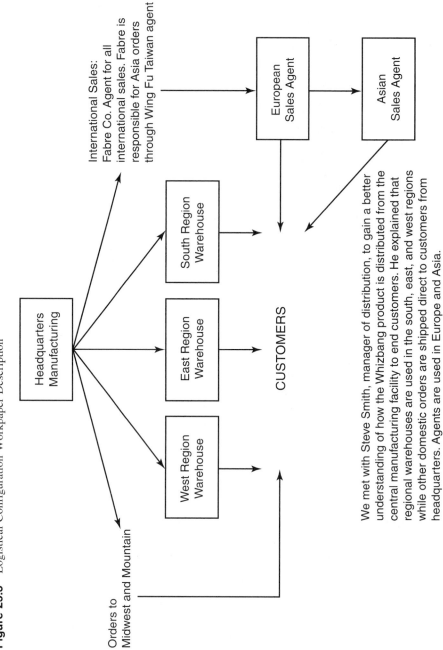

International Sales:
Fabre Co. Agent for all international sales. Fabre is responsible for Asia orders through Wing Fu Taiwan agent

Headquarters Manufacturing

West Region Warehouse

East Region Warehouse

South Region Warehouse

European Sales Agent

Asian Sales Agent

CUSTOMERS

Orders to Midwest and Mountain

We met with Steve Smith, manager of distribution, to gain a better understanding of how the Whizbang product is distributed from the central manufacturing facility to end customers. He explained that regional warehouses are used in the south, east, and west regions while other domestic orders are shipped direct to customers from headquarters. Agents are used in Europe and Asia.

Figure 25.4 Foreign Representative Selection Factor

◆ Current status and history of foreign representative company
  • What are the backgrounds of the principal officers?
  • Are its bank and trade references adequate?
  • How many field sales or distribution personnel does the representative have?
  • In what other countries does the representative operate?
  • What has been its sales volume growth for the past five years? What is the growth per employee?
  • What are the short- and long-range growth and expansion plans?
◆ Product and customer mix
  • What is the typical customer profile? Are competing companies represented?
  • Are the other product lines compatible? Would there be any conflict of interest?
  • Are there any minimum sales volumes needed to continue representation?
  • What types of customers are currently contacted by the representative?
  • Who are the key accounts, and what percentage of gross receipts do they represent?
◆ Facilities and equipment
  • Are there adequate warehouse facilities?
  • What is its method of stock control?
  • Does it use computers, and are they compatible with ours?
  • What types of communications facilities (fax, Internet, telephone) does it have?
  • Can the representative handle product repairs and spare parts?

• *Problems with Foreign Representatives.* When an organization in one country establishes distribution operations in another, it will almost always seek the help of foreign representatives to handle sales and local distribution. Distances and cultural differences encourage this practice but can be a challenge for an organization to select appropriate persons to represent it in the foreign country. An organization should perform a fairly thorough background check before appointing a foreign representative. Figure 25.4 contains some factors to consider. This type of list should be tailored by each exporting organization to its own needs, and internal auditors should determine if these types of background investigations have been performed.

• *Currency Translation Accounting Issues.* In many instances, sales revenues and distribution costs will be in a foreign currency, which can go up or down in value in relation to the company's home-country currency. These changes in exchange rates can fluctuate quickly due to such external events as a war in a nearby country or the failure of a major business in the country. Strong accounting rules for recording and handling foreign currency gains and losses can cause problems to the organization distributing to foreign countries. An extensive discussion of these issues is beyond the scope of this book.

• *Shipping and Transportation Problems.* Shipping internationally raises problems both in terms of distances and in terms of the associated costs, custom duties, and import/export controls. An organization should be aware of the special considerations needed and contract with specialized agents to handle specific local customs and laws.

Special sales and distribution organizations may handle a company's export operations, or, because of tax and other laws, an organization may establish its own freestanding, captive corporation. Such legal entities may represent little more than "the lower left-hand drawer on the controller's desk" or otherwise consist of a small group of specialists, and any captive export companies should be included in the risk-assessment model.

In other situations, an organization may use an outside export marketing company (EMC) or trading company to handle sales and distribution. An EMC acts as the export department for multiple producers of goods or services, transacts business in their behalf, and acts as the foreign representative. The EMC may specialize either by product or foreign market or both and often has its own network of foreign representatives to handle all foreign distribution sales and activities.

A major disadvantage in using an EMC is that an organization can easily lose control over its foreign distribution and sales activities. There should be a formal contractual arrangement with the company, regular status reports back to the organization, and a right to audit EMC operations for the contracting company. Because the EMC is an outside entity often representing many other companies, close communication with any EMC is essential.

An organization that distributes and sells internationally may become closely involved with its own government's foreign trade operation. In the United States, for example, it may use the services of the Export Import Bank to provide financing or credit guarantees. Such agencies often have a primary objective of promoting foreign trade but also may enforce national export laws by restricting trade licenses or controlling the granting of trade credits.

(iv) Partnerships and Changing Distribution Patterns.   The successful and aggressive company implements new technological concepts in such a manner that it increases company growth and resultant profits. The former American Hospital Supply and its implementation EDI sales terminals at customer sites (discussed in Chapter 24) and, similarly, the U.S. retailer Wal-Mart, are examples. Wal-Mart revolutionized the whole customer distribution process in 1986 with its Quick Response system.

Wal-Mart is a large retailer with a large chain of general merchandise stores scattered throughout the United States. The traditional method for replenishing goods to these stores was for the store to track sales activity through cash register receipts and to transmit that activity back to a distribution center, where sales were matched against inventory. Once this was a manual process that involved stockkeeping and inventory counts at the local store, but by the mid-1980s many chain-type retailers had automated these processes with the sales activity transmitted back from point of sale (POS) terminals to central warehouses. The warehouses would then match the reported sales against their model inventory for each store, and when inventory dropped below some recommended level, would pull the inventory from the warehouse and ship it to the stores during a regular delivery cycle.

The warehouse would review inventory records and place orders with suppliers when quantities appeared to be running low. Orders were placed through traditional purchase orders, discussed in Chapter 24. The suppliers would ship to the distribution center upon receipt of the order and the merchandise would remain at the distribution center until more demands came in from the remote stores. This "supplier to warehouse to network of stores" distribution process has been widely used over time. Its many control and paperwork-processing steps increased costs as well as processing time.

Wal-Mart entered into partnership arrangements with key suppliers, instituting a procedure whereby sales data from their stores was transmitted directly to the supplier. This data once was considered confidential information, but Wal-Mart decided to share individual sales of given products per register with the supplier, as well as inventory levels and replenishment rules for each store. Sales data was transmitted at the end of the day to all of the partnership suppliers, who matched this data against the agreed-upon stocking levels. When stocks appeared to drop, the partnership supplier shipped the goods to the branch stores without any form of specific authorization or purchase order and simply informed central operations of the shipments through an EDI transaction after the fact. When the goods were shipped, the partnership supplier updated its inventory level records for that store and then initiated a request for payment from Wal-Mart headquarters. The process eliminated many stockkeeping and ordering steps. The trust and responsibility for prompt and accurate shipment was given to Wal-Mart's key partnership suppliers.

Figure 25.5 shows the concepts behind the Wal-Mart Quick Response system. These types of partnership arrangements cause significant changes in many distribution patterns. Traditional paperwork-based control procedures are being replaced with more trust-based systems in many organizations today.

The auditor should be aware of newer distribution partnership arrangements, many of which are implemented using EDI (as discussed in Chapter 24). These approaches can produce significant savings to an organization, but can result in significant control problems if not managed and monitored correctly. In many cases, these approaches were first initiated by some systems designer going over the normal boundary and trying to do something unique. They often require a radical rethinking of traditional systems controls, but only work if there is some level of ongoing management review. As we move into the twenty-first century, internal auditors can expect to see more such distribution partnering arrangements, through telecommunications and information systems technology.

(b) INTERNAL CONTROL CONSIDERATIONS

The overall distribution process can be nearly as risky as the handling of cash because for many organizations their end products are almost as valuable as hard cash. An electronics manufacturer who builds some type of component that is subject to theft can subsequently see the stolen goods, sold over the "gray market," reappear as a component in a customer's product line. A food distributor without good distribution controls faces the risk of the foodstuffs not arriving at customers in a prompt manner, causing the distributor losses through spoilage.

As with other operational auditing areas, any discussion of distribution-related internal controls reflects back to the Treadway Commissions Committee of Sponsoring Organizations (COSO) model of internal control, initially introduced in Chapter 2. That model looked at controls for accurate and fair financial reporting, controls for compliance with laws and regulations, and controls to promote the effectiveness and efficiency of operations. Distribution internal audit procedures are separated into financial, operational, and information systems–related controls, which we consider here in terms of the three COSO elements.

(i) Distribution Process Financial Reporting Controls. Distribution costs are usually not an element of an organization's financial statements. Rather, they are operational costs included with overall transportation costs. As a result, excessive costs or poor control may not receive the same attention from senior management as do more direct

Figure 25.5 Wal-Mart Type Quick Response Distribution System

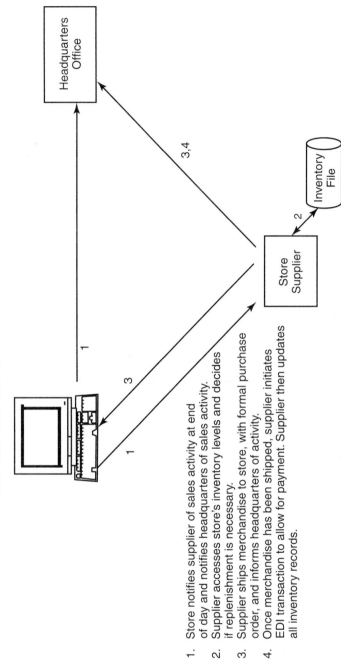

Point of Sale Terminal at Store

Headquarters Office

Store Supplier

Inventory File

1. Store notifies supplier of sales activity at end of day and notifies headquarters of sales activity.
2. Supplier accesses store's inventory levels and decides if replenishment is necessary.
3. Supplier ships merchandise to store, with formal purchase order, and informs headquarters of activity.
4. Once merchandise has been shipped, supplier initiates EDI transaction to allow for payment. Supplier then updates all inventory records.

costs and may sometimes be treated as little more than a ''cost of doing business,'' with little attempt at close analysis.

Adequate internal controls will allow an organization to recognize these costs and often to develop some improvements or cost savings. Distribution-related internal controls can be further broken down into two more detailed elements. First, controls must be in place to track and report the actual distribution costs of the product or service. Second, the organization's internal reporting system should be constructed so that management can easily see and measure the distribution costs.

Controls for accurately tracking and reporting distribution costs are very similar to those for manufacturing assembly costs, which are outlined in Chapter 23. There we talked about the importance of monitoring all shop floor assembly costs and other related costs. When a manufacturing organization does not accurately record the time required for small manufacturing steps, it will lose track of overall product costs and relative profits. Similar to the ''job ticket'' concepts outlined in Chapter 23 to record the time associated with small assembly steps, a method or procedure for tracking distribution costs should be developed. While it may not be necessary to record the time and labor required to move a single part from an assembly area to a manufacturing test area, for example, every part and all distribution steps that entail significant costs should be captured, recorded, and reported. Distribution costs are even more significant when the organization absorbs the shipping costs of sending the product to customers. Even if customers are charged for ''shipping and handling,'' actual costs should be monitored to determine if the shipping costs to customers represent their true costs.

The controls adopted depend on the distribution requirements used by the organization both for receiving goods and moving them to a production facility, and then shipping them to the ultimate consumer. The whole idea is to capture the appropriate costs and summarize and report them as appropriate. Figure 25.6 lists some representative manufacturing distribution cost internal controls for an organization involved in small assemblies and shipments. Similar but less extensive controls should be used for an organization involved only as a distributor, who warehouses and ships the product.

The second element of distribution internal controls involves the reporting system, which should be designed so that management can see and understand the relevant distribution costs. Again here, the controls and reporting procedures discussed in Chapter 23 are applicable. Capturing and reporting costs is often made easy through the use of bar coding. ''Swiping'' bar-coded labels as goods are received as well as preparing and then reading bar-coded labels for operations within the organization can allow easy monitoring of the movement of goods throughout the facility. The identification of the item transported, the costs of moving it, and its location at any time can be determined. Bar-coding techniques and their internal controls are discussed in the next section.

Procedures should be in place so that all goods involved in the distribution process can be easily tracked and their costs identified. In many instances, the distribution services to an organization can supply this information. Major shippers, such as DHL or Federal Express, have databases for their bar-coded shipping labels so that customers can call the company to locate a parcel. In addition, this provides data to produce billings to companies for these distribution services.

(ii) Effectiveness and Efficiency Internal Controls. As important as it is to move these goods as effectively and efficiently as possible, there should also be procedures for tracking the location of the goods at any time, assuring that the goods reach their intended

Figure 25.6   Representative Distribution Cost Internal Controls

25.06.01	Since time is money for a distribution process, the movement of goods both within a facility and staged for shipment should be date- and time-stamped for subsequent analysis.
25.06.02	The organization should have an understanding of its floor space allocations costs as well as all direct and indirect costs involved in the distribution of the products.
25.06.03	A numbering system should be in place, whether by part number, work-in-process assembly, or some other lot number, to identify both the type of item being distributed as well as the specific lot or grouping.
25.06.04	Whether through the use of bar-coding scanners or input to some other system, the movement of all lots of distribution products should be recorded as they pass through each logical area.
25.06.05	Standards should be in place for the various time intervals for products or lots to move through the distribution or production process. When items exceed standards by exceptional amounts, procedures should be in place to locate them, determine causes, and take corrective actions.
25.06.06	Controls should be in place to prevent the theft or improper use of lots involved in the distribution process.
25.06.07	If distribution requires transfer to outside contractors and when finished goods are shipped to end customers or distributors, controls should be in place to assess the efficiency of those moves.
25.06.08	Efforts should be employed to package all lots in the distribution process to minimize potential product damage and to minimize packaging waste.
25.06.09	Distribution system records should be reconciled with other related systems, such as receiving and inventory. Any differences should be reconciled and adjusted promptly.
25.06.10	If outside contractors or dealers are involved in the distribution process, the effectiveness and efficiency of those arrangements should be monitored on a regular basis.

destinations. "Improper locations" include those in which goods are misrouted, stolen by employees or transportation agents, or improperly used in operations. Improper use includes the allocation of a part to a different production process where there is a shortage, or the cannibalization of an assembly to support other shop floor needs.

An organization needs some type of monitoring mechanism to allow it to keep track of its goods. Aircraft have radar transponders to allow control towers to "see" and identify them, terrestrial vehicles use GPS satellite monitoring systems, and some industrial chemicals contain industrial "tags" to allow for their specific identification when subjected to detailed analysis. However, bar coding is often the most cost-effective way to monitor and track material distribution for almost any type of business enterprise.

Bar coding refers to horizontal bar labeling systems now found on many products. The code represents a product code or some similar identifying number that can be easily read by an electronic scanner. Most consumers encounter this technology during their visits to the grocery store. Products will contain small, bar-coded marks or labels. Passing the groceries through a scanner, a point of sale (POS) terminal captures the product price and prints out a detailed bill for the items purchased for the consumer. This same technology can be used for essentially any good as long as it is possible to attach a bar-coded label. Thus, in addition to individual parts, with their own bar-coded labels, entire sealed trucks often have a bar-coded tag to identify the truck's total contents. Even skiers on a mountain slope increasingly wear lift tickets with bar codes to tell lift operators the skier has a valid ticket for that day.

For a manufacturing (or some similar) organization, setting up a bar-coding system is relatively easy. Often, purchased parts and supplies come with the vendor's bar code label for the vendor's distribution controls. Since this coding is standardized, an organization needs only to secure a file of product numbers and their descriptions from the vendors. These can then be input to distribution system files. When the goods move across the shop floor or elsewhere, a scanner will pick up the bar-coded number, match that number to the description on the file, update the distribution logistics information in the controlling system, and report the results as appropriate. If an organization is building new products, it is quite easy to create bar-coded labels for them. Many automated systems are available, and the labels can even be printed on a small personal computer printer.

The Universal Product Code (UPC) makes bar codes unique, across product lines and across industries. Thus, someone cannot pass a can of tuna fish past a scanner with the objective of passing it off as a video monitor. All the codes are different, and the scanner will give a beep or even stop when it finds an error. This scanned data is passed to on-line systems where the location of the material can be tracked and its status monitored.

Table 25.1 shows some of the primary functional areas in a distribution area controlled by bar coding. Some of these functions were discussed in Chapters 23, on manufacturing resource planning, and 24, on purchasing and receiving. The internal control benefits from the use of bar coding are wide, but the most major reasons for installing the technology are increased inventory accuracy, improved space utilization in the warehouse facility,

Table 25.1 Functional Distribution Areas Controlled by Bar Codes

Functional Area	Bar-Coding Characteristics
Receiving	• Basic receiving routines, including processing for unplanned inboard orders • Advanced shipment notice and purchase order receiving
Storage/Put-Away	• Dedicated, random, or hybrid storage • System and operator location selection • Crossdocking • Put confirmation via radio terminals
Inventory Management	• Routing and exception-driven cycle counting • Rules-based stock rotation, including Last In First Out (LIFO) or First In First Out (FIFO)
Picking	• Release prioritization • Order, wave, and batch-picking • Pick confirmation via radio terminals
Shipping	• Order consolidation and staging • Trailer load sequence management • Shipping checklists • Manifests and bills of lading

and allowing for better order or manufacturing lot tracking. Current bar codes only represent single lines of descriptive numbers or digits, and industry is rapidly moving to something called two-dimensional bar codes. Here, lines of characters are stacked in a tight array so that some 2,500 characters of data can be packed into a 1 inch square symbol.

(iii) Compliance-Related Internal Controls.   The third internal control element is compliance with laws and regulations. There were once many distribution- and transportation-related legal requirements, when transportation and distribution were heavily regulated fields. With the ongoing deregulation of the transportation industry—at least in the United States—the number and extent of laws and regulations has declined, and compliance in this area is not as great of a concern.

However, one distribution area where compliance with laws and regulations is critical is the handling of environmentally hazardous materials, due to stringent environmental rules and an increased general concern about the potential dangers from various substances. Organizations are required by law to protect these types of materials when they're stored in warehouses, to maintain proper security of the hazardous materials when they're transported, and to provide reference library information on corrective actions that should be taken in the event of an employee's or customer's exposure to the hazardous material.

While most important for the distribution and warehousing process, compliance with hazardous material rules is also very important for many manufacturing processes, for research and engineering, and throughout the workplace. Although the subject of environmental controls as well as performing internal audits in these areas is beyond the scope of this book, some of these environmental audit concerns are discussed in Chapter 34, on the changing role of audit activities.

International shipping is another area in the distribution process where compliance with laws and regulations is critical. In addition to the need for controls to prevent the bribery of foreign government officials and compliance with such things as anti-boycott laws, provisions should be in place to ensure appropriate controls over foreign dealers and agents.

(c) INTERNAL AUDIT ACTIVITIES

Because the distribution process involves many small transactions, such as individual freight or mail shipments, or minor routing over a plant floor, senior management often loses sight of the significant savings possible through a minor adjustment in distribution processes. Too often this distribution process is summarized with the transportation controls discussed later in this chapter. Distribution audits of plant materials operations are somewhat different from reviews of the transportation function. A different type of shipping container, although incrementally more expensive, might yield overall savings to the organization through fewer products being damaged while in transit. Through the internal audit analyses, management can see such cost saving or improved profitability opportunities.

(i) Financial Audit Considerations.   Financial-related audits of distribution functions should focus on potential cost savings that can be realized by giving greater attention to the many small transactions associated with a typical distribution process. While some of these areas were discussed as part of Chapter 23, on manufacturing controls, others apply strictly to the distribution process. A major audit concern here is that management often neither has a good understanding of the true costs of distributing its products nor has the systems in place to capture those costs.

Internal audit should understand how distribution costs are collected and reported throughout the organization. An organization should have a process in place to track the movement of goods throughout their facility. This may range from a paper ''move ticket'' manual system to a modern bar code scanning system. However, the organization often will not use this distribution tracking system for any type of cost control, but only for logistical purposes.

If the distribution costs appear significant and if the control system can monitor the costs associated with product distribution at any point in time, internal audit should review those costs, which can then be matched to estimated actual costs to determine the system's accuracy. Even if the system does not track costs, internal audit should develop some estimates of the actual distribution costs. These can include the costs of staging the product before moving it from the receiving area and placing it in inventory, the costs of maintaining the product or materials in inventory, the in-transit costs of moving the product through various areas of production, and the costs of shipping the product to its final destination.

Audit sampling can determine the average costs associated with these distribution steps. Often, if the organization lacks good reporting tools, this type of cost-analysis review may highlight some areas requiring significant management attention. Figure 25.7 outlines some cost-review procedures, which point to areas where the auditor can assess the actual costs of distributing inventory and products. These procedures are based on the concept of understanding the cost structure and then estimating the true costs on a sample basis.

This type of review might recommend improved controls to measure the true costs of distribution. With improved reporting procedures, management can better understand their true distribution costs, and develop better or more efficient distribution procedures.

(ii) Operational Audit Procedures. An organization can realize some significant cost savings through the rapid and efficient movement of its products and materials, both within the company and to external customers. The cost savings come through the recognition of the old ''time is money'' proverb, as well as through the reduction of distribution errors resulting in both operating efficiencies and increased customer satisfaction.

Because the distribution process can be so broad and varied, it is difficult to suggest just one general operational audit program for the distribution function. An internal auditor should first break down the distribution process to its more detailed functions before identifying areas for a detailed operational audit program and approach. An organization that manufactures some product in its plants by purchasing piece parts and additional raw materials has a much different distribution problem than has a distributor of finished products. The latter is essentially a wholesaler, interested in moving the goods, which arrive in bulk quantities, from the shipping dock to a warehouse, where they will be picked, packed, and shipped to the ultimate customer. The manufacturer has a much more complex distribution problem in moving the goods through, perhaps testing any key components, performing necessary assembly, and moving them on to other remote warehouses or to the final customers.

The objectives of any distribution process or function should be to minimize the time required to move the goods (whether within a manufacturing facility or to others), to maintain control over that distribution process, to operate the distribution function in a cost-effective manner, and to increase overall satisfaction for the process. Because of this wide variety of areas for operational audits of the distribution process, this chapter contains no single set of audit procedures. Rather, Figure 25.8 lists some potential audit approaches and areas for review of the distribution process. Using the basic approach to operational auditing discussed in Chapter 21 as well as the earlier Chapters 7 and 8 discussions on evaluating risk and planning internal audit activities, internal audit can develop specific, distribution-related operational programs.

(iii) Computer Audit Procedures.   Because specialized automated systems may also control the distribution function, such as the generation of bar code tags for goods moved in-transit or the scanning and input of bar-coded records of incoming materials or products, many of the computer audit procedures discussed in Chapter 24 are applicable here. Internal auditors should understand the automated systems used to tag and track goods in-transit, which may require an understanding of the system used to develop and print bar code labels or any other distribution tickets. (See Chapter 17, Information Systems Application Controls.)

Internal audit may find opportunities here for using computer-assisted audit procedures (CAATs), discussed in Chapter 12. Received goods, for example, pass through a

Figure 25.7   Distribution Cost Review Procedures

25.06.01	Develop and document and audit understanding of the number of steps involved in the product distribution process. These might include receiving to inspection, inspection to the warehouse stock, stock to production location #1, etc.
25.07.02	Document the procedures used for measuring the costs of distributing the product both internally and to customers; are these procedures adequate?
25.07.03	Analyze the carrying costs incurred when storing and moving or shipping the product, both internally and to customers. If cost estimates have been prepared, assess their validity. If there is no costing system in place, develop estimates, including: • Floor space allocations and labor costs required for moving the product • Capital investment costs involved with storing and holding distribution materials • Other costs associated with the distribution process, such as bar code scanning systems
25.07.04	Determine the adequacy of the move ticket control system. Select a sample of items from production records and trace them to their actual locations, noting any exceptions. Similarly, select a sample of items in staging areas and in transit and trace them back to production control records.
25.07.05	Estimate the actual costs of distribution through a sample of materials in transit. Select a regular product and production line and estimate the actual costs of material distribution associated with the product. Assess the reasonableness of distribution costs based on published benchmarking statistics.
25.07.06	Observe any bottlenecks or delays in the distribution process. Make recommendations for improvements as appropriate.
25.07.07	Assess the adequacy of the management reporting system covering distribution costs. Determine that distribution costs are properly included with other costs of product production.
25.07.08	Review budgets and incurred costs for distribution, monitoring, and transportation. Comment on the adequacy of this process.

Figure 25.8 Distribution Process Operational Audit Opportunities

The following are potential areas where internal audit can develop operational audits of the distribution function. The internal auditor should refer to Chapter 21, on operational auditing, as well as to other chapters for help in developing specific audit programs.

A: Review of Distribution Paperwork Accuracy. To check the accuracy of the distribution move tickets and other paperwork controlling the shipment of materials, a sample should be selected from bar code scanning or other distribution system materials and compared to the actual material on the shop floor. Similarly, a sample of in-transit goods should be selected and traced back to control systems to assure accuracy of quantity and content.

B: Review of Warehouse Utilization. If the organization has multiple storage warehouses, particularly in remote locations or states, the total cost and efficiency of these storage units could be examined. Rather than multiple remote warehouses, could the organization realize efficiencies by shipping the product directly to the customer from the point of production? Based on the cost of maintaining the additional warehouses, could any be eliminated? If multiple storage locations are needed, are they in the most optimal locations based on customer demand, shipping factors, and other considerations?

C: Investigation into Advanced Distribution Approaches. Could better use be made of newer distribution technology such as 2-D bar codes to carry additional information? Could improved shipping methods be employed, such as just-in-time approaches, where the goods are not delivered until needed?

D: Distribution Security. The review would focus on the security over goods in-transit and getting ready for shipment to the ultimate customers. Audit procedures could include inspections of goods while in-transit, particularly during off-shifts. The review might also focus on reported losses, both during in-facility moves and shipments to customers. Overall security procedures as well as corrective actions taken should be investigated.

E: Distribution Packaging and Waste. An environmentally oriented review could focus on the types of packing materials used, whether they are recycled, and whether there are negotiations with vendors to use recyclable packing materials. The efficiency of packaging methods should also be examined to determine if the packing helps to reduce loss or damage.

The above are only a few examples to illustrate the types of operational audits that can be developed.

scanner for the generation of bar code labels. We may assume that these systems work according to specifications, but an extract file from the scanning system matched against inventory records can attest that all incoming goods are correctly recorded. Similarly, CAATs can help audit the movement of in-transit goods and their transfer from one production system to another as part of the overall distribution process.

25-3 TRANSPORTATION ISSUES

Although an organization may transport its products through the use of organization-owned trucks, often outside parties—including common carrier trucks, railroads, ships or barges, airlines, and commercial freight companies including the U.S. Postal Service—provide transportation services. Transportation here means the procurement of purchased goods, shipments to customers, or internal transfers of goods and materials. The overall importance of the transportation function depends on the range of operations of the particular organization, but it often represents a substantial operating cost. It is an area where an organization can gain a significant strategic advantage through the skillful exploitation of modern methods. The use of an outside transportation provider is a type of procurement that has many special complexities, and like any other operational activity presents opportunities for initiating effective control procedures.

In the United States, transportation was a heavily regulated area for much of the twentieth century. Government agencies awarded routes, regulated rates that carriers could charge, and required a massive level of report filings. Beginning in the 1980s, this regulatory structure began to crumble. Today transportation is much more of a free market where carriers are allowed to compete with one another. For the shipper the result has been many new opportunities and flexibilities.

Because the cost of moving goods is often relatively small compared to the overall cost of those goods, these transportation costs are sometimes all but ignored. And, because costs are often individually relatively small, it is easy for improper transportation charges to be presented and paid. Internal auditors often can review transportation procedures and make cash saving recommendations. However, they may find it more cost-effective to have an outside contractor perform the detailed review, often on a contingent fee contract basis, and concentrate their efforts on the larger issue of identifying improvements for the overall transportation system.

(a) OUTSIDE CARRIER TRANSPORTATION FUNCTIONS AND PROCEDURES

Transportation in its most basic sense deals with moving goods and materials from their place of origin to another location in the most efficient manner. This is different from distribution procedures because distribution usually refers to the internal transportation of goods, whereas transportation often uses outside providers and includes the shipment of raw commodities, work-in-process materials shipped to another location, parts, finished products, or any other tangible item. Transportation efficiency means the combination of price, other terms, timing, and physical conditions that best serve the organization's interests. This section will primarily discuss transportation service obtained from outside parties. In-house transportation services will be discussed later, and in-house transportation activities should continually be reviewed as to an alternative to securing that service from an outside group.

The functions of the transportation group, commonly called the traffic department, fall into two general areas. The first is concerned with the development of transportation policy and performing studies and investigations that pertain to major transportation decisions. What mode of transportation should be used for different requirements and in alternative situations? What routings are best? What new approaches can be developed to reduce transportation costs?

Day-to-day operations are carried on with regard to the transportation policies and key decisions. These are the activities concerning daily carrier relations, shipment follow-ups, and the like, including the maintenance of transportation status records. These activities may lend themselves to decentralization to field offices or other lower-level organizational components. The basic operational cycle here is similar to the purchasing cycle steps discussed in Chapter 24. These operational stages of the transportation function and the particular objectives associated with them can be the basis for looking at the structure of internal controls and related significant control problems in this area. The first stage is to determine needs for transportation services, including questions as to the validity of the need itself and whether other operational approaches could eliminate or modify the asserted transportation need. For example, could delivery be made at a closer location or could a storage point be established to eliminate a larger number of small shipments? There may also be a question of whether the need has been accurately defined. Is any asserted urgency realistic? Could the goods wait and be included with a regularly scheduled shipment? In many of these situations the traffic department should be able to provide advisory counsel.

Although the determination of transportation need may be the basic responsibility of other operating units, the transportation function has a professional interest in this process and to some extent a share of the responsibility. Once these needs have been established, the heart of the transportation function is to study and determine specific transportation arrangements to best satisfy the defined needs. Typical considerations are for the best method of transportation and the best selection of carriers, including:

- *Savings to Be Achieved by Using the Proper Commodity Rates.* Published tariffs are specific to the nature of the goods transported and the rates for those goods. When working in a regulated environment, a transportation professional can often look at the goods to be shipped, then at the published rates, and suggest how to classify them for a preferable rate. In an increasingly nonregulated environment, many of these rate issues are negotiable.

- *Decreasing Costs through Shipping in Carload or Truckload Quantities.* Substantial savings may result through bulk shipments. These potential savings should be communicated to others interested in shipping the goods to allow them to make proper decisions.

- *Possibilities of Pooling Shipments with Other Shippers.* Although this approach may create added risks due to insurance restrictions and the natures of the goods to be shipped, sometimes pooling with other shippers can result in significant savings.

- *Possibilities of Arranging Stopovers or Other Transit Privileges, Often at a Small Extra Cost.* The traffic representative may be able to obtain extra services for premium rates.

In order to expedite shipments, the traffic specialist should know published delivery schedules and should negotiate these, when practicable, with the carriers used.

There often may be customer preferences in connection with outbound shipments. The effective transportation function should make every effort to satisfy these. Often, the availability of special equipment can be the decisive factor in the selection of the transportation carrier. The traffic department should have some knowledge as to its options here. The relative costs of different modes of transportation in relation to existing operational needs can be a significant factor in the transportation decision.

For repetitive shipments, the same decisions would normally apply until some significant dimension of the evaluation has changed. In all situations, the importance of this step from a control standpoint is that this is where the transportation decision is actually made and it should reflect the greatest possible degree of efficiency and good judgment. The evidence here should indicate that all factors have been recognized and evaluated.

The actual transportation arrangement is the next step in this process. This may at the same time include the notification to all interested parties of shipping arrangements, including vendors, customers, or the actual carriers. In the case of a common carrier, the selected routing may be included on the purchase order, and for outgoing shipments, the proper bills of lading should be prepared by the traffic function or other organization personnel. The control objective is to have a clear and timely notification of the underlying transportation decision. In the case of repetitive shipments, there should be standard routing instructions.

On an ongoing basis, the transportation function should follow up on the specific execution of the transportation arrangements. The extent of this follow-up depends on the urgency of the need for the materials transported. In some cases, this may require the monitoring of actual loading operations and interim reports on the progress of the shipment up to the point of actual delivery to the final destination. This close supervision would be necessary, for example, if the organization were shipping some type of hazardous or extremely high-value materials. The failure of these materials to arrive at a destination at given times should then initiate follow-up efforts. The control objective here should be that the follow-up effort is adequate given the circumstances.

If, according to the applicable agreements, the transportation cost is to be absorbed or paid by the customer or vendor, the problem of the validity of the settlement is theirs, subject only to any claims against the carrier involved. In many other situations, the basis of purchase or sale may be that the cost of transportation is to be borne by the organization, which will ultimately be billed by the carrier, the vendor, or the customer who has paid for it. While the accounts payable function actually remits the funds, the traffic department will review and approve them. One reason for this practice is that accounts payable does not have transportation rate information. More importantly, the review and approval of freight costs require special expertise, and a special effort is warranted to assure against overcharge.

The normal practice for transportation billings is for the transportation department to make a general review of these bills for accuracy and the basis of the billing prior to payment. Transportation usually conducts a full audit of the rates on a more thorough basis at a later time. This second review in many cases is subcontracted to an even more specialized outside service group, which reviews all transportation billings over a period of time and looks for potential savings through the identification of tariff or billing errors. This is similar to the arrangements made with outside groups for smaller parcel deliveries.

The handling of claims against carriers is another broad area of transportation department responsibility. Claims are generally of two broad types: those arising out of incorrect billings and those for damage to goods while being transported. In both cases, these claims are handled by the transportation department. The internal control concern is that the operating group originally making the claim should promptly record and transmit it to the traffic department. These operating groups would include receiving, inspection, and accounts receivable activities. The traffic department must then establish adequate controls over the filing of these claims and their subsequent follow-up. From an internal control standpoint, the payment of claims should be controlled through the regular financial accounts.

Similar to other operational activities, the effectiveness of the traffic department and its transportation activities is closely related to its relative status in the organization. While the transportation function could argue for a relatively higher-level status as a separate, independent function, because of its close relationship to purchasing, it often is part of the purchasing department. There is no harm in this arrangement as long as the role of the transportation group is not restricted. A major difference between the two is that purchasing involves buying and bringing goods to the organization whereas transportation involves primarily outbound and intraorganization shipments. Distribution involves the overall planning for moving the products, both internally and to the final customers.

The transportation function is normally decentralized, and in a larger organization will cover operational activities involving the entire organization, including its subsidiaries and other components. Although these decentralized groups may report on a line basis to the local management, there should be a strong functional tie to the transportation control group. The objective here is to centralize those aspects that need a total organization approach and at the same time to give local operating management the direct support it needs.

The effective transportation group can make significant contributions to overall organizational welfare. These potentials are often lost sight of in actual organization situations due to the volume of the usual traffic department's day-to-day work. It is important, however, to foster a close collaborative relationship between the transportation group and the other operating activities including:

1. Decisions regarding the building of a new plant or the relocation of an existing facility. These decisions are significantly affected by available transportation alternatives and their related costs. Also pertinent is the impact on vendor supply, transfers of partially processed materials from one facility to another, and any special customer service requirements.

2. The utilization of plant capacity and the location of particular types of production processes. These involve the same types of considerations as do the location of warehouses that depend on proximity to plants, vendors, and customers.

3. New approaches to the use of existing transportation services, such as negotiating for innovative approaches with air freight vendors. These have important marketing implications. Also, the increased volume of transportation services may be a basis for pressing for further rate reductions.

4. New methods of shipment. New methods may materially reduce handling costs, such as in the use of alternative air freight carriers or special containers for small parts.

5. The careful study of common carrier rate structures. Such study may indicate different ways in which the organization can qualify for lower rates—for example, different size shipments, the use of different commodity classifications, and the like may impact tariffs.

Of course, the efficiencies of a well-administered operational activity are significant and should be fully exploited. The purpose here is to demonstrate that there are additional potentials to be studied and adequately explored. Both senior management and internal audit should measure the effectiveness of the organization's transportation activity. It may initially seem that the nature of transportation services is so interrelated with other organization activities that it is not practicable to set up meaningful goals and objectives, and thus, that it is not really practicable to measure the effectiveness of the transportation group. However, there are normally fertile audit opportunities with an operational group such as transportation. At lower levels, standards for individual performance are normally covered through personnel and expense budgets. At a higher level, it desirable to develop plans to provide more value for transportation expenditures. These can be reductions of cost or other types of added value to organization operating activities. Normally, these plans are expressed in terms of specific projects to be studied and are then grouped in the best possible fashion. These plans then provide the basis for a periodic reporting of accomplishments with adequate backup to support any claimed savings.

(ii) In-House-Controlled Transportation Functions. Today, costs can be saved by hauling for compensation, for wholly owned subsidiaries or for others, as allowed under the Motor Carrier Act of 1980. Before this act, private fleets of trucks were restricted to hauling only their own goods. Also under the old rules—although it was permissible for a subsidiary to haul for another subsidiary—it had to be gratuitous. Under the 1980 reform, an organization may become involved in for-hire transport for unrelated companies, or obtain contract carrier authority to haul for its subsidiaries. In the past, subsidiaries often approached freight movement methods independently, and these regulatory changes have created opportunities for joint freight operations.

(b) INTERNAL CONTROL CONSIDERATIONS

Although the age of railroads as the dominant carriers for many goods has long since passed, replaced by trucks and other modes of transportation, transportation regulations have gone away much more slowly. The rules are changing and evolving into a much more free-market environment. Perhaps this lack of rules makes strong internal controls over the transportation function even more important.

Unless a company is shipping a commodity like crushed rock used for construction projects as its major product, transportation is often a more minor cost of the product when compared to the actual costs of production. As a result, organizations often all but ignore many of their transportation costs. When they do subject them to any analysis, the tendency is to look at the major cost categories, ignoring smaller shipments costs, such as the use of overnight parcel service rather than slightly slower and more cost-effective methods (such as two-day delivery) or alternative methods such as sending the same documents by fax or e-mail. Close attention to all shipments can improve the overall control environment and can also reduce costs for the organization.

(c) INTERNAL AUDIT ACTIVITIES

The role that internal audit should follow here is similar to the one outlined for audits of the distribution processes, discussed earlier in this chapter, as well as for the purchasing function discussed in Chapter 24. In summary, this should include:

1. Understanding the transportation process
2. Reviewing the efficiency of the administrative operations and related compliance with current policies and procedures
3. Appraising the effectiveness of existing transportation-related policies and procedures

4. Determining how transportation can increase its contribution to the total organization welfare

(i) Transportation-Related Financial Audit Considerations. Audits of the transportation function are areas where the modern internal auditor can make effective use of the audit sampling techniques discussed in Chapter 13. For example, an auditor may use an automated process to calculate shipping costs based on the customer's postal ZIP code. If the system matching routine or customer address records are in error, the shipping process will assess incorrect shipping charges to the organization or its customers. Because there will often be a large number of transactions, it is difficult to determine the total number of errors found over a period of time. Audit sampling, where the results of a properly selected sample can be used to estimate the overall effect to the incidence of error in the population, can highlight the extent of such errors to management. While an internal auditor will understand the use of this analytical tool, other members of management often may not.

An auditor would review the actual transportation costs paid compared to the true costs of the shipments. This is a situation where an organization often uses an automated procedure to establish shipping costs, even though a portion of those costs may be in error. Shippers such as United Parcel Service (UPS) in the United States base their rates on a combination of the weight of the merchandise shipped and the ZIP code destination of the parcel. Automated shipping systems look at these two values and assign the transportation or shipping charges. However, the entry of a one-digit error in the ZIP code—say, entering 55404 instead of 75404 in the shipping program—will result in an incorrect and often higher shipping charge. Although the amount of the error is often small, a large number of these errors could result in a substantial loss recovery. If the organization, for example, has paid UPS for shipping a package to ZIP 55404 at $10.35 while actually shipping it to 75404 at $7.35, it can submit the proper documentation to the shipper and receive a credit or refund.

While recoveries from errors of this type can be large in the aggregate, they represent many small error amounts requiring careful analysis. Internal audit may not be making effective use of its time by making the type of detailed analysis required to define a substantial error-recovery amount. The best approach here is to use audit sampling to select a series of transactions to determine if there appears to be a potentially significant number of distribution errors. If this appears to be an area for a distribution cost recovery, internal audit might recommend that management contract with an outside cost-recovery audit firm to do the actual detailed analysis. These firms typically operate on a contingency basis, where their fees are based on a percentage of the errors discovered and costs recovered through a claim to the shipper.

(ii) Transportation-Related Operational Audit Program. The typical distribution function of a larger organization presents opportunities from operational auditing service to management. A transportation function will be involved in such a large number of transactions and contractual arrangements with service providers that effectiveness and efficiency may sometimes be ignored. Because of pressures to ship a product to a customer in a very short time period or because of the mass of transportation arrangements to be made, controls can be ignored or even bypassed. Transportation arrangements can be made without adequate consideration given to least-cost suppliers or routes, loss or damage claims can be forgotten, or other controls can be ignored.

Figure 25.9 outlines procedures for an operational review of the transportation function. These steps focus on transportation's arrangements with outside shippers, while the review procedures for operational audits of the distribution function, discussed earlier, emphasized more strategic areas. Although these two areas have been treated separately in this chapter to emphasize the differences, operational reviews of distribution and transportation can be combined into unified audits.

(iii) Transportation Function Computer Audit Activities.   Because the transportation function primarily deals with making arrangements with outside shippers, whether they be railroads, trucking firms, or package shippers such as UPS, transportation typically does not employ any particularly unique computer systems. Any specialized system may be little more than a microcomputer system to track freight claim losses and the like. In other cases, transportation will use, or its support systems will have, interfaces with company systems such as accounts payable (for settling freight bills) or production (for scheduling outgoing transportation needs). Many computer audit activities in this area are similar to the general application review concepts discussed earlier.

As always, an internal auditor should understand the supporting systems in the transportation area and, based on risk assessments, should review the internal controls covering more critical application areas. An evolving control risk area here is that transportation functions are increasingly making arrangements with outside providers to share computer systems data. A transportation provider may request access to the organization's system files to gain information on goods scheduled for shipping and the like. Similarly, the transportation function may give access to the transportation company's system to allow them to track the status on shipped items or to trace any that may be missing. Proper information systems security procedures should be in place to provide an adequate level of protection.

25-4 DISTRIBUTION AND TRANSPORTATION SAMPLE AUDIT FINDINGS

A: Uneconomic Use of Remote Product Warehouses.   Remote finished goods warehouses are used for the Whizbang product line in the south, east, and west regions. Products from the central and mountain regions are shipped directly to customers from the headquarters plant. Inventories in these three product warehouses averaged $XXX each over the past year, representing some 120% of the annual forecasted shipments for those regions. We were advised that these remote product warehouses were constructed because of problems in securing prompt shipping in those regions. We were also advised that shipping arrangements have not been reevaluated in the last five years and that adequate shipping arrangements using headquarters might be available at present. The three warehouses are each in leased facilities with a total annual cost for the three, including fixed and salary costs, of $ZZZ.

Recommendation.   A study should be initiated by the distribution department to determine if the three remote product warehouses are still economically justified. The study should look at the total costs of maintaining these finished goods warehouses, including the carrying cost of the products. As an alternative, distribution should consider the current costs of shipping the Whizbang product directly from headquarters, as well as any extra costs associated with keeping increased inventory levels there.

Figure 25.9   Operational Audit Procedures for Transportation Activities

---

25.08.01   Develop a general understanding of the transportation function and its organization structure. Establish that the transportation department is independent of the accounts payable department.

25.08.02   Review standards and published procedures for shipping function operations, including:
  • Standards of relationships with carriers. Formal procedures should be in place outlining how arrangements should be made with carriers. In addition, the extent of authority for local transportation arrangements should be defined.
  • Transportation's responsibility for coordination with user organizational groups. This responsibility should be defined, with such definition including their jurisdiction responsibility for all arrangements with outside truckers.
  • Authorized levels of approval and follow-up responsibilities. These should be defined.

25.08.03   Procedures for making transportation arrangements should be reviewed including:
  • Who initiates, what approvals are necessary for particular types of arrangements and in what amounts.
  • How the making of the transportation arrangement is finalized.

25.08.04   On the basis of actual tests, verify and appraise the extent to which transportation procedures are complied with and whether the procedures appear to be adequate.

25.08.05   When there are unusual types of arrangements, does it appear that these are questioned and discussed?

25.08.06   Are the internal operations being carried on in a manner consistent with established organizational responsibilities, policies, and procedures? If not, what are the causes? What kind of corrective actions seems to be warranted? This part of the review would include such questions as whether organizational responsibilities should be modified or whether better training and supervision of the existing people are needed.

25.08.07   Are internal records and files of various types adequate in terms of special purpose and relation to other records and procedures? Are they being maintained efficiently?

25.08.08   Is the operational cycle adequately controlled as to authorization, assignment to personnel, making of transportation arrangements, follow-up, and completion so that the status of individual transportation assignments can be easily determined?

25.08.09   Are official transportation documents properly safeguarded and controlled?

25.08.10   Is the selection of carriers reviewed and approved with reasonable frequency by a higher-ranking member of the traffic department?

25.08.11   Are adequate records maintained of business given to individual carriers, and what efforts are made to evaluate carrier performance?

25.08.12   Are procedures adequate to determine whether charges for organization are valid, and are portions chargeable to vendors or customers properly controlled?

25.08.13   Are billings in accordance with originally authorized transportation arrangements, and, if not, are proper deductions made? Are weights properly confirmed?

25.08.14   When claims are to be made, are they adequately recorded for subsequent follow-up and control? Is the follow-up of claims adequate?

25.08.15   Test a representative number of transportation decision actions by following through all steps in the operational cycle. The sample should be picked at random from the original input of authorizations to make transportation arrangements. Points of special interest at all stages would include:
  • Compliance with all policies and procedures
  • Reasonableness of timing at the various stages
  • Evidence of care and maximum protection or organization interests, as well as evidence of good teamwork in the total traffic group
  • Effectiveness of internal records and related procedures
  • Any matters to be investigated in the review of other operational activities, including any evidence of favoritism to individual carriers.

25.08.16   Appraise the relations with both carriers and organization personnel, with a focus on the reduction of transportation costs.

B: Freight Claims Are Not Settled Promptly.   Claims for goods damaged in transit are sent to the customers experiencing the damage. Some of the claims may be due to poor company packing and others due to shipper mishandling. Although we promptly refund the customers for damaged goods, we found that the reasons for the claims are not investigated in a timely manner. In addition, based on a transportation department investigation of two years ago, we found that most claims were due to shipper mishandling. At the time of our review, we found some 1,320 freight claims over the past six months had not been investigated and no freight claims had been filed. In addition, we found no procedure in place to monitor the loss ratios for the various shippers currently used.

Recommendation.   Greater attention should be given to investigating causes and then filing loss reports for damaged shipments to customers. If resources are lacking in the transportation department, a cross-functional team should be established to clear up the backlog. Once the problem has been corrected, transportation should establish procedures to resolve damage claims on an ongoing basis and to monitor the loss or damage rates by the various shippers.

CHAPTER 26

Engineering, Research, Quality, and Quality Control

26-1 INTRODUCTION: OPERATIONAL AUDITS OF TECHNICAL AREAS

Technical functions present a challenge to many auditors who are trained in areas such as accounting, information systems, or even manufacturing controls. Internal auditors often have difficulty in understanding the specialized functions and language of areas such as engineering or research. In addition, personnel in these technical areas are usually not accustomed to working with internal auditors and may meet their questions with indifference or even hostility. As a result, auditors often ignore these technical areas when considering and planning the areas for review.

Significant resources are devoted to these technical areas in many organizations, and auditors can assist both overall and technical management by recommending improved controls. Many control concepts remain the same whether a technical function or a more traditional area of the organization.

This chapter considers four broad areas in the modern organization: research, engineering, total quality management (TQM), and quality control. Research is the process of searching for new techniques or basic products using scientific investigation. Once identified through research, the engineering function will then design a product, as well as procedures to allow its manufacture. Both of these functions are typically associated with a manufacturing type of organization, although some service organizations may also have both functions as well. Each uses its own language and follows specialized procedures, but the auditor should never ignore these areas because they are considered too specialized or of ''no audit interest.'' An internal auditor will often find areas where improvements can be made.

Although both are included in this chapter, TQM and quality control represent two quite different functions. Quality control determines that products meet standards and are properly inspected for defects before their ultimate delivery. Quality control is often part of the overall production process.

The TQM function is still both unique and relatively new to many organizations. In response to international competitive pressures and general concerns that customers are not being properly served, organizations establish total quality programs whereby employees in all areas take steps to eliminate errors and perform high-quality work. The auditor can assess whether program objectives are being met and assist the TQM team in performing quality-oriented reviews. TQM activities are also discussed in Chapter 33.

26-2 ENGINEERING FUNCTION

The engineering function in the typical industrial organization is responsible for the design of products and processes for their manufacture. It may cover a wide spectrum of activities, broken down in terms of specific sub-areas in the manufacturing process. Different groups of engineers might concentrate on the design and operation of products, manufacturing processing approaches, plant layouts and other facilities, equipment, tooling, or work methods. In each of these areas there will be different degrees of specialization. Some engineering functions perform fairly basic research, including the search for new materials or new processes that might eventually contribute to the further development of products. Other engineers will perform no real product design, but may be involved with improving existing processes, including facilities and equipment.

The engineering function is important, and in many organizations—such as in aerospace manufacturing—it is perhaps the *most* important factor for operational success. The engineering function provides product design and translates concepts into production operations that make the products customers want. Engineering activities should be performed efficiently and effectively, and there should be close cooperation between engineering and other activities affected by engineering services.

Because many auditors lack technical skills, engineering functions often provide a particular challenge due to their technical nature. However, auditors can perform effective reviews of the engineering function if they have an understanding of the control framework and organizational structure within that framework. It is not necessary for an internal auditor to understand the specific design or procedural techniques that engineers use. All functions in the organization, whether technical, financial, administrative, or something else, should follow a set of basic control practices. Internal audit can assist management by evaluating those practices within the engineering function.

(a) ENGINEERING PROCESS CYCLE

Most engineering work tends to follow a general cycle where the engineer identifies, or is asked to identify, a problem or an area for change. The engineer then works to develop alternative solutions to the task, tests them to select the best, and implements the best solution. In many respects, this process is similar to the tasks performed by an auditor. A unique feature of the engineering process, however, is that the good engineer should be innovative in developing optimal solutions. The engineer is often developing something entirely new, whether a product, process, or technique. While auditors should also be developing creative solutions, they must rely more on established standards. However, there are still similarities.

The auditor should keep these general concepts of a problem-solving process in mind when reviewing the activities of engineering functions.

(i) Types of Engineering Functions in Organizations.   Many persons in a modern organization may have a job title of "engineer." Some may not have a formal engineering degree but have a job title name that includes the expression "engineer." For example, some more advanced information systems programmers may be called "systems engi-

neers,'' or the individuals responsible for the heating and air conditioning systems are called ''plant engineers.'' These persons do not have the same professional backgrounds or credentials associated with the types of engineers discussed in this chapter; college-trained specialists responsible for the design and manufacture of the organization's products.

The typical medium-to-large-sized manufacturing organization may have three different engineering functions: design, manufacturing, and industrial engineering. Engineers in each have specialized responsibilities and follow unique procedures. In a smaller organization, many of these separate functions may be combined in a small group or even in a single individual engineer.

(ii) Design Engineering Procedures. Design engineering is responsible for the overall design of products that will achieve management objectives and that can be placed into the manufacturing process. They will take basic known processes or component parts, including the current versions of existing products, and develop new or improved products from them. After developing the product or function, design engineering will perform tests to determine if it meets established design objectives. Following this, they may work with manufacturing engineering to place the product into production.

Design engineers usually do not just go to their engineering laboratories and ''invent something.'' Typically they work on specific projects, funded and approved by engineering or upper management. The design engineering process usually follows these steps:

- *Determine design need.* Numerous factors may influence the need for new design work. For example, either management or the engineering staff may determine that certain products or features are no longer competitive, or outside factors may force a design change. Management may have established goals to move in certain directions, or engineering may feel that a given product could be improved to enhance overall profitability. In any case, a general need is identified, and funds are budgeted for the engineering function to do some preliminary exploratory work.

- *Develop preliminary proposal.* Based upon the initial identified need, design engineering would typically make some very preliminary quick and dirty estimates of the project objectives, the project costs in terms of both resources and time, and its expectation of success. This proposal would be routed through engineering management for approval.

- *Develop and approve project proposal.* After a review of the preliminary proposal, a more formal project proposal document would be developed. This would more clearly identify the objectives, costs, and risks associated with the proposed project. Upper or engineering management, depending upon the size of the project, would next formally approve the project. This approval should clearly identify the authorized funding, the expected deliverables, and the anticipated duration of the project.

- *Begin work on project.* Depending on the size of the project, design engineering may add additional staff, acquire additional equipment, or otherwise assemble the resources to begin work on the project. The work here may consist of basic designs, the construction of prototypes, or other efforts. This is the classic ''engineering'' portion of the project.

- *Periodically report on project progress.* Following the project-reporting system in place, design engineering should periodically and regularly report to management on project progress, indicating the total resources expended to date, accomplishments against project milestones, and estimated costs to complete. Good microcomputer-based project-control software is available to assist here.

- *Develop and test alternative solutions.* Design engineering work requires the formulation of alternative solutions, coupled with tests to determine the best of them. In some cases, these alternatives are developed through the actual construction of prototypes in the engineer's laboratory. Today, they are more frequently developed through computer-based mathematical models or simulations.

- *Present preferred solution to management.* The design engineer's basic task is complete with the presentation of the recommended solution to management. Frequently, this will result in a new project where the engineer is asked to enhance the recommended solution or to develop something with changed objectives.

This design engineering process is very much a project-oriented task, where the engineer is given a general objective and asked to find the best solution. This process sometimes results in totally new products. However, much design engineering work results in only incremental improvements to existing products or processes. Sometimes, several groups of design engineers will be working in parallel to improve something, and their various smaller improvements may be combined to create a totally new product. Internal auditors should be able to relate to this same process. These are the same basic steps that an internal auditor would follow in developing computer-assisted audit software or in developing the best solutions for many audit tasks.

Because design engineering work may yield new products or even unexpected new discoveries, design engineers should always keep detailed laboratory notes documenting what they tested, and the results. These notes provide documentation to allow engineering and the overall organization to support research findings or to potentially defend patent rights.

Automation is changing the manner in which design engineers work. While once engineers had to build prototypes of many of their designs, computer-aided design (CAD) software allows them to build these models in a simulated manner on a display screen. Similarly, the design engineer once worked very closely with draftsmen to develop various views of the product. Today, automated design software has replaced this process. Detailed drawings, as well as parts lists, are maintained on computer files for easy retrieval and modification if necessary.

Many design engineering projects end up as false starts or canceled efforts. In some cases, the design engineering group may decide that original project objectives are not feasible for one or another reason. They might then recommend the project be canceled. In other situations, management may decide to drop a project due to excessive costs, slower progress than expected, or just changes in strategy. In other situations, engineering may develop a product or process that appears to meet all objectives but may not be placed into production for a variety of other management reasons. Those products that do pass all of the tests are readied for conversion to production, usually the role of the manufacturing engineer.

(iii) Manufacturing Engineering Procedures.   The manufacturing engineer has the task of taking an approved engineering design and making any modifications necessary to easily and efficiently place it into production. For example, a design engineer may specify on the design drawing that a given manufactured component requires six separate parts. The manufacturing engineer realizes that two of these six parts should be assembled before bringing everything to the production shop table. This assembly might take place as a separate step or could be performed by an outside subcontractor. These manufacturing engineering changes are designed to make the final product easier or more cost-effective to manufacture.

The manufacturing engineer must also take engineering revisions to a product and place them into production when appropriate. This can become a challenge when the product is very complex or is manufactured in a continuous production line. In the latter case, the manufacturing engineer must identify the appropriate point in the continuous production line to insert the product revision.

Manufacturing engineers are often concerned with maintaining adequate records for product and vendor source controls. For example, an organization may manufacture some type of machine that uses either vendor-supplied parts or even raw metal for fabricating other components. If an installed machine component failed at some future time, the organization might want to go back through its records to determine which vendor supplied the raw materials or components that failed. These records might help the organization to decide on a design change, to file a claim against that vendor, or help in any potential litigation actions.

The auditor will usually find manufacturing engineers in only larger organizations or those with particularly complex products. In many organizations, the design engineers also have manufacturing engineering responsibilities.

(iv) Industrial Engineering Procedures.   The industrial engineer is a third type of engineer in the manufacturing organization. This engineer is totally involved with procedures, many of them involving labor operations, on the manufacturing shop floor. Industrial engineers got their start in the early days of the twentieth century when they used stopwatches to record how much time each step of a manufacturing process took. These were called *time-and-motion studies*. They then developed improved manufacturing processes to reduce the time required to manufacture the products.

With increased automation in all aspects of production, the amount of labor content has decreased, and the need to perform industrial engineering time-and-motion studies has also diminished. Industrial engineers today are interested in improving the flow of materials through production line processes and in improving overall efficiencies. Although larger organizations may have separate industrial engineering functions, their role and that of manufacturing engineers as described previously is often similar, if not the same.

An industrial engineering function may be involved in other manufacturing process ancillary functions, such as manufacturing quality control, as discussed later in the chapter, or maintaining accident records and running the plant safety program. When internal audit encounters an industrial engineering function in the course of a review, interviews may be necessary to better understand that function's particular responsibilities.

(b) ENGINEERING PROCESS INTERNAL CONTROL CONSIDERATIONS

Although the term ''internal control'' is familiar to most managers, accountants, and others involved in organization operations, it may not receive the same type of recognition from the typical engineer. Engineers think of ''controls,'' but in terms of procedures to monitor a process to make sure that it does not function out of control. For example, a motor on an item of automated production machinery will have a governor control that keeps the motor operating at the correct speed. Engineers build this type of control into many of their products and processes.

Internal controls should also be important to the engineer. Costs over engineering projects should be properly controlled and allocated to other activities in a correct manner.

Engineering-related internal controls can be divided into the following broad areas:

- Controls over Engineering Projects
- Controls over Engineering Resources and Products
- Engineering-Related Cost Accounting Controls

The following paragraphs will briefly discuss each of these control areas. While internal audit should have a broad understanding of the overall engineering process, these areas of internal control that are specific to the engineering function should receive a significant amount of internal audit's attention when reviewing engineering-related activities.

(i) Controls Over Engineering Projects.   Engineering activities, particularly those for design engineering, are typically organized into separate, defined efforts called *projects*. While organizations may use other terms, they will still follow this project concept. An engineering project is a defined activity with its own objectives, budgets, and allocated resources. Controls over these project activities are the major area of internal control for most engineering functions.

The auditor unfamiliar with the concept of engineering projects should think of the information systems development life cycle (SDLC) process described in Chapter 18. Those procedures for developing information systems were originally developed, in the early days of computer systems, from the concepts of engineering project management, which normally consists of the following elements:

- *Project Objectives.* Projects should have a clearly stated set of objectives approved by management. This is the stated purpose of the engineering project against which the engineering efforts should be measured.

- *Project Budget and Plan.* Financial budgets and time-based plans should be developed and approved by management for all engineering projects. Both should contain sufficient detail to allow the engineers working on the project to have a road map and for management to understand the costs of the endeavor.

- *Project Recording and Reporting System.* A project plan is of little value unless there is some mechanism in place to capture actual project costs and to report on those costs as well as on actual project accomplishments. This requires some form of both labor and materials reporting systems, as well as mechanisms to measure actual results against plans and the original objectives.

- *Project Review and Adjustment Process.* An engineering project requires some facility for a management review of progress and for appropriate adjustments to budgets, plans, or even initial objectives when required. This review and adjustment process will continue at periodic intervals during the life of the project.

The preceding steps describe the basics used for most engineering projects, whether large or small. Internal control issues include proper management authorizations of the process and proper communication of results to appropriate levels of management. Many of the internal audit steps described in the next section describe similar procedures for reviewing project controls.

(ii) Controls over Engineering Resources.   In addition to recording time and accomplishments against engineering projects, the typical engineering activity is involved with controlling a variety of other resources, including the designs of the final engineering effort or even actual products. In many instances, the engineering drawings (now often computer design files) that are the result of an engineering project may be the only output from an expensive and resource-intensive effort. Because there may often be a high degree of confidentiality associated with these drawings, a strong set of internal controls is important.

An engineering project will often define a new competitive product or direction which the organization will want to keep confidential until released. The auditor should look for strong physical security controls over engineering work products, whether they are actual prototypes, engineering drawings, or even project status reports. The drawings defining the product (or even discarded scrap) may reveal the new product to improper persons. In addition, if the engineering function uses CAD or other computer-based systems, logical security controls as described in Chapter 19 would also apply.

Drawings and reports might be described as intellectual products associated with an engineering effort. In addition, many engineering efforts require other supplies and materials necessary to design and build the new product. Procedures must be in place for defining these requirements and then purchasing them. Depending upon the nature of the project, existing procedures such as the purchasing procedures described in Chapter 24 can be used here. In other instances, due to confidentiality reasons, special purchasing arrangements must be used. However, in all cases the same purchasing and inventory control procedures described for other areas of the organization should also be used here. Just because the materials are needed for the engineering function does not mean that their controls should be outside of normal good operational and financial controls.

(iii) Engineering-Related Cost Accounting Controls.   Many engineering activities support other organizational activities, and engineering labor and related costs associated with those activities should be properly allocated to the benefiting activities or departments. Internal auditors should look for appropriate cost accounting controls and procedures, as were discussed in Chapter 22.

Particular attention should be given to cost accounting controls over any nonproject engineering activities. Even if the engineer is charging time and other resources to a defined engineering project, efforts may be directed to other nonauthorized projects or to other support activities. Neither of these nonauthorized activities is necessarily wrong in all cases. However, appropriate cost accounting reporting tools should be in place to record these other activities, or the prime project may bear unnecessary costs more properly allocated to other benefiting activities.

Cost accounting for engineering activities is really no different than other cost accounting, but it is an area where control procedures may be weaker. Internal audit should be sensitive to the need for appropriate engineering-related cost accounting controls.

(c) ENGINEERING PROCESS INTERNAL AUDIT ACTIVITIES

As previously discussed, many internal audit functions have avoided reviews of engineering-related functions because they have viewed them as too specialized. In some instances, engineering areas were not even considered for review because internal audit's risk-assessment procedures did not recognize audit risks associated with its engineering functions.

A strong message of this chapter is that internal audit should consider reviews of engineering and other technical-related functions whenever the assessment of control risk justifies those reviews. Internal audit will not be expected to understand the intricacies of various engineering procedures, but should look for a strong set of internal controls over the engineering process. Management will expect such controls and internal audit should review this area for appropriate control procedures.

The following sections discuss financial, operational, and computer audit control procedures for a review of the engineering function in an organization. While this chapter discusses the engineering function in total, internal audit will often find it more effective to break down any planned reviews into more easily defined units. For example, based upon the risk analysis, internal audit can consider a review of a key engineering project rather than performing a review of the entire design engineering function.

(i) Engineering Process Financial Audit Considerations.   The primary area of financial audit concern for the engineering process is in financial controls over engineering projects. As a first step, internal audit should gain an understanding of the engineering project control process in place by discussing procedures with a manager responsible for engineering project control as well as reviewing the types of published procedures and reports used to manage engineering projects. Project management is a complex process including many phases or activities. The Project Management Institute[1] has defined these various processes, as shown in Figure 26.1, that are necessary for effective project management. These processes apply to a wide range of projects from engineering product development efforts to building construction projects, or to internal audit project management.

Based on internal audit's understanding of the engineering project-control process, a review of the project's financial controls over one or several key projects is a next important step. The projects reviewed could be selected on a random basis, but a risk-based selection is best. The risk selection factors should include the project's budget size, management's concerns over the project, and its complexity. Figure 26.2 is an example of a risk-based selection approach. Figure 26.3 outlines the procedures for a review of engineering project management financial controls.

If internal audit discovers that engineering project-management controls are significantly deficient, an overall review of project-management procedures may be needed. While internal audit can simply report to management that there are no engineering project controls, a better approach is to review overall procedures and to report actual project-management exceptions.

(ii) Engineering Process Operational Audit Approaches.   Chapter 21 discussed the overall approach to operational auditing, which identifies a wide variety of areas for

---

[1] Project Management Institute, 130 South State Road, Upper Darby, PA 19082.

Figure 26.1 Overview of Project Management Knowledge Areas and Project Management Processes

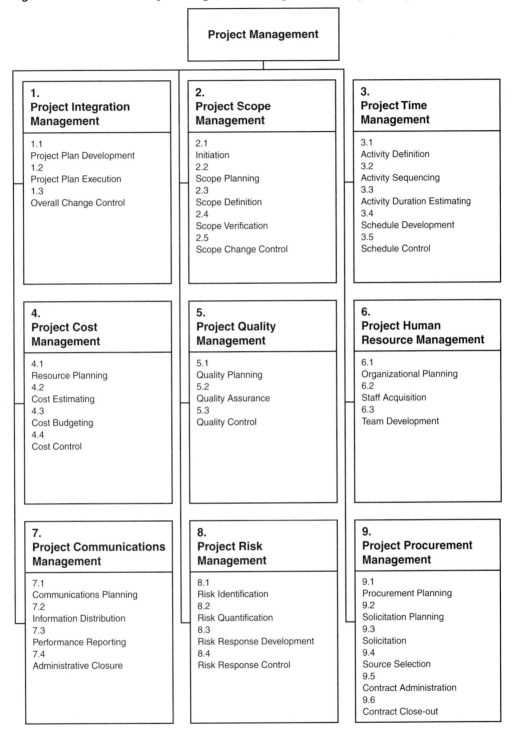

Source: Reprinted from *A Guide to the Project Management Body of Knowledge*™ with permission of the Project Management Institute Headquarters, Four Campus Blvd., Newton Square, PA 19073-3299 USA, a worldwide organization of state-of-the-art in project management.

Figure 26.2   Risk-Based Audit Selection for Engineering Projects

Audit Selection Consideration	Score
1. Project background and history	
a. Is the project based on an enhancement to existing products?	1.0 to 2.0
b. Project covers revisions to correct past problems?	2.0 to 5.0
c. New project along existing product/production lines?	5.0 to 8.0
d. New project utilizing newer or untested technologies?	8.0 to 10.0
2. Project size	
Rate project between 1.0 and 10.0 based on its relative size, in terms of budget, assigned staff size, and other resources assigned to the project when compared with other projects planned or in process for the engineering function.	1.0 to 10.0
3. Project duration and relationship with other efforts	
a. Is this a freestanding project expected to last less than 3 months?	1.0 to 2.0
b. Is this effort planned for up to one year in duration?	2.0 to 4.0
c. Is this a multi-year project effort?	5.0 to 8.0
d. Is the successful completion of this effort necessary for other projects?	6.0 to 10.0
4. Project complexity	
Based on discussions with engineering management and others, rate each of the project review candidates on a 1.0 to 10.0 complexity scale. While the auditor can develop impressions regarding complexity, engineering management should be the final authority.	1.0 to 10.0
5. Project-management concerns	
a. Is this a normal project with no known special considerations?	1.0 to 3.0
b. Has a responsible manager requested an audit review of project?	3.0 to 6.0
c. Was an audit review requested by senior management or the board?	9.0 to 10.0
Review each engineering project in process and select higher scoring efforts for audit.	

potential control and efficiency improvements and makes recommendations to management. Internal auditors can often make effective recommendations in virtually any area of the organization's operations.

Engineering and related technical areas often cause internal audit some operational review problems. Many engineering and related research areas are so specialized that internal audit may feel too intimidated to make conventional recommendations for control improvements. An internal auditor may be faced with comments along the lines of, "You don't understand engineering. We always do it this way!" The auditee may then proceed to barrage the internal auditor with a variety of comments using technical terminology to further confuse the issue.

When faced with this situation, internal audit should not attempt to evaluate how engineering functions are performed but should focus on project management and other key internal control issues surrounding these technical engineering operations. Internal audit should not be concerned with which specific steps were performed to complete as engineering design, but should determine that engineering has a structured approach to this design and that all work is appropriately documented and subjected to supervisory review. This is really a project-management review where the operational and financial elements are closely connected.

Figure 26.4 outlines operational audit steps for reviews of an engineering function, emphasizing the protection of assets and the need for appropriate levels of documentation. Internal audit should find them useful in any operational review of engineering functions, whether design, industrial, or manufacturing engineering.

(iii) Engineering Process Computer Audit Procedures. Computer systems are essential for the modern engineering function. Engineers no longer sit at drafting tables developing their designs, but use computer-aided design (CAD) software tools. This is a field that is rapidly evolving. The first computer-aided design tools allowed the engineer to, for instance, input the necessary equations for a bridge design. The computer system then performed the calculations but did not show the designer the final bridge product.

Current generations of automated design systems have a much stronger graphical emphasis. Rather than just working with the equations, the engineer can graphically design the structure with the computer system performing the necessary calculations. Figure 26.5 is an example of this type of computer-aided design. Even newer software, using parallel processing techniques, allow the engineer to first design the bridge and then to simulate

Figure 26.3 Audit Procedures for Engineering Project Management Financial Controls

Obj. 26.03.01	All projects should be authorized and approved by proper levels of management.
Obj. 26.03.02	Project plans should include appropriate estimates for all planned project expenditures.
Obj. 26.03.03	When project plans call for the expenditure of capital, planning should be linked to the organization's capital budget.
Obj. 26.03.04	A project reporting system should be in place to capture all relevant project costs and to measure these cost against established budgets.
Obj. 26.03.05	Procedures should be in place to assure timely reporting of progress against project plans, with approvals by at least one level above the individual reporting.
Obj. 26.03.06	Project progress, including appropriate expenditures for materials and resources, should be reported to appropriate levels of management on a periodic basis.
Obj. 26.03.07	Procedures should be in place to adjust project work and expenses in light of any management-authorized changes.
Obj. 26.03.08	Project expenditures should properly tie to relevant organization financial accounts.
Obj. 26.03.09	At the completion of project efforts, financial procedures should be in place to close out all open project tasks, to assign remaining resources to other areas, and to document and close down the project effort in an orderly manner.
Obj. 26.03.10	Financial reviews should be in place after completion of the project to assess whether project financial goals have been achieved.

Figure 26.4   Operational Steps for Review of an Engineering Function

Audit _____ Location _____ Date _____		
AUDIT STEP	**INITIAL**	**W/P**
1. Develop an overall understanding of the engineering function, including its organization structure, reporting relationships, mission, and management expectations.		
2. Develop an understanding of the project initiation, planning, and approval process; assess appropriateness of control procedures.		
3. Meet with director of engineering function to understand the major mix of projects in process for engineering. If lacking an understanding of technical aspects of key projects, request supporting materials for review or request a more general briefing on the project objectives.		
4. Assess the appropriateness of engineering project work documentation procedures, including such matters as the use of computer-aided design (CAD) procedures and engineering work notebooks.		
5. Request a walking tour of the engineering work areas. If questions arise about the nature of work observed and the role of special equipment, request explanations.		
6. Based on discussions with management, reviews of engineering procedures, and observations, prepare a detailed flowchart of the process from new project initiation through its turnover to production; obtain acknowledgment on the correctness of this chart.		
7. Obtain an understanding of the engineering revision control process as the work is developed, turned over to manufacturing/production, and modified due to customer and other requests. Assess integrity and control procedures in place.		
8. Select several projects that are listed in control reports as "completed" and review documentation records to determine that all work records have been filed and that work has ceased on the projects.		
9. Based on an observation of the engineering work area, select several projects in process and trace them back to authorization records to determine whether they are valid development projects; investigate any discrepancies.		
10. If appropriate, select several pieces of test or computer equipment, trace their fixed-asset tags back to property records, and assess whether the equipment is assigned to projects as authorized.		

Figure 26.5 CAD Drawing Example

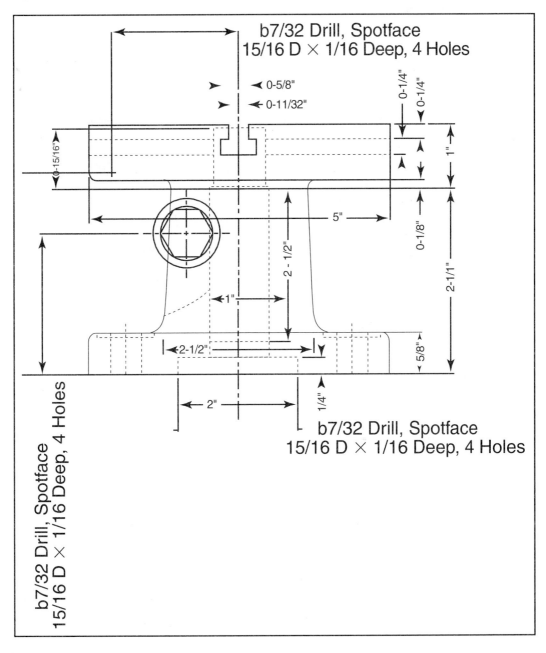

its performance, testing, perhaps, whether the computer-designed bridge could stand up in earthquakes of varying magnitudes.

These automated design systems of today are often based on specialized and ever more powerful engineering workstation machines. In the future, however, we may see these automated design systems gravitate back to larger computer systems due to the very large memory and processing requirements needed for various specialized simulations. No matter where located, internal audit should consider the physical and logical security controls surrounding these systems.

The auditor should also have an understanding of other engineering-related computer applications in use. For example, an engineering design system may provide preliminary bills of material to the type of manufacturing resource planning system discussed in Chapter 23. Reviews of the engineering-related application controls in this instance could be part of the auditor's overall review of the systems discussed in Chapter 17. Similarly, other engineering systems may provide input to various accounting systems. A key issue here is to determine whether controls over the engineering-related feeder systems are consistent with those surrounding the primary applications.

Engineering information systems are often good candidates for computer-assisted procedures. While an attempt to perform these procedures over automated design files may be difficult and not all that effective, audits of the engineering project-management function are often good candidates for computer-assisted audit procedures. Automated audit procedures can go through engineering project planning detail files and can calculate such items as differences between ledger and project-planning budgets or potential project-planning data errors.

(iv) Sample Audit Report Findings and Recommendations

A: Nonauthorized Project Work Being Performed.   During the walk-through of the new products laboratory, internal audit observed work on a new dock-loading machine. When we inquired about this project, we were advised that it was a ''special'' project that the design engineers were working on during their lunch hours and spare time. We found no authorization for this dock-loading machine. Subsequent observations of the engineering laboratory showed ongoing activity on the project. Engineering product design management advised us that they were informally working on a ''bootleg'' prototype to convince upper management of the merits of this new product. Evidently, time spent on the loader is charged to other authorized projects.

Recommendation. All engineering projects should be authorized by appropriate levels of management. If deemed appropriate, special design projects should be established for experimental design projects such as the dock loader.

B: Engineering Drawings Not Properly Secured.   We determined that engineering drawings stored on the computer-aided design system were properly backed up with key files stored in an off-site location. However, we also observed that numerous interim drawings are printed from the system and stored on open tables in the engineering office areas. Although these may not be final version product drawings, they could provide a competitor with an understanding of new product plans. The engineering laboratory area is open during evening hours and accessible to other second- or third-shift employees.

Recommendation. All hard-copy versions of engineering drawings should be stored in a locked, secure facility during evening hours. Engineering management should issue a policy letter to all design engineering personnel, reminding them of the importance of security over engineering designs.

26-3 RESEARCH FUNCTION

Research activities are closely related to engineering. Research exists basically for the purpose of generating new knowledge, which then, at a proper stage of development, should provide input to the development functions in the organization.

Research is often classified as either "pure" or "applied." Pure research is a search for new phenomena, using scientific method or just assumptions to discover something new. Because of its costs and risks, most organizations are unable to fund pure research activities. Rather, they will rely upon the pure research activities of academics or outside entrepreneurs who also sell services, and then will apply this basic research to their own processes. Only the largest organizations typically fund their own pure research. Although the transistor and laser were developed largely through organization-sponsored research, the then benefiting organization, Bell Laboratories, probably had many other failures. Another large organization, IBM, has funded pure research that led to their scientists winning Nobel prizes but provided few immediate new product benefits for IBM.

Applied research takes the results of existing basic research and applies it to other or better products. In some instances the applied researchers will attend technical conferences or review specialized journals to get their basic understandings, or they may purchase the work from a pure researcher in another company or research institution. As an example, in the 1950s a U.S. company then called the Haloid Corporation purchased a process called xerography from an inventor. The company eventually became the Xerox Corporation, and the research allowed for the development of the original Xerox copy machine, whose concept is so pervasive today.

Even though the area is often quite technically oriented, a research function may especially need the administrative and control type of assistance that internal audit can provide.

(a) NATURE AND IMPORTANCE OF THE RESEARCH PROCESS

New knowledge can be of any type and pertain to any kind of human activity. Research activities will pertain to some aspect of organization operations and should have as their central purpose the development of new knowledge to increase the profitability of the organization. Although the broader spectrum can include production, marketing, personnel, and the like, this section is concerned only with the technical type of research, which applies to products or production operations. The objective in all cases is to develop new knowledge that will be useful in some way. This may include reducing manufacturing costs, adding or strengthening the operational characteristics of a product, or perhaps developing other innovations.

The research process is rather different than the engineering design process described in the previous section. In engineering design, known or existing technologies are used to improve a product, process, or procedure. Although requiring strong analytical and innovative skills, the design engineer usually uses known technologies to build a product or process. In research, however, the scientist takes some basic principles and finds new or different ways that they may be applied. In some instances, however, the research effort is never translated into a practical product.

Another way to view the research role is in terms of its degree of proximity, in a time and developmental sense, to actual production utilization. Management may ask to what extent a new research project will reduce costs or increase revenues. These evaluations are often difficult because of the long time periods that are frequently involved, the uncertainty as to how the application will actually work out, and a lack of knowledge about the market demand for the new product or process. There may also be uncertainty as to whether the new knowledge can be implemented at a reasonable production cost level.

Even when the application being sought is fairly well known, with a pretty good idea of its potential value in evidence, it is often difficult to measure progress toward the achievement of the research objectives. For example, the time needed to find a solution to a problem may be a month or several years, or it may prove to be an unsolvable problem, at least in terms of an acceptable cost. Thus, it is difficult to say at a particular stage of the research how far it is toward completion. This evaluation is still more difficult when researchers have personal attachments to their particular projects and consciously or unconsciously have biased or erroneous views. Sometimes solving the stated research problem is not the total answer. Equally pertinent is whether and to what extent there is justification for further research costs to be expended.

All the above factors combine to make the management and control of a research activity a challenging area. The potential benefits or profits from the results of any research activities can be high, but the costs can be high as well. Most high-cost research activities also involve a risk that they will not necessarily result in a positive gain to the organization. Internal audit, while not expert in the areas of specialty research, can assist management by reviewing the internal controls covering these development activities.

(i) Organizational Status of the Research Department.   The size of the research department and its organizational status will depend directly on the kind of business the organization is in and how important the research function is to organization success. In an organization whose products have a significant technological basis, the research activity will typically have a high-ranking organizational status. This is necessary to attract the right kind of research professionals and to enable the department to interact with other operational and staff functions in an effective manner. Although the activities of the research department are closely related to engineering and production, research is normally independent of both. It is essential that research should be able to operate in a detached manner, free from the pressures of day-to-day regular operations.

In a large, multiunit organization, the research function is usually centralized, rather than distributed to the separate operating units. This is because the central or corporate organization can often take a broader view of overall organization goals and more easily fund a long-range research effort. It is also logical to exploit the economies of scale and to have a centralized research function serving all operational groups. The exception is where the organization has decentralized operational components which are in very different kinds of businesses with different research needs.

To a considerable extent, the special managerial and control problems that relate to engineering activities are applicable to research functions. Persons working in research often have stronger ties to their professions than to the organization. Unless properly managed and motivated, researchers can become more interested in the results of their research as an achievement of professional excellence and less concerned with either the cost of that achievement or its ultimate potentials in a profit-and-loss sense. From a control standpoint, the best solution is to have strong underlying project authorization and control procedures, combined with continuous monitoring and interaction with responsible managers of the other organization activities. This interaction can have the benefit of focusing on optimal directions for the research effort and securing a better organizational goal commitment from research personnel. The support for this collaborative effort should come from top management.

(ii) Measuring Research Department Activities.   The need for research in many industries is so great that ways must be found to deal with the problems. The basis for that need in its simplest terms is competitive survival. If a technology-based organization is to be competitive, it must be competitive in terms of its research efforts. Assuming that the direction of the organization's research effort has been established, the problem then takes on a new importance. Management must manage and control this research effort to which the organization has committed itself. The organization must achieve the research results that it needs to support its competitive objectives while accomplishing those objectives at a price that it can afford.

Any research activity requires strong project-management controls similar to what has been described for engineering projects. Perhaps the major difference between the two is that engineering will initiate a project to build a *better* machine or process while research will attempt to develop a *new* device. Both efforts face risks, but engineering is usually able to more easily demonstrate the results of its efforts to management. Unless research efforts result in demonstrable success, management may have difficulty envisioning the results of what can be very resource-intensive endeavors. Research function reports indicating that they are "almost there" on a project goal will not satisfy management over any length of time.

The previously described engineering process, starting with determining the design need and developing a preliminary proposal, is also applicable to research projects, but several other steps must be factored into this process. First, a research project should define some measurable interim milestone goals. Because the project may extend over a longer period, time-based objectives should be established. The research function would be asked to provide detailed reports on progress against these objectives, as well as the associated costs. The objectives should be developed in terms understandable to appropriate members of senior management.

A second important control in the research process is the need to understand when a project may not work and when to cut losses and drop the effort. This, of course, applies for all organization efforts, but it is even more important for research efforts where those involved can become too enthusiastic about their projects. In addition to periodic reports, research projects should receive periodic functional and financial reviews. In addition to the progress of the research project, these reviews should include inputs to determine the progress of any competitors, as well as the changing attitudes of potential customers.

Research projects are designed to give an organization a competitive edge, and any such advantage could be lost quickly if competitors become aware of a new research direction and start on similar projects themselves. Progress reports should be distributed to only a select group of managers with appropriate confidentiality and security controls.

(b) CONTROL CYCLE OF THE RESEARCH PROCESS

The nature of research operations has an interesting and important control impact on the internal organizational structure of the research function. The challenge for management is to exploit the benefits of normal organizational structures in the way of assigning work responsibilities, but at the same time to protect as much as possible the basic creativity and productivity of the individual researchers. Because of creativity needs, research personnel are often allowed more than the usual degree of independence and freedom from administrative work. This does not mean, however, that the research department can operate without basic controls.

Similarly, where goals may be difficult to achieve, productivity is often hard to measure. However, there should be measures in place to allow management to assess progress. Research activities frequently do not fit into traditional organizational structures, and management must be aware of their special needs and find the right balance between completely structured and completely unstructured types of organizational approaches.

Once approved, research projects should be subjected to proper implementation controls, including close administration over progress, with frequent reevaluations to assess whether initial goals are being met or whether those goals require some level of redefinition. This process is very similar to procedures for the design engineering process discussed earlier in this chapter.

Perhaps in no other area of operational activity is there such a need for a clear definition of organizational mission as in research. Lacking this, research efforts can go off in nonproductive directions based on the more restricted judgement or personal interests of individual researchers. At the same time, this mission can be too restrictive. The focus of research may be so narrowly directed that it overlooks more general areas that may offer greater rewards. There is a risk that tight mission statement controls may unduly restrict the creativity of the researcher—often a priceless ingredient. The determination of a particular research mission must come about through an effective interaction between organization management, other personnel, and the research group. In this interaction, consideration should be given to all pertinent factors, including:

- *New Research Needs.* The scope of the needs for new knowledge and the specific ways the new knowledge may benefit the organization must be considered. The organization may want to match or exceed a competitor who has a new process or they may want to develop an all new process. The scope should be clearly defined.

- *Expectations of Achieving Research Success.* The technical possibilities and probabilities of satisfying needs through planned research efforts—together with realistic estimates of the time and cost resources required—must be considered. The expectations of success must be matched against the risk of failure, and both must be compared to expected costs.

- *Organization Research Capabilities.* The total research capabilities of the organization in terms of its personnel and other resources must be considered. In addition, the alternative merits of competing research projects within those total capabilities and funding constraints must be considered.

These factors would normally be discussed on a preliminary and informal basis, and then, depending on the scope and required investments of the proposed projects, should be further documented and reviewed with senior management for approval. This research-planning process may focus on a single major project or an overall combination of projects for a given period. From a control standpoint, there should be orderly and comprehensive interaction, and from it should emerge a reasonably adequate definition of the composition and magnitude of the research project. This definition should clarify the extent of involvement in basic research as well as applied research.

The overall research mission process is similar to other strategic planning processes. The idea is to assemble some top operational, financial, and research personnel to discuss options and to propose a direction for new products, processes, or ideas. Since they may be discussing matters which, if successful, could impact both the organization and its competitors' future prospects, these discussions should be kept quite confidential. While preliminary cost estimates will be extremely tentative at this point, care should be given to developing the best cost and resource estimates possible. The proposed projects should then be taken to senior management for approval.

With the objective defined and the project authorized, the research department is ready to initiate actual work. At this point the project should be broken down into its various component elements and a determination made as to the requirements for facilities, personnel, equipment, materials, and supporting services, with cost estimates for each. This would be followed by direct operational assignments to the component organizational units and personnel of the research department. At the same time, records should be established to cover the various detailed operational activities for the project. In all cases, there should be appropriate consultation with the personnel to whom project assignments are made so that responsibilities and operational objectives are well understood.

The actual research effort would then go forward in the form of testing, compilations of data, analysis, and interpretations. Time spent on the various work elements should be recorded and accumulated, other costs also recorded, and periodic reports issued covering total costs incurred in relation to work accomplished. The project-planning and reporting system used by the engineering function, as discussed previously, might be appropriate for these records. During this time, there may be interaction with other personnel, both within the research group itself and in other organization activities. For the purpose of providing additional information as needed. It also serves to inform other interested parties of problems encountered and progress made so that there can be a useful interaction to encourage a more meaningful pursuit of the research objectives.

Because a research project may lead to a new product or process that is patentable, or that is similar to but different from a competitor's patented item, it is important that detailed records be kept for all research activities. This involves the researcher's keeping detailed notebook-type records of all work, the results of any findings, and summary descriptions of any discussions or interactions with others. This type of documentation is similar to an auditor's workpapers, as was discussed in Chapter 11. It should protect the organization as well as the individual researcher from any claims that the work was somehow improper.

The nature of the research process makes it essential that individual projects are reevaluated at appropriate intervals. Normally, these points were previously determined, at the time the project was defined and authorized. At the designated reevaluation points, consideration must be given to costs expended, results achieved, the estimated costs to complete, and the current expectations as to final benefits. Reevaluations should include participation by management, the research group, and the other persons who took part in the original project decisions. The conclusions may be to cut the project, to continue with it as it is, to make modifications, or to expand the project. If in the latter case new funds are required, these would again have to be subject to the same considerations as were discussed previously for new projects. New authorizations would typically be subject to the same kind of original approval requirements.

All projects should be reviewed at specific points in time—monthly or at least quarterly, depending on the size and criticality of the project. Since the precise scope of individual projects sometimes overlaps and may represent a continuing type of evolution, the project reviewers may want to consider these efforts in terms of an overall program. This may simplify the administration of the project-control effort. This periodic reevaluation approach, coupled with the redefinition and amendment of projects, provides an effective way to keep the research effort under reasonable and proper control.

(c) RESEARCH FUNCTION INTERNAL AUDIT ACTIVITIES

In many respects, an internal audit review of the research activity offers some of the greatest potential rewards in a very real operational auditing sense. At the lowest level, internal audit can verify compliance with stated operational procedures, including the authorization of research projects and the accuracy of the cost records and reports that cover the work. At the next level, it may be possible for internal audit to appraise the level of administrative efficiency in terms of the way people are performing their jobs. It is also possible to evaluate the extent of collaboration with groups outside the research function and to assess the tangible results of that collaboration leading to a recommendation to curtail, modify, or expand specific projects. At the highest level, it may be possible to evaluate to a reasonable extent the total research effort on the basis of what it has cost and what it has produced. The achievement of these internal audit goals is not easy because of the specialized areas covered, but they can be largely accomplished by an internal auditor, even though not a technically trained engineer or scientist.

As was discussed for the engineering function, an internal auditor may face some significant challenges in announcing and attempting to perform a review of the research function. Research personnel, all the way through top functional management, are often highly educated in their own specialized fields. Internal audit may face a combination of expressed annoyance and arrogance. After defining the need for a review through internal audit's risk-analysis process, the planned audit should first be discussed with the organization management responsible for the research function. Internal audit should take care to discuss its concerns and planned audit objectives, and should emphasize that they will endeavor not to delay any research activities and to primarily emphasize internal controls.

The actual audit procedures for financial, operational, and computer audit activities are similar to those discussed for engineering processes. The sections following only discuss some differences in these audit procedures.

(i) Research Function Financial Audit Considerations.

A research function should use project-management techniques very similar to those described for the engineering process. A prime difference is that for reasons of confidentiality, project reporting will often not be as open as for engineering projects. Research projects may use code names to disguise the activity from outsiders, and members of the research team may be operating under conditions of confidentiality. Internal auditors who simply send the research project manager an engagement letter announcing the planned audit may encounter major objections on many levels. Some advance discussion with management is often necessary.

Whether the internal audit risk-assessment analysis points to a review of the overall research function or of a specific research project, the internal auditors should carefully review the planned objectives of the review before proceeding further. The auditors may then want to discuss the audit plan with a member of management responsible for research. If internal audit properly explains that it is assessing internal financial controls over research projects, it should receive no objections. However, a given research project may be in a key development phase, and management may ask internal audit to postpone the review. If reasonable, the planned audit should probably be postponed.

Internal audit should recognize that the boundary between research function financial and operational controls is very thin and what may appear to be a financial control to one person will an operational control to another. When announcing the review, internal audit should make the point clear that it may be reviewing some project controls of an operational nature that have financial implications as well. The actual review of research project management controls is very similar to the audit procedures for reviews of engineering project management financial controls, as described in Figure 26.3. A major difference is that internal audit will probably not find a large number of projects in process at any point in time and individual research project selection may not be necessary. However, for any project reviewed, internal audit should find the same types of authorization, project-reporting, and project-review controls described for engineering projects.

(ii) Research Function Operational Audit Procedures. Operational audit procedures for a review of the research function are also similar to those discussed for the engineering function, and the audit procedures described in Figure 26.4 will also apply here. If anything, security, documentation, and housekeeping processes are more important here due to the confidential nature of many research projects. Internal audit will typically have to tread very carefully when reviewing these research activities. Even more than engineering functions, the research function may question the qualifications of the internal audit team.

In addition to the operational audit security- and documentation-related audit steps described in Figure 26.4 and also applicable for research, internal audit may also want to review procedures surrounding the research function personnel area as part of its operational review. Confidentiality issues can be critical here, and more extensive pre-employment background checks perhaps should be performed for various key researchers. In addition, members of the research function may argue that they have need to publish their work in professional journals, even though this may potentially risk research project confidentiality.

Figure 26.6 contains audit procedures for reviews of research function personnel matters. These steps should be included with the Figure 26.4 engineering-related audit procedures for an operational review of the research function. As with engineering processes, internal audit should not attempt to second-guess actual research procedures but should continue to look at the basic internal controls.

(iii) Research Function Computer Audit Procedures. A research function will typically make extensive use of computer systems to maintain documentation, perform specialized computations or modeling, and simulate various processes. In addition, a research function will have the same project-management system needs described for engi-

Figure 26.6 Objectives for Review of Research Function Personnel Procedures

Obj. 26.06.01	All research projects should be authorized, funded, and approved by proper levels of management.
Obj. 26.06.02	A clear line of demarcation should be in place between research activities and those applicable to normal production products; care should be taken to assure that costs are properly classified between these two.
Obj. 26.06.03	A project-management reporting system should be in place so that research activities, including progress goals, are reported to appropriate levels of management on a regular basis.
Obj. 26.06.04	Research work areas should be orderly and well secured, such that work is secure from outside interference and observation.
Obj. 26.06.05	Procedures should be in place to assure that all research work is documented in a manner to protect the organization from any potential future patent claims.
Obj. 26.06.06	Research personnel should be required to sign confidentiality and ''noncompetitive'' agreements to assure that their research products will remain within the organization.
Obj. 26.06.07	The same budgetary, project, and capital authorization controls and procedures in place throughout the remainder of the engineering organization should also apply to the research function.
Obj. 26.06.08	Researchers attending technical conferences and publishing in professional journals should obtain approval, in advance, for these activities and should report on their results through published summaries or copies of the published materials.

neering operations, and the audit procedures described in Figure 26.4 can be of use to internal audit performing operational audit reviews of the research function.

Research workstations, as well as the previously discussed engineering workstations, often provide some unique control exposures. Their users, highly educated and skilled research scientists, may have strong analytical skills but not a proper understanding of system controls. A specialized, controls-oriented review of the research computer system would often be of value, pointing out any areas where controls need improvements.

General guidelines for reviews of specialized workstation client-server systems were discussed in Chapter 16. These procedures emphasize the need for appropriate evaluations of the specialized application software used for research-related activity. The research function may use very specialized software to perform computations, develop graphic models, and perform other research-oriented activities. While internal audit may not understand some of the specialized computational techniques in use here, the audit procedures emphasize good general controls.

(iv) Sample Research-Related Findings and Recommendations

A: Research Results Not Properly Maintained.   As part of the review of the research laboratories, we observed activities surrounding Project ZZ. We observed considerable experimentation but saw little evidence of the researchers assigned to this project preparing documentation covering their experiments. When we asked to see the documentation prepared for the multiple experiments surrounding Project ZZ, we were advised that little attention was given to documenting failed tests. The researchers assigned were primarily looking for successful results.

Recommendation. Complete research documentation covering the results of all tests should be prepared by the responsible researchers. These research workpaper notes should then be reviewed and approved by research management. These procedures will result in better management of the overall research effort.

B: Research Fixed Assets Not Properly Authorized. In our review of research project expenditures, we identified several items of test equipment that were charged as expenses as part of research efforts but which should have been capitalized as fixed assets. For example, a test oven was purchased for Project ZZ activities. Its high cost and anticipated future use indicate that it should have been capitalized as a fixed asset.

Recommendation. Research function management should review organization capitalization policies and inform staff members of these procedures. All major research function expenditures over the last year should be reviewed to determine if classifications were proper. Reclassifications should be made as appropriate.

C: Program Library Controls Require Improvements. In our review of research workstation computer system controls, we observed that many of the researchers have programming skills and that they frequently make changes to their research diagnostic programs. We were advised that these program changes are made to improve research calculations and to improve the presentations of research results. However, we observed that these program changes are made as part of research efforts and with no management approval. This creates a risk that programs may be modified inappropriately and may yield incorrect research results.

Recommendation. All research workstation program libraries should be secured to prevent unauthorized program access or modifications. Lacking strong logical security controls over these systems, source libraries should be placed on a single, secured file server with a designated person or function responsible for library updates. Other researchers should operate only from approved source versions of this program library.

26-4 ORGANIZATION'S TOTAL QUALITY MANAGEMENT PROGRAM

Until recent years, when organizations began to recognize the importance of quality programs throughout their operations, quality concerns were generally a manufacturing- or engineering-related responsibility. Quality-management and control procedures typically involved the inspection and monitoring of processes to attempt to minimize errors. This function was usually called *quality control* or *quality assurance,* and is discussed in the section following.

It is necessary to understand what is meant by the concept of quality in the modern organization. Quality can be defined in terms of customer perceptions of an organization's products relative to their expectations. That is, the buyers of an organization's products, whether manufactured goods or services, expect a certain level of quality. Even if an organization manufactures a product that will work 99.9% of the time, customers may expect a higher success rate and may then perceive that the organization is producing goods of poorer quality.

In order to improve the quality of its end products, many modern organizations have initiated programs to raise the level of quality throughout their organizations. These efforts have been organized to cover all functions of the organization, ranging from the manufacturing floor to the accounting department to the mail room. These quality programs involve at least some participation by employees throughout the organization, and are often called total quality management (TQM) programs.

Total quality management programs are new, but very important to the modern organization. Many organizations facing competitive pressures have installed these programs with the objective of improving their product or service quality. Although their objectives and expectations may be high, total quality programs can be very expensive to the modern organization. This section briefly discusses the concepts of total quality management as well as approaches to auditing that function. Because total quality management programs are new to the modern organization, they have not often been candidates for internal audits. This is again an area where internal audit can make an effective contribution through a review of TQM controls.

Internal auditors may have a potentially dual role and interest in the organization's TQM program. Since quality management is an operational area within the organization, internal audit needs to understand and potentially subject quality management to the same types of operational reviews that are performed in many other areas of the organization. However, internal audit may play a somewhat different role in the organization's TQM process. Many TQM activities are similar to the operational reviews performed by internal audit. Rather than viewing quality management as an interloper, internal auditors are increasingly participating in their organization's TQM programs. They may assist quality management in assessing the organization's quality programs or may even take on some of these quality programs themselves. This newer, evolving TQM role for the modern internal auditor is discussed in Chapter 33.

(a) TOTAL QUALITY PROGRAMS IN THE ORGANIZATION

Organizations have historically established fairly loose quality standards, assuming that as long as some percentage of products was produced with no errors, there was no problem. This is the concept behind the classic quality control programs discussed in the next section. However, the competitive pressures of today's global economy require that the modern organization produce its products with zero defects. This concept of zero defects means that the organization must meet customer requirements the first time it produces the product, and this must be repeated every time, with nonperformance considered unacceptable.

The concept of zero defects is not particularly new. Zero-defect programs were initiated in the United States in the early 1960s during the space travel program's efforts to place a man on the moon. In order to improve the quality of manufactured goods, many organizations asked their employees to sign a zero-defects pledge in which they agreed to try to make no mistakes. This author recalls being asked to sign such a pledge as a 1960s U.S. Army Vietnam-era draftee. The problem with many of these zero-defects programs was that there was little follow-up beyond the initial pep talks and employee brochures. Organizations and their employees soon dropped into philosophies that their quality was good enough and that inspection functions would catch any important errors.

Competitive pressures have forced many modern organizations to realize that a system of producing products that are almost correct and then correcting them later just does not work. Inspections and subsequent rework add to the overall cost, and competitors are producing outputs that are right the first time. For example, manufacturing organizations in Japan adopted strong quality programs starting in the early 1950s. Over the years, their high-quality products have captured many worldwide markets. Established organizations, particularly those in the U.S. manufacturing sector, have seen their market shares erode because of the high quality of competing Japanese products and have adopted quality programs.

W. Edward Deming was an early pioneer in this TQM movement. He went to Japan after World War II and taught the principles of TQM to the recovering, postwar Japanese industries. While he was well received there, other industrial nations such as the United States paid little heed to Deming until recently. The Deming philosophy for TQM has been refined over the years. Deming has summarized his recipe for TQM in what he calls his Fourteen Points and Seven Deadly Diseases[2] which are summarized in Figures 26.7 and 26.8. The Fourteen Points outline some of the necessary changes an organization must make in order to establish a TQM program. Seven Deadly Diseases suggest things that will prevent an organization from becoming a quality operation and point to other internal problems within organizations.

This growing interest in quality is perhaps best illustrated by the active competition in the United States for the Malcolm Baldrige National Quality Award. Sponsored by private industry but governed by the National Institute for Science and Technology (NIST), up to six awards are given annually to major manufacturing and service organizations, as well as to small businesses. Organizations apply for the award themselves and must go through a tough assessment of their TQM programs and the differences those programs have made in the competitive strength of the award applicant. Figure 26.9 shows the categories and point scores used for awarding a recent Malcolm Baldrige Award. Customer satisfaction is a major category here and should be a key element of any organization's TQM program.

In recent years, many authors and consultants have described various approaches to TQM. These approaches all have similar objectives but differ in method. Management, after attending one seminar or another, may adopt that seminar's TQM approach. However, most of these TQM approaches consist of the following elements:

- Formal programs to achieve organization quality
- Quality education and implementation management
- Quality-improvement benchmarking.

This chapter will not attempt to discuss the unique elements of each of the various TQM approaches, but the overall, general approach of TQM as implemented in many organizations. Internal audit should spend some time with the team responsible for TQM in internal audit's organization, attend selected quality seminars, and read selected literature to gain a better understanding of this important program in the modern organization.

(i) Programs to Achieve Organization Quality.   An objective of TQM is to create quality by eliminating the root causes of potential errors from the beginning of any process.

---

[2] Mary Walton, *The Deming Management Method* (New York: Perigee Books, 1986).

Figure 26.7 W. Edward Deming's 14 Points

1. *Create constancy of purpose for the improvement of products and services.* Rather than just making money, the organization's role should be to provide jobs through innovation, research, constant improvement and maintenance.
2. *Adopt a new philosophy of quality.* A new "religion" is needed where mistakes and negativism are unacceptable.
3. *Cease dependence on mass inspections.* A company typically inspects products as they come off of production, and defective products are either scrapped or reworked. In effect, workers are being paid to make defects and then to correct them. Quality comes not from inspections but from an improvement of the process.
4. *End the practice of awarding business on the price alone.* The lowest price vendors frequently supply goods of a low quality. Purchasing selections should be made on the basis of best quality, and long-term supplier relationships should be established to improve quality.
5. *Constantly and continually improve the system of production and service.* Quality improvement is not a one-time effort.
6. *Institute training.* Workers often cannot do their jobs correctly because no one has told them how.
7. *Institute leadership.* Leading consists of helping people to do a better job and learning by objective methods who is in need of individual help.
8. *Drive out fear.* Employees are afraid to ask questions even when they do not understand what is right or wrong. It is necessary for better quality and productivity that people feel secure.
9. *Break down barriers between staff areas.* Staff departments or units often compete with each other or have goals that are in conflict. Efforts are needed to get everyone on the same program.
10. *Eliminate slogans, exhortations and targets for the workforce.* These never help people to do a better job. The work force should put up its own slogans.
11. *Eliminate numerical quotas.* Quotas take account only of numbers, not the quality of materials. They are usually a guarantee of inefficiency and high cost.
12. *Remove barriers to pride of workmanship.* People are eager to do a good job, but too often misguided supervisors, faulty equipment and defective materials stand in the way.
13. *Institute a vigorous program of education and retraining.* Both management and the workforce need to be retrained in new methods, including teamwork and statistical techniques.
14. *Take action to accomplish the transformation.* A top management team should develop a plan of action to carry out the quality mission. A critical mass of people in the company must understand the overall quality program.

This requires a strong program of *error prevention,* where all employees must look at all of the processes they perform and identify all possibilities for error. Every member of the organization must take ownership of their work outputs and become involved with a process of preventing errors before they occur.

TQM is based on the premise that all work is a process, whether traditional manufacturing operations, service related functions, or internal office administrative activities. This process-oriented concept requires all members of the organization to rethink how they perform their jobs.

A process can be defined as a set of continuous operational steps such as the operations in a highly mechanized chemical manufacturing plant, where raw materials come in the door and finished products are delivered at the end of the production line. Virtually all operational activities can be defined in a similar manner. For example, the secretary preparing a letter can view the boss as the supplier and the recipient of the letter as the customer. However, since the boss initially defines what is to be said in the letter, the boss's input to create the letter is also part of the same process. Both must understand their responsibilities to avoid errors.

A key element of TQM is to understand the various processes used in the organization. The next step is to use that model. There are typically five TQM steps using this process model.

1. *Define the process.* Each unit within the organization should define the various processes performed by that unit. This may be as simple as weighing the letter to determine the correct postage for a mail room unit. Processes can be much more complex for other units.

2. *Identify the outputs and process customers.* This step often requires some analysis. Many organization units, particularly those in staff functions, do not think of their work in terms of having customers. However, virtually all processes have some types of outputs and customers for them. For example, a data-processing operations center produces output reports, terminal displays, or data files from its various applications. The customers here may be the ultimate users, or other applications receiving the output reports.

Figure 26.8 W. Edward Deming's Seven Deadly Diseases

1. *Lack of constancy of purpose.* A company that is without constancy of purpose has no long-range plans for staying in business. Management is insecure, and so are employees.
2. *Emphasis on short-term profits.* Looking to increase the quarterly dividend undermines quality and productivity.
3. *Evaluation by performance, merit rating, or annual review of performance.* The effects of these are devastating—teamwork is destroyed, rivalry is nurtured. Performance ratings build fear, and leave people bitter, despondent, and beaten. They also encourage mobility of management.
4. *Mobility of management.* Job-hopping managers never understand the companies that they work for and are never there long enough to follow through on long-term changes that are necessary for quality and productivity.
5. *Running a company on visible figures alone.* The most important figures are unknown and unknowable—the multiplier effect of a happy customer, for example. Diseases 6 and 7 are pertinent only in the United States.
6. *Excessive medical costs.* Lack of proper safety and health programs will lead to excessive medical costs.
7. *Excessive costs of warranty, fueled by lawyers that work on contingency fees.* Our legal system encourages lawyers to bring charges on what appear to be questionable matters. Caution is important.

Figure 26.9   Malcolm Baldrige Award Scoring Criteria[1]

Customer-Driven Quality

Quality is judged by the customer. All product and service attributes that contribute value to the customer and lead to customer satisfaction and preference must be addressed appropriately in quality systems. Value, satisfaction, and preference may be influenced by many factors throughout the customer's overall purchase, ownership, and service experiences. This includes the relationship between the company and the customers—the trust and confidence in products and services—that leads to loyalty and preference. This concept of quality includes those that enhance them and differentiate them from competing offerings. Such enhancement and differentiation may include new offerings, as well as unique product-product, service-service, or product-service combinations.

Customer-driven quality is thus a strategic concept. It is directed toward market share gain and customer retention. It demands constant sensitivity to emerging customer and market requirements, developments in technology, and rapid and flexible responses to customer and market requirements. Such requirements extend well beyond defect and error reduction, merely meeting specifications, or reducing complaints. Nevertheless, defect and error reduction and elimination of causes of dissatisfaction contribute significantly to the customers' views of quality and are thus important parts of customer-driven quality. In addition, the company's approach to recovering from defects and errors is crucial to its improving both quality and relationships with customers.

Leadership

A company's senior leaders must create clear and visible quality values and high expectations. Reinforcement of the values and expectations requires their personal commitment and involvement. The leaders must take part in the creation of strategies, systems, and methods for achieving excellence. The systems and methods need to guide all activities and decisions of the company and encourage participation and creativity by all employees. Through their regular personal involvement in visible activities, such as planning, review of company quality performance, and recognizing employees for quality achievement, the senior leaders serve as role models reinforcing the values and encouraging leadership in all levels of management.

Continuous Improvement

Achieving the highest levels of quality and competitiveness requires a well-defined and well-executed approach to continuous improvement. Such improvement needs to be part of all operations and of all work unit activities of a company. Improvements may be of several types: (1) enhancing value to the customer through new and improved products and services; (2) reducing errors, defects, and waste; (3) improving responsiveness and cycle time performance; and (4) improving productivity and effectiveness in the use of all resources. Thus, improvement is driven not only by the objective to provide better quality but also by the need to be responsive and efficient—both conferring additional marketplace advantages. To meet all of these objectives, the process of continuous improvement must contain regular cycles of planning, execution, and evaluation. This requires a basis—preferably a quantitative basis—for assessing progress, and for deriving information for future cycles of improvement.

Figure 26.9 (*Continued*)

Full Participation

Meeting the company's quality and performance objectives requires a fully committed, well-trained and involved workforce. Reward and recognition systems need to reinforce full participation in company quality objectives. Factors bearing upon the safety, health, well-being, and morale of employees need to be part of the continuous improvement objectives and activities of the company. Employees need education and training in quality skills related to performing their work and to understanding and solving quality-related problems. Training should be reinforced through on-the-job applications of learning, involvement, and empowerment. Increasingly, training and participation need to be tailored to a more diverse workforce.

Fast Response

Success in competitive markets increasingly demands ever-shorter product and service introduction cycles and more rapid response to customers. Indeed, fast response itself is often a major quality attribute. Reduction in cycle times and rapid response to customers can occur when work processes are designed to meet both quality and response goals. Accordingly, response time improvement should be included as a major focus within all quality improvement processes of work units. This requires that all designs, objectives, and work unit activities include measurement of cycle time and responsiveness. Major improvements in response time may require work processes and paths to be simplified and shortened. Response time improvements often "drive" simultaneous improvements in quality and productivity. Hence it is highly beneficial to consider response time, quality, and productivity objectives together.

Design Quality and Prevention

Quality systems should place strong emphasis on design quality—problem prevention achieved through building quality into products and services and into the processes through which they are produced. Excellent design quality may lead to major reductions in "downstream" waste, problems, and associated costs. Design quality includes the creation of fault-tolerant (robust) processes and products. A major design issue is the design-to-introduction cycle time. To meet the demands of ever more rapidly changing markets, companies need to focus increasingly on shorter product and service introduction times. Consistent with the theme of design quality and prevention, continuous improvement and corrective actions need to emphasize interventions "upstream"—at the earliest stages in processes. This approach yields the maximum overall benefits of improvements and corrections. Such upstream intervention also needs to take into account the company's suppliers.

Long-Range Outlook

Achieving quality and market leadership requires a future orientation and long-term commitment to customers, employees, stockholders, and suppliers. Strategies, plans, and resource allocations need to reflect these commitments and address training, employee development, technology evolution, and other factors that bear upon quality. A key part of the long-term commitment is regular review and assessment of progress relative to long-term plans.

Figure 26.9 *(Continued)*

Management by Fact

Meeting quality and performance goals of the company requires that process management be based upon reliable information, data, and analysis. Facts and data needed for quality assessment and quality improvement are of many types, including: customer, product and service performance, operations, market, competitive comparisons, supplier, employee-related, and cost and financial. *Analysis* refers to the process of extracting larger meaning from data to support evaluation and decision making at various levels within the company. Such analysis may entail using data individually or in combination to reveal information—such as trends, projections, and cause and effect—that might not be evident without analysis. Facts, data, and analysis support a variety of company purposes, such as planning, reviewing company performance, improving operations, and comparing company quality performance with competitors.

A major consideration relating to use of data and analysis to improve competitive performance involves the creation and use of performance indicators. Performance indicators are measurable characteristics of products, services, processes, and operations the company uses to evaluate performance and track progress. The indicators should be selected to best represent the factors that determine customer satisfaction and operational performance. A system of indicators tied to customer and/or company performance requirements represents a clear and objective basis for aligning all activities of the company toward common goals. Through the analysis of data obtained in the tracking processes, the indicators themselves may be evaluated and changed. For example, indicators selected to measure product and service quality may be judged by how well they correlate with customer satisfaction.

Partnership Development

Companies should seek to build internal and external partnerships, serving mutual and larger community interests. Such partnerships might include those that promote labor-management cooperation, such as agreements with unions, cooperation with suppliers and customers, and linkages with education organizations. Partnerships should consider longer-term objectives as well as short-term needs, thereby creating a basis for mutual investments. The building of partnerships should address means of regular communication, approaches to evaluating progress, means for modifying objectives, and methods to accommodate changing conditions.

Public Responsibility

A company's customer requirements and quality system objectives should address areas of corporate citizenship and responsibility. These include business ethics, public health and safety, environment, and sharing of quality-related information in the company's business and geographic communities. Health, safety, and environmental considerations need to take into account the life cycle of production, distribution, and use of products. Plans should include problem avoidance and company response if avoidance fails, including how to maintain public trust and confidence. Inclusion of public responsibility areas within a quality system means not only meeting all local, state, and federal legal and regulatory requirements, but also treating these and related requirements as areas for continuous improvement. In addition, companies should support—within reasonable limits of their resources—national, industry, trade, and community activities to share nonproprietary quality-related information.

---

[1] 1992 Award Criteria, Malcolm Baldrige National Quality Award.

3. *Determine the requirements for outputs.* After defining the customers for a process, its owner must attempt to define what these customers really want. This usually requires interviews, surveys, or other analyses. Although it is easy to assume what the customer wants, an analysis may reveal different answers. Output requirements should be defined in measurable units if possible.

4. *Identify the inputs and suppliers.* Once the process outputs have been defined, this step is often easier. However, the process owner must consider all of the various inputs that flow into a process, such as commodities from outside suppliers, intermediate production items from earlier processes, and formal decisions from managers.

5. *Determine the requirements for the inputs.* This step considers what is needed to allow the process to be completed in a quality manner. This may involve quality standards for materials supplied to a manufacturing process, or a requirement that all inputs to an automated accounting system are in balance using correct account numbers.

Quality can be achieved only if the owner of each process demands that all suppliers meet the organization's input requirements in order, in turn, to produce quality outputs. This can be relatively easy if the supplier is an internal function. It is also fairly easy if a significant portion of the supplier's business is with the organization. However, an organization faces a much greater challenge in trying to impress smaller suppliers on the importance of its TQM program.

Once the organization has defined its work processes, the next step for TQM is a program for process improvement. The idea here is not to install a series of fixes, patches, or appraisal inspections to correct problems, but to understand the basic process and install appropriate corrections. This is a continuous process where problems are identified, solutions to those problems are defined and implemented, and the success of those improvements is measured and evaluated. The result may be a need for further analysis or a revised solution.

A TQM program is of little value unless the organization has a formal commitment to improving quality. This commitment must be an organization-wide process, starting with senior management and cascading through all levels of the organization. When assessing the progress of a TQM effort, internal audit should look for a strong level of commitment starting with support from the top and continuing through active and ongoing efforts to improve the quality of all processes.

(ii) Quality Education and Implementation Management. A successful TQM program requires both commitment and ongoing management direction. The three major components for managing the quality process are a *quality steering committee, quality councils,* and what can be called *process improvement teams.* A TQM organization for a multiunit manufacturing organization may have committees and teams that span multiple levels of the organization. They can be partially staffed with permanent positions, but are generally extra efforts in addition to normal job duties.

The quality steering committee should be comprised of members of upper management as well as representatives from other groups and levels. This would be the senior committee responsible for setting the overall direction of the organization's TQM effort. Their responsibilities would be to:

- Define the initial strategies and objectives of the total quality management program.

- Define the organization structure and responsibilities for all members of the TQM effort.

- Establish a quality-improvement education program.

- Develop and promote organization-wide quality-awareness programs.

- Monitor the progress of all elements of the quality program for consistency and effectiveness.

While the steering committee would typically be responsible for the overall guidance and direction of the TQM program, most quality improvement efforts take place within what are often called *quality councils*. These committees would be established at all levels of an organization. They would implement improvement programs designed to eliminate errors in the work process. They would probably also implement a quality-awareness program within their function and determine that members receive the appropriate level of TQM education to help them to implement the program.

The process improvement teams are the front line troops responsible for identifying areas at all levels where quality can be improved, and then for developing the means to improve that quality. The teams would use a process-improvement model as described in Figure 26.10 and would set quality and productivity goals. The teams would also be responsible for proposing and implementing quality-improvement changes, many of which might be implemented through fairly low-level, low-cost types of changes. For example, the team might identify that a small change in the plant floor layout, as well as a couple of minor changes in the order-scheduling system, could improve the time required for shipping completed goods. The costs here would be relatively minor compared to the value of the results.

More significant quality improvements identified by the process-improvement teams might be passed up through the councils or the overall steering committee for consideration. The more senior committees can usually request capital funding or otherwise implement more significant changes. The basic idea behind a TQM program is that all members of the teams should identify, analyze, measure, and recommend solutions for quality improvements within their own units and throughout the organization.

An essential factor for the success of any quality program is that all employees assume ownership of the quality process and receive adequate training including quality-awareness, quality-improvement, and team-building concepts. Figure 26.11 outlines TQM course descriptions that would normally be required for all members of the organization involved in the process-improvement teams. The idea is to build a level of enthusiasm for the process, get the members talking in a common language, and encourage active participation in the quality program.

(iii) Quality-Improvement Benchmarking.   A quality-improvement program needs some means to measure its progress and determine its results. Change for the sake of change is of little value. The organization should monitor the TQM process changes in terms of improvements in results as well as improvements in comparison to competitors. The latter is called benchmarking. The TQM program should try to see how it compares with other organizations that are generally viewed as successful. Based on this comparison,

Figure 26.10   Elements of Quality Management

I. Quality Control

Depending on the significant processes or functions of the organizations, develop procedures to measure quality through the following general techniques:

- *Inspection.* Processes need to be reviewed on an ongoing basis; this is similar to the internal audit process.
- *Testing.* In addition to reviewing through inspection, appropriate procedures for testing the produce or process may be needed.
- *Equipment calibration.* This is more common in a manufacturing process, but the equipment used to monitor the process must be closely calibrated.
- *New product controls.* The best place to establish a quality process or product is before it has been released to production; this is similar to preimplementation auditing.

II. Quality Assurance

The purpose of the overall quality process is to satisfy the customer—whether the outside buyer of a manufactured product or an internal customer in another department. Procedures necessary to establish a process include:

- *Identifying customer objectives.*
- *Developing quality processes*
- *Establishing systematic controls to monitor quality*
- *Measuring conformance to quality requirements continually*

III. Quality Planning

A process should be in place to ensure an ongoing planning of quality processes. Elements include:

- *Identifying the customer.* In many instances, an organization fails to realize who are its key customers. For example, an organization may concentrate on selling to its independent dealer network, forgetting who are the end purchasers from those dealers.
- *Identifying customer requirements and translating to needs*
- *Developing the quality product or process*
- *Measuring the established requirements against the developed product or process*

IV. Quality Measurement

A procedure should be in place to measure the results of any quality effort. Measures include:

- *Quality costs.* Cost is always one of the best ways to measure the results of a quality initiative, whether through reduced costs because of fewer production inspection failures or more efficient materials procurement.
- *Customer feedback.* Surveys, complaint letters, or any variety of techniques can be used here. In all cases, a process should be in place to measure quality from the standpoint of the customer.
- *Company's business continues.* A final, long-term measure of quality.

---

the organization can perform a self assessment and goals can be established to improve its quality program.

Another way to measure the progress of TQM improvements is through various statistical measurements, including control charts, histogram measurements, and other statistical control measurements similar to those discussed in Chapter 11. These are similar to the quality-control diagrams described in the next section of this chapter. The essential difference with TQM is that an organization would use these charts as a measure to

Figure 26.11   Quality Assurance Familiarization Course Outline

I. *Concepts of quality management.* This section would introduce members to the ideas and theories of the pioneers of the quality movement—Deming, Juran, Crosby, etc.—and how those concepts apply to the organization.

II. *Quality management teamwork.* Although it may be organized differently depending on the organization, all attendees should understand the quality structure in their organization and how they relate to the overall organization.

III. *Establishing quality measurement goals.* The focus here is on how quality program initiatives and processes are established for various procedures.

IV. *Measurements and analysis.* Once a quality program has been established, procedures need to be in place to measure its performance. All employees should understand how these tools can be installed, used, and improved upon.

V. *Installing continuous improvement.* Formal processes should be in place to take corrective actions once some measure of quality appears to be below standard. All members of the organization should understand how they can help to initiate and install improved processes.

VI. *Rewards of quality.* The organization's quality improvement incentive programs would be explained, including how all employees can qualify to participate.

determine if any errors still exist, while a quality-control function uses these same measures to determine if errors are within tolerable limits.

(b) TOTAL QUALITY PROGRAM INTERNAL CONTROLS

Total quality management programs are so different for staff and line functions in many organizations that management often does not think of them in terms of their associated internal controls. Programs are often organized following the philosophical concepts of TQM, with little concern about internal control. However, an organization can become so consumed with its TQM program that some controls may be weakened. For example, an organization may decide, as part of its TQM program, that various paperwork forms and procedures are slowing down operations and increasing costs, and they may eliminate some paperwork even though it has strong control purposes. As an outside reviewer and not a member of the TQM team, internal audit can ask questions about any procedures that may have been eliminated in an organization's enthusiasm to improve or simplify processes. There must be a balance between the TQM-related efficiencies and good controls.

In management's enthusiasm to establish a TQM program—often in response to competitive pressures—a TQM program can be established without giving proper consideration to budgets or internal controls. In addition, since the program may be run as an additional task in the course of an employee's normal workday, proper consideration may not be given to the costs associated with the TQM program, including the use of resources such as floor space or computer time. The major cost is often the personnel time allocated to the TQM program. Hours may be spent on TQM activities and charged to normal work projects, distorting the true cost of the TQM program.

An organization should build internal controls around its TQM program similar to those over engineering projects, as discussed earlier in this chapter. Budgets should be established for all levels of the TQM program, and time and expenses should be measured against those budgets. In addition, senior management should establish a measurable set of objectives for the TQM organization, allowing them to assess the quality of the TQM program itself.

(c) AUDITING THE ORGANIZATION'S TOTAL QUALITY PROGRAM

Internal auditors are often asked to participate in a review team as part of the organization's TQM program. This section discusses procedures for reviewing controls within the organization's TQM function. Although an organization may be expending significant resources in researching and promoting its TQM program, management may consider it too new or too important for an internal audit review. However, when consideration is given to the total impact of the TQM effort, it could end up fairly high in any internal audit risk ranking. A TQM program certainly is a potential candidate for financial or operational control reviews.

Because some TQM quality-improvement review activities can seem very similar to internal audit's operational reviews, internal audit must take care that its review does not appear to be based on competitive rivalry. A professional internal audit organization should not even consider a review based on this motivation, but a planned and announced review could give the wrong impressions. At a minimum, internal auditors who have recently been participants in a TQM review team should not be part of any effort to go back and review the TQM effort.

Reviews of the TQM function should be planned with care. Internal audit can explain to the quality steering committee that the review is designed to identify and improve internal controls over the TQM process just as those teams work to improve other organization processes.

(i) Total Quality Program Financial Audit Considerations. As discussed in a previous paragraph, the financial controls over a TQM function should be similar to the financial controls found in an engineering-control function. Audit steps are also similar to those described for engineering in Figure 26.4. However, internal audit will encounter some different control considerations in an organization-wide TQM function. Because a TQM effort takes the entire organization into consideration, the financial-control procedures will often cross multiple departmental lines, adding complexities to the review process.

Control procedures for a financial review of an organization's TQM function are general because there is no one commonly accepted way of organizing TQM financial controls. However, internal audit should always consider some of the basic concepts of the organization's financial control structure when embarking upon a review of the financial controls of the TQM function.

(ii) Total Quality Program Operational Audit Procedures. An operational review of an organization's TQM program will probably focus on the effectiveness and efficiency of the TQM program, as well as on recordkeeping issues. Because of the many similarities between a TQM program and internal audit functions, an operational review will often follow many of the procedures outlined in Chapter 33, on internal audit quality-assurance reviews. These are peer reviews of an internal audit department itself. They normally are conducted by a specialized group within the internal audit function or by qualified outsiders such as internal auditors from another organization or a public accounting firm. The type of review approach used is very similar to the operational review of a TQM function.

A good first step for internal audit when planning a review of the organization's TQM function is to attend all levels of the quality education offerings, not as a participant but as an observer. That is, internal audit does not want to prepare for participation in the TQM programs but to understand and observe the approach used.

The quality of the education efforts is a good starting point in a TQM operational audit. Some organizations send their staffs to outside providers for this education. This can be expensive and may not address the needs of the organization. The other alternative, of course, is to use in-house instructors to present the materials. The risk here is that the organization may not have the appropriate training resources or skills to effectively impart TQM concepts to the overall organization.

The assigned audit team should do some research and reading on the TQM approach used. The program will often be based upon the writings of one or another TQM experts, such as W. Edward Deming, cited earlier, or Phillip Crosby.[3] Internal audit should study these books, as well as others on the topic, to gain a general understanding of the organization's approach to TQM. In addition, as would be part of any audit, internal TQM standards and other materials should be reviewed.

As stated previously, a major focus of an operational review of a TQM function is its own controls over records and procedures. Because a typical TQM program places considerable pressure on all teams to show improvements, results may be reported up to the quality steering committee with a bias toward the positive. The TQM program should be able to identify these reporting or performance problems through its own procedures, but an independent internal audit review would be able to attest to top management that the TQM program is working as expected.

Figure 26.12 outlines procedures for an operational review of the organization's TQM function. While these steps could be used for a review of the entire TQM program, internal audit might be more effective in initially reviewing a single unit. In this way, it can report its findings to both the quality steering committee and to top management.

(iii) Total Quality Program Computer Audit Procedures. Total quality management programs are sufficiently new to many organizations that they have not established any form of specialized computer systems. However, any TQM program will require a fair amount of recordkeeping for the various recorded statistics and assignments made as part of the program. These records will usually be stored on some type of a database, often located on a microcomputer system or some other workstation device. The TQM group may require the support of a programmer to develop database structures and output reports.

Internal audit should determine what types of computer applications are used to support the TQM program and consider an application review of these systems. Procedures for these reviews were discussed in Chapter 17.

TQM systems may operate on a freestanding workstation computer system. This

---

[3] Crosby, Phil, *Quality is Still Free,* New York: McGraw-Hill, 1995. This is Crosby's most recent book on the topic. He originally wrote *Quality is Free*, also by McGraw-Hill in 1978.

Figure 26.12   Objectives for an Operational Review of the TQM Function

Note: These internal audit objectives are roughly based on Deming's 14 Quality Management Points as described in Figure 26.7. An internal auditor should use these to assess the effectiveness of the organization's TQM program.

Obj. 26.16.01   Management should exhibit a long-term commitment to its TQM program, as exhibited in references to it in strategic plans and other materials.

Obj. 26.16.02   Evidence should be in place to demonstrate that all levels of personnel have subscribed to the organization's TQM program through documented acknowledgments after a formal training session as well as through other evidence.

Obj. 26.16.03   Formal programs should be in place to monitor quality of products through the uses of statistical methods rather than mass inspections; documented records should demonstrate the results of these programs.

Obj. 26.16.04   Procedures should be in place in all organization processes such that they are continuously monitored for quality and that problems are corrected as they occur.

Obj. 26.16.05   Training programs should be in place so that both existing and new personnel are trained in the organization's TQM philosophy; records should be in place to evidence that activity.

Obj. 26.16.06   Formal programs should be in place to allow personnel at all levels to report problems and suggest improvements; evidence should be in place to demonstrate the success of the program.

Obj. 26.16.07   Cross-functional teams should be in place to monitor quality problems and to take corrective actions where needed.

Obj. 26.16.08   Reward and recognition programs should be in place at all levels to provide incentives for active participation in the TQM program.

Obj. 26.16.09   Partnering programs should be in place to extend the organization's TQM program to key suppliers and to establish communication regarding the program with key customers.

Obj. 26.16.10   The results of the TQM program should be in place through product defect records, surveys of customer satisfaction, or overall organization performance. These results should be monitored with evidence of corrective actions taken as required.

raises a variety of security and integrity-control concerns, as much of the data gathered by the TQM teams may be confidential in nature. The audit should consider assessing these controls as part of any TQM-related review, whether financial or operational. Procedures for workstation control reviews were discussed in Chapter 20.

(iv) Sample Quality-Related Findings and Recommendations

A: Quality Improvement Expected Benefits Not Compared to Costs.   Internal audit surveyed the TQM process-improvement activities in various areas of the organization. We generally found good progress in following TQM methods and in identifying ways to improve the overall quality of operations. However, we also found instances where the costs of developing improvements were not matched to any value to be received from the expected benefits. In particular, we found that over 5,000 hours of TQM team efforts have been expended on the Axylotl Enhancer product line. This is an obsolete technology with a very limited market today. However, we observed no attempt to match TQM costs with expected benefits.

Recommendation.   The quality steering committee should establish guidelines requiring a TQM improvement cost-versus-benefits analysis whenever expected TQM project efforts will exceed 1,000 hours.

B: Accounting Systems Group Not Participating in TQM Programs.   We reviewed the TQM education records to determine if all units of the organization are participating in the TQM evaluation program. We found that members of the accounting systems development group had neither participated in any TQM classes nor were involved in any process-improvement efforts. The manager of this group stated that normal system-development demands prevented this group from participating in TQM projects.

Recommendation.   Members of the quality steering committee should work with the accounting systems group and overall information systems management to gain the active participation of this group in overall TQM efforts. In addition, the quality steering committee should monitor the level of participation in TQM efforts by various departments and should take appropriate corrective actions when necessary.

C: Manufacturing Punch Press Benchmarking Records Inaccurate.   We reviewed the rejected item improvement records for various manufacturing units. We found a high rate of rejected items in the assembly unit and were advised that poor materials from the punch press section were the cause in many instances. We also found that punch press management denied any problem and pointed to their own product quality records. Internal audit observed the punch press operations. Several operators told internal audit that their inspection reports typically showed no errors but that they did not really test their outputs for errors. Because they were previously strongly criticized for high error rates, they ignored quality procedures and reported results with no errors.

Recommendation.   The manufacturing quality council group should meet with punch press operations management and emphasize the need to produce higher-quality parts and to accurately report production results. All members of the group should participate in a special TQM refresher course to reinforce the overall importance of this important quality program.

26-5 MANUFACTURING QUALITY-CONTROL FUNCTION

Although the overall TQM program outlined in the previous section is very important to the organization, most manufacturing or process-oriented functions still need a specific quality-control function to monitor and measure the extent of manufacturing processing errors and to take corrective actions where appropriate. There is a need to sample goods produced from a production process and to determine if quality standards are being met.

Quality control is a sampling and measurement process to determine if production goods are in compliance with established standards. The concept applies to all outputs produced in a large volume, allowing a quality-control evaluator to sample those goods and assess whether they are in compliance with standards. This section discusses procedures, internal controls, and approaches to auditing this quality-control function.

Quality control activities are usually part of the production process, but they extend into the engineering function and may also include other activities. In its simplest terms, quality control has as its mission the achievement of specified quality levels for all products. Statistical sampling methods are often used to measure this quality level.

The need for quality control arises because of the variability found in all parts of the production process, starting with the materials themselves and extending to various aspects of processing and finally to the completed product. Variability at the different stages must be kept within certain ranges so that the final product will conform to a given range of specifications and be able to function in the manner desired. Individual components must comply with acceptable ranges for length, thickness, width, weight, finish, texture, durability, and the like. Determining these specifications and their ranges of acceptable variability leads into some basic management decisions. Unless the smallest component in the illustration meets specifications, the final assembly may not meet overall specifications.

Just as a well-designed sample is important in order to reach a valid audit conclusion, quality-control sampling must also be built around appropriate procedures. However, quality-control sampling is often more of a challenge because of the complexities of the underlying processes. In addition, factors including marketing needs, production conflicts, and costs must be balanced to yield a sound and profitable quality-control operation.

Quality control is often a relatively small and not very visible function in the modern organization, an area often ignored in internal audit's risk-evaluation approach and not even considered for review. However, quality control is an important activity and should be considered as part of the audit universe of auditable entities.

(a) CYCLE OF QUALITY-CONTROL OPERATIONS

Quality control is often viewed only as the manufacturing process where completed products are inspected for final acceptability before delivery to the customer. This is only a minimal part of a comprehensive quality-control function. The broader spectrum of activities involved in the quality-control process can be viewed as follows:

- *Receiving Department Inspection Functions.* Chapter 24 discussed the inspection function of a receiving department. As discussed there, quality control is often responsible for the inspection of materials and components when first received by the organization. This inspection is concerned with protecting the quality level of the final products and is often responsible for acceptance and vendor payment authorization.

- *Intermediate Types of Inspections.* As materials and subassemblies are transferred from one operational group to another, quality control may perform inspections. These interim inspections protect quality levels and ensure a proper transfer of accountability for material quality as it moves to successive work areas.

- *Inspections During the Production Process.* There is often a need to check on how well interim processing operations are being carried out. This type of quality inspection is particularly important for continuous-process operations such as consumer grocery products or automotive assembly lines.

- *Final Inspections of Finished Products.* As products are released by the production department for shipment to customers or transfer to stores, there is often a need for a final inspection. At this point, total efforts of the production department are validated in the form of good final products.

- *Future-Directed Quality-Improvement Programs.* Actions may be taken in various areas which will have a bearing on the quality of the later production. Examples might include training sessions on the importance of quality controls, product design reviews, processing-improvement reviews, or studies of the reliability of the equipment used. These programs are very close to the TQM procedures discussed in the previous section and might also involve the examination of vendor facilities and their related production operations.

Quality control at its lowest level is responsible for catching defects or substandard conditions after the fact, and then getting those items out of the flow of otherwise good products. This differs from the TQM programs discussed in the previous section, where the emphasis is on eliminating errors in the first place.

Considerable organizational resources can be expended in maintaining a quality-control group and function, but expense could be many times greater were quality performance to deteriorate. Non-acceptable products cause a loss of material, labor, and support services that have now been wasted, subject only to any scrap recoveries. The most important cost here is incurred when an unsatisfactory product is delivered to a customer. This cost may range from loss of customer satisfaction to legal liabilities due to the defects. In some cases, a human life may be at stake. Thus, the quality of product has a major impact on the overall welfare of the organization, and quality control is a function that needs careful attention.

(i) Quality-Control Methods and Procedures.   Management must first establish certain quality standards over its products and processes. These standards are normally based upon minimum tolerated levels of error rather than on any attempt to achieve zero defects, as was discussed in the previous TQM section. Quality control samples actual production against these tolerable limits for defects and a single defective item may result in a rejection. However, if a representative sample reveals that there are problems with an entire production line, quality control would reject the error items but also recommend adjusting the parameters used in the entire production process.

A quality-control function would typically work very closely with manufacturing engineering, as was described previously. In some organizations, manufacturing engineering is actually responsible for quality control. In any case, the quality-control function needs to have a strong and complete set of product and production standards. These are the plus or minus tolerances to dimensions and measures that allow the product to work according to its overall specifications.

The types of deviations allowed here are generally not evident to the consumer. For example, a food-processing production engineer may decide that a product, such as canned vegetable soup, will meet specifications if the salt content is 0.025 mg per liter. Quality control, working in conjunction with the process engineers, may establish a standard that the salt content can be between 0.0245 and 0.0255. The assumption here is that the ultimate consumer of the soup product could not detect any difference in the salt content if it were within that range. However, if a batch was found to be outside of these limits according to a quality-control test, the batch would be rejected and the problem investigated and corrected.

Quality control would work closely with engineers and production specialists to establish standards, and then establish testing procedures to measure performance against these standards. These tests would take place at various points in the production process. Ideally, they should be performed as early as possible to avoid excessive waste or scrap. Other tests would be performed throughout the production cycle to determine that the final product is in compliance with specifications.

The quality-control function has an ongoing responsibility to measure errors and report results to management. A control chart approach might be used by a quality-control function to measure its activities in terms of the number of samples taken from production. It also shows the several key quality dimensions with each sample. This type of chart shows the activities of quality control, but more important, it shows any potential trends in product quality.

(b) QUALITY-CONTROL FUNCTION INTERNAL CONTROLS

The quality-control function should be monitoring accomplishments against established standards and then recommending corrective actions when necessary.

In general, a quality-control function needs to concentrate on three broad areas of internal control, as follows:

- *A System of Quality Standards.* No matter which industry and what processes used, a quality-assurance function needs to have a strong set of documented standards for all areas under its measurement. Quality control must work very closely with manufacturing and engineering functions to determine that these standards are both achievable and necessary for achieving product or process acceptance. The quality standards should also be coordinated with the needs of marketing and others. To go back to the ''salt in vegetable soup'' example discussed earlier, it is of little consequence that the salt content is within manufacturing limits if market research finds that consumers report the product tastes too salty.

- *An Appropriate System of Quality Testing.* There are really two related internal control issues here. First, quality control must have a consistent and representative method to select products for sampling. In many areas, 100% of the output cannot be tested, and quality control must devise testing techniques that yield representative samples of the populations tested. Once sampled, quality testing should be performed in a high-quality and consistent manner. The results should be documented similar to the earlier discussion of the research function.

- *Procedures to Communicate Results and Implement Change.* A strong quality-control function is of little value if no one pays attention to the results of that testing. Some quality-control functions publish extensive sets of charts and graphs describing the tests they performed. However, if no action is taken based upon these test results, the quality-control function will be of little value. Quality control should have the authority to implement change based upon the results of their tests, or they must have communication channels to management that can make those changes.

Because quality control is a technical-testing type of function, it must use many of the same operational and documentation procedures discussed previously in the engineering-related sections of this chapter. In some organizations, internal audit may even be able to learn some acceptance sampling techniques from quality control. Quality control is an established discipline, and older organizations have been using it for many years.

(c) AUDITING THE QUALITY-CONTROL FUNCTION

Quality control is another area that often is not included in the internal auditor's universe compilation of auditable entities. This may be because it often does not appear to be a major organization function. In some instances, there may not be a formal quality-control function, but those activities would be performed by other units of the organization. For many organizations, however, quality control is very important. Sometimes even customer contracts specify quality tolerance limits. If not effectively tested, the organization may be subject to a loss of business or even penalties.

Some quality-control functions miss the attention of internal audit because they are only classified as a support function along with the plant electrician or other support staff. However, depending upon the business and products, quality control can be a very important function in the organization. Internal audit should have a good understanding of the role of quality control in the product testing and acceptance process. This may be an area for a special audit or part of a review of other functions.

Many of the audit procedures described here are similar to audit procedures for engineering and TQM programs described previously in this chapter. However, this does not mean that reviews of quality-control functions are not important. Internal audit should modify other engineering-related audit procedures when necessary to perform appropriate reviews of the quality-control function.

(i) Quality-Control Financial Audit Considerations.   The typical quality-control function does not have the same type of project-management authority as was discussed for engineering process functions. Quality control typically operates as a staff function supporting normal manufacturing or production processes. The costs of quality-control testing are normally built into the cost of products typically through adding these costs to overall production overhead. Quality control often uses statistical techniques to select the item to be tested, but the cost of those tests should not be applied to just the items selected. The costs associated with this testing should be applied to the entire manufacturing process.

Audit procedures for financial reviews of production overhead processes were discussed along with other production process audit procedures in Chapter 23. Internal audit here should attest that the costs of the quality-assurance function are properly compiled and reflected in overall production overhead costs. This might include the direct costs of quality-control labor as well as the fixed asset and operating costs of the equipment used to support the testing effort.

Test equipment can be a major cost to a quality-control function. Many products require quite sophisticated devices to detect errors or irregularities. Internal audit should consider the fixed-asset financial controls discussed in Chapter 27 when reviewing the financial controls over the quality-control function.

(ii) Quality-Control Operational Audit Approaches.   An organization will rely upon its quality-control function to monitor the ongoing quality of production, to perform tests as appropriate, to document the results of those tests, and to make suggestions to improve overall quality. Similar to other technical functions discussed in this chapter, quality control is a unique area with its own language and procedures. Its use of statistical techniques for acceptance testing is an example. With the exception of the engineers, internal audit may be the only unit in the organization that understands the requirements for this type of attribute testing.

In order to perform an operational review of the quality-control function, internal audit must have a good understanding of the procedures used as well as of management expectations for that function. The procedures used can vary considerably with the types of processes as well as the industry. Although the two examples discussed previously are involved in an ingredient-based process, the quality-control procedures required for a pharmaceutical process will be far different from the vegetable soup process.

Figure 26.13 outlines general audit procedures for an operational review of an organization's quality-control function. Internal audit must expand and modify these procedures based upon the types of items tested and the industry, but these procedures focus on the quality-control internal control considerations discussed above.

(iii) Quality-Control Computer Audit Procedures.   Most organizations with quality-control functions do not have a need for specialized computer applications supporting those quality-control efforts. A quality-control function might have a need for database applications to keep records of the quality testing results as well as statistical applications to assist in testing procedures. These may operate on the main production system or on

Figure 26.13   Audit Procedures for the Quality Control (QC) Function

1. Develop a general understanding of the role of QC in the organization, its relationship to manufacturing, and to other processes in the organization.
2. Review the process for establishing and issuing QC standards within the organization and assess whether this process seems sufficient.
3. Taking a recently issued sample of QC standards, review documentation to determine how that QC standard was established including:
   √ The use of equipment, industry, or trade group standards
   √ Standards established through QC or other internal research
   √ QC standards established through management mandate.
4. Using the same selected group of standards, review how they were implemented including documentation and training, when appropriate. Measure and assess the related controls.
5. Assess procedures for monitoring quality controls and for taking corrective actions when necessary.
6. Review a sample of QC performance charts issued in several past periods, select any that were reported as out of range, and review subsequent actions to correct the reported deviation.
7. If the organization and its QC function are involved in any ISO initiative (e.g. ISO 9000), assess and document that role with an emphasis on the completeness of appropriate documentation.
8. Review the role of QC in communicating its standards and good quality practices to others in the organization. Assess that role in light of any quality assurance or related activities in the organization.

a separate workstation system. The computer audit procedures here are essentially the same as discussed in the previous section on TQM computer audit procedures.

A quality-control function may use a variety of computer applications or specialized systems to support testing efforts. Some of these may be constructed along the lines of the integrated test facility computer-assisted audit procedures discussed in Chapter 12. While that chapter discussed how to build an integrated test, the audit here should be concerned with the controls built around any such quality-control testing applications. A major concern here may be over the integrity of the programs used and the test data collected.

(iv) Sample Quality Control Findings and Recommendations

A: Quality Control Testing Standards Are Not Current.   We reviewed the standards used by the quality-control department to monitor the results of tests over the shoe polish production lines. We found that although there have been recent changes to improve production processes for shoe polish lines A and B, quality-control standards have not been updated to reflect those production changes. As a result, virtually every quality test performed over those lines showed no significant problems. However, the tests would not have determined if these products are being produced according to the new standards.

Recommendation.   Quality-control testing standards for the above product lines should be updated to reflect production changes. Procedures should be established to ensure that changes to production processes are reflected in quality-control standards.

B: Quality-Control Program Change Controls Weak.   The quality-control function uses a Xeon RKJ microcomputer system with relational database software to record testing results and to produce graphical reports of test results for management. We reviewed both general controls over the system and controls over the database application. We found that there was no procedure in place to control access to system files or to control changes to data files. The machine is in a relatively open area and various production personnel could improperly change quality test results. The organization's employee bonus system—which rewards unit leaders with no production rejects—might cause someone to make an improper change.

Recommendation.   A password-based logical security software system should be implemented to protect quality control system files and data. In addition, a more formal program change procedure documenting and dating all program changes should be implemented.

26-6 IMPORTANCE OF TECHNICAL FUNCTION AUDITS

As discussed in the introduction, audits of technical functions such as engineering or research are often ignored or avoided by internal auditors because of a fear that they will have trouble understanding these unfamiliar technical areas. However, internal auditors do not need to have a strong understanding of the technical processes and procedures behind the engineer's work efforts. Rather, internal audit should concentrate on basic controls such as those over the management of engineering projects. This way, internal audit can provide strong support to management by assessing controls over these important functions.

This chapter has also discussed a new area: audits of the organization's total quality management (TQM) function. This is a new area for many organizations, and should yield positive results to the modern organization if properly directed. However, many organizations have implemented TQM programs with much show but little substance. Management may not realize whether their TQM functions are accomplishing as much as anticipated. A review of both the functional effectiveness and the controls for this function could provide management with useful insights. Of course, a properly directed TQM program should be important to the organization, and internal audit should participate in these reviews when possible.

Reviews of technical areas are an important area for internal auditors. Internal audit's real skill in performing strong operational reviews should show itself with these types of technical reviews. When an internal audit's organization has engineering or related technical activities, they are good areas for the consideration of risk-based audit reviews.

CHAPTER 27

Fixed Assets and Capital Projects

27-1 INTRODUCTION: AUDITING FIXED-ASSET ACTIVITIES

At first inspection, fixed assets and asset-related activities are areas of limited auditor concern. Internal auditors often assume that their organization's fixed assets amount to little more than existing physical plants or investments that provide limited audit opportunities. However, as with many other operational audit areas, there are numerous issues surrounding the whole process of acquiring fixed assets, controlling them, and disposing of them at the end of their useful lives.

This chapter discusses operational audits of an organization's fixed-asset property control procedures, primarily the operational aspects of fixed-asset and construction project auditing. Chapter 30 discusses some related financial-management issues covering fixed assets and construction projects.

27-2 FIXED ASSETS

The fixed-assets entry on a financial statement balance sheet represents the recorded value of physical property, equipment, and other durable purchased goods. Many commodities purchased by an organization are of limited value and life—for example, office supplies. These commodities are simply written off as an expense at the time they are purchased. However, other purchased goods are of too high a value to write off against current profits and also have determinate useful lives. These goods are recorded as fixed assets on the organization's financial statements and are then written off over their useful life periods.

For internal audit, fixed assets are an important area of control concern. Decisions must be made whether to record the item as an asset or to write it off as an expense. If recorded as an asset, further decisions must be made as to its recorded value and its life expectancy. These decisions can affect the profitability and recorded financial strength of the organization.

This section discusses control procedures over the acquisition, maintenance, recording, and disposition of real property, physical plants, and other fixed assets. Included are programs and approaches for financial, operational, and computer applications. Subsequent sections of the chapter cover the capital-acquisition process and fixed-assets property controls.

(a) FIXED-ASSETS CONTROL CYCLE

Fixed assets—goods that typically have relatively high values and useful lives longer than a year—are recorded in the financial statements of the organization at their purchase price and then written off or depreciated over their useful lives until they are scrapped or otherwise disposed of. While this appears to be a relatively simple process, the organization is faced with a number of decisions over the recognition and recording of fixed assets that can impact the profitability and financial strength of the organization. An internal auditor should have a good general understanding of alternative fixed-asset accounting methods as well as management's established policies for fixed assets.

Several important decisions are required to properly record and account for a fixed asset. First, the organization must have policies for classifying items as fixed assets. Sometimes, this is a relatively simple decision, such as for a piece of production machinery that involves a major investment for the organization and is expected to be in use for an extended period of time, perhaps 10 years. The decision is often more complex, however. Estimates must be made regarding the useful life of the asset, the rate at which the asset will decline in value over time (called the rate of depreciation), and the salvage value at the end of the asset's useful life.

Records must be maintained for this property so that the current, depreciated value can be determined on an ongoing basis. These property records are also important for internal control purposes. An organization will purchase assets over time but should identify them to record the organization's ownership. Procedures should also be in place for periodic inventories of these assets, and to ensure that they are properly disposed of when they have exceeded their useful lives. This disposition may require the recognition of a gain or loss depending upon whether the asset was ultimately sold for more or less than its depreciated value at the time of the sale.

In the United States, an organization may keep two sets of books for fixed assets—one for financial accounting and the other for tax purposes. Following financial-accounting rules, an organization will depreciate or write off the value of a fixed asset in equal increments over its estimated life. However, tax rules often allow that write-off to take place on a rapid or accelerated basis. In Canada, these rules are part of what is called ''Capital Cost Allowances.'' While a section following discusses these accelerated-depreciation accounting methods, tax accounting is not within the scope of this book.

A special class of fixed assets not discussed in any detail here is mineral resources that are mined or otherwise extracted. Oil may be extracted from a well or gold from a mine. However, the organization can only estimate the value of that mineral source when it starts its extraction process. It then takes an annual depreciation-type charge against the value of the mineral resource. This is called the depletion allowance. There are many rules and complex accounting and tax procedures involved in accounting for mineral resources that are beyond the scope of this book.

(i) Fixed-Asset Capitalization Decisions.   Generally accepted accounting principles determine what types of goods are to be declared as fixed assets and what are to be written off as expenses. Organization policies should properly classify and record these fixed assets. The declaration of goods as assets with periodic write-offs for depreciation is usually called *fixed-asset capitalization*. This decision is influenced by several factors, including generally accepted accounting principles (GAAP) and good business practices. In addition, there may be somewhat conflicting tax rules. Internal auditors should be aware

of these capitalization policies and take steps to determine that they are being followed for all property, plant, and equipment purchases.

An organization should establish capitalization policies that normally state the classes of goods treated as assets, as well as the number of years for their assumed useful lives. For example, the organization's policy may state that all purchased delivery vehicles are to be treated as fixed assets and written off over a three-year period. Similarly, certain items of production equipment are to be written off over a 10-year period. An organization does not have complete freedom to establish these capitalization policies. Tax rules and GAAP accounting guidelines constrain decisions here. However, an organization has some flexibility to make capitalization decisions within these overall rules. Any capitalization policy should be comprehensive enough to cover all types of fixed assets that might be used by the organization.

The decision to capitalize a purchase should normally be part of a request for funds to purchase the item. The organization might normally have a capital equipment request that requires approval by an appropriate level of management. Large items, such as a request for a new plant, would be reviewed by a senior management committee, as discussed in the next section. However, there are often many other smaller items that should also go through a formal review and approval process. Management establishes a budget for the amount of funds available for these types of purchases, and the capital requests are prioritized and then matched against available funds.

In this approval process, the funding request states the cost of the item and estimates the annual savings that may result from the capital acquisition as well as its expected life. The expected annual savings multiplied by the expected life is called the *payback period*. This payback concept is discussed in greater detail in Chapter 30.

The capital goods request and budgeting process for larger fixed assets is usually done annually. Operating units submit their capital requests for management review and ranking. Because capital may be scarce or management may not wish to incur additional debt to acquire an item, it may be rejected in this budget review even though it would provide a positive payback. Management's top priority is to preserve and promote the overall financial health of the organization. An investment that may provide future expected returns may be viewed as too risky or may distort short-term financial performance.

Many small-dollar-value items may be treated as fixed assets rather than expensed items. Examples include fixtures in a retail store or tooling in a manufacturing organization. The decision to classify the item as an asset should be supported by the fixed-asset classification policy. The proposed item would be reviewed by local or unit management and a decision made to treat the purchase as a fixed asset or a current-period expense (usually less than one year). For smaller items, the financial effect is about the same. If the purchase price is relatively small, and if it is purchased for cash rather than financed over multiple periods, it might also be depreciated over a short period or even in a single year. The major advantage to treating the item as a fixed asset is that it will be recorded on property-control records, techniques for which are discussed later in this chapter.

Another management decision that must be made regarding fixed assets is whether to lease the proposed assets. With leasing, an outside financial organization acquires the title to the asset and then leases or "rents" it back to the requesting organization for a predetermined period of time. The annual lease fee for the asset becomes the equivalent of a depreciation expense to the organization. However, at the end of the leasing period, the property will revert back to the leasing company. The organization may have the option to purchase the asset at an agreed-upon price.

Why would an organization lease an asset rather than purchase it? The reasons range from an uncertainty over its useful life to tax or financing considerations. Financial-accounting and -reporting rules often drive the decision. These leasing considerations are discussed in more detail in Chapter 30 on financial management. Management's decision to lease or buy a fixed asset is based on some of the following factors:

- *Useful Life of the Asset to the Organization.* Leasing first became very popular during the 1970s when larger organizations acquired mainframe computer systems. These machines were very expensive, but technology was moving so fast that a computer system could easily become obsolete in a few years. Rather than purchase the system, the organization might lease the computer for perhaps five years. Annual lease expenses are generally less than the purchase price. The organization then considers acquiring a newer, more advanced machine on expiration of the lease. The leasing company benefits as it typically can find a smaller or less progressive organization to take the computer system at the expiration of the original lease. Useful life decisions continue to influence leasing decisions for organizations today.

- *Financial Balance Sheet Considerations.* When a fixed asset is acquired, it appears on the balance sheet in the asset column at its total purchase price, including taxes, delivery, and installation costs. It is offset by the amount due for the item, which appears as a liability or, if paid in cash, as a reduction of cash accounts. If a liability, the amount due in the current year appears as a current liability. Banks and other organizations who evaluate the financial strength of organizations use these balance sheet figures to calculate ratios of financial strength. In the United States, organizations sometimes move their fixed-asset transactions off their balance sheets through lease arrangements. Although accounting standards require that capital lease expenses be reported as a footnote to their financial statements, this arrangement is sometimes preferable to balance sheet entries.

- *Ability to Pay.* Ability to pay may dictate the lease decision. A young married couple often must rent their first residence rather than purchase it due to limited financial resources or credit history. If they take a loan to purchase it, the finance company may place higher requirements upon them. In a rental situation, the arrangement can be terminated easier after an extended nonpayment of rent. In a similar manner, some organizations do not have the financial strength to purchase a capital asset and instead will lease the item.

Choosing leasing over purchasing can also result from income tax rules and other financial considerations. Leasing is a popular alternative, and the auditor should understand some of the overall processes surrounding a leasing arrangement.

Whether purchasing, capitalizing, or leasing an asset, the organization may be faced with other decisions. For example, an item of production equipment may require additional accessories to make it functional. Although GAAP and tax rules limit their flexibility, organizations may face a decision regarding which of these additional items should be treated as a current expense and which should be treated as an addition to the asset to be expensed over time. Lower-level management may even be tempted to add inappropriate items to the fixed-asset account because of their more limited impact on current expenses.

The auditor should look for overall management policies covering what should and should not be added to the fixed-asset account. Internal audit should also be aware of potential abuse in this area, particularly for smaller items, which may be missed during higher-level, financial statement external auditor reviews.

The fixed-asset capitalization decision process should be based on sound policies and an understanding of GAAP and tax rules to guide the organization concerning what to capitalize and under what terms. These decisions can impact the overall financial strength of the organization.

(ii) Fixed-Asset Depreciation Accounting. When an item is acquired as a fixed asset, it is written off or depreciated over its estimated life. This periodic depreciation charge becomes an expense during the recorded life of the asset. The company first records the purchase price of the fixed asset, including shipping, taxes, and installation. This is known as the starting book value. The organization should estimate the expected productive life of the asset as well as its salvage value at the end of its useful life. The difference between the initial book value and the salvage value is divided by the number of years of expected life to determine the annual depreciation charge.

$$\text{ANNUAL DEPRECIATION CHARGE} = \frac{\text{Initial Book Value} - \text{Salvage Value}}{\text{Expected Life}}$$

Assume that a fixed asset is acquired for $125,000, inclusive of delivery and installation costs, and is estimated to have a useful life of eight years, after which it might be sold as scrap for about $8,000. The annual depreciation charge would be calculated as follows:

$$(125,000 - 8,000)/8 = \$14,625$$

As the eight-year period passes, the annual depreciation charge is applied to calculate the book value at any time. For example, at the end of the third year, the net book value of this example asset would be:

$$125,000 - (14,625 \times 3) = \$81,125$$

If the organization changes its mind and disposes of the asset at the end of that third year, it recognizes a gain or loss based on what it receives compared to the net book value at that time.

Often, an organization will argue that a fixed asset loses its value faster in the earlier years of its life than in later years. Income tax rules also allow some assets to be depreciated in a faster manner. Various calculations are used for determining accelerated depreciation annual charges. Figure 27.1 provides examples of some of these depreciation-calculation methods, which can help the auditor understand what an auditee means by such terms as the ''sum of the years'' depreciation method. Although Figure 27.1 provides some examples of these calculations, a typical accounting textbook will offer explanations of these alternative depreciation calculations and their accounting treatments.

Because assets are acquired at different points in time and because many have different expected lives, detailed depreciation calculation record-keeping is essential. In the past, organizations maintained manual records or journal books of their fixed assets with year-by-year depreciation calculations for each. Today, the task is much simpler, with fixed-asset computer applications used to calculate individual depreciation amounts

Figure 27.1   Depreciation Methods Calculation Examples

I. *Depreciation Methods Based on Time*
1. *Straight-Line Method.*   Annual depreciation charges are the total cost minus the salvage value divided by the expected life of the asset. Assume an asset costs $12,000 and has an estimated life of five years and a salvage value of $2,000. Depreciation for the first year D_1 is:

$$D_1 = \frac{\$12,000 - \$2,000}{5} = \$2,000$$

2. *Accelerated Depreciation: Sum of Years Digits Method.* The fraction used for the annual depreciation charge is the number of years remaining for the life of the asset, less its salvage value, divided by the sum of all of the years left in the life of the asset. In the above example, the first year's depreciation would be based on 5 (the number of years remaining) and 15 (the sum of $1 + 2 + 3 + 4 + 5$). This is an accelerated depreciation with the largest depreciation charges in the early years. Annual depreciation charges for the above example would be:

$$
\begin{aligned}
D_1 &= 5/15 \times (12,000 - 2,000) = &\$3,333 \\
D_2 &= 4/15 \times (12,000 - 2,000) = &\$2,667 \\
D_3 &= 3/15 \times (12,000 - 2,000) = &\$2,000 \\
D_4 &= 2/15 \times (12,000 - 2,000) = &\$1,333 \\
D_5 &= 1/15 \times (12,000 - 2,000) = &\underline{\$667} \\
& &\underline{\underline{\$10,000}}
\end{aligned}
$$

3. *Accelerated Depreciation: Declining Balance Method.* A constant percentage, based on *double* the straight-line rate is applied to the recorded balance of the asset. In the asset value example, the DDB% is $(100\% / 5 \text{ years}) \times (2) = 40\%$. This calculation brings the down to the salvage value very quickly. However, it must never reduce the asset value below the salvage value. In the above example:

$$
\begin{aligned}
D_1 &= 40\% \times (\$12,000) = \$4,800 \\
D_2 &= 40\% \times (\$12,000 - \$4,800) = \$2,880 \\
D_3 &= 40\% \times (\$12,000 - \$4,800 - \$2,880) = \$1,728 \\
D_4 &= 40\% \times (\$12,000 - \$4,800 - \$2,880 - \$1,728) = \$592
\end{aligned}
$$

Depreciation cannot be taken for D_5 since that would reduce asset to below the salvage value.

II. *Service-Quantity Method.* This depreciation is based on the actual use or utilization of an asset over its estimated productive life. The depreciation charge will vary by the estimated units used for a period. Assume the above asset was estimated to have a life of 25,000 productive units. The estimated cost by unit would be

$$\frac{(\$12,000 - \$2,000)}{25,000 \text{ units}} = \$0.40$$

If 4,000, 9,000, 8,000, 2,000 and 2,000 units were used over those five years, the depreciation calculation would be:

$$
\begin{aligned}
D_1 &= \$0.40 \times 4,000 = \$1,600 \\
D_2 &= \$0.40 \times 9,000 = \$3,600 \\
D_3 &= \$0.40 \times 8,000 = \$3,200 \\
D_4 &= \$0.40 \times 2,000 = \$800 \\
D_4 &= \$0.40 \times 2,000 = \$800
\end{aligned}
$$

and then summarize them to yield the annual depreciation expense. Quite inexpensive microcomputer-based software applications are available to calculate depreciation, or spreadsheet software can be programmed to accomplish the same thing for small organizations. However, these automated fixed-asset systems are not found in all organizations. Some argue that their fixed-asset activity is just too small to justify an automated system, and they continue to keep manual records.

In a manual system, the records will often be part of the property control documents discussed later in this chapter. The auditor will always want to review these records and test the appropriateness of the calculations.

(iii) Asset Property Records. The automated systems or manual records used to maintain fixed-asset records represent a key element of maintaining control over fixed assets. Whatever the record-keeping system, it must identify each fixed asset and indicate its recorded physical location. Management—as well as auditors—may want to review a property record and then locate the actual item for comparison purposes. Similarly, it should be possible to trace an item from its physical locations, such as on the shop floor, back to fixed-asset records.

The technique typically used to control the actual physical item is an asset or property tag, often a small metal plate with the organization's name and an identifying number for that fixed asset, which ties back to the formal fixed-asset records. Today, the property tag may be a plastic label with a bar-coded number, affixed with very strong adhesive.

Property tags should be attached to the fixed asset at the time it is acquired or placed in service. The tags should be firmly attached, perhaps riveted if an older metal tag, and should be in an inconspicuous location on the asset. Property tags establish the ownership of the fixed-asset item and tie back to the property records. They are particularly useful when two similar items of equipment are purchased at different times. The fixed-asset records contain the purchase information regarding the fixed asset, depreciation calculations, and other significant data. Often, an organization may have a system with two or more database records for the major fixed-asset items. The first has been discussed and contains purchase price and subsequent additional capitalized cost data. It also contains depreciation assumptions and all accrued depreciation, a record of the property tag number, and sometimes a note as to where the property is located. These records are often maintained by the organization's fixed-asset or general accounting function.

A second set, often part of the same database, contains maintenance records for the particular fixed-asset items, which cover the normal repairs necessary to keep the fixed-asset item operable. An example would be the checkups service calls performed on automobiles at various points of their accumulated mileage. Similar records are necessary for production equipment.

Maintenance that represents substantial work may be classed as a betterment to the base fixed asset. Although the maintenance-type records are necessary, they should also be recorded in the fixed-asset records since the betterment should be capitalized and depreciated over the remaining estimated life of the particular asset. Strong policies are needed here to define the classification of repairs as either betterments or maintenance expenses. Good records are necessary to tie capitalized betterments to fixed-asset property records.

Maintenance records are often maintained by the various groups within an organization responsible for classes of fixed-asset equipment. For example, information systems might maintain records for owned and capitalized data-processing equipment while the transportation department would have the records for the organization-owned vehicles. The fixed-assets database should maintain close ties between these property-maintenance records and the prime fixed-asset records.

In the United States, a third set of records covers the tax obligations for various fixed-asset items. These include tax basis records where different methods of depreciation and asset life calculations are used. Also included are personal property–type tax payments to local taxing authorities. These tax records can be a supplement to the main fixed-asset records or can exist as a separate set. If the latter, care must be taken to reconcile the tax records with the regular fixed-asset records on an ongoing basis. In Canada, accounting-based depreciation for financial statement purposes is usually only converted to tax records at year-end, and the two never coincide.

(b) FIXED-ASSETS INTERNAL CONTROL CONSIDERATIONS

Fixed assets are a financial statement item, and both management and outside auditors have a strong concern that they are properly classified and reported. Internal auditors are more concerned with fixed-asset controls, including proper recordkeeping. Controls over fixed assets may cause the organization some general internal control problems as well as some unique problems due to the nature of fixed assets, as follows:

- *Fixed-asset acquisitions and dispositions are irregular.* Many accounting transactions take place on a regular, periodic basis. Except for the largest of organizations, however, there may be only minimal fixed-asset activity in a given accounting period. This means that procedures may not be followed consistently.

- *Many decisions depend on accounting judgment.* Whether to include other costs such as delivery charges with it, and what to use as estimates for the useful life and salvage value, are some of the decisions that must be made. There may even be a need for a lease-versus-buy decision. The results of these decisions may impact the current-period profitability and financial structure of the overall organization.

- *Inventory records and maintenance records must be maintained over an asset's life.* A fixed asset, whether a major item of production equipment or office furniture, must be identified in organization fixed-asset records and must be maintained in good working order. The organization has a stewardship responsibility over these fixed assets.

- *Double accounting systems may be needed.* Fixed assets are unique in that two sets of books may be maintained over depreciation charges due to tax regulations. While not a problem in Canada, this situation creates some unique recordkeeping and tax accounting concerns in the United States.

Because of these unique attributes, the organization needs to establish strong internal controls over the authorization of fixed assets, fixed-asset recordkeeping, and accountability for fixed assets. Internal control should go beyond just accounting records and should include procedures within maintenance facilities to perform necessary repairs and enhancement. There is also a need to maintain physical security controls over fixed assets. This includes attaching identification tags on all items and performing periodic full or partial physical inventories.

Perhaps the strongest type of internal control procedure needed for fixed assets is a set of management-approved policies outlining such matters as what types of items can be capitalized, levels of approval for asset acquisition, and guidelines for what should be included as part of a fixed asset. While GAAP accounting and tax rules establish some limits, management still has some flexibility in establishing specific guidelines. While these fixed-asset internal control procedures are generally part of the overall control procedures in operation within the accounting department, some fixed-asset accounting decisions may be the responsibility of other personnel in the organization.

Because they involve limited activity in many organizations and because many fixed assets, such as office furniture, do not represent a high-risk area, fixed-asset internal controls can often easily be ignored. An organization will frequently only devote major attention to the controls over major capital construction projects. Internal audit can support management by assessing internal controls over fixed assets and fixed-asset records on a periodic basis.

(c) FIXED-ASSETS INTERNAL AUDIT ACTIVITIES

Internal auditors have a strong need to review the financial, operational, and data-processing controls over the organization's fixed assets. However, because fixed assets are a fairly static activity, internal audit will probably not review this area on a regular or even annual basis. Given that internal audit has limited time and resources, management often has numerous other "hot" areas that are perceived as having a greater need for internal audit reviews than do the fixed assets.

Internal audit should place fixed asset controls in its audit-planning risk model (see Chapter 8). Factors to be considered when deciding to schedule a review of fixed-asset functions and records might include the following.

- Have there been major changes in the organization's fixed assets? An example of a fixed-asset change might be the closure of a production facility.
- Have other audits indicated potential problems with fixed asset records? Examples might be the frequent identification of fixed assets in the field as not properly tagged.
- Is the organization under pressure to improve profitability or balance sheet strength?
- Have there been changes to systems or policies covering fixed assets?

The entire fixed-assets function or its separate financial, operational, or computer systems aspects should be included in the internal audit risk model for planning consideration. With a proper risk model, reviews of fixed-asset activities will rise to the top of the list of potential audit candidates from time to time.

(i) Fixed-Assets Financial Audit Considerations.

Internal audit's basic objective for performing a financial audit of the organization's fixed assets is to affirm the correctness of the net fixed-assets total on the financial statement balance sheet. This includes the total of all fixed assets net of accumulated depreciation. This may sound like a simple task, but the fixed-asset balance will typically include a large number of items that have been recorded at different points in time and with different depreciation rates and expected lives.

A first step in a financial audit is to develop an understanding of procedures for the management authorization of fixed-asset expenditures and for their classification. An internal auditor will review these procedures for their adequacy, review fixed-asset records (whether recorded through an automated or manual system), and verify that a sample of fixed assets is correctly recorded. The fixed-asset financial-audit process is outlined in Figure 27.2. Some of these same steps, covering the authorization and classification of fixed assets, are applicable to operational audits of the fixed-assets function, discussed in the following section.

The audit program steps in Figure 27.2 calls for selecting a sample of recorded fixed assets and determining that they exist and are properly recorded in the fixed-asset records.

Figure 27.2   Fixed Assets Financial Audit Program Steps

Audit _____ Location _____ Date _____

AUDIT STEP	INITIAL	W/P
1. Determine that detailed property records are maintained for individual facilities and equipment.		
2. Review policies and procedures in place to properly calculate and record depreciation of fixed assets.		
3. Capital expenditures should be approved in advance by proper management, with appropriate policy distinguishing between capital expenditures, repairs, and maintenance.		
4. Responsibilities for maintaining detailed property records should be segregated from those maintaining both the general ledger and the actual custody of the assets.		
5. Select a sample of additions from the fixed-assets acquisition register and review records for: • Recorded acquisition costs should agree to invoices with appropriate treatment of taxes and freight. • Recorded asset acquisition date should agree to the invoice paid date.		
6. Select a sample of asset repairs and maintenance account items and determine that these charges were properly expensed.		
7. Determine that depreciation is being calculated consistently and accurately through sample recomputations.		
8. Determine that fixed-asset deletions are properly supported by selecting activity from deletion records and tracing them to supporting documentation.		
9. Select a sample of fixed assets that have been designated as retired: • Determine accumulated depreciation and any associated gain or loss was correctly calculated. • Trace the retirement gain or loss to proper general ledger accounts. • Ensure the retired asset was removed from the books in proper month.		
10. Determine that adequate security procedures and controls are in place to protect fixed-asset records.		

The size of the sample to be reviewed can be decided either by attribute sampling or by monetary unit valuation. Attribute sampling allows the auditor to test for errors in fixed-asset transactions, but, as discussed in Chapter 13, care must be used in defining the critical fixed-asset attributes to be tested. An internal auditor can, for example, determine that the sampled fixed asset was properly authorized and classified. A broader range of attribute errors can result in too many errors in the initial sample and the need to expand sample size due to essentially immaterial errors. The outcome of this type of attribute-sampling test, correctly organized, allows the auditor to state that fixed assets are correctly classified and recorded.

With monetary unit sampling, also discussed in Chapter 13, the selection would be based on the net book value of the fixed assets, using files from the automated fixed-asset system. The objective for this type of test is to assess whether the net book values of the selected assets are fairly stated.

While the auditor may want to select a statistical sample for an attribute or variables test, in many instances the primary concern is to assess the compliance of fixed-asset records with established procedures. The auditor may decide that such a formal statistical sample yields too large a sample for the scope of the planned audit work. If only reviewing controls over fixed assets and not expressing an opinion on the overall fixed-asset balance, a more limited judgmental sample may be sufficient.

Once a sample has been selected, the auditor should review the adequacy of records to support the existence of the asset, determine whether appropriate items associated with the asset have been capitalized, and determine that depreciation calculations and accumulations are correct. The objective is to assess the accounting treatment and calculations for the sampled assets in order to evaluate the fixed-asset accounting controls.

The final step in a financial audit of fixed assets is to assess the adequacy of the recorded fixed-asset balance. This step depends on the results of the tests of accounting controls over sampled fixed assets as well as on the overall accumulation process. Assuming significant control problems or errors among the individual fixed assets selected have been identified, a good next step is to review the fixed-asset accumulation process. This may simply involve a review of the controls over the automated fixed-asset application, discussed below. If manual procedures are used, the auditor should review the process with an emphasis given to any adjusting entries.

Internal auditors should test selected asset items to determine their existence and condition. A full physical inventory of all fixed assets would usually be very expensive and time-consuming. (An inventory of fixed assets is discussed in the following section.) An internal auditor performing a financial review and not wishing to examine inventory, given there was evidence of fraud or misrepresentation, can instead choose a limited sample of fixed assets for verification. Once these are selected, the auditor should determine that the stated assets exist, are in appropriate working condition, and are tagged per organization standards.

When testing accuracy of depreciation calculations, again, the auditor need not recalculate the depreciation values for all of the fixed assets. Rather, if the organization is using manual methods, internal audit should review the methods of calculation and test several sample items to determine whether they are accurate. If using an automated system, internal auditors should understand the accumulation process and verify the final calculation records for any unresolved but reported error items. This financially oriented review of fixed-asset records, coupled with reviews of depreciation calculations and observations of actual fixed assets, will give an internal auditor assurances that fixed-asset records are correctly stated.

(ii) Fixed-Assets Operational Audit Procedures.   An operational audit of fixed assets is very similar to the financially oriented review previously described. Here, internal audit would test for the existence of fixed assets, might assess whether they have been properly classified, and would review local facility–level records used to keep track of maintenance and other fixed asset–related activities. A test for existence implies an inventory or some other procedure to attest to these fixed assets.

Because fixed assets may spread throughout the organization, a complete physical inventory is logistically difficult. Fixed assets may range from a major item of transportation equipment to portable computers (which can easily be moved from one location to another) to machine tooling, which is separate from other production equipment and difficult to identify. Although physically tagged, these items can be very difficult to locate.

Figure 27.3   Fixed-Assets Sample Inventory Audit Procedures

Audit _____ Location _____ Date _____

AUDIT STEP	INITIAL	W/P
1. Develop a strategy and plan for the fixed-assets inventory—are all assets to be counted or only certain classes or geographic locations?		
2. Based on plan, obtain a listing of the fixed assets for the areas to be inventoried; also, review recent asset additions and retirements.		
3. Obtain an understanding of the fixed-asset identification or tagging procedures—how are fixed assets identified?		
4. Schedule fixed-asset inventory and make arrangements that assets will normally not be moved on inventory day. In the case of assets such as a truck, make special arrangements for counting.		
5. In the areas to be inventoried, count each asset by checking it off against the fixed-asset lists. Once the asset has been counted and matched to the listing, attach a colored tape to the equipment, marking it as counted.		
6. If the tagged asset does not appear to match the description in inventory records, note the difference for follow-up. Mark the asset.		
7. If an asset is tagged but not in the inventory listing, note the tag number, description of the asset, and its location for follow-up. Mark the asset.		
8. Search the area inventoried for other apparent fixed assets with no tags. Inquire as to their status and description with local management, and describe them as above for resolution.		
9. After area has been counted, physically search for any missing items that were on list but not in area; describe the open items for follow-up.		
10. Complete inventory by reconciling missing assets or other items that appear to be mislabeled.		

If there is an ongoing program to inventory fixed assets, perhaps on a cyclical basis, and to verify their condition, internal audit may only want to review the appropriateness of the control procedures. Often, internal audit will find that fixed-asset inventories are seldom performed or are performed in a very perfunctory manner. Fixed-asset operational audit procedures can verify that they exist, and should try to determine that the asset represents at least its recorded book value. That is, financial controls might indicate an asset life over an extended period of time. However, a physical inspection may reveal the item is ready for scrap. If the operational review indicates potential problems regarding the condition or existence of the sample assets, internal audit might discuss these findings with management and recommend either a more complete inventory or a more extensive operational test of fixed assets.

Figure 27.3 outlines some the steps to take a sample inventory of fixed assets for an operational review. This type of inventory audit verification can be a difficult and time-consuming procedure for an organization with many geographically remote units or for a manufacturer with many different production-related assets. The auditor may want to verify these assets physically or ask personnel at remote locations to verify the fixed assets on behalf of internal audit through confirmation procedures. Once the assets are identified, internal audit should tie these inventoried assets to fixed-asset records to determine whether they exist and are correctly classified in terms of their condition or potential use.

Fixed-asset inventories often yield discrepancies, either because the asset cannot be located or because it does not correspond to its recorded description. These preliminary audit findings should be discussed with appropriate levels of management. The fixed-asset inventory procedures often also point to a need to review maintenance, repairs, and replacements control. As part of operational audit procedures for fixed assets, internal audit should review control procedures. Steps to review fixed-asset controls are outlined in Figure 27.4.

Figure 27.4   Fixed-Asset Operational Audit Controls Review Procedures

1. Procedures should be in place for all fixed assets to be periodically inspected and inventoried.
2. Physical assets should be physically protected, as appropriate, and covered by adequate levels of insurance.
3. Assets should be tagged with semipermanent markers to indicate that they are organization property. Procedures should be in place to formally cancel those markers when the assets are retired.
4. Fixed assets included in periodic inventories should be reconciled to financial records.
5. Procedures should be in place to ensure that when assets are moved, their new location is updated in fixed-assets records.
6. Appropriate maintenance procedures should be in place, along with records of that activity, to record both regular and emergency repairs to fixed assets.
7. Procedures should be in place to report on problems or needs for repairs for all fixed assets and production equipment in particular.
8. Fixed assets that have exceeded their useful, productive lives should be retired and either sold, transferred, or disposed of in a productive manner.

(iii) Fixed-Assets Computer Audit Procedures. In a very small organization, fixed-asset records may be manual, with little need for specific computer audit procedures other than to determine that controls to transfer fixed-asset information to other automated accounting systems are adequate. However, most cases today are automated. Internal audit may want to review the automated fixed-asset system and should consider performing a controls review when risk analyses of critical applications indicate a need for one. Often, internal auditors find that their risk analyses pinpoint other, more critical applications for review and ignore fixed-assets systems. However, risk criteria may be weighed in a manner that discourages a review of the fixed-assets control applications. Even if they may not initially appear on criticality lists, fixed-assets control systems may be a worthwhile application for a controls review, particularly if there is a large fixed-asset base as a balance sheet account.

Fixed-Assets System Application Reviews

Organizations have a common need to record the book values of fixed assets and deduct depreciation over their estimated life. Fixed-asset procedures are often similar from one organization to another, and many organizations use purchased software to account for their fixed assets. This is often true whether a large organization using a mainframe system or a smaller entity using only microcomputers.

A first step, then, in planning computer audit procedures for a review of the fixed-assets system is to develop an understanding of the nature of the application. While a major component of fixed-assets systems is the database to record descriptions of the assets, such systems can also calculate depreciation, keep separate tallies for tax accounting, and communicate with the organization's general ledger systems.

Figure 27.5 is a flowchart of a simplified fixed-assets system with typical interfaces to other supporting systems shown. The auditor should understand the controls over inputs to the system as well as general access controls. These follow the same general application-review procedures that were outlined in Chapter 17.

Fixed-Assets System Computer-Assisted Procedures

A fixed-assets system is a good candidate for computer-assisted procedures to verify the contents of data files and to recalculate various fixed-asset results. Because fixed-asset data is often reported at a high level, many smaller recording and calculation errors within a fixed-asset file can be ignored. An internal auditor may provide some useful input to management by using computer-assisted procedures to recalculate various fixed-asset depreciation and book values.

Based on the nature of the fixed-assets file structure, the auditor can use audit software, a fourth-generation retrieval language, or even a report writer supplied by the software vendor to perform computer-assisted tests of fixed-asset records—the types of tests that might check for unreasonably long product lives, negative book values due to improper depreciation calculations, or improper asset classifications. Figure 27.6 lists some potential computer-assisted tests for a review of a fixed-assets system. The overall computer-assisted procedures outlined in Chapter 12 should be used to prepare these audit tests.

Figure 27.5 Automated Fixed-Assets System

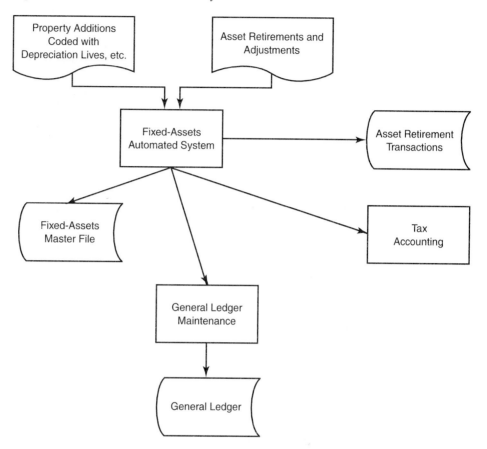

Figure 27.6 Fixed-Asset System Potential CAATs

- Match transaction files recording fixed-assets additions as well as fixed-asset deletions to the master fixed-assets database. All additions should be included and all deletions should no longer be on fixed-asset records.
- Based on the organization and the fixed-asset classification scheme, search fixed-asset records for potentially misclassified items (e.g., real property classified as office equipment), and research the potential reported differences.
- Using CAAT software, independently review the fixed-assets file, comparing the results for assets and accumulated depreciation to general ledger records.
- Compare recorded book values and accumulated depreciation amounts to identify any assets with negative book values.
- Review the recorded lives of fixed assets on files to identify any with unreasonable installation dates due to input errors or potentially excessive depreciation times.
- Survey recorded fixed-asset salvage values to determine if any appear unreasonable per organization procedures.
- As a general rule, survey various coded fixed-asset codes to identify any unusual items or assets missing proper code classification.

(iv) Audit Report Findings and Recommendations.

A. Controls Not in Place over Fully Depreciated Fixed Assets.   During internal audit's review of fixed-asset tags on the shop floor, we identified several significant equipment items where tags were missing or the control numbers on those tags could not be traced to fixed-asset system records. Local management advised us that this equipment was either fully depreciated or idle and thus not carried on the fixed-asset ledger. Failure to maintain records on this old equipment could result in its becoming lost or stolen.

Recommendation.   Fully depreciated fixed assets or assets in idle status should be appropriately coded and either maintained on the automated fixed-assets system or in a separate file until they are formally scrapped and removed from the facility. Once removed, their asset tags should be removed or obliterated.

B: Fixed-Asset Values Do Not Reflect Property Improvements.   In our inventory of fixed assets, we identified several items of production equipment that appeared to have had substantial repairs or refurbishments even though fixed-asset records only showed the original acquisition costs. Our investigations revealed that these repairs were charged to current period expenses even though the refurbishments extended the useful lives of the fixed assets reviewed. We further found that organizational procedures covering these transactions were unclear.

Recommendation.   Policies should be developed to define what types and values of fixed-asset refurbishments should be capitalized and depreciated over the remaining life of the asset and which should be expensed in the current period. As a check to determine that this accounting is proper, the policy should define an amount over which management should review expenditures and determine whether the refurbishments should be expensed or capitalized.

C: Fixed-Assets Inventory Procedures Are Needed.   In our limited review of fixed-assets inventory, we found a significant number of items from our sample that were not at their recorded locations and were only located with the assistance of local management. We also found that the property control department has taken no steps in recent periods to inventory these fixed assets even though property control has a responsibility to establish such control procedures.

Recommendation.   Management should take cyclical inventories of recorded fixed assets on a regular basis. For those assets in remote locations, formal confirmation letters to local management should be used. All differences should be investigated and fixed-assets records adjusted appropriately. Also, control procedures for reporting the physical movement of significant fixed assets should be reemphasized.

27-3 CAPITAL CONSTRUCTION PROJECT PROCESS

Major construction projects require the commitment of capital for facility construction as well as the managerial decisions and control procedures covering the projects. They also may involve the day-to-day care and utilization of individual pieces of equipment used to support ongoing construction projects. Operational audit activities in this general area are often closely related to financial audit concerns. The focus of this section, however, is on the activities pertaining to major construction projects requiring major capital investments. The financial-management issues of capital budgeting are discussed in Chapter 30. A capital construction project—which might be a new plant, a specialized type of equipment, or a mineral-extraction facility,—requires a major commitment of time and resources. These projects normally take place outside of normal organization operations and in many instances under contractual arrangements where internal audit's project involvement will be limited.

Internal auditors often become involved in construction projects only when management requests them, often well after the fact. This is a quite specialized area, and not many auditors have construction project audit skills—when these construction project audit skills exist, internal audit needs to make management aware of them. Audits of capital construction projects can be an effective but very specialized way to serve the total interests of management.

Physical and financial considerations are closely interrelated in capital construction projects. In a physical sense, tangible assets are committed for the support of organization operations. These tangible assets include land, construction materials, equipment, and other supporting materials. Capital construction projects provide an organization with facilities that may include the buildings and furniture for offices, the direct production of goods and services, and the support of operations. It is necessary to ascertain that capital construction projects actually meet management's needs and are carried out following good operational control procedures. Financial-controls concerns include whether the capital construction projects represent the best use of the organization's capital, whether they are constructed at the lowest possible cost, and whether they are ultimately utilized in a manner that results in maximum profitability for the organization. Supplementary financial-control concerns involve the proper accounting for the expense and asset elements of projects and, once placed in operations, the proper accumulation of depreciation expenses. These physical and financial control objectives overlap but are nevertheless recognizable as dual aspects of the problem of effectively controlling the capital construction projects processes. This chapter primarily discusses operational control procedures while Chapter 30 contains a section that addresses capital asset financial controls. Major construction projects are often not directly managed by an organization but are contracted to others. Internal audit may become involved in these efforts as a reviewer of the separate contractor.

(a) CONTROL CYCLE FOR CAPITAL CONSTRUCTION PROJECTS

The capital construction project process usually requires major expenditures and needs strong management and control efforts, especially because expenditures currently made will often not be recovered until after an extended period of time. The assets acquired may also be with the organization for many years, and during that time it may be relatively difficult or expensive to make major changes. As major investments, these projects need ongoing physical care and control.

The capital construction project process can be viewed in terms of the individual steps in the project's total control cycle. These individual steps could become the basis for internal audit's examination of controls over these operational activities and typically include:

1. A determination and initial justification made by the operational groups with primary needs or responsibilities.

2. Analysis and appraisal by upper management on its merits, with a resulting preliminary approval or rejection.

3. A more detailed analysis of total estimated costs, long-range expected returns, and potential contractual arrangements to initiate the construction effort for final management review and approval or rejection of the project.

4. Initiation of the actual construction or acquisition of the approved capital asset. Necessary financing would be obtained at this time. This is a major step involving a choice of funding alternatives such as issuing equity or taking on additional long-term debt.

5. Institution of strong project-management controls during the period of construction. Assuming an outside contractor will perform the work, provisions to allow internal audit to review project control procedures should be defined in the contracts.

6. Plans set for disposition at the end of its life or required need.

7. Establishment of procedures on completion of the project.

These same control cycle steps are appropriate for many capital construction projects, such as a new plant facility. The following sections discuss this control cycle in terms of a major capital project such as a new production plant.

(i) Determination of Capital Project Needs. The first step, the proposal, may be for the manufacture of new products or an expanded capacity for current products. The purpose of the project may be to increase capacity, improve the quality of production, or facilitate other aspects of operational activities. This proposal requires a careful study of all of the related factors and alternatives. The result will be a request for capital submitted to upper management for formal approval. The points covered in such a proposal normally include:

- *Description of the Proposed Construction or Acquisition Project and Its Purpose.* This detailed study provides justification and should provide sufficient data on current and proposed procedures to help management evaluate the decision.

- *Estimated Cost of the Proposed Construction Project.* For purchased assets such as land, buildings, or equipment, these estimates should include both the basic purchase price as well as any necessary professional fees, installation costs, and capitalized interest costs. If the proposed project involves constructed assets, the estimates should include materials, direct labor costs, overhead costs, indirect overhead costs, and capitalized interest costs.

- *Estimates of Time and Any Additional Nonconstruction Costs to Be Incurred over the Life of the Project.* A project-management system that monitors all such costs as well as the timing for when they are expected to be incurred allows for better management of the project.

- *Extent to Which the Proposed Capital Expenditures Are within an Already Approved Capital Budget.* In addition to the timing considerations, an organization should have a formal process for budgeting capital expenditures, normally summarized in the profit plan process discussed in Chapter 30, and including individual detailed monthly or weekly project budgets. Normally, this determination of needs would be summarized, approved by management, and then placed in the capital budget for future periods. However, there may be instances where the project is requested due to emergency conditions. For example, a regulatory ruling may require the immediate acquisition of pollution-control equipment, which may require the deferral of other budgeted capital projects.

- *Economic Justification for the Proposed Capital Expenditures in Terms of Costs, Anticipated Revenue, and Expected Profitability.* Included here also would be comparisons to present facilities, if any, and other alternative capital projects that were considered but rejected. This usually involves a detailed economic analysis.

- *The Projected Discounted Cash Flow Estimates for the Total Period of Acquisition and Service.* Discounted cash flow analysis projects expenses and revenues for a project over time, then discounts them back to the present based on the estimated cost of money. This technique allows management to estimate when payback will be realized from the investment. The idea is that $100 of cost savings, which will not be realized until a year into the future, is worth less than $100 today because, if received today, the $100 could have been earning interest. Although management's need for a facility often dictates acquisition decisions, discounted cash flow analysis is an important analysis tool useful for internal auditors.

- *Reasons for This Amendment, and Its Effect on Previous Profitability Projections (if a Supplement to a Previous Project).* The auditor should give particular attention to any capital project additions. Sometimes, an operating unit will secure approval for a small capital project and then change its nature through a series of supplemental amendment requests.

- *Approvals of Necessary Levels of Management.* There should be a formal approval process where appropriate levels of local and regional management review and approve all such capital project requests before submission to senior management. This process should be based on project size or scope.

Project proposal formats should be prepared in a format specifically designated by the particular organization and should also include a supporting financial analysis in accordance with applicable procedures and policies. Normally, the organization's central group, which has direct or functional responsibility for such capital projects as construction or fixed-assets control, would have worked with the local group to prepare the project proposal. In addition, there should have been some preliminary coordination with senior management.

The control considerations at this stage are, first, that the organization's project proposal requirements have been properly met. A second control consideration goes beyond any single proposal and should include the auditor's appraisal of the adequacy of the existing overall construction project control procedures. Possible improvements to this process may include additional information that would be helpful in later review stages or other data to provide a better financial analysis.

(ii) Capital Project Management Review and Approval. After the preliminary proposal and local-level management approvals, the project proposal next moves to more senior management levels. The levels involved will depend on the size of both the particular organization and the project. There will often be a review by a senior management committee, approval by an authorized executive, and, for major projects, review and approval by the board of directors. This review and approval process should include a detailed examination and evaluation of the proposed capital expenditures based on a review of the documentation submitted as well as other available materials and the experience and judgment of operational and staff executives. The impact on other organization activities and objectives also needs consideration. The higher-level review normally includes:

- *Assessment of Total Resources Available for Capital Expansion.* An organization may have established an internal capital budget, with funds generated through internal cash flows, for these types of projects. However, larger projects may require the organization to obtain financing through the sale of securities or through borrowing. Included in the consideration of the total resources potentially available should be both the amount of debt or equity capital the organization can reasonably expect to raise under current conditions and attitudes regarding how much risk the organization wishes to assume through such capital investment. This risk evaluation includes the level of debt servicing that may be required.

- *Organization Strategy.* The degree of support for capital expansion depends on the extent to which the proposed investment supports the strategic or long-term profit plans of the organization. Although these strategic plans may change over time, the facility proposals should be consistent with current plans.

- *Projected Profitability Contribution of the Project.* The project documentation includes the projected costs and revenues that have been developed to establish the projected profitability of the proposed capital expenditure. Cost and revenue data assumptions are subjected to additional review and analysis to further appraise their validity. This same management review should include a detailed examination of the assumptions as well as the various cost and projected revenue estimates.

- *Acceptability of the Rate of Return.* An organization has a cost of capital based on the interest cost of its debt plus the cost of equity capital determined by the market valuation of the stock. Figure 27.7 provides a simplified example of how

Figure 27.7 Simplified Average Cost of Capital Calculation

Capital Component	Proportion of Total Capital (a)	Cost After Tax % (b)	Weighted Average Cost of Capital (c) = (a) × (b)
Short- and long-term debt	0.20	3	0.60
New equity investments	0.10	10	1.00
Retained earnings	0.30	9	2.70
Depreciation provisions	0.40	7.5	3.00
Weighted Average Cost of Capital			7.30

such a cost of capital value might be calculated. An objective here is that the rate of return for the proposed project should at least match the cost of capital rate of the new investment. However, this measure will not work in all cases. Often, the anticipated benefits are too ''soft'' to just use the rate of return. Other management priorities may drive the project.

- *Judgment Factors.* In addition to the financial analysis, there should always be an independent decision by management as to the desirability of the proposed capital expenditure. This decision reflects management's judgment based on experience and other perceptions and goes beyond the basic supporting analysis.

- *Assessment of Priorities.* Each construction project generally competes with other projects for final approval. Although an organization may appear to have sufficient funds available, there are always alternative ways to utilize the organization's resources. The objective here is to find investments that best serve the organization's interests. Although not part of the formal capital project evaluation process, these capital budgeting projects should include an evaluation of the merits of each capital project proposal, along with a final assessment of priorities.

An adequate set of policies and procedures assures that all proposed projects receive fair and consistent consideration. Second, the organization should make these policies and procedures effective in actual practice through a careful and rigorous review effort.

(iii) Detailed Planning and Project Final Approval. Some projects are so complex that a more detailed planning step becomes necessary. The nature of tasks to be accomplished in this step will vary and could include:

- Preparation of requests for proposals to solicit bids from contractors to assist on various aspects of the project

- Obtaining preliminary approval from legal authorities for the planned construction or filing appropriate zoning variance requests and the like

- Obtaining quotes on any specialized items of equipment needed for the project

- Meeting with investment bankers or other advisors to describe the potential project and the anticipated financing needs

The various financial assumptions included in the preliminary proposal should receive a far more detailed analysis based on any additional estimates for various project costs.

The usual course for construction projects is to request tenders for the project and to evaluate the bids. This step should allow the team to develop a detailed project plan with timelines and cost estimates that may uncover some unknown factors that might not make the original proposal as attractive as initially assumed. In that case, the project team may recommend dropping the proposed project. Otherwise, the detailed plan should be summarized and submitted to senior management for final approval.

(iv) Acquisition of Facilities.   In addition to the evaluation of construction projects, an internal auditor may become involved with evaluating the controls surrounding the acquisition of the facility. This section discusses some of these considerations for the acquisition of fixed assets, including both major capital projects and other facilities that have been classified as fixed assets.

Assuming that the project has received final approval by the proper levels of management, a next stage is to acquire the facilities or assets covered by the project. This acquisition can be accomplished in various ways: by purchase, lease, construction, or any combination of approaches. The purchasing department may handle the entire acquisition or only specific portions. However, when major facilities such as buildings are to be acquired, the acquisition will normally be handled by a facility-construction group. The price paid for the acquisition may be a quoted vendor price, be the result of direct negotiation, or be based on actual cost. (These alternative approaches are discussed briefly in Chapter 24, on purchasing.) Since facility acquisitions normally involve so much money, the particular purchasing approach adopted is important. This problem is discussed in greater depth later in this chapter.

Facilities and other fixed assets can also be leased. The advantages achieved through leasing include lower capital requirements and greater possibilities for accelerating and maximizing the tax deductibility of the current expenditures. The decision to lease rather than purchase requires a careful analysis and consideration of all related factors. In addition, it requires competent legal assistance to cover the different conditions that have to be dealt with in protecting the organization's interest.

Lease financing is complicated by many financial and tax-related options. A detailed discussion of leasing procedures is beyond the scope of this book. If internal auditors encounter a leasing arrangement that raises questions, the auditor should seek an explanation of the terms and other details from someone on the organization's legal staff or from an outside source such as a specialist in the external audit firm.

The organization could also deem it best to construct the particular facility or capital asset with its own personnel and resources. In such situations, the complexity of the project will determine whether the work is done by a regularly established operational unit or a special group created for this purpose. Normally, when an organization does its own construction, it will still purchase many items, use a number of subcontractors, and lease various types of supporting equipment. The key control concerns involve the management of the project. Designated personnel, or an assigned general contractor, should have the responsibility for supervision and for the resulting costs of the project. For a construction project, for example, portions of the work—such as plumbing, electrical work, or cement work—may be subcontracted directly by the organization. In other instances, a general contractor may elect to perform portions of the work directly and subcontract for others.

Construction activities present some special concerns and challenges to internal audit. They typically involve large amounts of money and require the services of outsiders who are not aware of the organization's internal control procedures. Audits of construction activities are discussed in greater detail later in this chapter.

There are numerous control concerns surrounding larger construction and facility-acquisition projects. Adequate consideration should be given to the alternatives available in such areas as financing, timing, technology, and construction options. Particular attention should be given to any outside sources selected for the project. They should be both capable and reliable and should receive a reasonable basis of compensation. These considerations are particularly important because there is little recourse (such as sending it back) with an unacceptable construction project. Operational schedules and commitments to customers may depend directly on the performance of contractors on a construction project.

Another concern is control over the progress of the project, both from timing and cost standpoints. Specific controls are needed to monitor such projects so that any delays in scheduled completion and cost overruns can be detected on a timely basis, thus providing an opportunity for prompt corrective actions. The project control mechanisms discussed in Chapter 26 are applicable to larger engineering projects. Although facilities projects discussed here are typically even larger and involve more outside contractors, many of the control procedures are similar.

At times, the capital asset may be no more complicated than any regularly purchased item, and at others may require extensive examination and testing to determine acceptability. This is particularly true for projects that were initiated because of legal or regulatory mandates such as environmental clean-up projects. These projects may require acceptance testing at interim stages as well as at final completion. Acceptance testing is an important step in the determination of when the project is complete and when payment is due. Testing and acceptance steps will, therefore, normally be defined with great precision in a construction project. The terms of acceptance must be clearly defined in advance and the designated steps carried out properly. The testing must be done in the manner specified, with appropriate care, and be evidenced by appropriate approvals or other documentation. Any qualifications arising from the test results can be extremely important in the event of any subsequent performance failures and the related collection of damages.

The most important control process during any capital project, whether construction or acquisition, is a strong system of project management. Management should assure itself that the project-control system in place breaks down the work effort into identifiable steps, measures both progress and costs against those steps, and constantly reports on the cost and time remaining to complete the effort. If an outside contractor is responsible for the project, these detailed control steps are largely outside of the organization's control. Nevertheless, an organization should closely monitor the project's progress. These concepts are the same for all projects, whether a new device, a computer information system, or a major plant. Project-management fundamentals were discussed in Chapter 26.

(v) Administering Completed Facilities.   Once the construction project has been completed and accepted, the organization has the ongoing responsibility to maintain the asset. At the same time, there is a broader managerial responsibility to get the maximum value from the facility. This is often handled by a facilities-administration organization responsible for both physical and accounting matters. Although facilities administration goes rather beyond capital projects and construction, it has been included here because of the close relationship between construction projects and the maintenance of those completed projects. Some of the facilities-administration control concerns include:

- Providing adequate facilities for various types of assets, as required
- Protection from physical threats such as fire, humidity, excessive heat or cold, dust, and the like

- Adequate security from theft

- Appropriate insurance coverage

- Safety protection for employees

- Adequate preventive maintenance and repair activities

- Maintaining adequate records for maintenance, repair, and other work

- Established accountability to organizational components, including records for location, availability, and maintenance requirements

- Accurate accounting records for depreciation and other facilities costs

These administrative matters extend into the broader problems of operational care and control discussed later in this chapter. The detailed work may be handled by a property accounting function, but management should review these records for correctness.

(vi) Retirement of Fixed-Asset Facilities. Although some types of facilities may be used almost indefinitely, such as a major mineral-extraction facility, in most cases there comes a time when the particular facility needs to be abandoned, replaced, or modified substantially. This can be a simple, clean-cut action or a complicated one. An individual small machine may be removed and then scrapped or sold. At the other extreme, a multiple-building production facility may be sold or remodeled. The certain decisions and activities involved vary in degrees of complexity, depending on the particular facility, including:

- *Determination That the Particular Item Should Be Retired.* Management may determine that the ongoing costs of the facility are no longer justified by the benefits being received. This determination is often made as part of the decision to discontinue an entire line of business or to acquire a new facility.

- *Determination of What Is to Be Done with the Old Facility.* A decision may be made as to whether the facility will be transferred to another organization component, put in storage, scrapped, sold, or somehow incorporated in the construction of a new asset. Again, this decision may be made as a part of the new facility proposal.

- *Physical Implementation of the Retirement.* The particular asset, if an item of equipment, may be taken out of service and transferred to another location for other use or disposition. For a smaller asset, such as a machine, the disposition may be within the jurisdiction of the scrap department. Controls over scrap are discussed in Chapter 23. The disposition of a large facility may be so important or unique that it is handled in a special manner.

- *Accounting Implementation of the Retirement.* At this stage, the fixed-asset records must reflect the retirement. Physical and depreciation records need to be adjusted so that accounting records are properly reconciled. Any gain or loss from the disposition needs to be recognized for income purposes based on recorded book values.

The retirement of physical assets is both an operational and an accounting-related matter. Based on financial accounting principles, an asset may have been depreciated from its original purchase price to a relatively low salvage value. The disposition or sale for scrap may actually involve an accounting gain. However, in the United States, tax rules may affect the accounting for the retired asset as well as any replacement asset. An internal auditor may not be aware of these often quite complex tax rules but should obtain assurances that the organization's accounting function is quite aware of the tax and accounting implications of the disposition.

From a control standpoint, the auditor should determine that retirements are properly approved, as evidenced by an established policy or based on appropriate management approvals. There is always a danger that an unauthorized person will ''write off'' a fixed asset without proper authorization. A related concern is that these discontinued assets may be sold at less than market value on a less-than-arm's-length basis. Controls should be in place so that overall organization interests are maximized in every transaction.

(vii) Post-Implementation Reviews of Facility Projects. The final phase of the facilities construction and management cycle should include a management review and appraisal of the completed project. Although an individual internal auditor will typically not be involved with a single project from its construction, through its ongoing maintenance, and into its final disposition, internal auditors may become involved at all levels. At the end of its useful life, the individual facility project should be reexamined to determine actual and expected results over its life span. At the time the facility was proposed, expectations were established—along with supporting analyses—for certain results. Management now may have an interest in whether those expected results were actually realized.

Post-implementation reviews of facility projects are difficult to schedule. They raise questions as to when such an analysis should be made and whether it is feasible to perform such reviews at all. While the partial results for a new plant or substantial facility may be inconclusive, it is often of little value to wait many years to determine, for example, whether payback results have been achieved. The general results can often be reasonably appraised one or two years after the acquisition of the asset or the project completion, depending on the particular asset and the original estimated timing of the project completion. A judgment must be made regarding what is a reasonable time for demonstrating that the new facility is going to produce results along the lines originally projected.

This type of analysis always raises the problem of whether new developments since the date of the acquisition have significantly affected the outcome of the original plan. In many cases, subsequent developments substantially reduce the value of any post-implementation facilities review. Recognizing these limitations, good facility-management procedures should support such a review. A major benefit is that everyone can learn from past experience whether any aspect of the total procedure can be improved. This is especially true with regard to the kind of analysis and supporting documentation that was developed. It can also apply to the manner in which projects are initiated, reviewed, and finally approved. Feedback can result in modifications in the policies and procedures that will apply to future proposals. A second benefit is that the persons or organizational components that develop such proposals know that they may be subjected to a post-implementation review. This knowledge should serve as a motivation to be more thorough and objective in developing the initial support for a project. This is a useful check on overenthusiasm for a desired facility, which can lead to proposers being too optimistic in estimating future savings.

Because some capital projects require major investment decisions by senior management, an internal auditor may not be directly involved in the decision process; however, internal audit can play a significant role in reviewing supporting staff functions. An internal auditor can assist management in the administration and procedural support for the control of construction activities, the proper accounting for fixed-asset items, and their physical care and security. In particular, the auditor should determine that an effective project-management system is in place.

All fixed-asset acquisitions involve some overhead costs to the acquiring organization. Fixed-asset cost systems range from standard established prices for a small capital asset tool to the construction expenses associated with a major building where the organization's expenses are determined by the outside contractors. Two different types of questions are often involved. The first is whether the particular set of contractual arrangements was the best solution for the acquiring organization securing the facility at the lowest possible fair price. The second is whether the costs have actually been incurred in accordance with the established arrangements and whether costs incurred were properly accumulated to support the final recorded book value of the asset. The latter question requires a verification of supporting documentation, observation of completed items, and an assessment of whether reasonable value was obtained for the cost expenditures. Audit procedures for construction contracts are discussed later in this chapter.

(viii) Types of Facility-Acquisition Arrangements. There are numerous ways to negotiate with suppliers for facility-construction projects. Many of these pose control problems because in many instances, the costs controlled by the outside contractor are passed on as part of the contract. An internal auditor should be aware of these contractual arrangements before attempting any review. An organization's construction or facility acquisition costs can vary greatly due to some of the typical types of construction or acquisition arrangements, as follows:

- *Standard or Catalog Price.* This arrangement is used for smaller fixed-asset items where prices are published but supplier costs are not disclosed. The organization makes its acquisition decision on the basis of whether the purchase at the standard or catalog price is the best available. If there are alternative sources or substitute products available, the organization may make its own analysis of the acquisition's value content. Control concerns here are similar to those for routine purchasing, discussed in Chapter 24.

- *Negotiated Price.* When the acquiring organization has sufficient bargaining strength because of other available alternatives, prices are often negotiated. In such a situation, the costs of the supplier can play an important role, and in some cases, cost data may even be supplied by the vendor. Control concerns here include assuring that a fair price was negotiated, that other qualified suppliers were also allowed to bid, and that the entire transaction took place on an arm's-length basis.

- *Lump Sum with Redetermination.* In certain situations, it may be possible to negotiate a tentative price for the capital asset item subject to redetermination at some later date. Here, the organization has the right to review the internal records of the supplier to verify or appraise the propriety of the cost data used for the redetermination. The scope of this review varies and is detailed in the contract terms. This type of pricing arrangement preserves the incentive and overall benefit of a fixed-price arrangement, but also gives consideration to uncertainties or inadequacies of the preliminary cost data.

- *Cost Contracts with a Fixed Profit Percentage.* This type of contract allows the contractor to pass all actual costs to the organization, plus an allowance for profit based on those costs. The rationale for this arrangement is that costs cannot be determined in advance but must ultimately be fully recovered, and that the contractor needs to recover a profit based on a percentage of the costs incurred. This arrangement protects the contractor, but has the defect that the acquiring organization does not assure contractor motivation to control or reduce costs. In fact, the result may be just the opposite, and it should be employed only as a last resort.

- *Cost-Type Contracts with Limitations.* In this arrangement, limitations are placed either on the costs incurred or on the profit. One approach is to fix a maximum price that would be applicable if and when costs and agreed-upon profit exceed that maximum point. Another is to cover all costs but to provide for a fixed profit fee. These approaches provide protection to the acquiring organization but do not fully solve the problem of cost minimization.

- *Cost-Type Contracts with Incentives.* This arrangement attempts to motivate better cost performance by setting up incentives based upon costs, profits, or some combination. It can compare cost performance with previously established cost estimates, and then with either savings and cost overruns (or both) shared in a designated manner. The incentives may also be related to the extent to which the contractor completes the work in accordance with agreed-upon time schedules or cost savings.

- *Time and Material Contracts.* Some contracts may take the form of fixed rates for particular kinds of services, with final compensation depending on hours expended, plus supplementary material costs. The rates used may or may not include profit and overhead. These contracts are used in connection with certain kinds of installation work, excavations, or other specialized tasks.

There can be many variations in larger fixed-asset contract arrangements, depending upon the terms negotiated by both parties. In general, the complexity of contract terms will increase as the size of the overall fixed-asset project increases. As mentioned previously, an internal auditor may need to consult with the organization's legal counsel to verify the understanding of the contract.

The control of costs incurred by large facility contracts often varies greatly and may lead to a dependence on the contractor's cost data. In many instances, these costs may be verified by an independent public accountant engaged by the project owners. Without this independent verification, the need increases for an independent review of the validity of those costs. Construction costs for a building facility are typical of these kinds of situations.

(b) FACILITY CONSTRUCTION INTERNAL CONTROLS

When costs are the basis for compensation to the contractor, the auditor needs to consider the following various factors determining contract-term validity.

- *Identification of Allowed Costs to Be Incurred.* The starting point in any review is the identification of the specific cost components defined in the contract. All costs incurred must ultimately be evaluated in terms of their relationship to the end product.

- *Services to Be Provided by the Organization.* Individual contract items may be provided by either the contractor or the benefiting organization. Therefore, what is to be done and what is to be supplied by each party needs to be clearly defined. Examples might be the testing of soil, obtaining building permits or licenses for new construction, or providing computer equipment or software.

- *Identification of Costs to Be Charged Directly to the Project.* Of central importance is the necessity of a clear understanding of what costs are to be charged directly to the contract. These might include direct or indirect labor, specialized equipment purchases or rentals, materials, and services that are acquired by the contractor directly for the project. These items should be clearly defined with prices at the actual net costs to the contractor—or, in the case of contractor's own equipment, at prevailing market rates. General contractors normally bid for a project on the basis of their own estimates of costs. Cost overruns are usually the contractor's responsibility unless they are due to changes requested by the contracting organization.

- *Definition of Costs to Be Reimbursed as Overhead.* There may be many elements of cost for services performed by various indirect service groups within the contractor's organization. These might include support engineering, office services, or contractor data-processing services. Many of these costs incurred are normally recovered through the contractor's profit. However, these items should be defined in the contract. The types of costs that can be recoverable as well as those that can't should be agreed upon as part of the contract.

- *Overhead Cost Allocations.* Although normally the responsibility of the general contractor, there may be instances when project needs are served by internal organizational components that also serve other organization business units. In this situation, the allocation of costs between internal operations and the contract must be fair and equitable. There may be a tendency to shift cost allocations when conditions change to maximize performance. Just as contractor costs may be improper, the function responsible for the contract should also monitor its own internal costs to ascertain that these overhead allocations are valid.

- *Controls over Premium Costs.* In rare instances, a contract may call for some type of premium or incentive costs, raising questions as to whether these premium costs are justified. An example would be the use of higher-cost forms of transportation to accelerate delivery. Another is the use of overtime labor. Problems can arise because of uncontrollable developments and the resulting need to spend extra amounts to prevent possible future delays. However, these premium costs may also be due to contractor inefficiency or desire to avoid penalties for the delay of promised completion. The propriety of such payments should always be carefully established.

- *Do Costs Reflect Adequate Levels of Prudence?* Implicit in all is the requirement that the cost claimed be both authorized for recovery and actually incurred in accordance with the contract and a reasonable level of prudence. The contractor should not be reimbursed for inefficiency or negligence, and all aspects of the cost-recovery effort should be completed in good faith and with integrity.

(i) Facility Construction Financial-Control Considerations. Although project cost verifications are usually performed by an independent public accountant, both parties may agree to an internal audit review to validate the costs that will become the basis for the compensation in accordance with the terms of the construction contract. In a broader sense, an operational audit is concerned with helping to make the construction project more efficient and recommending steps to promote lower organization costs. This review might be carried out in part by accounting personnel or entirely by internal audit. In any event, internal audit should be interested directly or indirectly in all aspects of the review.

- *Precontract Participation.* A contract is often finalized and work actually begun before the internal audit's review begins. By that time, the opportunity has been lost to suggest contract conditions and controls that might better define relationships with the contractor. It would be efficient for internal audit to participate in the development of the contract, particularly in defining and monitoring the validity of costs. This can be accomplished even before any bids are solicited to ensure they will be on a comparable basis. The general bases of cost reimbursements should be defined in the precontract bid such that questions, if any, can be raised and clarified. For a major project, it may be desirable for a survey team, including internal audit, to visit potential contractors and their major subcontractors prior to approval of the actual contract to clarify any areas of misunderstanding and to develop more intelligently the planned audit coverage. An understanding of the contractor's organization and mode of operation can be useful in a later review of actual costs claimed.

- *Establishing Initial Contractor Relationships.* The internal auditor should establish a relationship with the contractor's on-site and/or remote offices promptly after the signing of the contract to help determine that the contractor follows good control procedures. This early auditor presence may serve to identify areas where organization services could be utilized to reduce the contractor requirements.

- *Labor Costs.* In a typical construction contract, a major portion of the costs incurred will relate to labor. Thus, a number of labor cost matters at the job site require careful attention, including:
  - The reasonableness of staffing levels recruited at the proper levels of skill
  - The adequacy of work records, including the accuracy of field payrolls
  - The adequacy of supervision, including controls over absenteeism
  - The quality of work practices, including general order and efficiency

At a contractor supervisory level there may be similar problems of effective labor utilization in the area of administrative supervision and control. At this administrative level, controls over proper direct charges and overhead allocations are especially important.

- *Material Costs.* Also of great importance is the efficient use of materials. These include:
  - Supporting material purchase documentation, including purchase orders, supplier's invoices, and receiving reports
  - Reasonable evidence of propriety of quantities ordered
  - Fairness of material prices, including charges for any materials internally transferred by the contractor

- Reasonable established standards for purchased materials
- Prudent use of materials for the contact project, as well as adequate protection from weather or theft of equipment and materials awaiting use
- Proper follow-up of claims against vendors

- *Equipment Rentals.* Necessary equipment over and above that which is supplied by the organization is often either rented by the contractor for use on the project or provided directly at agreed-upon rates. Items of auditor interest in this area include:

    - Supporting documentation in the form of rental agreements
    - Determination that items included in the rental rate are not also being charged as additional costs—as, for example, fuel or maintenance costs
    - An assessment of whether there is excessive equipment, as judged by the amount of equipment idle time
    - Possibilities that costs can be reduced through purchases rather than rental of equipment

- *Subcontractors.* In most cases, the contractor will subcontract portions of the work, such as electrical or plumbing. These expenditures can be of major significance and require adequate standards of subcontractor control. The same types of problems exist here as with the general contractor. Normally, these activities fall outside of the responsibility of internal audit as the general contractor has the responsibility for subcontracted work. Through inquiries, the internal auditor should determine that there are adequate procedures for the solicitation of bids, a continuing appraisal for the most appropriate type of subcontractor arrangements, and a review and appraisal of the actual implementation. These arrangements will be subject to approval by the general contractor, and internal audit should review these arrangements when possible.

- *Other Costs.* Any other costs charged at the job site should be reviewed for their propriety and reasonableness as to types of cost and expenditure. Costs generated at intermediate field offices or at the contractor's home office should also be reviewed most carefully. With these latter items, it is often difficult to determine whether the charges are proper as either a direct charge or as an overhead allocation. More intensive reviews in this area are often desirable to identify any potentially controversial cost-related issues.

- *Project Administration.* Although an examination of contract costs will tend to indicate the overall level of efficiency with which the construction contract is being carried out, internal audit should also look at the contract administration process to determine any additional controls to benefit the contract process. The benefits here might include the possible reduction of current costs charged to the contract, improved quality in the administration of the construction effort, and suggestions for improving the quality level while also realizing more reasonable cost levels. If these operational activities are not covered in the contract, organization management will be charged with the primary responsibility for them. However, internal audit can frequently provide additional assistance as a result of specific contract review activities. In such an effort, the auditor should work closely with the responsible organization representatives.

- *Control of Change Orders.* Even though contract negotiation will attempt to testimate all required steps, processes, and costs, changes to a contract are often necessary. This will require the authorization of change order covering some aspects of the existing contract specifications. These changes may involve significant costs. In any event, the decisions to make such changes should be considered as new contractual commitments that modify the existing contract and need to be handled with care. They should be supported by the appropriate levels of approval. Where these changes involve the loss of value of previous work performed, the decision to make the change requires special consideration. The reduction or expansion of the contract's scope may also affect maximum contract limits and originally agreed-upon incentive rights.

These aspects must be carefully considered. Also, an adequate procedure is needed to communicate and implement the changes so that the proper adjustments can be made to scheduled procurement of labor, materials, and equipment.

- *Winding up the Contract.* The organization will usually desire the earliest possible completion of the contract. The contractor may or may not be similarly motivated, depending on whether any incentive provisions are applicable or whether contractor personnel are needed elsewhere. In some cases, there can be delays that require special pressures on the contractor by the organization. When the construction is actually brought to completion and the organization has determined that it can accept the facility, the major operational problem is to be certain that all items that can be returned are so handled, and that proper credits have been made to the contract. At the same time, contractor-owned equipment needs to be removed and the premises cleaned up in an adequate manner. Finally, there is the need for a careful determination that the facility is complete in terms of the agreed-upon specifications.

(ii) Facility Construction Operational Control Considerations.   Facility construction capital projects represent major but infrequent efforts for most organizations. They are major because of their size as compared to other ongoing activities. More important, they will usually involve various outside contractors and control procedures that are not part of day-to-day operations. Although not always that common for a contracted job, there should be an appropriate level of administrative and internal accounting controls in place to manage the facility construction project and to achieve the best use of organization resources.

Although capital project internal controls cover a wide variety of areas—as discussed in the previous sections—an internal auditor may sometimes find it easy to think of them in terms of, first, the overall organization's operating controls to govern such projects and, second, the specific administrative controls over the particular project. These operating controls should be in place for all asset acquisitions, as discussed earlier. Specific administrative project controls for an organization's own projects were discussed in a different context in Chapter 26, on engineering and research activities. An internal auditor should always recognize, however, that controls over externally contracted work will be somewhat different.

Capital Project Operating Controls

Operating controls in this context are the broad policies and procedures that allow management to plan, budget, and engage in capital construction projects in a controlled manner.

These would start with some very general policies on the acquisition and disposition of major productive assets and should contain guidance for deciding which types of costs should be capitalized and whether to purchase or lease. There will be many variations in these decisions that cannot be spelled out in detail in a specific policy, but there should be some guidance on the levels and types of approvals needed.

The prior sections described the overall capital project process. A strong process includes formal capital asset planning and budgeting procedures. The more significant the project to the overall operations of the organization, the more thorough and formal should be the evaluation process. However, all projects should be included as part of a short- and long-range capital-asset planning process and evaluated for their estimated return on investment, their reasonableness given organization capabilities, and the risk of failure, and also be evaluated against other proposed projects to allow management to establish priorities. All capital projects should be examined both for their technical and their financial aspects.

Based upon appropriate approvals, the organization should have a formal approval mechanism where the project, depending upon its size and complexity, is subject to formal project controls. In addition, formal procedures should be in place to monitor the project over the course of its operation and to evaluate it after completion to assess and compare the final costs and benefits as compared to original plans.

Capital Project Administrative Controls

Capital project administrative controls refer to the particular control group assembled to build or supervise the installation of the project. This is an area where many major projects can go awry as management may delegate the project to a group that has had little experience with this size of endeavor.

Organizational controls may vary somewhat with the size of the project but are always important. The extent of these controls should be based upon:

- The significance of the capital project to overall organization size and operations
- The technological sophistication and planned installation time frames for the contemplated project
- The past experience of the organization with similar capital projects

These factors would help to determine the need for any special organization teams or structures assembled for the project. Persons from other units within the organization with experiences on similar projects could be brought in to help. However, perhaps the most important organizational internal control is the need for a clear designation of project management responsibility. Although these responsibilities should be described in the contract terms, various parties still may be second-guessing each other, and neither management nor any outside contractors will have a clear idea of who is in charge of the overall project. This project management should have responsibility for the overall accounting, administrative, and technical monitoring of the project.

Project controls are extremely important. A typical project involves a large number of separate but parallel efforts, following different time schedules, which must all come together in order to complete the project. An overall project control system should be in place for each effort and include:

Figure 27.8 Critical Path Example

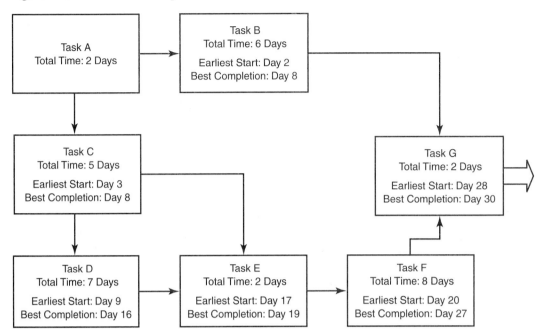

Project Sequence A - C - D - F - G Represent the Critical Path

- *A detailed project plan, using critical path notation, to outline sub-task interdependencies.* This type of plan would show the expected efforts required and elapsed times. An example of this type of chart is shown in Figure 27.8.

- *Formal commitments for all resources to be included in the project.* This might include formal contracts with vendors and commitments for other organizational resources.

- *Detailed cost estimates for each project sub-task, as well as estimates by type of expense.*

- *Formal systems to collect and approve all project disbursements, as well as reports of time expended.* For internal time reporting, labor cost charging mechanisms including an allocation of overhead should be established.

- *Procedures or systems to accumulate and transfer costs to appropriate capital and expense ledgers.*

- *Periodic project status reporting, including cost accumulations by sub-task and type of expenditure.* The cause of responsibility for significant variances should be reported, as well as ongoing estimates for costs to complete.

- *Defined project acceptance criteria for various stages as well as periodic formal technical reviews.*

For major capital projects the organization is directly executing, this type of project-control mechanism is the most important internal control. Lacking these controls, cost estimates can be missed, technical objectives may not be achieved, and management may not be aware of these problems until the project is in trouble. Internal audit should pay close attention to this project-control mechanism in any review of such major projects.

(c) FACILITY-CONSTRUCTION INTERNAL AUDIT ACTIVITIES

A review of a facility-construction capital project is an area where internal audit can be a significant help and resource to management. While this basic phrase has been used elsewhere within this book, it is most appropriate here because of the nonrecurring nature of facility-construction projects for an organization that just does not construct new plants, for example, on a regular, annual basis. These projects are often outside of the normal management control system. While the project team can report back that everything is under control, internal audit can review the controls surrounding the project from all of its aspects and independently report any problems or concerns to management for corrective action.

This chapter has discussed many of the control elements surrounding a major capital construction project. While an internal auditor may not have the skills to understand construction techniques and procedures, the skills gained in reviewing other financial and project-control activities will greatly aid internal auditors in performing financial, operational, and computer application reviews of a capital project facility-construction project. Materials in Chapters 26 (on engineering projects), 30 (on financial management), and in the previous sections of this chapter on fixed assets will somewhat aid the auditor in these reviews.

(i) Facility-Construction Financial Audit Procedures.   A large facilities project can present a real challenge to management and the internal auditor in attempting to monitor financial controls. There will typically be one prime contractor as well as numerous subcontractors, each having various materials and other needs, and, due to project time constraints, there may be strong pressures to approve payments with no undue delays to allow the project to move according to its schedule. This may be true even though requirements for making progress payments have been spelled out in the construction contract. The special nature of this type of project may mean that normal organization disbursement procedures will be bypassed. The large sums involved in many such projects add to the risks that improper payments are made or that unnecessary materials are purchased.

Many facility-construction projects are established with a financial controls team located on-site at the project and somewhat outside of the normal accounting organization. An individual may be assigned the task of project controller with the responsibility to review, approve, and pay all project expenses. This person is typically an employee of the general contractor and is responsible for authorizing all financial transactions associated with the project according to the general terms of the agreement and management's criteria. In addition, the person should obtain advance approval for any unusual, unplanned expenditures.

In addition to understanding the project cost system and controls in place, the internal auditor should perform a detailed review of purchase invoices to determine, among other matters, that:

- All purchase documentation includes evidence indicating the materials or services were received as billed.
- Purchase invoices are properly classified.
- There is no evidence of unusual or improper payments to contractors and suppliers.
- Actual costs do not exceed budgeted amounts by anything more than minor, explainable variances.
- Purchases are from vendors according to the terms of the contract and do not represent a potential conflict of interest.

Internal auditors should also determine that entries to organization accounting ledgers and systems are proper. This can be accomplished by tracing construction project transactions to the financial records of the organization. These internal audit procedures are outlined in Figure 27.9.

Figure 27.9 Construction Project Audit Program Example

Audit _____ Location _____ Date _____

AUDIT STEP	INITIAL	W/P
1. Determine a proper separation of responsibilities exists for all transactions. Persons ordering goods must be separate from those approving payments for the goods.		
2. Time and expense budgets should be prepared for all phases of the project and actual performance against those budgets should be managed.		
3. All major purchases must be authorized by an approved purchase order and must be formally received by a responsible member of the project management team.		
4. Damaged materials should be properly accounted for and surplus materials should have a proper accounting disposition.		
5. Working under the constraints of bargaining unit rules, procedures should be in place to monitor construction labor time and to control requests for overtime.		
6. The project controller should have authority over any necessary construction petty cash fund and this fund should be reconciled on a regular basis.		
7. All project costs should flow into the organization's financial systems with clear visibility of the costs and how they compare to established budgets.		
8. The construction site should have appropriate perimeter security, both during work and off hours.		
9. Safety and first aid facilities should be available on the construction site.		
10. The construction project should receive proper inspections by appropriate architects or engineers. Reports should be filed for management review on a regular basis.		

Other audit steps here include determining that a proper separation of duties exists so that no person can control all phases of processing a transaction such that errors can go undetected. Because the site controller often has less than full-time responsibilities for the project, there may be a danger that the controller has delegated both approval and data-entry responsibilities to a clerical-level person without adequate review. This could occur while the project controller is working on other matters.

Internal auditors should also take steps to assure that the project status reports communicated to management tie in to the financial records. In addition, the nature of many of these special projects may well require the project controller to have signature control over a special checking account and a petty cash fund for emergency purchases. An internal auditor should closely reconcile this checking account with supporting invoices, reconcile the petty cash account, and review supporting documentation.

(ii) Facility-Construction Operational Audit Procedures. Operational audit procedures here will concentrate primarily on the condition of the construction site and the protection and safeguarding of materials at the site. The auditor should look for proper security controls as well as adequate receiving procedures similar to those outlined in Chapter 24. In addition, there should be proper controls to prevent unauthorized persons from entering the construction area. While implementing these controls can be relatively easy if the construction site is within the organization's main facilities, it can be a challenge for a separate, freestanding construction project, particularly in a remote location.

Just as proper controls should be in place over the receipt of both goods and services, similar controls should be in place to prevent unauthorized goods and materials from leaving the site. Workers should properly sign out and unauthorized persons—both outsiders and members of the organization who do not have a need—should be prohibited from the construction site.

A basic knowledge of health and safety concerns can help the auditor to observe and make appropriate recommendations. For example, an internal auditor might observe that construction workers are not wearing hard hats on the site or that safety signs are not posted. Internal auditors should consult others in the organization or other sources with construction safety knowledge to follow up on any potential problems if specific regulations appear to be violated.

Internal audit will often find it effective to review operational controls along with the financial controls outlined in Figure 27.9 because of the close relationships between the two. For example, the financial review may raise questions about some purchased construction material and the auditor may want to go to the site to verify these purchases.

(iii) Facility-Construction Computer Audit Procedures. Since good project-control software is readily available, there should be no reason for the construction project to lack an adequate project-reporting system. Ideally, this software should be linked with the time and disbursement reporting systems used for the project as well as with main organization systems. The auditor should again be interested in reviewing input and output controls, as discussed in Chapter 17.

If the project-reporting system operates on a microcomputer networked to central servers, the auditor should give particular attention to access and output controls. In this environment, it can be easy for a manager under time pressures to alter file data. Similarly, because interfaces may be through a modem-based transmission or even a mailed diskette, the auditor should determine if sufficient protective and detective controls are in place to prevent these problems.

Computer-assisted audit procedures are often not particularly cost-effective for these types of audits, because they are not regular audits and their reporting systems may have unusual file structures. Internal auditors might be able to recalculate or verify project-reporting file records, but the audit project may not be worth the programming effort unless it is a large project or the organization is involved in a series of construction projects.

(iv) Audit Report Findings and Recommendations.

A: Cash Disbursements Are Not Properly Authorized. In our review of cash disbursements supporting the project, we found several without adequate documentation. A series of transactions labeled only ''Special Hardware Store Tools'' lacked any form of detailed invoice beyond a cash register charge slip. We could not locate the purchased tools.

Recommendation. All disbursements, no matter how small the miscellaneous purchases, should be properly documented with a detailed invoice.

B: Authorization Not Obtained for Related-Party Transactions. Our review of electrical contractor invoices revealed that the contractor had purchased significant amounts of construction materials from a subsidiary of that contractor without evidence of competitive bids and without prior management authorization. We also found that the prices paid for these materials exceeded normal market prices.

Recommendation. Purchases between related parties should only be allowed after prior management authorization.

C: Construction Assets Are Not Adequately Protected. Internal audit visited the construction site after hours and found copper pipe materials stored outside with no lighting and protected only by a low fence. As the materials were not directly visible from the site guard's office, they could be subject to theft without detection.

Recommendation. Construction materials that must remain outside should be protected by adequate fencing and lighting and receive periodic visits by the site guard. Whenever possible, however, valuable construction assets should be secured at the construction site.

27-4 FIXED-ASSET AND CAPITAL-PROJECT FUTURE DIRECTIONS

Fixed assets and capital construction projects are areas for operational auditing often ignored because of either low transaction volumes or the special nature of construction projects. However, internal auditors should at least consider both as part of the annual audit-planning risk analysis. In many industries, a review of fixed assets will not rank as that high of a risk in any given year due to low transaction volumes. In other industries, such as transportation, fixed assets are continually purchased, retired, and upgraded. Depending upon the organization and industry, they will and should eventually raise to a higher position in this risk ranking list, and then be considered for review.

Capital projects are often special projects that management or internal audit may not view as normal audit projects. However, due to their special nature, internal audit can often make a significant contribution through recommendations that improve controls and actually result in cost savings to the organization.

Other fixed asset–related areas were not covered in this chapter due to space limitations. One of these is an analysis of lease or buy options. The auditor should be aware of decision criteria to make appropriate recommendations. Another area not covered in this chapter is the whole field of ''soft assets'' such as computer programs and intellectual property. This is an area filled with internal audit opportunities and will be discussed in a future edition.

CHAPTER 28

Sales, Marketing, and Advertising

28-1 SALES, MARKETING, AND ADVERTISING FUNCTIONS

For many organizations, the sales, marketing, and advertising functions represent a wide area of importance. Although marketing was once viewed narrowly as including only sales functions, it now typically includes broader activities that go beyond basic sales efforts. Marketing functions are now found in many organizations that were once not even considered true sales organizations in the past. For example, the typical public accounting firm that once provided services through low-key, relationship-based sales efforts now has some type of marketing function to help sell its services to existing and potential new clients.

Just as sales and marketing have often been combined and treated as a single area in the traditional organization, advertising is often thought of as a component of marketing. While advertising responsibilities may be combined with marketing functions in some organizations, advertising has some unique control aspects that suggest it should receive special attention. In particular, many advertising functions are contracted out to specialized agencies that perform the creative work of advertising and deal with the various media vendors who present that advertising.

Internal auditors have historically reviewed the selling function within their organizations; however, the marketing department was considered to be responsible for little more than advertising, and internal auditors often gave only minimal attention to the marketing and advertising functions in their organizations.

Today, management often views marketing and related advertising programs as key components in the strategic planning process. In recognition of the sales, marketing, and advertising functions' greater scope and the concerns of management, internal auditors should have an interest in these areas beyond reviews of financial controls. While sales organizations tend to be procedures-oriented, the typical marketing function has unique characteristics requiring creativity, special personnel skills, and other intangible qualities. Because of this, the role of internal audit might appear to be less fitting than in more traditional operational audit areas such as engineering, inventory control, or shipping. Internal audit is in an excellent position to conduct an independent review and appraisal of these important areas. Internal audit must realize, however, that the creative core of the marketing function must be properly recognized and adequately preserved.

Internal control reviews of the sales, marketing, and advertising functions can make a significant contribution to the organization. Internal audit can often identify areas of cost savings through financial- and operational-oriented reviews. Marketing- and advertising-related functions, in particular, are often concerned with future-oriented issues where it is difficult to measure current performance against anticipated future benefits. In addition, some marketing and advertising activities are somewhat experimental, with approaches tried and then discarded. Internal audit should recognize the creative nature of marketing and seek to identify good control practices within this environment. As a first step, however, internal audit must have a good understanding of the particular sales, marketing, and advertising functions in the auditor's organization.

This chapter discusses approaches for auditing the sales, marketing, and advertising functions, including product planning. While these functions may be located in the same department, actual audit procedures differ. Although these activities, such as advertising, are often performed by outside contractors, internal auditors should at least consider reviewing the contractual arrangements for these activities.

28-2 UNDERSTANDING MARKETING ACTIVITIES

The ongoing success of any organization depends on satisfying the needs of customers in an effective manner, either through a tangible product or in the form of some kind of service. The product or service may be used by individuals, companies, or government units, all referred to as the customers. The purpose of the marketing function is to accomplish this need-satisfaction in the most effective and economical manner possible. In more specific terms, this means attracting and satisfying customers in a manner that contributes to the overall profit of the organization.

One can better understand how a marketing organization might function for a given organization by considering some examples.

- *A Consumer Products Organization.* Consumer products are sold directly or through intermediaries to consumers who purchase and use them. Often, an organization has established brand names that it must promote as well as new products it wishes to introduce. Many new products are introduced only after a marketing research that identifies how consumers will react to the new product. The products must then be advertised through various means, such as print advertisements or television commercials. In addition, it may be necessary to market the products through dealers by offering the dealers various promotional incentives. The marketing function is responsible for either performing these functions or managing outside sources—such as advertising agencies—in doing so.

- *An Industrial Products Organization.* This type of organization typically markets components or raw materials to other industrial companies. Some marketing requirements, such as advertising, are similar to those of a consumer products organization, but there are also some significant differences. For example, industrial marketing may involve selling through trade shows, as well as installing certain products at customers' sites for testing. Markets may encompass the world rather than limited national entities. The marketing function may become involved in customer service and support for specialized products.

- *A Service-Oriented Organization.* In many instances, service organizations may not have a formal function called "marketing," but they will have some other department with responsibilities for marketing. For example, a university is interested in marketing its programs to prospective students as well as selling itself to donors, potential faculty members, and officials who have the ability to dispense grant funds. Despite what it is called, this is a marketing function.

In any type of organization, the marketing function initially identifies particular types of customer needs, where the organization has some capability for satisfying those needs, and where there is a reasonable expectancy that this can be done profitably. Policies, programs, and procedures must then be developed that will provide the means for actually achieving the identified purpose. Finally, all of these plans must be implemented in an efficient manner. This is the typical marketing function. It centers on these issues but also acts in partnership with the production, engineering, financial, and other functions to support general management goals.

(a) MARKETING PROCESS

A starting point for understanding the marketing cycle requires an evaluation of the organization's resources and capabilities in this area. Internal audit should understand what products will be supplied and to which markets. These questions are at the highest level of an overall process where management should also be asking the question, "What business are we in?" Some have argued that United States railroads lost their passenger business in the 1950s because they never asked or perhaps incorrectly answered this type of question. They should have answered the question with a response to indicate they were in the *passenger transportation business.* They provided transportation services using trains as the main option. Other options for passenger transportation were buses and airplanes. Unfortunately, they kept thinking that they were just in the *railroad passenger business,* and so slowly saw their market share disappear.

The same questions may be addressed at lower levels. Here, management may use an analysis of their marketing process to decide, for example, whether they should build an economy model of an existing, higher-priced product. Management might question the range of products that should be offered and the types of customers who might purchase them. The idea is to determine how existing resources could be best used to exploit potential market opportunities.

Understanding the strategic marketing process should be an initial step in internal audit's review of the marketing function. Internal audit may find this product or market strategy to be formally documented. However, a formal published plan may not exist for reasons of confidentiality, and internal audit will have to discuss the strategy with appropriate levels of management.

A review of marketing can take place on several levels within an organization. Internal audit can review the marketing strategic planning process for the entire organization, a separate division, a functional product line, or a specific product. It can be a separate audit or can be combined with a review of sales or related functions. Each review scope requires an understanding of the organization's marketing capabilities, market requirements, and marketing decision and evaluation process.

(i) Scope of Marketing Capabilities. Internal audit needs to understand experiences gained and results already achieved in marketing particular types of products. Prior success with a cosmetic product, such as lipstick, should normally be a sound basis for the introduction of a similar cosmetic product. Similarly, contacts established with a particular group or industrial market provide a good base for expanding a product line to include similar items. This capability has a number of important dimensions, including a familiarity with the kinds of problems that are involved in the particular market. Also important are the contacts that have been made with the customers for other products. A reputation that can be transferred to new products should have been established with customers.

(ii) Understanding Market Requirements.   Market requirements for existing or new products must also be considered. Many organizations think of these requirements in terms of strategic business units (SBUs). Within a given organization, an SBU is a single business or group of related businesses that have their own responsible managers and distinct mission. An SBU typically has its own competitors and can be planned and organized independently of other units in the organization. Market requirements would be defined in terms of the overall organization's SBUs.

The Boston Consulting Group (BCG) developed an approach, some years ago, to classify SBUs in terms of a business portfolio matrix. Using this approach, each SBU is classified and plotted in terms of its annualized growth rate as well as its relative market share. Figure 28.1 shows this type of business portfolio matrix. The vertical axis shows the relative annual growth rate while the horizontal axis shows the market share on a log scale for each SBU relative to the share of the industry's largest competitor. A relative market share of 2.0 means that the SBU has twice the share of the strongest competitor in that market.

Figure 28.1 shows the various organization SBUs plotted as circles, where the size of a circle relates to the SBU's dollar sales. The BCG business portfolio matrix is then

Figure 28.1   Boston Consulting Group Portfolio Matrix

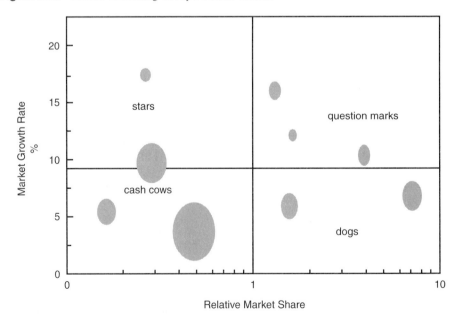

divided into four quadrants. These quadrants relate to the relative cash flow situation of each SBU as follows:

- *Cash Cows.* These are the lower left quadrant SBUs, which have a large market share but relatively low growth. They tend to generate cash the organization can use to finance other SBUs and other purposes.

- *Stars.* These are high-growth, high-market-share SBUs. They often use cash from the cows because it is necessary to support the rapid growth. When the growth of these SBUs eventually slows down, they typically become cash cows.

- *Question Marks.* These are problem SBUs. They demonstrate high growth but still have relatively small market shares. It should be an objective of the marketing function to move these SBUs into a star position.

- *Dogs.* These are often called cash traps. They are low-growth, low-market-share SBUs that may generate enough cash to maintain themselves but not enough for other organization purposes.

Once internal audit understands how a given or planned SBU fits within the organization, internal audit may want to evaluate its growth and market share data. The BCG business portfolio approach should help internal audit to better understand why management is promoting one SBU over another. It may also point out areas where management may be devoting too many resources to a given SBU when it appears to have minimal prospects of moving from a dog to a star status.

Internal auditors launching a review of the marketing function should discuss the nature of their products and how they are offered to and demanded by the marketplace (i.e., the customer). Strategies and even some controls will vary based on the various levels of customer demand. Types of demand include:

- *Total Demand Believed to Exist for the Product.* This information can often be obtained on an industry basis through trade groups or through the financial reports of publicly owned competitors. At the same time, current demand should be projected to estimate future demand. However, the potential growth of a particular market is difficult to estimate since it involves a judgment of both what customers will want and what the competition may offer.

- *State of Competition.* Projected market demand establishes market potential, but does not answer the question of how much of that potential can be obtained for a particular organization unit. Considerations include the overall competitive climate, whether it is conservative or aggressive, and the nature of any barriers to market entry. Requirements for capital, technical know-how, and sales outlets are also factors used to determine ease of entry.

- *Timing Requirements.* Important questions center around the time required to penetrate a market with enough volume to be profitable. In many cases, customer acceptance must be earned in the face of already established loyalties. These actions typically require a considerable period of time. The organization should have strong planning and forecasting skills to estimate these timing requirements.

- *Transportation Feasibilities.* The geographical dimensions of the market will directly determine the transportation costs involved in supplying customers with the product. In the case of a small consumer products organization, the problem may be relatively simple. In the cement industry, however, transportation costs would be a major factor.

- *Capital Requirements.* The time and effort required to penetrate new markets must finally be translated into the cost of securing the needed market volume. Funds are required to finance the various promotional and developmental activities that frequently extend over long periods of time. Operating losses must be expected before profitable operations can be achieved.

The above are just examples of considerations. Internal audit can develop others depending upon the nature of the organization. The key point here is that internal audit should develop a good understanding of the market requirements and conditions in the organization to be reviewed.

(iii) Marketing Research Process.   Marketing decisions cannot be made in a vacuum. Marketing management must have input from the customers to whom it plans to sell its product to better understand what will motivate them to buy. While some organizations make these decisions based on educated guesses, others perform some type of market research to help them with decisions. Marketing research for many organizations is performed by specialized outside organizations who have the research skills and procedures in place to evaluate a new product or to determine if consumers may be willing to purchase it. Although there are many different types and approaches to marketing research, common techniques include:

- *Surveys.* Considerable knowledge about potential customer interest can be obtained by just asking them through a survey. This type of research often uses mail questionnaires or telephone interviews. A key point here is that the questions be well structured, allowing the survey to gather the desired data.

- *Focus Groups.* This is often a highly structured form of survey where potential customers are brought together to show them a new product or to ask them their attitudes about such a product. The consumer responses to the focus sessions are often recorded for later analysis. Sometimes, focus group attendees are asked to sign nondisclosure statements before they are shown unannounced products.

- *Test Marketing.* Here, a new product is introduced to a representative submarket just as if it were being introduced on a total market basis. The quality of advertisements, product packaging, and other product features are introduced to the representative submarket in order to determine marketing strategies and customer acceptance.

- *Specialized Research.* Other techniques used to help support a marketing decision range from market share analyses of existing competitors to consumer psychological motivational research, product testing, and other research areas. Market stratification research is an important area here. Organizations will attempt to determine appropriate segments of the total market to be considered unique or targeted markets. Some organizations will perform this type of research themselves, but most will typically contract with outside researchers.

Marketing research is an area in which an internal auditor should devote extra attention when performing an operational review because considerable resources can be wasted by the organization if research is poorly conducted, if there is a lack of analysis and follow-up, or if costs are not adequately controlled.

(iv) Finalizing the Market Research Evaluation.   Market strategy should be based on a comparison of existing capabilities and the assessment of market opportunities based on available market research. In financial terms, this requires the balancing of projected costs and expected revenues at a level of risk that is acceptable to the organization. This evaluation should help to make the decision whether to market the product or service.

An internal auditor should look for some formal documentation in this area, covering the level of market research for each given product line and the resultant marketing decision. For most organization and product decisions, this is typically more than just a yes or no decision. For example, it may seek to establish itself in a broadly based market or try to carve out a particular market niche. This strategy is based on research finding a sector of a market in which to establish a strong position. The product developed may then be especially designed to fit that smaller market sector due to some unique operational characteristics.

An objective with niche markets is to create a situation where competitors may not think it worthwhile to compete in the particular sector. In today's global economy, nearly every product can find some type of unique niche. For example, an organization having trouble competing in the overall United States market might select some regional area as its niche. Another organization might ignore the United States market and specialize in Latin America.

The marketing planning process must be subject to continuous reappraisal as market conditions change. In addition, an organization's capabilities will be changing as experience is gained or as it grows in size. Organizations should also constantly review the general state of the economy, consider particular types of markets and changing customer preferences, and study the current and projected profitability of alternative products and market approaches.

While internal audit will often not have the necessary information or skills to evaluate an overall marketing plan, internal audit should look for established planning standards; all plans should be prepared in compliance with these standards and approved by management.

(v) Marketing Process in Perspective.   The marketing function is an important part of the entire management process. Products must be properly engineered and efficiently produced, people with proper skills must be recruited and administered in an effective manner, and in all cases the costs generated must be controlled so that adequate profits are earned. At the same time, the products or services must be sufficiently useful and attractive to consumers that they will be purchased at desirable prices and in adequate quantities. In order to encourage purchases, the products must be presented in an effective fashion to exploit product potentials and to overcome any customer reluctance. Each of these functions is important, and none of them can fail without dragging down the total effort. In many respects, the marketing function has claims to special importance because marketing cannot be standardized to quite the same extent as other functions such as sales, manufacturing, or accounting. Hence, auditing the marketing function may be more difficult and often requires special types of expertise.

There is often confusion about the roles of marketing and selling. In some organizations, the term *marketing* has replaced the term *sales*. The difference is that the marketing process is directed both to identifying customer needs and to satisfying those needs through an overall sales effort. Selling involves promoting organization products with less concern given to more abstract customer needs. In a classic study of marketing, Theodore Leavitt[1] explains these two orientations:

> *Selling focuses on the needs of the seller, marketing on the needs of the buyer. Selling is preoccupied with the seller's need to convert his product into cash; marketing with the idea of satisfying the needs of the customer by means of the product and the whole cluster of things associated with creating, delivering and finally consuming it.*

The importance of the marketing function can perhaps be seen most clearly in an individual organization. A marketing strategy is often part of the core of the organization's strategy. Decisions in this area must combine intangible creative factors with objective analysis through market research and related support from engineering, production, personnel, and financial-control areas. Proper weight should be given to the marketing point of view, but it still should not dominate the role of other related functions. Maintaining this balance is the difficult job of top management. The combined difficulty and importance of marketing creates opportunities for internal audit in this area of management service.

(vi) Product Demand and Basic Marketing Tasks.   In addition to understanding the complementary roles of sales and marketing, internal auditors should try to understand the demand status of the organization's products. Demand will or should determine how an organization markets and sells its products. For example, if a product or commodity is in very short supply, there may be little need for elaborate marketing or sales programs. Customers will demand the product whether or not it is actively marketed.

Although economists and others may classify demand in different terms, professionals involved in the marketing process often think of demand in terms of basic demand states. The eight basic states of demand, each of which has its own unique marketing challenges, are:

1. *Negative Demand.* This is a situation in which customers avoid a product. For example, some consumers have negative feelings about certain types of food. When an organization has a positive supply of a product but faces negative demand, its marketing department has the challenge of attempting to reverse that negative demand.

2. *No Demand.* Sometimes the market is uninterested or indifferent toward a product, such as when there is a major technological change in a field and little demand for the old product. Marketing may apply what is called stimulational marketing to try to develop a new interest in a product. For example, personal computers that have become obsolete due to major technological changes have been marketed as home game machines.

3. *Latent Demand.* Consumers here may have a need for a product or service that currently does not exist. This presents an opportunity for the innovative organization to develop such a product and for the marketing function to use what is called developmental marketing to promote it. Major marketing efforts are often built around attempts to transform latent demand into active demand.

---

[1] Theodore Leavitt, ''Marketing Myopia,'' *Harvard Business Review* (July-August, 1960).

4. *Faltering Demand.* This is the situation where demand for a product or service is falling. Remedial efforts can be applied through a program of remarketing to reinvigorate the demand. For example, an entertainer who has lost his following may require remarketing.

5. *Irregular Demand.* Product demand will vary but the product supply will either be constant or not correspond to the demand cycles. Marketing must work to synchronize demand with supply. For example, an airline has a constant supply of aircraft but faces low demand over weekends. It will typically discount tickets over the weekend to stimulate demand during that period.

6. *Full Demand.* In some instances, demand for the product is essentially equal to available supply. The marketing function only needs to develop a program of maintenance marketing and watch for any changes that could alter this situation.

7. *Excess Demand.* This is where demand exceeds supply. Prices may be raised or other steps taken to reduce demand. This process of formally discouraging sales is called demarketing. The organization may want to promote substitute products.

8. *Unwholesome Demand.* This is the extreme end of excess demand. In the 1970s, several United States speculators tried to corner the commodities market for silver. As a result, many persons thought that the price of silver was going to keep rising and rising. They took extreme steps to purchase silver goods and commodities with the expectation that prices could only increase at even greater rates. Although market forces eventually took care of the silver boomlet, countermarketing techniques often can be used to discourage product demand.

All of these different demand states may exist for an organization's various products at various points in time. Thus, the sales and marketing functions may be using what initially appear to be inconsistent marketing approaches for its various products in a single time period. An internal auditor should develop an understanding of the various demand states of an organization's products in order to better understand the sales and marketing techniques being used.

(b) MARKETING INTERNAL CONTROL CONSIDERATIONS

Major organization resources can be expended in attempting to market products and services. However, if improperly planned or executed, substantial resources can be wasted. Poorly organized marketing efforts can impact the overall health of the organization because significant funds may be expended on marketing efforts with no resultant increase in sales.

Similar to other activities discussed throughout this book, the marketing function can be viewed in terms of a total internal control cycle with individual operational stages. Marketing controls are closely related to sales function controls (discussed later in this chapter), but marketing has its own unique internal control characteristics. The marketing internal control framework is applicable to the organization as a whole or can apply to a review of the marketing activity at a division, subsidiary, or any other unit that has this function. An internal auditor should think of marketing-related internal controls in terms of individual operational stages or steps in the marketing function control cycle, as discussed below.

- *Determination of Product and Market Strategies.* This is the initial stage where internal audit may be concerned with how market needs are evaluated, how a determination is made as to which particular needs will be satisfied, and in what manner all of this will be accomplished. Although internal audit might expect to find strong, documented research results to support management's market need evaluations, these may sometimes lack appropriate analysis and documentation.

- *Product Planning and Development.* The broad product and marketing strategies are translated into the planning and development of specific products for ultimate production by the organization. At this stage in the cycle, decisions are made in such areas as pricing, marketing approaches, and distribution channel planning. Again, the process requires extensive analysis, which should be developed in conjunction with other appropriate organizational units. For a manufacturing organization, planning and development budgets are usually tied to similar budgets in the manufacturing and engineering areas.

- *Sales Promotion and Advertising.* Potential purchases must be informed about the products through effective marketing communications, such as the use of advertising media. Typically, outside parties are involved in the advertising portion of this step; advertising-related internal controls are discussed later in this chapter. However, all sales promotion efforts should have approved budgets, documented evidence that the promotions actually occurred, and some feedback mechanism to evaluate these efforts.

- *Sales and Distribution.* Sales efforts must be made through selected distribution channels. Systems must be in place to properly record sales. If a tangible product is being marketed, adequate but not excessive inventories may need to be maintained. Procedures must be in place to distribute the product to the customer. Sales internal controls are discussed later in this chapter, and the distribution function was discussed in Chapter 25.

- *Customer Support.* A sale typically involves a range of customer support activities starting with order handling and billing, including customer familiarization and warranty service as well as the handling of possible claims and adjustments. This is also an area where internal controls can break down. Adjustments can be applied incorrectly or the customer may not even be billed due to an internal control weakness. Some of these internal control considerations are discussed later in this chapter.

Strong marketing function internal controls as well as a good general marketing strategy are important to the modern organization. History provides many examples of organizations that have drifted downhill by taking for granted the continuing merits of a previously practiced strategy. Others have expended massive resources on marketing efforts with no gain in sales. The result may be a financial loss or a need to withdraw from a market due to poor marketing efforts.

The organization's marketing strategies should be formally documented and approved by the proper levels of management. In addition, definitive steps should be taken to periodically assess the need for modifying existing product or market strategies. These definitive steps include special studies and ongoing research efforts. The real vitality of these strategy reevaluations can be evidenced by product or market changes actually made over time. In our dynamic world, a lack of change is likely to be proof of inadequate analysis.

Marketing is also an area in which internal audit may find many financial internal control abuses. Organizations sometimes spend large amounts on efforts that are not justified, including:

- *Excessive Marketing-Related Entertainment Expenses.* The potential for abuse in this area is high. Marketing representatives may claim that they are entertaining important contacts and will spend large sums to do so. The marketing gains may be marginal, and marketing personnel may ignore appropriate entertainment cost controls.

- *Improper Payments to Agents.* In the United States, the Foreign Corrupt Practices Act (FCPA) became law because of furor over large payments to foreign agents to influence sales and marketing efforts. This is an internal control area discussed in Chapter 2 and again in Chapter 31.

- *Improper or Excessive Use of Outside Consultants.* The world of marketing is filled with numerous special consultants available for hire. While some may provide added value to the marketing effort, their use is sometimes inappropriate.

As a basic internal control over these abuses, marketing management policies must clearly define those practices that are wasteful or prohibited. Strong procedures and guidelines should be in place covering travel and entertainment expenses, the use of consultants, and other marketing-related outside expense areas. All activities in this area should be appropriately documented and be approved in advance. Internal audit should look for a strong set of internal controls over the marketing process. These can be tested for effectiveness through the audit procedures outlined in the following sections.

(c) MARKETING FUNCTION INTERNAL AUDIT ACTIVITIES

The overall marketing function is often ignored by auditors. Internal audit typically reviews sales procedures and may examine marketing-related special expenses. However, the entire area of marketing—including such matters as the development of market plans, the selection of outside vendors, and the allocation of marketing expenses—is a good area for internal audit review. This section covers some financial and operational audit procedures specific to the marketing function. The sections describing product planning, advertising, and sales later in this chapter are all related, and internal audit should have a good understanding of marketing policies and procedures in order to perform effective reviews in those other areas as well.

Internal audit will typically concentrate on two areas in reviews of the overall marketing process. First, internal audit should perform financial reviews of this area with an emphasis on budget controls and marketing-related expenses. This will be similar to the disbursement-related control procedures discussed in Chapter 22, ''Accounting Systems and Controls,'' but should have a strong emphasis on some of the unique types of marketing-related expenses.

There are many aspects of operational reviews of the marketing function. This section will focus on audits of the marketing process, including related research. These areas are often left to the attention of professionals in the marketing function with minimal attention by general management. While internal audit should not hold itself out as an expert in this area, reviews of marketing-related financial, operational, and information systems controls can provide value to marketing and general management.

(i) Marketing Function Financial Audit Considerations. A financial review of the marketing function should include a consideration of the budgeting process and the appropriateness of marketing-related disbursements charged against those established budgets. In many respects, these financial audit procedures are little different from the procedures of Chapter 22 and in other specific areas such as Chapter 26, on engineering. Here, internal audit will review financial controls as they apply to marketing-related functions.

Figure 28.2 outlines some of the financial audit procedures an internal auditor might use in reviewing marketing function budgets and disbursements. An internal auditor may find some resistance when questioning various transactions in these areas—for example, when a top marketing executive submits what appears to be excessive or inappropriate expense vouchers. Internal audit should always act as an independent entity and raise these types of issues with appropriate levels of management.

Marketing is an area where financial and operational audit procedures may tie closely together. For example, internal audit may identify a disbursement to an outside marketing consultant which appears to have been properly approved by management and paid according to contract terms. The transaction might satisfy the auditor's general financial objectives that the transaction was properly authorized and processed; however, an internal auditor may want to determine whether the work was appropriately performed and the results reviewed by management.

(ii) Marketing Function Operational Audit Procedures. A good starting point for operational reviews of the marketing function is to understand the marketing programs that are used to introduce a new product to the public. Internal audit should then review selected marketing research projects to determine whether there has been a complete project plan describing the objectives of the research effort, the expected type of results, and timetables. Although an internal auditor will not be an expert in marketing research, a review of market research project plans should show projects with clearly stated objectives that have been properly approved by management.

Internal audit procedures for reviews of marketing research as well as of general strategy are described in Figure 28.3. Internal audit should look for evidence of documentation as well as management review and approval of these documented strategic marketing plans. Internal audit should pay particular attention to the level of documentation that was developed for projects that never evolved beyond the earlier phases of marketing plans. In addition, internal audit should review sales statistics for new products in order to trace them back to strategic marketing plans. Particular attention should be given to any new approaches that do not appear to be as successful as anticipated. While internal audit should not just second-guess poor marketing strategy decisions, failures often point to inadequate initial planning.

Marketing strategy and market research are areas that are best left to highly skilled creative professionals. Internal audit's role in reviewing this area is to determine that:

- Strategic plans are properly documented and follow departmental standards.
- Adequate attention was given to an analysis of various market and product alternatives.

Figure 28.2 Marketing Function Financial Audit Procedures

Audit _____ Location _____ Date _____

AUDIT STEP	INITIAL	W/P
1. Obtain an understanding of how the budgeting process operates within marketing; determine that it is consistent with other organization budgeting procedures and note any differences.		
2. Determine that standard organizational systems, such as accounts payable or G/L accounting, are used in marketing processes. If unique financial systems are used, describe the process and document its interface with other financial applications.		
3. Determine that marketing activities are clearly identified and charged to appropriate marketing accounts.		
4. Obtain a list of all marketing projects either in process or completed over the past year and select several for detailed review, with selection based on project size or known potential risks.		
5. If not organized by marketing project or account, discuss procedures used by marketing management to monitor marketing budgets and costs; comment on potential control weaknesses.		
6. Obtain plan versus actual performance reports for marketing projects selected and obtain reasons for any significant differences.		
7. Using the list obtained in Step 4 above, select one or more projects for a detailed review of expense transactions, with an emphasis on expenses from outside sources, such as consultants and travel and entertainment. Review related transaction details and supporting invoices.		
8. Assess whether a process is in place to properly charge travel and entertainment expenses to appropriate marketing projects. If formal procedures are not in place, determine that expenses are appropriately tied to related marketing projects.		
9. Obtain current list of general ledger reports covering marketing operations; trace marketing expenses reviewed to general ledger entries and discuss the reasons for any reported differences with accounting management.		
10. Summarize and document any potential financial audit marketing management concerns, discuss with management as appropriate, and consider as potential audit report findings.		

Figure 28.3   Audit Procedures for Reviews of Marketing Research

Audit _____   Location _____   Date _____

AUDIT STEP	INITIAL	W/P
1. Through discussions with marketing management, document the overall process for marketing research, including procedures for establishing research objectives and developing research approaches.		
2. Select several research projects in process and assess whether the procedures described in step 1 are being followed.		
3. Review documentation procedures used for marketing research projects; review several completed projects to assess whether documented results are clear and describe the activities performed, conclusions drawn, and corrective actions—if any —taken as a result of the research.		
4. From a detailed review of one or more research projects, determine that expenses associated with the project should be clearly classified as "research" rather than promotional or other expenses; discuss any potential concerns with management to obtain their insights.		
5. Based on the results of several marketing research projects, assess whether corrective actions were taken; if not, obtain reasons for the lack of responses to research findings.		
6. Determine that clear channels of communication exist between research activities and other organizational activities such as sales or product development.		
7. If marketing research is performed through focus group sessions led by outside consultants, determine that the marketing function has a strong understanding of the focus group procedures used, the persons selected for participation, and that the results of the sessions are reviewed in detail.		
8. Determine that the organization performs a regular costs-versus-benefits analysis on its marketing research efforts and performs corrective actions as required.		

- Market research efforts are well controlled and performed according to preestablished plans and budgets.
- Strategic planning activities have been communicated to and approved by management.

Internal audit can make a significant contribution in this overall area by asking questions about the levels of documentation and the overall procedures for marketing strategic planning. A review and understanding of this area will allow internal audit to review the product-planning and development portion of the overall marketing function.

(iii) Marketing Function Computer Audit Procedures.   While many other functions in the organization rely on specialized systems for support, internal audit will often encounter few systems in the marketing area. At most, the marketing function may use specialized databases to record market research and other product promotional activities, statistical analysis software to analyze marketing data, and various economic modeling software packages. Of course, marketing activities would use other organization financial systems. While internal audit should develop a general understanding of the types of automated systems used to support marketing functions, there is usually little need for specialized computer systems control reviews in this area.

Internal audit will typically have no need to perform specialized computer audit procedures in the marketing area. There may be a need to examine an area such as marketing-related entertainment disbursements. However, this is not a marketing-related computer audit procedure but an example of the type of computer-assisted retrieval procedure discussed in Chapter 22. Of course, if an internal auditor finds that certain specialized systems are used in the marketing area that appear to raise questions, internal audit should develop a general understanding of them, evaluate the risk, and perform appropriate review procedures, as has been discussed throughout this book.

(iv) Marketing Function Sample Audit Report Findings

A: Entertainment Expenses Exceed Guidelines. Organization travel and entertainment procedures specify that business entertainment expenses should identify all persons attending an event, their business affiliations, and the business purpose of the event. In a review of 20 entertainment vouchers, we found the following:

- Business purposes were not documented on 12 of the 20 vouchers.
- Two expenses were documented only as ''Company dinner for 10'' with no indication of the names of attendees.
- Three luncheons appeared to be for employees, with no indication of a business purpose.

Recommendation. Marketing management should be reminded of the documentation required for organization travel and entertainment prior to their approval. Violators also should be advised of the requirements and closely monitored to determine whether corrective actions have taken place.

B: Questionable Use of Marketing Research Consultants. Our review identified a contract signed earlier this year with XYZ Consultants, Ltd., for $45,000 for ''market research.'' We could find no detailed engagement letter describing the work to be performed and only very general explanations of the value of this work in our discussions with management. XYZ Consultants evidently completed their work but filed no reports. The contract was approved by the marketing research department.

Recommendation. All contracts with outside consultants should be documented, with a formal engagement letter describing the work to be performed and the expected deliverables. Formal procedures should be implemented for marketing research efforts.

28-3 PRODUCT PLANNING AND DEVELOPMENT

Product planning and development can be considered the operational stage of the product marketing process. Although closely related, there are significant differences between marketing strategy, which was previously discussed, and the product-planning and development process. This operational area covers the implementation of a strategic product plan and is concerned with the actual products that are to be introduced. Both a conceptual plan and an implementation effort are necessary if the organization's resources are to be used effectively.

This is the phase of the marketing process at which the results of strategic planning are translated into actual new product introductions. This is also the phase at which existing products are promoted and enhanced to continue or increase their demand. Although marketing research efforts in many organizations are centralized, the product-planning function is often divided into broad product categories. Thus, internal audit may perform one review of the marketing strategic-planning function but may find it necessary to review multiple product line departments in order to understand controls over the product-planning and development function.

(a) NATURE AND SCOPE OF PRODUCT PLANNING AND DEVELOPMENT

Product planning and development typically extends from some basic product research to the actual management of individual products or product lines. These efforts are designed to assist in the overall promotion of a product. A certain level of product-related research will take place as part of this process and may include developing better materials for use in the products, better functional characteristics, or new ways to produce them at lower cost or better quality. Such research will normally be carried on by a research activity, as discussed in Chapter 26. Research is mentioned here because it is an initial step in the product-planning and development process. The product-planning and development group will typically place pressure on research functions to develop new and improved products.

As new or improved technology is developed, efforts must be made to apply that technology to existing products. For example, new types of materials may open the possibility for a range of items previously made from more expensive materials. Similarly, the release of a new version of a computer operating system may all but force a software publisher to tailor an existing product to that new operating system. In all such situations, the product-planning and development group should endeavor to explore these possibilities.

Many product-development efforts cover expanding the range of customer services available. These efforts may reach back to supporting research efforts but often result from the imaginative thinking of the product planner. Using the automotive industry as an example, the addition of high-quality audio systems on certain luxury automobiles involves minimal technical efforts, but, based on research, may be designed primarily to increase customer appeal.

(i) Forecasting Market Demand.

The product-planning and development stage is often the time when some market research efforts are expanded. In this phase, product planners go through formal analyses to forecast demand for their products. Some of this demand forecasting is directed toward learning more about how customers are responding to new types of product developments. Such research can precede the development of a new product and can be conducted periodically during current product life cycles.

Demand refers to the total units of a product to be acquired by defined customer groups within a time period and a specified geographical area. Market demand is based on both the total market demand for all products of a given type and on the expected market share of the product being forecast. Market share is a function of the expected

Figure 28.4   Relative Demand Concept

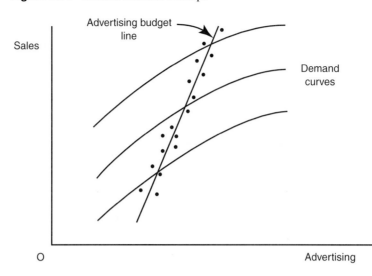

number of buyers, a product's price, and a variety of other factors. This relative demand concept is shown in Figure 28.4. Although the figure shows one period of time, these forecasts are then extended over future periods.

Forecasts of market demand are extremely important to an organization. In a manufacturing organization, for example, the demand forecasts will drive the production-planning system, as discussed in Chapter 23. An organization may hire additional staff based on anticipated sales gains or may make capital investment decisions based on the anticipated profitability of a product line.

Demand will also plot changes over time. There is normally a cycle of market acceptance that begins with product introduction, rises slowly during the early promotional stages, rises more sharply with expanding acceptance, then slows down as market saturation is approached, levels off, and finally trends downward as newer products begin to overshadow it. The exact shape of this demand cycle as well as the total elapsed time will vary. An effective product-planning and development effort will project demand over the life of existing products and, at the same time, will try to define new or enhanced products that will fill any gaps produced by aging products.

(ii) Product-Planning Organizational Considerations.   Product planning and development needs to have adequate organizational support because of the greater than normal need for collaboration with other organizational activities in the product-development effort. This can be accomplished by placing the product-planning and development group at a relatively high administrative or marketing level. Coordination is further assured through product-planning committees, including representation from other staff and line groups. The product-planning and development group might initiate programs while responding to suggestions from other groups such as research, engineering, production, sales, and finance. This effort focuses on the effective implementation of existing product and marketing strategies, and provides an opportunity to identify any need for major changes in the basic strategy.

After new products have been approved, production, promotional, sales, and financial profitability evaluation activities pertaining to those products are often distributed to the responsible functional groups. At the same time, there is a need to look at the combined activities on an individual product basis. The solution has been to create product managers who are assigned one or more individual products and are charged with the responsibility of coordinating the functional pieces for total management of these individual products. These product managers typically have no line responsibility over the production, promotional, sales, or financial organizational components but are charged with an overall product profit-and-loss responsibility. Despite the limitations of authority, this product-management approach has been successful for many organizations.

Internal audit should consider a review of this overall product-management process. The potential cost of poorly controlled or improper product introductions should justify such a review. Care should be taken to look at controls in the separate organizational functions. For example, product managers are often placed in ''fire fighting'' problem-solving situations. While the product manager has the authority to override certain functional department decisions in order to promote various product initiatives, this process should be clearly understood and documented.

(b) PRODUCT-PLANNING AND DEVELOPMENT INTERNAL CONTROLS

Although an internal auditor will encounter few unique accounting processes in the product-planning and development function, this function is responsible for delivering significant product-related statistics to management which they will use to make some overall product-related decisions. Control procedures must verify that the statistical analysis techniques used are valid, test results are properly documented, and the data is communicated to management without any bias.

Another internal control covers adequate procedures for a proper, periodic analysis of existing products as well as programs to enhance or replace aging products. Internal audit may want to review and evaluate the extent to which these programs are being carried out. An accurate assessment of the effectiveness and efficiency of controls surrounding these factors is not that simple. Internal audit may find that benchmarking-like comparisons with competitor products will provide a useful guide as to whether a product-planning and development effort has been well conceived and executed.

(c) PRODUCT-PLANNING INTERNAL AUDIT ACTIVITIES

Internal audit should consider reviews of the product planning function as part of overall audits planned for the marketing and sales functions. This requires a review of the overall demand forecasting process, which is the heart of product planning.

The demand or market-forecasting process helps an organization maintain a sustained sales and profitability growth rate. Through a review of this area, internal audit can provide valuable input to management. While there are limited financial and computer technology–related controls issues, internal audit will typically encounter numerous areas for operational reviews here. Items for internal audit to consider include:

- *Product-Development Standards.* There should be an ongoing process to review existing products, to assess inputs from customers and the sales force, and to suggest improvements to products. A successful organization will review all of its products, even the identified winners, on an ongoing basis. Otherwise, a product can lose market share because of management's failure to recognize needed changes.

- *Demand-Forecasting Procedures.* Internal audit should understand the demand-forecasting process, including how sales statistics and information on market share are gathered as well as how these forecasts are communicated to decision-makers within the organization and to various automated systems requiring this data.

- *Marketing Statistical Analysis.* By its nature, a marketing-planning and development function may gather a fair amount of statistics on current products as well as on the competition. Many of these rely on extensive regression-analysis techniques to better define the data. While an internal auditor may not have the statistical skills to review this data or judge the appropriateness of derived decisions, the auditor should determine that there is a formal process for gathering data, that procedures are documented, that appropriate backup copies of data are maintained, and that management appears to understand and properly respond to the results of these analyses.

- *Computer Systems Controls.* Marketing demand forecasting is often an area supported by computer systems applications. Internal audit should understand both application controls and, if the processing is done on a client-server workstation, general controls for that market-forecasting system. Chapters 16 and 17 discussed these types of controls.

(i) Product-Planning Financial Audit Considerations.   A review of the product-planning and control function is primarily an operational review with no significant financial-control issues. Although internal audit should have a clear understanding of how the demand-forecasting process and the results of various other statistical analyses feeds into other key systems—some of them accounting—financial auditing procedures in this area include reviews of the allocation of product-planning costs and the appropriate allocation of those costs to various marketing efforts.

The financial control issues in this area are budgeting and other basic system controls where the product-planning departments will use other systems, such as budgeting, to perform its functions. Financial audit control procedures were discussed as part of general accounting systems control issues in Chapter 22.

(ii) Product-Planning Operational Audit Procedures.   Operational audit steps for reviewing the product-planning function are outlined in Figure 28.5. This is sometimes a difficult area to review because it may be fragmented over product lines. In addition, because coordination is necessary across other functional boundaries, internal audit may find that some control procedures are also distributed.

Many of the audit activities in this area will involve understanding the standards and procedures that have been established to support the product-planning function and then testing them to determine whether these standards and procedures are being followed. Much of this type of review will entail an assessment of available documentation used to support the group's conclusions. Internal audit should similarly assess the documentation and procedures used for this statistical analysis work.

Figure 28.5   Operation Audit Procedures: Review of Product Planning Function

Audit _____   Location _____   Date _____

AUDIT STEP	INITIAL	W/P
1. Meet with product planning team to identify strategies, review how function fits in overall organization, talk about recent accomplishments and future plans, and discuss budgets and staffing. Refine detailed audit objectives based on the session.		
2. On a test basis, determine that the product planning group is operating in compliance with general organization procedures in such areas as travel expenses, desktop computer security, and project budget reporting.		
3. Review the long-term objectives of the product planning function. Discuss with group management the consistency of these with overall organization goals.		
4. Review processes in place to establish priorities and allocate funding for alternative product planning projects.		
5. Product planning will divide its efforts between sales or market development for its current products of either product development or diversification of new products. Based on discussions with management and reviews of performance records, assess where product planning resources are needed. Comment as appropriate.		
6. Review the number of planning efforts over the past year that have been viewed by management as successes as opposed to failures. Review the product-planning decision process to arrive at these efforts. Comment as appropriate.		
7. Through interviews and reviews of documentation, determine that the planning process has an appropriate level of checkpoints to measure progress in any research effort. Also determine if procedures are in place to stop work when appropriate.		
8. Review and comment on the level of research performed by organization personnel versus outside consultants.		
9. Assess the level of communication with product planning and other related functions in the organization. Comment on any perceived weaknesses in this process.		

The product-planning department should be able to explain clearly these statistical processes to an auditor who may be only somewhat familiar with statistical decision theory. If internal audit does not understand these processes, there is a strong chance that some key members of management may also not understand. If the product-planning analyst dismisses an auditor's question with a comment that ''everyone'' knows the answer, internal audit should determine if in fact ''everyone'' in organization management does know and actually understands the concept. This is often a prime area for internal audit comments.

(iii) Product-Planning Computer Audit Procedures.

This area is often supported by computer statistical and database applications often operating on client-server type workstations. The key point for internal audit to consider is that such functions are often operated independent of any centralized information systems function. Thus internal audit may have to perform general controls over these workstation processors, including a review of the LAN security and backup procedures.

Internal audit might also consider a review of the applications used to support this function. Typically, specialized applications for statistical analyses are based on specialized purchased software packages, and it may not be necessary to perform a controls review of those applications unless the organization has made some significant alterations. There may often be a risk, however, that control problems exist even if management has advised internal audit of minimal concerns. For example, they may have installed a standard software package but bypassed standard access controls. Internal audit should always evaluate relative audit risk (as was discussed in Chapter 7) when deciding to perform this type of review.

An internal auditor should also consider any special interface controls where other systems interface with product planning–related applications. There should be adequate interface controls between these systems with appropriate balancing and reconciliation procedures in place, where feasible.

(iv) Product-Planning Sample Audit Report Findings

A: Product-Planning Results Are Incomplete.   The product-planning group produces a series of demand-forecasting reports covering all major product lines. However, the reports only show updated data on the three major product lines: A, B, and C. Data for all other more minor product lines is updated semiannually. However, all of this data is summarized together to produce a single set of totals. The minor product lines, taken together, are equal to more than product line C. The summary reports that have current dates include older data, which might result in incorrect decisions.

Recommendation.   Data included in demand-forecasting reports should be regularly updated for all product lines to report current results. If it is more cost-effective to defer the update of minor product lines, the report should be modified to display the differing dates.

B: Statistical Forecasting Techniques Are Not Documented.   Product-planning projections are based on a statistical algorithm developed by an outside consultant under contract. This algorithm has been incorporated into the projection programs, but there is no documentation to explain the calculations and any underlying assumptions. There was no requirement in the consultant's contract for adequate testing of the externally developed routines and for their documentation. In discussions with forecasting group management, internal audit was unable to obtain satisfactory explanations of these routines, the underlying assumptions, and the testing and reliability-assessment procedures performed. Reliance on this undocumented forecasting program code may result in improper decisions.

Recommendation.   A comprehensive set of quality-assurance tests should be performed for the statistical software and both user and technical documentation should be prepared for the above-mentioned statistical algorithms. If the forecasting technical staff is unable to prepare this documentation, the consultant should be contracted to prepare it. All future contracts should require sufficient documentation as a condition of project acceptance.

28-4 SALES PROMOTION AND ADVERTISING

Once a product has been planned, developed, and produced, it is available for sale. Products, of course, refer to all types of goods, including industrial, consumer products manufactured on site, items manufactured by others under license, and service-oriented products. In most instances, a substantial effort is necessary to familiarize potential customers with the product to support a successful sales effort. This familiarization process is part of the sales promotion function, which includes the many forms of advertising activity. Internal audit will find common characteristics of all sales promotion activities as well as more detailed auditor concerns relating to advertising and to other types of sales.

The common objective of all sales promotion activities is to induce sales. These activities may result in immediate sales or may only plant an idea that will later contribute to making a sale. Advertising tomorrow's special sales offerings at a department store is at one end of the spectrum, and institutional advertising of a public-relations nature is at the other. In some instances the results achieved can be immediately measured with some reasonable degree of accuracy, but more often they have an intangible characteristic that defies accurate measurement and evaluation. Usually, other factors and new situational developments make it impossible to say exactly how much a particular sales promotional effort contributed to the sales actually achieved. The lack of precision here makes it possible for many claims to be made as to the actual contribution, some of which are often overenthusiastic and unrealistic by more conservative standards.

Despite problems in measuring the effectiveness of sales promotional activities, organizations generally must continue with them. Not only do managerial instincts support the wisdom of much of the sales promotional effort, but actions by competitors require an individual organization to do likewise. As a result, large sums of money are expended for advertising and other types of sales promotion. Management must decide how much to spend, what particular types of sales promotion activities should be used, and how to determine that maximum value has been received for these expenditures. The claims of the suppliers of sales promotion services must be evaluated, and there must be controls to ensure prudent promotional expenditure levels. Part of the mission of internal audit is to help management answer these difficult questions.

(a) SALES PROMOTION ORGANIZATIONAL CONSIDERATIONS

Adequate controls for the sales promotional activity vary with the level of expenditures and the type of sales promotions. Internal audit should gather basic information on how advertising and sales promotion activities are conducted within the organization. For example, many organizations will hire an outside advertising agency for all advertising placements while some have a separate in-house function to perform these tasks. Internal audit should understand the basic types of sales promotion. For example, an organization selling to retail stores may have what is called a *cooperative advertising program,* where distributor rebates are given for advertisements for distributor products placed by the retailer. This special arrangement may be controlled through the regular advertising and sales promotion function or may be handled by a separate group charged with monitoring that cooperative advertising activity. In order to effectively plan and perform sales promotion and advertising audits over these types of activities, internal audit needs to understand these various types of procedures in operation.

(i) Advertising and Agency Relationships. A characteristic of advertising is that it is usually accomplished through outside agencies. These agencies are separate business entities that stand between the organization and the placement media, including magazines, newspapers, radio, and television stations. Advertising agencies have established relationships with the media and are normally responsible for payments to them for space or time used. They also study organization advertising needs, determine how advertising outlays can best be utilized, propose specific advertising programs, and implement approved programs through the creation of effective presentation and supporting production materials. Although agencies may have other organization contacts, they work primarily with the organization's sales promotion function.

An advertising agency should be fairly reimbursed for its efforts. The agency should be able to pay its suppliers, cover its operating expenses, and also earn a fair profit. There may be a problem as to how this "fair level of compensation" will be determined. Traditionally, the major basis of compensation has been a percentage discount given by media to the agencies, a discount not directly available to the organization itself. This percentage allowance may also be supplemented by special services such as artwork, copy, and market research studies. Although these arrangements once applied primarily to consumer goods, today they also apply to all organizations that do media-type advertising—commercial, industrial, or not-for-profit.

This basic media allowance arrangement has been good in the sense that the agency is protected by an assured stream of revenue. It may be bad, however, in that there is built-in incentive for an agency to encourage use of various advertising media. Even when advertising budgets really need to be expanded, there could be a concern that the agency-recommended increase is somewhat motivated by the direct relationship to increased agency discount allowances. There may also be a concern that the amount of revenue obtained through the media allowances does not correlate with the scope of work performed by the agency. However, it can cost just as much to produce an advertisement that will run only once as for one that will run over an extended period. Industrial or not-for-profit advertising often involves the same level of media usage as with consumer advertising.

Some larger organizations have a tailored compensation arrangement with agencies that is negotiated to compensate for the scope of services actually performed. An internal auditor should understand the nature of these agency arrangements and exercise care to ensure that these arrangements are properly carried out.

(ii) Agency Selection and Operations. Although the actual choice of an agency is usually a high-level management decision, internal audit can be helpful in reviewing and commenting upon the various agent-compensation arrangements. This is especially important because internal audit may be reviewing the agency billings later. The fact that a new agency is being selected at all is usually because of dissatisfaction with the previous agency. Here, too, any internal audit experience with the previous agency, through audit report comments about billings and other matters, may have been a contributing factor to the decision to make the change.

After a new agency has been selected and the contract finalized, the new agency prepares and presents a proposed program that includes their basic creative approaches, alternative types of copy, media to be used, timing of usage, and estimated costs. After the necessary negotiations, the agreements reached become an action plan that may still be subject to future changes in the light of new developments. This action plan is very important from a control standpoint because it details both what is to be done and the extent of lead times and commitments that have to be respected in making any later changes.

The agency then proceeds to implement the agreed-upon advertising program. This includes creative work for the development of ideas and supporting copy, preparation of mats and plates, final selection of media, and relations with media. An agency's responsibilities also include accounting, billing and collection, and general administration. From the standpoint of the organization contracting with an outside advertising agency, major control concerns include the following:

- All advertising agency work should be carried out in a capable, professional manner and be properly coordinated with the organization.

- Billings for media services should only cover advertising properly authorized by the organization, at the best available rates, as well as other services properly authorized under the contractual agreement. Those costs should reflect good value.

- The internal operations of the agency—including the agency procurement of materials and services—should be carried out efficiently and in a businesslike manner.

- The relations of the agency with dealers and customers covering any cooperative advertising should be carried out in an efficient and well-controlled manner.

An advertising agency is an outside vendor whose performance is critical to the overall success of the organization. While management cannot monitor day-to-day operations inside the agency, it should watch for evidence of poor controls as well as for any other potential problems. Any questions or problems should be resolved as early as possible. Sometimes, internal audit can assist management in resolving any questions about agency operations by requesting and analyzing the data.

(b) ADVERTISING INTERNAL CONTROL CONSIDERATIONS

Management's concerns over the control of advertising expenses may be significant due to the large sums of money expended in many organizations. The key control here is close monitoring of all advertising activities, whether performed internally or externally. In addition to monitoring procedures, financial controls must be established, beginning with budgets allocated to individual agencies for particular products, or special-purpose programs.

Management should look for project control reports similar to those discussed in Chapter 26. Although Chapter 26 discussed engineering-type projects, the same needs exist for advertising. Even though many internal and external personnel involved with advertising activities may argue that they should be exempt from timekeeping and reporting because they are ''creative,'' these project controls should still apply.

Advertising internal control concerns and control procedures should include the following:

- Advertising program progress should be continuously monitored with updated reports, including summaries of agency preparatory work and commitments to outside suppliers and to media. This will allow management to consider whether advertising programs should be expanded, modified, or curtailed in the light of costs and new conditions.

- The extent to which advertising agency compensation is earned through actual advertising usage, including insertions in periodicals and broadcast media time, should be closely reviewed. Although an organization typically cannot review all advertising placements, they should be reviewed on a test basis.

- The actual advertising billings payable and the adequacy of the supporting documentation should be closely monitored. Whenever the organization has questions about such billings, more documentation should be requested from the agency before initiating payment.

- Agency operations and billings should be closely reviewed to ascertain that they are consistent with previously established agreements and budgets.

These internal control concerns are satisfied in two ways. The first is through the adequacy of the records and any documentation or explanations of related procedural controls supplied to the organization by its advertising agencies. Review of these records is typically a joint responsibility of the advertising and accounting departments. A second type of financial control could be accomplished through a field review of the operations of the agency itself. This review may be accomplished by organization advertising personnel, but can often be handled in part by the internal audit department, which is the organization's controls specialist.

Agency reviews are often not feasible because the agency will prohibit access to its detailed records. However, internal audit can insist on reviewing detailed copies of agency worksheets, invoices, and other documentation in order to assess billings and other control activities. The organization should request "right to audit" clauses in all advertising agency contracts. Even when this is not acceptable, internal audit should remind advertising management on a regular basis about their potential control concerns and audit requirements. If there are questions, internal audit should explain to an agency their audit requirements and typical audit procedures.

Although these comments generally relate to working with outside agencies, many organizations have internal advertising programs that can potentially present significant control problems. For example, cooperative advertising programs, through which an organization reimburses others when they place ads for the organization's products, can lead to abuses if not properly controlled. Reimbursements should not be granted until there is verification that the cooperative advertisements have actually been placed. Frequently, however, a key salesperson may insist that the cooperative payments should be made to help the organization's customer. The internal control system should prevent this.

(c) INTERNAL AUDIT AND ADVERTISING AGENCY FINANCIAL CONTROLS

While both the advertising and accounting departments should establish their own internal control procedures, internal audit should consider scheduling reviews of all advertising agency activities as well as a general review of the advertising function within the organization. As part of these reviews of advertising activities, internal audit should appraise the adequacy of advertising records maintained within the organization. Internal audit can carry out a similar appraisal through a review of agency operations, including the agency records, which would be expected to tie to organization records.

Because internal audit may be visiting outside agencies as part of a planned review, care must be taken in planning the review and discussing the procedures to be performed with advertising management in the auditor's organization. If the auditor's objectives are clearly defined and consistent with management concerns, there should be few problems. If problems are encountered or concerns are expressed by advertising management, the matter can be discussed with the auditor's management. There must be a strong level of support for any review of outside advertising agency activities.

(i) Advertising Financial Audit Considerations.   An internal auditor should be concerned with the manner in which advertising budgets are established and costs are collected and charged to those budgets, and the extent and accuracy of the financial procedures used to monitor advertising costs. These concerns may extend to the outside agencies, and include a mix of financial and operational audit issues.

As a first step, internal audit should review established advertising budgeting procedures in order to assess whether they are being followed. An advertising budget may be established through determining sales objectives for a product line and then estimating the costs for required advertising activities. Advertising budgets are sometimes just established through a lump-sum type of appropriation, where a percentage of the prior year's sales, or some other factor, becomes the advertising budget.

The actual costs of advertising would be measured against that budget. Internal audit needs to understand the source of these costs and then to verify them when appropriate. For example, an audit step might be to determine if copy development costs appear reasonable and do not represent a duplicate for similar advertising copy developed previously. Media placement should also be reviewed to determine if the advertisements were actually placed as billed.

Many advertising departments are involved with a fair amount of financial analysis to justify their advertising expenditures and to sometimes convince upper management that profits will increase if advertising expenditures are also increased. These types of financial analysis exercises can be self-serving. Internal audit should consider reviewing any such analyses for reasonableness and raise questions as appropriate.

Figure 28.6 contains some audit procedures for a review of the financial aspects of the advertising function. This includes steps for auditing records at the advertising agency. However, internal audit must have been given the contractual right to audit records on-site at the agency. If that is not part of the contract and the agency refuses, internal audit should point out this need to management, potentially as an audit finding, with a recommendation that the right be included in a future contract.

(ii) Sales Advertising Operational Audit Procedures.   The many types of advertising activities reflect an operational cycle of common control points. In order to design and plan an operational review of the advertising function, internal audit needs to have a good understanding of the overall advertising processes. Some of these control points were discussed in the prior section on financial audits of the advertising function. They can be summarized through the following points:

- *Determination of Objectives.* The starting point for any operational audit of advertising is to determine the objectives of the organization's advertising function. The advertising function should be able to answer such questions as:

Figure 28.6 Financial Audit Procedures for Review of Advertising Function

Audit _____   Location _____   Date _____

AUDIT STEP	INITIAL	W/P
1. Review and gain an understanding of the advertising budgets for each of the programs and agencies. Review supporting systems and reports that will support those budgets.		
2. Review procedures for purchasing media, materials, and services. Based on transaction tests, determine that purchases are approved, are assigned to the correct programs, and are matched with advertising budgets.		
3. Review procedures for the presentation of bills by the advertising agency or special service contractors. Determine that billing represents work performed and that it is monitored by management.		
4. If agency contractors request deposits for special programs and work performed, assess that procedures are in place to monitor those contracts and to request refunds when work is not completed on a timely basis.		
5. If prime advertising work is subcontracted to other providers, review these arrangements on a sample test basis to determine that prime contractor markups are reasonable and that subcontractor work is managed and appropriate.		
6. Review selected contractual arrangements for media placement, whether for print, television, or other. Through samples of magazine ads or other techniques, determine that the advertising is being delivered.		
7. For a sample accounting period, trace all advertising development and media placement costs to appropriate ledgers and to the general ledgers; determine accounting is correct.		
8. Review procedures for matching advertising expenses to established budgets, and determine a process exists for monitoring budget performance and taking corrective actions if needed.		

- Whom are we endeavoring to influence?
- Where are these customers located?
- How can we reach them most effectively?
- Internal audit should understand and evaluate the effectiveness of the different ways used to accomplish advertising activities. Management's decisions consider available alternatives, balancing costs and expected results. Where there has been previous experience with particular approaches, that evidence should be utilized. Specific approaches and a determination of goals at a given level of cost should result from this evaluation.
- *Approval of Budgets.* Budgets always play a key role in assuring adequate planning and control. Any proposed advertising program should be subjected to detailed management review and approval. As was discussed in the previous section, this

approved budget and program should set expenditure limits for the implementation of the program.

- *Determination of Suppliers.* Approved advertising programs require the procurement of varying amounts of goods and services from outside parties such as advertising agencies, media sources, and designers. Portions of these procurements can be handled through the regular purchasing department. In many instances, however, this type of procurement is so specialized that it is best handled by the advertising group itself. In either event, the principles of sound purchasing, discussed in Chapter 24, are applicable. The advertising group should seek to deal with financially sound suppliers, to utilize competitive bidding to the extent practicable, and to strive for reliable vendor performance. In cases where there is an extended and complicated relationship, the mutual understandings should be defined in a proper contractual form.

- *Procurement of Products or Services.* The products or services used in advertising efforts may be one-time acquisitions or be used over extended periods of time. The organization should be concerned that maximum value has been provided by these vendors, with quality performance at economical cost levels. A second concern is that the service to be provided was actually received. Many types of advertising services relate to some form of consulting where deliverables are intangible. Others relate to services that are difficult to monitor, such as advertisements in foreign-language journals or on radio stations. Formal monitoring procedures or some form of evidential matter are needed to protect the organization's interests.

- *Advertising Settlement.* The settlement stage of advertising agency placements requires a determination that all billings are in accordance with previously agreed-upon terms, including prices, specifications, and the timing of deliveries. In many instances there may be extra charges, and questions of propriety must be carefully examined.

- *Evaluation of Results.* The final step in this control cycle is to attempt an evaluation of what was accomplished, to the extent that such an evaluation is practicable. The results can provide an important guide to continuing advertising activities.

Figure 28.7 outlines selected operational audit procedures for reviews of the advertising function. Because advertising efforts may be so varied across product lines within a given organization, the controls procedures should be individually appraised for each major advertising effort. This appraisal should focus on the adequacy of existing controls and procedures as well as on the care and vigor with which they are implemented. In advertising functions, there are often crises and special emergencies that require deviations from established organization control procedures. However, reasonable efforts must be made to enforce appropriate levels of controls, and any deviations should be carefully documented and approved by the proper level of management.

This examination of advertising operational controls provides internal audit with a good basis to appraise the effectiveness of this function in its support of other business activities in the organization. Reviews of advertising agency relationships provide an excellent opportunity for internal audit to provide special input to management.

(iii) Advertising Function Computer Audit Procedures. Similar to other sections in this chapter, the typical organization will not have one automated ''advertising

Figure 28.7 Operational Audit Procedures for Review of Advertising Function

Audit _____ Location _____ Date _____

AUDIT STEP	INITIAL	W/P
1. Meet with product directors and the heads of advertising to gain an understanding of overall advertising strategies, directions, and scope.		
2. Review samples of advertising media to gain an understanding of the advertising strategies; if the material reviewed does not appear to be consistent with the strategies described in Step 1, resolve differences.		
3. Review advertising agency contracts covering major components of the advertising program. ✓ Determine that contracts appear to cover all aspects of advertising activity. ✓ Advertising should be tied to product performance with procedures in place to monitor effectiveness. ✓ Contracts should be reviewed periodically, with an objective of placing them open for competitive bids if results are inadequate.		
4. Review procedures in place for auditing print and sound media, including a review of records maintained for those tests. Determine that the advertising media audit provider used documentation procedures similar to internal audit.		
5. Tour advertising media production facilities and assess whether these areas appear to be neat and well organized. Trace a sample of media advertising material to formal purchase orders and to the specific contract .		
6. Review human resources policies covering advertising, determining that staff members are assigned to specific campaign areas, that their efforts are charged against those programs, and that controls appear otherwise adequate.		
7. Review security procedures covering advertising activities, both in the office and for materials handled by outside agencies and providers.		
8. Determine that management has a formal program in place to review the results of advertising and to make adjustments when appropriate.		

system.'' Rather, accounting systems will be used to support advertising budget and financial-analysis work, as discussed in the prior section on sales promotions. Similarly, various workstation-based tools may be used for advertising-related financial analysis. As previously discussed, an internal auditor should understand the application's controls and review these control procedures when internal audit determines there is an appropriate level of risk.

One area where there has been much recent progress is graphical systems for producing advertisement copy. Rather than relying on the graphic services of an advertising agency or an internal copy artist, powerful microcomputer-based systems can be used to design the copy and then prepare it for actual production. However, this type of application is usually implemented on a client-server workstation with network connections to a publisher.

An internal auditor should be interested in the backup, security, and access controls over that system. Even if it has no relationship to a financial system, its files include designs that take a considerable effort to develop. Just as internal audit was advised to be interested in the controls over computer-aided design files in the early days of information systems (as discussed in Chapter 26), similar controls should be employed for this type of system.

(iv) Advertising Audit Sample Report Findings

A: Agency Billings Are Not Properly Documented.   In our review of approved billings from the ADDCO agency, we found numerous instances of bills that were approved and paid with only minimal supporting documentation. In addition, a sample of billings was traced to internal records at the ADDCO agency. We found these billings to be supported by agency timesheets but no documentation for the type of work. Organization policies require all invoices to be adequately supported by documentation or other evidence before payment is approved.

Recommendation.   Advertising department management should establish procedures that require adequate documentation from advertising agencies before processing invoices for payment. All agencies should be reminded of this requirement.

B: Cooperative Advertising Billings Poorly Controlled.   Salespeople in the PRODCO division are allowed to give their customers a cooperative advertising allowance of 30% of the costs of local advertising placed for PRODCO products. We reviewed customer requests for payment for cooperative advertising and found that 22% of them lacked appropriate supporting documentation. In addition, all of these were approved by the responsible salespersons. PRODCO accounts payable procedures require that all disbursements should be supported with adequate documentation supporting the purchase and the receipt of the goods or services.

Recommendation.   Controls over cooperative advertising should be strengthened. Approvals for payment should be transferred to the accounts payable department, and no payment should be authorized without adequate support.

C: Graphics Design Computer System Needs Better Controls.   A specialized workstation computer has been installed along with software to produce camera-ready advertising copy. We found that these files and programs are not being backed up on a regular basis by either the department or the network administrator in accordance with corporate information systems procedures. The advertising department has not designated a staff member to perform these back-ups.

Recommendation.   Members of information systems department computer security staff should work with advertising to help establish back-up procedures in accordance with information systems procedures. Advertising should designate one member of its staff to take responsibility for file back-ups and appropriate off-site storage.

28-5 SALES ACTIVITIES

Sales promotion and advertising efforts set the stage for actual product or service sales. Unless sales are achieved in adequate volume and at proper prices, the organization cannot realize the revenues or earn the profits needed for its ongoing survival and progress. It is, therefore, most important that the sales effort be wisely planned and effectively carried out. This involves the determination of how products are to be sold and through which channels of distribution. Supporting sales efforts can then be developed and executed. The sales effort is the vital final phase of the overall marketing process. However, the character and effectiveness of this sales process is determined, to a large extent, by the marketing considerations discussed earlier in this chapter.

Although many of the marketing functions discussed previously in this chapter have primarily operational control implications, the sales process has financial and operational control implications. For example, if sales are not properly recorded due to control weaknesses, inventory and production will be negatively impacted and overall profits will suffer.

This section focuses on some of the specific aspects of the basic sales process. Whether considered as the final step in the marketing process (as discussed in this chapter) or as the first step in an accounting process (as discussed earlier), sales activities are critical. Internal audit should give proper attention to reviewing this function.

(a) DISTRIBUTION CHANNELS AND THE SALES PROCESS

An organization usually has a number of alternatives in deciding how to sell its products. One of these alternatives is to deal directly with the user or consumer. A manufacturer of industrial equipment may sell directly to factories using that equipment or a manufacturer of some consumer good may sell via direct mail to the ultimate consumer. In these situations, the sales contact with the customer will be through the organization's own sales representatives. In other cases, sales will be made through intermediate parties such as brokers, agents, dealers, or distributors. An organization will weigh the relative advantages and costs, subject to what it can afford, to determine which types of distribution channels should be selected and in what combinations. Of course, these determinations would always be subjected to continuing reevaluations based upon experience and changing conditions.

A small organization or a small division of a larger one may, at some point, have no alternative but to depend upon a particular sales distribution approach. However, most organizations have some choice in the type and mix of distribution channels used. Internal audit should understand how various products are sold and the control implications associated with each. Examples of sales distribution approaches include:

- *Direct Sales to Final Consumers.* This distribution approach is where the product is sold directly to the ultimate consumer. For consumer goods, the organization may advertise in magazines or catalogs and then take orders mailed or phoned in. Control procedures are somewhat simplified here since the organization has control over the complete sales cycle. However, the organization must take responsibility for all aspects of the cycle, ranging from order entry to shipping and billing. For a consumer product, the volume of transactions may be large, and an internal auditor may have to develop review procedures using statistical sampling to select items for review.
- *Industrial Sales.* Suppliers to manufacturers or other industrial organizations may

use salespersons or catalogs to advertise their products. Purchase quantities are often substantial and may be extended over a period of time. These types of sales are usually quite formal, with the customer requesting a bid based on specifications, the supplier organization submitting a quote, and the customer accepting the terms and conditions of the quote and issuing a formal purchase order.

- *Sales through Agents and Outside Salespersons.* Many organizations use outside salespersons to sell their products. These may include salaried sales employees, outside salespersons on commission, or independent agents selling under some type of contractual arrangement. Many salespersons receive their compensation through commissions and other incentives. Although this is often an effective method for general sales, management may encounter problems with this arrangement. For example, a salesperson may book less than firm orders during the current period to receive commission credit for a sales contest. The same salesperson may subsequently cancel or defer the order after the end of the contest period.

- *Sales through Wholesalers or Distributors.* Perhaps the most common method of sales for a product-oriented, non-retail organization is to sell to wholesalers or distributors, who will purchase the products in bulk quantity for resale. The organization may use its own sales force or a catalog to sell goods in this manner. While formal quotes and purchase orders are often not developed for these types of sales due to the regular processing of these transactions, internal audit should expect some formal control procedures over this type of sales process.

- *Indirect Sales through Outside Organizations.* Sales are sometimes transacted through various types of contractual arrangements, such as when an organization contracts to sell a predetermined amount of products to a limited group of customers. Sales would be made on an ongoing basis under the terms of the contract.

- *Nonconventional Sales Arrangements.* Organizations are increasingly selling goods using various nontraditional methods. For example, organizations are increasingly placing sales order transactions through the use of electronic data interchange (EDI) technology, as was discussed in Chapter 24. In some cases, the orders may be placed automatically, based upon unit sales and inventory levels. Consumers may shop for goods through their home television sets or through the Internet. These newer or evolving arrangements may raise control concerns.

The various types of distribution channels used have differing control implications, including controls over the availability of inventories and product inventory excess and obsolescence concerns. Other concerns include the efficiency of distribution systems for satisfying customer needs, the level of product and other distribution costs, and other types of inventory controls. Alternative approaches through which costs can be minimized should always be considered, assuming an adequate quality of services and benefits is maintained.

Distribution is often complicated because the organization may use intermediaries or agents who are independent parties and not subject to direction in the same manner as employees. Although common interests should lead to common actions, there may be differences of judgment. Actions that benefit the core organization may not benefit the intermediaries. However, if compensation and reward systems are properly constructed, both the prime organization and its sales agents can benefit from this type of cooperative arrangement.

(i) Organization of the Sales Effort. A basic requirement for the review of any sales effort is an understanding of how the function is organized. An aspect of this is the question of how many individuals can be effectively supervised, and hence how many supervisory levels will be necessary. A retail store where all salespeople work under one roof makes levels of supervision relatively easy. An organization where the sales staff travels out to potential customers creates additional supervision problems. Most of the comments in this section will be oriented to the latter type of situation.

Although the levels of supervision represent one dimension of a sales organization, a second dimension concerns the breadth of the sales department. In other words, how broad should the product line sales responsibilities of individual salespersons be? Sales department salaries, commissions, and other expenses often suggest utilizing individual salespersons for a greater range of products while serving a customer. However, the broader the line, the less effective the job the salesperson can do for particular products. There is also a question of how product line management, charged with ultimate responsibility for individual product profits, can be assured that it receives an appropriate sales effort in comparison with other organization products.

The physical location of salespeople is both a control and a logistical issue. The need for the supervision of sales personnel suggests more centrally located sales groups, while factors such as better contact with customers, reduction of travel costs, and resistance to too much time away from families may push the organization in the direction of regional, smaller district or even home-based offices. The location of sales offices is tied to a broader problem of the extent to which the sales effort should be decentralized. Under a centralized approach, all sales personnel, regardless of physical location and the number of intervening levels of supervision, will report on a direct line basis to the central sales executive. Under a decentralized approach, individual subsidiaries, divisions, or departments may have a broader profit responsibility that will include direct-line control over their own sales personnel. In this case, the central sales group may have a dotted-line functional responsibility, primarily in the way of policy. The particular arrangement selected by an individual organization will depend on the organization's approach to decentralization and other special considerations that push the organization toward greater or lesser centralized control of its activities.

The organization may find it advantageous to establish field sales offices of one kind or another away from the central headquarters. In a large sales operation, the field sales office organization may involve several levels, with certain field offices reporting to higher-ranking field offices, operational entities that can be important in an overall organization sense.

Two kinds of problems are usually involved. The first centers about the extent to which the operations conform to policies, procedures, budgets, and other types of designated controls established by the central sales office. Also involved may be controls established by other organization groups, such as personnel or accounting. A second group of problems goes beyond basic controls and deals with the general level of operational efficiency and effectiveness. This includes general housekeeping, quality of supervision, office hours observed, contacts with visitors, and the total management climate. The field sales office often is a geographically detached operation that has no day-to-day contacts and observation by higher-level management, as will exist at a central headquarters location. Therefore, an independent reviewer, such as internal audit, can play an important role in appraising the adequacy of the operation and its potential for improvement through periodic visits.

Regardless of how the sales effort is organized, management should endeavor to maximize the performance of the sales staff at a minimum cost. Questions here that are typically of interest include:

- *What type of qualifications are required of the sales personnel?* Questions include experience, special skills, educational levels, and product understanding. Answers depend on the complexity of the products sold, the value of individual items, the customers to be dealt with, and the opportunities for career advancement.

- *What kinds of training are needed?* This is related to the preceding question and applies to new recruits and to established sales personnel. In many situations, there is a need for continuing training to cope with new products or sales approaches.

- *How shall salespeople be compensated?* At one extreme is a fixed salary, with straight commissions at the other extreme. Other related issues involve the overall levels of compensation, the earnings potential of assigned territories, and the protection of territorial jurisdictions.

- *How shall sales personnel be coordinated and controlled?* Questions include the extent to which higher organizational levels should supervise the personnel for whom they are responsible, their accessibility to these lower-level personnel, and the reporting levels. Information is needed for control purposes and to utilize properly sales and customer reaction intelligence gathered from the field.

- *What is the best method to motivate sales personnel?* In addition to compensation, awards, and other monetary perquisites, sales personnel can be motivated through management policies and controls such as travel scheduling. The manner in which these controls operate has a great deal to do with how effectively salespeople are actually motivated.

- *What is the best method of assuring customer goodwill?* Although the organization wants to make sales, it is in its long-range interest that those sales be made in a manner that assures continuing customer goodwill. For example, the pressures of increasing commissions or meeting established sales objectives can lead to salespeople overselling the product. Although the organization may currently have the benefit of the sale, negative effects may prevent further sales.

The management of the sales effort, no matter what type of business and sales method, presents strong management challenges to the organization. Internal audit should have a good understanding of how the sales function is organized and how the sales staff is compensated and controlled. The questions raised in the preceding text should assist internal audit in better understanding how the overall sales effort helps design specific audit tests.

(ii) Dealers, Agents, and Franchisees.   In many situations, the organization will not sell to the ultimate customer through its own sales personnel but will use dealers or agents. The advantages gained include better geographic representation and the greater motivation that is often achieved through dealers' running their own businesses. In other cases, the volume of sales is not sufficient to support the use of in-house salespeople. In these situations, sales efforts will take the form of assisting intermediaries in dealing with the ultimate customers. Although the organization makes its direct sales to dealers, there should be a broader recognition that the organization's interests are not well served until the intermediary actually makes sales to the end customer. There should be an emphasis here on helping the intermediaries to run their businesses in a manner that will best assure these sales.

The formality of these arrangements can vary greatly. In a wholesale-to-retail type of sales arrangement, the organization simply sells products at wholesale prices to qualified distributors, who then resell them to retail customers. Similarly, the organization can operate through independent agents, who often do little more than take customers' orders. Other arrangements can be more complex. The dealers may operate under specific contracts, through which they have obligations to buy certain quantities and types of goods. They may also operate as franchisees, where the prime organization sells them the right to use the organization's name and products. These arrangements often involve extensive undertakings and are supported by strong contractual terms.

Sales representatives from the prime organization have a responsibility to assist their intermediaries in such matters as making individual sales, providing sales training, or developing sales promotional materials. The management counsel provided may typically cover how to order the right products in the right quantities; how to store products; how to display them effectively; how to train and manage personnel; plus business operations, facilities maintenance, and the like. The extent of this support depends upon the type of sales arrangement and the contractual agreements. The organization representative must be able to help dealers or agents to do what is in their own ultimate self-interest in a way that preserves the motivation and goodwill of those dealers. Unless this can be done with reasonable success, the alternative may finally be to sacrifice the potential advantages of this type of marketing arrangement and to revert to direct organization-controlled sales and distribution.

Internal audit should have a good understanding of the various dealer, agent, or franchisee sales arrangements that may exist in the organization. The various contractual terms here are often important. Internal audit may want the right to visit dealer or agent sites to examine records to determine if various agreements are satisfied. This requires that all agreements have a "right to audit" clause. These kinds of dealer sales office arrangements can present significant audit risks because the dealer, although sometimes relatively small, is conducting business as the representative of the parent organization. Customers in these situations often do not recognize that they are dealing with an independent dealer. Internal audit may want to consider reviews of selected numbers of these dealers to determine that contractual terms and proper procedures are followed. In addition, internal audit can review the accuracy of dealer inventory or sales performance representations.

(iii) Credit Policy Management. Credit policy management is, to a large extent, a problem associated with overall organization financial management. Too easy a credit policy may cause the organization to sell to customers who do not pay. The result is the write-off of uncollectible receivables. Too tight a credit policy may discourage sales, with a resultant reduction in cash flow. The extension of credit should be conducive to generating new customers and expanding sales from existing customers, with proper consideration given to the financial resources of potential customers, to organization and customer cash-liquidity problems, and to the overall service associated with the credit provided to customers.

Related credit policy considerations include the procedures through which credit extensions are made responsive to all the changing needs of different types of customers.

In this connection, goodwill and product loyalty are typically generated by a continuing appraisal of customer credit needs, stable and dependable availability of credit to customers, the fairness of the administration of credit policies and procedures, and a demonstrated interest in customer welfare.

(iv) Other Sales Promotion Activities.

The typical organization is often involved with many types of promotional activities other than those through advertising agencies. The number and kinds of these are limited only by the imagination and ingenuity of the sales promotion personnel. As a result, there may be a wide range of special control problems associated with them. They are often more complicated because they may operate through multiple levels of the product distribution process. That is, a particular promotion may involve final consumers but may be administered through jobbers, dealers, or agents. This multiple-level process often introduces potential control concerns.

Special arrangements can vary considerably depending upon the nature of the products, markets, dealers, or customers. These arrangements pose potential control concerns that require auditor understanding and attention. Some of the more common types of promotions and their related special control problems are as follows:

- *Contract Sales Promotion Services.* An organization often acquires promotional services beyond those provided by its advertising agencies. Depending upon the organization and industry, these might include such diverse services as a sales demonstrator at an industry trade show, the display of organization signs, or even skywriting. Common problems may be the fairness of the initial arrangements, the quality of the services performed, and the evidence that the services were actually rendered. Because such promotions are often ad hoc ideas, controls can potentially be weak and vendor arrangements may be at a less than ''arm's length'' basis. Internal audit should treat such promotional arrangements much like any other procurement except that more may be required to determine that the purchase arrangements were properly approved and documented.

- *Furnished Display Materials.* Some sales organizations, particularly those involved in retail, provide racks or signs to dealers to help sell their merchandise. Control problems include the prudent acquisition of the display materials, the care with which they are handled and protected while awaiting use, the manner in which they are distributed, and the effectiveness of their subsequent care and use. Frequently, the controls over the purchase and custody of these materials can be weak. They may be viewed as ''free'' goods by employees who steal or otherwise misuse them. When distributed to outside parties, there may be waste because the materials often come at no cost to the recipients. In some cases, these display materials may be sold to the recipients, and in that case, further controls are necessary to assure proper billing and collections. Depending on the cost of the materials and the volume involved, the possibilities for waste could be significant. It is important, therefore, that there be appropriate policies, records, and procedures for handling such display materials. Similarly, the implementation of any display materials program should be managed in a careful manner.

- *Free Samples.* Control problems here are similar to those of display materials. An added problem is that the free samples are normally desirable items for many persons, and hence are more easily diverted from their intended purpose. Internal audit should look for inventory and distribution controls over such goods. Although they will be ultimately given away, they should be viewed as valuable inventory within the organization. Just as employees would not be allowed to take regular inventory off the shelves, free samples also should be controlled to prevent any potential abuse.

- *Premiums.* There are many types of promotional premiums, ranging from vouchers for other purchases given with the purchase of an item to free accessories given with the product. One such promotion is airline frequent-flyer miles. In other cases, customers submit something as proof of purchase to obtain the premium. In all cases, control problems include enforcement of the conditions specified, proper accounting (including recognition of any liabilities due to unclaimed premiums), and the administration of the premium program in an efficient manner.

- *Coupons.* In certain businesses, usually retail, a popular type of sales promotion is to give coupons which then entitle the customer to a reduced price for their next purchase of the particular product. The dealer or agent who has accepted the coupon then claims reimbursement from the sponsoring organization or from a centralized coupon-processing organization. Concerns here include control over the creation of the coupons; the proper distribution of coupons to the persons who, it is hoped, will use them; and controls to prevent the coupons from being used improperly. For example, a dealer may submit coupons for reimbursement even though the dealer has neither purchased nor sold the proper amount of the products. Other controls are needed to cancel used coupons to prevent their reuse. There are many problems here because of the large number of people involved and the difficulty of enforcing the kind of controls that are often required.

- *Combination Sales.* Frequently, combinations of several products from different manufacturers may be offered at a specially reduced price. For example, a computer manufacturer may bundle a software package with purchase of the basic computer. The final seller may, however, abuse the arrangement by breaking up the combination and selling the individual components at their full prices. A concern here is that one manufacturer may be liable for the costs of product support for both. A control for this risk is sufficient visibility for the intended arrangement. This can be accomplished through advertising as well as by controlling serial numbers or otherwise marking the individual products.

- *Special Discounts and Allowances.* A common type of sales promotion is to establish a temporary special price by an announcement in some manner to dealers or to the ultimate consumer. The retailer or distributor is protected through a purchase allowance or a rebate payable upon their showing proper evidence of the sale under the stated conditions. A key control problem is the adequacy of the evidence that the specified allowance conditions have been carried out. Another complication is that when allowances apply to inventories on hand, there must be adequate controls over the accuracy of the affected inventory.

- *Contests.* Another popular type of sales promotion is the awarding of prizes to salespeople, dealers, distributors, and others on the basis of designated actions. In some cases, the contest may involve ultimate consumers and will seek additional sales through a purchase requirement for eligibility in the contest. Control problems with contests center around the necessary assurances that the specified conditions have been met. The administration of the contest is often placed in independent hands to complete integrity for the entire effort.

- *Shows and Presentations.* In many businesses, the introduction of new models and lines is supported by various types of trade shows and promotional meetings. These types of presentations also may include display materials, special discounts, and other special arrangements. Proper attention must be given to controls for this type of marketing.

- *Consignment Marketing.* Consignments are really not sales initially, as the goods are shipped to a dealer who is not required to pay for them until sold. This may sometimes be a method of normal distribution (as discussed in Chapter 25) or such a distribution may be used to promote sales as part of a special promotion. In either event, controls over the consigned goods are very important. It is easy to lose track of them and, therefore, not realize when the goods have been sold.

Although the above categories list some common types of sales promotions, these efforts can take other forms as well. When reviewing sales promotion and advertising activities, internal audit should pay particular attention to these types of promotions, as they pose a number of control concerns. The first is that each promotional project should provide reasonable promise that it will achieve results that justify the expenses incurred. Sales promotional people may be overly optimistic and enthusiastic about expected results from a promotion. Internal audit should look for a formal plan for the sales promotion effort, including budgeted expenses, estimated timings, and expected results. Internal audit should also look for a program of ongoing management reporting of actual results measured against such promotional plans.

A second area of control concern is whether promotional projects are implemented in a manner that prevents excessive cost and waste. All too often, the peoples involved with promoting a new product are so concerned about the promotional effort that they will ignore good cost-control procedures. The overall promotion effort suffers when special payments and allowances are diverted or otherwise appropriated without achieving originally intended conditions. Nevertheless, many promotional projects that involve special discounts, free samples, prizes, and the like are vulnerable to fraud or abuse. Internal audit should determine that these programs were designed with adequate controls and that these controls are being followed.

Finally, internal audit should assess whether the actual promotional project is carried out. Many sales promotion programs have been sound in concept and designed with good administrative controls, but the promotion failed because of a lack of care and discipline in their administration. All sales promotion projects require a continuing critical evaluation to identify and correct any potential problems. Although these controls and reviews are the prime responsibility of marketing management, internal audit can provide significant service through risk-based reviews of sales promotion projects.

(v) Pricing Control Concerns.   This area of internal control concerns is directly related to distribution channel control concerns. Pricing is a function for which marketing and finance have responsibilities. Product pricing control concerns were discussed in Chapter 22 as part of the discussion of accounting systems and controls. However, pricing is discussed here because it plays such an important role in the organization's relations with its distribution intermediaries. These intermediaries are interested in product prices as they directly affect sales volumes, market shares, and profits. Depending upon the channels of distribution used, the prices to intermediaries are set so the intermediary will be motivated to provide a vigorous sales effort. An organization must carefully weigh various cost and volume considerations and endeavor to fix pricing levels that achieve proper margins and meet budgetary goals. However, competitive pressures may prevent the achievement of either desired pricing stability or uniformity.

There are complex legal aspects to setting pricing levels and establishing overall pricing policy. While the assistance of a lawyer may be required when problems arise, an internal auditor should have some general knowledge of such matters. In the United States, many pricing related statutes have been in effect for years. For example, the Sherman Act of 1890 outlaws monopolies and contracts that cause a restraint of trade. The Clayton Act of 1914 outlaws price discrimination where it tends to lessen competition or create a monopoly. The Robinson-Patman Act of 1936 specifies the types of price discrimination that are Clayton Act violations, such as quantity discounts or other price differentials unless they reflect costs of manufacturing and selling goods. These laws allow a seller to discriminate in price, however, to meet a legitimately lower price of a competitor. There is other related legislation, such as the Federal Trade Commission Act of 1914, that also regulates unfair competition. In the United States and other countries, it is important that management be familiar with any relevant statutes so that marketing policies adhere to the law.

Beyond legal requirements, management has many other concerns about the pricing of its products. The price assigned impacts the competitive position of the organization as well as its long-run profitability. There should be a fairly detailed analysis of direct and indirect costs as well as of the prices of competing products. Internal audit would probably not question management's pricing decisions provided that they are supported by adequate analysis, justification, and management communications. Even if the price of an item is below cost, internal audit should not necessarily question the selling price provided it is supported by adequate analysis and management is aware of the pricing impact. An organization may underprice a product to gain market share or to gain a competitive position. Internal audit is fully correct in questioning whether a pricing decision may be illegal, however, if the pricing analysis appears to be deliberately missing key cost elements or if cost analyses communicated to management appear to be flawed.

Perhaps the most important concern over pricing—discussed in more detail in the following section on internal controls—is that the prices actually charged reflect management's intentions. From the lowest level of consumer retail goods to major industrial items, there is a tendency for sales personnel to violate established price rules and offer unauthorized discounts to promote sales. While sales personnel at all levels may have the flexibility to make price adjustments, there should be clearly stated adjustment limits and policies covering the levels of management approvals required to make further adjustments. Also, systems should be established to track any price adjustments and to measure their effect on overall profitability.

(b) SALES DEPARTMENT INTERNAL CONTROLS

The role of sales personnel as well as their sales approaches may vary widely from one organization to another. In some situations, products do not represent major commitments and sales are generated on a day-to-day or month-to-month basis. In others, sales may take the form of contractual relationships where considerable negotiation and customer evaluation forms part of the sales effort. In all cases, however, the sales function should have the objective of meeting or exceeding sales forecasts and doing this in a well-controlled manner. This section will consider several of the most important areas of internal control that should be in place over the sales function.

The sales process will vary with the type of industry or the sales approach. The types of internal controls over sales in a retail environment, however, are similar to controls over a high-end sales environment, such as the sale of industrial manufacturing equipment. In all cases, sales orders should be properly documented, there should be controls over sales invoices and prices, and there should be adequate procedures for handling customer credits. The comments in this section are intended to cover a generic sales function.

(i) Sales Orders.   Many types of sales are not taken from open stock but require custom manufacturing or preparation prior to customer shipment. Before an organization goes through this manufacturing or preparation process, the sale should be supported by a sales order document with appropriate customer authorization. This could be a purchase order submitted by the customer, an EDI transaction, an order prepared by the organization's salesperson, or a formal contract outlining the terms of the sale. The document should be authorized by appropriate management to bind that customer to the purchase. The sales order is an important document that allows the organization to recognize the sale and to begin taking steps to ship the goods ordered.

Goods should not be shipped, however, based solely upon the receipt of a sales order. The organization should have a formal process to review all sales orders, with an appropriate person in the organization giving approval to orders over specified monetary amounts. In addition, the credit function should review and approve all orders based on the customer's past credit history, current account balances, and reported credit performance.

The price at which the goods will be shipped should be generally determined at the time of receipt of the customer order. This is also the point at which management should review and approve any discounts or allowances that may have been given by a salesperson. Any exceptions to standard list prices or published discounts should receive approval by appropriate levels of management. Any exceptions to standard prices allowed by the sales department should be properly documented and approved.

As a final step, the sales order should be properly recorded in organization records. This includes entry into customer accounts as well as entry into manufacturing inventory or shipping records to provide control over the order. This step typically makes use of automated order-entry systems.

(ii) Sales Invoices.   All sales and shipments of goods should be documented through some form of invoice to the customer. This document is used to record sales, relieve inventory, calculate sales commissions, and for other purposes. Invoices should be controlled, prenumbered documents, and with adequate controls over any voided documents.

A packing slip, which is a nonpriced copy of the sales invoice, typically goes with the shipped goods and forms the basis for the customer's acknowledgment of receipt of goods. There should be frequent reconciliations between the total of invoices generated by the sales billing function and total charges to customer accounts to determine that all goods invoiced have been billed to customers. Controls should be established to ensure that all sales are billed and that all invoices are recorded as accounts receivable. Invoices should also be compared with both the original customer order and shipping records to determine that unit prices, extensions, discounts, credits, and any special terms have been properly recorded on the customer invoice. This control process should be the same whether for a manufacturing organization shipping custom-made goods on account or a retailer selling open stock items and dealing primarily in cash. The latter may not have formal customer invoices, but the reconciliation takes place through balancing cash charge slips and in registers to recorded sales.

(iii) Credit Memoranda.   The sales process often results in returned goods or in requests from customers for price adjustments. This is a final step in the sales internal-control cycle. There should be a formal approval process for making customer-requested adjustments due to incorrect prices, damaged goods, or a failure to invoice per agreed terms. All approved adjustments should become credit records to the billing system.

The organization should have effective controls over returned goods. Credits should not be issued just because the customer returned the goods. Rather, the organization should have a procedure for authorizing returns in advance, with a notification to the receiving function to properly handle the returned goods. Whether a returned good or a price adjustment, organizations issue credit memos to cover the matter. These are often good for future merchandise purchases or cash. Because of the latter, the organization should establish suitable controls over these valuable documents.

(c) SALES FUNCTION INTERNAL AUDIT ACTIVITIES

An internal auditor should understand the sales distribution approaches used in the auditor's organization. Each will have its own distribution control concerns, ranging from financial transaction controls to operational controls over the sales and distribution process.

Financial, operational, and computer systems audits of the sales process are closely related to other areas such as shipping, accounts receivables, and collections. Shipping issues were discussed in Chapter 25 on distribution and accounts receivable procedures, and in Chapter 22, on accounting systems. While an internal auditor may want to include audit procedures from those two chapters for a comprehensive audit of the sales, billing, and collection process, a separate review of the sales function can also be of value.

(i) Sales-Related Financial Audit Considerations.   An internal auditor should have basic objectives to ensure that sales are properly approved, that there are appropriate reviews over customer credit status, that goods shipped are properly billed, and that any adjustments are correctly recorded. Internal audit can assess the adequacy of these procedures through a detailed review of the sales process, including the selection of a sample of sales transactions to determine whether they were properly approved and are accurate. Figure 28.8 outlines some audit procedures for a financially oriented review of the sales function.

Segregation of duties is a major area here that an internal auditor should examine when reviewing sales. There are risks that a salesperson can offer special terms, that merchandise can be inappropriately accepted for return, or that a customer can be granted credit beyond prudent limits. Proper controls should be in place to prevent and detect any exceptions to sales control procedures.

The term *audit risk* has been used throughout this book to describe the basis for an internal auditor's selection of alternative areas or candidates for review and for determining the sizes of items to be sampled for selection and review. The evaluation of audit risk was discussed in Chapter 8. A similar concept of risk is found in the sales process itself.

Figure 28.8   Audit Program Extract: Financial Review of Sales Function

Audit _____   Location _____   Date _____

AUDIT STEP	INITIAL	W/P
1. Gather statistics for sales activity over the past 12 to 18 months. Observe trends and the mix of sales between various products and customers (e.g. normal billing versus deferred contract, etc.)		
2. Review the systems used for recording sales. Perform tests, as appropriate, to determine that sales are correctly recorded.		
3. If direct selling methods are used, document process and review selected individual sales records to determine that overall organization procedures are being followed.		
4. Determine an appropriate separation of responsibilities exists between sales accounts receivable and accounting to maintain control over sales records.		
5. Review procedures for pricing products sold. If standardized pricing lists/books are used, determine that updates are communicated to all staff members on a regular basis.		
6. Discuss policies in place for allowing discounts or allowances. Assess whether controls are adequate and are being followed.		
7. Review procedures in place for authorizing returns. Trace return activity to individual salespersons to determine if there is any abuse of this policy.		
8. Develop an understanding of the sales commission or bonus program. Review controls and determine if records indicate that salespersons are compensated according to their level of actual sales performance.		
9. Review the process, if any, for preparing sales quotes. Compare sales results to product profitability quotes and salesperson commission compensation.		
10. Perform a detailed analysis of sales over a recent period. Compare sales to such things as inventory purchases, production expenses, selling expenses, collections, and overall profitability. Discuss any unusual variances with management and comment on any internal control weaknesses.		

Management assumes a risk when it accepts a sales order from a new or unqualified customer. It also assumes a risk when it grants credit to an established customer who may not pay for the merchandise due to other pressures. Internal audit should be aware of these business risks and consider them when making selections of specific items to be reviewed.

A major internal audit concern in the sales area is that all sales should be properly recorded and recognized. There is a temptation for units to recognize sales prior to credit approval or prior to actual shipment. Also, goods may be loaned or placed on consignment with a customer but improperly recorded as a sale. Since the sale was not actually completed, no cash has been received and the goods may soon be returned. This is a difficult area for auditor review. Internal audit can not easily detect these errors through an accounts receivables confirmation test, as was discussed in Chapter 22, but in many instances, the customer will be unaware of the recording error. If the goods were not shipped until the first of the month but were recorded as a sale at the end of the prior month, the customer responding to a confirmation may just view it as a minor bookkeeping error and would respond favorably to the confirmation. However, if the goods were loaned to a customer and not recorded, confirmation will not be possible. There are no recorded sales to confirm. Internal audit must just look for strong internal control procedures to prevent this throughout the organization.

A second area of concern is whether the items sold were properly priced. While pricing files are typically part of automated systems, internal audit should consider performing tests to determine whether the calculated prices are correct and whether they take into account various discounts or surcharges.

(ii) Sales Function Operational Audit Considerations. The prior discussion points to the fact that financial and operational audit considerations over the sales function are closely related. When reviewing the sales function, internal audit may spend most of the review time on operational audit issues. Financial audit issues would often be covered in separate reviews of the accounts receivable function, as discussed in Chapter 22, or in reviews of the sales process, including the flow of goods from inventory to sales, as discussed in Chapter 25.

A first step for the operational auditor is to develop a general understanding of the sales process, which includes the order-entry, shipping, and billing cycle. This process includes the actual initial entry of the sale, which may occur through a salesperson calling on a customer or through an order generated by an advertisement. Internal audit should consider developing a similar chart for the organization under review. Figure 28.9 outlines some audit procedures for reviewing a sales function.

Figure 28.10 illustrates some of the operational audit steps for a review of the sales process. These procedures emphasize review of the sales documents described in the flowchart. While that chart shows many of them as manual, paper documents, they could also be transactions input into automated systems. Reviews of these systems are described in the following sections.

(iii) Sales Function Computer Audit Procedures. The sales function often has some type of order-entry systems for recording sales and processing invoices for shipped goods. This type of system can take many forms, depending on the size of the organization and the nature of the sales process. A very small organization may have a microcomputer LAN-based database or spreadsheet system to record its sales. As an organization becomes more complex, internal audit will typically find some form of order-entry and order-processing system with linkages to accounts receivable, shipping, and the general ledger.

As an initial step in reviewing controls over an automated sales system, an internal auditor should develop a flowchart for the basic sales order-entry system and significant system interfaces. The next step, as has been described repeatedly throughout these chapters on operational auditing issues, is to evaluate the application controls. Procedures for performing this type of review were discussed in Chapter 17, on application reviews, as well as in Chapter 16, on data-processing general control reviews. Particularly important

Figure 28.9   Operational Audit Steps for Review of Sales Function

Audit _____   Location _____   Date _____

AUDIT STEP	INITIAL	W/P
1. Obtain a sales function organization chart, including any outside sales agents; determine who is responsible for making sales decisions and approving special pricing or compensation terms.		
2. Through discussions with sales function management, document the nature of customers for that sales function; review sales status reports to determine if reporting system supports those customer types.		
3. Describe the sales process used by the group, developing process flowcharts to describe the basic sales steps; identify potential strengths and weaknesses in the process.		
4. Determine that proper separations of duties exist in all aspects of the sales process, including the following: • Persons opening mail are separate from persons recording cash. • Special sales discounts and terms are approved by management. • Goods do not leave warehouses without proper sales documentation. • Recorded sales activity is reconciled to cash receipts regularly.		
5. Determine that overall physical security covering the sales area is adequate. Assess security through observation.		
6. Review procedures for maintaining pricing lists and communicating that information to customers and sales staff; perform tests to determine that lists are correct.		
7. If an outside sales force is used, review procedures for reporting sales calls activity as well as promotional costs; assess the control procedures in place for this process.		
8. Based on observations and reviews of control reports, assess that procedures appear adequate for: • Tracking leads and updating customer information • Granting/revoking credit • Handling complaints • Maintaining histories of customer transactions		
9. Determine that training programs, procedural guidance, or other techniques are in place to assure that proper ethical procedures are followed.		
10. Assess the controls over the reporting procedure for the function; provide a proper level of sales status for senior management.		

are general controls related to overall logical security. The nature of a sales system application could lead to improper manipulation of data files.

Sales systems present prime opportunities for the use of computer-assisted audit techniques, which will support operational and financial audit procedures. Recorded sales can be analyzed to determine whether they were properly priced, whether any discounts granted were appropriate, or whether credits appear to be applied to proper accounts. Figure 28.10 lists some potential computer-assisted audit techniques to support operational or financial reviews of an automated sales and order-entry application. Chapter 12 provided some general guidance on developing these computer-assisted procedures.

(iv) Sample Sales Audit Report Findings

A: Dealers Not Following Accounting Guidelines.   According to the organization's basic dealer agreement, all dealers are to keep accounting records of consigned goods received, special orders placed, returns, and adjustments. They are to use these records to prepare a monthly settlement statement to be sent to district headquarters for commission checks. We reviewed a sample of dealers in regions 11 and 19 and found that these records had not been properly maintained and that commissions settlement check requests were only based on estimates. Regional sales representatives were not sufficiently reviewing these dealer claims to realize that commission requests were only based on estimates.

Recommendation.   All dealers should be formally reminded of dealer agreement policies. Regional representatives should be instructed to visit a broad sample of dealers on a regular basis and inspect dealer agreement records.

B: Product Sample Materials Not Properly Controlled.   We took a physical inventory of sample merchandise produced for product XX. Although this material is supposed to be given only to dealers who meet sales targets, we found that inventory stock withdrawals were taken by sales representatives without proper justification. We observed two sales

Figure 28.10   CAATs for a Review of Sales Function

- Review recorded sales file against appropriate product pricing files to determine if sales are made according to published price schedules; research reasons for reported differences.

- Review recorded sales files against product inventory status records at the time the sales were made to determine if sales are made for products not in stock. Assess propriety.

- Review discounts or special offers from sale files against a table of standard discount rates. Research reasons for reported differences.

- Match recorded sales by representatives to records of returned goods; investigate unusual activity, such as a high number of returns by one sales representative.

- Match recorded sales for one or more sample months against returns or cancellations in the first 10 working days of subsequent months. Investigate any unusual activity.

representatives who requested sample merchandise from stock clerks with no detailed justification. We also observed that the stock clerks did not adjust inventory records when they presented the samples to the sales representatives.

Recommendation. All sample merchandise should be maintained in the inventory-control system at some nominal value. Both sales representatives and stock clerks should be reminded of that value. Procedures should be strengthened to require formal inventory requests whenever sample goods are requested. Stock clerks should be formally reminded that their job requires them to maintain accurate records and that they could be subject to disciplinary procedures if they do not.

C: Credit Vouchers Not Properly Controlled. Credit voucher documents, which are used to request adjustments to customer accounts or refunds, are not numerically controlled. We observed that these documents are available in the supply room with no controls. In a sample of 90 credit vouchers tendered during the second quarter, we found that seven documents were not properly approved by a sales manager and that duplicate vouchers were applied to the same customer in four cases.

Recommendation. Numerical document controls should be placed over credit vouchers, and the documents should be stored in a secure location. All credit documents should be screened for valid authorizing signatures before processing.

28-6 SALES-MARKETING- AND ADVERTISING-RELATED AUDITS

The sales, marketing, and advertising functions of the typical organization have come of age in recent years in terms of management sophistication and overall management depth. Their broader dimensions and interrelationships with other organization activities have been recognized. No longer is the marketing function thought of only as the sales activity, but rather as linked to the central mission of the organization. It has now become the focal point of a total management effort. As such, internal audit should have reappraised its own role in relation to these broader sales and marketing functions.

The role of internal audit in these sales, marketing, and advertising areas can involve three different levels of activity. At the most elementary level, there is a need to consider financial controls. This is the concern with accountabilities for products sold, accounts receivable, and cash received in payment, as discussed in Chapter 22. At a second level, internal audit should be concerned with the extent of compliance with sales and marketing policies and procedures as a component of overall administrative operations and controls. Examples here would be the administration of an established plan of compensating sales personnel or the adequacy of the development and use of sales data.

The third and highest level involves some of the important policy determinations of the type described in this chapter. In these areas, internal audit can take a strong role in assessing risks and planning major operational and financial audits in various organization situations. This third area provides a great potential for internal auditing service. Internal audit has the capacity to provide a rational analysis of various sales and marketing practices from a detached vantage point, combined with an opportunity to see the sales and marketing operations close-up. Of course, special audit skills need to be developed in the appreciation of the creative and dynamic dimensions of the sales and marketing functions. This will require some special care, but if properly handled, the stage can be set for increased levels of internal audit service to management.

CHAPTER 29

Payroll and Personnel

29-1 INTRODUCTION: THE HUMAN RESOURCES FUNCTION

This chapter deals with controls over the payroll function and the activities of the personnel or human resources department. (We will hereafter use the more common term, ''human resources.'')

The payroll function involves more than just the issuance of employee paychecks at the end of a time period. It must work closely with human resources to ascertain that compensation is correct and that deductions—including taxes, employee benefit payments, and employee-requested deductions—are properly calculated. Payroll has a responsibility to report and remit these funds to the various governmental or other agencies. Although the calculation of compensation is an accounting function, because of confidentiality and control requirements, payroll is often a separate group in all but the smallest organizations.

Human resources has the responsibility for hiring, administering benefits for, and otherwise supporting all personnel in the organization. In addition, other specialized functions such as pension plan and medical program administration often compose the department. Payroll and human resources functions are essential to maintaining the quality of the workforce in the organization. Internal audit needs to understand the controls and procedures surrounding these functions.

This chapter begins with a discussion of the payroll process and the controls that surround it. The payroll section builds on the basic financial controls discussed in Chapter 22 but also includes payroll department operations. The next sections discuss some controls and responsibilities surrounding other human resources functions. Finally, since they may be either part of human resources or administered separately, supporting employee benefits such as pensions and medical plans are discussed.

The human resource function provides assistance and services to people in the organization at all levels. Because auditors are employees and because of confidentiality, some audit functions have avoided reviews of this area. However, internal control reviews of payroll, human resources, and employee benefits can make important management contributions, including potential cost savings. When all factors are considered, internal audit risk models may also point internal audit to this area.

29-2 PAYROLL AND STAFF COMPENSATION CONTROLS

Payroll and staff compensation includes regular salaries and wages as well as incentive payments such as sales commissions. Audit control considerations are important for payroll because:

1. Salaries and wages usually represent one of the largest segments of an organization's operating costs.
2. These expenditures involve people and, consequently, inevitable people problems.
3. They relate so closely to various operational problems of all organization activities and the efforts to achieve effective labor utilization.

There are also interrelated legal considerations such as minimum wage legislation, unemployment insurance taxes, various quota-related regulations, and government-sponsored pension programs. Payroll costs are at the heart of total organization operations.

Many of the basic financial controls discussed in Chapter 22 apply to payroll. In fact, payroll can be considered as a special type of accounts payable process. Internal audit's concern is with how payroll data are initially developed and subsequently processed because of the opportunities for fraud in connection with these activities.

Although most payrolls today are internally automated or prepared by a specialized outside service function, this chapter is concerned with the basic problems and issues that relate to payrolls regardless of the means by which the payrolls are processed. Computer application controls, in their broader sense, were discussed in Chapter 17.

The following section covers controls and procedures over the preparation and issuance of employee payrolls and other forms of compensation. There are a variety of special internal control and audit concerns here, as well as opportunities for computer-assisted auditing.

(a) PAYROLL PROCESS

Since payrolls have to do with employees and their compensation for work performed, the first requirement is evidence that the individual compensated is a properly authorized employee, officially employed and not subsequently terminated prior to the starting date of the current payroll period. Such evidence is subject to independent verification by the human resources department. The second requirement is evidence for the work performed. In the case of salaried employees, documentation of work done will vary depending on the organizational status and the level of the employee. For salaried employees, there are often records generated by established time-clock procedures. In other cases there may be records maintained by supervisors. At higher levels, controls depend more on general observation and the integrity of the individual. Human resources records provide the most reliable up-to-date existing salaries. Overtime compensation records should be maintained by supervisors for adequate approvals.

In many facilities, the amount of time spent on individual projects, job orders, or other specific work assignments must be recorded. Such records have historically been prepared by employees and subsequently reviewed and approved by supervisors. Today, this process is often automated, with a magnetic encoded job card to record employee starting time and to record time spent on various individual jobs. Supplementary records allow for a cross-check for accuracy of the total time, and for any cost-accounting allocations. For employees who work on different jobs with different classifications and bases of compensation, control issues involve the risk of rate manipulation as well as the effective utilization of labor. For payroll purposes, however, the time record authorization by a responsible supervisor is a key control.

Employees of different categories are often paid on different time period bases. Hourly labor is often paid on a weekly basis, certain salaried on a semi-monthly or biweekly basis, and more senior salaried members on a monthly basis. At the end of the designated payroll periods, the preparation of the payroll is usually automated to determine what is owed and payable to each employee for work performed during the payroll period. The key aspects of this preparation are as follows:

- *Accumulation of Work Evidence.* Time cards and all other records of work activity must be accumulated and receive proper approval from supervisors. Errors must be identified, corrected, and processed. Also required is the summarization by individuals and organizational components. When prepared manually, the clerical accuracy of this summarization must be assured by various internal controls, including the segregation of clerical work and responsibility. Determination of bona fide employees is established through cross-references to human resources records.

- *Application of Rates.* Existing pay grade rates, union contracts, or organization job grade scales are used to calculate compensation. When the authenticity of the rates has been adequately established (again, through human resources records), the necessary calculations are made and the resulting amounts computed. Usually, these rates are maintained in the payroll system master files.

- *Accounting Distributions.* The amounts payable for services performed must be allocated to proper operational activities in conformance with the established accounting requirements of the organization. Although it is possible, and sometimes necessary, to defer the determinations of these distributions, this process should be completed as soon as is practicable.

- *Application of Deductions.* Payroll deductions include income taxes, government benefit plans such as social security, union dues, retirement savings plans, and health plan contributions; they must be properly described on pay vouchers and applied to the employee accounts.

- *Determination of Net Pay.* The difference between the basic compensation earned and all deductions is the net pay due to individual employees. There must also be adequate controls to tie payroll system control totals against detailed payroll input data.

Although at one time employers paid their employees in cash, organizations today pay each individual by check or automatic funds transfer to reduce the risk of handling cash and, of course, to provide an automatic record of receipt by the employee.

Employees are often paid by a direct deposit to their checking accounts through electronic fund transfer (EFT) systems. The employer, or an outside provider, transmits the net pay amounts and checking account identification numbers to a clearing house bank that then transfers net pay amounts to the employees' bank accounts. Employees receive a pay voucher outlining their deductions and the net pay amount.

The checks or deposit advices are distributed to employees either on the job or through the mail. However, it is important that this delivery be made directly to the various individuals so that there is no opportunity for any diversion or manipulation by some intermediary. Identification of the recipient is important and receipts should be obtained where payment is made in cash. In the event that individuals are not available at the time of a direct regular distribution, the checks should be taken back to a designated cashier location, and the individuals affected should then be required to present themselves in person to receive payment.

(b) PAYROLL INTERNAL CONTROL CONSIDERATIONS

While often voluminous, time-constraint-bound, and extensively involved with the details of varying rates, calculations, and deductions, the payroll process in principle is straightforward and subject to basic internal control considerations. The handling of, or access to, any cash should be entirely separate from the creation of any part of the records that support that cash payment. More important, the process should be partitioned among departments so that a cross-check control exists. Controls over various stages can help manage voluminous detail, especially important in the payroll department, where the payroll or input to the automated payroll system is prepared.

The payroll function can incorrectly pay an individual, incorrectly process various deductions (including taxes), or incorrectly allocate payroll costs. There are controls built into the process to prevent or detect these potential errors. For example, if paid too little, an employee will almost certainly protest, but if too much, there may not be a reaction at all. If deductions are remitted incorrectly, the organization may be subject to a penalty or even legal action.

Payroll can also be subject to fraud. If an employee in a plant quits, the direct supervisor, rather than process the resignation, might instead misappropriate the resigned employee's checks on an ongoing basis. This can be difficult to detect without proper controls. Similarly, if check stocks are used but not protected, someone can steal check forms and cash them as fraudulent paychecks. Without detailed bank reconciliations of pay records, such theft can be difficult to detect. The large amount of cash processed through a payroll makes it an attractive target for fraudulent activity. Also, the many transactions associated with a payroll point to a need for strong internal controls.

These sections cover internal controls and audit activities over the payroll function. Later sections discuss controls over human resources and employee benefits functions. Internal auditors must always remember that these separate control areas are interrelated. Separate functions in the modern organization are involved in the employee benefit and compensation process, including:

- *Operating Departments.* Supervisors from operating units are responsible for approving employee time records as well as initiating pay rate changes and any additions or deletions to payroll records.

- *Human Resources Department.* This group is responsible for maintaining overall employee pay rates based upon established job classifications and evaluations submitted by operating departments on individual employees.

- *Timekeeping Function.* This is the group that takes submitted hourly pay data and prepares it for submission to payroll processing. Among other things, it reviews the labor data and codes or classifies it to proper distribution accounts. This function today is being replaced with automated labor collection systems on the job site.

- *Payroll Processing.* This group processes and distributes the actual paychecks. Once an extensive manual effort, automated systems now carry much of the burden. Many organizations have contracted this function to an outside service provider.

- *Payroll-Related Accounting Functions.* While the payroll function authorizes the release of funds for payrolls, taxes, and the like, actual payments are often handled by another accounting function, usually an automated system today. (See Chapter 22.)

As the above implies, the persons who authorize the pay records should not be the same as those who prepare the pay. Although human resources and payroll functions may be organized differently in every organization, internal audit should always look for these basic separation-of-duties controls.

(c) PAYROLL INTERNAL AUDIT ACTIVITIES

Today, the operational aspects of the payroll function are often ignored by auditors. In the past, internal auditors who frequently looked at the automated payroll system often found little or nothing after two or three reviews were performed over the years. As a result, they may have removed the payroll function and its supporting automated system from their risk models. Payroll may then never come up for audit. Although still viewed as a low-risk audit by both auditors and management, payroll systems can present significant audit risks. Payroll systems change as do the human resources handling the pay processes.

(i) Payroll Financial Audit Procedures. Financial and operational audit procedures for payroll are closely intertwined. Although some might argue that the financial audit controls described here are operational or that the operational and information systems controls described in the following two sections belong with financial controls, this section describes some primarily financial-related audit procedures for reviews of the payroll function. The internal auditor should consider all in an integrated review of the payroll function. The functions are described separately here, keeping with the overall format of this book.

Understanding how payroll is organized is key. A simplified flowchart describing the overall payroll process from time sheets to the distribution of checks is illustrated in Figure 29.1. While the flowchart should describe the overall pay process, internal audit should also consider the exceptions to that process—for example, sales commissions or executive pay.

An internal audit of any separate executive pay function may be viewed as a ''hands off'' area by members of senior management. This pay group is often the responsibility of the compensation committee of the board of directors, and internal audit may want to clear any planned review of executive pay with that group. Frequently, the external auditors will be asked to review this area as part of their annual review for preparation of the proxy statement for publicly held companies.

The pay and benefit policies and procedures include such matters as how authorized vacation entitlements, sick pay rules, and pay compensation grades are established. This data will assist internal audit in assessing compliance when reviewing payroll records.

Many of the controls discussed in Chapter 22 for a review of an accounts payable function are also applicable to payroll. However, the accounts payable function is normally disbursing funds to outsiders. Payroll is regularly disbursing funds to inside persons, including members of the payroll function. This points to areas for increased control evaluation scrutiny. The following objectives help to ensure that authorized persons receive authorized pay:

Figure 29.1 Simplified Payroll System

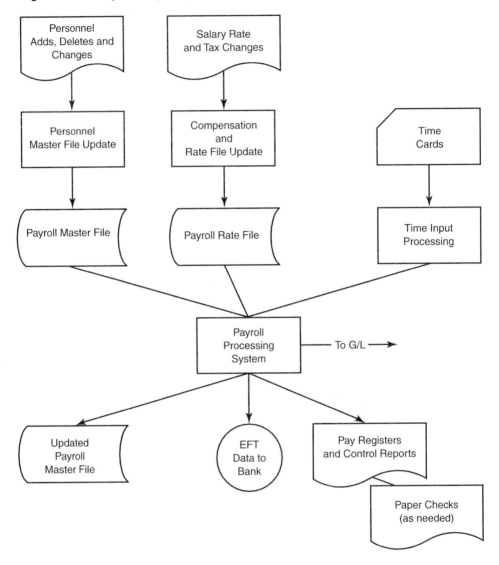

- All additions, deductions, changes in rates, and deductions to pay records should be properly authorized.
- Employee time data should be accurately processed, calculated, and distributed.
- All payroll-related taxes and deductions should be calculated accurately, in accordance with appropriate rules and regulations.
- Payroll payments should only be made to bona fide persons at authorized rates of compensation.

- Pay records should be properly classified and summarized in correct classification accounts.

Representative financial audit procedures for a review of the payroll function are outlined in Figure 29.2. Payroll files also are good candidates for computer-assisted audit procedures. For example, internal audit can perform a computer-assisted test to check if anyone has received an excessively high number of overtime hours. Sample computer-assisted tests of a payroll system are outlined in Figure 29.4.

Figure 29.2   Payroll Financial Audit Procedures

Audit _____ Location _____ Date _____

AUDIT STEP	INITIAL	W/P
1. Determine that formal procedures, including approvals, are in place to add, delete, or change any employee payroll records. Select a sample of recent payroll-maintenance activity and determine changes were appropriate and authorized.		
2. Determine that authorization procedures are in place for changes to established pay rates and job classifications.		
3. Review payroll bank account procedures; determine that account signatories are required to be approved and that formal procedures are in place for establishing, reconciling, and monitoring payroll bank accounts.		
4. Review procedures for processing employee tax and benefit programs as well as other claims, such as garnishments. On a test basis, trace several pay deduction options from request forms to payroll records to actual disbursements.		
5. Examine control procedures for a payroll cycle, determining that the source of pay information (e.g., time cards) is checked for accuracy and approval prior to processing.		
6. Review controls surrounding a payroll-processing cycle to determine that all accounts are balanced prior to disbursement of checks.		
7. Trace and balance records from a payroll-processing cycle to employee-specific and general financial accounts to payroll accruals, including holidays, vacation, sick leave, group insurance, and workman's compensation.		
8. Determine that payroll bank accounts are reconciled by someone independent of the payroll function; review the results of a sample reconciliation.		
9. Inquire whether persons involved in the processing of payroll are covered by fidelity bonds.		
10. Determine that there are periodic reconciliations made of net and gross pay amounts with amounts on tax returns and the general ledger.		

When the organization completes a periodic payroll, the total amount of that payroll is deposited in the special payroll imprest account, and all checks are drawn on it. This provides protection against an altered check drawing down the overall checking account balance. In the past, internal audit was often responsible for reconciling payroll imprest checking accounts, once a major task for many smaller internal audit functions that today is viewed as a violation of the Objectivity Standards for the Professional Practice of Internal Auditing and has all but disappeared from internal audit normal activities.

A periodic review of this reconciliation process might include a review of controls over the reconciliation or the performance of an actual cycle. A sample of canceled payroll checks can be examined to compare their signatures to those in human resources records.

Other financial accounting procedures should be part of the payroll process. For example, pay should be properly distributed to correct accounts, unearned vacation pay should be correctly accrued, and withholding tax records should be correct. The accounting should follow GAAP, discussed in Chapter 22. The financial-accounting procedures, generally performed by external auditors, are beyond the scope of this book. Internal auditors should discuss any planned financial-accounting tests with their external auditors to assure that audit tests are consistent and appropriate.

(ii) Payroll Operational Audit Procedures.   As discussed in the prior section, there is a tight interrelationship between financial and operational audit procedures over the payroll function. One payroll audit procedure is the payoff test, which determines that only authorized employees are receiving paychecks.

An appropriate person personally distributes all or a sample of paychecks to employees who must acknowledge their receipt, and after having ascertained that the signature meets employee records, releases the paycheck. Steps for an auditor payoff test are outlined in Figure 29.3. This procedure is difficult today since many employees have their pay electronically transferred to their bank accounts. The objective of verifying that only active employees are on the payroll can be accomplished by having them sign a pay receipt and then taking corrective actions in the subsequent payroll.

Internal audit will probably find that most checks in the sample payoff are delivered to valid employees. Any checks or pay receipts that remain undelivered and/or any excuses claiming that the employee is out sick (or whatever) should cause concern. The checks should be held until physically delivered to the actual employee, or a stop should be placed on subsequent bank transfers.

Direct deposit options can reduce paycheck fraud. However, this can lead to another type of fraud involving collusion. A supervisor could split the difference with a former employee who continues to receive the automatic paycheck deposits. Internal audit could verify that a sample of employees paid through automatic deposit are current employees.

(iii) Payroll Computer Audit Procedures.   For some good reasons, many organizations today use either purchased software packages or an outside payroll-processing service bureau for their payroll systems. Tax and benefit rates and laws frequently change, requiring payroll system changes. An outside group that specializes in payroll processing can be more efficient, and an organization typically derives no competitive advantage from an in-house payroll system.

If an outside service bureau is used in the United States, internal audit may want to ask for a service auditor's report, described in Chapter 16, which discusses the general and application controls in place. This report would be prepared by an external auditor

Figure 29.3 Payroll Payoff Test Audit Procedures

1. Reevaluate risks and other audit-related information to assess whether a payoff test may be justified.
2. Develop plans for the payoff test, including departments or functions to be tested as well as the timing of the tests.
3. Discuss plans for the payoff test with senior financial management, explaining the plans and timing for the review. Based on discussion, make adjustments to audit plans as necessary.
4. Make arrangements with the information systems function for the payoff test. All actual payroll checks for that period should be delivered directly to internal audit.
5. For checks deposited directly in employee bank accounts, make arrangements to secure a special list of employees receiving direct deposits who will be included in the payoff test.
6. Develop a payoff test report, listing all employees included in the test and whether they are to receive a check or direct deposit, and leaving a space for their signature.
7. If checks or pay advices are normally mailed to employee homes, make an announcement at about the time when employees normally receive their checks that they *must* pick up their checks or pay advices on the day of the test. Otherwise, notify supervisors on payroll day that internal audit will distribute pay vouchers for that day *only*.
8. On the day of the test, all employees in the department tested should be requested to visit the internal auditor's work area, to state their names and supply employee or other identification, and to sign the payoff test report. After a comparison of that signature with the identification and a visual check—if a photo ID is available—internal audit should distribute the payroll check or voucher.
9. If any checks or vouchers were not retrieved on the test day, determine if the employee is on excused absence and make arrangements for the employee to pick up the check from internal audit upon return.
10. If a check is not picked up and the employee is not on authorized leave, investigate whether this represents a ghost employee or some other potentially fraudulent situation. It may be necessary to consult with human resources management, or the legal department in these cases.
11. For those payoff test reports signed by employees, compare signatures to employee records on a spot test basis. Discrepancies should receive more detailed investigation to determine if there may be fraud.
12. If designated employees on payroll records cannot be identified, consider the possibility of fraud. The status of these fraudulent employees should be investigated, whether they are a former employee who physically left the organization at some earlier time or if they represent ghost employees. An attempt should be made to determine who has been receiving past pay remittances, and legal authorities should be consulted.

under contract to the payroll-processing service bureau. Service auditor reports are part of auditing standards in the United States, but not in many other countries.

A purchased payroll software package offers pay calculation programs and periodic updates of tax rates and other changes. Assuming that the organization has not modified the vendor-supplied program and has installed all updates, and assuming that controls over data-processing operations are strong, internal audit may find the risks here to be low. Controls over purchased software packages were discussed in Chapter 17.

Internal audit should examine payroll application controls if they have not been recently reviewed. Along with the steps for reviewing this type of application discussed in Chapter 17, the internal auditor should give particular attention to the following areas.

- *Controls over Program Changes.* A payroll program could yield improper or unexpected results if improperly modified. There should be particularly strong controls over the program change process for payroll application, including the program source code and any of its table files.

- *Logical Security Controls.* The logical security controls to prevent improper access to computer system files discussed in Chapters 17 and 19 are particularly important for a payroll application where data can be improperly manipulated.

- *Computer Program Update Procedures.* As payroll is subject to frequent mandated tax rate and processing changes, the systems-development group must be aware of these changes and have procedures in place to test and implement them within required time periods.

If the organization still has an in-house-developed payroll system, a review of the extent of payroll change activity and the hours expended to implement those changes may warrant an audit recommendation to consider a purchased package.

Whether purchased or in-house-developed software, a legacy mainframe or workstation-based system, virtually all use some type of employee master file with pay and human resources–related information on employees and a pay master file with year-to-date pay and deduction records. Incorrect or inappropriate file data due to either poor maintenance procedures or even improper manipulation can be assessed using various types of retrieval software to access these records. (See Chapter 12 for a discussion of computer-assisted auditing.)

Figure 29.4 describes some potential computer-assisted procedures for audits of payroll and human resources files. The exact test performed, of course, will depend upon the objectives of the planned audit. Due to the confidentiality associated with payroll and human resources data, internal audit should give particular care to maintaining the security and confidentiality of any extracted payroll data. The auditor may not want to include data-retrieval reports in normal workpapers, which may be open to review by other members of the internal audit staff. They can be referenced in normal workpapers but retained in a secure location.

(iv) Payroll Sample Audit Report Findings.

A: Payroll Input Forms Are Not Properly Approved. Payroll changes transmitted from field locations are sent directly to the payroll operations department for processing. Organization payroll procedures specify that certain changes, such as more than 12 hours of overtime pay per week per employee, are to go to line management for approval prior to processing.

Figure 29.4 Payroll and Human Resources Computer-Assisted Audit Procedures

The following are potential computer-assisted audit procedures for a review of payroll and human resources systems and functions. The auditor should have access to audit-retrieval software (see Chapter 12) when developing this software, as well as access to appropriate file layouts.

1. *Ghost Payroll Test.* Match by last name and employee number all employees on the most current pay register file with employees listed on HR department files; investigate any differences.
2. *Duplicate Employee Test.* Sort both payroll master and HR files by last name, looking for any potential duplicates. For family members, determine they are in accordance with family member hiring rules. For potential duplicates, investigate.
3. *Missing Deductions Test.* Based on a discussion with HR management, determine data items that are required for employees (such as certain tax deductions) and screen files to determine that all codes have been entered in the system.
4. *Payroll Footings Test.* Use audit software to recalculate certain deductions and summarize all file and payroll systems computed totals for a pay period. Reconcile difference to payroll records.
5. *Payroll Test Deck.* Using the "Test Deck" methods described in Chapter 12, obtain an extract version of the current pay files and process a series of "can't happen" transactions against this file. Verify that processing controls are adequate to protect or detect such matters.

In our audit sample, we found that virtually all special pay changes submitted by supervisors are going directly into payroll processing without line management approval. Payroll operations advised us that they do not submit these changes due to concerns that the employee pay may not be processed on a timely basis.

Recommendation. Payroll processing should establish procedures to expedite the processing of line management approvals of payroll exception transmittals. If schedules do not permit this review, consider either requesting the transmittals one day earlier or distributing paychecks one day later.

B: Payroll File Logical Security Controls. In reviewing the logical security access parameters established to protect payroll system files, we found that nearly 80% of the payroll department professional staff had been granted ALTER access to the payroll master file. Such access allows them to call up file records and to make possibly undetected changes. There is no satisfactory explanation for these access rights.

Recommendation. Logical security ALTER access rights over the payroll master file should be restricted to those persons allowed to change the master file. We feel this should be limited to at most two persons. All others should have only normal transaction entry access.

29-3 HUMAN RESOURCES FUNCTION

The human resources function is responsible for the overall administration of all employee records from the time the hiring relationship is first established until it is terminated. As such, human resources is all-inclusive and is interwoven with the total management process. There is work to be done, and people must be identified as to who can do that work. An effective match strikes the balance from two points of view: the needs of the organization to achieve its established objectives, and the personal needs of the people involved.

This close relationship can result in the human resources function extending its staff-stewardship role and infringing on the basic responsibilities of line managers. A related concern is that the function can develop policies and procedures that are detached from real operational conditions and needs and that do not support an organization-to-employee partnership. Human resources must work with other organization personnel in a close and collaborative manner.

Legislation requiring fair employment hiring practices, prohibiting discrimination based upon gender or age, and other related issues has increased the human resources record-keeping and policy-drafting requirements. Some of the specific U.S. laws are discussed in the sections following. In addition to legal statutes, the organization today faces the threat of litigation based upon claims of violations of these human resources–based statutes. This is a growing problem because many newer laws are drafted in a manner that encourages litigation, and courts often freely interpret these statutes. Human resources must have policies that are not in violation of these various laws, as well as programs to educate management on proper compliance with them.

(a) HUMAN RESOURCES DEPARTMENT FUNCTIONS

Human resources has a common focus on people problems as well as on the formal conditions of employment, the descriptions of the jobs performed, and the levels of compensation. It is not possible to cover all of these varying requirements completely in this general discussion, but this section specifies some of the general internal control considerations. The needs of an organization cover a wide spectrum, and human resources has a basic responsibility for the following:

- The identification of present and future human resources needs, normally forecast by operational functions with the human resources function providing guidance

- The inventory, analysis, and appraisal of current human resources to determine needs and the presence of any existing gaps

- Recruiting from outside of the organization as well as transfers, promotions, or training efforts from within, to help bridge the above-noted gaps

- Benefit program administration, employee welfare activities, governmental reporting, and any other ongoing administration of the current workforce

Many of these activities must also be considered in terms of the three major broad classes of employees in the typical organization: hourly paid labor, salaried personnel, and commission or contract workers.

The hourly paid group are eligible for overtime pay for work in excess of legal hour requirements, typically 8 hours per day or 40 hours per week. When part of production or support activities, this group is sometimes just called the labor force. Hourly clerical administrative employees are often called *nonexempt* since they are not exempt from legal overtime pay requirements. Other clerical workers who are salaried may also be eligible for overtime pay. Members of the hourly paid group often record their time through an automated time clock mechanism.

Historically, hourly paid employees in production were often unionized. An independent labor bargaining unit places additional complexities and constraints on the administration of the hourly paid labor force. Changes in the type of work, location of plant facilities, and attitudes regarding unions have reduced the level of union membership for many industries. While hourly paid labor exists mainly in production, it also extends to other allied service, operational, and clerical activities.

Salaried administrative and clerical employees are less likely to be unionized. This workforce can be located practically anywhere in the organization and represents a large cross-section of employees ranging from advanced degree professionals to clerical workers. There are an increasing number of bargaining unit employees in this group. Various teachers and government employees are examples.

At some level in each organization, the salaried personnel are classified as management personnel. This group covers gradations that run from lower-level, first-line supervisors up to top management executives. Due to their perquisites the latter is sometimes a separate group of executive managers, classified as *officers* in organization records. The compensation committee of the board of directors usually is responsible for their overall salary administration.

Contractors and persons working only on commission are a growing and varied group of employees. These persons are paid for their actual services, at some preestablished rate, but often do not receive the same benefits as normal salaried employees. A sales associate may be classified as an employee eligible for health care and the organization's retirement program but compensated only on the basis of sales performance. A contractor may work side by side with normal salaried employees but neither will be considered as an employee nor be eligible for benefits. Contractors often work on "temporary" projects such as data-processing system development efforts. When the project is complete, the contractor leaves. Although a contractor can be independent, separate labor brokerage agencies often take responsibility for health care and other matters and largely manage the contract employees.

Because of the commonality of many principles of the human resources function among the above, this chapter discusses the more basic functions and internal control considerations first as a whole, with only limited reference to these separate groups. The chapter later returns to a discussion of some special problems pertaining to the individual groups.

(i) Identification of Human Resource Needs.   An organization has a structure that satisfies present needs. It reflects managerial judgments as to how the work is allocated and assigned to individuals and functions at all levels. Within this structure is the development of more detailed job descriptions corresponding to positions on the organization chart. Job descriptions are a key building block in the administration of any organization activity; they become the basis for specific requirements for hiring personnel in terms of their knowledge, skills, personality, and experience.

An analysis of personnel requirements can at the same time be extended into future

Figure 29.5 Sample Job Description

> **Accounting Supervisor**
>
> In this position, an accounting supervisor will:
> 1. Supervise an accounting department staff of at least three persons, providing training on journal voucher entry and the proper classification of accounts.
> 2. Approve all journal voucher entries within the limits set by the accounting manager and submit other items to the accounting manager for approval.
> 3. Research any unusual transactions within approval limits, documenting all activity and reasons for the decisions.
> 4. Balance, reconcile, and close out accounting month-ends within periods of responsibility.
> 5. Research special accounts and perform other accounting duties, as required, at the request of the accounting manager.
>
> Educational and experience requirements for accounting supervisors include:
> 1. At least two years of college, with an emphasis on accounting procedures.
> 2. A basic understanding of computerized accounting systems, including spreadsheet packages.
> 3. At least two years of company or other business accounting experience.

periods. Sometimes this future projection is limited in scope and informal, but if it is done in a systematic manner and extends at least through the planning period that is appropriate to the business, organizational requirements, budget constraints, and human resources needs can all be fairly determined. This is a process normally carried out at all levels and by all managers and is based on the organization's common policies regarding estimated growth, scope of business activities, and the like.

This human resources needs forecasting is normally not the responsibility of the human resources function, but it can provide overall guidance for formulating standard job descriptions, specifying responsibilities and requirements for each forecasted position. This determination process is particularly important when certain classes of employees are hired on an annual basis. For example, an organization may recruit a cadre of new college graduates each year. There is a limited time period to do this, and the human resources department responsible for the recruiting must know the forecasted needs to avoid hiring too few or too many.

Job descriptions list, in an established format, the minimum requirements of each position as well as the formal job responsibilities. Figure 29.5 is a job description for an accounting supervisor. All employees should be aware of their individual job descriptions.

A larger organization has many defined positions that must relate to one another, at least within an overall department, to allow both management and employees to understand how the duties and responsibilities of various jobs relate to one another. A job responsibilities matrix takes key responsibilities and requirements of a variety of position descriptions and summarizes them. Figure 29.6 shows a job responsibility matrix for the Figure 29.5 accounting supervisor and others in that same organization. The process of developing individual job descriptions and the overall responsibility matrix are closely interrelated. Internal audit should look for these types of documents in any organization.

Figure 29.6 Accounting Department Responsibility Matrix

	STAFF ACCOUNTANT	ACCOUNTING SUPERVISOR	ACCOUNTING MANAGER	CONTROLLER
JOB REQUIREMENTS				
1. Prepare J/Vs	x	x	x	x
2. Research and resolve J/V issues		x	x	x
3. Approve J/Vs		x	x	x
4. Balance and close unit's accounts		x	x	x
5. Train and supervise staff		x	x	x
6. Prepare and approve G/L entries			x	x
7. Develop accounting department budgets			x	x
8. Prepare consolidated statements				x
EXPERIENCE REQUIREMENTS				
Basic understanding of accounting	x	x	x	x
Two years college		x	x	x
Two or more company accounting experiences		x	x	x
BA or equivalent degree			x	x
CPA				x

(ii) Determining and Assessing Available Human Resources. Human resources should inventory available people resources to determine to what extent the organization is meeting its needs. This inventory has both current dimensions and projections through the same planning period used to identify future needs. Individuals are viewed first in terms of their capacity to fill current designated jobs and then in terms of what they could reasonably be capable of doing with further development. These needs and resources are compared through a time spectrum that encompasses the planning period, and estimates should be made at each key point in that time period, highlighting any excess or shortage of resources. The identification of personnel gaps during successive years of the planning period sets the stage for determining the nature and scope of the programs that must be carried out to close that gap.

A strong process for establishing employee performance goals based upon their job descriptions, and periodically evaluating their performance against these goals, is an important part of assessing human resource availabilities. A formal succession-planning process can properly identify high-performing employees and move them to other positions according to their demonstrated abilities. Human resources should take a leading role in setting up the appropriate programs, gathering the evaluation data collected, and using it to recommend new job placements based upon changing needs.

Organizations may also face the task of properly downsizing their personnel. This may involve offering early-retirement incentives to employees, terminating personnel, or changing job descriptions and compensation levels to better reflect revised job requirements. Downsizing must be handled with the best interests of the overall organization in mind but must not discriminate against any class or group of individual employees. Otherwise, the organization may face lawsuits alleging wrongful terminations.

The different approaches to bridging the current and projected gaps between personnel needs and resources fall into several major categories. One is through the recruitment of new personnel to the organization and another is to accelerate the development of the organization's own personnel. Hiring contractors and other nonstandard employees is a third approach and includes the process of totally outsourcing departments to an outside provider. These are areas where the human resources department can provide assistance.

(iii) Recruitment and Selection of Personnel. The recruitment process begins with an estimate of where prospective candidates are likely to be found. Particular trade skills tend to concentrate in geographical areas, managerial resources will often be greatest in urban centers, and persons with certain specialized training can best be found through the leading schools in that discipline. A concentration of industries in a particular geographic area may also be a source for new personnel.

Closely related is the question of how potential employees can best be contacted. Typical methods are newspaper advertising, employee referrals, trade journal advertisements, employment agencies, and recruitment visits to colleges. Usually, a reasonable amount of care and thought will determine the most appropriate approach for the particular kind of recruits being sought. This is often a difficult process that depends upon overall economic conditions in the industry, demand for the professional specialty, and the reputation of the organization.

Once potential candidates have been identified through a recruitment process, the next consideration is how the actual selection shall be made. There is no single best approach and a combination of techniques and practices should be used, subject always to important judgment factors. Since the potential new candidate often comes to the organization as an unknown, however, the organization should attempt to gather as much information as possible about that candidate. Sources of information the human resources department should use for all job candidates include:

- *Application Forms.* The usefulness of the application form is that needed information can be conveniently obtained along such lines as education, professional achievements, and work experience. The form requires the candidate to make factual representations, which can later be checked. In addition, there is often something learned from the way an application form is completed. While management-level applicants are more likely to submit their own resumes, it is often a good practice to require that all candidates complete the organization's application form to obtain a consistent set of candidate data.

- *References.* Written or direct contacts, with references furnished by the applicant, provide a good basis for asking probing questions about the candidate's qualifications. From a control standpoint, however, it must be remembered that the reference has usually been selected by the applicant, thus ensuring to a significant extent that the reference will be well disposed toward the applicant. The organization's hiring official, knowing this, must be frank and persuasive to obtain a fairly objective report. When possible, the employer should seek to find independent references.

Additional background reference checks in such areas as credit history, previous employment, and academic degrees may not provide any detailed information but will answer some basic questions. A college, for example, will verify that the candidate attended or graduated but will give no information as to grades. A previous employer will typically only attest that the candidate is still employed, left voluntarily, or was terminated.

- *Special Tests.* A variety of special tests have been developed to evaluate a candidate's personality and aptitudes for different types of work. Clinical tests by psychologists are also sometimes used. These provide a useful supplementary bit of input but need to be used with caution, particularly in areas where the validity of the testing techniques is questionable. However, if a given test is used consistently over time for a given broad class of employees, the human resources department should be able to track the future success of these candidates against their relative test scores.

Tests are particularly valuable for special aptitude areas. For example, an organization may give its secretarial candidates a test of their word-processing keyboard typing skills. A production worker may be tested on knowledge of a given skill area.

- *Personal Interviews.* Personal interviews between the applicant and organization officials are often the best indicator. Most managers have developed a reasonable competence in sizing up applicants on a face-to-face basis and determining whether they are likely to fit well into the particular job situation. It also works out best when the interviewer is able to induce the applicant to speak freely, thus also requiring the interviewer to be a good listener. However, it is easy to make mistakes and to be misled by favorable first impressions.

Because many line managers do not have the skills or experience to conduct effective interviews, it is often a good idea to have the human resources department initially interview all candidates. They can often see positive and negative traits that may not be evident to line management who are primarily interested in matching a candidate to a required set of skills.

From a control standpoint, policies and procedures should be in effect that will reasonably assure the matching of job opportunities with the best-qualified candidates. This means that each major type of job need must be separately evaluated and handled. It also means that all available means of evaluation be utilized, but at the same time handled with great care. Interviews especially need to be made by a number of qualified persons to provide an adequate cross-check.

Candidate recruitment can be expensive. Recruiting agents typically charge a significant percentage of the candidate's first-year compensation as their fee. While this approach might appear less practical, newspaper advertisements or Internet postings—along with the time required to screen candidate resumes, interview potential candidates, and reply to those rejected—can also be expensive when all cost factors are considered.

(iv) Training and Development.   Recruits often need additional training and development throughout their careers, and the problem is determining how much of it there should be and how it can be done most effectively. Some training is often initiated at the time of hiring, depending upon the requirements of the job and the qualifications of the new employee. The human resources department often has some responsibility for the training function.

As a minimum, training that provides instructions to carry out a particular job assignment is necessary. Thereafter, the training may be of a remedial or supplemental nature to assist the employee in taking on a more advanced assignment. In other cases, the training may be of a broader nature and pertain to the development of better human relations or administrative skills, or be for other managerial purposes. The objective in all cases is to foster a greater usefulness and capability on the part of the individuals trained. All of this training is over and above the development that comes about through normal job experience and as a result of regular supervisory input.

The achievement of effective training depends directly on the extent to which competence is developed in the learning process. This is a professional area that cannot be reduced to precise formulas, but there are important training principles that need to be understood and properly handled, including:

- *Receptivity of the Trainee.* The trainee should recognize the need for the particular assistance being offered, and desire it. The trainee must see the course materials as relevant and worthwhile in terms of individual goals and objectives.

- *Quality of the Training Materials.* The training materials should be tested and presented in a manner that is consistent with their quality. Human resources, as well as line management requesting the training, should review the material's content and quality.

- *Time Requirements.* The time requirements depend on the degree of difficulty of the training to be imparted and the capacity of the trainees themselves.

- *Participation and Involvement.* Trainees need to be involved and have some kind of two-way interchange. In some situations, it is possible to provide feedback whereby trainees can check on their progress. In a case-method approach, for example, the trainee is able to participate directly in the discussion. These participative processes have often been proven to be more effective than the conventional lecture approach.

- *Reinforcement.* This takes place during the actual training session when an automated teaching program confirms the mastery of a particular increment of training or where the employer specifically recognizes the trainee's increased knowledge and competence.

Without the development of well-planned and well-executed programs, or without care given to the above principles, training programs can become sterile activities that are not meaningful to trainees and are potentially a source of irritation and ridicule.

The blame for training program failures usually falls to one of two major groups. The first is the human resources department, which may not properly assume the responsibility for constructing or obtaining adequate training programs. The second group is management itself, which may delegate to others too much of the training function. Management at all levels should be responsible for assuring adequate levels of training, and must be sufficiently involved to be certain that it is being carried out effectively.

There are many important aspects to an effective employee-training program. Many of these are described in various texts on the subject. Internal auditors can gain more information through a discussion with the organization's training staff. Internal audit should always consider the following aspects:

- There is a need for continuous management involvement and support of overall training programs.

- The design of training programs must be properly coordinated with operational needs and based on adequate professional standards.

- Training programs should be designed and administered to ensure appropriate levels of motivation and interest.

A review of training policies and procedures by an outside reviewer such as an internal auditor can be rewarding. The benefits achieved are especially important considering the amount of time and money that are expended in these programs and their impact on human productivity.

(v) Overall Human Resources Administration Responsibilities.
The effective utilization of human resources includes the proper assignment to jobs in accordance with abilities and where utilization will most benefit the organization. Sufficient staff support should be assigned to ensure that all employees are working in accordance with their job descriptions. While management is directly responsible for its staff, it expects human resources to set standards, procedures, and policies that impact the entire workforce.

Controls are needed to prevent excess of human resources in certain classifications and shortage in others. The timing and duration of any excesses needs to be reviewed, as well as whether hiring and transfers are based on actual needs. Staff duties need to be reevaluated continually to determine whether they are appropriate. In a production environment, records of idle time need to be maintained and studied for trends and identification of the causes.

Organizations often benchmark or compare the number of workers assigned to various duties to the numbers assigned by their competitors. As long as the request for statistics are kept fairly general, other organizations will typically share this data on a reciprocal basis. For example, an organization may ask a competitor with 20% higher sales how many nonmanagerial employees work in the order-entry and processing department. With this data and some basic knowledge of the competitor's systems and procedures, the organization can assess its own personnel needs.

Figure 29.7 illustrates a benchmark calculation. It shows that the organization making the survey has too many order-entry personnel when compared to its competitors. This does not mean, of course, that the organization can just slash its order-entry staff to bring the numbers in line. However, it should closely examine procedures and supporting systems to see whether current staff levels can be justified or if changes would allow it to work with a smaller staff.

Personnel costs needs to be controlled in other ways. Overtime for nonexempt employees should be well controlled and have proper authorizations. Excessive overtime may be a symptom of improper scheduling of work, shortage of certain personnel, deficiencies in technical performance, and inordinate demands of customers, supervisors, or departments. The use of outside contractors also needs close scrutiny. Often, a manager may face a hiring restriction but will get around the restraint by bringing in contract employees ranging from hourly technical consultants to temporary clerical help. Although this approach can be cost-justified based upon short-term needs, it is often abused when it becomes a permanent situation.

Work measurement is a basis for improving the productivity of production employees. Work-measurement programs disclose such factors as outmoded work routines, poorly organized systems, excess staffing, and duplication. Through automated labor-collection systems and other means, work systems can be reviewed to develop preferred methods, improve systems, and determine the time required by the average worker to perform a task. Various systems are used, such as work sampling and time measurement procedures. The latter analyzes operations into basic motions or steps required (such as for general office routines) and then assigns each motion a predetermined standard time. The purpose is to reduce operating costs through improved work flow and work area layout and to increase operating controls through improving systems, restructuring tasks, and measuring employee and supervisory effectiveness. Paper simplification and office mechanization are additional methods to increase productivity and reduce costs.

These work measurement procedures are based on industrial engineering procedures, discussed in Chapter 26, developed to improve processes on the manufacturing shop floor. The same basic procedures can be performed in the office.

Constantly adjusting its mix of human resources and job skill requirements to improve overall effectiveness may require the organization to shift functions and job responsibilities to other regions or even other countries to take advantage of labor cost differentials. The organization may also need to eliminate positions due to changes in operations, product mix, or general reductions in organization operations. The organization may decide that an outside contractor can perform the function in a more cost-effective manner and outsource the entire function. Managing these changes presents significant challenges both to human resources and to line management.

Figure 29.7 Sample Benchmarking Worksheet: Order Entry

Benchmarking Measure	Our Company	Competitor A	Competitor B	Competitor C	Competitor D	Competitor E	Competitor Average	Our Performance vs. the Competition
Annual sales (mil.)	18,325	55,750	112,000	12,250	75,000	16,988	54,398	0.337
Percent estimated orders through O/E	98%	100%	75%	95%	50%	100%	84%	1.167
O/E sales	17,959	55,750	84,000	11,638	37,500	16,988	45,694	0.393
Average lines/order	6	10	3	25	12	12		
Hours/week—O/E operations	36	60	84	84	40	84	70	0.511
Total O/E department staff	8	12	12	11	6	13	11	0.741
O/E and management support staff	2	2	3	4	2	2	3	0.769
Productivity: O/E sales per O/E staff	2,993	5,575	9,333	1,663	9,375	1,544	5,498	0.544

(b) HUMAN RESOURCES INTERNAL CONTROL CONSIDERATIONS

Increasing regulations, threats of litigation, and good management practices all add to increasing responsibilities of the human resources function for various activities, each of which has the following important internal control implications:

- Job Analysis and Evaluation
- Compensation Administration
- Performance Evaluations
- Transfers, Promotions, and Terminations
- Employee Records and Reports
- Personal Guidance Activities
- Employee Benefit Plans
- Employee Services
- Workman's Compensation and Safety
- Labor Relations

A discussion of the internal control and other aspects of each of these topics could consume a separate book. The purpose of this section is to provide internal auditors with a general introduction to human resources internal control issues. This discussion should help internal auditors apply general principals of internal control—discussed in Chapters 2 and 4—for reviews of the human resources function. Internal audit may also want to refer to other material for additional background information.

(i) Job Analysis and Evaluation.   From an administrative standpoint, along with providing job descriptions, it is also necessary to rate individual jobs in terms of their relative difficulty and importance. Job descriptions and guidelines are formally documented in a human resources manual, where various job position factors or dimensions are identified. These factors must then be compared to those in other jobs to provide a job evaluation or rating.

Job classifications are used to establish general categories for building individual job descriptions and payroll and promotional classifications. Detailed sets of job specifications should be developed to cover each individual job grade. The individual jobs are normally grouped in a number of grades or other broad classifications. The number of such grades can be relatively large or small but usually it seems to work best when about 15 to 25 are used. At the same time, appropriate job titles need to be developed. Human resources is responsible for developing the job grades, function descriptions, and compensation classifications.

The job description and job responsibility matrix in Figures 29.5 and 29.6 are examples of job classification. Each of these jobs is assigned a job grade and a salary range with an upper, lower, and midpoint. As an employee moves closer to the upper limit, future increases would be limited. The employee, however, might be a candidate for promotion or reassignment.

Department managers should develop detailed descriptions for each of the jobs in their areas. The human resources function first establishes a series of overall administrative job grades, and other units, such as accounting, establish specific job grades within those general classifications. For example, there might be general job grades for junior, staff, and senior accounting positions. Within those general grades, the organization's controller might set up specific job descriptions for junior, staff, and senior positions in the cost-accounting, general-accounting, and tax departments. Following the same general job grade structure, the marketing department might set up a specific job description for a sales commission accountant. A general set of job classification and specific job descriptions are important controls for all organizations, and provide a basis for evaluating and compensating employees as well as justification for allowing or denying employee promotions.

The most difficult part of the job-analysis and evaluation procedure is the application of these general criteria to individual jobs. This is generally accomplished by the assignment of points in recognition of the degree to which the various criteria apply. A concern is with relative rankings of jobs. This determination is bound to involve a great deal of judgment, and it must be made with extreme care and objectivity. Both individual managers and the human resources department have responsibilities for this overall job rating process, shown in Figure 29.8. Each major job category is ranked according to this process to assist in making overall pay grade compensation decisions.

An overall job analysis and evaluation process allows employees to see where they fit in the organization and what management expects of them. It also provides a level playing field to prevent employee allegations of job bias or discrimination. Internal audit should look for an overall system and ongoing process for reevaluation.

(ii) Compensation Administration.   While the job-analysis and evaluation process is technically something that stands apart from compensation, in practice the two processes are closely interwoven. Compensation administration determines the general level of pay in the community and industry of which the organization is a part. The organization must meet or at least compete with those pay levels, which must be sufficiently high to attract human resources of the quality desired and in the proper numbers, but not so high as to create excessive costs and noncompetitive product prices. Overall compensation blends direct pay, performance-incentive pay, and employee benefits. Sometimes, an organization can offer less direct pay if it has a strong deferred compensation or benefit package.

Once general levels have been determined, compensation levels must be fixed for the job classifications and grades. Each grade should have a minimum and a maximum along with a specified pay midpoint. These ranges should provide flexibility in their application to individuals. At the same time, flexibility must be provided for giving merit increases during the time span that an individual job falls within a particular grade.

Compensation grades and ranges provide a basis for managing employee pay increases and for setting general guidelines for such increases. For example, an organization may decide to move all compensation grades up by 6%. An employee currently at midpoint in the compensation grade might also move up by the same 6%. However, if another is currently at 120% of the pay grade midpoint, human resources may dictate that increases must be a lower percentage, say 2%.

The job classification and compensation grades together provide an orderly framework by which an organization can reasonably evaluate and control the overall employee pay structure, but at the same time, problems can arise in actual practice. Specific individuals will, for example, feel strongly that the nature of their work calls for a higher job classification than has been assigned. In some cases, changing conditions may provide legitimate support for that position. In others, the problem may be that of a restless employee who is qualified to do more responsible work in a context where there is presently

Figure 29.8 Job Evaluation Elements

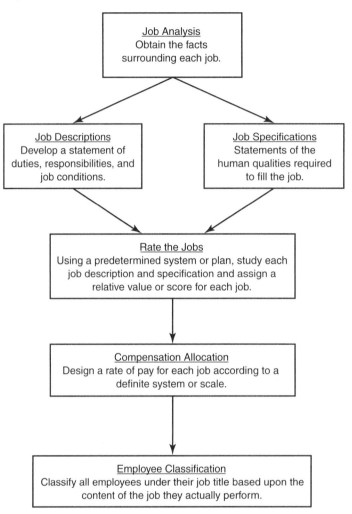

no opening for the employee's higher-level skills. Another problem arises when employees come to believe that periodic merit increases are automatically due to them rather than increases based upon outstanding performance.

In situations covered by collective bargaining agreements, job classifications and the related compensation typically are a contested part of the periodic contractual negotiations and are an issue in the subsequent administration of the contract. Unions often seek to establish multiple job classifications at different pay grades, which can limit management's flexibility in assigning workers to various jobs. Thus, job classifications and compensation are a sensitive point on many fronts in the resolution of conflicting individual and organization needs.

From an internal control standpoint, the essential requirements for the combined processes of job evaluation and compensation administration include at least the following:

- A plan of job classifications based on a well-thought-out set of evaluation criteria
- A level of general compensation, as applied to the various job classifications, that is reasonably competitive
- Individual job descriptions that are regularly reevaluated in terms of the existing job grades and classification criteria
- Regular reviews by the human resources and benefits functions as to the scope of compensation for individual employees
- An overall plan of grades and related compensation levels, which is appraised at appropriate intervals for changes in existing conditions

Internal audit should look for the above when reviewing the human resources function in virtually any organization. Even in an organization without a large human resources department, management should have these policies and procedures in place. The management of a smaller unit of a larger organization should implement the central organization's human resources procedures in the area of job descriptions and compensation ranges. Employees deserve to know where they fit into the organization and how management has defined their responsibilities.

(iii) Performance Evaluations.   Performance evaluation is in part a continuing process and usually a periodic undertaking. In its most basic form, it serves two key purposes. One is to provide a basis for determining the best possible future utilization of the individual. This might include a transfer, promotion, or increased compensation. The second purpose also has to do with achieving the most effective future utilization of the employee, but concentrates more on what can be done to help the individual overcome any existing limitations and to increase the individual's competence. In both cases, these are important line management responsibilities. Human resources provides supporting procedures and policies for evaluations.

Typically, there should be a policy whereby all managers and supervisors are required to perform at least an annual performance review for each of their employees. Human resources provides standard employee evaluation forms that indicate the various factors to be considered and the measures of performance to be evaluated. These factors, based upon individual job descriptions, might include job competence, personal qualifications, and the ability to work with others. Each of these factors is evaluated on the basis of a scale, which typically runs from unsatisfactory through acceptable, fair, good, very good, and outstanding. The performance review, prepared by the immediate superior, is then reviewed and approved by the next higher level of management. Following some established procedures, the completed review is shown to the employee, with his or her confirming signature required. The completed forms are then placed in files maintained by both the human resources function and by responsible management.

An effective performance-review program begins with a comprehensive and well-designed review process. Problems, however, often arise beyond the evaluation form and its related procedures. Sometimes, an individual supervisor may dislike the role of playing judge in the evaluation of subordinates. When required to reduce an evaluation to writing and share it with the subordinate, the needed degree of objectivity and candor may be difficult to maintain. As a result, reviewers sometimes rate all of their employees as ''above average,'' and the process falls short in terms of overall usefulness.

This failure to objectively rate direct subordinates is especially true as one moves up the managerial hierarchy, since it seems that the higher one goes, the less inclined managers are to complicate sensitive personal relationships by discussing performance evaluations. Human resources can play a useful role by reviewing evaluations and summarizing overall results. With these summarized results, line management can recognize the problem and make appropriate improvements.

An internal auditor should develop an understanding of the organization's performance-appraisal process and then determine whether that process is being correctly followed at all levels in the organization. In order to assess the quality of these performance appraisals, the auditor examines a sample of individual completed performance appraisals as well as the summary statistics. An objective is to ensure that there are human resources and management procedures in place to complete the evaluation and review process on a periodic basis, consistent with organization policy.

(iv) Transfers, Promotions, and Terminations.   In any organization, there is a changing pattern of available human resources and human resources needs. Some of the problems relate primarily to individual situations, whereas others arise from broadly based changes in human resources requirements. In all of these cases, the human resources function can serve as both a central source of information on available resources and as a planner and counselor in helping managers and supervisors solve their personnel problems. For example, a particular individual may not be working out in a current assignment. The human resources department can provide guidance to improve the situation, including finding another position in which the employee can be more effectively utilized. When someone leaves the organization or a new job is created, a job assignment may need to be filled. Human resources should be able to identify individuals in the organization who have the kind of experience and other qualifications that would make them eligible for consideration. In a larger organization, the human resources function is uniquely equipped to provide a list of such candidates and to help in making a final internal candidate selection.

An expansion of activity in a particular sector of operations may bring with it the need for a differently skilled workforce. Rather than ignoring the internal workforce and recruiting from the outside, the human resources department can make recommendations from within existing staff.

Conversely, a major cutback of operations may necessitate a substantial reduction of personnel in a particular department or division, or a computerized system may replace clerical tasks but expand needs in other areas. Human resources can develop plans to minimize disruptions and to satisfy the organization's overall needs.

The 1980s saw a considerable amount of organization combinations, restructurings, and downsizings. Plants closed or moved to other geographic areas and many workers were displaced. Large, traditional organizations were forced to rethink their strategies, move operations to lower-cost areas, or even shut down. At the same time, the decade saw a tremendous amount of growth in startup organizations and new industries. The human resources departments of these affected organizations played key roles in these restructurings.

When terminations are involved, there is a need for managing their impact. The human resources department must anticipate terminations whenever possible and develop equitable separation arrangements consistent with the organization's community and public-relations image. Legislation has also put some restrictions on termination processes. In the United States, federal laws require that an organization must formally give a 30-day notice before a plant is to be closed, offer certain health benefits for a specified period after termination, and provide procedures to allow employees to withdraw from their retirement plans. In addition, many organizations have established severance pay benefits based upon years of service as well as training or outplacement counseling to help find new jobs.

(v) Employee Records and Reports. Human resources department employee records serve as a major central source of information. They include the original employment application and supplementary investigation; individual job actions such as transfers, new assignments, compensation changes, or promotions; ongoing performance reviews and evaluations; and finally, when the employee leaves the organization, retires, or is terminated, the circumstances of this departure. These records enable the department to function effectively as a planning and counseling group.

Maintaining all employee records and the processing of all changes in employment status gives the human resources function the responsibility for reporting information desired by management, with respect to the composition of the workforce and its changes over time, or significant operational considerations such as information for the control of overtime, absenteeism, or turnover. Data may also be sought to monitor levels of compensation and trends. The latter might include such matters as the number and frequency of merit increases or the percentages of individuals in respective pay grades who are at or near their upper pay grade limits. Management may want to know how many people are being promoted from within as opposed to recruited from outside.

Organizations are subjected to a growing number of government compliance reporting requirements. For example, the U.S. government's Equal Employment Opportunity Commission (EEOC) mandates a series of reports on the organization's demographics and promotion activities by race. Human resources gathers this data from its own records and from operating departments. The Americans with Disabilities Act (ADA) of 1992 has the stated purpose of prohibiting all but the smallest of employers from discriminating in their job hiring based upon an employee's disability. Job descriptions and interview practices must be reevaluated to offer employment, if appropriate, to persons who may be blind or confined to a wheelchair. The act also allows persons who feel they were mistreated under its terms to sue the offending employer. Organizations must keep detailed records covering both their interview procedures and hiring practices to demonstrate compliance with the provisions of the act. Similar legislation exists in Canada. Human resources must keep abreast of these laws and develop programs and record-keeping facilities to remain in compliance with them. The employee record-keeping function is an important responsibility of the human resources department and should be reviewed by internal audit.

(vi) Personnel Guidance Activities. The responsibilities of the individual manager in developing and training subordinates have been stressed in the other chapters on operational auditing topics. There are occasions, however, when subordinates need a place to go that is independent of the primary supervisor-employee relationship. Questions may relate to the clarification of a particular human resources policy and its direct application to a specific aspect of the work relationship with the supervisor. Employee counseling services provide help with such problems as chemical dependencies, either in-house or through outside, organization-sponsored agencies. The human resources function should assume these responsibilities.

Other types of help include working out some aspect of a problem with a supervisor or exploring alternative job opportunities in other areas of the organization. Human resources can provide needed information and act as independent counselors. A worker can claim harassment based upon offensive sexual-related comments. Human resources must provide appropriate counsel on any recourse to the aggrieved employee and should initiate appropriate investigations of the matter. These functions require particular professional skills and a high sense of confidentiality and integrity with respect to the kinds of matters disclosed by individual employees. Also important is the necessity to retain a friendly but neutral attitude and to avoid becoming a partisan advocate. No matter what the final resolution, the human resources function should maintain adequate documentation over the entire matter. Human resources can protect the organization by potentially preventing employee litigation.

(vii) Employee Benefit Plans.   Employee benefits include health programs, retirement plans, insurance of various kinds, and employee product discounts. Human resources usually designs and administers these benefit plans. This is an area that is experiencing major changes in many organizations. Here too, government plays an increasing role in setting up regulations or requiring certain levels of minimum compliance.

Benefit plans require major organization concern and activity, and therefore have internal control ramifications. The plans are administered by human resources or some other organizational department, or sometimes outsourced to specialized providers.

(viii) Employee Services.   An employee benefit might be a special commercial discount program, such as at a local retailer. Human resources might issue discount cards to employees or attest that they are valid employees.

Other services benefit only certain classes of employees. Examples might be a stock option management program for executive employees or the availability of a credit union located on organization facilities. The credit union would be independent of the organization, managed by employees as an outside activity. The organization might provide office space, telephone lines, and other benefits, and human resources might process transactions between the payroll system and credit union records.

There may be sponsorship of employee athletic teams, first-aid services, or organization-sponsored charitable activities benefiting the surrounding community or schools. The distinction between these services and benefits is that benefits are usually available to all employees of a certain class or group as a condition of their employment. Services are necessary for the ongoing operations of the organization but are not benefits available for all. For example, many employees might not be interested in joining the company-sponsored baseball team. The team provides recreation for the employees and also benefits the organization through its image of community service.

There may be a large variety of employee services available. Whether this responsibility is assigned to separate administrative services groups or to human resources, these services are often administered through a consolidated operation to provide them to all participants at the lowest possible cost to the organization and in a way that suits operational needs.

Internal audit can review the controls and procedures covering these services and their utilization, potentially making cost saving recommendations. This chapter only considers these services to be part of the human resources function and related audit procedures in a general sense.

(ix) Workers' Compensation and Safety.   General problems of safety, also discussed in Chapter 23, are mentioned here because of their relationship with human resources. The administration of the workers' compensation program is also an important aspect of total human resources department activity. The issue of safety is a combination of effective protective devices, procedures, and education to promote greater safety consciousness. The careful selection of employees to avoid those who tend to be unduly prone to accidents or accident claims, together with the development of a staff service that educates employees on the desirability of safety and the means of best achieving safe conditions, combine with the need to reinforce each manager's responsibility for promoting safety in that manager's own area. The human resources department typically administers workers' compensation claims and is well positioned to develop an effective safety program. At the same time, information on this area should be communicated to all interested parties in meaningful reports. The final test, of course, is the extent to which accidents are actually eliminated.

Workers' compensation can be abused if not properly handled and can increase overall organization expenses and limit the available workforce. Both internal auditors and line management should be aware of potential abuses and consider contesting these types of claims if they doubt their validity.

(x) Labor Relations. Any discussion of human resources department activities would be incomplete without some recognition of its role in the handling of labor relations and the day-to-day problems of a workforce covered by collective bargaining agreements. A close interrelationship with collective bargaining units may exist, since the human resources department deals with a wide range of matters affecting covered employees and is often involved in the conditions out of which any union relationships may emerge. Human resources serves as both a sensor to any developing problems and a counselor to senior management on how particular problems can be neutralized. If a new collective bargaining unit is established, the role of human resources as a labor coordinator is even more important.

Current actions continuously set the stage for the renegotiation and modification of collective bargaining agreements. Interpretation of and compliance with individual contractual provisions must be continuous. Rules must be enforced and actions pursuant to these rules properly documented. Grievances should be dealt with in a fair and equitable manner. In all bargaining unit relationships, the human resources group must blend the organization-wide policies and procedures with the provisions of bargaining unit agreements.

The department has an even more important role in a non–bargaining unit organization. As part of union agreements, employers must often comply with certain union benefit and service programs. Retirement funding may be handled by the union, with the employer only deducting worker contributions through payroll or on the basis of hours worked. The nonunion organization wants to establish programs that are at least as attractive as those commonly required through collective agreements.

Internal audit typically does not have a role in reviewing contract compliance for collective bargaining agreements, but should at least be aware that these agreements exist and should consider them when making recommendations, particularly where professional employees are covered by a collective bargaining agreement.

(c) HUMAN RESOURCES DEPARTMENT INTERNAL AUDIT ACTIVITIES

As mentioned earlier, internal auditors have sometimes been reluctant to perform reviews in their human resources departments due to the confidentiality of employee records. Internal audit, line management, and human resources management might suspect potentially self-serving purposes in any review of the human resources department. In addition, the human resources department as a single function may be viewed as an area of relatively low risk when compared to other areas in the organization. Both of these assumptions are or should be incorrect. If audit objectives are properly defined and audit procedures well planned, any internal audit review of the human resources function should not become a self-serving review of human resources records. Rather, internal audit should take strong measures not to review records in any area that deal with internal audit.

Although the human resources function may have done little more than maintain employee records in the past, the preceding pages outline an expanded role, ranging from maintaining the employee review program and job grade salary standards to administering various employee special services. Internal audit should be able to identify areas of relatively high internal control risk where controls and procedures should be considered for review. However, any risk assessment and potential review of specific areas within the human resources function should focus on specific internal control concerns. For example, internal audit might review the administration of the performance evaluation function or compliance with various government reporting requirements. This approach is similar to that employed where internal audit does not just review ''accounting'' but separately considers such areas as accounts receivable and fixed assets.

As is the practice throughout these operational auditing chapters, this section covers financial, operational, and information systems procedures for reviews of human resource activities. Although the section on operational audits of the human resources function covers a broad spectrum, internal audit should use selected portions in planning any specific reviews of the various areas within the function.

(i) Human Resources Financial Audit Procedures.   Human resources does not typically have a large number of direct financial responsibilities. It is responsible for wage and salary planning and possibly for initiating authorized salary increases, but most of the financial and record-keeping responsibilities belong to the payroll function or line departments. Financial audit procedures for the human resources department relates to its own departmental procedures. Examples include departmental budget issues or compliance with travel and expense account standards. Audit procedures here have been discussed in other chapters as part of the financial audit issues covering many other functions.

The administration of employee benefit programs such as the pension plan or long-term disability programs may involve significant amounts of money, and these areas typically will be identified as having a high degree of audit risk. These programs are discussed in the following section.

(ii) Human Resources Department Operational Audit Programs.   Most audit risks surrounding a human resources department are strictly operational in nature and relate to the institution and administration of appropriate procedures, and reporting and record-keeping requirements. Selecting higher-risk areas within human resources for operational review can prove significant because many areas are not directly observed by management. That is, management can conclude that there is a problem in manufacturing because products did not get shipped on time or because there was a high production rejection rate in a given month. Similarly, they may conclude that there is a problem in accounting if a closing schedule was missed. However, problems in the human resources department are not always immediately evident.

Potential areas for an internal audit in the human resources department include:

- Salary Planning Standards and Procedures
- Employee Performance Review Procedures
- Employee Records and Reporting
- Governmental Compliance Activities
- Bargaining Unit Matters

- Employee Special Services Activities
- Overall Human Resources Department Standards and Procedures

Payroll and benefit plans are not included in this list as they are covered in separate sections of this chapter. Selected audit procedures for operational reviews of the human resources function are described in Figure 29.9.

Figure 29.9 Selected Audit Procedures for Review of Human Resources (HR) Function

Audit _____ Location _____ Date _____

AUDIT STEP	INITIAL	W/P
1. Review published H/R procedures to determine they are complete, current, and available to managers and employees with a need to know.		
2. Select a sample of organization employees and determine: • Employees are reviewed and evaluated consistent with policy. • Wages are consistent with pay grade procedures. • Employee records are complete regarding such matters as benefit elections, tax deduction selections, and the like.		
3. Using a CAAT or other procedures, identify employees who have not been evaluated per standards or whose compensation is above or below job grade ranges; investigate reasons.		
4. Determine appropriate procedures are in place for filing government mandated reports such as EEOC. Discuss the process and assess whether reporting is current.		
5. Review procedures for the recruitment, hiring, termination, and resignation of employees: • Determine that H/R sets standards for hiring and interviews candidates as appropriate. • Evaluate processes and expenses for recruitment; highlight any control weaknesses. • Determine if a process is in place for termination/resignation exit interviews; evaluate the supporting documentation. • Evaluate procedures to have new employees sign needed documentation such as Code of Conduct acknowledgment.		
6. Review procedures in place to encourage employee communication and feedback to questions.		
7. Review the procedures in place for employee discipline. Determine that all actions are documented and that procedures are consistent for all employees.		
8. Evaluate the adequacy of H/R records filing systems, including backup and security controls.		
9. Review procedures in place for employee promotions; determine that documentation is complete and consistent.		
10. If H/R has responsibility for other locations, determine that H/R coverage is adequate and consistent.		

As always, internal audit should properly define objectives and plan procedures when announcing any audit of the human resources function. Appropriate members of management should be made aware of the audit and its objectives.

(iii) Human Resources Function Computer Audit Procedures.

Human resources systems used to maintain profiles of all employees and to provide compensation and benefit data to supporting systems are usually in some form of database, with a set of records for each employee including key demographic and pay rate information. These systems and their related computer-audit activities were discussed in the previous section on computer audit procedures for the payroll function. Payroll and human resources systems are typically closely related, with the human resources system providing the pay rates that allow payroll to calculate the paychecks.

Internal audit should consider performing a review of controls over both of these systems, as discussed in the previous section and as outlined in Chapter 17. Particular attention should be given to logical security and program access controls for both of these systems. Other specialized applications might include a system to schedule the organization's automotive pool, a system to track continuing education activities, or one to perform salary planning to support the budgeting activities of other units. Internal audit should assess the criticality of any such applications and perform appropriate reviews.

(iv) Human Resources Sample Audit Report Findings.

A: Personal Use of the Company Airplane Not Being Reimbursed. We reviewed pilot flight logs for the company airplane for a three-month period and found numerous instances where two corporate officers used the aircraft to visit golf resorts with no indicated business purpose. The same two officers used the aircraft on several instances to transport family members for nonbusiness purposes. Organization policy states that all nonbusiness uses of the company airplane by officers should be reported to payroll in order to report the travel as employee benefits. These trips were not reported.

Recommendation. Procedures should be modified so that copies of flight logs are sent to the human resources special services function on a regular basis for analysis and follow-up to identify any personal, nonbusiness use of the company aircraft. Human resources special services should initiate appropriate executive payroll transactions. The policy on the personal use of the company aircraft should be recirculated to all officers.

B: Employee Terminations Need Better Analysis. In our review of employee records, we found that information systems database analysts experienced a turnover rate of 150% over the past year. We reviewed exit interview files for all of these past employees and found that ''better pay'' was the reason given by four of the six employees who had resigned. We also found that the human resources department had made no attempt to benchmark or otherwise gather comparative salary data for analysts in the area. Information systems management advised us that two of these positions have been open for an extended period due to the low salary. Requests to human resources for a status change have not been acted upon.

Recommendation. More attention should be given to reviewing average salary rates for professional employees, particularly for scarce technical specialists. Lacking comparative data, adjustments should be considered based upon the unfilled needs of line management.

C: Use of In-house Training Courses. The organization has incurred high costs in the last fiscal year for enrollment and travel expenses of individual employees for computer systems seminars sponsored by outside organizations. Based on the number of enrollees, we found that similar training could have been provided on a group basis through in-house courses. At least one of the seminar providers advertised the availability of an in-house course that would cost the same as six separate registrations and would save on travel costs.

Recommendation. The use of in-house training courses should be considered whenever cost-effective. The human resources training coordinator should review all requests for outside seminars and determine whether there might be savings by bringing the seminar instructors in-house.

29-4 EMPLOYEE BENEFITS PROGRAMS

There has been an ongoing development of programs to supplement the basic employee wage and salary compensation. In some cases, these programs have come out of legislation or union negotiations. In others, they have been devised to provide individual employees relief from problems, and in still others, to motivate employees to provide higher levels of service. The establishment of these types of programs by other, similar organizations has brought the competitive necessity to do likewise. All of these supplementary programs are referred to loosely as "fringe benefits." They are expensive to the organization and should be appraised to determine their worth in serving the organization's interests.

The nature and scope of fringe benefit programs cover a wide range. Some are closely related to basic compensation, such as bonuses paid out of profits, or stock option programs where the employee receives the benefit without any additional contribution. Or there may be savings programs where the organization matches employee contributions at some rate, or insurance coverage at below-market rates, or hospital and medical protection, vacations, paid holidays, and the like. Other programs are less significant and are not as closely identified with the basic compensation, such as credit services, food services that are partially subsidized, recreational services, and special types of counseling services. Some programs, while technically part of employee benefits, are hardly thought of as compensation at all. Examples would be organization newspapers, purchasing associations, and social centers. All, however, need sound standards of design and proper administering and control, usually by the human resources department.

Because of their cost as well as the legislative complexity surrounding some of them, employee benefits are an important area for internal audit reviews, often requiring knowledge of applicable laws and practices. While an internal auditor should not expect to become an expert in an area such as health claims or pension rules, many of the same basic rules on internal control discussed throughout this book apply here.

(a) EMPLOYEE BENEFIT PROGRAM ACTIVITIES

The number or type of benefit programs can vary considerably. Some are relatively minor as they impact only a limited group of employees, cost little, and present minimal risk. Others, such as health care programs initiated when health care was a relatively minor cost, represent today a major expense for the organization.

The benefit programs also involve direct relationships with employees and are based upon promises given to employees. Program costs and program controls must be carefully monitored. Important control considerations that need to be carefully assessed for all benefit programs include the following:

- The design of the program in terms of its costs and expected benefits
- The communication of the way the program is to operate, including especially the available alternatives for each participant
- The administration of the program—if the administration of that program has been outsourced to a specialized provider, the human resources function still should retain overall control
- There should be periodic reappraisals of whether the programs are achieving their proper objectives, and what possible modifications should be made; these reappraisals should be based upon human resources and management administrative and cost concerns as well as employee concerns

This section will cover some of the control issues surrounding three major types of employee benefit programs: health and disability insurance, pension programs, and investment and savings programs. Although these are specialized areas described in a variety of specialized texts, internal auditors should understand that all are areas in which costs and control risks are typically high.

(i) Employee Health and Disability Insurance.   Most larger organizations today have some type of group insurance programs in place to cover the medical-related costs of employees and their dependents. These plans typically cover one or more of the following areas:

- Sick pay when unable to work
- Hospitalization costs, including related physician fees
- Regular physician costs, including periodic physical examinations
- Drugs and medications
- Dental care
- Disability insurance to cover long-term illnesses and disablement
- Group life insurance programs

The programs offered are usually available to employees as well as their dependents. The organization subsidizes part of the costs, with a significant portion covered by the insurance program. Based upon estimated premiums from the insurance company and the amount the organization elects to spend on subsidizing the program, they will establish employee contribution rates. These are typically flat rates based upon whether just the employee or dependents participate in the program. Life insurance and disability program deductions are often based upon a percentage of gross pay and are used to purchase scaled coverages. Claims are paid by the outside insurance provider; exceptions such as sick pay are sometimes self-funded.

Employees typically elect which health programs they wish when they join the organization and then amounts are deducted against their payroll. Human resources, working with the payroll function, is responsible for accounting for these deductions and for remitting the total premiums to the health- or life-provider insurance company. When employee situations change or programs change, such change is processed by the payroll department.

Collection of employee contributions and remittance of total insurance premium checks is straightforward. Automated payroll systems show the deduction amounts on both the employee pay stubs and on separate registers. The organization is responsible for reconciling this list to insurance policy records, reporting any additions, deletions, or changes, and then paying the total insurance premiums. The processing of health claims becomes much more complex.

In the past, health plans allowed a participant to go to almost any health provider—with the exception of specific services excluded in the policy, such as faith healers—and then to submit a claim based upon the bill from that provider. Insurers found that some providers charge much higher amounts than others for the same services while others may order extensive laboratory tests or perform additional procedures. These practices have raised costs for the insurance company and, subsequently, for the organization responsible for the plan's insurance premiums. In response, organizations and insurers have modified programs with provisions, including:

- Requirements to receive medical care through health maintenance organization (HMO) group plans, where a group of physicians provides services at agreed rates

- Preferred-provider programs (PPO) where the plan negotiates fees with a series of physicians, and if the employee selects a different provider, plan reimbursement is less

- Coinsurance programs, where the employee pays a percentage of billed health care costs, with the program covering the balance

These arrangements lower costs to both the employer and the insurance company. However, since the costs from health claims are passed on to the employer, an organization typically has a high interest in determining that only valid claims are paid. This can be partially accomplished by having all claims routed through human resources to determine that the claimant is an active employee. The organization can insist that the plan's insurer give all submitted claims a close review. However, this may add to the cost of the plan and does not provide assurance that all claims paid are valid. Organizations will sometimes hire an outside specialist auditor to review these health claim payments. This type of review requires a special knowledge that is almost always beyond the knowledge of the typical internal auditor.

Life insurance and disability plans do not provide the same levels of cost overruns and concerns about possible fraud as in health insurance. There may be some question about disability claims, but most group insurance providers have procedures to screen for fraudulent claims, as they do for health claims.

(ii) Employee Benefit Pension Programs. Retirement plans are inducements to recruit new employees and to retain existing ones. The organization either makes all contributions or requires a portion of the plan to be funded by participating employee contributions. However, the employee must remain with the organization for a specified period of time, depending on national legislation regarding pension vesting, before the employee is eligible to receive any company contributions or earnings from the plan. The employer's contributions to a plan are not treated as taxable income to the employee. Some employee contributions are also often deferred from an employee's income tax assessment and become taxable after the employee starts to withdraw earnings from the plan. In the United States, this usually is no sooner than age $59\frac{1}{2}$ years.

Pension plans in the U.S. take the form of either what are called *defined benefit* or *defined contribution* plans. In Canada, a defined benefit is called a *money purchase plan*. In a defined benefit plan, the organization guarantees that, upon retirement, the plan participant will receive a specified amount or benefit, as outlined in the plan and usually based upon a percentage of the employee's salary during the years immediately before retirement. The amounts paid as benefits are based upon the employee's length of service, compensation level, and often on Social Security benefits. The employer's contributions to the plan will be based upon actuarial assumptions such as the employee's age upon enrollment.

In a defined contribution plan, the retirement benefits are based upon what the employer and the employee contribute to a plan. The employer agrees to contribute a certain amount to a plan each period over time and then agrees to administer that plan and pay out pension benefits based upon the plan's terms. Defined contribution plans can be based upon a variety of funding schemes such as stock ownership plans, where the company purchases its own stock in a protected program arrangement, or a deferred profit-sharing plan, where employer contributions are based upon a percentage of profits.

In the United States, defined benefit plans, common in the past, have been mostly replaced by defined contribution plans. They do not require complex life insurance–like actuarial assumptions, they are usually easier to administer, and government regulations are not as complex. Interestingly, the opposite is true in Canada. In the United States, government regulations dating back to about 1935 have regulated pension plan programs. The most comprehensive of these is the Employment Retirement and Security Act (ERISA) of 1974, which defines the rights and responsibilities of employers and employees. However, regulations and tax provisions regarding pension plans change constantly and knowledge of them is above the understanding of all but a limited set of professionals. Most organizations use a consultant or subscribe to a specialized information service to comply with ongoing pension plan regulation changes. In addition to the pension plan and related tax regulations, an organization faces a large set of complex financial accounting rules, which also require very special knowledge.

The actual process of investing the pension fund's resources is normally handled through a trustee arrangement with a financial institution or insurance company. It is common today for retirement plans to have a component based upon employee contributions, usually calculated through payroll deductions.

The plan administration function, sometimes part of human resources, is responsible for plan record-keeping for all participants, including their contributions and accrued entitlements, as well as the birthdate of each participant and the date they entered the plan. Other administrative duties include the payment of benefits to plan beneficiaries and other records concerning plan participants. The plan-administration function is also responsible for monitoring trustee activities, communicating with plan participants, and filing other reports.

Because of the strict government pension and tax regulations as well as financial accounting rules, pension plan administration is important. In addition to compliance with laws, the decisions of a pension plan administrator impact both current and future retiree pension plan participants. Although pension plan actuarial, tax, and financial-accounting rules are beyond the skills of most internal auditors, there are numerous operational audit issues surrounding the organization's pension plan.

(iii) Employee Benefit Investment and Savings Plan Activities. Investment or employee saving programs (such as stock-purchase packages) or profit sharing programs involve significant risk and should come to the attention of the internal auditor. In a stock ownership plan, employees can purchase the organization's common stock through payroll deductions. This stock can be purchased on the open market or from treasury stock held by the corporation. The plan may be administered by the finance department itself or by an outside brokerage that makes the open market purchases and prepares statements of employee stock-holding positions. The organization may deliver the actual stock certificates to the employee but more typically supplies them with just a monthly statement. Any stock dividends paid to stock held by the plan are reinvested, at the employee's option, in additional fractional shares. The organization may also contribute shares to employee accounts. In the United States and Canada, these will follow the rules of an employee stock ownership plan or ESOP, which outlines the company's allowed level of contribution and provides them with some income tax preferences.

Stock ownership plans provide employees with an opportunity to become partial owners of their companies. Employees can make stock purchases on the open market or accumulate shares through smaller fractional share purchases via payroll deductions. Stock ownership plans generally only apply to publicly held corporations. Private companies, such as partnerships, can also share ownership through the distribution of ''units'' of partnership interest. However, these partnership units are usually awarded in recognition of individual contributions rather than through voluntary pay deductions. A public accounting partnership is an example of the latter, where a new staff member cannot accumulate partnership units through payroll deductions but must be offered a partnership interest in recognition of performance.

An organization may offer certain classes of key employees the right to purchase specified numbers of shares of the organization's common stock at a specified price for a specified time. For example, the stock may be currently selling on the open market at $20 a share. Options would be awarded by the board of directors to give specific employees the right to purchase shares for a specified time—from one year to perhaps ten years—at that same $20 price. If the stock goes up to $40 three years later, an employee can exercise this option, purchase the number of shares awarded in the option from the treasury department at $20, and then immediately sell those same shares on the open market at $40. Some relatively complicated tax rules for the employer and employee are associated with this exercise of a stock option.

The compensation committee of the board of directors is responsible for authorizing stock option plans subject to votes of approval from the shareholders. The administration of the plans is normally performed by a unit of the treasury department. In addition to the more common options described above, there may also be special incentive-based options offered for certain qualified executives.

In employee savings programs, the employee elects to deduct a certain amount of pay and the organization contributes a matching percentage of the employee contribution based upon profits. These plans today form a portion of the organization's defined contribution retirement plan, although they may be separate from the pension plan. A substantial portion if not all of the employee contributions may be deferred from income taxes—that is, the contributions will not be taxable until the employee reaches retirement age and begins to withdraw the monies. An organization may have other, nonretirement employee savings programs. All require the deduction of pay from employees and the investment of those monies in either company stock, an investment mutual fund, or a money market fund.

(b) EMPLOYEE BENEFIT PROGRAM INTERNAL CONTROLS

All investment and savings programs that require the organization to deduct individual employee pay are the responsibility of both human resources and payroll. When the individual employee allows earned pay to be placed into some program where the benefits will not be realized until a future date, controls must be in place to ensure that the deductions are properly applied.

The organization must maintain accurate records of employee deductions as well as the organization's contributions to fund those employee benefits. Depending upon the nature of the benefit, the records may have to be maintained throughout the life of an employee's tenure with the organization, as well as afterwards if the benefits become vested. If a participating member of a retirement program, records must be maintained indicating when benefits are due to the retiree and the beneficiaries.

Record-keeping systems must have adequate controls to maintain the integrity of records and to prevent any improper manipulation. Problems with these supporting systems can result in improper calculations of plan benefits or funding assumptions.

The employee benefits portion of the organization must also manage these programs and supervise the specialist investment houses, insurance companies, and others who may provide these benefits. Since these areas are often specialized and involve legal and tax considerations, outside specialists provide needed advice and support. However, the cost associated with these consulting services should be reasonable and appropriately documented.

Retirement and savings programs require the organization to invest employee earnings into funds that will yield adequate returns with minimum levels of risk. Legislation places some limits on what can be invested. If benefit investments are to be placed in higher-risk investments, any resultant losses must be covered in some manner. Investment management also requires accurate accounting controls for all transactions, investment earnings, and disbursements.

Because the day-to-day activities of many benefit plans are relatively limited, large staffs to maintain those programs are usually not needed. However, the organization must administer and organize these benefit programs in a manner that preserves an adequate segregation of duties. Controls are also important because these benefit plans involve the issuance of checks to current or past employees.

(c) EMPLOYEE BENEFIT INTERNAL AUDIT ACTIVITIES

Internal audit has historically not been involved with audits of employee benefit programs because they are specialized programs and because they are somewhat outside an organization's day-to-day activities. Internal audit can nevertheless perform meaningful analyses and make recommendations to improve internal controls in this important area. This internal audit role has expanded in recent years as the costs of these services has increased and legal requirements have forced organizations to install appropriate reporting and control systems.

This does not mean that the internal auditor can review the appropriateness of health care benefit payments or the actuarial assumptions behind pension calculations. These reviews should be performed by qualified outside experts. Specialized firms are available to provide management with these review services. However, internal audit's basic understanding of accounting control procedures can affect important reviews.

Prior chapters have divided auditing issues into financial, operational, and computer systems–related audit procedures. Although such procedures could have been performed in an integrated manner, prior chapters have highlighted some of the unique differences associated with each. This chapter discusses internal audit issues for several specific areas of employee benefits. Health plans, pension programs, and savings plans are treated as whole topics, with no differentiation between financial, operational, or computer systems audit issues. Elements of all three apply to each of these areas.

(i) Employee Health Plan Audit Considerations. The typical organization establishes a health plan, offers that plan to its employees, and then remits insurance premiums based upon employee and organization contributions. The insurance provider pays employee claims submitted based upon the agreed terms of the plan as well as its decisions regarding their validity. The organization may require only a limited amount of staff support to administer its health plan internally.

The internal auditor should examine the plan, including its benefit provisions, the procedures for deducting employee contributions, and the organizations that actually review and pay health care benefits. If the organization actually reviews and processes its own health claims using an insurance company only as a coinsurance source for large claims, internal audit should take a critical approach to the entire process. The organization is assuming most of the risk, only relying on coinsurance to pay for major claims. This is not prudent.

Internal audit also should review the financial arrangements for admitting employees into the program, handling employee deductions, and paying the insurance company. This can be a relatively simple financial controls review to ensure that there are adequate balancing and reconciliation controls over the collection and remittance to the insurer of employee contributions. A portion of this review should cover the adequacy of procedures for adding new employees to the health care plan, processing changes in status, and removing departed plan members.

As discussed, the internal auditor almost certainly will not have the skills to review the adequacy or appropriateness of claims paid. However, internal audit should determine whether a formal process is in place to review all claims. Depending upon the size of the plan, it may be worthwhile for management to contract with a specialist health care auditor to review claims processing. These types of auditors are common in the United States. Internal audit can also develop a sense of the health claims process by reviewing any complaints that may have been filed with human resources by either employees or providers.

The internal auditor may want to discuss with human resources or line management any procedures that have been put into place to hold down health care costs. These can range from offering employees physical examinations at reduced rates to the active promotion of ''wellness'' programs across the employee base. The health care claims processor or outside consultants can provide these services. Often, these plans can be instituted at a minimum cost and will provide positive but hard-to-measure benefits that show their impact only after many years.

Long-term disability and group life insurance plans are other components of the overall benefits program. Since the funding and processing of transactions is similar to health care programs, similar audit procedures to health care premiums are appropriate. The level of risk for group life plans is often not high since the typical organization should not experience a high level of claims. Long-term disability may be another matter. Internal audit should review the number of long-term claims, with an emphasis on those that have been classified as permanent disabilities. If the number appears to be relatively high, the internal auditor can discuss with the insurance provider the procedures taken to determine the validity of these long-term claims. While the insurance company bear these costs, the organization ultimately pays for them through higher premiums.

Another area of health care audits worthy of attention is health benefits paid to retirees. Post-retirement health care programs may be an important area for review. Retirees move away, their circumstances change, and a few may be tempted to submit fraudulent claims. However, an audit request for information about the retiree's pension can cause stress for an older retiree. The internal auditor should discuss any planned review procedures for these claims with both management and the claims-processing company.

Internal audits of employee health care plans are often difficult to plan and execute. Specialized knowledge is required and other help is needed. Though typically audit procedures are limited to financial and operational processes, employee deductions, and transactions with the health care claims processor—internal audit must clearly define this limited audit scope—management may expect a more extensive review.

(ii) Employee Pension Plan Audit Considerations.   Strong legal requirements have been established for audits of pension plans. In the United States, these audits are defined by the Department of Labor as part of ERISA and require that ERISA audits be performed by an independent public accountant following guidelines established by the American Institute of Certified Public Accountants (AICPA). These are financial examinations which may include:

- Internal controls over transactions between the plan and the trustee handling the assets
- Tests and observations of trustee-held assets
- Reviews of the valuations of trustee-held assets
- Tests of income from trustee-held assets
- Tests of purchases and sales of fund assets

Because of the U.S. requirement that an independent public accountant perform audits of pension plans, internal audit is legally not allowed to perform these audits. However, it can support these external audit procedures, as described in Chapter 32.

Despite the requirements for an independent audit of an organization's pension plan, there is still a potential role here for internal audit. There may be a need for operational audits of the pension plan administration function. If totally in-house and not outsourced to specialists, this function would have separate functions responsible for plan records, benefits, investments, and the supporting information systems. Separation of duties is important here to prevent inappropriate entries in retirement records.

A starting step in an operational review of the organization's pension plan program would be a review of procedures for maintaining employee records. There must be complete records of all current and past plan participants with active accounts. That is, if a person worked for the organization 15 years ago, became vested, but subsequently left the organization, there is a need to maintain complete and accurate records of that person's pension contributions and status. Internal audit may want to consider testing these contributions through independent confirmation letters, similar to the approach discussed in Chapter 22 for accounts receivable balances.

Other steps for operational reviews of pension plans are outlined in Figure 29.10. Financial audit procedures would be part of reviews managed by independent public accountants, as required by law.

Figure 29.10 Pension and Employee Retirement Savings Plan Audit Procedures

1. Develop an overall understanding of pension plan procedures including:
   • Employee and employer contribution requirements
   • Rules for vesting
   • Periodic employee pension status reporting
   • Pension and profit sharing payment options
   • Overall administration of programs, whether administered by an outside provider or in-house.
2. If plans are administered by outside providers, obtain an understanding of internal controls of overall internal controls surrounding function. Obtain benchmarking or other studies to assess whether there may be efficiencies in outsourcing the process.
3. If using an outside contractor, meet with the administrators to determine if internal controls appear adequate and communication links are strong.
4. Select a sample of pension/employee savings deductions from a recent payroll cycle and review the deductions to determine the amounts deducted correspond to employee options and are correctly calculated and tie to pension plan summary records.
5. Select a sample of persons receiving pension payouts to determine:
   • Payments are consistent with plan options and are correct.
   • Individual and income tax reporting is correct.
6. With the full knowledge and cooperation of management, use external analytical sampling-based confirmation selection procedures to test pension payments. Follow-up on any returned mail or nonresponses.
7. Review pension record filing and storage procedures, particularly for employees that have left the organization and are vested. Determine that there are adequate procedures in place to secure and store records.
8. Assess general security procedures for all pension plan records.
9. Meet with legal council to assess whether adequate consideration has been given to the various pension-related tax rules.
10. If funds are invested by a bank or other outside provider, assess internal controls for making investment decisions, maintaining investment accounts, and distributing earnings or proceeds from investment activity.

(iii) Employee Savings Plan Audit Considerations. As described previously, many company profit-sharing plans today are part of the organization's defined contribution retirement program. The combination of organization and employee contributions forms the funding for the plan. Many operational audit control procedures here are the same as those described in the previous section for regular pension plan programs.

The other major component of employee savings plans is the stock option plans as well as other savings programs based on mutual funds, money market funds, and the like. Audits of these plans are a combination of operational and financial-related reviews. The internal auditor should test records covering these options to determine that all transactions are correctly recorded or that options are correctly granted per the terms of the offering. Since options have income tax consequences, all accounting records should correctly reflect these tax ramifications.

(iv) Employee Benefit Sample Audit Report Findings.
A: Employee Health Care Claims Not Reviewed. Internal audit interviewed human resources employees responsible for reviewing and paying submitted health care claims. We found that, other than determining that the claim was from a valid plan participant, no attempts were made to determine whether the physician's fees were reasonable or whether the procedures ordered were appropriate for the type of problem. We also found that, although the contract with the claims-processing organization gives us the right to audit, no attempt has been made to exercise this option.

Recommendation. An independent outside health care consultant should be hired to review a sample health care claim as processed. Appropriate changes should be included in the plan if the claims audit indicates areas where savings could be made.

B: Profit-Sharing Records Need Confirmations. We reviewed a sample of employee profit-sharing records in order to reconcile contributions, organization contributions, and any employee withdrawals. In order to confirm that the employee balance was correct for the records sampled, internal audit sent letters of confirmation to a selected sample of employees. We found several disagreements with fund balances, as outlined in an appendix to this report. While we were able to reconcile these exceptions, we found no ongoing program within the profit-sharing group to confirm independently their employee balances.

Recommendation. The profit-sharing group should establish a program to confirm independently employee balances in profit-sharing accounts on a regular basis. Once such a program has been established, internal audit will assume the role of managing those confirmations periodically, perhaps once per year.

29-5 PAYROLL AND HUMAN RESOURCES AUDITS IN PERSPECTIVE

The preceding discussion of the functions of the human resources department provides an opportunity to touch on certain broader human resource issues with which management is frequently challenged. These issues go beyond the purely operational functions of the human resources department. Many are in areas where internal audit can be of major assistance through its reviews.

At the same time, the internal auditor can, through better understanding of human resources procedures and control risks, be alert to the impact of operational problems.

Despite the comments in the introduction to this chapter about the reluctance of both internal audit and senior management to perform reviews of the human resources function, internal audit can improve the overall control environment within that function. Compliance with internal audit professional standards will ensure that internal auditors will not look at areas that are otherwise confidential. In addition, the various audit procedures in this chapter should provide some strong and significant areas for audit efforts.

CHAPTER 30

Financial Management

30-1 INTRODUCTION: THE FINANCIAL-MANAGEMENT FUNCTION

Over the years, financial management has emerged as a strong and important function supporting senior management. The area, historically operating in an accounting support role, has gone beyond this earlier base to include the responsibility for monitoring financial liquidity, managing capital resources, and coordinating and integrating total organization efforts for maximum profitability. This expanded role has resulted from the recognition that virtually all operations have a financial dimension. The development of financial-analysis techniques, combined with modern computer capabilities, has helped to make this new role possible. These factors are coupled with the broader and more management-oriented approach adopted by financial managers.

Financial management is a broad term, and this function can cover many aspects of the modern organization. This chapter discusses financial-analysis activities for such areas as pricing, treasury management, risk management, and budgeting. The internal audit–related issues regarding each of these topics could, perhaps, occupy separate chapters, if not entire books. However, the sections of this chapter should help to introduce internal auditors to some of these more significant financial-management issues.

Other financial management–related activities in the modern organization include employee health care plan management, pension fund accounting, governmental laws and regulations, and financial investment policies. Future supplements to this book may cover the internal auditor's concerns in some of these areas.

Although the various special financial-management functions in many organizations sometimes consider themselves to be somewhat special and beyond compliance with audit procedures, internal audit must be able to review these operations in the same way it reviews any other organizational activity. At the same time, an internal auditor should be able to identify and assess the higher-level financial policy dimensions of the other organization activities and include them in financial function reviews. The modern internal auditor should be vitally concerned with the broad area of financial management.

(a) FINANCIAL-MANAGEMENT ORGANIZATION

If financial operations are to effectively serve top management in various financial areas, there must be an adequate organizational setting. This includes the level at which financial-management operations are placed in the organization, the related communication channels with senior management, and the extent to which the financial operations are integrated with other functions. In the normal situation, a chief financial officer (CFO) reports directly to the chief executive officer (CEO) of the organization. This CFO will typically be responsible for both accounting and treasury operations, as well as for a variety of special financial activities. In many organizations, the CFO also has administrative responsibility for internal audit. That is, internal audit operates as an independent entity but is carried within the CFO's organization for budget and expense-reporting purposes.

Financial operations are sometimes split between the treasurer and the controller roles, with the responsible heads of these two groups reporting directly to the chief executive officer (CEO). Under this arrangement, the CEO has the additional responsibility of integrating these two important financial roles. Because this is likely to be a burden on the CEO, it is usually more satisfactory to have one CFO executive who coordinates and integrates the financial responsibilities.

Assuming there is a CFO responsible for all financial activities, the organization of financial operations still will vary. It is usually desirable to separate the roles of the treasurer and controller under a single CFO. The treasurer's role, among other activities, will cover the responsibility for the cash received and the subsequent disbursement or other utilization of that cash for organization purposes. This may also include responsibilities for bank relationships and investments as well as for real estate, financial asset management, pension funds, stock-purchase plans, and other financially based services.

The controller's role, on the other hand, will normally be concerned with accounting activities, including the preparation of financial status reports, the analysis and interpretation of financial data, and the development and administration of budgets and profit plans. These were discussed in Chapter 22. There may be other activities assigned here, including insurance, taxes, and liaison with outside auditors. Some of these additional responsibilities may also be assigned to managers reporting directly to the chief financial officer.

Financial-management activities can be classified and discussed in various ways. The approach in this chapter deals first with the activities that pertain most directly to current operations, including major accounting policies, report interpretation, and profit analysis. The next major section will discuss treasury operations and cash management. A following section will focus on budgeting, including a consideration of organizational relationships, the problems of determining and administering the capital expenditures program, and the problems of determining and satisfying the organization's capital needs.

(b) FINANCIAL POLICY RESPONSIBILITIES

Internal auditors need to understand an organization's basic financial policies and procedures, and the related controls that support them. While it is sometimes difficult to identify all such policy matters, an internal auditor should gain a general understanding of the more significant areas, including the following:

- *Credit Policies.* Very few organizations today operate on a cash basis. There is a need to establish the conditions for when and to whom credit is to be offered and at what levels. These decisions will depend on competitive pressures and marketing strategies, and overall market factors and legal restrictions will also be factors. An organization should typically make broad decisions at a high level regarding the granting of credit. Individual operating units would then set their credit policies based on this broad guidance.

- *Operational and Product-Costing Policies.* The typical organization should have policies defining how various costs are assigned or allocated. They should define consistent rules that allow for rational management behavior. For example, cost-allocation policies will determine how various costs are assigned to individual operations and then to products, affecting the values of inventories and what becomes the cost of sales for current accounting periods. Unless specified by policy, one organizational unit may be able to handle these allocations differently from another and report better or at least different results.

- *Capital versus Revenue Expenditures.* Capital expenditures are recorded as assets on the balance sheet and depreciated over time. Revenue-related expenditures are charged against current revenue on a period-by-period basis. The assignment of charges to either expense or asset accounts can substantially affect profits for an accounting period. While generally accepted accounting principles (GAAPs) and income tax rules provide some guidance here, an organization often has flexibility in making this type of decision. There is a need for firm policies based on dollar limits and the type of expenditure. Because of the many different types of expenditures encountered in the modern organization, there may be a tradeoff here between theory and practical considerations. Chapter 27 discussed some of the concerns and issues surrounding this type of decision.

- *Depreciation Rates.* Once depreciable assets are acquired, they must be written off over time through periodic charges to current operations. The manner in which this is done and the level of conservatism applied can vary greatly. Generally accepted accounting principles (GAAPs) provide the general guidelines for depreciation, but an organization has some flexibility in its interpretation of these guidelines. The rates used are not the same as those used for income tax purposes.

- *Deferment and Accrual of Various Expenses.* Portions of cash expenditures are often applicable to future periods and can be treated as a deferred item. Other current expenses can be treated as what is called an accrual because the debt has been recognized but actual cash has not yet been expended. The decision to defer the expense until a future period or recognize it at present may involve many different questions and levels of accounting conservatism. General accounting policies are needed. The aggressive organization will often try to defer as many expenses as possible to a future period in order to increase profits during the current period.

- *Accrual and Deferment of Income.* In some cases, income that has not yet been received but is fairly certain can be recognized as accruable. On the other hand, some income whose actual receipt is uncertain should properly be deferred to a future period and not accrued. In both cases, the selection of methods and the level of accounting conservatism create important estimation and policy problems. Strong financial policies should dictate what types and levels of income an organization can or cannot accrue.

- *Account Reserve Policies.* The possibilities of later liabilities or losses impacting existing assets may be so great that prudent accounting requires the creation of reserve accounts. Organizations sometimes use reserves to smooth fluctuations in reporting periodic results. How these reserves are set up and in what amounts can involve major policy determinations.

- *Consolidation of Subsidiaries.* Although the reporting of the consolidated results of subsidiaries is normally desirable, the decision to report those results separately or in a consolidated manner depends upon GAAP as well as various degrees of management judgement and conservatism. Both financial reporting and management structure decisions will influence accounting policies here.

The above are examples of major areas of accounting and financial policy. Internal audit should understand the organization's general financial and accounting policies and should apply them, as appropriate, to particular audit assignments. In some instances, the auditor will not find a written policy covering a specific area and may need to interview appropriate members of management to receive a policy interpretation.

In all these situations, internal audit should be concerned with the reasonableness of the particular policy, both in terms of generally accepted accounting principles and the level of business conservatism. Although some of the issues involve decisions made at a very high level, the standing of internal audit in the organization should provide a basis for raising questions about the adequacy or propriety of a given accounting policy and for making appropriate recommendations. In many instances, internal audit will not be able to present these matters as a ''finding'' following the Chapter 15 format for audit reports. However, the audit concern discussions with senior financial management are appropriate ways to raise these issues.

30-2 REPORTING AND FINANCIAL ANALYSIS

The modern organization typically has various functions that each generate a large number of internal accounting and status reports that may present complimentary or even contradictory information for the organization. The financial analysis function is responsible for analyzing these various trends and reporting to senior management the various numbers and data generated by accounting and other functions. Financial analysis, however, should be much more than just an accounting operation. For example, its work may involve analyses to decide on decisions regarding acquisitions, depositions, or other major investments.

Upper management will depend upon the information generated from its financial analysis function. The reports must contain a very high level of integrity, and many financial-analysis projects must be performed with a high level of confidentiality. If the financial-analysis function was analyzing the profitability of another organization with the possible objective of mounting a tender offer, that information could potentially kill the plan if word were to leak out. It might also subject both the organization and the individuals to violations of insider trading rules.

The financial-analysis function should be included in internal audit's universe of areas for potential audit review. This is an area where there are few financial transactions, but where decisions may impact many areas of organization operations. Internal audit should look for well-controlled processes here that follow the general directions of senior management. Although it is not a regular area for reviews, internal audit should perform sufficient work in this area to have a good understanding of controls surrounding the organization's financial-analysis function.

(a) FINANCIAL-ANALYSIS OPERATIONS

Financial analysis reports, together with their supporting details, can be a major means by which management is given the information for effectively controlling and guiding the organization. Some reports will deal with specific operational aspects, such as cost performance, product margins, or investment returns. Others may be concerned with over-all results of an individual profit center or of the organization as a whole. The scope of individual reports will range from a basic format to the inclusion of various kinds of special analysis. In some cases, the data they contain will be predominantly financial, while in others the coverage will be a blend of operational and financial information. Although it is not practicable to cover all variations of financial-analysis reports in this discussion, it is useful to emphasize certain aspects of good financial-analysis reports and their supporting analyses. These reports should follow five basic principles.

1. *Focus on User Needs.* The basic purpose of all financial reports is to serve the managerial needs of the particular users of those reports. Hence, the starting point is an understanding of those needs that arise out of the specific operational responsi-bilities of their users. Related also to the level of responsibility is the element of time. Management may require a summarized ''flash'' type of report that gives them rapid interim information before the more complete reports are ready. These interim reports must reflect anticipated final results as accurately as possible, given the time constraints. The financial-management function has the task of producing this type of specialized report. The financial-analysis group should make a constant effort to structure the scope of requested reports in terms of the persons using them.

2. *Ease of Interpretation and Use.* The reporting objective of ease of interpretation and use needs special emphasis. There is a natural tendency for those who prepare financial-administration reports to develop them in terms of their own professional standards and capabilities. While those reports may become satisfying to the makers, they may not be useful to their recipients. The key report elements that need attention relate to the clearness and simplicity of the information presented. In addition, report formats including the headings, overall arrangement, and appropriate supplementary analytical information should be of value to users.

3. *Respect for the Responsibility of the Individual Manager.* Each manager within a given sphere of responsibility deserves a reasonable opportunity to perform a job before the next level of management becomes involved in any reported problems. When reports covering certain problems are exposed to various levels of management simultaneously, the first or front line manager lacks the opportunity to assess causes and to develop immediate or planned solutions. Sometimes, a proper approach may be a difference in timing of the release of special analytical reports so that the first line manager can initiate appropriate corrective actions.

4. *Quality Analysis.* Reports quite commonly include analytical comments, either as a part of the basic report or as a separate attachment. Such supplementary analysis must be meaningful to the user. A good approach is to supply the user with any additional information that may help the user to understand the reported problems. In addition, the analysis must be accurate, without bias, and should help the reader to make the best possible decisions.

5. *Emphasis on the Future.* One purpose of financial reports is to provide historical

information for records and later reference. A more important purpose of financial-analysis reports, however, is to be a constructive force for current action. In part, the latter is accomplished by looking at the past and interpreting its implications. This can sometimes be accomplished by developing forward estimates and projections that can also be combined with historical data. For example, the actual results for previous time periods can be used to provide future period estimates, enabling managers to take actions to improve future results.

Going beyond the preparation of financial reports, an objective of financial analysis is to provide additional information that can be meaningful to management in other important dimensions. Despite the nature of the analysis, whether the profitability of a unit or the performance of a competitor, the analysis should provide clear information as to what actually happened.

In the course of various reviews, an internal auditor will be faced with many financial reports covering a wide range of topics or areas. Their format will vary greatly depending on factors such as management requests, information systems design, or regulatory requirements. The previously discussed five factors are important principles for the review of almost any information report, and should be considered when reviewing a report from some area of operations or when considering the requirements for a new information system.

Any financial analysis should identify and measure the relative significance of the different factors that were the causes of overall results. The focus should be on evaluating the performance in relation to some kind of an implicit or explicit standard. This could be a comparison to management goals, competitor's results, or overall market indicators.

Good analysis should provide guidance to the user as to what actions might serve the larger organizational interest. The success of financial analysis at this stage depends directly on how well the preceding purposes have been achieved. The analyst may want to also follow up on any reports issued to determine management's questions, planned actions requiring further details, or suggestions for improvement.

In many respects, an internal auditor can think of a financial-analysis project and its resultant reports as a process similar to an internal audit and its audit report, as was discussed in Chapter 15. A major difference is that the analyst's report discusses just financial issues, while the auditor typically includes operational recommendations.

The preceding general discussion of the nature of financial analysis and the resultant reports leads to a brief examination of the basic concepts behind two financial-analysis approaches: profit analysis and accounts receivable management. Neither of these are comprehensive treatments of the subject area, but are introductions for the modern internal auditor. Other texts are available for more comprehensive treatments of this type of information. Also, these are just two examples of many areas in which a financial analyst might work.

(i) Profit Analysis.   Because profits and profitability are the central issue in so many operational and policy decisions, the financial manager is concerned with all means to better measure profitability. Of course, profit analysis has certain limitations that need to be understood. One of these is that profits frequently do not provide adequate recognition of other forces and developments that are of vital concern to the future welfare of the organization. A given organization unit may, for example, be showing adequate profits but may at the same time be losing its relative sales position by failing to provide adequate service support for products sold; by pressuring customers into arrangements that may later be canceled; or by producing products of marginal quality. Although eventually these other factors will be reflected in declining profits, the current profit results may not be affected. Hence, profitability standards need to be supplemented by other types of operational standards. Business history is filled with examples of organizations that failed in the long run despite their short-term profitability.

A second limitation of the profits concept of financial analysis is that it comes out of an accounting process that may itself have certain basic deficiencies. Illustrative of these is that the costs of depreciable assets are recorded on a historical rather than current value basis, that allocations of costs may be unavoidably arbitrary, and that average costs cloud the impact of fixed, variable, and incremental costs. What all this means is that normal accounting data are frequently not directly useful as the major basis for decision making. The data must be adjusted and restructured in various ways by the financial analyst. This does not mean that accounting data are not important, but they must be used with special care and presented in a way that will reduce any limitations as much as possible.

A commonly used technique of profit analysis is the separation of fixed and variable costs and the projection of these costs at different levels of sales volume to show the resultant profits, including the point at which there is a break-even of profit and loss. In diagram form, this analysis is shown in Figure 30.1. Conceptually, this diagram illustrates that fixed costs and variable costs result in a varying total cost pattern under different sales volume conditions, and that profits are a function of the extent to which sales cover those total costs. In practice, it is very difficult to measure fixed and variable costs accurately because all costs are variable to different degrees in the long term, and because this degree of variability will fluctuate over time. Also, sales estimates represent a changing

Figure 30.1 Break-Even Analysis

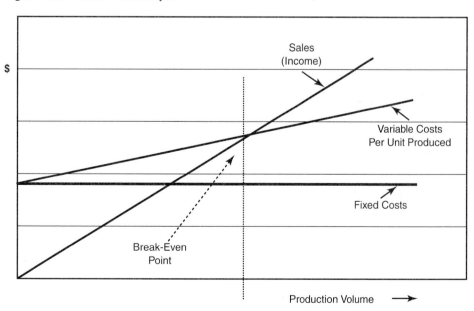

mix of products and prices over different levels of volume. However, this type of analysis can be useful for some basic profitability decisions.

What is pertinent to a particular decision is what additional revenues will be generated under the proposed course of action, and what additional costs will be incurred. The extent to which these incremental revenues exceed the incremental costs is a measure of the worth of that particular course of action. Estimating these incremental revenues and costs is difficult, especially when the estimate must be projected over longer future periods. Nevertheless, incremental profit analysis is an approach that is useful in performing a profitability analysis. Decision makers too often can be unduly influenced by irrelevant past costs, and thus fail to think in the necessary future incremental terms.

Figure 30.2 is an illustration of an incremental profit analysis to determine if a product line should be dropped. While this is a very limited analysis, it shows the various steps the financial analyst might present to support the recommended decision. Here the analysis shows that product 1 should be dropped. This sample report might be supported by materials and files which would describe how the analyst arrived at the numbers presented.

(b) FINANCIAL-ANALYSIS INTERNAL CONTROL CONSIDERATIONS

The financial-analysis function often plays a key role in helping management make key decisions. Its analysis may point out that a given operation or product is not carrying its portion of overall organization overhead costs. As a result, management may decide to shift some costs, which then might have the effect of making that product unprofitable. Errors or the use of bad assumptions in the analysis might cause management to drop as unprofitable a product that otherwise appeared to have promising prospects. For this reason alone, an organization should establish strong internal controls over its financial-analysis function.

A financial analyst is typically given an area or project to review. The project may come as a result of the analyst's ongoing review of other financial reports or because management requested a special review in some area. The overall process is similar to the research and design-engineering processes discussed in Chapter 26. This

Figure 30.2 Profitability Analysis

Item	Product 1	Product 2	Product 3	Product 4	Total
Units Produced	10,000	300,000	250,000	200,000	760,000
Selling Price/Unit	$235	$12	$75	$125	
Total Sales	$2,350,000	$3,600,000	$18,750,000	$25,000,000	$49,700,000
Manufacturing Cost/Unit	$186	$3	$54	$85	
Total Manufacturing Cost	$1,860,000	$900,000	$13,500,000	$17,000,000	$33,260,000
Net Realizable Value/Unit	$49	$9	$21	$40	
Total Realizable Value	$490,000	$2,700,000	$5,250,000	$8,000,000	$16,440,000
Overhead @ 20%/Unit	$47	$2	$15	$25	
Total Overhead @ 20%	$470,000	$720,000	$3,750,000	$5,000,000	$9,940,000
Profit/Unit	$2	$7	$6	$15	
Total Profit	$20,000	$1,980,000	$1,500,000	$3,000,000	$6,500,000
Profit/Selling Price	0.85%	55.00%	8.00%	12.00%	

Figure 30.3   Financial-Analysis Sample Audit Finding

As part of our audit review of Eastern European manufacturing operations, we reviewed the financial results of the ExCommie Division with operations in Russia, Moldovia, and Georgia. We found that this division, which manufactures heavy tractors for local agricultural markets, has been reporting favorable results to corporate headquarters. We reviewed the results of operations at the ExCommie Division and found that the operation may not be as profitable as reported. This is perhaps because there has not been a sufficient analysis of the results of operations. Our limited financial analysis revealed the following:

- *Product lines are combined to show misleading results.* Product results from the previously named Commissar product line have been combined with the NewAge line. These two lines are reported together as the Russki line. Our very limited financial analysis indicated that the Commissar line, when considered by itself, is very unprofitable. However, when combined with the profitable Russki line, moderate profit margins are being reported.

- *Variable costs are being reported as fixed.* We found that certain costs of production including certain space allocations are being charged to overall fixed costs of production rather than to the benefiting product lines. When we inquired why these costs were not better identified with the benefiting product lines, we were told that corporate standards did not require this separation.

The results of our financial analysis are shown in the appendix to this report. It points to a lack of more detailed financial-analysis guidance from headquarters international accounting as well as a failure of headquarters personnel to periodically visit ExCommie Division operations to help improve reporting and profitability analysis.

process is also similar to many types of internal audit reviews, and financial analysis has often been viewed as a potential career path for financially oriented internal auditors.

Some of the internal control concerns over the financial-analysis function can be considered in light of the example audit report finding illustrated in Figure 30.3. The report suggests that the division's profits are not adequate at present and might get worse in the future.

This example report is similar to many reports prepared by financial analysts. These are the types of reports that might result in a management decision to downgrade or otherwise change Division XYZ's operations in order improve overall profitability. Some of the key internal controls that should be in place over this type of example report and over the overall financial analysis process that creates these types of reports include the following:

- *Sources of the Analysis Data.* The analyst should determine that complete and correct sources are used for the data used in an analysis. Appropriate references should be used for all of these sources. While other supporting information systems would provide much of this input, there must be consistency in the system calculation approaches and the reporting periods used. Control procedures should be in place to assure that the reports are based on fair and representative sources. All data sources should be well documented and include explanations of why alternative sources and recording periods were or were not used.

- *Software Analysis Tools Used.* Financial analysts do much of their work using one or another of today's many powerful internet or microcomputer software tools. Spreadsheets or internet search tools are perhaps the best examples of these. Spreadsheets were discussed in Chapter 14 in terms of their potential for automating internal audit processes. This software should be used by properly trained persons following good application controls. Chapter 17 discussed information systems application controls that should also be in place in a financial analysis system, although in that chapter they are presented in the context of more typical production information systems.

- *Assumptions and Other Factors Used.* Any type of financial analysis requires some assumptions on the part of the analyst. For example, the analyst assumes various levels of growth and cost-increase factors and also assumes the rate of growth for the overall industry for the division's significant products. Minor changes in any of these assumptions could change the picture painted by this report. An analysis report is often more valuable if the analyst runs several different versions, each using different factors and assumptions.

- *Documentation and Retention of Analysis Results.* Copies of key programs, input files, and other materials used to develop the financial-analysis reports should be retained in a secure location for a reasonable period of time after the analysis report has been delivered to management to allow for reprocessing if necessary. Although this type of financial-analysis report may be a one-time effort, the results from the analysis report could cause significant organization changes. The application should be documented following the guidelines described for computer systems application documentation in Chapter 17.

- *Output Reporting Formats.* Many financial-analysis reports can be produced in formats that yield misleading or difficult-to-interpret results. Any financial-analysis report should be in a format that is easy to understand and gives correct impressions. Graphical format reports present a particular problem here. Many software packages contain graphical reporting capabilities that allow the analyst to produce visually striking presentations, and it is very easy for an analyst to use scales and formats in such manners that distort the analysis. Figure 30.4 provides several examples of ''bad format'' graphical reports. Management of the financial-analysis section should establish general standards for graphical presentations to discourage the release of misleading formats.

(c) FINANCIAL-ANALYSIS DEPARTMENT INTERNAL AUDIT ACTIVITIES

When developing its risk-analysis evaluations and internal audit plans, the financial-analysis function in the organization should be considered as an area for internal audit review. The type and frequency of any review, of course, will depend upon available audit resources and the relative risks associated with the financial-analysis function compared to other functions in the organization.

As was discussed for reviews of engineering functions in Chapter 26, internal audit may face challenges in announcing and attempting to perform a review of the organiza-

Figure 30.4 "Bad Format" Graphical Report Examples

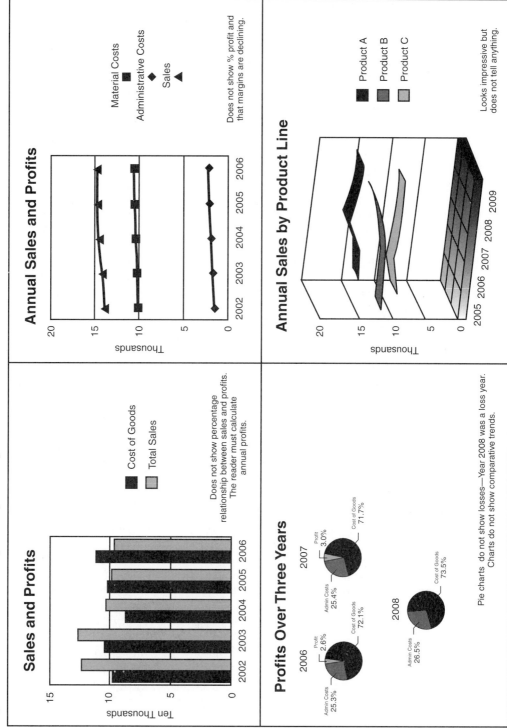

tion's financial-analysis function. Financial analysts are usually highly skilled professionals, and internal audit may face a combination of expressed annoyance and arrogance. After defining the need for a review through the auditor's risk-analysis process, internal audit should take care to discuss the planned audit, its concerns, and its objectives with the management of this function.

Any review of a financial-analysis function should not be made to second-guess the results of its analytical activities. Rather, internal audit should evaluate the financial, operational, and information systems controls that are in place within the analysis function. The actual audit procedures are similar to those discussed for other financial processes, but the sections following discuss some differences in these audit procedures.

(i) Financial-Analysis Financial Audit Procedures.

The financial-analysis department is a reporting function that controls no assets or significant financial transactions. The group may work on projects whose results may suggest that management should make significant changes or introduce restructuring to the overall organization. Internal audit should recognize that many of these projects can be highly confidential. In the course of preliminary discussions, if senior management asks internal audit to defer a planned review in this area due to the critical and confidential nature of certain projects in process, internal audit should certainly give appropriate consideration to that request.

As with internal audits in virtually all areas, the auditor's first step should be to develop an understanding of the functions and processes used by the financial-analysis function. Although the preceding departmental descriptions have characterized the financial analysis function as a group that primarily does analytical work leading to financial and operational recommendations, some analyst groups may do little more than review standard output reports and develop additional reports from them. Internal audit should understand and document the normal processes that are the responsibility of the financial-analysis group. Special emphasis should be placed on the financial-analysis projects performed by this type of function. Financial analysis projects typically involve a very small staff and are often highly time-dependent.

If the financial-analysis function does little more than review existing reports and issue some analytical summary reports based upon those reviews, internal audit may want to develop review procedures to test the relative cost and value of the group. Today, powerful report-retrieval languages are available and may be used by persons in the same organization to develop these types of special reports. The ubiquitous microcomputer spreadsheet programs provide a strong example. Many persons in the modern organization have become skilled in the use of these tools and may not need the help of a financial-analysis group. Management may not have considered this organizational change, but internal audit can certainly highlight this through a survey of other end-user financial-analysis work.

If the financial-analysis function typically performs special financial-analysis projects, internal audit should select several recent projects for a review of the financial and project-management controls surrounding those efforts. The review should emphasize the overall controls in place over those projects but should exercise extreme care not to second-guess the results of the past analysis. It is easy to look at a financial-analysis project that recommended an acquisition that turned out bad due to totally external factors and then to critique that analysis in a post-mortem, ''you should have thought of that'' fashion. This type of internal audit review adds little value and can often be counterproductive.

Figure 30.5 contains representative procedures for a review of selected financial-analysis function projects and processes. These procedures have financial, operational,

Figure 30.5 Audit Procedures for Review of a Financial-Analysis Function

1. Obtain organization charts and determine responsibilities for the financial-analysis function.
2. Understand the nature of the financial-analysis work performed.

   - Internal cost analysis procedures, such as production-process cost analysis
   - Comparative costs analysis, such as evaluations of alternative vendor proposals
   - Internal operations financial analysis, such as lease-versus-buy reviews
   - Financial statement reviews, whether for organization financial reporting or competitor analysis

3. Review published procedures, if available, covering the financial-analysis function, or discuss requirements and expectations with responsible members of management.
4. Determine that standards exist for the completion and retention of workpaper-type documentation covering the analysis work. If primarily composed of microcomputer spreadsheet files, the standards should cover automated file retention as well.
5. Understand the project management system in place to assign financial-analysis projects, to monitor times spent on projects, and to complete them. Assess whether project controls appear adequate.
6. Select a sample of financial-analysis reviews performed over the past six months for further review. If the sample selected is not confidential and not ''public,'' make arrangements with senior management for those reviews.
7. For each sample selected, obtain the following:

   - The original management request for the analysis project
   - The extent and sources of the data used for the analysis
   - Workpapers and other documentation covering the analysis work
   - The completed report, including any presentation materials

8. On an even more limited sample basis, reperform some of the calculations that were necessary to complete the financial analysis. If computer system spreadsheets or other automated functions were used, assess whether appropriate system functions were used.
9. If internal audit's analysis results in different conclusions, review the discrepancy, if any, with persons who performed the original financial analysis to resolve differences.
10. Review output reports or presentation materials as a result of the analysis. Assess whether:

    - Conclusions summarized in the analysis are consistent with detailed analysis work
    - The analysis is complete and unambiguous

and computer systems–related aspects. The latter two components will be briefly discussed in the sections following.

(ii) Financial-Analysis Operational Audit Procedures. Operational audit procedures for a review of the financial-analysis function should emphasize security, documentation, and housekeeping processes due to the potential confidential nature of many financial-analysis projects. Internal audit should look for some of the same procedures that are used for documenting and reporting the results of audits. In many organizations, this may be an easy task because members of the financial-analysis group may have once worked in the internal audit department. In other instances, the assigned auditor may have to tread carefully when reviewing these financial-analysis activities, as skilled members of that staff may choose to challenge the qualifications of internal audit.

In addition to the operational audit documentation and housekeeping-related steps included in Figure 30.5, internal audit may also want to emphasize procedures surrounding financial-analysis security. Confidentiality issues can be critical here, and both analytical work in process and output reports can cause damage to the organization if placed in the wrong hands.

Figure 30.6 contains audit procedures for reviews of financial-analysis security controls. These steps can be structured as a separate review or could be part of an overall review of the financial-analysis function. Management may request a special review of financial-analysis security if they perceive there has been a leak of sensitive organization financial data. These same audit procedure steps are applicable to security-related reviews of other areas, such as the treasury function, discussed later in this chapter.

(iii) Financial-Analysis Computer Audit Procedures.

As discussed previously, the modern financial-analysis function will typically make extensive use of microcomputer-based systems to perform the specialized computations or modeling necessary for financial-analysis projects. In addition, an internal auditor will typically encounter the same types of computer hardware as were discussed in Chapter 14, on automating the internal audit function. These computers or workstations may be freestanding devices, tied to others on a local area network (LAN) or to a client/server or legacy mainframe system. Nevertheless, because of confidentiality concerns the financial-analysis group often takes full responsibility for these systems, including program library maintenance, applications controls, and file backups.

End user–controlled computer systems used for financial-analysis purposes often provide some unique control exposures. Their users may have strong analytical computer skills but lack a proper understanding of systems controls. A review could point out any areas where controls need improvements.

A type of application software very common for financial analysis work is the microcomputer spreadsheet. Internal audit should have a good understanding of spreadsheet system controls and operating procedures for using the software. This software will be encountered in many areas of the organization in addition to financial analysis. Figure 30.7 contains some suggested control guidelines for the use of microcomputer-based spreadsheet software.

(iv) Sample Audit Report Findings and Recommendations.

A: Standards Are Lacking for Graphical Format Financial Reports.   The financial-analysis function often produces graphical format reports as a result of its analytical review projects. These charts are developed in a bar, line, or pie-chart format, depending upon a decision by the individual analyst responsible for the project. In our review of the graphical reports generated from several projects, we found inconsistent graphical reporting standards. For example, units of measure were not consistent on both axes of charts and were occasionally improperly labeled. Some started from zero and others from a higher value. A visual examination of a sample of these reports might cause the reader to draw incorrect conclusions.

Figure 30.6 Audit Program Example: Financial Analysis Function

Audit _____ Location _____ Date _____		
AUDIT STEP	**INITIAL**	**W/P**
1. Understand the overall purpose of the financial-analysis function including whether it is to: • Produce analytical reports from internal documents and readily available information such as daily stock prices, based on established schedules. • Produce analytical reports, under management direction, requiring independent research sources. • Independently produce reports using independent research for proposals to management.		
2. If the group is preparing reports under management direction, evaluate the control procedures over that report preparation, including the level of documentation prepared and control procedures used to assure adequate documentation.		
3. If the group is performing independent research, assess the number and types of reports produced as well as the costs to prepare them. Discuss this process with members of management to determine their satisfaction with the function.		
4. Determine that adequate project control procedures are in place, including project time reporting and database search cost controls to capture the costs associated with the financial-analysis function.		
5. If the financial-analysis function is used for such projects as assessing potential acquisition candidates or sales, determine that adequate security controls exist over both computer systems and the physical facility to protect research materials and other work products.		
6. Determine that all members of the financial-analysis group have had adequate human resources background checks and that they were asked to sign statements prohibiting such things as insider trading.		
7. Review the group's expenditures for outside consultants or research databases; discuss the appropriateness of any unusual expenditures.		
8. Determine that procedures are used by management to measure the productivity of the financial analysis group.		

Recommendation. Financial-analysis management should develop standards for the format and labeling of its graphical format reports. All such reports should be reviewed for compliance with these standards before their release to management.

B: Financial-Analysis Department Requires Better Security. The internal audit team walked through the financial-analysis area after hours and found report drafts sitting in

Figure 30.7 Microcomputer Spreadsheet Controls

---

1. Assess the extent that microcomputer spreadsheet packages are used by individuals for financial report preparation and generation.
2. Determine that the organization has standards for the types and versions of software used and that training programs, either on-line or classroom, are offered to acquaint new system users.
3. Determine that standards exist for all spreadsheet-developed reports including:

   - Requirements for standard report formats, including report titles and general formats and naming conventions.
   - File version control procedures requiring that appropriate versions are maintained for all key reports.
   - File naming conventions and backup procedures such that all files used to generate key reports are archived for possible later retrieval.

4. Select several financial reports that were generated by individuals on their microcomputers and used for overall analysis and decision making to determine:

   - Spreadsheet software self-audit functions have been used to determine potential logic errors in calculations.
   - Any macro functions used are supported by documentation to describe the calculations or other logic used.
   - Adequate control procedures exist for data that is input to build spreadsheet-based financial reports whether transferred from other microcomputer systems, downloaded from other systems, or manually input from other sources.
   - Procedures should be in place to review all reports produced for obvious errors and overall controls.

5. Review the level of backup procedures in place requiring that adequate versions of key reports are backed periodically for retrieval and disaster recovery purposes. Using several key reports issued as examples, determine that adequate levels of backup copies exist.
6. Determine that adequate information security procedures exist for user microcomputers containing spreadsheet files and reports.

---

the open on desks, microcomputer systems that were not logged off, and various reports stored on office area tables. There are no office procedures and standards for department security. The financial-analysis department is in a separate room that can be locked, but it remains unlocked until after 11:00 P.M., when the cleaning crew finishes its work. This open atmosphere could expose the organization to unauthorized persons having access to data.

Recommendation. Financial-analysis management should develop and enforce office security standards covering the storage of work in progress and the signing off of computer systems. The standards should emphasize a "clean desk" approach to office security. Arrangements should be made with the building maintenance function so that the financial-analysis area is locked at all times. Cleaning crew supervisors should be responsible for locking or unlocking this area.

30-3 TREASURY OPERATIONS AND CASH MANAGEMENT

The treasury department is an important but often misunderstood function in the modern organization. Some internal auditors with accounting backgrounds tend to view treasury as a high-level accounting function but may be uncertain of its exact duties. Others view the treasury department as the group responsible for dealing with banks or financial markets. Still others associate the treasury department with the entry on the organization's balance sheet called "treasury stock" but are not too clear of what that function does besides taking custody of stock that is not available on the open market. As a result, treasury operations and their related task of overall cash management are not always included as areas for internal audit review.

This section discusses some of the significant functions of the treasury department in the modern organization. While the scope of treasury operations can be quite broad, this section discusses the very important functions of liquidity and cash management, foreign exchange management, and both equity and debt obligations.

Subject to a formal risk analysis, internal audit should consider, from time to time, a review of selected treasury function control procedures. As with many other reviews discussed in the chapters of this book, a review of the treasury function may present a challenge to internal audit. In many organizations, the office of the treasurer is a relatively small function in terms of the number of personnel involved in its operations; however, that function has a very important role in managing the financial health of the organization.

(a) TREASURY DEPARTMENT ORGANIZATION

Virtually every organization, whether a corporation with stock on the open market or a private partnership, has some person designated as the treasurer of the organization. The person designated as the treasurer is responsible for many bank and lending-related matters, and is also one of the persons whose signature appears on a stock certificate.

The treasurer of an organization is typically a high organization officer, often with a position on the board of directors. The treasurer often reports to the CFO along with the controller, or this officer may report directly to the president in a position that is of equal stature to the CFO. However, the CFO or controller in a modern organization typically has a relatively large staff to handle such matters as paying bills and collecting funds. The treasury function is usually much smaller in terms of its personnel headcount. That small size should not limit the auditor's review activities of the treasury-management function.

Although there may be other areas that audit management may decide are more critical, this chapter discusses review procedures for important aspects of treasury management: cash management and issued securities and debt management.

(i) Cash Management.
The management of cash is perhaps the most important activity of the treasury department. It is the focal point of the broader problem of working-capital management, including receivables, inventory, and payables. All of these involve the total financial liquidity of the organization. Cash management also relates to the problem of capital needs and how desired funds can be obtained. In the simplest terms, cash management has to do with the most efficient utilization of cash, including consideration for all other related needs of the enterprise. It covers all the means to increase cash availability, how cash flows can be regularized to minimize the need for outside borrowings, and the investment of surplus cash to maximize supplementary earnings.

Chapter 22 discussed various accounting systems, including the cash and accounts receivable financial processes. Actions that provided effective controls over the uses of cash were discussed in that chapter. All relate to an objective of increasing the availability of cash and form a basis for an overall treasury cash-management function. The objectives of this function, which is part of the overall responsibility of the treasurer, can be summarized as follows:

- Billings to customers should be made as quickly as possible after determining what is actually being shipped to the customer.
- Every possible legitimate means should be used to accelerate payment from the customer.
- Control over collections should be achieved at the earliest possible time by, for example, routing collections to a regional location or using a lockbox account system.
- Transfers of cash balances should to be made promptly so that funds in excess of needed minimum balances are accumulated in key accounts for investment purposes.
- Disbursements should be controlled so that the organization meets but does not accelerate the stipulated terms of payment.

To the extent that these actions involve procedures under the organization's control, appropriate policies and procedures should be established and then effectively enforced and monitored. Where bank actions are involved, the advice of the organization's banks should be solicited. Assistance in achieving maximum availability of cash is a proper part of good banking service.

The operational requirements of each individual organization business unit will determine the relative cash inflows and outflows over time. It is essential that the financial manager understand the nature of these various flows and be in a position to appraise their relationships and any possibilities of modifying them. The starting point for this type of financial management is to develop a cash budget that identifies and summarizes the aggregate results. From such an overview, it may then become clear whether shortages will exist at various points. With these special cash needs identified, consideration can then be given to what other courses of action might be taken to eliminate any potential cash problems. Figure 30.8 shows an example of such an organizational cash budget with spreadsheet-type notations.

The courses of action that should be taken, when consideration is given to any penalties involved, would have to be determined by management on the merits. The important cash-management concept here, however, is that the various possibilities are explored so that the organization can decide on what is best. If there are still shortages in the availability of cash, that need would be known through the cash budget so that plans can be made to obtain funds from bank lines of credit or other sources. Such plans would be implemented only at the time the funds are actually needed. However, the financial manager should be aware of the potential cash needs and prepared to deal with them.

Under the procedures previously outlined, all cash not needed to maintain minimum balances and any established imprest funds should be routed to a central cash depository, either a single or group of banks. Determinations should be made by the cash-management function as to the size of balances to provide adequate support for the total organization

Figure 30.8 Monthly Cash Budget Example

Cash at Beginning of Period	<u>$XX</u>
<u>Cash Receipts</u>	
Receipts from Cash Sales	+r1
Cash Receipts from A/R Billings	+r2
Royalties and Miscellaneous Income	+r3
Cash from Borrowings	+r4
Other Cash Receipts	<u>+r5</u>
Total Cash Receipts for Period	RR
Estimated Cash Balance at End of Period	+$XX +RR
<u>Cash Disbursements</u>	
Payroll	
Hourly Payroll	+d1
Salary Payroll	+d2
Sales Commissions and Bonuses	+d3
Accounts Payable Vouchers	+d4
Sales and Excise Taxes	+d5
Real Estate and Personal Property Taxes	+d6
Federal and State Income Taxes	+d7
Major Lump Sum Payments	+d8
Social Security and Employee Taxes Withheld	+d9
Interest	+d10
Capital Expenditures	+d11
Repayments of Debt	+d12
Dividends to Stockholders	+d13
Other Disbursements	<u>+d14</u>
Total Cash Disbursements for Period	DD
Cash at End of Period	XX + RR − DD

operations. Advantageous buying developments might lead to greater cash requirements, or a pending strike might cause a major reduction in sales. Available cash beyond reasonable reserves, however, should be used in a productive manner by investment in interest-bearing securities. The choice of these particular securities is determined to a major extent by the length of time the money will be invested and the general state of the money market. Normally, the objective would be to maximize the return within the constraints of an acceptable level of risk and an assured liquidity of the securities or money-market funds. In many cases, this liquidity can be achieved with securities such as Treasury bills that have maturities corresponding to the expected time needs of the organization.

(ii) Other Treasury-Function Activities. In addition to cash management, the treasury function is responsible for a variety of other organization financial activities. The treasury function has an overall objective of financing organization operations at the lowest possible cost. In accordance with these objectives, its activities might include:

- Managing the issuance of debt or equity securities issued by the organization
- Ensuring that adequate other financial services are available
- Protecting the organization from the effects of foreign exchange rate fluctuations

Not all these activities apply to all organizations. A governmental or not-for-profit organization would not issue stock to the public. A small, local organization might have no foreign exchange concerns. However, all organizations are interested in financing operations at the lowest possible cost.

The treasury function of a publicly held organization does not just issue stock. The number of shares issued must be approved by the stockholders under the management of the board of directors. Issues of stock that will be publicly traded must also be approved by government regulatory authorities, such as the Securities and Exchange Commission (SEC) in the United States. For publicly traded stock, the organization will also use an outside registrar, such as an independent bank, to keep shareholder records. A similar situation is true if the organization has publicly traded debt securities such as bonds. The treasury function is primarily responsible for maintaining its own records of the securities issued, maintaining an inventory of treasury stock, and paying either dividends or interest on the debt securities.

Smaller or private organizations do not have to deal with the requirements of publicly traded securities. However, their treasury function still has an important role. A small, closely held organization often will have issued a limited number of shares or partnership units to its owners. The treasury function is responsible for maintaining these owner records, processing any distributions, and recommending adjustments to the securities issued and to be issued. This securities-control process is an important function of treasury, no matter what its size. The various certificates issued are not just pieces of paper, but negotiable instruments with value.

Overall financial planning is perhaps the most important treasury function. Working with bankers, organization strategic planners, and other members of senior management, the treasury function is responsible for assessing the organization's capital needs and recommending the best approach to satisfying these needs. This often requires a very complex set of decisions; as long- and short-term interest rates fluctuate, stock will be more easily sold at some times than at others, and the organization must keep its overall capital structure in balance. Both bonds and stock certificates have their own advantages and risks.

This section is not intended to be a comprehensive discussion of corporate finance. The interested internal auditor should consult a book on finance to gain more background information. This section only introduces some treasury activities from an internal audit perspective.

Bonds and Debt Instruments.   As part of its cash-management function, an organization may have some larger cash needs beyond what might be available from a bank. If an organization is sufficiently large and financially strong, it may issue bonds to the public. A bond is a long-term debt instrument that contains a promise by the organization to pay a stated rate of interest to the bondholder at specified intervals, usually twice a year, and to pay back the face value of the bond at the end of a specific period of time. In order to issue the bond, the organization, an investment banker, and a banker who will act as a trustee will work together to develop a certificate of indenture which outlines the bond's many conditions, including the exact terms of interest payments, how the repayment of the bond's principal amount will be managed, and the organization's rights to repay the bond early. Bonds may be issued for various periods of time such as 10 years, 20, or even longer periods. The indenture also outlines the rights of the bondholder in the event the organization becomes bankrupt. These concepts are essentially the same no matter whether the organization is a publicly held company or a governmental entity.

A bond issue presents substantial risks for both the issuer and the purchaser. Both sides are betting on the prospects for long-term interest rates as well as the long-term health of the issuer. As a result, various provisions are placed in the indenture agreement to protect both. For example, an organization may promise to repay the face value of the bond after 10 years. The bondholder wants some assurance that funds will be available after those 10 years. The bankers may insist that the organization create what is called a *sinking fund* to repay the bond. That is, in addition to the interest payments, the organization will be required to place funds into a type of escrow fund to ensure that monies are available at the end of the 10 years. In other cases, certain organization assets may be pledged to the bondholders. In the event the organization goes into default, the bondholders can take possession of the pledged assets.

The face-value interest rate is a particularly important element on any bond. Long-term interest rates are usually higher than the short-term rates because the lender faces the greater uncertainty of not having use of the money until the expiration of the bond at some time in the future. Both sides, the lender and the borrower, are betting that long-term interest rates will change in their favor over time. Assume, for example, that long-term interest rates are 7% for a high-quality 15-year bond. If interest rates for similar-quality 15-year bonds go up over time to 9%, the issuer of the 7% bond will be able to pay a low rate of interest on the loan to the disadvantage of the bondholder. If interest rates drop, however, the organization must continue to pay the high 9% rate of interest on this bond, even though it could borrow money at lower rates from other sources. The only alternative is to pay off the bondholders through bond maturity at the 9% rate, if this is allowed in the bond indenture, and then seek new, lower-rate sources of funding. An organization will often try to insert what is called a *call provision* in its bond indenture. The provision allows it to call in all the issued bonds, paying the lenders the bonds' face amounts. The organization can then refinance the bond issue at the current, lower rate. This is similar to a home mortgage refinancing for an individual. However, the lenders who purchase the original bond may resist this call provision. They want the protection of the higher-interest income over the life of the bond.

The long- and short-term rates that organizations must pay on their debt obligations are a market-driven function over which the individual organization has little power. The rates for "risk free" government long- and short-term bonds tend to dictate the individual rates an organization must pay. Lenders look at what rate they will receive under the conditions of no risk and then determine how much more they want to receive based on an organization's perceived ability to repay. Many factors go into these interest rate strategies, and any detailed discussion is beyond the scope of this book.

In addition to paying the interest on the bonds issued, the treasurer of an organization has a responsibility to monitor financial markets, to make adjustments when allowed, to work with senior management to assess capital needs, and to go to the bond market as needed. This is a field that requires very specialized financial knowledge, and the treasurer should obtain good investment banking advice to make these financing decisions.

The treasury function has an interest in working with other members of management to keep the organization financially strong and to not issue more debt than the rating agencies feel the organization can afford to repay. The treasurer has an important role in the organization in working to keep the organization financially strong and any debt ratings high. This requires close coordination with the organization's controller, who is responsible for important measures of organization financial strength such as the ratio of accounts receivable to cash and the levels of inventory. Of course, both the treasurer and controller will work under the overall leadership of the CFO.

Stocks and Equity Ownership.   The treasury function is also responsible for the issuance of any stocks or other securities to the investing public. These instruments go under the general name of *equities*. That is, they represent claims of ownership on the organization. When an organization first incorporates, its ownership is stated in terms of a certain number of shares of stock in that organization. For a small or private company, these shares are usually not traded publicly through any of the recognized exchanges. The treasurer of the organization is responsible for issuing these shares and keeping shareholder records. For some privately owned companies that have incorporated, the owner may have 100% of the shares. However, over time some of these shares may be distributed to loyal employees or heirs. In a larger organization, a percentage of the shares may be sold to the public. A board of directors, composed of elected shareholders, is responsible for overall management of the organization, including the issuance of any additional shares.

The treasurer is responsible for keeping the stock records. When the organization is profitable and the board of directors declares a dividend, the treasury function is also responsible for disbursing the dividend payment. In addition, when an organization incorporates, it structures its organization into a certain number of shares, some of which are retained by the owners, some sold to the investing public, and the remainder held as what is called *treasury stock*. This latter stock is typically held for various organizational purposes. For example, an organization may sell some additional shares to the public at a later date, may give options to purchase these shares as an incentive to key employees, or may use the shares to acquire another company. In addition, when a company has an excess of cash and when the board of directors feels the shares are priced too low given the value of the company, the board may authorize the treasurer to purchase additional shares on the open market. These repurchased shares go into the treasury stock account.

The treasury function is usually responsible for monitoring shareholder records and the ownership status of the organization. An organization may be at risk that some other investors, not always friendly, may attempt to purchase a very large interest in the company for purposes of potential control. The treasurer should monitor this type of shareholder activity and advise the CFO and the board of what appear to be unusual transactions.

While this discussion has focused on what are called common stocks, some organizations may have issued different types or classes of stock. One type of stock encountered from time to time is called *preferred stock*. This is an issue of stock that is somewhat of a hybrid between common stock and a bond. That is, preferred stock has a stated rate of interest or amount for its dividend. The organization must pay these dividends on its preferred stock before it is allowed to pay common stock dividends. The treasurer is again responsible for disbursing these dividend payments.

Although preferred stock dividends are almost always in cash, sometimes the board will authorize what is called a stock dividend on the common stock. For example, they might pay shareholders a 3% stock dividend. A holder of 100 shares would receive three additional shares from the treasury stock account. A dividend of this type does not really represent cash value to the shareholder. If an organization is worth $1,000,000 and has 100,000 shares outstanding, after the issue of 3,000 shares as a stock dividend, the company would still be worth the same $1,000,000. However, shareholders may perceive greater value for the stock. In any case, the treasurer is responsible for the recordkeeping for this stock dividend. An organization may make other similar adjustments in its shareholder records. They may, for example, declare a 100% dividend or a two-for-one stock split. Stock records must be adjusted to reflect this action.

Under the direction of the board of directors and the CFO, the treasury function has overall responsibility for these stock records and transactions. They will have a similar responsibility in a partnership type of organization where various persons have relative levels of interest as partners. A significant difference with a partnership, however, is that the partners generally cannot sell their interests on the open market like shares of stock but must sell them back to the partnership. Also, the distribution of income for a partnership is often much more complex. However, the treasury function would have overall responsibility for this bookkeeping and accounting.

Foreign Exchange Currency Management.   Although a treasury function may be involved in numerous other activities, an important task for many is the management of foreign currency exchange risks. A United States–based manufacturer may establish a sales office in France or a sales distributor may buy products from Indonesia. For both, the organization will deal with others in the local currencies of those countries. Since the rates of exchange between the U.S. dollar and those countries can change over time, the organization is subjected to foreign exchange risk. That is, they may accept an order from a foreign country when one dollar is equal to 3.55 units of the local currency. They will take an order for a $100,000 product, writing out the order in terms of 355,000 units of the local currency. Economic conditions and other factors could cause that exchange rate to change to 3.65 by the time the U.S.–based organization ships the order, sends the bill for 355,000 local currency units, and receives payment. The customer pays the 355,000, but the U.S. company receives only 3.55/3.65, or $97,726. It has taken a foreign currency translation loss of $2,740. For products with a relatively thin margin, this loss can be significant.

The treasury function is normally responsible for taking steps to control foreign currency gains and losses. The typical approach is to estimate whether the exchange rate will go up or down and then to enter into some type of hedge transaction. Futures markets allow the organization to buy a contract for delivery at a future date to buy or sell the foreign currency at some fixed exchange rate. In the case described, the organization might enter into a transaction to sell dollars at a future date, about the time this sale transaction is to be completed, at a contracted future rate of 3.55. This will cost the organization a small commission charge on the futures contract, but the expected exchange rate losses can be minimized.

This type of transaction works fine unless the treasurer estimates wrong and the exchange rate moves down to beyond 3.35 rather than up to 3.65. Currency exchange losses can be large. If managed poorly, the organization can be faced with significant losses. The losses can be even greater if the function attempts to hedge losses through instruments popularly called *derivatives*. These are complex trading instruments tied to such things as stock market or currency indexes. While they can provide protection, an

Figure 30.9   Foreign Exchange Rate Complexities

> **I.** U.S. Headquarters sells shipments of tools to its international subsidiaries:
> $50,000 of tools to Germany @ $1.00 U.S. = 0.5495 Marks
>   (Germany records sale at 90,83)
> $25,000 of tools to Brazil @ U.S. $1.00 = 0.8658 Reals
>   (Brazil records sale at 2145 Reals)
> $15,000 of supplies to Argentina @ $1.00 = 1.0001 Argentine
>   (Argentina records sale at 15,002 Pesos)
> **II.** Germany ships components to United States and sells to both Brazil and Singapore:
>   12,500 Marks of components to the U.S. @ 1 Mark = 0.5495
>   (Germany records sale at 12,500 Marks in its books and at U.S. $6,869)
>   10,000 Marks of tools to Singapore @ 1 Mark = Singapore $0.3260
>   (Germany records sale at 10,000 Marks and at U.S. 5,495)
> These translations can continue, but every international operation will record sales in its own
> local currency and then will translate total sales to U.S. dollars.

improper guess can result in huge losses. In the mid 1990s, several major and well-respected organizations reported huge losses because of their derivatives trading.

Foreign currency exchange management can become particularly complex if the organization has units in different countries which all do some business with one another. For example, Figure 30.9 shows the exchange rate complexities of an organization that sells to subsidiaries in the United Kingdom, Brazil, and Argentina. These trade with each other as well as with another subsidiary in Singapore. In addition, Germany sells back to the parent in the United States. A centralized treasury function has a significant challenge in managing the economic risk of selling products in a currency different from that in which manufacturing costs are denominated.

The shrinking of our world and the globalization of many business operations has made foreign currency management an increasingly common task for the treasury function. An organization with foreign currency exposures needs to apply appropriate protection for the risk of currency exchange rate losses through the use of these various hedging techniques.

(b) TREASURY OPERATIONS INTERNAL CONTROL CONSIDERATIONS

The typical organization treasury function is small in terms of its overall number of responsible personnel when compared to the size of the overall accounting organization. A treasury function does not have a large number of transactions compared to the controller's accounting department, which must send out bills, collect and record payments, pay bills, and close the books periodically. The treasury function typically performs more limited, but nevertheless significant, functions in the organization. Treasury function internal controls are important as the group has some direct responsibilities to the board of directors and outsiders, including investors and lenders.

Depending on the type of organization and its capital structure, a treasury function can be expected to have different internal control processes. That is, a private, not-for-profit organization has no need for controls over treasury stock, while this will be a key component for a publicly traded company. However, despite its organization structure, a treasury function has the important control responsibilities of monitoring and conserving its cash, keeping good records over shareholders and investors, and providing advice to management on ways to maximize financial returns to the organization.

Accurate investor and debtor record-keeping procedures are, perhaps, the most critical control area for the treasury function. Although the treasurer will use banks and investment bankers to act as registrars for the stock, indenture agents for any bonds, and provide other record-keeping support, the treasurer should closely coordinate investment-related activities with these agents. The treasurer is typically responsible for maintaining an active level of contact with these independent agents and reconciling their records with organization records.

Treasury stock is another area where controls are important. The treasury function has an inventory of stock that has not been issued, but which would represent value if placed in the hands of outsiders. The treasurer cannot just issue or repurchase this treasury stock on the open market. All such transactions generally must be approved by the board of directors. Corporate minutes should clearly show these actions. Similarly, the treasurer should have a detailed set of documentation records recording this security-related transaction activity.

A good set of documentation over all treasury-function activities is the most important internal control in this area. In addition, there should be a formal chain of responsibility for approving the more major of these transactions. In some instances, the approval will be by the CFO; by the president of the organization for others; and by the board for the most significant. The treasurer is often the authorized signatory for many different types of transactions that could obligate the organization for large amounts of money. These significant transactions should be reviewed on a continuous basis.

(c) TREASURY DEPARTMENT INTERNAL AUDIT ACTIVITIES

As mentioned previously, internal audit functions often ignore the office of the treasurer. However, internal audit should focus on basic controls within the treasury function similar to those discussed in other chapters covering such complex areas as engineering in Chapter 26 or manufacturing-related systems in Chapter 23. We have argued in these chapters that a professional internal auditor can perform an effective and worthwhile review in these specialized technical areas, with a focus on internal controls, even though the auditor may not necessarily have strong skills in those specific technical areas. Similarly, internal audit should consider reviews of various areas within the treasury function as part of its risk-assessment and audit-planning process.

Internal audit must understand the responsibilities and processes within the organization's treasury function and establish appropriate audit objectives. If internal audit has not performed any significant reviews within the treasury function, a first step is for a senior member of the internal audit department to schedule a meeting with the organization's treasurer or some other senior member of that organization to gain a general understanding of treasury function operations. Based on the review, internal audit can assess the relative risks and develop a detailed plan for areas of potential review.

Discussions with senior members of the treasurer's office will typically reveal a variety of different activities in the treasury function as potential candidates for internal audit review. The procedures sections following will focus on three of these many and varied activities. The financial audit procedures section will discuss reviews of foreign currency trading; the operational audit section will briefly discuss audits of the treasury stock-management function; and the computer audit section will discuss reviews of systems for controlling stock options, another treasury function not discussed in this chapter.

(i) Treasury Operations Financial Audit Procedures. Although there are many different financial processes and operations in the modern treasury function, this section will focus on audits of the organization's foreign currency trading operations. The controls over the treasury function's management of foreign currency exchange risks is a particularly important risk area.

As discussed, exchange rates fluctuate between various countries in ways that the typical organization can neither manage directly nor even understand. However, the treasury function has a variety of options available to control or hedge the risk of currency-exchange losses. Figure 30.10 provides foreign currency transaction audit procedures.

These types of strategies can protect the organization from fluctuations in foreign currency exchange rates. Sometimes, a treasury function will enter into some type of hedging transaction that makes a huge trading profit as well as providing organization operations with exchange rate protection. This ''easy money'' sometimes creates a temptation for the organization treasury function. All too often, then, the treasury function may be tempted to try the same type of transaction again but to even increase the amount of the trade to make an even greater trading profit.

Treasury functions have often fallen into this foreign currency trading trap. In the short run they may make nice profits, but are always at risk that the exchange rates may move in the other direction. This could turn a highly profitable leveraged transaction into a significant loss for the organization. All too often, senior management may not be aware of the nature of these foreign currency trading transactions and the potential risks that they may carry. This is an important area for potential internal audit review. Figure 30.10 contains audit procedures for consideration in a review of an organization's foreign currency trading and hedging operations.

(ii) Treasury Stock Operational Audit Procedures. Management of the treasury stock account can be an important area of operational control within an organization's treasury function. For example, mismanagement of this account could, at a minimum, embarrass the board if the treasury function somehow issued more shares than authorized or otherwise improperly controlled these shareholder records. The treasury function has a particularly important responsibility to maintain appropriate records for their treasury stock account.

Although auditors once might have included a physical review of stock certificates as part of this type of review, today treasury stock, similar to virtually all stock certificates, is usually managed through entries into computer system records. However, some smaller organizations may have physical possession of at least a portion of their treasury stock account in the form of canceled certificates purchased on the open market and returned to the treasury. Internal audit should gain an understanding of how this overall process works, who is responsible for maintaining stock records, and the key control points.

Internal audit should document the overall process for the issuance and control of all securities, including both equities and debt instruments, with an emphasis on the treasury stock account. This is an area usually covered by outside auditors in their review of the fairness of the financial statements. However, their review will emphasize the correctness

Figure 30.10   Audit Program Example: Foreign Currency Transactions

Audit _____ Location _____ Date _____		
AUDIT STEP	**INITIAL**	**W/P**
1. Understand the type and extent of foreign currency transactions used: are they the result of normal business, foreign operations, or financial market trading?		
2. For each basic transaction type (foreign sale, investment, etc.) document the accounting steps surrounding the booking and currency adjustments.		
3. Determine the basis for establishing daily exchange rates, as required, and the documentation to support the rates used.		
4. Select a sample of recent foreign currency transactions and determine that proper exchange rates were used and were properly documented.		
5. If any foreign cash is used, determine that controls over its security are adequate and that any disbursements use proper exchange rates.		
6. Review procedures for hedging foreign currency transactions, such as buying or selling local currency denominated transactions to reduce exposure to changing exchange rates.		
7. If any major areas of business take place in countries with extremely high inflation or widely fluctuating exchange rates, discuss any special procedures to manage those transactions.		
8. Inquire whether financial derivative transactions are used and assess the magnitude and levels of risk. Assess whether appropriate members of senior management understand the levels of risk.		
9. Review controls over letters of credit issued to support foreign currency transactions and assess the adequacy of those controls.		
10. Determine if any barter transactions are used for foreign business and assess the level of internal controls and documentation surrounding those transactions.		

of security balances as they appear on the financial statements. Internal audit should emphasize control procedures within the treasury function, including such areas as the recording of transactions, recordkeeping, and document controls. The director of internal audit should coordinate the planned internal audit review with the external auditors, who may be planning their annual review in this area. Figure 30.11 outlines operational review objectives for a review of treasury stock accounts.

(iii) Treasury Operations Computer Audit Procedures.   Treasury functions, historically, did not have many significant computer applications of their own. Shareholder

Figure 30.11   Procedures for Review of Treasury Stock Function

1. Through interviews with treasury department managers, obtain an understanding and document procedures for treasury stock. For example, determine if treasury stock is recorded at par value or some other recognized approach.
2. Review treasury stock accounts to determine the amount and extent of this stock. Review controls over business transaction procedures to determine that:

   - Treasury stock is properly recorded or classified
   - Overall capital gains or losses are not recognized in treasury stock accounts
   - Adequate accounting and administrative systems exist to maintain treasury stock records

3. If treasury stock is issued for employee stock options or company acquisition transactions, review the internal control procedures supporting these transactions. For example, treasury stock issuance should be properly recorded so that it is recorded with the stock's registrar and treasury stock account adjusted.
4. When the organization declares a dividend on its publicly held stock, review the internal control cycle procedures to determine that dividends are not paid to the treasury stock accounts.
5. If the organization is involved in a stock buyback program, review the internal controls over that program. In particular, determine that audit trails are adequate when stock is purchased from individual stockholders:

   - Returned stock is properly canceled and the certificates destroyed
   - Payment is issued to the former owners at the agreed upon purchase price
   - Treasury stock accounts are adjusted to reflect the buy back transactions

6. Assess whether overall internal controls over the treasury stock function appear adequate.

records were maintained by outside registrars, and other activities were not viewed as significant enough to justify their own computer systems. Treasury applications often just did not get the same priorities as other areas, such as accounts receivables and the general ledger. Today, a series of specialized, microcomputer-based applications are often used to support an organization's treasury function. The applications may include treasury stock records, general shareholder records, foreign currency exchange transactions, and others. Internal audit should gain an understanding of the various types of applications used to support treasury operations. These will often be freestanding, separate systems, but other applications may also support various treasury operations. For example, an organization may have some type of treasury-administered employee profit-sharing system. Such a process may be controlled by the treasury function, but the automated records may reside in the payroll or human resources system. Internal auditors should gain a general understanding of these supporting treasury applications.

Once internal audit has an understanding of any area of operations and of the supporting automated systems, internal audit should assess risks to determine the more significant of these applications. These should then become candidates for application control reviews.

Treasury-related applications are also good candidates for the use of computer-assisted procedures. For example, a larger organization may decide to offer stock option rights to certain key employees. Internal audit, in wishing to evaluate the correctness of those outstanding option records, could develop a computer-assisted procedure to evaluate file records and to perform recalculations as required. The computer-assisted audit techniques discussed in Chapter 12 are applicable here.

Another information systems–related audit area that could impact internal auditors is the use of outside service providers for significant treasury functions. For example, a registrar organization will keep security holder records or a bank will maintain duplicate sets of pension plan records for purposes of disbursing pension payments. While these types of outside institutions typically provide record-keeping and data-processing services for a large number of other clients, internal audit may want to inquire into the computer systems controls in place over those operations. This is particularly true if the provider of the services is relatively small compared to the organization, or if there has been a pattern of errors or problems. While internal audit generally would not find it cost-effective or permissible to visit that provider to review controls, it may want to request a *service auditor's report* covering these systems controls. This is a report typically prepared by an outside, external audit organization and made available to all users of the service facility. These service auditor reports were discussed in Chapter 16 as part of an overall discussion on reviews of data-processing operations.

(iv) Sample Treasury Audit Findings and Recommendations

A: Futures Contracts May Expose the Organization to Excessive Risks.   The treasury department makes use of various futures contracts to protect the organization from the risk of foreign currency exchange rate fluctuations. Internal audit reviewed all such transactions over a one-year period and found that the transactions have protected the organization from currency fluctuations and have also earned a small profit. We also found that some positions taken over the past six months have exceeded the transactions that they were designed to cover. Based on our discussions with senior treasury management, they do not seem to be aware of these exposed positions and the related risks. A significant but unexpected change in exchange rates could expose the organization to significant losses.

Recommendation.   The foreign currency trading operation should limit its activities to providing protection from potential currency fluctuations as part of a normal business operation. If management wishes to actively engage in currency trading, the function should be established as a separate profit center. Otherwise, transactions should be limited to coverage of normal business. A weekly report should be developed for distribution to senior management to report foreign currency positions and the related potential exposures.

B: Cash-Management Procedures Require Improvement.   The organization has no central "sweep" operation to move cash from its separate sales offices to central bank accounts. Although most cash is received in the form of checks or EDI transactions at central sales receipts offices, cash sales for spare parts and other miscellaneous transactions take place at district sales offices. These units are required, per procedures, to make nightly deposits to their local bank account and then to transfer the cash weekly to central accounts. However, we found that a sample of these district offices missed their central deposit cutoffs 12% of the time over a three-month period. In most cases, the deposits were late by only one day, while in others the central office had to call the district office to initiate the transaction. The organization loses cash availability because of these delays.

Recommendation.   The organization should establish a centralized sweep account system where all monies are automatically transferred from local accounts to a centralized source. If district offices have other cash needs that are currently satisfied by monies in local sales receipt accounts, separate accounts should be established for that purpose.

30-4 ORGANIZATION PLANNING AND BUDGETING

Planning and budgeting are basic management functions that should occur at all levels of management. Current operations merge into and overlap with the organization's planning role through the development of an annual budget or profit plan. Although these are key control components of current operations, the finance function has a strong role in helping to set planning parameters and to assist in organization-wide planning and budgeting activities. The financial manager also has a key role in helping to develop the organization's annual budget and in monitoring planning performance down to individual profit centers.

In years past, many organizations made little use of any budgetary process, perhaps having a financial officer develop a projected profit-and-loss statement and then all but disregarding it. Today, it is unusual to find any larger organization that does not make substantial use of detailed operational budgets covering all organization activities. These budgets are typically built from the bottom up, and come together as an integrated final result in which all the individual pieces are linked. That is to say that the expense budgets of individual cost centers and the revenue budgets of the revenue-producing components come together in profit center budgets, to the extent that intermediate profit centers exist, and these are summarized in the total budget of the organization. These detailed and aggregate budgets combine the operational and financial dimensions of various activities, as will the later reports covering actual performance.

(a) BUDGETING AND PLANNING ORGANIZATION

The responsibility for the overall budgetary process is sometimes delegated to a special organizational component reporting directly to the chief executive officer or to an intermediary responsible for planning or administration. More commonly, however, the responsibility for coordinating and administering budget activities rests with the chief financial officer. Internal audit should be aware of the budgeting process and of the budget levels authorized. With proper consideration given to overall audit risk, a review of the total planning and budgeting process should be considered when reviewing financial operations.

If budgets are properly developed, they provide an opportunity for individual managers to measure the effectiveness of the operations for which they are responsible. Plans for improving the operational results, if achieved, can well justify the entire budgeting process. Once this planning has been accomplished, the budget becomes a major basis of control for the managers who developed it and for the entire organization. However, both planning and budgetary control must be carried out in a proper manner. When budgets are viewed primarily as a control device, the planning role of budgeting is likely to be significantly undermined. Budgets may be prepared to show expected or favorable results rather than to support sometimes uncertain planning.

A basic requirement of the budgeting process is that it should be organized along the same lines as the accounting system. That is, there should be corresponding budgeting and accounting system units. If general ledger accounting reports are prepared on an individual department basis, it does little good to prepare budgets at an overall higher-business-group level. In addition, the organization needs a well-designed accounting system and a supporting report structure that recognizes the established scope of organizational responsibilities and accountabilities. These same organizational responsibilities can then be used in connection with the establishment of budgetary responsibilities and objectives.

A key component in any budgeting and reporting system is the distinction between the controllable and noncontrollable factors. Managers at all levels have the ability to control certain expenditures in their budgets but are all but powerless to control others. For example, a manager at a line unit can restrict overtime hours or reduce hiring to control labor costs. However, that same manager has little control over allocations for administrative overhead costs, which perhaps come from a central headquarters. It is usually not appropriate to measure a manager's performance by budget variations over these uncontrollable items. Although the line is not always totally clear between controllable and noncontrollable factors, and although it is sometimes not practicable to eliminate all noncontrollable items, the budgetary and accounting structures should focus on controllable responsibilities.

The actual performance, as developed by the accounting system, should be reported in a manner that is easily comparable with the budgetary data. If this were otherwise, there would be no possibility of using the budgetary process for either planning or control purposes. When there is a high degree of decentralization of operations to individual profit centers, the accounting and budgetary structures can combine particularly well to provide the basis for effective financial and general management control. When this is done, the control exercised by the central management is enhanced through budgets and profit plans. This in itself brings financial operations actively into the managerial control system.

The decision to create profit centers on this type of a meaningful basis requires close collaboration with financial operations to determine the feasibility and practicability of profit measurement. The problem that frequently exists is that the profit centers share common facilities or services, and the costs and profits can be difficult or impracticable to determine with accuracy. In other situations, profit centers sell products or furnish services to each other, raising the problem of determining meaningful transfer prices. Financial operations must play an active role both in determining which profit centers should be set up and in developing the policies and procedures by which their operations are measured and evaluated. The latter aspects become part of the administration of both budgets and profit plans.

(i) Developing the Budget. A question raised frequently is whether budgets should be developed from the top down or from the bottom up. The answer is both. Eventually, an integrated organization budget should represent the mutual agreement of all levels of management. In achieving this final result, some budget factors—such as overall limits or growth factors—must come down from the top while others, such as an assessment of local needs, come from lower levels. Where there are gaps or conflicts, they must be negotiated. Budget objectives coming from senior management should represent overall organization objectives such as sales goals, cost expansion limitations, hiring constraints, or profit goals. Certain other assumptions—such as the level of expected general business activity, estimated industry sales, the expected level of inflation, and labor cost level assumptions—should be developed and approved on an organization-wide basis. The individual organization activities would then develop their own budgets within the framework of those objectives and assumptions.

The development of budgets is the primary responsibility of the line and staff organizational components that are responsible for those particular activities. This responsibility should not be shifted to the finance group, which should only have a responsibility to provide assistance where needed. This assistance usually takes the form of providing needed historical data and developing forms, systems, and procedures for the development of the budgetary data. Finance personnel should neither dominate the budget process nor set the objectives. Otherwise, the commitment by the responsible managers may not be genuine, and the result will be a budget based on form rather than substance.

In developing their respective portions of a budget, individual managers are always faced with the problem of how much of a challenge to take. The easy approach is to start with the budget levels from the prior period and factor up or down. These are often levels that will be relatively easy to achieve, but managers can be too optimistic and set objectives that are unrealistically high. On balance, objectives should be set at levels that are difficult to achieve but still attainable. The objectives must be backed up by sound plans to achieve those objectives.

In setting budget objectives, risks should be adequately understood both by the individual managers and by their superiors. This often raises the question of how the budget will be used later as a control device. If organizational experience has demonstrated that the budget will be used in a rigid manner and that blame will be assessed in a punitive way when there are budgetary shortfalls, individual managers will tend to build protection into their budgets. However, if higher-level management uses the budget in a control sense, with an understanding of potential changing conditions, the individual manager will have the confidence to go on the line at budget-development time with realistic and attainable objectives.

The detailed budgets prepared within the framework of certain organization-wide assumptions will move upward through the several organizational levels and eventually come together in the total organization budget. At any stage, there may be gaps between the objectives proposed by the individual managers and those sought by the managers at the next higher level. These gaps must be resolved in some manner, and how this is accomplished is critical to the success of the overall budgetary process. Perhaps the wrong action here is for higher-level managers to arbitrarily change the lower-level budgets to match their own ideas. Under a proper procedure, there should be a meaningful joint probing of the issues, supplemented by a reexamination of the underlying buildup of the budget with the responsible manager's subordinates. If the budget levels are revised, there should be a sound basis for the revision as well as agreement by the lower-level managers who are going to be faced with the responsibility of performing in accordance with those revised objectives.

If the budget has been properly developed along the lines just described, it now becomes a useful means of controlling operations at all levels. When managers are committed to budgetary objectives, they should seek every proper means to achieve those objectives. However, conditions do change and efforts toward compliance with the budget can become so intensive that they lead to actions that are not in the organization's interest. The budget should have a reasonable amount of flexibility. It should be a guide and not a straitjacket. In dealing with budget-adjustment situations, there is a need for close management cooperation coupled with a concern for what can and what should not be done to reverse a current or projected budgetary deficiency.

In its simplest form, an organization's budget will look quite similar to a household budget where known income, known expenses, and other estimated costs are scheduled. Microcomputer spreadsheets, as were described in Chapter 14, can be an effective tool for developing these types of budget documents. Often, however, an automated system linked to the organization's other automated accounting applications will be used for budgeting. Figure 30.12 is an example of a summary budget document for a small- to medium-sized organization. This would be supported by one or several levels of more detailed budgets at operating-unit levels.

When conditions develop that are different from those existing at the time the budget was approved and finalized, procedures should be in place to make budget adjustments. There are various ways in which this kind of a situation can be handled. One is to adjust the budget to reflect the new conditions. An alternative approach is to leave the original budget objectives as they were, but to explain the effect of the changed conditions as a part of the supplementary variance analysis. In the case of deficiencies that are of a reasonably controllable nature and a measure of bad performance, adjustments of the budget are usually considered to be undesirable. To do so would in effect relieve the manager of responsibility for poor performance and eliminate the pressure to recover a budget deficiency in the future months. When the variance causes are clearly noncontrollable and of a really significant nature, the case for a budget adjustment has considerable merit.

Flexible budgets adjust for volume changes. Although most frequently used in a manufacturing operation, they are useful in any operation where costs or other factors may vary in ways that impact the entire budget. For example, an organization might adjust its sales budget to reflect changes in industry volume, thus focusing on the level of its penetration versus the competition in an available market. Figure 30.13 shows an example of a flexible manufacturing overhead budget for the same example organization.

(ii) Profit Plan.   The profit plan is like a budget in many respects, but is different in that it concentrates on a longer time horizon and is not as detailed or precise as a budget. Moreover, the profit plan typically does not involve lower-level managers to the same extent as the annual budget. There can be various alternatives in its timing. It can be developed just prior to the development of the annual budget, in which case the annual budget then becomes the detailed implementation of the first year of the previously finalized profit plan.

The time horizon of modern business is being continually extended. One of the reasons for this is that we are able, through the use of automated quantitative tools, to probe the future more effectively. With this longer planning horizon, it becomes increasingly necessary that management think more carefully about its future directions. What new demands are developing? What new technologies will be available? What new markets will exist? What new operational approaches will be possible? In short, management must consider the revenue opportunities, the possibilities for increased productivity, and the basis for continuing growth and increased profitability. Although these determinations are basically general management responsibilities, the considerations have significant financial-management dimensions. What will the alternative actions cost? What are the revenue potentials? What kind of funds will be required to support these endeavors? In attempting to answer some of these questions, the finance group must become actively involved in the total profit-planning process.

A profit-planning exercise is sometimes initiated through a statement by the chief executive officer regarding the scope of the total plan and how it is to be formulated. The supporting policies and procedures as well as the subsequent coordination of the total development process may, in some cases, be assigned to the chief financial officer, in conjunction with an officer responsible for planning. The finance group will typically be

Figure 30.12 Organization Budget Example

	Jan.	Feb.	Mar.	Apr.	May	Jun.	Jul.	Aug.	Sep.	Oct.	Nov.	Dec.	Total
Professional Salaries													
Commissions													
Taxes and Benefits													
Travel													
Meals and Entertainment													
Seminars and Meetings													
Professional Expenses													
Total Professional Expenses													
Administrative Labor													
Administrative Overtime													
Taxes and Benefits													
Office Equipment and Supplies													
Computer Systems													
Telecommunications													
Total Office Expenses													
Floor Space Allocations													
Rent, Light, and Power													
Insurance and Taxes													
Other Expenses													
Total Corp. Allocated Expenses													
Total Monthly Budget													

Figure 30.13 Manufacturing Overhead Flexible Budget

| Hours | 10,000 | 12,000 | 14,000 | 16,000 | 18,000 | 20,000 | 22,000 | 24,000 |
Percentage of Capacity	50%	60%	70%	80%	90%	100%	110%	120%
Indirect Labor								
Supervision—Salary	3,600	3,600	3,600	3,600	4,000	4,000	4,000	4,000
Supervision—Hourly	3,000	3,600	4,200	4,800	5,400	6,000	6,600	7,200
Material Handlers	2,100	2,520	2,940	3,360	3,780	4,200	4,620	5,040
Setup Labor	175	210	245	280	315	350	385	420
Overtime Premium							2,805	3,060
Idle Time	5,275	4,220	3,165	2,110	1,055			
Employee Benefits	1,953	2,185	2,417	2,649	2,969	3,201	3,433	3,665
Total Indirect Labor	16,103	16,335	16,567	16,799	17,519	17,751	21,843	23,385
Indirect Materials								
Supplies	1,700	2,040	2,380	2,720	3,060	3,400	3,740	4,180
Scrap Losses	700	840	980	1,120	1,260	1,400	1,540	1,680
Maintenance	2,000	2,080	2,160	2,240	2,320	2,400	2,480	2,560
Total Indirect Materials	4,400	4,960	5,520	6,080	6,640	7,200	7,760	8,420
Other Overhead								
Depreciation	950	950	950	950	950	950	950	950
Space and Power	1,225	1,225	1,225	1,225	1,225	1,225	1,225	1,225
Other Allocations	360	360	360	360	360	360	360	360
Total Other	2,535	2,535	2,535	2,535	2,535	2,535	2,535	2,535
Overhead Budget Total	23,038	23,830	24,622	25,414	26,694	27,486	32,138	34,340

closely involved in the profit-planning process, both in working with other organization activities and in developing the portion of the profit plan covering its own activities. Plans submitted by the individual line and staff operational activities will then be reviewed and will finally come together as a total profit plan for the organization.

The subsequent administration of the approved profit plan will vary. In some organizations, quarterly or semiannual reports of progress may be required. In others, these interim reviews focus on the performance as covered by the annual budget, with the longer-range profit plan viewed as little more than a reference item. In either case, a major formal review would come at the time the next profit plan is developed or formally revised—often annually. At that time, the new plan should be adequately reconciled with the plan presented the previous year and satisfactory explanations provided for changes and new directions. Again, the well-developed planning materials become an important basis for high-level management control.

(iii) Capital Budgeting. In the development of the profit plans just discussed, management should also consider the kinds of facilities necessary to achieve planned operational results. These facilities may be a necessary prerequisite for expanded operations, new product directions, or cost savings, and will require the development of both cash and fixed-asset or capital budgets. This budget planning will reflect the greater cash needs at the time of constructing or purchasing facilities, followed by anticipated cash availabilities when the facilities investment is retired in later years. Because of the major costs of very large capital facilities, an organization often must borrow funds or sell securities to finance the project. Those capital expenditures should be planned carefully and with full consideration given to all the various aspects of the total management effort.

This section focuses on the financial policy aspects of the capital budgeting process. The finance group would be very concerned with capital expenditures because of their major tie to the ongoing profitability of the organization. A further concern arises through the impact of capital expenditures on capital needs, both in terms of maintaining adequate short-term liquidity and in terms of the soundness of the longer-term capital structure. These concerns are all the greater because decisions made covering capital expenditures have such a long-term impact.

This section will briefly discuss the capital budgeting process, including procedures for evaluating a capital project and monitoring short- and long-term capital needs. Both of these topics can be the subjects of specialized books, and the treatment here will be brief. Internal auditors can use this information to perform general operational reviews of these processes, but additional reference materials or professional help may be needed to fully understand the capital budgeting process.

Financial Evaluations of Capital Projects.   Management decisions to make a capital expenditure normally evolve through a series of stages. While not be the same for every organization or for every capital project, internal audit would expect to find a fairly orderly process leading to the development of a capital project. A capital evaluation process typically goes through five basic steps, as follows:

1. *Coordination with Organization Strategic Plan.* In some instances, the decision to embark on a capital project may have been initially identified in the organization's strategic plan. The organization's strategy may have given consideration to potential new capital assets, their costs, and their expected return. This information would be used to support a strategy for a proposed capital asset project. That same strategic plan should, presumably, have given consideration to whether providing the needed facilities was within the financial capabilities of the organization. That is, the approved strategic plan provides a kind of general approval for the capital asset acquisition. This general approval often then remains valid until there are developments that require a revision of the strategies or until the original assumptions behind the strategic plan are found to be incorrect.

2. *Developing the Capital Expenditure Budget Plan.* When the future-directed profit plans are being developed, strategies may involve the addition or replacement of capital assets. These projected needs must be carefully analyzed to be sure that aggregate capital expenditures do not exceed the financial capabilities of the organization. Proper priorities must be established between the competing needs of individual organization components. Thus, the development and finalization of profit plans typically takes place in conjunction with the development of the capital budget. While a capital budget covers estimates for the total cost of the capital projects, the applicable portions of this plan are also reflected in the annual budgets. However, none of these budget and planning-related actions normally constitutes authorization for the actual capital expenditures.

3. *Delegation of Project Approval Authority.* Actual capital expenditures are often approved in the form of charges against established facilities or capital expenditure projects. The organization should have policies covering the required approval levels for projects at various monetary levels. A particular divisional profit center might, for example, have an authority of up to some specified amount but might delegate a lesser authority to a lower-level department. An important subsequent control concern over these approval authority delegations is a concern that projects are not deliberately broken up to keep them at lower-level authorized limits. There is also a risk that capital expenditures will be charged to expense accounts to avoid capital approval restrictions. A complimentary control to this practice may be the resulting unfavorable impact on the profit performance of the particular organization component.

4. *Development and Submission of Specific Projects.* Specific project accounts for these capital expenditures should then be developed and processed in accordance with established organization procedures. These projects should be reviewed by responsible line and staff personnel and approved, modified, or rejected by those individuals previously authorized. These projects will pertain to the types of capital expenditures covered in the capital budget, and if not, should be supported by appropriate explanations of the special circumstances.

5. *Later Control and Evaluation.* Approved projects should be subjected to continuing review for progress and conformity with authorized cost levels. If and when it becomes evident that there will be overruns beyond a designated percentage, a review of the entire project may be initiated or a supplemental project established. As discussed previously, post-completion audits should also be considered, subject to risk, after completion of the projects. These matters were discussed in more detail in Chapter 27.

The financial evaluation of individual capital projects typically includes an analysis of the expected profitability of the proposed capital asset, consistent with established organization measures such as the level of return on investment (ROI). An established ROI objective constitutes a benchmark commonly used as a cutoff point for minimum acceptability of every proposed project. Another key aspect of this financial evaluation is a comparison to the expected profitability of competing projects so that they can be ranked as to their respective levels of attractiveness. The objective here is to allocate the organization's capital resources in a manner that will yield the greatest potential return. Of course, there will always be cases when a project is approved for special reasons despite its relative ranking. Illustrative of this would be compliance with governmental regulations, safety requirements, or competitive threats. All choices, however, should be on the basis of maximizing long-run profitability.

Evaluation of Capital Asset Profitability.   In the usual evaluation of individual project profitability, several considerations are involved. One concerns the accuracy of the estimates used for building the project's financial assumptions. These estimates include the cost of the facilities and the time required to make them operational. They also include the estimated benefits that will be derived from the use of the facilities. The accuracy of these estimates is dependent both on the degree of certainty inherent in the particular estimate and the skills of the people doing the estimating. Where new processes are in-

volved or when revenue projections extend a number of years into the future, these estimates will necessarily be more difficult.

There also may be problems regarding the objectivity of the profitability estimates.
When the management of a particular organizational component has concluded that a
given facility is what is needed, it is very easy to present that proposed capital expenditure
in its most favorable terms. For these reasons, the supporting estimates and related analyses
must be subject to especially careful review and appraisal. This type review can be a
strong challenge to an internal auditor reviewing the materials.

Several different approaches are typically used to evaluate capital project profitability. Although some of these testing approaches have a high degree of complexity based
upon the required assumptions or the actual mathematics, an internal auditor performing
reviews in this area should gain a general understanding of these various approaches.
Some of the most commonly used capital project evaluation approaches are as follows:

- *Payback.* This type of evaluation predicts the number of years required to recoup
  the cost of an investment project. It is not really a measure of profitability, but
  rather a measure of liquidity and risk exposure. Nevertheless, payback is frequently
  used to measure the relative desirability of competing capital investment proposals.
  The payback period is calculated by determining the number of years required for
  the projected cost savings or revenue benefits, on an ''after-tax'' basis, to equal
  the amount of the proposed capital investment. Assuming that the estimates are
  sound, payback is a very simple and well-understood measure, as shown in Figure
  30.14. Its limitations, however, include the fact that there is no consideration for
  how long or in what amounts there will be benefits to the organization after the
  payback point. This means also that there is no measure of overall profitability
  or return on investment. Payback calculations are useful but are only a crude
  measure.

- *Accounting-Method Capital Evaluations.* This type of evaluation attempts to
  project the profitability of the proposed investment through normal accounting
  processes. That is, the estimated income expected to be earned as a result of the

Figure 30.14   Financial Payback Calculation Example

Year	Asset A Cash Outlays	Earnings from Asset A	Net Cash	
1	($450,000)	0	($450,000.00)	
2		$85,000.00	($365,000.00)	
3	($1,250)	$155,000.00	($208,750.00)	
4		$285,000.00	$76,250.00	**BREAK-EVEN**
5		$320,000.00	$396,250.00	

> Assuming a $450,000 investment, as shown,
> and the earnings as a result of the asset shown,
> the break-even point will be during year 4.

project is related in terms of percentage yield or return on the investment being made. The computation may include the yield either before or after depreciation and taxes. Internal audit should understand these assumptions, as they can greatly alter the results of the analysis. On the investment side of the computation, the amount used may alternatively be the original investment amount or the average investment over the life of the asset. These alternative approaches can lead to some confusion, and this is one of the disadvantages of using this measure. Moreover, the averaging of the investment may not fairly measure the use of the asset. The most important limitation, however, is that the method gives no consideration to the time element for the return of the invested funds.

- *Time-Adjusted Methods.* Time-adjusted methods correct a major deficiency of the previously discussed accounting method by taking into consideration the time-based value of money. Although several alternative calculations are frequently used, these methods recognize that funds have an interest-earning potential over time. Similarly, the sooner monies invested are returned for other management uses, the sooner they will have additional earning capability. The basic approach here is that all fund outflows and inflows pertaining to the project are adjusted through the use of interest rates to a single point in time. This approach allows all projects to be evaluated on a comparable basis.

  The two commonly used time-adjusted methods are the discounted cash-flow method and the present-value method. The discounted cash-flow method provides for the determination of the rate which, when applied to the expected later inflows of cash from asset utilization, will make those inflows equal the original investment. This determined rate can then be compared with the rates calculated for other projects and with the required ROI rate. This rate should normally be higher than the organization's cost of capital, which is defined as its combined cost of outside financing from debt and equity, where the cost of equity is developed from the relationship of the market price of the stock to current earnings per share. Figure 30.15 is an example of the discounted cash-flow method of evaluation.

  In the present-value (PV) method, the expected future cash flows are discounted at a predetermined rate, and the resulting present value is obtained and compared with the original investment. Since any difference will be in terms of dollars, those dollars must be related to the original investment to develop an index of profitability. The index can then be compared with an index for other projects. Figure 30.16 is a simplified example of a present value type of calculation. On balance, the discounted cash-flow approach is simpler and is more commonly used. However, microcomputer software and even powerful hand-held calculators have very much simplified these calculation tasks.

(b) BUDGETING AND PLANNING CONTROL CONSIDERATIONS

Management should have a concern that the quantitative tools and financial guidance provided by the budgeting and planning group leads to sound decisions by the other operating units of the organization. That is, the budgeting and planning function in the modern organization is a significant component of the overall control environment, and

Figure 30.15 Discounted Cash-Flow Example Calculation

Discounted cash flow is the reverse of compound interest. It allows an organization to take into account the time value of money when costs are discounted by an assumed interest/inflation rate.

For each year of a project's life, its *cash flow* will be the annual income minus expenditures.

$$\text{The } present\ value = discount\ factor \times cash\ flow$$

$$\text{Discount factor} = \frac{1}{(1 + k)^n}$$

k = the forecasted interest rate
n = the number of years from the start date

Year	10%	11%	12%	13%	14%	15%
1	0.9091	0.9009	0.8929	0.885	0.8772	0.8696
2	0.8264	0.8116	0.7972	0.7831	0.7695	0.7561
3	0.7513	0.7312	0.7118	0.693	0.675	0.8575
4	0.683	0.6587	0.6355	0.6133	0.5921	0.5718
5	0.6209	0.5935	0.5674	0.5428	0.5194	0.4972

The net present value for a $350,000 investment over five years that will provide a cash flow of $100,000 per year is as follows.

Year	Cash Flow	Discount Factor @ 10%	Present Value
0	($350,000)	1.0000	($350,000)
1	$100,000	0.9091	$90,910
2	$100,000	0.8264	$82,640
3	$100,000	0.7513	$75,130
4	$100,000	0.6830	$68,300

Net Present Value of Investment — **($33,020)**

its budgeting processes represent significant control procedures. Internal audit should understand the organization's overall planning and budgeting process, any potential problem areas, and the nature and scope of the techniques and procedures used by this financial-management group. Many financial procedures are based on quantitative methods, rather than just on managerial intuition alone. What is needed is a competent understanding of these financial approaches, combined with the proper use of experience and judgment.

Budgeting and planning procedures become a strong internal control in an organization only if the actual results of the planning are monitored against the plan on a regular basis, and corrective actions are taken as appropriate. All too often, operating units go through elaborate annual planning exercises but then pay little attention to progress against these budgets. This failure to follow up on performance is sometimes justified by changes in the organization that cause significant budget variances. For example, a major operating unit is sold. This action may cause management to ignore the reported variances due to this event. However, this type of event should force the planning and budgeting function to work with operating units to recast their budgets. Otherwise, the annual budgets will

Figure 30.16 Present Value Calculation

Assume that the interest rate for money is 4.0%. If $1.00 is invested at the 4.0% rate over a period of 5 years, the value of the $1.00 will grow through compound interest (interest on interest). For example, in year 2, the value would be $1.04 + ($1.04 × .04) = $1.082. Over 5 periods, this $1.00 would grow as follows:

Period	Value at 4%
0	$1
1	$1.04
2	$1.08
3	$1.13
4	$1.17
5	$1.22

In order to receive $1.00 after 4 periods, assuming the 4% rate, we would need to invest less as follows:

$$\frac{\$1.000}{\$1.170} = \frac{x}{\$1.000}$$

$$x = \$0.855$$

$0.855 is the *present value* of $1.00 at four periods in the future given these rates.

remain as just an annual exercise and not a strong component in the overall control structure.

While the sale of a major operation or some similar action can have a major impact on the financial structure of an organization, many other less significant changes will take place over the course of a year or operating period. Often, it is not cost-effective to redo budgets and capital plans based on the results of that less material activity. However, the budgeting and planning group should design its reports and procedures to accommodate these more minor changes. The published reports of actual performance against established budgets should reflect these minor financial and organizational changes. Upon the advice of the budgeting and planning group, senior management should make the decision on whether to redo budgets.

Internal audit should understand this overall budgeting process, including decisions to either prepare new budgets or to recognize that ongoing budgeted variances are caused by these recognized organizational changes. Departmental budgets and capital expenditure plans are a good starting point for reviews in other areas. Internal audit should secure these budget schedules as part of any review, ask questions regarding the assumptions behind them, and then identify potential control problems through reported budget variances. This approach can sometimes give internal audit a unique opportunity to review financial-management activities and to make appropriate balanced judgments.

(c) BUDGETING AND PLANNING INTERNAL AUDIT ACTIVITIES

Internal audit's interest in the total budget process has a number of important dimensions. The first of these is when the auditor reviews the overall total budget process, including planning, departmental budgeting, and capital budgeting. This generally can be accomplished through in-depth reviews of the activities of the budget department. For operating budgets, this would include the design of basic budget policies and procedures, the scope of instructions issued to operating units, the timing of the development of the various parts of the budget, the manner in which the budget department coordinates the development of the budget, and the way in which the budget is finalized. Other areas for review should include the procedures and the types of reports used to evaluate budgetary performance, the nature and extent of more formal budget reviews, the manner of adjusting budgets, and the general overall controls and efficiency of the budget department. Since the budget process is such an important means of developing good management at all levels in the organization, internal audit reviews should seek to identify specific ways in which that total process can be more effective.

A second kind of internal audit interest in the budgeting process arises in connection with a detailed review of any budget line item or staff operational activity. At this point, the auditor would be interested in the budget estimate and any backup materials as a source of information about the plans and objectives of the particular operational activity. The auditor's review might also include subsequent budget performance reports to identify any new problems and conditions that have been encountered. Finally, the auditor should be interested in the manner in which the budget is being used as a basis for effective managerial control, the kinds of budget review meetings held, what was accomplished, and evidence of other efforts to counter significant budget variances.

Third, internal audit should have a direct interest in the budgeting process because of the need to develop and administer the budget covering the internal auditing department, as was discussed in Chapter 7. This firsthand involvement in organizational budgeting has an additional benefit in that internal audit will have an opportunity to observe directly the way the total organization budget procedures are designed and administered.

(i) Budgeting and Planning Financial Audit Procedures.   Based upon a risk-analysis evaluation, internal audit should consider performing a review of the overall organizational budgeting and planning process. This review should include the preparation of parameters to guide planning, the design of planning tools to aid users in the budgeting process, and procedures for following up on budget performance. These procedures are closely interrelated with the operational audit procedures discussed in the next section, and the audit procedures presented in this section will cover both. Although capital budgeting audit procedures have some unique aspects, these are not covered here but were discussed in Chapter 27.

Budgeting is normally a multi-step process for an organization. Senior management simply does not ask its operating units to prepare their budgets and then operate throughout the balance of the period following those projected budgets. Similarly, senior management typically does not tell its operating units that "this is your budget" and then expect them to work under that budget with no feedback. The budget process is typically an iterative process for the modern organization, with many steps and revisions along the way. An important first step for the internal audit team initiating a review of the overall budgeting process is to develop an understanding of that process. This can often be accomplished through the preparation of flowcharts describing the budget process. The questions asked in preparing the chart will allow the assigned internal auditors to gain a general understanding of how the process works, of key control points, and of any potential control weaknesses.

Individual departments in the organization understand their own new product plans, expected sales, and other factors that would not be of concern to the budgeting function. However, those same departments may not have any knowledge of other significant factors such as the ''burden'' rate for taxes and employee benefits that must be applied to wage hours, the space occupancy charges for common area space, or various management-directed goals or limits. The central budgeting function should play the important function of accumulating the data, combining it when appropriate, and then communicating it to the separate operating units. Internal audit should attempt to understand these procedures and to test whether the data gathered and related calculated factors are accurate. For example, the budget department may have provided guidance to its operating units that floor space should be charged at $26.25 per square foot when preparing operating budgets. Internal audit might want to look at the assumptions that were used to arrive at this charge, as well as at the actual and planned costs included in the cost calculation.

As part of a review of this area, internal audit should develop a strong understanding of the financial procedures in place to compile the individual budgets and to communicate those results both back to the operating unit that prepared them as well as to senior management. This should be a well-controlled process that allows management at all levels to make necessary adjustments and to communicate the resultant budget to all interested parties. At a most basic level, internal audit should determine that the budget process is working.

(ii) Budgeting and Planning Operational Audit Procedures.   As discussed in the previous section, the operational and financial controls over the budgeting and planning process in the modern organization are closely interrelated. Operational controls over the budget process include areas such as the gathering of key statistics to prepare budget-planning materials, the distribution of appropriate budget-planning guidance to the operating units, review procedures over budget performance reports, and the retention of budgeting and planning data. All these areas might be included in a review of the budgeting and planning function, along with the financial-control aspects of the review discussed in the previous paragraphs.

The internal audit team should gain an understanding of the budget-planning documentation guidance distributed to the various operating units. This can be an area where the budgeting function, because it is too close to the process, could issue budget instructions that contain ambiguities or requirements that could result in an incorrect budget preparation. Internal audit should consider performing a detailed review of these budget instructions to determine if they are consistent with overall management objectives, are free of ambiguity, and will yield correct results. In addition, internal audit should review the overall process that the budget function uses to review submitted unit budgets and assess the appropriateness of the budget department's review of completed unit budgets as part of their review.

Figure 30.17 contains audit procedures for a review of an organization's budgeting and planning function. These operational and financial audit procedures should be useful to the auditor no matter whether the organization has a separate budgeting and planning function or if the responsibility for budgeting rests elsewhere within the financial-management organization.

Figure 30.17 Audit Program Example: Budget Planning Operations

Audit _____ Location _____ Date _____		
AUDIT STEP	**INITIAL**	**W/P**
1. Review published procedures to understand the overall budget planning process. Determine if procedures are regularly updated and distributed, and that a facility is in place to respond to questions.		
2. Review documents and meet with groups responsible for preparing materials for periodic budgets to ascertain that they fully understand procedures.		
3. Assess whether guidance given to operating units for submitting budget planning data in a clear and consistent manner was sufficient.		
4. Using the groups selected for the budget preparation inquiries, review procedures in place for preparing the planning data, maintaining backup documentation, and preparing revision requests as necessary.		
5. Review the process for reviewing, approving, and making adjustments as required to submitted budget materials and determine that materials receive adequate control reviews.		
6. Assess control procedures in place for inputting control procedures to production systems and for monitoring periodic plans versus actual reports.		
7. Where significant budget procedures exist, review procedures for communicating those differences to appropriate levels and taking corrective actions.		
8. Review controls in place for initiating a new budget planning cycle including the preparation of new budget instructions consistent with relevant business process changes.		

(iii) Budgeting and Planning Computer Audit Procedures. The typical organization will use one or more automated systems to support its budget-planning process. One system might be used to take the actual results from general ledger reports and provide the user with a facility, usually an on-line mechanism, to input changes to the budget for future periods. In earlier times, this type of system might have produced a ''turnaround'' document for later batch input. In either case, this is the typical budget-planning system. Once summarized budgets have been approved by management and users submitting their planning data, the budget package is either transferred to the general ledger system for ongoing plan versus actual reporting, or it will remain as a freestanding system.

A budget-planning system presents a challenge to its users as well as to auditors. While not a complex application when compared to many others discussed in these chapters, a budget-planning system has a control risk due to its infrequent usage. The system may be used quarterly or even as infrequently as once a year, and there may be a tendency to ignore or only temporarily fix system problems and wait for the next time the system is needed. This is the "there's plenty of time" type of thinking. Unfortunately, correction of the problems is often deferred until just before the system is needed again. The control problems continue uncorrected and the problems occur once again.

Internal auditors often get caught in a similar trap. Management may ask internal audit to review the controls over its budget-planning system in advance of a new budget cycle but with little lead time. If performed, the review will not cover key control points. Or if the review is not performed in a short time period, as requested, management may accuse internal audit of being unresponsive to the needs of management. Following the risk-analysis procedures discussed in Chapter 7 and the review procedures discussed in Chapter 17, internal audit should assess control risk and plan a review of the budget-planning system at an appropriate time during the course of the year.

(iv) Sample Budget Process Findings and Recommendations

A: Depreciation Calculation Factors. Depreciation policies established by the treasurer's office have not been modified despite changed conditions. Our review found that eight planned items of capital equipment were being depreciated over 10 years even though the organization's current plans for usage of the equipment were only six years. This longer-term depreciation increased the production group profit plan due to lower depreciation expenses, but was in violation of organization policies.

Recommendation. Improved coordination over the planning for fixed-asset depreciation is needed between production, the budgeting and planning office, and the treasurer's office. These depreciation factors should be closely reviewed by all parties before budget plans are completed.

B: Logical Security over Budget Planning Factor Files. The budget department uses a budget factors file that contains such factors as planned salary increases or floor space occupancy rates. These factors are used to develop the budget-planning data for all departments. We found that logical security over update access to this file was very limited. Virtually all members of the budgeting organization had update access to the file. Without proper management control, changes could be introduced to the budget factors file that would impact the budget plans of other departments.

Recommendation. Logical security controls over the budget-planning file should be increased. Assignments to update this file should be limited to responsible members of the budget department who have the authority to make such budget-factor changes. The department security administrator should review these access levels on a periodic basis and make adjustments as needed.

30-5 RISK-MANAGEMENT OPERATIONS

Risk-management or insurance operations are important areas of operations that are often ignored in the course of other business dealings. These functions are sometimes part of the finance organization but may separately report to other senior organization officers. Although an important area of operations, risk management is often ignored by internal auditors when performing their risk evaluations and developing audit plans. This may be a mistake. It should at least be considered as part of internal audit's analysis to determine potential candidates for control evaluations and audits.

This section contains a general discussion of an organization's risk management function, the group responsible for maintaining programs to evaluate risk, to develop strategies to shield the organization against those risks—usually through the acquisition of insurance policies—and to work with insurance brokers and manage insurance contracts where appropriate. Risk management helps the organization to acquire protection from major hazards such as fires or business interruptions. This is another one of those important but often overlooked areas that should receive internal audit's attention.

(a) RISK-MANAGEMENT FUNCTIONS

The management of risks, including obtaining an appropriate level of insurance coverage, is an important activity that is frequently the responsibility of the finance organization. The modern organization faces a large number of risks due to hazards such as fires, illegal acts caused by employee dishonesty, or lawsuits by customers or employees. Insurance policies or appropriate self-insurance programs can provide some protection from these risks. However, insurance has its own costs and management must decide when the potential risk of loss is greater than the cost of appropriate insurance coverage.

A risk-management or insurance function in the modern organization is only one component of a total organization effort to manage risk. Business operations unavoidably involve risk. Profits are, indeed, the reward for the assumption of risk in committing capital to selected operational areas. When risks can be eliminated or minimized through various actions, the prudent business manager should weigh the costs and determine a course of action to best serve organization interests. One of the ways to accomplish this is by purchasing insurance coverage for losses of such assets as cash, inventory, and facilities. Insurance can go further, however, to cover such items as the collectability of accounts receivable or loss of profits due to interrupted business operations, or to provide life insurance coverage of key officers. The responsibility of the risk-management group is to recommend to management the options for insurance protection purchase. Subsequently, the risk-management group has the responsibility for administering the approved insurance policies. In a large, complex organization, a great deal of expertise is typically required by the people who administer this activity.

As mentioned previously, risk-management functions often are not reviewed by internal audit. This is because internal auditors frequently do not have a sufficient understanding of the function to perform an appropriate type of review. While this section will only introduce internal audit to the risk-management function in the modern organization, it points to areas for possible future audit activities.

(i) Risk-Management Operations.

The development of insurance policy starts with an inventory of the types of risks to which the organization is subject. Although to some extent risks may be unavoidable, there is usually a way that they can be substantially reduced if the organization is willing to pay the costs of preventive measures, insurance, or both. Fire insurance is a good example of this type of protection. To limit the risk of fires, the organization might choose to install alarms and establish programs to move hazardous, flammable materials outside of the facility. This can limit the danger of a fire and even possibly reduce the cost of an insurance policy. However, because of the many things that could cause a fire and the large losses that could result from a fire, the prudent manager almost always shares a significant portion of the risk of a fire through an insurance policy.

In most high-risk situations, an organization will decide to pay the cost for insurance. In a few other circumstances, they may decide either that the cost of insurance is too high or the risk is not that great. For example, a multilocation manufacturer may face the risk of potential storm damage to its manufacturing facilities, but the properties may be so widely dispersed in a geographical sense that the organization may conclude that it will assume directly the risk of storm damage hazards. The organization could either absorb losses directly into operations when and if that storm damage occurs or, even better, accrue reserves for future losses at customary insurance rates and then charge any future actual losses to those reserves. The risk here, of course, is that covering any losses from current cash could be devastating to the organization—or, that they will not accrue sufficient reserves to cover any actual losses. For example, that storm damage may be considered to be a once-every-100-years type of event. An organization could start the accrual today, and that same disastrous storm could occur tomorrow and again the following year. Insurance companies have reserves as well as their own reinsurance programs to provide them with coverage for these types of unexpected events. Outside insurance policies are almost always the answer for these types of situations.

The insurance or risk-management function appraises the risks and determines the particular features that are desired in the way of insurance coverage. Considerations might cover what inclusions and exclusions are needed, what ranges of dollar limits, or whether a deductible provision for auto damage is acceptable. Similarly, do we want liability coverage at the $100,000 level, $300,000 level, or $500,000 level? In all these determinations, a major level of professional competence is required for the identification and evaluation of the various issues and alternatives. In addition to the insurance department, counsel can be obtained from insurance agents and brokers.

- *Administering the Risk-Management Activity.* The decision to seek insurance coverage in a given area provides the basis for the actual procurement of the coverage and selecting the carriers to be used. In making the selection of an insurance provider, a number of factors should be considered, including the range of the coverage that a particular carrier can offer, its financial resources, its reputation as to the efficiency and fairness with which claims are settled, and the rates charged. Insurance brokers, who usually represent a number of carriers, are often helpful in appraising the various alternatives. As a basis for the final negotiation for the purchase of insurance coverage, the risk-management group will need complete data as to the value and location of the organization's assets, as well as other pertinent operational data. The objective here is maximum leverage in achieving the most advantageous rates possible.

- *Ongoing Risk-Management Administrative Activities.* During the life of insurance policies, there is a need for a varied range of ongoing administrative responsibilities. For some types of insurance, coverage should be adjusted periodically on the basis of regular reports and the status of the insured assets. In other cases, changes in coverage may be linked to operational developments such as new facilities purchased and old ones retired. Usually, coverage is automatically adjusted in such situations, but there must be notification within a given period for the purpose of adjusting future billings. Adequate procedures must be designed so that the various operational developments are identified and properly reported to the carriers. As billings are received for insurance coverage, they must be carefully reviewed for the accuracy of rates charged and correctness of the coverage provided.

All these review activities must also be closely tied to the regular processing of the invoices for payment, and the proper distribution of costs to the various operational activities affected.

- *Handling Insurance Claims.* The insurance group will also play an active role in the reporting of developments that provide a basis for a claim by the organization under the existing coverage. This claim-reporting requires the cooperation of the operational activities directly affected. It is especially important because the carrier must usually be given the opportunity to take any steps that may assist it in reducing the final loss claim. The risk-management group should work with the affected operational groups in developing the actual claim, and after its submission to the carrier, coordinate any later review and negotiation that precedes the ultimate settlement. These settlement activities must be closely coordinated with accounting and operations.

- *Educational Role of the Risk-Management Group.* The cost of insurance is closely related to the loss experience of a particular organization. If losses run at a high level, higher rates must be charged by the insurance carriers to maintain their own profitable operations. In an extreme case of high losses, a carrier may even elect to cancel the coverage completely. These possibilities make it very important that operations are carried out in a way that will minimize losses, thus reducing the amount of claims filed. Risk management may want to develop educational materials that describe various precautions or preventive measures. Departmental personnel can also make periodic field visits to ascertain firsthand what problems may exist and provide direct counsel to operational managers. The liaison also makes possible a more up-to-date understanding of insurance needs and possible alternative solutions.

(b) RISK-MANAGEMENT CONTROL CONSIDERATIONS

An impressive thing about the risk-management and insurance function is that it relates in some way to almost every phase of the organization operations, and that it has an interest in each level of those operations. This makes it a necessity that this function maintains effective coordination with the highest level of management as well as with basic accounting and other financial-management activities. The effectiveness of the risk-management department is, therefore, dependent on combining professional expertise with good coordination of all organization activities. The department must have a strong set of control procedures in place over its operations, be prepared to respond to the needs of the various operational activities, and take the initiative in suggesting new alternatives and approaches. The appraisal of this insurance activity centers on the extent to which the risk-management group is carrying on this total coordination.

Management often assumes that risk management is correctly performing its very important tasks. That is, organization management may have reviewed the business-interruption coverage at some point in time, and unless there is a need to change the level of coverage, that same management will assume that policies are being renewed regularly. They will also assume that the risk-management function will advise them if changes are required. There can be a significant problem if the organization has a need for that same business-interruption insurance and finds that the policy is now inadequate or has expired for nonpayment of the premium. Controls are very important here.

(c) RISK-MANAGEMENT INTERNAL AUDIT ACTIVITIES

Although an important specialized function in the typical organization, risk management is again one of those areas that is usually not included in internal audit's planned review activities. As it happens, internal audit often only comes across the risk-management or insurance problems as it reviews various other operational activities. For example, internal audit may find that a production facility is in a storm-prone area or may be told that a particular facility is "essential" to organization activities. When the auditor asks about the level of storm damage or business-interruption insurance, the local unit may not be able to give the auditor appropriate answers. This provides further input for the specific review of the activities of the risk-management function to determine that the function has developed sound policies and procedures and that they are being carried out in an effective, well-controlled manner.

(i) Risk-Management Operations Financial Audit Procedures. Risk management is another area where financial and operational audit activities are closely interrelated, and any internal audit review will probably include procedures in both. In keeping with the organization of these chapters, separate sections discuss each, although the audit procedures here will be included in the section following, on risk management operational audit procedures. The financial audit activities covering the risk-management function include steps to determine that insurance policies are paid in a timely manner and that those costs are then allocated to the benefiting departments. Operational audit activities in the area of risk management include the adequacy of procedures to select insurance carriers, the handling of claims, and the risk-assessment selection itself.

While insurance carriers typically send bills for policy renewals, the organization should have procedures in place to determine that all policies up for renewal are actually reviewed and that those policies are current. An effective way to handle this is to maintain a database of outstanding insurance policies and to use it to pull the policies just prior to renewal to determine if the policies are still correct. Internal audit can select a sample of these policies outstanding and read the summarized policy terms to assess if they still appear to be accurate. This may require visits to the locations covered by the policies.

The risk-management group typically does not have a budget to cover the costs for all organization insurance policies. Rather, the costs of those insurance policies usually are distributed to the benefiting departments or groups. Internal audit should develop an understanding of this allocation process and perform appropriate tests to determine that distributions are proper and accurate.

(ii) Risk Management Operational Audit Procedures. The line between financial and operational audit procedures is often very thin, and, regarding risk management, it is difficult to define what is a financial audit procedure and what is operational. A review of the risk-management function, however, should contain many procedures that are often considered to be primarily operational. For example, an important operational audit step would be a review of the procedures used to identify risks and then to decide whether appropriate steps were taken to decide to accept that risk or to seek outside insurance.

Internal audit should review the procedures used by the risk-management function to assess risks. There should be a formal process in place not too different from the internal audit risk-evaluation process discussed in Chapter 8. Once the organization has identified a

Figure 30.18   Sample Risk Evaluation Calculation

Assume that ExampleCo has two production plants, each in different cities. Insurance examiners have determined that each plant has a 1/40 chance of having a major fire in any given year. The overall loss probabilities for these two plants in any year are:

Risk that both plants will have a fire: $(1/40) \times (1/40) = 1/1600$

Risk that one plant will burn, but not the other: $(1/40)(1 - 1/40) = 79/1600$

Risk that either will burn, but not both: $1/40 + 1/40 - 1/1600 = 79/1600$

potential risk, the risk-management group should go through a formal process to determine whether to accept those risks or purchase insurance. This analysis should consider the costs of the projected loss and the expectation of a probable loss. Although many different approaches can be used for this type of analysis, an example calculation is shown in Figure 30.18.

Internal audit should also review the process for selecting insurance providers. Despite a general need to select the most cost-effective insurance provider, insurance departments may sometimes be tempted to use an insurance company that is not necessarily the lowest-cost provider because the organization has had a history of working with that company or an agent representing it. Internal audit should look for a competitive bid process or some similar evidence that the organization has selected the most cost-effective approach to securing its insurance coverage.

Because internal audit has traditionally not reviewed the organization's risk-management function, and because the assigned auditors will be reviewing a very specialized area, it may encounter some resistance from the risk-management organization. However, despite the specialized nature and language of insurance coverage, internal audit should be quite successful in this type of review if it just considers basic internal control principles. Selected audit procedures for a review of the risk-management function are discussed in Figure 30.19.

(iii) Risk-Management Computer Audit Procedures.   Risk management is an area where the typical organization does not have many unique or specialized computer systems. Internal audit, performing an overall review in this area, should probably find some type of a database system to keep track of the various outstanding insurance policies, including their general coverages, premium amounts, and renewal dates. The group will probably have a database to control and monitor its open and outstanding insurance claims. Similarly, internal audit may also find a spreadsheet package for evaluating insurance risks and for determining whether to seek outside insurance coverage.

These risk-management applications will not necessarily be good candidates for computer-assisted procedures. Review activities here should probably be limited to developing an understanding of the automated systems used to support the risk-management function and then performing general and specific application control reviews as would be deemed necessary to support the overall audit. Procedures for these types of reviews were discussed in Chapters 16 and 17.

Figure 30.19   Procedures for Auditing the Risk-Analysis Function

---

1. Develop a general understanding of the mission or responsibilities of the risk-analysis function. Are they actively involved with assessing risks and developing strategies for risk protection or are they primarily just insurance agent coordinators?
2. If the role of risk analysis is primarily to delegate business to outside agents, after completing other steps in this survey, consider recommending whether efficiencies could be gained by outsourcing much of the function.
3. Does the risk-analysis function go through a formal assessment process to identify all significant and insurable risks within the organization? Does this process consider both known and unknown risks?
4. Are risk analyses performed on a regular, periodic basis throughout the organization or only when requested? If the latter, assess the adequacy of this process.
5. What is the basis for any formal risk analyses performed such as benchmarking surveys against databases, probable loss studies, or the like? Based on records of risks analyzed, do these procedures appear to be applied consistently?
6. Once risks have been identified and analyzed, does risk analysis use a variety of response techniques ranging from acquiring insurance to working with the responsible area to build controls? Do these seem appropriate?
7. When outside insurance providers are used to cover the risk, are a variety of outside providers used to carry the insurance and are competitive approaches used to determine the most cost-effective providers?
8. Assess the role of the risk-analysis function in negotiating contracts with insurance providers. Based on a review of recent contract negotiations, assess whether competitive bidding was encouraged.
9. Given the role of risk analysis in identifying risks and negotiating with insurance carriers, review their role in assessing damages and processing claims. Has proper attention been given to the separation of duties controls and does their role appear sufficient?
10. Does/should risk analysis play any role in communicating risk exposures to other members of the organization? Assess the adequacy of their role here.

(iv) Sample Risk Management Findings and Recommendations

A: Competitive Bids Are Not Used for Insurance Brokers.   The organization has a need for fire, property damage, and hazard insurance at each of its geographic sites. Despite the fact that this is a relatively price-competitive area for purchases of insurance, we observed that the same insurance broker is used for all policies and that there has been no attempt to obtain competitive bids on this insurance coverage. Organization policy requires at least three competitive bids on all contracts of this size. In addition, we feel the organization could potentially realize savings on its insurance costs through the solicitation of competitive bids.

   Recommendation. Requests for competitive insurance policy bids should be periodically solicited for new insurance coverages. While it may not be cost-effective to secure bids at every policy renewal, the bidding process should be used from time to time to determine that insurance costs are competitive and are giving desired levels of service.

B: Controls Need to Be Improved on Self-Insurance Programs.   The organization has decided to accept the risks and is self-insured for losses or damage to shop tools, both company- and employee-owned. An employee can file a claim for a tool that was lost or damaged during the course of normal work activities. We found that these employee damage claims are paid without question as long as they are less than $100. Although no records are maintained for these claims, we reviewed canceled checks for the insurance account and found that certain employees appear to be filing repetitive claims. All of these were paid with no detailed analysis.

Recommendation. A controls system should be established to screen for such abuses as potential duplicate or repetitive claims for damaged employee-owned tools. All such self-insured claims should be entered on a database established to monitor this activity. Potentially repetitive loss claims should be forwarded to direct the employees' supervisors for investigation before making payment.

30-6 OTHER FINANCIAL-MANAGEMENT ACTIVITIES

Internal audit will find a large number of other financial activities in the modern organization that are potential candidates for review. In some instances, internal audit will be introduced to an area for potential review because management requests such a review. For example, the organization may be a retailer with a large amount of construction activity to build new stores and related support facilities. Management may be concerned about the administration of the various construction contracts, and request that internal audit perform a review of contract administration. This could be considered to be primarily an operational review or, depending upon the objectives of the requested audit, an essentially financial review. This is one example of the many financial-management reviews that could be performed by internal audit.

In addition to management reviews, internal audit should be aware of other financial-management activities in the organization and should consider these areas as potential audit candidates if they represent a significant audit risk. Although they may vary by the size and type of the organization, some of the financial-management areas that could be potential candidates for review include:

- Tax department operations
- Employee stock options administration
- Profit-sharing and pension fund administration
- Organization investments in joint ventures or acquisitions

The above list could easily become much longer depending on the type and nature of the organization. The first step for internal audit when considering an area for risk assessment and potential audit is to gain a general understanding of the function's operations. This understanding, gathered through interviews and observations, will allow the auditor to have enough data and information to perform a risk-analysis assessment of the operation and then develop appropriate audit programs covering financial, operational, and information systems operations.

PART FIVE

SPECIAL AUDIT ACTIVITIES

CHAPTER 31

Loss Prevention and Fraud Investigation

31-1 INTERNAL AUDITOR ROLES AND RESPONSIBILITIES

As a major component of their service to management, internal auditors have a responsibility to help protect the assets of the organization. As has been discussed in the preceding chapters, auditors often perform this service by evaluating existing systems of internal controls and making recommendations to improve those controls. Control often breaks down and assets are lost or damaged when employees, acting under otherwise good faith, do not follow good control procedures. However, there is another side to the protection of assets through good control procedures. Sometimes employees and others may willfully violate control procedures for their own benefit or for other reasons. They may do this by performing a fraudulent or otherwise illegal act.

Internal auditors and others in the organization have a role in helping to prevent illegal acts and in detecting them when they occur. Two types of control procedures are usually in place here; loss prevention and fraud investigations. Loss prevention is a term frequently used today for the modern organization's internal protection functions. The loss-prevention function in a retail organization, for example, consists of the persons who apprehend shoplifters and turn them over to local police. While generally a separate organization from internal audit, both organizations should work together closely to help protect organization assets. This chapter will initially describe a typical loss-prevention function in a modern organization and how internal audit can either work with them or take responsibility for some of their functions in the smaller organization.

Dictionaries define fraud using such terms as "deceit, trickery, sharp practices or breaches of confidence used to gain some unfair or dishonest advantage." Fraud is committed when someone operates outside of the rules. As a very elementary example of a fraud, an employee responsible for opening mail containing payments in the form of checks and occasional cash who steals some of that incoming cash, changing records or taking other actions to avoid detection of the theft, is guilty of a fraud. Normally frauds are larger incidents, but the employee altering records to steal small amounts of cash or the buyer that agrees to a "side deal" for personal benefit are both guilty of frauds. Internal audit often plays a key role in helping to detect and investigate frauds in the organization. Working with the loss-prevention organization, the legal staff, and others, internal audit often becomes very involved in supporting fraud-related investigations that become necessary within the modern organization. This chapter will discuss fraud and fraud-investigation techniques, a knowledge of which is an important component in the modern internal auditor's set of skills.

The modern internal auditor, however, should approach fraud-related reviews with a level of caution and conservatism. Internal auditors should never think of themselves as Agent 007 or some other detective figure when investigating fraud. The Standards for the Professional Practice of Internal Auditing provide thorough guidance on the deterrence, detection, investigation, and reporting of fraud. These matters were originally introduced as part of SIAS No. 3 and exerpts from the standards are included in the Chapter 5 discussion of professional standards. The reader may wish to consult those materials again.

31-2 LOSS PREVENTION

The loss-prevention function in the modern organization represent the organization's internal police. However, an effective loss-prevention function should be more than just the plant guards who check employee badges at the entrace or determine that everyone is parking their cars in the correct areas. A modern loss-prevention organization is responsible for establishing control procedures to protect against the loss of assets, to detect incidences where those losses could occur, and to identify and apprehend persons responsible for taking or attempting to take organization assets.

A loss-prevention function is usually separate from internal audit in the modern organization, but the two often work together very closely. Internal auditors need to understand how their loss-prevention function operates and how to coordinate activities. In some smaller organizations without a formal loss-prevention function, internal audit may be called upon to assume some of the duties of a typical loss-prevention function. While these duties should not reduce internal audit's other many important services to management, as discussed in previous chapters, the modern internal auditor should understand the role of a loss-prevention function and should assume appropriate responsibilities in that area when necessary.

(a) LOSS-PREVENTION FUNCTION IN THE ORGANIZATION

While internal audit departments have a direct reporting relationship to the audit committees of their boards of directors as well as a dotted-line relationship to the organization's financial function, loss-prevention functions do not always follow as consistent a pattern. Many loss-prevention departments have evolved from an organization's building security function, the plant guards. Rather than loss prevention, they were called ''building security'' or some similar name. These persons often had law enforcement backgrounds, wore police-like uniforms, and represented internal security to the organization. When a theft or similar act occurred, they were called upon to help out. In the early days, the role of loss prevention often involved little more than apprehending the individual, writing up the incident, and calling the local police if necessary.

Over the years, the roles of these facility security functions have changed. Just as internal auditors have changed from a group once responsible for detecting errors in books and records to a group that recommends improved controls, security functions now often recommend procedures to prevent thefts and other losses rather than to just catch the malefactor after the fact. With this changed emphasis, security functions began to be known as *loss-prevention functions*. Loss prevention often works very closely with internal audit, and some organizations today have loss prevention even reporting to the director of internal auditing.

Although loss prevention's goals and objectives are different from those of internal audit, the modern internal auditor should understand the role of loss prevention in the modern organization and how loss prevention relates to internal audit. In most instances, these two activities should be coordinated. In others, there should be a strong sharing of information between the two in order to create a more effective organization. Internal auditors should also understand that all loss-prevention functions are not the same—often depending upon the organization's area of business operations. These differences also arise because loss-prevention functions do not follow the same set of professional standards as are found for internal audit. Chapter 5 discussed the professional practices for internal auditing, and any credible internal audit organization must follow those standards. Loss-prevention functions follow a mixture of control and legal protection standards, but do not have the same common body of knowledge as is communicated through the standards of The Institute of Internal Auditors. Because loss prevention's functions will differ according to the type of organization where it operates, we will consider loss-prevention activities as they operate in two major business areas; consumer products and industrial manufacturing organizations.

(i) Loss Prevention in Consumer Products Organizations. The need for a formal loss-prevention function is perhaps greatest in a consumer products or services organization, and in a retail sales organization in particular. In these companies, customers generally walk into stores unescorted to examine merchandise for potential purchase but a very small minority of these customers may be attempted to steal those goods. Closely monitoring every customer to determine if he or she is attempting to steal something is neither very effective nor does it encourage new customers. Most people are honest and would be offended if the scrutiny were too close. What is needed are procedures to prevent customers and others from stealing and to detect and identify those who do. This is the role of loss prevention in the consumer service or retail organization.

Loss prevention is generally responsible for working with management in a sales organization to help design stores, develop store procedures, and install systems to prevent theft, both by customers and employees. Depending upon the size and nature of the organization, loss prevention's role in the design of stores may include such things as reviewing plans and making recommendations for the following:

- Clear lines of sight throughout the facility so that a thief cannot operate behind a counter or rack without fear of detection.
- Store entrances clearly observable by personnel within the store.
- Cash collection stations in protective areas appropriate to the nature of the business.
- Storage areas located in secure rooms such that merchandise cannot leave these rooms without detection either through store or back door entrances.

Many of the above are just principles of good store design, and a loss-prevention function is generally not responsible for deciding how these ideas will be implemented in a new facility. However, the effective loss-prevention function should review new facility layouts and make recommendations to others responsible for the actual design and implementation of new store facilities. This is an example of how a modern loss-prevention function can move beyond the role of ''store policeman'' and offer advice to management to help prevent losses.

An effective loss-prevention function in a consumer service or retail organization should also help to establish effective procedures with the organization to prevent losses. This might include a store ''hot line'' system allowing sales personnel to report potential shoplifting, procedures for labeling and pricing all merchandise, and procedures for inspecting the personal effects of employees as they leave the store during the evening. These ''hot line'' operations will be discussed in Chapter 35, on business ethics and social responsibility. Again, loss prevention will not be directly responsible for implementing all of these types of procedures, but it may make recommendations to store operations management and actually directly implement only some of them. As an example of the latter, the pickup of merchandise that does not go through the normal sales process, such as goods returned for repair, can cause control problems as other goods could leave by that same route. Loss prevention may work with store management to develop a better procedure for customer pickup of repaired or lay-by merchandise by suggesting, for example, that all such merchandise be distributed over a pickup desk upon presentation of a customer receipt. In this instance, loss prevention will then actually staff such a function.

Loss prevention's third major responsibility in a customer service or retail organization is to help develop and implement procedures to prevent losses. This may involve procedures to apprehend a shoplifter and report the matter to local police, to make certain that cash from point-of-sale stations is properly delivered to a cashier function, and to establish procedures for the approval of customer personal checks. In this role, loss prevention may play a direct role in a retail organization with large stores by actually having a physical presence at the store. In organizations with smaller units, such as a chain of drive-in restaurants, loss prevention will be responsible for establishing the procedures to be used by all units. They may also visit these units from time to time to determine that procedures are being followed.

An internal audit function operating in a retail organization should be aware of these loss-prevention activities and should periodically review them to determine that they are operating in an effective manner. In a typical commercial or retail organization, internal audit will be performing audits of individual stores on a periodic basis. Among other areas for review, the internal auditors performing the store review should review the loss-prevention activities at that store. If the loss-prevention function separately reports to the director of internal audit, those concerns should be discussed directly with internal audit's loss-prevention counterparts. However, they always should be included in audit reports, as with any other deficiency in the unit.

(ii) Loss Prevention in Industrial Organizations.   While the loss-prevention function often has the reputation as the in-house police force in a retail organization, they are often viewed as the plant or front gate guards in industrial organizations. This perception is not true for the modern loss-prevention function. Just as the previous paragraphs have described the expanded role of loss prevention for the retail organization, an effective loss-prevention function should have a much more important role in the modern industrial organization. It is often responsible for developing safety and security facilities, establishing asset-protection programs within the organization, and helping with investigations of potential wrongdoing.

In a modern industrial facility, safety can be a major concern. Management is concerned that all of its employees operate in a safe work environment and follow procedures to prevent accidents, which can slow production, create dissent within the workforce, and be very expensive to the organization in terms of insurance or workman's compensation program claims. Direct factory management is responsible for establishing procedures for a safe workplace. The modern loss-prevention function is often responsible for monitoring safety practices on an ongoing basis and reporting potential problems to appropriate levels of management. It may also take the responsibility for preparing accident reports and for initiating the filing of reports to insurance carriers.

Environmental concerns are closely related to industrial safety and are often a responsibility of the modern loss-prevention function. The United States and many other industrial countries have strong laws covering environmental matters. For instance, the plant facility is prohibited from dumping industrial wastes down rivers or drains, and cleaning substances and other chemicals used around the workplace must be safe. Where contact with them might cause a problem, workers need access to antidotes and protective mechanisms on an immediate basis. A modern loss-prevention function often may have the responsibility of helping to implement an environmental controls program and then monitoring it to determine that procedures are followed.

Asset protection in a retail organization is perhaps a much easier task for a loss-prevention function than are similar programs in industrial facilities. Depending upon the nature of the goods manufactured or used for operations, both employees and others may be tempted to steal goods. Thefts may range from a hand tool used in the manufacturing process to an integrated circuit chip used in an electronics facility to an entire truckload of finished goods shipped to a fraudulent address. Many activities here might be considered outright frauds and will be discussed later in this chapter. Loss prevention often has a very important role in helping to investigate such frauds. It has a more important day-to-day role in helping to prevent both major and minor thefts from occurring. While procedures will vary considerably depending upon the nature of the organization, the modern loss-prevention organization might be responsible for implementing procedures such as:

- Establishing and manning a metal-scanning device at employee exits to prevent the theft of goods; this is similar to airport passenger security systems.

- Monitoring delivery trucks arriving or leaving from facility gates and reviewing paperwork to document the outbound shipments.

- Reviewing employee desk and office areas during off shifts to determine that no key drawings or other confidential documents are left in the open.

The above are just a few of the things that a modern industrial loss-prevention function might do to minimize organization asset losses. These activities should be subject to management review and any findings should be reported to facility management. Internal audit should develop a good understanding of the types of procedures performed by loss prevention and might make suggestions for improvements based upon internal audit's understanding of internal control procedures. In addition, internal audit may want to modify some of its operational audit procedures in light of relevant loss-prevention activities.

A third important area of activity for the modern loss-prevention function in an industrial organization is the investigation of potential or actual wrongdoing. This activity takes a rather different direction from apprehension in a retail environment, where many of the problems are the result of shoplifters or employees trying to steal merchandise. In a manufacturing facility, employees and outsiders still may try to steal, but they will often use methods that are more difficult to detect. For example, a dishonest shipping clerk may make arrangements with a truck driver to steal merchandise by loading it on a truck as otherwise legitimate merchandise. This may be difficult to observe and will only become apparent after a physical inventory when losses are detected. In such a situation, management may ask loss prevention to perform an investigation. They may do such things as arrange to have an informant hired as an employee on the shipping dock to observe and report any improper procedures. In this role, loss prevention is acting as a detective, a role rather different from internal audit in most circumstances.

Internal audit should be familiar with the activities and the capabilities of loss prevention in these areas. While both loss prevention and senior management may want to keep any such investigation activities highly confidential, internal audit should be aware of these capabilities and request help where appropriate. In particular, loss prevention investigation and apprehension activities may be useful to internal audit in the types of fraud investigations discussed later in this chapter.

(iii) Other Loss-Prevention Activities.   Although the preceding sections have discussed loss-prevention functions in retail or manufacturing organizations, loss-prevention functions can or should operate within many industries. Any industry handling assets that can be subject to theft, such as a bank or a securities firm, will or at least should have a loss-prevention function. Internal audit should gain an understanding of the capabilities of that function and develop a mechanism for an informal exchange of information where appropriate. Loss prevention and internal audit should become close allies, sharing information with each other and coordinating activities when appropriate.

Sometimes, internal audit will find that the organization's loss-prevention function still operates in the "parking lot guard" mode of earlier days. The director of internal audit may initially want to discuss this with the head of loss prevention and suggest a more active approach for loss prevention. Using experience gained from other organizations, internal audit may suggest improvements to make loss prevention a more effective component of the organization's internal control structure. If these recommendations are received favorably, internal audit can work with loss prevention to suggest areas to improve loss prevention's control procedure activities. If loss prevention does not want to change and if a risk-based analysis indicates that a stronger loss-prevention function could be a more effective component of the internal control structure, internal audit may want to suggest changes to more senior management. If there continues to be a lack of interest, internal audit may want to perform an operational review of the loss-prevention function, as discussed below, and to report findings and recommendations to improve the function.

(b) LOSS PREVENTION INTERNAL AUDIT ACTIVITIES

The loss-prevention function in the modern organization is very much part of the control structure, with a special role similar to internal audit. Internal audit and loss prevention can and should work closely together on many projects and in many areas. In some instances, internal audit may find itself involved in turf battles with loss prevention. Loss prevention may feel that it should have responsibility for some area while internal audit has different perceptions. This is particularly true when loss prevention becomes engaged in investigations that may seem similar to normal operational audits. If loss prevention reports to the director of internal audit, as has been discussed, these territory conflicts should not be a problem. Both organizations should have their own charters and plans. The director of internal audit, with the approval of senior management, should resolve any conflicts so that both functions operate for the greater good of the organization.

Problems sometimes arise when loss prevention reports through a different channel in the organization, perhaps to the head of plant operations. Both groups may have their own plans and should work on projects in a cooperative manner. However, there frequently may be conflicts—in particular when some operational group has a control-related concern and calls on loss prevention rather than internal audit for help. When appropriate, loss prevention should pass the request on to internal audit. However, sometimes a loss-prevention function in its enthusiasm may start on an examination that should have been handled by internal audit. Close communications between the two groups should prevent any conflicts, and requests for work should be passed in both directions, depending upon the nature of the request. It is important that each understand the other's responsibilities and capabilities.

As a separate operational component of the overall organization, internal audit may want to consider the loss-prevention function as a potential candidate for an operational review. This is particularly true if loss prevention is a separate organization with its own reporting relationships. It would then be considered in the audit-planning risk rankings, as was discussed in Chapter 8. If loss prevention, as an audit candidate, has been selected, the sections following discuss procedures for an operational audit of the loss prevention function.

If loss prevention also reports to the director of internal audit, this may pose a dilemma for the internal audit function. Internal audit can review its counterpart loss-prevention function, but disputes must be resolved by the director of internal audit, who would be responsible for both functions. Whether the audit came out clean or revealed some internal control concerns, the audit might be subject to comments or concerns by others in the organization about the level of independence and objectivity shown in the review. If loss prevention is a separate but independent component of the internal audit organization, any reviews of loss prevention might be best performed as an internal audit quality-assurance review. These reviews will be discussed in Chapter 33.

(i) Operational Audits of the Loss-Prevention Function.   Although loss prevention may be a separate organization with similar requirements for independence and objectivity as is found for internal audit, the loss-prevention function still should be considered a candidate for a periodic operational review by internal audit. Because internal audit should normally operate in a very cooperative basis with them, loss prevention may first ask "why?" when informed that internal audit plans to perform a review of its operation. However, internal audit management should justify the planned operational review through a formal risk-analysis process, as was discussed in Chapter 8. Senior management often places a high degree of trust in its loss-prevention function to provide adequate protection over organization assets. It often will understand loss prevention less than it understands the capabilities and services performed by internal audit.

Even if loss prevention reports through the director of internal audit, an operational review of loss prevention still may be justified. However, rather than announcing the operational review through the formal audit-scheduling procedures (as discussed in Chapter 7), the review of loss prevention may be treated similar to an internal audit quality-assurance review, as will be discussed in Chapter 33. However, the loss-prevention review should result in a formal audit report with appropriate findings and recommendations.

What types of operational review procedures should internal audit perform in a review of its loss-prevention function? This somewhat depends upon the specific industry and the associated risks. Any review should emphasize loss prevention's basic procedures, ranging from hiring practices, documentation of procedures, and coverage of high-risk organizational activities to loss prevention's investigation follow-up procedures. Although there may be many other areas that can be included in this type of review, Figure 31.1

Figure 31.1 Loss Prevention Operational Audit Procedures

31.01.01 Develop an understanding of the loss-prevention function, its responsibilities, and its reporting responsibilities within the organization. Assess whether loss prevention reports at a sufficiently high level.

31.01.02. Review personnel files for members of the loss-prevention organization to determine whether reference checks and other standard background investigations have been performed for new additions to the loss-prevention staff by the human resources organization.

31.01.03. Obtain an understanding of the loss-prevention annual project-planning process for ongoing activities and obtain a copy of the most recent plan. Also obtain an understanding of how loss-prevention responds to emergency situations and special projects requested by senior management.

31.01.04 If loss-prevention plans or operations do not cover certain major areas within the organization, such as receiving dock operations or employee product purchases, determine why these areas are not covered or determine what other functions in the organization have this responsibility.

31.01.05 Assess whether loss-prevention has a risk-analysis process in place to provide proper coverage of high-risk areas within the organization.

31.01.06 Determine if loss-prevention has documented procedures for normal operations, including investigative techniques, coordination with external authorities, follow-up, and preparing adequate project documentation.

31.01.07 Select several loss-prevention investigations or special projects completed over the past year and review documentation to assess compliance with loss-prevention standards.

31.01.08 Interview several members of senior management, including the director of internal auditing, to assess their feelings regarding the effectiveness of the loss-prevention function. Discuss any concerns with the director of loss-prevention to obtain clarification.

31.01.09 Assess whether loss-prevention has established appropriate communication links with other functions in the organization responsible for related activities such as internal audit or ethics.

31.01.10 Evaluate mechanisms in place to supply "tips" to loss-prevention and their procedures for investigating the matters and taking action if appropriate.

31.01.11 Review loss-prevention budgeting and cost-accounting procedures. Assess whether appropriate attention was given to the costs of various loss-prevention projects.

31.01.12 Depending upon their overall activities and charter, evaluate the appropriateness loss-prevention programs in place to educate employees and management on loss-prevention control procedures.

describes some basic control procedures for an operational review of the loss-prevention function.

Although an operational review of the loss-prevention function may cause some ill feelings, particularly if significant control weaknesses are detected, this can be a very valuable type of review for senior management. Internal audit normally performs operational reviews in many parts of the organization, providing management with its assessments of control strengths and weaknesses. Internal audit also reviews itself through the quality-assurance reviews that will be discussed in Chapter 33, and external auditors also assess the quality of internal audit, as will be discussed in Chapter 32. However, no separate or outside organization normally reviews the loss-prevention function. Internal audit, of course, should take care to make this type of review as constructive as possible, since the two organizations must cooperate very closely on other investigatory matters.

(ii) Loss Prevention Sample Audit Report Findings

A: Background Checks Lacking for Loss-Prevention Personnel. Although the human resources function has regular procedures for performing background checks for all new employees, we found that loss prevention does not perform these types of background checks. Rather, the director of loss prevention advised us that members of its staff, particularly the part-time guards, are hired from local police departments, which presumably have performed their own background checks. Others are hired by the director of loss prevention through contacts with other loss-prevention groups. There is no assurance that local police departments or others have performed background checks over these important employees.

Recommendation. All loss prevention employees, whether full- or part-time, should be subjected to the same human resource background check procedures as other employees. Procedures should be established to give all potential new loss-prevention employees this form of background check, and follow-up reviews should also be performed on existing members of the staff.

B: Loss-Prevention Activities Not Properly Documented. We found that loss prevention has no formal procedures documenting its activities and describing how loss prevention should be contacted by others in the organization when there are potential problems. Rather, loss prevention relies on its professional experiences to perform various procedures as well as on the knowledge of others regarding its utilization. As a result, we observed that two members of the loss prevention staff used totally different approaches in documenting similar loss-prevention investigations. One used very good procedures similar to audit workpapers while the other used only sketchy notes. Similarly, we found that management of the product ZZZ manufacturing line has had no contact with loss prevention despite the significant losses detected there in the last physical inventory. When interviewed by internal audit, the manager of the product ZZZ line, a new hire, was only generally aware of loss prevention and whom to contact for help.

Recommendation. All loss-prevention procedures should be formally documented following a set of consistent procedures. In addition, loss prevention should make these procedures available to other managers in the organization and should initiate a formal process to acquaint other departments with the capabilities and procedures used by loss prevention.

C: Plant Gates Not Properly Protected.   Loss prevention is responsible for monitoring access to both the front visitor's entrance and employee parking lots. Entrances to the employee parking lots are open throughout the day, and employees show their identification badges when they enter the plant through the rear entrances. Loss-prevention procedures call for all visitors passing through the front gate to stop and state their business to the guard, who will call ahead to determine if the visitor appears to be authorized. We observed that the front entrance gate is open virtually all of the time and the guard waves all visitors through unless the visitor specifically stops with a question. We also observed that the loss-prevention guard at the front entrance does not normally check badges or otherwise determine the business of visitors. As a result, unauthorized persons could enter the plant facility without challenge.

Recommendation.   Loss prevention should improve the overall plant entrance procedures. The gate to the front entrance should be closed and all visitors required to stop and state their business. The guard should then have procedures to call the persons being visited and to issue a visitor's badge before allowing the visitor to enter the facility. The employee entrance should be closed except for normal starting and ending times, with employees instructed to use the controlled main entrance at other times. Finally, the main-entrance guard should be instructed to challenge all visitors for proper identification and should control access to the remainder of the facility through a button-controlled type of interior door lock.

31-3 FRAUD

Both business-related publications and the more popular press contain frequent accounts of white-collar crime or management fraud. A company may declare bankruptcy, and subsequent news accounts may reveal that a member of management has defrauded the company through some type of side deal. A contractor may be accused of rigging construction bids in order to gain additional business. A local government official entrusted to invest pension plan funds may make arrangements in a less-than-arms-length transaction. In many cases, particularly when a company failure harms investors, the question always raised is, ''Where were the auditors?''

Although the popular press is increasingly filled with accounts of management fraud, there are no good statistics to indicate that fraudulent activities are increasing. In the United States, one need only think of the robber barons of the 1880s or the various schemes promoted in the 1920s. Due to increased information sources, we hear more about fraudulent activities these days. Financial-reporting requirements and computer databases mean that more data is available to outside reviewers. Financial reporters are able to comment on and explain complex fraudulent activities because of their increasing sophistication. In addition, our society has become much more aware of what are good ethical business practices.

Internal auditors can play a key role in the detection of and protection from fraudulent activities in the modern organization. Although many modern internal auditors will argue that they are responsible for assessing the operational effectiveness of organizations and are not policemen, management continues to look to internal audit to be sensitive to situations that might create an opportunity for fraud and then to test for potential fraudulent practices. Internal auditors should be aware of situations that could encourage fraudulent activities and should modify their procedures to look for controls that might encourage improper acts.

(a) FRAUD-DETECTION INTERNAL AUDIT ACTIVITIES

Fraud is an ever-present threat to the effective utilization of resources in an organization, and the risk of fraudulent activities should always be an important management concern. Existing fraud needs to be detected and potential fraud prevented to the extent practicable. Management at all levels has the primary responsibility for implementing and operating effective fraud-detection and -prevention control procedures. However, management will need assistance and quite properly looks to auditors, especially to its internal auditors, for assistance.

The question is then the extent to which internal audit is directly or indirectly responsible for detecting and preventing fraud. It is impossible for an internal auditor to detect and prevent *all* fraudulent activities. Even if internal audit performed very detailed transaction-level reviews, there could be unrecorded transactions, forgeries, and collusion that might not be discovered. In the absence of a known fraud that must be investigated, it is too costly to go beyond reasonable levels of fraud prevention while performing normal audit reviews. As discussed in earlier chapters, it is possible to overcontrol, and judgment is a basic ingredient in determining the nature and scope of auditor fraud-control efforts. Internal audit is faced with the challenge of giving fraud-detection activities the balanced attention they deserve while achieving the total range of internal auditing services. This challenge also includes helping all parties of interest to understand the desirability of properly balanced fraud-control efforts. This position has been consistently taken in all previous editions of this book.

(b) INTERNAL AND EXTERNAL AUDITOR RESPONSIBILITIES FOR FRAUD

In earlier days, the internal auditing profession was more directly concerned with fraud. As discussed in the opening chapters, this concern was part of internal audit's then-existing major orientation toward protective-type services, including compliance controls, accuracy of records, and the preservation of physical assets. This orientation reflected management's dependence on internal auditors for assistance in the detection of existing fraud. The situation began to change as the nature and scope of internal auditing services broadened to include a greater emphasis on fraud prevention versus fraud detection. All concerned parties generally decided that it was more beneficial to develop good systems of internal controls and managerial procedures that would reduce the possibilities of fraud rather than perform exhaustive reviews of transactions in order to look for detailed accounting records that might appear fraudulent.

The shift away from fraud detection through better systems and procedures helped to make it possible for internal auditors to provide more constructive services via operational auditing activities. Over time, these fraud-detection services became a proportionately smaller part of the total work of internal audit. However, internal auditors should always be conscious of their very real responsibilities for helping to prevent and detect fraud. Today the pendulum has swung back somewhat to a greater interest in fraud prevention and detection by internal auditors. Management has been held increasingly accountable for various white-collar crimes, such as improper payments or embezzlement. The Foreign Corrupt Practices Act, the Organizational Sentencing Guidelines discussed below, and other legislative initiatives have heightened the need to have better systems of internal control. In attempting to have a strong fraud-prevention and -detection program, management has often called on its finance personnel, internal auditors, investigators, and external auditors for assistance. Internal audit often finds that an increased amount of resources needs to be devoted to this area.

This emphasis on fraud is reflected in the Standards for the Professional Practice of Internal Auditing, which were discussed in Chapter 5. Section 280 of those standards states:

> *In exercising due professional care, internal auditors should be alert to the possibility of intentional wrongdoing, errors and omissions, inefficiency, waste, ineffectiveness, and conflicts of interest. They should also be alert to those conditions and activities where irregularities are most likely to occur. . . . Internal audit cannot give absolute assurance that noncompliance or irregularities do not exist. Nevertheless, the possibility of material irregularities or noncompliance should be considered whenever internal audit undertakes an internal auditing assignment.*

The Standards do not state that internal audit is *responsible* for the detection of fraud. They do require, however, that internal auditors be alert for potential fraudulent conditions, recognize that they can exist, and consider the possibility of fraud when performing audit assignments. As the Standards point out, an internal auditor cannot give *absolute assurance* that there were no irregularities in an area reviewed. Internal audit should make this point clear in its charter, approved by the audit committee of the board. Nevertheless, this incorrect perception often places internal audit in a difficult situation when fraudulent activities are detected subsequent to a review where internal audit found no fraud. When these events occur, management often asks ''Where were the auditors?''—expecting internal audit to have somehow discovered such matters.

The American Institute of Certified Public Accountants (AICPA) has similarly changed its approach to fraud over the years, with resultant changes in public accounting standards. In the early 1990s there was strong emphasis by external auditors on the detection of fraud because audits primarily involved cash records. Early auditing textbooks indicated that the detection and prevention of fraud errors were among the main objectives of an audit. This gradually changed over the next three decades until accounting literature began to emphasize that external auditors *did not have any direct responsibility* for the detection of fraud. There were many reasons for the change. In particular, the growth of business entities in size and complexity required external auditors to use sampling and testing techniques rather than detailed reviews of all transactions, making it especially difficult to detect irregularities. In addition, the inability of an external auditor to detect fraud involving unrecorded transactions, theft, and other matters made the profession more cautious. This became more important as lawsuits were filed against accounting firms, holding them responsible for losses resulting from frauds. At the same time, there was a growing trend toward strengthening systems of internal accounting control that could help prevent fraud and related deficiencies.

As an example of the AICPA's earlier approach to fraud, in 1951 the organization adopted a position in its Statements on Auditing Procedures that read:

> *The ordinary examination incident to the issuance of an opinion respecting financial statements is not designed and cannot be relied upon to disclose defalcations and other similar irregularities, although their discovery frequently results. . . . If an auditor were to attempt to discover defalcations and similar irregularities he would*

have to extend his work to a point where its costs would be prohibitive. It is generally recognized that good internal control and surety bonds provide protection much more cheaply. . . .

In effect, that early auditing standard stated that the external auditor was *not responsible* for the detection of fraud. This position was criticized by many for its attempt to relieve external auditors of any responsibility for the detection of fraud. In recognition of this, the AICPA issued Statement on Auditing Procedures No. 30 in 1960, which was subsequently incorporated into the AICPA's Statement on Auditing Standards (SAS) No. 1 in November 1972. Section 110.05 of that Statement said:

The responsibility of the independent auditor for failure to detect fraud (which responsibility differs as to clients and others) arises only when such failure clearly results from non-compliance with generally accepted auditing standards.

This standard again somewhat left external auditors off the hook on fraud-related matters. In light of increased litigation against accountants and the concern of external auditors that there may be material misstatements as a result of fraud, the profession then developed SAS No. 16, which superseded SAS No. 1 as it dealt with the auditors' responsibility for fraud. This stated in part:

. . . under generally accepted auditing standards, the independent auditor has the responsibility, with the inherent limitations of the auditing process, to plan his examination to search for errors or irregularities that would have a material effect on the financial statements, and to exercise due skill and care in the conduct of that examination.

This Statement required external auditors to look specifically for irregularities that may have a material effect on the financial statements. This standard still did not relieve the pressure on external auditors to detect and report on fraudulent activities. There was a series of well-publicized major frauds in the United States in the 1970s that were not detected by external auditors reviewing those financial records. External auditor responsibilities have changed in recent years, as discussed below.

(i) Current External Audit Fraud Responsibilities and the "Expectation Gap." By the late 1980s, a series of dramatic financial failures coupled with recent "clean" external auditor opinions caused investors, newspaper and television commentators, and even members of the U.S. Congress to again ask the question, "Where were the auditors?" Initially, the public accounting profession defended its then-current standards by stating that, as public accountants, they were not expected to find the frauds. They performed their audits of the companies that soon were placed in bankruptcy following the clean audit opinions, but the auditing standards did not point them to anything that might cause them to discover the fraud. Their audit reports followed the Standards as they then existed, which allowed the auditor to state that financial statements were "fairly presented" in accordance with generally accepted accounting principles. These external auditor reports did not talk about other problems. This whole matter became known as the "expectation gap," where investors and users of audited financial statements *expected* the audited financial statements to give them more information about the potential problems. There was a gap between these expectations and actual delivery.

As a result of public clamor about the lack of content in audited financial statements, the AICPA released eight new Statements on Auditing Standards (SASs) in 1988. These came to be known as the *expectation gap standards,* and they covered such matters as a revised audit report, communications with audit committees, new internal control standards, and the auditor's responsibility for detecting and reporting errors and irregularities. The Standard on internal control, SAS no. 55,[1] was discussed in Chapter 2, "Fundamentals of Control." Others are more of interest to external auditors than to internal auditors and more information regarding them can be found in a book on public accounting auditing. SAS No. 53, *The Auditor's Responsibility to Detect and Report Errors and Irregularities,* is of interest here in order to better understand the external auditor's responsibility for detecting fraudulent financial reporting.

We previously discussed SAS No. 16, which admitted that the external auditor had some responsibility to search for fraud in the course of a normal financial audit. SAS No. 53 now requires an auditor to "design the audit to provide reasonable assurance of detecting errors and irregularities." It also states that external auditors should "exercise . . . the proper degree of skepticism to achieve reasonable assurance that errors and irregularities will be detected." This professional skepticism requires the auditor to assume that management is neither honest nor dishonest. The SAS goes on to list 21 factors, summarized in Table 31.1, that should be considered, in combination, by the external auditor to assess the risk that errors and irregularities may cause the financial statements to contain significant misstatements. Many of these do not point directly to fraudulent acts but to problems where the organization's financial statement could contain nonfraudulent but significant errors.

SAS No. 53 suggests that external auditors should take a very skeptical view of management when they perform their financial statement reviews. This is rather contrary to internal auditors, who are aware of the possibility of dishonest acts but also primarily act to serve management. Despite the issuance of SAS No. 53, external audits generally have not taken the totally skeptical stance suggested by the auditing standard as they continue to service their client management and boards of directors. However, internal audit should be aware of these audit standards and of how they may tend to reduce the external auditor's expectation gaps.

(ii) Foreign Corrupt Practices Act.   Despite all of the clamor about potential fraudulent activities, there has been very little general legislation that establishes laws against fraudulent practices. In the United States, most frauds are prosecuted under the mail or wire fraud statutes, which essentially make it illegal to send anything with an intent to deceive. One United States act, however,—the Foreign Corrupt Practices Act (FCPA)—particularly addresses fraudulent activities. Although first passed in 1972 and modified slightly in 1976, the act continues to be a major statute prohibiting certain fraudulent activities. The FCPA also has a record-keeping section that was discussed in Chapter 2, on internal control.

---

[1] American Institute of Certified Public Accountants, Statements on Auditing Standards No. 53, *The Auditor's Responsibility for the Detection of Errors and Irregularities* (New York: AICPA, 1988).

Table 31.1 SAS No. 53 Factors That May Cause Irregularities

Management Characteristics
- Management operating and financing decisions are dominated by a single person.
- Management's attitude toward financial reporting is unduly aggressive.
- Management (particularly senior accounting personnel) turnover is high.
- Management places undue emphasis on meeting earnings projections.
- Management's reputation in the business community is poor.

Operating and Industry Characteristics
- Profitability of entity relative to its industry is inadequate or inconsistent.
- Sensitivity of operating results to economic factors (inflation, interest rates, unemployment, etc.) is high.
- Rate of change of entity's industry is rapid.
- Direction of change in entity's industry is declining, with many business failures.
- Organization is decentralized without adequate monitoring.
- Internal or external matters that raise substantial doubt about the entity's ability to continue as a going concern are present.

Engagement Characteristics
- Many contentious or difficult accounting issues are present.
- Significant difficult-to-audit transactions or balances are present.
- Significant and unusual related-party transactions not in the ordinary course of business are present.
- Nature, cause (if known), or the amount of known and likely misstatements detected in the audit prior period's financial statements is significant.
- It is a new client with no prior audit history or sufficient information is not available from predecessor auditor.

The FCPA was initiated in the aftermath of the United States presidential election of 1972, which was surrounded by a series of allegations of illegal and questionable acts that eventually resulted in the resignation of the president. The events were first precipitated by a burglary of the Democratic party headquarters then located in a building complex known as Watergate. The resulting scandal and related investigations became known as the "Watergate" affair. Investigators found, among other matters, evidence of various bribes and other questionable practices that were not covered by legislation. (As an aside, that "gate" suffix has continued to be used by the press to label almost any allegation of improper activity. For example, in 1992, when the new Clinton administration fired members of the White House travel office and tried to bring in political friends to run the function, the scandal became known as "Travelgate.")

In 1976, the Securities and Exchange Commission (SEC) submitted to the United States Senate Committee on Banking, Housing and Urban Affairs a report on its Watergate-related investigations into questionable and illegal corporate payments and practices. The report recommended legislation to prohibit bribes and other questionable payments. In response to the recommendations, the Foreign Corrupt Practices Act (FCPA) was enacted in December 1977. The FCPA contains provisions specifying requirements for necessary books and records, internal accounting control, and bribery prohibitions. Chapter 2 discussed the provisions of the act as they pertained to basic internal control requirements. The focus here is the effect of the FCPA on possible fraud and other types of corrupt practices.

The act requires organizations to "make and keep books, records, and accounts, which in reasonable detail, accurately and fairly reflect the transactions and dispositions of the assets of the issuer." This provision applies to United States organizations that have securities registered under Section 12 of the Securities Exchange Act of 1934 and does not apply to nonpublic companies. It was adopted as a result of SEC comments that illegal payments disclosed in SEC filings were often hidden by either the falsification of records or maintenance of incomplete records. The provision requires that issuers keep records that accurately reflect their transactions. The phrase "in reasonable detail" was added to give effect to concerns by the accounting profession that no accounting system could achieve complete freedom from error. While there is no exact definition of "in reasonable detail," the intent of the rule appears to be that records should reflect transactions in conformity with accepted methods of recording economic events, preventing off-the-books slush funds and payments of bribes.

The act also requires that companies with registered securities maintain a system of internal accounting controls that should be sufficient to provide reasonable assurances that transactions are authorized and recorded to permit preparation of financial statements in conformity with generally accepted accounting principles. Accountability is to be maintained for assets and access to the assets permitted only as authorized. Also, recorded assets are to be physically inventoried periodically, with any differences analyzed.

Because the cost of fully controlling each organization transaction cannot be justified in the face of potential risks, the act uses the term "reasonable assurances" when mandating its accounting control requirements. Management must estimate and evaluate these cost-versus-benefit relationships, exercising judgment as to the appropriate steps to be taken. Although the concept of cost-versus-benefit decisions is not mentioned in the FCPA, based upon the conference committee's minutes, it is apparent that Congress intended that management have the right to make some cost-versus-benefit decisions as to its internal controls.

The bribery provisions of the act, which are applicable to both issuers of securities and all other United States domestic concerns, prohibit giving bribes to a foreign official. The maximum penalty for violation of the bribery prohibitions by an organization is $1,000,000, and for individuals who participate in bribes, the punishment is a fine of not more than $10,000, or imprisonment not to exceed more than five years, or both.

The purpose of the bribery payment must be to influence a foreign official to assist an organization in obtaining business. The offer or gift must be intended to induce the recipient to misuse an official position, such as to direct business to the payer or a related client. Excluded from the definition of foreign officials are government employees whose functions are clerical or ministerial in nature. Thus, so-called "grease payments" to minor officials to get their help in expediting some process are permissible.

Various groups may be involved in determining the organization's compliance with FCPA standards. The controller or CFO is responsible for the financial-control system of the organization, while the external auditors are involved through reviewing management's representations of its control system. Legal counsel is interested because of the need for interpretations of compliance with the act. Internal audit should be very involved because of the responsibilities for the evaluation of internal control. Also, in many organizations, the board of directors and its audit committee have taken an active part in directing reviews of internal controls. Although these activities were initiated to assure compliance with the FCPA, they have continued because of a general management recognition of the importance of good internal controls.

Many years have passed since the FCPA was first introduced, and both internal auditors and other members of management sometimes all but forget about it. After its initial introduction in the mid 1970s, the FCPA received considerable attention in business and auditing publications, and some consulting firms developed quite a business in providing compliance procedures for dealing with the act. However, in subsequent years there has been minimal enforcement activity, and the FCPA is often all but forgotten by members of management. Nevertheless, the FCPA remains an active statute and defines an area where an organization can encounter significant legal problems if it is involved in fraudulent activities that may come under the act.

(iii) Treadway Commission and COSO. Even though the FCPA, with its record-keeping requirements, was passed in the late 1970s, internal control failures and other incidents of management fraud continued through the early 1980s. A series of accounting professional organizations, including the IIA and the AICPA, formed a commission in the early 1980s to consider the problem of fraudulent financial reporting and to recommend some improvements. This group became know as the Treadway Commission—named after its chair—and issued its report in 1987.[2] The Treadway Commission developed a long list of recommendations to improve the integrity of financial reporting, including the following:

- Senior management must identify, understand, and assess the factors that may cause the company's financial statements to be fraudulently misstated.

- Organizations should maintain an effective internal audit function, staffed with an adequate number of qualified personnel.

- Internal auditors should consider the implications of their nonfinancial [operational] audit findings on the company's financial statements.

- Audit committees should have adequate resources and authority to discharge their responsibilities.

The above are just a sampling of a long list of recommendations from the Treadway Commission report. Another was that "The commission's sponsoring organizations should establish a body to guide public companies in internal control." This recommendation was strongly accepted by the accounting profession and resulted in the Committee of Sponsoring Organizations (COSO) report, which was discussed in Chapter 2. Other portions of this report discussed standards to improve the integrity of financial statements. The Treadway Commission report did not discuss fraud in the context discussed elsewhere in this chapter; however, it provides some important foundation blocks that will help organizations improve the integrity of their financial statements.

(iv) Organizational Sentencing Guidelines. The preparation of fraudulent financial statements and other violations of the FCPA are clearly illegal acts. However, before 1992, the courts viewed violations of the act as white-collar crimes, with less importance than more traditional criminal acts such as robbery or kidnapping. As a result, executives

---

[2] National Commission on Fraudulent Financial Reporting, *Report of the National Commission on Fraudulent Financial Reporting,* 1987.

responsible for the preparation of fraudulent financial statements that harmed many investors were often punished with little more than a slap on the wrist. Often, an employee found guilty of embezzling company funds for personal benefit may have received a harsh prison sentence, while an executive who approved improper financial transactions that improved that executive's annual bonus may not have even been punished for the action. The same situation with another executive and another company but a different geographic area might have resulted in a prison sentence for the executive. In the United States, this all changed with the introduction of the Organizational Sentencing Guidelines.

In 1992, the United States Congress passed a law requiring certain minimum and maximum fines and prison sentences for various acts of white-collar crime. This has come to be known as the Organizational Sentencing Guidelines. The Guidelines cover punishments for both individuals and organizations who are found guilty of violations of various federal statutes. In recent years, due to the increasing size of the United States government and its regulatory agencies, the number of laws and regulations with statutory criminal punishments has grown quite large. Some of these include the following:

- *Laws Covering an Organization's Relations with Outside Parties*
    - Laws covering relations with competitors, including the Sherman Act, the Clayton Act, and the Robinson-Patman Act
    - The Copyright Act of 1976
    - Collection practices laws, including the Civil Rights Act, the Fair Debt Act, and the Fair Credit Reporting Act
    - A large group of acts covering gift-giving and -receiving, including the Ethics Reform Act of 1989, the Federal Election Campaign Act, Illegal Bribery and Illegal Gratuity Act, the FCPA, and the Hobbs Act
    - Procurement- and contracting-related laws, including the Civil Rights Act, the Walsh-Healy Act, and the Davis-Bacon Act of 1931

- *Laws Covering an Organization's Relations with Government Agencies*
    - General laws covering gift-giving, lobbying, and relations with foreign governments
    - Criminal violations of tax statutes
    - Criminal violations of regulations from various Federal agencies, including the SEC, DOE, and OSHA

- *Labor Related Laws* (Including Employee Benefits)
    - Various wage and hour laws, as well as laws covering relations with unions
    - The Worker Adjustment and Retraining Notification Act
    - Labor-Management Reporting and Disclosure Act
    - Americans with Disabilities Rehabilitation Act
    - Equal Employment Opportunities Act
    - Immigration Reform and Control Act
    - ERISA and COBRA

- *Other Federal Laws and Regulations*
    - Records-Retention Regulations
    - Product Liability Laws
    - Tariff and Trade Regulations

The above list is not all-inclusive. Its purpose is not to define but only to illustrate many of the regulations in effect today. Many of these have been on the books for years, but the courts have taken little enforcement action against organizations or the individuals managing those organizations. The Organizational Sentencing Guidelines have somewhat changed this. Now, if an organization or its management is found to be guilty of a violation of one of these federal statutes, the judge often has no choice but to impose punishments following the Organization Sentencing Guidelines.

The guidelines also specify a series of mitigating factors that allow a judge to substantially reduce a fine or other punishment. For example, if the organization has a formal employee Code of Ethical and Business Conduct and a formal process to monitor compliance with the code, and has established investigation and disciplinary procedures, the judge is allowed to substantially reduce any punishments under the Organizational Sentencing Guidelines. These mitigating factors very much point to the need for an organization to establish a formal ethics and compliance system. The sentencing guidelines and compliance programs will be discussed again in more detail in Chapter 35, "Business Ethics and Social Responsibility."

The purpose of this book is not to brief internal auditors on the specifics of all of the various laws and regulations in addition to the FCPA, previously discussed. Many of those laws cover some very large, total organization issues beyond the scope of most operational audits. In other instances, an internal auditor can meet with the organization legal staff to gain a greater understanding of the elements of one or another law or regulation. However, internal auditors should be aware of the Organizational Sentencing Guidelines and how they might increase punishments if the organization or its key managers are in violation of one or another law.

(c) INTERNAL CONTROLS TO PREVENT AND DETECT FRAUD

Regardless of differing opinions on whether internal auditors and external auditors have a responsibility to detect fraud, management tends to look to them in fraud matters. As discussed previously, when a fraudulent act is committed, the question is invariably asked: "Where were the auditors?" or "When was the last audit?" Even though they may not want it, this responsibility is placed on auditors to explain why their last examination did not reveal the fraud, or at least disclose the internal control weakness that led to the fraud. The auditors' responsibility is thus seen as doing their work in such a professional manner that, if fraud exists, the chances are that it will be exposed. In addition, management expects both internal and external auditors to identify opportunities to provide more prevention, since prevention is preferable to detection where frauds are concerned.

There are, of course, limits to the ability of any organization to prevent fraud. No system of internal control can prevent an employee from stealing cash that he handles, and no controls can prevent a purchasing agent from colluding with her supplier. Also, no control can be expected to disclose a fraud the instant it is committed. However, management looks to the auditors to be imaginative in the application of comprehensive and well-thought-out audit programs so that, if fraud exists, there will be a reasonable assurance that it is discovered. Moreover, they especially look to internal auditors to detect or help prevent fraud because of their deeper involvement in the total activities of the organization.

(i) Consideration of Fraud in Operational Audits. Internal audit is in a unique position to identify potentially fraudulent situations during the course of other audit projects. Internal audit's ongoing reviews and presence in the organization can play a strong role in preventing fraud and other illegal acts. Internal audit should always have a supplemental objective of considering controls to prevent fraud, as well as procedures to potentially detect fraud as part of all operational audits planned and performed. While these fraud-detection and -prevention control procedures should not be the major control procedure in all audits, they should always be given greater emphasis when the audit covers an area with a higher potential risk of fraud. These preventive and detective fraud-audit procedures could take place, among other areas, as part of the following types of general reviews:

- *Automated Systems Reviews.* Reviews of automated systems should consider the extent to which fraud prevention and detection are given some consideration, along with other operational objectives. Reviews should consider such areas as program-to-program balancing, file-change procedures, and access controls. Because of the technical complexity, computer-based fraudulent acts can be difficult to detect and severe in their impact. Computer-assisted audit procedures, as were discussed in Chapter 12, can often be useful here.

- *Reviews of Potentially Fraudulent Operational Activities.* Auditors should always be alert to the possibilities of fraud in their reviews of operating activities carried out by organizational personnel. This should include a constructive evaluation of managerial capabilities and performance. Internal audit should always have a skeptical eye, but auditees should never be accused of potential wrongdoing in the course of these internal audits. Rather, the matter should be clearly documented and discussed with management and appropriate authorities. The emphasis for these types of operational audits should always be on internal control improvements.

- *Participation in Formal Fraud Investigations.* Auditors should offer to cooperate with loss prevention and other organizational personnel that have been assigned responsibilities in connection with the investigation of actual or suspected fraud. For example, if the organization has a formal loss-prevention security function, as discussed previously, internal audit should arrange to work with it in various investigations, as appropriate.

- *Special Fraud Audits.* Internal audit may be requested by management to carry out special assignments relating to fraud or potential fraud. These fraud investigations will be discussed in more detail later in this chapter.

In all of these efforts, an internal auditor should seek directly and indirectly to balance fraud-oriented efforts with the audit's other objectives. Unless engaged in a special investigation or a specific fraud audit, an internal auditor should not focus on potential fraud-detection activities at the expense of the prime objectives of an audit.

With the current increased emphasis on preventing, detecting, and investigating fraud, internal audit is often faced with the problem of resources to perform fraud-related procedures along with other audit work. Normal coverage of areas on a recurring basis may be disrupted by fraud audit investigation efforts. In some instances, internal auditors have had to curtail operational auditing and their resultant recommendations for cost savings due to management demands for fraud or loss prevention–related reviews. This can be especially frustrating when it has taken many years to develop an operational auditing capability with demonstrated results.

In order to accomplish overall audit objectives with available resources, audit priorities must be set carefully in coordination with management. Based on previous experience, an estimated amount of time should be budgeted for special fraud-related audits throughout the year as well as fraud work in some specific audits. In some cases, the fraud-related functions performed by internal audit may be better handled by others, such as the loss-prevention function, law officials, or other departmental personnel. To make time available for both fraud and operational audits, it may be necessary to lengthen the cycle for audit coverage. Overall, internal audit has to weigh the benefits of various audit efforts to arrive at the best utilization of audit time. The objective is that there should be time available both to perform normal audit procedures and to carry out any requested fraud-detection responsibilities.

(ii) Warning Signals for Fraud. Although internal auditors occasionally carry out direct assignments in the investigation of suspected or actual frauds, the greater number of auditor fraud-oriented efforts are usually part of broader audit assignments. These fraud efforts may take the form of specific procedures included in a broader audit program or considered as part of normal review activities. Internal audit should also always be alert to potential areas for fraud when carrying out various other audit assignments. This general alertness requires an understanding of the various areas, conditions, and developments that provide potential fraud warning signals.

Internal audit must always be aware of the overall organizational climate and its potentialities for fraud. An internal auditor should be especially alert for sensitive areas that may, in some instances, disclose potential wrongdoing. The following are examples.

- *Insufficient Organization Working Capital.* A weak balance sheet with limited working capital may indicate such legitimate problems as overexpansion, decreases in revenues, transfers of funds to other organization units, insufficient credit, or excessive expenditures. However, an internal auditor also should be on the lookout for diversions of funds to personal use through such methods as unrecorded sales and falsified expenditures.

- *Rapid Turnover in Financial Personnel.* The recent loss of key accounting or other financial personnel may signify inadequate performance and result in weaknesses in internal controls. In addition, the departure of these financial managers calls for a review of their accountability for funds and other resources upon termination of employment.

- *Use of Sole-Source Procurements.* Good procurement practices encourage competition to assure that the organization is obtaining the required materials or equipment at the best price. Sole-source procurement, if not adequately justified, may indicate potential favoritism or buyer kickbacks.

- *Excessive Travel Costs.* An internal auditor should always be on the lookout for unauthorized or personal trips, entertainment, travel costs in excess of those allowed by the organization, or unsupported travel expenses. This type of behavior may indicate that unapproved funds are available to one or more persons.

- *Transfers of Funds between Affiliated Companies or Divisions.* A pattern of transfers of funds between affiliated companies or divisions may indicate unauthorized borrowings, a cover-up of shortages, or inadequate controls over funds.

- *Changes in Outside Auditors.* In some instances, the change in outside auditors may indicate differences of opinion as to the appropriate method of handling certain transactions. There may be a reluctance on the part of management to disclose significant problems or events.

- *Excessive Consultant Costs or Legal Fees.* These may be indicative of abuses in having services performed on the outside, favoritism, and undisclosed problems within the organization which require extensive legal work.

- *Downward Trends in Key Financial Figures and Ratios.* The use of ratio, change, and trend analysis may indicate problems in certain areas which require follow-up. For example, a significant change in the ratio of current cash plus accounts receivable to sales may indicate that some recorded sales are not being properly collected. Other downward trends could be symptomatic of significant losses, diversion of funds and resources, and inadequate controls over operations.

- *Reported Conflicts of Interest.* Internal audit should always be aware of any rumors or allegations of conflicts of interest pertaining to outside employment, vendor arrangements, and relationships between employees. Company transactions with officers or employees should be carefully scrutinized. Calls made to an 800 number employee ethics hot line, as discussed in Chapter 35, may provide this type of information.

- *Unexplained Shortages in Physical Assets.* Inadequate physical storage may lead to pilfering or other diversion of such assets as tools or inventory. Shortages in assets should be analyzed carefully to determine their cause.

- *Management Control by Few Individuals.* Domination of an organization by one or a few individuals may provide the opportunity for diversion of assets or other manipulations. This concern is particularly true when there are large staffs in place but all major decisions are made by those few individuals.

- *Collection Difficulties.* Problems in collecting receivables should be analyzed to determine whether there may be fictitious sales or even diversions of funds received from collections. This is an area where auditor confirmation letter requests can be valuable.

- *Many Bank Accounts.* The use of a large number of bank accounts, in excess of what appears to be normally needed, may indicate a possible diversion of funds or cover-up of illegal transactions. Transfers among these accounts, and to personal bank accounts, should be reviewed carefully.

- *Late Reports.* Financial or even operational reports may be consistently delayed so that the preparer can manipulate data to cover up fraudulent actions.

- *Copies Used for Payments to Creditors.* Rather than making payments based on original invoices, copies may be used to hide duplicate payments and kickbacks.

- *Shortages, Overages, and Out-of-Balance Conditions.* While these conditions may be symptoms of larger internal control problems, they may also point to potential fraudulent activities. When reviewing various accounts or systems, explanations should be obtained as to significant variances. If an internal auditor receives an answer that some out-of-balance condition is ''under investigation,'' the auditor should follow up on the matter to determine resolution.

- *Checks or Other Documents Written in Even Amounts.* Internal audit might encounter a check for $10,000 or $35,000 in a review of inventory purchases when it would normally be expected to be in odd amounts, such as $10,261.34 or $35,322.28. Such transactions might be worthy of more detailed inspection.

The above list of characteristics is neither all-inclusive nor does it indicate areas that always may point to fraudulent activities. An internal auditor must always look for potentially unusual transactions or activities that cannot be easily explained. If the auditor's questions about such areas are not easily answered, further investigation may be warranted. If the unusual items from the more detailed investigation indicate the possibility of some form of fraudulent activity, the auditor should initiate the process for an investigation, as discussed below.

(iii) Representative Types of Fraudulent Financial Activities.   While no single particular type of fraud is always most common in one situation and not in another, an internal auditor should understand some of the more common types of fraud. While fraudulent acts will only be limited by human imagination, most frauds have to do with a person taking funds or items of value for personal gain. Some of the more common types of fraud can be classified as follows.

- *Nonrecording of Revenues.* When an employee has control over both the sale and collection of cash, it is relatively easy to pocket the cash without recording the sale. This can also occur when the employee handles receipts of cash and also does the record-keeping.

- *Withholding Receivable Collections.* A person may gain access to improper cash receipts by temporarily withholding collections on an account, or keeping the amount received and later writing off the account as a bad debt. In some cases, shortages are made up by using new cash receipts, and the latter shortage then covered by still later receipts. This type of action is known as "lapping."

- *Theft of Materials.* Sensitive materials and equipment with high resale value may be susceptible to pilferage, especially if not adequately secured. Theft losses may be covered up by arbitrary write-offs, transfers between departments, or inadequate inventory-taking procedures. In some cases, building release passes are forged, or there may be collusion of security guards with individuals.

- *Diversion of Securities, Key Documents, or Software.* This type of theft could occur through unauthorized access, or where someone was able to remove the securities or materials without being detected. The theft of a customer list or some valuable negotiable instrument can be a significant exposure for an organization.

- *Padding Payrolls.* In some situations, a payroll clerk or supervisor may be able to carry nonexistent or terminated people on the payroll, and then later get access to the check used for payment to those individuals. These are known as *ghost payroll employees.* In other cases, the payroll clerk may overstate an employee's wages in return for a share of the excess. This procedure was more common in the days of manual payroll systems and is more difficult now that most are automated.

- *Misuse of Credit Cards.* Organization-owned credit cards may be used to make personal purchases or may be lent to others in return for favors. Also, expenses paid for by organization credit cards may be simultaneously claimed and reimbursed by check.

- *Falsification of Disbursement Documents.* Cash disbursements may be supported by documents that are false or improperly altered. Warehouse receipts may be forged, or receiving reports may be falsified. Copies of invoices or receipts may be submitted for duplicate payments.

- *Payment of Personal Expenses.* Miscellaneous expenses of a personal nature not authorized by the organization may be submitted for reimbursement. These may include entertainment, expenses of a spouse, equipment bought for personal use, and unauthorized travel.

- *Purchase Kickbacks.* Arrangements may be made with vendors to purchase from them in return for special favors or money. In some cases, vendors may specifically offer bribes to members of the purchasing department.

- *Misuse of Petty Cash Funds.* Funds may be used for personal or other unauthorized purposes. In some cases, supporting documents may be forged or falsified to cover the shortage. While large amounts are not involved at any one time, this type of fraud can become large over an extended period of time.

- *Transfers of Assets.* Transfers of funds between bank accounts in various divisions or affiliated companies could be used to camouflage unauthorized expenditures or use of funds. While the transfers may represent legitimate business activities, they also may be a warning sign.

- *Excessive Allowances to Customers.* In order to develop a fraudulent relationship with some vendor or outside third party, sales allowances or discounts may be overstated. Also, preferred customers may be charged less in return for favors.

- *Conflicts of Interest.* Conflicts or the appearance of them may occur in various parts of an organization involving relatives, employees with an outside interest, or dealings with related companies. While an outside business relationship with a relative does not necessarily indicate fraudulent activity, it can represent a ''red flag'' requiring further investigation.

- *Bribes and Other Improper Payments.* Payments to obtain business may be made to foreign officials, in violation of the anti-bribery provisions of the Foreign Corrupt Practices Act, as discussed earlier in this chapter.

- *Misappropriation of Receipts.* Through having incoming customer checks made payable to an employee rather than the organization, the employee can gain access to the cash while the customer will still receive their goods or services.

The above list of representative types of fraud is not all-inclusive but represents some of the more common types of fraudulent activities that an internal auditor may encounter in the course of operational audit activities.

Specifically with respect to bribes, an internal auditor might examine certain accounts that are frequently used for disguising the bribe as a legitimate business expense. These may include entertainment, travel, advertising, consulting services, engineering services, selling costs, legal fees, and individual expense accounts. An examination of relevant documents may give an indication of a bribe, such as the name of the bribe recipient appearing on copies of airline or delivery tickets. This information may be compared with endorsements on checks. Loans made to individuals may in reality be bribes. Items such as automobiles and boats may be purchased by an organization to be used as bribes. Significant events and transactions related to obtaining large sales contracts with large contractors or foreign governments should be examined. Through these and other audit steps, internal audit should attempt to determine any potential for bribes or other improper payments.

(d) PERSONAL CHARACTERISTICS FOR FRAUDULENT BEHAVIOR

In addition to unusual transactions or activities, an internal auditor should be aware of personal characteristics that may point to improper activities. Of course, there is no specific profile of the white-collar criminal that would identify such a person to an internal auditor. Although a prior criminal record would indicate the need for observation, many white-collar criminals have had no prior record of criminal activity. In many instances they are members of middle class, well-educated families with status in the community. An internal auditor may, however, find some early warning signals of personal behavior, as are listed below, that may require close watching. These will often not show up until internal audit has initiated the fraud-related review and has initiated a detailed review of various personal characteristics.

- *High Personal Debts or Financial Losses.* This characteristic will not normally come out of audit interviews but might surface through comments or discussions with others. The pressure of having to meet large debts can often drive a person to fraudulent activities.

- *Expensive Lifestyles.* Frequent vacation trips to expensive locations or possessions far greater than would be expected based upon an individual's salary can be a warning signal of improper personal behavior.

- *Extensive Gambling Habits.* Persons with this trait may not exhibit particularly lavish lifestyles but are often involved with heavy gambling on sporting events or other matters. Debts from gambling losses can cause a person to act improperly.

- *Excessive Use of Alcohol or Drugs.* In addition to heightening the potential for fraudulent activities, these traits may point to the need for employee counseling, as was discussed previously. These habits, particularly illegal drugs, force individuals into situations where they have high demands for cash. This often can result in some type of fraudulent or illegal activity.

- *Extensive Overtime and Skipping Vacations.* Individuals often conduct personal frauds through schemes that require them to be on the job all of the time. Although organizations should always have policies requiring that vacations be taken, this is not always the case. The employee who never takes vacation or always works excessively late may be signaling possible improper activities.

- *Domination of Specific Activities.* Sometimes an individual may insist on taking complete responsibility for some activity that could be easily delegated or shared with others. This might be an indication of some type of fraud surrounding that activity.

- *Questionable Background and References.* The organization's human resource function should have screened for these types of problems. If any questions were raised there, they could point to the possibility of future improper behavior.

Fraud is so directly the product of individuals and their operational situations that it is impossible to cover all possibilities. Just because an individual exhibits one or several of these traits does not mean that the individual should be a suspect for potential fraud or a candidate for a fraud audit. Rather, these traits point to circumstances where the individual *might* have a higher motivation to engage in fraud. An internal auditor should be aware of these potential situations and carefully review the activities of individuals who might come under suspicion.

An internal auditor should always remember that a suspect of a fraudulent act should not be considered guilty until actually proven guilty. Even more so, an internal auditor can not assume that just because an employee exhibits warning traits that the person is guilty of something. The employee in question should be treated with respect and any investigation should not be initiated just on the basis of circumstantial impressions.

31-4 FRAUD AND LOSS-PREVENTION INVESTIGATIONS

Fraud and loss-prevention matters should not be reported in the typical audit finding and recommendations approaches described in sample audit reports and used as examples throughout these chapters. Although audit reports are for the exclusive use of auditees and their management, through the use of copy machines, an audit report can easily become a semi-public document available to other members of the management team. The auditor normally describes the facts, discusses what is wrong, and concludes with recommendations for improvement. A fraud-related investigation is different. Although a formal security function is best suited for investigations, in smaller organizations an internal auditor is frequently asked to perform the fraud-related investigation to determine the facts and then to present the results of the investigation to appropriate levels of management. The person or persons conducting the fraud is confronted by management for a more detailed investigation. If an immediate confession is obtained, the person may be terminated. However, in many instances the accused may deny the allegations. Formal proceedings, possibly including a legal action and trial, may follow.

Even though a formal audit report will not be published, internal audit should conduct the review in the same manner as a normal audit. If there is any other significant change here, the workpapers and other materials should be prepared in greater detail than normally used with conventional internal audits. For example, it may be a good idea to take contemporaneous notes of interviews with auditees in order to capture questions and responses. These workpapers may end up as evidence in a legal proceeding at some future date, and all details of the investigation should be documented.

If internal audit becomes directly involved in the investigation of the fraudulent activities, either alone or with loss prevention, some special techniques are needed to identify the activity and to interview the persons potentially involved in the fraud in order to obtain more information. While this type of investigative activity can become a special skills requirements area, the following sections discuss procedures for identifying fraudulent activities, conducting an investigation, and interviewing suspects.

(a) IDENTIFICATION OF FRAUDULENT ACTIVITIES

Fraudulent acts may be disclosed in various ways. Internal auditors may discover potential fraudulent activities during the course of a review where there were no planned procedures to look for fraud. Documents may contain questionable items which, when followed-up, disclose irregularities. Employees or outsiders may make allegations or bring up items of a suspicious nature during discussions. In some instances an employee who has committed or participated in a fraud may come forth and make a confession to an internal auditor, assuming the purpose of an otherwise planned audit was really to investigate that person's fraudulent activity. In many other instances, management may specifically request that internal audit review some sensitive area for a possible wrongdoing, such as a potential conflict of interest. There may be just general warning signs which require close attention by internal audit as indicators of potential fraud.

Internal audit needs to be on the alert for any leads that indicate potential irregularities. General audit experience as well as a good understanding of the organization's lines of business are necessary to effectively recognize and identify these leads or danger signals when found. This takes auditor curiosity and imagination to separate the normal from the abnormal. Being independent from day-to-day operations and personnel, internal auditors are often in a good position to recognize irregularities or questionable behavior. However, an internal auditor should always act with a degree of prudence and should not always assume fraud first when faced with an error or other internal control breakdown.

As soon as some type of fraud is suspected, the situation should be reported to the proper organization officials. Generally, more senior management is interested in obtaining information about fraud anywhere in the organization, and they should be alerted about the suspected type and characteristics of any fraud at an early stage before there is a chance of unfavorable publicity. This early reporting gives top officials an opportunity to provide input as to how the investigation will be conducted, and to make key decisions as to the disposition of the case. Normally, cases are not dropped without the concurrence of management. Informing management will also allow them to become aware of the control deficiencies that enabled the irregularities to occur.

Once a fraud has been reported or discovered and interested parties feel it potentially may be genuine, a report should usually be made to the organization's bonding company under the provisions of existing surety bonds. This bonding organization may be of assistance in the investigation and determination of action to be taken based on evidence available. A notification report should also be made to the legal counsel and to any special investigators in the organization, such as the loss-prevention group. The director of internal auditing should, of course, also be informed of all suspected frauds.

In some instances, the immediate supervisor and other managers of the employee about whom there is the complaint should be informed. Depending upon the nature of the suspected fraud, the identified employee may be temporarily relieved of duties to either aid in the investigation or to prevent further manipulation. Generally, the suspected employee should not be informed of the suspicions until strong evidence has been gathered. While the matter is still under investigation, the employee may be assigned to other work. It may be necessary to take immediate control over the employee's records to prevent their alteration or destruction. However, the employee should not be accused of the fraud or suspended until the organization has gathered clear proof of the wrongful act. Otherwise, the organization may be held liable for a wrongful termination suit.

As soon as the preliminary facts are reviewed, a plan of action should be developed and an auditor or investigator designated to be in charge. It is especially important to start the investigation as soon as possible to prevent the destruction or alteration of records, to obtain any confessions, and to gather evidence that can be used for any eventual legal actions.

Internal auditors assigned to the fraud investigation should initially attempt to determine the types of records and supporting documents that may need to be reviewed. To prevent the need for detailed checking, it may be preferable to interview key personnel and witnesses prior to performing the review. The type of evidence necessary to prove the case should be discussed to assure that the data obtained are pertinent.

Resources needed should be carefully reviewed. In many cases, the work will require professional investigators because of the questioning involved or due to other factors. Discussions with law-enforcement officials may be necessary. Once others are brought into the investigation, internal audit's role should be carefully defined, both for helping to perform the investigatory work and for writing any reports.

(b) CONDUCTING THE INVESTIGATION

Before conducting any fraud-related investigation, internal audit must first coordinate the efforts of all parties involved. In an individual case this may involve internal auditors who carry out various audit tests, including following the paper trails; the investigator who conducts interviews, interrogates witnesses, and gathers other evidence; the legal counsel who provides technical advice and support; and prosecuting attorneys who perform early case review and provide guidance on evidence needed. Close communication should be encouraged among all of these parties during the fraud investigation.

There are no audit procedures that are unique to fraud situations. Each case is different and requires its own study and analysis to determine the best approach. In a case involving the lapping in accounts receivable, in which the employee evidently diverted collections to personal use during the early months of a year, a confirmation of accounts should perhaps be performed. In another case involving theft of sensitive equipment, a physical inventory should be taken which is both observed and reconciled by internal audit. In both cases, internal audit would be responsible for making inquiries of selected employees to obtain explanations of circumstances surrounding the irregularity. Internal audit often must rely on judgment in selecting the best procedures for gathering evidence, and must also be imaginative enough to try to detect such items as the falsification of documents, forged signatures, or evidence of collusion. It should be emphasized that as soon as internal audit begins investigating a fraud, internal audit's normal cooperative role of reviewing controls as part of routine auditing is changed. Internal audit now assumes duties more like that of a detective, gathering evidence to determine whether there is a fraud, who committed the fraud, the extent of loss, and information on how the fraud was perpetrated. Internal audit must investigate all discrepancies, believing no explanations until they can be proved, and must routinely suspect possible collusion. Speed is essential in such an investigation to prevent destruction of records and to obtain evidence for interviewing witnesses.

In these matters, internal audit should always be on the lookout for any diversion of funds to personal use. Although certain practices followed by an employee may be wasteful or not in the best interests of the organization, an individual may not benefit personally and prosecution may be difficult. Transfers of funds between accounts and divisions of the organization should be examined closely, as well as personal withdrawals in various forms. These activities may just represent bad judgment or bad management, and not necessarily indicate fraud.

Internal audit should attempt to concentrate efforts on those areas that are most likely to provide specific evidence as to the suspected fraud. To conserve time and resources, test checks should be limited as to their detail and should emphasize the areas of concern. Once the actual fraud is uncovered, other activities of the malefactor employee may have to be examined to detect possible additional fraudulent actions. As the investigation proceeds, information obtained by interviews with employees should be used to help determine audit emphasis. Internal audit should begin to develop answers to the following questions and plan any additional work accordingly.

- Have cash, securities, or other assets been stolen?
- Can the defalcation be easily determined, or does it require extensive tracing of transactions through the records?
- What documents and other evidence are needed to prove both shortages and the intent of the fraudulent actions?
- How far back does the shortage go?
- Do records indicate that there have been prior shortages that have not been thoroughly investigated or have been covered up?
- Has management been aware of any wrongdoing and taken any action?
- How many persons are involved?
- What is known or can be learned about the suspect's habits and finances?
- Do personnel files indicate employment background verification?

Internal audit must take extreme care to carefully document all work and to handle records in an appropriate manner. If a matter does eventually end up as a criminal case, defense attorneys can destroy a carefully constructed set of evidence by pointing out that some workpaper notes are neither signed nor dated, raising the question of when they were prepared, or that a computer file was not properly copied, raising the question of possible alteration of records. Many of the previous chapters of this book have talked about proper methods for workpaper preparation and other auditing procedures. In a fraud-related investigation, internal audit should take extreme care to follow such procedures.

(c) FRAUD-AUDITING INTERVIEWING TECHNIQUES

Interviewing and making inquiries of employees and outsiders is an especially important procedure in conducting fraud- and loss-prevention–related investigations. Information made available by employees and other witnesses, or by the suspected defrauder is often the key to the investigation. Internal audit or others assigned to perform interviews have to plan interviews carefully to obtain the maximum evidence and benefit for the investigative effort. In larger organizations, this interview task is often given to the loss-prevention department, as discussed earlier, or to others who may be more experienced in this type of interview process. However, internal audit is also often requested to at least help in this form of investigative work. At smaller organizations, the task may be often 100% handled by internal audit.

If the fraud investigation originated through some other employee blowing the whistle, the source of the complaint should be interviewed, if possible, soon after the allegation is made. If the source desires secrecy, extreme care should be taken to ensure there will be complete confidentiality as to the source of the information. If the source has some documentary support for the allegation, this should be requested at the time of the interview. If the allegation is general in nature, the complainant may be able to refer the investigator to other personnel or records for more information. In some cases the allegation should be put in writing.

Because of the desire of many individuals to not get involved or because of fears of retribution, a direct employee report of a fraudulent act by another employee is unusual in the modern organization. Employees may report these matters in the manner of anonymous letters to senior management or even through the informal organization rumor mill.

The Organization Sentencing Guidelines, discussed earlier, strongly encourage—and many modern organizations have developed mechanisms for—employees to report improper acts anonymously and without fear of retribution. The normal mechanism for this is either a ''hot line'' toll-free telephone-reporting systems or some form of mail-in reporting system. Both of these will be discussed in Chapter 35, ''Business Ethics and Social Responsibility.'' Some organizations even have formal reward systems to encourage employees to report acts of wrongdoing.

Any allegation of fraud or potential wrongdoing, whether directly reported by an employee or through an anonymous mechanism, should be evaluated as soon as possible on the merits of the allegation. Internal audit, loss prevention, the law department, or whomever is responsible for following up on reported wrongdoings should preliminarily review the allegation in detail and survey all available evidence. The fraud-investigation team should then determine the action to be taken, which may include the following:

- *Further action should be dropped because allegation is unsupported.* Sometimes an improper act is reported because someone just wants to get even or because an otherwise innocent act appears improper in the eyes of some other employee. This type of action should be the exception to the rule because, if nothing is done, employees will see little value in reporting any fraudulent act.

- *The matter should be turned over to management for administrative action because there appears to be no intent to defraud.* An employee may be reported in violation of some travel expense accounting rule because of sloppy personal recordkeeping or a misunderstanding of certain rules. The appropriate action may be just administrative discipline.

- *The reported matter is considered to be an abuse or a wasteful management action rather than fraud, and recommendations should be made for improvements in procedures.* This is the situation where the investigators find some potential problems but not necessarily fraudulent acts. This may result in a detailed operational audit, with its finding and recommendations.

- *A full-scale investigation may be recommended with possible prosecutory action based upon the results.* The allegation may point to willful employee misconduct. This is the type of matter that does not appear to be initially criminal in nature, but the organization should start the investigation to gather more evidence.

- *There appears to have been a serious fraud where law enforcement and legal help should be consulted at once.*

Internal audit or other fraud investigators should make an early determination as to when any interviews will be conducted. If early in the examination, the information gathered from them may enable the interviewer to pinpoint the approach and limit the extent of a comprehensive review of books and records. However, even if all parties are asked to pledge confidentiality, the investigators face a risk that there may be some breach, with the news getting out that an investigation is in process. The persons guilty of the fraud may then destroy records or take other preventive actions. In these instances, the investigators may wish to perform preliminary reviews and audits of the records in order to obtain information for conducting meaningful interviews. It is sometimes preferable to conduct an interview with the suspects early in the process, while the suspected persons are still on the job and unaware of the fraud-related nature of the review. Later, they may be unavailable to answer questions as the review progresses. In some cases, however, it may be necessary to remove a suspected employee from his or her position because the person's duties involve the handling of assets or controlling records where there is a possibility of hiding the fraud or for further misappropriation of assets. This puts the suspected employee in a defense-related position where he or she may seek outside legal help who will advise them to curtail any interviews.

Legal precedent supports the authority of internal audit or another designated fraud investigator to question individuals about organization-related duties and actions while they are employed. This procedure is based on the employee's stewardship responsibility to the organization. If an official investigation is begun to gather evidence for prosecution, however, the requirements for informing a suspect of his or her rights must be observed. When there are any questions on this, prosecuting officials or the legal staff should always be consulted. An organization can lose all rights to prosecute if this matter is not handled properly, and the accused person may even be able to take legal actions against the organization. Many internal auditors have grown up in an environment of private detective movies and novels. This may sound exciting, but such tactics should never be used as part of an internal audit fraud-related investigation.

In conducting the actual interview, internal audit or other designated investigators should prepare an outline of the questions to be asked. The interviewer should be prepared for both affirmative and negative responses to key questions and should avoid creating the impression that the purpose of the interview is to seek a confession or conviction. It is preferable to appear in the role of one merely seeking the truth. The interviewer should be tactful when replies to questions do not agree with the facts obtained and should point out the inconsistencies and ask for additional explanations. The fraud interviewer should listen carefully to whatever the interviewee has to say and then relate questions to specific transactions and documents of interest. The skill of the interviewer is often a determining factor in obtaining information to use in the investigation. The key to a successful fraud investigation interview is to use one or more interview techniques, relying on an ability to size up the suspect and determine the approach that will work best. Many fraud examiners carefully organize their interviews following some very structured, well-phrased questions, as follows:

- *Open-Ended Questions.* This type of question is broad and unstructured, letting interviewees give answers as they see fit. Open-ended questions are intended to establish good communications and obtain the viewpoints of the interviewee. An example is, ''Do you think management is concerned about inventory controls in the parts crib area?''

- *Restatement Questions.* The purpose of restatement is to check the listener's understanding of what was said and to encourage the speaker to continue. The interviewer takes a statement that the interviewee has just made and rephrases it as a clarifying question. An example is, ''You say that the mail clerk sometimes hands envelopes to the accounting clerk without checking for receipts of cash?''

- *Probe-Oriented Questions.* The purpose of probes is to obtain more specific information. The speaker is asked to explain in more detail when the responses are not sufficient. An example is, ''Do you have any other information that would explain how this happened?''

- *Closed-Response Questions.* This type of question is used when it is desired to lead the interviewee to express an opinion in one way or another. An example is, ''Do you record transactions daily or wait until near the end of the month?'' The use of closed questions requires the interviewer to have background knowledge of the subject. This method is useful when it is desired to have the interviewee think through several alternatives and arrive at a conclusion.

- *Yes-No Response Questions.* This is a form of closed question that allows the interviewee to answer either ''yes,'' ''no,'' or ''I don't know.'' This type of question does not elicit much information, and is generally less valuable than questions that require more detailed answers.

As part of a fraud investigation, the employer has a right to ask a suspect to prepare a written statement explaining the employee's actions, whether or not a confession to the work-related allegations. This form of statement will be useful as evidence for recovery or even prosecution. While there may be no confession, the suspect should be willing to explain his or her version of the facts. In some instances, suspects may be willing to formally describe their versions of the matter after the conclusion of interviews, when the suspect feels that the tone and direction of the questions has made the interview subject to misinterpretation and the suspect wants to restate matters.

Any confession, if made, must be voluntary and not made under threat. The interrogation and subsequent confession may provide leads to additional fraudulent activities or to other individuals involved. Depending upon the nature and severity of the suspected fraud, the fraud-investigation team should involve members of the legal staff or even outside counsel in the interrogation process. The process may lead to criminal action against the suspect or, if the interview and resultant action is handled incorrectly, to legal action against the organization for damages, defamation of character, and the like.

Fraud investigations and interrogations should not be taken lightly. Even if the organization is small, with a limited legal staff or no loss-prevention function, internal audit should seek outside help and counsel before charging ahead with interrogations and making allegations. While the purpose of the activity is to discover the perpetrator of the fraud, the investigators should be very sensitive to the rights of the accused persons. The principle that an individual is considered innocent *until proven guilty* should always apply.

(d) CONCLUDING THE FRAUD-RELATED AUDIT

At the conclusion of a fraud-related investigation, whether performed by internal audit or others, internal audit should make a careful analysis of the related internal controls that were violated or that were not strong enough to prevent the matter. While no controls will be strong enough to prevent a fraud by a group of employees operating in collusion, internal audit should be concerned with the following general questions:

- Was the cause of the problem ineffective internal controls or controls that were not functioning?

- Could the type of fraud committed occur elsewhere in the organization?

- Are additional preventive controls economically justifiable?

- Would any proposed expansion of controls fit into the normal pattern of the business and be accepted by employees, or would they be unworkable?
- How could normal audit programs and procedures be revised to detect a fraud of this nature?

Based on the facts in the case, decisions have to be made on whether the employee will be dismissed, whether management will seek prosecution, and whether management will ask for restitution. In addition, if the employee is prosecuted and found innocent, management must decide on alternative strategies for subsequent action.

Internal auditors must be aware that it is very difficult in some cases to get a district attorney to prosecute. Decisions as to whether or not to prosecute may depend on the amount of the fraud, the type of crime, the type of evidence gathered, and in some cases the workload of the district attorney and current political considerations. It is especially frustrating for the fraud investigator or auditor to complete an investigation, provide the evidence to the district attorney's office, and then have them decline to prosecute.

The surety organization that provides bonding insurance should be consulted regarding restitution. This is generally desired to reduce the amount of the loss. Since any restitution may affect the criminal prosecution, the district attorney's office and the surety organization should be closely informed.

The final report of the investigation presents the evidence gathered and conclusions reached. It provides management with a summary of action taken as a result of leads and serves as a basis for decisions on how to handle the employee. A description is included of the process followed in committing the fraud. The amounts and dates of each item involved should also be included for submission to the surety organization. Evidence should be retained for use in the prosecution, if needed. The report should attempt to identify the cause for the irregularity. If there are weaknesses in controls, recommendations for corrective action should be made.

Figure 31.2 is an example of a final report covering the internal audit investigation of a purchasing fraud in a smaller organization. Generally, this type of written report on the fraud should include the following elements:

- The source of fraud discovery, whether a regular audit, complaint, anonymous tip, or confession
- The nature of the fraud, such as a theft or misappropriation of funds
- The source of the fraud, whether an employee, manager, outside accomplice, or a combination through collusion
- The estimated loss from the fraud, stated as an audited amount, a suspected amount, or an admitted amount
- The methods used to conceal the fraud, such as lapping or forgery
- The length of time the fraud has been in effect
- Effect of the fraud on the organization's financial statements and how the loss or potential loss will be reported
- Method to prevent or control the deficiency in the future, as well as recommendations for future action
- Prosecution action as a result of the fraud, whether it was waived or is pending, and whether there was a sentence or the suit was settled through restitution.

Figure 31.2   Example Audit Report on Purchasing Fraud

AUDIT FINDING XX-ZZ: INVESTIGATION OF PURCHASING IRREGULARITIES

Internal audit was advised, through an anonymous tip, that one of the electronic goods buyers may be involved in illegal purchasing activities. It was alleged that certain goods were purchased, using normal procedures, for deliveries at one of the distribution centers and then "sold" to a fictitious customer to the benefit of the buyer. The source for this information appeared to be good. After a discussion with very senior management, internal audit began a project to determine if these allegations were true.

Over a three-month period, we investigated the purchasing activity for the buyer in question. We found that certain high-demand products were ordered by this buyer for delivery to the main distribution center. Concurrent with delivery, the distribution center received a "special" purchase order for a large shipment of the same electronic goods. The goods then left the distribution center per normal procedures.

We reviewed these special shipments and found that the customer, Whiz-Bang Products, had only recently established a relationship with our company. We found that Whiz-Bang had not been set up as a normal customer, but no credit investigation research could be found in our files for this company. We further found that the mailing address for Whiz-Bang was the home address of the buyer's brother-in-law. We also found that virtually all shipments to Whiz-Bang over a six-month period had been disputed with claims of damages, improper products, or incomplete quantities. Our accounts receivable function accepted these claims and issued credits.

During the period of our review, we also followed the truck carrying one of these special purchase order shipments. We found that the truck, a leased van, delivered the products to a discount merchandiser. The billing for these goods was again disputed by Whiz-Bang, claiming that these goods were damaged in transit. This claim, along with all similar Whiz-Bang claims over the past year, were accepted by the same supervisor in the accounts receivable department. After a detailed interview with the accounts receivable supervisor, we were advised that the same buyer had paid the supervisor to accept these Whiz-Bang claims because "the company is really having a tough time."

The supervisor has been suspended, with no charges, in exchange for further cooperation on this investigation. We brought the matter to our legal department, who brought it to the county attorney. The buyer has been suspended and is awaiting formal criminal charges. We estimate the total loss for this purchasing fraud and illegal shipment fraud to be over $650,000 for the current fiscal year.

To avoid a recurrence, we recommend that procedures be strengthened for all "special" purchase orders to require at least two levels of approval before release for shipment. In addition, disputed shipment claims should be controlled by a single individual in accounts receivable, who should be responsible for reporting disputes in process and overall settlement history. This should prevent a single individual from approving adjustments for a single customer.

This type of fraud-related report should be kept confidential and should not go through internal audit's normal audit-report process. Its purpose is to inform senior management of the nature of the fraud and what might be done in the future to prevent such a matter from reoccurring. This is a report that may be of interest to the audit committee of the board of directors if the fraud is of sufficient size. The materials in this report may provide the basis for any questions or responses to reporters or others regarding the nature of the fraud. However, if the fraud is sufficiently large and important, legal counsel and public relations specialists should be consulted before a summarized version of the report is prepared for outside dissemination.

31.5 LOSS PREVENTION AND FRAUD IN PERSPECTIVE

The need to assist management in the prevention and detection of losses and fraud presents a real challenge to internal audit. Although these activities cannot be planned or even predicted, there must be sufficient time planned in the internal audit budget to provide for these activities. Because of its importance to management, the prevention and detection of fraud usually will take precedence over other work. As such, careful planning and assessment of priorities is needed to assure that the broad responsibilities of internal auditing are met. For the short term, it may be necessary to do fewer operational audits to handle investigations. It may also be necessary to devote significant resources to studying the risk of fraud in an organization and to devise preventive measures. In the long term, the amount of time devoted to fraud measures should decrease, and internal audit should coordinate closely with management to assure that there are sufficient resources and time available to perform meaningful operational auditing.

Loss-prevention and fraud-related special reviews allow internal audit to demonstrate its competence to management, and beneficial findings in all areas of internal auditing will help in accomplishing this objective. Internal audit and management should work together to achieve the proper balance between fraud-oriented objectives and other broader internal audit needs and services. Internal audit must always be alert to the prevention and detection of fraud.

CHAPTER 32

Coordination with External Auditors

32-1 IMPORTANCE OF EXTERNAL AUDIT COORDINATION

Organizations receive their major auditing services from two different sources: internal audit and independent external auditors. Although each audit function has very distinct responsibilities, there are many common objectives which can be a basis for coordination between these two distinct audit functions. Since both audit functions work with the same organization records and personnel, there is a possibility of unnecessary duplication of effort or avoidable excessive demands on organization personnel without some level of coordination. These coordinated audit efforts should provide more effective audit coverage for the organization served.

Every internal audit function should have an objective to coordinate work with their external auditors. This is not to state that they must work together on projects or that they must follow the same general audit approach for their various projects. Rather, each should be generally aware of what the other is doing and plan work to avoid any obvious duplication of effort. While an internal auditor understands the differences between his or her goals and objectives and those of external auditors, often many members of management do not. Persons who are not acquainted with the audit process sometimes think that an auditor is an auditor is an auditor. That is, they may have the impression that all auditors are really about the same, even though the internal auditor plays a unique role in day-to-day audit processes.

This chapter discusses approaches for internal auditors to develop a better working relationship with external auditors. While internal audit cannot dictate to external auditors the extent to which they should coordinate their work, both management and the board of directors (via its audit committee) generally will endorse this coordination. Internal audit cannot, of course, speak directly for the company's external auditors, but must endeavor to understand their special needs, requirements, and concerns in order to achieve an effective coordinated audit effort.

This chapter discusses the official support for audit coordination, including the American Institute of Certified Public Accountants (AICPA) Statement on Auditing Standards (SAS) No. 65, "The Auditor's Consideration of the Internal Audit Function in an Audit of Financial Statements,"[1] as well as the Institute of Internal Auditors (IIA) Professional

---

[1] American Institute of Certified Public Accountants, "Statement on Auditing Standards No. 65." (New York: AICPA, 1991).

Standard No. 550, "External Auditors."[2] These audit standards provide guidance to external and internal auditors in working together and coordinating their efforts. The two audit groups have some fundamentally different responsibilities, however, and internal audit management should be aware of them and communicate them to management in the event of questions. Internal audit should *never* be viewed as a subset of or junior partner to the external auditors.

32-2 OFFICIAL SUPPORT FOR AUDIT COORDINATION

An internal auditor can better understand the current environment—for coordinating the internal and external auditing efforts—through consideration of internal and external audit coordination since 1941, when the first edition of this book was published. At that time, internal auditing departments had most often been linked closely to the work of their external auditors. Historically, concerns about the growing magnitude of independent audit responsibilities and the cost of this effort caused external auditors to recommend the creation of internal auditing departments to their clients. Under these earlier situations, internal auditing activities tended to be viewed by all parties as a support function that was directly supportive of the external auditor's objectives. Additionally, these early internal auditing departments were often largely staffed by personnel drawn from public accounting practice. Early internal audit work often consisted of work considered by external auditors to be necessary but time consuming. For example, internal auditors working in support of their external auditors might reconcile certain checking accounts or perform test counts of inventories, both resource-consuming tasks. This was often viewed by external audit as necessary but low-level work. With internal audit's help on these audit procedures, the net result was typically a close, coordinated effort between the internal and external auditors, but with internal audit playing a subordinate role.

In 1941, The Institute of Internal Auditors was founded and the internal auditing profession moved toward modern operational auditing, as is discussed in these chapters, with its stronger emphasis on management service. This diversion from the earlier financial statement–oriented internal audit activities weakened the linkage to external auditors and, in turn, the closeness of their coordination. In some cases, the two audit groups operated totally autonomously, with only the most perfunctory contact and coordination. The changing atmosphere of the 1970s and 1980s, however, along with the enactment of the Foreign Corrupt Practices Act of 1977, the later Treadway Commission report, and the Committee of Sponsoring Organizations (COSO) standards, have again generated a much greater emphasis on the adequacy of an organization's system of internal accounting control. These initiatives, and COSO in particular, were discussed in Chapter 2, on the fundamentals of control.

These internal control developments have once more swung the pendulum back toward a closer coordination effort between internal and external auditors in many organizations. Although internal and external auditors have different primary missions, there are important common interests, and close coordination between internal and external auditors should be strongly considered by internal audit management. If an organization's internal audit management wants to promote coordination with the objective of overall efficiency

---

[2] The Institute of Internal Auditors, "Standards for the Professional Practice of Internal Auditing." (Altamonte Springs, Fl.: IIA, 1995).

and resource savings, and if the external auditors do not, senior management should be consulted for resolution. Conversely, if external audit wants to coordinate its efforts with internal audit and the latter does not want to cooperate, that internal audit management may be subject to serious questions from senior management.

(a) AICPA SUPPORT FOR AUDIT COORDINATION

External auditors in the United States are governed by the standards established by their professional organization, the American Institute of Certified Public Accountants (AICPA) which is responsible, among other matters, for defining educational and examination standards for external auditors, for defining audit reporting requirements, and for establishing auditing standards. These auditing standards are published in what are called Statements on Auditing Standards (SAS) documents. The AICPA's SAS standards are similar to the internal audit standards discussed in Chapter 5. However, since the investing public, owners, and government regulators rely upon the work of and reports by external auditors, the AICPA's standards carry a much greater level of importance. Similar standards exist for most national public accounting groups. The Canadian Institute of Chartered Accountants, for example, has its own auditing standards. These external audit standards outline, among other matters, the extent of reliance that an external auditor can place upon internal auditors in a financial statement review.

The AICPA's major pronouncement in the area of internal audit coordination is its Statement on Auditing Standards No. 65, "The Auditors Consideration of the Internal Audit Function in an Audit of Financial Statements." This SAS was released in 1991 and supersedes their earlier SAS No. 9, "The Effect of the Internal Audit Function on the Scope of the Independent Auditor's Examination." The AICPA's Statements on Auditing Standards provide the basis for what external auditors call Generally Accepted Auditing Standards (GAAS), the overall basis for their audit work.

The original SAS No. 9 (no longer in effect) and the new SAS No. 65 each treat audit coordination somewhat differently. The opening sentence of the older SAS No. 9 stated, "The work of internal auditors cannot be substituted for the work of the independent auditor; however, the independent auditor should consider the procedures, if any, performed by internal auditors in determining the nature, timing, and extent of his own auditing procedures." This older guidance had been criticized by both internal and external auditors. Much of the criticism focused on SAS No. 9's very general nature and on its failure to adequately recognize the proper high-level partnership relationship that has existed between the internal and external audit functions in the typical large organization. In addition, SAS No. 9 provided little definitive guidance to external auditors on how much reliance they could place on the work of internal auditors and the extent to which they could reduce their planned procedures based upon this internal audit work.

Because of its relatively general and cautious language and because of other changes in auditing standards, SAS No. 9 was superseded by SAS No. 65. This new audit standard better describes the role of both auditors, areas for joint audit participation, and external auditor responsibilities for financial statement audits. Paragraphs 2 and 3 of the new SAS define the roles of external and internal auditors as follows:

> Paragraph 2. *The [external] auditor's responsibility, when performing an audit in accordance with generally accepted auditing standards, is to express an opinion on the entity's financial statements. To fulfill this responsibility, the auditor maintains*

independence from the entity. The independent auditor cannot have a financial interest in the entity or have other relationships that might impair auditor objectivity as defined by the profession's independence rules. The auditor is also required to obtain sufficient competent evidential matter to provide a reasonable basis for the opinion.

Paragraph 3. Internal auditors are responsible for providing entity management and its board of directors with analyses, evaluations, assurances, recommendations, and other information that assists in the effective discharge of their responsibilities. To fulfill this responsibility, internal auditors should maintain objectivity with respect to the activity being audited but they are not independent of the entity.

The SAS goes on to discuss procedures for external auditors to obtain an understanding of the internal audit function, to assess internal audit competence and objectivity, to coordinate work with internal auditors, and to evaluate the effectiveness of this work. The SAS suggests ways in which this audit coordination can be accomplished, including:

- Holding periodic meetings
- Scheduling audit work
- Providing access to workpapers
- Exchanging audit reports and management letters
- Documenting responsibilities related to the audit
- Discussing possible accounting and auditing problems

SAS No. 65 strongly suggests, but does not mandate, that external auditors should consider the work of internal auditors when performing their financial statement attest work. While the earlier SAS No. 9 only suggested that the external auditor should gain an understanding of the internal auditor's work but could not rely upon it for purposes of forming an audit opinion, SAS No. 65 now states that external auditors can rely upon certain work performed by internal auditors. Before making this decision, however, they must gain an understanding of the activities of the internal audit function, including its competency and objectivity. They can then coordinate their work with internal audit. However, the auditing standards still correctly place the final responsibility for financial statement reviews on the external auditor—the independent public accountant.

Internal auditors should have an understanding of the key elements and requirements of SAS No. 65. This will enable internal audit to better understand external audit's decision process when deciding whether to use or not to use internal audit as part of its annual reviews. The SAS contains a flowchart, summarized in Figure 32.1, which directs the external auditor to use the following steps in considering whether to use internal audit in his or her work.

1. *Obtain an understanding of the internal audit function.* An external auditor will want to gain an assurance that internal audit reports to proper levels in the organization, that audits are adequately planned, with measurements for plan performance, that internal audit has a quality-assurance process, and that audits are completed in accordance with IIA standards. In other words, an external auditor would want to determine if an internal audit organization was following many of the standards and practices outlined in chapters of this book.

Figure 32.1 SAS No. 65 Decision Flowchart

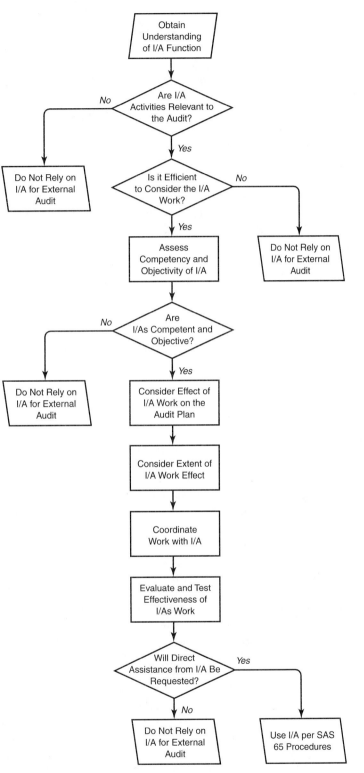

2. *Assess the competence and objectivity of internal audit.* In addition to understanding the organizational structure of an internal audit function, an external auditor would want to assess the competency of individuals working in internal audit and the quality of their work product. This would include a consideration of the staff's educational levels, their professional experience as internal auditors, professional certifications, such as CIAs or CPAs, and programs for continuing professional education. This review step would also include an assessment of quality of workpapers and audit reports as well as the degree of supervision over internal audit activities.

3. *Consider the effect of internal audit on the external auditor's plan.* The external auditor should determine how internal audit might contribute to the overall audit objectives through testing and other procedures. This recognizes that the external auditor has a prime responsibility for forming the opinion on the fairness of the financial statements reviewed.

4. *Plan and coordinate work with internal audit.* Once the external auditor has determined that the internal audit function meets the external auditor's quality standards, audit work can be planned and coordinated. This is discussed in greater detail later in this chapter.

5. *Evaluate and test the effectiveness of internal audit's work.* Per the standards, external auditors cannot just plan for internal audit to perform certain procedures and then rely upon the results of that work with no further review. Just as internal audit management should review the work of auditors assigned to a project, external auditors are also required to evaluate the work of the internal auditors working with them on a project.

6. *Use internal audit to provide direct assistance to the external auditor.* The SAS allows external auditors to have internal auditors provide direct support on an audit assignment. This has been a common practice, as discussed in this chapter, but SAS No. 65 confirms this practice.

SAS No. 65 defines the overall rules of the external auditor's use of internal audit resources to support the external auditor in his or her very important attestation as to the fairness of the organization's financial statements. The SAS does not say that the external auditors *must* use internal audit in their financial statement audits; however, it sets the basic rules that external auditors should use when evaluating an internal audit function and making a decision to use this very important resource. The internal audit function that follows the standards and guidance discussed in earlier chapters of this book should find no trouble in meeting an external auditor's requirements. If an internal audit function and its management want to support external audit in its annual financial statement reviews, internal audit management should discuss these SAS No. 65 measurement standards with their external auditors.

Internal audit should always remember that it has a unique and very important mission in its service to management. In many instances, internal audit management may not want to devote its resources to supporting the external auditors. However, internal audit should never place itself in a position where an organization's external auditors advise management that they cannot use internal audit due to SAS No. 65 problems. When internal audit does work for their external auditors on their financial statement audit, internal audit must always realize that the external auditor has the ultimate responsibility of attesting to the fairness of the organization's financial statements. Although SAS No.

65 provides guidance to external auditors for audit coordination efforts, it also clearly defines the unique role of the external auditor. Paragraph 21 states, in part:

> *The responsibility to render an opinion on the financial statements rests solely with the [external] auditor. Even though the [external] auditor's work in obtaining an understanding of the internal control structure, assessing control risk, and performing substantive procedures may be affected by the work of the internal auditors, the [external] auditor should perform sufficient procedures to provide reasonable assurance that the financial statements do not contain material misstatements.*

(b) INTERNAL AUDIT SUPPORT FOR AUDIT COORDINATION

Audit coordination from the standpoint of internal auditors is covered by The Institute of Internal Auditors in their Standards for the Professional Practice of Internal Auditing, previously referenced and discussed in Chapter 5. Standard 550, titled "External Auditors," provides that guidance.

The IIA Standards recognize that "the scope of internal audit work encompasses both financial and operational objectives and activities," while the scope of the external auditor's work, determined by their professional standards, "is designed to obtain sufficient evidential matter to support an opinion on the fairness of the annual financial statement." The IIA Standards then state that while oversight of the work of the external auditor is generally the responsibility of the audit committee, the director of internal auditing should coordinate internal and external audit efforts, and that the purpose of the coordination is both to ensure adequate audit coverage and to minimize duplicate efforts.

As was discussed in Chapter 6, the responsibilities of the audit committee of the board of directors typically include the coordination of the total audit effort, both for the internal auditing department and the independent public accountants engaged to carry out the annual external audit. The director of the organization's internal audit function is typically charged with the responsibility for managing this coordination. Guideline 110.01 of the Statement on Internal Auditing Standards states, in part:

> *The director of internal auditing should communicate the results of evaluations of the coordination between the internal and external auditor to senior management and the board along with any relevant comments about the performance of the external auditor.*

Just as external auditors have their own standards in SAS No. 65 outlining practices for coordination with internal auditors, the standards of The Institute of the Internal Auditors outline some standards of practice and participation for internal auditors. The director of internal audit should make sure that the external audit team is aware of internal audit's standards and of the audit department's compliance with those standards. This may require some educational efforts on the part of internal audit. Sometimes, an external audit firm will be aware of internal audit standards in only a very general manner but will not understand the scope and comprehensiveness of those standards. Materials such as the discussion of internal audit standards outlined in Chapter 5 may help to educate the external auditors.

External auditors may have sometimes encountered internal audit functions that are not in compliance with the standards of The Institute of Internal Auditors. They might then assume that all internal audit functions are the same and are deficient in their standards. When discussing any external-internal audit coordination, the director of internal audit should describe and discuss internal audit's level of compliance with audit standards.

Audit coordination can often be a very effective process that contributes to the overall control environment of the organization. Other times, there may be coordination problems when an external auditor chooses, for whatever reason, to operate in a manner that ignores or circumvents internal audit. Internal audit's director may have to discuss coordination problems with either the external audit engagement partner or even, as was mentioned in Chapter 6, the audit committee of the board.

Internal audit will generally find it is able to work closely with its external auditors to develop efficient and effective audit services for the overall organization. The subsequent sections of this chapter will discuss the various components of effective audit coordination and suggest ways in which both internal and external audit can coordinate their different but equally important tasks.

32-3 FOUNDATIONS FOR EFFECTIVE AUDIT COORDINATION

Effective coordination of internal and external audit activities starts with an understanding of the primary and secondary responsibilities of each. These internal audit understandings, in turn, generate the kinds of coordinated efforts that are supportive of the needs of the two audit groups and of organization management, the overall client for these audit services.

Before an internal audit organization can effectively coordinate its work with external audit, it must have its own clearly defined role in the organization. Starting with Chapter 1, on the foundations of internal auditing, this has been the message throughout this book.

(a) PRIMARY INTERNAL AUDIT COORDINATION RESPONSIBILITIES

Chapter 1 described internal auditing as an independent appraisal function established within an organization to examine and evaluate activities with the objective of assisting organization management in the effective discharge of its responsibilities. At the same time, internal audit should seek to assist the organization in achieving a more productive use of its resources.

Internal audit operates independently but is still a member of the overall management team in the organization. It has a responsibility to review and assess the overall system of internal control in the organization, as was outlined in Chapter 4, 21, and other chapters of this book. Although internal audit is free to review any area of the organization, management will often suggest areas that require more internal audit attention. These areas of emphasis will often be defined in the internal audit department's mission statement, as was discussed as part of the foundations of internal auditing in Chapter 1.

This is a broad but still very unique responsibility within the structure of the organization. Internal audit reports to the audit committee of the organization's board of directors and may also report functionally or administratively to a high level of senior management. Either of these can set some broad objectives governing internal audit activities.

Although internal audit is charged with a broad set of objectives and responsibilities reporting to senior management and the audit committee, external auditors have an even broader responsibility because their reports are directed to investors, bankers, and members of public interest groups. While internal audit is an independent entity within the organization, outsiders may not always view internal audit as *totally* independent. Those outsiders—investors, lenders, and others—often look to the external auditor to provide that independent assessment regarding the fairness of financial statements and other matters. These differences and the primary responsibilities of internal audit have been discussed throughout this book, starting in Chapter 1.

(b) PRIMARY RESPONSIBILITIES OF EXTERNAL AUDITORS

The typical modern organization operates in an environment in which it must interrelate in various ways with stockholders, customers, creditors, governmental agencies, and various other regulatory organizations. In these interrelationships, the modern organization must provide information and representations about its strength and ability to operate as an ongoing entity. These representations usually center around its financial statements, as expressed in periodic balance sheets, cash flow statements, and the results of operations or the income statement. These financial statements are the responsibility of the organization preparing them. However, financial statements could contain errors or be prepared in a manner that misrepresents actual results. These financial statements need to be reviewed by someone who is outside the organization. That outside reviewer, through independence and special expertise, can examine the supporting data and then attest that the financial statements are fairly stated and in accordance with generally accepted accounting principles. Although an external auditor may also provide other services to the organization, the primary mission of the external auditor is to provide this independent opinion as to the fairness of the presentation of those statements.

(c) OTHER COMMON AUDIT RESPONSIBILITIES

In addition to the common responsibility for assessing the system of internal accounting control, both internal and external audit functions have other common audit responsibilities. Some of these may result in conflicts. Internal audit, for example, should be interested in the organization's overall welfare, including that the external auditor provides service in a manner that renders good value for the fees charged and that minimizes interference with other ongoing organizational activities. Internal audit here should have the same basic interest in the external auditor as in any other vendor, with the special capability in this case of better understanding the manner in which this particular vendor product or service is provided.

　　While external auditors are interested in the overall welfare of their client organization, they cannot examine *every* system or account in that client organization, and must assess overall risks when performing their audit. This will include an SAS No. 65 assessment of the internal audit function. Management will often look to the external auditor for counsel in evaluating the effectiveness of the internal audit function, including the range and quality of its various services. The external auditor knows also that management will normally be expecting—if not insisting—that the external auditor give all possible consideration to the work of internal auditors while carrying out his or her financial statement audit.

　　While only the external auditors can sign a financial statement audit report in such a manner that the report is recognized by outsiders, internal audit often has the time and resources to perform certain necessary audit activities in a manner that is more cost-effective than external audit. For example, external auditors have a requirement to solicit independent confirmations of customer accounts receivable balances. The most effective way to perform this procedure is to make a selection from an automated accounts receivable file and to produce the confirmation requests using computer-assisted software. Internal audit can often do a more cost-effective job producing these confirmations to assist its external auditors. External audit might only set the selection criteria and supervise the results of the confirmation process. The result of this cooperative effort would be a cost-effective accounts receivable confirmation using the selected resources of both audit groups.

(d) PROBLEMS THAT LIMIT AUDIT COORDINATION

In some organizations, senior management may make a decision to limit internal audit's participation in the external audit process. This may be precipitated by external auditors who are sometimes guilty of requesting internal auditors to perform extensive reviews of areas that would normally only receive minimal external audit attention. While this will increase external audit assurances, it may not be the most efficient use of internal audit resources. Management needs to be advised that limited internal audit resources cannot complete their own plans if they are constantly responding to external audit requests. Although a decision may have been made to limit internal audit participation in external audit work, internal audit should continue to coordinate work through such things as sharing audit plans and audit reports.

External auditors base much of their audit selection work on the concept of materiality. For example, they may ignore audit procedures on certain balance sheet accounts because they will determine that any misstatements to those accounts are not material to the overall financial statement results. To many internal auditors accustomed to extensive audit testing, external auditor procedures based on very small sample sizes or limited inquiry and observation procedures will appear inadequate or even inappropriate. These issues can cause problems in auditor coordination. It is important that each understand the scope and objectives of the other in order to promote more effective coordination.

There are many other problems that can impact internal and external audit coordination. Most can be resolved, however, by close coordination between the director of internal audit and the public accounting firm partner responsible for the audit engagement. Even if management has restricted any joint internal-external audit projects, internal audit has an obligation to review plans and activities with the external auditor in order to achieve a level of coordination.

(i) Right Attitude by Each Audit Group.

Although internal audit will find an ample basis for generating an effective coordination effort, there is a further need of having a "right attitude" on the part of each internal and external audit group. This right attitude goes beyond an understanding of the common interests just described and pertains to the sincerity and cordiality with which the two audit groups view each other. Audit professionals are human beings just like any other individuals. They can therefore be subject to the same problems of pride, jealousy, distorted self-interest, inertia, lack of self-confidence, and other counterproductive forces. Too often, these problems unduly prevent an effective coordination effort. Both parties should be alert to the danger and encourage a more substantive approach to the problem. A healthy and friendly attitude is a necessary basis for cooperative efforts.

Some of these coordination problems were discussed previously and are often due to the fee-based work of external auditors compared to the salaried compensation of internal auditors. An internal auditor earning, for example, $40,000 per year cannot understand why an external audit staff member may be billing his or her time at $125 per hour. The internal auditor does a quick calculation and assumes that this external auditor must be receiving annual compensation in excess of $250,000. The internal auditor forgets that external auditors are not able to bill out 100% of their time, and that their audit firms have many other costs which are built into an individual's billing rate. Both internal and external audit staff members are often compensated with comparable salaries. The difference is that internal auditors typically do not charge their time to other departments at an external audit type of billing rate.

(ii) Establishing an Understanding at Senior Management Levels. The effective coordination of internal and external audit efforts requires the understanding and support of senior management, typically the chief financial officer, the chief executive officer, and the chairman of the audit committee of the board of directors. The chief financial officer (CFO) is usually the person who has the most direct interface with the external audit firm engagement partner. The CFO most often has line responsibility for the accounting and financial control activities that make up the system of internal accounting controls. These activities culminate in the financial statements that are reviewed by the external auditor. The CFO typically first works with the external auditor in coming to an agreement on the nature and scope of the external auditor's review.

The extent to which the CFO stresses the importance of internal audit's input and the possibilities of greater utilization through effective coordination can become a major determinant of how much consideration is given to a coordinated effort by the external auditor. The CFO usually has responsibility for managing the overall costs of audit activities, including the fees charged by the external audit firm, as presented in their annual proposal. As part of the initial negotiation over the scope of work to be performed and the proposed fees, the CFO can insist on certain levels of internal audit participation to help reduce external audit fees. This influence is, of course, all the more powerful when the CFO plays a dominant role in the negotiation of the external auditor's fees.

Traditionally, the chief executive officer (CEO) has assigned to the CFO the responsibility for accounting and financial control activities, including the preparation of the financial statements and arrangements with the external auditors. The enactment of the Foreign Corrupt Practices Act in 1977, as was discussed in Chapter 2, has tended to more deeply involve the CEO in these areas. In addition, the Securities and Exchange Commission in the United States may soon require the CEO to sign a management report attesting to the adequacy of the system of internal accounting control. Because of this, many CEOs have become more deeply involved in the work of their external auditors, and, in turn, the coordination of the work between internal and external auditors. Needless to say, the deeper the involvement of the CEO in this coordination effort, the more serious is the approach to the audit coordination process.

The expanding role of the audit committee of the board of directors was discussed in Chapter 6. The audit committee, under the leadership of its chairman, often takes the direct responsibility for engaging and approving the terms of the engagement of the external auditors. In many organizations, the audit committee has also taken an active role in coordinating internal and external audit efforts. This more active role is a direct result of the internal control recommendations published by the Committee of Sponsoring Organizations (COSO) of the Treadway Commission internal control model, also discussed in Chapter 2. This expanded audit committee role does not mean that the contributions of the other key parties are not extremely important. Effective coordination starts at the previously mentioned director of internal auditing, external audit engagement partner, and the CFO. However, the involvement of the audit committee under the leadership of a strong audit committee chairman adds a very important force for achieving effective internal and external audit coordination arrangements.

In order to achieve effective coordination of internal and external audit activities, a proper understanding by all involved individuals is very important. Especially needed is an understanding of the responsibilities and interests of each audit group in order to coordinate the audit effort in a manner that will achieve all major objectives. It is especially important that there is a high-level professional relationship between the two audit partners, internal and external audit. This relationship includes the understanding that internal audit does not function primarily to assist external audit and that external audit resources should also be devoted to providing services to management for achieving operational objectives.

32-4 MOTIVATING SUCCESSFUL AUDIT COORDINATION

There are several key motivating factors necessary for the effective coordination between internal and external auditors. Some of these factors tend to overlap, and they range from relatively low-level to those of high-level importance. Coordination at a lower level may, for example, be as basic as ensuring that representatives of the two audit groups do not arrive at a given location simultaneously, each with different objectives but seeking to examine some of the same records or interview the same employees. Coordination can also involve internal audit performing specified work directly under the supervision of members of the external auditing firm. In this instance, the motivation often is to reduce external audit staff time and thus reduce the cost of the external audit. On the other hand, the motivating factor can be one of higher-level cooperative assistance. This might include the coverage of defined portions of the audit work by internal audit with a later, relatively limited review of that work by the external auditors. Coordination could include also the exchange of findings and related information, together with joint discussions and agreement as to further follow-up on the correction of identified deficiencies. Motivation at higher levels does not ignore the more elementary types of benefits, but it also focuses on the deeper common interests of achieving an effective system of internal controls.

(a) RESPONSIBILITIES FOR INTERNAL-EXTERNAL MOTIVATION

The preceding discussions have stressed the importance of involving key individuals in both the internal and external audit organizations in an effective audit coordination effort. However, internal audit has a special responsibility because of its unique opportunities to provide leadership in the audit motivation and coordination effort. These opportunities are the result of internal audit's greater in-depth involvement with total corporate operations. In many organizations, internal audit is in an especially advantageous position to know and understand various potential audit problems. Further, internal auditors often will have a good professional understanding of the work of external auditors, or will at least generally understand the external audit standards. Internal audit, therefore, can often take the initiative in proposing and helping to work out arrangements that will better satisfy external audit's needs.

Internal audit's responsibilities may also extend to exerting reasonable pressure on various members of management to ensure their support in working with the external auditors. This is often necessary because some members of management may not understand the differing roles of internal and external audit. Internal audit should attempt to explain to its line management the differences in audit scope and objectives.

Internal audit often needs to negotiate various planned audit projects with external auditors. For example, if internal audit has performed a review in an area where external audit now plans to visit, internal audit should question why external audit cannot rely on the work of internal audit. Sometimes, internal audit may want to question a planned area of review if they have reasons to believe that external audit does not understand the audit risks in the area to be reviewed. External auditors often perform only a very limited risk assessment as part of their planning work and may decide to perform procedures that may not be all that necessary. Internal audit, because of its close knowledge of the organization, can suggest alternative audit approaches. This may even result in audit fee savings to the organization.

Internal audit must recognize, however, that external auditors are *independent,* and, thus, can perform their reviews in any area they feel necessary for performing their attest function. Internal audit can only recommend changes. However, if the external auditors are performing work that does not appear to be cost effective in the professional judgment of internal audit, this should be discussed initially with the external audit engagement partner. If the matter cannot be resolved, internal audit should bring these concerns to senior organization management.

When internal audit has serious reservations about some planned external audit procedure, an effective way to challenge that work is to request some documentation covering their risk assessment of the area to be reviewed or the tests performed. External auditors should go through a similar set of risk assessments as was discussed in Chapter 8 for internal auditors. Where there is a difference of opinion or where internal audit has performed a risk assessment over the same area but with different results, internal audit may want to go to senior management to raise these concerns. However, internal audit must always recognize that the external auditor is independent. If there is a serious dispute over audit procedures or other matters, the organization can always retain a new external auditor. This is a serious step, however, and should not be done casually.

(b) CONSTRAINTS LIMITING EFFECTIVE AUDIT COORDINATION

Many potential constraints can stand in the way of an effective audit coordination effort. These can range from very low-level, personnel-related conflicts to very significant management- or audit approach–related differences, all of which can prevent the effective coordination that should otherwise develop at a working level. Barriers to effective coordination concern anything that directly or indirectly weakens the overall audit effort.

There are several key types of constraints that can limit audit coordination. Many are based on the overall competency and charter of the internal audit function. As has been discussed previously, external auditors are required to assess the competency and objectivity of the internal audit function per their SAS No. 65. Some of the SAS No. 65 factors they should consider include:

- *Independence of the Internal Audit Function.* Chapter 1 discussed the necessity that internal audit should be an independent function within the organization.

However, external auditors have somewhat different standards for their assessment of independence. For example, an internal auditor may be totally independent in action but may also be a cousin or some other distant relative to a key member of the organization's management. External audit might not view that auditor as independent. Similarly, the internal audit function may report to the chief financial officer of the organization or even a lower-level accounting director with only minimal connection to the audit committee. External auditors may not consider that internal audit function to be independent from the pressures of their direct management.

• *Adequacy of Internal Audit Standards.* As discussed previously, SAS No. 65 requires that external auditors obtain an understanding of the internal audit function, including its standards. If internal audit follows the standards of The Institute of Internal Auditors or a related internal audit standards-setting group such as the General Accounting Office (GAO) for governmental auditors, there is a basis for coordination. However, if such standards are not followed in spirit or action, external audit may decide to severely limit any internal audit coordination. In all fairness to external auditors, their professional reputations are always on the line, and the work of internal audit must meet adequate professional standards. A real constraint can exist, however, when internal auditors are not sufficiently objective to recognize the need to perform their own work using proper standards and practices. Sometimes, internal audit may expect a level of external audit reliance on their work beyond that which is justified. For example, internal audit may have performed a review in a given area but not properly documented it through adequate workpapers. External audit may have to reperform some of these tests due to this inadequate audit documentation. They may feel that it is easier to just do all of the work themselves.

    Although the problem of achieving proper standards typically relates to internal audit, the problem can also exist in reverse. For various reasons, the work of external audit may not always meet the desired standards. For example, an external auditor may not have an adequate understanding of data-processing controls. While this is a significant problem that must be communicated to senior management, internal audit also may decide to limit any coordination activities in this area. There may be other situations where internal audit may look upon such coordination with considerable skepticism. This is particularly the case when internal audit believes its competence and understanding of a specialized area is superior.

• *Possible External Auditor Organizational Deficiencies.* The condition can sometimes exist where partner-level persons responsible for the audit support effective coordination but where that message never reaches lower-level personnel assigned to the engagement, such as in-charge auditors or managers based at different locations. The typical public accounting firm often has somewhat autonomous offices in various cities. If an audit engagement uses resources from multiple city offices, messages to coordinate the engagement with internal audit can sometimes be lost. Major problems can also exist in the form of overly rigid budgetary controls, where audit fee or schedule pressures do not allow sufficient time for properly planning internal audit participation. The public accounting firm may set its own budgets and schedules without consulting with internal audit. Internal audit management may not be aware of any plans for coordination until it has already made other plans for audit resources. These practical problems can become significant barriers to effective internal-external audit coordination.

- *Potential Legal Liability of External Auditor.* Another significant constraint to effective coordination is that external auditors are increasingly faced with legal responsibility for losses due to audit failures. A frequent assertion made in legal proceedings is that injured parties relied on the ''clean'' opinion of external audit, and the financial deficiencies that were disclosed later could have been identified if there had been a proper external audit effort. If internal audit standards or work quality is weak, the external audit team may be reluctant to place much reliance on the work of internal audit. Undue reliance by external audit on internal audit work could potentially be asserted or believed to be one of the bases for the failure to discover an audit deficiency.

As a result of these constraining factors, external auditors sometimes may be extremely cautious about entering into a significant audit coordination effort. If they do not see compliance with the internal audit standards, or see inadequate procedures, they may decide not to work with the internal audit department in a coordinated manner. However, they should always communicate these concerns to the organization's management. If the concerns are valid, internal audit should consider improving its standards and procedures so that its work will be accepted by the external auditors in the future.

The AICPA's SAS No. 65, as discussed previously, defines the factors external audit should consider when using the work of internal auditors. Since external audit is ultimately the party that will express an opinion on the fairness of the organization's financial statements, they also must make the final decision on using the work of internal auditors. Sometimes, external audit will fail to properly coordinate audit efforts despite the adequacy of internal audit standards and procedures. The director of internal audit should determine the reasons for this failure. If the two parties cannot resolve the matter, both may want to bring their dispute to senior management or, if necessary, to the audit committee.

32-5 COMPONENTS OF EFFECTIVE COORDINATION

Once decisions have been made to coordinate internal and external audit efforts, the specific components or types of coordination practices must be defined. These coordination activities will vary with the size and complexity of the organization as well as with the size of the two audit groups. For some organizations, certain coordination activities will take place in relatively simple forms between the two audit groups while each pursues its own mission. These same coordination activities may be a major part of a comprehensive coordination effort in other organizations.

Both the IIA Standards and SAS No. 65 outline various audit coordination activities that might be considered under the following 10 broad categories:

1. Exchange of audit documentation
2. Face-to-face sharing of information
3. Use of common methodologies
4. Collaborative work assistance

    5. Cooperation in training personnel

    6. Supportive follow-up of audit findings

    7. Joint planning

    8. Segmented audit work

    9. Joint reporting to higher organizational levels

   10. Cross-evaluation

(a) EXCHANGE OF AUDIT DOCUMENTATION

The exchange of audit documentation is a very basic type of coordination. The two major types of such documentation are workpapers and audit reports. The flow of those documents should be between the internal and external auditor.

- *Exchange of Workpapers.* The sharing of internal audit workpapers with external audit is probably the most common coordination effort in practice. The logic here is that external audit must examine those workpapers as part of its determination of the extent to which it can rely on the work of internal audit. In some cases, an internal auditor might be reluctant to expose workpapers that are not of the desired standards of professional quality; however, that is a problem that needs basic correction on its own merits. Typically, no really good reason can exist for internal audit withholding working papers from external audit.

  The reverse type of action—making the workpapers of external audit available to internal audit—is a slightly different problem. Some external auditors may feel in principle that such availability is not compatible with their independent status and broader responsibilities to the outside world. Also, external audit may in some cases not be too proud of the quality of some of its own workpapers. In still other instances, there may be timing problems due to the review procedures within the external audit firm. Generally, however, such availability should be extended by external audit, except in cases of a confidential nature. Even then, external audit should provide copies of selected extracts. Freer availability seems to be an increasingly accepted practice. Internal audit management should try to request access to selected external workpapers as part of the coordinated planning process.

- *Exchange of Reports.* The exchange of reports between the internal and external auditors seems to be a reasonable and typically general practice. The flow of reports from internal audit involves the same principles covered under workpapers. Internal audit reports should be distributed automatically to external audit. They constitute an important means of keeping external audit properly informed of internal audit findings and other audit activities. In some cases, certain internal audit reports may be of a confidential nature or not really within the concerns of external audit. However, this would be a very unusual situation.

  In a typical external audit engagement, narrative-type reports in addition to the regular audit opinion letter are less common and vary with the terms of the individual audit engagement. Such narrative reports often cover special controls reviews or supplemental management advisory comments. These narrative reports are normally of interest to internal audit, although some external audit reports may be confidential. Otherwise, the reports should be available to internal audit. It is normally a standard practice to make that distribution.

(b) FACE-TO-FACE SHARING OF INFORMATION

It is desirable for internal and external auditors to at least cooperate to the extent of responding to day-to-day questions from each other. This allows the exchange of needed information with relatively little effort. Examples might include information about a new auditing standard, organization changes, or the status of a new computer system that was under development. More extended requests might require extra efforts to provide responses, and at that point the factors of cost and effort required need careful consideration.

The face-to-face sharing of information reaches a more comprehensive level when there is an ongoing sharing of overall audit-related information from one audit group to the other. Typically, internal audit is more likely to run into matters that would be of interest to external audit during internal audit's more detailed and broader coverage of operational activities. Typically also, external audit depends very much on such a flow of useful information, and this level of cooperation is generally understood by both parties to be important. Internal audit can be an effective sensing group, alerting external audit to developments that bear on external audit's total audit effort, including the assessment of control risk.

Although external audit is less likely to develop information that is useful to internal audit, there is the same need and the same mutual benefit in that reciprocal action. A particularly important input source here is the nonconfidential discussions that external auditors typically have with senior organization officers, and which can sometimes be made available to internal audit. However, many of these discussions may be highly confidential, and internal audit should not press their external audit counterparts for information that is not public in nature. More important, external audit can supply internal audit with information on such matters as new accounting and auditing standards.

(c) USE OF A COMMON METHODOLOGY

In many situations, internal audit should try to follow technical and documentation procedures similar to those of the external auditors. The most common examples are the format and indexing schemes of workpapers, audit sampling procedures, and audit procedures followed for specialized audit areas. Alternative sampling approaches were discussed in Chapter 13. Some external audit firms have strong technical support in this area and may endorse one approach over another. Because that sampling approach may be supported by external auditor–supplied computer programs and other materials, it is often efficient for internal audit to use the same approach. One rationale here is that this makes it easier for external audit to review and utilize the work of internal auditors.

Some internal auditors, however, may view such common procedures as relatively unimportant. In any event, it must be recognized that internal audit's objectives are broader than those of external audit, and there is often a need for different approaches to specific audit tasks. Probably the best approach is to recognize that such a common methodology may be most useful in financial auditing situations, but that judgment needs to be exercised in its actual application. Certainly, common approaches should not be carried to such an extreme that they get in the way of individual efforts for developing meaningful and useful audit results. A common methodology is a tool to be used with reasonable care and caution.

(d) COLLABORATIVE WORK ASSISTANCE

In some instances, external audit may request direct assistance from internal audit in performing its work. Here, internal audit does not share independent work efforts with the external auditors but works directly under the supervision of them, essentially as part of the latters' staff. As previously discussed, this was a more common practice in earlier years, when the emphasis on the coordination effort was primarily to reduce external auditor hours and fees. In its lowest-level form, the internal auditors assigned might function as junior helpers. In a more sophisticated form, however, the two audit groups might work together under a single administrative head on a project such as an inventory observation, because of the need for tight audit coordination and control. This same situation might also exist in the case of a fraud investigation.

Any such collaborative work arrangement must be handled with extreme care. Internal auditors should generally resist any direct assignment that implies a second-class work status that is not in keeping with their own professional competence. The problem can be solved sometimes by having internal audit function serving as an assigned consultant, or with the clear understanding that the arrangement involves equals working on a temporary basis to meet a clearly recognized need. Another solution is to put the best qualified person in charge of the joint work effort, regardless of whether an external or internal auditor, and regardless of who is to ultimately be in possession of the workpapers involved.

(e) COOPERATION IN TRAINING PERSONNEL

Quite commonly, both the internal and external audit groups have training capabilities that are useful for both audit groups. External audit, which serves many clients, is especially likely to have developed training programs of various types, which can be useful to the internal auditors of their clients. In other instances, however, internal audit may be conducting training sessions or developing other training materials that are unique to the particular client organization. The external audit firm may want to utilize such materials for its staff members working on that particular audit. An example here might be when the training relates to special production processes or computer systems that need to be used by external audit. In actual practice, however, because internal and external auditors have different primary missions, it is often more advantageous for each to develop and administer its own training programs.

When training materials of one audit group are used by the other, such usage is usually provided without extra charge because of the common interests served. In recent years, however, some external auditing firms have developed training programs for internal auditors as a separate business venture, to provide a supplementary source of professional income. Such training programs are less directly linked to the audit coordination program. Internal audit should weigh these materials on their individual strengths and should always select the best source for internal audit training, even if delivered by another public accounting firm.

(f) SUPPORTIVE FOLLOW-UP OF AUDIT FINDINGS

Both the external and internal audit groups will be developing findings and recommendations affecting the activities of the organization under review. Although the line organization personnel individually and collectively have the basic responsibility for the consideration of such recommendations and the related corrective actions, both audit groups have a common interest in the nature and scope of all reported deficiencies and in the later corrective actions. Both auditor groups should be alert to all deficiencies and should work in a coordinated manner to monitor corrective actions over the reported operational procedures. Also, the auditors should be very interested in the overall audit findings monitoring system and how effectively it is being administered.

As previously discussed, external audit's primary interest is in the fairness of the presentation of the financial statements, and external auditors will not be involved with the underlying operational procedures in the same depth as internal audit. Hence, external audit will normally have fewer audit findings and recommendations pertaining to those operational procedures. In addition, an external auditor will be less involved in the follow-ups to audit recommendation than will internal audit. However, the particular findings and recommendations made by external audit normally have great visibility with organization management. As a result, the initiation of any findings and subsequent follow-up by external audit should be viewed with special concern by all parties of interest.

External and internal auditors should cooperate in every possible way to share information on anything bearing upon the current and evolving effectiveness of the organization's operational procedures, especially in the areas pertaining to the system of internal control. By working together, they best assure the implementation of needed corrective actions.

(g) JOINT PLANNING

When the internal and external auditors work cooperatively to achieve effective audit coordination, they will find that they need to sit down together to plan their respective audit programs in advance of the actual audit efforts. As discussed in Chapter 6, the planning process involves the audit committee and the two audit groups. Typically, it extends over a number of years and should be expressed partially in the budget approved for the upcoming audit year. Although external audit will normally participate to some extent in that long-range planning process, its own plans focus more sharply on the need each year to develop the proposal for the following year's engagement, which requires the approval of the stockholders and the board of directors. Typically, that proposal is made just following the completion of the annual audit.

Chapter 7 discussed the planning process, where internal audit develops an audit universe of all entities or units subject to audit, performs a risk analysis against that universe to select candidates with the highest audit risks for review, and develops a current and long-range audit plan based upon that risk evaluation. External auditors should perform a similar risk assessment based upon the scope of their review at a given organization. The concept of audit universe is different for external audit. Their universe will often be based upon various balance sheet accounts or financial transactions, while the internal audit universe is usually based upon operational areas or processes in the organization. However, these risk-assessment processes and audit plans based on the separate audit universes should be coordinated.

The result of this coordination is a continuing planning process whereby audits for future years are added to the plan and activity in current years further refined to the extent practicable preceding the performance of actual audit work. Through joint planning, the needs of each audit group can be reconciled. On the one hand, internal audit determines risk-based audit plans with an understanding of external auditor needs for the next year. External audit, then, makes its risk-based judgment of what needs to be done to satisfy the audit responsibilities, with consideration given to the support expected from internal audit. In making that judgment, proper weight should be given to the size of the internal audit staff, its demonstrated capabilities, and the extent to which it can be available for this audit work.

The benefits derived from this coordination are essentially the same as those obtained from any kind of advance planning. Auditors, like any other managers, need to determine in advance what they want to accomplish and how they will make that desired future become reality. This is true irrespective of whether such agreed-upon plans can and should be modified when changing conditions so require. The coordination of these risk-based audit plans results in the achievement of overall audit objectives and provides the most essential foundation for an effective coordinated audit effort. This should be a standard practice in the well-managed internal audit organization.

(h) SEGMENTED AUDIT WORK

While the advance planning between internal and external auditors provides the essential foundation for an effective coordination effort, its benefits are best achieved when the planned audit work involved is divided in a fashion that is most suited to the needs and skills of each of the two audit groups. The goal here is to divide the planned audit work in such a way that each audit function can deal with segments of that audit work in an independent manner. This segmentation is often best achieved by assigning to each the primary audit responsibilities for an individual plant, department, division, company, or procedural area. Similarly, various information systems areas can be divided up in a like manner. The audit group with primary responsibility for an area can then plan the required audit effort in greater detail and execute that plan with staff under its own supervision. At the same time, workpapers, reports, findings, and recommendations can be shared in the manner previously discussed. Also, the audit work of internal audit can be subject to further review as is necessary to satisfy external audit, as part of their overall evaluation of the fairness of the final statements.

Advanced audit planning, together with plan segmentation, can become the most sophisticated and most effective type of coordination between the two professional audit groups. It provides the best possible basis for an ongoing coordination while the two audit groups, as respected professional partners, proceed with their work, respond to new developments, and work together under the overall leadership of an audit committee to achieve the best possible total audit effort. This professional partnership typically exists in the better-managed larger organization, but it can work no matter what the size of the engagement and audit staff involved. An example of such a coordinated audit plan, based upon a hypothetical company, is shown in Figure 32.2.

(i) JOINT REPORTING TO SENIOR MANAGEMENT

An especially significant aspect of an effective audit coordination effort is the trend toward joint reporting to higher-level organization management. This joint reporting is typically directed to executives, senior management committees, or the audit committee of the board of directors. This joint reporting can take several forms. It can, for example, be a joint management discussion based upon separate reports from the two audit groups. It may

Figure 32.2   Internal-External Coordinated Audit Plan Example

ExampleCo Internal Audit and Debit and Credit, LLP, will participate in the following joint review activities during Fiscal Year 20X1:

Audit Area	Debit and Credit Responsibility	Internal Audit Responsibility
1. Review changes in internal control environment	Review I/A W/P	Perform Audit
2. New Automated Accounts Receivable System		
2a. Computer Systems Controls Review		Perform Audit
2b. Develop Confirmation CAAT		I/A to Develop
2c. Confirm Customer Receivables	D&C Resp.	
3. General Ledger Account Analytical Review	D&C Resp.	
4. New XYZ Manufacturing Plant Operations		
4a. Document Material Control Procedures		Perform Audit
4b. Test New Manufacturing Cost System	Review I/A W/P	Perform Audit

> Note: This is only an extract of what should be a much more detailed plan outlining the separate responsibilities for internal audit and the external audit firm responsible for the year-end financial audit.

also come about through a joint assignment to the two audit groups, where both have had a substantive role in the review. The two audit groups may then present a single joint report or coordinated individual reports. Needless to say, this assumes that there is a high level of cooperative collaboration between the two groups. Joint reporting requires a sophisticated level of coordination between internal and external auditors.

(j) CROSS-EVALUATIONS

The two audit groups have professional backgrounds that are very similar in many areas. This, together with the fact that they see a great deal of each other's work, provides a strong basis for effective cross-evaluation. Of course, as defined in SAS No. 65, external audit is expected to evaluate the work of internal auditors when they rely upon that work. Moreover, external audit's self-interest in having good internal auditing, combined with their close access to senior management, can help to get better organizational status and resources for internal audit. Internal audit should encourage cross-evaluation by external audit and make full use of it.

Evaluation of the external audit effort by internal audit is also inevitable and useful, although it may cause some differences or problems. In some situations, external audit may not really welcome evaluation by the internal audit group. A more healthy attitude, however, is to recognize that there is always room for improvement and that very often internal audit can make a good, objective evaluation. Moreover, the acceptance of constructive cross-evaluation is more consistent with the professional partnership approach described throughout this chapter. It can be expected that there will be more of the two-way evaluation in the future. This has been an accepted practice in many larger organizations, and may become a standard procedure in the future.

32-6 COORDINATION IN PERSPECTIVE

The common interests of internal and external auditors in their assessments of the adequacy of the system of internal control, as a basis for achieving their respective primary missions, provide substantial motivation to achieve an effective coordination effort. Clearly, effective coordination makes good sense for all parties. Clearly also, effective coordination serves the overall interests of the organization. The challenge for all is to understand and support those factors that contribute to the achievement of effective coordination. For internal audit, it is important to understand the primary missions of each audit group while building on the strong common interests as foundations for the achievement of those primary missions. It is also important for internal auditors to demonstrate their compliance with standards of professional excellence to provide the needed basis for effective coordination between two mutually respected professional partners. Only then can the coordination effort support the achievement of an integrated audit process for maximum organizational welfare. There is the need for an effort by all parties of interest—especially of the internal and external auditors themselves—to foster effective coordination. It needs also to be recognized that effective coordination is a continuous process. The potential rewards, however, clearly warrant the efforts that may be expended.

CHAPTER 33

Internal Audit Quality-Assurance Reviews

33-1 INTRODUCTION: THE IMPORTANCE OF QUALITY ASSURANCE

Internal auditors have a special role in their service to the management of the modern organization. As has been described in many chapters of this book, internal auditors will visit a unit or component of an organization, review its controls, and make recommendations for improvements. The modern internal auditor uses the Standards for the Professional Practice of Internal Auditing, described in Chapter 5, as well as the supporting practices and procedures discussed throughout this book. The director of internal audit will have communicated these standards and practices to all members of the internal audit staff. Other members of the organization—that is, the auditees—should have a basic understanding that internal audit is following a set of good practices when it performs its reviews. However, no one regularly "audits the auditors" to see that they are following good practices and their own professional standards.

The effective modern internal audit function should look at itself from time to time to determine if all of its own components are following good internal audit practices and procedures. This is best accomplished if internal audit goes through an "audit the auditors" type of review over its own functions. The Standards for the Professional Practice of Internal Auditing refer to what are called *quality-assurance reviews*. Standard 560 calls for the director of internal auditing "to establish and maintain a quality assurance program" to appraise the quality of the audit work performed through ongoing supervisory reviews, reviews by internal audit of its own work, and reviews by external parties.

Internal audit quality-assurance reviews are a special type of audit—more than a normal management assessment of operations or an external auditor SAS No. 70 review, as was discussed in Chapter 32. While the IIA Standard 560 calls for three levels of review, this chapter will primarily focus on reviews of internal audit performed by persons outside normal internal audit operations, including members of other organizations or even a specialized department within internal audit. These reviews allow an internal audit function to assess the quality of its own procedures and its compliance with internal audit standards. This chapter describes the elements that should be included in an internal audit quality-assurance program and describes how internal audit can establish a program to perform these reviews.

33-2   WHO BENEFITS FROM QUALITY-ASSURANCE REVIEWS?

The internal audit function in a modern organization sometimes operates outside of other mainstream organization functions. Internal audit certainly reports to very senior levels of management, including the audit committee of the board, and has contact with all other functions in the organization through its operational and financial reviews. However, as a very specialized function, internal audit is not always considered when other organization performance measurement policies and procedures are established. This is not to suggest that internal audit is ignored. However, a new program of employee incentive pay, a major quality-assurance initiative, or some other employee benefit does not always consider the unique aspects of the internal audit function. These programs are often focused on the organization's main functions, whether they are manufacturing, distribution, or financial. As a very key function in the organization, however, internal audit needs a way to measure itself and to establish incentives to do a better job. This is one of the real benefits of an internal audit quality-assurance review.

While internal audit itself is the prime beneficiary of these reviews, other stakeholders in an organization also benefit from a strong program of internal audit quality-assurance reviews. These reviews allow internal audit to demonstrate to management that it is doing a good job or taking corrective action to improve if necessary. Other parties, such as regulatory agencies, also may benefit from these reviews. They will provide them with a basis to better utilize the work of the internal audit department.

(a)   BENEFITS TO INTERNAL AUDIT

The main beneficiary of any internal audit quality-assurance review program will be the internal audit function itself. As discussed, internal audit operates somewhat differently from many other functions in a modern organization and often cannot measure itself by that organization's normal measures of success, such as sales, production, or administrative efficiencies. An external reviewer who understands the internal audit process and who has had exposure to other organizations can review internal audit operations with both the perspective of internal audit's compliance with professional standards and by how its operations compare with other similar internal audit organizations.

A review of compliance with internal audit standards also is valuable. As outlined in Chapter 5, these standards are quite comprehensive, covering all aspects of internal audit operations. While an internal audit function should have a program in place to follow these standards in all of its auditing activities, compliance with one or another specific standard may slip through inattention or just the pressure of completing audit projects. A quality-assurance review will allow a reviewer outside of day-to-day internal audit activities to assess how good a given audit function is doing in complying with internal audit standards. This can be a valuable benefit to the modern internal audit function.

The other area where internal audit can benefit from a quality-assurance review is from the reviewer's comparison of an internal audit function with other internal audit organizations. Internal audit management does not always know how well it compares to other internal audit functions in terms of such things as its use of audit automation, efficiency in performing audit tests, or travel policies. Directors of internal audit can gather some of this information through their professional contacts at Institute of Internal Auditors meetings or other personal or professional contacts. However, these contacts do not always provide the same level of objectivity that would be found through the work of an independent reviewer who looked at several internal audit organizations. Even though one-on-one professional contacts are valuable, there can be a tendency for professional peers in different organizations to gloss over some faults or weaknesses when comparing their relative activities.

Internal audit quality-assurance reviews, performed by either outside parties or by a specialized function in the larger internal audit department, can add significant value to the internal audit organization. The review may point to areas where some internal audits had been performed in a manner not fully in compliance with standards or where efficiencies could have been achieved by using different audit procedures. For example, the sample selection approach used in a given audit may have been too large. Although the audit's results were correct, a smaller sample might have produced the same audit conclusions but with greater efficiency. As a result of such quality-assurance reviews, internal audit management may be able to take the recommendations and improve its own overall operations.

(b) BENEFITS TO MANAGEMENT

Several levels of management, ranging from the managers directly responsible for areas reviewed to the audit committee of the board, are all potential beneficiaries of internal audit quality-assurance reviews. Although an internal audit team should certainly not show its latest quality-assurance review report to the auditee management of the next audit project, the findings of a good program of quality-assurance reviews should result in better and more efficient audits. All members of management—and managers directly responsible for units audited, in particular—will benefit from an efficient and effective internal audit organization. A program of quality-assurance reviews should help to ensure ongoing audit efficiency and effectivity.

Senior management realizes even greater benefits from a strong program of internal audit quality-assurance reviews. As has been discussed throughout this book, internal audit is a strong component in the system of internal control that should be in place in the modern organization. Senior management, up through the audit committee of the board, should understand the overall principles of internal control, but it may not fully understand the workings of a modern internal audit function. By sharing the summarized results of an internal audit quality-assurance review with various levels of senior management, it can have a greater confidence in the quality of the reviews performed. This is a major benefit to the overall organization.

(c) LEGAL AND REGULATORY REVIEW REQUIREMENTS

As society increasingly recognizes the importance of internal audit as a key component in organizational control and governance, various laws and regulations rely upon the work of internal audit. Chapter 31 as well as Chapters 34 and 35 talk about some of these laws and regulations in effect in the United States. Two with a major impact are the Foreign Corrupt Practices Act (FCPA) and the Organizational Sentencing Guidelines (OSG). The FCPA, among other matters, requires that organizations maintain good systems of documentation over their internal controls. The OSG calls for a strong organizational compliance program as one of its measurements for reducing the punishments for an organization found guilty of wrongdoing. Both of these measures assume a strong internal audit function.

An effective program of quality-assurance reviews will help to strengthen that internal audit function.

Although the well-managed organization should have systems and controls in place to prevent and detect any criminal acts, in the complex world of today even the best-intentioned organization can potentially run afoul of some law. As will be discussed in Chapter 35, if an organization is convicted of some wrongdoing, the judge is often compelled to use the OSG to determine the punishment. Those OSG penalties can be very much reduced if the guilty organization has an effective compliance program in place to prevent future occurrences. Internal audit is a key component of any such compliance program, and the results of a strong program of quality-assurance reviews might be used to demonstrate to a prosecutor that internal audit has effective programs in place. Although a director of internal auditing would certainly not want to develop a program of quality-assurance reviews only for these very protective reasons, the results of the reviews would benefit both the judge making a sentencing decision and, of course, the organization.

33-3 ELEMENTS OF A QUALITY-ASSURANCE REVIEW

The decision of both who performs the internal audit quality-assurance review and what areas are reviewed will determine the overall success of this process. A review by persons who do not really understand the internal audit process and its operating standards will accomplish little. Similarly, a review that is not well organized and that misses key areas of internal audit operations will not appropriately assess the overall quality of internal audit policies and procedures. There is no ''one size fits all'' rule for these quality-assurance reviews, however. Internal audit functions vary in size from fairly small organizations serving the operations of one business and one facility to very large organizations spanning diverse business operations across the globe. The director of internal audit is often the key person responsible for designing and managing the internal audit quality-assurance process. This review approach will be subject to the approval of senior management in the organization and the audit committee of the board.

In developing a quality-assurance review approach, the director of internal audit needs to make three basic decisions. First, some general requirements and review objectives should be established. Second, appropriately qualified persons must be designated to perform the review. The third decision is to decide how the results of the review will be communicated to management and used to improve internal audit operations. Each of these will depend upon the size of the internal audit department, its responsibilities within the organization, and senior management's interest in this review process. While there is no one correct answer, the paragraphs following will discuss some of the alternatives available to the modern internal audit function.

(a) REQUIREMENTS FOR INTERNAL AUDIT QUALITY-ASSURANCE REVIEWS

An internal audit quality-assurance review should be a formal audit process not unlike many of the other audit procedures outlined in other chapters of this book. The review should be properly planned, follow a formal plan or audit program, and be performed by qualified reviewers who can exhibit an appropriate level of independence. Whether performed by a special unit of internal audit charged with performing such reviews or by an outside reviewer such as a public accounting firm, the review should follow the same standards of independence and objectivity found in any internal audit. The only significant difference here is that the quality-assurance review will focus its efforts on internal audit procedures. The establishment of these requirements is an important first step necessary to launch an internal audit quality-review function.

Although management may want to vary the content of any review to reflect local concerns within an organization and its internal audit function, the review should concentrate on the internal audit organization's compliance with the Standards for the Professional Practice of Internal Auditing, as was outlined in Chapter 5. These standards have been codified in five major areas, and any quality-assurance review should assess compliance with the principles outlined in these standards, as follows:

> *100 Independence.*   The internal audit department should operate as an independent entity within the organization and also should exhibit both independence and objectivity in all of its activities.
>
> *200 Professional Proficiency.*   Audits should be adequately staffed with knowledgeable professionals who exhibit due professional care in completing their audit assignments. Audit projects should be properly supervised and the staff performing the work should receive appropriate levels of continuing education.
>
> *300 Scope of Work.*   Audits performed should achieve their established goals and objectives. The work should emphasize compliance with established policies, procedures, and laws in addition to other audit objectives.
>
> *400 Performance of Audit Work.*   All audits should be properly planned, various evidential data should be examined and evaluated, and the results of the review should be communicated to proper persons in the organization.
>
> *500 Management.*   All audits completed by the department should have proper management controls, ranging from a good system of departmental policies and procedures to appropriate relationships with internal auditors.

The specific details behind how the quality of internal audit operations will be measured depends upon many factors, including the size of the internal audit department, directions by senior management specifying more emphasis on one area over another, and other factors. Nevertheless, all internal audit activities should be measured against compliance with these standards.

A quality-assurance review is usually initiated through a detailed review of compliance with internal audit procedures. This would include such matters as an evaluation of the risk-assessment planning process, reviews of other planning documents, staff assignment procedures, a review of selected workpapers and reports used in actual audits, and all other planning and administrative materials used by internal audit in the course of performing its audit assignments. The purpose of this review approach is to measure the overall quality of internal audit's own procedures. While the specific procedures to be performed will vary with the size and activities of the internal audit department and its various activities, Figure 33.1 outlines the general procedures to be performed in a review of internal audit quality-assurance review.

In addition to reviewing workpapers and administrative procedures, the quality-assurance review should focus on the auditees who either request reviews or have reviews performed in their areas. An internal audit function contributes little to the quality of procedures in the overall organization if auditee management has serious concerns about the nature of the work performed, including the appropriateness of the audit conclusions

Figure 33.1 General Procedures for a Quality-Assurance Review of Internal Audit

33.1.01 Define the areas to be included in the internal audit QA review—whether the entire function or just a separate function, such as a manufacturing or geographic area; such as the ABC and DEF manufacturing divisions.

33.1.02 Define the time period for the audits to be included in the QA review—whether from the conclusion of the last QA review or for the 12-month period prior to the announcement of the audit.

33.1.03 Determine who will be performing the QA internal audit review and ascertain that the reviewer understands both IIA standards and supporting internal audit department procedures.

33.1.04 If internal audit has not had such a quality-assurance review within the last 24 months, take steps to assure that both members of the internal audit staff and management understand the purpose and nature of the QA review.

33.1.05 If the QA review team plans to survey or interview auditees outside the internal audit department, make some preliminary plans to inform all affected persons.

33.1.06 Based on internal audits completed and in-process, develop a general strategy for the number and types of audits to be selected for review. If special knowledge areas are to be included, such as computer security or automated design, determine that appropriate resources have been allocated.

33.1.07 Decide if the QA review will be on a top-level basis, checking for compliance to general standards or planned to include detailed reviews of selected audits, including workpaper reference checks or reperformance of tests.

33.1.08 If problems are encountered in the course of the planned QA review, such as audits requiring a more detailed review, procedures should be prepared to evaluate the QA review's scope or schedule.

33.1.09 Develop a general procedure for the format and nature of the QA final audit report.

33.1.10 Develop a strategy for reporting the results of the QA review to other members of the internal audit department and to selected members of senior management.

reached and how those conclusions were communicated to management. These matters will be discussed later in this chapter in the section titled ''Auditee Interviews and Surveys.'' The idea is not to determine that a representative group of auditees necessarily *like* the internal auditors who performed one or another review in their area but to assess whether the reviews were performed in an appropriately professional manner.

As a result of these review procedures and auditee surveys, the quality-assurance reviewer should summarize his or her results and prepare a report for the director of internal auditing. Based upon these report recommendations, a plan for improvement or corrective action should be established. In some cases, if the reviewers found that certain reviews did not follow good internal audit procedures, a program of ongoing review or corrective action should be established. If the quality-assurance review points out the need for such improvements as increased continuing education, a plan for corrective action should be established. The paragraphs following describe in greater detail the procedures performed in quality-assurance reviews.

(b) WHO PERFORMS THE QUALITY-ASSURANCE REVIEW?

Although a director of internal audit may see the value of a quality-assurance review, an independent party is often needed to perform the review. This is often fairly easy in a large, multi-unit internal audit department where a team of centralized "corporate" internal auditors as well as others from differing divisional units can perform quality-assurance reviews of other divisional units. Although there is always the possibility for certain jealousies and nonobjective appraisals, an in-house quality review, if properly managed, can be performed inexpensively as well as effectively and efficiently. For larger internal audit departments, in-house resources should be devoted to performing periodic quality-assurance reviews.

Some internal audit departments are either not large enough to perform a separate quality-assurance review or may face other challenges that prevent them from having members of their organization perform quality-assurance reviews. A five-person internal audit group, for example, cannot realistically conduct a quality-assurance review with one member of the staff reviewing the other four. Internal audit management has two basic options here. They can either develop a self-assessment type of review and have all members of the smaller staff evaluate themselves, or they can contract with an outside party to perform the review.

The options available for outside parties to perform a quality-assurance review include public accounting firms, consultants who specialize in such reviews, or internal auditors from other organizations. As another option, The Institute of Internal Auditors has a review program where it will schedule a team of professionals to perform the review. In addition to very small internal audit groups, some larger internal audit functions may find these outside source review approaches to be attractive. The following section will discuss each of these alternatives.

(i) Reviews by Members of Internal Audit.

A larger internal audit organization can perform quality-assurance reviews using designated members of the department. In many respects, an internal auditor who is familiar with the organization, its procedures, and industry—but also understands general internal audit procedures—is often the best, most qualified person to review internal audit operations. Just as internal audit performs a review of another function, such as the purchasing department, the purchasing department could review itself by assigning certain people from the organization to perform this task. However, unless the purchasing department had experience performing such self-assessments, the results of their review could be viewed as self-serving. Internal audit has an advantage over a function such as purchasing, as internal audit regularly exhibits its independence through its standards and other review activities. A larger internal audit function can perform its own effective quality-assurance reviews if it can demonstrate to others, both inside and outside of internal audit, that it is acting as an independent party.

Larger internal audit functions can establish effective quality-review programs internally by designating certain members of the organization the responsibility to perform quality-assurance reviews throughout the department. The internal audit department must be large enough to allow one auditor, or a small specialized group of auditors, to perform the quality-assurance reviews separate from normal audit activities. In a large internal audit department, there may be enough activity to justify a full-time quality-assurance function. In addition to the reviews, it could perform other activities such as developing audit procedures. This internal-review arrangement will not work if members of the regular audit staff are regularly pulled from the normal schedule and asked to review their peers.

Although internal auditors have standards that require them to act independently, quality reviews of themselves can be viewed by some persons as either self-serving exercises or as programs to "get" one or another persons in the audit department. As mentioned, the reviews should be performed by an independent function within the internal audit organization and should otherwise follow normal internal audit procedures. That is, the internal audit quality-assurance function would schedule each of its reviews in the same manner as internal audit plans and schedules any normal audit. If it were doing a quality review of a separate organizational unit's internal audit function, it would schedule and announce the review as any normal audit. Once the review was completed, the manager responsible for the unit reviewed would respond to the audit report as would any other auditee. Copies of the final report would go to the director of internal audit, who could take further action as necessary. Figure 33.2 shows how a quality-assurance review function might be organized in a very large internal audit department. This is a particularly effective way to organize internal audit when the audit functions are distributed throughout the organization. An outside quality-assurance reviewer would probably not get to all of the geographically remote units in the course of a single review. An in-house set of quality-assurance reviewers could.

(ii) Quality-Assurance Self-Assessment Reviews.   In a self-assessment review, the internal auditors directly responsible for regular audit activities will perform a review of their own operations. The internal auditors would not be from a specialized function within internal audit but normal "line" members of the internal audit staff and its management. Using an established set of self-assessment procedures, various regular members of the internal audit department would step back, look at their own operations, and effectively

Figure 33.2   Quality Assurance in the Internal Audit Organization

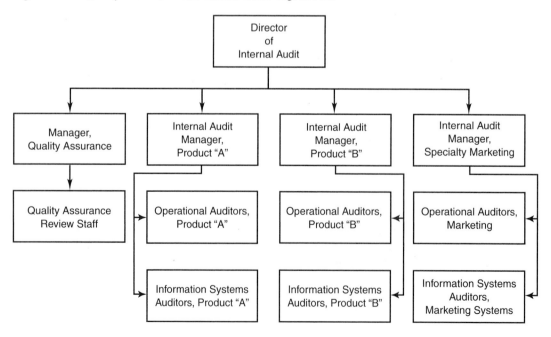

audit themselves. This work would often be headed by a line manager or even by the director of internal audit, with audit staff support to gather any necessary details.

Self-assessment reviews are often the most realistic way for a very small internal audit staff, perhaps with less than 10 members, to review its own operations. The staff might postpone normal scheduled audits and block out time to perform the self-assessment review. Time could be allocated for this type of review when the staff was not otherwise busy with scheduled audits.

A self-assessment review by the same internal audit staff responsible for normal audit procedures almost appears as if the auditees are auditing themselves! However, this is often the only way to review the quality of internal audit procedures in a small organization. Budget limitations might prevent hiring outsiders to perform the review and a small audit department could not justify the people resources. Members of the staff would be asked to step back and review all of the procedures performed in the course of a series of audits, including planning, workpaper documentation, audit report content, and a variety of other matters. The audit steps performed would follow the general procedures described in Figure 33.1 as well as questionnaire-based approaches discussed later in this chapter. Rather than writing a report about itself, as is often done when persons outside of normal internal audit operations perform this type of quality-assurance review, findings from the self-assessment review are often shared through a series of introspective review meetings. Here, internal audit management and all parties involved would take steps to improve operations based upon the self-assessment review findings. For a smaller internal audit organization, self-assessment is usually a cost-effective way to measure quality assurance. People are often their own best critics!

(iii) Reviews by Members of Public Accounting Firms.   Many of the major public accounting firms today have established specialized functions to provide services to internal audit departments, both for their audit clients and others. One of these functions is called *outsourcing,* wherein the public accounting firm will take over total management of the internal audit function by bringing in its own management team to run the internal audit function. Internal audit outsourcing has received considerable attention in recent years, and will be discussed in Chapter 34.

Another available external audit firm service is to perform a specialized quality-assurance review of an internal audit function. Although the danger of a conflict of interests exists, these reviews are most often performed by the organization's external auditors for an internal auditor of a client, often at the request by the audit committee of the board or by senior management. Public accounting firms also offer these services to other organizations, not their normal audit clients. These public accounting–based reviews often will emphasize the need for strong standards and documentation of the internal audit work performed. The major weakness with these quality-assurance reviews is that the external auditor reviewers may not always have a strong understanding of the internal audit process. While the engagement partner that "sells" review may have a general understanding of the internal audit process, often the staff members who perform the work do not.

For a small internal audit department that does not have the resources to bring in its own auditors from another organization unit, or does not want to incur the expense of hiring an independent firm to do the work, a public accounting firm can be a good resource for performing a quality-assurance review. If they are also responsible for the financial statement audit, they will have some insights and know the people, making the job easier. If a public accounting–managed quality-assurance review of an internal audit function is proposed, either by senior management or external audit, the director of internal audit should ask the following general questions:

- *What are the qualifications of the staff who will perform the actual review?* "Qualifications" here refers to knowledge of the internal audit process, including a strong understanding of the operational approach used by internal auditors and the Professional Standards for Internal Auditing, as outlined in Chapter 5. Internal audit should be wary of external audit firms that do not demonstrate that level of understanding.

- *If a financial statement audit client, how will this review differ from SAS No. 70 review procedures?* Chapter 32, "Coordination with External Auditors," discussed Statement on Auditing Standards (SAS) No. 70, which outlines the procedures a public accounting firm should perform in order to rely upon the work of its client's internal auditors. The external auditor is effectiveiy asked to review the performance and work of the internal audit group before relying on that work to help gather data to express his or her audit opinions. Recognizing this SAS No. 70 requirement, internal audit should ask the question of how a proposed external audit quality-assurance review will differ from an external auditor's normal SAS No. 70 work. While an internal audit quality-assurance review should be more comprehensive, the external auditor may be tempted to just repackage portions of the SAS No. 70 work as a separate quality-assurance review.

- *Will the review findings be presented to internal audit or to senior management?* External auditors normally serve the audit committee of the board rather than a separate unit within the organization, such as internal audit. Even though the director of internal audit has arranged for the external auditor to perform the quality-assurance review, an external auditor may be tempted to report findings directly to the audit committee. This is particularly true in the case of a financial statement of an audit client. In a quality-assurance review, internal audit is looking for observations and insights to help improve its operations. This understanding should be established in advance.

As discussed, an external audit firm can often be a very good source to perform a quality-assurance review. However, many public accounting firms do not have a specialized internal audit review function; only some of the major firms have established this level of expertise. Even if an organization's external auditors do not have an internal audit review function, in the interest of "client service" many firms will gladly agree to perform such a review. The director of internal audit should approach such offers with caution for the reasons outlined above. This does not mean that they would be unable to perform an appropriate internal audit quality-assurance review. Rather, internal audit should advise the potential external audit reviewer about its compliance with internal audit standards and should provide them with an outside reference on internal audit standards and procedures, such as that found in this book.

(iv) Reviews by Other Qualified Parties. An internal audit function that does not want to devote resources to performing its own quality-assurance review but also does not want to contract with a public accounting firm to do the work can find other quite qualified persons to perform the review. Several small consulting firms have been established to work with internal audit functions and perform quality-assurance reviews. The director of internal audit can obtain more information about these types of firms by consulting with other directors of internal audit or requesting help through The Institute of Internal Auditors.

Many of these specialized internal audit consulting firms are headed by former directors of internal audit from larger organizations who have retired or left their positions for a variety of reasons. They are often extremely qualified to perform internal audit quality-assurance reviews, as they understand the process of internal auditing better than many other potential consultants. Before asking such a firm to provide quality-assurance review services, the director of internal audit should ask for a client list and should then independently contact several of the organizations where the consultants have performed QA reviews. Since a consulting firm will only give its successes as references, it is often helpful to make some independent inquiries to determine the satisfaction that other organizations may have had with a given consulting firm.

Before contracting with the outside firm to perform a quality-assurance review, the director of internal audit should follow the same basic procedures that should be used whenever an outside consultant is engaged. These start with such basic matters as requesting a formal proposal outlining expected fees and deliverables, deciding who will do the work, and defining time requirements for both. These matters are outlined in Figure 33.3.

Figure 33.3   Requirements for an Internal Audit Quality-Assurance Review Contractor

33.3.01 What is the basis or approach for the contractor's review of internal audit functions?

33.3.02 What are the professional credentials of the team that would be assigned to the review? How many hours of on-site review work will be performed by the designated leads as described in the proposal?

33.3.03 What are the contractor's professional qualifications for the review? How many members of the review team assigned to the engagement are members of the IIA or have CIA certifications?

33.3.04 How many similar reviews has the contractor performed in the past 24 months? Will the contractor release any of these names as references?

33.3.05 Will the review be based on the IIA auditing standards? How much consideration will be given to internal audit department and corporate standards and procedures that support the IIA standards?

33.3.06 Approximately how many audits completed over the past 18 months will be included in the QA review?

33.3.07 Will the review be focused on headquarters-based audits (corporate audit) or on reviews performed by other parts of the audit organization, such as certain subsidiary audit operations?

33.3.08 How much attention will be given to specialty audit areas such as information systems security or quality assurance? What are the contractor's qualifications for those reviews?

33.3.09 How much time does the contractor anticipate in reviewing audit results with auditees?

33.3.10 What type of QA report does the contractor propose to release? Will the distribution of that report be controlled by the director of internal audit?

33.3.11 Will a complete set of QA workpapers be made available to internal audit?

33.3.12 What procedures does the contractor employ if the proposed QA review appears to require more resources than proposed?

They outline the same basic process as when the organization contracts with a public accounting firm for consulting services or the like. They are particularly important here since specialized internal audit consulting firms are often small and relatively informal, and expectations from the quality review may not be met unless the process is defined in advance.

33-4 LAUNCHING THE QUALITY-ASSURANCE REVIEW PROCESS

The director of internal audit should take the lead in launching a quality review program in the internal audit organization if such a function is not already in place. If not, the director may find that other interested parties—such as senior management or the outside auditors—may initiate this review process. While it does not matter who starts the review process in terms of the overall content of adequately performed internal audit quality-assurance reviews, internal audit will often realize a strategic advantage if the director of internal auditing initiates the process. If the outside auditors, for example, suggest such a review to members of the audit committee of the board, all parties will have the underlying question, ''What's wrong with internal audit?'' In addition, if internal audit initiates the process, they will have much greater flexibility to suggest the most appropriate parties to perform the review. When an organization's external auditors propose an internal audit quality-assurance review, the implication is that they will probably be contracted to do the work.

Internal audit may initiate a quality review process by proposing the activity as part of the annual budgeting and planning process. A basic program can be outlined and resources allocated for either creating a separate quality-assurance review function in the organization or contracting the review process to an outside provider. If such a process is not already in place, the director of internal audit should not think of this as a one-time process but a continuing mechanism to assess the quality of overall internal audit performance. While any outside contractors should clearly understand that they do not have an annuity for these reviews once they receive the first assignment, internal audit should think of this quality-assurance review process as an ongoing program rather than a one-time review.

When a director of internal audit proposes a program of internal audit quality-assurance reviews to senior management, there may be mixed messages received in return. If the work is planned to be performed by a specialized in-house group, the question may be asked why existing audit staff can not be pulled off of other audit work to perform the reviews. The director of internal audit needs to emphasize the importance of performing these reviews independently and in a manner that will not limit other planned audit activities. If the review is planned to be performed by a consulting firm specializing in such reviews, internal audit may have to explain why they would be preferable to the outside auditors. In either case, the director of internal audit may find that convincing management of the need for the reviews and the approach to be used will require some ''selling.''

An internal audit quality-assurance review process will be readily accepted by management if internal audit presents a good plan to perform these reviews on an ongoing basis, if the reviews will allow auditees to provide some inputs regarding their impressions of the overall internal audit process, and if the quality-assurance review process points to an improved internal audit function in the organization. In addition to selling management on the need for such a quality-assurance function, internal audit management should inform all levels of the internal audit staff of the plans to form the function. Care should be taken to emphasize that the reviews are not intended to be witch hunts but will be designed to improve the overall quality of all audits performed. Properly explained, the process should be enthusiastically accepted by members of the internal audit staff.

Although an overall plan of performing QA reviews over a period of time is needed, this chapter will emphasize the procedures necessary to perform a single, comprehensive review of an internal audit function. The necessary steps are to set the review of objectives of a given review, to review internal audit staff procedures, to survey or interview a selected group of auditees, and to report the results of the review to internal audit management and other interested parties. The following sections assume the quality-assurance review process will be performed by either outside parties or by a specialized, independent group within the internal audit function. A section following discusses self-assessment reviews directly performed by members of an internal audit function on their own audit activities. These self-assessment reviews are most appropriate for a smaller organization.

(a) DETERMINING QUALITY-ASSURANCE REVIEW APPROACHES

An internal audit function launching a quality-assurance review program needs to make some basic planning and organizational decisions. In addition to deciding who will be performing the reviews, internal audit management must decide upon the scope, depth, and breadth of the reviews to be performed. *Scope* here implies the amount of detail to be included in any review. Should the review include primarily internal audit administrative procedures or should it extend to detailed reviews of such areas as computer audit practices or audit sampling approaches? *Depth* here refers to the amount of detail to be included in the quality-assurance review of any area. With an extended scope, the quality-assurance reviews might go down into the detailed audit procedures performed in each audit reviewed. It is one matter to determine that a selected audit project to be reviewed has a planning memo, a set of workpapers, and an audit report on files. In an extended scope review, the quality-assurance reviewers might examine the detailed audit procedures performed for each audit selected for the review. This might include a detailed review of workpapers and even the reperformance of some tests.

Breadth, as used in this chapter, refers to the number of units to be included in any quality-assurance review. Should the quality-assurance review be just restricted to the larger centralized audit function at headquarters or should it extend to remote units? In other organizations, the geographically remote units may be subject to quality-assurance reviews but headquarters will not. In other instances, internal audit management will just review domestic units and not go overseas or will review one operating division but not others. Auditees may or may not be surveyed depending upon the review approach selected.

Decisions should be made as to the frequency of planned quality-assurance reviews. In a large, geographically disbursed organization, a quality-assurance function will probably not be able to review every internal audit unit every year. The selection of who to review—and how often—should depend upon the criticality of the internal audit function reviewed. The same risk-assessment techniques introduced in Chapter 7 can be useful in helping internal audit management decide which areas are to be included as part of annual quality-assurance review plans. If a given area was subjected to an earlier quality-assurance review and areas in need of corrective action were identified, the quality-assurance review function may want to schedule an additional follow-up review in that area.

Even if an outside consultant, such as a public accounting firm, is used to perform its quality-assurance reviews, internal audit management should take a major role in deciding on the scope, depth, and breadth of the quality-assurance reviews to be performed by the quality-assurance reviewers over a specified, often a one-year time period. Internal audit management should take the lead in specifying the types of reviews to be performed as well as the expected outputs from those reviews. Sometimes outside reviewers will have a tendency to do the work according to their own agenda. Management should make it known that the director of internal audit is responsible for setting the quality-assurance review approach subject to risk-analysis studies and various other inputs from organization management.

While these comments have assumed that the director of internal audit will have a strong input into the quality-assurance review process, the role of that same director in administering and reviewing internal audits also should be considered to be within the scope of any review of overall quality-assurance procedures. For example, if internal audit standards call for the director to sign the engagement memo and if the director ignores this duty, the quality-assurance review should highlight this discrepancy. This scope allows the review to assess the overall quality of performance by the entire internal audit function. The director of internal audit should assure the quality team performing the work that it has an obligation to effectively assess the overall quality of the internal audit function, including that of the director.

Once the reviews have been selected, an approach established, and a plan developed, senior internal audit management should inform all members of the organization of the quality-assurance review plans. For a larger internal audit organization with multiple units, that communication could take the form of a formal memo announcing the review plans and the need for cooperation. A sample memo is shown as Figure 33.4. A similar note should be directed to auditee groups that may be asked to participate in interviews or

Figure 33.4 Quality-Assurance Review Announcement

MEMO

TO: XYZ Division Internal Audit Staff
From: Tom Goodguy, Quality Assurance Manager
Date: May ■■, ■■■■
Subject: Quality-Assurance Review

As part of our established internal audit procedures, the internal audit quality-assurance department periodically selects areas for review to assess compliance with department and general internal audit standards. Since we have not performed a review in your area for over two years, the XYZ Division internal audit function has been selected for a quality-assurance review starting May XX, XXXX. I will be directly managing this review and will be assisted by two staff members.

Please send me a current schedule of internal audits completed over the past year, as well as a copy of your current audit plan. We will select two audits completed over this period and will request a set of the workpapers in advance.

We plan to arrive at the XYZ Division internal audit offices on the morning of May XX and would like to meet with the internal audit management team at that time, and we will then advise you of the areas selected for detailed review. We expect that our fieldwork will require no more than two weeks. At the end of our fieldwork, we will meet with XYZ internal audit management to discuss our initial findings and recommendations.

Thank you for your cooperation and please contact me if you have questions.

Tom Goodguy

---

surveys. All parties need to be informed of the objectives of the quality-assurance review program. Even if internal audit has an ongoing review program, a notice similar to Figure 33.4 will remind organization members that the review program is starting another new, often annual cycle.

(b) AN EXAMPLE QUALITY-ASSURANCE REVIEW OF AN INTERNAL AUDIT FUNCTION

The quality-assurance review team can now begin its review of the internal audit function. This section describes how a quality-assurance review might be performed. The example assumes the quality-assurance reviewers are members of internal audit's overall organization, such as described in the Figure 33.2 organization chart, but that they are scheduled to review an internal audit department at a separate, semi-independent division of the organization, called Axylotl Specialties, an independent unit that is 75% owned by the headquarters company, with the remaining 25% held by outside investors. Assume Axylotl Specialties' internal audit function ultimately reports to the headquarters director of internal audit but does not have day-to-day audit project–related contact with the headquarters audit staff. As with many decentralized organizations, the Axylotl Specialties internal audit function has been asked to follow general guidance from headquarters but has the freedom to establish some of its own local procedures based upon the unique audit risks found in this business. In addition, ABC Specialties has its own audit committee.

This quality-assurance example review will follow the general procedures outlined in Figure 33.1 and assumes that the headquarters review team has had little contact with Axylotl Specialties. While this example assumes that the group to be reviewed is an independent unit of the parent corporation, these same basic procedures can be used by a variety of different reviewers and for varying internal audit units.

(i) Quality-Assurance Review Preliminary Planning.   The internal audit quality-assurance review team should follow some of the same procedures here that it might use if it were performing a normal internal audit, as has been described in previous chapters of this book. These might include the following:

- *Announce the Planned Quality-Assurance Review.* The planned review should be announced to organization management as well as to all members of the internal audit staff that might be impacted by the review. Members of the internal audit staff, in particular, might become quite offended if they do not know about the planned review and its objectives. The review announcement should contain a strong message that the purpose of the review is not to ''get'' anyone on the internal audit staff but to help the overall internal audit organization to become more efficient and effective.

- *Assign Resources to Perform the Review.* Concurrent with or even prior to announcing the review, decisions need to be made regarding who is to perform the review. If performed by an outside provider, objectives and review schedules should be defined. An internal audit quality-assurance review should have designated persons who will be performing the work and who will not be distracted by other projects.

- *Meet with Internal Audit Management.* In a larger internal audit organization, the director of internal audit often is responsible for initiating the review by scheduling it with the specialized function within internal audit that will perform the work or by contracting with an outside provider. Other members of the internal audit management team may not have that much knowledge about the planned review. Before starting the actual work, the review team should meet with appropriate members of audit management to advise them of its review approach and to discuss any special considerations that might impact the review approach. For example, the quality-assurance team may schedule a review at a separate, divisional internal audit function. Local internal audit management may explain some special considerations that might suggest that the reviewers avoid looking at one or another area. If the request is reasonable, the quality-assurance team should honor it.

- *Meet with Other Members of Management.* Organization management is normally quite aware of their internal auditors' work products through internal audit's presence in various operational areas or through audit reports. They may not be aware of the objectives of an internal quality-assurance review. This is the time for the review team leaders to meet with appropriate members of local management to explain their review objectives. The review team should also request some input from management regarding any of their concerns about the performance of internal audit. For example, management may feel that certain audit reports took far too long to issue or that members of the audit organization have not been acting in a professional manner. This type of input may point the review team to an examination of completion times for those audits mentioned or a review of training records for the audit staff.

After completing these first steps, the quality-assurance team should be ready to perform the actual review. Assuming that it has established a starting audit program, it may want to modify the scope and extent of its planned review based upon these inputs. If a branch unit audit manager has indicated a very critical audit is in process during the time of the review, the review team may want to avoid that review area so as to not disrupt other internal audit operations.

(ii) Quality-Assurance Internal Audit Review Procedures. As had been discussed, an internal audit quality-assurance review is an independent assessment of the audit department's performance in compliance with internal audit professional and audit departmental standards. There is no single approach that applies to all internal audit departments and all reviews. Generally, a review will investigate internal audit office procedures and organization standards and then will focus on individual completed audits to determine if the standards have been followed. This section will discuss reviews of audit department procedures. The section following will discuss approaches for reviewing completed audits.

Figure 33.5 describes some of the major review steps for a quality-assurance review of internal audit operations. The reviewers here need to understand specific internal audit departmental procedures. This requires an initial study of documentation and other materials as a first step, just as internal auditors would review available documentation as a first step in their operational audits. Even if members of the same overall audit organization are performing the quality-assurance review, the review team should still review this internal audit documentation. It will reacquaint them again with operations and will allow

Figure 33.5 Audit Program Extract: Internal Audit (I/A) Quality-Assurance Review

Audit _____ Location _____ Date _____

AUDIT STEP	INITIAL	W/P
1. Review I/A department procedures to determine if adequate emphasis is devoted to accuracy and quality issues. Highlight areas for potential improvement.		
2. For current and past years, review the risk analysis and planning process. Assess whether appropriate attention was given to broad range of risks in organization.		
3. Review the most current year of the completed audit plan: • Assess reasons for audits either never launched or still in process. • Review the hours recorded for completed audits and compare to original plans. Document and determine reasons for major variances. • Review the extent of special, nonplanned audits performed over past year and assess reasonableness.		
4. Select a sample of audits completed of the past years and pull their complete workpaper files to ascertain: • Workpapers are in good order and follow I/A department standards. • Audit programs support the risks identified, audit scope, and the work performed. • All potential findings have been carried to the final audit report or otherwise received appropriate disposition. • Appropriate audit reports or other communications were prepared following good internal audit standards.		
5. Based on workpapers reviewed and other materials, assess I/A's use of audit automation, audit sampling, and other advanced techniques.		
6. Interview key auditees from several audits completed to assess their impression of the professionalism of the I/A department.		
7. Review I/A budgeting, travel expense, and time reporting procedures to determine the reasonableness and thoroughness of accounting procedures.		
8. Review the continuing education activities within the I/A department to determine that appropriate attention is given professional training.		
9. Review staff turnover within the department. If this seems high, investigate potential causes. If little turnover, discuss with the director plans for auditor career growth.		

them to better define their audit tests. This documentation standards review may also point to additional areas to emphasize in their detailed testing procedures. For example, the reviews may find that internal audit's standards for auditor project timekeeping are extremely complex. Because of this complexity, they may see a red flag that might suggest that auditors may have trouble completing the time reporting and therefore may not keep accurate time records. This might be an area for more detailed review.

Items reviewed within the internal audit department should be selected on a test basis. While this might not be an appropriate area to perform detailed statistical sampling test selection approaches, the review team should use judgmental sampling in the various areas reviewed. That is, internal audit might not care to reach an attributes sampling–type of conclusion, as was discussed in Chapter 13, and the review teams should take care to make representative selections of all areas sampled. For example, if the quality-assurance reviewers are interested in whether internal audit has been performing an adequate risk-analysis in various areas of the organization, the review team might judgmentally select several areas of overall organization operations and determine if an adequate risk-analysis had been performed in those areas selected as part of the annual planning process.

The actual quality-assurance review procedures to be performed are essentially the same as for all other audit procedures described throughout this book. The reviewers should identify an area from their established review program, select a representative sample of actual items in that area, review or test the items selected, evaluate the tests, and document the results. The quality-assurance review team should take the same care in selecting and documenting its work as it would expect members of the internal audit staff to follow in its regular audits. As with normal internal audits, when the review team finds what appear to be significant exceptions, it should discuss these potential findings with the internal auditors being reviewed to determine that there are no extenuating circumstances behind the potential findings. This is the same process normally followed in any internal audit, except that here the reviewers are auditing the auditors.

(iii) Reviews of Individual Completed Audits.   In addition to reviewing overall audit group procedures, a quality-assurance review should always include a detailed review of a sample of completed audits. This review should not be made to second-guess the findings of the auditors who performed the work but to determine that the review followed good internal audit standards throughout all of its aspects, including planning, test procedures performed, workpaper documentation, and the completed audit report. While the steps described previously reviewed internal audit department standards, this phase of a quality-assurance review will assess compliance with these standards in the completion of actual audits.

Normally, a quality-assurance review team should select a representative sample of materials from completed audits over perhaps the past one-year period. This sample should include all types of audits, including operational, financial, information systems, and other types of special reviews. A good starting point here is to look at an audit project report listing completed audits. From this, the review team should select the sample and pull the workpaper files and any other related data to describe the audit procedures performed, the conclusions reached, and the method for communicating those audit conclusions. This is not a process to second-guess the auditors who performed the review. The reviewers should read enough of the workpapers to understand the audit objectives, the approaches used, and the conclusions reached. If the internal section reviewed has what appears to be a good process where audit supervisors or others review all workpapers and appear to ask appropriate questions prior to the completion of normal audits, the quality-assurance review team can look at this sample review and satisfy itself it is working for all of the audits selected.

Once a review selection has been made, the quality-assurance reviewers should examine a sample of completed audit workpapers. This exercise should very much depend on the reviewers' understanding of departmental procedures, as discussed in the Figure 33.5 review steps. Here, in a review of individual workpapers, quality assurance should determine if those standards are being followed and if good auditing practices are used. The number and extent of areas that might be included in such a review will vary with the overall type and scope of the audit. They might include the following:

- *Audit Sampling Procedures Used.* Chapter 13 discussed procedures for the use of both statistical and nonstatistical sampling procedures. The internal auditors who did the actual work may have made a decision to only pull a limited judgmental sample when a better audit result might have resulted from the use of some type of statistical sampling approach. An appropriate quality-assurance comment is that the auditor in charge of the review did not appear to have considered statistical sampling techniques.

- *Compliance with GAAP or other Accounting Standards.* While internal auditors will generally not be performing financial audits, many audits have some financial accounting ramifications. In many cases, these reviews may have been performed for the external auditors who would be responsible for reviewing the work and signing off on the conclusions developed. However, if the financial accounting procedures performed were strictly part of internal audit's review, the quality-assurance reviewer might want to consider the appropriateness of the financial accounting procedures as documented in the workpapers.

- *Appropriate Consideration of Information Systems Risks.* Operational audits sometimes do not consider the information systems risks associated with the area reviewed. For example, an operational or financial review might rely upon the outputs of an information system, with no attention given to the controls surrounding that system. An appropriate quality-assurance review point is to comment on the assessment of information systems risks.

- *Use of Computer-Assisted Audit Techniques.* Chapter 12 discussed the use of computer-assisted audit techniques to introduce efficiencies into the process of gathering audit evidence. If the audit workpapers reviewed do not show evidence of any considerations on the use of these techniques when the data reviewed might suggest this use, this may be an area for a review comment.

- *Use of Other Audit Automation Techniques.* Chapter 11 discussed the preparation of workpapers to document audit activities. While many of the areas discussed in this chapter are appropriate for a quality-assurance review, the chapter emphasized some of the automated techniques that could be used to make the audit and workpaper-preparation process more efficient. Again, this is an area for potential quality-assurance review and comment.

The above are just a limited example of the many specific areas that might be included in a quality-assurance review of completed workpapers. The quality-assurance reviewers need to go through the selected workpapers in some detail and determine if best practices were followed during the review.

In some instances, the quality-assurance reviewers may want to discuss the work with the internal auditors who completed the review and prepared the workpapers. While the audit workpapers should speak for themselves, the internal auditors who did the work can often provide additional background information on their reviews. While a need to ask specific questions about the audit procedures not documented in the workpapers may point to lack of documentation, these questions are sometimes necessary for clarification purposes. Also, the quality-assurance reviewers will often want to interview or survey the actual auditees.

The actual audit report and its findings are also part of the quality-assurance review of the completed audit workpapers. The reviewers should determine that all points covered in the workpapers and identified as potential report findings have been included in the final audit report or otherwise given proper disposition. While the purpose of quality-assurance review is not to act as an after-the-fact ''English teacher'' who looks for style and small grammatical errors and the like, the reviews should assess whether the report has been clearly written and is in accordance with internal audit department standards. The reviewers may want to consider the elapsed time between report issuance and fieldwork completion. Too long of a delay in this report production may indicate some overall internal audit quality problems. The review of workpapers should include all of the steps documented in the internal audit process, from risk-assessment and initial audit planning to the release of the final report, including auditee responses.

(iv) Quality Assurance versus Ongoing Quality Monitoring. Chapter 11, on preparing workpapers, discussed the need for a manager or some other person in an internal audit supervisory position to review and initial all workpapers prior to the completion of an internal audit. This is a function very similar to the quality-control workpaper review function found in most public accounting firms but different from the formal quality-assurance process described in this chapter. The purpose of a workpaper review is to assess the audit work in process often before the completion of the audit fieldwork. A staff internal auditor will complete some portion of an internal audit—a test of signatures on some operational transaction, for example—and then give the workpaper to the in-charge auditor for review to determine if the test was properly performed and properly documented. This function is typically performed by internal audit field management and not by the independent quality-assurance reviewer.

In many internal audit organizations, a more senior member of internal audit management may review all completed audit workpapers prior to the release of the draft report. This type of review focuses on the appropriateness of the audit conclusions reached to support audit report findings. In a very large organization, this type of review may be performed by a member of the quality-assurance function, since they understand standards and are accustomed to these types of reviews. However, internal audit management will be responsible for understanding the scope and extent of the audit work performed and the nature of the audit report conclusions reached. Quality assurance usually takes a broader view of the audit work performed and does not focus on the specific issues included in individual audits.

The point here is that a given set of audit workpapers may be reviewed two, three, or even four times during the course of a review. The first review will be by the supervisor or in-charge auditor in the field as detailed audit tests are completed and initial conclusions developed. A second review may be by internal audit management prior to their release of the report. A potential third level of review would take place if the audit work was performed for an external audit firm as part of its financial audit work. Each of these three parties would review the workpapers and initial and date the workpaper sheets reviewed.

The quality-assurance review of workpapers is somewhat different. Often, it does not go into the level of detail found in any of the above-mentioned reviews. Rather, as discussed previously, quality assurance may randomly select a series of completed audits and review them for compliance with professional and audit department standards. That quality-assurance review takes place on a random basis and typically well after the completion of the audit report and its fieldwork. The other levels of reviews discussed take place during the course of the audit or soon thereafter. In addition, this chapter has emphasized that a quality-assurance review should not second-guess the audit work performed. The other levels of review will closely scrutinize the work and may suggest changes to the work in process or to the audit report findings.

(v) Auditee Interviews and Surveys. A quality-assurance review should include interviews or surveys with a sample of auditees who are the users of internal audit services. This process can take two different forms. The reviewers may want to interview both the auditees and users of audit reports as part of a quality-assurance review of selected internal audit projects. As an alternative, quality assurance may want to survey organization management to better understand their impression of internal audit's services. Each of these surveys of persons outside of the internal audit department can have different dimensions and each may point to different potential conclusions.

Benchmarking is a different type of internal audit survey. This is where reviewers interview persons from audit departments in other organizations. The idea here is not to just review the quality of one or another individual audit but to assess how the entire internal audit department stacks up with similar internal audit functions in other organizations. This type of exercise is most meaningful when data is gathered from internal audit organizations of a similar size and in a similar industry. While some internal audit benchmarking is often done on an internal audit director to internal audit director level through informal professional contacts, quality assurance–sponsored internal audit benchmarking often formalizes this process and provides a better understanding of what internal audit departments in other organizations are doing.

Although the material discussed here is presented in the context of internal audit quality-assurance review work, internal audit management should consider the use of these survey and interview techniques for all audit work. An internal audit process often works outside of normal business processes, and internal audit should be able to gain considerable value from assessing what auditees thought of an audit just completed. Although the following sections are addressed to an internal audit quality-assurance function, some of these same concepts are applicable also to general internal audit management.

Quality-Assurance Auditee Interviews

After reviewing workpapers and other materials from a completed audit, the quality-assurance team will often find it valuable to interview some of the auditees. These are the persons whose functions were reviewed as part of the completed audit selected in the quality-assurance review. The idea here is to assess the level of internal audit professionalism as seen through the eyes of the auditees. Even though the quality-assurance team may have found the selected workpapers to be well organized and the audit report well written, internal audit has a potential quality problem if the auditees—the subjects of the audit—did not regard the internal auditors who performed the review as high-quality professionals. Many factors can cause this type of feeling. For example, the field audit team may have worked late into the evening one day but arrived at the audit site late in the morning the following day. Because auditees do not know the team was working late, the auditees might resent the auditor's work habits. Quality-assurance interviews with selected auditees might reveal this type of information.

Auditee interviews are usually initiated following a quality-assurance workpaper review. While not every auditee identified in the workpapers should be contacted, the review team might consider taking a small set of these persons to participate in an interview. Even though quality assurance may want to talk to several auditees identified in a single set of workpapers, all quality-assurance interviews should involve only one single auditee at a time. This one-on-one approach allows an auditee to be more open in expressing concerns regarding an audit.

Quality-assurance auditee interviews can provide much information about the quality of the internal auditors performing a review, but they can present difficulties. First, an auditee may not give totally honest responses to the interviewer's questions. The auditee being interviewed may not want to hurt the members of the audit team and will be reluctant to express honest opinions. Even worse, if a group of auditees are interviewed together as a focus group, there is a danger the session will transform itself into some form of a feeding frenzy where a large amount of negative but unsupported bad news is communicated.

Figure 33.6 outlines the types of questions a team of quality-assurance reviewers might ask a series of selected auditees. The interviewer should clearly state the purpose of the review is to measure the overall quality of the audit procedures performed and not to ''get'' anyone. The auditee being interviewed should be assured that all responses will be kept confidential—similar to the procedures followed in a normal audit. If appropriate, the interview responses should be summarized to capture total auditee impressions regarding the review.

Internal Audit Quality-Assurance Surveys

Interviews, as discussed above, are generally limited to a small group of auditees involved with only a limited number of audits included in a quality-assurance review. In some instances, quality assurance may find some value in surveying all auditees in a given division, department, or larger organizational unit that has had contact with internal audit. This approach usually works best when quality assurance is reviewing the internal audit department in some geographically remote unit where the quality-assurance team has little knowledge of local internal audit operations. The survey might be mailed out prior to the arrival of the quality-assurance review team, with instructions to mail back the responses. If this is done in advance, the internal audit quality-assurance team may be able to identify some potential concerns before the initiation of the actual quality-assurance review.

Figure 33.6 Internal Audit Quality-Assurance Survey Letter

As part of our effort to maintain the highest level of professionalism, we are asking you to help review our performance in a recent audit performed in your department. We are interested in the _____ audit that took place between mm/dd/yy and mm/dd/yy and was led by _____ .

Please take a few minutes to answer the following questions. If necessary use additional sheets and send your response in the enclosed envelope.

1. Did you understand the purpose and objective of the audit? Did you receive a formal letter announcing the audit?
2. Did the audit start when it was planned and finish as you expected?
3. Did the internal audit team maintain a Professional attitude consistent with your department, in terms of such matters as their work hours, dress, and attention to work during the day?
4. Did the audit team appear to understand the area they were reviewing? Did they ask questions when appropriate? Did those questions appear excessive?
5. Was the audit performed so as not to hinder your normal work activities?
6. Were matters of audit concern, particularly those that were included in the final audit report, discussed with you in the course of the review?
7. Did the audit conclude with a formal exit meeting? Were the auditors' matters of concern discussed with you and did you have an opportunity to respond as appropriate and to provide additional data when necessary?
8. Was the audit report for the review delivered in a timely manner and did it reflect the final closing meeting and any additional clarifications that you may have added?
9. Were the audit recommendations in the final report appropriate and helpful?
10. In general, what was your overall opinion of the audit?

The overall survey would have the same types of questions as in Figure 33.6. If this is to be sent to a separate unit of the organization, which may have its own separate internal audit function, the survey might be directed to all members of management that might have come in contact with internal audit rather than just to those who have been subjected to audits. This way, the quality-assurance team will be able to determine if some members of the organization who have never been included in an internal audit feel they should be so included. The quality-assurance team conducting the survey should carefully classify the survey data to identify trends or issues.

Internal Audit Benchmarking

Sometimes an internal audit quality-assurance team may want to determine how the practices in the internal audit function reviewed compare with those in other functions outside of their organizations. While a standard tenet of The Institute of Internal Auditors has been "Progress through Sharing," benchmarking is an expanded version of that sharing. In a traditional sharing exercise, the director of internal audit or some other member of audit management may call directors of internal audit in other organizations to ask how they do something or to inquire as to their policy regarding some audit task. Benchmarking is a much more formal task where the best practices from a series of internal audit organizations are surveyed.

Although benchmarking is used to measure nonaudit practices across different companies, it is also a very effective tool for the quality-assurance review team. Although the quality-assurance team may have its own impression as to the best way to perform some audit procedure, it will often have no supportive evidence to show that its suggested approach is the best and is even used by other leading organizations. Quality-assurance benchmarking provides a way to assess how other internal audit departments are dealing with similar situations. For example, the quality-assurance team may find that the internal auditors reviewed are seldom using statistical sampling techniques in their reviews even though departmental standards call for its use as a suggested optional procedure. A good way to convince the audit managers and supervisors involved to use statistical sampling is to point out that a benchmarking survey has found that such sampling is used successfully by the internal audit departments in a series of leading and generally respected internal audit department organizations.

Benchmarking is a useful technique that can be used by internal audit in a variety of areas. Today, it is most frequently used by overall organization quality-assurance functions to compare cross-organizational practices. It is a useful technique for internal audit quality-assurance reviews.

(c) REPORTING THE RESULTS OF THE QUALITY-ASSURANCE REVIEW

As has been discussed, an internal audit quality-assurance review is an internal audit review of internal audit. Thus, the quality-assurance review should follow many of the same procedures from a normal internal audit, including planning, fieldwork, documentation of results, and then the audit report. A quality-assurance review is of little value unless its results are reported to internal audit management and others in some type of audit report. Depending upon the size of the internal audit department and the scope of the quality-assurance review, the completed review might follow a normal internal audit report, as was discussed in Chapter 15. That is, the quality-assurance reviewers should prepare a draft report with their quality-assurance review findings; the audit group reviewed would have an opportunity to respond to those findings, outlining the corrective actions steps they plan to take; and the final product would be a quality-assurance report similar to regular internal audit reports.

A key difference between an internal audit quality-assurance report and a normal internal audit report is the report distribution. This report will normally be addressed to the director of internal audit with few if any persons outside of the audit department on its distribution list. Since the report may cover some very specific and technical details of problem areas identified by the quality-assurance team, it may go into far greater detail than should be included in a well-drafted internal audit report. The quality-assurance review team is responsible for discussing areas where the internal audit area reviewed can improve its procedures; internal audit itself is responsible for making certain that appropriate corrective actions are taken.

The director of internal audit is normally responsible for deciding if persons outside of internal audit should receive a copy of the internal audit quality-assurance report. The director, for example, may want to give a copy of the report to a selected number of senior managers and often will give a copy to the external auditors. Quality assurance, however, should not assume that it can distribute the compiled report as desired. The director of internal audit is responsible for determining that all aspects of the internal audit department follow good practices and that any appropriate corrective actions are taken.

33-5 USING SELF-ASSESSMENT TO IMPROVE PERFORMANCE

A smaller internal audit department or an organization that has not devoted formal resources to performing formal, quality-assurance reviews should still take steps to monitor the quality of its internal audit activities. The quality of the internal audits performed can be measured through self-assessment surveys, which can take many forms, ranging from an open discussion in response to a ''How are we doing?'' type of question raised at a departmental session, through the completion of a formal self-assessment review or questionnaire. While the open discussion will give the director of internal audit some information on how well the small audit department is doing, a self-assessment survey is most useful.

The idea is to ask each member of the internal audit department to complete a survey where they will respond to questions regarding their audit practices and how well they think that they, the individual auditors, as well as the department in total, think they are doing. Despite the size of the internal audit organization, all members of the team can evaluate how they feel they are performing as individuals, how they are performing as a team on their audit assignments, and how the overall audit department is performing in the eyes of each individual auditor. Each member of the audit department would be asked to complete a survey, tailored to the individual internal audit department, which emphasizes compliance with internal audit standards and the overall perceived quality of the work performed. Figure 33.7 shows a portion of this type of survey, which is designed for completion by all members of the internal audit staff. A limited number of users of internal audit services might also be polled through this type of survey.

A small internal audit organization may be faced with the question of who should complete the survey. If the internal audit department consists of the director of internal audit and perhaps only a staff of six, that director would know which of the internal audit staff completed the surveys based upon the nature of some criticisms or even the handwriting. These types of surveys are best run independently. The director of internal audit might ask the human resource department in the organization to mail out the surveys and to compile the mailed-in results. This way, the survey responses would not be easily connected with the staff members completing them and staff members would feel more free to express their opinions regarding the quality of internal audit department operations.

Once the survey results have been tabulated by the responsible nonaudit party, the director of internal audit should share them with the audit staff. Although this type of assessment will not result in a formal findings and response type of audit report, members of the audit staff can collectively decide on various areas for internal audit improvement and should take steps to change internal audit operations as appropriate. Although not as comprehensive as the formal internal audit quality-assurance review described earlier in this chapter, an independent self-assessment review is a good exercise for the smaller internal audit department to evaluate the quality of its performance.

Figure 33.7   Quality-Assurance Self-Assessment Survey

	YES	NO	NEEDS REVIEW
1. Is the technical proficiency and educational background of internal audit staff members sufficient to perform assigned reviews?			
2. Is a sufficient amount of supervision given to all audits?			
3. Does the staff comply with the Professional Standards when performing its work?			
4. Are staff members skilled in dealing with people and communicating effectively?			
5. Does each internal auditor exercise due professional care when performing audits?			
6. Do internal auditors review the reliability and integrity of financial and operating information when performing reviews?			
7. Do internal auditors regularly appraise the economy and efficiency in which resources are employed?			
8. Are internal audits planned in advance?			
9. Is a risk-assessment procedure used to plan and select audits?			
10. Are workpapers prepared to support all audit work?			
11. Do internal auditors adequately collect, analyze, interpret, and document information to support audit results?			
12. Are workpapers reviewed by a member of audit management prior to the issue of the audit report?			
13. Do internal auditors adequately communicate the results of audit work through formal audit reports?			
14. Are proposed audit report findings discussed with the auditee prior to the release of the formal report?			
15. Are audit reports, along with auditee responses for corrective action, issued in a timely manner?			
16. Is there a formal follow-up procedure to ascertain that appropriate action has been taken on reported audit findings?			
17. Are key findings from audit reports communicated to senior management on a periodic basis?			
18. Are the costs and time spent on each audit collected and measured against established audit plans?			
19. Is there a formal set of policies and procedures covering internal audit operations?			
20. Are workpaper and audit report records adequately maintained?			
21. When an audit requires special skills, such as for information systems controls, are adequately trained auditors assigned?			
22. Are computer-assisted audit procedures used when appropriate?			
23. Are audit sampling techniques used when appropriate?			
24. Is there a regular continuing education program to provide training to all audit staff members?			
25. Is audit work coordinated with internal auditors to avoid any duplication of effort?			

33-6 FUTURE DIRECTIONS FOR QUALITY-ASSURANCE REVIEWS

Quality-assurance reviews are powerful tools that allow an internal audit department to measure how well it is performing. Internal auditors often review many other areas and freely make constructive suggestions, but they often do not take the opportunity to review themselves. A formal program of quality-assurance reviews will allow internal audit to better assess its own performance. As has been discussed, these reviews can be performed by a specialized function within internal audit, by various qualified outsiders, or by means of a self-assessment survey. Who performs the review will depend upon the size and organization of the internal audit department, as well as on management's commitment to this type of review program.

In addition to reviewing how an individual internal audit department is doing and how well it is operating in compliance with internal audit standards, the modern internal audit department often needs to assess how it is performing when compared to the better or more respected internal audit functions in other organizations. This is where the concept of benchmarking is useful. An internal audit quality-assurance function can meet with other internal audit groups and determine how those groups are performing. Similarly, the well-run internal audit function should hold itself open to share its ideas and practices with other internal audit functions who are doing their own benchmarking. Benchmarking, briefly mentioned in this chapter, will be discussed in greater detail in Chapter 35 and is another tool to allow an internal audit function to assess the overall quality of its practices and procedures.

No matter what specific approaches are used, the effective modern internal audit function needs to have an effective quality-assurance program in place. This will allow internal audit to comply with the Professional Standards for the Practice of Internal Auditing, as described in Chapter 5, and will otherwise allow internal audit to act as a strong, effective function in the organization.

PART SIX

INTERNAL AUDIT FUTURE DIRECTION

CHAPTER 34

Changing Role of Audit Activities

34-1 INTERNAL AUDITING IN THE CONTEMPORARY ORGANIZATION

One hundred years ago, as we moved from the nineteenth to the twentieth century, much like every such hundred-year transition in the past, society took time to stop and look back at where they were and where we were going in the future. This same introspective approach is useful today for the internal audit professional. The previous chapters of this book discussed the many and varied roles of the modern internal auditor, roles that originally were defined by Vic Brink in his first edition some 60 years ago and have since continued to grow and evolve. Subsequent editions of this book talked about some of these changes.

While it is only human to think of one's current times as the most important and most exciting ever, we would argue here that the internal auditor today is truly on the threshold of series of changes that will alter the way internal auditors are viewed by senior management, their total organization, and society in general. In the past, after the concept of the modern internal auditor was established, many of the changes that followed in the internal audit profession were primarily driven by technology factors. Business computer systems did not exist at the time of Brink's first edition, but their use has grown and evolved in the years since in ways internal auditors of the past could not even speculate. Similarly, business processes have changed radically. We are now in a global marketplace, and the nature of the products and services produced has changed dramatically.

This chapter will consider some of the ways internal auditing is changing today. These range from new requirements for internal audit leadership in newer review areas such as compliance with ISO 9000 quality and ISO 14000 environmental management standards, to increased internal audit involvement in acquisitions, divestitures, restructuring, and other organizational change issues.

34-2 EXPANDING NEEDS FOR AUDITORS

Once an organization's internal audit function is established and recognized, senior management often threatens to ''send in the auditors'' when there are allegations of misconduct, significant control problems, or security violations. Internal audit has often been viewed as the shock troops who come in, find the source of the problem, and recommend an effective solution to management. If needed, they can even take over operations for a short period of time. While this type of role was often very effective, it has caused many persons to view internal auditors as the "management cops" who were not there to provide service to management but to investigate frauds or act as the internal police. While that role still may have a place in some situations, the role of internal audit is very much changing in the modern organization.

Internal auditors are increasingly asked to serve management and their organizations in a variety of new and nontraditional ways. These often include becoming involved with the newer management programs taking place in the modern organization, such as the expanded internal control concepts following the Committee of Sponsoring Organizations (COSO) report of the Treadway Commission, which were discussed in Chapter 2, as well as the ISO quality and environmental management standards. Internal auditors can use their basic internal control–oriented skills to review these areas and to provide management with some assurance as to their worth.

(a) AUDITING QUALITY STANDARDS

Chapter 26 described operational, financial, and information systems audits of an organization's quality function, along with similar reviews of the organization's engineering and research functions. The engineers and technicians responsible for those functions have been responsible for monitoring their own standards and often perform what they call "audits" to assess compliance with these standards. Many of these "audits" are far too specialized for the modern internal auditor who has concentrated on rather broader control issues in these areas. Increased global competition and international standards, however, have caused many organizations to take a much stronger look at the quality of their products and processes.

Nearly every organization has tried, in media advertisements and sales presentations, to claim "highest quality." However, an automotive manufacturer in Japan wants a greater level of assurance of that advertised quality when buying a manufactured part from a company in Iowa beyond just reading a trade magazine advertisement. It needs some assurance that the quality of those Iowa-manufactured automobile assemblies is high, but the Japanese buyer cannot justify a trip to Iowa to observe and understand those quality standards. An internationally recognized set of quality standards, called ISO 9000, has provided a solution to this problem. However, organizations cannot just say that they are "in compliance" with internationally recognized quality standards; rather, they need some type of audit or third-party confirmation. This is the same problem as with financial standards. Although an organization can state that it has correctly followed the generally accepted accounting principles (GAAP) financial accounting standards and that its financial statements are fairly stated, a CPA is needed to independently attest that those standards are being followed.

Quality-assurance auditors play a role similar to independent CPAs. Although their audits are often performed by specialized outside consultants, this is an area where internal audit can make a significant contribution to an organization. This is an evolving role for the modern internal auditor; while there may be a need in these situations to have a fairly strong understanding of manufacturing processes, internal auditors do have the skills needed to make strong contributions.

(i) ISO 9000 Standards Overview.   The standards for quality, ISO standards, were developed by an international set of industry leaders and issued by the International Organization for Standardization. ISO is a Geneva, Switzerland–based group founded in 1946 to promote the development of international standards in many areas. ISO membership represents over 90 countries, and it is composed of some 200 specialized technical committees who develop and set standards in a wide variety of areas. Since many organizations have defined "quality" in different ways using different terminology, in 1979, ISO started to develop a set of standards for the quality-assurance process and quality management. Following the document numbering of these pronouncements, these standards came to be known as ISO 9000.

Detailed information on ISO standards can be found through many specialized books such as Stamatis[1] or through publications by national quality organizations such as American Society for Quality (ASQ),[2] the major quality-control professional organization in the United States. The goal of these quality standards is not to define quality procedures for specific products, materials, or manufacturing processes, but to define a documentation process and management methods to allow an organization to maintain its quality standards. ISO 9000 talks about procedures rather than the end product. The goals of these standards are for an organization to take the following quality standards steps.

- Define a quality system that is appropriate and applicable to the organization.
- Demonstrate to customers the organization's commitment and management system to maintain that quality system.
- Allow the organization to compete credibly in international markets.
- Maintain compliance with standard safety and product liability regulations and procedures.
- Reduce overall operating costs following well-defined, results-oriented goals.
- Establish programs to continue to implement improvements that were the result of quality-improvement gains.
- Work with suppliers as partners using second-party audits to minimize supplier surveillance.
- Provide an environment to launch a "continual improvement" program such as the total quality management (TQM) program discussed in Chapter 26.
- Involve all employees in these programs by educating them in the importance of quality systems and their effect on the organization and its customers.

The concept here is to develop very specific quality standards and procedures, to document those standards in such a manner that they represent current practices, being continually updated with further improvements, and serve as a training vehicle for the entire organization. While internal auditors generally would not be directly involved in this process, which is the responsibility of the organization's quality-assurance function, internal audit should have a good understanding of ISO documentation requirements when required for internal audits. That documentation can be considered on four levels.

---

[1] Stamatis, D. H., *Understanding ISO 9000 and Implementing the Basics to Quality Controls* (New York: Marcel Dekker, 1995).

[2] American Society for Quality, 611 East Wisconsin Ave., Milwaukee, WI.

1. Top-level ISO documentation—statements of company philosophy and policy. This is a *why* type of documentation describing top-level quality philosophy.

2. Quality procedures describing the *what, when, where,* and *who* aspects of the organization's quality program. This level of documentation describes the organization's quality principles and strategy.

3. Specific quality-oriented work instructions. This is the *how* level of quality documentation describing work practices.

4. Finally, at the lowest or more basic level, an organization needs records and other documentation to provide *proof* of their quality program and its results.

A major component of any ISO 9000 program is the documentation that the organization has maintained to both build their quality program and to describe that program to management, customers, and other interested parties. Through this documentation, an organization can attest that they follow recognized quality standard practices and quality documentation procedures. With ISO 9000 compliance certification, an organization in one country can rely on the value of a supplier's quality standards even if that supplier is in another country across the globe.

ISO 9000 does not require every organization to follow the *same* quality standards. A quarry supplying crushed rock to road construction firms will have different needs for quality standards than a pharmaceuticals manufacturer. However, both should have documented quality standards, following the four levels described from policy manuals to detailed work records. Similarly, ISO 9000 does not require that every organization follow the *highest* quality standards, but only that they document their level of quality. An organization could, in theory, decide that their quality is third rate and be willing to admit that. To follow ISO 9000 standards, they must be able to document why their quality is third rate and not fifth rate or worse. The whole idea behind ISO 9000 certification is that an organization confirms that it has established a set of quality standards and has documentation to describe those standards.

Although an organization has developed standards that attest to its level of quality standards and procedures, an independent auditor must attest to those quality procedures. The ISO and related national quality standards organizations have established certification standards for quality auditors who visit an organization seeking ISO 9000 certification to review and attest to their quality standards. This process is very similar to the role of the CPA, licensed by a state board of accountancy, who follows AICPA-developed auditing standards and reports on the fairness of an organization's financial statements. Many organizations today, both in manufacturing and other industries, seek this ISO 9000 certification.

(ii) Internal Auditors as ISO 9000 Auditors.   For many organizations, the ISO 9000 quality certification process has historically not involved internal auditors. Quality programs were first developed and introduced by classic ''industrial engineers'' and have been viewed as shop-floor-type processes rather than steps that would involve ''the auditors.'' This is changing! As an increasing number of organizations become involved in this entire ISO certification process, they need specialists who understand ISO standards and its audit certification process, and can assist their organizations in preparing for an ISO review. While ISO 9000 standards require the auditor certifying quality processes to be independent from the organization, internal auditors can assist their organizations to prepare for a formal ISO outside review by examining documentation, test results, and other audit procedures. This is a true service-to-management type of review, where internal audit attempts to understand what has been done and to make suggestions to improve processes.

Quality auditing follows a set of standards, developed in the United States by the ASQ. That professional organization has its own certification examination allowing an auditor to be designated as a certified quality auditor (CQA) as well as a certified quality lead auditor. In addition to passing the examination, the CQA is expected to have designated levels of experiences and education. Figure 34.1 outlines the knowledge requirements for a CQA. While there are many similarities to the CIA and the CPA examination requirements, the CQA body of knowledge covers some very special quality areas. The internal auditor whose organization is involved with obtaining ISO 9000 certification should develop an understanding of ISO 9000 requirements and their audit requirements. While this does not necessarily point to still another examination, an involved internal auditor should develop an understanding of the overall process.

(b) ENVIRONMENTAL MANAGEMENT SYSTEM AUDIT NEEDS

Environmental control issues are becoming increasingly important on a worldwide basis. There is a worldwide recognition that organizations cannot just drain industrial or human waste into a nearby river, burn it while watching the smoke drift away, or bury it with no concern that it might seep back into the water supply. Strong environmental rules have been established throughout the world to encourage people and organizations to create a cleaner and safer environment. Those violating the rules or standards may be subject to penalties ranging from large fines to public approbation. Depending upon the organization, its industry, and even its geographic location, the management of these environmental risks can be very complex. Rules are difficult to follow and subject to interpretation, but regulations require a high level of documentation to attest that the environmental procedures are working. Although there are many rules and regulations, it is not in society's interests to have large cadres of ''environmental police'' to monitor these rules. Rather, organizations are encouraged to ''self-police'' their environmental compliance standards. As a result, organizations have established what are called environment management systems (EMS), which have some close analogies to the systems of internal control discussed throughout this book. An EMS is a series of control procedures designed to provide the organization as well as outsiders with assurances that the company's environmental control system is working.

Standards have been established, similar to the ISO 9000 quality standards, to monitor the success of an organization's EMS. These standards come under the designation of ISO 14000 and define the procedures that an organization must have in place to attest that they have an effective EMS. ISO 14000 procedures were first released in 1996 and are supported by a set of guidance materials similar to ISO 9000. Figure 34.2 summarizes some of the principle requirements of ISO 14000. The emphasis is very much on documentation standards.

Audits of EMS procedures under ISO 14000 will become increasingly important to internal auditors. While many organizations have industrial engineers and others on their staffs who have a good understanding of the manufacturing and other processes covered by ISO 9000 quality standards, there is presently a wide need for knowledge about EMS procedures. Because an important aspect of an EMS audit under ISO 14000 involves a review of supporting documentation and the control systems in place to manage environ-

Figure 34.1 Certified Quality Auditor (CQA) Body of Knowledge

I General Knowledge, Conduct, Ethics, and Audit Administration
  A. General Knowledge
    1. Characteristics of audits including quality, systems, and compliance audits
    2. Understand qualitative and quantitative audit methods as well as subjective evidence
    3. Use of standard ASQ auditing terms and definitions
    4. Changes and trends in auditing practices
  B. Professional Conduct and Ethics
    1. ASQ Code of Ethics
    2. Standards of performance for an auditor
    3. Auditor's responsibilities
      (a) In unethical activities
      (b) In unsafe activities
      (c) In audit-related conflict-of-interest situations
  C. Audit Administration
    1. Audit program objectives
    2. Methods for building credibility of audit function
    3. Management of the audit function
II Audit Preparation
  A. Audit Plan Preparation and Documentation: Purpose, Scope, and Resources
  B. Audit Resources: Credentials, Expertise, and Accountability
  C. Sources of Authority for Conducting Audits
    1. Industry and national/international standards
    2. Organization, hierarchy, contract, and regulatory
  D. Requirements Against Which to Audit: Standards, Contract, Specifications, and Policy
  E. Importance and Utility of Quality Documentation
    1. Appropriate, adequate, accurate, and current
    2. Prior audit information
  F. Checklists, Guidelines, and Log Sheets
    1. Tailored for specified audits and appropriate use
    2. Update existing documents
  G. Development of Data-Collection Methods: Criteria for Selecting Appropriate Tools
  H. Audit Plan Communication and Distribution
III Audit Performance
  A. Conducting the Opening and Entrance Meeting
    1. Agenda: purpose, objective, scope logistics, standards, and schedule
    2. Working papers
    3. Responsibilities and roles, including attendees
  B. Audit Team Management
    1. General auditing strategies
    2. Purposes and uses of data-collection methods
    3. Methods for verifying documents and records: tracing, sampling, and physical determination
    4. Calibration principles and practices: traceability to recognized standards

Figure 34.1 (*Continued*)

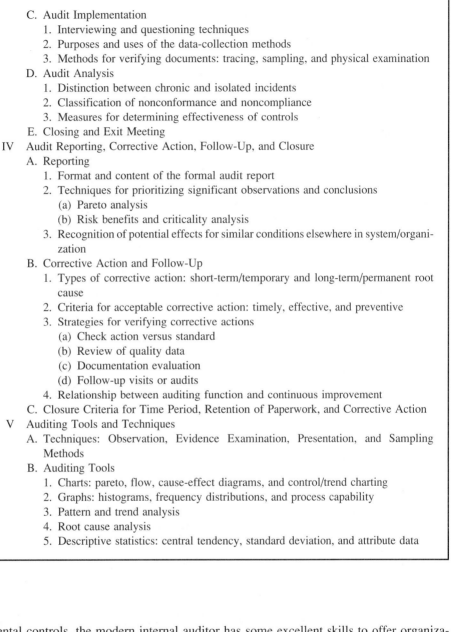

> C. Audit Implementation
>   1. Interviewing and questioning techniques
>   2. Purposes and uses of the data-collection methods
>   3. Methods for verifying documents: tracing, sampling, and physical examination
> D. Audit Analysis
>   1. Distinction between chronic and isolated incidents
>   2. Classification of nonconformance and noncompliance
>   3. Measures for determining effectiveness of controls
> E. Closing and Exit Meeting
> IV Audit Reporting, Corrective Action, Follow-Up, and Closure
> A. Reporting
>   1. Format and content of the formal audit report
>   2. Techniques for prioritizing significant observations and conclusions
>   (a) Pareto analysis
>   (b) Risk benefits and criticality analysis
>   3. Recognition of potential effects for similar conditions elsewhere in system/organization
> B. Corrective Action and Follow-Up
>   1. Types of corrective action: short-term/temporary and long-term/permanent root cause
>   2. Criteria for acceptable corrective action: timely, effective, and preventive
>   3. Strategies for verifying corrective actions
>   (a) Check action versus standard
>   (b) Review of quality data
>   (c) Documentation evaluation
>   (d) Follow-up visits or audits
>   4. Relationship between auditing function and continuous improvement
> C. Closure Criteria for Time Period, Retention of Paperwork, and Corrective Action
> V Auditing Tools and Techniques
> A. Techniques: Observation, Evidence Examination, Presentation, and Sampling Methods
> B. Auditing Tools
>   1. Charts: pareto, flow, cause-effect diagrams, and control/trend charting
>   2. Graphs: histograms, frequency distributions, and process capability
>   3. Pattern and trend analysis
>   4. Root cause analysis
>   5. Descriptive statistics: central tendency, standard deviation, and attribute data

mental controls, the modern internal auditor has some excellent skills to offer organizations.

In 1997, The Institute of Internal Auditors announced they were developing membership guidance for ISO 14000 EMS audits and let it be known that their objective was to take a leading role in this area. Internal auditors in the future can expect to see considerable additional guidance on EMS audits, an area where internal auditors have many of the necessary skills to provide effective service to management.

Figure 34.2 ISO 14000 Major Requirements

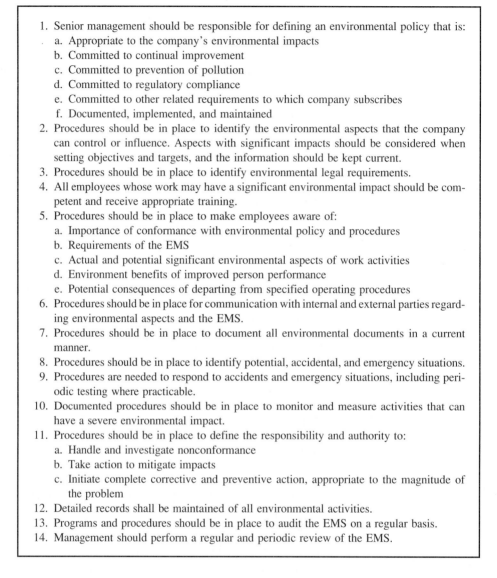

1. Senior management should be responsible for defining an environmental policy that is:
    a. Appropriate to the company's environmental impacts
    b. Committed to continual improvement
    c. Committed to prevention of pollution
    d. Committed to regulatory compliance
    e. Committed to other related requirements to which company subscribes
    f. Documented, implemented, and maintained
2. Procedures should be in place to identify the environmental aspects that the company can control or influence. Aspects with significant impacts should be considered when setting objectives and targets, and the information should be kept current.
3. Procedures should be in place to identify environmental legal requirements.
4. All employees whose work may have a significant environmental impact should be competent and receive appropriate training.
5. Procedures should be in place to make employees aware of:
    a. Importance of conformance with environmental policy and procedures
    b. Requirements of the EMS
    c. Actual and potential significant environmental aspects of work activities
    d. Environment benefits of improved person performance
    e. Potential consequences of departing from specified operating procedures
6. Procedures should be in place for communication with internal and external parties regarding environmental aspects and the EMS.
7. Procedures should be in place to document all environmental documents in a current manner.
8. Procedures should be in place to identify potential, accidental, and emergency situations.
9. Procedures are needed to respond to accidents and emergency situations, including periodic testing where practicable.
10. Documented procedures should be in place to monitor and measure activities that can have a severe environmental impact.
11. Procedures should be in place to define the responsibility and authority to:
    a. Handle and investigate nonconformance
    b. Take action to mitigate impacts
    c. Initiate complete corrective and preventive action, appropriate to the magnitude of the problem
12. Detailed records shall be maintained of all environmental activities.
13. Programs and procedures should be in place to audit the EMS on a regular basis.
14. Management should perform a regular and periodic review of the EMS.

34-3 INTERNAL AUDITING AND ORGANIZATIONAL CHANGE

In the past, organizations were typically fairly cohesive, keeping their staffs and operating units together, whether in good or bad times. Although mergers, acquisitions, or divestitures have always been part of corporate life in the western world, in recent years these organizational changes and restructuring have become much more common. Major corporations may merge, consolidating some business units, divesting others, and all but ignoring still others. In this environment, internal controls can easily break down as traditional control systems may be bypassed or may no longer be fully functional in the face of organizational change.

This situation can become particularly acute when senior management has mandated massive downsizings (e.g. layoffs) with resultant surviving employee feelings of insecurity. Employees at all levels often feel bitter, betrayed, and disheartened. While the organization's ultimate objective may be to save its own life through the cutbacks, the soon-to-be-terminated employees may not be very sympathetic to this argument. While not necessarily acting dishonestly, they may frequently look the other way when faced with control-related problems.

Internal auditors have the skills to assist management in these types of corporate restructuring transactions. Even if the internal audit department is not at all weighted towards "CPA type" balance sheet auditing, it can provide significant service to management in stepping in and becoming the eyes and ears of senior management for these types of downsizing transactions.

(a) RESTRUCTURING, REENGINEERING, AND OTHER MOVEMENTS

A management technique that became very popular starting in the late 1980s has variously been called *restructuring, reengineering,* or *rightsizing.* The whole idea was to go through the entire organization, examining each job function and deciding what might be done to make each of these jobs or functions more efficient. In many instances, this process looked at organizational procedures, where Employee I completed Form A, which was passed to Employee II who used it to create Form B, which then went on to Employee III, etc. The whole idea of reengineering was to look at these detailed procedural processes, eliminate redundancies, and make the overall process more efficient. Often, the reengineering analysts found that, with minimal changes, Form A could be modified and then go directly to Employee III, eliminating the need for Employee II and Form B. As a result, the very mention of reengineering struck terror in employees, who felt their jobs might be eliminated. That feeling of terror was perhaps justified in many instances as the emphasis of reengineering, more and more, was to use an ax rather than a scalpel to primarily eliminate overall employee headcount with not too much attention given to job functions.

While these reengineering studies were largely performed by outside consultants, their role of studying individual job processes is very similar to some of the internal controls-based process analysis and improvement studies performed by internal auditors. Perhaps, in their role of assisting management at all levels, senior management has perceived their internal auditors as being too nice to perform an "eliminate X% of the jobs" type of a reengineering study. Nevertheless, the modern internal auditor may be the best and most qualified person in the organization to perform a reengineering type of study. Historically, internal audit understands and documents processes and then reviews the control procedures performed by each member of the team.

(b) DIVESTITURES, ACQUISITIONS, AND ORGANIZATIONAL CHANGE

Internal auditors and others frequently talk about how much is changing at their company and other companies. They see major companies splitting apart, spinning off the pieces as separate entities, acquiring other organizations, or otherwise changing the nature of their business operations. These changes can have traumatic effects on the audit organization and can cause some major individual career disruptions. Often, the whole process may be very difficult. Whenever we go through this type of process—and they seem to occur in waves—auditors talk about how bad things are ''right now.''

Massive and ongoing organizational changes have always been a major component of business, at least through much of the history of the United States as well as elsewhere in the world. In the 1870s, railroads forced out river and coastal steamship lines and then those railroads combined, went bankrupt, and otherwise reorganized. We have experienced similar waves of organizational changes over the years with technology and marketing-demand factors driving those changes. These changes can impact internal audit departments today as senior management decides, for example, to bring the company private, and because of fewer SEC reporting requirements, to downsize internal audit. An internal auditor may say, ''How can this be? Internal audit is much too important!'' However, right or wrong, management may make this decision and alter the size and structure of internal audit.

While often a difficult time, periods of organization change are also a time when internal audit can provide some major services to management. Internal audit is a function that understands the organization, is independent, and can provide a well-controlled approach to helping with organizational change. Examples where internal audit can help with major organization changes include:

- *Acquisition ''Due Diligence'' Reviews.* When Company A acquires Company B, A does not have complete knowledge about B's operations. As part of the acquisition negotiations, B may state that its inventory is 1% excess or obsolete or may make assertions about other matters. The acquiring company A will often want someone to come out to review the more significant of B's procedures in some detail, performing what is called a ''due diligence'' review. A representative from A will visit B, review records or make observations, and report results back to management. While audit-type procedures can be followed here, no testing or detailed analysis is performed. The objective is for the reviewer to raise ''flags'' if things are not consistent with expectations. Internal auditors are often good candidates to perform these types of reviews.

- *Shutdown Operations Managers.* When a unit closes and many jobs are lost, remaining employees will often demonstrate their bitter feelings through theft of goods or sloppy business practices. Internal auditors are often ideal persons to come into the unit and take the role of acting controllers during this time period. While they probably will not be at the exit door to check parcels, knowledge of their presence in the organization often encourages employees to do the right thing more frequently.

- *Special Financial or Operational Analysts.* Organizational change often requires considerable detailed analysis to determine the costs of winding down a project, to recalculate employee severance benefits, or to attend to other matters. Again, because of their analytical skills, internal auditors are ideal persons for these types of reviews.

The above are examples of areas where internal auditors can perform special services to management to assist with organization changes and the often resultant turmoil that surrounds those changes. The director of internal audit should remind senior management of the special skills that internal audit can bring to the overall organization in light of significant changes.

34-4 MANAGEMENT VIEWS OF THE AUDIT FUNCTION

Prior to about 1950, management frequently viewed its internal auditors as little more than accounting specialists who often primarily helped the organization's external auditors. During those times, many internal auditors tried to assume the more professional role as defined by Vic Brink, but too many others still kept their old habits. The role of internal audit changed over the years, and management began to recognize internal audit's evolving and expanded role of service to management. Now, internal audit is almost always viewed as an essential component of the modern organization. It has become so important a component, however, that senior management will sometimes search for what they think might be a more cost-effective internal audit arrangement; they frequently consider such approaches to improving internal audit performance as bringing in outside persons to perform internal audit functions.

The concept of bringing in nonemployees to operate key organizational functions became very popular starting in the 1990s. It has extended to all functions in the modern organization, including internal auditing. This section will discuss some of these trends, which go by such names as *outsourcing* or *rightsourcing,* using outside internal audit specialists as contractors, or many other variations. These are very important trends impacting many internal audit professionals today.

(a) OUTSOURCING: INSIDER OR CONTRACTOR?

Although organizational trends come and go, the 1990s have been a decade where many have questioned why they needed specialists in "non-mainstream" areas when they could potentially contract for the services from specialists outside the organization. The basic concept is that while every organization may occasionally need a plumber to repair a plugged drain, they do not need to keep a plumber on the payroll just in case that drain may become plugged. Rather, they will call a plumber when such services are required—or, if there are continuing needs for such services, will contract for these plumbing services. Under negotiated contract terms, the plumber may agree to do plumbing maintenance work X hours per month, agree to be on call and on site within Y hours, or agree to some other limited but nonemployee service status.

The role of the internal auditor, both as an employee of the organization and as an independent reviewer of management's actions, is changing. Senior management today, with increasing regularity, hires outside persons to perform some or even all of internal audit's functions. Often, internal audit will bring in individuals with special technical or audit skills not as employees but as short-term contractors to perform specialized audit tasks. An organization may be installing a new UNIX operating system–based computer network. Even though members of the internal audit department will be able to get up to speed regarding the new system, an outside contractor might be able to come in and provide some short-term help to the audit department. These contractors often work as members of the internal audit department for only a short-term basis to perform designated audit tasks. They are not inside employees but are working independently or through a contracting or temporary help agency; and they generally will leave the organization's internal audit department when their designated contract task is finished or when the contract term otherwise ends.

In many other instances, the CFO or the audit committee will hire an outside firm, usually a major public accounting firm, to come in and totally manage the company's internal audit function. In this situation the outside organization will usually take over total management of internal audit, but may keep some of the existing audit staff and bring in others from their organization to provide additional or specialized staff support when needed. This process often is called *outsourcing*. Here, the audit committee usually replaces the director as well as others in internal audit with persons from the outside organization to handle internal audit functions. In the eyes of the organization's senior management, their internal audit function still exists, but its operation has been turned over to a specialized outside provider.

In the eyes of a staff internal auditor who has just lost a job due to this type of action, the feeling is that internal audit has been eliminated. Senior management, on the other hand, looks at these actions in a favorable manner, seeing this as a way to improve overall organizational efficiency or to reduce costs. Properly managed by both the internal management and the firm performing the outsourcing, these actions can yield economic or efficiency benefits to the organization. Handled poorly, the actions will hurt the many internal auditors who have been outsourced and, perhaps more importantly, will damage the welfare of the entire organization.

The use of contractors to perform certain internal audit functions as well as the possibility of outsourcing the entire audit function have changed the way many traditional internal auditors think about their careers. While management will generally view these moves as cost savings or productivity improvements, many internal audit professionals view these actions as a disturbing threat to their profession. However, these actions are really nothing new. For years, internal audit departments have brought in persons with secretarial or other special skills from temporary help agencies, for example, to help in a "time crunch" situation. Similarly, organizations have outsourced entire functions. The employee cafeteria operation is a typical example. Although organizations once ran their own kitchens, few would think it reasonable today to have an in-house food-service staff. Even as these actions have taken place for other functions, today the use of contractors to perform certain internal audit services and the concept of outsourcing the entire internal audit function are very much growing and evolving trends.

(i) Contracting Specialized Internal Audit Services.   The most common and perhaps least radical way to use outside audit services today is to use contractors. Audit departments typically have special needs where the existing staff lacks the necessary skills. There may be a need for auditors with specialized knowledge, usually of a more recent nature, to provide support to the entire organization. Examples might be persons who can understand and evaluate computer network security, including firewall facilities, or specialists to initially help evaluate the organization's environmental management system under ISO 14000. Hiring persons to join the internal audit staff may be difficult in the short run as these specialists are often in high demand, and training a member of the existing internal audit organization may take too long. The solution, at least for the short run, is to hire specialists to perform the special function.

While hiring contractors to perform specialized internal audit functions can often be a very cost-effective solution, the process needs careful management attention. First, the director or others in internal audit must locate professionals with appropriate credentials and then independently verify those credentials. All too often, there may be charlatans posing as consulting experts who do not have the credentials but are looking for a quick assignment to carry them over other job breaks. Finding the most qualified contractors is often difficult; the persons brought in as internal audit contractors must have appropriate credentials and other references. Another component of this problem is the lack of a ready labor marketplace for contractors with audit skills, making a search through diverse sources a likely necessity. Internal audit specialized contracting will be more successful, however, if the following steps are taken.

1. Define the contractor's project with as much precision as possible. Rather than just saying that a UNIX network specialist is needed, internal audit should take care to define in a fairly extensive level of detail the knowledge requirements, such as the level of network detail needed, planned review procedures, and the expected duration of the contracted assignment.

2. Locate sources for finding contractors. Public accounting firms can be of help, as can temporary help agencies specializing in technical personnel. The Internet is a growing marketplace where an organization can post its needs and expect to receive a wide variety of responses.

3. Define the terms of the engagement. Contractors will often demand a relatively high hourly rate, but since they are usually receiving no health care, retirement plan, or the like, that higher rate may be justified. If the contractor is coming in from out of town, work schedules and travel expense allowances, if any, should be decided in advance.

4. Obtain and verify contractor references. Even though the contractor may only be working on the assignment for a few months, it is important that references are checked and are strong.

5. Once a contractor has been identified—and as part of the hiring—carefully define the nature of the project, the expected deliverables, and due dates.

6. Inform members of internal audit and others about the contract assignment, making it convenient for the contractor to perform the required task.

7. During the project, closely monitor the contractor's progress. Because of the short-term nature of most assignments, it is extremely important that tasks are accomplished on schedule and per the plan. Quick adjustments must be made as necessary.

8. At the conclusion of the contract, determine that all expected reports, workpapers, and other materials are complete and turned over to internal audit. Generally, the process should conclude with extensive, in-depth reviews of the contractor's performance.

The previous are general guidelines for most jobs where internal audit contractor resources are used. While not too different from the management of normal audit projects, contract management requires special attention because of the critical, short-term nature of these projects and because a new person is generally being brought into the organization. Contracting for internal audit services can be very effective if other members of the audit staff can learn the techniques used and can potentially use those skills internally for a subsequent review in the same area.

The contract process is often a good way to evaluate the individual doing the audit work. If that person has the skills and approach that may make a good match for the organization, the director of internal audit may consider offering a full-time assignment to the contractor auditor. When there does not appear to be a good fit, the contractor auditor is free to better market services elsewhere, and the organization can search for help that better meets its needs.

(ii) Managing the Outsourcing of Internal Audit.

The public accounting firms that contract to outsource internal audit functions will generally use two different approaches. While they will always secure the agreement of the audit committee and CFO, some will replace the director of internal audit with a public accounting firm manager, will retain some members of the existing internal staff, and then will bring in their own personnel to conduct the program of internal audits. In other instances, the director of internal audit will be retained but much of the staffing, planning, and audit performance work will be the responsibility of the outsourcing contractor. The arguments for either arrangement are that the outsourcing firm has a pool of specialists who can perform the required audit work during their ''less busy'' times of the year. The theory is that the public accounting type of financial auditor, who is normally busy with December 31st corporate closings during the first quarter, is less busy by midyear and then can help with internal audits.

The problem with outsourcing is that, like many outside consulting engagements, the impressive-sounding objectives at the beginning of the review can quickly become forgotten after the outsourcing deal has been signed. Even though it was hinted that some high-level public accounting staff members with specialized knowledge would be doing certain internal audit financial reviews during their ''less busy'' times, the outsourcing firm may, in the end, assign less experienced junior staff members for the same work. Although the nature of an outsourcing engagement is that numerous and multiple persons will be assigned, the outsourcing staff can soon appear to be passing through revolving doors. If considering an internal audit outsourcing arrangement, the organization should demand some continuity. Problems of these types can occur. It is essential that someone in the organization closely manage any outsourcing arrangement!

The challenge here is determining who should manage the outsourcing. Although the independent public accounting firm that made the outsourcing arrangements should have the professional integrity and skills to manage such an outsourcing arrangement, someone from inside the organization should closely monitor the outsourced internal audit's activities and performance. The question here is who should do that work. The soon-to-be-former director of internal audit who has been told that the job is about over will not be the best choice here. With a strong understanding of overall project management as well as the terms of the outsourcing engagement, the CFO may be the best person to closely review the activities and performance of the outsourced internal audit function.

Figure 34.3 contains some management guidelines for reviewing the performance of an outsourced internal audit function. These questions point to the greatest potential weaknesses in the outsourced internal audit function. If no one is monitoring how that outsourced function goes about identifying risks, performing the reviews, and reporting the results, the performance of the outsourced function will probably be less satisfactory than the original internal audit function that the audit committee decided to outsource. The organization's CFO as well as the engagement partner reponsible for the financial audit, whether or not it is the same firm, should closely review the performance of the outsourced internal audit group. The idea is not to build a ''case'' against them but to closely monitor their performance in the same manner as any other organizational function. Once an internal audit function has been outsourced, all concerned should remember that the arrangement probably will not last forever. Depending upon the terms of the contract

Figure 34.3   Guidelines for Reviewing Outsourced Internal Audit Functions

34.03.01	Does the outsourced audit function (audit contractor) prepare an annual plan, updated quarterly, that is consistent with management's wishes?
34.03.02	Are audit contractor plans developed based on a formal risk analysis that has received review and approval by senior management?
34.03.03	Does the audit contractor exhibit flexibility in audit planning and scheduling such that it can easily schedule a new requested audit or modify others due to scope changes?
34.03.04	Does the audit contractor formally report its progress on scheduled audits including any new issues identified or other audit execution problems?
34.03.05	Does the audit contractor formally report the names, titles, and backgrounds of the persons assigned to audit projects and is their actual participation, including levels of effort, monitored for selected audit projects?
34.03.06	For specialized audit projects, such as information systems or special industry areas, does the audit contractor assign qualified persons to perform the audit work?
34.03.07	Is the turnover of audit contractor personnel assigned no worse than would be expected under normal or pre-outsourced conditions?
34.03.08	Does the audit contractor provide organization management with sufficient notice when there are planned changes in the audit contractor staff or when the contract team will be off-site at a contractor training session or the like?
34.03.09	Based on inspections by nonaudit contractor specialists, is the workpaper documentation prepared by the contractors sufficient? Also, is it delivered to the organization on a regular basis?
34.03.10	Are the reports prepared by the audit contractor meaningful with appropriate recommendations? Are those reports delivered on a timely basis?
34.03.11	Based on periodic formal or informal surveys, are other members of organization management satisfied with the audit contractor team?
34.03.12	Does the audit contractor engagement partner meet with management on a regular basis and does that person appear to have an understanding of the audit team and audit in progress?

and the level of satisfaction with the outsourced function, the arrangement should be submitted for rebid from time to time. It may even become a better idea to bring the function back in-house after a period of time. The major concern here is that the outsourced internal audit function should be managed by the organization in a manner similar to the way it manages any major service or consulting contract.

(iii) Contracting, Outsourcing, and Their Impact on Internal Auditors.   The internal audit professional today needs to realize that contracting and outsourcing are concepts that have become much more common in the workplace, both in the United States and elsewhere in the world. An immediate implication of this is that many internal audit professionals may very well spend some time in their audit careers working as contractors. If an auditor has good skills and professional credentials, this can become a very interesting and profitable career direction. In many instances it may result in improved annualized basic compensation, although with far fewer if any company-paid benefits. The professional who works in this manner should view the arrangement in a positive manner. The contractor-auditor may have a greater degree of professional flexibility and can really show off professional skills.

Similarly, an internal audit department outsourcing action does not mean the end for all members of the audit staff. Typically, what will happen in the short run is that the firm taking over management of the internal audit department will look at the skills and responsibilities for each member of the audit organization and will ask many to remain. In some cases little will change except that the individual auditor will now be working for the outsourcing firm, receiving a paycheck from a different source, and may have a new supervisor in the short run. Often, things like benefits and vacation time will prove even better, and the outsourced internal auditor may have expanded career opportunities. The public accounting firms who are active in outsourcing internal audit functions today may well offer an individual greater opportunities in terms of training programs and career advancement.

Despite these positive words, there are numerous negative factors surrounding this trend to specialized contracting work for individual internal auditors. First, contractor-auditors will be closely observed and evaluated for their performance and professional skills. If an individual is working on an hourly basis, on a one-year contract, and if that contractor-auditor is not necessarily that skilled or efficient, management could easily decide to end the arrangement at contract termination and bring in someone new. This is not so easy when an individual is a regular, full-time employee who goes through the classic annual performance review. People usually are not just terminated on the basis of that one performance review, and they may go through an extended and elaborate process prior to separation from the organization. The contractor-auditor also must keep in mind that no job lasts forever but only as long as the terms of the current contract. If a contractor-auditor is good, the current arrangement may be extended or similar jobs will arise with other organizations looking for contractor-auditors. The successful contractor-auditor must always operate at 100% efficiency, keep his or her professional and technical skills current, and keep that resume current.

Who loses in this contractor-auditor or outsourcing approach? Generally it will be the internal auditor who has not taken the time or effort to build a portfolio of professional skills and credentials. The auditor that once decided the CIA examination was too much work and not worth the effort may now regret that decision. Similarly, the auditor who has generally avoided much responsibility in the organization, has been cited in past performance reviews for late audits, or is generally viewed as a weak link in the internal audit organization, may not have a place in a new, outsourced internal audit organization.

Operating as a contractor-auditor is a change in working style that will impact many professionals as we move into the twenty-first century. While not all organizations will use this approach, internal auditors can expect this to be much more common.

34-5 DEFINING INTERNAL AUDIT'S CHANGING ROLE

The 1960s science fiction author Robert Heinlein frequently used a character called ''the auditor'' in his novels as an individual who observed events, listened in on the conversations of others, informally gathered facts, and provided third-party attestation on a continuous basis for many of the events in a story. In some respects, society today is looking for auditors to play this wider attestation role. For example, the AICPA has recognized this potentially wider role for their CPA members and has released a series of Attestation Standards. These standards are similar to the numbered SAS auditing standards discussed in prior chapters. Although there is still some controversy surrounding the CPA's role in nonfinancial attestation audits, areas that have been discussed for potential reviews include:

- *Audit Reviews of Computer Software.* A considerable amount of software today is purchased rather then developed in-house. For example, no organization today would develop its own payroll system when many other versions are available for purchase.

- *Audits of Industrial Monitoring Equipment.* The users of certain types of specialized industrial equipment pay for services based on their level of usage; the monitors that are dropped into oil well drilling shafts are an example. Although no standards have been established, this is a potential area for independent auditor reviews.

- *Reviews of Circulation Activities.* There are fairly well-established procedures for independent organizations to audit the mail circulations of various magazines. With the growing interest in publishing through the Internet and other vehicles, usage here will be an area for independent audit reviews.

The whole concept behind these nonfinancial attestation projects is that CPAs have been rendering opinions on the fairness of financial statements for years, those opinions are generally well recognized and respected, and the feeling has been that the independent public accountant has the expertise and general approach to give formal, independent opinions in other areas. Although there are many professional and technical issues surrounding these attestation reviews, the CPA's roles and responsibilities for attestation reviews will become better defined in future years.

Internal auditors also should have a similar role in future attestation reviews over nonfinancial, nonorganizational operational issues. While internal auditors are not independent in the style of the CPA auditor or the ISO registered standards auditor, they can take a nontraditional role for their organizations in developing audit opinions for organization clients and customers regarding nontraditional audit areas. The internal audit's role here will almost certainly change and expand in future years.

CHAPTER 35

Business Ethics and Social Responsibility

35-1 INTRODUCTION: EVOLVING BUSINESS TRENDS

The control of industrial waste is just one example of how attitudes have changed over the years. Organizations that once made most decisions based only on the maximization of profit and return to shareholders are also frequently forced to question whether their decisions are fair or ethical to all interested parties. As an example, many organizations have established employee codes of conduct to provide guidance on appropriate types of normal business conduct, and organizations have established ethics offices to oversee these matters. The COSO internal control standards, discussed in Chapter 2, and the Organization Sentencing Guidelines, outlined in Chapter 31, have encouraged if not required the establishment of ethics offices.

This chapter outlines the responsibilities of an ethics function and how internal audit should coordinate efforts and otherwise work with that function. From the perspective of internal audit, an ethics function has similar objectives to the quality function described in Chapter 26: to improve organization operations and procedures. Internal audit should work with their organization's ethics office, or, if one does not exist, suggest the need to establish such a function when appropriate. Of course, the function also should be part of internal audit's universe of auditable entities, and based upon appropriate risk analysis, should be a potential review candidate.

35-2 IMPORTANCE OF BUSINESS ETHICS

Starting in the late 1970s, some almost spectacular business failures, particularly in the United States, were shown by investigators, regulators, and journalists to be the result of unethical behavior on the part of business managers and CEOs. Historically, failures are nothing new and ethical lapses have occurred since the early days of business and trade—at least over the past 1,000 years. However, today's lapses often seem different, as access to information widely publicizes them and more people may be hurt due to the increasing number of people with stock market investments, bank accounts, and other financial interests. The 1880s Robber Barons' attitude of ''Let the public be damned!'' is not acceptable in today's society.

In response to societal changes, government legislators and regulators have established rules for businesses to follow that encourage ethical business behavior. Such rules can be found in the Organizational Sentencing Guidelines, introduced in Chapter 31 and discussed in greater detail in this chapter. Internal auditors should be aware of its requirements and potential impact. In addition, the new and evolving COSO report internal control standards model for use in the modern organization emphasizes business ethics as a foundation component of an organization's internal control environment. These standards are to be used by both internal and external auditors.

Management is also interested in having better ethical standards. Some disturbing societal trends are replacing traditional values. While this book or this chapter is certainly not intended to be a sociological study, this chapter will briefly explore some of these issues.

(a) ORGANIZATIONAL SENTENCING GUIDELINES ENCOURAGEMENT

Various laws or rules in the United States and other countries result in potential legal action if they are violated. First, of course, are civil laws or rules, where anyone who causes harm can be sued in a civil court of law. Rules that cover criminal acts in the United States exist on federal and state or local levels. Violations of federal criminal laws are generally regarded as the most serious and include:

- Theft

- Embezzlement

- Bribery

- Copyright and trademark infringement

- Fraud through the use of mail or communications wires

- Insider trading of publicly traded securities

- Money laundering

Federal judges are appointed for life and operate in separate judicial districts where one judge's sentencing procedures may differ from another. While one judge may sentence a convicted felon to prison, another may give only a relatively minor sentence of probation. These sentencing discrepancies have in past years been particularly common for nonviolent, "white collar" types of convictions. This problem of inconsistent and inappropriate punishment was greater when the convicted party was a "legal citizen"—a corporation, rather than an individual. Corporations cannot be put in jail, and judges' punishments were often very subjective. Some imposed significant fines on the organization, others imposed mandatory donations to charities, and still others gave little more than a formal dressing down to senior management in the courtroom, or gave probation.

To establish more consistent sentencing, the U.S. Congress established and authorized the U.S. Sentencing Commission in 1984 to provide federal crime sentencing guidelines that judges are required to follow. Guidelines for individuals became effective in 1987, but they did not apply to corporations except for some antitrust issues. Guidelines for organizations became effective in 1991 and cover a variety of organizations, including partnerships, associations, unions, pension funds, governments, and not-for-profit organizations.

The guidelines specify a rather severe set of punishments that could result in very onerous fines for an organization. These fines may escalate through a series of multiplier factors if the organization is found particularly culpable—for example, if the organization found out about the crime itself and tried to cover the matter up. On the other side, fines could be reduced significantly if the organization had in place guideline-mandated programs such as for the detection and correction of criminal acts as they occur. These programs are called *compliance programs.*

The Organizational Sentencing Guidelines specify seven specific activities that should be considered when a sentencing judge decides whether or not a convicted organization has an effective compliance program in place. These seven steps are described in the ethics compliance programs paragraphs following. Organization law departments or legal advisors should know these requirements, and the organization must take steps to meet them. The compliance requirements point to many elements found in today's organization ethics function. As a result, law departments today communicate these requirements to their senior management and suggest that ethics functions be established.

(b) COSO INTERNAL CONTROL STANDARDS

The COSO report and its internal control standards, discussed in some detail in Chapter 2 and referenced elsewhere throughout this book, stress the need for strong ethical standards in the organization. The COSO model of internal control is built around a foundation called the *control environment,* which sets the overall tone of the organization to influence the control consciousness of its employees (see Chapter 2 and Figure 2.3). A significant factor is the component of integrity and ethical values.

Although the report has an extensive discussion of the issue of ethics, the following paragraph from COSO report illustrates the report's emphasis on ethics functions:

> *Managers of well-run enterprises have increasingly accepted the view that "ethics pays"—that ethical behavior is good business. Positive and negative examples abound. The well-publicized handling by a pharmaceutical company of a crisis involving tampering with one of its major products was both sound ethics and sound business.[1] The impact on customer relations or stock prices of slowly leaked bad news, such as profit shortfalls or illegal acts, generally is worse than if full disclosure is made as quickly as possible.*

Along with the Organizational Sentencing Guidelines, COSO is a strong influence to promote organizational ethics functions. An internal auditor reviewing internal control procedures should consider the ethical environment in the organization and whether it has an appropriate ethics function in place.

---

[1] The reference is to the U.S. medical products company Johnson & Johnson, which faced a massive crisis in the 1980s when some malefactor inserted a deadly poison in bottles of one of its widely distributed products, which resulted in the death of several people. The company had to decide whether to treat this as an isolated incident or take more drastic corrective actions. Using its statement of ethical values as justification to recall and pull the entire product line, it averted a more serious crisis and received favorable publicity for its actions.

Figure 35.1   Changing Employee Values

100 Years Ago	Now
• Hard Work	• Salary and Status
• Self-Control	• Self-Fulfillment
• Self-Reliance	• Entitlement
• Perseverance	• Short-Term Views
• Honesty	• "Don't Get Caught"

(c) CHANGING PERSONAL VALUES

The other major factor that has encouraged the establishment of ethics functions is the changing values of members of the workforce. Many managers decry the lack of such classic values as "hard work" by many of their employees. A document published by The Institute of Internal Auditors on building an employee code of business conduct[2] describes these changing values, summarized in Figure 35.1. The need to return to such basic values as hard work and employee honesty has encouraged human resource functions in many organizations to develop programs to improve personal value practices among all members. Establishing a code of business conduct and an education program for all employees is one of the methods organizations employ.

35-3 ETHICS FUNCTIONS IN MODERN ORGANIZATIONS

Many organizations today have established formal ethics functions, often formed from members of their legal department, in response to the Organizational Sentencing Guidelines and its requirements for an effective compliance program. Human resource functions have also been involved with establishing or staffing an ethics function because of their ongoing need to provide guidance to employees and to answer their questions. Codes of business conduct were in place at many organizations long before this ethics function trend.

In the United States, organizations first started establishing ethics functions in the late 1980s, particularly if an organization was in trouble either because of a violation of some government regulation (often contract procurement laws) or bad publicity due to some other action. The ethics function was a way for the organization to communicate correct guidance and to promote ethical behavior for all employees. Internal audit functions often have not been involved in the early phases of these ethics functions.

Ethics offices, which go by such department names as business ethics or the ombudsman office, generally are responsible for the employee code of business conduct, have a "hotline" type of function to report violations, and maintain education and compliance-monitoring programs. The paragraphs following discuss some of the components in the effective ethics function.

---

[2] Wayne G. Moore and Mortimer A. Dittenhofer, How to Develop a Code of Conduct (Altamonte Springs, Fl.: The Institute of Internal Auditors Research Foundation, 1992).

(a) EMPLOYEE CODES OF CONDUCT

Employees needs to know "the rules"— what is expected of them and what the basic policies and general guidelines are for employee behavior. Formal policies such as the hours of work or vacation policies are generally communicated to employees through human resource manuals and other documents. However, the employee today must follow many other rules to remain in compliance with the law or such matters as relationships with suppliers, rules that are not easily documented in a manual. Organizations solve this by issuing an employee code of business conduct, a general document that gives employees guidance on the type of conduct it expects the employee to follow.

Codes of conduct often cover complex areas where there are many specific legal or organization rules. Rather than giving the employee a detailed set of these rules, organizations find it more effective to communicate the general flavor of the rules to employees, and support this with instructive materials. Two examples of code of conduct guidance should help explain this concept.

- *Personal Investments.* There are a variety of insider trading rules and conflict-of-interest policies regarding how employees should make personal investments. An employee code of business conduct could summarize personal investments with this statement.

  We are all expected to make our personal investments in a way that avoids the use, for personal gain, of any nonpublic material information obtained through the course of our work. Although we may invest in companies that do business with our company, we may not be personally involved in decisions relating to those companies.

- *Relationships with Suppliers.* Similarly, this is an area filled with laws as well as detailed policies developed by many larger companies. Although available in various manuals, some general guidance should provide a statement on how to deal with suppliers, such as the following.

  Helpful, friendly, professional relationships are essential to any business. While maintaining such relationships with our suppliers, we must maintain an honest, objective, and efficient procurement process.

Both of the above statements were adapted from actual codes of business conduct. Each have been followed up in the actual codes by a few instructive questions and answers. The idea is to communicate the spirit of a complex set of rules in a manner that all employees should understand. An employee who works in a specific area covered by a code of conduct general rule, such as the procurement office, should understand more details; all employees should understand the general concepts that govern good employee behavior.

There is no one set of specific topics that should be included in an employee code of conduct, nor is there one standard format. Each organization should develop its own code of conduct dependent on the industry and organizational culture. Figure 35.2 is a table of contents from an employee code of business conduct.

One important element of any code of conduct, however, should be a process that requires the acknowledgment by all employees that they have received their organization's code, have read and understood it, and agree to abide by it. The acknowledgment can be evidenced either by signing a paper document or using an electronic means. If an employee is in violation of some significant guideline in the code and claims ignorance of it as a response, the organization can point to that acknowledgment. Organizations

Figure 35.2   Sample Code of Business Conduct Table of Contents

I. INTRODUCTION
   A. Purpose of This Code of Conduct
   B. Our Commitment to Strong Ethical Standards
   C. Where to Seek Guidance
   D. Reporting Noncompliance
   E. Your Responsibility to Acknowledge the Code
II. FAIR DEALING
   A. Our Selling Practices
   B. Our Buying Practices
III. CONDUCT IN THE WORKPLACE
   A. Equal Employment Opportunity Standards
   B. Workplace and Sexual Harassment
   C. Alcohol and Substance Abuse
IV. CONFLICTS OF INTEREST
   A. Outside Employment
   B. Personal Investments
   C. Gifts and Other Benefits
   D. Former Employees
   E. Family Members
V. COMPANY PROPERTY AND RECORDS
   A. Company Assets
   B. Computer Systems Resources
   C. Use of the Company's Name
   D. Company Records
   E. Confidential Information
   F. Employee Privacy
   G. Company Benefits
VI. COMPLYING WITH THE LAW
   A. Inside Information and Insider Trading
   B. Political Contributions and Activities
   C. Bribery and Kickbacks
   D. Foreign Business Dealings
   E. Workplace Safety
   F. Product Safety
   G. Environmental Protection

should update their codes of conduct on a regular basis and also to periodically ask employees to reacknowledge the code.

(b) TELEPHONE HOTLINES

The concept that a manager's office is always open and that any employee can schedule time to come in to talk and register any concerns often works better in theory than in practice. A manager's style or office location can sometimes discourage such openness. When the employee does get to see the manager, that manager's body language or other traits may discourage the employee from speaking openly about an ethics concern. In other instances, employees may be reluctant to come in because the manager herself may be the cause of the concern. Employees need a mechanism to anonymously report violations of company policy, the law, and/or other matters. This reporting can be accomplished through ''suggestion box'' type letters, electronic e-mail notes, or calls to a designated telephone operator. The latter approach, using a toll-free 800 number, is perhaps the most common and has come to be known as a telephone ''hotline.''

A hotline is available to all employees who seek guidance about some matter, perhaps a human resources question, or to report some violation of the law or company policy. Callers may talk to a manager in the organization's ethics function, a specialized operator, or an outside organization with that responsibility. They can report their concerns anonymously, and the call-takers will record the conversation and either report the matter to appropriate persons in the organization or seek resolution or guidance in response to the caller. The hotline operators may simply use their on-hand references to answer a question such as, ''How many days of vacation am I allowed if I have worked $7\frac{1}{2}$ years?''

Although a hotline number allows employees to seek help and guidance for a whole series of day-to-day work issues, its real purpose as part of an organization compliance program is as a mechanism to allow employees to report infractions of the law or other improper acts. An employee who observes illegal acts, such as a fellow employee taking an item of merchandise out of the building or a supervisor charging a business dinner expense to a government contract when no contract discussion took place, may feel reluctant to confront either the fellow employee or the supervisor. A hotline type of number allows the employee anonymity.

Matters reported through the hotline number should record as much information as possible about the incident. This is where an operator hotline is superior to a recorded message or a post office box for anonymous notes. The operator can get more information to pass on to appropriate persons for resolution. A hotline program is of no value if the organization takes no further action. Regarding an alleged theft, the organization might investigate inventory records to determine if the item is missing, take steps to improve facility security to prevent repeat incidents, or even closely observe the work practices of the alleged thief. The idea is not to accuse the alleged thief based upon the anonymous tip, but to keep alert for other improper acts by that employee and others. While the reported employee cannot be considered guilty until proven so, the organization may want to take steps to assess whether it may have a problem. If the reported theft was an item of significant value, the matter should be reported to legal authorities.

The example of reported fraudulent errors on a contract expense report may raise other issues. In the United States, if the matter involved a federal government contract, the supervisor who directed the employee to make the false entry may be guilty of a criminal act. The organization should take this reported incident seriously and investigate it through its contract compliance office or legal function.

A telephone hotline allows employees to ask a wide range of questions or to report a variety of potentially illegal or improper acts. Even false reports should receive at least a cursory investigation. An organization that records the alleged illegal act and then does nothing about it may be worse off than if it had never heard about the matter.

A typical hotline should have some mechanism to provide an answer or report the disposition of the call back to the originator. A vendor, for example, may have invited an employee to participate in a vendor-sponsored event that is not directly covered by existing policy. The matter should be researched and the answer either communicated to the employee directly or through some form of organization-wide communication. Often, hotline operations will give callers a "case number" to allow them to be anonymous. The original caller might call the hotline back after a designated period of time, give the case number (which would be known only to that person) and then receive disposition information or acknowledgment that investigation is underway.

Even a smaller organization that cannot justify the toll-free telephone line should develop procedures—such as a suggestion box in the human resources department or a post office box—to allow employees to report incidences of potential wrongdoings. A hotline program should be an important element of an organization's compliance program.

(c) ETHICS COMPLIANCE PROGRAMS

Compliance programs are a major component of the Organizational Sentencing Guidelines and the COSO internal control standards. Although each describes them slightly differently, both require organizations to have programs in place to ensure that published standards and procedures are followed. It is of little benefit to the organization to have published rules that are ignored. This becomes more important to the organization in light of the Sentencing Guidelines where an organization, if convicted of a Federal law violation, will have its penalty reduced if it has an effective compliance program in place. The Organizational Sentencing Guidelines specify seven steps necessary for a compliance program to be considered "effective."

1. The organization must have established compliance standards to be followed by its employees and other agents that are reasonably capable of reducing the prospect of criminal conduct.

2. Specific individuals within the higher-level personnel of the organization must have been assigned overall responsibility to oversee compliance with such standards and procedures.

3. The organization must have used due care not to delegate substantial discretionary authority to individuals whom the organization knew, or should have known through the exercise of due diligence, had a propensity to engage in illegal activities.

4. The organization must have taken steps to communicate effectively its standards and procedures to all employees and other agents, by requiring participation in training programs or by disseminating publications that explain in a practical manner what is required.

5. The organization must have taken reasonable steps to achieve compliance with its standards, by utilizing monitoring and auditing systems reasonably designed to detect criminal conduct by its employees and other agents and by having in place and publicizing a reporting system whereby employees and other agents could report criminal conduct by others within the organization without fear of retribution.

6. The standards must have been consistently enforced through appropriate disciplinary mechanisms, including, as appropriate, the discipline of individuals responsible for the failure to detect an offense. Adequate discipline of individuals responsible for an offense is a necessary component of enforcement; however, the form of discipline that will be appropriate will be case-specific.

7. After an offense has been detected, the organization must have taken all reasonable steps to respond appropriately to the offense and to prevent further similar offenses,

including any necessary modification to its program to prevent and detect violations of the law. Self-reporting is a key component in the philosophy of the Guidelines.

Step 5 mandates the hotline approach described previously in this chapter. Some matters tie clearly to basic organizational policy, while others may be difficult to implement. The Guidelines go on to recognize that these compliance program attributes will never be fully implemented in all organizations. As discussed in the Guidelines, some of the more important considerations in designing an organization compliance program include:

- *The Size of the Organization.* The larger organization should have a more formal program than the smaller organization.
- *The Likelihood That Certain Offenses May Occur.* A bank or organization in the securities industry can expect a greater likelihood of some employee violating a federal law than perhaps a commercial food processor, and therefore should have a stronger compliance program in place.
- *Prior History of the Organization.* If punished for a past offense, an organization should install a program to prevent recurrences.
- *Applicable Government Regulations and Industry Standards.* No matter what its size or past history, an organization in a heavily regulated industry would be expected to follow applicable standards.

Although the Guidelines do not state that each organization *must* have the same type of compliance program in place, internal audit should play a strong role in ensuring that the organization has effective compliance programs in place to mitigate the strong punishments mandated by the Organizational Sentencing Guidelines.

35-4 INTERNAL AUDIT AND THE ETHICS FUNCTION

An effective ethics program sponsors an employee code of conduct and allows employees to report violations of the code. This function answers many of the types of issues that have been subjects of internal audit recommendations over the years. Yet rather than being the initiator for ethics functions, internal audit tends to suggest individual exception conditions. Ethics functions have been instituted because of the need to have programs in place to comply with the organizational sentencing guidelines.

Most ethics functions have been sponsored by organizations' law departments. Earlier ones at U.S. defense contractors were sponsored by the sales and contracting function involved with government-related procurement activities. Other organizations have started ethics functions sponsored by their human resource functions.

Even though legal and human resource functions have taken the lead in starting the first ethics departments, there is still a role here for internal audit. On a year-by-year basis, based on membership statistics of the Ethics Officer's Association (EOA), the growth of new ethics functions in U.S. corporations has been almost exponential. The EOA is the professional organization established for heads of organization ethics functions.[3] Despite

---

[3] Ethics Officer Association, Bentley College, Waltham, MA 02154–4705.

this rapid growth, many organizations still have no ethics function or effective compliance programs. Working with the legal department, human resources, and others, internal audit can help establish such a new ethics function. If the organization has such a function, internal audit should develop close ties with the ethics department. This section describes how internal audit might promote the creation of an ethics function where one is lacking or develop appropriate contacts with an established one. When the organization has an established ethics function, internal audit may consider it as a candidate for review if so ranked through internal audit's risk-analysis process.

(a) HELPING TO LAUNCH THE ORGANIZATIONAL ETHICS PROGRAM

Organizations often have established ethics functions after they have found themselves in trouble. For example, a defense contractor might have been accused of overbilling due to some type of government-sponsored audit or it may be pulled into a product liability lawsuit because employees incorrectly documented product test results. In the aftermath of these incidents, senior management often looks at the factors that caused the situation and takes corrective actions to prevent a repeat of the incident leading to an ethics initiative. Internal audit is in a good position to offer to help based upon internal audit's general understanding of the COSO model of internal controls, described in Chapter 2, and the components of the Organizational Sentencing Guidelines, described in Chapter 31. As a specialized area of corporate governance, this offer will generally be accepted.

In other instances, organizations launch what they call ethics functions, though these functions do not contain the key components described earlier in this chapter. For example, some organizations have published a code of conduct, which has been distributed to their new hires, and consider this their ''ethics function.'' This is not a true ethics function, as it does not contain the general guidelines of having a facility to accept reported cases of noncompliance, procedures for taking appropriate actions when there are breaches in compliance, or an established education program to communicate ethical practices to all employees. In many cases, senior management does not realize the key components that may be lacking. Often, human resources has launched a code of conduct, calling it the ''ethics initiative'' or some such name and no one in the organization has questioned this assertion.

Internal audit can point out the key components that are missing through a formal review of this established ''ethics function,'' following the steps outlined in the Figure 35.3 questionnaire. However, in many cases the limited function will be so lacking that a formal review will not be necessary. The director of internal audit can discuss the deficient, ad hoc ''ethics function'' with members of the legal staff or appropriate senior management. Extracts from the Organization Sentencing Guidelines and other published materials can support internal audit's concerns. A strong argument here is that the Guidelines call for an *effective* compliance program. A poor program gives false assurance to management and is perhaps worse than no program at all.

A much greater challenge occurs when the organization has made no attempt to establish an ethics function and is not concerned with any need to establish such a program. Internal audit can educate members of management on the risks and the need to establish an ethics function, and can act as a catalyst to establish such a function if a preliminary risk analysis indicates the need. The risk is that the organization may violate some U.S. federal criminal law and be all but penalty fined into bankruptcy. The typical manufacturer involved with regulatory-related business could be more at risk of violation than a small

Figure 35.3 Ethics Function Assessment Questionnaire

1. Does the organization have a formal code of business conduct?
2. Is the code of conduct regularly updated to reflect current business activities?
3. Is the code distributed to all employees?
4. Are all employees required to acknowledge the acceptance of the code?
5. Are permanent records maintained of employee code acknowledgments?
6. Are there formal programs in place to educate employees on the ethical issues covered in the code as well as on other compliance issues?
7. Do employees have an effective mechanism to confidentially report violations of the code or other questionable acts?
8. Is there a process in place to investigate reported compliance violations?
9. Are reported compliance violations subject to disciplinary action and programs of corrective action?
10. Does the organization have a formal ethics office or ombudsman program?

restaurant chain with a limited number of locations. Internal audit needs to point out potential risks and, if appropriate, suggest the organization establish an ethic function.

(b) AUDIT COORDINATION WITH THE ESTABLISHED ETHICS FUNCTION

If an ethics function has been established without internal audit involvement, the director of internal audit should become acquainted with the ethics officer to set up close connections between that ethics function and the internal audit organization. Although they each have unique roles, each party should work to support the other.

A first step in this coordination might be to introduce the audit committee of the board to the organization's ethics function and its officer or director. The director of internal audit can suggest that the ethics function present its program to the audit committee. The ethics officer can present a summary report to the audit committee on a periodic basis, perhaps semiannually. Internal audit should facilitate this communication. Some boards of directors have established separate ethics committees in addition to their audit committees, usually when there has been some legal or regulatory crisis. Although the board's ethics committee will have its own relationship with the ethics function, internal audit should ensure close communication.

A significant internal audit role is in helping to make the compliance monitoring function work more effectively. Step 5 of the sentencing guidelines for a compliance program is to establish ''monitoring and auditing systems reasonably designed to detect criminal conduct.'' While internal audit review objectives are not normally designed to detect criminal conduct, they do detect violations of internal control standards and other policies or procedures and can therefore support this guideline step.

Internal audit can work with ethics to perform a series of legal and compliance-type reviews similar to other regular internal audit reviews but emphasizing the auditee's compliance with certain laws and regulations. Figure 35.4 illustrates some of the issues that might be included in a legal and compliance review of a chain of retail stores. Such compliance may be with required health and safety regulations, its obtaining of various operating licenses, and with various sales and local tax-exemption rules. While none of

Figure 35.4   Legal and Compliance Review Audit Procedures

35.04.01	Review published procedures and other directives for references to legal compliance requirements.
35.04.02	Meet with representatives of general counsel's office to gain understanding of ongoing organizational legal issues.
35.04.03	Determine if the organization is under a consent decree or other legal restrictions.
35.04.04	Meet with representatives of controller's department, sales and contracts, or other functions in the organization that may have legal compliance concerns or vulnerabilities.
35.04.05	Develop a list of legal and compliance areas to test as well as an approach for testing. The list should be risk based, where violation of national rather than local law can be viewed as higher risk and a violation with a high risk of detection can be higher risk; an example of the latter would be OSHA rules, where a safety inspector could visit on a random basis and impose a fine.
35.04.06	Working with legal counsel, obtain *attorney-client privilege* on the matters to be reviewed. That way, internal audit will not have a responsibility to report violations of illegal acts to outside authorities but only to counsel. This privilege will prevent an authority from issuing a subpoena to review the auditor's workpapers.
35.04.07	Determine which locations and departments to review to measure compliance for the audit. If a 100% level test does not appear to be cost effective, consider statistical sampling random selection techniques to make the selection.
35.04.08	Consider scheduling the actual audits either on a surprise basis or with only a minimal announcement. Do not announce details of the specific legal compliance areas to be reviewed in advance.
35.04.09	For the locations selected, test compliance for the selected areas on a *yes* or *no* compliance test basis. There should be no room for explanations or ''shades of gray.''
35.04.10	Depending upon the nature of the violation, report the violation to local management for corrective action prior to completion of the fieldwork. Explain the ''compliance with the law'' nature of the audit to local management.
35.04.11	If a violation appears to be a serious legal issue beyond such ''minor'' matters as the failure to post an EEO legally required poster, report the matter to the legal counsel.
35.04.12	Report compliance violations in a summarized manner in the audit report itemizing the number of the violations detected as compared to the number of locations visited.
35.04.13	If significant and pervasive violations were found, report the matter to the legal counsel and appropriate members of senior management.
35.04.14	Schedule a follow-up review to include at least the major problem sites visited in the first review to measure the level of corrective action.

the matters described in the figure are issues that probably would result in criminal prosecutions under federal laws, they illustrate areas to check for compliance with existing laws and regulations. The product of this review will be similar to that of other audits described throughout this book. The differences are that, since this review is a component of the ethics function's compliance program, internal audit should work closely with ethics in developing the audit program and schedule, and the ethics function should be on the distribution list of the published compliance audit reports produced.

(c) AUDITING THE ETHICS FUNCTION

The ethics function should not be exempt from the same types of operational or financial reviews that internal audit performs in all other segments of the organization. Different from marketing or design engineering, which may be subject to an operational and financial review based on an identification of potential audit risks, the ethics function should nevertheless be included in the same risk-analysis model used by internal audit for its annual planning, discussed in Chapter 8. Although there should be minimal risks for the well-organized ethics function, an occasional internal audit review may be more similar to the quality-assurance review, as was discussed in Chapter 33. Indeed, the team that performs internal audit quality-assurance reviews might be the most appropriate to review the quality and overall control procedures in place in the ethics function.

The purpose of an internal audit review of the ethics function is to assess whether that ethics department is following good internal control procedures, making effective use of its resources, and following its department charter or other organization documents authorizing the ethics function. While every ethics function may be a little different, internal audit should gain a detailed understanding of how the function operates and the procedures normally performed. As the organization's *ethics function,* internal audit should expect to find the ethics department procedures at least as good as internal audit regarding compliance with such areas as travel expense policies. Other ethics functions areas may point to areas where internal audit can suggest improvements. For example, the ethics department's code of conduct normally should have an acknowledgment form or process where employees indicate that they have read and understand the code. An ethics function may not have established appropriate procedures here to ensure that all current and new-hire employees go through this acknowledgment process or it may not have a good filing system for those responses. Internal audit can assess this process and recommend improvements where appropriate.

Figure 35.5 describes some general audit procedures in a review of an organizational ethics function. Because of the close, ongoing relationship that should exist between the ethics function and internal audit, if an operational review of ethics does come up as part of audit's risk analysis, the director of internal audit should discuss the planned review with the ethics director in some detail to explain the reasons for and the objectives of the planned operational review.

Privacy and confidentiality may become an issue in this type of review. A call to the hotline may have pointed to some form of potential employee malfeasance, which ethics will want to keep highly confidential until the matter is resolved. Despite internal audit's ongoing exposure to other sensitive areas and issues in the organization, the director of the ethics function may be reluctant to have internal auditors review certain materials. The director of internal audit should point out internal audit's ongoing exposure to other sensitive information and the requirements that it follow appropriate professional standards. Assuming these matters can be resolved appropriately, an operational review of an ethics function will give management additional assurances as to the integrity of controls in the ethics function, a component of operations where most managers have had little exposure or experience.

Figure 35.5 Organizational Ethics Function Sample Audit Program

Audit _____ Location _____ Date _____

AUDIT STEP	INITIAL	W/P
1. Obtain a general understanding of the ethics function organization, its charter, and its responsibilities.		
2. Assuming the ethics function is responsible for the code of conduct, assess whether the code is current and whether there is a process in place to periodically update the code.		
3. Review procedures for obtaining employee formal acknowledgment of acceptance of the code and for maintaining records of that action. Select a sample of several new hires and long-term employees to determine they have acknowledged the code.		
4. Assess the procedures in place allowing employees to report ethics violations as well as procedures in place to investigate and correct reported violations. • Determine complete information is recorded for all ethics calls.		
• Procedures should allow employees to report anonymously but still obtain follow-up status information about their reported incidents.		
• Security procedures should keep call records confidential.		
5. Select a sample of reported ethics incidents from call logs and assess the adequacy of follow-up and disposition procedures.		
6. Review the adequacy of procedures in place to track reported ethics incidents and report trends to senior management.		
7. Assess the adequacy of ethics function security over its files, other records, and general office matters.		
8. Develop an understanding of other ethics function activities, such as support of the compliance program, and assess adequacy.		
9. Assess adequacy of the ethics department training program to introduce the function to all employees. Determine whether programs are available and are used by all employees and others such as contractors.		
10. Review ethics function compliance with other company procedures such as the travel policy, expense reporting, and other matters.		

35-5 SOCIAL RESPONSIBILITY

Social responsibility concerns are unique in that internal audit must deal with relatively intangible areas that combine certain values, existing in their own right, with other values that directly relate to organizational self-interest and profitability. That is, an organization and its managers should see their social responsibilities both in terms of good citizenship and as necessary components of organizational welfare. In this connection, social responsibilities and business ethics have common roots but involve differing problems and objectives. Social responsibility should be a concern of internal auditors as part of a dedicated professional effort to serve management.

Understanding the nature and scope of the problems of social responsibility in order to identify potential management action is crucial. Internal auditors can assist management in carrying out a business social responsibility program. This section will briefly deal with some of these broader social responsibility areas.

(a) SOCIAL RESPONSIBILITY ISSUES IN THE MODERN ORGANIZATION

''Social responsibility'' is a general term that covers the obligation of an organization and its managers to help serve the broader needs of society over a wide range of physical and intangible considerations for which there is no common agreement. Different views as to the nature and scope of social needs combine with different priorities for their satisfaction. In general terms, social needs involve such broad issues as physical safety, the quality of living standards, freedom of choice, opportunities for self-expression and development, and respect for fellow human beings. These needs, as individually and collectively expressed, define the responsibilities of all participants—both individually and collectively. Any evaluation of these needs and responsibilities is directly related to the nature and scope of social expectations, which have changed over the years in terms of both their range and intensity. Modern society now has a broader variety and higher level of these needs and wants those needs to be satisfied more quickly.

Organizational social responsibility concerns cover a wide range but typically include the following:

- *Neglect of Various Aspects of the Physical Environment.* This is a worldwide set of concerns covering such matters as air pollution, contaminated bodies of water, commercialization of the countryside, inadequate sanitation, and the like. An example is the pumping of industrial waste into a river or lake, making that lake unfit for drinking, bathing, and fishing.

- *Waste and Destruction of Natural Resources.* Concerns here center around the destruction of wildlife, the loss of natural areas supporting that wildlife, the defilement of land surfaces through mining or other construction activities, destruction of forests, dissipation of energy resources, and the like. An example is strip-mining operations where the land is not restored after the extraction of minerals.

- *Lack of Physical Security.* At issue here is rising crime and violence and the insecurity of people both in their homes and on the street. An example is the incidences of mugging, vandalism, burglary, and murder found in some larger cities.

- *Protection of Human Rights.* The concern here is for minority groups that directly or indirectly have been denied legal and social rights believed to be due all human beings. The plight of minority groups in certain countries of the world is illustrative.

- *Freedom of Opportunity and Self-Development.* At this higher level are the concerns for the total fulfillment of self-expression and for healthy economic and spiritual growth for all peoples.

The foregoing social expectations have always existed. What is new, and at the same time of major significance, is that in recent years these expectations have been dramatically accelerated. To attempt to address some of these concerns, governmental regulatory bodies have imposed a large number of rules and restrictions on various organizations. The regulations are often both complex and difficult to implement, and the punishments for not complying with them can be both severe and arbitrary. It is in this environment that the business organization finds itself as it seeks to maintain needed profitability and sound growth. Managers and internal auditors serving those managers must find solutions if the organizations are to survive.

While social responsibility concerns all responsible members of the society, the problem for the business organization is further compounded by the varying ways in which society views the business organization. Normally, correcting the problems of society comes from the people themselves through the established government; this is especially true in democracies. Because citizens are not often satisfied with the traditional process, they may see the business organization as a convenient way of achieving faster social action. Various pressure groups attempt to influence the business organization to take actions for solving perceived social problems. Their methods may involve new laws and governmental regulation, or appealing to the emotions of the public, or perhaps infiltrating and pressuring boards of directors. The organization must decide the extent to which it should yield to or resist these varied pressures, in addition to deciding the proper role the organization should play in a free society.

There are two basically different viewpoints. At one extreme is the view that in a free enterprise system the proper role of the organization is solely to make a profit. With businesses competing for consumers of its products, society thereby is able to vote on how all resources should best be utilized to satisfy its needs. If the organization tries to administer to social needs, it not only takes on a role for which it is not properly qualified, but also impairs its capability to carry on its basic profit-making role. According to this view, the business organization should concentrate on achieving profitability and leave to government the job of responding to broader social needs.

An opposing view is that society creates the business organization to serve its needs and, therefore, the business organization has a direct responsibility to society. Put another way, the business organization is a citizen and as such has the same responsibilities as every other citizen. Indeed, it can be argued that, because the business organization controls so many assets and people, its responsibility as a citizen is all the more genuine. This view does not necessarily relieve government of its responsibilities, but it does attribute a major responsibility to the organization itself. Indeed, if this view is carried to the extreme, responding to social needs often becomes a higher priority than profitability.

What, then, should the organization do in the face of such conflicting views? If the organization operates under the grace of a charter granted by the society, organization management has a primary responsibility to satisfy society in return for its continuing existence. At the same time, unless the organization is profitable, management will have failed in its responsibilities to the investors and creditors who have provided the organizational resources. Moreover, organizational managers who do not achieve profitability are replaced by others who do. Businesses must be profitable to survive and to avoid liquidation. Management's challenge is to satisfy both types of needs. That is, the business organization must be sufficiently responsible to public pressures and at the same time be profitable enough to protect its existence and to assure its health and survival. A special challenge of the organizational manager is to reconcile these often conflicting forces by finding the proper middle ground. This longer-range reconciliation, called "enlightened self-interest," requires at least partial involvement in developing actions for satisfying a range of social responsibilities.

(b) PROBLEMS OF SATISFYING SOCIAL RESPONSIBILITIES

A policy decision for satisfying social responsibilities, sound as it is, presents difficulties.

- *Questions of the Right Priorities.* Individuals, and in turn the groups those individuals work through, have widely differing views as to the merits and relative priorities of various social needs. Any decision in this area is therefore always bound to be controversial, applauded by some and condemned by others. In this connection are questions of both propriety and feasibility.

- *High Emotional Content of Social Issues.* Many if not most social responsibility issues tend to have exceptionally high emotional content, coupled with correspondingly decreasing objectivity. Individual social needs are frequently viewed with missionary zeal and lead to demands that are both unsound and impractical.

- *Limited Capacity for an Impact.* Frequently, the particular social problems involved are so great that the capacity of an individual organization to deal with them is unavoidably minuscule. While the concept that "every little bit helps" applies, this is inevitably true irrespective of the large resources of the particular organization.

- *Susceptibility to Manipulation.* Because social causes have such high emotional content, it is always tempting to use them in a manipulative sense to achieve other personal goals and objectives. In this way, social causes become political footballs or covers for more sinister objectives. Some groups may see this pressure as an opportunity to discredit both the organization and the free enterprise system.

- *Difficulties in Social Program Implementation.* Decisions to satisfy social responsibilities, even though often theoretically sound and appealing, are typically hard to implement in terms of corrective action. Here also, the choice of methods for that implementation are usually exceedingly controversial and typically emotional.

- *Difficulties of Corrective Action Measurement.* The difficulties of program implementation just indicated are compounded by the fact that results are hard to measure and evaluate. Again, the evaluation of what has been accomplished in the way of corrective action is exceedingly controversial and subject to further emotional manipulation. The difficulties here apply to both input and output.

- *Special Problems of Cost versus Benefit Analysis.* The difficulties of measurement are further compounded by the complicated interrelationships of the various costs and benefits. For example, a decision to close a plant because of the pollution it causes may at the same time deprive workers of needed employment. Equating all of these varying costs and benefits thus becomes almost impossible and again always very controversial.

- *Problems of Organization Credibility.* In many cases, well-intentioned efforts to discharge social responsibilities are challenged by hostile groups as misguided or improper commercialism—often for the sole purpose of discrediting management or the organization itself. Managers are therefore often disillusioned and demotivated to continue meritorious programs. Even when it does persevere, management faces special problems in demonstrating that its efforts are sincere and credible.

The challenges of satisfying social responsibilities should not be viewed as unduly pessimistic or discourage definitive action. Such definitive action must be taken within the framework of enlightened self-interest. It is necessary, however, that management fully understand these special problems and give appropriate consideration when developing action programs.

(c) BUILDING THE ORGANIZATION'S SOCIAL RESPONSIBILITY PROGRAM

Each action program to deal with a particular organization's social responsibilities, within the framework of enlightened self-interest, has its own distinctive problems. Controlling considerations include the types of relationships existing between social needs and organizational goals and objectives. A second consideration is the level of available organization resources. Proper responses must be evaluated in terms of the particular management's philosophy and approach. These programs can usually be grouped as those that are internal in nature and those external, with some unavoidable overlap. *Internal* programs may include:

1. *Consideration of Social Responsibility in All Ongoing Managerial Decisions.* All business decisions, both in the areas of policy and implementing action, have components that involve types of social responsibility. The organization needs a program to give continuing consideration of such issues in the decision process. Especially illustrative are decisions relating to new facilities and the resultant possibilities of noise, pollution, and accidents.

2. *Special Research for New Approaches.* In addition to the ongoing day-to-day decisions, there should be special efforts to minimize or eliminate undesirable features. Illustrative would be attempts by the automotive industry to reduce the impact of engine exhausts. Here were both direct profit benefits and a demonstration to the public of the sincerity of industry efforts.

3. *Special Social Responsibility–Related Training.* Many opportunities exist whereby organizations can train needed workers and at the same time reduce the numbers of the disadvantaged who would not otherwise qualify, such as persons lacking basic needed skills. In the United States, the organization may be able to obtain some government help to support this type of initiative.

4. *Incorporation of Social Responsibility Issues in Management Policies.* To a major extent, an organization can augment its social role by incorporating such intentions in its public statements and internal policies and procedures. Social responsibil-

ity–oriented plans can also be incorporated in managerial objectives at all organizational levels. This coverage needs to be supported actively by all levels of management and be made visible to the general public.

5. *Identification of a Specific Organizational Responsibility.* A special department is sometimes devoted to studying and reviewing all pertinent outside developments, maintaining liaisons with people active in this area, preparing plans for effectively dealing with the existing problems, and working with those people charged with the responsibilities of actual implementation. This approach often better assures proper attention is given to social responsibility developments.

External programs focus more directly on people outside the organization itself, and include:

1. *Donating Money or Other Resources.* Perhaps the easiest way of supporting social causes, financial support can be on a one-time basis or as part of a continuing program. Decisions as to the cause to be supported, the amounts, and the timing of contributions should be based on informed management judgments.

2. *Organization Employee Assistance and Counsel.* Business enterprises can make officers and employees available to provide advice and counsel to social causes and to the organizations directly involved. In some cases, the organization can provide individuals to directly manage socially oriented activities for limited periods of time. Employees can also be encouraged to engage in such activities in a private, volunteer capacity.

3. *Profit-Based Involvement.* On a profit basis, the organization can take on particular socially oriented jobs and use its own managerial skills as a substitute for governmental institutions for such things as building public facilities, running training programs, and actually operating institutional units. Although profit margins may be fixed at below-normal levels, there is still reasonable compensation.

4. *Working with Government.* A potentially rewarding type of action, assistance here can pertain to the shaping of particular legislation and related regulations. While the relationship with government has been typically adversarial, a more enlightened view might be to better understand the problems faced by government and to help to ensure that resulting legislation and regulatory efforts will be sound and effective. An appreciation on the part of both government and business of their underlying common interests and a more vigorous effort to work together as partners can achieve those common interests.

5. *Effective Communications to Outsiders.* In the last analysis, the outside public has the multiple roles of customers, investors, sources of legislation, and participants in all existing social problems. It follows therefore that the business organization should help that public better discharge its multiple responsibilities. Especially important is to help the public to better understand the impact on business—and in turn thereby on the society itself—of actions taken in response to asserted social needs. The challenge here is to make the voice of organization heard and to do it in a way that is both sound and credible to the public. In part, this points to the need for an effective public relations department, but it also represents a challenge for all organizational managers.

Organizations will encounter problems initiating programs to satisfy their social responsibilities even if senior management realizes that certain programs should be implemented. In addition, management may often encounter resistance within the organization due to the wide range of values and views as well as the emotional content regarding various social responsibilities. It is inevitable that subordinates will often feel quite differently about decisions made by senior management. In many cases the socially oriented actions will be seen as being directly at odds with the employees' own views. Although this resistance can never be fully overcome, the understanding of its existence will result in a better implementation.

A related problem is that senior managers may give official support to the legitimacy of social responsibility policies and procedures but then do nothing. When subordinates, who may be already at odds with the policies involved, detect that lack of dedication, the forces for effective implementation are immediately undermined. There is a need for a better understanding of the social responsibility program at all levels, which points to the need for better communication. In particular, a social responsibility program may cause some confusion with the organization's regular reward system. Traditional performance measurement and reward systems in organizations have been based on elements of volume, cost, revenue, and profitability. The injection of social responsibility considerations conflicts to some extent with those long-accepted standards. The result is a combination of differing measures of performance, under conditions where the impact of the social program is unavoidably intangible. Under these circumstances, the evaluation of performance and the determination of related rewards become more difficult, especially with already controversial social issues. In total, this difficulty can often significantly undermine an effective implementation of social responsibility programs.

Internal audit can alert management to areas to improve social responsibility activities and then perform reviews of those activities. In more practical terms, internal audit can assist management through a series of specific steps, including:

- *Basic Social Responsibility Operational Auditing Activities.* Given a basic objective to provide better services to society, it follows that operational auditing activity can be similarly beneficial. In an attempt to identify every possible opportunity to expand sources of revenue and to reduce costs, audits can be expanded to consider compliance with identified social responsibility issues.

- *Reporting on Consumer Interests.* The normal range of operational auditing provides an opportunity to identify problem areas in protecting customer or consumer interests. Illustrative would be the observation of promotional programs in action, the review of sales activities, customer responses, and the review of warranty programs. Operational audits can include surveys where an internal auditor can be particularly alert to the levels of customer satisfaction.

- *Legal Compliance Audits.* Compliance with legal requirements has always been a part of the internal auditor's interests. Figure 35.4 describes procedures to follow in a legal and compliance review in a retail or distribution organization. Similar procedures would be used for other industries. These requirements should include compliance with socially oriented legislation such as fair employment practices, pollution and disposal standards, and the like.

- *Public Citizenship Responsibilities.* Internal auditing services can be made available directly to local philanthropic or public groups. The volunteering to perform an operational audit of a community charitable organization is a positive expression of direct citizenship service by the auditor's organization.

• *Direct Review of Organization Social Responsibility Efforts.* Where an organization has set up a special department or office to deal with social responsibility activities, a review of the operations of that group can be a normal extension of the regular internal auditing effort. Similarly, the internal auditor should consider reviews of the progress or final results of particular organization-sponsored social programs. The procedures here will be the same as those in the financial or operational audits in other areas described throughout this book.

• *Social Evaluation Audit.* In this type of review, internal audit might look at the various programs the organization has established, how they are being performed, how the organization compares to other organizations in the community, and what needs or opportunities might exist for other potential organization activities. Figure 35.6 provides procedures for this type of social evaluation audit. This is the type of review, however, that internal audit should only perform if requested to by senior management.

Internal auditing can be effective with respect to social responsibility issues by being alert to special aspects that pertain to the particular dimension of social responsibility, and by making specific reviews of activities and programs of a social responsibility nature. The independence of internal audit, combined with special analytical skills, provides a

Figure 35.6 Social Evaluation Audit Procedures

Audit _____ Location _____ Date _____

AUDIT STEP	INITIAL	W/P
1. Meet with the ethics officer, H/R director or other responsible persons to understand specific social issues impacting the organization.		
2. Based on the interviews, select several significant social programs that have involved the organization over recent months; if there are no such programs, determine the reasons for no participation.		
3. Based on the ethics officer-related interview or other management inputs, select several programs to review.		
4. Meet with managers responsible for selected programs; determine current budgets, planned activities, and other promotions of the programs.		
5. For selected social/philanthropic projects, perform a detailed financial review to determine that all expenditures are backed by receipts and that all expenditures appear to be related to the program.		
6. Meet with recipients of the philanthropic funds, newspaper editors, or others to assess their impressions of the organization's social efforts.		

major opportunity to render important assistance in this new critical area of management concern. Hopefully also, internal auditors can make some contributions in the development of such newer approaches as social accounting and the social audit.

35-6 FUTURE TRENDS IN ETHICS AND SOCIAL AUDITING

The beginning of this chapter discussed how social responsibilities and business ethics issues had common roots in social values and that the problems were closely interrelated. In both cases, they involved objectives that were both directly rewarding and increasingly a needed part in achieving organizational welfare. Internal audit must understand these combined problems and provide appropriate internal audit services to management. Moreover, predictions for the future indicate the further intensification of all of those needs. What this means is that internal audit's social responsibility and business ethics activities represent a new challenge and a new potential area for organizational service.

INDEX